Estate Planning and Wealth Preservation

STRATEGIES AND SOLUTIONS

KATHRYN G. HENKEL

Partner, Hughes & Luce, L.L.P.
Dallas, Texas

ABRIDGED EDITION
FOR STUDENT USE ONLY

WARREN, GORHAM & LAMONT
OF RIA

To
May and Jack

Author's Note
to Revised Student Edition

This abridgement of *Estate Planning and Wealth Preservation: Strategies and Solutions* retains all material of major pedagogical interest but omits those chapters that are of more interest to the practicioner than to the student. To make the volume a more manageable size, the endmatter tables and index have been deleted. The cumulative tables and index, which includes references to the omitted chapters, will appear in the student supplements.

Preface

This book is intended to serve as a practical guide to estate planning for substantial estates. It aims to provide (1) guidance on which techniques may be suitable to accomplish particular goals, (2) how-to explanations accompanying the technical discussions regarding each method, (3) an understanding of the theory underlying each technique, and (4) plain English summaries that are suitable as a resource in communicating difficult subject matter to clients. It is meant to be advanced and comprehensive, but as easily accessible as the complexity of the subject and the limitations of the author's brain allow.

Part I deals with the fundamentals of transfer taxation and selected aspects of income taxation which are integral to estate planning. Chapter 1 gives an overview of each of the transfer taxes, in order to impart a clear understanding of the impact and interrelationship of those taxes. Chapters 2 through 7 are details discussions of various elements of the transfer tax system, including the transfers included in the gift and estate tax bases, powers of appointment, the basics of planning for married couples (including use of the unified credit, the marital deduction, formula wills, and equalization techniques), the generation-skipping transfer tax, important aspects of income taxation of estates, trusts, and beneficiaries, and coordination of nontestamentary transfers with the entire estate plan.

Part II deals with the tax effectiveness of lifetime gifts. The part begins with Chapter 8, which discusses the dramatic difference in tax rates between gifts and estate transfers, the circumstances calling for gifts, and how to choose the best gifts. Chapter 9 covers the law dealing with retained powers and interests, and explains how to give the donor maximum control keeping the property out of her estate and income tax bases. Chapter 10 contains a discussion of the rules applicable to tax-free gifts, including tuition and medical payments, annual exclusion gifts, and gifts using up the donor's unified credit. Chapter 11 is an explanation of the mysteries of the actuarial tables, laying a predicate for later discussions of actuarially valued transfers, and attempting to impart an instinct for the tables and how they are likely to work in particular situations.

Part III addresses assets which sprout added value and/or added rules at a person's death—life insurance, annuities, and qualified plans. The chapters discuss a variety of techniques to deal with these assets, ranging from basic to highly sophisticated, and provide suggestions for appropriate choices in specific circumstances.

Part IV is a guide to business entities for estate planners. Separate chapters discuss partnerships, limited liability companies, S corporations, and C corporations. Since a details discussions of the tax consequences of each entity would take (at least) a whole book apiece, these chapters concentrate on the aspects of taxation of those entities which an estate planner is most likely to encounter. Chapter 20 on choice of entity gives a comparative treatment of each entity with respect to a large number of tax and non-tax issues.

Part V covers non-charitable actuarial techniques, including qualified personal residence trusts, grantor retained annuity trusts, private annuities, and some less commonly used techniques. These chapters include analyses of when such techniques are likely to present the best opportunities, and technical discussions of the specific requirements and ramifications of each technique.

Valuation planning is the subject of Part VI, which contains chapters on discounts, and on Sections 2703 and 2704, which contain special rules relating to the valuation of property in specific circumstances. These chapters should be helpful to the planner dealing with family entities, as well as other difficult-to-value assets.

Part VII deals with estate freezing techniques, including loans, leases, installment sales, and preferred interests. The chapters in this part cover the income tax ramifications of the various techniques in detail, as well as the transfer tax effects. The chapter on preferred interests contains a technical discussions of Section 2701 for those who desire a deep understanding, as well as a briefer executive summary for those who are more interested in how to avoid the application of the statute at all than in its effects if it does apply.

Charitable planning is an area of passing importance to many wealthy individuals. Part VIII begins with a chapter on outright gifts, which includes the various limitations and special rules applicable to the income tax deduction of charitable gifts, as well as the transfer tax implications. Chapter 33 contains an in-depth discussion of charitable remainder trusts, proceeding from basic trusts to more complex and sophisticated structures, along with recommendations about when each structure is likely to be useful. Following are chapters on charitable gift annuities, charitable lead trusts, and other charitable split-interest gifts. These include technical requirements, income tax effects, and best use of the techniques. Chapter 37 is a discussion of private foundations, including income tax limitations, excise taxes, and opportunities for use. The part ends with a chapter on custom-designed charities for those wealthy individuals who either cannot or do not want to use private foundations, but who desire foundations tailored to their specific needs.

Part IX assists the planner with particular family configurations. Chapter 39 discusses marital property agreements, which estate planners are often asked to draft and negotiate. Chapters 40 and 41 explore special issues applicable to blended families (with children of more than one marriage) and to unmarried couples, and provide suggestions for addressing the special problems and taking advantage of the special opportunities inherent in those situations.

Part X helps in planning for the elderly, disabled, seriously ill. The chapters on the elderly discusses Medicare and Medicaid issues, nursing home and home care options, and other matters which concern senior citizens. The chapter on disability needs discusses issues of a person with special needs as a lifetime matter (the brain-damaged or emotionally disturbed, for example), as well as the individual who wants to plan for the possibility of disability related to illness or accident. The chapter on pre-mortem planning lists a variety of options to consider in planning for a person whose death is expected to occur in the short term.

Planning which can be done to maximize post-mortem choices and opportunities is discussed in Part XI. The chapters address the issues of providing liquidity to pay taxes, expenses, debts, and other cash obligations at death, whether and how to take advantage of the deferred payout of estate taxes under Section 6166, the pros and cons and ins and outs of disclaimers, and the application of Section 2032A, dealing with special valuation of certain agricultural property. Chapter 49 is an advanced treatment of material which is covered in basic form in Chapter 4. It deals with sophisticated planning for the marital deduction and unified credit, as well as other funding and apportionment issues. Chapter 50 explains other post-mortem elections and how to plan for their availability.

Part XII contains chapters on planning for executives, directors, and major owners of publicly traded and potentially publicly traded companies, including a basic treatment of the securities restrictions that impact estate planning. Chapter 52 deals with international issues, including a basic treatment of the income and transfer taxation of nonresident aliens, discussion on situs rules, a detailed discussion of qualified domestic trusts, and coverage of the rules on taxation of foreign trusts. Chapter 53, finally, is a wide-ranging discussion of asset protection, which is also an issue of concern to many wealthy individuals. It includes such techniques as gifts, spousal transfers, family entities, use of exempt property, creation of trusts which will maximize protection for the beneficiaries, and the use of asset protection trusts in foreign and domestic jurisdictions.

The book generally assumes, unless otherwise noted, that all individuals and taxable entities are taxable at the maximum income tax rates and the 55 percent transfer tax rate. The book addresses federal taxes, and does not purport to discuss the various state tax consequences of the techniques discussed, except as specifically noted. Section or §, without a specific reference, refers to the Internal Revenue Code.

The material in the text is generally updated through early to mid-1977. The legislative changes contained in the Taxpayer Relief Act of 1997 are contained in blue pages.

It is with humility that this effort is launched. Accordingly, suggestions, comments, and corrections from readers are welcome and will be received in that spirit.

KATHRYN G. HENKEL

Acknowledgments

Many individuals have contributed, directly or indirectly, to the success of this book, and I am truly grateful to all. I take the opportunity to mention a few.

I would like to acknowledge Alan J. Bogdanow, a former managing partner of my law firm, Hughes & Luce, L.L.P., for agreeing to commit the firm's resources to this endeavor. I also want to publicly thank all the people at the firm who shared in the adventure. I am particularly grateful to my partners, Karen K. Suhre and Jon L. Mosle, for their insightful comments and gentle corrections regarding the chapters on employee benefits and securities, respectively. I appreciate the assistance of Renn G. Neilson, who reviewed the corporate and choice of entity chapter, Matthew L. Larsen, who carefully proofread and reviewed many chapters, and W. Bradley Bickham, who researched a variety of issues. I am indebted as well to two of our secretaries, Kelly Menn and Sharron D'Arcy, who spend countless hours of their own time over many months typing the manuscript, and who never once failed in good cheer, enthusiasm, and excellent work.

I reserve a special bouquet for my colleague, Elizabeth R. Turner, in appreciation of her fantastic editing of the entire first draft, her countless invaluable contributions on a wide range of subjects, and her effective and competent assumption of more client responsibilities than I had a right to expect of a person of her years (which allowed me to finish this project before the turn of the millennium).

Special thanks are also in order for my secretary, Joyce Barto, who coordinated the word processing efforts, worked efficiently and pleasantly with all the various people involved in the effort, deciphered thousands of pages of my intolerable handwriting without complaint, and devoted two years of her life to this work along with me. Without exception, she applied her customary high standards to the work product, maintained a cheerful, professional, optimistic, and dedicated attitude, and made my life run more smoothly in many ways during the process.

I acknowledge all the personnel at Warren, Gorham & Lamont who contributed their talents to the book, and especially Bruce Furst, my editor, and Jeff Hall and Marie G. Simon, my copy editors, for their hard work, faith in the mission, good humor, and patience with a novice author.

I express sincere appreciation to my mother, Dolores Grundy, who read the manuscript from the viewpoint of an intelligent layperson and made many very helpful suggestions.

I am grateful to my daughters, Stephanie and Carolyn, for their involuntary but good-natured sacrifices of part of my time and attention for the duration of the writing, and for affording me endless laughter and joy.

Last, but certainly not least, I thanks my partner and friend, Vester T. Hughes, Jr., both for his encouragement and support of this undertaking, and for his many years of showing me the way.

Summary of Contents

Table of Contents

5   Generation-Skipping Transfer Tax

6   Income Taxation of Trusts and Beneficiaries

7   Nontestamentary Transfers

Part II THE POWER OF LIFETIME GIFTS

8 Tax Economics of Lifetime Gifts

9   Donor's Retention of Control and Interests

10   Tax-Free Gifts

11 Split-Interest Gifts—Understanding the Actuarial Tables

PART III ASSETS PROVIDING DEATH BENEFITS

12 Life Insurance

13   Commercial Annuities

14   Qualified Plan and IRA Benefits

PART IV FAMILY BUSINESS AND INVESTMENT ENTITIES

15 Family Business and Investment Entities

16 Partnerships

17   Limited Liability Companies

18   S Corporations

19   C Corporations

20   Choice of Entity

PART V   NONCHARITABLE ACTUARIAL TECHNIQUES

21   Qualified Personal Residence Trusts

23   Private Annuities

24   Other Actuarial Techniques

PART VI   VALUATION PLANNING

25   Valuation Issues

26   Section 2704: Rights That Lapse and Restrictions on Liquidation

27   Section 2703: Buy-Sell Agreements, Options, and Noncommercial Restrictions

PART VII   ESTATE FREEZING TECHNIQUES

---

28   Loans

29   Leases and Leasebacks

30   Deferred Payment Sales

31   Preferred Equity Interests

32   Outright Charitable Gifts

34   Charitable Gift Annuities

35   Charitable Lead Trusts

36   Other Charitable Split-Interest Gifts

37   Private Foundations

38 Designer Charities

PART IX PLANNING FOR MARRIAGE AND OTHER FAMILY ARRANGEMENTS

39 Marital Property Agreements

40 Special Issues for Blended Families

41   Special Issues for Unmarried Couples

PART X   **ADVANCED MATURITY, DISABILITY AND SERIOUS ILLNESS**

42   Special Issues of the Elderly

43   Disability Planning

44   Pre-Mortem Planning

Part XI PLANNING FOR POST-MORTEM CHOICES

45 Providing Liquidity for the Estate

46 Deferred Payout of Estate Taxes

47   Disclaimers

48   Special Use Valuation of Farms and Ranches

49   Wills With Marital Deduction Provisions—Drafting, Funding, and Apportionment

50   Other Post-Mortem Elections

PART I

Fundamentals

CHAPTER 1

Overview of the Transfer Taxes

¶ 1.01 INTRODUCTION

Three taxes can be imposed on the transfer of a person's property during life
or at death—the gift tax, the estate tax, and the generation-skipping transfer
tax (GSTT). These three taxes are called "transfer taxes" because they are excise taxes imposed on the transfer of property. Much estate planning involves
minimizing, or even eliminating, transfer taxes.

The computation of each transfer tax is different. Gift and estate taxes are
assessed as part of a unified graduated rate system. Generation-skipping transfer taxes are imposed on a different set of taxable transfers, using a flat rate.

The Economic Growth and Tax Relief Reconciliation Act of 2001
("EGTRRA"), which was passed in June 2001, provided numerous changes in
the transfer tax system. Relevant specific details are noted below. The most
difficult item for planners to contend with is the repeal of the estate tax and
generation-skipping transfer tax for deaths and transfers occurring in the year
2010, followed by their reinstatement under laws applicable in 2001 for years
after 2010. This is because EGTRRA has a sunset provision indicating that all
of its provisions will expire in 2011 and the law will revert to the status quo
ante.[1]

Some think that the law will sunset as planned. Some think it won't. The
discussions below address both eventualities.

¶ 1.02 GIFT AND ESTATE TAXES

[1] Terminology

A person who makes a gift during his lifetime is called a "donor." A "gift," in
gift or estate tax parlance, is a transfer of property made for less than adequate

---

[1] EGTRRA § 901.

consideration.[2] Certain gifts are transfer tax-free.[3] All other gifts are called "taxable gifts."

A deceased person is known as a "decedent." The "probate estate" includes all items which are subject to administration in the probate court. The "gross estate" and "taxable estate" may include many items which are not part of the probate estate.[4] The estate tax applies to property that is part of a decedent's taxable estate.

Transfers of property made by taxable gift or through a taxable estate are "taxable transfers." In order to compute the tax on any taxable transfer, it is necessary to determine the "tax rate" and the "tax base."

[2] Gift Tax—Payment and Return

The gift tax is payable by the donor,[5] although a donee can be liable for the tax where the donor fails to pay.[6] The gift tax is generally due on April 15 of the year following the gift, and the gift tax return (Form 709) is also generally due on that day.[7] However, an automatic extension of time for filing the gift tax return (but not for paying any gift tax due) is granted until the due date of the donor's income tax return (including extensions, if the donor checks the appropriate box on an application to extend the time for filing the donor's income tax return).[8] If a donor dies before a gift tax return reporting his or her gifts in a particular year is due, the executor of the donor's estate is responsible for filing the gift tax return and paying any gift tax due. In that case, the due date for filing the gift tax return and paying gift tax is the same as the due date (including extensions) for filing the donor's estate tax return if that falls earlier than the date the gift tax return would otherwise be due.[9]

---

[2] Adequate consideration is measured by the tax laws. The definition varies with the situation. The technical definition of the term often (but not always) matches its common-sense meaning.

[3] See Chapter 10 for a description of tax-free gifts.

[4] See Chapter 2 for a description.

[5] IRC § 2502(c).

[6] IRC § 6901.

[7] IRC §§ 6075(b)(1), 6151(a).

[8] IRC § 6075(b)(2).

[9] IRC § 6075(b)(3).

[3] Estate Tax—Payment and Return

The estate tax is payable by the executor of the estate,[10] and may be apportioned among various recipients of the property subject to the tax. Payment of the estate tax is required nine months after the date of death, unless an extension of time for payment is sought and granted.[11]

The estate tax return (generally, Form 706) is generally due nine months after date of death.[12] An extension for one six-month period for good cause shown may be granted.[13] Only executors who are abroad may be granted an *additional* extension of time to file the estate tax return.

For estate tax returns due after July 25, 2001, regulations generally allow an automatic six-month extension of time to file upon an estate's filing of a Form 4768, "Application for Extension of Time to File a Return and/or Pay U. S. Estate (and Generation-Skipping Transfer) Taxes."[14] The application for automatic extension must be filed with the IRS on or before the due date for the estate tax return,[15] and must include an estimate of the amount of estate tax and generation-skipping transfer tax due.[16] The automatic extension applies only to filers of Form 706.[17] Thus, estates filing Form 706-A, Form 706-D, or Form 706-NA still need to file Form 4768 to request a discretionary extension of time to file those returns. Individuals filing Form 706-QDT would be required to request additional time in accordance with the procedures set out in the instructions for that form.

[4] Transfer Tax Rate

Gift and estate taxes form the two parts of a "unified" transfer tax system. This means that these taxes are imposed at graduated rates on the cumulative amount of taxable transfers made by one person, counting transfers made both during life and at death.

The combined gift and estate tax rate tables for (a) the years 2002-2009, and (b) years beginning in 2011 are contained in Tables 1-A and 1-B to this

---

[10] IRC § 2002. Transferees are liable for estate tax that is unpaid. IRC §§ 6324(a)(2), 6901.

[11] Treas. Reg. § 20.6081-1(e).

[12] IRC §§ 6075(a), 6151(a).

[13] Treas. Reg. § 20.6081-1(a).

[14] Treas. Reg. §§ 20.6081-1(b), 20.6081-1(f).

[15] Treas. Reg. § 20.6081-1(b).

[16] Treas. Reg. § 20.6081-1(a). Note that the regulations do not elaborate on this estimate, so presumably, an estimate that later turns out to be inexact will not jeopardize the estate's qualification for the automatic extension.

[17] Treas. Reg. § 20.6081-1(b).

chapter. In the year 2010, the top gift tax rate will be 35 percent,[18] and there will be no estate tax.[19] If EGTRRA does *not* sunset after all, then the 2010 rules would also apply in years following 2010.

[a] Unified Gift and Estate Tax Credits

The "unified credit" (sometimes known as the "gift tax credit" or the "estate tax credit," as the case may be) allows an individual to make a certain amount of taxable transfers free of transfer tax.[20] What amount is this? It depends on the year in which the transfers are made, and the type of transfer. The amount increases over the period 2002 through 2009.

How the credits work. The gift and estate taxes technically start at 18 percent of the first dollar of taxable gifts, and are imposed at graduated rates as cumulative gifts grow higher.[21] For example, in 2002, the amount of transfer tax which would be due on the first $1,000,000 transferred before the unified credit is applied is $345,800; therefore, in 2002, the unified credit actually operates as a credit against gift and estate taxes of $345,800.[22] In technical terms, the amount of the unified credit in any year is the "applicable [gift or estate tax] credit amount."[23] The applicable credit amount is the amount of credit required to exclude a certain amount of transfers from transfer tax. The amount excluded is called the "applicable [gift or estate tax] exclusion amount."[24]

The amount of the applicable gift and estate tax exclusion amounts in the years 2001 forward is included in Table 1-C at ¶ 1.04[3].

Beginning in 2004, the applicable gift and estate tax exclusion amounts are not the same. The applicable estate tax exclusion amount increases as indicated in Table 1-C, at ¶ 1.04[3], while the gift tax exclusion amount remains at $1,000,000 for all years after 2001.[25]

The estate tax is repealed in 2010, and is reinstated in 2011 under 2001 rules.[26] Therefore, in 2011 and thereafter, the applicable gift and estate tax exclusion amount will be $1,000,000 (the amount to which the exclusion amount

---

[18] IRC § 2502.

[19] IRC § 2210(a).

[20] IRC §§ 2001, 2502, 2505.

[21] IRC §§ 2001(c), 2502.

[22] For a period before 1977, a $30,000 gift tax exemption was available. There is a small loss of unified credit (maximum $6,000) of 20 percent of any amount of the $30,000 exemption which was used in the period from September 9, 1976, through December 31, 1976. IRC §§ 2010(b), 2505(b).

[23] IRC § 2010(c).

[24] IRC § 2010(c).

[25] IRC § 2505(a)(1).

[26] IRC § 2210.

would have increased under 2001 law). If, however, Congress subsequently acts to prevent EGTRRA from sunsetting, the estate tax would be repealed in 2010 and thereafter, and the gift tax exclusion amount would remain at $1,000,000.

The applicable exclusion amounts are allowed in addition to tax-free gifts,[27] gifts which qualify for the marital or charitable deduction, gifts which are deducted from a decedent's estate as qualified family-owned business property,[28] and gifts of permanent qualified conservation property.[29] The applicable exclusion amounts are sometimes casually referred to as the gift or estate tax "exemptions."

> **EXAMPLE:** Mom gives $200,000 to Child. This transfer will use $200,000 of her gift tax exemption. This is the only taxable gift she ever makes. At her death, $800,000 of her taxable estate will pass free of estate tax if Mom dies in 2003.

Use of the unified credit on a taxable transfer is mandatory. That is, if a taxable transfer is made, any available unified credit must be applied against it.[30]

Effect of increases in the unified credit. Increases in the unified credit protect the entire increase in an applicable exclusion amount from transfer tax only to the extent that a person's additional gifts do not increase his cumulative gift tax bracket beyond the bracket containing the increased applicable exclusion amount (39 percent in 2002 through 2003). Hence, the increasing unified credit does not necessarily allow a person to transfer the increased exclusion amount tax-free.

> **EXAMPLE:** By the end of 2001, Dad has made $4,000,000 of taxable gifts, which puts him in the 50 percent gift tax bracket for 2002. Suppose Dad makes $325,000 of taxable gifts in 2002. Even though the tax exclusion amount increases by $325,000 in 2002, Dad's gift tax is $42,250: ($167,500 (50 percent of $325,000), less unused unified credit of $125,250 (additional unified credit resulting from the increase in the exempt amount from $675,000 to $1,000,000)).

[b] Taxable Transfers in Excess of the Unified Credit

After the unified gift or estate tax credit is used, gift or estate tax is imposed at graduated rates, ranging from:

---

[27] Discussed in Chapter 10.

[28] Qualified family-owned business property is discussed in Chapter 50.

[29] Permanent qualified conservation property is discussed in Chapter 50.

[30] Rev. Rul. 79-398, 1979-2 CB 338; Tech. Adv. Mem. 8132011 (Apr. 24, 1981).

- 41 percent on the amount of total transfers in excess of $1,000,000 and less than $1,250,000, to
- the maximum rate applicable to transfers in excess of the maximum-bracket amount.

The maximum rates and maximum-bracket amounts vary from year to year, and are set out in Table 1-C at ¶ 1.04[3].

For deaths occurring and gifts made in 2010, there will be a 60 percent tax rate for taxable transfers in excess of $10,000,000 but less than $17,184,000. This is the amount necessary to bring the transferor's total effective transfer tax rate to 55 percent, less the unified credit.[31] The "bubble" has the effect of phasing out the benefit of the graduated rate structure, completely eliminating it at the phase-out amount. Said another way, when a person's total taxable transfers have reached the phase-out amount, the cumulative gift and estate tax paid by that person during his lifetime and by his estate at his death will be a flat percent of his total taxable transfers, less the unified credit.[32]

Thus, if Mom makes taxable gifts of $17,184,000 in 2011, her tax calculation is:

$1,290,800	on first $3,000,000 (from table)
+ 7,801,200	55 percent of excess over $3,000,000
− 220,550	unified credit
+ 359,200	5 percent of $7,184,000
$9,230,650	

This calculation will result in a tax of 55 percent of the total amount of gifts, less the unified credit, if all gifts were made when the current rates applied. For example, Mom's tax liability of $9,230,650 is $17,184,000 (total gifts) × 0.55 tax rate, less $220,550 (unified credit).

[5] Transfer Tax Base

[a] Gift Tax Base

The gift tax base for a particular gift is the value of that gift, plus the total value of all taxable gifts previously made by the donor.[33]

---

[31] IRC §§ 2001(c)(2), 2505.

[32] More precisely, transfer tax would be 55 percent of the transfers if the current gift tax rates were applicable to all gifts included in the transfer tax base. Because gift tax rates were different in the past, the actual amount paid may not be exactly 55 percent of the total transfer tax base.

[33] IRC § 2502.

[b] Estate Tax Base

The estate tax base is the total value of all taxable gifts made by the decedent after 1976, plus the value of his taxable estate.[34]

[c] Critical Differences in Tax Bases

Gifts made before 1977 are included in the gift tax base, but not in the estate tax base. An even more critical distinction between the gift and estate tax bases also exists. The gift tax base consists only of property actually transferred to the recipient, and does not include money paid to the IRS as gift tax. The estate tax base includes both the property transferred to the recipient and the estate tax, and therefore is much more onerous.

This difference is not intuitively obvious. It results from the fact that the donor pays the gift tax in addition to the gift, and the executor pays the estate tax out of the transferred property. Hence, a donor paying 50 percent on a gift of $10,000,000 pays $5,000,000 tax for the privilege of transferring $10,000,000. An executor paying 55 percent on an estate of $10,000,000 pays $5,000,000 in order to transfer $5,000,000.[35]

In technical terminology, the gift tax is "tax-exclusive," and the estate tax is "tax-inclusive."

[6] Gift Tax Calculation

Here is the four-step formula for calculating gift tax for gifts made after 2001 —

Step one. Use the combined gift and estate tax rate table to calculate a tentative tax on the gift tax base, including the current gift.[36]

Step two. Use the combined rate table to calculate a tentative tax on gifts made in prior years, including the generation-skipping transfer tax on direct skips, as if the current rate table applied. Only for gifts made after 2010, add a surtax of 5 percent of the amount of the gift tax base that ex-

---

[34] IRC § 2001(b)(2). Gifts which are included in the taxable estate are not included again as taxable gifts in the estate tax computation. IRC § 2001(b). See Chapter 2 for a description of taxable gifts that are included in the taxable estate.

[35] See Chapter 8 for a thorough discussion of the ramifications of the difference in bases.

[36] IRC § 2502(a)(1). If any generation-skipping transfer tax was or is payable on gifts that were direct skips, (explained in ¶ 1.03[1][a]), include the amount of the generation-skipping transfer tax in the amounts of the gifts. Only for gifts made after 2010, add a surtax of 5 percent of the amount of the gift tax base that exceeds $10,000,000 and does not exceed $17,184,000. IRC § 2001(c)(2).

ceeds $10,000,000 and does not exceed $17,184,000.[37] (Do not use the gift tax actually paid, which may or may not match the tentative tax resulting from use of the current table.)

Step three. Subtract the tentative tax on prior taxable gifts from the tentative tax on the current gift tax base (that is, subtract the number calculated in step two from the number calculated in step one).[38]

Step four. Subtract the donor's remaining gift tax credit[39] from that number.[40]

Voilà—the result is the amount of the gift tax.

Note: The effect of the calculation is that the current gift is taxed as the last gift when the graduated rates are applied to the total gift tax base.

> **EXAMPLE:** Stephanie has made no taxable gifts. In 2000, she makes gifts of $500,000, and therefore uses $155,800[41] of her unified credit. In 2003, she makes taxable gifts of $750,000, bringing her total gift tax base to $1,250,000. How is the tax computed for 2003?

Step one:	Tentative tax on $1,250,000[a]	$448,300
Step two:	Less tentative tax on $500,000[b]	(155,800)
Step three:	Tentative tax on 2002 gift	$292,500
Step four:	Less unused gift tax credit	(190,000)
	Gift Tax Due	$102,500

[a] From tax table in Table 1-A at ¶ 1.04[1].
[b] From tax table in Table 1-A at ¶ 1.04[1].

[7] Estate Tax Calculation

Here is the four-step formula for computing the estate tax for decedents dying after 2001—

---

[37] IRC § 2001(c)(2).

[38] IRC § 2502(a).

[39] The remaining gift credit is the applicable gift tax exclusion amount, less previous taxable gifts. The gift tax credit is further adjusted for gifts made in late 1976, if the reduction described in note 10 applies. IRC § 2502.

[40] IRC § 2505.

[41] From tax table in Table 1-A at ¶ 1.04[1].

Step one. Use the combined gift and estate tax rate table to calculate a tentative tax on the sum of the taxable estate and the taxable gifts made after 1976 (other than gifts included in the taxable estate).[42]

Step two. Calculate gift taxes payable on taxable gifts (including generation-skipping transfer tax payable on direct skips) made after 1976 (other than gifts included in the taxable estate), using the rate table existing at date of death.[43] The gift tax payable under the existing table is the correct number to use, even if the gift taxes actually paid were a different number.[44]

Step three. Subtract the number calculated in step two from the tentative tax on the estate tax base calculated in step one.[45]

Step four. Subtract the full estate tax credit for the year of death[46] and any other available credits[47] from that number.[48] Subtract the unified credit even if it was wholly or partly used during lifetime. (This is because the taxable gifts sheltered by the credit during life are all added to the estate tax base; to make things come out even, any credit previously used must also be allowed.)

EXAMPLE: Mom made taxable gifts of $750,000 in 1996. Mom dies in 2002. Her estate is $1,250,000. Calculation of estate tax:

Step one:	$1,250,000	Estate
	+ 750,000	Taxable Gifts
	$2,000,000	
	$ 780,800	Tentative Tax on $2,000,000[a]
Step two:	Taxable Gifts	$750,000
	Tax on $750,000	$248,300

---

[42] IRC § 2001(b)(1). Generation-skipping transfer tax payable on lifetime direct skips are added to the amount of the gift. Only for decedents dying after 2010, add a surtax of 5 percent of the amount of the estate tax base that exceeds $10,000,000 and does not exceed $17,184,000. IRC § 2001(c)(2).

[43] IRC § 2001(b)(2). Pre-1977 gifts are taken into account in determining the amount of gift tax payable on post-1976 gifts. Tech. Adv. Mem. 9642001 (Nov. 30, 1994).

[44] Only for decedents dying after 2010, add a surtax of 5 percent of the amount of the post-1976 gift tax base that exceeds $10,000,000 and does not exceed the $17,184,000. IRC § 2001(c)(2).

[45] IRC § 2001(b).

[46] Or, the reduced estate tax credit if the reduction described in note 10 applies.

[47] Credits against estate tax include: the unified credit, IRC § 2010; the credit for state death taxes, IRC § 2011; the credit for tax on prior transfers, IRC § 2013; the credit for foreign death taxes, IRC § 2014; and, the credit for death taxes on remainders, IRC § 2015. The only credit against gift tax is the unified credit. IRC § 2505.

[48] IRC §§ 2010–2015.

	Less Unified Credit	345,800
	Tax on Taxable Gifts	$ -0-
Step three:	Step one	$780,800
	Step two	- -0-
		$780,800
	Unified Credit	-345,800
		$435,000

Proof: The table tax on $2,000,000 of transfers is $780,800 – $345,800, or $435,000. Mom's tax on $2,000,000 of taxable transfers is $-0- + $780,800, or $780,800.

ᵃ From tax table in Table 1-A at ¶ 1.04[1].
ᵇ From tax table in Table 1-A at ¶ 1.04[1].

The effect of the calculation is that the taxable estate is calculated as the last transfer when the graduated rates are applied to all taxable transfers made by the decedent after 1976.

EXAMPLE: In 1999, Carolyn had made no taxable gifts. In 2000, she made taxable gifts of $500,000, using $155,800[49] of her unified credit. She dies in 2003 with a $750,000 estate. Assume that no credits are available except the unified credit.

Step one:	Tentative tax on $1,250,000ᵃ	$448,300
Step two:	Less gift tax payable on $500,000	-0-
Step three:	Tentative tax on estate	448,300
Step four:	Less unified creditᵇ	(345,800)
	Estate Tax Due	$102,500

ᵃ From tax table in Table 1-A at ¶ 1.04[1].
ᵇ As explained in ¶ 1.02[1][a], the unified credit for 2003 is $345,800.

The calculation may be more complicated if certain fact patterns exist involving gifts that (1) were actually made by one spouse, but were treated for tax purposes as made one-half by each spouse and (2) are included in either spouse's estate.[50]

[8] Distinction With a Difference

If the two tax numbers in the gift tax and estate tax examples involving total taxable transfers of $1,250,000 turned out the same, why is the estate tax more onerous? In the gift tax example, Stephanie's recipient actually got $1,250,000. The gift tax was imposed on Stephanie. The $102,500 tax in the estate tax ex-

---

[49] From tax table in Table 1-A at ¶ 1.04[1].
[50] These fact patterns are discussed in Chapter 8.

ample was imposed on Carolyn's taxable estate, so that her beneficiaries actually received $1,147,500. So—the same amount of tax is due for a different amount transferred, depending on whether the transfer is made by gift or by an estate transfer.[51]

¶ 1.03 GENERATION-SKIPPING TRANSFER TAX

Before the generation-skipping transfer tax (GSTT) was enacted, wealthy families used generation-skipping trusts to transfer huge amounts of property free of estate or gift tax. The GSTT was enacted in 1986 for the purpose of curtailing this practice. It is imposed on "generation-skipping transfers" (GSTs). It is a separate tax, imposed independently of, and in addition to, gift and estate taxes. The transfers to which it applies may or may not be transfers which are also subject to estate or gift tax.

The generation-skipping transfer tax is repealed in the year 2010, and thereafter if EGTRRA does not sunset.[52] The following subsection applies to transfers occurring in years 2002–2009, as well as 2011 and thereafter if EGTRRA sunsets in accordance with its current provisions.

[1] Generation-Skipping Transfers

There are three types of GSTs—"direct skips," "taxable distributions," and "taxable terminations." These transfers will be explained by example. Let's say Mom is in the first generation, Child is in the second generation, and Grandchild is in the third generation.

[a] Direct Skips

GSTT applies to a taxable transfer[53] by Mom to a person in Grandchild's generation or below (a skip person).[54] This kind of transfer is called a "direct skip."[55] For example, if Mom writes a check to Grandchild, she makes a direct skip.

---

[51] Opportunities created by this difference are explained in Chapter 8.

[52] IRC § 2664.

[53] Defined in ¶ 1.02.

[54] IRC §§ 2601, 2611(a)(3), 2612(c).

[55] IRC § 2612(c).

A direct skip will always be a transfer for gift or estate tax purposes, although it will not necessarily be a transfer which actually generates a gift or estate tax.

> **EXAMPLE:** Mom gives $11,000 to a trust for Grandchild's sole benefit. The gift is a direct skip, even if it qualifies for the gift tax annual exclusion, or if it is a taxable gift on which no gift tax is payable due to use of the gift tax credit.

GSTT on a direct skip by gift is paid by the transferor.[56] If the direct skip is made from a trust or trust equivalent, the trustee or trustee-equivalent is liable for the tax.[57] Generally, if the GST occurs as a result of the death of the transferor, the GSTT is paid by the transferor's executor.[58] It is apportioned to the property included in the direct skip, unless the transferor otherwise directs.[59] The tax on a direct skip by gift is due on April 15 of the year after the gift is made.[60] The tax on a direct skip by estate transfer is due when the estate tax is due.[61] In the case of a direct skip by gift, the GSTT is added to the amount of the gift for purposes of the gift tax.[62]

[b] Taxable Distributions and Taxable Terminations

These terms refer, generally speaking, to transfers from trusts.[63] For GSTT purposes, a person has an "interest in a trust" at a particular time if that person is permitted to receive distributions from the trust at the time in question.

Suppose Mom establishes a trust. The GSTT will generally apply to a distribution from the trust to any beneficiary in Grandchild's generation or below, if anyone in any older generation can receive distributions at the time. Such a distribution is called a "taxable distribution." The GSTT would also generally apply to the termination of an interest of a beneficiary in Child's generation

---

[56] IRC § 2603(a)(3); Treas. Reg. § 26.2662-1(c)(1)(iii).

[57] IRC § 2603(b)(2); Treas. Reg. §§ 26.2662-1(c)(1)(iv), 26.2662-1(c)(vi), example 2.

[58] Treas. Reg. § 26.2662-1(c)(1)(v); but see Treas. Reg. § 26.2662-1(c)(2) with respect to liability for GSTT when property is held in a trust arrangement (such as life insurance) on the date of death of the transferor.

[59] IRC § 2603(b); Treas. Reg. § 26.2662-2(c)(v).

[60] IRC §§ 6075(b)(1), 6151(a); Treas. Reg. § 26.2662-1(d)(1)(i).

[61] IRC § 6151(a); Treas. Reg. § 26.2662-1(d)(1)(i).

[62] IRC § 2515.

[63] Transfers from "trust equivalents" are also included. IRC § 2652(b)(1). These include legal life estates and other arrangements similar to trusts.

or above, if the remaining current beneficiaries are in younger generations. This termination would be called a "taxable termination."[64]

> **EXAMPLE:** If Mom creates a trust which can distribute to both Child and Grandchild during their lifetimes, both Child and Grandchild hold interests in the trust. A distribution to Grandchild during Child's life is a taxable distribution. The death of Child during Grandchild's life is a taxable termination.

A taxable distribution or taxable termination will generally not be a taxable transfer for gift or estate tax purposes.[65] The gift or estate tax transfer will usually have been made on the initial transfer to the trust or at some later point.

The tax on a taxable distribution is paid by the recipient.[66] It is due on April 15 of the year after the taxable distribution.[67] If the trust pays the tax, the trustee is making an additional taxable distribution.[68] The tax on a taxable termination is paid by the trust.[69] It is due on April 15 of the year after the taxable termination.[70]

[2] GST Tax Calculation

The tax is calculated by multiplying the tax rate times the tax base.

[a] GST Tax Rate

The GSTT is imposed on each taxable transfer at a rate equal to the top estate tax rate in the year of transfer.[71]

[b] GST Tax Base

The tax on direct skips, like the gift tax, is tax-exclusive. It is imposed on the amount of property actually transferred to the recipient.[72] The tax on taxable distributions and taxable terminations, like the estate tax, is tax-inclusive. It

---

[64] IRC §§ 2601, 2611(a)(1), 2611(a)(2), 2612(a), 2612(b).

[65] See Chapter 5 for certain exceptions.

[66] IRC § 2603(a)(1).

[67] IRC § 6151(a); Treas. Reg. § 26.2662-1(d)(1)(ii).

[68] IRC § 2621(b).

[69] IRC § 2603(a)(3).

[70] IRC § 6151(a); Treas. Reg. § 26.2662-1(d)(1)(ii).

[71] IRC §§ 2001, 2602, 2641.

[72] IRC § 2623.

is imposed on the value of property actually distributed to, or remaining in trust for, the skip persons, plus the tax.[73]

[3] GSTT Exemption

Each individual is allocated an exemption from GSTT. The GSTT exemption was $1,000,000 in 1999, and is indexed annually for inflation.[74] The indexed amount for transfers made in 2002 is $1,100,000.[75] The exemption will continue to be indexed through 2003. For transfers occurring in 2004 through 2009, the exemption will be the same as the applicable estate tax exclusion amount.[76] The GSTT is repealed for transfers made in 2010 and thereafter,[77] subject to sunsetting of EGTRRA in 2011.[78] See further discussion in Chapters 1 and 5 of this treatise.

Each individual can allocate his exemption to whatever transfers he chooses.[79]

[4] Grandfathered Trusts

Certain transfers from trusts that were irrevocable on September 25, 1985, are grandfathered from the GSTT. The same is true of direct skips occurring at death and certain transfers from trusts which are included in the taxable estate of a person who was mentally incompetent to change the disposition of his property on October 22, 1986, and never regained his competence.[80]

---

[73] See Chapter 5 for a detailed explanation. The calculations are similar to those for the gift and estate taxes, discussed at ¶ 1.02[3] above. IRC §§ 2603, 2621, 2622.

[74] IRC § 2631(c).

[75] Rev. Proc. 2001-59, 2001-52 IRB 623.

[76] IRC § 2631(c). See Table 1-C at ¶ 1.04[3].

[77] IRC § 2664.

[78] EGTRRA § 901 (sunsetting provision).

[79] IRC § 2631(c). The exemption and its allocation are discussed in Chapter 5.

[80] Tax Reform Act of 1986, Pub. L. No. 99-514, § 1433(b)(2)(C), 100 Stat. 2085, 2731 (1986), amended by Technical and Miscellaneous Revenue Act of 1988, Pub. L. No. 100-647, § 1014(h)(2), 102 Stat. 3342, 3567 (1988). The grandfather rules, as part of a more complete analysis of the GSTT, are discussed in Chapter 5.

¶ 1.04 REFERENCE MATERIALS

[1] Table 1-A: Gift and Estate Tax Rates—2002 through 2009

The following table applies to 2002 through 2009.[81]

If the amount with respect to which the tentative tax to be computed is:	The tentative tax is:
Not over $10,000	18 percent of such amount
Over 10,000 but not over $20,000	$1,800, plus 20 percent of the excess of such amount over $10,000.
Over 20,000 but not over $40,000	$3,800, plus 22 percent of the excess of such amount over $20,000.
Over 40,000 but not over $60,000	$8,200, plus 24 percent of the excess of such amount over $40,000.
Over 60,000 but not over $80,000	$13,000, plus 26 percent of the excess of such amount over $60,000.
Over 80,000 but not over $100,000	$18,200, plus 28 percent of the excess of such amount over $80,000.
Over 100,000 but not over $150,000	$23,800, plus 30 percent of the excess of such amount over $100,000.
Over 150,000 but not over $250,000	$38,800, plus 32 percent of the excess of such amount over $150,000.
Over 250,000 but not over $500,000	$70,800, plus 34 percent of the excess of such amount over $250,000.
Over 500,000 but not over $750,000	$155,800, plus 37 percent of the excess of such amount over $500,000.
Over 750,000 but not over $1,000,000	$248,300, plus 39 percent of the excess of such amount over $750,000.
Over 1,000,000 but not over $1,250,000	$345,800, plus 41 percent of the excess of such amount over $1,000,000.
Over 1,250,000 but not over $1,500,000	$448,300, plus 43 percent of the excess of such amount over $1,250,000.
Over 1,500,000 but not over $2,000,000	$555,800, plus 45 percent of the excess of such amount over $1,500,000.
Over 2,000,000 but not over $2,500,000	$780,800, plus 49 percent of the excess of such amount over $2,000,000.
Over 2,500,000	$1,025,800, plus 50 percent of the excess of such amount over $2,500,000.

---

[81] IRC § 2001(c)(1).

Beginning in 2003, the tentative tax will be adjusted to reflect the decreasing top tax rates for cumulative transfers over $2,000,000.[82]

[2] Table 1-B: Gift and Estate Tax Rates—2011 and Thereafter

The following table applies for transfers made in 2001, as well as 2011 and thereafter if EGTRRA sunsets:

Column A	Column B	Column C	Column D
Taxable amount over—	Taxable amount not over—	Tax on amount in Column A	Rate of tax on excess over amount in Column A
$ —	$ 10,000	$ —	18%
10,000	20,000	1,800	20%
20,000	40,000	3,800	22%
40,000	60,000	8,200	24%
60,000	80,000	13,000	26%
80,000	100,000	18,200	28%
100,000	150,000	23,800	30%
150,000	250,000	38,800	32%
250,000	500,000	70,800	34%
500,000	750,000	155,800	37%
750,000	1,000,000	248,300	39%
1,000,000	1,250,000	345,800	41%
1,250,000	1,500,000	448,300	43%
1,500,000	2,000,000	555,800	45%
2,000,000	2,500,000	780,800	49%
2,500,000	3,000,000	1,025,800	53%
3,000,000	10,000,000	1,290,800	55%
10,000,000	17,184,000	5,140,800	60%
17,184,000	—	9,451,200	55%

[3] Table 1-C: Selected Transfer Tax Rates and Exemption for 2001 and Thereafter

---

[82] IRC § 2001(c)(2).

Year	Estate Tax Maximum Rate	Gift Tax Maximum Rate[a]	Flat Rate GSTT[b]	Maximum Estate and Gift Rates Begin When Cumulative Taxable Transfers Exceed	Estate Tax Exemptions[c]	Gift Tax Exemption	Generation-Skipping Transfer Tax Exemption
2001	%[d] 55	55% (35.48%)[e]	55% (35.48%)	$3,000,000	$ 675,000	$ 675,000	$1,060,000
2002	50%	50% (33.33%)	50% (33.33%)	$2,500,000	$1,000,000	$1,000,000	$1,100,000
2003	49%	49% (32.89%)	49% (32.89%)	$2,000,000	$1,000,000	$1,000,000	$1,100,000 adjusted for inflation from 2002
2004	48%	48% (32.43%)	48% (32.43%)	$2,000,000	$1,500,000	$1,000,000	$1,500,000
2005	47%	47% (31.97%)	47% (31.97%)	$2,000,000	$1,500,000	$1,000,000	$1,500,000
2006	46%	46% (32.57%)	46% (32.57%)	$2,000,000	$2,000,000	$1,000,000	$2,000,000
2007	45%	45% (31.03%)	45% (31.03%)	$1,500,000	$2,000,000	$1,000,000	$2,000,000
2008	45%	45% (31.03%)	45% (31.03%)	$1,500,000	$2,000,000	$1,000,000	$2,000,000
2009	45%	45% (31.03%).	45% (31.03%)	$1,500,000	$3,500,000	$1,000,000	$3,500,000
2010	-0-	35%	35%	N/A	N/A	$1,000,000	N/A
2011 and following years	%[c] 55	55% (35.48%)[d]	55% (35.48%)	$3,000,000	$1,000,000	$1,000,000	$1,100,000, adjusted for inflation from 2002

[a] Although gift tax rates are nominally the same as estate tax rates, gift tax rates are actually much less, since the estate tax is imposed on the transferred amount plus the tax, and the gift tax is imposed on the transferred amount only. Nominal rates are on the top. Rates computed on the same basis as the estate tax rate are in parentheses.

[b] Simplistically—Rates not in parentheses apply to distributions from, and terminations in favor of, a grandchild-level beneficiary from a trust which includes an older-generation beneficiary. Rates in parentheses apply to transfers directly to a grandchild-level beneficiary or a trust for a grandchild-level beneficiary. "Grandchild-level" means the generation of a grandchild or more remote descendant.

[c] The estate tax exempt amount is the applicable number below, less taxable gifts made during the deceased person's lifetime, and certain administrative expenses occurring at death.

[d] 60 percent for cumulative transfers between $10,000,000 and $17,184,000.

[e] 60 percent (37.5 percent) for cumulative transfers between $10,000,000 and $17,184,000.

CHAPTER 2

Taxable Gifts and the Taxable Estate

¶ 2.01 INTRODUCTION

Gift taxes are imposed on taxable gifts. Estate taxes are imposed on items included in a decedent's taxable estate. Both "taxable gift" and "taxable estate" are terms of art. Taxable estate means the "gross estate," less estate tax deductions.

¶ 2.02 GIFTS

A gift generally includes any property transferred during the donor's lifetime for less than adequate consideration.[1]

[1] General Rule

Adequate consideration generally means the fair market value of transferred property. The fair market value of the property is the price at which the property would change hands between a willing buyer and a willing seller, neither being under any compulsion to buy or to sell, and both having knowledge of relevant facts.[2] Thus, if Mom sells Blackacre to Child for $100, and Blackacre is actually worth $250, Mom has made a gift to Child of $150.[3]

---

[1] IRC § 2511.

[2] Treas. Reg. § 25.2512-1.

[3] Treas. Reg. § 25.2512-8.

While, in many cases, it will not take a rocket scientist to decide whether a gift has been made, sometimes the determination is much more complicated. For example, certain exceptions to the common-sense understanding of value and adequate consideration exist, and there is inherent uncertainty in valuation of many kinds of property.

[2] Special Rules on Valuation and Consideration

[a] Failure to Pursue Advantages

In 1984, the United States Supreme Court held that the failure to charge adequate interest on a demand loan constituted a continuing gift in each year that the loan remained outstanding.[4] The *Dickman* case, in which the Court made this holding, was statutorily superseded with respect to loans of money.[5] However, it still forms the basis of numerous IRS positions that failure to pursue certain advantages results in a gift. Some examples of deemed gifts follow.

[i] **Inadequate interest on loans.** If Mom simply lends money to Son interest-free or sells property to Son using a low interest rate on any purchase-money indebtedness, her failure to charge adequate interest is a gift in many circumstances. Adequate interest is defined by statute; however, its precise meaning in any given circumstance varies with the situation.[6]

[ii] **Failure to exercise business rights.** The failure to exercise ownership rights in a business may or may not be considered a gift, depending on the circumstances. For instance, is the failure to exercise rights related to equity subject to the same analysis as failure to charge adequate interest on a loan? This question was addressed by the Tax Court in the *Snyder*[7] case. In *Snyder*, a woman held Class A preferred stock, which carried a seven percent noncumulative dividend. The Class A stock was convertible to Class B preferred stock, which had a seven percent cumulative dividend and additional rights (including the right to redeem the preferred stock for a note in the amount of the stock's par value plus accumulated dividends). The Tax Court held that

---

[4] Dickman v. Comm'r, 465 US 330 (1984).

[5] IRC § 7872.

[6] IRC §§ 483, 1272, 7872. Interest-free and no-interest loans and installment sales are discussed further in Chs. 28 (loans) and 30 (sales).

[7] Snyder v. Comm'r, 93 TC 529, 546-547 (1989); see also Tech. Adv. Mem. 8726005 (Mar. 13, 1987) (IRS advised that failure to convert nonparticipating preferred stock to common stock was a gift when the corporation's contractual financing documents prohibited it from paying dividends for a substantial period).

the woman's annual failures to convert her Class A preferred stock to Class B preferred stock constituted continuing gifts to the common shareholders in the amount of the preferred dividends that could have been paid by the corporation or accumulated to pay the redemption price, less dividends actually paid. The IRS unsuccessfully took the position in this case that the taxpayer's failure to convert her stock and redeem the cumulative preferred stock for a note was a gift in the amount of the foregone interest that she could have earned on the note if she had redeemed the stock.

Importantly, the Tax Court held that, as a general matter, the *Dickman*[8] holding cannot be directly applied to an equity instrument, because an equity investor ordinarily does not have rights analogous to those of a lender. This would appear to indicate that the failure of a controlling stockholder to cause dividends on his stock to be paid would not necessarily result in a gift.

The IRS, however, has taken the position that a failure to exercise a right to purchase stock under a buy-sell agreement,[9] or to compel a controlled corporation to pay a noncumulative dividend on the controlling shareholder's preferred stock,[10] is a gift.[11]

[b] Marital Rights

Relinquishment of spousal rights generally does not constitute consideration for transfer tax purposes.[12]

EXAMPLE: Husband transfers $100,000 to a trust for Wife in exchange for her surrender of her spousal right to support. The couple remain married. The transfer is a gift, even if her support rights are actually worth $100,000.

However, a transfer made to a spouse or former spouse in settlement of marital or property rights or for reasonable child support for minor children is considered made for adequate consideration, provided that it occurs pur-

---

[8] 465 US 330 (1984) (discussed above).

[9] Priv. Ltr. Rul. 9117035 (Jan. 25, 1991). Son had a first refusal right to purchase Dad's shares for $1,370.45 per share. He intended to forego that right and allow an ESOP to purchase Dad's shares for their actual fair market value of $5,502.49 per share. The IRS position was that the Son's failure to purchase Dad's stock for the option price was a gift to Dad of the difference between the ESOP's purchase price and the option price, where Son's financial position would have enabled him to purchase the stock.

[10] E.g., Tech. Adv. Memo. 8723007 (Feb. 18, 1987) (reasoning that, even if there were sufficient business reasons not to declare dividends, he could have taken subordinated debt of the corporation instead) and Tech. Adv. Mem. 8403010 (Sept. 30, 1983).

[11] The results in these rulings are questionable. The purpose of including them here is not to indicate that they are correct, but to indicate the types of transactions attacked by the IRS as gifts by failure to exercise rights.

[12] IRC § 2043(b)(1); Treas. Reg. § 25.2512-8.

suant to a written property settlement agreement which is entered into within one year before or two years after a divorce or legal separation.[13]

> EXAMPLE: Pursuant to a written property settlement agreement entered into within a year of divorce, ex-wife pays ex-husband $2,000/month for the support of their 14-year old son. This payment is not a gift if the amount is reasonable.

> EXAMPLE: Pursuant to a written property settlement agreement entered into within a year of divorce, Carol transfers an interest in the family business to her 30-year old son. This is a gift.

[c] Actuarial Interests

Actuarial tables published by the Treasury Department are generally used to value interests that are limited in time, such as life estates and interests for a term of years.[14] If the actuarial tables apply, they conclusively establish the value of the time-limited interest, regardless of the actual facts.

> EXAMPLE: Uncle gives Niece a life estate in Blackacre. Niece is 50 years old, but she has an illness causing her actual life expectancy to be three years. Her life estate will be valued according to the tables. If the applicable interest rate is 10 percent, a life estate for a 50-year old would be worth 84.743 percent of the value of the entire property; an interest for a term of three years would be worth 24.8685 percent of the property. Hence, if the property is worth $100,000, Uncle will be treated as giving Niece a gift of $84,743, even though her life expectancy predicts that she will actually receive only $24,868.50.

The news here is not all bad. Whenever an artificial rule varies from the actual facts, danger generally exists of falling on the wrong side of an arbitrary line. However, opportunity usually also exists for positioning on the right side of the line. For example, in this case, if Niece makes a gift to a friend of a remainder interest to take effect after her death, she will make a gift that is actually worth much more than its taxable value.[15]

[d] Gift Exclusions

Certain gifts are excluded from the tax base. These are primarily the annual exclusion of $10,000 per donee per year, and certain tuition and medical payments.[16]

---

[13] IRC §§ 2043(b)(2), 2516.

[14] Treas. Reg. § 25.2512-5.

[15] Opportunities to take advantage of the actuarial valuation rules are discussed in Ch. 11.

[16] IRC § 2503(b), (e). Tax-free gifts are discussed in Ch. 10.

[e] Chapter 14 Transfers

In certain situations, a transferor may be deemed to make a taxable gift when there is no actual gift or may be deemed to make a more valuable taxable gift than he is in fact making. These special rules are contained in Chapter 14 of the Internal Revenue Code. They apply to—

Retained interests in businesses. If a person transfers common stock, or an equivalent interest in a business entity, and he or his spouse or ancestors retain a preferred interest in the entity, the Chapter 14 rules may apply.[17]

Retained interests in trusts. If a person transfers an interest in a trust, and he or his spouse or ancestors retain certain types of interests in the trust, the rules may apply.[18]

Property subject to buy-sell agreements or other restrictions. The rules may apply to certain buy-sell agreements and restrictions on the sale and use of property which are not consistent with arm's-length transactions.[19]

Lapsing rights and restrictions on liquidation. The rules apply to certain lapses of rights in business entities, and to some transfers of interests in business entities, if those entities have certain restrictions on liquidation of a person's interest in the entity, and/or certain restrictions on liquidation of the entity itself.[20]

[f] Exercise, Release, or Lapse of a General Power of Appointment

A general power of appointment is the power in Person A to transfer property of another (usually a trust) to himself, his creditors, his estate, or creditors of his estate without adequate consideration. If the holder of a general power of appointment over property transfers the property to another person, releases the power, or allows the power to lapse, he may make a taxable gift.[21]

[g] Gift Made by an Agent

The IRS should respect a gift made by an agent if the gift was authorized under the power of attorney and state law.[22] State law may require the power of attorney to specifically grant the agent authority to make gifts of the

---

The $10,000 annual exclusion is indexed, beginning in 1999. IRC § 2503(b)(2). See Ch. 10 for further discussion.

[17] IRC § 2701. This is further explained in Ch. 31.

[18] IRC § 2702. This is further discussed in Part V.

[19] IRC § 2703. This is discussed in detail in Ch. 27.

[20] IRC § 2704. These are discussed in Ch. 26.

[21] IRC § 2514. Powers of appointment are discussed in greater detail in Ch. 3.

[22] Tech. Adv. Memo. 9513001 (Nov. 28, 1994).

principal's property and, if a gift is made to the agent, the authority to make a gift of the principal's property to the agent.

[h] Net Gift

Sometimes, a gift is made, subject to the condition that the donee pay the gift tax. In such a case, the amount of the gift is the gross amount transferred, less the gift tax owed by the donee. The transfer is treated for income tax purposes as a sale, resulting in a gain if the amount of gift tax for which the donee agrees to be liable exceeds the basis of the property transferred.[23]

> EXAMPLE: Dad gives Blackacre to Son, on condition that Son pay the gift tax. Blackacre has a value of $100, and a basis of zero. If Dad is in the 55 percent gift tax bracket, the gift tax payable on the transfer will be $35.48.[24] Dad will also have a taxable gain of $35.48, resulting in capital gains tax at 28 percent of $9.93. Here, $35.48 = (.55/$1.55) ($100). Algebraically, the formula for determining the amount of the net gift tax is: net gift tax = [gift tax rate/(1 + gift tax rate)] (gross gift). Here, $35.48 = [(.55/$1.55) ($100)].

[3] Complete and Incomplete Gifts

For transfer tax purposes, a gift occurs only when the gift is complete. The exact time a gift is complete is important. For instance, the value of a gift is determined on the date that the gift occurs. Various other tax provisions relate to the time of a gift (e.g., the availability of the $10,000 annual exclusion for gifts made within a calendar year, or the inclusion of gift taxes in the estate with respect to a gift made within three years of death).

Certain retained powers will render a gift incomplete.[25] For example, if a person transfers property in trust, but retains a power to determine who will actually receive the property, the gift is incomplete, and will not be considered a taxable event until it is complete.[26] The gift might be completed, for ex-

---

[23] Diedrich v. Comm'r, 457 US 191, 194-200 (1982), aff'g 643 F2d 499 (9th Cir. 1981).

[24] $100 value of Blackacre less $35.48 tax = $64.52 received by donee. Fifty-five percent × $64.52 = $35.48. Decimals are rounded.

The capital gains rates have been changed for certain sales. IRC § 1(h). See Ch. 6 for discussion.

The $10,000 annual exclusion is indexed, beginning in 1999. IRC § 2503(b)(2). See Ch. 10 for further discussion.

[25] Treas. Reg. § 25.2511-2.

[26] Treas. Reg. §§ 25.2511-2(b), 25.2511-2(c). There is an exception for a power limited by a fixed or ascertainable standard (such as the health, support, education, or maintenance of the permissible distributees). Treas. Reg. §§ 25.2511-2(b), 25.2511-2(c), Treas. Reg. § 25.2511-2(g).

ample, by a distribution of the property to a beneficiary.[27]

¶ 2.03 TAXABLE ESTATE

The composition of a person's "estate" depends on what kind of estate is under consideration—the "probate estate," or the "gross estate." The gross estate includes both the probate estate and certain nonprobate assets. The "taxable estate" means the gross estate, less applicable estate tax deductions.

[1] Probate Estate

The probate estate consists of the deceased owner's property which, under applicable state law, is subject to the probate process. The disposition of this property is determined by the deceased owner's will. If the will does not dispose of it, or the owner dies without a will, the property will pass by the laws of intestacy.

> EXAMPLE: Carol owns a share of stock, which is registered in her name. On Carol's death, the share will be a probate asset.

"Nonprobate assets" are assets which are not subject to probate proceedings.[28] The disposition of these items is not determined by the deceased owner's will (unless the estate is the beneficiary); rather, it is generally determined by beneficiary designation or form of title. For example—

Nonprobate Asset	Disposition on Death of Owner
Life insurance	Beneficiary designation governs
Retirement plan, including IRA, § 401(k) plan, pension or profit-sharing plan, nonqualified plan	Beneficiary designation or plan provision governs
Asset held as joint tenant with right of survivorship	Surviving joint tenant takes
Payable on death account	Named payee takes
Nominal trust account (a type of bank account title—no actual trust)	Named beneficiary takes
Revocable trust	Trust instrument governs
Tenancy by the entirety (special form of joint tenancy between spouses)	Surviving spouse takes

---

[27] Treas. Reg. § 25.2511-2(f).

[28] Aspects of nontestamentary transfers are discussed in Ch. 7.

[2] Gross Estate

The "gross estate" means the assets which are considered part of a decedent's estate for federal estate tax purposes. It includes assets that are subject to the probate process, as well as some assets that are not subject to probate, and may even include property that the decedent did not own. A list of the types of includable property follows.

[a] Section 2033: Property Owned by the Decedent at Death

Property which the decedent owned is generally included in the gross estate.[29] Few people find this surprising. Thus, if Carol owns a share of stock when she dies, the share is included in her gross estate.

If a minor or incapacitated plaintiff dies, are tort settlements paid on account of his death in trust or annuity form or to a next friend for his benefit includable in the plaintiff's estate? Such items have been held includable where the plaintiff and his estate were the sole beneficiaries.[30] Wrongful death proceeds, which are not attributable to pain and suffering or reimbursement for medical expenses, are not generally includable in a decedent's estate. This is because the wrongful death action does not generally arise until after the decedent's death, and the proceeds accrue to the survivors, even if the decedent's will determines who takes.[31]

[b] Section 2042: Life Insurance

The proceeds of life insurance are included in the insured's gross estate under two circumstances.

[i] Section 2042(1): Proceeds are payable to the insured's estate. If the insured's estate is a beneficiary of the policy, the proceeds payable to the estate will be included in the gross estate.[32]

[ii] Section 2042(2): Insured has incidents of ownership in the policy. Regardless of the identity of the beneficiary, the proceeds will be included in the insured's gross estate if the insured possessed any of the incidents of ownership of the policy at his death, either alone or with another person.[33]

---

[29] IRC § 2033.

[30] Arrington v. United States, 34 Fed. Cl. 144 (1995), aff'd, 79 AFTR2d 97-1341, 97-1 USTC ¶ 60,260 (Fed. Cir. 1997).

[31] Rev. Rul. 75-127, 1975-1 CB 297; Priv. Ltr. Rul. 9622035 (Mar. 4, 1996).

[32] IRC § 2042(1).

[33] IRC § 2042(2).

This is true even if another person was the policy owner, according to the life insurance company's records.

"Incidents of ownership" are the rights to the economic benefits of the policy. Some incidents of ownership are, for example, the power to: change the beneficiary; change the time or manner in which the beneficiary or owner receives the beneficial interest of the policy or the proceeds; borrow against the policy; pledge the policy as collateral for a loan; choose whether to receive dividends or apply them to premiums; surrender the policy; determine the form in which proceeds are to be paid; or, change the owner.[34]

> EXAMPLE: Carol buys a life insurance policy on her life, naming herself as the owner. Face value of the policy is $100,000. When she dies, the $100,000 is includable in her gross estate.

If an insured assigns a policy, but retains the right to get it back under certain circumstances, he has a reversionary interest in the policy. If the value of the possibility that the policy or proceeds may return to the insured or his estate or may be subject to a power of disposition by him exceeds five percent just before the insured's death, the proceeds will be includable in his estate.[35]

> EXAMPLE: Mom assigns life insurance policy on Mom's life to Trust. Trust agreement provides that if Dad predeceases Mom, the policy will be distributed to Mom. Mom's actuarial chance of surviving Dad is 60 percent. Even if Mom in fact predeceases Dad, the policy proceeds will be included in her estate.

An insured does not have to possess all of the incidents of ownership in the policy, or even a majority, in order for policy proceeds to be included in his estate; one incident of ownership is sufficient.

Community property policies present an exception to the rule. The incidents of ownership in a policy owned as community property are generally considered held one-half by each spouse, even if (say) Husband is listed by the insurance company as policy owner. The powers held by Husband as agent for Wife under the community property laws are not considered incidents of ownership.[36]

Under certain circumstances, incidents of ownership held by a corporation will be attributed to the insured.[37]

[c] Section 2039: Annuities

The gross estate includes the value of certain annuities or other payments that a beneficiary receives because he survives the decedent. Such an asset is

---

[34] Treas. Reg. § 20.2042-1(c)(2).

[35] Treas. Reg. § 20.2042-1(c)(3).

[36] Treas. Reg. § 20.2042-1(c)(5).

[37] Treas. Reg. § 20.2042-1(c)(6).

includable if the decedent was entitled to receive all or part of the annuity or other payment for her life, or for any period determined with reference to her death, or for any period which did not in fact end before her death.[38]

> EXAMPLE: An annuity is payable to Mom for Mom's life, with a 10-year minimum period. Mom dies within the 10-year term, and Child receives the payments for the rest of the 10-year period. The value of the annuity is includable in Mom's gross estate. Would this answer be different if the annuity would not start paying until Mom was 65 years old, and Mom was 40 when she died? No, it is still includable, since Mom had the right to receive payments in the future.[39]

An annuity or other payment is includable under Section 2039 only to the extent of the portion that was purchased by the decedent.[40] Any contribution by the decedent's employer or former employer is considered made by the decedent if the contribution was made because of her employment.[41]

> EXAMPLE: Mom is a participant in her company's retirement plan. The company makes annual contributions and Mom makes voluntary contributions. The plan provides that, on Mom's retirement, Mom will receive an annuity for her life. When she dies, any remaining amount in her account will pass to her beneficiaries. On Mom's death, the entire amount remaining in her account will be included in her estate.

Death-only benefits. What if, in the above example, Mom's company also has an executive death benefit plan in place which provides that, if Mom dies while she is employed, her beneficiary will receive $100,000? No other benefit is provided by the plan. Is the $100,000 includable in Mom's estate if she dies during her employment? If the plan is viewed alone, the $100,000 should not be includable, because no benefits to Mom are provided in the agreement.[42] However, the IRS may attempt to aggregate this plan with the retirement plan, finding an overall agreement to provide lifetime income and a death benefit to Mom.[43] If the IRS is successful in aggregating, the entire $100,000 will be includable.

Numerous kinds of annuities exist. Each has its own set of tax consequences.[44]

---

[38] IRC § 2039(a).

[39] Treas. Reg. § 20.2039-1(b).

[40] IRC § 2039(b).

[41] IRC § 2039(b).

[42] Estate of Fusz v. Comm'r, 46 TC 214 (1966), acq., 1967-2 CB 2; Rev. Rul. 76-380, 1976-2 CB 270.

[43] Treas. Reg. § 20.2039-1(b)(2), example 6.

[44] More on annuities can be found at the following places: Ch. 13—commercial annuities; Ch. 14—employee annuities; Ch. 22—grantor retained annuities; Ch. 23—private annuities; Ch. 33—charitable remainder annuities; Ch. 34—charitable gift annuities; Ch. 35—charitable lead annuities.

[d] Section 2036(a)(1): Gifted Property Where Donor Retains a Prohibited Interest

Generally, if a donor makes a gift and retains possession, enjoyment, or the right to income of the gifted property, the property will be included in her taxable estate on her death.[45] Thus, if Mom gives a boat to a trust and retains the right to use the boat rent-free, the boat is included in Mom's gross estate.

Property is also includable if the donor relinquishes a prohibited interest within three years of her death.[46] Thus, if Mom relinquishes the right to use the boat rent-free two years before her death, the boat is included in Mom's gross estate.

[e] Sections 2036(a)(2) and 2038(a)(1): Gifted Property Where the Donor Had a Prohibited Power

If a donor gives an interest in property and, at the date of his death, has either retained the right, alone or with others, to designate who will possess or enjoy the property or its income, or had the right to alter, amend, revoke, or terminate the donated interest, the property will be includable in his estate.[47]

EXAMPLE: Mom gives property to a trust for her children. She is trustee, and retains the right to determine the timing, amounts, and recipients of distributions, unlimited by any standard related to health, support, maintenance, or education. The trust is includable in her estate.

EXAMPLE: Mom transferred property to a trust, and retained no interest or power. Three years later, she became successor trustee, with the unlimited right to determine which of her descendants received the trust assets at her death. She died with this power. The trust is includable in her estate.

If a donor's power to determine beneficial enjoyment of property is limited by an ascertainable standard related to the health, education, support, and maintenance of the beneficiaries, the power will not cause the property to be included in her estate.[48]

EXAMPLE: Mom gives money to a trust for her children. She is trustee of the trust. She is to distribute for the health, support, maintenance, and education of the children until the youngest is 25. Then the trust terminates in favor of the children. Mom's powers of distribution will not cause the trust assets to be included in her estate.

---

[45] IRC § 2036(a)(1).

[46] IRC § 2035(d)(2).
IRC § 2035(a).

[47] IRC §§ 2036(a)(2), 2038(a)(1).

[48] See, e.g., Estate of Budd v. Comm'r, 49 TC 468 (1968), acq., 1973-2 CB 1.

If a donor gives shares of a "controlled" corporation and retains the right, directly or indirectly, to vote the transferred shares, the donor will be deemed to have retained the right to determine enjoyment of the transferred shares.[49] A corporation is "controlled" if, on any "relevant date," the decedent and his family[50] owned, or had the right to vote (either alone or with others) stock possessing at least 20 percent of the total combined voting power of all classes of the corporation's stock. A "relevant date" is any date after the gift is made which is less than three years before the donor's death.[51]

Even if the decedent only had the right to vote the stock in a fiduciary capacity, the stock is still generally includable in the decedent's estate.[52]

> EXAMPLE: On Day One, Mom gives voting stock of a corporation to a trust. She is trustee, and so has the right to vote the shares. Mom's father owns 50 percent of the voting stock of the corporation. If Mom dies on Day Two, the stock that she transferred to the trust will be included in her gross estate.

> EXAMPLE: On Day One, Mom gives voting stock of a family corporation to a family limited partnership. She is general partner, and so has the right to vote the shares. The stock will be included in Mom's estate.

PRACTICE POINTER: People sometimes forget about Section 2036(b), since it does not arise every day. If donor gives stock of a family corporation and serves in a capacity such as trustee of a trust or general partner of a partnership which owns the stock, the trust agreement, partnership agreement, or other governing instruments should name an alternate person to vote the entity's shares of the corporation.

Property is also includable in the donor's gross estate if the donor relinquishes a prohibited power over the property within three years before her death.[53]

[f] Section 2037: Certain Gifted Property if the Gift Takes Effect at the Donor's Death

Gifted property is included in the donor's estate if:

---

[49] IRC § 2036(b)(1).

[50] Shares owned by the decedent's family are attributed to the decedent. IRC § 2036(b)(2). For this purpose, a decedent's family means the decedent's spouse (unless the spouse is legally separated from the decedent by a court order), children, grandchildren, and parents. IRC § 318(a)(1).

[51] IRC § 2036(b)(2).

[52] Prop. Reg. § 20.2036-2(c).

[53] IRC § 2035(d)(2).
IRC § 2035(a).

- the recipient must survive the donor to obtain possession or enjoyment of the property through ownership of the interest;
- the donor retains a "reversionary interest" in the property; and
- the value of the reversionary interest just before the donor's death is over 5 percent of the value of the property.[54]

A "reversionary interest," generally, is a right to the return of the gifted property under designated conditions without paying adequate consideration.

EXAMPLE: Child transfers property to a trust. The trust provides that no distributions can be made until the first of Child's death or Mom's death. If Child dies first, the trust is to remain in place for the benefit of Mom. If Mom dies first, Child gets the property back. Suppose Child dies first. If Child's chance of getting the property back exceeded 5 percent immediately before her death, the property is included in Child's estate.

Reversionary interests may be included in a person's estate under Section 2037 or Section 2033. It makes a big difference which section applies.

EXAMPLE: John gives the income from Blackacre to Paul for Paul's life. The property is to return to John or his estate at Paul's death. Legally speaking, John has a reversion in Blackacre. As the property does not meet the Section 2037 tests for inclusion, the actuarial value of John's reversion will be included in John's estate under Section 2033, as an interest he owned at death. Now suppose that the income from Blackacre is to be accumulated and that the property will pass to Paul outright if he survives John. If John's interest exceeds 5 percent right before his death, Section 2037 will pull Blackacre into John's estate at its full value—not at the value of the reversionary interest alone.

How do we tell whether a reversionary interest is worth more than five percent of the property value? The value is generally determined by the Treasury's actuarial tables.[55]

A reversionary interest includes the possibility that the property will return to the donor or his estate, or may be subject to a power of disposition by him, but does not include those possibilities if they relate only to income from the property.[56] The possibility must be a legally enforceable possibility, and does not include the possibility that the donor may inherit the property from another person.[57]

---

[54] IRC § 2037(a).

[55] IRC § 2037, Treas. Reg. § 20.2037-1(c)(3).

[56] IRC § 2037(b).

[57] Treas. Reg. § 20.2037-1(c)(2).

Even if gifted property meets all the above tests under Section 2037, it is not includable in the donor's estate if the recipient has a general power of appointment over the entire property during the donor's lifetime.[58]

EXAMPLE: Take the example above involving Child and Mom. If Mom had the power during Child's lifetime to distribute the trust property to herself at her discretion, the trust would not be included in Child's estate if Child died first.

[g] Section 2035: Gifts Made Within Three Years of Death

[i] **Gift included in estate.** A gift made within three years of the donor's death may be included in the donor's gross estate. The gifted property will be includable only if it would have been includable in the donor's estate under Section 2036, 2037, 2038, or 2042 (described in subparagraphs [b], [d], [e], and [f] above) if the property had been retained by the donor.[59]

EXAMPLE: Mom gives a life insurance policy on her life to Child one year before her death. The proceeds of the policy are included in Mom's estate, because if she had not transferred the policy, the proceeds would have been included in her estate under Section 2042 (see subparagraph [b] above).

EXAMPLE: Mom transfers land to her son one year before her death. The land is not included in her estate, because if she had retained the property, it would have been included in her estate under Section 2033 (property owned by the decedent), and not under Section 2036, 2037, 2038, or 2042.

Exception. Property gifted within three years of death is not included in the donor's estate if the gift qualifies for the $10,000/year gift tax annual exclusion,[60] a gift tax return is not required, and the gift does not consist of a life insurance policy.[61] Additionally, the tax-free payment of tuition or medical expenses[62] within three years of death is not an includable gift.[63]

Exception. Generally, for purposes of IRC §§ 303(b) (discussed in Chapter 45), 2032A (discussed in Chapter 48), certain tests under IRC § 6166 (discussed in Chapter 46), and subchapter C of IRC Chapter 64 (relating to liens for taxes), the gross estate includes the value of all property transferred

---

[58] IRC § 2037(b). Powers of appointment are described in Ch. 3.

[59] IRC § 2035.
IRC § 2035(a).

[60] The $10,000/year annual exclusion is discussed in Ch. 10.

[61] IRC § 2035(b)(2).

[62] The gift tax exception for tuition and medical payments is discussed in Ch. 10.

[63] IRC § 2035(b)(2).

by the decedent within three years of death.[60] However, the transferred property is not included even for these purposes if the gift qualifies for the $10,000 year gift tax annual exclusion[61] or the exclusion for payment of tuition or medical expenses,[62] the donor is not required to file a gift tax return for the year of gift with respect to transfers to the donee, and the gift does not consist of a life insurance policy.[63]

[ii] Section 2035(c): Gift tax included in estate. Gift tax paid by the donor or the donor's estate on gifts made by the donor or the donor's spouse within three years of the donor's death is always includable in the donor's estate, regardless of whether the gift itself is included.[64] The effect of this rule is to subject taxable gifts made within three years of death to the estate tax rates instead of the lower gift tax rates.[65]

[h] Section 2044: Property for Which Decedent's Spouse Took a Marital Deduction

If a marital deduction was allowed in a deceased spouse's estate for property passing to a QTIP trust[66] or for non-trust property in QTIP form, the trust assets or the property, as the case may be, will be includable in the surviving spouse's estate.[67]

[i] Section 2040: Property Held in Survivorship Form

[i] General rule. The gross estate generally includes property held by the decedent and any other person as joint tenants with right of survivorship (JTWROS), or as tenants by the entirety, or in any other form in which the property passes to the survivor by reason of the form of ownership.

EXAMPLE: Mom sets up a bank account as JTWROS with Child. Child makes no contribution to the account. If Mom dies first, the entire account is includable in her estate.

---

[60] IRC §§ 2035(c)(1), 2035(c)(2).

[61] The $10,000 annual exclusion is indexed, beginning in 1999. IRC § 2503(b)(2). See Ch. 10 for further discussion.

[62] The gift tax exception for tuition and medical payments is discussed in Ch. 10.

[63] IRC § 2035(c)(3).

[64] IRC § 2035(c).
IRC § 2035(b).

[65] See Ch. 8 for a further discussion.

[66] QTIP trusts are explained in Ch. 4.

[67] IRC § 2044.

[ii] Exceptions.

Property which never belonged to the decedent. Property which originally belonged to the survivor and was never given to the survivor by the decedent is not included in the decedent's estate.[68] If property originally contributed by more than one person is involved, each person's share of the property, for estate tax purposes, will generally be his proportionate share of capital contributions.[69]

> EXAMPLE: Mom sets up a bank account as JTWROS with Child. Child makes no contribution to the account. If Child dies first, no part of the account would be included in Child's estate.

> EXAMPLE: Mom and Child each contribute $10,000 of money earned from their respective careers to buy real estate as JTWROS. If Mom dies, one-half of the real property is included in her estate.

If the decedent gave the survivor the money that went into the JTWROS property, then the decedent will be considered to have made the contributions of the gifted property.[70]

> EXAMPLE: Mom puts money into a bank account held in the names of herself and her son as JTWROS, or as a "payable on death" account which is payable to her son. Her son makes no contribution. On Mom's death, the entire account is included in her estate. If, instead, Mom had made two-thirds of the contributions in the account, and her son had made one-third of the contributions with money given to him by Mom, the entire account would still be included in Mom's estate.

Survivorship interests of husband and wife. If a decedent owned property as JTWROS or tenants by the entirety with his spouse, one-half of the joint property is included in his estate, regardless of who originally owned the property.[71]

> EXAMPLE: Dad owns $1,000 as his separate property. Dad puts the $1,000 into a bank account titled as JTWROS or tenants by the entirety with Mom. If either Mom or Dad dies, one-half of the account will be includable in his/her estate, regardless of the fact that it was Dad's separate property.

There is an issue as to whether the above rule applies to survivorship interests created before 1977. Several courts have held that the general rule applies to those interests (i.e., the entire property is included in the prede-

---

[68] IRC § 2040.

[69] Treas. Reg. § 20.2040-1(a).

[70] IRC § 2040.

[71] IRC § 2040(b).

ceasing spouse's estate, except to the extent of property attributable to original consideration furnished by the surviving spouse).[72]

[j] Section 2041: General Powers of Appointment

Property is generally included in the decedent's gross estate if he had the power, alone or with others, to appoint the property to himself, his estate, his creditors, or creditors of his estate.[73]

[k] Old Transfers

Property which was transferred in the past may be grandfathered from some of the above rules. In such cases, other rules apply, as the following table indicates. These situations are not often encountered.

Transfers	Special Rules Apply to:
Gifts made within three years of death (Section 2035).	Persons dying before 1982 (Section 2035(d)(1)).
Gift tax on gifts made within three years of death (Section 2035(c)).	Persons dying, and transfers made, before 1977. (P.L. 94-455, Sections 2001(a)(5), 2001(d)(1)).
Transfers with retained interest (Section 2036(a)(1)).	Transfers made before 3/4/31 (Section 2036(c)).
Transfers with retained power (Section 2036(a)(2)).	Transfers made before 3/4/31 (Section 2036(c)).
Transfers of corporations controlled with retention of voting rights (Section 2036(b)).	Transfers made before 6/23/76 (P.L. 95-600, Section 702(i)(1).
Transfers taking effect at death (Section 2037).	Generally, gifts made before 9/7/16.
Transfers taking effect at death (Section 2037).	Certain reversionary interests in transfers made before 10/8/49 (Section 2037(a)).
Revocable transfers (Section 2038).	Transfers before 6/23/36 (Section 2038(a)(2)).
Annuities (Section 2039).	Agreements entered into before 3/4/31 (Section 2039(a)).
Powers of appointment (Section 2041).	Powers created on or before 10/21/42.

---

[72] See discussion in Ch. 4.

[73] Powers of appointment are discussed in Ch. 3.

[l] Reciprocal Trusts

If two people make transfers to trusts or trust-like arrangements that are not otherwise includable in the transferors' estates, they may still be includable if they are reciprocal.

> EXAMPLE: Sister transfers property to a trust giving income to Brother for life, remainder to her children. Brother transfers an identical amount of property to a trust giving income to Sister for life, remainder to his children. Each is treated as the settlor of the trust established by the other, so the trust established by Brother is included in Sister's estate, and the trust established by Sister is included in Brother's estate.[74]

The trusts will be "uncrossed" if they are interrelated, and the arrangement, to the extent of mutual value, leaves the settlors in approximately the same economic position as they would have been in had they created trusts naming themselves as life beneficiaries.[75]

There is a question whether trusts will be considered crossed if the settlors retain powers which would cause the trusts to be included in their estates if the trusts were uncrossed, but do not retain economic interests.

QUESTION: *Sister transfers property to a trust for Brother's children, giving Brother the right to distribute the assets of the trust in his sole discretion. Brother transfers property to a trust for Sister's children, giving Sister a reciprocal right. Are the trusts uncrossed, causing the trust established by Sister to be included in Brother's estate, and vice versa?*

ANSWER: The IRS, the Tax Court, and the Federal Circuit say yes.[76] The Sixth Circuit says no.[77]

The IRS has taken a position that the reciprocal trust doctrine applies even where the grantor of the crossed trusts was not the beneficiary/powerholder. In Private Letter Ruling. 9235025,[78] the IRS addressed a situation in which Dad had left trusts for the benefit of each of his two sons. Each son, as trustee of his brother's trust, had an unrestricted power to distribute trust property to his brother. The IRS said that the trusts would be "uncrossed," and each brother would be treated as having a general power of appointment over the trust established for his benefit.

---

[74] United States v. Grace, 395 US 316 (1969).

[75] United States v. Grace, 395 US 316 (1969); Rev. Rul. 74-533, 1974-2 CB 293.

[76] Bischoff v. Comm'r, 69 TC 32 (1977); Exchange Bank & Trust Co. of Fla., 694 F2d 1261 (Fed. Cir. 1982).

[77] Estate of Green v. United States, 68 F3d 151 (6th Cir. 1995) (1 dissent).

[78] May 29, 1992.

Private Letter Ruling 9235025 relied in part on a New York state surrogate's court decision. In *Matter of Estate of Nathaniel Spear, Jr.*,[78.1] the decedent's will created a trust for each of his two grandchildren with income for life and a contingent remainder interest. Both grandchildren were co-trustees of each trust with absolute discretion to invade corpus for the benefit of the life income beneficiary. Although the court decided the case on other grounds, the court stated that "these reciprocal powers are the equivalent of a general power of appointment.

A similar application of the reciprocal trust doctrine can be found in an earlier letter ruling. Private Letter Ruling 8029001[78.2] involved two trusts established by a father for each of two daughters. Each sister was sole trustee of the trust for the benefit of the other. The IRS ruled that "the reciprocal nature of the control and beneficial enjoyment in these two trusts must be recognized as giving [the beneficiary of one of the trusts] a degree of control over the trust of which she is not the designated trustee . . . . By applying the reciprocal trust doctrine to this two-trust configuration, the donor (or her sister) is considered trustee of which she (or her sister) is the income beneficiary.

The applicability of the reciprocal trusts doctrine in the gift tax context is discussed in Chapter 10.

¶ 2.04 ESTATE TAX VALUATION DATE

For estate tax purposes, an asset is valued at date of death or, at the executor's election, as of the alternate valuation date. The alternate valuation date is the earlier of six months after date of death or the date the asset was disposed of.[79]

¶ 2.05 ESTATE TAX DEDUCTIONS

The gross estate, less allowable deductions, constitutes the taxable estate. The following deductions are allowable.

[1] Consideration Given for Gifts

If the decedent's estate includes property that was transferred for inadequate consideration, whatever amount of consideration was paid is deductible.[80]

[78.1] 553 NYS2d 985 (Sur. 1990).

[78.2] Feb. 12, 1980.

[79] IRC § 2032. More on the alternate valuation date is included in Ch. 50 on postmortem planning.

[80] IRC § 2043.

(More precisely, only the estate tax value of the asset, less the consideration paid, is includable.)

> EXAMPLE: Suppose Mom sells property worth $1,000,000 to Child for $600,000, thus making a gift of $400,000. If the property is included in Mom's estate, the includable value of the property will be its estate tax value in Mom's estate, less the $600,000 that Child paid.[81]

It should be noted that a waiver of marital rights is not treated as deductible for these purposes, except for certain transfers made pursuant to a divorce decree.[82]

> EXAMPLE: Husband gives Trust $1,000,000. As consideration, Wife relinquishes her right to support, which is valued at $600,000. Husband and Wife remain married. If the gift is included in Husband's estate, there will be no deduction for Wife's waiver of her support rights, even though the waiver actually had value to Husband.

[2] Administration Expenses, Debts, and Taxes

[a] General Rule

Deductions are allowed from the gross estate for: funeral expenses; administration expenses of probate property; claims against the estate; unpaid mortgages on, or any indebtedness in respect of, property included in the estate; and, administration expenses of nonprobate property included in the gross estate, to the extent that such expenses are paid before the expiration of the assessment period for estate tax.[83]

[b] Exceptions

The following are not deductible:

- Income taxes on income received after the decedent's death;
- Property taxes accruing after the decedent's death; and
- Estate, succession, legacy, and inheritance taxes.[84]

However, at the executor's election, the estate may deduct any estate, succession, legacy, or inheritance tax imposed by a state, the District of Columbia, or a foreign country on a transfer which is eligible for the charitable

---

[81] IRC § 2043(a).

[82] IRC § 2043(b).

[83] IRC §§ 2053(a), 2053(b).

[84] IRC § 2053(c)(1)(B).

estate tax deduction. The tax savings must accrue to the charity. The election operates as a waiver of the foreign tax credit.[85]

> EXAMPLE: Dad leaves real property in a foreign jurisdiction to charity, and the rest of his estate to Child. The foreign assets generate a death tax in the foreign country of $100,000. The executor can elect to deduct the $100,000 as a charitable deduction if the $100,000 not paid to the IRS will all go to the charity, and not to Child. If the executor does deduct the $100,000, he cannot also take a credit for foreign taxes on the $100,000.

[3] Losses

The estate is entitled to deduct casualty losses incurred during the estate administration arising from fires, storms, shipwrecks, other casualties, or theft.[86]

[4] Charitable Bequests

An estate tax deduction for qualifying charitable bequests is allowed.[87] The charitable estate tax deduction is unlimited.[88]

[5] Marital Bequests

A marital deduction is allowed for qualifying marital bequests.[89] The marital deduction is unlimited, so any amount of property (including the entire estate) can pass to the spouse free of transfer tax.

¶ 2.06 ESTATE TAX CREDITS

There are several credits allowed against the estate tax. They are:

- The unified credit.
- The unified credit of $192,800.[90]
- The state death tax credit.[91] (In states with "sponge taxes," the tax is

---

[85] IRC § 2053(d).

[86] IRC § 2054.

[87] IRC § 2055.

[88] It is discussed in detail in Part VIII.

[89] IRC § 2056. The marital deduction is discussed in detail in Ch. 4.

[90] IRC § 2010. Discussed in Chs. 1 and 4.

[91] IRC § 2011.

designed to be the maximum it can be without increasing the total amount the estate owes to the state and federal governments.)
- The credit for estate tax on property which was taxed in the estate of another decedent within ten years before the second decedent's death.[92]
- The credit for foreign death taxes.[93]
- The credit for death taxes on remainders.[94]

---

[92] IRC § 2013.
[93] IRC § 2014.
[94] IRC § 2015.

Powers of Appointment

¶ 3.01 INTRODUCTION

Powers of appointment are among the most important tools in the estate planner's box. They provide great flexibility in long-term trusts, and can be used to accomplish many tax and substantive objectives. This chapter explains what they are and how the holder of a power is taxed.

¶ 3.02 DEFINITIONS

First, some terminology.

[1] Power of Appointment

A "power of appointment," sometimes called a "power," is the power to affect the beneficial ownership of property which one does not own—usually property owned by a trust. A power of appointment may be exercisable during the exercising person's lifetime (a "power by deed"), or by will (a "testamentary power"), or both. For example, if Trust A owns Blackacre and Mom, at her discretion, can direct the trustee to distribute Blackacre to Brother or to Sister, Mom has a power of appointment over Blackacre.

Sections 2041 and 2514 deal with the estate and gift tax consequences of powers of appointment. These sections refer to a power created by someone other than the person who can exercise the power. If the person who can exercise the power is the same person who created the power, that retained power is governed by Section 2036(a)(2) and/or Section 2038, as well as Section 2511. This chapter deals solely with a power created by someone other than the person who can exercise it. Retained powers are dealt with in Chapter 2, which discusses the inclusion of gifted property in the donor's estate.

> **EXAMPLE:** Mom creates a trust and retains a power of appointment. The trust assets are included in Mom's estate under Section 2036(a)(2). This chapter does not address this power of appointment. However, if Grandma created the trust and gave Mom the power of appointment, the tax rules applicable to the power would be found in Sections 2041 and 2514, and therefore the discussion in this chapter would apply.

[2] Dramatis Personae

Any question concerning a power of appointment will involve certain persons and elements. They are—

Holder. The person who can exercise the power of appointment is known as the "holder" of the power or, sometimes, as the "donee" of the power.

Creator. The person who created the power of appointment is the "creator" or "donor" of the power.

Object. The people (or entities) who are the permissible beneficiaries of the power of appointment are the "objects."

Appointee. A person who has received the appointed property is an "appointee."

Taker in default. A person who is entitled to receive property subject to a power of appointment if the power is not exercised is a "taker in default."

> **EXAMPLE:** Mom creates a trust. She gives Child the power to appoint

among Child's descendants. If Child does not exercise the power, the trust property will pass to Sibling. Child appoints one-half of the trust property to Grandchild. Mom is the creator of the power. Child is the holder. Child's descendants are the objects of the power. Grandchild is an appointee. Sibling is a taker in default with respect to the one-half of the trust property that was not appointed to Grandchild.

[3] Things One Can Do With a Power of Appointment

The holder of a power may use or not use the power in the following ways—

Exercise. If Mom wants Child to have Blackacre for no consideration, how does she transfer it? If Mom owns Blackacre herself, she gives or transfers it to Child. If, instead, she has a power of appointment over Blackacre, she "exercises the power of appointment in favor of" Child.

Appoint. Another way of saying that Mom "exercises the power of appointment in favor of Child," is that she "appoints the property to Child."

Release. If Mom gives up her power of appointment without exercising it, she "releases" it.

Partial exercise or release. Most powers do not have to be exercised or released in an all-or-nothing fashion. If the holder exercises/releases the power over a portion of the property, she "partially" exercises/releases the power.

Lapse. Some powers of appointment expire after a certain period of time, or on certain events. The expiration is a "lapse."

[4] General Power of Appointment

Generally speaking, property subject to a general power of appointment is subject to gift and estate taxation on its exercise or release, or upon the death of the holder.[1] The definition of a general power of appointment varies, depending on whether the context is state law property rights, income taxation, or transfer taxation.

[a] State Law Definition

For state law purposes, a person holds a "general power of appointment" over property if she can appoint the property to any one or more of herself, her estate, her creditors, or creditors of her estate.[2] What if Mom has a power to appoint among her descendants, and she owes her child $1,000? Can Mom appoint to the child? If she can, does she have a power to appoint to her

---

[1] IRC §§ 2041, 2514.

[2] Restatement (Second) of Property § 11.4 (1984).

creditors? Yes, and no. A power to appoint to one's creditor is the power to appoint to the creditor in his capacity as such—that is, to satisfy the holder's debt.[3] If Mom appoints $1,000 to the child under a non-general power of appointment, her debt to the child would remain outstanding. If she could appoint property to the child in satisfaction of her debt, that would be considered appointing to herself (since she would be paying off her debt by the appointment).

A general power of appointment is a property right under state law. The tax law definition of a general power has certain exceptions, described below. The state law definition of a general power of appointment generally does not include the tax law exceptions.[4] Accordingly, a power can be a general power under state law and a limited power for tax purposes. The consequences of having a general power of appointment under state law can therefore ensue, regardless of whether the power is considered general or limited for tax purposes.[5]

[b] Income Tax Definition

The existence of a general power of appointment has income tax ramifications. The income tax has rules that are not parallel to the transfer tax rules. Hence, a person may have a general power for income tax purposes but not for transfer tax purposes, and vice versa.[6]

The primary income tax consequence of the possession of a general power of appointment is found in Section 678. Under this section, the holder is taxable on income from the property that the holder can appoint to himself if—

- The holder has the power alone to appoint such property to himself or had such a power but released or modified the power while retaining certain interests in or powers over the trust, and
- The trust is not the kind of trust that is taxable to the creator of the trust.

The IRS position is that a lapse of a power is treated as a release for this purpose.[7]

---

[3] Treas. Reg. § 20.2041-1(c)(1). A power is not treated as a general power just because a permissible appointee may in fact be a creditor of the holder. Treas. Reg. § 20.2041-1(c)(1).

[4] Restatement (Second) of Property § 11.4, reporter's tax note (1984).

[5] Restatement (Second) of Property § 11.4, cmt a. (1984); see also discussion in Ch. 53 on asset protection.

[6] Chapter 6 discusses the income tax rules in detail.

[7] E.g., Priv. Ltr. Rul. 9034004 (May 17, 1990); Priv. Ltr. Rul. 8521060 (Feb. 26, 1985).

EXAMPLE: Dad creates a trust for Child, giving Child the right to withdraw contributions to the trust for 30 days after they are made. Dad contributes $10,000 to the trust, and Child does not withdraw any of the contribution. For income tax purposes, the IRS believes that Child has released a general power of appointment over the trust. The IRS takes the position that Child is taxable on the income attributable to Dad's $10,000 contribution to the trust.[8]

EXAMPLE: Assume the same facts as the preceding example, except that Dad has retained powers over the trust sufficient to cause him to be taxed on the trust's income. Dad will be taxable on the income attributable to his $10,000 contribution as long as he holds the power which causes him to be taxable on trust income. After that, Child will possibly be taxable on the income attributable to the $10,000 contribution.[9]

If the holder has a joint power, requiring the consent of another to exercise, the holder will not be treated as having a general power for income tax purposes. Note that this is different from the transfer tax definition of a general power, which includes certain joint powers.

EXAMPLE: Assume the same facts as the next-to-last example, except that Child cannot withdraw contributions to the trust without the consent of Uncle. Child should not be taxable on income attributable to the $10,000 contribution.

[c] Transfer Tax Definition

For transfer tax purposes only, certain exceptions to the above general state law definition of a general power of appointment exist.

[i] Effect of power to invade trust for health, education, maintenance, and support (HEMS). If the holder's power to appoint property is limited to distributions for his own HEMS, the power is not considered a general power of appointment.[10]

---

[8] Rev. Rul. 67-241, 1967-2 CB 225; Priv. Ltr. Rul. 8142061 (July 21, 1981). In the latter ruling, the IRS indicated that the limited duration of the power should be taken into account in determining the share of income, deduction, and credits allocable to the powerholder. For example, under the IRS's reasoning, if Child, who is the life beneficiary of a trust, has the right to withdraw a $10,000 contribution during the month of December, Child is only taxable on a pro rata part of the trust's income for the year. For all years following, Child would be taxed on all the income attributable to the $10,000 contribution, since Child has a lapsed power.

[9] IRC § 678(a). But see Priv. Ltr. Rul. 9321050 (Feb. 25, 1993), coming to the opposite conclusion without explanation in a case in which a wife proposed to establish a Crummey trust for her husband.

[10] IRC § 2041(b)(1)(A).

EXAMPLE: Mom establishes a trust for Daughter. Daughter is trustee, and her only power is to make distributions to herself for educational purposes. Daughter does not have a general power of appointment for transfer tax purposes.

[ii] Effect of joint power. A general power of appointment is still a general power even if it's exercise requires the consent of another person. However, exceptions to this rule exist in the following cases—

Exception: Exercise of power requires consent of creator. If the holder can appoint property to herself only with the consent of the person who created the power, the power is not considered a general power.[11]

EXAMPLE: Mom establishes a trust, naming Child as trustee. Child can distribute to herself only if Mom consents. Child does not have a taxable general power as long as Mom must consent.

Exception: Consent of adverse party required. If A can only appoint property to himself with the consent of a person having a "substantial interest" in the property, and if the distribution to A would be adverse to that other person, A's power will not be considered a general power.[12] "Substantial," for this purpose, means not insignificant.[13] A person's interest is "adverse" to the holder, in this instance, if the exercise of the power in favor of the holder, her estate, her creditors, or the creditors of her estate would diminish the person's interest.[14]

EXAMPLE: Mom establishes a trust which gives income for life to Child, remainder to Grandchild. Child can appoint the property to herself, but only with Grandchild's consent. Child does not have a general power for transfer tax purposes, as long as Grandchild has a substantial interest in the trust.

Let's analyze the above example. Child has a power to appoint the assets of the trust to herself, but only with Grandchild's consent. To the extent that the power is not exercised, Grandchild will receive the trust assets on Child's death. To the extent that the power is exercised in favor of someone besides Grandchild, Grandchild will get nothing. Hence, Grandchild's interest is adverse to Child's. Accordingly, the consent requirement will cause the power held by Child to be considered a limited power if Grandchild's interest is substantial.

---

[11] IRC § 2041(b)(1)(C)(i).

[12] IRC § 2041(b)(1)(C)(ii).

[13] Treas. Reg. § 20.2041-3(c)(2).

[14] Treas. Reg. § 20.2041-3(c)(2).

The above example is an illustration of the general principle that a taker in default of appointment has an interest adverse to an exercise of the power.[15] However, if the taker in default has only a remote contingent chance of actually getting anything even if the power is not exercised, his interest may not be substantial enough to be adverse.

> EXAMPLE: In the above example, suppose that the trust provided that on Child's death, the trust assets would go to all of Mom's descendants except Grandchild, unless Grandchild were her only living descendant. In that case, Grandchild would take. If Mom has 20 living descendants, all younger than Grandchild, Grandchild's interest is probably not substantial. If Child and Grandchild are Mom's only descendants, Grandchild's interest probably is substantial.

The IRS has taken the position that if a person's actuarial interest in the trust, assuming maximum exercise of discretion in favor of the person, is less than five percent of the trust's value, the person's interest is not substantial.[16] The fact that a power must be exercised jointly does not by itself mean that the holders have adverse interests.[17] Neither does the fact that the joint holders are all objects of the power.[18]

> EXAMPLE: Mom establishes a trust for her children, Son and Daughter. Son and Daughter can terminate the trust in favor of themselves on a fifty-fifty basis at any time, but both must consent to the termination. On the death of either Son or Daughter, one half of the trust terminates in favor of the deceased sibling's children. If Daughter dies first, one half of the trust will be included in her estate, due to her joint power to appoint that half to herself. Son does not have an adverse interest in that half. If he and Daughter had terminated the trust just before Daughter's death, he would have gotten one half of the trust; in the absence of the exercise of the power, he still gets only one half of the trust.

If, however, a joint powerholder will have the power to appoint the property to himself after the other powerholder's death, he will be considered to have a substantial interest that is adverse to the exercise of the power in the other powerholder's favor.[19]

> EXAMPLE: The same facts as in the previous example apply, except that on the first sibling's death, the trust is continued, but the surviving sibling will have the unrestricted power to distribute the entire trust to himself. If Daughter is the first to die, the property subject to the power will not

---

[15] Treas. Reg. § 20.2041-3(c)(2).

[16] Priv. Ltr. Rul. 8911028 (Dec. 16, 1988).

[17] Treas. Reg. § 20.2041-3(c)(2).

[18] Treas. Reg. § 20.2041-3(c)(2).

[19] Treas. Reg. § 20.2041-3(c)(2).

be included in her estate. She will not be deemed to have a general power, since Son's interest would have been adversely affected by the exercise of the power during Daughter's lifetime.

Exception: Joint general power exercisable in favor of the holders. If, after the application of the joint power rules above, a joint holder's power is a general power and is exercisable in favor of the other holder(s), that joint holder's power will be considered a general power over a fraction of the property. The fraction will be: one, divided by the number of holders who are objects of the power.

EXAMPLE: Mom establishes trust for the benefit of Son and Daughter. Son and Daughter can jointly terminate the trust in their own favor, in any proportions that they like. At the death of the first sibling, one-half of the property will continue to be held for that sibling's children. Son and Daughter each have a taxable general power over one-half of the trust.

The requirement that one person consent to a second person's exercise of a power does not elevate the first person to the status of a co-holder of the power.[20]

[d] Hidden General Powers

A general power of appointment is not always clearly labeled as a "general power of appointment" or "power to appoint to any person or entity, including the holder, his estate, his creditors, and the creditors of his estate." Various other powers or rights may also be considered general powers.

EXAMPLE: Mary is the trustee of Trust *M*. She is not a beneficiary. As trustee, Mary has the power to distribute trust income or principal to the beneficiaries, and to encumber or mortgage trust property should she deem it necessary or essential for any purpose. She also has the power to deal with any person, including herself. In 1994, the IRS took the position that such an administrative power would give Mary a general power of appointment, under the theory that she had the power to use trust property as security for loans to herself, not pay back the loans, allow the property to be foreclosed, and thereby appoint the property to her creditors(!).[21]

---

[20] Rev. Rul. 79-63, 79-1 CB 302.

[21] Tech. Adv. Mem. 9431004 (Apr. 26, 1994). The IRS said that administrative powers exercisable by a beneficiary-trustee may be deemed general powers of appointment if they are not exercisable in a fiduciary capacity and if they affect beneficial interests. The power given the trustee in the ruling situation, however, was exercisable in his capacity as trustee. In this situation, the trustee had actually pledged assets of the

EXAMPLE: Mary is the beneficiary of Trust *M*. The trustee must distribute trust income and principal as Mary requests for her support, maintenance, comfort, and welfare. Mary is considered to have a general power of appointment.[22]

EXAMPLE: Mary has a legal life estate in property *X*. The will granting the life estate gives her the power to sell, mortgage, and otherwise dispose of the property at such times and on such terms as she may deem proper. This power has been deemed to include the power to consume the property and therefore to constitute a general power of appointment.[23]

[e] Conditional General Powers

If a decedent would have received a power of appointment had a condition occurred before her death, the assets subject to the conditional power would not normally be included in her estate. However, if the occurrence of the condition was within the decedent's control, the decedent will be considered to have possessed the general power, even if she did not trigger the condition.[24]

---

trust for a personal loan and used the proceeds for personal purposes. The executor of the deceased trustee's estate and the beneficiaries of the trust reached a settlement regarding the issue of the trustee's liability, which the IRS believed was collusive. However, the IRS stated that, independently of these actual facts, the power of a trustee to borrow from the trust constituted the ability to appoint the trust property to the trustee's creditors. If the IRS is correct, self-dealing powers exercisable in a fiduciary capacity could be used to pull the assets of a non-beneficiary trustee into his estate.

[22] See, e.g., Lehman v. United States, 448 F2d 1318, 1320 (5th Cir. 1971). Generally, powers to invade trust property for one's "comfort," "welfare," or "happiness" will constitute general powers of appointment. Treas. Reg. § 25.2514-1(c)(2). Ultimately, state law will govern whether a power of invasion for particular reasons will be viewed as subject to an ascertainable standard related to health, education, maintenance, and support (HEMS), and therefore, not a general power, or as not subject to that standard, and therefore a general power. What constitutes a general power in one state may be a limited power in another. See, e.g., Best v. United States, 902 F Supp. 1023 (D Neb. 1995) (holding that under Nebraska law, power to invade for amounts reasonably necessary for decedent's comfort would be limited to invasion for HEMS purposes). A drafting solution to this is always to use the statutory HEMS language for beneficiary-trustees and grantor-trustees, and to give powers that are not limited by the statutory language to an independent trustee.

[23] Renfro v. United States, 78-1 USTC ¶ 13,241 (ED Tex. Mar. 2, 1978); see also Phinney v. Kay, 275 F2d 776 (5th Cir. 1960); Rev. Rul. 77-30, 1977-1 CB 291.

[24] Estate of Kurz v. Comm'r, 76 AFTR2d 95-7309 (7th Cir. 1995) (power to withdraw 5 percent of marital trust on exhaustion of second trust was a general power of appointment when there were no barriers to decedent's exhaustion of second trust).

[f] Reciprocal Powers May Equal a General Power

The IRS has taken the position that, if two beneficiaries of different trusts each have powers to distribute to each other, unrestricted by a standard related to health, maintenance, support, and education, the trusts will be "uncrossed," and each beneficiary will be considered to have a general power of appointment over the trust of which he is a beneficiary, even if a third party was grantor of the trusts.[25]

[5] Limited Power of Appointment

A "limited power of appointment" (sometimes called a "special" power of appointment) is (1) any power of appointment that cannot be exercised in favor of the holder, her creditors, her estate, or creditors of her estate and (2) for transfer tax purposes only, any general power of appointment that fails to qualify as a general power for tax purposes due to the above-discussed exceptions.

¶ 3.03 TRANSFER TAX CONSEQUENCES OF GENERAL POWER OF APPOINTMENT

[1] General Rules

For transfer tax purposes, a general power of appointment over property is considered the same as absolute ownership of the property. If the holder exercises or releases a general power of appointment during her life, she makes a gift.[26] If a holder had a general power of appointment over property at the time of her death, the property is included in her estate.[27]

If a person owns property directly and transfers it on certain terms, the property will be included in her estate under Sections 2035-2038.[28] If the holder of a general power of appointment over property exercises or releases the power during her life on such terms, the property will be includable in the holder's estate.[29] The exercise may also be a gift, depending on its terms.

EXAMPLE: Mom exercises a general power of appointment over property

---

[25] Priv. Ltr. Rul. 9235025 (May 29, 1992).

[26] IRC § 2514(b).

[27] IRC § 2041(a)(2).

[28] Chapter 2 describes these sections. They relate to certain transfers made or powers relinquished within three years of death (IRC § 2035), transfers where the transferor retains taxable retained interests and/or powers (IRC §§ 2036, 2038), and certain transfers taking effect at the transferor's death (IRC § 2037).

[29] IRC § 2041(a)(2).

by appointing it to New Trust. She retains the right to the income of New Trust for life. New Trust is includable in her estate, since it was created by the exercise of a general power with a retained income interest. Mom's exercise is also a gift of the remainder interest, unless she retains a power that would render the gift incomplete.[30]

EXAMPLE: Mom establishes a trust. Child is trustee; in her capacity as trustee, she can also distribute principal to herself for any reason. Child has a general power of appointment, and the trust assets will be includable in her estate if she dies while she holds it. If Child during her lifetime releases the power to distribute to herself, but retains a power of appointment among her children, the assets will still be included in her estate, because they would have been includable under Section 2036(a)(2) (retained power to determine beneficial enjoyment of property) if she had owned the trust assets and transferred them subject to the retained power.

[2] Lapses and Releases

[a] General Rule

A release of a general power will generally be considered a gift, to the extent that the transfer would have been a gift if the holder had actually owned the property.[31]

EXAMPLE: Mom creates Trust X, giving Child a general power of appointment by deed. On Child's death, Grandchild or Grandchild's estate will receive any property that Child did not appoint. If Child releases the power, Child makes a gift of the remainder interest to Grandchild (the taker in default). The release is treated as if Child owned the property in Trust X and gave the remainder interest to Grandchild.

If the holder lets a general power over property lapse, the lapse will generally be considered a release of the power.[32] If, after the lapse or release, the holder retains powers that would be described in Sections 2035-2038 if the holder had been the property owner, then the property will be taxed in her estate.[33]

EXAMPLE: Mom has a power to appoint property to herself or to any of her descendants. In default of appointment, it goes to her children. Mom releases the power to appoint to herself, but retains the power to appoint to her descendants. Mom dies. The trust property is included in her estate, just as if she had given away property while retaining a power of

---

[30] Incomplete gifts are discussed in Ch. 2.

[31] IRC § 2514(b).

[32] IRC §§ 2041(b)(2), 2514(e).

[33] IRC § 2041(a)(2). See n.28 for a list of these powers.

appointment. If Mom had released her entire power, her release would have been a gift to the takers in default.

[b] Exception

If a person allows his general power(s) of appointment to lapse in any year, then to the extent that the total lapse does not exceed the greater of $5,000 or five percent of the total value of property with which the general power could be satisfied, the lapse will not be considered a gift.[34] A power which is so limited is called a "five-or-five power." It is an important kind of power in certain generation-skipping trusts.

> EXAMPLE: Mom establishes trust for Child. Each year, Child can withdraw the greater of $5,000 or five percent of the value of the trust assets on the date of withdrawal. Child has no other withdrawal powers. The lapse of the power in any year will not be considered a gift by Child to the trust.

The five-or-five power is only a gift tax exception, not an estate tax exception. If a person has a five-or-five power immediately before his death, the assets which the holder could have appointed to himself on the date of his death will be includable in the holder's estate, even if the power lapses at his death.[35] The five-or-five power exception only applies to powers that have lapsed or been released during the decedent's lifetime. For this reason, some drafters make their lapsing powers exercisable for only a short time each year.

> EXAMPLE: Carol has a five-or-five power to withdraw assets of a trust on December 31 of each year. If she does not withdraw, the power lapses. The thought is that if Carol dies on any day except December 31, the assets will not be included in her estate because she did not have the power to withdraw at the time of her death.

[3] Grandfathered (Pre-October 22, 1942) Powers

Powers of appointment created on or before October 21, 1942 are subject to a different set of rules than those described above. Grandfathered general powers of appointment are not included in the holder's gross estate unless the holder exercises them.[36]

---

[34] IRC § 2514(e).

[35] Treas. Reg. §§ 20.2041-3(d)(3), 20.2041-3(f), example 2.

[36] IRC § 2041(a)(1).

PRACTICE POINTER: A holder of a grandfathered general power should not exercise the power unless he is comfortable with subjecting the property to transfer taxation.

¶ 3.04 TRANSFER TAX CONSEQUENCES OF LIMITED POWER OF APPOINTMENT

[1] General Rule

A limited power of appointment will not cause the property to be included in the holder's estate, if someone other than the holder created it.

> **EXAMPLE:** Mom establishes a trust. Child can appoint the trust assets among his descendants. He has no other power. Child has a limited power of appointment. If Child dies, the trust is not includable in his estate.

[2] Holder With Beneficial Interest in Trust

If the holder has a limited power of appointment and a beneficial interest in a trust, and exercises the power during his lifetime, does he make a gift of his beneficial interest? This is an important issue, since, as a practical matter, a holder of a power of appointment will usually also be a beneficiary of the trust.

> **EXAMPLE:** Mom establishes a trust, giving Child the right to income of the trust and the limited power to appoint the trust assets during Child's lifetime among Child's descendants. Child appoints the property to Grandchild. The regulations say that Child has made a taxable gift of her income interest, regarding it as a disposition of property (Child's income interest), rather than an exercise of the power.[37]

> **EXAMPLE:** Same facts as above, except that Child's ability to receive distributions is strictly in the discretion of the trustee or is limited by a HEMS standard. The IRS has taken the position that Child's exercise of his limited power in either situation is also a gift.[38]

If the IRS is correct, the exercise of an inter vivos limited power will almost always result in a gift. Is the IRS correct? The regulations say that the exercise of the power results in a taxable gift under the general gift tax rules,[39]

---

[37] Treas. Reg. §§ 25.2514-1(b)(2), 25.2514-3(e), example 3; Accord Estate of Regester v. Comm'r, 83 TC 1, 8 (1984).

[38] Priv. Ltr. Rul. 8535020 (May 30, 1985), Priv. Ltr. Rul. 9451049 (Sept. 22, 1994).

[39] IRC § 2511; Treas. Reg. §§ 25.2514-1(b)(2), 25.2514-3(e), example 3.

rather than the power of appointment rules. The history of these regulations and the cases that have considered them is enlightening.

The corresponding regulation under the 1939 Code[40] said that the lifetime exercise of a limited power of appointment by a holder of an income interest, a limited power of appointment by deed, and a general power of appointment by will was a taxable gift of the holder's income interest under the general gift tax rules and a relinquishment of her testamentary general power.

In 1956, the Court of Claims decided *Self v. United States*,[41] holding that the exercise of a limited power of appointment by a holder who had an income interest in the trust and only a limited power of appointment was not a taxable gift. The Court of Claims distinguished the regulation, pointing out that it applied only where the powerholder had both a lifetime limited power of appointment and a testamentary general power. The Court of Claims disagreed with the regulation, to the extent of any implication that a beneficiary with an income interest and a limited power made a gift by exercising the limited power.

In 1958, the Treasury re-promulgated the regulation in substantially the same language.[42] Treasury Regulation § 25.2514-3(e), example 3, promulgated at the same time, stated that if a person had an income interest and a limited power, the exercise or release of the limited power "would not constitute a transfer for purposes of the gift tax."

In 1979, the IRS officially indicated that it would not follow *Self* to the extent that the case was contrary to the regulations, and announced its position that a person with an income interest and a limited power of appointment would make a gift on the lifetime exercise or release of the power.[43]

The Treasury amended Treasury Regulation § 25.2514-3(e), example 3 in 1981 by adding what is now the last sentence. For the first time, the regulations explicitly stated that the holder of a life income interest and a limited power made a gift under Section 2511 by exercising the power.[44] The preamble to the regulations did not report that this was a change—rather, it stated that the additional sentence was added to "emphasize" the point.

The issue went to the Tax Court in 1984, in a case where a life income beneficiary with the right to income and a limited power of appointment had exercised the power during lifetime in 1974. The Tax Court said that the holder made a taxable gift of the income interest by exercising the limited

---

[40] Treas. Reg. § 108.

[41] 142 F. Supp. 939 (Ct. Cl. 1956).

[42] Treas. Reg. § 25.2514-1(b)(2).

[43] Rev. Rul. 79-327, 1979-2 CB 342; see also Priv. Ltr. Rul. 7921069 (Feb. 27, 1979).

[44] TD 7776, 1981-1 CB 478.

power.[45] The court explicitly disagreed with *Self*, agreed with the revenue ruling, and upheld Treasury Regulation § 25.2514-1(b)(2), without addressing Treasury Regulation § 25.2514-3(e), example 3.

In 1985, the IRS took a step further and stated, in a private ruling, that the holder made a gift by exercising a lifetime power of appointment when the holder was a potential beneficiary of a discretionary trust but had no measurable rights (such as an income interest for life).[46] The fact that the holder's ability to receive distributions was completely subject to the discretion of the trustee was considered irrelevant to the existence of a gift. The IRS determined that trustee's discretionary control over the distribution was merely a factor to be taken into account in determining the value of the gift. This ruling goes further than *Estate of Regester*, which relied on the fact that the decedent had the right to receive all trust income for her life, and suggested that the outcome might be different if the decedent had not had the unrestricted right to enjoy trust income for life and to make a lifetime transfer of her income interest.[47]

In 1994, the IRS privately ruled that a trust beneficiary who held an income interest and a contingent remainder interest, as well as a limited power of appointment, made a taxable gift of her interests under Section 2511 when she exercised the limited power during life. The IRS also stated that, even if no taxable gift had been made under Section 2511, the beneficiary had made a gift under Section 2514. The IRS's theory, which it based on *Jewett v. Commissoner*,[48] was that since the beneficiary had a contingent remainder interest, her limited power was actually a general power because she could appoint the subject property to herself by not exercising her limited power.[49] The IRS stated that it believed that *Self* had been, in effect, overruled by *Jewett*.[50]

Later in 1994, the IRS privately ruled on a situation in which two daughters were each the beneficiaries of a separate trust. Each daughter had the power with a co-trustee to make distributions to herself pursuant to a HEMS standard, after taking into account her other resources. Each daughter also had an inter vivos and testamentary limited power in favor of family members

---

[45] Estate of Regester v. Comm'r, 83 TC 1 (1984).

[46] Priv. Ltr. Rul. 8535020 (May 30, 1985).

[47] Estate of Regester, 83 TC 1, at 6-7; see also Walston v. Comm'r, 8 TC 72, 83-84 (1947), aff'd, 168 F2d 211 (4th Cir. 1948) (ruling that the taxpayer did not have an income interest in property she appointed to her brother, and so no gift was made).

[48] 455 US 305 (1983).

[49] *Jewett* held that a beneficiary who disclaimed a contingent remainder interest had made a gift because the disclaimer was untimely. Interestingly enough, the Supreme Court in *Jewett* only addressed general powers of appointment in dicta, and neither the Ninth Circuit nor the Tax Court mentioned IRC § 2514.

[50] Priv. Ltr. Rul. 9419007 (Feb. 3, 1994).

other than herself. Each daughter planned to appoint the assets of her trust to the other daughter. The IRS said that each daughter would make a gift of her right to receive HEMS distributions. The value of this interest was said to be readily ascertainable. The IRS expressly declined to apply the reciprocal trust doctrine to characterize these exercises as gifts.[51]

What is the meaning of all this? The impact is best illustrated by some examples.

> EXAMPLE: During Dad's life, he is entitled to receive all of the income of Trust X. Dad also has a limited power to appoint assets of Trust X to his children. If Dad exercises this power during his lifetime, the regulations and the Tax Court's decision in *Estate of Regester* indicate that he has made a taxable gift of his income interest. *Self* provides contrary authority, albeit before the regulations were amended to reach a different result.

> EXAMPLE: During his life, Dad may receive distributions of income and principal of Trust X for any reason in the discretion of Trustee. Trustee is unrelated to Dad and has no interest in Trust X. Dad also has the power to appoint assets of Trust X to his children. If Dad exercises this power during his lifetime, the IRS might take the position[52] that Dad has made a gift to his children. Assuming that this position were upheld, the amount of the gift is unclear.

> EXAMPLE: Dad may receive distributions of income of Trust X for his HEMS. Dad also has a power to appoint the income and principal of Trust X to his children. If Dad exercises this power during his life, does it result in a taxable gift? The regulations indicate that Dad's failure to distribute the income to himself is not a taxable gift under Section 2514.[53] However, the IRS might take the position that Dad has made a gift of his ascertainable right to receive distributions for HEMS in the future under Section 2511.[54]

Dealing with the uncertainty: Is the IRS right or wrong? In exercising a limited power during life, the holder must take the IRS position into account. What does the holder do in the face of this uncertainty? If the issue arises at the planning level, the issue addressed by the regulations can be avoided by not giving the beneficiary the right to receive income. One solution to the other issues might be to give a power of appointment to a nonbeneficiary special trustee rather than the beneficiary—or, to give the power separately to both the life beneficiary and the special trustee, and let the special trustee exercise it alone if the law does not develop favorably and he wishes to do so.

---

[51] Priv. Ltr. Rul. 9451049 (Sept. 22, 1994).

[52] Based on Priv. Ltr. Rul. 8535020, above.

[53] Treas. Reg. § 25.2514-3(e), example 2.

[54] Based on Priv. Ltr. Rul. 9451049, above.

If the prospective beneficiary will need more rights, or the situation arises in the context of an irrevocable document, one must decide whether to take a chance that the IRS is wrong. If the holder has an income interest, the regulations and the Tax Court say there is a gift. On the other hand, the Court of Claims has said there isn't. Can the holder exercise the power, and take the position that there is no gift? Yes, but he intentionally disregards the regulations, which are presumed to be correct.[55]

If the holder's beneficial interest is discretionary, or limited by an ascertainable HEMS standard, the only authority in each situation saying the exercise is a gift are the private letter rulings issued in 1985 and 1994, respectively. The IRS does not appear to have tried to assert the theory adopted in those rulings in any reported cases or revenue rulings.

[3] Creator Has Retained Interest/Power

If the creator of a power of appointment did not make a completed gift upon establishing the trust, and the holder of the power exercises it, the creator may be deemed to have made a gift upon the holder's exercise of the power.

> **EXAMPLE:** Mom puts property in a revocable trust and gives Child a general power of appointment over the trust. When Child withdraws for his own benefit, Mom makes a gift to Child.

[4] Exercise Without Regard to Rule Against Perpetuities

Most states have a "rule against perpetuities," which says that a trust can only last for 21 years after designated lives in being at its creation (or some variation in length). A person who exercises a limited power of appointment may (depending on state law and the terms of the power) be permitted to appoint the property in further trust and give the new beneficiaries a limited power of appointment. However, in most states, the rule against perpetuities limits how long this can go on. Even in the few states that allow powers of appointment to continue the trust indefinitely, families cannot avoid transfer tax by exercising limited powers of appointment at each generational level.

If a holder (say, Child) exercises any power of appointment by creating another power of appointment which allows its holder (say, Grandchild) to extend the original trust beyond a permitted period under the traditional rule against perpetuities, certain consequences will ensue. If the exercise is of the sort that would have resulted in the property being included in Child's estate if she had owned and given away the appointed property, the property will be

---

[55] National Muffler Dealers Ass'n v. United States, 440 US 472, 477 (1979).

includable in her estate.[56] If the exercise is not of that sort, it will be a taxable gift.[57]

There is a technique built around this rule called the "Delaware tax trap." Mom gives property to a trust for Child. Trust gives Child a power of appointment that can be exercised without regard to the rule against perpetuities (something which may be doable under Delaware law). Then Child can either choose to exercise it in such a fashion, causing an estate or gift transfer, or Child can choose not to exercise it in such a fashion, causing the trust to be governed by the generation-skipping transfer tax, rather than the gift or estate tax. This enables Child to decide, after the trust's creation, whether it is more advantageous to have an estate or gift tax apply or the generation-skipping transfer tax apply[58] to the transfer of the trust assets to someone other than Child.

[5] Exercise of Limited Power Over Grandfathered Generation-Skipping Trust

Suppose a person holds a limited power of appointment over a trust that is old enough to be grandfathered for generation-skipping transfer tax purposes. Can he exercise the limited power so as to extend the term of the trust for another generation or two? Yes, and such an exercise will not affect the grandfathered status of the trust, as long as the applicable rule against perpetuities is respected.[59] It is usually smart to exercise limited powers of appointment over grandfathered trusts to make them last as many generations as possible.

---

[56] IRC § 2041(a)(3).

[57] IRC § 2514(d).

[58] Situations in which one tax may be preferable over another are discussed in Ch. 5.

[59] Treas. Reg. § 26.2601-1(b)(1)(v)(B). If there is no applicable rule against perpetuities, the regulations provide a rule. See Ch. 5 on the Generation-Skipping Transfer Tax.

CHAPTER 4

Optimizing the Tax Attributes of Married Couples

¶ 4.01 INTRODUCTION

A cornerstone of estate planning for couples is making the best use of the tax attributes of both Husband and Wife. For this purpose, "tax attributes" means the spouse's annual exclusion amount, unified credit, generation-skipping transfer tax exemption, and run-up the brackets to $3,000,000, and to $10,000,000.

NOTE: For illustrative purposes, we will assume in this chapter that Husband is the first spouse to die and thus Wife is the surviving spouse. In the case of gifts, it is assumed that Husband transfers property to Wife. The principles, of course, operate the same way if the situation is reversed.

Suppose Husband and Wife do not wish to pay transfer taxes at the first death. A basic estate plan will take advantage of both spouses' unified credits and will leave the remaining property to or for the benefit of Wife in a manner that qualifies for the marital deduction.

¶ 4.02 TRANSFERS THAT QUALIFY FOR THE MARITAL DEDUCTION

The taxable estate is determined by subtracting allowable deductions from the gross estate. The estate tax marital deduction is a deduction from the gross estate for property passing to the spouse in a qualifying form.

EXAMPLE: Husband has gross estate of $1,000,000. He leaves all of it in a qualifying form. His taxable estate will then have a value of zero: $1,000,000 (gross estate) less $1,000,000 (marital deduction).

Any transfer of property by Husband to Wife, during his lifetime or at his death, will be free of transfer tax if it is transferred in a form that qualifies for the unlimited marital deduction.[1] Marital deduction transfers must be structured in one of several ways.

[1] Outright Gift or Bequest

This type of disposition is generally made in a form such as: "I, Husband, leave my estate to my Wife."

When might this type of disposition be especially desirable? One instance might be for transfers of a principal residence. This is because, if Wife later sells the house, she may be able to qualify for a tax-free rollover of gain,[2] and/or the $125,000 exclusion of gain for taxpayers over 55.[3] Most marital deduction trusts are not eligible for these benefits.[4]

Although the trust would not be eligible for these benefits, can the trust distribute the residence to Wife immediately prior to the time the trust would have entered into the contract of sale, let her make the sale, and render these benefits available to her? The answer is "yes," in the case of the Section 1034 tax-free exchange, but generally "no," in the case of the Section 121 gain exclusion. This is because Section 121 requires Wife to have owned the house and used it as her principal residence for three out of the five years before the sale.[5] However, Wife will be deemed to meet this holding and use requirement, provided that (1) the sale of the house occurred within two years after Husband's death, (2) Husband had owned and used the house as his principal residence for three out of the five years preceding the sale, and (3) Husband had made no other election.[6]

The second category of items usually left outright to the surviving spouse, instead of in trust, is household and personal effects. The motivating factor in this instance is ease of administration. That is, it may be troublesome for a trustee to account for and keep track of such items.

[2] QTIP Trust

"QTIP" stands for "qualified terminable interest property." A QTIP trust is a trust for the benefit of Wife which meets the requirements described below. It will qualify for the marital deduction to the extent that Husband or his

---

[1] IRC §§ 2056(a), 2523(a).

[2] IRC § 1034.

[3] IRC § 121.

[4] A trust with a general power of appointment by deed would qualify. Rev. Rul. 85-45, 1985-1 CB 183 (referencing Rev. Rul. 66-159, 1966-1 CB 162).

[5] IRC § 121(a)(2).

[6] IRC § 121(d)(2).

executor elects.[7] The trust must be held for the benefit of Wife during her lifetime; at her death, it can pass to persons chosen by Husband.[8] The people who will receive the property after Wife's death are called the "remainder beneficiaries."

[a] When Is a QTIP Trust a Good Idea?

An outright gift is uncomplicated and makes sense in many situations. However, the QTIP trust is by far the most popular marital deduction gift among the affluent, especially for estate transfers, because of the additional flexibility and protection it provides. In addition, the availability of a partial QTIP election and a reverse QTIP election provides additional options for maximizing the benefits of both spouses' generation-skipping transfer tax exemptions and other transfer tax attributes.

> **EXAMPLE:** Husband leaves property to a testamentary QTIP trust, providing that Wife is the life beneficiary, and his children are the remainder beneficiaries. The QTIP format allows Husband's executor the flexibility to choose, with knowledge of the facts existing after Husband's death, whether it is best to qualify all, any part, or none of the property for the marital deduction. The QTIP trust assures that any property left in the trust on Wife's death goes to Husband's chosen beneficiaries, rather than a second husband or other person outside the family. It can also provide protection from subsequent divorcing husbands and creditors of Wife during her lifetime.

PRACTICE POINTER: If limitations on Wife's interest are important to Husband, he can hedge Wife's rights with restrictions contained in the will or trust instrument. However, if Wife is the sole trustee, or the sole managing trustee, she will, as a practical matter, have control over the trust assets. If she does violate the terms of the trust, the remainder beneficiaries will have the right to sue her; however, they may be reluctant to do so, since lawsuits tend to be expensive, troublesome, and destructive to family relations. If Husband is serious about restricting Wife's powers, it may be appropriate to name another trustee or co-trustee.

If Husband leaves property to a QTIP trust, what rights can/must Wife have?

---

[7] The fact that an election is necessary is beneficial, because it is sometimes better not to elect to qualify a transfer for the marital deduction. See Chs. 49 and 50 on post mortem elections.

[8] IRC §§ 2056(b)(7), 2523(f).

[b] QTIP Requirement: All Trust Income Distributed Annually to Wife

Wife must receive all income of the trust, at least annually.[9] The term "income" means income as determined under applicable state law fiduciary accounting principles, rather than taxable income for income tax purposes.[10]

Can the trustee avoid paying income to Wife by investing all of the trust's assets in property that does not produce trust accounting income (for example, growth stocks or raw land)? Generally, not without Wife's consent.[11] Hence, a provision giving Wife the power to require the trustee to make the trust productive of income is usually part of the boilerplate in a QTIP trust document. This requirement can raise difficulties in certain situations.

> EXAMPLE: Second Wife is income beneficiary of a QTIP trust; children of the first marriage are the remainder beneficiaries. Wife would like to maximize income earned by the trust. The trust's major asset is an interest in a family business that does not pay dividends. The business interest would be hard to sell. The required QTIP provision allowing Wife to force the trustee to make the trust productive of income could lead to unpleasant consequences for all of the beneficiaries.

In the foregoing commonly encountered example, what's good for Wife isn't necessarily what's good for the remainder beneficiaries. Should a QTIP trust always be avoided in such a situation? No, not necessarily. However, the practical ramifications of the requirement should be examined, and solutions should be considered if the issue looks problematic.[12]

Stub period income. The stub period income between the surviving spouse's date of death and the last income payment is apparently not required to be distributed to the surviving spouse's estate.[13] However, the amount of stub period income will be included in the surviving spouse's gross estate.[14]

Current income interest. The IRS has privately ruled that a bequest of a vested remainder interest, subject to a third party's life estate, could not

---

[9] IRC §§ 2056(b)(7)(B)(i), 2056(b)(7)(B)(ii)(I).

[10] For example, taxable income would usually include capital gains; accounting income usually would not. Taxable income is determined by the Internal Revenue Code; accounting income is usually determined by the applicable state law regarding principal and income of trusts.

[11] Treas. Reg. § 20.2056(b)-5(f), Treas. Reg. § 20.2056(b)-7(h) example 2.

[12] Chapter 40, dealing with estate planning in the blended family, discusses this subject in detail.

[13] Treas. Reg. § 20.2056(b)-7(d)(4); Howard Estate v. Comm'r, 910 F2d 633 (9th Cir. 1990), rev'g 91 TC 329 (1988); Shelfer Estate v. United States, 78 AFTR 2d 96-5177, 96-2 USTC ¶ 60,238 (11th Cir. 1996), rev'g 103 TC 10 (1994).

[14] Treas. Reg. § 20.2044-1(d)(2).

qualify for QTIP treatment, since the income interest would be delayed until the third party died.[15]

Annuity in lieu of income. Can a QTIP trust pay an annuity to Wife rather than the amount of the income? The answer is generally "no," under the present regulations. A gift or bequest of an annuity to the spouse which is payable from a trust or other group of assets passing from the decedent, or a direction to the executor to purchase an annuity for the spouse, will not qualify for the marital deduction.[16] However, an exception exists in the case of

- decedents dying before October 25, 1992 and
- decedents dying after October 24, 1992, if (1) the property passes pursuant to a will or revocable trust executed before October 25, 1992 and (2) either the decedent was not competent to change the will or trust on October 24, 1992 and never regained competence, or the decedent died before October 24, 1995 and did not change his will or trust after October 24, 1992 so as to increase the amount of the marital deduction or alter the terms by which the interest passed to the surviving spouse.[17]

The IRS has requested comments on the application of the income requirement to annuities.[18] A provision in a QTIP trust that the spouse receives the greater of the annuity payment or the income in any year should be okay.

[c] QTIP Requirement: Wife Is Sole Beneficiary During Her Life

No one but Wife can receive distributions during her lifetime.[19] Does this mean that Wife can't have a power of appointment in favor of others[20] during her lifetime? That's right.

What if Wife wants to let the kids have some of the QTIP property while she is alive? Isn't there a way? If a transfer to the children during Wife's lifetime seems appropriate, some options (discussed in the following subsections) are available.

[i] Assignment of wife's interest in the trust. Wife can assign her interest

---

[15] Priv. Ltr. Rul. 9604003 (Oct. 10, 1995); Priv. Ltr Rul. 9717005 (Apr. 25, 1997).

[16] Treas. Reg. §§ 20.2056(b)-1(f), 20.2056(b)-1(g), example (7).

[17] Treas. Reg. § 20.2056(b)-7(e).

[18] Preamble to TD 8522, 1994-1 CB 236, issuing final and proposed marital deduction regulations.

[19] IRC §§ 2056(b)(7)(B)(i), 2056(b)(7)(B)(ii)(II).

[20] A power of appointment allows Wife to transfer the trust property during her life and/or to determine who will receive trust assets on her death. Powers of appointment are more fully discussed in Ch. 3.

in the trust to the children, if the trust is not a spendthrift trust.[21] The assignment will be deemed a taxable transfer of both the assigned income interest and all other interests in the trust, except to the extent that the transfer qualifies for one of the normal exceptions from gift tax.[22]

> EXAMPLE: QTIP trust holds assets worth $750,000. Wife gives her income interest in the trust to Child. Because of the special rule, she is deemed to have made a gift of the entire $750,000, not just the value of her income interest. Does this result make any sense? Well, yes. The entire trust would have been included in Wife's gross estate if she had died without making the assignment. She cannot avoid transfer tax on the entire value of the trust by giving her income interest away during her lifetime, except to the extent that the usual transfer tax exceptions apply.

Wife's right to recover gift tax from income interest assignee. If Wife assigns her income interest, she has the right to recover the gift tax paid on the remainder interest from the assignee.[23] However, she may waive this right. If she reserves the right, does she make a gift of the entire value of the property or the value of the property less the gift tax that she is entitled to recover? It seems that the answer would be the value of the property, less the gift tax. If she in fact does not recover the gift tax, then perhaps she makes an additional gift when her right to recover it expires. The authority on these points, however, is not clear.

The original proposed regulations provided that the amount of Wife's gift would be computed according to the usual computation applicable to net gifts (gifts on which the donor requires the donee to pay the gift tax).[24] This calculation would result in a gift of the value of the transferred property less the value of the gift tax reimbursement.[25]

The IRS subsequently developed a theory, however, that the statute giving the wife the right of reimbursement could be viewed as shifting the gift

---

[21] A "spendthrift trust" does not mean that any trust beneficiary is a spendthrift. It means that the beneficiaries cannot assign their interests in the trust. Many trusts include spendthrift trust provisions, mostly because spendthrift trusts are protected from the beneficiaries' creditors to some extent, and may be protected from a beneficiary's own excesses, as well. Spendthrift provisions are further discussed at ¶ 4.02[2][d] and Ch. 53.

[22] IRC § 2519. These will be the tuition and medical exceptions, IRC § 2503(e), and transfers qualifying for the gift tax annual exclusion, IRC § 2503(b). These transfers are more fully described in Ch. 10.

[23] IRC § 2207A(b).

[24] Former Prop. Reg. § 25.2519-1(a).

[25] If a donor makes a net gift, the value of the gift is considered the property transferred less the gift tax. Former Prop. Reg. § 25.2519-1(a). See, e.g., Rev. Rul. 75-72, 1975-1 CB 310.

tax liability to the recipient, and that payment of gift tax by a person who is liable for the tax by statute should not have the effect of reducing the amount of the gift for gift tax purposes (as is the case with net gift treatment).[26] It is not totally clear what, if any, decision was reached on the point.

The final regulations deleted the proposed regulation on that issue and reserved that section in anticipation of subsequent proposed regulations.[27] However, an example in another part of the regulations indicates that the value of the gift will be the entire value of the interest, without reduction for gift tax recovered.[28] The regulations do not address the consequences, if any, of Wife's actual recovery of the gift tax.

Assignment of fractional income interest. If Wife assigns a fractional part of her income interest, the corresponding fraction of the trust is deemed to be assigned.

> **EXAMPLE:** QTIP trust holds assets worth $750,000. Wife assigns one-half of her income interest to Child. Wife is treated as having given one-half of the trust assets away.

[ii] Purchase of remainder interest. Wife can buy the remainder interest in the trust from the children, if (1) the trust is not a spendthrift trust and (2) the children's interests are vested.[29] If the purchase is made for cash, this transaction will result in money being transferred to the children, rather than trust property. If the children's interests are contingent, or any child is a minor, court approval of the purchase may be necessary. In a court proceeding, a guardian ad litem or other personal representative will probably be appointed by a court to represent the minor, unborn, and unascertained beneficiaries. If Wife pays the children the fair market value of the remainder interest,[30] it seems that she should not be viewed as making a taxable gift to the children.

Some courts, however, have held, as a matter of law, that the actuarial value of a remainder interest sold by a parent to a family trust (which was not

---

[26] See, e.g., Rev. Rul. 80-111, 1980-1 CB 208.

[27] Preamble to TD 8522, 1994-1 CB 236; Treas. Reg. § 25.2519-1(c)(4).

[28] Treas. Reg. § 25.2519-1(c)(1), § 25.2519-1(g)(1).

[29] "Vested" is the opposite of "contingent." "Vested" means that the interest will take effect without regard to any contingencies. For example, suppose Mom establishes a trust to pay income to Child for her life. The trust provides that the remainder after Child's life goes to Grandchild, but if Grandchild is not alive at Child's death, the interest goes to Grandchild's estate. Grandchild has a vested interest. Suppose, instead, that if Grandchild is not alive at Child's death, Brother will take the remainder. Grandchild has an interest which is contingent on his being alive at Child's death.

[30] The fair market value of a remainder interest is normally determined by multiplying the total value of the trust assets by a factor contained in the Treasury's actuarial tables.

otherwise includable in the parent's estate) or to family members was not adequate consideration for the transfer of the remainder interest. Rather, the purchaser of the remainder interest would have to pay the parent the entire value of the property in order to avoid a deemed gift by the parent.[31]

Those cases have been widely criticized.[32] However, since they exist, is there an opportunity to use them to a taxpayer's advantage? If their reasoning applies to the purchase of a remainder interest, as well as the sale, then a parent purchasing the remainder interest in property would be required to pay the children the full value of the property—an estate planning coup.

In the particular case of a purchase of a remainder interest in a QTIP trust, the IRS may also take the position that, since the surviving spouse is essentially already deemed to own the entire QTIP property for transfer tax purposes, the payment of any purchase price by the spouse is a gift. The theory would be that payment of the purchase price of an asset the surviving spouse is already deemed to own under Section 2044 (the remainder interest in the trust) depletes the surviving spouse's estate by the entire amount of the purchase price without a corresponding addition to her estate (the value of the purchased remainder).

Section 2702 implications. It should be noted that all of the above cases involved transfers which predated the effective date of Section 2702. That section, which specifically addresses a transfer of an actuarial interest by a person who also retains an interest in the trust, supersedes this case law in situations involving the sale of a remainder interest by a person who retains a life estate. However, if Wife buys the remainder interest, she will own both the income and remainder interests in the property; these interests will normally merge under state law, so that she will end up owning the trust assets outright—Section 2702 would not appear to apply. If the interests do not merge under local law, Section 2702's special gift tax valuation rules, discussed in Chapters 22 and 24, may apply to the transaction.

[iii] **Loans.** The trust can lend money to the children; the transaction must be on fair market value terms. A private letter ruling has approved this

---

[31] Gradow v. United States, 11 Cl. Ct. 808 (1987), aff'd, 897 F2d 516 (Fed. Cir. 1990); accord Parker v. United States, 894 F. Supp. 445 (ND Ga. 1995), aff'd without op., Parker v. United States, 74 F3d 1253 (11th Cir. 1995); Pitman v. United States, 878 F Supp 833 (EDNC 1994); Magnin v. Comm'r, 71 TCM 1856 (1996); contra, Estate of D'Ambrosio, 101 F3d 309 (3d Cir. 1996), rev'g 105 TC 252 (1995), cert. denied, 117 S. Ct. 1822 (1997); Wheeler v. United States, 97-2 USTC ¶ 60,278 (5th Cir. 1997), rev'g 77AFTR 2d 96-1411, 96-1 USTC ¶ 60,226 (WD Tex. 1996). See also United States v. Allen, 293 F2d 916 (10th Cir. 1961), cert. denied, 368 US 9448 (1961) (sale of parent's retained income interest in trust to child for actuarial value).

[32] See, e.g., Pennell, Cases Addressing Sale of Remainder Wrongly Decided, 22 Est. Plan. 305 (Sept./Oct. 1995).

technique in fairly extreme circumstances.[33] Once the loan is made, can everyone wink at each other and just forget about collecting it? No, not without tax consequences. If it can be demonstrated that the loan is a sham in the first place, Wife may be deemed to have assigned the interest when the loan is made.[34] Suppose the loan is initially bona fide, but, as time goes by, the child never fully repays it, the trustee does not enforce the trust's right to repayment, and Wife does not enforce her rights to require the trustee to pursue the child. When the statute of limitations expires on the trustee's right to collect the loan, and on Wife's right to sue the trustee for not trying to collect, Child will have in essence received a gift, if he in fact could have repaid the loan. Wife may be deemed to make an assignment of the interest when she allows her rights to expire, triggering tax on the entire principal and interest outstanding at that time.[35]

[iv] **Payment for services.** The trustee can pay the children a fair price for services actually rendered to the trust. However, consideration must be given to state trust laws which prohibit a trustee from self-dealing. Hence, if the beneficiary receiving the payment is the trustee, and the state's self-dealing rule is not or cannot be waived in the trust instrument or by the beneficiaries, state law may prohibit both loans and payment of compensation (except for services as trustee) to the trustee-beneficiary.

[d] Optional QTIP Provision: Spendthrift Trust Clause

A spendthrift clause will make the trust interests to which it applies nonassignable. Omitting the clause will provide flexibility to make tax-motivated (and other) gifts of trust interests. Including the clause will afford the protection that is provided by the creation of an inalienable interest.[36] This can include protection from subsequent husbands, subsequent divorces, Wife's creditors, overly importunate charities, family members, or what-have-you.

So—should a spendthrift provision be included in a QTIP trust? It's a tradeoff, requiring a judgment in each situation of which advantage is more important—the ability to transfer the trust interests versus the protection such a clause offers.

The best of both worlds, however, may be to include the spendthrift clause and to appoint a non-beneficiary special trustee who has the ability to distribute to Wife for reasons beyond health, education, maintenance, and

---

[33] Priv. Ltr. Rul. 9418013 (Feb. 2, 1994).

[34] Rev. Rul. 77-299, 1977-2 CB 343.

[35] E.g., Estate of Lang v. Comm'r, 613 F2d 770, 773-774 (9th Cir. 1980); Rev. Rul. 81-264, 1981-2 CB 185.

[36] See Ch. 53 on asset protection for a discussion.

support (the "HEMS" standard). This trustee does not have to have any other powers over the trust. This way, if it is desirable for Wife to make gifts, the special trustee can distribute funds to her, and she can then make the gifts.

If we choose the special or independent trustee route, should we provide in the trust document that this trustee can distribute to Wife for the purpose of making gifts to others? It's probably best not to tie a distribution (or the ability to make a distribution) to the condition that it be used to make a gift. That's very close to the power to distribute to persons other than Wife—which is a definite no-no, even if Wife's consent is required. If Wife wants a distribution to make a gift, and the special trustee approves, the special trustee should just distribute to her. If she then chooses to do something else with the money instead of giving it to the approved recipient, so be it. That can be weighed the next time the circumstance arises.

[e] Optional QTIP Provision: Spouse-Trustee

Wife can be trustee, if her powers to distribute to herself are limited to distributions for her own HEMS.[37] She can have complete control over the asset management.

[f] Optional QTIP Provision: Spouse's Right to Invade Principal

Wife can have the power, in her individual capacity, to direct the trustee to distribute the principal of the trust for her own HEMS.[38] A trustee other than Wife can distribute principal to Wife, in his sole discretion, unlimited by a standard. That trustee should not be a beneficiary of the trust, since a distribution to the Wife not covered by the standard could be a taxable gift by the beneficiary, even if it is made in a fiduciary capacity.

[g] Optional QTIP Provision: Testamentary Limited Power of Appointment

At Wife's death, the property remaining in the trust passes to persons chosen by Husband when the trust was created. Husband can choose to give

---

[37] Astute technicians will note that, since the QTIP trust is taxable in Wife's estate, there is no gift/estate tax reason to limit her invasion rights to HEMS. However, giving discretion to her in excess of that standard will turn the QTIP trust into a trust with a lifetime general power of appointment. This will (a) at best, eliminate the flexibility to elect not to qualify any or all of the trust as marital deduction property, and (b) at worst, create a trust which does not qualify for the marital deduction in Husband's estate (if it does not meet all the separate requirements of a general-power-of-appointment marital deduction trust), but is includable in Wife's estate. Exceeding the HEMS standard can also vitiate the trust's protection from creditors.

[38] See preceding footnote.

Wife a testamentary limited power of appointment - that is, a power to change the beneficiaries by her will. This power can be limited to whatever class of beneficiaries Husband likes. For example, he can give her a power to appoint to and among his descendants, his descendants and charities, his descendants and their spouses, or any other class.

[h] QTIP Requirement: Timely Filed Election

A timely election must be made by Husband, if he is alive, or by his executor, if he is not, to qualify the trust for QTIP treatment.[39] The election is made on the gift or estate tax return, as the case may be.

[3] Annuity Includable Under Section 2039

Certain annuities that are not receivable as proceeds of life insurance policies may qualify for the marital deduction, to the extent that the annuities were purchased with Husband's funds. For this purpose, amounts contributed to the purchase price by Husband's employer or former employer are considered contributed by Husband if the contributions were made by reason of Husband's employment. Eligible annuities are those which are receivable by Wife by reason of surviving Husband, provided that Wife's rights arise under any form of contract or agreement entered into after March 3, 1931 which granted Husband the right to receive an annuity or other payment for his life, for any period which could not be determined without reference to his death, or for any period which did not end before his death. An example would be an annuity payable under Husband's employee benefit plan. This kind of annuity will qualify for the marital deduction if Wife is the only person who is eligible to receive benefits during her lifetime and no contrary election is filed by the executor.[40]

[4] Other Marital Deduction Forms

Other less commonly used forms of marital deduction transfers also exist, and are occasionally useful in particular situations.[41] However, the above—outright gifts, QTIP trusts, and employment-related annuities—are the big three.

---

[39] IRC §§ 2056(b)(7)(B)(v), 2523(f)(4).

[40] IRC § 2056(b)(7)(C).

[41] These include the general power of appointment trust, IRC § 2056(b)(5); estate trust, Treas. Reg. § 20.2056(e)-2(b); life insurance or annuity with general power of appointment, IRC § 2056(b)(6); and, charitable remainder trust, if the surviving spouse is the only noncharitable beneficiary, IRC § 2056(b)(8).

[5] Marital/Charitable Dispositions

Sometimes, an interest is left to the surviving spouse, with the remainder after certain events passing to charity. The interests left by such dispositions must technically qualify for both the marital and charitable deductions in order for these deductions to be available. If the dispositions do not qualify technically for both deductions, the fact that all of the property will necessarily pass either to the spouse or to charity will not suffice to make the disposition deductible.[42]

¶ 4.03 BASIC PLANNING TO UTILIZE BOTH SPOUSES' UNIFIED CREDITS

Basic planning for married couples who expect to have a combined estate over $600,000 usually includes a bypass trust and marital deduction gift. That is, Husband will leave his exempt amount ($600,000 if he hasn't made any taxable gifts during his life) to a "bypass trust" for Wife. The bypass trust is so called because it bypasses (that is, is not included in) Wife's estate when she subsequently dies. Husband will leave the residue of his estate to Wife in a form that qualifies for the marital deduction.

> **EXAMPLE:** Husband has $1,000,000. Wife has no property. Neither Husband nor Wife has made any taxable gifts. Husband dies. If he leaves the entire $1,000,000 to Wife, his death will trigger no estate tax, due to the unlimited marital deduction. When Wife dies, assuming no change in value, she will have a $1,000,000 estate, which will generate a tax of $153,000.[43]
>
> If, instead, Husband leaves $600,000 to a bypass trust, and the rest of his estate to Wife, no tax will be due on his estate, because $600,000 is exempt and the rest qualifies for the marital deduction. On Wife's subsequent death, the $600,000 will not be taxed because it is in a trust which bypasses her estate, and the $400,000 will be covered by her exemption—so the couple has saved $153,000 for the children. If, in the interim between Husband's death and Wife's death, the bypass trust has increased to a million dollars, a billion dollars, or any other amount, it is still entirely free from estate tax on Wife's death.

¶ 4.04 BYPASS TRUSTS

What does a bypass trust look like? Essentially, it can be similar to the QTIP trust, except that it is even more flexible. Income does not have to be distributed annually; rather, it can be accumulated for later distribution when the

---

[42] E.g., Roels v. United States, 928 F. Supp. 812 (ED Wis. 1996) (spouse's interest terminated in favor of charities on her remarriage).

[43] IRC § 2001(c)(1).

beneficiaries need it. The bypass trust can have additional current beneficiaries (like the children) during Wife's lifetime (thus allowing distributions to the children free of gift tax). Any power that Wife has to distribute to herself, whether in her capacity as trustee or under a power of invasion held by her as an individual, must be limited to distributions for her HEMS, in order to avoid inclusion of the trust in her estate.[44] However, she can have the power, unlimited by any standard, to distribute or appoint trust property to people other than herself during her lifetime or at her death.[45]

Suppose Husband would choose to leave his entire estate to Wife outright, if taxes were not a concern. He is using the bypass trust for tax reasons only, and wants the minimum possible restrictions imposed on Wife. In such a case, Wife could (1) be trustee of the bypass trust, (2) have a power to distribute to anyone she likes (except herself) at her discretion, and (3) have the power to distribute to herself for her own HEMS. However, the one power she cannot have is the power to make distributions to herself for purposes unrelated to her own HEMS. People do not always want to allow distributions to their spouses in excess of the HEMS standard. But, in this case, where the Husband wants as few restrictions as possible, such distributions can be authorized by a non-beneficiary special trustee who has no other powers over the trust.

The preceding paragraph describes the bypass trust with minimum limitations on Wife; the various powers and interests which could be held by her can be scaled back to any degree and in any combination. In fact, she is not required to have any rights or powers in the trust at all.

Is there a situation in which tax (as opposed to personal) reasons would favor an outright gift to the spouse, rather than a bypass trust, when the unified credit is still available at the first death? Yes. If Husband's estate is less than $600,000, and Wife's estate, including property left to her by Husband, is never expected to be more than $600,000, use of a bypass trust may be contraindicated. This is because, in this instance, the use of the bypass trust is not expected to save estate taxes, and property in the bypass trust at the second death will not receive a new income tax basis at Wife's death, whereas property that Wife owns outright will.

---

[44] IRC § 2041(b)(1)(A).

[45] Note, however, that the regulations provide that the exercise of a limited power of appointment which is unrestricted by a standard will be a gift by the wife if she is a trust beneficiary. Treas. Reg. § 25.2514-3(e), examples 1, 5. The value of the gift depends on the extent of the wife's beneficial interest in the trust, and may be virtually impossible to determine. See discussion in Ch. 3.

¶ 4.05 TAX AND EXPENSE APPORTIONMENT IN MODEL PLAN

Some expenses can be deducted only for estate tax purposes. Others can be deducted only for income tax purposes. Some can be deducted on either the estate tax return or the income tax return, but not both. Chapter contains a discussion of the most efficient way to allocate these expenses in different situations.

There is a standard way to apportion taxes and expenses at the first death of two spouses when: (1) the goal is to have zero estate tax at the first death, and to get as much property into the bypass trust as possible consistently with zero estate tax; (2) all property is initially passing to a bypass trust or marital deduction gift; and (3) the ultimate beneficiaries of all trusts after the surviving spouse's death are the same. In this plan, if the same people are generally expected to take the property passing from any source, the apportionment clause will be expected to have no substantive effect, as far as burdening one ultimate beneficiary more than another with taxes and expenses. However, it will have an effect on the amount of tax. The "right" clause allocates items which are chargeable to principal and deducted for estate tax purposes to the marital deduction bequest, other principal items to the non-marital bequest, and items which are properly chargeable to income under state law to income.[46]

¶ 4.06 WHO OWNS THE MARITAL PROPERTY?

Often, spouses do not precisely know, or especially care, which of them is the owner of the various items of marital property. However, for estate planning purposes, it can be important.

[1] Common Law States

In most states, the ownership of the marital property is determined in a manner similar to the ownership of nonmarital property. That is, the owner of any particular property is the spouse who earned it, whose property produced it, or who received it from other parties. The non-owner spouse may have rights in the property on the dissolution of the marriage by death,[47] divorce,[48] or functional equivalents of divorce.

---

[46] The income allocation is subject to the issues of the Hubert case, described in Ch. 49. These issues relate to whether expenses allocated to income will reduce the marital deduction.

[47] For example, widow's allowance, year's support, or right to an elective share.

[48] For example, equitable division, alimony, or spousal support, which may be secured by various interests in the property.

[2] Community Property

Several states (California, Texas, Louisiana, Washington, Arizona, Idaho, Nevada, New Mexico, and Wisconsin) provide that certain types of marital property are owned as community property. Three types of property may exist in marriages in these states—the separate property of Husband, the separate property of Wife, and the community property of the spouses.

In community property states, all marital property is generally considered community property except: property acquired before marriage; property that is acquired by either spouse by gift, devise, or inheritance; earnings from separate property, in some states; proceeds of disposition of separate property; property acquired as separate property when the marital domicile was in a common law state, at least for some purposes; personal injury proceeds, in some states; and property which the spouses agree is separate by a valid marital property agreement. Separate property which is commingled with community property may be magically transformed into community property, if the separate property cannot be traced or otherwise proven to be separate. In some states, the spouses can agree that a spouse's separate property is community property.

Community property is generally owned 50 percent by each spouse during the marriage. On the death of one of the spouses, the community property is generally divided in half—50 percent belongs to the deceased spouse's estate and 50 percent belongs to the surviving spouse. On divorce, all or part of the community estate may be awarded to either spouse and, depending on the particular state law, it may not necessarily have to be divided on a 50-50 basis.

There are a number of additional ramifications of holding property as separate or community. Community property (both halves) may be liable for certain debts of either spouse. On the death of one spouse, both halves of the community property receive a new income tax basis. The new basis for the property will equal twice the estate tax value of the decedent's half of the property, which may be more or less than the pre-death basis of the property.[49] Thus, the new basis, commonly referred to as a "step-up," may equally as well be a "step-down."

[3] Why the Nature of Marital Property Ownership Matters

The ownership of marital property may be important for a variety of reasons unrelated to estate planning,[50] but for our purposes, understanding the own-

---

[49] IRC §§ 1014(a), 1014(b)(6).

[50] These may include, for example, the determination of which spouse can manage the property, which spouse's creditors can reach the property, and which spouse receives the property on divorce.

ership of the property enables us to determine whether we can or should make use of both spouses' tax attributes.

¶ 4.07 USE OF BOTH SPOUSES' TAX ATTRIBUTES—BEYOND THE BYPASS TRUST

A husband and wife may wish to arrange the ownership of their marital property in such a way as to maximize tax advantages for the family as a whole. On the other hand, they may not. Tax minimization may or may not be consistent with the best arrangements for creditor protection, divorce protection, or division of property among children who are not all mutual children of the couple. Let's take a look, using the following Global Example, at the different tax results when the marital estate is equally divided, and when it is mostly owned by one spouse.

GLOBAL EXAMPLE

Suppose Father and Mother live in New York, a common law state. Son, Daughter-in-law, and their Child live in Texas, which is a community property state. Father has built an estate of $20,000,000 from his earnings as an investment banker. Son has built a $20,000,000 estate from his earnings as a movie star. Mother and Daughter-in-law have never worked outside the home. All property in both cases was earned during the marriages and the marital domiciles have never changed. THEREFORE, according to the respective state laws, Father has a separate estate of $20,000,000, Mother has no estate, and each of Son and Daughter-in-law has a community estate of $10,000,000.

These two couples' estates are similar, in that they both consist of $20,000,000, all earned by the husband during marriage. However, the transfer tax consequences of the different patterns of ownership will vary dramatically, particularly if either wife predeceases her husband.

[1] Gift Tax Annual Exclusions[51]

Equal estates. A gift to Child of $20,000 made by Son and Daughter-in-law will automatically qualify for both spouses' annual exclusions, even if only one of them writes the check. Assuming no further gifts by Son or Daughter-

---

[51] The $10,000 gift tax annual exclusion is discussed in detail in Ch. 10.

in-law to Child during that year, no gift tax return will be required because of such a gift.[52]

Unequal estates. If Father gives $20,000 to Child, Mother will need to elect to treat Father's gift as made half by her (gift-splitting), in order to use her annual exclusion.[53] Father must file a gift tax return, and both spouses must sign the consent.[54]

PRACTICE POINTER: The gift tax return preparer in the above situations should note that Son's and Daughter-in-law's returns (if they filed returns) would look exactly the same. Father's and Mother's returns will not be identical in form, although they will show the same amount of gift made by each spouse.

[2] Unified Credits

Equal estates. Son and Daughter-in-law will each be able to use the full unified credit, thereby enabling the first spouse to die to give $600,000 to a bypass trust (or in some other manner which will be free of further tax at the surviving spouse's death), no matter which spouse dies first.

Unequal estates. If Father dies first, he can use his unified credit by leaving $600,000 to a bypass trust. If Mother dies first, she will be unable to use any of her unified credit, since she does not have any estate. Father can change this, if he wants to, by giving Mother $600,000 during their joint lifetimes in such a way that it will be included in her estate. If he is inclined to do this, how should he go about it?

EXAMPLE: Father could accomplish this goal by giving Mother an outright gift. If Mother then dies first, she can leave the $600,000 to a bypass trust for Father or others.

EXAMPLE: Father could give Mother a life insurance policy on his life, with a value at date of gift of $600,000. If she predeceases him, only the value of the policy on her date of death (not the face amount) will be in her estate. The face amount will be out of Father's estate, if he lives for at least three years after the assignment, and Mother does not leave the policy to him or give him any incidents of ownership of the policy.[55]

EXAMPLE: If Father does not want to make an outright gift to Mother, he could give $600,000 to a QTIP trust for her. The IRS has ruled that, if: Father funds a QTIP trust for Mother during their lifetimes; Mother dies before Father; and, the remainder after her life is left in a bypass trust for

---

[52] IRC § 6019(1).

[53] IRC § 2513. This is permissible, even though Mother has no actual estate.

[54] Treas. Reg. §§ 25.2513-1(c), 25.2513-2(a)(1), 25.6019-2.

[55] Treas. Reg. § 20.2031-8.

Father, the bypass trust will not be included in Father's estate at his subsequent death.[56]

[3] Graduated Transfer Tax Rates

The gift and estate tax rates, after the first $600,000, begin at 37 percent for transfers in excess of $600,000 (but less than $750,000), and top out at 55 percent of transfers in excess of $3,000,000 (60 percent for the bubble between $10,000,000 and $21,040,000[57]). Stacking[58] the estates can prevent the utilization of the trip through the brackets by the estate of the first spouse to die. Since the couples in our global example do not have estates in the right range for this to be a factor, we will visit another couple, to illustrate this point.

> EXAMPLE: Husband and Wife each have an estate of $3,000,000. Husband dies. Wife dies one year later, and no values have changed. If Husband leaves everything to Wife except the unified credit amount, he will leave her $2,400,000 ($3,000,000 less unified credit of $600,000). The estate tax on that $2,400,000 at Wife's death will be $1,320,000, as it will all be taxed at 55 percent. If, instead, Husband leaves his entire estate to a trust that does not qualify for the marital deduction, and is not includable in Wife's estate, his taxable estate will be $3,000,000. The estate tax on this property will be $1,098,000. The difference in tax between the non-stacked estates and the stacked estates is $222,000.

In the above example, the $222,000 amount is the immediate dollar benefit of having the first $2,400,000 after the unified credit is used[59] taxed at the lower brackets, assuming that the alternative would be taxation on Wife's death of Husband's entire estate at 55 percent. If Husband's estate takes advantage of this bracket trip, his estate tax must be paid, generally, nine months after the date of his death.

So...should we stack the estates, once the unified credit has been used? The considerations involved in deciding whether to pay the tax at the first death versus the second are similar to those involved in making lifetime gifts versus estate transfers.[60] In the above example, if Husband's estate pays the estate tax of $1,098,000, the bypass trust for Wife will receive $1,902,000 from Husband's estate, after estate tax. So, both Husband's $1,902,000 after-tax

---

[56] Priv. Ltr. Rul. 9140069 (July 10, 1991).

[57] The bubble is discussed in subparagraph [4], infra.

[58] "Stacking" the estates means leaving the first spouse's estate to the other spouse in such a fashion that both estates are taxed at the second death. Two smaller estates will often pay less total tax than one "stacked" estate (which consists of both smaller estates).

[59] At $3,000,000, the 55 percent rate begins.

[60] See discussion in Ch. 8.

estate and his $1,098,000 estate tax will be out of Wife's estate, along with income and appreciation of the $1,902,000 occurring after Husband's death and before Wife's death. However, Wife will not have the use of the $1,098,000 tax money, and her ability to access the $1,902,000 will be determined by the terms of the will or trust.

Using a QTIP trust for the marital bequest will allow the executor the flexibility to choose whether or not to pay the tax, or any part of it, at the first death. Thus, the stacking decision can generally be postponed for 15 months after Husband's death.[61]

[4] Avoidance of Surtax

There is a gift and estate tax marginal rate of 60 percent on transfers over $10,000,000 and less than $21,040,000. This bubble serves to partially eliminate the benefit of the unified credit and the graduated rates in estates exceeding $10,000,000, and totally eliminates these benefits in estates exceeding $21,040,000.

Returning to our Global Example—

Equal estates. If Son and Daughter-in-law die simultaneously,[62] each will have an estate of $10,000,000, and neither estate will be subject to any surtax. Total estate tax will be $9,896,000.

Unequal estates. In contrast, the total tax on one $20,000,000 estate is almost $11,000,000—a difference of over $1,000,000.

Should Father consider making a $10,000,000 lifetime gift to Mother to equalize their estates and avoid the surtax?

Let's look at the following equalizing measures.

[5] Equalizing Measures

[a] Equalization Clause in Will

An equalization clause is sometimes used in wills to deal with deaths that occur simultaneously or in close succession. Such a clause will limit the marital deduction gift to the amount necessary to equalize the estates. For instance, in the Global Example, Father's will could provide that, if Mother dies with

---

[61] The QTIP election must be made on the Husband's estate tax return. The return is due nine months after death (IRC § 6075(a)), but the due date can usually be extended for six months.

[62] The principle described in this example is not limited to simultaneous deaths. This fact pattern is used to isolate the principle discussed, without having to consider post-death changes in the estate.

him or within six months after his death,[63] he bequeaths to her (or a QTIP trust for her benefit) whatever amount is necessary to equalize their estates, and leaves the rest to other beneficiaries. Father must die first for the equalization clause to accomplish anything.

[b] Equalization by Lifetime Gift

In the Global Example, if Mother dies first, an equalization clause will not do any good, since she has no estate to leave Father. Most younger, and even middle-aged, couples do not want to make equalizing gifts of major proportions. This is often for nontax reasons. For some couples, however, such gifts can be quite advantageous.

Suppose, in the Global Example, that Father and Mother are in their eighties. Mother is diagnosed with cancer and has a life expectancy of three years. It might make sense for Father to go ahead and give Mother (or a QTIP trust for Mother) an equalizing gift, in case she should die before he does. Even if Father in fact then dies before Mother, no adverse estate tax consequence should ordinarily ensue as a result of the marital gift.[64]

[6] Aspects of Lifetime Equalizing Gifts

Again, using the Global Example, Father should be aware that, if the couple subsequently divorces, any outright gift from Father to Mother will be her separate property. If the gift is in trust, the principal can be maintained for the family, but she must still maintain the minimum rights necessary for the marital deduction (in a QTIP trust, the right to income for life, the right to require investment of the assets in income-producing property, and no possibility of distributions to others during her lifetime).

Suppose Father gives Mother an interest in the family business. Does the gift qualify for the marital deduction if the business entity documents provide that Mother must sell her interest to the business or to Father if a divorce occurs? Yes, the gift will qualify for the marital deduction as long as the

---

[63] If Mother does survive for longer than six months, a marital deduction gift will probably be desirable. Six months (or death as a result of a common disaster, if later) is the maximum period which Mother can be required to live in order to receive benefits, consistent with qualifying the gift for the marital deduction if Mother does outlive Father by a substantial period. IRC § 2056(b)(3).

[64] In specific circumstances, qualification for certain tax benefits related to estates which substantially consist of closely held businesses (IRC § 6166), farms and ranches (IRC § 2032A), or stock which is to be redeemed on death (IRC § 303), could be affected by such a gift. IRC § 2035.

ultimate purchase price and terms are at fair market value, measured at the time of sale.[65]

The above-discussed ways of making an equalizing gift also apply to larger gifts.

PRACTICE POINTER: There is a limit to the extent that equalizing gifts make any difference. Once Wife's estate, including amounts given or left to her by Husband, reaches the lesser of one-half of Husband's remaining estate or $21,040,000, further gifts to her do not help guard against the wasting of tax benefits which could occur if she predeceases Husband. This is because additional transfers by either spouse will be subject to the same marginal rate. Therefore, an equalizing gift above that amount is not necessary or helpful.

[7] Putting Property in Survivorship Form

Suppose, in the Global Example, that, in 1997, Father and Mother put Father's property in joint tenancy with right of survivorship (JTWROS) or tenancy by the entirety form (both forms being referred to as "survivorship property"). The estate of a decedent dying after 1981 includes one-half of any survivorship property owned with the decedent's spouse, regardless of which spouse's funds were used to purchase the property.[66] Hence, if Mother dies first, one-half of the survivorship property will be included in her estate. All of the property will then belong to Father again.

[a] Disclaimer of Survivorship Property

Can Father disclaim the one-half of the property included in Mother's estate and thereby use Mother's tax attributes, if he was the actual contributor? Generally, yes, at least if (1) the survivorship property did not consist of a bank account or brokerage account and (2) the survivorship feature could have been unilaterally terminated by either spouse during the spouses' joint lifetime.[67]

[b] Basis of Survivorship Property

Whether or not Father can disclaim, will one-half of the survivorship property get a new basis at Mother's death? Generally, yes; however, the

---

[65] Priv. Ltr. Rul. 9606008 (Nov. 9, 1995).

[66] IRC § 2040(b). Compare *Gallenstein* issue, with respect to joint tenancies formed before 1977, discussed below.

[67] AOD 1990-06 (Feb. 7, 1990); Prop. Reg. § 25.2518-2(c)(4)(i). See Ch. 47 on disclaimers for a discussion.

property will not get a step-up in basis if Mother received her interest from Father by gift within one year of her death.[68] Presumably, for this purpose, the date of receipt of her interest would be the date(s) that the property was placed in survivorship form, at least to the extent that the titling of the property constituted a completed gift to her. It is possible to have survivorship property which was not the subject of a completed gift during Father's lifetime. For example, the proposed disclaimer regulations take the position, in the case of joint bank accounts and joint brokerage accounts, that there is no completed gift during the spouses' joint lifetime of property in the account, if the contributing spouse could unilaterally withdraw the funds and thereby deprive the other spouse of the property.[69] If there has been no completed gift of such an interest during Father's lifetime, Section 1014(e) should not apply to the interest on Mother's death.

[c] Joint Tenancy Created Before 1977

The Sixth Circuit, in *Gallenstein v. United States*,[70] the Fourth Circuit, and two district courts have held that spousal joint tenancies with right of survivorship created before 1977 are fully includable in the estate of the first spouse to die, except to the extent that the surviving spouse contributed to the property's purchase price. As a result, the surviving non-contributor spouse gets a basis step-up in the entire property (and not just in one-half the property) to its value on the date of the deceased spouse's death.[71]

The *Gallenstein* issue is as follows. Before 1977, under Section 2040(a) a predeceasing spouse's estate included the value of all property in which the decedent held an interest as JTWROS with his spouse, except any part of the interest shown to have originally belonged to the surviving spouse and not received from the deceased spouse for less than full consideration.[72] In 1976, Section 2040(b) was enacted. It provided that spouses who created JTWROS after 1976 would include one-half of the value of such JTWROS property in the estate of the first spouse to die, regardless of which spouse furnished the consideration. In 1978, the statute was amended to allow spouses to elect to

---

[68] Generally, property included in a decedent's estate receives a new basis for income tax purposes of its estate tax value. IRC § 1014(e), however, says that, if A gives appreciated property to B, and then B dies within one year and leaves the property to A, no increase in basis is allowed on B's death.

[69] Prop. Reg. §§ 25.2518-2(c)(4)(iv), 25.2518-2(c)(5) example 13.

[70] 70 AFTR2d 92-5683 (6th Cir. 1992).

[71] Gallenstein v. United States, 70 AFTR2d 92-5683 (6th Cir. 1992). Patten v. United States, 97-2 USTC ¶ 60, 279 (4th Cir. 1997), aff'g 77 AFTR2d 96-1877, 96-1 USTC ¶ 60, 231 (WD Va. 1996); Anderson v. United States, 96-2 USTC ¶ 60,235 (D Md. 1996).

[72] IRC § 2040(a).

apply the Section 2040(b) "50 percent rule" to JTWROS property created before 1977, in exchange for treating the election as a gift resulting from the fictitious severance and re-creation of a joint interest. In 1981, Section 2040(b) was amended by repealing the sections enacted in 1978 allowing an election for pre-1976 property and by making the 50 percent rule mandatory rather than elective, effective for estates of decedents dying after 1981. This series of laws has been interpreted by the courts (but not the IRS) to apply the 50 percent rule of Section 2040(b) to JTWROS property created after 1976, and the general pre-1977 rule of Section 2040(a) to JTWROS property created before 1977. This interpretation can result in 100 percent inclusion of pre-1977 JTWROS property in the predeceased spouse's estate. The surviving spouse's basis in the property is equal to the value of the property in the decedent's estate. This allows the surviving spouse to receive a step-up in the basis of the property at no federal estate tax cost, due to the availability of the unlimited marital deduction. The IRS has argued unsuccessfully that Section 2040(b) applies to spousal JTWROS property of decedents dying after December 31, 1981, regardless of when the JTWROS was created.

[8] Tax Basis Revocable Trust

A plan has been suggested to make use of the nonpropertied spouse's tax attributes and to achieve a new basis in all of both spouses' property on the death of the first to die. The plan makes use of the so-called "Tax Basis Revocable Trust."

The plan starts with contributing all (or any part) of the spouses' property to a revocable trust for their mutual benefit. In our Global Example, Father owns all of the marital property and Mother owns none. Father gives his property to the revocable trust. He retains the power to revoke the trust. After either spouse dies, the survivor can revoke the entire trust. The trust provides that Mother has the power during Father's life to direct the trustee of the trust to pay debts and taxes attributable to her property on her death. She can exercise the power by filing the direction with the trustee and giving notice to Father during her lifetime. If she does exercise the power, Father can avoid it by revoking the trust during her lifetime. If Mother predeceases Father and she has exercised her power, and Father did not revoke the trust during her lifetime, Father's power to revoke the trust after Mother's death is subject to the trustee's duties to pay Mother's estate's obligations.

The theory is that if Mother dies before Father, the entire trust will be includable in her estate as general power of appointment property, and the trust assets will, therefore, receive a new basis as of the date of Mother's death. Through disclaimer by Father, Mother's unified credit, generation-skipping transfer tax exempt amount, and graduated rate brackets can be used.

The IRS considered such a plan in 1992, and concluded that the property did not receive a new basis, due to Section 1014(e).[73] That section says that if A gives appreciated property to B, and then B dies within one year of the gift and leaves the property to A, there is no step-up in basis of the property on B's death. The Technical Advice Memorandum said that this situation should obviously operate on the same principle, because the donor spouse had not surrendered dominion and control over the property within one year before his death.[74]

It seems that this arrangement could be vulnerable under several theories. Section 2041(b)(1)(C)(i) says that a power of appointment that is only exercisable in conjunction with the creator of the power will not be deemed a general power of appointment. This power of appointment itself is supposedly exercisable by Mother alone and in all events. In practice, however, it requires Father's consent to exercise. If Mother exercises it by filing her notice with the trustees and Father does not like it, all he has to do is revoke the trust and get the property back, as long as Mother is still alive.

Under the same line of thinking, the power could also be defined as a special, rather than general, power by reason of Section 2041(b)(1)(C)(ii), which says that a power held by person A is not a general power if it is exercisable only in conjunction with person B, who has a substantial interest in the property subject to the power, if the value of B's interest would be decreased by the exercise of the power in favor of A.

This technique may be analogous to the non-spousal joint account rules. Generally, if Mom puts money into a joint account with Child, Child would have the right to withdraw for his own benefit. Mom also has the right to withdraw for her own benefit. If Mom predeceases Child, the entire account will be in her estate.[75] If Child predeceases Mom, nothing would be included in Child's estate, since there has been no completed gift.[76]

Some suggestions have been made to address the issues described above, although the suggestions have potential to cause more problems than they solve.[77] Suggested in the footnoted articles is a joint trust which would, among other things, require both spouses' consent to

---

[73] Tech. Adv. Mem. 9308002 (Nov. 16, 1992).

[74] See Paul M. Fletcher, Drafting Revocable Trusts to Facilitate a Stepped-Up Basis, 22 Estate Planning 100 (Mar./Apr. 1995), and Paul M. Fletcher, Tax Basis Revocable Trusts, 51 J. Miss. Bar, No. 1, at 23-29 (1995), for a discussion of the TAM by the taxpayer's co-counsel.

[75] IRC § 2040.

[76] Treas. Reg. § 20.2040-1(c), example (3).

[77] See Michael D. Mulligan, Income, Estate and Gift Tax Effects of Spousal Joint Trusts, Est. Plan. 195 (July/Aug. 1995), and Michael D. Mulligan, More on the Income, Estate and Gift Tax Effects of Spousal Joint Trusts, Est. Plan. 36 (Jan. 1996).

revoke, restrict distributions to the settlors to the minimum possible amount, and bar distributions of principal to one of the spouses. According to the articles, the techniques are risky, possibly resulting in a worse situation than straightforward estate planning would have produced.

CHAPTER **5**

Generation-Skipping Transfer Tax

¶ 5.01 INTRODUCTION

In the days before the generation-skipping transfer tax (GSTT) existed, people would sometimes avoid estate and gift tax at their children's level by passing family property to their grandchildren rather than their children. Even more popular were transfers to "dynastic" trusts benefiting children, grandchildren, and succeeding generations for as long as state law would permit. Such trusts, known as generation-skipping trusts, were the foundation of estate planning for large estates in pre-GSTT days. Vast fortunes descended for 100 years or more with no estate or gift tax. The GSTT was enacted in 1986 in response to this perceived loophole.[1]

The GSTT now applies to (1) generation-skipping transfers occurring before 2010, and (2) generation-skipping transfers occurring after 2010 (due to

---

[1] A previous version of the GSTT was enacted in 1976, and then retroactively repealed by the Tax Reform Act of 1986.

the sunsetting of the Economic Growth and Tax Reconciliation Act of 2001 (EGTRRA)).[2]

The GSTT applies, logically enough, to certain transfers by persons in higher generations to or for the benefit of persons in lower generations.[3] The tax is imposed at a flat rate equal to the maximum estate tax rate.[4] The GSTT is imposed in addition to estate and gift taxes. The effects of the GSTT are dramatic (although not necessarily more severe than successive transfers through estates).

The wealthy are in a position to avoid the GSTT to a certain extent by taking advantage of some of the techniques described in this chapter. To the extent that they can't avoid it, enormous taxes will be imposed on family fortunes as they pass down the generations. The GSTT could be the death knell of family dynasties.

This chapter deals with domestic application of the GSTT. The application of the GSTT to nonresident aliens is discussed in Chapter 52.

¶ 5.02 DEFINITIONS

To understand the GSTT, one must first become familiar with some terms.

[1] Transferor

The person who makes the transfer that is immediately or ultimately subject to the GSTT is the "transferor." Thus, if Mom gives property to a trust for the benefit of Child and Grandchild, Mom is the transferor.

The transferor may change as estate or gift tax is incurred with respect to trust[5] interests.[6] A trust may have multiple transferors. If it does, the portion of the trust attributable to each transferor's contributions is treated for GSTT purposes as a separate trust.[7]

---

[2] IRC § 2664, EGTRRA § 901.

[3] IRC § 2600 et seq.

[4] IRC §§ 2602, 2641.

[5] The term "trust" includes an arrangement (other than an estate) which has substantially the same effect as a trust. IRC § 2652(b)(1).

[6] See ¶ 5.03[6] below.

[7] IRC § 2654(b)(1).

[2] Member of the Family

Certain generation assignments are determined by reference to family relationships. For purposes of this chapter, we'll call these people in those relationships "members of the family." The following people are the members of the transferor's family: descendants of the transferor's grandparents; the transferor's spouse; the transferor's ex-spouse; descendants of the spouse's and ex-spouse's grandparents; and the spouses and ex-spouses of all categories of persons previously listed in this sentence.[8]

[3] Interest

[a] Who Has an Interest?

[i] **Individuals.** An individual has an "interest" in a trust if he is at the time a permissible distributee of income or principal from the trust.

> **EXAMPLE:** Trustee of Trust *A* can distribute to Child and Grandchild. Both Child and Grandchild have interests in Trust *A*.

[ii] **Charities.** A charity has an interest in a trust only if (1) it has a present *right* to distributions (as opposed to being a permissible distributee of discretionary distributions), or (2) the trust is a charitable remainder trust.[9]

[b] Ability to Have Support Obligation Satisfied as an Interest

If an individual's support obligations may be satisfied through *mandatory* distributions of trust income or principal, then that individual is deemed to have an interest in the trust. If support obligations may be satisfied through *discretionary* distributions, however, the individual will not be deemed to have an interest in the trust.[10]

> **EXAMPLE:** Child is the parent of Grandchild. Trust *A* provides that the trustee shall distribute income and principal for Grandchild's support, without regard to Child's duty or ability to support Grandchild. Grandchild is a minor. Child has an interest in the trust. If Trust *A* con-

---

[8] IRC §§ 2651(b), 2561(c) (dealing with persons whose generation assignment is determined by relationship to the transferor).

[9] IRC § 2652(c)(1).

[10] Treas. Reg. §§ 26.2612-1(e)(2)(i), 26.2612-1(f), example 15.

tained the word "may," instead of "shall," Child would not have an interest.

[i] Court-ordered support obligations. Suppose Child is a divorced parent who has judicially or contractually imposed child support obligations exceeding the basic state-law standards of parental support. What if the trust allows those child-support obligations to be satisfied from trust funds? The regulation providing that Child has no interest solely due to the trust's ability to satisfy his obligations speaks of "support obligations," and does not specify whether "support" means the basic state-law standard of support or whether it includes a broader standard imposed by a court (or a contractual settlement agreement incident to divorce). If the term "support obligations" means basic state-law standards, and the trust permits trust funds to be used to make Child's child support payments of $10,000/month, Child may have an interest in the trust, because trust funds could be distributed on Child's behalf. For instance, if the child support order requires Child to pay for Grandchild's summer vacation in France, then the trust's payment of those expenses may be considered a distribution to Child rather than to Grandchild.

[ii] Custodial accounts. Where an individual's support obligations may be satisfied through distributions from an account established under the Uniform Gifts to Minors Act, Uniform Transfers to Minors Act, or similar state law, the individual will not be deemed to have the right to receive current distributions from the account.[11]

> **EXAMPLE:** Grandma establishes a custodial account for her grandchild under the Uniform Transfers to Minors Act. The parents of the grandchild do not have an interest in the custodial account, even though distributions from it might satisfy their support obligations. The theory underlying this rule presumably is that, if distributions were made in satisfaction of the parents' obligations of support, the grandchild could sue to recover the amount of the distributions.

[iii] Mandatory support provisions. Some transferors to trusts like to provide that a Grandchild will (not may) be supported in Grandchild's accustomed lifestyle, without regard to Child's duty to support Grandchild. Nevertheless, in certain of those situations, it will be important that Child not have an interest in the trust (e.g., a grandchild's annual exclusion trust).[12] Can we accomplish these two objectives?

---

[11] Treas. Reg. § 26.2612-1(e)(2)(i). Note that the account, rather than the grandchild, is viewed as the skip person to whom the transfer is made, because the account is a trust equivalent for GSTT purposes. Treas. Reg. § 26.2652-1(b)(2), example 1.

[12] See discussion at ¶ 5.04[1].

In such a case, it is often a practical solution to provide that distributions cannot be made in satisfaction of Child's legal obligation of support *under state law*. The state law support obligation is often limited to basics, whereas the definition of "support" in a trust instrument can be much broader. For example, such a provision might not allow the trustee to buy groceries for Grandchild, yet allow the trustee to pay Grandchild's tuition at Harvard.[13]

[c] Disregarding GSTT-Avoidance Interests

If any significant purpose of creating an interest in a trust is the postponement or avoidance of the GSTT, the interest will be disregarded.[14]

EXAMPLE: Grandma establishes a trust for Grandchild and names the President of the United States, who is ten years younger than Mom, as a permissible beneficiary. If the President is respected as a beneficiary, the GSTT will be postponed until the President's interest terminates or property is distributed to Grandchild. Depending on the facts, however, the IRS might take the position that the President's interest was created to postpone or avoid GSTT, and therefore, should be disregarded.

EXAMPLE: Mom establishes a trust for Grandchild and names Nanny, who is ten years younger than Mom, as a current beneficiary. Nanny is a long-time family employee. Nanny's interest in the trust should be respected, unless there is evidence that a significant purpose of creating her interest was to postpone or avoid GSTT. It is possible that the IRS and the courts will use hindsight as evidence of the original intent—for example, by examining whether substantial distributions were actually ever made to Nanny.

[d] Look-Through Rules

If a corporation, partnership, estate, trust, or other entity (except a charity or governmental entity) holds an interest in property, individuals who have a beneficial interest in the entity are treated as having an interest in the property.[15]

EXAMPLE: Mom owns a receivable from Corporation. The stock of Corporation is owned by a trust for Grandchild. If Mom forgoes payment due

---

[13] Some states require a parent to furnish a child with a college education if the parent is financially able to do so and college is realistic for the child; however, no state requires the parent to send the child to an expensive private school as part of the statutory or common law obligation of support.

[14] IRC § 2652(c)(2); Treas. Reg. § 26.2612-1(e)(2)(ii).

[15] IRC § 2651(f)(2).

on the loan, then under certain circumstances, she may be treated as having made a gift.[16] If so, the gift will be a direct skip and may give rise to GSTT.

[4] Skip Person

The GSTT applies to transfers to skip persons, directly or through a trust. A "skip person" with respect to a transferor includes:

- A family member who is in the generation of the transferor's grandchildren or a younger generation—e.g., the transferor's grandchild and step-grandchild (and their spouses);[17]
- A person who is more than 37½ years younger than the transferor and is not a member of the transferor's family;[18]
- A trust, if the only beneficiaries who have interests in the trust are skip persons (or skip persons and charities, if the trust is a charitable remainder trust);[19] and
- A trust that has no permissible current beneficiaries and that can never distribute property to anyone but skip persons[20] (e.g., a trust that must accumulate income until Mom's grandchild is 21 and then terminate in favor of the grandchild or other skip persons).

[5] Non-skip Person

A "non-skip person," not surprisingly, is a person or trust who is not a skip person.[21] Thus, any person in a generation above the transferor's grandchild's generation is a non-skip person, and a charity or a governmental entity is a non-skip person.[22]

---

[16] See Chapters 2 and 31.

[17] IRC § 2613(a)(1).

[18] IRC § 2651(d).

[19] IRC §§ 2613(a)(2)(A), 2652(c)(1).

[20] IRC § 2613(a)(2). According to the regulations, this means that it can be actuarially ascertained that there is less than a 5 percent probability that a distribution to a non-skip person will ever occur. Treas. Reg. § 26.2612-1(d)(2).

[21] IRC § 2613(b).

[22] IRC § 2651(f)(3).

[6] Skip Persons and Non-Skip Persons—How to Identify

[a] Family Members

Generations are determined by relationship[23] to the transferor, in the case of a family member.[24] The transferor's spouse and ex-spouses are assigned to the transferor's generation.[25] A spouse or ex-spouse of a relative of the transferor (by blood or adoption) is assigned to the same generation as the relative.[26] A family member who is a member of more than one generation is assigned to the youngest applicable generation.[27]

> **EXAMPLE:** Mom (the transferor) has adopted her granddaughter. The granddaughter is assigned to the grandchild's generation, even though she is also Mom's adopted child.

[b] Other Persons

A person who is not a member of the transferor's family is assigned a generation based on the difference between his age and the transferor's age—a person who is no more than 12½ years younger than the transferor is in the transferor's generation; a person who is more than 12½ years younger than the transferor (but no more than 37½ years younger) is in the transferor's children's generation, and so on every 25 years.[28]

[c] Look-Through Rules

Persons who have interests under the look-through rules[29] are assigned generations accordingly.

> **EXAMPLE:** Mom establishes Trust *X*. Trust *X* can distribute funds to Trust *Y*, which can currently distribute to *A* and *B*. *A* and *B*, who are unrelated individuals, have interests in Trust *X* under the look-through rules. *A*, who is 35 years younger than Mom, is a non-skip person. *B*, who is 40 years younger than Mom, is a skip person.

---

[23] Relationship includes relation by blood, half-blood, adoption, marriage, or former marriage. IRC §§ 2651(b)(3), 2651(c).

[24] IRC §§ 2651(b), 2651(c).

[25] IRC § 2651(c)(1).

[26] IRC §§ 2651(b), 2651(c)(2).

[27] IRC § 2651(f)(1).

[28] IRC § 2651(d).

[29] Discussed at ¶ 5.02[3][d].

[d] Generation Assignment Changes

Can generation assignments be changed by marriage, divorce, or adoption? Yes, in some cases; no, in others. As a general rule, generation assignments can be altered by bringing a nonfamily member into the family by marriage or adoption. Otherwise, generation assignments will not be affected by family changes.

[i] **Marriage.** If Mom's boyfriend is 40 years younger than she is, then transfers by Mom to Boyfriend or his children will be generation-skipping transfers.[30] If Mom marries Boyfriend, however, Boyfriend and his children will no longer be skip persons.[31]

[ii] **Divorce.** If Mom's step-grandchildren are 15 years younger than Mom, can she step up their grandchildren's generation assignment to her children's generation by divorcing her Husband (i.e., their grandfather), and having the unrelated person rules apply? The answer is no.[32] If Mom and Husband divorce, Husband and his descendants will retain whatever generation assignments they had when Mom and Husband were married.[33]

[iii] **Adoption.** If Mom is 40 years old, and she adopts an unrelated three-day-old baby, the baby is in her child's generation.[34] If Mom adopts her three-day-old biological grandchild, the adopted child remains in the grandchild's generation.[35]

¶ 5.03 GENERATION-SKIPPING TRANSFERS (GSTS)

There are three types of GSTs—direct skips, taxable distributions, and taxable terminations.[36] Each has a variety of different tax effects.

---

[30] IRC § 2651(d).
[31] IRC § 2651(c)(1).
[32] IRC § 2651(c)(1).
[33] IRC § 2651(b)(2).
[34] IRC § 2651(b)(3)(A).
[35] IRC § 2651(f)(1).
[36] IRC § 2611.

[1] Direct Skips

A transfer of an interest in property that is subject to gift or estate tax and made directly to a skip person is a "direct skip."[37] A transfer can be "subject to gift or estate tax" even if no tax is actually payable. This could happen, for example, if Mom makes a gift to a grandchild that uses her unified credit or that qualifies for the annual exclusion.[38]

> **EXAMPLE:** Mom's gift of $10,000 to Grandchild is a direct skip. Even if the transfer qualifies for the gift tax annual exclusion or uses the unified credit, it is still a direct skip.[39]

[a] Predeceased Ancestor Exception

The predeceased ancestor rule applies in certain situations where deaths occur "out of order."

Note. As a working definition, the term "transferor group," in the following discussion, refers to the transferor, the transferor's spouse, and the transferor's ex-spouse.

[i] Descendants of members of the transferor group. The predeceased ancestor exception generally applies when a descendant of a member of the transferor group has predeceased the transferor. In such a case, the descendants of the predeceased person will "move up" a generation.[40]

> **EXAMPLE:** Mom transfers property to Grandchild. Child (Grandchild's parent) is deceased at the time. Under the predeceased ancestor exception, Grandchild will "move up" to Child's generation, so that the transfer will not be a direct skip.[41]
>
> The predeceased ancestor does not have to be the transferor's child. Thus, if Mom transfers property to Great-Grandchild, and if Child and

---

[37] IRC § 2612(c)(1).

[38] Treas. Reg. § 26.2652-1(a)(2).

[39] In some cases, a gift which qualifies for the annual exclusion or for the tuition and medical expense exclusion will not attract a GSTT. IRC § 2642(c). However, it will still be defined as a "direct skip."

[40] IRC § 2651(e)(1); Treas. Reg. § 26.2612-1(a)(2)(i).

[41] The predeceased ancestor exception applies even if Grandchild is adopted by a sibling of Child. See Priv. Ltr. Rul. 199907015 (Nov. 20, 1998).

Grandchild are deceased at the time, the transfer to Great-Grandchild will not be a direct skip, due to the move-up rule.[42]

[ii] Eligible collaterals. In limited situations, the predeceased ancestor exception applies to collateral relatives. An eligible collateral relative is a person who *is not* a descendant of a transferor group member, but who *is* a descendant of a parent of a transferor group member.[43] In such a case, the collateral transferee will "move up" a generation if the transferor has no living lineal descendants at the earliest time that the transfer (from which an interest of the transferee is established or derived) is subject to gift or estate tax imposed upon the transferor.[44]

> **EXAMPLE:** Great-Uncle Joe has no living descendants. His sister has one deceased child and one living grandson by the deceased child. If Joe makes a gift to his sister's grandson, the predeceased ancestor provision will apply, Joe's grandnephew will be considered to be his nephew for purposes of the GSTT, and the transfer will not be considered a direct skip.

[iii] Ninety-day survival rule. For purposes of the predeceased ancestor exception, if Child (for example) dies within 90 days after Mom's transfer to Grandchild or a lower generation descendant, Child will be treated as predeceasing Mom to the extent that the governing instrument or local law provides that Child is deemed to predecease Mom.[45]

> **EXAMPLE:** Mom dies. She leaves her estate to Child, but provides in her will that if Child does not survive her by at least 90 days, Child will be treated as predeceasing her, and Grandchild will take the estate. If Child dies 60 days after Mom dies, Grandchild will "move up" a generation, and the transfer to Grandchild will not result in a GSTT.

---

[42] Treas. Reg. § 26.2612-1(a)(2).

[43] IRC § 2651(e).

[44] IRC § 2651(e)(2).

[45] Treas. Reg. § 26.2612-1(a)(2)(i).

Practice Pointer: Provide that any descendant (or eligible collateral relative) of the transferor must survive the transferor for at least 90 days in order to take his/her bequest.

[iv] Transfers to trust after a beneficiary dies. The predeceased ancestor exception can apply to transfers to a trust in which the deceased ancestor once had an interest.

> **EXAMPLE:** Mom transfers property to a trust for Child and Grandchild. Child dies two years later, while Mom is still alive. Child's death is a taxable termination, and Mom will "move down" a generation with respect to the property in the trust at Child's death.[46] If Mom makes new transfers to the trust after Child's death, those transfers will be deemed to be made to a separate trust, and Grandchild will move up a generation for purposes of those new transfers, which would otherwise be considered direct skips.[47]

[v] Effect of disclaimers. The predeceased ancestor exception only applies when the ancestor in question is actually deceased (or actually dies within 90 days of his own ancestor, as discussed above). Subject to the 90-day rule, the predeceased ancestor exception does not apply if the ancestor is actually alive and is simply treated as if he were deceased under local law for other reasons.[48]

> **EXAMPLE:** Mom dies. She leaves her estate to Child, or if Child does not survive her, to Grandchild. Child disclaims his interest in Mom's estate. Child's disclaimer causes him to be considered to have predeceased Mom under state law. The transfer of Mom's estate to Grandchild is still a direct skip. Grandchild does not move up a generation.

[b] Transfers Subject to Withdrawal Powers

A transfer to a trust that gives a skip person withdrawal powers is not a direct skip unless the trust is otherwise a skip person.[49] Accordingly, if Mom contributes $30,000 to a pot trust for Mom's descendants, and the trust pro-

---

[46] IRC § 2653(a).
[47] Treas. Reg. § 26.2612-1(a)(2)(i).
[48] Treas. Reg. § 26.2612-1(a)(2)(i).
[49] Treas. Reg. § 26.2612-1(f), example 3.

vides that Son, Daughter, and Grandchild each have a right to withdraw $10,000, the transfer is not a direct skip to any extent.

[c] Look-Through Rules

The look-through rules that generally apply to entities[50] do not apply in determining whether a transfer to a trust is a direct skip.[51] Said another way, a transfer to a trust is not a direct skip unless the trust itself is a skip person.

> **EXAMPLE:** Mom gives property to trust. Trustee can make current distributions to Son and Grandchild in any proportion. The look-through rules do not apply to cause Mom's transfer to be treated in part as a direct skip to Grandchild.

[d] Direct Skips Resulting from Disclaimers.

A disclaimer can result in a direct skip. If the transferor's remaining GSTT exemption[52] is not sufficient to cover the transfer of the disclaimed property or is not allocated to the property, a GSTT will be due. The GSTT will be payable from the disclaimed property, in the absence of a contrary apportionment clause specifically referring to the GSTT and directing that it be paid out of other property.[53] Many apportionment clauses specifically direct that the GSTT on a direct skip be paid out of the residuary estate, which may not be desirable in the case of disclaimers.

> **EXAMPLE:** Mom leaves her residuary estate in equal shares to Son and Daughter. If a child predeceases Mom or disclaims, that child's share is to go to the deceased or disclaiming child's children. Daughter disclaims, creating a direct skip from Mom's estate to Daughter's children. If the apportionment clause in Mom's will directs that GSTT on all direct skips is paid by the residuary estate, then Son will bear one-half of the GSTT with respect to the direct skip to Daughter's children.

Practice Pointer: In a case of direct skips resulting from disclaimers, it might be appropriate to provide for payment of the GSTT on the direct skips out of a source other than the entire residuary estate (such as the disclaiming child's nondisclaimed share of the residuary estate or the direct skip property itself).

---

[50] Discussed at ¶ 5.02[3][d] above.

[51] IRC § 2612(c)(2).

[52] The GSTT exemption is discussed at ¶ 5.05 below.

[53] IRC § 2603(b).

[e] Payment of Tax on Direct Skips

The tax on a direct skip is payable, generally, by the transferor (in the case of a lifetime gift) or by the transferor's estate (in the case of a direct skip taking effect at the transferor's death).[54] If a direct skip occurring at the transferor's death is made from nonprobate property, the executor has a right to recover the tax.[55]

[f] Taxable Amount

The amount of a direct skip is generally the amount that the transferee actually receives.[56] However, the IRS has ruled that a reduction in the amount actually received by the transferee due to payment of interest on an underpayment of GSTT applicable to a direct skip does not reduce the amount of a direct skip.[57] Similarly, according to the IRS, neither the interest payable on an estate tax underpayment nor the interest earned on an estate tax overpayment affects the taxable amount of a direct skip residuary bequest.[58]

[2] Taxable Distribution

A distribution of property to a skip person from a trust that can currently distribute to a non-skip person is a taxable distribution.[59] For example, if the trustee of Trust *Q* has discretion to distribute income or principal to the transferor's child or grandchild, a distribution to the grandchild from Trust *Q* is a taxable distribution.

[a] Predeceased Ancestor Exception

The predeceased ancestor exception[60] does not normally apply to taxable distributions. However, it will apply if the predeceased ancestor is dead at the

---

[54] Treas. Reg. § 26.2662-1(c)(1).

[55] Treas. Reg. § 26.2662-1(c)(2)(v).

[56] IRC § 2623.

[57] Priv. Ltr. Rul. 9822001 (Sept. 18, 1997).

[58] Priv. Ltr. Rul. 9822001 (Sept. 18, 1997).

[59] IRC § 2612(b). The qualification that non-skip persons be current distributees arises from the provision that distributions to skip persons will not be considered taxable distributions if the distributions also come within the definition of "direct skips" or "taxable terminations."

[60] Described at ¶ 5.03[1][a] above.

earliest time that the transfer establishing the beneficiary's interest is subject to gift or estate tax imposed on the transferor.[61]

> **EXAMPLE:** Grandpa has one deceased Child and one living Grandson by the deceased Child. If Grandpa establishes a trust for Grandma and Grandson, a distribution to Grandson during Grandma's life will not be a taxable distribution, because Child was deceased when the trust was created.

[b] Deemed Distributions—Withdrawal Rights

If estate or gift tax is imposed on a beneficiary with respect to a trust interest, that trust interest is treated as being distributed to the beneficiary to the extent that the interest is subject to estate or gift tax.[62]

> **EXAMPLE:** Mom contributes $27,000 to a new trust. Son, Daughter, and Grandchild each have a right to withdraw $9,000. The rights of withdrawal lapse at the end of the year. In this case, a lapse of a general power of appointment is a gift to the trust to the extent that it exceeds $5,000.[63] Assume that no beneficiary has a power of appointment that would prevent the lapse from being considered a taxable gift, and that applicable law would not result in a beneficiary's interest being available to his creditors on account of the lapse. Mom makes no other transfers to any beneficiary in that year. For GSTT purposes, the lapses will be treated as a $4,000 distribution from the trust to each beneficiary.[64] The deemed distribution resulting from the lapse of Grandchild's withdrawal right will be a deemed taxable distribution to Grandchild, followed by a deemed taxable gift by Grandchild to the trust of the lapsed amount.[65]

A skip person's exercise of a withdrawal right over a trust may also result in a taxable distribution.

---

[61] IRC § 2651(e).

[62] Treas. Reg. § 26.2612-1(c)(1). The regulations provide that a transfer is subject to estate or gift tax if a gift tax is imposed, without regard to exemptions, exclusions, deductions, and credits, or if the value of the property is includable in the decedent's gross estate under IRC § 2001. Treas. Reg. § 26.2652-1(a)(2).

[63] IRC § 2514(e).

[64] Four thousand dollars ($4,000) represents the excess of that beneficiary's gift ($9,000) over $5,000, which is exempt because it falls within the five-or-five power exception. See Chapter 3 for a discussion of five-or-five powers.

[65] Treas. Reg. § 26.2652-1(a)(5), example 5. A situation like that described in this example can cause a planning nightmare, since the trust will be deemed to have four transferors (Mom, Son, Daughter, and Grandchild) after the lapse. For ways to avoid this, see Chapter 10.

EXAMPLE: Mom contributes $27,000 to a new trust. Son, Daughter, and Grandchild each have a right to withdraw $9,000. Unexercised rights of withdrawal lapse at the end of the year. If Grandchild allows his right to lapse, the lapse will be treated as a taxable distribution from the trust only to the extent that it exceeds $5,000.[66] However, if Grandchild exercises his withdrawal right over $9,000, then the entire actual withdrawal (not just $4,000) is treated as a taxable distribution.[67]

Summary of effects of withdrawal powers. The lapse of a skip person's withdrawal right (in excess of a five-or-five power) is a taxable gift by the skip person (although it will be incomplete if the skip person retains a limited power of appointment or if the lapse renders the lapsed amount subject to the skip person's creditors).[68] If the lapse is a completed gift, it will also be a taxable distribution from the trust (or a direct skip from the trust, as the case may be).

The exercise of a skip person's withdrawal right is a taxable distribution (or direct skip, as the case may be).

If the donor wants to avoid a generation-skipping transfer in such situations, his GSTT exemption must be allocated to the trust or the trust must be structured to qualify for the GSTT annual exclusion requirements.[69]

[c] Distribution From One Trust to Another Trust

If a distribution is made from one trust to another trust, a taxable distribution will only occur if the distributing trust *is not* a skip person and the recipient trust *is* a skip person.[70]

EXAMPLE: Mom creates a pot trust for her grandchildren that lasts until the youngest is age 25. At that point, the trust divides into a separate trust for each then living grandchild. The division of the pot trust assets into separate trusts is not a taxable distribution (or other taxable transfer).

EXAMPLE: Mom creates a pot trust for her children and descendants of a child who died prior to the trust's creation. The trust lasts until her youngest child is age 25. Any distributions to a deceased child's descendant who is under age 18 are made to a separate trust for that descendant.

---

[66] Treas. Reg. § 26.2652-1(a)(5), example 5.

[67] Treas. Reg. § 26.2612-1(f), example 13.

[68] Which could happen if state law treats the lapse as a transfer to the trust by the beneficiary-powerholder, resulting in a self-settled trust.

[69] See Chapter 10 and discussion at ¶ 5.04[1] below on GSTT annual exclusion.

[70] Treas. Reg. § 26.2612-1(c)(2). Technically described, the look-through rules do not apply to determine whether a taxable distribution has been made.

The trustee's distribution of property to a trust for a minor descendant of the deceased child will not be a taxable distribution.[71]

EXAMPLE: Mom creates a pot trust for her descendants. The trust lasts until her youngest child is age 25. At that point, the trust property is divided among Mom's children and descendants of any deceased child, with each individual's share being held in a separate trust for the benefit of that individual and his or her own descendants. All of Mom's children are alive at the time she creates the pot trust. When the pot trust terminates, any share allocated to a trust for a child of Mom and that child's descendants will not result in a taxable distribution, because the child (a non-skip person) still has an interest in the trust. Any allocation to a trust for a grandchild of Mom and the grandchild's descendants should be considered a taxable distribution because the distributing trust is not a skip person and the recipient trust itself is a skip person (that is, a non-skip person has an interest in the trust).

[d] Multicharacter Distribution

A distribution that could also be characterized as a direct skip or taxable termination[72] will not be considered a taxable distribution.[73]

EXAMPLE: Mom creates a trust for the benefit of Child and Grandchild. The trustee may distribute income and principal to either Child or Grandchild in the trustee's discretion. Trustee distributes all of the trust assets to Grandchild. Although this distribution could be viewed as a taxable distribution, it is also a taxable termination[74] and will be treated as such.

[e] Tax on Taxable Distribution

The tax on a taxable distribution is payable by the distributee.[75] A deduction is allowed for expenses incurred by the distributee in connection with the determination, collection, or refund of the GSTT on the distribution.[76] If the trust pays the tax with respect to a taxable distribution, the tax payment will

---

[71] The transfer is eligible for the predeceased ancestor exception because the deceased child was dead at the time Mom created the trust. IRC § 2651(e)(1).

[72] Taxable terminations are discussed at ¶ 5.03[3] below.

[73] IRC § 2612(b).

[74] See ¶ 5.03[3] below.

[75] IRC § 2603(a)(1).

[76] IRC § 2621(a)(2).

be considered an additional taxable distribution made on the last day of the taxable year in which the original taxable distribution was made.[77]

[3] Taxable Terminations

A termination of a person's interest in a trust is a taxable termination if (1) the only persons left with an interest in the trust are skip persons, or (2) no beneficiaries of the trust have an interest and there is less than a five percent likelihood that a distribution to a non-skip person will ever occur.[78]

> **EXAMPLE:** Mom establishes a trust for the life of Child, with the remainder on Child's death to be held in trust for Grandchild and Great-Grandchild. Child's death during Grandchild's life is a taxable termination of Child's interest. If the trustee subsequently distributes the entire trust property to Great-Grandchild, the distribution is a taxable termination of Grandchild's interest.[79]

A taxable termination will typically occur if a termination of any non-skip person's interest in a trust occurs, unless (1) the property in the trust is the subject of a taxable transfer for estate or gift tax purposes on the termination, (2) a non-skip person still has an interest in the trust, or (3) it can be actuarially ascertained that the probability that a distribution will ever be made to a skip person is less than five percent.[80]

Since a charity does not have an interest in a trust unless the charity is entitled to distributions, one cannot defer a taxable termination by including a charity as a discretionary distributee.[81]

[a] Predeceased Ancestor Exception

The predeceased ancestor exception[82] applies to a taxable termination if the predeceased ancestor was dead at the earliest time that the transfer that es-

---

[77] IRC § 2621(b); Treas. Reg. § 26.2612-1(c)(1).

[78] IRC § 2612(a); Treas. Reg. 26.2612-1(d)(2).

[79] Treas. Reg. § 26.2612-1(f), example 9.

[80] Treas. Reg. § 26.2612-1(b)(1). Regarding condition (3), the statute uses the phrase "at no time may a distribution be made from the trust to a skip person." However, Treas. Reg. § 26.2612-1(b)(1)(iii) provides that distributions to skip persons that are theoretically possible, but actuarially highly improbable, are disregarded.

[81] IRC § 2652(c) (applicable to trusts other than charitable remainder trusts or pooled income funds).

[82] Described at ¶ 5.03[1][a] above.

tablished the beneficiary's interest was subject to gift or estate tax imposed on the transferor.[83]

> **EXAMPLE:** Grandpa has one deceased child and one living grandchild by the deceased child. If Grandpa establishes a charitable lead trust with his grandchild as the remainder beneficiary, the termination of the trust in favor of the grandchild will not be a generation-skipping transfer, because the child was deceased on the establishment of the CLT.

[b] Exception if Estate or Gift Tax Is Imposed on the Termination

A taxable termination does not include any termination to the extent that a transfer subject to estate or gift tax occurs with respect to property held in the trust at the time of termination.[84]

> **EXAMPLE:** Mom establishes a trust for the life of Child, with the remainder on Child's death to be appointed to anyone Child chooses, including his estate. In default of appointment, the trust property will be held in trust for Grandchild. Child dies without exercising his power of appointment. No taxable termination occurs, because the trust property is included in Child's estate due to his general power of appointment.

> **EXAMPLE:** Mom establishes a revocable trust. When she dies, the trust assets that pass to Grandchild are included in her estate. This transfer is a direct skip, not a taxable termination.

> **EXAMPLE:** Dad dies, leaving a trust for Mom for her life, remainder to grandchildren. Dad's executor elects QTIP treatment for the trust. On Mom's death, the transfer to grandchildren is a direct skip,[85] unless Child (grandchildren's parent) is deceased at Mom's death. In that case, the transfer would not be a direct skip, due to the predeceased ancestor exception.

> If Dad's executor had not made the QTIP election, or had made a reverse QTIP election, Mom's death would constitute a taxable termination unless Child was deceased at Dad's death.

---

[83] IRC § 2651(e)(1).

[84] Treas. Reg. § 26.2612-1(b)(1)(i).

[85] Treas. Reg. § 26.2612-1(f), example 5.

[c] Tax on Taxable Termination

The tax on a taxable termination is payable by the trustee.[86] The taxable amount is the value of the trust property in which the terminating beneficiary had an interest, less deductions similar to the estate tax deduction for expenses of administration, debts, and taxes.[87]

[4] Certain Transfers of Property Previously Subject to GSTT

A transfer that would otherwise be considered a generation-skipping transfer will not be treated as such if (1) the property transferred has already been subject to GSTT; (2) the previous recipient was in the same generation as, or a lower generation than, the current recipient; and (3) the transfer does not have the effect of avoiding GSTT.[88]

> **EXAMPLE:** Grandma transfers $100,000 to a trust for Great-Grandchild, paying GSTT on the direct skip. Great-Grandchild dies, and, under the terms of the trust, the trust property passes to Grandma for life, then to other great-grandchildren. No additional GSTT should be imposed at Grandma's death if the transfer at that time does not have the effect of avoiding GSTT. Presumably, the transfer would not have the effect of avoiding GSTT unless it were pre-arranged as a scheme to (for example) turn what would have been a taxable termination at Grandma's death into a direct skip at the date of transfer—as would occur, for instance, if Great-Grandchild had three days to live when the initial transfer was made.

This section will rarely apply in practice, partly because of the move-down rule, which operates to move the transferor down a generation after a GST anyway.[89]

[5] After a GST Occurs

[a] Transferor Moved Down a Generation

Once a GST takes place with respect to property in a trust, the transferor will be given a new generation assignment. She will be deemed to be in the

---

[86] IRC § 2603(a)(2).

[87] IRC § 2622.

[88] IRC § 2611(b)(2).

[89] Discussed at ¶ 5.03[5][a].

first generation above the highest generation of any person who has an interest in the trust.

> **EXAMPLE:** Mom establishes a trust that provides for successive life interests in Child, Grandchild, and Great-Grandchild. Child dies, causing a taxable termination. Mom will be moved down to Child's generation. This means that Grandchild will become a non-skip person, and subsequent distributions to Grandchild will not be treated as taxable distributions. When Grandchild dies, there will be a taxable termination of his interest, and Mom will be moved down to Grandchild's generation.

[b] Change in Exempt Portion

The exempt portion of a trust may be affected by a GST.[90]

[c] Basis Adjustment

[i] **General rule.** The basis of property that is the subject of a GST is increased (up to its fair market value) by a portion of the GSTT. That portion is the amount of GSTT attributable to the property's appreciation. The property's appreciation is the excess of its fair market value over its basis at the time of the GST. This basis rule applies after taking any adjustment for gift tax paid on the appreciation into account.[91]

> **EXAMPLE:** Mom gives Blackacre to Grandchild. Its value is $100 and basis is zero. GSTT on the direct skip is $50. The GSTT is added to the gift for gift tax purposes,[92] so the total gift is $150. The amount of appreciation, however, is still $100 (since the added "gift" has no appreciation element) . The gift tax attributable to the $100 of Blackacre appreciation is $50, and the basis of Blackacre in Grandchild's hands is increased by this $50 (i.e., the gift tax attributable to appreciation) pursuant to the gift tax rules.[93] For purposes of determining the GSTT paid on the appreciation of property subject to the direct skip, the basis is considered $50, and an additional $25 basis step-up for GSTT will be allowed [($100 value of prop-

---

[90] IRC § 2653(b). See ¶ 5.03[7] below for an explanation.
[91] IRC § 2654(a)(1).
[92] IRC § 2515.
[93] IRC § 1015(d).

erty less $50 new basis after gift tax step-up) times 50 percent GSTT rate]. Thus, the total basis step-up (for gift and GST tax) is $75.

[ii] Taxable termination occurring at death. A special basis adjustment applies to a taxable termination taking place at the same time as, and as a result of, an individual's death. The basis of property included in such a transfer will receive the same adjustment it would have received if it had been included in the individual's estate. This basis adjustment only applies to the portion of the trust on which GSTT is paid (the nonexempt portion).[94]

> **EXAMPLE:** Mom gives Blackacre to a non-exempt trust for Child, remainder to Grandchild. Child dies, causing a taxable termination. If Blackacre is worth $100 at Child's death (or alternate valuation date, as the case may be), the new basis of Blackacre is $100.

[6] Multiple Transferors and Changes in Transferors

Many trusts have more than one transferor. In such a trust, the portions attributable to each transferor's contributions are treated for GSTT purposes as separate trusts.[95]

If any part of a trust is subject to estate or gift tax with respect to a beneficiary, the beneficiary who was subject to the tax is treated as the new transferor of that portion of the trust.[96]

> **EXAMPLE:** Mom establishes a trust with successive life estates for Child and Grandchild. Child dies, holding an outstanding withdrawal power over half of the trust. Child will be the new transferor of the half of the trust property that is included in his gross estate. Thereafter, if a distribution of any of that half of the trust assets is made to Grandchild, the distribution will not be a taxable distribution—Child is the new transferor, and Grandchild is not a skip person with respect to Child. The half of the assets that was included in Child's estate will generally receive a new basis of fair market value at the date of Child's death (or the alternate valuation date, if applicable). Since the half of the trust that was not included in Child's estate was the subject of a taxable termination occurring on and as a result of Child's death, that half will get a similar basis adjustment, to the extent that the trust was not exempt. Mom will still be treated as the transferor, and she will move down a generation.

---

[94] IRC § 2654(a)(2).

[95] IRC § 2654(b)(1).

[96] IRC § 2652(a)(1); Treas. Reg. §§ 26.2652-1(a)(1), 26.2652-1(a)(5), example 3.

If Aunt Louise subsequently contributes to the trust, her contribution and the earnings attributable to her contribution will be treated for GSTT purposes as a separate trust.

[7] Comparison of Taxable Amounts of GSTs

The GSTT on taxable terminations and taxable distributions is tax-inclusive[97] and on direct skips is tax-exclusive.[98] This may not be intuitively obvious from a reading of the statute, so we'll review a few examples. The concept is the same as that regarding the difference between gift and estate taxes, discussed in Chapters 1 and 8.

The statutes define the "taxable amount" of both taxable distributions and direct skips as the value of the property received by the transferee.[99] However, in the case of a taxable distribution or taxable termination, the tax is imposed on the distributee and measured by the amount of distributed property (meaning that the tax is included in the base), or on the trust and measured by the entire terminated interest (including the tax). The tax on a direct skip is imposed on the transferor (meaning that the tax is only imposed on property actually received by the skip person).[100]

Let's look at some actual fact situations to compare taxes payable on different types of transfers. The examples are based on the exemption and rates applicable in 2002. The exemption and rates change in the future, as described in Chapter 1. However, the concepts applied remain the same.

> **EXAMPLE:** Trust distributes $1,000,000 as a taxable distribution. The taxable amount is $1,000,000. The distributee is liable for the tax, so she pays tax of $500,000 and receives $500,000 net.

> **EXAMPLE:** Trust for the life of Child, remainder to Grandchild, has $1,000,000. Child dies. The amount of the taxable transaction is $1,000,000. Trustee pays $500,000 to the IRS and $500,000 to Grandchild.

> **EXAMPLE:** Mom dies and leaves $1,000,000 to Grandchild as a direct skip. GSTT is imposed on the transfer based on the amount actually received by Grandchild. Estate pays $333,333 to the IRS, and Grandchild receives $666,667.[101]

---

[97] IRC §§ 2603(a)(1), 2603(a)(2), 2621, 2622.

[98] IRC §§ 2603(a)(3), 2623.

[99] IRC §§ 2621(a), 2623.

[100] IRC § 2603.

[101] The math for computing this amount is:

EXAMPLE: Mom gives $1,000,000 to Grandchild as a lifetime direct skip. The taxable amount is $1,000,000. The tax is payable by Mom, so Mom pays $500,000 of GSTT. Because the transfer is a direct skip by gift, the GSTT is added to the amount of the gift, resulting in the gift tax being tax-inclusive with respect to the GSTT. In this case, the $500,000 of GSTT will be added to the gift, resulting in a total taxable gift of $1,500,000, with gift tax payable of $750,000. So, Mom pays $1,250,000 of gift tax and GSTT to the IRS, and Grandchild receives $1,000,000.

¶ 5.04 GIFTS EXCLUDED FROM GSTT

A special GSTT exclusion for certain nontaxable gifts is available. The exclusion is in addition to the GSTT exemption, which is discussed in the next section.

[1] Annual Exclusion Gifts to Skip Persons

If Mom makes an outright gift to Grandchild[102] that qualifies for the gift tax annual exclusion,[103] the gift is not subject to GSTT.[104] If, however, she makes an annual exclusion gift to a trust for Grandchild, the trust must contain the following two provisions in order to qualify for exclusion from GSTT:[105]

- No distribution may be permitted from the trust to anyone except Grandchild during Grandchild's life.[106]

Bequest + GSTT = $1,000,000;
GSTT = .5 (Bequest);
Bequest + .5 (Bequest) = $1,000,000;
1.5 (Bequest) = $1,000,000;
Bequest = $1,000,000 ÷ 1.5;
Bequest = $666,667;
GSTT = $1,000,000 − $666,667; and therefore
GSTT = $333,333.

[102] Or any other skip person.

[103] The annual exclusion is indexed. IRC § 2503(b)(2). The indexed amount for 2002 is $11,000. See Chapter 10 for further discussion.

[104] IRC §§ 2642(c)(1), 2642(c)(3)(A).

[105] IRC § 2642(c)(2).

[106] IRC § 2642(c)(2)(A).

- If the trust is still in existence at Grandchild's death, the trust assets must be includable in Grandchild's gross estate.[107]

[2] Qualifying Tuition and Medical Expenses

If Mom pays the tuition and medical expenses of a skip person in such a fashion as to qualify the payments as tax-free gifts,[108] those gifts will not be subject to GSTT.[109] If a trust pays the medical expenses and tuition of skip persons, those payments will not be subject to GSTT, provided that the payments would have qualified as tax-free payments under the gift tax rules had they been gifts by an individual.[110]

> **EXAMPLE:** Mom has created two trusts that benefit Child and Grandchild. One is exempt from GSTT and the other is nonexempt. Normally, the trustee might make distributions to Grandchild from the exempt trust and distributions to Child from the nonexempt trust. However, the trustee might want to make Grandchild's GSTT-free tuition and medical expense payments from the nonexempt trust, thereby preserving the exempt trust for other uses.

[3] Section 529 Plans

Certain transfers to and from Section 529 plans are excluded from GSTT. The GSTT aspects of these plans are described in Chapter 10.

¶ 5.05 EXEMPTION PLANNING

Each person has an exemption from GSTT, which she can decide when and how to allocate.[111] The exemption for 2002 is $1,100,000.[112] It will adjust for

---

[107] IRC § 2642(c)(2)(B). The IRS has ruled that a scrivener's error that causes the trust to violate this rule may, in appropriate circumstances, be reformed in state court in order to establish compliance and qualify for the exclusion. Priv. Ltr. Rul. 200114026 (Jan. 5, 2001).

[108] This gift tax exclusion, under IRC § 2503(e), is discussed in Chapter 10.

[109] IRC §§ 2611(b)(1), 2642(c)(1), 2642(c)(3)(B).

[110] IRC § 2611(b)(1) ; Priv. Ltr. Rul. 9823006 (June 5, 1998).

[111] IRC § 2631(a).

[112] See Appendix A.01, Table of Indexed Amounts, in the supplement.

inflation in 2003. In 2004, the GSTT exemption will convert to the same amount as the estate tax exemption.[113] In 2010, the GSTT is repealed.[114] If EGTRRA sunsets, the GSTT exemption will be $1,000,000 in 2011 and thereafter. If it does not, the GSTT is repealed for 2011 and thereafter.

The numbers in this section are based on the 2002 exemption and rates. Subsequent differing amounts do not affect the application of the concepts discussed.

In 2002, a lifetime gift of the entire exemption amount for both spouses ($1,100,000 per spouse) will generate a current gift tax of $82,000 for a couple who have never made any taxable gifts, and $1,100,000 for a couple who are already in the 50 percent transfer tax bracket.[115]

Unlike the unified credit, which must be allocated to gifts in the order in which they are made,[116] the GSTT exemption can be allocated as the transferor chooses.[117]

A lifetime gift of the exempt amount to a dynastic trust[118] is a good idea for those who can afford both the gift and the gift tax. Not only will the exempt amount of property be removed from the transfer tax system for so long as it remains in the trust, but the income from (as well as any appreciation of) the trust property will also be free of transfer tax as long as it is kept in the trust. The trust property can grow enormously by the time state law requires the trust to terminate.[119] The dramatic effects of the exemption are shown in the diagram at ¶ 5.11[1], Exhibit 5-A: Using the GSTT Exemption.

[1] Mechanics

The exemption can be allocated to the property actually transferred, in the case of a direct skip. In any other case, the exemption must be allocated to a trust.

> EXAMPLE: Mom makes gift of $50,000 to Grandchild. She can apply $50,000 of her exemption to the transfer. However, if Mom makes a transfer of $100,000 to a trust for the benefit of Child and Grandchild, and the trust distributes $50,000 to Grandchild (a taxable distribution),

---

[113] IRC § 2631(c).

[114] IRC § 2664.

[115] Computed according to the table contained in IRC § 2001(c), as required by IRC § 2502(a).

[116] Rev. Rul. 79-398, 1979-2 CB 338; Tech. Adv. Mem. 8132011 (Apr. 24, 1981).

[117] IRC § 2631.

[118] Dynastic trusts are discussed at ¶ 5.07 below.

[119] If the trust is situated in a jurisdiction with no rule against perpetuities, and powers of appointment are not exercised, even state law limitations will not require an eventual tax.

Mom cannot apply $50,000 of exemption to the taxable distribution and render it exempt. If $50,000 of Mom's exemption is allocated to the trust, the taxable distribution will be one-half exempt (assuming the value of the trust is still $100,000 just before the distribution). To render the taxable distribution wholly exempt, either (1) $100,000 of exemption would have to be allocated to the trust, or (2) the trust would have to be severed into exempt and non-exempt trusts and $50,000 of exemption applied to the exempt trust.

The exempt portion of a partially exempt trust is a fraction. The numerator is the amount of exemption allocated, and the denominator is the value of the trust property or other direct skip. The value to be used in the denominator of the fraction is determined by specific rules.[120] Generally, however, the value is the fair market value of the property as of the effective date of allocation of exemption.[121]

The "applicable fraction" and the "inclusion ratio" of a trust are fancy phrases for the "exempt portion" and the "nonexempt portion," respectively. The applicable fraction is the amount of exemption allocated to the trust, divided by the fair market value of the trust on the effective date of allocation. The inclusion ratio is one minus the applicable fraction.

[a] Procedure for Allocation—Gifts

[i] **Direct skips.** The exemption is automatically allocated to a direct skip made during the transferor's lifetime unless the transferor elects otherwise.[122] The automatic allocation is irrevocable after the due date of the return reporting the transfer.[123] Some practitioners like to make the allocation on the gift tax return for purposes of the record. An affirmative allocation to a direct skip is made on Form 709, Schedule C, Part 3. An election not to allocate the exemption is also made on a timely filed gift tax return. Alternatively, the timely filing of a gift tax return, together with payment of the GSTT with respect to

---

[120] See discussion at ¶ 5.05[2].

[121] Treas. Reg. § 26.2642-2(a).

[122] IRC § 2632(b).

[123] Treas. Reg. § 26.2632-1(b)(1)(ii).

the direct skip, will prevent automatic allocation of the exemption.[124] An election not to allocate the exemption is generally irrevocable.[125]

[ii] Indirect skips. The exemption is automatically allocated to indirect skips for transfers made and estate tax inclusion periods ending (1) after 2000 and before 2010, and (2) if EGTRRA is extended, after 2010.[126]

[A] *Defined.* The concept of an indirect skip was introduced by EGTRRA in June 2001. It is defined as any transfer of property subject to the gift tax (other than a direct skip) made to a GST trust.[127]

[B] *GST trust—general rule.* A GST trust is any trust that could have a generation-skipping consequence with respect to the transferor *unless* the trust meets one of six exceptions, as described in ¶ 5.05[1][a][iii] below.[128]

[iii] GST trust—exceptions. The following trusts are *not* considered GST trusts, and the exemption will *not* be automatically allocated to them.

Trust required to distribute to non-skip person under age 46. Automatic allocation does not apply if the trust instrument provides that more than 25 percent of the trust corpus must be distributed or may be withdrawn by any individual non-skip person(s): (1) before the individual is age 46; or (2) on one or more dates that will occur before the individual is 46; or (3) to the extent that regulations provide, on an event that may reasonably be expected to occur before the individual is age 46.[129]

> **EXAMPLE:** Mom establishes trust for Child, remainder to Grandchild. The trust corpus is to be distributed to Child in thirds on his 30th, 35th, and 40th birthdays, and so is not a GST trust. If regulations permit, the trust would not be a GST trust if (for example) Child could withdraw one third of the assets of the trust when Child graduates from high school or gets married.

Trust required to distribute to non-skip person at an older person's death. No automatic allocation will be made if the trust instrument provides that more than 25 percent of the trust corpus must be distributed to, or may be withdrawn by, an individual(s) who (1) is a non-skip person and (2) is living on

---

[124] Treas. Reg. § 26.2632-1(b)(1)(i).

[125] Treas. Reg. § 26.2632-1(b)(1)(ii). A transition rule, however, permitted an election made on or before January 26, 1996 to be revoked until July 24, 1996. Treas. Reg. § 26.2632-1(b)(1)(iii).

[126] IRC § 2632(c); EGTRRA § 561(a).

[127] IRC § 2632(c)(1).

[128] IRC § 2632(c)(3)(B).

[129] IRC § 2632(c)(3)(B)(i).

the date of death of another person(s) designated by name or class who is more than 10 years older than such individual.[130]

> **EXAMPLE:** Mom's trust for Child and Grandchild provides that two thirds of the trust corpus must be distributed to Child on Mom's death.

Trusts included in non-skip person's estate if he dies prematurely. No automatic allocation will be made if the trust instrument provides that, if an individual(s) who is a non-skip person dies on or before a date or event described in the two preceding exceptions, more than 25 percent of the corpus must be distributed to the non-skip person's estate or pursuant to a general power of appointment held by the non-skip person.[131]

> **EXAMPLE:** Mom's trust for Child and Grandchild says that if Child dies before his 30th birthday or before Mom dies, more than 25 percent of the corpus passes to Child's estate.

Trust includable in non-skip person's estate if he dies on the date of transfer. The trust will not receive an automatic allocation if any part of the trust would be included in the estate of a non-skip person (other than the transferor) if that person died immediately after the transfer.[132]

> **EXAMPLE:** Mom's trust for Child and Grandchild gives Child a general power of appointment by will over 10 percent of the corpus.

Charitable lead annuity trust (CLAT) or charitable lead remainder trust (CRT). Exemption will not be automatically allocated to a CLAT or a CRT.[133]

CLUT. No automatic allocation will be made if the trust is a charitable lead unitrust that must distribute principal to a non-skip person if that person is alive when the payments terminate.[134]

> **EXAMPLE:** Mom establishes a CLUT that must pay an annuity to charity for ten years, and then distribute principal to Child if he is alive.

[iv] Rules of the game. The following are the applicable special rules for applying the described exceptions in ¶ 5.05[1][a][iii].

Withdrawal rights. Property is not considered part of the gross estate of a non-skip person, or subject to a right of withdrawal by the non-skip person,

---

[130] IRC § 2632(c)(3)(B)(ii).

[131] IRC § 2632(c)(3)(B)(iii).

[132] IRC § 2632(c)(3)(B)(iv).

[133] IRC §§ 2632(c)(3)(B)(v), 2632(c)(3)(B)(vi).

[134] IRC § 2632(c)(3)(B)(vi).

solely because the non-skip person holds a right to withdraw limited to the maximum annual exclusion amount for the year.[135]

> **EXAMPLE:** Mom's trust for Child and Grandchild gives Child a *Crummey* withdrawal right of $11,000 per year. This will not in itself prevent automatic allocation to the trust. If, however, as a result of hanging withdrawal powers,[136] Child's withdrawal rights increase to $15,000 in a particular year, then the trust may become a non-GST trust that would not receive an automatic allocation.

Powers of appointment. It is assumed that powers of appointment held by non-skip persons will not be exercised.[137]

> **EXAMPLE:** Mom transfers property to a trust for Child and Grandchild. The trust must distribute all of its assets to Child on his 40th birthday, unless Child exercises his limited power of appointment before then. It is assumed that Child will not exercise the power, and the automatic allocation will not be made.

Estate tax inclusion periods (ETIPs). The automatic allocation is deemed made at the close of the ETIP, if any, at the value of the property at the time of the close.[138]

[v] Election out (or in). A taxpayer may elect that the automatic allocation will not apply to (1) an indirect skip or (2) any or all transfers made by such taxpayer to a particular trust.[139] The taxpayer may also elect to treat any trust as a GST trust with respect to any or all transfers made by the taxpayer to that trust.[140]

An election out of automatic allocation to an indirect skip will be timely if it is filed on a timely filed gift tax return for the year in which the transfer was made or deemed made.[141]

---

[135] IRC § 2632(c)(3)(B).
[136] Discussed in Chapter 10.
[137] IRC § 2632(c)(3)(B).
[138] IRC § 2632(c)(4).
[139] IRC § 2632(c)(5)(A)(i).
[140] IRC § 2632(c)(5)(A)(ii).
[141] IRC § 2632(c)(5)(B)(i).

An election to treat all transfers made to a particular trust, or to treat a non-GST trust as a GST trust, may be made on a timely filed gift tax return for the calendar year in which the election is to become effective.[142]

[vi] Effective dates. The automatic allocation of exemption to indirect skips applies to estate and gift tax transfers made after 2000 and to ETIPs closing after 2000, subject to the sunsetting of EGTRRA in 2011.[143]

Practice Pointer: Until EGTRRA, the general rule was that allocations would not be automatically allocated, except to direct skips. Now the general rule is that the exemption will be automatically allocated, unless an exception applies or an election out is made. In order to minimize annual angst over automatic allocation:

- File a gift tax return for any transfer to a trust and elect out or in, without worrying about whether the automatic exemption would or would not apply in that year; or
- If the exemption should never be applied to a particular trust, make a one-time election out.

---

[b] Procedure for Allocation—Transfers at Death

[i] Executor's allocation of exemption. The executor's allocation is made by the executor on Schedule R, Part 1, of the transferor-decedent's estate tax return. This schedule requires information similar to that required by the gift tax return.[144]

[ii] Automatic allocation—general rule. Any exemption that (1) was not allocated during the transferor's life or (2) was not specifically allocated by the executor after the transferor's death, will be automatically allocated, as of the due date of the estate tax return, in the following manner:

- First, pro rata, among direct skips occurring at death;
- Second, pro rata, among trusts with respect to which a taxable termination may occur or from which a taxable distribution may be made.[145]

EXAMPLE: Mom dies, leaving $300,000 outright to each of her three grandchildren, and $1,000,000 to each of three trusts for her children and their descendants. The automatic allocation would allocate $300,000 of

---

[142] IRC § 2632(c)(5)(B)(ii).

[143] EGTRRA §§ 561(c)(1), 901.

[144] See Treas. Reg. § 26.2632-1(d)(1).

[145] Treas. Reg. § 26.2632-1(d)(1).

Mom's exemption to each direct skip and the remaining exempt amount equally to each of the trusts.

[iii] Exceptions to automatic allocation rule. Exemption will not automatically be allocated to (1) a trust that will be subject to gift or estate tax at a beneficiary's level before any GST may occur with respect to the trust or (2) a trust from which no GSTs have occurred during the nine-month period following the transferor's death and from which no future GSTs can occur with respect to the trust.[146] This second exception permits disclaimers to occur that will avoid GSTT, without a waste of exemption.

EXAMPLE: Mom leaves trust to Grandchild for life, remainder to Charity. Grandchild has no descendants. Grandchild executes a qualified disclaimer, resulting in Mom's estate passing to Charity under state law. No GST will occur, and no exemption need be allocated to the trust.

[c] Formula Allocation

Unless the amount of the transfer is absolutely unquestionable, it is a good idea to allocate exemption by a formula that takes into account any adjustments due to changes in the transferred property's valuation and changes in allowable deductions against the property. A sample formula allocation is included at ¶ 5.11[2], in Exhibit 5-B: Sample Exemption Allocation Language.

Formula allocations are generally not permitted with respect to CLATs[147] except to adjust asset values to those finally determined for tax purposes.[148]

[d] Void Allocations

An allocation of exemption to a trust is void to the extent the amount allocated exceeds the amount needed to make the trust fully exempt.[149] An allocation to a trust is also void if the trust has no "GST potential" at the time of allocation. A trust is considered to have "GST potential" if there is any possibility of a GST being made from the trust, even if the possibility is so remote as to be negligible.[150]

---

[146] Treas. Reg. § 26.2632-1(d)(2).

[147] CLATs are discussed in Chapter 35.

[148] Treas. Reg. § 26.2632-1(b)(2)(i).

[149] Treas. Reg. § 26.2632-1(b)(1)(i).

[150] Treas. Reg. § 26.2632-1(b)(1)(i).

[e] Improperly Executed Allocations

When allocations have been made in an improper manner, the IRS has occasionally been lenient if the taxpayer's intent was reasonably clear.[151] For example, the IRS has ruled that a GSTT exemption allocation was timely where the donor sufficiently indicated on the return itself an intent to allocate exemption to the donor's gifts to an irrevocable trust, even though the donor completed portions of the form applicable only with respect to direct skips and failed to attach a notice of allocation to the return.[152]

An allocation of exemption to testamentary trusts has also been respected as substantially compliant, despite the fact that the allocation was made on Part 2 of Schedule R (pertaining to direct skips) of the Form 706.[153]

EGTRRA gave the IRS authority to grant 9100 relief with respect to improperly executed allocations until 2011, when EGTRRA sunsets.[154]

[2] When to Allocate—Effect on Value for Exemption Allocation Purposes

There is a time for everything under the heavens[155]—a time to allocate, and a time not to allocate. The time of allocation can have an effect on how much of the trust is exempt and/or how much exemption it takes to render a trust totally exempt.

[a] Gifts

Exemption is automatically allocated to property transferred by direct skip during the transferor's lifetime and to certain indirect skips, unless the transferor elects otherwise on a timely filed gift tax return.[156] Except for these instances, the exemption is not automatically allocated to any property during the transferor's lifetime. The transferor, however, may choose to allocate exemption to other property on any gift tax return.

[i] **Timely allocation.** If an allocation is made on a timely filed gift tax return for the year of the gift (or is automatically allocated), the allocation will

---

[151] E.g., Priv. Ltr. Ruls. 9712009 (Dec. 18, 1996), 199919027 (May 14, 1999), 200017013 (Jan. 20, 2000).

[152] Priv. Ltr. Ruls. 200017013 (Jan. 20, 2000), 199909034 (Dec. 4, 1998), 200040013 (June 29, 2000).

[153] Priv. Ltr. Rul. 9534001 (May 1, 1995).

[154] IRC § 2642(g); EGTRRA § 901.

[155] Ecclesiastes 3:1.

[156] See discussion at ¶ 5.05[1][a] above.

be effective on and after the date of the gift. In that instance, the value of the property (for purposes of determining how much is exempt from GSTT) will be its value for gift tax purposes.[157] A timely allocation becomes irrevocable on the due date of the return.[158] However, any automatic allocation to an indirect skip will be treated as made, and the value will be determined, as of the close of any ETIP.[159]

[ii] **Late allocation.** An allocation made on any other return is known as a "late" allocation. Making a late allocation is not improper, like filing a late gift tax return might be. "Late" is simply the term applied to an allocation that is made to a gift after the date for which a timely gift tax return for that gift could still be filed.

> EXAMPLE: Mom makes gift in Year One. Depending on whether an extension(s) of time to file the gift tax return is granted, Mom can generally make a timely allocation by April 15, August 15, or October 15 of Year Two. Any allocation after that will be "late."

A late allocation is effective and becomes irrevocable on the date the return making the allocation is filed, and the value of the property for purposes of using the exemption will generally be its value on that date.[160]

> EXAMPLE: Mom gives Corporation A stock to a new trust for Child and Grandchild on July 15 of Year One. Its value is $100/share on that date. If she files a timely gift tax return in Year Two, she will need to allocate $100/share of exemption to completely exempt the trust. If she does not do so, and allocates her exemption on November 15 of Year Two, she will need to use the value of Corporation A stock on November 15 of Year Two (or on November 1, if she makes the special election to do so).

First-day-of-month election. The transferor can generally elect the first day of the month during which a late allocation is made to a trust as the valuation date.[161] The transferor makes the election by stating that she is doing so on the gift tax return on which the allocation is made, and by indicating the valuation date and the fair market value of the trust assets on that date.[162] This rule alleviates the practical problem of making an allocation when the property is to be valued on the very day of filing the return.

---

[157] IRC § 2642(b)(1); Treas. Reg. §§ 26.2632-1(b)(2)(ii), 26.2642-2(a)(1).

[158] Treas. Reg. § 26.2632-1(b)(2)(i).

[159] IRC § 2632(c)(4).

[160] Treas. Reg. §§ 26.2632-1(b)(2)(ii)(A), 26.2632-1(d)(1); IRC §§ 2642(b)(1), 2642(b)(3).

[161] Treas. Reg. § 26.2642-2(a)(2).

[162] Treas. Reg. § 26.2642-2(a)(2).

EXAMPLE: Mom gives Corporation *A* stock to a new trust for Child and Grandchild on July 15 of Year One. Its value is $100/share on that date. Mom allocates her exemption to the Year One trust on Wednesday, November 15 of Year Two. The GSTT value for exemption purposes will be the mean of the high and low values of Corporation *A* stock on November 15 of Year Two. Hence, the market has to close before the value on November 15 of Year Two will be known. By that time, it might be too late in the day to file the return. Mom can choose November 1 of Year Two as the valuation date, if she likes.

No "first-day-of-month" election for life insurance on deceased insured. The election to value the gift as of the first day of the month of filing a late allocation cannot be made with respect to a gift of a life insurance policy or to a trust holding a life insurance policy, if the insured individual died before the actual filing date.[163]

EXAMPLE: Mom transfers $12,000 to trust on January 1 of Year One. Trust purchases insurance policy on Dad's life. On July 1 of Year 3, the policy has a value of $5,000. Dad dies on July 3 of Year Three. The face value of the policy is $100,000. Mom cannot file a late allocation in July of Year Three, thereby choosing July 1 as the valuation date and $5,000 as the value of the policy. Instead, the value will be $100,000—that is, the actual value on the date of filing the return that makes the late allocation.

[iii] Remedial provisions for incorrect allocations. Congress has directed the Treasury to promulgate regulations providing extensions of time to make exemption allocations, and, in appropriate cases, elections not to allocate.[164] The IRS has authority to treat late elections as made on a timely basis with respect to requests pending on or filed after 2000 and before 2011 (due to the sunsetting of EGTRRA).[165]

The IRS is also directed to allow an allocation of exemption when a taxpayer has substantially complied with the allocation requirements but did not quite get it right.[166] The substantial compliance relief applies to estate and gift

---

[163] Treas. Reg. § 26.2642-2(a)(2).

[164] IRC § 2642(g)(1).

[165] EGTRRA §§ 564(b)(1), 901.

[166] IRC § 2642(g)(2).

tax transfers made after 2000 (and before 2011, if EGTRRA is not extended).[167] Comparable relief for earlier transfers may be available.[168]

[iv] **Retroactive allocations.** Retroactive allocation may be available for a nonexempt trust that has a non-skip person beneficiary who dies after 2000.[169] Specifically, the transferor can retroactively allocate any of his unused GSTT exemption (at the time of the beneficiary's death) to any previous transfers to the trust on a chronological basis,[170] if the following circumstances exist:[171]

- a non-skip person had a present or future interest[172] in the trust;
- the non-skip person was a lineal descendant of any grandparent of the transferor, the transferor's spouse, or the transferor's former spouse;
- the non-skip person was assigned to a generation below the transferor's generation; and
- the non-skip person predeceased the transferor.

If the retroactive allocation is made on a timely filed gift tax return for the year that the non-skip person died, then the transfers will be valued for allocation purposes as if the allocation had been made in the years of transfer.[173] The allocation will be effective just before the non-skip person's death, and the amount of unused GSTT exemption will be determined just before the non-skip person's death.[174]

> **EXAMPLE:** Mom contributes $1,000,000 to a trust for Child, remainder to Grandchild. She does not allocate exemption, because she believes that the trust will be used mostly for Child. Two years later, Child dies. At that time, trust property is worth $2,000,000. Mom may allocate any exemption she has left to the original transfer to this trust. If she allocates $1,000,000, the trust will be fully exempt.

---

[167] EGTRRA §§ 564(b)(2), 901.

[168] IRC § 2642(g)(1); EGTRRA § 564(b)(2).

[169] EGTRRA § 561(a).

[170] Subject to sunsetting of EGTRRA in 2011.

[171] IRC § 2632(d)(1).

[172] A person has a future interest in a trust if the trust may distribute income or corpus to the person at any future date. IRC § 2632(a)(3).

[173] IRC § 2632(d)(2)(A).

[174] IRC §§ 2632(d)(2)(B), 2632(d)(2)(C).

[b] Transfers at Death—General Rule

The percentage of a taxable transfer that is exempt is a fraction equal to the amount of exemption allocated, divided by the value of property transferred. What value is used in the denominator—estate tax value, date of distribution value, or some other value? The rules are quite complex, so we'll do both a technical explanation and a simplified set of instructions.

An allocation to a transfer made at death or to a trust included in the transferor's estate will be effective at date of death, and the value for allocation purposes of the property transferred is determined by the regulations.[175]

[c] Transfers at Death—Explanation for Technophiles

Under varying circumstances, the GSTT value of a transfer at death for purposes of allocating the exemption will be its date of distribution value, its estate tax value, or a different value. Generally speaking, the value will be the estate tax value of the property.[176] However, special rules apply to pecuniary payments, and to residual transfers after pecuniary payments.

The following Global Example will be used to illustrate the rules concerning transfers at death.

GLOBAL EXAMPLE

Mom has $1,000,000 GSTT exemption available. Mom dies with an estate of $1,100,000. She leaves a bequest of $100,000 to Grandchild, residue to Trust. Since Mom's death, the entire estate has appreciated by 50 percent, so the total value of the estate on date of distribution is $1,650,000. The executor wants the bequest to Grandchild to be totally exempt, and the residuary estate to have the highest exempt portion possible, consistent with that. How does he do that?

[i] Pecuniary payment funded in cash. The payment will be valued at the cash amount.[177] In the Global Example, if the Grandchild's bequest is paid

---

[175] Treas. Reg. § 26.2642-2(b)(1). Special rules apply to IRC § 2032A property. Treas. Reg. §§ 26.2642-2(b)(1), 26.2642-4(a)(4). See Chapter 48 on Special Use Valuation of Farms and Ranches for a discussion.

[176] Treas. Reg. § 26.2642-2(b).

[177] Treas. Reg. § 26.2642-2(b)(2)(i).

in cash, allocation of $100,000 of exemption will render the Grandchild's bequest fully exempt.

[ii] **Pecuniary payment funded in kind.** The value of the pecuniary payment will be the pecuniary amount *if* payment must be made with property on the basis of (1) date of distribution values, or (2) values that reflect appreciation and depreciation since date of death of all assets that could have been used to fund the payment.[178] Otherwise, the value will be the date of distribution values of the assets used to satisfy the payment.[179]

Using the Global Example, the following results will be obtained, depending on funding requirements:

- *Date of distribution funding.* If the governing instrument or state law requires date of distribution funding, then the assets used to fund Grandchild's bequest must be valued at their date of distribution values. This means that, if Stock *X* has appreciated from a $100,000 estate tax value to $175,000 on date of distribution, the executor can fund Grandchild's bequest with $100,000 of Stock *X* and allocate $100,000 of exemption to render the bequest wholly exempt.
- *Fairly representative funding.* If the estate as a whole has appreciated 50 percent, and "fairly representative" funding is required, then the executor could fund Grandchild's bequest with $150,000 of stock, using only $100,000 of exemption.
- *Estate tax value funding.* If the governing document requires the bequest to be satisfied with assets at their estate tax values with no "fairly representative" requirement, then the executor could fund the bequest with stock using its estate tax value of $100,000. Grandchild would actually receive $175,000 of Stock *X*, and $175,000 of exemption would have to be used to exempt the bequest. The exempt amount of the residuary bequest would also be affected.[180]

[iii] **Residual transfer after pecuniary payment.**

[A] *Pecuniary payment meets two special requirements.* If the pecuniary payment:

- (1) carries "appropriate interest," *or* (2) is distributed or irrevocably set aside within 15 months of death, *or* (3) is allocated its pro rata share of income earned by the fund from which payment is to be made during the period before distribution pursuant to requirements imposed by the governing instrument or local law, *and*

---

[178] Treas. Reg. § 26.2642-2(b)(1).

[179] Treas. Reg. § 26.2642-2(b)(2)(ii).

[180] See ¶ 5.05[2][c][iii] below.

- if payable in kind, is required to be satisfied with property on the basis of (1) date of distribution values, or (2) values that are fairly representative of the appreciation and depreciation in value of all assets available to fund the payment from date of death to the funding date,

then property used to fund a residual bequest will be valued at the estate tax value of the assets available to fund the pecuniary payment, reduced by the *actual amount* of the pecuniary payment.[181]

In the Global Example, if the bequest to Grandchild meets the above special requirements, then Grandchild's bequest will be totally exempt, with use of $100,000 of exemption. The residual trust will receive $1,550,000, and will be 90 percent exempt ($900,000 remaining exemption/$1,000,000 estate tax value of amount available to fund pecuniary bequest, reduced by amount of pecuniary bequest).

[B] *Pecuniary payment does not meet of first special requirement, but meets second requirement.* In that case, the value of the residual transfer will be the estate tax value of all property available to fund the pecuniary payment less the *present value* of the pecuniary payment.[182] The present value is determined by discounting the pecuniary payment, using the Section 7520 rate at the death of the transferor, for the period between the date of the transferor's death and the date of the pecuniary payment.[183]

In the Global Example, if the bequest to Grandchild does not meet the first special requirement, but (1) meets the second requirement and (2) the present value of the pecuniary bequest is $75,000, Grandchild's bequest of $100,000 is 100 percent exempt (using $100,000 of exemption) and the residual bequest is 88 percent exempt ($900,000 exemption/$1,025,000 estate tax value of entire estate less present value of pecuniary bequest).

[iv] Pecuniary bequest does not meet second requirement. If the pecuniary payment (1) is payable in kind and (2) is not required to be satisfied with assets at date of distribution value (or with assets reflective of the appreciation and depreciation in all assets available to fund the pecuniary bequest), the GSTT value of property used to fund the residuary transfer will be its value at date of distribution.[184]

In the Global Example, if Grandchild's bequest is payable in kind and is required to be satisfied at estate tax values, without regard to appreciation or depreciation, then the executor can fund the bequest with $100,000 of stock at estate tax values. Grandchild will receive $175,000 of stock, and $175,000 of

---

[181] Treas. Reg. § 26.2642-2(b)(3)(i).
[182] Treas. Reg. § 26.2642-2(b)(3)(i).
[183] Treas. Reg. § 26.2642-2(b)(3)(i).
[184] Treas. Reg. § 26.2642-2(b)(3)(ii).

exemption must be used to make the bequest exempt. The residual bequest will be valued for GSTT purposes at $1,475,000 (i.e., the actual value of assets used to fund the distribution), and the bequest will be 56 percent exempt ($825,000/$1,475,000).

[v] **Appropriate interest.** "Appropriate interest" means interest that meets the following three requirements:

- The interest is payable for the period from the transferor's date of death (or from the date specified under local law for the payment of interest) to the date the pecuniary bequest is funded.[185]
- The interest rate must be at least equal to the statutory rate applicable to pecuniary bequests under local law, or, if there is no such rate, 80 percent of the rate applicable under Section 7520 at the death of the transferor.[186]
- The interest rate cannot exceed the greater of (1) the statutory rate applicable to pecuniary bequests under local law or (2) 120 percent of the rate applicable under Section 7520 at the death of the transferor.[187]

Practice Pointer: If the dispositive instrument is a revocable trust, rather than a will, and the statutory rate applicable to pecuniary bequests is desired, incorporate the statutory rate, as it may not otherwise apply to nonprobate dispositions.

[vi] **Irrevocably set aside.** "Irrevocably set aside" means segregated and held in a separate account.[188] The "entire payment" must be set aside.[189] (Note that if the pecuniary bequest is based on a formula, the "entire payment" may not be determinable after 15 months.)

[d] One-Size-Fits-All Provisions

The evil to be avoided by this bewildering labyrinth of regulations is an executor stuffing property that has appreciated since death into an exempt trust at its date-of-death value. Most estate planners are familiar with Revenue Procedure 64-19,[190] which addresses a similar abuse in a marital deduction context.

---

[185] Treas. Reg. § 26.2642-2(b)(4)(i).
[186] Treas. Reg. § 26.2642-2(b)(4)(i)(A).
[187] Treas. Reg. § 26.2642-2(b)(4)(i)(B).
[188] Treas. Reg. § 26.2642-2(b)(4)(ii).
[189] Treas. Reg. § 26.2642-2(b)(4)(ii).
[190] 1964-1 CB 682.

The following drafting suggestions should simplify the lives of people trying to thread their way through this regulatory maze. These provisions are not custom-fitted to each individual situation, but they will allow the exemption to be efficiently utilized, whether the pecuniary transfer or the residual transfer is intended to be fully exempt:

- Provide that pecuniary payments payable in kind will be funded at date of distribution values, or values reflective of general appreciation and depreciation of the assets available to fund the pecuniary payment.
- Provide that all pecuniary payments bear interest at the local statutory rate. If, however, there is no statutory rate, use the Section 7520 rate at the death of the transferor. Make the interest payable for the period from date of death (or date specified under state law requiring payment of interest) to date of funding.

If these provisions apply, then a pecuniary payment will be allocated exemption equal to the pecuniary amount. Residual transfers will be valued for exemption allocation purposes at the estate tax value of all assets available to fund the pecuniary payment, less the amount of the pecuniary payment.

In the Global Example, if Grandchild's bequest is payable in cash or in kind, and the pecuniary bequest must be funded at date of distribution values, Grandchild will receive $100,000. If the pecuniary bequest must be funded at fairly representative values, the Grandchild will receive $150,000. Either way, the bequest will use $100,000 of exemption and will be completely exempt. The residual trust will receive $1,550,000 if Grandchild's bequest was satisfied at date of distribution values. Otherwise, it will receive $1,500,000. Either way, it will be 90 percent exempt ($900,000 remaining exemption/$1,000,000 estate tax value of estate, less amount of pecuniary bequest).

If it is too late to change a governing document that doesn't meet either the interest requirements or the share-of-income requirement, fund or set aside the pecuniary bequests within 15 months from date of death.

[e] Statute of Limitations

After allocation of exemption has been made to a trust, the percentage of the trust that is exempt from GSTT becomes final as follows:

- For direct skips, at the expiration of the statute of limitations with respect to the direct skip;[191]
- For other GSTs, at the later of (1) the expiration of the statute of limitations for the first GSTT return filed using the exempt percentage or (2)

---

[191] Treas. Reg. § 26.2642-5(a). Often, the same as the expiration of the gift or estate tax statute of limitations, but possibly differing due to the existence of an ETIP or other reasons.

the expiration of the statute of limitations for the transferor's estate tax.[192] If no estate tax return is required, the period is determined as if a return were required and were timely filed.[193]

[f] Estate Tax Inclusion Period

[i] **Definition.** The ETIP is any period during which a trust created during the transferor's lifetime would be included in the estate of the transferor or the transferor's spouse (other than pursuant to the three-year rule)[194] if either died. The ETIP will involve a trust in which the transferor or the transferor's spouse has an interest or power causing estate inclusion. If the transferor makes a gift that would be included in her estate if she died immediately after making the gift (other than because of the three-year rule),[195] the trust will have an ETIP. The ETIP is generally the period between (1) the date of the gift and (2) the earliest of:

- the transferor's death,
- the date of a GST (but only with respect to the property involved in the GST), or
- the time at which property will cease to be included in the transferor's or transferor's spouse's estate (other than under the three-year rule) if either of them were to die.[196]

[ii] **Allocation of exemption—general rule.** If a trust has an ETIP, an allocation of exemption cannot be effective until the end of the ETIP.[197]

---

[192] Treas. Reg. § 26.2642-5(b)(1). This seems to mean that the earliest the statute will run will be three or six years after the transferor's estate tax return is filed, and the latest will be the expiration of the statute for the first return reporting a taxable distribution or taxable termination, if later. See, however, Treas. Reg. § 26.2642-2(a)(1), which provides that the value of the exempt portion of trust is determined by the value of the property as finally determined for gift tax purposes in cases of inter vivos transfers where a timely allocation of exemption is made. For such transfers, the value of the transferred property would appear to become final at the expiration of the gift tax statute of limitations if there is no ETIP.

[193] Treas. Reg. § 26.2642-5(b)(2).

[194] The three-year rule, discussed in Chapter 2, provides that certain gifts made within three years of the transferor's death are included in her estate. IRC § 2035.

[195] For example, a gift to a qualified personal residence trust, grantor retained annuity trust, or grantor retained income trust. These trusts are discussed in Chapters 21, 22, and 24, respectively.

[196] For example, if the transferor has retained an income interest for five years, the expiration of the five-year period.

[197] IRC § 2642(f).

EXAMPLE: Mom establishes a qualified personal residence trust, retaining an income interest for the shorter of her life or ten years, remainder to grandchildren. Assume the value of the remainder interest at the date of the gift is $40,000, and the value of her income interest is $60,000. The gift tax will be based on a gift of $40,000. However, Mom cannot exempt the trust from GSTT by allocating $40,000 of her GSTT exemption on the creation of the trust. The allocation can only be effective at the earlier of Mom's death or the end of the ten years; the value of the trust assets at that date will determine the amount of the direct skip, which takes place at that time.[198]

If exemption is allocated prior to termination of the ETIP, the allocation cannot be revoked, even though it is not effective until the termination of the ETIP.[199] If the ETIP terminates upon the transferor's death, the value of the property for GSTT exemption purposes will be its value for estate tax purposes.[200] If the ETIP terminates during the transferor's life, the value of the property for GSTT exemption purposes will be its value as of the termination.[201]

If the transferor's spouse consents to split a gift with the transferor, the spouse will be considered the transferor of one half of the property for GSTT purposes.[202] This will subject the trust to an ETIP if the spouse has interests or powers that would cause the trust to be included in the spouse's estate if the spouse were the actual transferor. If the transferor's spouse dies during the ETIP, his executor can allocate exemption to the portion of the trust of which he is treated as the transferor.[203] If the trust is still subject to an ETIP because of the transferor's rights or powers, the allocation will not be effective until the ETIP terminates.[204]

Exceptions. The following are exceptions to the above:

- If the transferor establishes an inter vivos QTIP trust for her spouse and makes a reverse QTIP election, she can effectively allocate her exemption to the reverse QTIP trust at the outset.[205]
- A trust will not be treated as having an ETIP solely because the transferor's spouse has a withdrawal power over property transferred to the trust, if (1) the power is limited to the greater of $5,000 or 5 percent of

---

[198] IRC § 2642(f)(1).

[199] Treas. Reg. §§ 26.2632-1(c)(1), 26.2642-1(b)(2).

[200] IRC § 2642(f)(2)(A).

[201] IRC § 2642(f)(2)(B).

[202] IRC § 2652(a)(2).

[203] Treas. Reg. § 26.2632-1(c)(5), example 3.

[204] Treas. Reg. § 26.2632-1(c)(5), example 3.

[205] Treas. Reg. § 26.2632-1(c)(2)(ii)(C). The reverse QTIP election is discussed at ¶ 5.05[6][a] below.

the value of the transferred property and (2) the power expires within 60 days of the transfer to the trust.[206]

- If the possibility of inclusion of property in the transferor's or the transferor's spouse's estate can be ascertained actuarially to be less than five percent, the property will not be considered includable in either estate for purposes of the ETIP rules.[207]

Practice Pointer: The existence of an ETIP affects the ability to allocate GSTT exemption; it is largely irrelevant to a trust that is not intended to be exempt. The only other issue affected by the ETIP is that, if the transfer to the trust is a direct skip, the direct skip will be deemed to take place at the close of the ETIP rather than at the date of transfer.[208]

EXAMPLE: Mom gives a life insurance policy to a trust for Grandchildren, and retains, in her individual capacity, incidents of ownership in the policy. Since the trust will be included in her estate if she dies, the trust is in an ETIP. A direct skip will take place on the termination of the ETIP, rather than on the transfer to the trust.

[3] Selecting the Exempt Property and Deciding When to Use the Exemption

[a] General Considerations

First, it is best to allocate exemption when the value of the property is low. Second, other things being equal, one is better off using the exemption sooner rather than later, because income and appreciation of the transferred property can begin accumulating outside of the GSTT system earlier.

[b] Which Type of GST to Choose

As a general rule, it is more tax-efficient to allocate the exemption to a trust that is expected to have taxable terminations and taxable distributions, rather than to allocate it to direct skips. This is because direct skips are tax-exclusive and the other GSTs are not. In practice, however, GSTT exemption is often allocated to direct skips, even if that allocation is less efficient, because

---

[206] Treas. Reg. § 26.2632-1(c)(2)(ii)(B).

[207] Treas. Reg. § 26.2632-1(c)(2)(ii)(A).

[208] IRC § 2642(f)(1).

the transferor or executor (for whatever reason) does not want to pay generation-skipping transfer tax at the date of transfer. For example, the person may
feel that the law might change or that he needs the money that would otherwise be used to pay GSTT.

[c] Trusts for the Primary Benefit of Non-Skip Persons

It is rarely a great idea to allocate exemption to a trust that is virtually
certain to be included in a non-skip person's estate. In fact, an allocation to a
trust that has no GST potential at all with respect to the allocating transferor is
void.[209] However, an allocation to a trust that has negligible GST potential is
effective.[210] It is also not wise to allocate exemption to a trust from which substantial distributions to non-skip persons are expected, if there is a better alternative.

The broad new automatic allocation rules provided by EGTRRA[211] can
catch us unawares in this regard. The exceptions from automatic allocation are
designed to include trusts that are intended primarily for non-skip persons.
However, the exceptions are very specific in their application, and therefore,
do not cover many trusts that a person might want to omit from the automatic
allocation.

[d] Special Use Property

The special use value of property (valued under Section 2032A) is its
value for purposes of determining the exempt portion of a trust funded with
the property, if the recapture agreement includes GSTT as well as estate tax.[212]
If recapture occurs, the exempt portion will be redetermined as of the transferor's date of death.[213]

[4] Assuring Treatment as Separate Trusts

Many times it will be important for different interests in trusts to be treated as
separate trusts, and not as parts of one larger trust.

---

[209] Treas. Reg. § 26.2632-1(b)(2)(i).
[210] Treas. Reg. § 26.2632-1(b)(2)(i).
[211] Described at ¶ 5.05[1].
[212] Treas. Reg. § 26.2642-2(b)(1).
[213] Treas. Reg. § 26.2642-4(c)(4).

[a] Separate Shares

Separate shares of certain trusts are automatically treated as separate trusts for GSTT purposes. These include (1) trusts with multiple settlors, (2) trusts with shares that constitute substantially independent and separate shares for different beneficiaries from the beginning,[214] and (3) trusts that begin to qualify for the predeceased ancestor exception after the inception of the trusts.[215]

[b] Pecuniary Amounts Payable From Trust Included in Estate

If a person has a current right to receive a mandatory pecuniary payment from a trust that is includable in a deceased transferor's gross estate (including a testamentary trust), the pecuniary gift will be treated as a separate gift (not a distribution from the trust as a whole) if it meets the following two requirements:

1. (a) The trustee is required to pay appropriate interest to the pecuniary legatee; or (b) the gift is distributed or irrevocably set aside within 15 months of the transferor's death; or (c) the trust or local law specifically requires the trustee or executor to allocate to the pecuniary gift a pro rata share of the income earned by the fund for which the pecuniary payment is to be made between the date of death of the transferor and the date of payment; and
2. If the pecuniary amount is payable in kind, it must be funded at date of distribution values, or in a manner fairly reflecting net appreciation or depreciation in value of the assets available to fund the pecuniary bequest from the valuation date to the date of funding.[216]

If both of the above requirements are not met, the pecuniary gifts will be treated as if they were part of the trust as a whole.

EXAMPLE: Revocable trust provides an outright gift of $100,000 (payable in kind) to Grandchild, and a residuary trust that provides income to Child for his life, remainder to Grandchild. If the above two requirements are not met, the distribution of the $100,000 to Grandchild will be a taxable distribution rather than a direct skip.

---

[214] Treas. Reg. § 26.2654-1(a)(1).
[215] Treas. Reg. § 26.2612-1(a)(2)(ii).
[216] Treas. Reg. § 26.2654-1(a)(1)(ii).

Practice Pointer: To avoid having to worry about this complex rule:

- Provide that pecuniary amounts payable in kind must be satisfied at date of distribution value or at a value fairly reflecting changes in the value of all assets that are available to fund the pecuniary bequest.
- Provide that all pecuniary bequests bear the statutory interest rate on bequests for the statutory period, or, if there is none, the Section 7520 rate for the period from date of death to date of funding.
- If the trust is already irrevocable, and does not contain the above provisions, distribute or set aside pecuniary gifts within 15 months of date of death.

These are the same easy provisions that can be used in responding to the Byzantine regulations determining the exempt percentage of a transfer at death.[217]

---

[c] Avoiding Partially Exempt Trusts

Generation-skipping trusts, ideally, will be wholly exempt or wholly non-exempt from GSTT.[218] This arrangement enables a trustee to make investments and distributions suitable to a trust that is not going to be subject to GSTT or to one that is, as the case may be. It also can make the accounting simpler and enables the trustee to make distributions either to skip persons without paying GSTT or to non-skip persons without wasting exemption. A sample formula to avoid establishing partially exempt trusts is at ¶ 5.11[3], Exhibit 5-C: Trust Division Language.

It will often be desirable to know how to separate a trust into one wholly exempt and one wholly nonexempt trust. This separation is called a severance.

[d] Severance of Trust Included in Transferor's Estate

In essence, a trust that divides into separate shares on the settlor's death is treated as one trust for GSTT purposes unless certain conditions are met.[219] This rule also applies to amounts that pour into a revocable trust from the probate estate.[220] However, the severance of a trust included in the transferor's gross estate will be recognized under certain circumstances.

---

[217] See ¶ 5.05[2][d] above.

[218] That is, they will have an inclusion ratio of zero or one.

[219] IRC § 2654(b).

[220] Treas. Reg. § 26.2654-1(a)(5), example 3.

First, if the will or revocable trust agreement directs that a trust be divided into separate trusts upon the transferor's death, the trusts created as a result of the division should be treated as separate trusts for GSTT purposes.[221]

Alternatively, if the governing instrument or local law grants discretionary authority to sever the trusts, the trusts will be treated as separate trusts for GSTT purposes if:

- the terms of the new trusts provide in the aggregate for the same succession of interests and beneficiaries as are provided in the original trust;
- the severance occurs, or a judicial proceeding to reform the trust is commenced, before the due date of the transferor's estate tax return (including extensions actually granted); and
- either the new trusts are severed on a fractional basis or, if the will or revocable trust agreement requires that any severance be made on a pecuniary basis, the pecuniary amount would be treated as a separate share if it were paid to an individual.[222]

Each trust does not have to have the same beneficiaries as the original trust to provide for the same succession of interests. For example, if Dad established a testamentary trust providing that income is paid to Mom for her life and the remainder goes one half to Child and one half to Grandchild, the executor could divide the trust into two trusts—one providing income to Mom for life, with the Child as remainder beneficiary, and the other providing income to Mom for life, with Grandchild as the remainder beneficiary.[223]

A fractional severance of a testamentary trust made at the discretion of an executor or trustee, or pursuant to a reformation, need not be funded with a pro rata share of each asset. The trusts may be funded on a non-pro rata basis if funding is done on the basis of the fair market value of the assets on date of funding or in a manner fairly reflecting the appreciation and depreciation in the value of the assets.[224]

The IRS has authority under Section 9100 to recognize belated severances.[225]

---

[221] Treas. Reg. § 26.2654-1(b)(1)(i); Priv. Ltr. Rul. 200040010 (Jan. 28, 2000) (IRS accepted court's finding that revocable trust agreement provided for creation of separate trusts for grandchildren at testator's death).

[222] Treas. Reg. § 26.2654-1(b)(1)(ii). See ¶ 5.05[4][a] above.

[223] Treas. Reg. § 26.2654-1(b)(4), example 1.

[224] Treas. Reg. § 26.2654-1(b)(1)(ii)(C)(1).

[225] See, e.g., Priv. Ltr. Rul. 199939024 (July 1, 1999) and Priv. Ltr. Rul. 200040008 (June 22, 2000).

[e] Qualified Severances

Before 2001, numerous complex requirements existed in order for a trust to be severed for GSTT purposes.[226] Trusts could not be severed after they had commenced unless they met the separate share rules.[227] As of January 1, 2001, in addition to the pre-existing permitted severances, severances can be made at any time after a trust has commenced.[228]

A qualified severance is the division of a single trust by any means available under local law or the governing instrument into two or more trusts.[229] The single trust must be divided on a fractional basis, and the terms of the new trusts, in the aggregate, must provide for the same succession of beneficiaries as the original trust.[230]

If a trust is partially exempt, the severance will only qualify if the single trust is divided into two trusts. One trust must receive a fractional share of the total value reflecting the exempt portion and the other trust, the non-exempt portion. Thereafter, the trust receiving the exempt fraction of value will be wholly exempt and the other trust will be non-exempt.[231]

The Secretary is authorized to promulgate regulations permitting other qualified severances.[232] A qualified severance may be made at any time pursuant to forms and regulations prescribed by the Secretary.[233]

[5] Effect of Withdrawal Powers in Exempt Trusts[234]

Withdrawal, or *Crummey* powers, are commonly used in generation-skipping trusts. An extensive discussion of the issues presented by such powers is contained in Chapter 10. Here, however, is a brief summary of these issues.

A trust that is intended to be an exempt generation-skipping trust should not expose the beneficiaries to estate or gift tax that would render use of the GSTT exemption pointless. Hence, it ordinarily should not have a withdrawal power held by a non-skip person that lapses to a greater extent than $5,000 or

---

[226] See Treas. Reg. § 26.2654(a)-1.

[227] See Treas. Reg. § 26.2654(a)-1.

[228] IRC § 2642(a)(3); EGTRRA § 562(a). The rules will return to the more complex set of provisions in 2011, due to sunsetting of EGTRRA.

[229] IRC § 2642(a)(3)(B)(i),

[230] IRC §§ 2642(a)(3)(B)(i)(I), 2642(a)(3)(B)(i)(II). Presumably, Treas. Reg. § 26.2654-1(b)(4), example 3 would apply in determining whether the trusts provide for the same succession of beneficiaries.

[231] IRC § 2642(a)(3)(B)(ii).

[232] IRC § 2642(a)(3)(C).

[233] IRC § 2642(a)(3)(C).

[234] Withdrawal, or "Crummey" powers, are discussed at length in Chapter 10.

5 percent of the property subject to the withdrawal right in any year. This is because any amount that lapses in excess of this limit will be either (1) a current gift by the powerholder to the trust, or (2) taxable in the powerholder's estate, depending on the trust provisions.[235] This will result in the powerholder being treated as the new transferor of a portion of the trust for GSTT purposes and will waste the original transferor's exemption.[236]

> **EXAMPLE:** Trust holds insurance policy on Mom's life. The annual insurance premium is $20,000. Mom pays the $20,000 and allocates $20,000 of her exemption to the trust. The primary beneficiary, Child, is given the power to withdraw $20,000. The power to withdraw lapses entirely after 30 days. Because of the five-or-five rule, the lapse of the first $5,000 has no gift or estate tax consequences. Child is treated as the new transferor for gift, estate, and generation-skipping transfer tax purposes, of 15/20ths of $20,000, or $15,000. If the $20,000 is the only asset of the trust, Mom will be the transferor of 25 percent of the trust, and Child will be the transferor of 75 percent of the trust. Hence, either (1) Child immediately makes a taxable gift (not eligible for annual exclusion) of $15,000, or (2) 75 percent of the trust will be included in Child's estate when he dies (or will be a gift from Child to the extent that the property is distributed to others during Child's lifetime), depending on whether (a) Child has retained a power that would make his gift incomplete, or (b) the lapsed amount is subject to Child's creditors. Use of Mom's GSTT exemption on this trust would be a waste to some extent because Child will make a taxable transfer on disposition of the property during his life or at his death.

Query: Can Mom allocate $5,000 of her exemption to the above trust and make that portion of the trust wholly exempt? We can't count on it. On the date of premium payment, Mom is the sole transferor of the entire trust. The lapse of Child's power will render Child the new transferor of ¾ of the trust. The portions attributable to Mom's transfer and Child's transfer will be treated as separate trusts—$5,000 in Mom's trust and $15,000 in Child's trust. If Mom allocated exemption on a timely filed return, exemption would be automatically allocated, effective as of the date of transfer (before the separation into two trusts is deemed to have occurred), rendering the entire trust ¼ exempt. On the lapse of Child's power, Child's deemed separate trust would be ¼ exempt, and Mom's deemed separate trust would be ¼ exempt. In order to render her own portion of the trust totally exempt, she would have to file a late allocation, using whatever value her deemed separate trust has at the allocation date. Child must use his own exemption to render his deemed trust exempt.

---

[235] IRC §§ 2041(b)(2), 2514(e).

[236] IRC §§ 2652(a)(1), 2653(a)(1); Treas. Reg. §§ 26.2611-1, 26.2612-1(c)(1), 26.2652-1(a)(6), example 5. See Chapter 10 for an extensive discussion of this issue.

Practice Pointer: In the case of an exempt generation-skipping trust that is a *Crummey* trust, it will often be appropriate to give the beneficiary a hanging power,[237] in order to avoid the lapse issues. Even then, if the powerholder dies during a period in which he has any unlapsed withdrawal right, a portion of the trust will be includable in his estate and he will be treated as a new transferor.[238]

> **EXAMPLE:** Trust holds insurance policy on Mom's life. The single premium payment is $20,000. Mom pays the $20,000 and allocates $20,000 of her exemption to the trust. The primary beneficiary, Child, is given a hanging power to withdraw $20,000, which lapses in the amount of $5,000 on December 31 each year. At the end of Year Two, Child dies, holding a $10,000 withdrawal right (a total of $10,000 having lapsed in Years One and Two). Since $20,000 of GSTT exemption was allocated to the trust, the GSTT exemption is partly wasted, because 50 percent of the trust ($10,000/$20,000) is included in Child's estate.

Practice Pointer: If there is any substantial likelihood that the powerholder will die before the power completely lapses, or if there is another good use of the annual exclusion, it may be best not to make an exempt generation-skipping trust a *Crummey* trust.[239]

[6] Using Full Exemption of First Spouse to Die

Let's suppose Wife dies without having made any taxable gifts. Husband survives her, and Wife's will follows a common pattern of disposition of a married person's estate—that is, she leaves the applicable exclusion amount for the year in question ($1,000,000 in 2002) to a bypass trust that will be excluded from Husband's estate, and leaves her remaining estate in a manner qualifying for the marital deduction. Her executor allocates the applicable exclusion amount ($1,000,000 in 2002) of GSTT exemption to the bypass trust. How does he avoid wasting the remaining amount (which is $1,100,000 less

---

[237] That is, a power which lapses annually at the five-or-five rate. Crummey trusts and hanging powers are fully described in Chapter 10.

[238] IRC § 2041(a)(2).

[239] Another consideration in this decision is whether the lapse of a Crummey power is a transfer of property for state law property purposes. If so, part of the trust may be subject to the powerholder's creditors.

$1,000,000, or $100,000, in 2002) of the transferor's GSTT exemption? Four alternatives are discussed below.

[a] Reverse QTIP Election

If the marital deduction gift is in the form of a QTIP trust, the executor can make a reverse QTIP election.[240] This is an election to treat Wife as the transferor of the QTIP trust for GSTT purposes (despite the fact that the trust will be included in Husband's estate), so that her remaining exemption ($100,000 in 2002) can be allocated to it. What if the QTIP trust contains more than the remaining exemption amount? A partial reverse QTIP election is not available.[241] Hence, if a reverse QTIP election is to be made, the reverse QTIP amount must be held in a separate trust from its inception.[242] The division of one trust into separate trusts for this purpose cannot be done after the fact, and, hence, either (1) the reverse QTIP trust must qualify as a separate trust without a severance or (2) the QTIP trust must be severed into two trusts and the reverse QTIP election made for one of them before the due date for making the election. Thus, it is smart to include a formula in the will or revocable trust establishing two separate trusts from the outset—one exempt and one nonexempt trust. An example of such a formula is at ¶ 5.11[4], Exhibit 5-D: Reverse QTIP Election Language.

The reverse QTIP election is made on the return on which the QTIP election is made. If a protective QTIP election is made, a protective reverse QTIP election must also be made if reverse QTIP treatment is desired.[243]

The reverse QTIP election is the solution most often used to utilize the first spouse's full exemption because it is the only method that does not involve payment of estate tax at the first death.

[b] Partial QTIP Election

If Wife's executor is willing to incur some estate tax, and Husband wants to retain the benefits of the trust, a partial QTIP election can be made. In such instance, Wife's remaining exemption can be allocated to the non-QTIP trust. The exempt part should be put in a separate trust.

EXAMPLE: Mom dies in 2003, leaving $1,000,000 to a bypass trust and $2,000,000 to a QTIP trust. The executor allocates $1,000,000 of GSTT exemption to the bypass trust. It will take $163,951 of estate tax to get an

---

[240] IRC § 2652(a)(3).
[241] Treas. Reg. § 26.2652-2(a).
[242] Treas. Reg. §§ 26.2652-2(a), 26.2654-1(b)(1).
[243] Treas. Reg. § 26.2652-2(b).

additional $100,000 into a nonexempt marital trust. (Tax on $163,951 is $63,951. Remaining amount is $100,000.) This will leave $2,000,000 – $163,951, or $1,826,049, to pass to the QTIP trust. Hence, the executor can make a partial QTIP election for $1,826,049/$2,000,000 of the property passing to the QTIP. If Mom's GSTT exemption is allocated to the marital trust as a whole, the trust will be partially exempt—not an ideal result. However, if the QTIP trust is then separated into two trusts—one of $1,826,049 and one of $163,951, and the will apportions estate tax to the non-QTIP trust, then the non-QTIP trust will have $100,000 after tax, and an allocation of Mom's remaining exemption to the $100,000 trust can render it completely exempt.

A partial QTIP election might be desirable to run up the estate tax brackets in the predeceasing spouse's estate where the surviving spouse doesn't want to disclaim (for example, where no disclaimer trust for the surviving spouse[244] has been set up under the deceased spouse's will or where the surviving spouse does not want to give up a testamentary power of appointment over the assets).

A sample provision for making a partial QTIP election is at ¶ 5.11[5], Exhibit 5-E: Partial QTIP Election Language.

[c] Disclaimer Trust for Transferor's Surviving Spouse

A disclaimer is a decision not to accept property that would otherwise be transferred to the disclaimant. A qualified disclaimer is not treated as a gift by the disclaimant for tax purposes.[245] It must meet certain requirements,[246] which are discussed in Chapter 47. Suppose Wife's will provides that, if Husband disclaims property, the disclaimed property then passes to a trust which is to be used for Husband's benefit only if he is without other resources.[247] Husband can disclaim $100,000, plus an amount equal to the estate tax that will be generated as a result of the disclaimer. The total amount will then pass to that trust. If the tax apportionment clause provides for payment of taxes out of property passing to the disclaimer trust, part of the disclaimed property will be used to pay these taxes. The executor can then allocate $100,000 of GSTT exemption to that trust. The exempt $100,000 trust will probably never make a distribution to Husband (so the exemption probably will not be wasted or inefficiently used). It will still give Husband a safety net, however, should he ever need it.

---

[244] As discussed in ¶ 5.05[6][c] below.

[245] IRC § 2518.

[246] IRC § 2518.

[247] IRC §§ 2518(a), 2518(b)(4)(A); Treas. Reg. §§ 25.2518-3(a)(1)(ii), 25.2518-3(a)(2), 25.2518-3(c).

Practice Pointer: Specific drafting in anticipation of such a disclaimer must be done in order to use this technique, and it only works with the surviving spouse. In the case of a disclaimer by anyone other than the surviving spouse, the disclaimed property must pass to someone other than the disclaimant. Moreover, even the surviving spouse cannot have a power of appointment over the disclaimed property. If the trust receiving the disclaimed property gives the surviving spouse a power of appointment, he should disclaim the power of appointment.

---

[d] Ordinary Disclaimer

Husband can disclaim in favor of a generation-skipping trust.

[e] Partial Election and Diversion of Non-QTIP Amount to Bypass Trust

Wife's will can provide that, to the extent the executor does not elect QTIP treatment, the non-QTIP portion passes to the bypass trust.[248] This technique prevents Husband from having to receive income from the non-QTIP portion.

[7] Drafting and Administration of Exempt Trusts

Trusts that are exempt from estate tax or GSTT, usually due to their qualification for the unified credit and/or the GSTT exemption, should be drafted and administered to maximize their tax advantages, if that is consistent with nontax goals.

[a] Mandatory Distribution of Income

A requirement that all income be distributed is not usually an ideal provision in an exempt trust, as it can seriously limit the trust's tax-avoidance capabilities. Such provisions, however, are sometimes found in existing trusts, and some trusts must distribute all of their income to qualify for certain tax advantages.[249] If the trustee is administering an exempt trust that must distribute all its income, and the income beneficiary doesn't object, the trustee could invest in growth assets, so as to minimize required distributions.

---

[248] Treas. Reg. § 20.2056(b)–7(d)(3)(i).

[249] E.g., QTIP trusts and qualified subchapter S trusts.

[b] Qualified Subchapter S Trust

A qualified subchapter S trust (QSTT) is not an ideal exempt vehicle, because the trust must distribute all its income.[250] If the S corporation does not pay dividends, the beneficiary will still be liable for tax on his undistributed share of S corporation income.[251]

[c] Accumulation Trusts

To distribute or not to distribute? That is the question. If an exempt trust gives the trustee discretion to accumulate or distribute income and the trust holds income-producing property, the decision must be made each year to accumulate or distribute. The attraction of accumulating income in an exempt trust will be reduced by the high income tax rates on trusts, unless the beneficiaries are in the highest income tax bracket without regard to trust distributions.

However, one should be careful of making distributions from trusts that are not going to be subject to estate or generation-skipping transfer tax. Distributions may ease the income tax pain in the short term, but the long-term advantages of sheltering income from estate tax and GSTT are lost.

> **EXAMPLE:** Exempt Trust *A* provides for discretionary distributions to Child for life, remainder to Grandchild. Trust has taxable income of $100,000. If the income is accumulated, income tax is about $39,000. If Child dies one year later, there is no estate tax or GSTT. Grandchild receives about $61,000.

> **EXAMPLE:** Same facts as above, but income is distributed to Child, who is single and has no other taxable income. Income tax is approximately $26,000. When Child dies one year later, leaving her estate to Grandchild, the estate tax on the remaining $74,000 of income equals $37,000. Total income and estate tax equals $63,000. Grandchild receives $27,000.

Moral. In the above example, the family could have saved about $24,000[252] in taxes if the trustee had not made the distribution. Before making distributions from a trust that is exempt from gift, estate, or generation-skipping transfer tax, the trustee should seriously consider the transfer tax effect as well as the income tax effect.

---

[250] IRC § 1361(d)(3)(B).

[251] IRC §§ 1361(d)(1), 1361(c)(2)(A)(i), 1366. Taxation of income from an S corporation is discussed in Chapter 18.

[252] Total income and estate tax of $63,000 when income was distributed less income tax of $39,000 if it had not been distributed.

[d] Investments

To avoid high trust income tax rates, which can partially offset the transfer tax savings available with exempt trusts, a trustee could make investments designed to produce capital growth rather than current income.

[8] Life Insurance

Life insurance, which is planned to achieve generation-skipping objectives, will usually be held in an irrevocable life insurance trust (ILIT). ILITs are discussed in detail in Chapter 12. Contributions of premiums to the ILIT, or payments of premiums on its behalf, will generally constitute gifts.

[a] Term Insurance

Term insurance is "pure" insurance—it provides only a death benefit and has no investment feature. Its value at any point is the unearned premium for the policy year. Hence, its value decreases over the policy year as the premium is earned.

Term life insurance has potential for use of hindsight in allocating the exemption. The donor makes the gift of the premium amount to an ILIT in Year One. If the donor subsequently dies in Year One, or before the gift tax return is due in Year Two, the executor can file a timely allocation of exemption in Year Two, and use the premium payment value (rather than the policy proceeds) as the exempt amount. If the donor is alive on the due date of the gift tax return in Year Two, the donor can file a late allocation for the Year-One gift before the next year's premium is paid, reporting the premium at its lowest value for the year. The best use of this technique involves filing a late allocation the day before the premium is due in Year Two, when the premium for Year One has been almost totally earned.

EXAMPLE: Trust created by Mom in 2002 holds a term policy insuring Mom's life in the face amount of $1,000,000. Annual premiums on the policy are $100,000 and are due April 17 each year. On April 17, 2003, Mom contributes $100,000 to Trust, which the trustee uses to pay the premium. If Mom dies before her 2003 gift tax return is due, her executor should be able to allocate $100,000 of Mom's exemption on a timely filed gift tax return for 2003, and thereby exempt the entire $1,000,000 policy proceeds from GSTT. If Mom is living when her 2003 gift tax return is due on April 15, 2004, she can file a late allocation on April 16, 2004 when the value of the policy is only, say, $1,000 (due to all but one day's premium having been earned).

[b] Other Life Insurance

Whole life, universal life, variable life, etc. are types of life insurance policies that have an investment feature; as a result, they may increase in value over the policy year. Hence, the second part of the term insurance technique (making a late allocation at the end of the year) may not work as well, because the value of the policy may have gone up rather than down by the end of the year.

[9] Charitable Lead Annuity Trusts

Special rules exist for allocating GSTT exemption to charitable lead annuity trusts.[253]

[10] Nonresident Aliens

Special rules also apply for nonresident aliens who are planning for the GSTT.[254]

¶ 5.06 TRANSFERS IN EXCESS OF THE EXEMPTION AMOUNT

A nonexempt generation-skipping trust will be exposed to either gift and estate tax or GSTT, depending on the terms of the trust. The chart included at ¶ 5.11[6], Exhibit 5-F: Comparative Tax Analysis of Various Transfer Methods, shows a comparison of the different aspects of the various kinds of transfers. Often (but not always), a taxable termination or taxable distribution will result in as much or more tax than an estate transfer would. The following subparagraphs address different drafting options.

---

[253] See Chapter 35 on charitable lead annuity trusts for a discussion.
[254] See Chapter 52 on international issues for a discussion.

[1] Formula General Power of Appointment

A formula general power gives the beneficiary a general power of appointment[255] over part of the trust—perhaps, the part in excess of the transferor's unused GSTT exemption at his death.

[a] Advantages

If amounts in excess of the exemption are subject to a testamentary general power of appointment, the assets will be included in the estate tax system. This consequence will often be better than or as good as inclusion in the GSTT system from a transfer tax standpoint.

[b] Potential Pitfalls

[i] **Unnecessary estate tax.** One serious disadvantage of this approach is that, under certain circumstances, the trust could unnecessarily attract a transfer tax. This could happen, for example, if the GSTT is re-enacted after its repeal, but existing trusts are grandfathered from the re-enactment. Another case would be a trust that passes to a beneficiary in the same generation as, or a higher generation than, the powerholder, in an estate-taxed transfer that would not have been subject to GSTT.[256]

Some difficulties might be cured with more fine-tuned drafting of the governing instrument. For example, the instrument could provide that the trust is subject to a testamentary general power only to the extent that the GSTT would otherwise be applicable or, perhaps, only to the extent that the GSTT would result in a higher tax than the estate tax. Although this special drafting might result in the most exact approach to dealing with minimizing the tax on nonexempt trusts, it could also result in some practical difficulties.

Often, the actual amount of the estate tax (1) will depend on elections made by the executor and beneficiaries, (2) will depend on what administrative expenses are incurred, and (3) may depend on whether any beneficiaries disclaim. Thus, it may not be possible to ascertain to what extent the beneficiary had a general power until months or years after the beneficiary has died. Elections such as deferral of estate tax[257] and special use valuation[258] can be ren-

---

[255] A general power of appointment is one which gives the holder the ability by will, or during life, or both, to appoint the assets of the trust to the holder, his estate, his creditors, or the creditors of his estate, subject to certain exceptions. IRC § 2041. See Chapter 3 for a detailed discussion.

[256] IRC § 2612(a).

[257] IRC § 6166.

[258] IRC § 2032A.

dered unavailable (or available) if trust assets are included in the estate. The IRS has recognized certain general powers that were measured by a formula relating to the amount that overall estate and GST taxes were lowered as a result of the power's existence.[259]

[ii] Diversion of assets. Another disadvantage is that an exercise of the general power of appointment may result in the assets being diverted to someone outside of the family. However, if the transferor is willing to give the beneficiary a broad limited power of appointment over the trust (a common provision in dynastic trusts), the diversion could occur anyway. In such circumstances, no additional problem from that standpoint exists with a general power, except to the extent that creditors of the beneficiary are able to reach the property subject to a general power and would not have been able to reach property subject to a broad limited power.[260]

One option sometimes used to minimize the diversion difficulty when creditor problems are not expected is a general power of appointment giving the beneficiary a power to appoint only to the creditors of his estate.

[iii] Creditor exposure. A third disadvantage is that the existence of the general power of appointment may render the trust assets subject to the beneficiary's creditors. This will always be true of a general power that can be exercised during the beneficiary's life, at least if the beneficiary is bankrupt.[261] In the case of a general power that can be exercised only by will, the trust will ordinarily not be subject to creditors by reason of the power unless a state statute makes it so or the power of appointment is exercised.[262] The exercise, of course, cannot happen until the beneficiary's death.

---

[259] E.g., Priv. Ltr. Ruls. 9527024, 9110054.

[260] This distinction is further analyzed in Chapter 53 on asset protection.

[261] 11 USCA § 541(a); Restatement (Second) of Property § 13.6 cmt. c.

[262] Restatement (Second) of Property at § 13.4 (if the holder exercises a general power of appointment by will, the assets appointed are subject to claims against the holder's estate); id. at § 13.2 (if the holder does not exercise a testamentary general power of appointment that was created by another person, the assets subject to the power will be subject to payment of claims of the holder's creditors or claims against the holder's estate only to the extent provided by statute); 5 American Law of Property § 23.16 (A. James Casner ed. 1952 & Supp. 1977) (property subject to a general power of appointment is subject to the holder's creditors only if the holder exercises the power, if a statute enables creditors to reach the property, or if the power is exercisable during the holder's lifetime and the holder is bankrupt).

[2] Special Trustee Who Can Grant a General Power

Some estate planners provide that a trustee or special trustee can grant and remove a general power of appointment over the nonexempt portion of the trust.

[a] Advantages

This technique allows more flexibility than the formula of general power. Additionally, the beneficiary begins with a limited power, so if the GSTT goes away, the trust will not be subject to tax in his estate, as a trust subject to a general power would be.

[b] Potential Pitfalls

[i] **Fiduciary issues.** Will the discretion to grant and remove a general power of appointment render the fiduciary liable if it turns out in hindsight that he made a choice that resulted in more tax? Or, if his choice resulted in different beneficiaries getting the property? In such cases, exculpatory language may be appropriate.

[ii] **Monitoring.** If the best choice is to grant the beneficiary a general power, someone will have to think about and implement this decision before the beneficiary's death. The situation will need to be monitored.

If this method is selected, the decision to grant or withhold a general power should be considered carefully because the inclusion or noninclusion of trust assets in an estate may affect other estate planning (e.g., the availability of a Section 6166 or Section 2032A election),[263] as well as the beneficiary's asset protection planning.

[3] Planning for a Child With No Descendants

In structuring a disposition to a child with no descendants, an automatic reaction will often be that it is not worthwhile to leave the child's share in trust. This is a decision to be made carefully. Apart from the considerable nontax advantages of trusts, an exempt trust may enable the child to pass more property tax-free to her beneficiaries than if the property were included in her estate. Even if the trust is in excess of the exempt amount, she would be able to

---

[263] These provisions, giving special treatment to certain business interests, require certain percentages of the estate to consist of such interests. They are discussed in Chapters 46 and 48.

pass assets to beneficiaries in her generation or above with no estate tax, which an estate transfer could not accomplish in many situations.

> **EXAMPLE:** Mom leaves $1,000,000 to Daughter. Daughter dies and leaves the $1,000,000 to her Sister. At the 50 percent rate, Daughter's bequest to Sister will generate $500,000 estate tax. If Mom had instead left the $1,000,000 in a trust giving Daughter a limited power of appointment, Daughter could have appointed the entire $1,000,000 to Sister without generating any estate tax.

[4] Avoidance of GSTT on "Use" Assets

A trust that contains tangible assets that are enjoyed by personal use may not be subject to GSTT until the trust's termination, if no beneficiary has a right to distribution of the assets.

For example, suppose Trust for the benefit of all descendants of the settlor's parents and the spouses of those descendants contains residences, recreational property, art, jewelry, automobiles, antique furniture, silver, crystal, and china. The trust does not allow distribution to any beneficiary until the termination of the trust. Rather, it allows each beneficiary to use the assets for a portion of time each year. The trustee coordinates the use of the property, and pays expenses that are not allocable to any specific beneficiary's use (e.g., real property taxes). Each beneficiary pays expenses occasioned particularly by his use (e.g., daily maid service provided especially for his visit to the trust residences). Such a trust may not be subject to GSTT until it terminates. Since no distribution at all is made, it is hard to say that any taxable distribution is made during the trust term. What about taxable terminations? A taxable termination involves the termination of a beneficiary's "interest" in a trust.[264] An "interest" is a current right to receive distributions.[265] Since no beneficiary has a current right to receive distributions until the trust's termination, no beneficiary should have an interest that can be the subject of a termination until the trust ends.

---

[264] IRC § 2612(a).

[265] IRC § 2652(c)(1).

¶ 5.07 DYNASTIC TRUST

The dynastic trust is very popular in planning for large estates. A "dynastic trust" is a trust that is designed to last for the longest period allowable under the rule against perpetuities.[266] How long is that?

[1] Traditional Rules Against Perpetuities

[a] Common Law Rule

The common law rule, coming down from centuries ago in England, provides that a trust is void from the outset unless the beneficiaries' interests must vest,[267] if at all, no later than 21 years after the death of identified persons, all of whom must be alive at the date of transfer to the trust. For example, under the common law rule, a trust can be drafted to last 21 years after the death of all of the donor's descendants who are living at the date of the creation of the trust.

The specified people whose lives will determine the maximum period of the trust are the "measuring lives." The measuring lives do not have to be related in any way to the beneficiaries of the trust—however, they do have to be ascertainable with relative ease.[268] Therefore, one cannot, for example, use all persons living in New York City on the date of creation of the trust as measuring lives.

For people who are serious about generation-skipping, and don't mind getting fancy, the British royal family can be used, since its genealogical records are painstakingly kept and publicly available. The usual royal measuring lives are the descendants of George V (Queen Elizabeth's grandfather) who are alive on creation of the trust. (Although Queen Victoria had many more descendants, some of her descendants were lost in the Russian revolution and, therefore, their continued existence or dates of death cannot be ascertained.) Some people who prefer an American slant use the descendants of Joseph and Rose Kennedy, since the Kennedys are such a large family. At the moment, it is probably reasonably easy to trace the Kennedys—100 years from now, who knows?

---

[266] The "rule against perpetuities" is a law prohibiting trusts from lasting forever. The rule does not *require* the trust to last for its maximum legal duration; it *permits* the trust to last for that period.

[267] "Vest" means that the beneficiaries have an immediate fixed right to enjoy the trust property either now or in the future. That is, a vested beneficiary's interests are not subject to any contingencies.

[268] See Restatement (Second) Property § 1.3.

Up-to-date genealogical records are not always easy to obtain, even for the royal family. It may cost money to determine which members of the measuring group are still living or when they died. For people who don't want to deal with tracing outside families, a satisfactory set of measuring lives can often be found somewhere within the donor's family (although the tracing problems may actually be more difficult if the family members lose track of each other).

[b] Uniform Statutory Rule Against Perpetuities

The Uniform Statutory Rule Against Perpetuities (USRAP), which has been adopted in many states, provides that compliance with the common law rule is sufficient.[269] In addition, a trust will be valid if all interests in the trust actually vest within 90 years.[270] In some states, the trust is valid if all interests vest on the later of the common law period and the 90-year period. In other states, certain "later of" clauses are statutorily converted to the common law period.[271]

[2] Adaptations of the Rule

Some states have adopted relaxed rules against perpetuities.[272] It has become fashionable to consider establishing trusts that will be exempt from GSTT in those jurisdictions. Some factors to look at before leaping include the following.

[a] Nexus

Establishment of a substantial connection between the trust and the desired jurisdiction may be necessary. The creator of a trust can generally designate that the laws of any state will govern the trust, even though that state has no other connection with the trust, with respect to matters of administration (for example, trustee compensation and trust investments).[273] As to matters of public policy (such as the validity of clauses limiting the trustee's liability, the validity of spendthrift clauses, and, in some cases, authorization of self-dealing

---

[269] USRAP § 1(a)(1), 8B ULA 333 (1990).

[270] USRAP § 1(a)(2), 8B ULA 333.

[271] USRAP § 1(e), 8B ULA 333.

[272] Including, e.g., Alaska, Delaware, Florida, Idaho, Illinois, Maine, Maryland, New Jersey, Ohio, Rhode Island, South Dakota, Virginia and Wisconsin.

[273] 2A Austin W. Scott & William F. Fratcher, The Law of Trusts §§ 606, 611 (4th ed. 1987); Restatement (Second) of Conflict of Laws §§ 268, 277.

by the trustee), the creator's designation that a particular state's laws will govern is effective only if the state has some substantial connection with the administration of the trust.[274] The rule against perpetuities goes to the validity of the trust, and thus might be considered a matter of public policy. A "substantial connection" may involve a connection between the creator and the designated state, a trustee in the designated state, substantial assets located in the designated state, or beneficiaries in the designated state.

Factors constituting a substantial connection to "State X" may include, among others, a trustee who is a resident of State X, the physical presence of trust assets in State X, and administrative activity in State X.

Some state statutes provide their own nexus rules, which may require minimal or no connection. However, these rules cannot necessarily be relied on if a challenge is brought in another state or in federal court.

> **EXAMPLE:** State X, which has no rule against perpetuities, provides that it will consider a trust a resident of State X if the trust instrument so provides. There is no other connection of State X to the trust. If the validity of the trust is litigated in State Y, State Y may not recognize the trust as valid if State Y would require adherence to a rule against perpetuities.

[b] Local Taxes

Establishment of a connection to a particular state can result in exposure of the trust to that state's income and other taxes.

[c] Restraints on Alienation

Some states have prohibitions against restraints on alienation that may have a practical effect similar to the rule against perpetuities. For example, state law may provide that a trust is void if it suspends the power of alienation of property beyond a certain time; however, the power of alienation with respect to property held in trust may not be considered suspended if the trustee has the power to sell the property.

[d] Special State Provisions

Local state laws (including tax laws) may apply to real property or businesses sitused in the trust jurisdiction.

---

[274] 2A Austin W. Scott & William F. Fratcher, The Law of Trusts §§ 606, 611, 622 (4th ed. 1987).

[e] Expense and Trouble

Some donors may not consider it worthwhile to go to the extra expense and trouble of establishing a trust in another state for the sake of benefiting or controlling people who would otherwise take the trust assets 100 or more years from now. Such a donor can probably allow the trust to last for 100 years or so even using a common law rule.

[f] Private Trust Companies

The particular state may permit formation of a private trust company. Thus, an interested client may form his own trust company to act as the resident trustee of a perpetual or very long-term trust in the state involved. Capital requirements, application fees, and other provisions may apply.[275]

[3] Uncertainties of the Future

It is difficult (arguably impossible) to draft a trust with much specificity for an environment 100 years or more in the future. It boggles the mind to consider an attorney drafting a trust in 1902 (before the advent of cars, planes, television, radio, plastic, computers, income tax, estate tax, GSTT, etc.) and trying to specifically address situations that would exist in the world in 2002. A trust that may last until the year 2100 or beyond should incorporate great flexibility, in light of the unpredictability of the tax system, social conditions, etc. in the distant future.

Flexibility will often involve provisions like the following:[276]

- Income and principal distributions are discretionary.
- A beneficiary-trustee can be appointed, with ability to make distributions to herself for health, education, maintenance, and support (HEMS), and other distributions fitting the exceptions to the definition of a "general power of appointment." A settlor-trustee can be appointed with power to make distributions for a beneficiary's HEMS.
- A special trustee, who is not a beneficiary, a settlor, or a person acting in a reciprocal relationship[277] with a trust established for or by a benefi-

---

[275] For an illustrative discussion, see Duncan, "Forming a Private Trust Company, Elements and Process," Trusts & Est. 36–45 (Aug. 1997).

[276] Some of these powers may have income tax consequences to the settlor or beneficiary, depending on the trust's structure. Each situation must be considered individually.

[277] Why is the reciprocal arrangement important? Suppose, for example, A establishes trust and names B the special trustee. B establishes a trust and names A as special trustee. A and B could each be deemed to be special trustee of the trust he established. Bischoff v. Comm'r, 69 TC 32 (1977); Exchange Bank & Trust Co. of Fla., 694 F2d 1261 (Fed.

ciary or settlor, can be appointed to make distributions unrestricted by the HEMS standard and to terminate the trust, if this flexibility is desired.

- The beneficiary may have inter vivos and/or testamentary limited powers of appointment.

[4] Powers of Appointment

Taxable transfers from a non-grandfathered dynastic trust will be subject to GSTT, unless GSTT exemption is allocated to the trust and the trust is wholly exempt. If a donor establishes an exempt trust in a state without a rule against perpetuities, he should be aware that gift tax, estate tax, or GSTT can still be imposed if a beneficiary exercises a power of appointment that may, under local law, postpone vesting for a period determined without reference to the date of creation of the trust.[278]

> **EXAMPLE:** Mom creates Trust *X*, which is governed by Idaho law, holds no real property, and is not subject to the rule against perpetuities. Child, a beneficiary of Trust *X*, exercises a power of appointment by appointing assets to New Trust for the benefit of Grandchild. If the provisions of New Trust give Grandchild a power to postpone vesting or suspend the absolute ownership or power of alienation of property for a period without reference to the creation of the original trust (which will be the case if New Trust is subject to no rule against perpetuities), Child would be considered to have made a taxable gift or estate transfer, as the case may be.[279]

Trusts can be drafted to prohibit an exercise that can be considered an estate or gift tax transfer. Some, however, think it adds flexibility to not prohibit such an exercise because, if such an exercise is allowed, the beneficiary can choose to (1) exercise the power in that fashion and thereby put the trust into the estate or gift tax system or (2) not exercise the power and leave the trust in the GSTT system.

> **EXAMPLE:** *A* established valid Trust *X* for the benefit of *B*. Trust *X* gives *B* a power of appointment that can be validly exercised under local law to create other powers of appointment that suspend vesting for a period as-

---

Cir. 1982) . Contra Estate of Green v. United States, 68 F3d 151 (6th Cir. 1995). The IRS has taken the position that such trusts can be uncrossed even if neither *A* nor *B* is the settlor. Priv. Ltr. Rul. 9235025 (May 29, 1992). See discussion of reciprocal trusts in Chapter 2.

[278] IRC §§ 2041(a)(3), 2514(d).

[279] IRC §§ 2041(a)(3), 2514(d).

certainable without reference to the date of creation of Trust *X*. *B* validly exercises his power of appointment by creating a trust that gives *C* the power to appoint the property to trusts that can last in perpetuity. *B*'s exercise of the power of appointment is treated as an exercise of a general power of appointment, because he exercised the power in a manner that could postpone vesting for a period that can be ascertained without regard to the creation of Trust *X* (in this case, forever). The GSTT regulations consider transfers to a trust by the exercise of a general power of appointment to be contributions to the trust.[280] If *B* did not exercise his power in such a manner, his exercise would be considered the exercise of a limited power of appointment.[281]

The rules of Sections 2041(a)(3) and 2514(d) can have undesirable results in states with no rule against perpetuities. Suppose the first powerholder, *A*, exercises his power over a perpetual trust in a fashion that allows *B* to exercise a further power. Unless *A* limits *B*'s power to a period determined with reference to the date of creation of the original trust, *A*'s exercise will be a general power. For example, if *B* can create another power that allows the trust to continue in perpetuity, *A*'s exercise will necessarily be considered a general power, whether *B* ever creates such a power or not. To avoid this problem, states are adopting statutes that only permit powers of appointment to be exercised in favor of trusts which last for a period of time dating from the date of the creation of the first power (e.g., 1,000 years). The same result could be achieved in a no-rule jurisdiction by drafting such a limitation in the trust instrument.

Practice Pointer: Even if a trust is established in a no-rule state, certain exercises of a power of appointment can subject an otherwise exempt trust to estate or gift tax.

¶ 5.08 GRANDFATHERED TRUSTS

The GSTT does not apply to any generation-skipping transfer under a trust that was irrevocable on September 25, 1985 (i.e., a "grandfathered trust"), as long as nothing was actually or constructively added to the trust after that date.[282] The GSTT also does not apply to certain transfers occurring as the result of

---

[280] Treas. Reg. § 26.2601-1(b)(1)(i).
[281] IRC §§ 2041(a)(3), 2514(d).
[282] Treas. Reg. § 26.2601-1(b)(1)(i).

the death of a decedent who was incompetent on October 22, 1986 and at all times thereafter.[283]

[1] Perpetuities Period

The perpetuities period is the period of any life in being at the creation of the trust plus 21 years (plus, if applicable, a reasonable period of gestation). An exercise that postpones or suspends vesting, absolute ownership or power of alienation for 90 years or less from the date of creation of the trust is deemed to be within the above rule. If a power is exercised by creating another power, it is deemed exercised to whatever extent the second power could be exercised.[284]

In this regard, the two-prong vesting rule in the USRAP (referring to the later of the common-law period or the 90-year period) is not respected by the GSTT regulation. The exercise of a limited power that may extend the trust for the longer of the two periods can destroy grandfathering and result in a taxable transfer. Hence, exercise of limited powers of appointment over grandfathered trusts in USRAP states should be crafted either to meet the common law rule or to use the 90-year period, and should not use the longer of the two periods.[285]

[2] General Powers of Appointment

The GSTT regulations take the position that the transfer of property pursuant to the exercise, release, or lapse of a general power of appointment created in a pre-September 25, 1985 trust is not a transfer under the trust, but rather is a constructive additional transfer by the powerholder occurring when the exercise, release, or lapse of the power becomes effective.[286] This section of the regulations applies with respect to any exercise, release, or lapse of a general power of appointment that occurs after November 18, 1999 with respect to a grandfathered trust. While two courts have rejected the position adopted by the

---

[283] Treas. Reg. § 26.2601-1(b)(3). The incompetency exemption does not apply to property transferred by gift or by means of death to the incompetent decedent or trust includable in his estate after August 3, 1990. Omnibus Budget Reconciliation Act of 1990, Pub. L. No. 101-508, § 11703(c)(3), 104 Stat. 1383 (1990).

[284] Treas. Reg. § 26.2601-1(b)(1)(v)(B).

[285] For a more complete discussion of this concept, see J. Dukeminier, The Uniform Statutory Rule Against Perpetuities and the GST Tax: New Perils for Practitioners and New Opportunities, 30 Real Prop. Prob. ¶ Tr. J. 185 (Summer 1995).

[286] Treas. Reg. § 26.2601-1(b)(1)(i)(v)(A).

regulations,[287] both cases involved fact situations occurring before the regulations were promulgated. Accordingly, the final regulations were not at issue in either of the two cases, and thus were not declared invalid.

[3] Limited Powers of Appointment

The exercise of a limited power of appointment will not be considered a constructive addition to a grandfathered trust, as long as the power is not exercised in a way that can postpone or suspend vesting, absolute ownership, or power of alienation of any interest beyond the perpetuities period.

Practice Pointer: It will usually be smart to exercise all limited powers of appointment over grandfathered trusts so that they can continue to exist for the maximum period allowed by the rule against perpetuities.[288] Do not, however, exercise those powers in such a way as to enable the trust to last beyond the perpetuities period.

---

[4] Incompetent Person

A grandfathering exception to the GSTT exists if a person was under a disability to change the disposition of his property on October 22, 1986, and never regained his competence. In such a case, the GSTT generally does not apply (1) to a GST under a trust, to the extent that the trust consists of property included in the incapacitated person's gross estate or reinvestments of such property or (2) to a GST that is a direct skip that occurs by reason of the incapacitated person's death.[289] However, the incompetency exemption does not apply (1) to property transferred by gift or by means of the death of another person to the incapacitated person or the exempt trust after August 3, 1990,[290] or (2) to property transferred by the incapacitated person during his life after October 22, 1986.

If a trust is grandfathered because of the transferor's incompetency, it will be important to preserve evidence that the incompetency existed on October 22, 1986 and at all times thereafter. The regulations address evidentiary requirements in situations where there has not been a court adjudication of in-

---

[287] Simpson v. United States, 183 F3d 812 (8th Cir. 1999), Bachler v. United States, 281 F3d 1078 (9th Cir. 2002) .

[288] Unless, of course, this would be in conflict with important nontax objectives.

[289] Pub. L. No. 100-647, § 1014(h)(2).

[290] Omnibus Budget Reconciliation Act of 1990, Pub. L. No. 101-508, § 11703(c)(3), 104 Stat. 1383 (1990).

competency.[291] If the transferor became able to change or revoke his will or revocable trust after October 21, 1986, the exception will not apply.[292]

[5] QTIP Trusts

If a QTIP trust is grandfathered, the trust is treated as if a reverse QTIP election was made. This means that the failure of the executor or estate beneficiaries to exercise their right of recovery of estate tax paid on account of the QTIP trust or a waiver by the spouse of the right of recovery is not a constructive addition.[293] Hence, the estate taxes imposed on the grandfathered QTIP trust on the death of the surviving spouse can be paid out of other assets without jeopardizing the grandfathered status of the trust. However, the failure of the spouse to demand the income required to be paid to her may be considered a constructive addition.[294]

Practice Pointer: It is generally a good idea, in such circumstances, to provide that estate taxes imposed on a grandfathered QTIP will be borne by other assets which are not exempt from GSTT.

---

[6] Permitted Changes in Grandfathered Trusts

Occasionally, it will be desirable to reform a grandfathered trust—to create separate shares for beneficiaries with conflicting interests, to enable the trust to be a qualified S corporation shareholder, to change trustees, etc. Before reforming the trust, the GSTT ramifications should be considered.

Regulations have been issued addressing the types of changes that may be made to a grandfathered trust without affecting its exempt status.[295] The rules contained in the regulations apply only for GSTT purposes, and would not apply in determining, for example, whether a modification would result in a gift for gift tax purposes, would cause inclusion of the trust assets in anyone's

---

[291] Treas. Reg. § 26.2601-1(b)(3)(iii).

[292] Treas. Reg. § 26.2601-1(b)(3).

[293] Treas. Reg. §§ 26.2601-1(b)(1)(iii)(A), 26.2601-1(b)(1)(v)(C).

[294] See Priv. Ltr. Rul. 9052023 (Sept. 28, 1990).

[295] The regulations appear to permit more extensive modifications to grandfathered trusts than were previously permitted under the old standard applied by the IRS. Under the old standard, changes in the quality, value, or timing of any of the powers, beneficial interests, rights, or expectancies originally provided for under the terms of the grandfathered trust would cause the trust to lose its exempt status. Priv. Ltr. Ruls. 200046002 (July 21, 2000), 200046004 (July 21, 2000).

gross estate, or would result in the realization of gain.[296] The regulations apply with respect to changes made to a grandfathered trust on or after December 20, 2000, although the IRS has indicated that it will not challenge the exempt status of a grandfathered trust that was subject to any trustee action, judicial construction, settlement agreement, modification, or other action prior to December 20, 2000, provided that action satisfies the requirements of the regulations.[297]

Under the regulations, the following actions will not destroy grandfathering.

[a] Construction Proceedings

A court order in a construction proceeding that resolves an ambiguity in a trust instrument or corrects a scrivener's error will not cause the trust to lose its grandfathered status, provided that the judicial action involves a bona fide issue and the court's decision in the matter is consistent with applicable state law, as it would be applied by the highest court of the state.[298]

[b] Settlements

A court-approved settlement of a bona fide controversy relating to the trust administration or construction of the trust instrument will not endanger a trust's exempt status, provided that the settlement is the product of arm's-length negotiations, and the settlement is within the range of reasonable outcomes under the trust instrument and applicable state law addressing the issues resolved by the settlement.[299]

[c] Trust Extensions

A trustee's distribution of trust principal to a new trust, or the retention of trust principal in a continuing trust, will not cause the new or continuing trust to be subject to the provisions of Chapter 13 of the Internal Revenue Code, provided:

- The original trust instrument or state law applicable at the time the original trust became irrevocable authorizes the trustee to make distributions to a new trust or retain trust principal in a continuing trust without the consent or approval of any beneficiary or a court.

---

[296] Treas. Reg. § 26.2601-1(b)(4)(i).

[297] Treas. Reg. § 26.2601-1(b)(4)(ii).

[298] Treas. Reg. § 26.2601-1(b)(4)(i)(C).

[299] Treas. Reg. § 26.2601-1(b)(4)(i)(B).

- The terms of the new or continuing trust instrument cannot postpone or suspend the vesting, absolute ownership or power of alienation of an interest in property being postponed or suspended beyond the perpetuities period.[300]

[d] Modifications

A modification to a trust instrument (including a distribution to a new trust or retention of trust principal in a continuing trust, settlement, or construction proceeding not otherwise excepted under other provisions of the regulations) will not cause a grandfathered trust to lose its grandfathered status, provided that the modification does not (1) shift a beneficial interest in the trust to any beneficiary who occupies a lower generation than the person or persons who held the beneficial interest before the modification, or (2) extend the time for vesting of any beneficial interest beyond the period provided in the original trust instrument. A permitted modification may be made either by judicial reformation or by a nonjudicial reformation that is valid under state law.[301]

A shift in beneficial interest to a lower generation will occur if the modification could cause an increase in the amount of a generation-skipping transfer or the creation of a new generation-skipping transfer, with the determination being made by considering the effect of the instrument before and after the modification. A shift in beneficial interest to a lower generation will be presumed if the effect of the modification cannot be immediately determined. A modification that is administrative in nature and has the indirect effect of increasing the amount transferred to a lower generation (e.g., a modification resulting in lowered administrative costs or income taxes) will not be considered to shift a beneficial interest in the trust to a lower generation.[302]

The IRS has issued proposed regulations that would, among other things, permit accounting income to include capital gains in certain cases.[303] These regulations would be effective for taxable years beginning on or after date of publication of final regulations. The proposed regulations would permit the trustees of grandfathered GSTT trusts to convert income interests to unitrust interests or to make equitable adjustments between income and principal without affecting the trusts' grandfathered status.[304]

---

[300] Defined at ¶ 5.08[1] above.

[301] Treas. Reg. § 26.2601-1(b)(4)(i)(D)(*1*).

[302] Treas. Reg. § 26.2601-1(b)(4)(i)(D)(*2*).

[303] Prop. Reg. §§ 1.643(a)-3, 1.643(b)-1.

[304] Prop. Reg. §§ 26.2601-1(b)(4)(i)(D), 26.2601-1(b)(4)(i)(E), 26.2601-1(b)(4)(ii).

There is still some uncertainty regarding particular modifications. For example, the IRS will not rule on the consequences of changing a trust's situs from the United States to a foreign location.[305]

Practice Pointer: Certain hidden dangers may exist with seemingly innocuous modifications. For example, a change in a trust's situs may cause a loss of grandfathered status if the new state's rule against perpetuities would lengthen the permitted duration of the trust.

¶ 5.09 COMPARISON OF METHODS OF TAXABLE TRANSFER OF PROPERTY

Because of the tax-exclusive nature of the GSTT, direct skips are subject to less tax than taxable terminations or taxable distributions. Similarly, gifts are subject to less transfer tax than estate transfers. Various combinations of transfers are less expensive than others.

[1] Apples-to-Apples Comparison of Rates

The following scenarios illustrate the total transfer tax cost of transferring $200,000 to a grandchild by various methods. All of the examples assume (1) a 50 percent estate and gift tax rate applies to all transfers subject to such taxes; (2) no exemptions or exclusions are available; (3) no expenses or other deductions are allowable; and (4) there is no change in the value of assets from one date to another. The value of deferral of tax payment is not calculated.

All tax rates are computed on a tax-inclusive basis for comparability.

[a] Gift to Child Followed by Gift to Grandchild

Grandparent gives $300,000 to child. Grandparent pays gift tax of $150,000. Child gives $200,000 to grandchild and pays gift tax of $100,000. Total transfer tax is $250,000. Thus, it costs $250,000 to transfer $200,000 to grandchild. Total transfer tax rate is 56 percent ($250,000/$450,000). The approximate total transfer tax on any amount to be transferred to a grandchild in this manner is determined by multiplying the amount that the grandchild will

---

[305] Rev. Proc. 2002-3, 2002-1 IRB 117 (Jan. 7, 2002).

receive by 1.25. In this scenario, $200,000 gift to grandchild times 1.25 equals $250,000 tax liability.

[b] Gift to Child Followed by Bequest to Grandchild

Grandparent gives $400,000 to child. Grandparent pays gift tax of $200,000. Child dies and leaves grandchild $400,000. Estate tax is $200,000, and grandchild receives $200,000. Total transfer tax is $400,000. It costs $400,000 to transfer $200,000 to grandchild. Total transfer tax rate is 67 percent ($400,000/$600,000). The approximate total transfer tax on any amount to be transferred to a grandchild in this manner is determined by multiplying the amount that the grandchild will receive by 2. In this scenario, $200,000 gift to grandchild times 2 equals $400,000 total transfer tax.

[c] Bequest to Child Followed by Gift to Grandchild

Grandparent dies and leaves child $600,000. Estate tax is $300,000. Child gives $200,000 to grandchild and pays gift tax of $100,000. Total transfer tax is $400,000. It costs $400,000 to transfer $200,000 to grandchild. Total transfer tax rate is 67 percent ($400,000/$600,000). The approximate total transfer tax on any amount to be transferred to a grandchild in this manner is determined by multiplying the amount that the grandchild will receive by 2. In this scenario, $200,000 gift to grandchild times 2 equals $400,000 total transfer tax.

[d] Bequest to Child Followed by Bequest to Grandchild

Grandparent leaves child $800,000 under his will. Estate tax is $400,000. Child dies and leaves grandchild $400,000 under his will. Estate tax is $200,000, and grandchild receives $200,000. It costs $600,000 to transfer $200,000 to grandchild. Total transfer tax rate is 75 percent ($600,000/ $800,000). The approximate total transfer tax on any amount to be transferred to a grandchild in this manner is determined by multiplying the amount that the grandchild will receive by 3. In this scenario, $200,000 gift to grandchild times 3 equals $600,000 total transfer tax. Note, however, that, if child dies within ten years of grandparent, a previously taxed property credit is available under Section 2013 for estate tax paid on grandparent's death. Such a credit will not be available in any other double transfers.

[e] Gift to Trust Followed by Taxable Termination or Taxable Distribution

Grandparent gives $400,000 to a trust providing income to child for life, remainder to grandchild. Grandparent pays gift tax of $200,000. Child dies. Taxable amount is $400,000. GSTT is $200,000. Total transfer tax is $400,000. It costs $400,000 to transfer $200,000 to grandchild. Tax rate is 67 percent ($400,000/$600,000). The approximate total transfer tax on any amount to be transferred to a grandchild in this manner is determined by multiplying the amount that the grandchild will receive by 2. In this scenario, $200,000 gift to grandchild times 2 equals $400,000 total transfer tax.

[f] Bequest to Trust Followed by Taxable Termination or Taxable Distribution

Grandparent dies and leaves $800,000 to a trust providing income to child for life, remainder to grandchild. Estate tax on this amount is $400,000. On child's death, the taxable amount is $400,000, and GSTT is $200,000. It costs $600,000 to transfer $200,000 to grandchild. Total transfer tax rate is 75 percent ($600,000/$800,000). The approximate total transfer tax on any amount to be transferred to a grandchild in this manner is determined by multiplying the amount that the grandchild will receive by 3. In this scenario, $200,000 gift to grandchild times 3 equals $600,000 total transfer tax.

[g] Direct Skip by Gift

Grandparent gives $200,000 to grandchild. GSTT is $100,000. Because GSTT is added to the gift,[306] total gift is $300,000. Gift tax is $150,000. Total transfer tax is $250,000. It costs $250,000 to transfer $200,000 to grandchild. Total transfer tax rate is 56 percent ($200,000/$450,000). The approximate total transfer tax on any amount to be transferred to a grandchild in this manner is determined by multiplying the amount that the grandchild will receive by 1.25. In this scenario, $200,000 gift to grandchild times 1.25 equals $250,000 total transfer tax.

[h] Direct Skip Subject to Estate Tax

Grandparent dies and leaves grandchild $600,000 under his will. Estate tax is $300,000. GSTT is $100,000 (50 percent of amount received by grandchild, or 33⅓ percent of total amount). Net amount received by grandchild is $200,000. Total transfer tax is $400,000. It costs $400,000 to

---

[306] IRC § 2515.

transfer $200,000 to grandchild. Tax rate is 67 percent ($400,000/$600,000). The approximate total transfer tax on any amount to be transferred to a grandchild in this manner is determined by multiplying the amount that the grandchild will receive by 2. In this scenario, $200,000 gift to grandchild times 2 equals $400,000 total transfer tax.

[2] Other Tax Aspects

Exhibit 5-F, at ¶ 5.11[6], contains a chart that compares the tax treatment of the various transfer methods.

¶ 5.10 ADDITIONAL READING

For more in-depth coverage of GSTT, an excellent source is Harrington, Plaine & Zaritsky, Generation-Skipping Transfer Tax (Warren, Gorham & Lamont 2d ed. 2001).

¶ 5.11 EXHIBITS

[1] Exhibit 5-A: Using the GSTT Exemption

EXHIBIT 5A

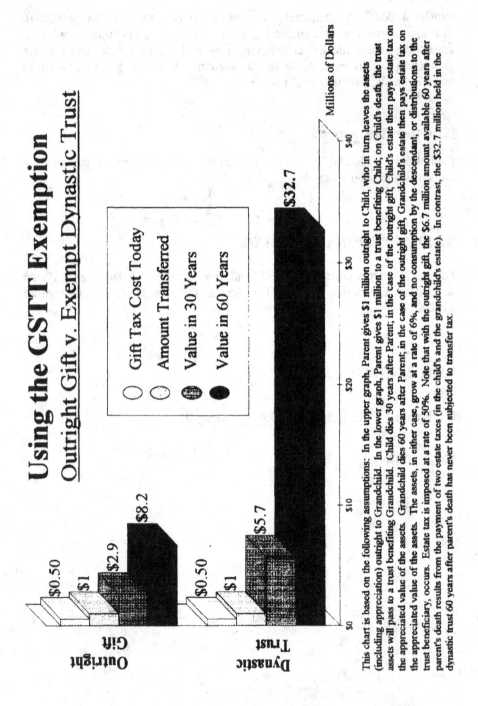

Using the GSTT Exemption
Outright Gift v. Exempt Dynastic Trust

Legend:
- Gift Tax Cost Today
- Amount Transferred
- Value in 30 Years
- Value in 60 Years

Outright Gift: $0.50, $1, $2.9, $8.2

Dynastic Trust: $0.50, $1, $5.7, $32.7

Millions of Dollars — $0, $10, $20, $30, $40

This chart is based on the following assumptions: In the upper graph, Parent gives $1 million outright to Child, who in turn leaves the assets (including appreciation) outright to Grandchild. In the lower graph, Parent gives $1 million to a trust benefiting Child; on Child's death, the trust assets will pass to a trust benefiting Grandchild. Child dies 30 years after Parent; in the case of the outright gift, Child's estate then pays estate tax on the appreciated value of the assets. Grandchild dies 60 years after Parent; in the case of the outright gift, Grandchild's estate then pays estate tax on the appreciated value of the assets. The assets, in either case, grow at a rate of 6%, and no consumption by the descendant, or distributions to the trust beneficiary, occurs. Estate tax is imposed at a rate of 50%. Note that with the outright gift, the $6.7 million amount available 60 years after parent's death results from the payment of two estate taxes (in the child's and the grandchild's estate). In contrast, the $32.7 million held in the dynastic trust 60 years after parent's death has never been subjected to transfer tax.

[2] Exhibit 5-B: Sample Exemption Allocation Language

The intent of this allocation is to allocate the decedent's entire GSTT exemption pro rata among skip persons 1 through 3 (as listed on Schedule R, Part 2), based on the net value for federal estate tax purposes that each such person actually receives, after taking into account taxes, expenses, debts and other charges. Hence, should the value of any direct skip as finally determined for federal estate tax purposes differ from the value of such direct skip as computed pursuant to this Notice of Allocation, whether due to adjustments by the Internal Revenue Service, ruling by a court of competent jurisdiction or for any other reason, then the executor hereby directs that the GSTT exemption for skip persons 1 through 3 (as listed on Schedule R, Part 2) be recomputed so that the GSTT exemption is allocated pro rata among all such skip persons on the basis stated in the preceding sentence.

The amount of the exemption from generation-skipping transfer tax allocated to the direct skips received by skip persons listed on Schedule R, Part 2 based on values as computed on the basis of values as returned is as follows:

Skip Person No. 1 $..........................
Skip Person No. 2 $..........................
Skip Person No. 3 $..........................

[3] Exhibit 5-C: Trust Division Language

Prior to the funding of any trust to be created under this Agreement to which property that is exempt or excluded from generation-skipping transfer tax and property that is not exempt or excluded from such tax is to be allocated, settlor hereby directs the trustee of such trust to divide (on a fractional share basis) the property that would otherwise pass to such trust and to establish separate trusts with identical terms to hold such property, so that property which is exempt or excluded from generation-skipping transfer tax shall be held in a separate trust from property which is not exempt or excluded from such tax. Trustee also has discretion to divide (on a fractional share basis) any trust created under this Agreement after it has been funded, and to establish separate trusts to hold such property, so that property which is exempt or excluded from generation-skipping transfer tax is held in a separate trust from property which is not exempt or excluded from such tax. Any such division shall be in accordance with the regulations issued pursuant to Chapter 13 of the Internal Revenue Code. With respect to any trust which has been divided into separate trusts as described in the preceding sentence, the trustee of such trusts, in making a discretionary distribution to the beneficiary of such trusts in accordance with the terms of such trusts, may make such distribution either all from one trust, all from the other trust, or part from one trust and part from the other trust, in trustee's sole discretion; provided, however, that settlor hereby recommends, but does not require, that trustee make discretionary distributions in accordance with the terms of such trusts (i) from the trust which is exempt or excluded from generation-skipping transfer tax, to the extent possible, if the beneficiary to whom such distribution is to be made is a skip person (as defined in section 2613 of the Internal Revenue Code); and (ii) from the trust which is not exempt or excluded from generation-skipping transfer tax, to the extent possible, if the beneficiary to whom such distribution is to be made is a non-skip person (as defined in section 2613 of the Internal Revenue Code); and provided, further, that settlor hereby directs that any death tax or administration expense of settlor's estate which trustee is authorized or directed to pay pursuant to this Agreement shall be charged first, entirely, or to the extent possible, to property of such trusts other than any property to which the generation-skipping transfer tax exemption allowed to any person pursuant to section 2631 of the Internal Revenue Code has been allocated.

[4] Exhibit 5-D: Reverse QTIP Election Language

I hereby authorize, but do not require, my executor, in my executor's sole and absolute discretion, to elect to treat any part or all of any amount passing to THE (QTIP) TRUST for which a qualified terminable interest property election is made as if such election had not been made, as allowed for purposes of Chapter 13 of the Internal Revenue Code.

Notwithstanding any provision of this will to the contrary, if:

(i) a valid election is made to qualify all or a part of THE (QTIP) TRUST for the marital deduction under section 2056(b)(7) of the Internal Revenue Code; and

(ii) a valid election is made to treat me as the "transferor" of part (but not all) of THE (QTIP) TRUST for generation-skipping transfer tax purposes pursuant to section 2652(a)(3) of the Internal Revenue Code.

My executor shall divide (on a fractional share basis) the property that would otherwise constitute THE (QTIP) TRUST into separate trusts. One of the separate trusts so created shall be THE (QTIP) EXEMPT TRUST, to hold the property to which all or any part of my generation-skipping transfer tax exemption allowed pursuant to section 2631 of the Internal Revenue Code is allocated, and the other trust so created shall be THE (QTIP) NON-EXEMPT TRUST, to hold the property which is not exempt from such tax. Any estate, gift or other transfer tax attributable to (or that would later be recoverable from) THE (QTIP) EXEMPT TRUST, under section 2207A of the Internal Revenue Code or otherwise, by reason of the death of my (spouse), shall instead be charged, to the extent possible, to THE (QTIP) NONEXEMPT TRUST.

[5] Exhibit 5-E: Partial QTIP Election Language

Attachment to Schedule

Pursuant to section .... of the Last Will and Testament of Decedent, the residue of the Estate of Decedent passes to The (QTIP) Trust, established under section .... of said will. (Surviving Spouse) has a qualifying income interest, as defined in Internal Revenue Code section 2056(b)(7) and the regulations thereunder, in such trust, and thus the trust is able to be qualified as a Qualified Terminable Interest Property trust. This election is being made with respect to a part of the trust, as defined by a fraction or percentage of the entire trust. This fraction or percentage is defined by the following formula, as allowed by regulation section 20.2056(b)-7(b)(2):

$$1 - (x + y)$$

- where x = the greatest amount that can pass free of federal estate tax in Decedent's estate, taking into account all relevant tax credits (including, but not limited to, (i) the unified credit provided by Internal Revenue Code Section 2010, (ii) the credit for state death taxes provided by Internal Revenue Code Section 2011, and (iii) any credit or reduction in adjusted taxable gifts provided by Chapter 14 of the Internal Revenue Code) and all other factors pertinent to the computation of the federal estate tax in Decedent's estate (including, but not limited to, any transfers of property included in the gross estate, to specific beneficiaries other than the surviving spouse, by will or otherwise), but only to the extent that the use of any such credit or the consideration of any such factor does not increase the amount of death taxes otherwise payable to any taxing authority by reason of Decedent's death; and
- where y = the total gross estate, less the sum of expenses of administration, indebtedness and taxes; losses; transfers for public, charitable and religious uses; and all property interests included in the gross estate transferred to specific beneficiaries, including the surviving spouse, by will or otherwise.

For the estate of Decedent, based upon the amounts as reflected in this United States Estate (and Generation-Skipping Transfer) Tax Return, Form 706, the fraction is .... However, if for any reason, the property or amounts in this United States Estate (and Generation-Skipping Transfer) Tax Return, Form 706, should change, then the fraction or percentage of property subject to this election shall change in accordance with the above formula.

[6] Exhibit 5-F: Comparative Tax Analysis of Various Transfer Methods

[Note: The following chart addresses tax analysis only. Of course, nontax aspects of the method of transfer, such as protection from creditors and divorcing spouses, should also be a part of the practioner's overall analysis.]

Tax Treatment	Estate Inclusion	Gift	Direct Skip	Taxable Termination	Taxable Distribution
Graduated Rate	yes	yes	no	no	no
Exemption	$1,000,000[a]	$1,000,000 plus $11,000[b]/year/donor/donee	$1,100,000[c]	$1,100,000[c]	1,100,000[c]
Basis Adjustment	fair market value	gift tax paid on appreciation	generation-skipping transfer tax paid on appreciation	fair market value for nonexempt portion, if at death	generation-skipping transfer tax paid on appreciation
IRC § 303	yes	no	yes, if at death	yes, if at death	yes, if at death
IRC § 6166	yes	no	yes, if at death	no	no
IRC § 2032A	yes	no	yes, if at death	no, but exemption amount based on § 2032A valuation	no, but exemption amount based on § 2032A valuation
IRC § 2032(a)	yes	no	yes, if at death	yes, if at death	no
Tax-Inclusive Rate for 2002	50%	33-⅓%; 46% for gifts which are direct skips	33-⅓%	50%	50%
Transfer Tax Deductions	IRC § 2053	none	none	IRC § 2053 type	expenses of determining tax
IRC § 2057	yes[d]	no	no	no	no

[a] Substitue the applicable exclusion amount for the year in question ($1,000,000 in 2002).
[b] The annual exclusion amount is indexed, beginning in 1999. For 2002, the indexed amount is $11,000. Rev. Proc. 2001-59, 2001-59 IRB 623 (2001). See Appendix A.01, Table of Indexed Amounts, in the supplement.
[c] The GSTT exemption is indexed, beginning in 1999. IRC § 2631(c). For 2002, the indexed amount is $1,100,000. Rev. Proc. 2001-59, 2001-52 IRB 623 (2001). Beginning in 2004, the GSTT exemption will be the same as the estate tax exemption, ranging from $1,500,000 in 2004 to $3,500,000 in 2009. EGTRRA § 521(c)(2); IRC § 2631(c).
[d] Until 2004. IRC § 2057(j).

¶ 5.12 SECTION 2057

The qualified family-owned business interest deduction (discussed in Chapter 50) is not available for GSTT purposes, according to the conference report to IRSRRA '98.

CHAPTER **6**

Income Taxation of Trusts and Beneficiaries

¶ 6.01 INTRODUCTION

QUESTION: *Do all Internal Revenue Code sections relevant to estate plan-ners have four digits and begin with 2?*

ANSWER: No. An estate planner must pay attention to the income tax, as well as transfer tax, consequences of her recommendations. This chapter covers the highlights of the income taxation of trusts and beneficiaries. Some trusts are subject to special income tax treatment (for example, charitable remainder trusts, pooled income trusts, etc.). The taxation of those trusts is discussed in their respective chapters. This chapter deals with trusts that are subject to the ordinary rules of subchapter J of the Internal Revenue Code. These trusts fall into three categories—simple, complex, and grantor trusts.

¶ 6.02 DEFINITIONS

[1] Simple Trust

Whether a trust is simple or complex is determined on a year-to-year basis. A simple trust in any year is a trust which requires that all its trust accounting income[1] be distributed currently, has no charitable beneficiaries or purposes, and does not make a distribution of principal during the year.[2]

[2] Complex Trust

A complex trust is any trust that is neither a simple trust nor a grantor trust. Many family trusts are complex trusts.

[3] Grantor Trust

A grantor trust is ignored for income tax purposes. Its items of income, deduc-tion, gain, loss, and credit are reported directly by the grantor or by a beneficiary.[3]

---

[1] See ¶ 6.02[4] for a definition.

[2] IRC § 651(a).

[3] IRC §§ 671, et seq.

[4] Income

It is critical to understand the different concepts of income which apply in trust administration.

[a] Accounting Income

The allocation of a trust's receipts and disbursements to income or principal is governed by state law and the governing instrument. Generally, income receipts will include such items as dividends and interest. Principal receipts will often include proceeds from the sale of assets, including capital gains.

[b] Taxable Income

Taxable income refers to items that are subject to federal income taxation. Taxable income has no relationship to accounting income. Accordingly, when "income" is considered in relation to trusts, it is important to know whether accounting income or taxable income is meant.

¶ 6.03 INCOME TAXATION OF COMPLEX TRUSTS

[1] General Rules

A complex trust is a separate taxable entity, and is taxed on its gross income, less deductions.[4] One of these deductions which is unique to trusts and estates is the deduction for distributions of distributable net income (DNI).[5]

[a] Distributable Net Income

DNI is taxable income of the trust, with the following modifications:

- No distribution deduction is taken.[6]
- No personal exemption is taken.[7]
- Capital gains are ordinarily (but not always) excluded.[8]
- Capital losses are not taken, except to the extent of capital gains which are included in DNI.[9]

---

[4] IRC § 641.

[5] IRC § 661(a).

[6] IRC § 643(a)(1).

[7] IRC § 643(a)(2).

[8] IRC § 643(a)(3).

[9] IRC § 643(a)(3).

- Tax-exempt interest is included, less certain expenses.[10]

There are extra adjustments for foreign trusts, and for trusts distributing to charity.[11]

[b] Distributions of Distributable Net Income

[i] In general. Distributions that carry out DNI are deducted by the trust and taxed to the beneficiary.[12] Moreover, if a trust has DNI, trust distributions will ordinarily "carry out" DNI whether they are in fact made from DNI or not.

> EXAMPLE: Trust has $200,000 of DNI, consisting of cash dividends. If trust distributes $50,000 of real estate to Child, the distribution carries out DNI, reducing Trust's DNI to $150,000 and adding $50,000 to Child's taxable income.

There are, however, exceptions to the rule that a distribution from a trust with DNI will carry out DNI. These exceptions include specific gifts and charitable distributions. First, under the specific gift exception, distribution of a gift of a specific sum of money (or of specific property) which is paid in three or fewer installments, and which is not restricted to being paid out of income, does not carry out DNI.[13] A typical pecuniary formula bequest is not a specific gift for these purposes.[14] Thus, if Trust provides that Beneficiary gets $50,000 in one lump sum when she is 30, this is a specific gift that does not carry out DNI. However, if Trust provides that spouse-beneficiary receives an amount equal to the minimum marital deduction needed to reduce the estate tax to zero, this is not a specific gift.

Under the charitable distribution exception, a trust distribution that qualifies for a charitable deduction does not carry out DNI.[15] The regulations further provide that a distribution to charity that does not qualify for a charitable deduction by reason of Section 642(c) is not eligible for a Section 661 distribution deduction.[16]

---

[10] IRC § 643(a)(5).

[11] IRC § 643(a)(6), 643(a).

[12] IRC § 662(a).

[13] IRC § 663(a)(1).

[14] Treas. Reg. § 1.663(a)-1(b)(1).

[15] IRC § 663(a)(2).

[16] Treas. Reg. § 1.663(a)-2. This regulation was upheld in Mott v. United States, 462 F2d 512 (Ct. Cl. 1972), cert. denied, 409 US 1108 (1973); United States Trust Co. v. United States, 803 F2d 1363 (5th Cir. 1986), rev'g 617 F. Supp. 575 (SD Miss. 1985); Estate of O'Connor v. Comm'r, 69 TC 165 (1979), appeal dismissed (2d Cir. 1980); Rebecca K. Crown Income Charitable Fund v. Comm'r, 98 TC 327 (1992), aff'd, 8 F3d 571 (7th Cir. 1993); Pullen v. United States, 45 AFTR2d 381 (D. Neb. 1979).

EXAMPLE: Trustee makes a distribution of unrelated business taxable income to charity. The distribution is only partially deductible as a charitable distribution under Section 642(c). The remaining part of the distribution is not deductible as a general distribution under Section 661.

[ii] **Character of DNI distributed.** Generally speaking, distributed income takes the same character in the beneficiary's hands as it had in the trust. And, unless the terms of the governing instrument specifically allocate different classes of income to different beneficiaries, a trust distribution carrying out DNI is deemed to consist of the same proportion of each class of income included in DNI as the total of each class bears to total DNI.[17]

EXAMPLE: Trust earns $100,000 in dividends and $200,000 in rent in 1996. Trust distributes $100,000 each to A and B. A and B will each include $33,333 of dividends and $66,667 of rent in his gross income.

Note that in order for an allocation mandated by the instrument to be respected, it must have economic effect independent of income tax consequences.[18]

EXAMPLE: Trust earns $100,000 in dividends and $200,000 in rent in 1996. Trust distributes $100,000 each to A and B. The trust instrument allocates all rental income to B. B will include $100,000 rent and A will include $100,000 dividends in each of their respective incomes.

EXAMPLE: Trust earns $100,000 of dividend income and $100,000 of tax-exempt income in 1996. The trust instrument provides that income is divided equally between A and B. It also provides that when distributions are made, taxable income will be distributed to A and tax-exempt income will be allocated to B to the extent possible. If $100,000 is distributed to A and $100,000 to B, each of A and B will include $50,000 of dividends and $50,000 of tax-exempt income in his own income. The allocation is not respected because it doesn't have "an economic effect independent of the income tax consequences of the allocation."[19]

EXAMPLE: Same as above, except that all tax-exempt income is to be distributed to or held solely for B, and all taxable income is to be distributed to or held solely for A, regardless of the fact that the amounts may differ. In this case, the allocations would have economic effect independent of the tax consequences of the allocation because the allocation might result in A getting a larger or smaller distribution than B. Thus, the allocations are respected and A would take $100,000 of dividend income and B would take $100,000 of tax-exempt income into his own income.

---

[17] IRC §§ 652(b), 661(b), 662(b).

[18] Treas. Reg. §§ 1.652(b)-2(b), 1.662(b)-1, 1.662(b)-2.

[19] Treas. Reg. §§ 1.652(b)-2(b), 1.662(b)-1, 1.662(b)-2.

The items of deduction entering into the computation of DNI are generally allocated in proportion to the trust's and beneficiary's shares of income, with certain exceptions. An example of an exception is a deductible reserve. Reserves for depreciation and depletion are shared by the beneficiary and the trust in proportion to the income of each, except to the extent that a reserve is established by the trustee pursuant to the governing instrument or applicable law. To the extent of the reserve, the trust gets the entire depreciation or depletion deduction.[20]

> EXAMPLE: Trust has oil income of $100,000. The depletion deduction is 15% of the income. If the trust has a depletion reserve of 15% of the income, then the trust will accumulate $15,000 pursuant to the reserve, and will take the $15,000 depletion deduction against that income. Even if the trust distributes the remaining $85,000 to the beneficiary, the trust will keep the deduction. The accumulated $15,000 will not constitute undistributed net income (as defined below), since it was offset by the depletion deduction.

[iii] Rules on deemed timing of distributions. Under the "65-day rule," the trustee can elect to treat all distributions made within the first 65 days of the taxable year as made within the previous year.[21]

Under the "required distribution rule," income which is required to be distributed is treated as distributed, whether it is in fact distributed or not.[22]

[iv] Treatment of capital gains. Sometimes, it will be desirable to make capital gains part of DNI. Capital gains are, however, not included in DNI unless: (1) the trust is terminating, (2) capital gains are required by the trust instrument or local law to be distributed, (3) the fiduciary routinely follows the practice of distributing capital gains, or (4) the fiduciary validly allocates capital gain to income on the trust books or by notice to the beneficiary.[23]

[v] Equalizing distributions. The aggregate income tax payable by the beneficiaries and trust can often be minimized by making distributions to the beneficiaries until their marginal brackets equal the trust's marginal bracket. How does this work? In any one year, a trust will receive a deduction from its income for distributions made during that year (or, if an election is made, within 65 days after year-end), and the beneficiary will include the distribution in her income (in all cases, limited by DNI).

---

[20] IRC § 642(e); Treas. Reg. §§ 1.167(h)-1(b), 1.611-1(c)(4).

[21] IRC § 663(b).

[22] IRC §§ 661(a), 662(a).

[23] Treas. Reg. § 1.643(a)-3(a); Rev. Rul. 68-392, 1968-2 CB 284.

The trustee will need to make a decision each year as to whether equalizing distributions should be made.

The beneficiary receiving a distribution will include the trust income carried out to her in her taxable year with which or in which the trust year ends.[24] Normally, trusts and individuals will be on a calendar year.[25] Hence, a distribution of DNI during Year One will be taxable to the beneficiary in Year One. If the trustee makes the election to treat distributions made during the first 65 days of Year Two as having been made in Year One, then the DNI so distributed is also deductible in Year One and, accordingly, taxable to the beneficiary in Year One.

[c] Undistributed Net Income

To the extent that DNI is not distributed, it is taxed to the trust. The after-tax amount is accumulated, and constitutes UNI ("undistributed net income").[26] When the UNI is ultimately distributed, it is an "accumulation distribution,"[27] and is subject to a "throwback tax."

[i] **Throwback tax.** The calculation of the throwback tax, with an example, is as follows.

EXAMPLE: Trust *X* has UNI of $100,000 in Year One and $200,000 in Year Two. It paid income tax in Years One and Two of $33,000 and $90,000. It makes a distribution of $150,000 of UNI in Year Three. Beneficiary's taxable income for the past five years is $300,000, $200,000, $100,000, $200,000, and $200,000. The following steps in the computation of the throwback tax will be illustrated by reference to this example.

Step one. The accumulation distribution is deemed made from each year's UNI beginning with the earliest year. Determine the number of years and the amounts in each year, using all of the UNI in an earlier year before proceeding to a later year. We'll call these years the "UNI years." Using the facts of the above example, the UNI for Year One is $100,000 and the UNI for Year Two is $50,000.

Step two. Add the income taxes paid by the trust attributable to the accumulation distributions. The sum is the deemed distribution. Thus, the amount for UNI Year One is $100,000 distribution plus $33,000 tax, or $133,000. And, the amount for UNI Year Two is $50,000 distribution plus $22,500 tax, or $72,500. Consequently, the deemed distribution is $205,500, consisting of the totals for UNI Years One and Two.

---

[24] IRC § 662(c).

[25] IRC § 645.

[26] IRC § 665(a).

[27] IRC § 665(b).

Step three. Ascertain the beneficiary's taxable income for the beneficiary's five taxable years preceding the distribution. Disregard the two years with the highest and lowest taxable income. We'll call the remaining three years the "Base Years." Using the facts of the example, each Base Year's income is $200,000.

Step four. Divide the deemed distribution by the number of UNI years. Here, $205,500 deemed distribution ÷ 2 UNI years = $102,750. Then, add this number to each of the Base Years' taxable incomes. Under our facts, each Base Year will now have $302,750 taxable income (i.e., $200,000 deemed base year income + $102,750).

Step five. Determine the average increase in the beneficiary's tax for the Base Years. Using our facts, the average increase in tax for the Base Years is $40,689.

Step six. Multiply the average increase in tax by the number of UNI years. Here, $40,689 × 2 = $81,378. Then, subtract the taxes deemed distributed to the beneficiary from that number. Here, $81,378 − $55,500 taxes deemed distributed = $25,878.

Step seven. The number calculated at the end of Step six is the throwback tax. Under our facts, the throwback tax is $25,878.

Bottom line. If the trust paid less tax in the UNI years than the beneficiary would have if the UNI had been included in her taxable income in the three Base Years, the beneficiary will owe an additional tax. If the trust paid as much as or more tax than the beneficiary would have owed in the hypothetical calculation, the beneficiary will not owe an additional tax.

PRACTICE POINTER: With the compression of the income tax rates on trusts (compared to the individual income tax rates), the throwback rule is less likely to be as important as it once was.

[ii] Exception for accumulations before beneficiary attains age 21. The throwback tax does not apply to income accumulated when a beneficiary is under 21.[28]

[iii] Exception for accumulations when trust was a grantor trust. The throwback tax does not apply to income accumulated when the trust was a grantor trust, since the income accumulated would not have been included in DNI.[29]

---

[28] IRC § 665(b).

[29] Grantor trusts are discussed at ¶¶ 6.05 and 6.06 below.

[d] Multiple Trusts Rule

If DNI is accumulated for the same beneficiary in more than two trusts in any year, then on the ultimate distribution of the UNI to the beneficiary, the distribution of UNI from the first two trusts is taxed under the usual rules discussed above. The distribution of UNI from the third and other trusts is taxed similarly to a corporate dividend—that is, the amount of the distribution does not include the taxes the trust originally paid, but the distribution is taxed to the beneficiary again, without crediting the amount of tax initially paid by the trust.[30] The multiple trust rule does not apply to a distribution from a trust if the amount accumulated in that trust in a particular year is less than $1,000.[31]

In the above example used in ¶ 6.03[1][c] suppose Trust 2 was a "third trust." The distribution of $50,000 from that trust would not be deemed augmented by the tax paid on that income. The amount taxable to the beneficiary is $50,000. No credit is available for tax paid by the trust.

The taxpayer beneficiary can choose which trusts are the "first" two trusts in any year. The choice does not have to be consistent from year to year.[32]

[e] Ordering Rules

If a distribution is made, it is characterized in the following order: first, DNI of current year; then UNI (beginning with the earliest UNI year); and, last, other amounts.

[i] Pot trusts. A "spray" or "pot" trust is one that can distribute to more than one individual at a time. Inequities can result, if the income tax considerations are not taken into account.

EXAMPLE: Suppose trust can distribute to Child *A*, *B*, or *C*, in any proportion. In Year One, trust has DNI of $100,000 and UNI of $100,000. Trust has no DNI in Years Two and Three.
Year One. If trust distributes $100,000 to Child *A* in Year One, the distribution will carry out DNI; accordingly, Child *A* will pay income tax on the distribution at her marginal rate (39.6 percent if she is in the highest bracket).
Year Two. If the trust then distributes $100,000 to Child *B* in Year Two, the distribution will carry out UNI. Child *B* will be taxed under the throwback rules, and generally will pay tax on the distribution only to the

---

[30] IRC § 667(c)(1).

[31] IRC § 667(c)(2).

[32] IRC § 667(b)(5).

extent that the trust paid less tax in the years of accumulation than Child
B would have if he had received the distribution in his three Base Years.
Year Three. Trust then distributes $100,000 to Child *C* in Year Three.
Child *C* pays no income tax on this distribution of principal.
Comparison. If all three of these distributions had been made in Year
One, Children *A*, *B*, and *C* would be considered to have each received
$33,333 of DNI, $33,333 of UNI, and $33,333 of principal.

PRACTICE POINTER: If the trust permits, in a particular year, consider distributing UNI to beneficiaries who were under 21 in the years of accumulation. In
succeeding years, distribute to other beneficiaries. This should prevent or minimize application of the throwback rules to any beneficiary.

[ii] **Tier system.** Inequities can also result from the tier system applicable
to complex trusts which are required to distribute all their income at least
annually. Distributions to beneficiaries who are required to receive the income
each year carry out DNI first. Other beneficiaries are only allocated DNI to
the extent that the first tier beneficiaries don't use it up.

EXAMPLE: In Year One, suppose Trust has $100,000 of DNI, has $50,000
of UNI, is required to distribute all its income to Child each year, and is
permitted to distribute principal to Grandchild. Suppose it distributes
$100,000 to Child and $100,000 to Grandchild in Year One. Child will
receive $100,000 of DNI, and Grandchild will be treated as receiving
$50,000 of principal tax-free and $50,000 of UNI taxed under the throwback rules.

[f] Capital Gains

Capital gains which are included in UNI lose their character as capital
gains, and are taxed at ordinary income rates, according to the throwback
computation.

PRACTICE POINTER: If capital gains are included in DNI, it will ordinarily be best
to distribute them in the year in which they are earned, so as not to lose their
character.

[2] Income Not Included in DNI

Income which is not included in DNI is taxable to the trust. If the after-tax
income is accumulated, it is not part of UNI and is not taxable to the beneficiary on distribution.

[3] Special Rules on Distribution of Property in Kind

[a] Distribution in Satisfaction of a Dollar Amount

If the trust is required to pay the beneficiary $10,000, it may distribute property having a fair market value of $10,000, if that is permitted by the trust instrument. This will be treated as a sale of the property to the beneficiary for $10,000, followed by a distribution to her of $10,000 sales proceeds. Gain or loss will be recognized by the trust on this deemed sale. Accordingly, the trust will be taxed on any gain. However, a loss will not be deductible by the trust, but will be available to the beneficiary if she ever sells the property for more than $10,000.[33] The beneficiary will take a new basis, which will be the trust's basis, adjusted for recognized gain or loss.[34] The beneficiary also will start a new holding period for the distributed property. The trust will receive a distribution deduction of $10,000, and the beneficiary will take the $10,000 into her income, if DNI of at least that amount exists. (The gain itself ordinarily will not generate DNI, since capital gains are usually not included in DNI. The capital gain will not be considered distributed to the beneficiary in this case, absent other facts.)[35]

[b] Other Distributions

If a trust makes a distribution of property, but does not do so in satisfaction of a specific dollar obligation, one of two tax treatments can apply.

[i] General rules. Generally, the beneficiary will take a carryover basis from the trust (or the fair market value of the property, if less),[36] and no gain or loss will be realized. The beneficiary will tack the trust's holding period. To the extent of DNI, the trust will receive a distribution deduction of its basis (or the fair market value of the property, if less) in the property, and the beneficiary will take that amount into income.[37]

[ii] Election to treat distribution as a sale. The trust can file an election to treat the distribution as if it were a sale.[38] In that case, the trust will realize gain or loss. A loss cannot be deducted, but can be used on an eventual sale

---

[33] IRC §§ 267(a)(1), 267(b)(6), 267(d). See explanation in Ch. 8.

[34] IRC § 643(e)(1).

[35] Rev. Rul. 68-392, 1968-2 CB 284.

[36] IRC § 643(e)(2).

[37] IRC § 643(e)(2).

[38] IRC § 643(e)(3).

of the property by the beneficiary for more than the fair market value on the date of distribution.[39] The beneficiary will take a new basis equal to the trust's basis, plus the trust's recognized gain or loss, and a new holding period will begin with the date of distribution. The trust can take a distribution deduction of the fair market value of the property distributed, and the beneficiary will take that amount into income.[40]

[c] Non-Pro Rata Distributions

If non-pro rata distributions are not permitted by the trust instrument and/or state law, and the trustee makes such a distribution with the agreement of the beneficiaries, the distribution will be treated as a pro rata distribution to the beneficiaries, followed by an exchange between the beneficiaries, resulting in the non-pro rata holdings. This deemed exchange will constitute a taxable transaction if no exception applies.[41]

[4] Sale of Appreciated Property Within Two Years of Transfer

If Mom contributes appreciated property to a trust, and the trust sells the property at a gain within two years, the trust's tax rate on the pre-transfer gain will be the higher of its own tax rate or Mom's tax rate (without regard to loss carrybacks and carryovers).[42] Special rules apply to short sales, substituted basis property, and installment sales.[43] Section 644, which imposes this rule, does not apply to property passing to the trust from a decedent or to the sale of the property after the transferor's death.[44]

PRACTICE POINTER: Section 644 was enacted in 1976, when income tax rates were steeply graduated. It was enacted to prevent a high-income taxpayer who wanted to sell appreciated property from giving the property to a trust just before the sale in order to lower the capital gains rate on the sale. Section 644 has limited application today, because a trust will reach the maximum capital gains rate at $1,650[45] of income, and the maximum ordinary income tax rate at $8,100.[46]

---

[39] IRC §§ 267(a)(1), 267(b)(6), 267(d). See explanation in Ch. 8.

[40] IRC § 643(e)(3)(A)(iii).

[41] Rev. Rul. 69-486, 1969-2 CB 159.

[42] IRC § 644(a).

[43] IRC §§ 644(d), 644(f).

[44] IRC §§ 644(e)(1), 644(e)(4).

[45] IRC §§ 1(e), 1(h). (1997 tables, as indexed for inflation.)

[46] IRC §§ 1(e), 1(h). (1997 tables, as indexed for inflation.)

[5] Losses

A trust can take ordinary and capital losses and net operating loss carryovers. However, it cannot distribute them to the beneficiaries, and thus the beneficiaries cannot deduct such trust losses, until the year that the trust terminates.[47] If a trust has expenses in excess of income in a particular year, the excess is not deductible unless it qualifies for a carryover and can be deducted in subsequent years, or unless the trust is in its termination year, in which case, the deductions can be carried out to the beneficiaries (to be deducted on their individual income tax returns).

¶ 6.04 TAXATION OF SIMPLE TRUSTS

The rules applicable to complex trusts generally apply to simple trusts as well. However, there are a few special rules. But, as a general rule, the tax treatment of such trusts is much simpler, since by definition, simple trusts must distribute all of their income currently and there are no distributions of principal.

A simple trust receives a distribution deduction for the amount of income required to be paid in the year of distribution.[48] Therefore, a simple trust, which must distribute all of its fiduciary accounting income currently, will only pay tax on items of taxable income that constitute principal for fiduciary accounting purposes (e.g., capital gains and income from wasting or depreciating assets, to the extent of depletion and depreciation reserves). For simple trusts only, extraordinary dividends and taxable stock dividends are excluded from DNI if they are properly allocated to principal.[49]

Income that is required to be distributed in Year One is treated as having been distributed in Year One, even if the distribution actually takes place in Year Two.[50]

¶ 6.05 HOW TO AVOID GRANTOR TRUST STATUS

The income, gains, loss, deductions, and credits of any trust established during the grantor's lifetime will be reportable by the grantor instead of the trust if certain rules set out in Sections 671–678 apply. Consequently, these rules must always be considered in drafting such a trust.

The grantor will not be treated as the owner of a trust for federal income tax purposes if all of the following seven statements are true:

---

[47] IRC § 642(h).

[48] IRC §§ 651(a), 652(a).

[49] IRC § 643(a)(4).

[50] IRC §§ 651(a), 652(a).

[1] Trust Is Irrevocable

A trust will be a grantor trust if the trust is revocable.[51]

[2] Grantor and Grantor's Spouse Have No Beneficial Interest

A trust will be wholly or partially a grantor trust if either the grantor or his spouse has a beneficial interest in the trust.[52]

[3] Trust Does Not Hold Life Insurance on Grantor or Spouse

A trust will be a grantor trust to the extent that premiums on life insurance actually held by the trust on the life of the grantor or his spouse can be paid from income.[53]

[4] Discretionary Distributions are Limited in Specified Manner

As a general rule, a trust will be a grantor trust unless the trustee's power to make distributions is limited in one of the following four ways.

[a] No Limitation for Trusts With Independent Trustees

The trustee can have full discretion regarding distributions if (1) neither the grantor nor his spouse can make any decisions regarding distributions and (2) a majority of the people who can make distribution decisions for the trust are not related or subordinate parties[54] who are subservient to the wishes of the grantor or his spouse.[55]

[b] Ascertainable Standard Limitation for Trusts With Non-Independent Trustees

Provided that the grantor or his spouse is not the trustee, the distribution limitation requirement will be met if the trustee's power to

---

[51] IRC § 676.

[52] IRC §§ 673, 677(a)(1), 677(a)(2).

[53] IRC § 677(a)(3).

[54] A "related or subordinate party" is any nonadverse party (defined at n.60) who is: the grantor's spouse, if living with the grantor; the grantor's mother, father, descendant, brother, or sister; the grantor's employee; a corporation or any employee of a corporation in which the stockholdings of the grantor and the trust are significant from the viewpoint of voting control; or, a subordinate employee of a corporation in which the grantor is an executive. IRC § 672(c).

[55] IRC § 674(c).

distribute income and principal among beneficiaries is limited by a reasonably definite standard,[56] such as health, support, maintenance, and education.[57] Accordingly, a trust with a related or subordinate trustee who is subservient to the wishes of the grantor or his spouse will meet the distribution limitation requirement if his power to distribute is limited by an ascertainable standard.

[c] Special Rule for Separate Trusts

The distribution limitation requirement will be met, even if the grantor or his spouse is the sole trustee, if: (1) the trust is a separate trust; (2) only one beneficiary is permitted to receive distributions during that beneficiary's lifetime, unless that beneficiary consents to a different distribution; and (3) either (a) the trust's termination date is reasonably expected to occur during that beneficiary's lifetime (e.g., a trust which terminates when the beneficiary is 35)[58] or (b) the beneficiary has a broad limited power of appointment (i.e., a power to appoint the trust assets during his lifetime or at his death, or both, to any person he chooses, other than himself, his estate, his creditors, or the creditors of his estate).

PRACTICE POINTER: Even though the permissible appointees of the beneficiary's broad limited power of appointment will, by definition, include the trust's grantor as long as he is alive, and therefore trust income could possibly be distributed to the grantor via an exercise of the power, the grantor will not for this reason be treated as the owner of the trust under Section 677.[59]

[d] Adverse Party Consent Required

The distribution limitation requirement will be met, regardless of who is the trustee, if any distribution of trust assets can be made only with the consent of an adverse party.[60]

---

[56] IRC § 674(d).

[57] IRC § 674(b)(5).

[58] IRC §§ 674(b)(5), 674(b)(6).

[59] Treas. Reg. § 1.674-1(c).

[60] An "adverse" party is any person having a substantial beneficial interest in the trust which would be adversely affected by the exercise or nonexercise of the power which he possesses respecting the trust. IRC § 672(a). A "nonadverse party" is a person who is not an adverse party. IRC § 672(b).

[5] No One Can Add Beneficiaries

As a general rule, a trust will be a grantor trust if anyone has the power to add to the trust beneficiaries, except to provide for after-born or after-adopted children.[61] A testamentary power of appointment does not violate this rule.[62] A power to assign or appoint during lifetime does not violate this rule if the assignment or appointment would be adverse to the assignor or appointor.[63]

[6] Certain Administrative Powers Are Not Granted

As a general rule, a trust will be a grantor trust if certain administrative powers, as discussed below, exist with respect to the trust.

[a] Power to Deal With the Trust for Less Than Adequate Consideration

A trust will be a grantor trust if anyone can, without an adverse party's consent, purchase, exchange, deal with, or dispose of the trust property for less than adequate consideration.[64]

[b] Power to Make Certain Loans to Grantor or His Spouse

A trust will be a grantor trust if anyone can, without an adverse party's consent, lend trust assets to the grantor without adequate interest and security, unless a trustee (who is not the grantor or his spouse) is authorized to lend to any person without regard to interest or security[65] and either (1) there is no such loan to the grantor or his spouse outstanding at any time during the year or (2) all loans to the grantor/spouse outstanding during the year are made with adequate interest and security, and are made by a trustee who is not the grantor/spouse or a related or subordinate trustee who is subservient to the grantor or his spouse.[66]

[c] Other Prohibited Powers

A trust will be a grantor trust if anyone acting in a nonfiduciary capacity can do any of the following without the trustee's approval:

---

[61] IRC §§ 674(b)(5), 674(b)(6), 674(c), 674(d).

[62] Treas. Reg. § 1.674(d)-2(b).

[63] Treas. Reg. § 1.674(d)-2(b).

[64] IRC § 675(1).

[65] IRC § 675(2).

[66] IRC § 675(3).

- Vote the trust's stock, if the trust's and grantor's position in the stock is significant from the viewpoint of voting control;[67]
- Control or veto the trust's investments, where the trust funds consist of securities of corporations in which the holdings of the grantor and the trust are significant from the viewpoint of voting control;[68] or
- Reacquire trust assets by substituting assets of equivalent value.[69]

[7] No Disqualifying Replacement Powers Held by Grantor or Spouse

A trust will be a grantor trust if the grantor or his spouse can remove and replace the trustee in such a manner as to cause it to be a grantor trust under any of the above tests.[70]

[8] Failing One of the Seven Tests

If the trust fails any of the above seven tests, further analysis is required to determine whether the trust is a grantor trust. The provisions of the trust will need to be studied, with a view to the application of Sections 671-677 and the regulations interpreting those sections.

[9] Estate and Gift Tax Considerations

If the grantor is trustee, the grantor's distribution powers must be limited by a standard related to health, maintenance, support, and education in order for the trust to escape estate taxation.[71] So, the grantor could have unfettered discretion to distribute income and principal of a separate trust without running afoul of the grantor trust provisions, but the trust assets would be in his estate if he died while holding these powers.

---

[67] IRC § 675(4)(A).

[68] IRC § 675(4)(B).

[69] IRC § 675(4).

[70] Treas. Reg. § 1.674(d)-2(b).

[71] IRC § 2036(a)(2); see also Estate of Budd v. Comm'r, 49 TC 468 (1968), acq., 1973-2 CB 1.

PRACTICE POINTER: It is possible, with multiple trustees, to split the powers of the trustees, and leave maximum permissible power in the grantor without sacrificing flexibility. For example, the grantor can be management trustee, and control the investment of the assets, while leaving part or all of the distribution powers to a distributing trustee. This division of powers works just fine in theory; in practice, it sometimes requires some fancy footwork when banks, brokers, etc. are trying to sort out the proper party to deal with the assets in any particular transaction.

[10] Trusts Which Are Treated as Owned by the Beneficiary

If the beneficiary has the right, by himself, to cause trust income or principal to be distributed to him, and the trust is not taxable to the actual grantor as a grantor trust, the trust will be treated for income tax purposes as owned by the beneficiary.[72] Additionally, if the beneficiary once had such a right and released or modified it, and the beneficiary has rights or powers that would cause the trust income tax items to be attributed to him if the beneficiary were the grantor, then the trust income tax items will be taxable to the beneficiary, unless the trust income tax items are taxable to the actual grantor.[73] This situation arises often with respect to Crummey trusts.[74]

¶ 6.06 PLANNING WITH GRANTOR TRUSTS

In some cases, a grantor trust, sometimes referred to as a "defective" trust or "intentionally defective grantor trust," will be appropriate. Generally, a grantor will not want to be taxable on the income of property transferred to a trust, and will arrange for the normal trust rules to apply by following the guidelines described in ¶ 6.05 above, or by other means. "Defective" planning involves intentionally violating one of the rules, so that a trust held for the benefit of another is taxable to the grantor for federal income tax purposes. Why would someone intentionally create a grantor trust? A defective trust provides a good opportunity for the grantor to, in essence, increase the value of property transferred to the trust with no additional gift tax.

> **EXAMPLE:** Defective grantor trust for child has income of $1,000. Grantor reports the $1,000 as his own income, and owes income tax of $396. By arranging for himself rather than the trust to be liable for this tax, he has enabled the trust to save $396 (if it would have been in the 39.6 percent bracket), and he has apparently made no gift under current law. If the grantor is in a lower income tax bracket than the trust would have been, so much the better.

---

[72] IRC § 678(a).

[73] IRC §§ 678(a)(2), 678(b).

[74] A more in-depth explanation is contained in Ch. 10 on tax-free gifts.

[1] When to Consider Using an Intentionally Defective Trust

When is defective status desirable? A grantor might want to pay the income taxes on the trust and thereby permit the trust from bearing that expense; or she might want to use the trust losses against her personal income; or she might want to be sure that the trust qualifies as a grantor trust in order to be a qualified S corporation shareholder; or she might want to take advantage of the lower rates applicable to individuals without making distributions.

[2] Possible Disadvantages of Defective Trusts

[a] Cash Flow Issues

A defective grantor trust can become problematic if the grantor owes the tax and does not have the cash to pay it, since distributions to him from the trust are not usually permitted. Under some state laws, a reimbursement can be required from the trust to the grantor for payment of those taxes. A bona fide loan from the trust to the grantor might also be arranged in appropriate circumstances.

[b] Payment of Income Tax as Gift

The IRS has made noises about treating the grantor's payment of income tax as a gift, either as it is paid or on the establishment of the trust, in an amount to be determined by a formula.[75] Private Letter Ruling 9444033[76] stated, in the context of a grantor retained annuity trust, that the trust contained a provision to reimburse the grantor for any income tax paid by the grantor attributable to income he did not receive. The ruling gratuitously stated that if there were no reimbursement provision, an additional gift "to a remainderperson" would occur when the grantor paid tax on income of the trust.[77] This ruling was subsequently withdrawn without comment and reissued without the paragraph containing the statement.[78] The IRS has not announced an official position on the issue.

---

[75] See Priv. Ltr. Ruls. 9413045 (Jan. 4, 1994), 9504021 (Oct. 28, 1994), 9416009 (Dec. 30, 1993), 9352004 (Sept. 24, 1993).

[76] Issued on August 5, 1994.

[77] The IRS informal policy is apparently not to issue GRAT rulings without a reimbursement condition, since any "gift" might constitute an impermissible contribution to a GRAT.

[78] Priv. Ltr. Rul. 9543049 (Aug. 3, 1995).

Many estate planning pundits think that the position stated in the withdrawn ruling will be difficult for the IRS to sustain without legislation.[79] They cite, for example, Technical Advice Memorandum 9128009.[80] In this Technical Advice Memorandum, the IRS determined that if the donor paid the entire gift tax on a split gift, he did not make a gift to his wife, since the liability was primarily his. However, one should be aware of the IRS's possible stance on this issue and let the grantor know of the risk. Some people don't like to live on the edge.

[3] How to Make a Trust Defective

The art is in including a provision that causes the trust's assets to be deemed to be owned by the grantor for income tax purposes, but not for transfer tax purposes. A trust is usually made defective in one of the following ways.

[a] Permit Grantor to Substitute Assets

The grantor is given a power (exercisable in a nonfiduciary capacity) to reacquire trust assets by substituting assets of equivalent value.[81] This power is popularly used. The Tax Court has held, and the IRS has agreed, that the retention of this power will not cause inclusion in the grantor's estate under Section 2038.[82] The IRS has since reached the same result under Section 2036.[83] The IRS, however, will not generally rule on whether a Section 675 power will make a trust defective, since Section 675 is an area under extensive study.[84]

[b] Permit Related or Subordinate Trustee to Make Discretionary Distributions

The trust will be defective if a trustee who is related or subordinate to the grantor, and subservient to the wishes of the grantor, can make discretionary

---

[79] E.g., Huffaker, Kessel & Sindoni, Is Income Tax Payment by Grantor-Owner of a Subpart E Trust a Taxable Gift? J. Tax'n 202 (Apr. 1995).

[80] Issued on March 29, 1991.

[81] IRC § 675(4)(C).

[82] Estate of Jordahl v. Comm'r, 65 TC 92 (1975), acq., 1977-1 CB 1.

[83] Priv. Ltr. Rul. 9247024 (Aug. 24, 1992), Priv. Ltr. Rul. 9227013 (Mar. 30, 1992).

[84] E.g., Priv. Ltr. Rul. 9548013 (Aug. 29, 1995); Priv. Ltr. Rul. 9337011 (June 17, 1993); Priv. Ltr. Rul. 8351139 (Sept. 23, 1983). The IRS considers the question of whether a power to substitute assets is exercisable in a nonfiduciary capacity to be a question of fact. Priv. Ltr. Rul. 9413045 (Jan. 4, 1994).

distributions (that is, distributions which are not limited by a reasonably definite standard).[85]

If the trustee is a related or subordinate party, a rebuttable presumption exists for income tax purposes that the trustee is subservient to the wishes of the grantor.[86] Does this cause an estate tax problem? There is no reported case requiring the inclusion of a trust in the grantor's estate solely due to the existence of a trustee who is merely presumed to be subservient to the grantor's wishes for income tax purposes. The grantor must actually control the trustee, by agreement or otherwise, for the trust to be included in the grantor's estate, if it would not otherwise be includable.[87]

> EXAMPLE: Suppose Trustee of a spray trust is a related party who is not actually controlled by the grantor. Because Trustee is related, she is presumed to be subservient to the grantor for income tax purposes. Hence, the trust will be a defective grantor trust unless the grantor chooses to submit evidence of Trustee's actual lack of subservience. Since Trustee is not actually subservient to the wishes of the grantor, the trust should not be included in the grantor's estate.

[c] Permit the Addition of a Beneficiary

The trust will be defective if a nonadverse party has the power to add a beneficiary, other than after-born or after-adopted children.[88] The person with this power should not, however, have the power to add the grantor as a beneficiary, for gift and estate tax reasons.

[d] Make Spouse a Beneficiary or Powerholder

The trust will be wholly or partially defective if the grantor's spouse is a permissible distributee or the holder of a power which would render the trust defective if the grantor held it.[89] Of course, if the spouse dies, the trust will suddenly cease being a grantor trust unless other arrangements are made to maintain its status.

---

[85] IRC § 674(a).

[86] IRC § 672(c).

[87] See Estate of McCabe v. United States, 475 F2d 1142 (Ct. Cl. 1973) (finding prearrangement between grantor, grantor's wife and trustee and thus retention of beneficial interest in trust by grantor for estate tax purposes). As an evidentiary matter, of course, the burden may be on the grantor's estate to show that actual control did not exist. Treas. Reg. § 20.2036-1(a); Estate of Wells, 42 TCM (CCH) 1305 (1981).

[88] IRC §§ 674(b)(5), 674(b)(6), 674(b)(7), 674(c), 674(d).

[89] IRC §§ 673, 677, 672(e).

[e] Use a Foreign Trust

If a U.S. grantor creates a foreign trust for the benefit of U.S. persons, the grantor will be taxed on the trust income.[90] So, such a foreign trust could be used as a grantor trust.

[f] Defective Means to Defective Ends

Other ways of making a trust defective involve estate tax problems—such as, retaining a reversionary interest worth more than five percent,[91] retaining a power to revoke,[92] or retaining a beneficial interest.[93]

Retaining the power to invest in life insurance on the grantor's life only results in grantor trust status to the extent that premiums on a policy actually held by the trust could be paid out of trust income.[94]

[4] Escape Hatch: Later Paths to Non-Grantor Status

It is a good idea in a defective trust to include a means to enable the trust to cease being a defective trust during the grantor's lifetime. This will involve reversing whatever means was chosen to make the trust a defective trust (e.g., releasing powers which cause defective status, having a related or subordinate trustee resign, domesticating a foreign trust). It should be noted, however, that the IRS has taken the position that, for income tax purposes, the cessation of grantor trust status during the grantor's lifetime constitutes a deemed transfer of the trust assets to the newly recognized trust (e.g., resulting in gain from the deemed sale of a partnership interest to the extent liabilities exceeded basis).[95]

[5] Reporting Requirements

Recently, the IRS issued alternative methods for reporting income of trusts that are treated entirely as grantor trusts. For purposes of these reporting methods, spouses who file jointly are considered a single grantor.[96] The alternative methods are available in tax years beginning in 1996 or thereafter.[97]

---

[90] IRC § 679.

[91] IRC §§ 673, 2037.

[92] IRC §§ 676, 2038.

[93] IRC §§ 677, 2036.

[94] IRC § 677(a)(3); Rand v. Helvering, 40 BTA 233 (1939), acq. in result, 1939-2 CB 30, aff'd, 116 F2d 929 (8th Cir.), cert. denied, 313 US 594 (1941).

[95] Rev. Rul. 77-402, 1977-2 CB 222; Madorin v. Comm'r, 84 TC 667 (1985).

[96] Treas. Reg. § 1.671-4(b)(8).

[97] TD 8633, 1996-4 IRB 20, amending Treas. Reg. §§ 1.671-4, 1.6012-3(a)(9), and 301.6109-1(a)(2).

[a] Traditional Reporting Method

Under the traditional method, the trustee files an income tax return (Form 1041) by the fifteenth day of the fourth month following the end of its tax year.[98] The items of income, deduction, and credit are not reported on the Form 1041, however, but are shown on a separate statement attached to the Form 1041 that identifies the grantor.[99] The grantor will then, in turn, report the information on his or her return. Methods for reporting in lieu of filing a Form 1041 are available.[100]

[b] Alternative Reporting Method #1 for Trusts With Single Grantor

The trustee furnishes the name and taxpayer identification number of the grantor, and the address of the trust to all payors[101] of the trust during the taxable year and (unless the grantor is a trustee of the trust) furnishes the grantor with a statement (1) informing the grantor that the information on the statement must be included in computing the grantor's taxable income and credits, (2) setting out all items of income, deduction, and credit for the trust for the taxable year, (3) identifying the payor of each item of income, and (4) providing all information necessary for the grantor to compute his taxable income with respect to the trust.[102]

[c] Alternative Reporting Method #2 for Trusts With Single Grantor

The trustee furnishes the name, taxpayer identification number, and address of the trust to all payors of the trust during the taxable year. The trustee then files all of the trust's Form 1099s (showing the payor and the grantor as payee) with the IRS. The trustee has the same obligations for filing the appropriate Form 1099s as a payor making reportable payments, except that the trustee must report each type of income in the aggregate and each item of gross proceeds separately. Unless the grantor is a trustee of the trust, the trustee must furnish the grantor with a statement similar to the statement

---

[98] IRC §§ 6012(a)(4), 6072(a).

[99] Treas. Reg. § 1.671-4(a); see also Instructions to Form 1041.

[100] Treas. Reg. § 1.671-4(b)(1).

[101] A "payor" of the trust is any person who is required under the Internal Revenue Code or regulations to make any information return (including Form 1099 or Schedule K-1) for the trust for the tax year. Treas. Reg. § 1.671-4(b)(5). For example, if Bank A pays interest on a savings account to a grantor trust, Bank A is a payor of the trust.

[102] Treas. Reg. §§ 1.671-4(b)(2)(i)(A), 1.671-4(b)(2)(ii).

described in Alternative #1, except that the statement does not have to identify the trust's payors.[103]

[d] Alternative Reporting Method #3 for Trusts With Two or More Grantors

The trustee furnishes the name, taxpayer identification number and address of the trust to all payors of the trust during the taxable year. The trustee must provide each grantor with the statement required by Alternative #2 with respect to that portion of the trust treated as owned by that grantor. The trustee must file the trust's Form 1099s with the IRS, reporting the items of income paid to the trust by all payors during the taxable year attributable to the portion of the trust owned by each grantor.[104] The trustee has the same obligations for filing the appropriate Form 1099s as a payor making reportable payments, except that the trustee must report each type of income in the aggregate and each item of gross proceeds separately.

[e] Trusts Which Cannot Use Alternative Reporting Methods

These alternative methods are not available for a common trust fund, a qualified subchapter S trust, a non-U.S. situs trust (or a trust with any of its assets located outside the U.S.), a trust with a single grantor who reports income on a fiscal year, or a trust with a grantor who is not a U.S. person.[105]

[f] How to Select an Alternative Reporting Method

If a trustee has been filing Form 1041s and wishes to switch to an alternative method, the trustee must file a final Form 1041. The trustee must indicate on the final 1041: "Pursuant to § 1.671-4(g), this is the final form 1041 for the grantor trust. . . ."[106]

¶ 6.07   TRUST HOLDING S CORPORATION STOCK

A trust may need to be a defective trust to qualify as a shareholder of an S corporation. Alternatively, trust assets could be transferred to an S corporation and, if the trust instrument has qualifying provisions, the trust could elect to be a qualified S shareholder trust or an electing small business trust. This would result in the trust's share of the income of the S corporation being taxed

---

[103] Treas. Reg. §§ 1.671-4(b)(2)(i)(B), 1.671-4(b)(2)(iii).

[104] Treas. Reg. § 1.671-4(b)(3).

[105] Treas. Reg. § 1.671-4(b)(6).

[106] Treas. Reg. § 1.671-4(g).

directly to the beneficiary, in the case of a QSST, or to the trust at the highest rate, in the case of an electing small business trust. Of course, numerous other ramifications of these elections exist.[107]

¶ 6.08 COMPARISON OF TRUST AND INDIVIDUAL INCOME TAX RULES

[1] Income Tax Rates

Individuals. The regular tax rates for individuals do not reach 39.6 percent until $271,050* ($135,525* for married filing separately).[108] The maximum tax on long-term capital gains is 28 percent for both trusts and individuals.[109] The maximum alternative minimum tax for both individuals and trusts is 28 percent.[110] However, trusts are, as a practical matter, rarely in an alternative minimum tax situation, since they do not often have significant tax preferences.

Trusts. All trust ordinary income over $8,100* is taxed at 39.6 percent.[111]

[2] Reduction of Itemized Deductions for High-Income Taxpayers

Individuals. For individuals whose adjusted gross income exceeds $121,200* ($60,600* for married filing separately), itemized deductions are reduced by the lesser of three percent of adjusted gross income exceeding that amount or 80 percent of the itemized deductions.[112] The reduction does not apply to the deductions for medical expenses, investment interest, casualty losses, or wagering losses.[113]

Trusts. The reduction does not apply to trusts.[114]

[3] Floor on Miscellaneous Itemized Deductions

Individuals. An individual can take certain itemized deductions only to the extent that they exceed two percent of his adjusted gross income.[115] These

---

[107] See Ch.18 on S corporations.

[108] IRC §§ 1(a)-1(d). All asterisked amounts in this section reflect the 1997 amounts, as indexed for inflation.

[109] IRC § 1(h).

[110] IRC § 55(b)(1)(A).

[111] IRC § 1(e).

[112] IRC § 68(a).

[113] IRC § 68(c).

[114] IRC § 68(e).

[115] IRC § 67.

deductions include all itemized deductions, except deductions for: interest; state and local taxes; GSTT on income distributions from trusts; environmental taxes; casualty losses; wagering losses; charitable contributions; medical expenses; impairment-related work expenses; estate tax on income in respect of a decedent; personal property used in a short sale; restoration of substantial amounts held under claim of right; cost of annuity payments which cease before the investment is recovered; amortizable bond premium; and cooperative housing corporations.[116]

Trusts. Trusts are also subject to this limitation, except that a trust is allowed to deduct the following without regard to the two percent limitation: (1) administrative expenses which were incurred as a result of the property being held in a trust; (2) distributions to beneficiaries; and (3) its personal exemption.[117] It is not completely clear what expenses are included as trust administrative expenses. The Sixth Circuit has held that investment advisory fees incurred by a nonprofessional trustee are not subject to the floor.[118] However, the Tax Court took the opposite view, and the IRS has nonacquiesced in the case.[119]

[4] Charitable Deduction

Individuals. An individual is subject to limitations on the deductibility of charitable contributions.[120] An individual does not get a charitable income tax deduction for amounts contributed to foreign charities, or to domestic charities for use outside of the United States.[121]

Trusts. A trust is entitled to an unlimited charitable deduction for charitable contributions required pursuant to its governing instrument, except against unrelated business taxable income (UBTI).[122] UBTI is subject to the same limitations as those that apply to an individual.[123] A trust can receive a charitable income tax deduction for a distribution to a foreign charity.[124]

[5] Personal Exemption

Individuals. The personal exemption for an individual is $2,650,* but is phased out at the rate of two percent for each $2,500 (or fraction thereof) by

---

[116] IRC § 67.

[117] IRC § 67(e).

[118] O'Neill v. Comm'r, 994 F2d 302 (6th Cir. 1993), rev'g 98 TC 227 (1992).

[119] 1994-2 CB 1.

[120] IRC § 170(b). These limitations are fully discussed in Ch. 32.

[121] IRC §§ 170(a)(1), 170(c)(2).

[122] IRC §§ 642(c), 681(a).

[123] IRC § 681(a).

[124] IRC § 642(c)(1).

which the individual's income exceeds a threshold.[125] The threshold starts at $181,800* (joint returns and surviving spouses), $151,500* (heads of households), $121,200* (other singles), and $90,900* (married filing separately).[126]

Trusts. A trust is entitled to a personal exemption of $300 (simple trusts) or $100 (other trusts), which is not subject to the phaseout.[127]

[6] Standard Deduction

Individuals. A nonitemizing individual is generally entitled to a standard deduction of $6,900* (married filing jointly), $6,050* (heads of households), $4,150* (other singles), or $3,450* (married filing separately).[128]

Trusts. A trust is not entitled to a standard deduction.[129]

---

[125] IRC § 151(d)(3).

[126] IRC §§ 151(d)(3)(C), 151(d)(4).

[127] IRC § 642(b).

[128] IRC § 63(c).

[129] IRC § 63(c)(6)(D).

CHAPTER **7**

Nontestamentary Transfers

¶ 7.01 EXPLANATION OF TESTAMENTARY AND NONTESTAMENTARY TRANSFERS

Some assets are part of a person's probate estate, are subject to the probate process, and pass according to the decedent's will.[1] These are called probate assets. An example would be property titled in a person's sole name, such as a stock certificate or a bank account.

Other assets bypass the probate process, and are not disposed of by the will. These are known as "nontestamentary" or "nonprobate" assets. Examples are revocable trusts, employee benefits, life insurance,[2] and some joint accounts.

Both testamentary and nontestamentary transfers are perfectly legitimate. Problems can occur when they are not properly coordinated. For example, the best drafted will in the world won't accomplish anything if the decedent's only assets are held in joint tenancy with right of survivorship. All of the property will pass outside of the will to the surviving joint tenant.

---

[1] Or according to the laws of intestacy, if he had no will. This concept is only footnoted, since persons with large estates should not die intestate. (It's simply not done.)

[2] Provided the beneficiary of the benefits or insurance is not the decedent's estate.

It is important in planning an estate to know exactly how assets[3] are held. Most people don't know the answer off the top of their heads, at least not with the specificity required to determine the disposition of the property. If practical, persons planning an estate should obtain evidence of the title of important assets.

¶ 7.02 REASONS TO AVOID PROBATE

Should special efforts be made to avoid probate? It depends on what a person's objectives are and on how onerous probate is in the jurisdiction(s) where it would be required.

[1] Privacy Concerns

Privacy concerns can be addressed by putting assets in a nonprobate format. Once a person dies, the will is probated and (in most jurisdictions) an inventory of the probate assets is filed with the court. Both the will and the inventory are matters of public record, and therefore can be examined by anyone who is interested. Some people do not care at all about the exposure of their wills and estates to the public eye; others find the prospect distasteful. Privacy is likely to be a significant concern to a person who has unusual dispositions in his estate plan or who is sensitive about the publicity of financial information after his death.

[a] Disposition of Assets

If Dad doesn't want the public to know how he is disposing of his property, a will is not the best dispositive vehicle for him. He might be better off, for example, putting the dispositive provisions of his estate plan in a revocable trust, which serves as a will substitute, but is not part of the probate proceedings. Why would Dad care whether anyone knew what he did with his estate? He might be concerned if he is disinheriting a child or otherwise treating one child differently from others. There may be gifts to employees or close friends that could be misconstrued by a scandal-hungry public. These kinds of arrangements can be made privately by nonprobate dispositions.

[b] Composition of Estate

Probate assets must ordinarily be listed on an inventory, which is filed in the public records. Often, people with substantial estates are not enthusiastic

---

[3] At least the significant assets.

about this. Assets held in nonprobate form will normally not have to be listed on a publicly available inventory.

> **EXAMPLE:** Husband and Wife have a substantial estate. At the death of one spouse, they do not want the survivor's property to become a matter of public record, partly for reasons of privacy and partly so that fortune hunters and other scoundrels will not be as likely to start pestering the survivor.

> **EXAMPLE:** Husband and Wife own an extensive art collection. They are worried that listing their art collection in the public records will attract thieves and other unscrupulous characters.

[c] Meeting These Two Different Privacy Concerns

[i] Disposition of assets. Privacy regarding the disposition of assets can be attained, even with probate assets. The device used to achieve this is called a "pour-over" will. It leaves the probate assets to a revocable trust or other entity whose terms are not subject to public disclosure.

[ii] Composition of estate. However, privacy with respect to the composition of the estate can only be attained by putting the assets into nonprobate form before the person's death. This is because whatever he owned at date of death in probate form will ordinarily be subject to inclusion in a probate inventory, regardless of whether it passes to a revocable trust or other nonprobate entity. Hence, re-titling the assets in nonprobate form during the person's life will be necessary in order to avoid listing the assets and their values in the probate records at his death.

[d] Use of Nominee Entities

Nominee entities are sometimes used for privacy purposes. For example, Dad may wish to sell property *A*, and he may not want the buyer to know that he is the selling party. Therefore, he may place the property into a nominee corporation, nominee partnership, or other nominee entity as his agent to sell the property for him as the undisclosed principal. Such nominee entities are commonly used to hold property for a person who does not wish to be known as the owner of the property, for whatever reason.

Nominee arrangements may protect a person's privacy during lifetime. However, when the person dies, the property owned by the nominee agent will have to be listed on the probate inventory. That is, if Dad has hired Corporation *A* to act as his agent to hold Blackacre and Dad dies, the probate inventory will have to disclose that Dad owned Blackacre and that the entity was merely an agent.[4]

Therefore, if the principal wants the beneficial ownership of property held by the nominee entity to remain unknown at his death, the principal could fund a revocable trust with the property and have a nominee entity serve as agent for the trust. Even if a revocable trust is not used, the principal must nevertheless find some means to get the property into nonprobate form. Use of the nominee entity alone will not do the trick.

[2] Avoid Expense and Trouble of Court-Supervised Proceedings

Probate assets normally require probate either in the state of the decedent's domicile (everything but real estate) or in the state where the property is located (real estate). The difficulty of probate will vary depending upon the particular state. Some states have quite onerous proceedings, where the executor must obtain court approval for virtually every action. This process can be very expensive, time-consuming, and cumbersome. Other states have quite streamlined procedures.

There is no question that the disposition of assets outside of probate or in a state with simplified probate procedures is usually less expensive and involves less red tape than probate proceedings in states with complex probate laws. This is because the executor (if one is necessary) will need to take fewer legal actions and obtain fewer court approvals. On the other hand, the judicial protection built into the more complicated probate systems is not present (at least to the same degree) in streamlined systems which allow the executor to operate fairly independently of court supervision or in nonprobate dispositions which typically have no judicial involvement.

What are the extra protections offered by probate? With supervised proceedings, it is more difficult for the executor to make off with assets, make mistakes borne of inexperience, or otherwise cause harm to the estate. The executor is also protected by court approval of his decisions, making him less vulnerable to lawsuits by the estate's creditors or beneficiaries.

The decision to go with a simplified administration or nonprobate route is based on a judgment regarding the tradeoff between extra expense and delay and extra protections. Most people will opt for the simplified administration and/or nonprobate dispositions if the extra expense and delay of probate are expected to be substantial.

---

[4] If the entity owned the property in its own right, and not just as agent, the property would not have to be included in the probate inventory. However, for income tax reasons, it will usually be important to use the agency structure. Otherwise, an entity level tax will be incurred on income from, or sale of, the property; or, in a pass-through entity, the tax will be incurred by the entity owner(s), who will normally not be the principal(s).

One exception might be the insolvent estate. In the insolvent estate, the executor will be responsible for paying the debts according to statutorily prescribed priorities of claims against the estate. Accordingly, he will probably prefer the protection of a court determination of priorities. If he pays the debts without court supervision, he will usually be personally liable for the consequences of a payment in the wrong order.

In states that have streamlined probate proceedings, extensive nonprobate planning to avoid expense and delay is not necessarily worthwhile. Putting assets into certain types of nonprobate forms will involve start-up costs, and certain formats will involve additional administrative burdens during the person's life. Wherever a person lives, nonprobate planning is usually a good idea if the person owns real estate in several jurisdictions. For example, a client who lives in Texas can provide for independent administration (which is very easy) with a will. But if she has real estate located in New York or California (or some other state with a complex probate system), she may wish to use, for example, a revocable trust to hold the real property located in those jurisdictions.

[3] Property Management in Case of Incapacity

Certain types of nonprobate formats allow management of one person's assets by another during the person's lifetime. For example, a person (i.e., grantor) can put property into a revocable trust and appoint another person as trustee to manage the property during any period of time that the grantor is incapacitated.

[4] Creditors

Property in the probate estate is subject to the claims of the decedent's creditors. Often, property that passes outside of probate is not subject to such claims, at least if placement of the decedent's property in nontestamentary form was not a fraudulent conveyance.

[5] Spousal Election

In states that require spousal elective shares, property in a revocable trust, as well as other nonprobate property, may not be subject to the spousal election to take against the will.

Let's look at some specific examples of nonprobate dispositions.

¶ 7.03 REVOCABLE TRUSTS

The revocable trust is one of the most popular nontestamentary devices. The person who establishes the trust is called the "settlor" or "grantor." The settlor transfers title to certain assets to a trust. "Revocable" means that the trust can be "revoked," or canceled, by the settlor. Whatever is held by the trust at the settlor's death passes according to the trust instrument—outside of the probate process. The trust is normally used as a substitute for a will. Hence, it will provide for the disposition of the person's assets at death; the terms of the disposition will then not be a matter of public record.

The revocable trust is usually accompanied by a pour-over will, which leaves everything which is still in the deceased settlor's name to the trust. If the revocable trust is not just an empty receptacle for the pour-over will, but actually contains assets, it is considered "funded."

[1] Making Use of Settlor's Knowledge

A funded revocable trust has an administrative advantage over probate. The settlor, who usually knows more than anyone else about the location of the records and the details of the property involved, is still alive when the trust is funded, and therefore can assist with the title transfers and other administrative matters. In the absence of this type of lifetime disposition, the executor is often left with the laborious task of plowing through the decedent's records to unearth the information necessary to administer the estate.

[2] Providing for Incapacity

The revocable trust should always be considered when incapacity is expected. If Mom becomes incapacitated and no plans have been made to deal with it, a court-supervised guardianship may be necessary to deal with Mom's property during her incapacity. Guardianships are notoriously expensive and time-consuming.

Prior to her incapacity, Mom could, instead, transfer her assets to a revocable trust. Then, after she becomes incapacitated, the revocable trust's trustee can manage the trust's assets for Mom's benefit free of court involvement.

Almost all of us will become incapacitated for some period during our lives, and none of us knows for sure whether or when the incapacity will occur. Hence, the revocable trust is an appropriate incapacity technique for anyone; however, it may be especially desirable for persons facing the imminent likelihood of incapacity. For example, a good candidate for a revocable trust would be someone who has been recently diagnosed with Alzheimer's disease and knows he must expect decreasing mental acuity. Other good prospects for a revocable trust would be someone who has been diagnosed with a terminal disease that is likely to cause unconsciousness or other physical or mental incapacity at some point, as well as someone who is facing a substantial risk of incapacity because of advanced age.

What if Mom, a person who needs incapacity planning, is worried about the expense and trouble of the revocable trust? Can an equivalent result be obtained by granting a friend or trusted person a power of attorney which does not terminate (or which becomes effective) on Mom's incapacity?[5] Maybe, but possibly not.

PRACTICE POINTER: One practical disadvantage of durable powers of attorney is that third parties are often reluctant to rely on them. The third party may want all sorts of extraneous evidence of Mom's incapacity, if that is relevant, or evidence of whether Mom was incapacitated when she initially signed the power. These same questions could equally as well be asked about a revocable trust. However, in practice, they almost never are. As a practical matter, it is frequently much easier to get third parties to rely on the authority of the trustee of a revocable trust than on the authority of an agent under a durable power of attorney.

[3] Privacy Offered by Revocable Trusts

The revocable trust will not be included in the court records, unless it is the subject of litigation, or a statute provides otherwise. In some states, however, the trustee may be required to file accountings with the court.[6]

If the trust is incorporated by reference in the will, a filing of the trust instrument may be required in the probate proceedings. Hence, such a reference in the will should be avoided, if possible.

As a practical matter, persons dealing with the trustee (e.g., banks, brokerage houses, and purchasers of trust property) may require copies of the trust instrument. Similarly, if litigation is instituted regarding the trust, a copy may need to be disclosed. Hence, it cannot be assured that the contents of the trust will always remain totally confidential, either during the settlor's life or after the settlor's death. A will, on the other hand, need not be revealed at all during the testator's life. The privacy issue, therefore, does not have a totally clear-cut resolution.

[4] Probate Avoidance and Rules of Interpretation

The revocable trust is usually not subject to court-supervised probate administration; it is generally administered and interpreted according to the laws relating to trusts, and not the laws governing estates.

---

[5] A power of attorney which does not terminate on the principal's incapacity is known as a "durable" power of attorney. See Ch. 43 on disability planning for more on powers of attorney.

[6] E.g., see Ga. Code Ann. § 53-7-180 (1997).

If the revocable trust contains real estate, however, care needs to be taken that the trust is valid and will be recognized in each state in which the real property is located. Additionally, the transfer of real property to the trust must be properly documented. Accordingly, especially where real estate is involved, consultation with local counsel is advised.

A person who executes and funds a revocable trust should almost always execute a will as well, to dispose of assets that were not transferred to the revocable trust and to accomplish things that cannot be done by a trust (e.g., appoint guardians for children and select an executor to receive and deal with claims and other matters associated with the probate estate). The will and revocable trust provisions should coordinate well. Both should have consistent tax clauses, as well.

[5] Creditors

Property in a revocable trust should not be subject to the deceased settlor's general creditors unless a state statute provides that it is available to creditors or the transfer to the trust was a fraudulent conveyance.[7]

[6] Spousal Election

Property in a revocable trust may not be subject to a spousal election against the decedent's dispositive plan.

[7] Tax Treatment During Settlor's Lifetime

During the settlor's life, the trust is ignored for income tax purposes. All items of income, gain, loss, deduction, and credit are reported directly by the settlor on his or her individual income tax return. In a similar fashion, transfers from the trust to other people will be considered gifts by the settlor, assuming that they would be gifts if made directly by the settlor. The IRS has taken the position, in some cases, that gifts from revocable trusts made within three years of the settlor's death are includable in the settlor's estate.[8]

[8] Tax Treatment After Settlor's Death

All assets of a revocable trust are included in the settlor's gross estate.[9] However, the trust will be subject to income tax as a trust, not as an estate. There are some significant differences, as discussed in the next paragraph.

---

[7] See Ch. 53 on asset protection.

[8] See Ch. 8 for an explanation.

[9] IRC § 2036.

[9] Differences in Income Tax Treatment Between Trusts and Estates

Revocable trusts normally become irrevocable on the settlor's death. There are several differences between the tax treatment of estates and irrevocable trusts which may make it advantageous to put certain property in one format rather than the other. Some of these are discussed in the following subparagraphs.

[a] Taxable Years

Trust. A trust must use a calendar year.[10]

Estate. An estate can use any taxable year, as long as it ends on the last day of a month.[11]

[b] Estimated Tax

Trust. A revocable trust which becomes irrevocable at the settlor's death must pay estimated tax unless (1) all of the trust was considered owned by the decedent for income tax purposes and (2) either the residue of the decedent's estate passes to the trust or, if there is no will admitted to probate, the trust is the primary entity responsible for paying debts, taxes, and administration expenses.[12] If both conditions are met, the trust does not have to pay estimated tax for any taxable year ending less than two years after the decedent's death. Any other trust must pay estimated tax from its inception.[13]

Estate. Estates do not have to pay estimated tax for any taxable year ending less than two years after the decedent's death.[14] Thus, if Mom dies on October 31, 1996 and her estate uses a calendar year, it will not have to pay estimated tax for the years 1996 or 1997.

[c] Estimated Tax Treated as Paid by Beneficiary

Depending on the facts, trust or estate income may be taxable to either the entity or the beneficiary. It may not be clear until after the taxable year has ended who will be taxable on the income. If a beneficiary does not receive a distribution until late in the year, or even in the following year (in the case of a trust), he may not have paid sufficient estimated tax for the year. To make matters worse, the entity may have paid the estimated tax on income that was

---

[10] IRC § 645(a).

[11] IRC §§ 7701(a)(23), 7701(a)(24).

[12] IRC § 6654(l)(2)(B).

[13] IRC § 6654(l)(1).

[14] IRC § 6654(l)(2)(A).

not ultimately taxed to it. It is helpful in such a case if the entity's estimated tax can be credited to the beneficiary.

Trust. The trustee may elect to treat estimated tax paid by the trust as paid by a beneficiary.[15]

Estate. An executor can only make this election in the last taxable year of the estate.[16]

[d] Personal Exemption

Trust. A simple trust has an exemption of $300. A complex trust has a personal exemption of $100.[17]

Estate. An estate has a personal exemption of $600.[18]

[e] Sixty-Five-Day Rule

Trust. A trust receives a distribution deduction for certain amounts of income distributed within the taxable year in which the income was earned.[19] Additionally, if trust income is earned in Year One, the trust can make distributions during the first 65 days of Year Two and elect to treat these distributions as made in Year One.[20] This election can be particularly useful, for example, when the trustee doesn't know exactly how much the trust income is until the year is over.

Estate. An estate receives a distribution deduction for certain amounts of income distributed within the taxable year in which the income was earned.[21] However, the sixty-five day election is not available to estates.

[f] Simple Trust Provisions

The "simple trust" rules for trusts that are required to distribute income currently do not apply to estates.[22]

[g] Throwback Rule

Trust. Ordinarily, when a trust distributes accumulated income, a calculation is made that may result in a "throwback" tax payable by the beneficiary. This throwback tax liability will arise if, in general, the beneficiary would have

---

[15] IRC § 643(g)(1).

[16] IRC § 643(g)(3).

[17] IRC § 642(b).

[18] IRC § 642(b).

[19] IRC §§ 651, 661.

[20] IRC § 663(b).

[21] IRC §§ 651, 661.

[22] IRC §§ 651, 652. These rules are explained in Ch. 6.

been taxed at a higher rate had the income been distributed rather than accumulated.[23] This is known as the throwback rule.[24]

Estate. The throwback rule does not apply to estates. Distributions carrying out accumulated income of an estate are not taxable to the beneficiary, regardless of the beneficiary's income tax status vis-à-vis the estate.

[h] Multiple Trust Rule

Trust. If income is accumulated in more than two trusts for the same beneficiary in the same year, some punitive income tax results can occur.[25]

Estate. An estate is not subject to the multiple trust rule.

[i] Separate Share Rule

Trust. Separate and independent shares of trusts are taxed as separate trusts.[26]

Estate. The separate share rule is not applicable to estates.

[j] Charitable Set-Aside Deduction

Trust. A trust is not eligible for a charitable set-aside deduction.[27] In order to take a charitable deduction in Year One, the trust must actually distribute the income to the charity by the end of Year Two.[28] If it does not distribute the income in that time period, it will be subject to tax on the income. It is not always possible or desirable to force out distributions of income. In such cases, it is necessary to incur a tax on trust income that is ultimately going to charity—not a good situation.[29]

Estate. An estate is entitled to an unlimited charitable deduction for income that is paid to or permanently set aside for charity pursuant to the terms of the will.[30] Thus, an estate can receive a charitable income tax deduction in Year One, even if the income earned in Year One is not distributed

---

[23] IRC § 667.

[24] See Ch. 6 for an explanation.

[25] IRC § 667(c). See Ch. 6.

[26] IRC § 663(c).

[27] Certain trusts created before October 10, 1969 or established by a will executed before October 10, 1969 are eligible for a set-aside deduction. IRC § 642(c)(2).

[28] IRC § 642(c)(2).

[29] For example, an actual case existed in Texas where the issue was which of two charities was going to take the assets of a trust. The income could not be distributed, since the proper distributee was not known, so tax had to be paid on the trust income. If the assets had been in an estate, instead of a revocable trust, no income tax would have been due.

[30] IRC §§ 642(c)(1), 642(c)(2).

to charity until the estate is closed. Accordingly, an estate may be a better format than a revocable trust if a charitable income tax set-aside deduction is important.

[k] Unrelated Business Taxable Income

Trust. A trust's charitable income tax deduction from unrelated business taxable income is limited to the deduction allowable to individuals.[31]

Estate. An estate's charitable income tax deduction is not so limited.

[l] Actively Managed Real Estate—Passive Loss Rules

When a person is engaged in a passive activity, normally, his losses from that activity cannot exceed his income from that activity and other passive activities.[32] Rental activities are automatically considered passive, subject to certain exceptions.[33] One of the exceptions allows a natural person who is involved in the active management of real estate to shelter up to $25,000 of nonpassive income with rental real estate losses, subject to a phase-out for people with incomes over a certain level.[34]

Trust. There is no active management exception for a trust.

Estate. If an individual actively participated in rental activities during his life, the exception will be available for those activities in the individual's estate for taxable years ending less than two years after the individual's death, reduced by certain amounts allowed to the surviving spouse.[35]

[m] Related Parties

[i] Disallowed losses.

Trust. Losses are disallowed on transactions between a trust and a beneficiary.[36]

Estate. Losses are allowed on transactions between an estate and a beneficiary.

---

[31] That is, it is limited to a percentage of unrelated business taxable income. The percentage depends on what kind of charity and what kind of property is involved. IRC §§ 642(c)(4), 681; Treas. Reg. § 1.681(a)-2.

[32] IRC § 469.

[33] IRC § 469(c)(2).

[34] IRC § 469(i).

[35] IRC § 469(i)(4).

[36] IRC §§ 267(a)(1), 267(b)(6).

[ii] Sale of depreciable property. If depreciable property is sold to a related party, gain is treated as ordinary income.[37]

Trust. For this purpose, an individual and any trust in which he or his spouse had more than a remote contingent interest are related parties.[38]

Estate. An estate and a beneficiary are not related for this purpose.

[n] Deductions for Depreciation and Depletion

Trust. The depreciation and depletion deductions of a trust are apportioned between the income beneficiary and the trustee on the basis of trust income allocable to each, except to the extent that the trustee maintains a reserve.[39]

Estate. The deduction for an estate is apportioned between the estate and the beneficiaries on the basis of estate income which is allocable to each.[40]

[o] Limitations on Holding S Stock

Trust. For two years after the settlor's death, a revocable trust that continues in irrevocable form after the settlor's death can hold S corporation stock which was already in the trust at the settlor's death.[41] The trust is also eligible for the two-year holding period if it was funded entirely with community property or if the only other owner of trust property is the decedent's spouse.[42]

Estate. An estate is eligible to hold S corporation stock as long as it is legitimately open.

¶ 7.04 LIFE INSURANCE

Life insurance will normally pass pursuant to a beneficiary designation, rather than pursuant to the will of the owner of the policy. In order to make sure that the life insurance coordinates with the estate plan, some planners like to name the owner's estate as the beneficiary of the policy; in that case, of course, the property would go through the owner's probate estate, and pass according to his will. That is not necessarily a bad thing. It does, however, expose the life insurance proceeds to the decedent's creditors, whereas proceeds passing to named life insurance beneficiaries may not be subject to the claims of the

---

[37] IRC § 1239(a).

[38] IRC § 1239(b)(2).

[39] Treas. Reg. §§ 1.167(h)-1(b), 1.611-1(c)(4).

[40] Treas. Reg. §§ 1.167(h)-1(c), 1.611-1(c)(5).

[41] IRC § 1361(c)(2)(A)(ii).

[42] Treas. Reg. § 1.1361-1(h)(1)(ii).

decedent's creditors.[43] To achieve both objectives—most states allow an unfunded revocable trust, or a trust under the will, to be named as beneficiary of a life insurance policy without having it treated as a payment of policy proceeds to the estate.

In any case, if substantial insurance is owned, the estate planner should be sure that the beneficiary designations of the life insurance are coordinated with the estate plan as a whole.

¶ 7.05 JOINTLY HELD ASSETS

Property held in certain forms of joint ownership will pass directly to the joint owner on one owner's death, thereby bypassing probate. These forms include: joint tenancy with right of survivorship, tenancy by the entirety, a payable on death account, or a trust account where there is no actual trust. Generally speaking, if A and B hold property pursuant to one of these forms, the rules discussed in the following subparagraphs will apply.

[1] Joint Tenants With Right of Survivorship

If A and B own property as joint tenants with right of survivorship and A dies, B will automatically take the property. State law varies as to what type of title is sufficient to result in a joint tenancy with right of survivorship, as opposed to joint tenancy without right of survivorship. What if Mom and Dad take property as joint tenants, without mentioning a right of survivorship? Some states presume that the property is survivorship property; others require survivorship language to be spelled out, or presume the opposite.

[2] Tenancy by the Entirety

Tenancy by the entirety is a nonprobate form of property ownership between spouses. It is only available in a few states. If the spouses own property as tenants by the entirety, the property will pass automatically on the first spouse's death to the surviving spouse.

[3] Payable on Death Account

If A holds an account which is titled as "A, payable on death to B," then in most states, the asset is indeed payable to B, and the property is not a probate asset.

---

[43] See Ch. 53 on asset protection.

[4] Nominal Trust Account

In many states, if A owns property in a trust account for B and there is no actual trust arrangement, the property will pass directly to B on A's death.

[5] Creditors' Rights

Statutes sometimes often provide that nonprobate assets held in joint ownership are subject to the decdent's debts and certain other estate obligations if the probate estate is insolvent. Additionally, these assets will usually be subject to the decedent's creditors if the transfer of title to a nonprobate form was a fraudulent conveyance.

[6] Joint Accounts Which Are Not Survivorship Accounts

Not all joint accounts will bypass probate. A tenancy in common is the classic example. A tenancy in common or joint tenancy without right of survivorship is a probate asset, and the decedent's interest in such property will pass according to his will.

¶ 7.06 EMPLOYEE BENEFIT PLANS AND IRAS

Employee benefit plans and IRAs are generally governed by beneficiary designation and do not pass pursuant to a will unless the beneficiary is the estate. Hence, it is important to coordinate the beneficiary designations of a person's significant benefit plans and IRAs with his or her estate plan as a whole.[44]

¶ 7.07 OTHER NONTESTAMENTARY TRANSFERS

[1] Annuities

Annuities usually pass outside of the owner's estate to a designated beneficiary.

[2] Texas Community Property

Community property is allowed to be held with right of survivorship in Texas.[45]

---

[44] Qualified employee plans and IRAs are discussed in detail in Ch. 14.

[45] Tex. Prob. Code Ann. § 451 (West Supp. 1996).

[3] Property Subject to Nontestamentary Dispositive Instruments

Uniform Probate Code Section 6-101 says that provisions in certain instruments are nontestamentary. So, the Uniform Probate Code does not invalidate such an instrument as not complying with the statute of wills.

The provisions are "that money or other benefits . . . due to, controlled by, or owned by a decedent before death must be paid after the decedent's death to a person whom the decedent designates either in the instrument or in a separate writing, including a will, executed either before or at the same time as the instrument, or later."

The instruments include an insurance policy, contract of employment, bond, mortgage, promissory note, certificated or uncertificated security, account agreement, custodial agreement, deposit agreement, compensation plan, pension plan, individual retirement plan, employee benefit plan, trust, conveyance, deed of gift, marital property agreement, or any other written instrument of a similar nature.

Read literally, this statute could easily render the statute of wills moot, since it would allow virtually any type of writing to operate as a beneficiary designation. Some courts have, however, held that the statute does not go that far.[46]

¶ 7.08 GIFTED PROPERTY

Some gifted property is included in the gross estate, but not included in the probate estate (since someone else owns it).[47]

¶ 7.09 FAMILY ENTITIES

Sometimes, family entities are used as nonprobate devices.

> EXAMPLE: Mom transfers her oil and gas interests to a family partnership in exchange for a partnership interest. On her death, the oil and gas interests themselves will not be subject to probate. However, her interest in the entity will.

Note that the family partnership will save the expense and trouble of running the oil and gas interests through probate, but may not meet privacy objectives.

---

[46] E.g., Hibbler v. Knight, 735 SW2d 924, 927 (Tex. App.—Houston (1st Dist.) 1987, writ ref'd n.r.e.) (contract between husband and wife purportedly leaving wife husband's entire estate was fundamentally testamentary in nature and was therefore invalid; statutory exception allowing nontestamentary contracts to convey property did not permit conveyance of entire estate).

[47] See Ch. 2 for a description.

¶ 7.10 TAX APPORTIONMENT

In a large taxable estate, the tax clause will govern more property than the dispositive clauses. It is critical to coordinate the tax apportionment clause with all transfers—both testamentary and nontestamentary. The general common law rule on death is that expenses and taxes are paid from the residue of the estate,[48] and that specific bequests and nonprobate assets are not reachable for these types of expenses unless the residue of the estate is insolvent.[49] Some states have differing apportionment statutes with respect to various assets. Many states allow a will or nontestamentary instrument to apportion tax, debts, and expenses to nonprobate assets, at least in the proportion to which they generate such expenses, debts, and taxes. This would be an important clause to have in a will or other nontestamentary instrument if the nontestamentary transfers are significant enough to cause difficulties if the taxes and expenses attributed to them are paid from the probate estate.

> EXAMPLE: Suppose Dad names his two daughters by his first marriage as the beneficiaries of a $2,000,000 insurance policy and names his second wife as the beneficiary of the residue of his estate ($1,000,000 before taxes). The will apportions all taxes to the residue. Wife will have to bear the estate taxes on the insurance proceeds received by the daughters, which will wipe out her entire inheritance if Dad is in the maximum estate tax bracket. Careful attention to apportionment must be paid.

The federal tax laws provide for apportionment of estate tax on certain nonprobate property to the recipients, subject to contrary provision by the will. If the gross estate includes life insurance proceeds, the beneficiary is liable to the estate for the fraction of the estate taxes represented by the amount of the proceeds divided by the taxable estate. Proceeds that qualify for the marital deduction are exempt from sharing in the tax.[50] (The statute does not address proceeds qualifying for the charitable deduction.) A federal apportionment rule also exists for power of appointment property that is included in the estate.[51] A similar rule exists for property included in the decedent's estate under Section 2036 (transfers with prohibited retained powers and interests).[52] A right of recovery for estate taxes also exists for QTIP property that is included in the surviving spouse's estate. However, the QTIP trust must bear tax at the marginal rate, not the average rate.[53]

---

[48] E.g., Guaranty Nat'l Bank v. Mitchell, 111 SE 2d 494, 496 (W. Va. 1959).

[49] E.g., Bigoness v. Anderson, 106 F. Supp. 986-988 (DDC 1952); Seattle First Nat'l Bank v. Macomber, 203 P2d 1078 (Wash. 1949).

[50] IRC § 2206.

[51] IRC § 2207.

[52] IRC § 2207B.

[53] IRC § 2207A.

If the person doing his estate plan does not want taxes and expenses apportioned in the manner provided by state and federal laws, the will or other dispositive document must provide differently.

PART **II**

The Power of Lifetime Gifts

CHAPTER **8**

Tax Economics of Lifetime Gifts

¶ 8.01 INTRODUCTION—COPING WITH CHANGE

Wealthy individuals can usually afford to make lifetime gifts. Whether they should, from a tax point of view, is not always an easy question. Consideration of the tax effects of gifts must take into account both currently scheduled and speculative changes in the transfer tax system.

Currently scheduled changes. Under the Economic Growth and Tax Relief Act of 2001 (EGTRRA), the gift tax exclusion amount remains at $1 million indefinitely. The estate tax and generation-skipping transfer tax exemptions, however, are:

Exclusion Amount	Year
$1,000,000	2003
$1,500,000	2004–2005
$2,000,000	2006–2008
$3,500,000	2009
Unlimited	2010
$1,000,000	2011 forward (estate tax)
$1,000,000 as adjusted for inflation	2011 forward (GSTT)

Additionally, the maximum transfer tax rates are:

Rate	Year
49%	2003
48	2004
47	2005
46	2006
45	2007-2009
0 (estate tax)	2010
35 (gift tax)	2010
55	2011 forward

Assets included in the estate receive a new basis of fair market value for decedents dying before and after 2010. Carryover basis applies, with certain exceptions, for decedents dying in 2010. Assets given as a lifetime gift take a carryover basis, plus a partial adjustment for gift taxes paid, for all years.[1]

Speculative changes. No one expects the law to remain in place as is. Speculations on the future exist as to exemption amounts, rates, outright repeal, and basis adjustments. Thus, an advisor to a person contemplating a gift must make a best guess as to the future of the various taxes.

For the small to middle-sized estate (under $7 million for a married couple, or $3,500,000 for a single person), the likelihood that increased exemptions will remain in place may be sufficient reason to restrict lifetime donative transfers to gifts that do not generate a gift tax, unless the prospective donor is expected to die before the exemptions fully phase in, or there is some other compelling reason to make the taxable gift. Persons with estates of this size are often not in a position to make gifts in excess of $1 million, in any case.

---

[1] If, however, the adjusted basis of the asset exceeds its fair market value at the time of the gift, then the donee must use that fair market value for determining loss.

For larger estates, an advisor must consider the likelihood of the estate tax disappearing. Many believe that Congress will not repeal the tax on larger estates. Many others believe that it will. Advisors who don't expect a complete repeal may wish to continue recommending gifts that generate a tax in appropriate circumstances. Those who do expect a complete repeal may not.

When should a taxpayer consider gifts, and what types of estate planning transfers are desirable?

Despite the current uncertainty, gifts that do not generate a tax will often still make sense for taxpayers of all means. Planning could include annual exclusion gifts, payment of educational and medical expenses, use of the $1 million gift tax applicable exclusion amount, and payment of tax on the income of grantor trusts.[2] These gifts can get appreciation and income out of the estate in case the estate turns out to be taxable, and take advantage of any favorable valuation advantages of gifts.

Estate freezing devices[3] (e.g., GRATs, sales to IDGTs, loans) are also still appropriate in many cases. These techniques involve little or no gift tax, move income and appreciation out of the estate, and take advantage of favorable gift tax valuation rules.

Additionally, gifts may still be a good gamble where property has a relatively minor value today but is expected to appreciate substantially in future years.

Taxable gifts by persons who are likely not to live until 2010 may also be advisable under appropriate circumstances.

For taxpayers who expect to outlive 2010 and have large estates, taxable gifts will often be a good idea if estate tax repeal does not come to pass. These individuals and their advisors should check their crystal balls, make the best prediction they can about the future of the estate tax, and act accordingly.

Advantages of gifts under current system. If one predicts that the estate tax will remain in place for a particular taxpayer, gifts are highly tax-favored. Why? Three reasons:

- The gift tax rate is generally much lower than the estate tax rate;
- Valuation of a transfer for gift tax purposes may be lower than the value for estate tax purposes;[4] and
- Any income and appreciation accruing from the gifted property from the date of the gift forward escape transfer taxation to the donor altogether.

---

[2] Discussed in Chapter 6.

[3] Discussed in Part VII, Chapters 28–31, on estate freezing techniques.

[4] For example, gifts may be eligible for discounting due to fractionalization of interests and other factors that may not always be available for estate transfers. Valuation is discussed in Part VI.

Of course, the gift tax must be paid in the year following the gift,[5] and the tax money is not thereafter available to earn income for the donor. However, strictly from a transfer tax point of view, at the maximum rates, the advantages of making lifetime gifts outweigh the effect of the forgone interest on gift tax paid, where consistent assumptions regarding the rate of return on assets are used and the value of the property does not decline.

Note: The material in this chapter assumes a 50 percent[6] maximum transfer tax rate, and that all transfers are taxed at that rate, unless otherwise noted. The actual maximum rates will vary slightly from year to year, but the concepts illustrated apply, regardless of the tax rate used.

¶ 8.02 TAX-EXCLUSIVE RATE

To understand the transfer tax system, it is essential to have a firm grasp of the concept of tax-exclusive rates and tax-inclusive rates, as well as the enormous difference this concept makes in the effective tax rate on a transfer. People often find it difficult to accept the notion that gift tax rates are lower than estate tax rates. This is unsurprising—the same rate table is used for both taxes,[7] and this table shows the same rates applying to the same amounts transferred.

So, how do estate tax rates successfully masquerade as their kinder, gentler sisters, the gift tax rates? The base to which the rates apply is different. The estate tax is imposed on the transferred property (before tax), and is payable out of the transferred property. The gift tax is imposed on the transferor, and is payable out of the transferor's other property. This difference means that the maximum gift tax rate is about half the maximum estate tax rate (even though the same rate table is used for both taxes).

This is easier to see by comparing the results of the following two situations, assuming a 50 percent rate. In situation one, Mom leaves $1 million to Child, the estate tax is $500,000, the tax is payable out of the $1 million be-

---

[5] The gift tax return is generally due on the due date of the income tax return for the year of gift. IRC § 6075(b). So, a gift made in 2003 would generally be reported on April 15, August 15, or October 15 of 2004, depending on the donor's due date for his income tax return. The gift tax is payable on the due date of the income tax return, without regard to extensions, even if an extension of time for filing the return has been given. IRC § 6151(a).

[6] For current year's marginal rate, see Appendix ¶ A.01, Table of Indexed Amounts, in supplement.

[7] IRC §§ 2001, 2502.

quest, and Child ultimately receives $500,000. In situation two, Mom gives $1 million to Child, the gift tax is $500,000, the tax is payable by Mom, and Child ultimately receives $1 million.

Thus, if Mom dies, it costs her $500,000 to transfer $500,000 to Child. If Mom makes a gift, it costs her $500,000 to transfer $1 million to Child. This is because the estate tax base includes the tax and the gift tax base does not. In other words, the gift tax is tax-exclusive, and the estate tax is tax-inclusive.[8] The difference in the two effective tax rates is dramatic. At the 50 percent rate, it costs $.50 in tax to transfer $1.00 by gift, and $1.00 in tax to transfer the same $1.00 at death.

Another way of viewing this difference is by looking at the costs of assuring that Child gets $1 million after the payment of the applicable transfer tax. If Mom dies and leaves $1 million to Child, the estate tax incurred to get the full $1 million to Child is $1 million, and the total cost of the bequest and tax is $2 million. If Mom gives $1 million to Child, the gift tax cost of transferring $1 million to Child is $500,000, and the total cost to Mom of the gift and gift tax is $1,500,000.

One last way of looking at this same situation is as follows. Again, Mom has $1 million. If she dies, bequeathing the money to Child, the estate tax is $500,000, and Child gets $500,000 after payment of the tax. If Mom had used the same $1 million to make the gift and pay gift tax during her life, the gift tax would have been $333,333—50 percent of the amount actually received by the child ($666,667).

If both taxes are computed as a percentage of the transferred property plus the tax (on a tax-inclusive basis), the maximum gift tax rate[9] is about 33⅓ percent and the maximum estate tax rate[10] is 50 percent. If both taxes are computed as a percentage of the transferred property only (on a tax-exclusive basis), the maximum gift tax rate[11] is 50 percent and the maximum estate tax rate[12] is 100 percent.

Practice Pointer: To realize the advantage of the difference in rates described above, the donor must survive for three years after the gift is made.[13]

---

[8] IRC § 2501 (tax applied to gifted amount); IRC § 2001 (estate tax applied to entire estate, including portion of estate used to pay tax).

[9] This example disregards the 60 percent bubble that existed until December 31, 2001. The bubble (i.e., the extra five percent of tax imposed on transfers between $10 million and $17,184,000) is scheduled to return with the scheduled sunsetting of EGTRRA in 2011.

[10] Disregarding the 60 percent bubble.

[11] Disregarding the 60 percent bubble.

[12] Disregarding the 60 percent bubble.

[13] IRC § 2035(c). See explanation at ¶ 8.04[2] infra.

¶ 8.03 INCOME AND APPRECIATION OF GIFTED ASSETS IS TRANSFER-TAX FREE

In addition to the difference in rates applied to the property actually transferred, the rate on the income and appreciation of the gifted assets after the gift is made is hard to beat. All the income and appreciation of the gifted property escape any further estate and gift taxation to the donor. This consequence argues, of course, for early gifts.

> **EXAMPLE:** Dad gives $1 million to Child. Gift tax is $500,000. The gifted property earns 5 percent per year after-tax, and Child does not consume any of the property or its income. Therefore, if Dad dies 20 years later, the gifted property, along with its earnings, will be worth $2,653,298 in Child's hands. No further transfer tax will be due at Dad's death. Total cost to Dad of making the gift, including gift tax, is $1,500,000. On the other hand, if Dad had waited until he died to transfer the property, estate tax on the $2,653,298 would have been $1,326,649, leaving $1,326,649 for Child.

Forgone earnings on the gift tax. Now, to be accurate, we should remember that the $500,000 gift tax paid in the above example could have earned income or otherwise grown for an additional 20 years in Dad's hands if the gift had not been made. If we assume the same 5 percent per year after-tax return on the entire $1,500,000, Dad would have had $3,979,947 at his death. Estate tax of 50 percent of that amount would be $1,989,973, leaving $1,989,973 for Child. Therefore, even taking the forgone earnings on the gift tax into account, Child would have received $663,324 more with the early gift and payment of gift tax than if Dad had held all of the property and income until his death 20 years later and then left it to Child.

This analysis illustrates the principle that, in considering the economic effect of a gift versus an estate transfer at maximum rates, the negative effect of forgone earnings on the gift tax will be less than the positive effects of (1) the rate differential on the initial gift and (2) transfer-tax-free earnings on that gift, provided that consistent assumptions are used (at least, if the property does not actually decline in value).

To further illustrate this point, the following table charts the difference between the amounts received by Child in the gift/inheritance scenarios where Mom has $1 million (which she wants to use to make a gift to Child and pay any transfer tax thereon) and Mom's death occurs at various alternative times during a 20-year period. For purposes of the table, it is assumed that (1) if Mom made a gift to Child on Date *X*, a gift tax of $333,333 would be due and the net gift to Child would thus be $666,667; (2) if Mom invested the $1 million or Child invested the amount of the gift, either could realize a 5 percent after-tax return; (3) Mom or Child would reinvest all earnings, and (4) a 50 percent estate tax would apply at Mom's death.

AMOUNT RECEIVED BY CHILD AFTER GIFT OR ESTATE TAX

Transfer by Gift on Date X	Transfer at Death Rather Than Gift	Death Occurs This Many Years After Date X
$500,000*	$500,000	On Date X
$533,333*	$525,000	1
$850,855	$638,141	5
$1,085,930	$814,447	10
$1,385,953	$1,039,464	15
$1,768,866	$1,326,649	20

* When the gift occurs within three years of Mom's death (i.e., the first two cases), the gift tax paid with respect to the gift on date X will be brought back into Mom's estate, thus increasing the cost of the lifetime transfer.

¶ 8.04 GIFT/GIFT TAX INCLUDED IN DONOR'S ESTATE

The situation becomes even less straightforward if a transfer is contemplated that may result in the gift or gift tax (or both) being included in the donor's estate.

[1] Gift Included in the Estate

Certain gifts may be included in the donor's estate if he dies within three years after the gift is made (three-year rule), or if he dies while retaining certain powers or interests in the gifted property.[14]

[a] Gifts Included Under the Three-Year Rule

This rule is discussed fully in Chapter 2. Summarizing here—gifts includible under this rule are gifts of property made within the three-year period prior to the donor's death which, had the donor not made the gifts, would have

---

[14] Discussed in detail in Chapter 2.

been includible in the donor's estate under one of the following sections:[15] Section 2036,[16] Section 2037,[17] Section 2038,[18] or Section 2042.[19]

What is the practical application of this formidable-sounding rule? The good news is that it does not apply to most situations. Consider a plain vanilla gift, either outright to the recipient or to a trust, that is not included in the donor's estate under one of the above sections. If the donor had not made the gift, the property would have been included in his estate under Section 2033 (property owned by the decedent), and so the gift would not be affected by the three-year rule. Also not affected are transfers of property that, if the donor had retained the property, would have been included in the donor's estate under Section 2039 (certain annuities), Section 2040 (property held in joint tenancy with right of survivorship), or Section 2041 (powers of appointment).

Notwithstanding the general rule, a gift made from any portion of a trust that was revocable by the grantor will not be subject to inclusion in the estate under the three-year rule unless it would have been so included if the transfer had been made directly by the grantor.[20]

So, when does the three-year rule come into play? As a practical matter, it usually arises with gifts of life insurance policies. If a donor gives away a life insurance policy on his life and dies within three years after the gift, the policy proceeds are included in the donor's estate.[21] The rule also applies for purposes of qualifying for certain tax advantages related to businesses.[22] It could also apply to include gifts made from irrevocable trusts if the grantor's retained benefits or rights would have caused the trust to be included in the grantor's estate under Sections 2036–2038[23] and the grantor surrenders those benefits or rights within three years of his death.

---

[15] IRC § 2035(a).

[16] This section applies when the donor has retained certain rights to income or possession of the transferred property or prohibited controls over its enjoyment.

[17] This section applies when the gift takes effect at the death of the donor and the donor retains at least a 5 percent reversionary interest.

[18] This section applies when the donor has power to amend, alter, revoke, or terminate enjoyment of the property.

[19] This section applies when an insured has incidents of ownership in an insurance policy on his life.

[20] IRC § 2035(e), applying to decedents dying after August 5, 1997. See AOD 1995-006 (Aug. 7, 1995) for treatment before that date. An example of such a transfer would be a gift of a life insurance policy on the grantor's life from the revocable trust.

[21] IRC §§ 2035(a), 2042.

[22] IRC §§ 2035(c) (relating to IRC §§ 303, 2032A, and 6166), 2057(c)(2)(a)(iii). See Chapters 45, 46, 48, and 50.

[23] Discussed in Chapters 2 and 3.

[b] Effect of Inclusion of a Gift in the Estate

If gifted property is included in the estate, that property's value at date of death (not date of gift) will be used to determine the estate tax, the estate tax rates will apply, and, if gift tax was paid, the total transfer tax will have been at least partially paid early in the form of gift tax. Other aspects of the estate plan could also be affected by estate inclusion.[24] However, the income earned by the gifted property between the date of gift and the date of death is still out of the estate, even if the property itself is included.

A gift that is included in the estate will not be included in the donor's adjusted taxable gifts for purposes of calculating the estate tax. So, any applicable exclusion amount or run-up the brackets used on the gift is restored to the donor. However, the same is not necessarily true for a non-donor spouse who elects to split the gift.

[c] Gift-Splitting

For purposes of discussing gift-splitting, we'll refer to the actual donor spouse as Husband and the electing non-donor spouse as Wife.

[i] Gift-splitting—in general. If Husband makes a gift of his separate property to someone other than Wife, the spouses can elect to "gift-split"— that is, to treat the gift for gift tax purposes as being made one-half by each spouse.[25] Gift-splitting is a good way to (1) use both spouses' annual exclusions, unified credits, or generation-skipping transfer tax exemptions, and (2) take advantage of the run-up the gift/estate tax brackets twice.[26]

[ii] Inclusion of split gift in the donor spouse's estate. For purposes of including a split gift in the donor's estate, the actual donor, and not the donor's spouse, is considered the donor of all property that he actually gifted.[27] Therefore, if the non-donor spouse dies within three years of the gift, the gift will not be includible in her estate. The actual donor's estate tax will be adjusted for gift taxes payable by both spouses on the split gift.[28] This adjustment cannot reduce the donor's estate tax below zero.

---

[24] E.g., qualification under IRC § 303 (described in Chapter 45), IRC § 2032A (described in Chapter 48), IRC § 2057 (described in Chapter 50), and IRC § 6166 (described in Chapter 46), all providing tax advantages for certain interests in businesses.

[25] IRC § 2513. This technique is more fully described in Chapter 2.

[26] If the surtax on transfers between $10 million and $17,184,000 returns as scheduled in 2011, gift-splitting can also avoid the surtax.

[27] Rev. Rul. 54-246, 1954-1 CB 179; see also Rev. Rul. 82-198, 1982-2 CB 206; Rev. Rul. 81-85, 1981-1 CB 452.

[28] IRC § 2001(d).

However, if a split gift is made which utilizes the non-donor Wife's unified credit and/or bracket run-up, and the property is included in the donor Husband's estate under the three-year rule, Wife's unified credit and run-up the brackets are not restored to her for gift tax purposes, although they will be available for estate tax purposes. If the property is included in Husband's estate for any reason other than the three-year rule, Wife's unified credit and run-up the brackets are not restored at all. These results, as more fully examined below, are true, even though the entire property is included in Husband's estate.

Inclusion as a result of three-year rule. If Husband dies within three years of making a gift that is subject to the three-year rule, the entire gift (not just his one half of the split gift) will be included in his estate.[29] In that case, Wife's one half of the split gift will not be included in Wife's gift tax base when her own estate tax is eventually computed,[30] but it will be included for her own subsequent gift tax purposes.[31]

> **EXAMPLE:** Husband owns an insurance policy on his life. He gives this policy to a trust. The value of the policy is $2 million. Husband and Wife elect to split this gift, and use both of their unified credits. Husband dies two years later. The entire face amount of the policy is taxable in his estate. Wife can make no further taxable gifts during her lifetime without paying gift tax, starting at the rate applicable to gifts over $1 million. However, at her death, the $1 million split gift will not be included in her adjusted taxable gifts, so her estate may be able to recoup the unified credit at that time.

Inclusion for other reason. If the entire amount of a split gift is included in Husband's estate for any reason other than the three-year rule, Wife's unified credit and run-up the brackets used in the split gift are wasted altogether.

> **EXAMPLE:** Husband establishes a grantor retained income trust, with himself as beneficiary for ten years, and with his nieces as remainder beneficiaries. Assume that the property transferred to the trust is worth $4 million, the retained annuity interest is worth $2,200,000, and the gifted remainder interest is worth $1,800,000. Wife splits the gift (treating $900,000 as given by her). Due to the Husband's retained interest, the trust assets will be includible in his estate if he dies within ten years after the gift.[32] If Husband dies during the 10-year term, and values remain the same, the entire $4 million will be includible in Husband's estate, but

---

[29] See note 24.
[30] IRC § 2001(e).
[31] IRC § 2502.
[32] IRC § 2036(a).

Wife's $900,000 gift will still be includible in her adjusted taxable gifts, so that $900,000 of her applicable exclusion amount is wasted.

It is true that, if this rule applies, Husband's estate will receive an adjustment (that cannot reduce the estate tax below zero) for gift taxes paid by both Husband and Wife.[33] Does this make everything okay? No, for three reasons. It does not compensate for Wife's loss of unified credit (since there are no actual taxes paid). The adjustment will have no effect if Husband's estate pays no tax (as will often be the case on the death of the first spouse to die). Moreover, even if Husband's estate is taxable, if Wife is not the beneficiary (through trusts or otherwise), the benefits of the adjustment accrue to other people.

This is a harsh rule. A couple considering a gift that has a substantial chance of being included in one spouse's estate[34] should seriously consider whether it is advisable to split gifts if the spouses have not reached the maximum gift tax bracket before the transfer.

Practice Pointer: If the nondonor spouse has used her unified credit and bracket run-up before the transfer, then this is a nonissue with respect to further gift-splitting, except to the extent that the 60 percent bubble is a factor.[35]

---

[2] Gift Tax Included in the Estate

Gift tax paid by the donor or his estate on any gift made by the donor or his spouse within three years of the donor's death is always included in the donor's estate, whether or not the gift itself is included.[36] The effect of this rule is to eliminate the rate differential between the gift tax and estate tax for taxable gifts made within three years of death. In effect, the tax-inclusive estate tax rate, rather than the more favorable tax-exclusive gift tax rate, is applied to taxable gifts made within three years of death.

Sometimes, people find this concept difficult to grasp. Here's the proof. Suppose, in scenario one, Dad (who is in the 50 percent bracket) makes a $1 million gift, pays gift tax of $500,000, and dies two years later, resulting in $500,000 gift tax being included in his taxable estate.

---

[33] IRC § 2001(d).

[34] E.g., a gift which would be included through application of the three-year rule, a qualified personal residence trust (QPRTs are discussed in Chapter 21), or a grantor retained annuity trust (GRATs are discussed in Chapter 22).

[35] The 60 percent bubble is discussed in Chapter 1. It applies to transfers after 2010, due to the sunsetting of EGTRRA. EGTRRA § 511(b).

[36] IRC § 2035(b).

Transfer Tax Payable When Gift Tax is Includable in Estate:

Gift tax	$500,000
Estate tax on gift tax	$500,000 × .50 = 250,000
Total estate and gift tax	$750,000

Suppose, in scenario two, Dad makes no gift at all. When he dies, both the property he would have gifted in scenario one ($1 million) and the money equal to gift tax on that property ($500,000) remain in his possession, and are therefore included in his estate.

Transfer Tax Payable if No Gift Had Been Made:

Estate tax	$1,500,000 × .50 = $750,000

[3] Gifting by Donors Who May Not Survive for Three Years

[a] Gifts May Still Be Advisable

If a person's three-year prognosis of survival is not optimistic, does it make any sense for him to make a taxable gift? It depends. If the property itself will be included in the estate, it may still be smart to make the gift despite the prognosis if (1) the property will generate significant income or appreciation before his death or (2) the property's value is less than its income tax basis, and a step-down in basis on death may be avoided.[37] The downside or cost of such a transfer is the forgone after-tax income (on the amount of the gift tax) that could have been earned between the required dates of payment of the gift tax[38] and payment of the estate tax.[39]

If the gift tax would be included in the donor's estate, but the gifted property would not, it may still be wise to give the gift (1) when the property is expected to increase in value or produce a significant amount of income before the donor's death or (2) if the gift tax valuation would be more favorable than the estate tax valuation. In this case, the cost of making the gift versus dying with the property is the loss of the income that could have been earned on the gift tax (adjusted for income and estate taxes) and, if the value of the gifted

---

[37] See ¶ 8.06 for limitations on avoiding a step-down.

[38] April 15 of the year following the gift, IRC §§ 6075(b)(1), 6151(a), or, if earlier, the due date of the donor's estate tax return. IRC §§ 6075(b)(3), 6151(a).

[39] Usually, nine months after date of donor's death, IRC §§ 6075(a), 6151(a).

property exceeds its income tax basis, the loss of a step-up in basis at the do-nor's death.[40]

[b] Special Considerations for Married Donors

In the case of a gift by a married donor who is not expected to survive for three years, it may be a good idea to have the healthier nondonor spouse pay the gift tax.

Here's the idea. Let's say the donor spouse is Husband. If Husband pays the gift tax, the gift tax will be included in Husband's estate if he dies within three years. No gift or estate tax marital deduction is available for the included tax, because the tax does not pass to Wife.[41] If Husband dies within three years, a marital deduction will also not be available for the estate funds used to pay the estate tax on the included gift tax, so the gift tax included will generate additional estate tax at the higher tax-inclusive rate.

Instead, if Wife pays the gift tax, the gift tax will not be included in Husband's estate. Wife's payment of Husband's gift tax should qualify for the gift tax marital deduction if Husband is a U.S. citizen. To repay Wife, Husband can leave the gift tax amount to Wife in his estate and receive an estate tax marital deduction.

The following two examples contrast the difference in tax consequences discussed above. The tax computations in the examples will change with adjustment in the maximum rates and the unified credit.[42] However, the concept still applies.

> **EXAMPLE:** In 2002, Husband, who has an estate of $8 million and has never made a gift before, makes a gift of $3 million to a trust for his children. This generates a gift tax of $935,000, which Husband pays. Husband dies later that year, leaving his entire estate to Wife, who has an estate of her own of $5 million. The gift tax is includible in his estate.[43] No marital deduction is available for this amount, because the tax didn't go to Wife. In addition, the amount eligible for the marital deduction must be reduced by the estate funds that are used to pay the estate tax on the $935,000, thus further increasing estate taxes. In all, since Husband has reached the 50 percent bracket, the inclusion of the $935,000 gift tax in the estate will cause about $935,000[44] in estate tax that would not oth-

---

[40] IRC §§ 1014, 1015.

[41] Priv. Ltr. Rul. 9128009 (Mar. 29, 1991).

[42] See Table 1-C at ¶ 1.04[3]. Both examples assume the use of 2002 rates and applicable exclusion amounts. For current rates and exclusion amounts, see Appendix ¶ A.01, Table of Indexed Amounts, in supplement.

[43] IRC § 2035(b).

[44] Additional estate tax computed as follows:

erwise have been due at Husband's death. Assuming no changes in value, on Wife's death, additional estate tax of $3,616,600[45] would be due, leaving a total of $4,513,400 passing to Husband's and Wife's descendants from Wife's estate.

EXAMPLE: Assume the same facts as the preceding example, except that Wife pays the $935,000 gift tax. The gift tax payment qualifies for the gift tax marital deduction, since it pays Husband's debt. Since Wife pays the gift tax, it will not be included in Husband's estate. Husband is leaving his entire estate to Wife, so there is no estate tax due at his death. She in effect gets the $935,000 gift tax payment reimbursed, and she gets $935,000 more from Husband's estate. Assuming no changes in value, on Wife's death in 2002, estate tax of $4,308,300[46] would be due, leaving a total of $4,756,700 passing to the couple's descendants from Wife's estate. This is $243,300 more than they would have received, had Husband paid the $935,000 gift tax.

- Amount included in gross estate = $5,000,000 + $935,000 = $5,935,000.
- Amount eligible for marital deduction = $5,935,000 − $935,000 − estate tax paid.
- Estate tax paid = .50 ($5,935,000 − marital deduction).
- If x = estate tax paid and y = marital deduction, then: $5,935,000 − $935,000 − x = y. $5,000,000 − x = y and x = $5,000,000 − y.
- Also, if x = .50 ($5,935,000 − y), then x = $2,967,500 − .5y.
- Combining equations: $5,000,000 − y = $2,967,500 − .5y and .5y = $2,032,500. Therefore: y = $4,065,000 and x = $935,000
- THUS: $935,000 gift tax × 1.0 = $935,000 additional estate tax.

[45] Estate tax per IRC § 2001(c) on Wife's estate of $5,000,000 + ($8,000,000 − $3,000,000 − $935,000 − $935,000).

[46] $4,308,300 is the estate tax per IRC § 2001(c) on Wife's estate of [($5,000,000 − $935,000) + ($8,000,000 − $3,000,000)].

Practice Pointer: If both spouses' three-year survival is questionable, the spouses can hedge their bets on inclusion of the gift tax by having each spouse actually pay half of the gift tax. Then, if only one spouse dies during the three-year period, only one-half of the gift tax will be included in the estate.[47]

CAUTION: Will these strategies work? The IRS may challenge the above strategies when the donor spouse gives the non-donor spouse the money to pay the gift tax. In 1997, the IRS ruled in such a situation that the "substance of the transaction" dictated that the gift tax be included in the donor's estate when he died within three years of the gift.[48] At least two courts have agreed with the IRS in a similar situation,[49] applying the step transaction doctrine to include gift tax paid in the donor husband's estate, where the wife served as a "mere conduit" for the donor's funds, even though she had no legal obligation to use the funds to pay the gift tax.

Practice Pointer: Have the non-donor spouse pay the gift tax with funds not given to her by the donor spouse, or at least not given in connection with the transaction.

¶ 8.05 SHIFTING INCOME TO LOWER-BRACKET TAXPAYERS

All asterisked amounts in this subsection are for the 2003 taxable year. For current year's amounts, see Appendix ¶ A.01, Table of Indexed Amounts, in supplement.

[1] In General

Another advantage of gifts is the ability to save income taxes for the family as a whole by shifting future income from donors in higher income tax brackets to donees in lower brackets. For example, if Dad is in the maximum income tax bracket, and his children are not, the family unit may save income tax if a transfer of income-producing property is made to the children or trusts for their benefit. More specifically, if Dad's daughter has taxable income and she is at least 14 years old (i.e., she is a non-"kiddie," as discussed below), she

---

[47] IRC § 2035(b).

[48] Tech. Adv. Mem. 9729005 (Apr. 9, 1997).

[49] Brown v. United States, 329 F3d 664 (9th Cir. 2003), aff'g 2001-2 USTC ¶ 60,424, 88 AFTR2d, 2001-6665 (CD Cal. 2001).

will not reach the 35 per cent income tax rate until she (or she and her husband) have $311,950*[50] of taxable income ($155,975* if filing separately).[51] The ordinary income of trusts is taxable at 35 percent of any amount over $9,350*.

[2] Kiddie Tax Considerations

A child less than 14 years old (for this purpose, known as kiddie) is generally taxed on unearned income at her parent's marginal rate, after her first $1,500* (or $750* plus certain itemized deductions, if greater).[52] The result is that the first $750* of income is not taxed, because of the standard deduction, and the next $750* is taxed at the kiddie's rate. Thus, it may make sense to give a kiddie enough property to produce $1,500* of income per year.

Which parent's income is used to compute the kiddie tax on income over $1,500* per year?

Manner of Filing	Income Used
Parents file jointly	Joint income
Parents are married, filing separately	Higher of the two incomes
Parents not married/legally separated	Custodial parent's income

Special rules are used to compute a kiddie's alternative minimum taxable income. The kiddie's exemption from alternative minimum taxable income for unearned income is the greater of $1,500* or the kiddie's share of the parent's unused exemption.[53]

Under certain circumstances, a parent can elect to include a kiddie's income on the parent's own return. How does this work? First, Parent adds to his return the amount of the kiddie's income, less $1,500*. Then, after computing the tax, Parent adds to his tax an amount for each kiddie equal to the lesser of $75* (which is 10 percent of $750*) or 10 percent of the excess of

---

[50] All asterisked amounts in this subsection are for the 2003 taxable year. The income tax rate table for trusts and estates for 2003 is attached as Table 8-A (located at the end of this chapter). For current year's amounts, see Appendix ¶ A.01, Table of Indexed Amounts, in supplement.

[51] IRC §§ 1(a), 1(d).

[52] IRC § 1(g) for 2003. For current year's amounts, see Appendix ¶ A.01, Table of Indexed Amounts, in supplement.

[53] IRC § 59(j). The kiddie's exemption from alternative minimum tax for unearned income is increased to $5,000, adjusted for inflation. IRC § 59(j), effective for taxable years beginning after 1997. The inflation-adjusted amount for 2003 is $5,600. For current amount, see Appendix ¶ A.01, Table of Indexed Amounts, in supplement.

the kiddie's gross income over $750*.[54] If EGTRRA sunsets, for taxable years beginning after 2010, the 10 percent number will increase to 15 percent.[55]

Can Parent take advantage of this election to offset the kiddie's capital gains and Parent's capital losses, or the kiddie's passive income with Parent's passive losses, etc.? Generally, no, because the election is only available if the kiddie's gross income for the year consists solely of interest and dividends.[56] However, if the child's dividend income includes capital gain distributions, those gains can be offset against Parent's capital losses.[57]

Additionally, to qualify for the election, the child's gross income must be more than $750* and less than $7,500*; no estimated tax payments for the year can be made in the name and social security number of the child; no backup withholding on behalf of the child can be made; and the parent of the child whose return will include the child's income must make an election.[58]

¶ 8.06 TAKING ADVANTAGE OF BASIS RULES

The income tax basis of property transferred by death, gift, or sale will often change as a result of the transfer. The basis rules need to be considered in determining the best method to transfer property—estate transfer, gift, sale to a related party, or sale to an unrelated party.

[1] Property Included in Estate

[a] Decedents Dying Before 2010

If a person dies with property in his taxable estate, the property generally takes a new basis for income tax purposes[59] equal to its fair market value at (1) the date of his death[60] or (2) if the alternate valuation date is elected for estate tax purposes, the earlier of the date which is six months after his death or

---

[54] IRC § 1(g)(7).

[55] IRC § 1(g)(7)(B)(ii)(II).

[56] IRC § 1(g)(7)(A)(i). If Parent really wanted to accomplish these offsets, he might have made sure that the kiddies received their income-producing property via a grantor trust. This solution, of course, would not accomplish income tax-shifting, which is the subject of this section.

[57] IRS Publication 929; IRS Form 8814.

[58] IRC § 1(g)(7)(A).

[59] IRC § 1014.

[60] IRC § 2031.

the date of disposition of the property by the estate.[61] This rule is often referred to as the "step-up in basis rule," but it is really a "change in basis" rule—it can result in a basis decrease as well as a basis increase. For example, if Mom's property, Whiteacre, is valued for estate tax purposes at $1,000, under the above basis rule, the property takes a new basis of $1,000 at Mom's death. If Mom had paid $100 for Whiteacre, no capital gains tax will be payable on the $900 increase in Whiteacre's value. On the other hand, if Mom paid $1,000 for Whiteacre and the property is valued at $100 for estate tax purposes, no deductible loss would be available to take into account the $900 decline in the value of Whiteacre, because the change-in-basis rule would assign a new basis of $100 to Whiteacre.

For basis purposes, the values represented on the estate tax return are presumptive only. The IRS has ruled that a beneficiary of a decedent's estate who inherited stock of a closely held corporation was not estopped from claiming a stock basis for income tax purposes that was different than the value of the stock used on the federal estate tax return.[62] The IRS noted that, as a general rule, Treasury Regulation § 1.1014-3(a) provides that the value of an asset as reflected on the estate tax return is *deemed* to be the asset's fair market value for purposes of Section 1014. However, the IRS also stated that an asset's estate tax value is only presumptively the asset's value, and thus the beneficiary may rebut the estate tax value with clear and convincing evidence to the contrary, unless the beneficiary is otherwise estopped by previous actions or statements.[63]

Community property. Both halves of community property will receive a new basis on the death of the first spouse to die.[64]

Income in respect of a decedent. There are some different rules in certain situations, the most important being the rule that items of income in respect of a decedent[65] do not receive a new basis on the owner's death.[66] The Internal Revenue Code does not define items of income in respect of a decedent; however, the regulations offer a definition keyed to the decedent's accounting system.[67] According to the regulations, such income includes:

---

[61] IRC § 2032(a). The alternate valuation date can only be elected if the total estate and generation-skipping transfer tax is decreased as a consequence—it cannot be elected solely to achieve a higher basis in the estate assets. IRC § 2032(c). See Chapters 47 on disclaimers and 50 on postmortem elections for practice pointers on this topic.

[62] Tech. Adv. Mem. 199933001 (Jan. 7, 1999).

[63] Rev. Rul. 54-97, 1954-1 CB 113.

[64] IRC § 1014(b)(7).

[65] Income in respect of a decedent is income that was earned by decedent before he died, but which is actually received after his death.

[66] IRC § 1014(c).

[67] Treas. Reg. § 1.691(a)-1(b).

- Accrued income of a cash-basis taxpayer;
- Income of an accrual taxpayer that accrues solely by reason of his or her death; and
- Income to which the decedent had a contingent claim at the time of his or her death.

[b] Decedents Dying after 2009

A carryover basis scheme will go into effect for deaths occurring in 2010.[68] It will continue thereafter if EGTRRA does not sunset. Otherwise, the current system will remain in place.

The new scheme is quite complicated, and is further described in Chapter 4.

[2] Basis Rules for Gifts

Generally, the donee receives a carryover basis from the donor, with certain modifications.

Appreciated property. Mom's Property has a value in excess of its basis. If Mom gives Property to her child, the child (under a carryover basis rule) takes Mom's basis,[69] except that the child gets to add the gift tax attributable to the appreciation element to his basis. The appreciation element is the excess of Property's fair market value over its basis at date of gift.[70] This basis is used by the child for determining both gain and loss on the subsequent sale of the gifted property.

Depreciated property. Mom's Property has a value less than its basis. The rule for determining the child donee's basis for determining gain on the later sale of the Property is the same as the rule for appreciated property—that is, the child uses Mom's basis under the carryover rule; of course, there is no gift tax adjustment, because there is no appreciation element. However, the child's basis for determining loss is equal to Property's fair market value at date of gift.[71]

---

[68] IRC § 1022.

[69] IRC § 1015(a). Spousal gifts are not generally subject to the rules described in this paragraph. The donee of a gift from one spouse to the other takes the donor spouse's basis in most circumstances. IRC § 1041.

[70] IRC §§ 1015(d)(1), 1015(d)(6). If more than one gift is made in a year, the basis increase is allocated proportionately to all gifts in accordance with rules prescribed in Reg. § 1.1015-5.

[71] IRC § 1015(a).

EXAMPLE: Mom has property worth $1,000. Its basis is $2,500. She gives it to Child. No gift tax is payable, due to the annual exclusion. Here's what happens if Child eventually sells the property at the following prices:

- Sale for $3,000—Child's basis for determining gain is $2,500, so Child has gain of $500;
- Sale for $700—Child's basis for determining loss is $1,000, so Child has a loss of $300; and
- Sale for $1,500—Any sale for a price between the fair market value of the property at date of gift and the basis of the property (here, between $1000 and $2500) generates neither gain nor loss.[72]

If Mom had, instead, died just before making the anticipated gift, and left the property to Child, Child would take a new basis of $1,000 for all purposes. Hence, when Child later sold the property, she would have a $2,000 gain on a sale for $3,000, a $300 loss on a sale for $700, or a $500 gain on a sale for $1,500. Thus, the gift before Mom's death gave Child a chance to use Mom's basis to reduce or eliminate gain on her eventual sale of the property at any amount greater than the fair market value of the property on the date of gift ($1,000).

[3] Sale to a Related Party

If property is sold to a related party, the seller cannot take a loss.[73] However, if the related purchaser should later sell the property to an unrelated party at a gain, she will be able to take advantage of the seller's disallowed loss to reduce that gain at that time.[74]

EXAMPLE: Mom holds Whiteacre, which has a value of $1000 and a basis of $2500. She sells it to Daughter for $1000. Mom cannot take her $1500 loss. Daughter will receive, in effect, a suspended loss of $1500. If Daughter eventually sells the property for $3000, she has a $500 gain, after applying the entire suspended loss. If she sells the property for $1500, she can apply $500 of the disallowed loss to offset her $500 gain. However, she may not use the remaining disallowed loss to match any other gain—it disappears at that point. Finally, if she sells the property for $700, she has a $300 loss.

Related parties for this purpose are defined in Sections 267(b), 267(c), 267(e), and 267(f). The definition is complex. Related family members of an

---

[72] IRC § 1015(a).
[73] IRC § 267(a).
[74] IRC § 267(d).

individual include the individual's siblings, spouse, ancestors, and lineal descendants.[75] However, in-laws, aunts and uncles, and nieces and nephews are *not* considered family members for this purpose. Hence, if Mom sells property to her son-in-law, the *unrelated* party rules (discussed below) will apply; on the other hand, if she sells it to her daughter, the *related* party rules apply.[76]

[4] Sale to an Unrelated Party

If Mom sells property to an unrelated party, she will ordinarily recognize whatever gain or loss is incurred, and the purchaser's basis will ordinarily be his cost.[77]

[5] Communication of Basis

If a person makes a gift, he should give the recipient evidence of the amount of his basis and the amount of gift tax paid on the appreciation. If a person sells property to a related party at a loss, he should give the purchaser evidence of the amount of his loss.

¶ 8.07 THE SCIENCE OF CHOOSING A GIFT

Because some assets make better gifts than others for tax purposes, choosing the right gift is important.

[1] Good Choices

Appreciating property. If Mom gives property that is likely to appreciate, she can take advantage of the low value at date of gift.

    Income-earning property. If Mom gives property that will generate income, all of the income after the date of gift will be transfer-tax-free.

---

[75] IRC §§ 267(b)(1), 267(c)(4).

[76] IRC §§ 267(b), 267(c).

[77] IRC § 1012.

[2] Not-As-Good Choices

Appreciated property. Appreciated property is property with a value exceeding its income tax basis. Appreciated property is generally valued for gift tax purposes at its fair market value, without regard to potential income taxes that would be imposed on the donee on a subsequent sale.[78] However, a capital gains tax will be imposed on the appreciation when the property is ultimately sold by the recipient, so gift tax is being paid (or unified credit used) on a higher value than is actually being given.

> **EXAMPLE:** Mom has property worth $600,000, with a basis of zero. Mom gives the property to Child. Mom uses transfer tax exemption of $600,000, but when Child sells the property, he will only receive $600,000 × .85 = $510,000, assuming a 15 percent capital gains tax rate.

Property subject to income tax. This is property that carries a deferred income tax obligation—that is, any property on which amounts of income tax will be owed on the value subject to gift tax.

> **EXAMPLE:** Mom gifts shares of Mutual Fund *A* to Child on November 15. Mutual Fund *A* declares dividends on November 16. Mom will pay gift tax on the value of the shares (including the money used to pay dividends), but since Child will pay income tax on the dividends, Child will only receive 65 cents (in 2003) after income tax of each dollar that Child must report as taxable income.[79]

Gifts of rights to income-producing property may also be treated as assignments of income, triggering immediate income tax to the donor. The general rule is that a gift of the right to income-producing property is not an assignment of income, and the donee will be taxed on the income from the property.[80] However, a gift of the right to income from personal services or a gift of a naked right to income from property, or of income which has been earned before the date of gift, is treated as an assignment of income, and the donor is taxed on the income.[81] Sometimes, the distinction between a gift of income-producing property and a gift of the right to income from property or income from services (especially those services resulting in the creation of property) is very unclear. In any event, this property concept is sometimes illustrated by saying that if the donor gives away the tree, the donee will be subject to income tax on the fruit, whereas if the donor keeps the tree and gives away the fruit, the donor is subject to the income tax on the fruit.

---

[78] IRC § 1015.

[79] Assuming Child is in the highest bracket; if not, the percentage will be higher.

[80] Blair v. Comm'r, 300 US 5 (1937).

[81] Lucas v. Earl, 281 US 111 (1930).

EXAMPLE: Dad gives a bond to Son. Son is taxable on subsequent interest payments. On the other hand, if Dad gives the right to interest payments on the bond to Son, and keeps the bond, Dad has made an assignment of income, and is subject to income tax on the present value of the future interest payments under the bond.

Research on the question of who is taxable on the built-in income from transferred property will generally involve looking under the topics of "assignment of income" and "who is the taxpayer."

¶ 8.08 GIFT TAXES—STATUTE OF LIMITATIONS (GIFTS MADE AFTER AUGUST 5, 1997)

Gifts can be made in any number of unintentional ways (e.g., a sale of property to a child, where the IRS successfully asserts that the child did not pay enough). By filing gift tax returns that adequately disclose gifts and possible gifts, a person can afford herself some protection from IRS attacks many years after gifts are made. The IRS cannot assert additional gift tax for a particular year if the statute of limitations has run for the year in question. Nor can it revalue the gifted asset for purposes of calculating the tax on subsequent gifts or for estate tax purposes.

[1] Statutory Period for Assessing Additional Gift Tax

The statute of limitations for assessing gift tax is normally three years after the gift tax return is filed (or due, if later).[82] The statute is six years after the return is filed (or due, if later) if the value of the gifts omitted from the gift tax return exceed 25 percent of the total gifts reported in the year in question.[83] If the statute of limitations has run, the value of the gift for all gift and estate tax purposes will be its value as finally determined for purposes of the gift tax.[84] The statute of limitations will not begin to run unless the gift has been adequately disclosed on a gift tax return.[85] If a gift is adequately disclosed on a

---

[82] IRC §§ 6501(a), 6501(b)(1).

[83] IRC § 6501(e)(2).

[84] IRC §§ 2001(f), 2504(c). Applies to gifts made after August 5, 1997. TRA § 506(e)(1), referring to Section 2001(f); Pub. L. No. 105-206, § 6007(e)(1), referring to Section 2504(c).

[85] IRC § 6501(c)(9), TRA § 506(e)(2). Applicable to gifts made after 1996. Section 6501(c)(a) applies to all gifts made after 1996, if the gift tax return for the calendar year was filed after December 3, 1999. Treas. Reg. § 301.6501(c)-1(f)(8). However, the IRS

gift tax return, the statute of limitations begins to run for all purposes on the date of filing of the return (or the date the return is due, if later).[86]

In order to revalue an adequately disclosed gift, the IRS must issue a final notice of redetermination of value within the statute of limitations for gift tax purposes. This rule applies even where the redetermination of value does not result in a gift tax being owed.[87] A taxpayer who is mailed a final notice may challenge the redetermined value by filing a motion for declaratory judgment with the Tax Court within 90 days of the date of mailing of the final notice.[88]

If the original gift tax return did not disclose the transfers, a late amended return that does disclose them may not operate to start the statute running,[89] although a timely filed amended return should start the statute.[90] An originally filed late (nonfraudulent) return should start the statute.[91] The statute of limitations does not run if the gift tax return is fraudulent.[92]

[2] Extensions by Agreement

If the statute of limitations is about to expire during an income tax or gift tax audit, or on audits of certain generation-skipping transfers, the IRS and the taxpayer may extend the statute of limitations by agreement. However, the statute of limitations on assessment of estate tax and of generation-skipping transfer tax occurring at the same time as and as a result of the death of an individual cannot be extended by agreement.[93]

[3] Adequate Disclosure

If a transfer is adequately disclosed on a timely filed gift tax return, then, once the period for assessment has expired, no further adjustments are permitted with respect to determining current gift tax liability or estate tax liability.[94]

---

has taken the position that similar requirements apply to *all* gifts made after 1996, regardless of when the gift tax return was filed. CCA 2002 21010 (Feb. 12, 2002).

[86] IRC §§ 6501(a), 6501(b)(1).

[87] Pub. L. No. 105-206, § 6007(e)(1).

[88] IRC § 7477.

[89] See Badaracco v. Comm'r, 464 US 386, 401 (1984).

[90] SCA 1998-024 (Sept. 9, 1998), citing principles of Haggar Co. v. Helvering, 308 US 389 (1940), that timely amended returns will generally be treated as valid returns (distinguishing the *Badaracco* principle that late-filed amended returns are generally nullities).

[91] IRC § 6501(a).

[92] IRC §§ 6501(c)(1), 6501(c)(2), 6501(c)(3).

[93] IRC §§ 2661, 6501(c)(4).

[94] Treas. Reg. §§ 20.2001-1(b), 25.2504-2(b).

The regulations provide a list of information that must be indicated on a gift tax return in order for the transaction to be considered "adequately disclosed."

Description of transaction. The listed information must completely and accurately describe the transaction, including:

- A description of the property transferred and any consideration received by the transferor;
- The identity and the relationship of the parties involved in the transaction;
- The value of the transferred property; and
- How the transferred property was valued, noting the use of any valuation discounts or adjustments.[95]

Gift in trust. If the property was transferred in trust, the taxpayer must provide a brief description of the terms of the trust or a complete copy of the trust instrument.[96]

Discounts. If an interest in any entity is transferred, the regulations ordinarily require a statement of the fair market value of 100 percent of an entity (without regard to entity discounts).[97] However, that disclosure is not required if (1) less than 100 percent of the interests in a non-actively traded entity is transferred and (2) the value of the interest in the entity is properly determined without using the net asset value of the entity as a whole. If the taxpayer does not disclose the fair market value of the entity as a whole, she bears the burden of demonstrating that the fair market value of the entity is properly determined by a method other than a method based upon the net value of the assets held by the entity.[98]

Lower-tier entities. If the entity subject to the transfer owns or controls other entities, information relating to lower-tier entities must be submitted only if the information is relevant and material in determining the value of the interest in the entity transferred.[99]

Valuation method. Taxpayers must submit a detailed description of the method used in determining the fair market value of the property transferred, including any financial data used in valuing the property transferred.[100] An appraisal satisfying specific requirements may be submitted in lieu of the detailed description and in lieu of information regarding tiered entities.[101]

---

[95] Treas. Reg. §§ 301.6501(c)-1(f)(2)(i)–301.6501(c)-1(f)(2)(iv).

[96] Treas. Reg. § 301.6501(c)-1(f)(2)(iii).

[97] Treas. Reg. § 301.6501(c)-1(f)(2)(iv).

[98] Treas. Reg. § 301.6501(c)-1(f)(2)(iv).

[99] Treas. Reg. § 301.6501(c)-1(f)(2)(iv).

[100] Treas. Reg. § 301.6501(c)-1(f)(2)(iv).

[101] Treas. Reg. § 301.6501(c)-1(f)(3).

Position contrary to authority. A statement must be attached to the return describing any position taken with respect to the transaction that is contrary to any proposed, temporary or final regulation, or any revenue ruling published at the time of the transaction (but not subsequent to the transaction).[102]

Transaction not in gift form. With respect to the disclosure of nongifts, if a transfer is made to a member of the donor's family (as defined in Section 2032A(e)(2)) in the ordinary course of operating a business, the transfer is deemed to have been adequately disclosed, even if it is not reported on the gift tax return, provided that the item is properly reported by all parties for income tax purposes. This exception only applies with respect to transactions conducted in the ordinary course of operating a business. It would not apply, for example, with respect to the sale of other property by a parent to a child.[103] For other transactions that are not considered to have been gifts, adequate disclosure may be made by attaching a statement (or providing the information on the return itself) providing certain specific information and explaining why the transfer is not a gift under the Code.[104]

If the taxpayer enters into a transaction with a related party and takes the position that the transaction is not a gift, he has a choice of whether to file a gift tax return adequately disclosing the gift or not. A taxpayer is not required to disclose a transaction that he (for supportable reasons) does not consider a gift on a gift tax return. If he chooses to file the return and adequately disclose the transaction, the statute will begin to run. If he does not, his transaction may escape notice by the IRS, but the IRS is free to attack it at any time the IRS does become aware of it.

Incomplete gifts. Adequate disclosure of a transfer reported as a completed gift will begin the running of the statute of limitations, even if the transfer is later determined to have been incomplete. On the other hand, where a transfer is reported as incomplete, the statute will not begin to run until it is reported as complete even if adequate disclosure is made.[105]

Failure to meet regulatory requirements. The detailed disclosure requirements set forth in the regulations serve as a safe harbor. If the requirements are not met, and, consequently, the IRS asserts that the limitations period is still open, all may not be lost. The regulations provide that a transfer is adequately disclosed if the return reports the transfer in a manner adequate to apprise the IRS of the nature of the gift and the basis for claiming the gift's

---

[102] Treas. Reg. § 301.6501(c)-1(f)(2)(v).

[103] Treas. Reg. § 301.6501(c)-1(f)(4).

[104] Treas. Reg. § 301.6501(c)-1(f)(4). Apparently, the "return" means the gift tax return.

[105] Treas. Reg. § 301.6501(c)-1(f)(5).

reported value.[106] Presumably, this standard could be met in ways that would not satisfy the requirements of the safe harbor found in the regulations.[107]

¶ 8.09 STATUTE OF LIMITATIONS—GIFTS MADE BEFORE AUGUST 6, 1997

The law on gifts made before August 6, 1997, is still relevant because IRS re-valuations of these gifts can affect the transfer tax payable for (1) gifts made after that period and (2) estates of decedents dying after that period. The rules on such gifts[108] are as follows.

[1] Statutory Period for Assessing Additional Gift Tax

The statute of limitations for assessing gift tax is normally three years after the gift tax return is filed (or due, if later).[109] The statute is six years after the return is filed (or due, if later) if the value of the gifts omitted from the gift tax return exceed 25 percent of the total gifts reported in the year in question.[110]

[2] What Starts the Statute?

A required gift tax return will generally start the statute of limitations running for gift tax purposes on its due date or its filing, whichever is later.[111] Expanding on this—

---

[106] Treas. Reg. § 301.6501(c)-1(f)(2).

[107] See Quick Trust v. Comm'r, 54 TC 1336, 1347 (1970) (interpreting "in a manner adequate to apprise the Secretary of the nature and amount of such item," as used in IRC §§ 6501(e)(1) and 6501(e)(2), to equate to a "clue"), aff'd, 444 F2d 90 (8th Cir. 1971); Wood v. Comm'r (Estate of Williamson), TC Memo. 1996-426, 72 TCM (CCH) 687 (1996) (interpreting the subject phrase more narrowly).

[108] Gifts made after August 5, 1997, for purposes of IRC §§ 2001(f) and 2504(c).

[109] IRC §§ 6501(a), 6501(b)(1).

[110] IRC § 6501(e)(2).

[111] IRC §§ 6501(a), 6501(b)(1).

[a] Return Not Required

A gift tax return reporting only annual exclusion gifts (unless they are split gifts) will not start the statute running because a gift tax return for such gifts is not required to be filed.[112]

If a return reports only annual exclusion gifts and they are all split gifts, the donor's return is required to be filed, and so will start the statute running with respect to him. The nondonor spouse is not required to file a separate return in this case and so the statute may not start for that spouse.[113]

[b] Required Return Reporting No Tax Due

A gift tax return that reports the use of part, but not all, of the unified credit will prevent the IRS from imposing an additional gift tax for the year of the gift once the statute has run. But, it will not prevent revaluation of the gift for the purpose of computing the gift tax for a future year. The revaluation can increase the gift tax payable on a subsequent gift because of the progressive rates. If the value of the previous gift is increased, the new gift can be taxed in a higher bracket.

> **EXAMPLE:** Dad makes his first taxable gift, reports it at $500,000, and uses that amount of his unified credit. The gift tax statute of limitations expires. Dad makes a gift of $400,000 in a subsequent year. The IRS can go back and revalue the $500,000 gift for purposes of taxing the second gift. If the IRS successfully revalues the gift at, say $700,000, then no additional tax would be due for the initial $700,000 gift, but the $400,000 gift made in the subsequent year will be taxable because total taxable gifts will then exceed the applicable gift tax exclusion amount.

[c] Required Return Reporting Tax Due

A gift tax return reporting gifts on which gift tax is actually paid will, after the statute has run for the year of gift, prevent the IRS from (1) imposing more gift tax for the year of gift or (2) revaluing the gift for purposes of computing future gift taxes.[114]

---

[112] IRC § 6019.

[113] Treas. Reg. § 25.2513-1(c).

[114] IRC § 2504(c).

[3] Statutory Period for Revaluing Gifts for Estate Tax Purposes

The IRS may be entitled to revalue all gifts made during lifetime for purposes of computation of the estate tax.[115] This is only a practical issue if the estate would be pushed into a higher bracket by the revalued gifts. If it would be in the same bracket regardless of the inclusion of further gifts, this is a non-problem.

[4] Situations Where No Statute of Limitations Applies

The statute of limitations does not run for any purpose if no gift tax return is filed for the year or if the return is fraudulent.[116] A late (nonfraudulent) return should start the statute.[117]

The statute of limitations does not run with respect to transfers valued under Section 2701 or Section 2702[118] unless the transfers are disclosed in detail on the return.[119] In such a case, if the original return did not disclose the transfers, an amended return that does disclose them may not operate to start the statute running.[120]

The IRS takes the position that the statute does not run with respect to any gift made after 1996 unless the gift was adequately disclosed on the gift tax return.[121]

[5] Extensions by Agreement

If the statute of limitations is about to expire during an income tax or gift tax audit, or on audits of certain generation-skipping transfers, the IRS and the taxpayer may extend the statute by agreement. However, the statute of limitations on assessment of estate tax, and of generation-skipping transfer tax occurring at the same time as and as a result of the death of an individual, cannot be extended by agreement.[122]

---

[115] Estate of Smith, 94 TC 872 (1990), acq. 1990-2 CB 1; Evanson v. United States, 30 F3d 960 (8th Cir. 1994); Levin v. Comm'r, 986 F2d 91 (4th Cir. 1993), cert. denied, 510 US 816 (1993) (all upholding IRS right to revalue); contra Boatmen's First Nat'l Bank v. United States, 705 F. Supp. 1407 (WD Mo. 1988) (denying IRS right to revalue).

[116] IRC §§ 6501(c)(1), 6501(c)(2), 6501(c)(3).

[117] IRC § 6501(a).

[118] Described in Chapters 21–24, and 31.

[119] IRC § 6501(c)(9).

[120] See Badaracco v. Comm'r, 464 US 386, 401 (1984).

[121] CCA 200221010 (Feb. 12, 2002).

[122] IRC §§ 2661, 6501(c)(4).

[6] Protective Filing of Gift Tax Returns

Under the pre-1997 law, wealthy persons who had transactions with, or were in business with, family members, often filed a gift tax return every year, using up the unified credit and paying tax, so as to start the statute of limitations running on inadvertent gifts.

[7] Effect of Gift Tax Adjustment in the Estate

Where the IRS revalues a gift and the revalued adjusted taxable gift is included in the estate tax calculation, the estate is entitled to deduct the adjusted amount of gift tax payable under the table in effect at date of death on the revalued amount.[123] This is true even though that amount of gift tax was not actually paid by the decedent and cannot be assessed or collected because the statute of limitations has run.[124]

¶ 8.10 ANY DISADVANTAGES OF GIFTS?

Of course, making a gift should always be carefully considered. Some reasons not to make a gift are discussed in the following subsections.

[1] Property Has Value in Excess of Basis

If the death of the owner and the sale of the property are both anticipated in the near future, the loss of any step-up in basis at death that a gift will entail may outweigh the transfer tax savings.

> **EXAMPLE:** The owner has used his estate tax exclusion amount and is not expected to live for three years after the date of gift, so the tax-exclusive gift tax rate will not be available. If the gift tax will be the same as the estate tax anyway, it may make sense for the owner to hold out for the step-up in basis.

> **EXAMPLE:** Husband owns Property X, with a basis of zero and a value of $5 million. Husband would like to give Property X to Child. Wife concurs. Husband is terminally ill. If Husband holds the property until he dies, and leaves it to Wife, his estate will get an estate tax marital deduc-

---

[123] IRC § 2001(b)(2).

[124] Estate of Smith, 94 TC 872 (1990), acq. 1990-2 CB 1; Stalcup v. Comm'r, 792 F. Supp. 714 (WD Okla. 1991).

tion for the property, and Wife will get a new basis of $5 million (if value is still the same), free of estate tax. Then, Wife can make the gift, and Child will take a $5 million basis, instead of a basis of zero plus gift tax paid.

If the difference between basis and value is large, and the donor does not anticipate the sale of the property during her lifetime, the difference between the gift and estate tax rates becomes less dramatic, but still significant.

EXAMPLE: Mom is in the 50 percent transfer tax bracket. She owns property with a basis of zero and a value of $50 million. She gives the property to Son and pays $2,500,000 gift tax. Son takes a new basis of $2,500,000 (reflecting gift tax paid on appreciation). Mom dies four years later. Son sells the property for $5 million immediately after her death. His capital gains rate is 15 percent. Total income tax ($.15 × $2,500,000 = $375,000) and transfer tax ($2,500,000) required to get the net proceeds of $4,625,000 to Son is $2,875,000.

Suppose, instead that Mom left the property, less $375,000, to Son when she died, and the facts were otherwise the same. Total income tax (zero) and transfer tax ($4,625,000)[125] required to get the same $4,625,000 cash proceeds to Son is $4,625,000.

[2] Donor Needs/Wants the Property

Good estate planning is not meant to create King Lear-type situations. The donor should never make a gift that leaves him financially or otherwise uncomfortable.

EXAMPLE: Suppose wealthy Donor has been advised to gift Property X, worth $10 million. Donor is not enthusiastic about this plan, because he is afraid he will ultimately need the property. What tax effects will occur if Donor does not gift Property X? If Donor does ultimately need Property X and eventually consumes all or part of it, the consumed amount will not be in his estate to incur a tax. On a let's-keep-things-in-perspective note, even if Donor does not in fact consume any of the property, and it is all ultimately taxed in his estate, tax savings aren't everything. A veritable plethora of red-blooded Americans would be tickled to get 50 percent of $10 million.

---

[125] Fifty percent ($4,625,000 asset plus $4,625,000 tax).

[3] Payment of the Gift Tax Is a Problem

A person considering a gift of land, a business, or whatever, may be willing to part with the property, but may not be in a position to pay the gift tax.

[4] Property Is Declining in Value

The property may decline in value before the donor's death. If the property actually declines in value, making a gift of it at a high value may or may not achieve the most tax savings vis-à-vis an estate transfer, depending on the actual numbers.

[5] Gifts Could Be Made Transfer-Tax Free if Left in Estate

If, as a result of higher exemptions, lower rates, estate going to charity, or other reason, the property is not expected to be subject to estate tax, then it may not make sense to incur a gift tax to transfer it.

[6] Adverse Income Tax Consequences

A gift can trigger income tax consequences in situations such as the following—

Liability in excess of basis. If the property is subject to a liability in excess of its basis, the transfer may be treated as a sale for the amount of the liability, and a gain will be recognized.[126]

> **EXAMPLE:** Mom owns office building, which has an adjusted basis of zero (because it has been fully depreciated), and is subject to a mortgage of $100,000. If Mom gives the property to Child subject to the liability, Mom will be treated as having sold the property for $100,000.

Section 306 stock. Preferred stock issued with respect to common stock will lose its Section 306 taint on the death of the owner, but not on a gift.[127]

Assignment of income. See discussion at ¶ 8.07[2].

---

[126] See Levine v. Comm'r, 634 F2d 12 (2d Cir. 1980).

[127] IRC § 306 stock is discussed in Chapter 19 on C corporations.

[7] Gifts Which Disqualify Estate From Certain Advantages

Certain tax advantages are available if business interests constitute a portion of the estate.[128] If a gift would reduce the estate below a qualifying amount, this fact should be considered in determining whether a gift is desirable. In addition, gifts are taken into account in certain computations under these sections.

Gifts of nonbusiness interests may also qualify an estate for these provisions in certain circumstances, which could be an advantage of gifting.[129]

[8] Donor and Donee Deaths out of Natural Order

If the donee of a gift predeceases the donor, estate tax may be paid earlier than expected (at best) or unnecessarily (at worst).

> **EXAMPLE:** Mom, who has a net worth of $5 million, gives Child $600,000. Child (who also has money of his own) dies one year later, and an estate tax is payable on the $600,000. This problem can be solved by putting the gift in trust for Child in such a manner that it won't be includible in his estate, at least to the extent that (1) the trust is exempt from generation-skipping transfer tax, or (2) the trust assets do not pass to a skip person at Child's death.

[9] No Donative Intent

Maybe Grandma can afford to make gifts, understands the advantages of gifts, and still doesn't have any interest in making any. Does this mean that Grandma is a bad person? Not in the least. After all, the tax savings benefit others, not her. Gift planning is not intended to make nice ladies miserable—it should help people take advantage of the rules if they want to do so.

[10] Relinquishing Control of Donated Property

One of the most common hurdles for potential donors is reluctance to transfer the control (as opposed to the value) of property. These problems and considerations are the subject of Chapter 9.

---

[128] IRC §§ 303, 2032A, 6166, and 2057, discussed at Chapters 45, 48, 46, and 50, respectively.

[129] See Chapter 44 on premortem planning for a discussion.

[11] Consistent Assumptions Are Not Applicable

The idea that gift tax is usually better than estate tax at the maximum bracket rests on the idea that consistent assumptions apply—i.e., that the gifted property will earn the same return whether or not the gift is made. If this is not the case, then it may not be better to pay the gift tax. For example, let's say that property is worth $100, the donor is in the 50 percent bracket, and the property will double in value before the donor dies, whether or not gift tax is paid. Below is a chart illustrating that the beneficiary is better off if the gift is made (assuming the donor lives for at least three years after the gift).

	Gift	No Gift
Property worth	$150	$150
Gift	100	–0–
Gift Tax	(50)	–0–
Property left after gift tax	$100	$150
Property doubles in value	x 2	x 2
	$200	$300
Donor dies—estate tax (50%)	–0–	(150)
Amount left for beneficiary	$200	$150

Suppose, however, that consistent assumptions are not appropriate. For example, in the above case, suppose that, if the donor makes the gift and pays gift tax, he and the donee will not have the money to invest in the next deal, which will earn 1000 percent instead of 100 percent. Then, the results are different. Using the above chart, here is the situation if the family missed out on a chance to invest in an asset which would have increased ten times in value due to not having the cash which was paid in gift tax.

	Gift	No Gift
Property worth	$150	$150
Gift	100	–0–
Gift Tax	(50)	–0–
Property left after gift tax	$100	$150
Property multiplies in value	× 2	× 10
	$200	$1500
Donor dies—estate tax (50%)	–0–	(750)
Amount left for beneficiary	$200	$750

¶ 8.11 REFERENCE MATERIALS

[1] Exhibit 8-A: Trusts and Estates Income Tax Rates

If Taxable Income Is:	The Tax Is:
Not over $1,900	15 percent of the taxable income
Over $1,900 but not over $4,500	$285 plus 25 percent of the excess over $1,900
Over $4,500 but not over $6,850	$987 plus 28 percent of the excess over $4,500
Over $6,850 but not over $9,350	$1,692 plus 33 percent of the excess over $6,850
Over $9,350	$2,567 plus 35 percent of the excess over $9,350

Note: This table reflects 2003 numbers, and is subject to indexing. For current amounts, see Appendix ¶ A.01, Table of Indexed Amounts, in supplement.

CHAPTER **9**

Donor's Retention of Control and Interests

¶ 9.01 INTRODUCTION

For good reasons, a prospective donor may not want to transfer assets without retaining some kind of control or interest in the assets. Can we accommodate this? Yes, to a certain extent. Aren't there all sorts of tax and other minefields in this area? Yes, but we have maps—we just need to step delicately around the mines.

¶ 9.02   CONTROL ISSUES

Let's say Mom is comfortable with transferring the beneficial interest in property to Children, but does not consider it wise to surrender control over the property. How much control must she give up in order to keep the gifted property out of her estate? Generally, she must give up some control—but not much.

[1]   Management Control Mechanisms

Mom can retain control of the management of gifted property without adverse estate tax consequences in the following ways.

[a]   Transfer Property to a Trust

Mom can give property to a trust and serve as sole management trustee of the trust, thereby retaining control over investment of the trust assets.[1] Mom can also arrange things so that as trustee, she has broad authority to invest in different kinds of assets. A trust can ordinarily be drafted to permit investments other than traditional trust investments.[2]

[b]   Transfer Property to a Partnership

Mom can transfer property to a limited partnership. Mom can then be the general partner of a family limited partnership and give away limited partnership interests to her children. Limited partners cannot generally participate in the management of the partnership if they want to maintain their limited liability.[3] However, they usually have the right to participate in major decisions, such as liquidation of the partnership.[4] If Mom transfers limited part-

---

[1] There is an exception to this if the trust holds voting stock of a family corporation, and Mom retains the right to vote the donated shares. IRC § 2036(b).

[2] Traditionally, trustees were limited in making investments by a "prudent man" rule—that is, a trustee had to invest as a prudent man would, emphasizing safety of principal. This was often interpreted to require very conservative investments. Some states have now liberalized the standard. In those which have not, this standard can usually be waived in the trust instrument. Some states have now adopted a rule allowing the trustee to invest the assets in accordance with modern portfolio theory. This means that no single asset is judged as prudent or imprudent on its own. Rather, the whole portfolio is examined, and if the portfolio as a whole is invested prudently, the fact that some assets were speculative will not necessarily be considered improper.

[3] E.g., Revised Uniform Limited Partnership Act, 119761, 6A ULA 1, § 303(a) (Supp. 1985) ("RULPA"); Texas Revised Limited Partnership Act, Tex. Rev. Civ. Stat. Ann. art. 6132a-1, § 3.03(a) (Vernon Supp. 1994) ("TRLPA").

[4] E.g., RULPA § 3.03(b)(6)(i); TRLPA § 3.03(b)(8)(A).

nership interests and retains management rights over the partnership assets as a general partner, are the gifted interests includable in her estate as a result of her general partner status? No, according to several IRS rulings.[5] The expressed underpinning of these rulings is the fact that state law provides that a general partner owes a fiduciary duty to the limited partners.[6]

PRACTICE POINTER: In an effort to decrease the value of gifted limited partnership interests, some drafters provide in their partnership agreements (in an attempt to override state law) that the general partner does not have a fiduciary duty to the limited partners in that particular partnership. Apart from the issue of whether such a provision is enforceable, it would seem to increase the risk of estate tax inclusion of the gifted interests in the general partner's estate. It also may create problems under Section 2703(b),[7] because such a provision would not typically be present in a transaction among unrelated parties.

[c] Transfer Property to a Corporation

Mom can transfer the property to a corporation and then give her children nonvoting stock or a minority interest in voting stock.

Gift of nonvoting stock. Mom can give Child any amount of nonvoting stock of a corporation, while retaining voting stock, and avoid inclusion in her estate of the gifted nonvoting stock. Doesn't the estate tax law say that gifted voting stock of a family corporation will be included in the donor's estate if the donor retains the right to vote it? Yes, very specifically.[8] In the "strange but true" category, however, a donor can give nonvoting stock without estate inclusion of the gifted stock, even if the donor retains all of the voting stock.[9] This technique can be used even with an S corporation, despite the fact that an S corporation can have only one class of stock. This is because an S

---

[5] Priv. Ltr. Rul. 9546007 (Aug. 17, 1995); Priv. Ltr. Rul. 9546006 (Aug. 14, 1995); Priv. Ltr. Rul. 9415007 (Jan. 12, 1994); Priv. Ltr. Rul. 9332006 (Aug. 20, 1992); Priv. Ltr. Rul. 9310039 (Dec. 16, 1992); Priv. Ltr. Rul. 9131006 (Apr. 30, 1991); Priv. Ltr. Rul. 8611004 (Nov. 15, 1985). If partnership income from a particular property is specially allocated to the contributing partner, however, the property may be included in the contributor's estate. Priv. Ltr. Rul. 8827003 (Apr. 4, 1988); Priv. Ltr. Rul. 8821005 (Feb. 22, 1988). Such an allocation may also cause problems under IRC § 2701. (See Ch. 31.)

[6] The theory is that she is legally obligated to manage the partnership in the best interest of the limited partners, and so does not have the sort of powers that would cause the limited partners' interests to be included in her estate.

[7] See Ch. 27 for a discussion of IRC § 2703.

[8] IRC § 2036(b).

[9] Rev. Rul. 81-15, 1981-1 CB 457, overruling Rev. Rul. 67-54, 1967-1 CB 269.

corporation can have two classes of stock which are identical except for different voting rights.[10]

Gift of minority voting stock interest. Mom can give away a minority interest in stock and retain a majority interest. Mom will then retain management control of the corporate assets.

[2] Distribution Control Mechanisms

Mom can retain some ability to control distributions without causing estate tax problems, depending on the structure of the entity involved.

[a] Use of a Trust

Mom can retain control over trust distributions and still avoid estate tax inclusion of the trust property as long as such control is subject to a standard relating to health, education, maintenance, and support of the beneficiary.[11] Also, a friendly third party can have the power to make decisions regarding other distributions. If, however, a third party trustee has the power to make discretionary distributions unlimited by a standard, can Mom retain the right to remove and replace that trustee with another independent party? Until recently, the IRS unsuccessfully took the position that the reservation of the power to remove and replace a corporate trustee with another corporate trustee would cause the trustee's powers to be attributed to the donor for tax purposes.[12] The theory is that the trustee will do whatever the donor tells him to do, if the donor can fire him. In Rev. Rul. 95-58, however, the IRS conceded that the donor's power to remove the trustee and appoint a successor who is not related or subordinate to the grantor will not cause the trustee's powers to be attributed to the donor.[13] The IRS has not officially given up on treating the settlor's power to remove and replace the trustee with a related or subordinate person as a power causing inclusion of the trust property in the settlor's estate.

---

[10] IRC § 1361(c)(4).

[11] See, e.g., Estate of Budd v. Comm'r, 49 TC 468 (1968), acq., 1973-2 CB 1. (Depending on the situation, further restrictions may be required for income or gift tax reasons. See Chs. 2 and 6.)

[12] E.g., Estate of Wall v. Comm'r, 101 TC 300 (1993), and Estate of Vak v. Comm'r, 973 F2d 1409 (8th Cir. 1992), Rev. Rul. 79-353, 1979-2 CB 325, as modified by Rev. Rul. 81-51, 1981-1 CB 458, revoked by Rev. Rul. 95-58, 1995-36 IRB 1.

[13] A party is related or subordinate to the donor if the person is: the donor's spouse, parent, descendant, sibling, or employee; a corporation or employee of a corporation in which the stock holdings of the donor and the trust are significant from the viewpoint of voting control; or, a subordinate employee of a corporation in which the donor is an executive. IRC § 672(e).

[b] Use of a Partnership

If Mom is the general partner of a family partnership, she may retain control over the timing and amount of distributions from the partnership to the limited partners, provided that (1) her distribution decisions serve the reasonable business needs of the partnership and (2) she complies with her fiduciary duties to the other partners[14]

In this regard, a partner cannot necessarily transfer the management rights incident to her interest. If Mom gives a partnership interest to Child, Child may have a status of an "assignee" of the partnership interest. An assignee is, generally, the holder of the economic rights in a partnership interest, without the management rights associated with the interest. An assignee may not be owed fiduciary responsibilities under state law for all or any purposes.[15]

PRACTICE POINTER: If an assignee is not owed fiduciary responsibilities under applicable state law or the partnership agreement, and Mom gives an assignee interest to a child while she is a general partner, she may no longer be protected from estate inclusion of the gifted interest by the fiduciary responsibility exception in certain circumstances.[16] Consider admitting the child as a limited partner if the donor is the general partner and has broad or unusual distribution powers.

[c] Use of a Corporation

If Mom is majority shareholder, she has the ultimate control (through her power to elect the board of directors) over the declaration of dividends. Since she is required to use reasonable business judgment, this power does not cause the gifted stock to be includable in her estate.[17]

[3] Fiduciary Issues

In general, the donor can retain broad controls over gifted property. However, as discussed below, the donor must enter into any fiduciary relationship with a real intention and effort to act in the best interests of the people who are owed the fiduciary obligations.

---

[14] See n.6 above.

[15] Griffin v. Box, 910 F2d 255, 261 (5th Cir. 1990); Bynum v. Frisby, 311 P2d 972, 975 (Nev. 1957); Kellis v. Ring, 155 Cal. Rptr. 297, 299-300 (Cal. Ct. App. 1979); accord, 7547 Corp. v. Parker & Parsley Dev. Partners, L.P., 38 F3d 211, 218-220 (5th Cir. 1994) (highlighting distinctions between assignees and limited partners in denying assignees standing to sue derivatively on behalf of partnership).

[16] Described in n.6.

[17] United States v. Byrum, 408 US 125 (1972).

[a] Trusts

A trustee has fiduciary duties of care and loyalty to the trust beneficiaries.

EXAMPLE: Suppose Dad's company is suffering financial reverses and needs a cash infusion. Dad, as trustee of his children's trust, lends trust funds to the business. The business pays him a large salary. Eventually, the business fails without repaying the trust. If the beneficiaries are willing to sue Dad, they might successfully bring an action for lack of due care (lending money to a business which wasn't creditworthy) and self-dealing (using trust funds to benefit himself).

Depending on the state trust law, provisions in the trust instrument may effectively exonerate the trustee from liability for self-dealing and negligence.[18] However, there may be limits, which are grounded in public policy, to the enforceability of such provisions.[19]

[b] Other Entities

Similar fiduciary principles apply to partners, directors, and, to some extent, majority shareholders.[20]

[4] The Need to Respect the Identity of the Entity and the Rights of Co-Interest Holders

What if the trustee/partner/director/shareholder does not act in accordance with the trust/partnership agreement/corporate documents, or the law applicable to the entity? Once in a while, a person may want to proceed with an action that is not permitted by the governing instruments or state law, feeling comfortable that the family members involved will never sue him. Engaging in impermissible actions gives the IRS, as well as creditors, an opening to dis-

---

[18] See, e.g., Texas Prop. Code Ann. § 113.059 (Vernon 1984); Restatement (Second) Trusts § 222, Perling v. Citizens & S. Nat'l Bank, 300 SE2d 649 (Ga. 1983).

[19] See New England Trust Co. v. Triggs, 135 NE2d 541 (Mass. 1956); InterFirst Bank Dallas, N.A. v. Risser, 739 SW2d 882 (Tex. App.—Texarkana 1987, no writ).

[20] See Tex. Rev. Unif. Partnership Act, Tex. Rev. Civ. Stat. art. 6132b-4.04 (Vernon Supp. 1994); 5A Zolman Kavitch, Business Organizations with Tax Planning, § 108.02[3] (1995) (generally, directors owe duties of obedience, diligence, and loyalty to the corporation they serve); Fix v. Fix Material Co., 538 SW2d 351 (Mo. Ct. App. 1976) ("shareholders in control are under a fiduciary duty to refrain from using their control to obtain a profit for themselves at the injury or expense of the minority, or to produce corporate action of any type that is designed to operate unfairly to the minority").

regard the whole arrangement as a sham or fraudulent conveyance, and can destroy the person's credibility with respect to other matters.[21]

If the donor wants to accomplish his goal of controlling the gifted property, he must respect whatever sort of arrangement he establishes.

¶ 9.03 BENEFICIAL INTEREST RETENTION ISSUES

Even if a potential donor will have ample assets left after making a gift, she may be worried about needing the gifted assets at some future time. The donor may want to retain an economic interest in the property. If Mom has these concerns, various techniques exist to address them.

[1] Salary

Mom may receive reasonable compensation for services she renders to a gifted business or a donee trust.

[2] Lease

Mom may lease real estate, equipment, or other property to a gifted business or donee trust on fair-market-value terms, and receive rental income.

[3] Sweetheart Deals

Although it goes without saying, let's say it anyway. Salary, rent, interest, and any other payments to Mom from the family entity must be comparable to payments third parties would make when dealing at arm's-length.

[4] Retained Interests—Horizontal Slices

Mom can make a gift and retain an income or annuity interest for life or for a term of years, through the use of QPRTs, GRATs, GRITs, and other acronymic techniques.[22]

---

[21] E.g., Para Technologies Trust v. Comm'r, 1994 RIA TC Memo. ¶ 94,366, 68 TCM (CCH) 294, 304 (1994) (holding that a business trust would not be respected as a separate taxable entity for federal income tax purposes since its officers and trustee disregarded the trust's form).

[22] See detailed discussion at Chs. 21, 22 and 24.

[5] Retained Interests—Vertical Slices

Mom can retain a fractional interest in property—for example, an undivided one-half interest in a farm.

[6] Retention of Preferred Equity Interests—(So Passé and Dangerous)

It was once in vogue for Dad to freeze the value of Dad's business interest by transferring common stock to his children and retaining preferred stock for himself (or doing something similar with partnership interests). This scheme allowed the children to enjoy any appreciation in the value of the business, while enabling Dad to retain other benefits from the entity. A complex set of special valuation rules enacted in 1990 makes this an undesirable strategy except in a few special situations.[23]

One of the best reasons to learn these special valuation rules is to know how to avoid inadvertently stumbling into a situation affected by them. A conscious choice to use the preferred equity freeze route comes under the heading of ultra-sophisticated estate planning; and, one must be thoroughly conversant with the special rules (discussed elsewhere in this book) to avoid some nasty tax surprises.[24]

WARNING: A donor may choose to retain rights in an entity pursuant to employment agreements, leases, loans, and other types of nonequity arrangements that give him rights to payments which have priority over dividends or other equity distributions. In appropriate cases, these payments may be recharacterized as preferred equity interests,[25] with some potentially horrendous gift tax results under Section 2701. Thus, it is critical that such arrangements be structured so that the interests retained do not resemble equity interests.

---

[23] IRC § 2701.

[24] These rules are discussed in more detail in Ch. 31.

[25] Numerous cases exist, mostly in the income tax area, which determine when such recharacterizations are indicated. Presumably, the type of analysis used in the income tax cases would also be applied in the IRC § 2701 context.

CHAPTER 10

Tax-Free Gifts

¶ 10.01   INTRODUCTION

Certain types of gifts can be made free of transfer tax. These gifts can be made in addition to "taxable gifts," which require use of the $600,000 exemption or payment of gift tax (if the exemption has already been used). These tax-free gifts are limited, either to a specific purpose (tuition and medical expenses) or to a specific amount ($10,000 per donor for each donee).[1]

Does it make any sense for a person with a very large estate to even bother with these gifts? Certainly. While tax-free gift planning for the extremely wealthy has some of the elements of going after Goliath with a slingshot, meaningful amounts of taxes can be saved even if the estate tax giant can't be slain.

> **EXAMPLE:** Grandma and Grandpa have eight grandchildren. Together, they can give $160,000 per year to the grandchildren, in addition to paying the grandchildren's tuition and medical expenses. These gifts, without use of their gift or generation-skipping transfer tax exemptions, would be entirely free of gift tax.

> **EXAMPLE:** Suppose that Grandma and Grandpa make the gifts discussed in the above example for ten years, that the gifted amounts earn five percent per year after taxes, and that Grandma and Grandpa also make tuition and medical expense gifts of $20,000 per year for the ten-year period. They will have transferred $2,313,086 tax-free. Even in a large estate, that's substantial money. Moral: Significant tax savings, like general life achievements, can be accomplished in small steps.

---

[1] The "donor" is the giver. The "donee" is the recipient.

The following section discusses the rules on these two types of gifts.

¶ 10.02 UNLIMITED GIFTS FOR TUITION AND MEDICAL CARE

A donor can make unlimited payments for tuition and medical expenses of any person(s) free of gift tax, without using up any exclusions or exemptions.[2]

> EXAMPLE: In 1995, Grandmother pays college tuition for four grandchildren ($75,000) and health insurance for the entire family ($25,000). In one year, she gives $100,000 away tax-free and uses none of her $600,000 exemption or annual exclusions.

Curiously, people tend to underuse this technique—many are not aware of it at all and those who are familiar with it often don't remember to take advantage of it before the bills have been paid. Remembering to use this exception is therefore a good opportunity for an affluent person to tweak his estate plan in an easy and inexpensive way.

Tuition payments are particularly attractive gifts for grandparents to make, because such gifts—

- Can remove a substantial amount from the grandparents' estates at no gift tax cost;
- Tend to be much appreciated by the children; and
- Constitute investments in the grandchildren as individuals.

While the simplicity of these gifts is appealing, there are, however, the following few limitations—

Payment to the medical or educational provider only. Payments must be made directly to a qualified educational organization or health care provider.[3] Thus, payment may not be made to the student or patient,[4] and giving money to a trust for future educational and medical expenses of the beneficiary will not work.[5]

Payment to a qualified educational organization only. Tuition payments must be made to an organization which normally maintains a faculty and curriculum and normally has a regularly enrolled body of students in attendance at the place where its educational activities are regularly carried on.[6] This means that payments to Harvard are okay, but payments to the piano teacher are not. In this regard, however, some schools arrange for extracur-

---

[2] IRC § 2503(e).

[3] Treas. Reg. § 25.2503-6(c).

[4] Treas. Reg. § 25.2503-6(c), example 4.

[5] Treas. Reg. § 25.2503-6(c), example 2.

[6] Treas. Reg. § 25.2503-6(b)(2).

ricular classes in piano, ballet, etc. Payments for these classes are made directly to the school, and the school then pays the teachers, as its independent contractors. Under this kind of arrangement, payment to the school for the piano lessons should be okay.

Payment for tuition only. The tax-free treatment does not apply to payments for room and board, books, fraternities/sororities, transportation to school, etc.[7]

Payment for qualifying medical expenses only. These include: medical care expenses (including diagnosis, cure, mitigation, treatment, or prevention of disease), transportation and certain lodging expenses necessary for such care; and health insurance.[8] Tax-free treatment is not allowed for items that are reimbursed by insurance[9] or for medical treatment for cosmetic purposes (except to correct disfigurement due to birth defect, accident, or disease).[10]

No gift tax return required. The donor is not required to file a gift tax return as a result of making qualifying payments of tuition and medical expenses.[11]

¶ 10.03   ANNUAL EXCLUSION GIFTS

Each person may give up to $10,000 per donee each year free of gift tax, without using any of his gift or generation-skipping transfer tax exemptions.[12] However, not just any old gift will qualify for the annual exclusion. Annual exclusion gifts must be gifts of "present interests." Nevertheless, a variety of forms of gift will qualify.

[1] Annual Exclusion—Outright Gifts

An outright gift involves giving the property directly to the recipient—for example, writing a check to the person.

[a] To a Competent Adult Donee[13]

An outright gift is simple, and there are no costs of establishing or maintaining a structure to administer the gifted property.

---

[7] Treas. Reg. § 25.2503-6(b)(2).

[8] Treas. Reg. § 25.2503-6(b)(3).

[9] Treas. Reg. § 25.2503-6(b)(2).

[10] Treas. Reg. § 25.2503-6(b)(3), § 213(d)(9).

[11] IRC § 6019(a)(1).

[12] IRC § 2503(b).

[13] "Competent" is used in its legal sense, to mean a person who is legally able to carry on his own affairs. "Incapacitated" means "not competent," in the same legal sense of the word.

[b] To a Minor or Incapacitated Donee

At the outset, it should be noted that an outright gift to a minor may be appropriate if the gift is of nontitled property (for example, a bicycle), or is of little value (say, $50 in cash), or if the child is almost the age of majority and it will be no problem for the child to own the property at that age. As discussed below, however, an outright gift to a minor or incapacitated person is seldom appropriate where titled property or property of substantial value is involved, because other forms of ownership are almost as easy to establish and much easier to administer.

[i] **Dealing with titled property.** Making an outright gift of titled property[14] to a minor or person under a legal disability in order to save the expenses of establishing a trust can be penny-wise and pound-foolish. If the property is sold or otherwise dealt with during the donee's minority or legal incapacity, a court will generally have to appoint a guardian to administer the property during that time. A minor's parents usually cannot deal with the minor's property, unless the court has appointed them guardians or conservators of the minor's estate and approved the proposed transaction.

PRACTICE POINTER: It is often not a good idea to transfer a limited partnership interest directly to a minor. While, in such cases, it is expected that the minor will not be called upon to do anything with the interest except hold it, an often-overlooked problem is that the consent of the limited partners may be necessary for certain partnership transactions. If a minor or incapacitated person holds the limited partnership interest, a guardian may have to be appointed solely to authorize a partnership transaction on the donee's behalf. This is generally a cumbersome and expensive process.

[ii] **Income taxation on income generated by the gift.** Income earned by an outright gift will be taxable directly to the donee on her own return.

[iii] **Death during donee's minority or incapacity.** What happens if a donor-guardian or donee dies when the donee is still a minor or incapacitated?

Donor-guardian dies. An outright gift will not be includable in the estate of the donor, even if he had been appointed guardian of the donee's estate. If he had been appointed guardian, a successor will be appointed by the court if a guardian is still necessary.

Donee dies. If the donee dies before she reaches majority or otherwise has

---

[14] "Titled property" is property whose ownership is evidenced by a written title. Examples of titled property include real estate, securities, and automobiles. Examples of untitled property include furniture and objects d'art.

her legal disabilities removed, the property is included in both her taxable and probate estates. Since a minor or incapacitated donee usually cannot make a legally recognized will, the property would normally pass by intestacy law.

[iv] **Distribution to donee.** An outright gift may be spent, sold, or otherwise disposed of by a child when she attains majority, and by an incapacitated person when and if she becomes legally competent.

[2] Annual Exclusion—Custodianship

A gift under the Uniform Gifts to Minors Act (UGMA) or Uniform Transfers to Minors Act (UTMA) to a person under 18 (UGMA) or 21 (UTMA) will qualify for the annual exclusion. A version of UTMA is in effect in at least 44 states and the District of Columbia.[15]

PRACTICE POINTER: Because of limitations on investments in some states and mandatory distribution by age 18 or 21, as discussed below, custodianships are recommended only for relatively small gifts or assets which would not be problematic for the child to control at 18 or 21 (e.g., a limited partnership interest in a family partnership).

[a] Level of Simplicity

A custodianship is easy and inexpensive to establish. Just title or retitle the property. For example, all that needs to be done is something similar to the following: "I, Marge Smith, give $5,000 to George Jones, as custodian for Jane Jones, under the Texas Uniform Transfers to Minors Act."

[b] Restrictions on Investments

Custodians are restricted to investments allowed by the relevant state statute. For example, UGMA allows transfers to custodianships only if the transferred property consists of securities, life insurance policies, annuity contracts, or money.[16] This rule is often problematic in the case of partnership interests. To be permitted investments, they must apparently come under the category of "securities." General partnership interests are not typically con-

---

[15] See Table of Jurisdictions, Uniform Transfers to Minors Act (1983), 8B ULA 47 (Supp. 1995).

[16] UGMA (ULA) § 2.

sidered securities.[17] Limited partnership interests are generally considered securities for purposes of federal securities laws.[18] Some states have resolved the problem by expressly permitting gifts of limited partnership interests under UGMA. UTMA does not prohibit any particular type of investment, as long as it is prudent.

[c] Appointment of Successor Custodians

Resignations and appointments of custodians can be cumbersome in some cases, depending on the relevant state statute. Resignations or appointments of successors may require court approval, and the class of people who can be successor custodians may be limited.[19]

[d] Distribution to Child

The custodianship property is available to the child at a time specified under state law. Typical distribution events occur when the child attains age 21,[20] or attains majority.[21] The definition of "majority" varies from state to state, but often includes the earliest that the child does one of the following: attains age 18, marries, enters military service, or has her legal disabilities removed by a legal proceeding.

[e] Income Taxation of Property

The income earned by the donated property is taxed directly to the child.

[f] Death During Custodianship

Donor-custodian dies. If a donor-custodian dies before the custodianship terminates, the custodianship property will be included in the donor-custodian's estate if state law permitted him to spend the custodianship property on the child for reasons other than health, education, support, and maintenance. UTMA and UGMA allow expenditures on behalf of the child that are not limited by these standards.[22] Hence, a custodianship will normally be

---

[17] See, e.g., Goodwin v. Elkins & Co., 730 F2d 99 (3d Cir.), cert. denied, 469 US 831 (1984).

[18] See, e.g., Siebel v. Scott, 725 F2d 995 (5th Cir.), cert. denied, 467 US 1242 (1984).

[19] E.g., TUTMA § 141.019; UGMA § 7; UTMA § 18.

[20] UTMA § 20(1).

[21] UGMA § 4(d).

[22] UGMA § 4(b); UTMA § 14(a).

includable in a donor-custodian's estate if he dies before the child is entitled to receive the property.[23] A successor custodian will be appointed, according to the procedures outlined in the state statute. This will not typically require a court proceeding.

Child-donee dies. If the child dies before becoming entitled to the property, the property is included in her taxable estate. The property will be part of the child's probate estate, and will usually pass by the laws of intestacy[24] (if she is a minor or doesn't have a will) or by the terms of the child's will (if she dies with a valid will).

[3] Annual Exclusion—Special Minor's Trust a/k/a The Section 2503(c) Trust

The annual exclusion is available for a gift to a qualifying trust for the benefit of a beneficiary who is under 21. As discussed in the following subsections, the trust must contain certain provisions.

[a] Trust Distributions Before Beneficiary is 21

The trustee's discretion to distribute trust property to the beneficiary must be substantially unrestricted.[25]

[b] Distributions After Beneficiary is 21

When the child reaches age 21, she must have a right to elect to receive the trust property for some period of time specified in the trust, although it is okay for the child to elect to extend the trust at the end of that period. Many of these trusts provide for an automatic extension, with the child's consent.[26]

[c] Administering the Property

The trustee will have the authority to administer the property. Successor trustees are chosen in accordance with the trust instrument.

---

[23] See, e.g., Rev. Rul. 57-366, 1957-2 CB 618; Rev. Rul. 59-357, 1959-2 CB 212; Rev. Rul. 70-348, 70-2 CB 193; Estate of Prudowsky v. Comm'r, 55 TC 890 (1971), aff'd, 465 F2d 62 (7th Cir. 1972) (per curiam).

[24] UTMA § 20; UGMA § 4(d).

[25] Treas. Reg. § 25.2503-4(b)(1).

[26] Treas. Reg. § 25.2503-4(b)(2).

[d] Income Taxation of Trust Income

Before the child is 21, the income of the trust is taxed according to the normal trust rules. Generally, income that is distributed currently is taxed to the child. Income that is not currently distributed (i.e., accumulated) is taxed to the trust in the year of ownership. Later, there is no additional tax on the ultimate distribution of this accumulated income to the child.[27] After the child has attained age 21, if she elects to maintain the property in trust, the income of the trust will be taxed directly to the child, whether or not it is distributed.

[e] Death During Trust Term

Donor-trustee dies. Because the trustee must be able to distribute property to the beneficiary for reasons other than the beneficiary's health, education, maintenance, and support, if the donor is the sole trustee, the trust property will be included in his estate if he dies before the beneficiary is 21.[28] Thus, if the donor wants to maintain maximum control without estate tax inclusion, he could divide the trustee's powers. That is, the donor could be management trustee and have a right to distribute trust property for the beneficiary's health, support, maintenance, and education, while another special trustee or co-trustee could be appointed solely to exercise the power to make unrestricted distributions of trust property to the beneficiary.

Donee dies. If the child dies before reaching age 21, the trust assets must pass to her estate or in accordance with the exercise or lapse of her general power of appointment. As a result, the trust assets will be taxable in her estate.[29] If the child dies during the trust term, either before reaching age 21 or during an extension of the trust term, the trust property will become part of her probate estate if the trust provides that it passes to her estate. Because of this, the common practice is to give the child a testamentary general power of appointment (a power by will to direct the property to her estate or creditors of her estate). This avoids probate of the assets in the child's estate (unless, of course, she exercises her general power of appointment by appointing the property to her estate). Whichever way the trust reads, if the child has the legal capacity to make a will and does so in a manner disposing of the trust assets, the trust property will pass to the beneficiaries under her will. Otherwise, the property will pass by intestacy (if the trust property went to her estate) or to beneficiaries whom the donor has specified (if the child had a general power of appointment, but did not exercise it). The fact that the child

---

[27] Technically speaking, the throwback tax (a tax on previously undistributed income) is not applicable to income accumulated before the beneficiary attains age 21. IRC § 665(b).

[28] IRC §§ 2036, 2038.

[29] IRC § 2503(c)(2)(B).

is too young to execute a valid will or validly exercise a general power of appointment is irrelevant; the trust will still qualify for the annual exclusion.[30]

PRACTICE POINTER: Section 2503(c) trusts are infrequently used today because the trust assets must be available to the beneficiary at age 21 and because custodianships are much simpler and Crummey trusts (discussed below) are more flexible.

[4] Annual Exclusion—Crummey Trust

Unlike a custodianship or Section 2503(c) trust, a Crummey trust can be established for the benefit of any individual, without regard to the individual's age.

The *Crummey* case established this method of using the annual exclusion and christened the technique with its joke-provoking name.[31] In the Crummey trust scenario, the gift is made to a trust and the beneficiary is granted a right to withdraw an amount equal to the value of the gift within some time period after the gift. Withdrawal periods as short as 30 days have been approved by the IRS.[32] The withdrawal beneficiary should be given reasonable notice of her withdrawal right[33] and a reasonable time within which to exercise the right. It is good practice to have the beneficiary sign the notice, affirming its receipt, and to keep the notices in the trust records. If the beneficiary is a minor, her guardian should have the right to withdraw the gift on her behalf.[34] This technique works even if the beneficiary has no actual legal guardian during the withdrawal period, as long as there is no legal impediment to the appointment

---

[30] Treas. Reg. § 25.2503-4(b).

[31] Crummey v. Comm'r, 397 F2d 82 (9th Cir. 1968); Rev. Rul. 73-405, 1973-2 CB 321.

[32] See, e.g., Priv. Ltr. Rul. 8813019 (Dec. 24, 1987); Priv. Ltr. Rul. 8517052 (Jan. 29, 1985); Priv. Ltr. Rul. 8134135 (May 28, 1981); Priv. Ltr. Rul. 8003033 (Oct. 23, 1979).

[33] Rev. Rul. 81-7, 1981-1 CB 474. Some practitioners issue an initial letter notifying the withdrawal beneficiary that she can withdraw contributions, and have the beneficiary waive notice of all future contributions. The IRS has taken a position that gifts will not qualify for the annual exclusion if the beneficiary does not get specific notice of the gift (i.e., the notice requirement cannot be waived by the beneficiary). Tech. Adv. Mem. 9532001 (Apr. 12, 1995). In the actual *Crummey* case, the withdrawal beneficiaries did not have notice of the gifts. Crummey v. Comm'r, 397 F2d 82 (9th Cir. 1968). What about group life insurance premiums, which are deducted from a semi-monthly paycheck? One notice per year, stating when the premiums will be paid and when they can be withdrawn, may be okay, when it is impractical to send numerous notices of repetitive transactions.

[34] See, e.g., Naumoff v. Comm'r, 1993 PH TC Memo. ¶ 83,435, 46 TCM (CCH) 852 (1983).

of a guardian.[35] However, some rulings suggest that if the withdrawal beneficiary is a minor, the withdrawal period should be long enough to permit the appointment of a guardian under state law.[36]

Certain aspects of Crummey trusts merit further mention.

[a] Trust Provisions

Except for the Crummey power of withdrawal, the provisions of the trust agreement are not subject to special limitations. They can be, and often are, quite flexible.

[b] Taxation of the Donor

[i] **Gift taxation.** Generally, the donor can take advantage of the gift tax annual exclusion as a gift to the withdrawal beneficiary. Why "generally"? This question leads us to the subject of giving withdrawal powers to more than one person. Since the beneficiary's power to withdraw secures the annual exclusion for the donor, multiple withdrawal powers are sometimes granted to obtain multiple gift tax exclusions. For example, if Jane contributes $100,000 to a trust, and ten different people are given the right to withdraw $10,000 each for thirty days, does Jane get credit for ten annual exclusion gifts? The answer is yes if the powerholders are the primary beneficiaries of the trust. The Tax Court has approved this technique even when contingent[37] beneficiaries held withdrawal powers.[38] However, the IRS has indicated its intent to deny exclusions for gifts to holders of withdrawal powers where:

- The powerholders have no beneficial interest in the trust other than their withdrawal powers;
- The powerholders hold only contingent remainder interests[39] or discretionary income interests;

---

[35] Rev. Rul. 73-405, 1973-2 CB 321; see also Rev. Rul. 81-6, 1981-1 CB 385.

[36] Priv. Ltr. Rul. 8022048 (Mar. 4, 1980), Priv. Ltr. Rul. 7922107 (Mar. 5, 1979).

[37] "Contingent" means that they will only receive an interest if a certain contingent event occurs—commonly, that they outlive another beneficiary.

[38] Estate of Cristofani v. Comm'r, 97 TC 74 (1991), acq. in result 1992-1 CB 1, 1996-10, IRB 1996-29.

[39] Estate of Cristofani v. Comm'r, 97 TC 74 (1991), acq. in result 1992-1 CB 1, 1996-10, IRB 1996-29; see also Tech. Adv. Mem. 9628004 (Apr. 1, 1996) (a total of 19 annual exclusions disallowed with respect to two trusts, including some exclusions attributable to withdrawal rights held by holders of vested remainder interests); Tech. Adv. Mem. 9141008 (June 24, 1991) (32 annual exclusions disallowed); Tech. Adv. Mem. 8727003 (Mar. 16, 1987). Some of this IRS authority relies on Estate of Cidulka v. Commissioner, 1996 RIA TC Memo. ¶ 96,149, 71 TCM (CCH) 2555 (1996), in which the Tax Court denied annual exclusion treatment to (a) gifts made each year to the donor's daughter-in-law, who routinely immediately transferred the gifts to the

- The facts show that the withdrawal right did not in substance exist; or
- There was an understanding that the powerholder would not exercise the withdrawal rights or would be penalized for doing so.

EXAMPLE: Grandpa creates a trust which can make unlimited distributions to any of his five children as long as any of the children live, except that property which is still subject to a withdrawal power can only be distributed to the holder of the power. At the death of the last surviving child, the trust assets will pass equally to Grandpa's grandchildren who are living at that time. In 1995, Grandpa gives $100,000 to the trust. Each of the five children has a right to withdraw $10,000 during the 30-day period following the gift. Grandpa is entitled to a gift tax annual exclusion of $50,000, assuming the gifts otherwise qualify.

Variation 1: Grandpa also gives a right to withdraw $10,000 each to the contingent remainder beneficiaries (his three grandchildren). Is he entitled to a gift tax annual exclusion of $80,000? The Tax Court has said yes. The IRS disagrees.

Variation 2: Grandpa also gives a withdrawal right to his two secretaries. He never tells them about their rights—or, he has them sign a waiver of their withdrawal rights as he presents their checks, and claims a $20,000 annual exclusion with respect to them. According to the IRS, Grandpa does not receive the annual exclusion in these situations. In addition, might it be possible that the IRS would take the position that these actions amount to criminal tax fraud and render Grandpa eligible for an all-expenses-paid stay at a designated federally owned location? The theory would be that if the withdrawal power is illusory, it might be fraudulent to claim the exclusion.[40]

[ii] Estate taxation. Even if the donor is the trustee, the Crummey power will not cause the trust property to be included in his estate.

[iii] Generation-skipping transfer tax. A Crummey power will not by itself enable property contributed to the trust to qualify for the GSTT annual exclusion. Contributions to a Crummey trust will qualify for the exclusion from GSTT only if the holder of the withdrawal power is the only person who can receive distributions during her life, and the trust assets are included in her estate.[41]

---

donor's son, and (b) gifts made to the donor's grandchildren, when the grandchildren's rights in the stock were not respected in practice.

[40] See Heyen v. United States, 945 F2d 359 (10th Cir. 1991). The Tenth Circuit affirmed the District of Kansas in upholding a civil fraud penalty imposed on a woman who gave shares of stock to 29 people and claimed annual exclusions for all of the gifts. Twenty-seven of the recipients signed blank stock certificates and returned them to her so that the stock could be reissued to her family.

[41] IRC § 2642(c)(2).

[iv] Income taxation. The Crummey power will not cause the trust income to be taxable to a donor-trustee.

[c] Taxation of Withdrawal Beneficiaries

In drafting Crummey trusts, most attorneys are careful to address the tax consequences to the donor. However, the tax consequences to the withdrawal beneficiaries are not always considered.

[i] Income taxation. A person who has a current withdrawal power will normally be taxed on the income attributable to the property she can withdraw.[42]

What about a former powerholder? Although the holder of a withdrawal power must have a real right to withdraw, the donor never intends that the withdrawal will actually occur. If the donor wanted the beneficiary to have the money immediately, he would just write her a check, rather than going through the Crummey complications. If (as intended) the withdrawal beneficiary does not withdraw, at the end of the withdrawal period, her right to withdraw will lapse. The IRS's position on the income taxation of a beneficiary with a lapsed power of withdrawal is as follows: A person who allows a right to withdraw property from a trust to lapse will nevertheless be taxable on trust income allocated to property she could have withdrawn if she has any powers over or rights in the property that would result, had she herself originally transferred that property to the trust, in her being taxed on trust income.[43] (That is, in almost any case where the powerholder is an actual or potential beneficiary of the trust.)[44] In general terms, this means the IRS believes that any income attributable to trust property formerly subject to a withdrawal power is taxed directly to the former powerholder, whether or not it is distributed.[45]

Let's recall *Variation 1* of the example above. In *Variation 1*, Grandpa established a Crummey trust for the benefit of his five children and contributed $100,000 to the trust. Each of his five children and three grandchildren had a right to withdraw $10,000, and each let this power lapse. What happens if the IRS is right about the income tax aspects of the lapsed powers? If the trust has $70,000 of taxable income in the year 2000, and makes no distribu-

---

[42] IRC § 678(a).

[43] An explanation of these powers and rights is contained in Ch. 6.

[44] IRC § 678(a)(2). E.g., Priv. Ltr. Rul. 9034004 (May 17, 1990).

[45] The technical theory is as follows: According to IRC § 678, if a person releases a power to withdraw property from a trust, but retains such control over or beneficial interest in that property as will subject a grantor of a trust to treatment as the owner, that person will thereafter be taxed on the income from that portion of the trust which he could have withdrawn. The IRS considers a lapse to be a release.

tions, then $35,000 (50 percent) will be taxed to the children, $14,000 (20 percent) will be taxed to the trust, and $21,000 (30 percent) will be taxed to the grandchildren, even though the grandchildren receive nothing in that year, and may never receive anything from the trust. This may not make for happy campers at the grandchild level. And, in fairness, grandchildren who don't like this arrangement are not just looking a gift horse in the mouth—they have real, current tax liability on their "share" of trust income, with no trust distributions to fund the payment of such tax liability (and, for that matter, no assurance that they will ever receive anything from the trust).

If the IRS is correct about the income taxation of Grandpa's trust, the children will also be taxed on a portion of the income, even if nothing is currently distributed to them. This will be a potential issue in any Crummey trust that does not make annual income distributions at least equal to each withdrawal beneficiary's liability for the income tax attributable to his deemed share of trust income.

Here's the problem. Crummey powers may result in some people being taxed on money that other people receive. For example, in Grandpa's Crummey trust, the children are taxed equally (even if some get more distributions than others) and the grandchildren are taxed currently (even though they may never receive anything).

Here's a partial solution. A separate trust with only one Crummey powerholder, who is also the sole beneficiary during her lifetime, will avoid part of this problem. In such a trust, if the IRS is correct, the powerholder or former powerholder will be taxed on the entire income of the trust, assuming all of the property was once subject to a withdrawal power. However, no distributions would be made to any person but that beneficiary during her lifetime, unless she consented. As undistributed income would still be taxable to the beneficiary, distributions to her to pay the tax may be warranted. Happily, taxability to the powerholder (instead of the trust) will often be the best tax result anyway, given the highly compressed trust income tax rates.[46]

Here's another possible solution. An alternative solution may be to make the Crummey trust a grantor trust[47] —that is, to structure the trust so that its income is taxable to the actual donor. The powerholder or former powerholder will not be taxed on the income of the trust while the actual donor is taxed on it.[48] Arguably, when the actual donor dies or otherwise ceases to be taxed on the trust income, the beneficiaries who have previously let their powers lapse will be taxed on the income from that point forward.[49]

---

[46] Chapter 6 discusses the income taxation of trusts and individuals.

[47] Described in Ch. 6.

[48] IRC § 678(b).

[49] But see Priv. Ltr. Rul. 9321050 (Feb. 25, 1993), coming to the opposite conclusion without explanation in a case in which a wife proposed to establish a Crummey trust for her husband.

As a practical matter, the gift and estate tax consequences to the powerholders who let their powers lapse are usually taken into account in planning, drafting, and administering the trust. However, the income tax consequences are often widely ignored, either because they are overlooked or because the return preparers disagree with the IRS's view of the taxability of the withdrawal beneficiaries. In these cases, the preparers usually report trust income in accordance with the general rules of subchapter J dealing with the income taxation of trusts and beneficiaries. A view held by many of these preparers is that the IRS has little reason to go after the withdrawal beneficiaries for income tax, since (1) the IRS will collect a tax from the trust (under the normal rules) that is usually greater than it would have been if the trust income had been charged to the withdrawal beneficiaries and (2) in any case, the amounts are often too small to be important to the IRS.

PRACTICE POINTER: Unless the income tax issues are judged not to be a problem, stick with a Crummey trust which is a separate trust with one withdrawal beneficiary, who is also the only person who can currently receive distributions.

[ii] **Gift and estate taxation of powerholder.** The lapse of a beneficiary's power of withdrawal will result in a taxable gift to the trust by the withdrawal beneficiary, unless (1) she has a limited power of appointment[50] over the lapsed property or (2) the lapse is subject to a "five-or-five" limitation.[51] The deemed gift will not ordinarily qualify for the annual exclusion, since there would usually be no present interest holder at that point.

[A] *Limited power of appointment.* A limited power of appointment is a power to change the disposition of the trust assets, within whatever limits the trust agreement sets, provided that the powerholder cannot appoint the assets to herself, her estate, her creditors, or the creditors of her estate. For example, if a beneficiary has the power to appoint the assets of a trust at her death to any one or more of her descendants, she can put a provision in her will directing the trustee to distribute trust assets to any one or more of her descendants.

---

[50] A general power of appointment, which is a power that is exercisable in favor of the powerholder, her creditors, her estate, or the creditors of her estate, will also work, but is not often used for reasons related to creditor protection and a desire to restrict benefits to a class of persons selected by the donor.

[51] See Priv. Ltr. Rul. 8517052 (Jan. 29, 1985); Priv. Ltr. Rul. 8545076 (Aug. 14, 1985). This means that the lapse of the power to withdraw in any one year is limited to the greater of $5,000 or 5 percent of the value of the assets which are available to satisfy the withdrawal power. IRC § 2514(e) provides that the lapse of a power to withdraw will not be considered a gift by the powerholder to the trust to the extent of the five-or-five limitation.

A limited power of appointment may be exercisable during the power-holder's lifetime (called an inter vivos power or power by deed), by the powerholder's will (a testamentary power), or both.

If a person gives property to a trust but retains a power of appointment over the trust, the gift is considered incomplete for tax purposes and, therefore, the transfer is not subject to gift tax until the property is distributed to a person other than the donor. If the donor dies before that happens, the gift to the trust will be included in his taxable estate.[52] Since a powerholder who lets her withdrawal power lapse may be considered a donor to the trust, giving her a limited power of appointment will render her "gift" to the trust incomplete. Therefore, the lapse will not be considered a completed gift until the earliest of the exercise of the power of appointment, a distribution of the assets subject to the power to another beneficiary, or her death.[53] If multiple powerholders exist, care should be taken that one beneficiary does not have a limited power to appoint another beneficiary's share of the trust assets.

[B] *Five-or-five power.* A current gift resulting from the lapse of a withdrawal power can be avoided by limiting the beneficiary's withdrawal power in any one year to the greater of $5,000 or five percent of the property available to satisfy the withdrawal power.[54] Because the $5,000 amount can only be counted once, the lapse of a five-or-five power can be problematic, if the powerholder is or may become the beneficiary of more than one Crummey trust.

> EXAMPLE: Child is beneficiary of two Crummey trusts. Each of these trusts has assets of $5,000, all of which is subject to Child's withdrawal power. Both powers lapse at the end of the year. Child does not get to let $10,000 lapse in one year without making a deemed gift.[55] She is limited to $5,000 in one year, and thus the lapse of both powers in the same year will result in her making a $5,000 gift to one of the trusts. Therefore, drafting of a power must be carefully handled when $5,000 may exceed the five percent measure. (If the trusts had each had $100,000, the entire $10,000 could have lapsed with no gift being made, since the five percent rule would have exempted the lapse of the aggregate withdrawal powers from treatment as a gift.)

[C] *Hanging power.* A five-or-five power limits the power to withdraw to the five-or-five amount in any one year. A hanging power limits the lapse of a power to withdraw (whatever the amount) to the five-or-five amount each year, and leaves any excess amount still subject to the withdrawal power.

---

[52] IRC § 2036.

[53] Treas. Reg. § 25.2511-2(b).

[54] IRC §§ 2514(b), 2514(e).

[55] Rev. Rul. 85-88, 1985-2 CB 201.

Thus, the hanging power is a gradually lapsing power, designed to keep the powerholder from ever making a gift to the trust as a result of letting her power lapse. If she lives until the power totally lapses, the property will not be includable in her estate as a result of the lapsed power. A hanging power lapses each year only to the extent of the five-or-five limitation, and will gradually disappear over the years, once gifts to the trust cease or diminish to a sufficient extent.

> **EXAMPLE:** Dad establishes a Crummey trust for the benefit of Child. Child has the power to withdraw all contributions to the trust. The power is a hanging power, which lapses in the five-or-five amount each December 31. Annual gifts to the trust are $7,000, and are made for three years. Child's Crummey power over trust principal will lapse as follows:

Year of Trust	Gift Amount	Lapse Amount	Balance Subject to Withdrawal After Lapse at End of Year	Computation of Previous Column
1	7,000	5,000	2,000	7,000 (gift) − 5,000 (lapse)
2	7,000	5,000	4,000	7,000 (gift) + 2,000 (hanging power from previous year) - 5,000 (lapse)
3	7,000	5,000	6,000	7,000 (gift) + 4,000 (hanging power from previous years) − 5,000 (lapse)
4		5,000	1,000	6,000 (hanging powers from previous years) − 5,000 (lapse)
5		1,000	0	1,000 (hanging powers from previous years) − 1,000 (lapse)

If Child dies before the end of the fifth year, the entire amount subject to the unlapsed withdrawal power is includable in her estate.[56]

WARNING: The IRS has privately ruled that a particular hanging power was ineffective.[57] The IRS objected to language in the power providing for a lapse of the greatest amount that was permissible without causing a gift to be made by the powerholder. To avoid this objection, the language in a hanging power should reference an amount which is fixed or determinable without regard to whether the particular lapse is a gift—say, the greater of

---

[56] IRC § 2041(a)(2).

[57] Priv. Ltr. Rul. 8901004 (Sept. 16, 1988).

$5,000 or five percent of the value of the assets subject to withdrawal.[58]

[D] *Considerations in trust design.* The following features relevant to trust design need to be reviewed in terms of hanging powers and nonlapsing limited powers of appointment:

Avoiding gift tax problems incidental to a lapse. The two most common ways to structure a trust so as to avoid gift tax problems incidental to a lapse are to (1) give the withdrawal beneficiary a testamentary power of appointment or (2) give the withdrawal beneficiary a hanging power of withdrawal. Which is preferable? Let's examine a fact situation.

> EXAMPLE: In year one, Dad makes gifts of $10,000 to Trust *A* and Trust *B*. In Trust *A*, Son has the right to withdraw $10,000. The right lapses at the end of the year. Son has a limited power of appointment by will over the trust assets. In Trust *B*, Daughter has the right to withdraw $10,000. Her withdrawal right lapses at a five-or-five rate. She does not also have a limited power of appointment. What are the effects of each arrangement? Both gifts qualify for the annual exclusion. The lapse of the withdrawal right will not result in a current gift by the child to either trust. This is because in Trust *A*, the gift caused by the lapse is incomplete, due to the testamentary limited power, and the gift by lapse in Trust *B* is covered by the five-or-five exception. The IRS will regard each child as the grantor for income tax purposes of his/her trust. The only difference is that (1) part of the property in Trust *A* will be included in Son's taxable estate, due to his retained power of appointment and (2) the property in Trust *B* will not be included in Daughter's taxable estate unless she dies before the withdrawal power lapses.

Conclusion. Using a hanging power will probably be more tax-advantageous, because it can enable the estate tax to be avoided at the child's level. It will also prevent the generation-skipping transfer tax (GSTT) from coming into play, since the lapse at a five-or-five rate avoids a transfer by lapse for GSTT purposes. However, the hanging power is more complicated and requires more monitoring than a limited power. Complexity is often the tradeoff for tax advantages in estate planning. This is such a case.

Hanging powers and trusts included in powerholder's estate. Here's a logical exercise—

- Major premise: The only purpose of a hanging power (as opposed to a vanilla Crummey power which lapses entirely within the year of gift with a limited power of appointment over the powerholder's lifetime) is to keep the trust property from being included in the beneficiary's estate due to the power's lapse.
- Minor premise: Certain types of trusts (e.g., marital deduction trusts,

---

[58] The particular lapse could still be a gift, for example, if other withdrawal rights exercisable by the beneficiary also lapse during the year.

grandchild's annual exclusion trusts, Section 2503(c) trusts) will by definition be included in the beneficiary's estate.

- Deduction: Hanging powers do not belong in such trusts. A nonlapsing power of appointment is appropriate in such a trust—either general, if a general power of appointment is desirable to qualify the trust for its special status, or limited, if a general power is not desirable.

Trusts with small expected contributions. Neither the hanging power nor the nonlapsing limited power of appointment will be necessary, if the contributions to the trust will never exceed the five-or-five limit per withdrawal beneficiary (after counting any other withdrawal powers held by each beneficiary), as the withdrawal power will lapse each year and the lapse will not be considered a gift.

Trusts which are exempt from GSTT. If GSTT exemption is allocated to a trust for child and grandchild, the donor will necessarily intend that the trust not be subjected to transfer tax at the child's level. A nonlapsing limited power of appointment will cause property subject to the power to be included in the child's taxable estate, unless it is accompanied by a hanging power or five-or-five power, and the power has lapsed at the child's death. Hanging powers and five-or-five powers are appropriate in GSTT-exempt trusts; however, a hanging power is usually desirable only if the donor is reasonably sure that the power will have time to lapse completely before the child's death.

Hanging power of withdrawal in combination with limited power of appointment. Should a beneficiary ever have both a hanging power and a limited power of appointment?

Only if the donor wants the beneficiary to have a limited power for reasons unrelated to transfer tax. The hanging power will prevent a current gift by lapse and prevent estate tax inclusion in the beneficiary's estate if the beneficiary outlives the withdrawal right. The limited power then serves a non-tax purpose—flexibility in letting the beneficiary modify the trust terms within the power's limits.

[5] Annual Exclusion—Other Issues

[a] Gift of Income Interest

A gift of an income interest in property may qualify for the annual exclusion. For example, if Michael gives Liz a life estate in Blackacre, the value of the life estate is generally eligible for the gift tax annual exclusion.[59]

---

[59] Treas. Reg. § 25.2503-3(b).

But, if Michael gives Liz a life interest in non-income-producing property, the gift may not qualify for the annual exclusion.[60]

[b] Gift of Partnership Interest

The IRS has issued a technical advice memorandum indicating that an outright gift of a partnership interest qualified for the annual exclusion, in a situation where: (1) the donee-partner had the immediate use, possession, and enjoyment of the partnership interest; (2) the donee-partner could at any time sell or assign his partnership interest; and (3) the general partner was subject to strict fiduciary duties which were equivalent to those of a trustee with discretionary authority to distribute or withhold trust income or property.[61]

The IRS also recently ruled that gifts of partnership interests qualified for the annual exclusion when the donees could sell their interests, subject to a right of first refusal held by the other partners.[62]

A gift of a partnership interest to a partner who has the unfettered ability to realize the value of the gift by selling the interest or withdrawing assets equal in value to the gift from the partnership should qualify for the annual exclusion. The question is whether a gift of an interest in the typical family partnership, which is laced with all manner of restrictions on withdrawal and sale, will also qualify.

PRACTICE POINTER: If Dad plans to use partnership interests to fund annual exclusion gifts to Child, it is safest from the point of view of securing the annual exclusion to avoid restrictions which, as a legal matter, prevent Child from realizing the value of the interest. However, eliminating restrictions for annual exclusion purposes is likely to run counter to Dad's other purposes, such as discounting and asset protection.[63] For these reasons, tradeoffs may be involved in designing partnership interests that will be used as annual exclusion gifts. Including a provision allowing the limited partners to sell, subject to a right of first refusal, would be good enough, according to the above letter ruling. If a first refusal is not acceptable for other reasons, and if other assets are available to take advantage of the annual exclusion, the other assets may be preferable choices.

---

[60] See Rev. Rul. 69-344, 1969-1 CB 225; Stark v. United States, 477 F2d 131 (8th Cir.), cert. denied, 414 US 975 (1973); Berzon v. Comm'r, 534 F2d 528 (2d Cir. 1976), aff'g 63 TC 601 (1975) (denying exclusion for income interest in closely held businesses with no likelihood of paying dividends).

[61] Tech. Adv. Mem. 9131006 (Apr. 30, 1991); see also Tech. Adv. Mem. 8611004 (Nov. 15, 1985).

[62] Priv. Ltr. Rul. 9415007 (Jan. 12, 1994).

[63] These concepts are discussed more fully in Chs. 25 and 53.

[c] Gift of Restricted Equity Interests

A gift of unvested stock or options may not qualify for the annual exclusion. Similarly, if the donee cannot exercise an option immediately or cannot sell restricted property, the annual exclusion may not be available.

[d] Gift to Non-Trust Entity Deemed Gift to Owners

Partnerships. At least one court has held that gifts of cash to a partnership qualified as annual exclusion gifts to the partners where the gifts increased the partners' capital accounts and the partners were free to withdraw their capital accounts.[64]

Corporations. A gift to a corporation is a gift of a future interest to the shareholders, and therefore does not qualify for the annual exclusion.[65]

[e] Gift Through Forgiveness of Loan

One fairly common method of making annual exclusion gifts is for A to lend B a large amount of money, and then for A to forgive the note each year to the extent of the amount which can qualify for the annual exclusion. The IRS has frequently challenged such transactions as being a gift of the entire amount loaned from the outset. The IRS's theory is that there is no intent to require repayment. The IRS has not had much judicial success with this approach. However, the courts have supported the IRS when the facts indicated no bona fide debtor-creditor relationship arose. The existence of such a relationship depends on factors such as whether there was (1) a note or other evidence of indebtedness; (2) interest imposed; (3) security or collateral; (4) a fixed maturity date; (5) a demand for repayment; (6) actual repayment; (7) the ability to repay; (8) records reflecting the transaction as a loan; and (9) consistency in reporting the transaction as a loan for tax purposes.[66]

[f] Reciprocal Gifts

Occasionally, someone will propose that several adults get together and make gifts to each other's children and/or children's trusts, in order that each adult can transfer more money free of gift tax.

EXAMPLE: Jack has three children. Jill also has three children. Can Jack

---

[64] Wooley v. United States, 736 F. Supp. 1506 (SD Ind. 1990).

[65] Rev. Rul. 71-443, 1971-2 CB 337; Hollingsworth v. Comm'r, 86 TC 91 (1986); Treas. Reg. § 25.2511-1(h)(1).

[66] Miller v. Comm'r, 1996 RIA TC Memo ¶ 96,003, 71 TCM 1674 (1996) aff'd, 97-1 USTC ¶ 60,277 (9th Cir. 1997); Deal v. Comm'r, 29 TC 730 (1958).

and Jill each give $10,000 to each of the six children in the group, resulting in each child receiving $20,000 tax-free? The IRS doesn't think so, and some courts agree with them.[67] The IRS would seem to be correct on this issue, since Jack has, in essence, paid consideration to Jill in return for her "gifts" to his children, and vice versa. (If *A* pays consideration to *B* to make a gift to *C*, *A* is considered to have made the gift to *C* for gift tax purposes.) The disallowance of exclusions applies only to the extent that the gifts are reciprocal. If, in this example, Jill has two children, she may claim annual exclusions to the extent that she gives more than her children get.

[g] Gift to Grandchild or Skip Person

Annual exclusion gifts to grandchildren or to trusts for their benefit are popular. By definition, these gifts are subject to GSTT unless they qualify for the special GSTT annual exclusion or GSTT exemption is allocated to them.[68] There is often no point in wasting generation-skipping transfer tax exemption or incurring generation-skipping transfer tax on an annual exclusion gift. If those gifts qualify for the special grandchild's annual exclusion, the gifts will neither use up any GSTT exemption nor result in imposition of the tax.[69]

Outright gifts, custodianships, and Section 2503(c) trusts all qualify for the special GSTT exclusion. So does a special variety of Crummey trust. During the beneficiary's life, she must be the only potential distributee, and the assets of the trust must be includable in her estate if she dies during the term of the trust.[70] So, the grandchild's annual exclusion trust can have no multiple holders of withdrawal powers and should have no hanging power.[71]

One misnomer needs to be cleared up. The "grandchild's trust" is a loose bit of jargon used by estate planners to describe such a trust. The trust does not actually have to be for the benefit of a grandchild; any skip person can be the beneficiary.[72]

---

[67] Schultz v. United States, 493 F2d 1225 (4th Cir. 1974), aff'g an unpublished opinion of the District Court for the Eastern District of Virginia; Tech. Adv. Mem. 8717003 (Jan. 17, 1987); see also Rev. Rul. 85-24, 1985-1 CB 329; Exchange Bank & Trust Co. of Fla., 694 F2d 1261 (Fed. Cir. 1982) (reciprocal custodianships for children).

[68] GSTT concepts are discussed in Ch. 5.

[69] IRC § 2642(c).

[70] IRC § 2642(c).

[71] See ¶ 10.03[4][c] above.

[72] IRC § 2642(c). A skip person includes any person at least two generations younger than the donor. See Ch. 5 for a discussion of the GSTT.

[h] Gift to Parents

Most people think of annual exclusion gifts in terms of gifts to descendants. If an affluent person's parents have modest estates, he may want to make annual exclusion gifts to them. Even if they don't need the money, this is a good way to build their estates to $600,000 each, and get that much out of the transfer tax system. If it would be sensible to utilize the parents' GSTT exemptions by leaving their estates to the donor's children, this technique can also serve to help build their estates to $1,000,000 each, after estate tax, so that they can maximize their use of the exemption.

    [i] Disposition of donated property on parents' deaths. There are two potential issues to consider here. First, if the parents leave their estates to the donor-child, nothing will have been accomplished. The child may or may not be able to re-address the problem after his parents' deaths by disclaiming the property, depending on who will receive the property if the child disclaims. Second, if one child is the donor, and the parents leave their estates equally to all their children, the child-donor may be disappointed. He may have been quite willing to make gifts to his parents, but not to his siblings.

PRACTICE POINTER: There are methods to prevent both of these problems. The donor-child might ask the parents to leave the gifted property to the donor's children in their wills. Alternatively, the donor-child could make the gifts via a Crummey trust, giving the parents a testamentary limited power to appoint the property among Child's descendants, and providing for distribution to Child's descendants in specified shares if the parents do not otherwise appoint. The limited power will prevent the parents from making a current gift due to the lapse of the Crummey withdrawal power.[73]

    [ii] Gift of life insurance. One interesting way for a child to make an annual exclusion gift to his parents is to give them a policy of life insurance on the child or the money to buy such a policy. This may be particularly appropriate if the parents are accustomed to being supported wholly or partially by the child. This would be a good plan if the parents worry about the child's predeceasing them and are not comfortable relying on the child's surviving spouse or children to take care of them. Leaving a bequest to the parents in the will is quite expensive. From a transfer tax standpoint, such a bequest costs $1.22 at the maximum rate to get each $1 to the parents.[74] Life insurance can be much more tax-efficient in this case.

    EXAMPLE: Child gives $20,000 to a trust for his parents. The trust pur-

---

[73] See ¶ 10.03[4][c][ii] above.

[74] See Ch. 8 for an explanation of the tax economics of lifetime gifts.

chases life insurance in the face amount of $100,000 on the child's life. If the parents outlive the child, they will have the life insurance proceeds to support themselves, and there will be no estate tax inclusion in the child's estate. If the child outlives the parents, then, on the surviving parent's death, the trustee can decide whether to let the policy lapse or to maintain it for the child's spouse and/or descendants.

[i] Gift Included in the Donor's Estate

The general rule is that annual exclusion gifts are not included in the donor's estate, even if they are made an hour before the donor's death.[75] However, this rule (like most others) has some exceptions. Hence, certain annual exclusion gifts will be includable in the donor's estate if the donor dies within three years of the gift. These are not garden-variety gifts—they generally include gifts of life insurance policies, as well as releases of certain interests in or powers over previously gifted property.[76]

[j] Delivery and Completion of Gift

Suppose it is December 31 of Year One, and a donor wants to be sure that the gift is made in Year One. Delivery is usually required to effectuate a gift.

Delivery of a check. Delivery of a check will be deemed complete on the earlier of (1) the date that the donor parts with dominion and control of the check under local law or (2) the date the donee deposits or cashes the check or presents the check for payment, if: (a) the drawee bank pays the check when it is first presented; (b) the donor is alive when the bank pays the check; (c) the donor intends to make a gift; (d) delivery is unconditional; and (e) the check is deposited, cashed, or presented in the calendar year in which the gift treatment is sought and within a reasonable time of issuance.[77]

Delivery of stock. A gift of stock is complete if the donor delivers a properly endorsed stock certificate to the donee or the donee's agent.[78] What if the stock is held in street name, or the certificate is at the broker's office? A properly executed stock power can be delivered instead of the certificate. However, in either case, if the donor delivers the certificate or stock power to the donor's bank or broker as the donor's agent, or to the issuing corporation or its

---

[75] IRC § 2035(b)(2).

[76] IRC § 2035(d)(2). See discussion in Ch. 2.

[77] Rev. Rul. 96-56, 1996-50 IRB 7, modifying Rev. Rul. 67-396, 1967-2 CB 351, which stated that a gift of the donor's own check was not complete until the check was paid or negotiated for value to a third person.

[78] Treas. Reg. § 25.2511-2(h).

transfer agent, to transfer to the donee's name, the gift is completed on the date the stock is transferred on the books of the corporation.[79]

¶ 10.04 UNIFIED CREDIT GIFTS

In addition to annual exclusion and medical and educational gifts discussed above, each person can transfer up to $600,000 free of transfer tax during his lifetime or at death.[80] The mechanism that makes this possible is technically known as the unified credit.[81] It makes sense to use the credit early, so that the income and appreciation from the gift will accrue outside of the donor's estate. The unified credit must be used on taxable gifts in the order in which they are made.[82] A taxable gift that uses the credit is tax-free in the sense that it requires no current payment of gift or estate tax. However, use of the credit during the donor's lifetime reduces the credit available at his death, on a dollar-for-dollar basis.

Unified credit gifts are discussed at length in Chapter 4.

---

[79] Treas. Reg. § 25.2511-2(h).

[80] IRC §§ 2001(c), 2010, 2505.

[81] The amount of gift tax that would be incurred on the first $600,000 of gifts without the credit is $192,800. The unified credit is technically a credit of $192,800 against gift tax due on $600,000 of gifts. This is discussed in more detail in Ch. 1.

[82] Rev. Rul. 78-398, 1979-2 CB 330.

Split-Interest Gifts—Understanding the Actuarial Tables

¶ 11.01   INTRODUCTION

Many estate planning techniques involve gifts of interests which are measured actuarially (e.g., annuity interests, unitrust interests, income interests, as well as remainders after the foregoing). Actuarially valued interests typically last for a life or lives, or for a term of years, or for the shorter or longer of both.

This chapter explains:

- How the actuarial tables work,
- How interest rates and facts affecting life expectancy are likely to affect the desirability of using these kinds of interests in estate planning, and
- When actuarial techniques are likely to prove useful.

Most actuarial techniques are known by their acronyms.[1] Each actuarial technique is discussed more fully in its own chapter. This chapter assumes the reader's familiarity with the referenced techniques.

Many of the creative opportunities using actuarial techniques will take advantage of situations in which the actuarial table value of an interest in property varies from its actual value.

¶ 11.02   DESCRIPTION OF THE ACTUARIAL TABLES

The Treasury publishes its own actuarial tables. The tables are contained in two books which are each the size of a telephone directory for a major city. The books are called Publication 1457, Actuarial Values, Alpha Volume (used for valuing remainder, income, and annuity factors) and Publication 1458, Actuarial Values, Beta Volume (used for valuing unitrust remainder factors). The tables published by the Treasury include:

---

[1] E.g., QPRT (qualified personal residence trust), GRIT (grantor retained income trust), GRAT (grantor retained annuity trust), GRUT (grantor retained unitrust), CRAT (charitable remainder annuity trust), CRUT (charitable remainder unitrust), CLAT (charitable lead annuity trust), and CLUT (charitable lead unitrust).

- Table S (showing the present worth of a life annuity, a life income interest, and a remainder interest based on a single life);
- Table R(2) (showing the present worth of a remainder interest after two lives);
- Table B (showing the present worth of an annuity, an income interest, and a remainder interest for a term of years);
- Table U(1) (showing the present worth of a remainder interest in a single life unitrust);
- Table U(2) (showing the present worth of a remainder interest in a two-life unitrust); and
- Table D (showing the present worth of a remainder interest in a term unitrust).

When the tables apply, both the IRS and the taxpayer must use them for valuing actuarially determined interests. In short, the table values depend on two factors: interest rates and life expectancies. Most of the tables assume annual payment of annuities and payment at the end of each period.[2] Minor adjustments are made for frequency of payment and for payment made at the beginning of the period.[3] Additional tables, also found in Publications 1457 and 1458, provide the factors needed to make these types of minor adjustments.

¶ 11.03 INTEREST RATES

[1] The 7520 Rate

Generally speaking, the interest rate that must be assumed in valuing an actuarial interest is determined by Section 7520.[4] The rate is derived from the "applicable federal rate" for the month in question. The applicable federal rates are published each month by the Secretary of the Treasury. They represent the average market yield during the one-month period on outstanding marketable obligations of the United States with remaining periods to maturity of three years or less (federal short-term rate), more than three years but not more than nine years (federal mid-term rate), and more than nine years (federal long-term rate).[5] The "7520 rate" is an interest rate (rounded to the

---

[2] Treas. Reg. §§ 1.7520-3(b)(1)(i)(A), 20.7520-3(b)(1)(i)(A), 25.7520-3(b)(1)(i)(A).

[3] Treas. Reg. §§ 1.7520-3(b)(1)(i)(A), 20.7520-3(b)(1)(i)(A), 25.7520-3(b)(1)(i)(A).

[4] IRC § 7520 applies for income, gift, and estate tax purposes. The regulations promulgated under IRC § 7520 are found in the income tax regulations, the gift tax regulations, and the estate tax regulations.

[5] IRC § 1274(d)(1).

nearest 2/10ths of 1 percent) equal to 120 percent of the federal mid-term rate in effect for the month in which the valuation date falls.[6] If a charitable deduction is allowable for any part of the property transferred, the taxpayer can elect to use the 7520 rate for either of the two months preceding the valuation month.[7]

The interest rates are an arbitrary measuring stick predicting how much income/growth an asset will experience in a certain amount of time. Since the interest rates are based on U.S. Treasury obligations, the applicable federal rate will usually be lower than the rate an individual would have to pay to borrow from a commercial source, and will often be lower than the rate the individual can earn on his investments. Even the 7520 rate will often be comparatively low. This means that assets which are expected to earn more than the 7520 rate are not always hard to find. The real actuarial value of an interest in an asset that is expected to earn more than the 7520 rate will, depending on what kind of interest it is, be more or less than its tax actuarial value.[8]

[2] Benefits of High and Low Interest Rates

Different levels of interest rates will have the following effects, other things being equal.

[a] When Interest Rates Are High

[i] Income interests. When interest rates rise, the value of an income interest is enhanced, and the value of a remainder interest following the income interest is depressed. Why? As interest rates rise, expected income will rise. A higher percentage of the value of the property in question will be attributed to the income interest, and a lower value to the remainder interest. Hence, in periods of high interest rates, desirable actuarial techniques will include QPRTs and old-style GRITs which invest in low-income, high-growth properties.

> EXAMPLE: Mom, who is 50 years old, creates a QPRT lasting for 20 years, with a contingent reversion if she dies during the 20-year term. If the 7520 rate is six percent, she makes a gift of 23.2503 percent of the value of the property she transfers to the QPRT. If the 7520 rate is nine

---

[6] IRC § 7520(a)(2).

[7] IRC § 7520(a).

[8] E.g., an annuity interest in an asset earning more than the 7520 rate will be worth less than the tax actuarial value, and a remainder interest after the annuity will actually be worth more.

percent, she makes a gift of only 13.3050 percent of the value of the property she transfers to the QPRT.[9]

[ii] Annuity interests. When interest rates rise, the value of an annuity interest is depressed, and the value of a remainder interest after an annuity interest is enhanced. Why? The value of fixed payments decreases as interest rates rise; the more income the property produces, the more is left for the remainder beneficiaries after the fixed annuity payments have been made. The charitable remainder annuity trust will be an attractive actuarial technique in periods of high interest rates. The charitable remainder will be allocated a higher percentage of the value of the property, increasing the charitable deduction.

> EXAMPLE: Mom, who is 50 years old, creates a CRAT with a seven percent annual payout to her during her remaining life. If the 7520 rate is six percent, she makes a charitable gift of 12.461 percent of the value of the property she transfers to the CRAT. If the 7520 rate is nine percent, she makes a charitable gift of 34.033 percent of the value of the property she transfers to the CRAT.

[iii] Unitrust interests. The value of a unitrust interest is substantially unaffected by changes in interest rates. Why? Since a unitrust interest is a percentage of the value of the property, as it changes from year to year, interest rate changes do not affect its value. However, where the unitrust payment is not made in the month the unitrust assets are valued (or is made more frequently than annually), the adjustment factors (which take into account the interest rate) will cause the value of the unitrust interest to change.

> EXAMPLE: Mom, who is 50 years old, creates a CRUT with a seven percent annual payout to her during her remaining life. The CRUT provides that the assets will be valued at the beginning of the year, but the unitrust amount will be paid at the end of the year. If the 7520 rate is six percent, she makes a charitable gift of 20.629 percent of the value of the property she transfers to the CRUT. If the 7520 rate is nine percent, she makes a charitable gift of 21.384 percent of the value of the property she transfers to the CRUT. Had the CRUT provided that the unitrust amount was payable in the same month that the assets were valued, the gift would have been 19.107 percent of the value of the property Mom transferred to the CRUT, regardless of the interest rate.

---

[9] Note that in either case, Mom has retained the right to income from the QPRT for the 20-year term plus the right to get the QPRT property back should she die during the term (i.e., a contingent reversion).

[b] When Interest Rates Are Low

When interest rates decline, the reverse effects of those noted above will occur. Attractive techniques during low-interest periods include grantor retained annuity trusts, charitable lead annuity trusts, and private annuities.

[c] Length of Term

The longer the income or annuity interest is expected to last, the greater effect a change in interest rates will have.

> EXAMPLE: Mom, who is 50 years old, creates a 10-year QPRT, with a contingent reversion if she dies during the term. If the 7520 rate is six percent, she makes a gift of 51.0808 percent of the value of the property she transfers to the QPRT. If the 7520 rate is nine percent, she makes a gift of 38.6412 percent of the value of the property she transfers to the QPRT. The gift at nine percent is about 76 percent of the amount of gift at six percent. If the QPRT had a 20-year term with a contingent reversion, the gift at nine percent would have been about 57 percent of the amount of gift at six percent. Part of this difference is due to the fact that Mom's contingent reversion is worth more in a 20-year QPRT than in a 10-year QPRT; the rest is due to the fact that the interest rate makes a bigger difference with a longer term.

[3] Effect of Expected Asset Returns Which Differ From Interest Rates

If the return on an asset to be transferred is expected to exceed the 7520 rate used in valuing the actuarial interests to be created, the CLAT, GRAT, and private annuity will be useful. In these techniques, the object is to get the maximum amount to the remainder beneficiary for the minimum transfer tax cost. The actuarial calculations of the gifted remainder interests are based on assumptions that the property transferred will earn exactly the 7520 rate. If the property actually earns more than the 7520 rate, then more property will be transferred to the remainder beneficiary than the value on which gift tax was paid.

If the income generated by an asset (as opposed to the return on such asset)[10] is expected to be less than the 7520 rate, QPRTs and GRITs will be attractive, since the tables will attribute more value to the income interest than the trust will actually realize or earn. QPRTs and GRITs are generally most attractive where the 7520 rate is high, little income is earned and the property grows in value.

---

[10] The income means interest, dividends, rent, etc. The return includes all of these items and capital appreciation.

¶ 11.04 LIFE EXPECTANCY

[1] Mortality Factors

The current tables are based on 1980 mortality factors. The tables must be revised every ten years to reflect the mortality data most recently available from the U.S. census.[11] The last revision was done in 1989. The mortality tables are based on broad statistical averages and will not match a given individual's true life expectancy, except by coincidence. The following mismatches result from the generality of the tables:

- *The tables do not differentiate by gender.* Women will therefore tend to have longer life expectancies, and men will tend to have shorter life expectancies, than the tables indicate.
- *The tables do not differentiate by race.* Hence, some races will tend to have slightly higher life expectancies than the tables indicate, and other races may tend to have somewhat lower life expectancies.
- *The tables do not reflect economic differences.* Affluent individuals will tend to have higher life expectancies than the tables reflect, and people in the lower economic classes will tend to have lower life expectancies.
- *The tables do not reflect lifestyle experience.* Life expectancies vary, depending on an individual's occupation, state of health, and other factors. None of these factors are reflected in the tables. For example, smokers will tend to have lower, and non-smokers higher, life expectancies than the tables indicate.

[2] Relatively Short Life Expectancy

If an individual is expected to die before his statistical life expectancy would indicate, the following techniques may be advantageous.

[a] Use of Private Annuity

Mom sells Son property for payments of $1,000 per year for her life. If her life expectancy, according to the tables, is 20 years, and the present value of 20 annual $1,000 payments (as determined under the tables) equals the fair market value of the property plus a return of the 7520 rate for 20 years, she will not have made a gift. If Mom in fact dies after two years, Son will have received a valuable property for only $2,000.[12]

---

[11] IRC § 7520(c)(3); Treas. Reg. § 1.7520-1(b)(2). The current mortality component table (80 CNSMT) can be found in Treas. Reg. § 20.2031-7(d)(6) and in Publication 1457.

[12] For a discussion of income tax and other consequences of this transaction, see Ch. 23 on private annuities.

[b] Use of Charitable Lead Trust for Life

Suppose Mom has a life expectancy of 20 years. If Mom puts property into a charitable lead trust for her life, with remainder after her life to Son, she will receive a gift tax charitable deduction based on payments to charity for her actuarial life expectancy of 20 years. If she actually dies after two years, she will have transferred most of the property to Son, at a small gift tax cost, reflecting 18 years of expected payments to charity which were never in fact made.[13]

[c] Use of Measuring Life of Another

Suppose Mom wants to transfer property to Son, and Mom herself is in hearty health. Can she use a charitable lead trust, basing the charitable annuity on the life of a person who is not likely to live long? There is no specific case on this, but the terms of the statutes and regulations do not appear to prohibit it.

[3] Relatively Long Life Expectancy

If an individual is expected to live longer than his actuarial life expectancy, a charitable remainder trust will be advantageous, since the charitable deduction will be based on fewer payments to the individual than are actually expected to be made.

¶ 11.05 WHEN THE TABLES DON'T APPLY

Planning opportunities arise because the requirement that the actuarial tables be used is a hard and fast rule. Both the IRS and the taxpayer must use the actuarial tables; neither is allowed to take the facts of an individual situation into account. However, in certain specified circumstances, the tables cannot be used to measure the value of an actuarial interest. In those circumstances, the value of an actuarial interest must be determined by special rules or by facts and circumstances, depending on the interest being valued.

[1] Pre-December 14, 1995 Transactions

The regulations under Section 7520, dealing with the circumstances in which the tables cannot be used, are effective for transactions occurring after De-

---

[13] For a discussion of charitable lead trusts, see Ch. 35.

cember 13, 1995.[14] Whether the tables applied to transfers before May 1, 1989,[15] depended on applicable case law and rulings. Whether the tables applied to transfers from May 1, 1989, through December 13, 1995, is said, by the preamble to the new regulations, to depend on applicable case law and rulings.[16] However, Section 7520 itself provides that the tables must be applied to transfers in all cases from May 1, 1989, forward, except where the Treasury regulations provide otherwise. Thus, a literal interpretation of the statute would result in the application of the tables in all cases from May 1, 1989, until December 14, 1995.

[2] Special Exceptions to Application of Tables

[a] Insurance Products

Special mortality tables are generally used to value annuities under Sections 72 and 101(b), dealing with the income taxation of life insurance, endowment and annuity contracts.[17] These tables are found in Treasury Regulation § 1.72-9 (as adjusted for various factors by other regulations under Section 72). They use longer life expectancies than the 1980 statistical tables. Hence, they will give a higher value to a life annuity interest, and a lower value to a remainder after a life annuity interest, than the Section 7520 tables would.

[b] Deferred Compensation

Section 7520 is not generally used in determining the income tax treatment of deferred compensation.[18] The Section 7520 tables do, however, apply in determining the estate and gift tax treatment of certain qualified plans and for purposes of determining excess accumulations under Section 4980A.[19]

---

[14] Treas. Reg. §§ 1.7520-3(c), 20.7520-3(c), 25.7520-3(c). Note that the other regulations under IRC § 7520 are generally effective with respect to transactions occurring after April 30, 1989.

[15] The effective date of IRC § 7520.

[16] TD 8630, 1996-3 IRB 19, corrected by Notice 96-22, 1996-14 IRB 30.

[17] Treas. Reg. §§ 1.7520-3(a)(2), 20.7520-3(a)(2), 25.7520-3(a)(2). Private annuities (including charitable gift annuities) are valued pursuant to IRC § 7520 for transfer tax purposes. See IRC § 7520(a); see also Dix v. Comm'r, 392 F2d 313 (4th Cir. 1968), aff'g 46 TC 796 (1966), acq. 1967-1 CB 2.

[18] IRC § 7520(b); Treas. Reg. §§ 1.7520-3(a)(1) (IRC § 401 et seq.), 1.7520-3(a)(3) (IRC § 83), 1.7520-3(a)(4) (IRC § 457), 1.7520-3(a)(5) (IRC §§ 3121(v), 3306(r)), 1.7520-3(a)(6) (IRC § 6058). Corresponding provisions are found in the gift and estate tax regulations under IRC § 7520.

[19] Treas. Reg. §§ 1.7520-3(a)(1), 20.7520-3(a)(1), 25.7520-3(a)(1).

[c] Pooled Income Funds

The Section 7520 tables are not used to value interests in pooled income funds. The present value of an interest in a pooled income fund is determined according to rules and special remainder factors prescribed in Treasury Regulation § 1.642(c)-6, and possibly the special rules on mortality found in Treasury Regulation § 25.7520-3(b)(3) if the person who is the measuring life is terminally ill on the date of transfer.[20]

[d] Tax Accounting, Low-Interest Loans, Certain Interests in Specially Valued Trusts

Section 7520 is not generally used to determine the taxable year of inclusion of gross income,[21] to value the gift/income tax treatment of loans with a below-market interest rate,[22] or to value certain retained interests in trusts that are specially valued at zero under Section 2702.[23]

[e] "Yet-To-Be Determined" Exceptions

The regulations allow the IRS to provide other situations in which the tables do not apply by issuing published revenue rulings.[24] This rule appears to be inconsistent with the statute, which requires new regulations to be issued in order for new exceptions to be created.[25]

Before the new regulations were issued, the IRS determined by private letter ruling that the annuity tables did not apply to an annuity interest in a trust, partly because the trustee had the power to invest in highly speculative assets without regard to the preservation of the trust principal.[26]

QUERY: Many practitioners have boilerplate provisions in their documents allowing the trustee to make investments which are riskier than traditional trust investments. Will the IRS try to use such provisions in trusts with actuarially determined interests to avoid application of the tables?

---

[20] Treas. Reg. § 25.7520-3(b)(2)(iv). A similar provision is found in the income and estate tax regulations under IRC § 7520.

[21] IRC § 451; see also Treas. Reg. §§ 1.7520-3(a)(3), 20.7520-3(a)(3), 25.7520-3(a)(3).

[22] IRC § 7872; see also Treas. Reg. §§ 1.7520-3(a)(7), 20.7520-3(a)(7), 25.7520-3(a)(7). Although exceptions to this may be provided for in the regulations issued under IRC § 7872, none currently exist.

[23] IRC § 2702(a)(2)(A); Treas. Reg. §§ 1.7520-3(a), 20.7520-3(a)(8), 25.7520-3(a)(8).

[24] Treas. Reg. §§ 1.7520-3(b)(5), 20.7520-3(b)(5), 25.7520-3(b)(5).

[25] IRC § 7520(b).

[26] Priv. Ltr. Rul. 9543049 (Aug. 5, 1994).

[3] Trust With Annuity Payout Higher than the 7520 Rate

The regulations also limit the use of the actuarial tables when both (1) the annuity is payable out of a trust or other limited fund and (2) the property is not expected to return the full amount of the annuity. The tables assume that all property yields the 7520 rate. Therefore, if the annuity payout is greater than the 7520 rate, after taking into account adjustments for frequency and time of payment, the principal will be assumed to gradually exhaust.[27] If the principal is assumed to completely exhaust before the annuity term ends, the standard tables cannot be used. If the term is measured by the life of one or more individuals, each individual is assumed to survive until age 110. Instructions for computing the likelihood of exhaustion are contained in the regulations.[28]

> EXAMPLE: John gives $1,000,000 to a charitable lead annuity trust, which will pay an annuity of 12 percent once a year at the end of each year for 20 years. The 7520 rate is seven percent. Under these assumptions, principal will have to be invaded to pay the annuity. According to the tables, the principal of the trust will be exhausted between the 12th and 13th year.

Although it might seem that a full charitable deduction would be allowed because the entire fund and all its earnings will eventually pass to charity, the regulations under Section 7520 indicate that this may not be so. A special 7520 annuity factor that takes into account the exhaustion of the property will need to be calculated by the IRS.[29] It would be helpful if the regulations gave an example showing how the factor is calculated, as they do with the exhaustion of property where a measuring life is used.

Pre-December 14, 1995, transactions. The sections of the regulations limiting use of the tables apply to transactions occurring after December 13, 1995.[30] For transactions occurring before December 13, 1995,[31] Revenue Ruling 77-454[32] applied, according to the IRS. It espouses a viewpoint on possible exhaustion of principal which is similar (but not identical) to that adopted by the new regulations. Many taxpayers felt that a 100 percent charitable deduction should be available in the above situation, since the entire principal was going to charity. This view was supported by the language of the old regulations.

---

[27] Even if the payout rate is exactly the same as the 7520 rate, the principal will be assumed to exhaust if the payout is more frequent than annually, or at the beginning of the period instead of the end.

[28] Treas. Reg. §§ 1.7520-3(b)(2)(i), 20.7520-3(b)(2)(i), 25.7520-3(b)(2)(i).

[29] Treas. Reg. §§ 1.7520-3(b)(2)(i), 20.7520-3(b)(2)(i), 25.7520-3(b)(2)(i).

[30] Treas. Reg. §§ 1.7520-3(c), 20.7520-3(c), 25.7520-3(c)

[31] For transfers made from May 1, 1989, through December 1, 1995, see subparagraph [1] above.

[32] 1977-2 CB 351.

[4] Interests With Bells and Whistles

An "ordinary annuity interest" is the right to receive a fixed dollar amount at the end of each year during one or more measuring lives or for some other defined period.[33] An "ordinary income interest" is the right to receive the income from, or the use of, property during one or more measuring lives or for some other defined period.[34] A "remainder or reversionary interest" is the right to receive an interest in property at the end of one or more measuring lives or some other defined period.[35] Interests which vary from the standard interests may be subject to being valued by a special annuity factor.

Thus, unless the income beneficiary has rights similar to those required of a QTIP income beneficiary, the tables cannot be used to value an income interest for a term of years or life.[36] One of these rights is the right to compel the trustee to invest in property that will produce income.[37] The regulations provide that the requirement is met if the income beneficiary may require the trustee to make the trust productive for purposes of applicable local law, even if the minimum rate of income required under state law to make a trust productive is substantially below the 7520 rate in the month of transfer.[38] Similar requirements also apply requiring protection of the remainder or reversionary holder's interest.[39]

The IRS has privately ruled that a state law requirement that a court approve the assignment of an interest did not constitute a restriction that would render the tables inapplicable because the requirement does not affect the holder's right to receive the entire interest.[40]

If an interest is subject to being valued by an annuity factor which is not published, the IRS will provide the special factor on request. If an interest cannot be valued actuarially, then the actual fair market value of the interest will govern.[41]

---

[33] Treas. Reg. §§ 1.7520-3(b)(1)(i)(A), 20.7520-3(b)(1)(i)(A), 25.7520-3(b)(1)(i)(A).

[34] Treas. Reg. §§ 1.7520-3(b)(1)(i)(B), 20.7520-3(b)(1)(i)(B), 25.7520-3(b)(1)(i)(B).

[35] Treas. Reg. §§ 1.7520-3(b)(1)(i)(C), 20.7520-3(b)(1)(i)(C), 25.7520-3(b)(1)(i)(C).

[36] Treas. Reg. §§ 1.7520-3(b)(2)(ii), 20.7520-3(b)(2)(ii), 25.7520-3(b)(2)(ii). See Ch. 4 for a description of those rights.

[37] Treas. Reg. §§ 1.7520-3(b)(2)(v), example 1, 20.7520-3(b)(2)(ii), example 1, 25.7520-3(b)(2)(ii), example 1.

[38] Treas. Reg. §§ 1.7520-3(b)(2)(v), example 1, 20.7520-3(b)(2)(ii), example 1, 25.7520-3(b)(2)(ii), example 2.

[39] Treas. Reg. §§ 1.7520-3(b)(2)(iii), 20.7520-3(b)(2)(iii), 25.7520-3(b)(2)(iii).

[40] Priv. Ltr. Rul. 9616004 (Dec. 29, 1995) (dealing with lottery winnings).

[41] Treas. Reg. §§ 1.7520-3(b)(1)(iii), 20.7520-3(b)(1)(iii), 25.7520-3(b)(1)(iii).

[5] Terminally Ill Measuring Life

Do the actuarial tables valuing interests depending on life expectancy apply if the person with the measuring life is known to have a very limited life expectancy? This question has been the subject of extensive litigation. At some point, if the actual life expectancy of the person with the measuring life is short enough, the actuarial tables cease to apply and the actual facts will be used to value an interest. There is conflicting authority on just what this point is.

[a] Transfers Before May 1, 1989

The IRS's view on the law was contained in Revenue Ruling 80-80,[42] which has been revoked for transactions occurring after December 13, 1995.[43] However, according to the IRS, it remains as authority for transactions occurring before December 14, 1995. The ruling says:

- The actuarial tables must be used to value actuarial interests unless the person's death is clearly imminent;
- If the possibility that a person may survive a year or more is not so remote as to be negligible, his death is not clearly imminent; and
- If the evidence indicates that the possibility that a person will survive for at least one year is negligible, the facts and circumstances will determine whether his death is clearly imminent on the valuation date.

Case law dealing with transactions during this period reached varying conclusions about use of the tables in the case of a terminally ill person who was the measuring life.

[b] Transfers After April 30, 1989, and Before December 14, 1995

The tables may have applied to all transfers taking place during this period. If not, general cases and rulings apply.[44]

[c] Transfers After December 13, 1995

[i] General rule. The final Section 7520 regulations, issued December 13, 1995, prohibit use of the tables if the individual is terminally ill.[45] "Terminally ill" means that (1) the individual with the measuring life is known to have an incurable illness or other deteriorating physical condition and (2) there is at

---

[42] 1980-1 CB 194.

[43] Rev. Rul. 96-3, 1996-2 IRB 14.

[44] See subparagraph [1] above.

[45] Treas. Reg. §§ 1.7520-3(b)(3), 20.7520-3(b)(3)(i), 25.7520-3(b)(3).

least a 50 percent probability that the individual will die within one year.[46] If the individual in fact survives for at least 18 months after the date of the transaction, the individual will be presumed not to have been terminally ill at the date of the transaction unless the contrary is established by clear and convincing evidence.[47] An elderly person suffering from the general infirmities of old age, but not from a specific incurable life-threatening illness, would not be considered terminally ill.[48]

If the donor (or other person whose measuring life is being used) is terminally ill within the above definition, then a special factor must be computed that is based on the 7520 rate and that takes into account the individual's actual life expectancy.[49]

PRACTICE POINTER: Note the difference between Revenue Ruling 80-80 and the regulations with respect to the one-year life expectancy test. Under Revenue Ruling 80-80's bright-line rule, if the person had more than a negligible possibility of living for one year, his death would not be treated as clearly imminent. However, if his possibility of survival for at least one year was negligible, the facts and circumstances would determine whether his death was clearly imminent. The new regulations, on the other hand, provide that if a person with an incurable condition has a 50 percent or lower expectation of living one year, the factual inquiry is over, and he will be conclusively presumed to be terminally ill. But, if the person actually lives for more than a year after the transfer, then a factual determination can still be made that he was terminally ill on the date of transfer. If he in fact survives for at least 18 months, then he will be presumed not to have been terminally ill on the date of transfer, but the contrary can still be shown by clear and convincing evidence.[50]

[ii] Exceptions: credit for previously transferred property and certain retained reversions. The tables are used even when a terminally ill person is the measuring life in the following two circumstances.

Credit for previously transferred property. The credit for previously transferred property is a credit which applies if *A* dies and leaves property to *B*, who subsequently dies within ten years of *A*'s death.[51] Where property included in the second decedent's estate is eligible for the previously transferred property credit, a special rule applies. If determining the federal estate tax liability of

---

[46] Treas. Reg. §§ 1.7520-3(b)(3), 20.7520-3(b)(3)(i), 25.7520-3(b)(3).

[47] Treas. Reg. §§ 1.7520-3(b)(3), 20.7520-3(b)(3)(i), 25.7520-3(b)(3).

[48] TD 8630, 1996-3 IRB 19.

[49] Treas. Reg. §§ 1.7520-3(b)(4), example 2, 20.7520-3(b)(4), example 1, 25.7520-3(b)(4).

[50] Treas. Reg. §§ 1.7520-3(b)(3), 20.7520-3(b)(3)(i), 25.7520-3(b)(3).

[51] IRC § 2013.

the first decedent's estate required valuation of the life estate received by the second decedent, then the value of the transferred property (for purposes of the previously transferred property credit allowable to the second decedent's estate) will be the value previously determined in the first decedent's estate.[52]

> EXAMPLE: Son dies, leaving Mother a life estate in Blackacre. The remainder interest in Blackacre passes to Wife outright, and qualifies for the marital deduction. The estate tax calculation of Son's estate will depend on a valuation of Mother's life estate. If Mother dies within ten years of Son, her estate's Section 2013 credit will be calculated using the value of her life estate as determined for purposes of Son's estate tax, regardless of Mother's state of health on Son's death.

There is also some case law suggesting that the tables will apply for purposes of the Section 2013 credit, regardless of the physical condition of either party, since the timing of transfers qualifying for the credit is not subject to abuse.[53]

Certain retained reversions. Under certain circumstances, property will be included in a decedent's estate if he transferred the property and retained a right to get it back for less than fair consideration, and the reversionary right was worth more than five percent of the value of the property immediately before the decedent's death.[54] The value of a decedent's reversionary interest for purposes of Sections 2037(b) and 2042(2) is determined without regard to the physical condition of the individual who is the measuring life.[55]

> EXAMPLE: Grandma, who is 90 years old, transfers insurance policy on her life to Grandson, a healthy 18-year-old, but retains a right to get the policy back if Grandson dies before she does. Grandma dies five years later. Under the actuarial tables, the chances immediately before Grandma's death that Grandson would predecease her were less than five percent, so the policy proceeds are not included in her estate. This would be true even if Grandson had become terminally ill during the five-year period after the gift and before Grandma's death.

The Treasury has asked for comments on whether reversionary interests should also be valued for purposes of Section 673 without regard to the physical condition of the donor or his spouse.[56]

---

[52] Treas. Reg. § 20.7520-3(b)(3)(ii). This exception was also stated in Rev. Rul. 80-80.

[53] See Ch. 50 for a discussion.

[54] IRC §§ 2037(a)(2), 2042(2).

[55] Treas. Reg. § 20.7520-3(b)(3)(ii). See Ch. 2 for a description of these reversionary interests.

[56] TD 8630, 1996-3 IRB 19, corrected by Notice 96-22, 1996-14 IRB 30. Section 673 treats the grantor of a trust as the owner of the trust's tax items if the grantor has

[6] Deaths in a Common Disaster

The tables do not apply if the decedent and an individual who is the measuring life die as a result of a common accident or other occurrence.[57]

> EXAMPLE: Brother and Sister are caught in a snowstorm on a mountain-climbing expedition. Brother falls down the mountain and dies. Sister is buried by falling snow two hours later. Brother's estate passes to a trust providing Sister an annuity for her life, remainder to his Wife. The marital deduction is not measured by the value of Sister's actuarial life expectancy at Brother's death.

¶ 11.06 ADDITIONAL READING

For an excellent article on the workings of the actuarial rules, see Lawrence P. Katzenstein, Lives in the Balance—Taking the Mystery out of Actuarial Valuations, 29 U. Miami—School of Law Philip E. Heckerling Inst. on Est. Plan. ¶ 1200 (1995). The article was written before the proposed regulations were finalized, but it contains very helpful explanations of the mathematics underlying the tables, how those mathematics translate into planning, and how to do actuarial calculations when the tables do not have a number for a specific set of facts.

---

a reversionary interest in the trust which is valued at more than 5 percent of the trust assets during the year in question.

[57] Treas. Reg. § 20.7520-3(b)(3)(iii).

PART III

Assets Providing Death Benefits

CHAPTER **12**

Life Insurance

¶ 12.01 INTRODUCTION

Life insurance is a tax-favored asset. Why? First, the increase in its cash value (its "inside buildup") accumulates tax-free, as long as it remains in the policy.

Second, in most cases, the proceeds pass to the beneficiary free of income tax and, if proper steps are taken, free of estate tax. Most of an estate planner's efforts regarding life insurance are directed toward keeping the proceeds out of the insured's estate. That being the case, this chapter first discusses the transfer taxation of life insurance policies and proceeds, including available techniques to minimize or eliminate the tax. The chapter then discusses other important issues pertaining to life insurance, including the income tax aspects of life insurance policies and proceeds, as well as factors to consider when selecting a life insurance policy.

¶ 12.02 TRANSFER TAXATION OF LIFE INSURANCE

[1] Estate Tax Considerations

Life insurance is generally included in the insured's estate if the proceeds are receivable by the personal representative of the insured's estate (whether or not the insured's estate is the designated beneficiary of the policy).[1] Life insurance is also taxable in the estate of the insured if the insured has any "incidents of ownership" in the policy.[2]

In community property states, however, only one-half of the proceeds payable to a decedent's estate or subject to the insured's incidents of ownership are includable in the decedent's estate, if the local community property law provides that one-half of the proceeds belong to the decedent's spouse.[3]

[a] Incidents of Ownership

"Incidents of ownership" include rights to name the beneficiary, surrender or cancel the policy, assign the policy, pledge the policy for a loan, or otherwise enjoy the economic benefits of the policy.[4] If the insured has an option to acquire an insurance policy on his life for less than the fair market value of the policy, he may have an incident of ownership over the policy.[5]

---

[1] IRC § 2042(1); Treas. Reg. § 20.2042-1(b)(1).

[2] IRC § 2042(2). See Ch. 2 for a further discussion.

[3] Treas. Reg. § 20.2042-1(b)(2).

[4] Treas. Reg. § 20.2042-1(c)(2).

[5] The IRS so held in Tech. Adv. Mem. 9128008 (Mar. 29, 1991) (insured could re-acquire assigned policy for an amount equal to the premiums paid by the assignee plus 10 percent per year) and Tech. Adv. Mem. 9349002 (Aug. 25, 1993) (insured could purchase policy for cash surrender value plus unearned premium on the repayment of a corporate note to her); but see Priv. Ltr. Rul. 9233006 (May 11, 1992) (insured did not have incident of ownership where he could purchase policy for its cash surrender value if certain events of independent significance occurred).

[b] Incidents of Ownership Held by Entities

[i] **Corporations.** Incidents of ownership may, in certain circumstances, be attributed to the insured from entities in which the insured has an interest.

If the insurance proceeds are payable to a corporation in which the insured holds an interest, the corporation's incidents of ownership in the life insurance policy are not attributed to the insured.[6] This rule avoids double estate taxation of the insurance proceeds, which are already indirectly included in the estate as part of the value of the deceased insured's stock. It would be unfair to tax the insured's estate both on the policy proceeds and on the newly appreciated shares, since the value of the shares takes into account the corporation's receipt and retention of the proceeds.

However, to the extent that the insurance proceeds are payable to someone other than the corporation, the proceeds will be taxable in the insured's estate if (1) he can personally exercise any incident of ownership in the policy (such as naming the beneficiary) or (2) even if he cannot personally exercise any incident,[7] the corporation's incidents of ownership are attributed to the insured because he is a controlling shareholder.[8] The insured will be considered a controlling shareholder only if, at the time of his death, he owned stock possessing more than half of the voting power of the corporation.[9] Moreover, the insured will only be considered the owner of stock that was legally titled in the name of: the insured; the insured's agent or nominee; the insured and another person jointly (but only to the extent that the consideration had been furnished by the insured); or a voting trust (but only to the extent of the insured's beneficial interest).[10]

Controlling shareholder of an S corporation. If an S corporation owns the policy and the insured is the life beneficiary of a qualified subchapter S trust (QSST) holding over one-half of the voting power of the S corporation, the question has arisen as to whether the insured will be treated as the owner of the S stock for both income and estate tax purposes or only for income tax purposes.[11] The IRS, in previously considering this issue, suggested that the electing income beneficiary of the QSST would be treated as the owner of the S stock for purposes of estate taxation of the life insurance policy, so that the proceeds would be included in his estate if the corporation had held an incident of ownership. This was dicta, however, since the rulings held that the

---

[6] Treas. Reg. § 20.2042-1(c)(6).

[7] For example, if all of the rights in the policy not held by the corporation are held by an irrevocable life insurance trust and other officers of the corporation have the rights to exercise the corporate rights in the policy.

[8] Treas. Reg. § 20.2042-1(c)(6).

[9] Treas. Reg. § 20.2042-1(c)(6).

[10] Treas. Reg. § 20.2042-1(c)(6).

[11] See Ch. 18 for a discussion of QSSTs.

corporations had no incidents of ownership in the policies.[12] The correct answer would seem to be that the income tax treatment of the shareholder is not relevant to the estate tax. This is consistent with the general treatment of the income tax and the transfer tax as not being *in pari materia.*

[ii] **Partnerships.** Incidents of ownership should not be attributed to a partner if the partnership is the beneficiary.[13] Otherwise, double estate taxation of all or a portion of the proceeds would result because of the inclusion of the insurance proceeds in the estate along with the partnership interest, the value of which was proportionately increased by the partnership's receipt and retention of the insurance proceeds.[14]

If the partnership is not the beneficiary, and the insured can actually exercise any incident of ownership, the policy will be includable in the insured's estate. Moreover, even if the insured cannot personally exercise any incidents of ownership, but the partnership can,[15] the insured might still be deemed to possess the partnership's incidents of ownership, regardless of the amount of his interest in the partnership.[16]

[iii] **Trusts.** If the insured has a power of appointment over an insurance policy on his life, the policy may be included in his estate, since the insured has the power to direct the recipient of the proceeds. The IRS recently issued and immediately withdrew a series of letter rulings regarding the incidents of ownership possessed by beneficiaries of trusts that owned life insurance on the beneficiaries' lives. The IRS withdrew the rulings, purportedly to consider the effect of special powers of appointment held by the beneficiaries over the assets of the trusts.[17]

Where the insured is merely the trustee, however, some courts have held that the power to exercise ownership solely in a fiduciary capacity (i.e., where the insured cannot benefit himself or his estate) will not result in inclusion of

---

[12] Priv. Ltr. Rul. 9511046 (Dec. 22, 1994); Priv. Ltr. Rul. 9348009 (Aug. 31, 1993).

[13] Rev. Rul. 83-147, 1983-2 CB 158.

[14] See explanation in the above paragraph applicable to corporations.

[15] For example, if the insured is a limited partner.

[16] Rev. Rul. 83-147, 1983-2 CB 158; GCM 39034 (Sept. 21, 1983) (both making an exception for group-term policies). These authorities involved general partnerships, and held that the general partner-insured held incidents of ownership in conjunction with the other partners. It is not clear how this theory would be applied if the insured were a limited partner.

[17] See Priv. Ltr. Rul. 9542007 (July 12, 1995); Priv. Ltr. Rul. 9541024 (July 12, 1995); Priv. Ltr. Rul. 9541023 (July 12, 1995); Priv. Ltr. Rul. 9541022 (July 12, 1995); Priv. Ltr. Rul. 9538035 (June 27, 1995).

the proceeds in the trustee-insured's estate.[18] Other courts have, however, held to the contrary.[19]

The IRS's position, where the insured is merely the trustee, is that the proceeds are only includable in the trustee-insured's estate if the insured transferred the policy or the consideration for the premiums to the trust and he participated in the plan to possess fiduciary incidents of ownership.[20] In other words, if the insured divests himself of incidents of ownership by giving the policy to his wife, and his wife later dies and leaves the policy to a trust of which the insured husband is a trustee but not a beneficiary, the proceeds should not be includable in the insured's estate, provided he cannot benefit from the policy and does not contribute property to the trust for the payment of premiums.

PRACTICE POINTER: Avoid the issue of inclusion of life insurance proceeds in the fiduciary-insured's estate by including a provision in the governing instrument (i.e., the trust, will, or power of attorney) that prohibits the fiduciary from exercising any incidents of ownership over policies on the fiduciary's life. A special trustee or co-trustee can be appointed to exercise the incidents of ownership, if that is permissible under state law.

[iv] **Buy-Sell Arrangements.**[21] Suppose that Lily and Travis are co-owners of Company, a business entity. Lily purchases insurance on Travis's life for the purpose of buying Travis's interest in the business on Travis's death. If Travis dies, the proceeds should not be included in his estate, assuming he had no incidents of ownership in the policy.[22] This is true even if Travis had also purchased a policy on Lily's life.[23] If Company purchases the life insurance on the shareholders, and the proceeds are payable to or for the

---

[18] E.g. Estate of Fruehauf v. Comm'r, 427 F2d 80 (6th Cir. 1970) (indicating that the same analysis is appropriate in the case of a deceased executor-insured); Estate of Hector R. Skifter v. Comm'r, 56 TC 1190 (1971), aff'd, 468 F2d 699 (2d Cir. 1972); see also Estate of Dawson v. Comm'r, 57 TC 837 (1972), aff'd, 480 F2d 917 (3d Cir. 1973), holding that when the insured was the sole residuary legatee under his deceased wife's will, IRC § 2042 did not apply upon the subsequent death of the insured during the estate administration because under the applicable state law, a residuary legatee's qualified equitable right to receive what is left of the estate after administration is inchoate in nature.

[19] E.g., Rose v. United States, 511 F2d 259 (5th Cir. 1975); Terriberry v. United States, 517 F2d 286 (5th Cir. 1975), cert. denied, 424 US 977 (1976).

[20] Rev. Rul. 84-179, 1984-2 CB 195.

[21] See Ch. 27 on buy-sell agreements for a more detailed discussion of buy-sell agreements.

[22] Rev. Rul. 56-397, 1956-2 CB 599.

[23] Rev. Rul. 56-397, 1956-2 CB 599.

benefit of Company, the proceeds would not be included in Travis's estate, even if Company were subject to a binding agreement to use the proceeds to purchase his interest in the entity.[24] (Note, however, that the proceeds will be reflected in the estate tax value of Travis's interest in Company.)[25] If proceeds are included in Travis's estate, but there is a binding agreement to purchase his interest in Company with the proceeds, then the interest in Company which is purchased with the proceeds will not be included in Travis's estate.[26]

[c] When the Insured Should Keep Incidents of Ownership

If someone besides the insured (or a person/entity whose incidents of ownership are imputed to the insured) owns all incidents of ownership in the policy, in the absence of other factors, the proceeds will not be taxable in the insured's estate. Hence, it will often not make sense for the insured to own the policy in such a manner that it would be included in his estate.

In some situations, however, it may make sense for the insured to own or control the incidents of ownership. For example, the insured may need to exercise the incidents of ownership of a policy to access the cash value of a policy or to pledge the policy as security for his personal debts. Or, the insured may want to control the incidents of ownership because he expects to keep the policy for less than three years and therefore an assignment of the policy or incidents of ownership would not remove the proceeds from his estate anyway. Or, the insured may not expect to keep the insurance until his death, and may not want to use his gift tax annual exclusion on, or make a taxable gift of, the policy or the premiums. Or, the policy may be payable to charity and thus render inclusion in the insured's estate of no net tax consequence.

[d] Transfer to an Irrevocable Life Insurance Trust Versus Transfer to an Individual Owner

In the case of an existing policy, it is simpler at the outset for the insured-owner to transfer the policy to an individual than to establish a trust owner. However, the disadvantages of allowing another individual to own the policy often outweigh the advantages. For example, if Insured's Child owns the policy, Child may or may not decide to continue paying the premiums, or may not in fact be able to pay the premiums. In a financial pinch, Child may decide to surrender the policy to get some cash. The policy will be subject to Child's creditors if it does not constitute exempt property, and it may constitute

---

[24] Estate of Knipp v. Comm'r, 25 TC 153 (1955), acq., 1959-1 CB 4, aff'd, 244 F2d 436 (4th Cir. 1957), cert. denied, 355 US 827 (1957); Rev. Rul. 83-147, 1983-2 CB 158.

[25] Rev. Rul. 82-85, 1982-1 CB 137.

[26] Estate of Tompkins v. Comm'r, 13 TC 1054 (1949).

marital property which can be divided in Child's divorce. These disadvantages can be eliminated, for the most part, through the use of an irrevocable life insurance trust (ILIT). For this and other reasons, an ILIT is often the preferred vehicle to own policies outside the insured's estate.[27]

[2] Gift Tax Considerations

[a] Valuation of the Policy

Existing policies. The value of an unmatured insurance policy for gift tax purposes is generally its replacement cost.[28] According to the regulations, however, when a contract has been in force for some time and the policy is not paid up, the replacement cost is not readily ascertainable. In such instance, the value is usually the "interpolated terminal reserve value" at date of transfer plus the gross premium that is still unearned.[29] The interpolated terminal reserve value must be obtained from the insurance company, and will usually approximate the cash surrender value of the policy.

New policies. The value of a new policy is the premium paid.[30]

Term policies. The value of a term policy is generally the unearned premium at date of transfer.[31] If an employee's interest in a group term policy is assigned, a gift is made to the assignee each time the employer pays a premium.[32] What is the amount of the premium allocable to the employee's coverage? According to the IRS, if the plan is nondiscriminatory and the employee is not a key employee, the Table I rates can be used. If those conditions do not apply, the cost is the actual cost allocable to the employee's insurance.[33]

Policy loans. In all cases, outstanding policy loans are subtracted from the above numbers to determine the policy value.

Imminent death/shortened life expectancy. If death is imminent at the date of transfer, or if the insured has medical problems which will significantly shorten his life expectancy at date of transfer, do the above rules still apply? It has been suggested from time to time that they may not.[34] For example, if

---

[27] ILITs are discussed in detail at ¶ 12.04.

[28] Treas. Reg. §§ 20.2031-8, 25.2512-6.

[29] Treas. Reg. §§ 20.2031-6(a)(2), 25.2512-6(a).

[30] Treas. Reg. § 25.2512-6(a), example 1.

[31] See Rev. Rul. 76-490, 1976-2 CB 300.

[32] See Rev. Rul. 76-490, 1976-2 CB 300.

[33] Rev. Rul. 84-147, 1984-2 CB 201.

[34] See Estate of Pritchard v. Comm'r, 4 TC 204 (1944), appeal dismissed, (6th Cir. 1945) (unpublished opinion) (when death is imminent, value approaches proceeds

an insured has terminal cancer and is expected to die within six months, the value of the policy may be its actual fair market value.[35]

An owner-insured with a short life expectancy must also remember that if he gives away a policy, the proceeds will be includable in his estate if he dies within three years after the gift.[36]

[b] The Community Property Problem

An unexpected (and unwelcome) gift of life insurance proceeds can occur in community property states. When a married couple purchases life insurance on the life of one spouse with community property and names someone other than the uninsured spouse as beneficiary, the uninsured spouse makes a gift of one-half of the proceeds to the beneficiary upon the insured's death (provided that, under applicable state law, the insured's death makes the transfer by the uninsured spouse absolute).[37]

¶ 12.03 INCOME TAXATION OF LIFE INSURANCE PROCEEDS

[1] General Rule

Life insurance proceeds generally do not constitute taxable income.[38] There are, however, a number of exceptions to this general rule.

[2] Transfer-for-Value Rule

Under the transfer-for-value rule, if a policy has been sold during the insured's life, then the proceeds will generally be taxable income to the beneficiary, except to the extent of the transferee's investment in the contract.

---

receivable on death, and is not based on investment features); Priv. Ltr. Rul. 9413045 (Jan. 4, 1994) (basing ruling that interpolated terminal reserve value was correct on representations that the insureds were not in danger of imminent death and did not have medical problems that would unexpectedly shorten their life expectancies).

[35] The fair market value of a policy on the life of a terminally ill person may not be difficult to determine. An active market actually exists for such policies. Numerous viatical companies, which are in the business of buying such policies, have been established since the emergence of AIDS.

[36] IRC §§ 2035(a), 2035(d)(1)–2035(2).

[37] Treas. Reg. § 25.2511-1(h)(5); Rev. Rul. 94-69, 1994-2 CB 241.

[38] IRC § 101(a)(1).

The following policy transfers are excepted from the transfer-for-value rule:

- Transfers to the insured;
- Transfers to a partner of the insured;
- Transfers to a partnership in which the insured is a partner;
- Transfers to a corporation in which the insured is a shareholder or officer; and
- Transfers in which the basis of the transferee is determined wholly or partly by reference to the transferor's basis (the "tacked-basis exception").

[a] Tacked-Basis Exception—Gifts (No Consideration Paid)

A gift of a policy falls under the tacked-basis exception because the transferee takes a carryover basis from the transferor.[39]

[b] Tacked-Basis Exception—Partial Gifts (Sales for Inadequate Consideration)

A sale for less than adequate consideration will be within the tacked-basis exception if the amount received by the seller is less than his investment in the contract.[40]

[c] Gift of Policy Subject to Outstanding Loan

Before assigning a policy with a large cash value, it may be desirable to borrow the cash value to reduce the value of the gift; such loans against the policy are nonrecourse, and are secured only by the policy and its proceeds. The policy owner receives no increase in his investment in the contract for repayment of a loan.

A gift of a policy subject to such a loan is a transfer for consideration. The amount of the loan, plus interest, is the consideration.[41] If the consideration does not exceed the transferor's investment in the contract, then the transfer comes within the tacked-basis exception.[42]

---

[39] IRC §§ 1015, 1041.

[40] Treas. Reg. § 1.1015-4(a) provides that a part gift/part sale results in a carryover basis if the consideration paid is less than the seller's basis, and a cost basis (determined without reference to the seller's basis) if it is the same or higher. See ¶ 12.07 for a discussion of the investment in the contract.

[41] See Crane v. Comm'r, 331 US 1 (1947); Treas. Reg. § 1.1001-2(c)(1), 1.1001-2(a)(4).

[42] Rev. Rul. 69-187, 1969-1 CB 45; Priv. Ltr. Rul. 8951056 (Sept. 27, 1989).

[d] Pledge of Policy

A pledge or assignment of a policy as collateral security does not constitute a transfer for value unless the policy is actually taken by the creditor in repayment of the loan.[43]

[e] Subsequent Transfers of the Policy

[i] General rule. Generally, once the policy has been transferred for value, the death proceeds (less the owner's investment in the contract) will be taxable income to the beneficiary, even if the policy is subsequently transferred in a tacked-basis transfer. The final transferee gets to count consideration paid by all previous owners in determining his investment in the contract.

[ii] Exception. However, a transfer of a policy to the insured, the insured's partner, a partnership in which the insured is a partner, or a corporation in which the insured is a shareholder or officer removes all taint from a policy which was previously transferred for value.[44]

¶ 12.04 IRREVOCABLE LIFE INSURANCE TRUST

Life insurance on a wealthy individual is usually held by an irrevocable life insurance trust (ILIT). A properly drafted ILIT can allow the proceeds of life insurance policies held in the trust to pass free of estate tax on the deaths of both the insured and the insured's spouse, while providing financial support for the insured's surviving spouse and descendants and/or liquidity for taxes in the insured's or surviving spouse's estate.

[1] Basics

A contributor to the ILIT (usually the insured) assigns an insurance policy to the trust. Or, in the alternative, the ILIT's trustee may buy the policy with trust cash (usually contributed by the insured). The insured is not the trustee and retains no benefits in the trust. During the insured's lifetime, premiums are paid by the trustee with trust cash, which may be received by the trustee as gifts from the insured. The beneficiaries of the trust do not contribute to it. At the insured's death, the insurance company pays the policy proceeds to the trust. The policy proceeds are thereafter held in trust for the benefit of the insured's spouse, descendants, or other beneficiaries, as the trust instrument provides. If liquidity is needed in the insured's estate, the trustee may use the

---

[43] Treas. Reg. § 1.101-1(b)(4); Priv. Ltr. Rul. 8628007 (Mar. 21, 1986).

[44] Treas. Reg. § 1.101-1(b)(3)(ii), 1.101-1(b)(5), examples 5, 7.

proceeds to purchase assets from the insured's estate or lend money to the insured's estate, if the trust instrument permits.

> **EXAMPLE:** Farmer has a dell worth $10,000,000. Farmer takes a wife and signs a will leaving the dell to her. Farmer gives cash to an ILIT, which buys a $5,500,000 joint and survivor life insurance policy on the lives of farmer and his wife, payable on the death of the survivor. Wife is the survivor, and values do not change. On her death, her estate will owe estate tax of $5,500,000 on the dell. What if her estate has no liquidity to pay the tax? Due to Farmer's good planning, Wife's executor will not have to look far. The ILIT will have $5,500,000 of life insurance proceeds. The trustee can buy part of the dell from the estate, or lend the estate money, so that the executor will be able to pay the estate taxes.

The usual way to transfer a policy and/or cash to pay premiums is by gift. One advantage of life insurance is that the gifts necessary to keep the ILIT out of the estate are measured by the value of the gifted premiums, or by the date-of-gift value of the policy, in the case of a gift of an existing policy. The gift is not the face value of the policy.

> **EXAMPLE:** Dad gives a trust $10,000, and the trustee uses it to buy life insurance with a face value of $100,000 on Dad's life. The value of the gift is $10,000. Suppose that in Dad's situation, the gift tax on the $10,000 is $5,500. If Dad dies that year, the trust will receive $100,000 of insurance proceeds, and the total transfer tax cost will be $5,500. If Dad had owned the policy himself when he died, the estate tax on the proceeds, at the 55 percent bracket, would have been $55,000, and his beneficiaries would have received $45,000.

[2] Use of Joint and Survivor Policies

Many wealthy couples do not need a policy to take care of the support needs of the surviving spouse; rather, their primary concern is to provide for the payment of estate taxes, for the replacement of assets left to charity, or for the support of their children and grandchildren, as the case may be. Hence, a popular technique is to purchase a policy which matures on the death of the survivor of the husband and wife.

Riders are also available for some joint and survivor policies: (1) to provide some benefit on the death of the first spouse to die (so that the cash can be used to fund future premiums or to buy a split-dollar policy which is being rolled out);[45] (2) to provide increased benefits to cover estate tax attributable to the policy if both spouses die within three years of obtaining the policy; and (3) to split the policy into two individual policies on a divorce.

---

[45] Split-dollar funding is described at ¶ 12.06.

WARNING: The premiums on a joint policy may turn into premiums on a single-life policy, and therefore increase, on the death of the first spouse. Some companies offer a rider to eliminate this result or to pay up the policy at the first death.

[3] Effective Use of the Unified Credit

Transfer of cash or a policy to an ILIT may be a good use of the unified credit, since it may be possible to purchase quite a bit of life insurance for premiums of $600,000 ($1,200,000 in the case of a married couple who use their combined credits of $1,200,000).

[4] Effective Use of the Generation-Skipping Transfer Tax Exemption

One good way for a couple to use the generation-skipping transfer tax (GSTT) exemption is to give up to $2,000,000 to a dynastic trust for the benefit of their descendants. The trust can then purchase a joint and survivor policy with the cash. Even if the couple are killed a week later, the insurance proceeds (which should be considerably in excess of $2,000,000) will be received tax-free by the beneficiaries.[46]

[5] Gift Tax Annual Exclusion Considerations

Structuring the ILIT as a Crummey trust with a hanging power may be appropriate, if the ILIT is being designed to hold (1) policies with premiums that have "vanished"[47] and are not expected to reappear; (2) policies for which the premiums are never expected to exceed the annual exclusion; or (3) term policies that the insured does not intend to keep in force after a certain point (e.g., when his children are all adults).[48]

---

[46] E.g., Estate of Headrick v. Comm'r, 93 TC 171 (1989), aff'd, 918 F2d 1263 (6th Cir. 1990), action on decision, 1991-012 (July 3, 1991).

[47] Premiums do not actually vanish. If premiums have "vanished," for a year, this means that the policy dividends/interest are sufficient to pay the premium, so that no out-of-pocket cash is required that year to maintain the policy. In subsequent years, depending on how the policy performs, the premiums may or may not reappear. They would reappear if the dividends/interest did not support the premiums—because interest or dividend rates were too low, expenses or mortality costs were too high, or a combination. A policy with "vanished" premiums is not the same as a "paid-up" policy, which is a policy subject to a contractual provision that no further premiums will be required to maintain the policy, regardless of the investment performance of the policy or the company.

[48] See Ch. 10 on tax-free gifts for a more complete discussion of Crummey trusts.

[a] Employer-Provided Policies

If the employee's interest in a group term or other policy owned by the employer is assigned to a Crummey trust, enough withdrawable property must be in the trust to satisfy the beneficiary's withdrawal right. Premiums for a group life insurance policy are usually deducted from the employee's paycheck, and the interest in the policy itself may not be able to be withdrawn by a trust beneficiary. Therefore, it might be prudent to keep at least one month's premium payment in the trust.

According to the IRS, if a beneficiary waives the right to notice of future withdrawal contributions, those contributions will not qualify for the annual exclusion unless the beneficiary had actual notice.[49] Does this mean that the trustee in a group term situation must send a Crummey notice after each paycheck? Surely not—no one would ever comply.

PRACTICE POINTER: A cautious but workable solution to the notice issue for premiums which are deducted from paychecks might be to write one notice letter per year, notifying the beneficiaries that $x per month will be contributed to the trust on the nth date of each month, and that they may withdraw within y days of the contribution.

[b] Trust for Spouse

If the trust holding life insurance on Husband's life is to be used for the benefit of Wife, Wife should not contribute to the trust. Should Wife be a Crummey powerholder? It is probably best if she is not for the reasons set out in detail in Chapter 3.

Summarizing the discussion in Chapter 3, the "five-or-five amount" is the greater of five percent of the value of the assets subject to the withdrawal power or $5,000. To the extent that Wife's power to withdraw trust assets in excess of the five-or-five amount lapses in any one year, she will make a gift to the trust, causing inclusion of all or part of the proceeds in her estate if she retains a taxable interest in or power over the gifted property. If she dies holding an unlapsed power, all or part of the trust will be includable in her estate. Inclusion of the proceeds in Wife's estate defeats the purpose of the ILIT, which is to remove the life insurance proceeds from both spouses' estates.[50]

If the ILIT is an exempt generation-skipping trust, (1) distributions to Wife will result in a waste of the GSTT exemption and (2) the estate tax

---

[49] Tech. Adv. Mem. 9532001 (Apr. 12, 1995).

[50] Simply keeping the proceeds out of the taxable estate of the insured spouse could be achieved by keeping the incidents of ownership in the hands of the insured and paying the proceeds on his death in a manner which qualifies for the marital deduction.

inclusion period (ETIP) will not generally expire until the trust would not be includable in her estate if she died.[51] The final GSTT regulations provide one exception to the ETIP rule. Wife's withdrawal power over a contribution to the trust will not subject the trust to an ETIP as long as the power is limited to the greater of $5,000 or five percent of the trust copus and the power expires within 60 days after the contribution is made.[52]

[c] Complications of Crummey Trusts

Crummey trusts have disadvantages in many ILITs. They can result in deemed gifts by the beneficiaries to the trust, inclusion of the trust assets in the beneficiaries' estates, and taxation of the beneficiaries on income of the trust after it is funded.[53] For policies requiring large premiums, for exempt trusts, and for spousal trusts, it will often make sense to use the unified credit and GSTT exemption on the ILIT and not clutter the picture with Crummey powers.

[6] Advance Funding of the Trust

In cases where the annual exclusion is not used to exempt premium payments from gift tax, it may be best to fund an ILIT with several years' premiums all at once for the following two reasons.

To avoid status as a modified endowment contract. Let's say the cost of acquiring a single-premium paid-up policy is $200,000. If the ILIT pays for it all at once, the policy will likely be a modified endowment contract (MEC), which has some substantial disadvantages.[54] If the donor gives the trust $200,000, and the trust pays the insurance company over a permitted period of years, this consequence can be avoided.

To minimize gift tax. Premiums paid over time will normally be larger in total amount than a single premium paid at the policy origination. In the previous example, if trust premiums were $35,000/year for seven years and cash equal to the annual premium was donated to the trust each year, total taxable gifts would be $245,000 (assuming that no gift tax annual exclusion was available). However, if the gift were made at the inception of the trust, only $200,000 would have to be transferred to the trust. The fact that the trust assets ultimately grow enough to pay the $245,000 does not increase the gift.[55] Accordingly, gift tax of $24,750 could be saved by the upfront gift to the trust.

---

[51] Treas. Reg. § 26.2632-1(c). These concepts are explained in detail in Ch. 5.

[52] Treas. Reg. § 26.2632-1(c)(2)(ii)(B).

[53] These issues are discussed in detail in Ch. 10.

[54] See ¶ 12.07[2][d][ii].

[55] Of course, the insured may be taxable on the income earned by the original $200,000 contribution. IRC § 677(a)(3).

[7] Three-Year Rule

[a] General Rule

If a donor gives an ILIT an existing policy, as opposed to the cash needed to purchase an equivalent new policy, then the donor must live for at least three years after the transfer in order to remove the policy proceeds from his estate.[56]

[b] Indirect Transfers

Indirect, as well as direct, gifts of policies can be covered by the three-year rule. The IRS considers each of the following indirect transfers to be subject to the three-year rule, thereby requiring the inclusion of the policy proceeds in the insured's estate if the transfer occurs within three years before the insured's death:

- A transfer of ownership of a policy on the life of the insured by the insured's controlled corporation.[57]
- A transfer by the insured of his controlling interest in a corporation holding a policy on his life.[58]
- A transfer of ownership of a policy on the life of the insured by the insured's controlled corporation coupled with the insured's disposition of his controlling interest in the stock, both occurring within the three-year period.[59]

[c] Avoiding the Rule With New Policies

The three-year rule is not an issue if the trust (and not the insured) pays for the new policy. Otherwise, if the donor-insured purchases a new policy and immediately gives it to the trust, the three-year rule is unnecessarily invoked.

[d] Avoiding the Rule With Existing Policies

Avoidance of the three-year rule is not as easy or straightforward as with a new policy. However, it is possible. Suppose Husband owns an insurance policy on his life, and wants to give the policy to an ILIT for the benefit of his children. Husband has a serious medical condition. Wife is younger than Husband and in good health. Can Husband avoid the three-year rule? Let's analyze some ideas.

[i] Partition the policy. If the policy is community property, the couple

---

[56] IRC § 2035(d)(2).

[57] Rev. Rul. 82-141, 1982 CB 209.

[58] Rev. Rul. 82-141, 1982 CB 209.

[59] Rev. Rul. 90-21, 1990-1 CB 1972.

can execute a partition agreement, partitioning the policy to Wife as her separate property, and an amount of cash equal to the value of the policy to Husband as his separate property. Wife can then give the policy to the children's ILIT.

[ii] Sequential gifts of policy. If the policy is Husband's property, he can give it to Wife, and she can transfer it to the children's ILIT. However, the IRS may take the position that Wife was only a straw person and that, in substance, the policy was really transferred by Husband.[60]

[iii] Sale of policy to children. Husband can sell the policy to the children for fair consideration.[61] This will remove the policy from his estate. However, the sale will invoke the transfer-for-value rule, which subjects the proceeds of the policy to income taxation.[62] The income tax rate may be less than the estate tax rate, so this solution may still be better than Husband's keeping the policy.

[iv] Sale to wife, with gift to ILIT. A sale of the policy to Wife for fair market value, followed by a transfer of the policy by her to the children's ILIT, may also work. The transfer-for-value rule does not apply to a transfer if the transferee's basis is determined, in whole or in part, with reference to the transferor's basis.[63] This will be the case with most interspousal transfers, since gain or loss is not usually recognized on a sale between spouses, and the purchasing spouse takes the selling spouse's basis.[64] If, however, indebtedness

---

[60] Interestingly, sometimes people react to this statement by saying that the IRS has given up on this argument, since the Headrick case decided the question in the taxpayer's favor. The Headrick case involved a different issue. After Headrick, the IRS formally gave up its position that a gift of cash to an insurance trust, followed by a purchase of a life insurance policy on the donor by the trustee, constituted a constructive transfer of the policy by the insured. Estate of Headrick v. Comm'r, 93 TC 171 (1989), aff'd, 918 F2d 1263 (6th Cir. 1990), action on decision, 1991-012 (July 3, 1991). The issue raised in our proposed transaction is: if donor gives a policy to person A, who immediately in a planned transaction gives it to person B, is this really just a gift of the policy by donor to person B? See Priv. Ltr. Rul. 9349002 (Aug. 25, 1993).

[61] The IRS has taken the position that, in the case of a transfer of a life insurance policy within three years of the insured's death, fair consideration is the amount of the death benefit. See Tech. Adv. Mem. 8806004 (Nov. 4, 1987) and Estate of Pritchard v. Comm'r, 4 TC 204 (1944), appeal dismissed (6th Cir. 1945) (unpublished opinion); but see Priv. Ltr. Rul. 9413045 (Jan. 4, 1994). If this valuation rule applies, there is no point in transferring a policy within three years of the insured's death. The analysis in this section assumes that value is determined in the normal way, except as specifically noted.

[62] IRC § 101(a)(2).

[63] IRC § 101(a)(2)(A).

[64] IRC § 1041(b).

against the policy exceeds Husband's basis in the policy, then Wife will take a cost basis in the policy, the transaction will not fit the tacked-basis exception, and the sale will render the proceeds subject to income taxation.[65]

[v] **Sale to ILIT.** A sale of the policy to the ILIT[66] may also work, without triggering the transfer-for-value rule, if the ILIT assets are treated as wholly owned by Husband for income tax purposes. Such a sale should be treated as a transfer to the insured for purposes of the transfer-for-value rule.[67] The IRS will not rule on this issue, as it involves an area under extensive study.[68]

[vi] **Sale to partnership.** In a 1993 private letter ruling, the IRS determined that a partner's transfer of an existing policy to a newly formed partnership was excepted from the transfer-for-value rule. The private letter ruling involved corporate shareholders who had a buy-sell agreement which was to be funded with cross-owned life insurance. That is, shareholder *A* would assign his life insurance policy to shareholder *B* and vice versa. Because these assignments would have been considered transfers for value, however, the shareholders formed a new partnership solely for the purpose of acquiring and holding their life insurance policies and then transferred the policies to the partnership. The IRS ruled that this transfer came within the exception for transfers to a partnership of which the insured is a partner.[69]

Is the sale of a policy to a partnership holding life insurance a good solution then? When substantially all of the organization's assets consist or will consist of life insurance policies on the lives of the members, the IRS will no longer rule on whether the organization will be taxed as a partnership or whether the transfer-for-value rule will apply to the transfer.[70] Solution: Use a partnership with an independent business purpose to hold the policies.

[e] Drafting in Contemplation of the Rule

If it is important not to have transfer tax imposed on the proceeds at the death of the first spouse to die, it may be prudent to provide in the ILIT's

---

[65] IRC § 1041(e). Whether this transaction could be recharacterized as in substance a transfer by Husband to the ILIT, with Wife's payment of consideration to Husband considered a gift to the ILIT, is yet to be determined.

[66] Discussed below.

[67] See Swanson, Jr. Trust v. Comm'r, 518 F2d 59 (8th Cir. 1975); Rev. Rul. 74-76, 1974-1 CB 30 (1976).

[68] Rev. Proc. 97-3, 1997-1 IRB 84; Priv. Ltr. Rul. 9413045 (Jan. 4, 1994).

[69] Priv. Ltr. Rul. 9309021 (Dec. 3, 1992).

[70] Rev. Proc. 96-12, 1996-3 IRB 30 (Jan. 16, 1996); Rev. Proc. 97-3, 1997-1 IRB 84.

governing instrument that the proceeds will be allocated to the spouse, or to a marital deduction trust, if the insurance policy held by the ILIT is included in the insured's estate.

[8] How to Unwind an ILIT

In order to keep the proceeds out of the insured's estate, the trust must be irrevocable. If the insured later decides that he doesn't like the trust any more, is he stuck with it? No, he's got several options.

[a] New ILIT Buys New Policy

If the insured is still insurable, he can establish a new trust to purchase a new policy. He can let the policy in the old trust lapse or surrender it for cash.

[b] Insured Buys Policy From ILIT

The insured can buy the policy from the ILIT for fair consideration, and contribute it to a new ILIT. The proceeds will be included in the insured's estate if he dies within three years of the contribution to the new ILIT.[71] The sale itself should not be a taxable event for income tax purposes, as long as the ILIT is a grantor trust.[72] And, the sale should not constitute a transfer for value for purposes of the exemption of policy proceeds from income tax, since the insured is deemed to be the buyer.[73]

[c] New ILIT Purchases Policy From Old ILIT

The IRS has privately ruled on a purchase of a policy from one ILIT by another ILIT. The IRS, in Priv. Ltr. Rul. 9413045, indicated that the policy would not be includable under Section 2035 in the estate of the trustee/insured who sold the policy, since the purchase was for adequate consideration. The IRS also ruled that the property of the transferee trust would not be includable in the estate of the insured under any other section of the Internal Revenue Code, and that a power in the trustee to withdraw trust property and substitute trust property of equivalent value under Section 675 was not an incident of ownership. The IRS declined to rule that the transferee trust was a grantor

---

[71] IRC § 2035.

[72] Rev. Rul. 85-13, 1985-1 CB 144; but see Rothstein v. United States, 735 F2d 704 (2d Cir. 1984).

[73] IRC § 101. The IRS will not rule on the issue. See ¶ 12.04[7][d][v] above.

trust or that the purchase by the new ILIT was excepted from the transfer-for-value rule, due to its being an issue under extensive study.

[d] Old ILIT Lends Money to New ILIT to Buy New Policy

If the policy in the old ILIT has cash surrender value and the insured is insurable, the trustee can cash in the old policy and lend money to the new trust to fund the purchase of a new policy. If the amount received exceeds the investment in the contract, this will result in a gain to the old ILIT (and hence taxable to the grantor if the old ILIT is a grantor trust). It will also result in the application of Section 7872 to the loan transaction, unless both the old and new trusts are grantor trusts.

[e] Sale to Partnership

Suppose that the insured is not the sole grantor of the new ILIT. The new ILIT forms a partnership with the insured. Then the old ILIT sells the policy to the new ILIT. The sale may be excepted from the transfer-for-value rule because it is a sale to a partner of the insured.[74] The IRS will not rule on this transaction.[75]

[f] Merger of ILITS

A new ILIT and the old ILIT could merge, and continue to hold the old policy, if such a transaction is permitted under state law.[76] Court approval of such a transaction may be required.

[g] Joint Policies

If the policy insures more than one person (e.g., a first-to-die or last-to-die policy), it is not clear how the transfer-for-value exceptions will apply.

QUERY: If a joint policy is transferred to one of the insureds, for example, is that an exempt transfer to the insured? If not, and the policy is transferred to both insureds, what percentage of the policy must each insured receive?

------

[74] Priv. Ltr. Rul. 9235029 (May 29, 1992).

[75] Rev. Proc. 96-12, 1996-3 IRB 30 (Jan. 16, 1996); Rev. Proc. 97-3, 1997-1 IRB 84.

[76] Priv. Ltr. Rul. 9348029 (Sept. 3, 1993) and Priv. Ltr. Rul. 9619047 (Feb. 7, 1996) approved mergers without adverse tax consequences in other contexts on the basis that no real substantive changes took effect.

[9] Zero Tax Plan

Under the "zero tax plan," a person leaves his entire estate to a charitable entity, or to a charitable lead trust that receives a 100 percent deduction, or to a charitable remainder trust with a life interest in the person's spouse—that is, his estate is left in such a fashion that no estate tax will be incurred. An irrevocable life insurance trust also buys life insurance on his life (or on the joint lives of him and his wife) with a face amount equal to the value of his estate. The idea is that, when he (or the survivor of him and his wife) dies, the ILIT beneficiaries will receive an amount equal to the value of his estate, tax-free. If the beneficiaries want any of the specific assets of the estate, the ILIT can purchase the assets from the estate for cash and hold them for, or distribute them to, the beneficiaries. (This is true even if a private foundation or split-interest charitable trust is the beneficiary of the estate, provided the estate administration exception to self-dealing applies.)[77]

This plan can also be used on a smaller scale to cover part of the estate tax.

[10] Spouse-Owned Policy

In the days before the unlimited marital deduction, spouse-owned life insurance was common.

Now, there is no estate tax reason to have spouse-owned policies. If the insured wants the spouse to receive the proceeds, he can just as well own the policy himself and name her the beneficiary. The purpose of the ILIT is to keep the proceeds out of both spouses' estates.

[11] Change of Carriers in Employer-Provided Policy

If an employer changes insurance carriers, an employee will generally have to assign his rights under this new policy and survive for three years after the new assignment to keep the new policy proceeds out of his estate. The fact that the employee may have completely assigned his rights in the coverage purchased from the old carrier is irrelevant. If, however, the original assignment was drafted to cover all replacement policies, the question remains as to whether the three-year rule will apply when the new policy is "assigned" when the employer changes carriers. The three-year rule should not apply in such a case, any more than it would if the trustee of the ILIT exchanged policies, since the insured's rights were irrevocably assigned as of the date of the

---

[77] See Ch. 37.

original assignment. The IRS has agreed with this position, as long as the new policy provides coverage essentially identical to the old policy.[78]

[12] Community Property Considerations

If an existing community policy is assigned to a trust of which the uninsured spouse is a beneficiary, the policy should be partitioned or otherwise converted to the separate property of the insured spouse first. The uninsured spouse should receive consideration for her half of the policy. Otherwise, she may be regarded as having made an indirect gift to the trust by a transfer of her one-half interest in the policy to the insured for no consideration, which is then followed by an immediate transfer of the policy by the insured to the trust. The same principle applies to any cash contributions to the policy.

If the policy premium is paid by the insured's employer or deducted directly from the insured's paycheck, a blanket partition of all monies used to pay the premiums to the insured, with an equal amount of cash to the spouse, may be effective.

¶ 12.05 USING A PARTNERSHIP INSTEAD OF AN ILIT

Some planners think it is easier to use a partnership rather than an ILIT to purchase life insurance.

> **EXAMPLE:** Dad and kids form a family limited partnership with Dad as one percent general partner and kids as 99 percent limited partners. Dad contributes the premium amount to the partnership, and the partnership buys a life insurance policy on Dad, naming the partnership as beneficiary.

[1] Gift Tax Issues

Since the premiums are being contributed to a partnership and not a trust, is the gift tax treatment of the premium contributions any different from a contribution to an ILIT? The gift will be reduced by at least the value attributable to Dad's interest in the partnership.[79]

Will Dad get the annual exclusion, since there is no Crummey trust? Gifts directly to partnerships do not generally qualify for the annual exclusion, since the partners do not usually have present interests in contributions to the partnership by other partners. However, the partnership agreement can probably be drafted to give the partners present interests in contributions, in the

---

[78] Rev. Rul. 80-289, 1980-2 CB 270.

[79] See Treas. Reg. § 25.2511-1(h)(1).

form of the immediate right to withdraw increases in their capital accounts due to contributions (such rights being the partnership equivalent of Crummey powers).[80] Or, Dad could take a bigger share of the partnership at the outset and then make gifts of partnership interests to the children. These gifts may qualify for the annual exclusion if the children-partners are not prohibited from availing themselves of the value of their partnership interests.[81] If trust partners are used, the trusts would also have to qualify as annual exclusion trusts.

[2] Estate Tax Issues

Will the insurance proceeds be included in Dad's estate? Dad's partnership interest will be included in his estate. Therefore, if the partnership is the beneficiary, that portion of the insurance proceeds allocable to Dad's partnership interest will be indirectly includable (as part of the capital value of such interest) in Dad's estate.[82] On the other hand, if the partnership is not the beneficiary, it is possible that the insurance proceeds will be directly includable in Dad's estate.[83]

[3] GSTT Issues

What about generation-skipping transfer tax considerations? The GSTT exemption cannot be allocated to a partnership. When the proceeds are paid to the limited partnership, they can be kept in the partnership for as long as the law allows. The partners will receive credits to their capital accounts in the amount of their pro rata portions of the proceeds. When a partner dies or gifts his interest, the transfer tax value of his partnership interest will take into account the added value of the insurance proceeds. If a partner is a trust which is exempt from GSTT, the trust's interest in the partnership (and not the policy) will be its asset, and thus it does not need to incur a GSTT on account of the life insurance until a taxable transfer otherwise occurs.

[4] Income Tax Issues

The partnership may not be recognized for income tax purposes if the insured, the trustee, and the general partner are all the same person.[84]

---

[80] Wooley v. United States, 736 F. Supp. 1506 (SD Ind. 1990).

[81] See Ch. 10 for further discussion.

[82] Rev. Rul. 83-147, 1983-2 CB 158; Priv. Ltr. Rul. 9623024 (Mar. 6, 1996).

[83] See discussion at ¶ 12.02[1][b][ii].

[84] See Treas. Reg. § 1.704-1(e)(2)(vii).

[5] State Law Issues

A partnership is not as stable an entity as a trust or corporation, since certain events will cause it to dissolve and wind up. If it is important to keep the proceeds out of the ultimate beneficiaries' hands for a time even if the partnership liquidates, trust partners can be used.

[6] Non-Pro Rata Distributions

It may be desirable to make distributions to some people and not others at particular times. This flexibility is commonly provided in trusts. In partnerships, non-pro rata distributions can cause some difficulties, even though they are not per se prohibited. A solution that avoids these difficulties might be to use trust partners. Then, pro rata distributions can be made to the trusts, and each trust can distribute to its beneficiary or not, as appropriate.

¶ 12.06 SPLIT-DOLLAR FUNDING[85]

"Split-dollar" is not a type of insurance. It is a method of paying for a policy, whereby two parties jointly pay the policy premiums and split the policy benefits. Generally, one party pays premiums in excess of the cost of pure insurance protection and owns the investment portion of the policy. The other party (the term portion owner) pays (or receives a gift or income in the amount of) the cost of pure insurance protection, and receives the death proceeds in excess of what is required to repay the owner of the investment portion (i.e., usually, the amount of the premiums the investment owner paid, the cash surrender value of the policy, or some similar measure). The term portion owner is often an ILIT or other third party, if the split-dollar funding is being used in an estate planning context.

The attractive feature of split-dollar funding in estate planning is the fact that the amount of the gift made to the third-party owner of the term portion of the policy is not measured by the premium—rather, it is measured by the cost of term insurance for a standard-risk insured, which will generally be significantly less than the premium cost, if the insured is young.

Split-dollar funding only works in a policy with an investment feature because if a pure term policy is used, the measure of the gift will approximate the total premium cost, except in the case of a substandard risk insured. Standard split-dollar arrangements also tend not to work well with older insureds because the cost of term protection is dramatically higher for an older

---

[85] Split-dollar funding of life insurance is a complicated subject. An excellent resource is Stanford Wynn, Split-Dollar Life Insurance, ABA Section of Real Property, Probate and Trust Law (1991).

person. The cost to an older insured or third-party owner of paying for, or being taxed on, the term protection can be prohibitive.

[1] When to Consider Split-Dollar Funding

A split-dollar funding arrangement with an ILIT as owner of the risk (or term) portion of the policy should be considered in accomplishing the following objectives.

[a] To Minimize Cash Outlay by Insured

Split-dollar funding may be appropriate if (1) the insured cannot or does not want to pay the premiums or make a taxable gift of the premiums and (2) the insured is willing to pay the price of partial estate taxation to make the transaction work[86] or is able to get a third party (usually his employer) to provide part or all of the funding.

[b] To Maximize Use of Unified Credit and GSTT Exemption

Split-dollar funding may be advantageous if the insured wants to leverage the unified credit or GSTT exemption by minimizing the taxable gift to, and maximizing proceeds received by, the exempt trust. Split-dollar funding of life insurance is one of the best ways to get the maximum amount of property into an exempt trust. This is because the gift tax cost per dollar of death benefit is minimized, due to the fact that the insured's employer[87] is paying part of the cost of the policy. The insured employee's gifts to the trust are usually limited to the annual cost of a one-year term policy on the life of a person his age.

[c] To Fund a Buy-Sell Agreement

Split-dollar funding can be useful if a buy-sell agreement funded with life insurance is contemplated. It leaves control of the policy with the entity. And, due to the fact that the entity will be reimbursed for its cost when an insured dies, split-dollar funding can ameliorate inequities caused by differences in costs of insuring different partners or shareholders.

[d] To Substitute for Employee Benefits

[i] Wealth transmission. Split-dollar funding can be a good idea if an insured employee is more interested in wealth transmission than salary con-

---

[86] This would be the result, for example, if an entity in which he had an interest owned the investment piece of the policy.

[87] Or other owner of the investment portion of the policy.

tinuation as an employee benefit. If an executive does not need a supplemental retirement plan, a split-dollar policy would usually get much more money to the beneficiaries than a salary continuation plan would, for the same cost to the executive. This is because the policy proceeds are exempt from income and estate taxes, if properly structured, whereas salary continuation payments are subject to both.

[ii] **Retirement funds.** Split-dollar funding is also marketed as an additional source of retirement funds. The idea is that the policy is transferred to the employee when he retires. The employee then surrenders or borrows against the policy to obtain retirement funds. The amounts contributed by the employer and received by the employee, pursuant to a split-dollar arrangement, are not subject to the limits and certain other requirements imposed on qualified plans, provided that they are unfunded plans maintained for a select group of management or highly paid employees. For this purpose, if the plan assets are subject to the employer's general creditors, the plan is unfunded. However, a split-dollar plan can be subject to some ERISA compliance procedures. These issues, however, are outside the scope of this book.

[2] The Basics of Split-Dollar Funding

[a] Economics of a Split-Dollar Policy Owned by Employer and Insured

There are many different kinds of splits of the premium, cash surrender value, and death benefits. We'll use the following example to illustrate split-dollar economics.

EXAMPLE: Corporation X, Dad's employer, buys a policy on Dad's life on a split-dollar basis. Corporation X retains the right to receive the greater of the total amount of premiums it paid or the cash surrender value of the policy when the policy is terminated or matures (i.e., the policy is surrendered or Dad dies). The incidents of ownership in the rest of the policy are endorsed over to Dad. Dad may be required to reimburse Corporation X for the economic benefit amount each year, the amount of the premium in excess of the increase in cash surrender value, or some other amount. If instead, Corporation X pays the entire premium each year, Corporation X's annual premium payment is in essence an interest-free loan to Dad of the economic benefit amount.

[b] "Economic Benefit Amount" Determined

The facts in the above example were addressed in the primary revenue ruling detailing the tax treatment of a traditional split-dollar policy.[88] Each year, the insured employee is treated as receiving as compensation an economic benefit from the split-dollar arrangement equal to the premium on a one-year term insurance policy on the life of a person his age, to the extent that he does not pay or reimburse the employer that amount. A positive economic benefit amount will exist each year, even if the premiums have vanished or the policy is paid up. The amount is the lower of the "P.S. 58" amount or the insurer's standard published rates. If the insured's employer pays the entire premium, and the insured does not reimburse the employer, the economic benefit amount will be taxable to the insured as compensation. The economic benefit amount will be taxable to the insured as a dividend if the insured receives the benefit in his capacity as a shareholder, rather than as an employee.[89]

The employee may be subject to income tax under other theories, as well. For example, in an equity split-dollar arrangement,[90] the IRS has taken the position that once the cash surrender value of the policy exceeds the amount that will be paid back to the employer (generally, the total premiums paid by the employer), the employee will have taxable income under Section 83 to the extent of the increase in cash surrender value each year.

[i] P.S. 58 amount. The "P.S. 58" amount is an amount reflected in a table issued by the government listing premium rates on 1-year policies.[91]

[ii] Standard published rates. If the insurer publishes rates for individual, initial issue, one-year term policies (available to all standard risks), and these are lower than the P.S. 58 rates, these insurer rates may be used instead.[92] Only standard, and not preferred, rates may be used.[93] The issuer's standard rates should always be considered, as they are often lower than the P.S. 58 rates.

---

[88] Rev. Rul. 64-328, 1964-2 CB 11.

[89] In an equity split-dollar plan, the employer retains the right to the return of its premiums. Cash surrender value which exceeds premiums paid belongs to the insured or third-party owner.

[90] Tech. Adv. Mem. 9604001 (Sept. 8, 1995).

[91] Rev. Rul. 64-328, 1964-2 CB 11; see also Rev. Rul. 79-50, 1979-1 CB 138.

[92] Rev. Rul. 66-110, 1966-1 CB 12.

[93] Priv. Ltr. Rul. 9452004 (Sept. 2, 1994); Priv. Ltr. Rul. 8547006 (Aug. 23, 1985); Priv. Ltr. Rul. 9604001 (Sept. 8, 1995) (cannot use nonsmoker rates).

[iii] Joint and survivor policy. If the policy is a joint and survivor policy, the P.S. 58 tables are not used. The IRS has not formally announced how the economic benefit of the coverage is determined; however, a formula derived from U.S. Life Table 38[94] is generally followed, as a result of the "Greenberg-to-Greenberg" letter, developing a method for converting individual P.S. 58 rates to survivorship P.S. 58 rates. After the first death, the individual P.S. 58 or one-year term costs may again become applicable. A joint and survivor policy is an excellent choice for split-dollar funding to maximize wealth transmission, because last-to-die premiums are often much less than individual premiums.

[iv] Split-dollar funding with an S corporation. It has been suggested that split-dollar funding involving an S corporation may result in the existence of a second class of stock if a stockholder-insured or his assignee is not required to reimburse the corporation each year for the economic benefit amount.[95] The theory is that a dividend is paid to one stockholder-insured, and not to the other stockholders, when the reimbursement does not take place.

The IRS has privately ruled, however, in the context of an employer-pay-all split-dollar policy, with no reimbursement, that the split-dollar arrangement did not constitute a second class of stock.[96] The theory was that the agreement was a fringe benefit, not a vehicle for the circumvention of the single-class-of-stock requirement. The life insurance agreement was analogized to payment of accident and health insurance premiums by an S corporation on behalf of "2 percent + shareholder-employees." The IRS has held in a public ruling that payment of such premiums would be disregarded for purposes of the single-class-of-stock requirement.[97]

[c] Ownership Alternatives for Split-Dollar Funded Insurance

Endorsement. The employer owns the policy and endorses the policy to allow the employee or ILIT to name the beneficiary of its interest in the proceeds.

Collateral assignment. The employee or ILIT owns the policy, and assigns an interest in the policy to the employer as collateral securing the

---

[94] The rates derived from US Life Table 38 are based on the actuarial assumptions of the P.S. 58 tables. The method for deriving these rates is from a letter known as the Greenberg-to-Greenberg letter, issued by the Chief of the Actuarial Branch of the Department of the Treasury on August 10, 1983.

[95] Priv. Ltr. Rul. 9331009 (May 5, 1993); Priv. Ltr. Rul. 9318007 (Jan. 29, 1993); Priv. Ltr. Rul. 9235020 (May 28, 1992).

[96] Priv. Ltr. Rul. 9413023 (Dec. 23, 1993).

[97] Rev. Rul. 91-26, 1991-1 CB 185.

employer's interest in the policy. The tax consequences are the same, regardless of whether the endorsement or collateral assignment method is used.[98]

Co-ownership. The employee or ILIT owns the policy, and absolutely assigns ownership rights to the employer, reflecting the employer's interest. This form can be used when it is important for non-tax reasons to avoid characterization of the arrangement as a loan (for example, if state law or federal regulations prohibit loans to directors and officers).

Undocumented. In this instance, an agreement exists between the employer and the owner of the policy. However, the employer has no agreement with the insured, and thus no actual interest in the policy itself. The employer merely has a contractual right against the owner to receive its share of the payments on the employee's death. This method is sometimes used to avoid attribution of a corporation's incidents of ownership in a policy to the controlling shareholder-insured. The theory is that the employer-corporation's position is that of an unsecured creditor of the employee, and thus it has no incidents of ownership in the policy itself. No primary authority exists on the taxation of this arrangement.[99]

Note that "undocumented" does not mean that the agreement is not reflected in any documents at all. In fact, the agreement between the employer and the owner of the policy should be in writing. There is, however, no document or agreement between the employee (or third-party owner) and the insurance company regarding the reimbursement of the employer.

[d] New Split-Dollar Products—Agreement Design Issues

The creation of new life insurance products has raised new issues in split-dollar agreements. For example, in a universal life policy, the owner chooses the amount of the premium, within certain limits: which owner will make the choice? Variable life allows a choice of investment funds within the policy: who will decide which fund should be used? In some joint and survivor policies the economic benefit of the coverage (and possibly the premium)

---

[98] Rev. Rul. 64-328, 1964-2 CB 11.

[99] The Tax Court, in Young v. Comm'r, 1995 RIA TC Memo. ¶ 95,379, 70 TCM (CCH) 357 (1995), held that an arrangement whereby the corporation had an unsecured contractual right to have certain loans made by the insurance company to it repaid out of the proceeds or cash value of the policy was not a split-dollar arrangement. However, under the facts of the case, the Tax Court held that the corporation's "functional" annual premium payments were not to be repaid, and that the initial premium payment, which was funded with a loan from the insurance company, was a mere bookkeeping transaction. This is a set of facts reflecting a type of leveraged arrangement which is occasionally used to try to achieve deductions for money used to fund the insurance purchase. The ruling's conclusion is not necessarily translatable to a standard nonleveraged undocumented arrangement.

increases after the first death: who will decide whether to continue the policy, purchase a first-to-die rider, or terminate the arrangement?

[3] Getting the Split-Dollar Policy Out of the Insured's Estate

In a split-dollar policy designed to be excluded from the insured's estate, a third-party owner (usually an ILIT) takes the place of the employee as the person entitled to receive death benefits in excess of the employer's share and to exercise incidents of ownership with respect to that portion of the policy. The following subsections discuss the income, estate, gift, and generation-skipping transfer tax consequences of a split-dollar policy with a third-party owner (for example, an ILIT).

[a] Income Tax Consequences

Even if a third party has the incidents of ownership in the policy, the employee will still be taxable each year on the economic benefit amount of the policy[100] to the extent that the employee does not reimburse the employer for those costs. The employee may also have taxable income under Section 83 once the cash surrender value exceeds the total amount returnable to the employer (usually, the total premiums the employer paid).[101]

[b] Gift Tax Consequences

Whether or not the employee reimburses the employer for the annual economic benefit amount, that amount will be treated as an annual gift by the employee to the third-party owner (i.e., ILIT, etc.).[102] If that owner is a Crummey trust, the trust should be sufficiently funded so that the holder of the withdrawal power actually has something to withdraw. This is an issue because the "gift" to the trust may not actually flow into or through the trustee's hands. An annual economic benefit will continue to exist even after the premiums have vanished or the policy is paid up.

Additionally, any premiums which are actually paid by the insured will be treated as gifts to the policy owner.

If the insured's interest in an existing policy subject to a split-dollar agreement is assigned, the gift tax value of the policy is the interpolated

---

[100] The economic benefit amount is discussed at ¶ 12.06[2][b] above.

[101] Tech. Adv. Mem. 9604001 (Sept. 8, 1995).

[102] See Rev. Rul. 78-420, 1978-2 CB 67.

terminal reserve value plus prepaid premiums, less the value of the employer's interest.[103]

[c] Leveraging the GSTT Exemption and Unified Credit

Split-dollar insurance is an excellent way to leverage the GSTT exemption and the unified credit. This is because the taxable gift on the original assignment or acquisition of the policy is reduced by the value of the employer's share of the policy, and the amount of the annual gift (which might otherwise be determined by the premium payments) is limited to the P.S. 58, U.S. Life Table 38, or standard one-year term rates, as the case may be, rather than the full amount of the premiums.

[d] Controlling Shareholder-Insured's Estate Tax Consequences

If the insured is a controlling shareholder of a corporation, and the corporation possesses incidents of ownership in a policy on his life, the policy proceeds, which are not payable to the corporation, will be included in the insured's estate due to his deemed incidents of ownership in the policy.[104] A deduction for the amount payable to the employer will be allowed.

Can the corporation's powers over the policy be limited so that it will hold no incidents of ownership that could be attributed to the insured? The IRS has ruled that a corporation had no incident of ownership which could be attributed to the controlling shareholder-insured when the corporation was prohibited from borrowing against the cash value of the policy and had no powers over the policy other than those incident to its security interest.[105]

[e] Noncontrolling Shareholder-Insured's Estate Tax Consequences

Since the corporation will receive a portion of the policy proceeds on the insured's death, the value of the shareholder-insured's equity interest in the corporation will increase indirectly due to the corporation's receipt of its share of the policy proceeds.

---

[103] Rev. Rul. 81-198, 1981-2 CB 188.

[104] Treas. Reg. § 20.2042-1(c)(6); Rev. Rul. 82-145, 1982-2 CB 213.

[105] Priv. Ltr. Rul. 9651017 (Sept. 18, 1996); Priv. Ltr. Rul. 9651030 (Sept. 20, 1996); Priv. Ltr. Rul. 9511046 (Dec. 22, 1994); see also Priv. Ltr. Rul. 9348009 (Aug. 31, 1993). Compare dicta in Priv. Ltr. Rul. 9037012 (June 14, 1990).

[f] Charitable Deduction for Assignments to Charity

Due to the limits on deductions of partial interests in property, there may be no income or gift tax charitable deduction for the donation to charity of a donor's interest in a policy subject to a split-dollar arrangement.[106]

[4] Consequences of Terminating a Split-Dollar Arrangement

In an employee-employer situation, usually the split-dollar funding arrangement is terminated when the employee retires. The termination can be handled in a number of ways.

[a] Cashout Terminations

The employer may cash in the policy, pay itself the amount due under the agreement, and distribute the excess, if any,[107] to the other owner.[108]

[b] Rollout Terminations

The rollout involves a distribution of the policy by the employer to the other owner, simultaneously with the other owner's payment to the employer of the value of the employer's share of the policy. The value of the employer's share will often be either the cash surrender value of the policy or the total amount of premiums paid, or the higher of the two.

If the other owner has insufficient cash on hand to buy the employer's portion of the policy, additional funds can be obtained in a number of ways, such as by borrowing against the policy, borrowing from other sources, withdrawal of funds from the policy, or receipt of a bonus from the employer.

If the policy is rolled out, the employee has taxable income to the extent that the value of the policy on rollout exceeds any premiums paid by him and, perhaps, any economic benefit amounts taxed as income to him during the life of the policy.[109] The employer is entitled to a compensation deduction of that same amount, and will also have a gain equal to the value of what it receives from the other owner on the rollout of the policy that is in excess of its basis.[110]

---

[106] IRC § 2522(c); see also Rev. Rul. 76-200, 1976-1 CB 308.

[107] Under a traditional arrangement, there will be no excess, as the employer will be entitled to the entire cash surrender value.

[108] The other owner will be either the employee or his assignee—usually, an ILIT.

[109] IRC § 83(a); Priv. Ltr. Rul 7916029 (Jan. 17, 1979); Priv. Ltr. Rul. 8310027 (Dec. 3, 1982). The employee is the taxpayer who has income, even if his part of the policy has been assigned to the third-party owner.

[110] Treas. Reg. § 1.83-6(b).

A rollout may occur at the employee's retirement. It also may occur sooner, since the tax consequences of a split-dollar arrangement with an older employee may become daunting. The annual economic benefit of the policy (the cost of one-year pure term insurance) will become very high as the employee gets older. And, the cost to the employee of paying this amount to the employer each year, or even of absorbing the income tax on the amount of the employer's premium payment treated as compensation, can become prohibitive.

[c] Crawlout Terminations

In a crawlout, the other owner makes the employer whole on a gradual basis. For example, after the cash premiums have vanished, the owner may write a check to the employer each year equal to the economic benefit of the policy in that year, slowly reducing its obligation to the employer. When the employer is repaid, the policy is distributed to the owner.

[d] Avoid Transfer-For-Value Rule Violations

In unwinding a split-dollar arrangement, one must be careful not to violate the transfer-for-value rule.[111] If an ILIT buys the policy from the employer, the rule should not be violated, because the trust will be a grantor trust for income tax purposes.[112] Accordingly, for income tax purposes, the transfer to the ILIT should be treated as a transfer to the insured.[113] However, the IRS will not rule on the issue.[114]

[5] Variations on Split-Dollar Arrangements

[a] Reverse Split-Dollar

This is just what it sounds like. The ownership roles of the employee (or third-party owner such as an ILIT) and employer are reversed. The purpose of the arrangement is to assist the employer in the acquisition of key person insurance coverage. The employee or ILIT owns the policy, and pays the premiums in excess of the P.S. 58 cost. On the employee's death, the employee's estate or the ILIT will receive the cash surrender value or amount of premiums paid, or the greater of the two. The employer pays the P.S. 58 cost (rather than the generally lower standard rates), and gets the excess death

---

[111] Discussed at ¶ 12.03[2] above.

[112] IRC § 677(a)(3).

[113] Swanson, Jr. Trust v. Comm'r, 518 F2d 59 (8th Cir. 1975).

[114] See ¶ 12.04[7][d][v] above.

benefit if the key person dies during the term of the arrangement. This way, the employer funds the premium cost of the insurance protection (as opposed to the investment portion of the policy). On the termination of the arrangement during the key person's lifetime, the employer receives no reimbursement. The policy is simply transferred to the employee or third-party owner. The owner should be a person who fits within the transfer-for-value exceptions. There is little official guidance on the taxation of this arrangement.[115]

Why would reverse split-dollar be interesting? It is generally useful with an older insured, because the holder of the term portion (whose portion of the proceeds is not designed to remain with the insured during the premium payment period) may be able to pay the higher of the P.S. 58 costs or the one-year term rates.

EXAMPLE: Dad is 68 years old. Dad's S corporation enters into a collateral assignment split-dollar arrangement with his ILIT, which owns the policy. The ILIT pays the premiums to the insurance company and the S corporation is required to pay to the ILIT each year an amount equal to the higher of the P.S. 58 costs or the standard one-year rates, which will be most of (and eventually more than) the premium. The premiums vanish in seven years. During the seven years, if Dad dies, S corporation will receive the proceeds in excess of the amount required to repay the ILIT for its net premium outlay, or the cash surrender value. Each year, Dad makes a gift to the ILIT of the amount necessary to fund its share of the premiums. At the end of the 7-year period, the reverse split-dollar arrangement is terminated. The ILIT retains the policy, and the S corporation terminates its interest in the policy.

The net result is that the insurance policy is held by the ILIT, with no further premiums due if the policy performs as expected. Very little gift tax has been paid—only the amount of gift tax payable on the ILIT's small share of premiums paid during the even years. As the P.S. 58 costs come to exceed the actual premium, dollars will be transferred free of transfer tax from the S corporation to the ILIT, as it transfers the excess amount to the ILIT each year. The usual tax and economic difficulties encountered in terminating a standard split-dollar arrangement do not exist, since the S corporation does not need to receive reimbursements for its premium investments during the insured's life (because all it ever purchased was pure insurance protection).

[b] Private Split-Dollar

In a private split-dollar arrangement, a trust, a partnership, or an individual (say, Child) pays all or part of the premiums and receives the greater of the premiums or cash surrender value (or some other agreed amount) at the

---

[115] Priv. Ltr. Rul. 9026041 (Mar. 30, 1990) (indicating that the full policy death benefit is included in the employee's estate, but the amount payable to the employer is deductible as a debt under IRC § 2053(a)(4)).

insured's death, just as the employer does in traditional split-dollar. Another individual or trust (say, ILIT) pays the remaining premiums and receives the death benefit in excess of Child's portion.

The question here is whether the principles of Revenue Ruling 64-328,[116] governing traditional split-dollar arrangements, apply to this situation. If they don't, then the arrangement might be taxed on a different basis—perhaps as an interest-free loan from Child to ILIT.[117] The IRS has, however, ruled on certain income tax consequences of such a transaction. In one ruling, A was the grantor and trustee of a revocable trust. The trust was the general partner of a limited partnership which was in the real estate business. The trust purchased a policy on the life of A. The trust and the partnership entered into a split-dollar arrangement. The trust paid the cost of term life insurance protection to the partnership, which paid the rest of the cost. The partnership was to receive the greater of premiums paid or cash surrender value, and the trust would get the rest. The IRS ruled that the trust would not be considered to have derived any economic benefit from the arrangement, and that, so long as the trust paid its share of the premiums, neither the trust nor the insured would be deemed to have received a partnership distribution.[118]

WARNING: The split of ownership rights should not involve the insured, as the insured's incidents of ownership would cause the inclusion of the policy in the insured's estate.[119]

In a private split-dollar arrangement that does not involve any employer-employee (or other compensatory) relationship, there is generally no taxable income to the insured on the annual economic benefit amount of the policy which is not paid by the insured. The annual economic benefit amount, however, may be deemed a gift to the third-party owner, as it would be in a traditional split-dollar plan.

[c] Private Reverse Split-Dollar

The IRS has ruled on at least one situation involving a private reverse split-dollar arrangement.[120] In that ruling, Husband created an ILIT, naming his wife and children as beneficiaries. It was funded with cash, which was used

---

[116] 1964-2 CB 11.

[117] See, e.g., Priv. Ltr. Rul. 9413023 (Apr. 1, 1994); Priv. Ltr. Rul. 9349002 (Dec. 20, 1993); Priv. Ltr. Rul. 9639053 (June 20, 1996) (specifically expressing no opinion on whether IRC § 7872 applies to split-dollar arrangements).

[118] Priv. Ltr. Rul. 9639053 (June 20, 1996).

[119] Rev. Rul. 81-164, 1981-1 CB 458; Rev. Rul. 79-129, 1979-1 CB 306.

[120] Priv. Ltr. Rul. 9636033 (Mar. 12, 1996).

to purchase an insurance policy on his life. The ILIT entered into a collateral assignment agreement with Wife. The ILIT agreed to pay the portion of the premiums equal to the lower of the P.S. 58 costs or the one-year term cost for standard risks. Wife agreed to pay the remaining premiums. Either party could terminate the agreement. If the agreement terminated during Husband's life, Wife would get the cash value of the policy. If the agreement terminated due to Husband's death, Wife would get the greater of the cash value, or premiums paid by her. The IRS ruled that the payment of premiums would not result in a gift to the trust by Wife (because the arrangement would result in her being reimbursed for the premiums) nor be deemed a gift to the trust by Husband (since he received nothing of value, compensatory or otherwise, on the payment of the premiums). The IRS also ruled that the proceeds would not be includable in Husband's estate.

[d] Equity Split-Dollar

Under this arrangement, the employer's share of the death proceeds is limited to the return of its premiums. Increases in the cash surrender value in excess of the premiums paid accrue to the benefit of the employee or third party owner. In other words, if the employee or third party owner receives all policy value in excess of the employer's premiums, the employee or third party is building equity in the policy with funds that the employer paid. There is little official guidance on the taxation of this arrangement. It might not be subject to tax until the policy is surrendered,[121] or it could be currently taxable as an "other benefit,"[122] or it could be viewed as restricted property and taxed when the restrictions lapse.[123]

The IRS has issued a technical advice memorandum addressing such an arrangement.[124] The IRS stated that the employee would be taxed on the increase in the cash surrender value each year which would not return to the employer on termination of the arrangement, as well as the economic benefit amount. This ruling has generated considerable comment because its result seems doubtful. The cash surrender value in any year depends on the investment, administrative, and mortality experience of the insurance company. As a result, the cash surrender value can increase in some years and decrease in others. Thus, if an increase in cash surrender value is taxed to the employee one year, and the cash surrender value decreases in the next year, does the employee have a deduction in that year? An increase in the cash surrender value would not be taxable to the employee if the policy were held entirely by

---

[121] IRC §§ 72(a), 72(e)(5); Treas. Reg. § 1.72-11.

[122] Rev. Rul. 66-110, 1966-1 CB 12.

[123] IRC § 83(e).

[124] Tech. Adv. Mem. 9604001 (Sept. 8, 1995).

him. It would seem that taxation of the employee on cash surrender value increases that occur while the employer holds the policy would be premature. If the technical advice memorandum is correct, then, in essence, the result will be the current income taxation of inside buildup. Some split-dollar plans provide that the employee's or third-party owner's interest will be forfeited under certain conditions (e.g., if the employee resigns his employment). Increases in cash surrender value of a policy subject to such a provision should not be taxable under Section 83.

[6] Forthcoming IRS Guidance

The IRS has informally indicated its intent to issue guidance on split-dollar arrangements, possibly as early as sometime in 1997.[125]

¶ 12.07 INCOME TAXATION OF LIFE INSURANCE CONTRACTS THAT HAVE NOT MATURED

Insurance policies do not just provide death benefits. During an insured's lifetime, a non-term insurance policy may increase in value. The insurance company may pay dividends to the owner of the policy or, at the owner's election, may apply them to the payment of future premiums or installments due on policy loans. If the owner needs to raise cash, he may borrow money against the cash surrender value of the policy or simply surrender the policy. These and other events that occur before the policy matures may have income tax consequences.

[1] "Investment in the Contract" Element

A critical fact in determining the income tax consequences of owning a life insurance contract is the amount of the owner's "investment in the contract." This concept is equivalent to the "basis" of other assets. Generally, the owner's investment in an insurance contract is the total amount of premiums or other consideration paid for the contract, reduced by total amounts ever received under the contract which were not included in taxable income.[126] The IRS, however, has taken a somewhat different view. It has privately ruled that, for purposes of determining gain on the sale of a policy, the investment in the contract must be reduced by the cost of insurance protection provided through

---

[125] Remarks by Treasury and IRS officials quoted in Daily Tax Report, Jan. 2, 1997, at G-1.

[126] IRC § 72(e)(6); Treas. Reg. § 1.72-6. For purposes of assignment or surrender of the policy, this apparently includes dividends which were applied to reduce premiums.

the date of transfer.[127] The cost of insurance protection approximates the total premiums paid, less the cash surrender value of the policy.[128]

[2] Policy Loans and Distributions

[a] Loans

Borrowing against a policy is not generally a taxable event. Interest on personal life insurance policy loans is not deductible.[129]

[b] Distributions

Distributions from a life insurance policy during the insured's lifetime are generally treated as nontaxable returns of basis until the investment in the contract has been recovered.[130] Once the investment in the contract has been recovered, further distributions are included in the gross income of the recipient.[131]

[c] Universal Life Policy Distributions

Cash distributions received as a result of a decrease in policy benefits during the first 15 years of a universal life policy may be taxed first as income, subject to a ceiling, under certain rules which are too arcane to contemplate without a specific set of facts.[132]

[d] Modified Endowment Contract

Cash accessed from a modified endowment contract (MEC) before the policy matures is generally subject to an "income-out-first" rule.

[i] **What Is a Modified Endowment Contract?** An insurance policy is a MEC if it is entered into after June 21, 1988, and the total premiums paid at

---

[127] Priv. Ltr. Rul. 9443020 (Jul. 22, 1994) (relying on Century Wood Preserving Co. v. Comm'r, 69 F2d 967 (3d Cir. 1934), and London Shoe Co. v. Comm'r, 80 F2d 230 (2d Cir. 1935), cert. denied, 298 US 663 (1936), both holding that this reduction in basis is appropriate for purposes of determining loss).

[128] Priv. Ltr. Rul. 9443020 (Jul. 22, 1994) (relying on Century Wood Preserving Co. v. Comm'r, 69 F2d 967 (3d Cir. 1934), and London Shoe Co. v. Comm'r, 80 F2d 230 (2d Cir. 1935), cert. denied, 298 US 663 (1936), both holding that this reduction in basis is appropriate for purposes of determining loss).

[129] IRC § 163(h).

[130] IRC § 72(e)(5). Exceptions are described in the following paragraphs.

[131] IRC § 72(e)(5).

[132] IRC § 7702(f)(7).

any time during the first seven contract years exceed the total net level premiums which would have been paid by that time if the policy provided for paid-up future benefits in the face amount of the policy after the payment of seven level annual payments.[133] An insurance policy is also a MEC if it is received in exchange for a MEC.[134] For instance, suppose Mom has a policy with a $1,000,000 face amount. The policy is a MEC if, at any time during the first seven years of the policy, the amount of the total premiums paid exceeds the total amount of premiums which would have been required to buy a $1,000,000 policy that is paid up after seven years. ("Paid up" means that no further premiums are required to continue the policy in effect, regardless of the investment performance of the policy or the company. An insurance professional will be able to calculate this amount.)

[ii] Consequences of MEC status. If a policy is a MEC, any distribution from the policy during the insured's lifetime will be treated as follows:

- The distribution will be treated as income, to the extent that the cash surrender value before the distribution exceeds the owner's investment in the contract;[135] for this purpose, distributions include policy loans and dividends retained by the insurer to pay principal or interest on a policy loan.[136]
- Any distribution in excess of the above income amount will be considered a nontaxable return of basis to the extent of the investment in the contract.
- Further distributions will be included in gross income.[137]
- Additionally, a ten percent penalty tax is imposed on any distribution that is treated as income unless (1) the recipient is disabled or at least 59 1/2 years old or (2) the distribution is part of a series of substantially equal payments made at least once a year for the recipient's life or life expectancy or the joint lives or joint life expectancies of the recipient and her beneficiaries.[138]

---

[133] IRC §§ 7702A(a)(1), 7702A(b).

[134] IRC § 7702A(a)(2).

[135] IRC § 72(e)(10).

[136] Conference Report to Accompany HR 4333, 100th Cong., 2d Sess. (1988), 1988-3 CB 473, 592.

[137] IRC § 72(e)(2)(B).

[138] IRC § 72(v). Although it is clear that distributions from a MEC held in trust will receive the same income tax treatment as MECs held by an individual (IRC § 72(e)(10)(A)(ii)), a trust which reports the inside buildup as income each year pursuant to IRC § 72(u) will not incur a penalty, since the income will already have been taxed.

PRACTICE POINTER: A lawyer usually does not have access to the information necessary to determine whether a contract is a MEC. It may be wise to obtain a representation from the insurance company that the policy will not be a MEC, if it matters. When does it matter? If the owner of the policy never borrows against the policy or withdraws cash value or takes an early distribution, MEC status will never be relevant. If accessing the cash value (through distributions or loans) will ever be necessary, MEC status will be undesirable, although not the end of the world. The consequence of MEC status is that the cash withdrawn or borrowed will be treated as income, to the extent that there is value in the policy in excess of the owner's investment in the contract, and a possible ten percent penalty. The policy will still be taxed as life insurance for all other purposes.

[iii] **Effective date of MEC rules.** If a policy was issued before June 21, 1988, it may be covered by the grandfather rules, which are quite complex.[139]

[3] Exchange of Policies

One policy can be exchanged for another policy on a nontaxable basis if both policies have the same insured.[140] The IRS has ruled that a single life policy cannot be exchanged for a joint policy insuring two lives on a tax-free basis[141] and that two single life policies on the lives of *A* and *B* cannot be exchanged tax-free for a second-to-die policy insuring both *A* and *B*.

¶ 12.08 SELECTING A POLICY

[1] Due Diligence

A number of books and articles exist which will familiarize the estate planner with due diligence techniques.[142] However, to do a thorough job, an insurance professional is needed, since much of the essential information is unavailable to those outside the insurance business. The estate planner can insure that the right questions are asked, however.

[2] Investment Aspects

Life insurance comes in many varieties and is a complicated financial product. It is worthwhile for the estate planner to invest some time and effort in

---

[139] Technical and Miscellaneous Revenue Act of 1988, Pub. L. No. 100-647, § 5012(e), 102 Stat. 3342 (1988).

[140] IRC § 1035(a); Treas. Reg. § 1.1035-1.

[141] Priv. Ltr. Rul. 9542037 (July 21, 1995).

[142] An excellent resource is Catherine R. Turner & Richard A. Schwartz, Life Insurance Due Care: Carriers, Products and Illustrations (ABA, Chicago 1994) (2d ed).

developing an acquaintance with the different types of policies and understanding how they work.[143]

A couple of common-sense observations may be in order. Most policy illustrations focus on how much the cash surrender value will increase over time at various performance rates. The cash surrender value is accessible instead of, not in addition to, the death proceeds. If the insured does not expect to access the cash value, these performance projections are not relevant. A person primarily interested in death protection may be paying for investment performance that will never benefit him or his family, provided that his expectations of dying with the policy intact are met. This sort of person may be better off with a term policy or a policy with minimal investment features.

Conversely, if a person buying a policy is only interested in investment performance, he is incurring the extra costs of insurance protection he really doesn't want in exchange for the tax-free buildup in value.

Charles Givens, in his book, "More Wealth Without Risk,"[144] makes a case that it is still smart to buy term and invest the difference between the cost of term and other more expensive insurance products. He maintains that a person is unlikely to get the best value on both insurance protection and investment performance in one package deal. Insurance industry professionals, on the other hand, make the case that life insurance policies are now financially efficient enough to compete with other tax-advantaged investments.

[3] Is It Life Insurance?

An insurance policy issued after 1984 must meet a very complicated set of tests throughout the life of the contract in order to constitute life insurance for tax purposes.[145]

Policies issued on or after January 1, 1985, that fail the tests can subject policy owners and beneficiaries to severe consequences. For example, the cash surrender value at death will be treated as taxable income at death and the income on the contract each year will be subject to current income taxation.[146]

The ordinary (or even extraordinary) person who is not privy to insurance company information cannot make the determination as to whether a contract complies with the rules. It may be prudent to get a guarantee from

---

[143] Some good resources are Lawrence Brody & Louis R. Richey, Insurance Products: Analysis, Taxation and Planning—How to Select What's Right for Your Client and the ABA Section of Real Property, Probate and Trusts' Insurance Counselor series.

[144] Charles J. Givens, More Wealth Without Risk 72—77 (1991).

[145] IRC § 7702.

[146] IRC § 7702(g).

the insurance company that the contract will constitute life insurance at all times during its life.

[4] Large Amounts of Life Insurance

[a] Limits on Amount Available

There are limits on the amount of life insurance that can be purchased on the life of a single individual or couple. This is because there are limits to the amount of risk that any one insurance company can or will retain on any one person (or couple).

> **EXAMPLE:** Dad wants to buy a policy with a face amount of $200 million. It may or may not be possible for Dad to acquire that much insurance, depending on his age, health, financial statement,[147] and other factors. In any case, any one company will have a limit of far less than $200 million. Suppose that Dependable Life Insurance Company is Dad's insurance company. Dependable may have a retention limit of, say, $20,000,000. If Dependable sells a $100 million policy to Dad, it will reinsure the amount in excess of its limit with other carriers (that is, it will place pieces of the policy with other companies).

[b] Ability to Pay Proceeds

When purchasing very large policies, it is especially important to determine if an insurance company appears able to pay upon the insured's death. A knowledgeable life insurance professional should be retained to evaluate the financial strength of the companies. If part of the policy is being reinsured, it will also be prudent to identify and review the strength of the reinsurers.

¶ 12.09 TERMINALLY OR CHRONICALLY ILL INSURED—ACCELERATED DEATH BENEFITS AND VIATICAL SETTLEMENTS

Some policies will pay an accelerated death benefit to an insured who is terminally or chronically ill.

The Small Business Jobs Protection Act added sections to the Internal Revenue Code which provide that amounts received under an insurance contract on the life of an insured who is a "terminally ill individual" or a "chronically ill individual" will be treated as life insurance payments, and therefore

---

[147] Dad's financial statement is relevant because (a) he will need money to pay for the policy, and (b) with large policies, the insurance companies may consider whether the financial statement indicates a need for the amount of insurance purchased.

will not be subject to income taxation in the hands of the insured, absent other factors.

[1] Terminally Ill Insured

An individual is terminally ill if he has been certified by a physician as having an illness or physical condition that can reasonably be expected to result in death within 24 months after the certification.[148] No restrictions apply to the amount of insurance proceeds that can qualify or to the use of the proceeds.

[2] Chronically Ill Insured

An individual is chronically ill, generally, if he is not a terminally ill individual and if he has been certified, within the preceding 12 months, by a licensed health care practitioner, as:

- Unable to perform on a substantially unassisted basis at least two activities of daily living (including eating, toileting, transferring, bathing, dressing, and continence) for at least 90 days owing to a loss of functional capacity;
- Having a similar level of disability as determined under regulations which may be issued; or
- Requiring substantial supervision to protect himself from threats to health and safety owing to severe cognitive impairment.[149]

When does an accelerated death benefit paid as the result of chronic illness qualify for the exclusion from income? Generally speaking, the payment must be for costs incurred by the payee (and not compensated by insurance or Medicare) for qualified long-term care services.[150] However, the contract may make payments on a per diem (or other periodic basis) without regard to actual expenses incurred during the period covered[151] up to $175 per day,[152] indexed for inflation for calendar years after 1997. The contract must comply with certain consumer protection provisions.[153]

---

[148] IRC § 101(g)(4)(A).

[149] IRC §§ 101(g)(4)(B), 7702B(c)(2).

[150] IRC § 101(g)(3)(A)(i).

[151] IRC § 101(g)(3)(A)(ii)(I), incorporating the requirements of IRC § 7702B(b)(1)(B).

[152] IRC §§ 101(g)(3)(D), 7702B(d).

[153] IRC § 101(g)(3)(A)(ii)(II).

[3] Viatical Settlements

The exclusion from income also applies to the proceeds of qualifying viatical settlements.[154] A qualifying viatical settlement is a sale or assignment of all or part of the death benefit under an insurance contract on the life of a terminally ill or chronically ill individual to a "viatical settlement provider." A viatical settlement provider must be (1) regularly engaged in the business of purchasing, or taking assignments of, policies on terminally or chronically ill individuals and (2) licensed in the state in which the insured resides or, if that state does not require licensing of viatical settlement providers, the provider must meet certain other specified requirements.[155]

[4] Business Insurance

The income exclusion for accelerated death benefits does not apply if the policyholder is not the insured and the policyholder has an insurable interest in the life of the insured because the insured is a director, officer, or employee of the policyholder or because the insured is financially interested in any trade or business carried on by the policyholder."[156] This exception generally excludes policies with a business purpose from the favorable income tax treatment.

¶ 12.10 ADDITIONAL READING

Other excellent sources of information and guidance in this are include both Tax Facts on Life Insurance (1997) (Deborah A. Miner, Ed.) and American Bar Association Section of Real Property, Probate and Trust Law, The Insurance Counselor Series (1989).

---

[154] IRC § 101(g)(2)(A).
[155] IRC § 101(g)(2)(B).
[156] IRC § 101(g)(5).

CHAPTER **13**

Commercial Annuities

¶ 13.01 INTRODUCTION

There are many types of annuities, each with its own set of rules. We are concerned with commercial annuities in this chapter. However, the basic concepts often apply to other types of annuities, as well. The specific differences will be pointed out in the chapters addressing the other types of annuities.

Why does an affluent person purchase a commercial annuity for himself? Usually, as a tax-advantaged investment; often, as a source of retirement income; sometimes, as an asset which is protected from creditors; but, preferably, not as a wealth transmission vehicle.

This chapter discusses how an annuity works and then explains the tax treatment. Since an annuity is primarily an income tax (rather than transfer tax) shelter, we'll summarize the income tax treatment first and then discuss the transfer tax treatment.

¶ 13.02 HOW AN ANNUITY WORKS

[1] Cast of Characters

The "purchaser" buys the annuity from the "seller"—say, an insurance company. The "owner" or "holder" owns the annuity policy. The "annuitant" receives the annuity payments and provides the measuring life for the term of the payments, if necessary. The purchaser, owner, and annuitant may all be the same person, and this chapter assumes they are except where it specifies otherwise. The "beneficiary" receives the remaining benefits, if any, at the annuitant's death.

[2] Terms of the Annuity Contract

The purchaser pays one or more premiums in exchange for the insurance company's promise to pay the annuitant a sum of money periodically, beginning at some date in the future and lasting for the annuity period. The "annuity period" is generally a term of years, or the life of one or two people, or the life expectancy of one or two people, or a combination of these. The "annuity starting date" is the first day of the first period for which an amount is received as an annuity.[1] So, the annuity starting date is not necessarily the date of the first payment.

> EXAMPLE: An annuity is payable for each full calendar year at the end of the year. If the annuity begins in 1997, the annuity starting date is January 1, 1997. The first payment will be made on December 31, 1997.

The annuity starting date may be immediate or deferred. The starting date of a deferred annuity will usually be a date occurring after the annuitant attains age $59^1/_2$ (or the annuitant's earlier disability or death), since earlier distribution will cause a ten percent penalty tax unless certain special exceptions apply. If the annuitant dies before the annuity starting date, a death benefit is paid—often, the greater of the premiums paid or the accumulation value of the contract. If the contract is surrendered during the first few years after it is purchased, there is usually a surrender charge imposed by the insurance company.

---

[1] IRC § 72(c)(4); Treas. Reg. § 1.72-4(b).

[3] Terminology

[a] Income on the Contract

The insurance company credits the premiums paid with earnings. These earnings result in income on the contract.

If the holder is a natural person, the income on the contract each year is not subject to income taxation, except to the extent it is received by the annuitant, holder, or beneficiary, or until the contract is transferred by the holder. "Income on the contract" in any year is the cash value of the policy (determined without regard to surrender charges) plus all distributions ever received under the contract, less the sum of net premiums paid for all years and all amounts included in gross income for prior years.[2] Income on the contract is analogous to the concept of unrealized appreciation.

For purposes of determining income on the contract, all contracts issued after October 21, 1988 by the same company to the same policyholder during any calendar year are treated as one contract.[3]

[b] Cash Value

For purposes of this chapter, the "cash value" of the contract at any time is the amount of cash the holder will receive if he surrenders the contract, without subtracting any surrender charge.

[c] Investment in the Contract

The "investment in the contract" is a concept comparable to the "basis" of other assets. Simplistically, it is the amount that has been paid for the contract, reduced by amounts previously received which were excluded from income.[4]

> EXAMPLE: Mary has paid $100,000 of annuity premiums. She has received one distribution of $5,000; $3,000 of that distribution was treated as a return of principal. If no special rules apply, Mary's investment in the contract (or basis in the policy) is $97,000.

Numerous special adjustments are made. Detailed rules for calculating the investment in the contract are contained in the regulations.[5]

---

[2] IRC §§ 72(u)(2), 72(e)(3)A).

[3] IRC § 72(e)(11); Technical and Miscellaneous Revenue Act of 1988, Pub. L. No. 100-647, § 5012(d)(2), 102 Stat. 3342 (1988).

[4] IRC § 72(e)(6); Treas. Reg. § 1.72-6.

[5] Treas. Reg. §§ 1.72-6, 1.72-7.

While the original owner's initial investment in the contract will generally consist of premiums paid, a successor owner computes his initial investment in the contract as follows:

- *Purchased contract.* If Child purchases an annuity contract from Mom, Child's initial investment in the contract is the consideration he pays.
- *Gifted contract.* If Mom gives an annuity contract to Child, Child's initial investment in the contract is the same as Mom's investment in the contract, plus any income recognized by Mom on the transfer.[6]
- *Contract acquired from decedent.* If Mom dies holding an annuity contract, and Child receives the contract as a result of Mom's death, Child's initial investment in the contract is Mom's investment in the contract; i.e., no change in basis (investment in the contract) occurs on Mom's death.[7]
- *Special adjustments.* The new owner makes the same adjustments for income on the contract described in ¶ 13.02[3][a] above for premiums paid, distributions received, etc. for the period that the new owner owns the contract.

[d] Amounts Received as an Annuity

Amounts received as an annuity are taxed under the annuity rules of Section 72. "Amounts received as an annuity" are amounts which are payable at regular intervals over a period of more than one full year from the date on which they are deemed to begin, provided that either the total amount payable or the period over which the payments may be paid can be determined as of that date.[8]

[e] Non-Annuity Distributions

We'll call any amount received under the contract that is not an amount received as an annuity, a "non-annuity distribution."[9] Non-annuity distributions (NADs) with respect to contracts entered into after August 13, 1982 include loans, dividends that are not left with the insurer, cash withdrawals, and amounts received on partial surrender of a contract.[10] Additionally, a

---

[6] IRC § 72(e)(4)(C)(iii).

[7] IRC § 1014(b)(9)(A); see also Rev. Rul. 79-335, 1979-2 CB 292, revoking Rev. Rul. 70-143, 1970-1 CB 167.

[8] Treas. Reg. § 1.72-1(b).

[9] Treas. Reg. § 1.72-1(b). See ¶ 13.03[2] below for a discussion of the taxation of non-annuity distributions.

[10] IRC § 72(e)(5)(B); Treas. Reg. § 1.72-11.

transfer of an annuity contract issued after April 22, 1987 for less than adequate consideration will generally result in a deemed NAD.[11]

[4] Kinds of Annuities

The purchaser of an annuity has a number of structural choices. They are as follows.

[a] Ordinary or Variable Annuities

[i] **Ordinary annuity.** An "ordinary annuity" is a promise to pay a fixed amount periodically for the annuity period.

> EXAMPLE: Phil buys an ordinary annuity from Insurance Company. He pays Insurance Company a lump sum premium of $100,000, and the company agrees to pay him $1,000/month for life.

The fixed amount may vary with time or a specific economic indicator (e.g., it may increase by a certain percentage each year, or it may vary with increases in a specific stock market index). However, the amount does not vary based on the performance of particular assets in which the insurance company has invested the premium payments.

The premiums become a part of the insurance company's general assets. As a bookkeeping entry, the premiums paid on a particular annuity are credited each year with interest or dividends, reflecting the general performance of the insurance company. The premiums are also debited each year with a charge reflecting the general expenses of the insurance company. The owner hopes that the net amount will be positive; in fact, a minimum positive amount may be guaranteed.

Like an insurance policy's cash surrender value, the increase in the annuity's cash value is irrelevant if the annuity is paid out to the holder in accordance with its schedule. The cash value is only relevant for determining the amount that can be withdrawn instead of distributed as an annuity, as well as for determining the amount paid to the beneficiary if the holder dies before the annuity starting date.

The insurance company's obligation to make the payments is backed by the insurance company's general assets. If the insurance company fails, the holder may lose his investment.

[ii] **Variable annuity.** Like an ordinary annuity, a variable annuity is also a contract to pay an amount to the annuitant at periodic intervals. However, the premiums paid for a variable annuity will actually be deposited in a

---

[11] IRC § 72(e)(4).

separate account for the owner. The amount of the annuity or other benefits will depend on the performance of the investments in that account. The owner can direct those investments, usually by choosing among various funds offered by the insurance company.

Unlike an ordinary annuity, a variable annuity is not backed by the insurance company's general assets—its payment depends solely on the performance of the fund. A variable annuity contract is a security, subject to federal securities laws, and cannot be sold by a life insurance agent unless she is licensed to sell securities under federal (and possibly state) law. The account is similar to a trust account in that it is not part of the insurance company's general assets—that is, if the insurance company fails, the account will still belong to the holder and will not generally be available to the company's creditors.

[b] Immediate or Deferred Annuities

[i] Immediate annuity. An immediate annuity contract is usually purchased with a single premium. The annuity starting date is one year or less from the date of purchase. The contract provides for a series of substantially equal periodic payments to be made at least annually during the annuity period.[12]

[ii] Deferred annuity. Most annuities purchased as investments or for retirement income are deferred annuities. A deferred annuity is any annuity that is not an immediate annuity.

> EXAMPLE: Phil buys a deferred annuity from Insurance Company. He pays Insurance Company $100,000, and the company agrees to pay him $10,000/year beginning on his 65th birthday.

[5] Pricing of Annuities

There are two parts of the cost of an annuity: (1) the initial premium(s) and (2) the annual charge to earnings levied by the insurance company. The annual charge will affect the surrender value of the annuity and, perhaps, the amount of premiums needed to keep it in force. Other things being equal, the value of an annuity will vary inversely with interest rates. That is, when interest rates increase, the value of an annuity will decline and the purchase price of a new annuity will be relatively low. When interest rates decline, the opposite will occur.

Another factor that can affect the price/value relationship of an ordinary annuity is the financial health of the insurance company.

---

[12] IRC § 72(u)(4).

Besides the annual charge, an annuity contract usually also provides for a surrender charge of a percentage of the surrender value if the annuity is surrendered in the first several years; this percentage may decline over the years. If the annuity is bought strictly as an investment, it must generally be held for a certain number of years to make economic sense.

[6] Exposure to Creditors

Under some state laws, annuities are exempt from creditors of the holder, annuitant, and/or beneficiary.[13]

¶ 13.03 INCOME TAXATION OF ANNUITIES

In the case of an annuity held by an individual, the income on the annuity contract is not generally taxed until distributions are made. However, when annuity distributions taxable as income are made, they are taxed as ordinary income, regardless of whether the income on the contract consisted of ordinary income, capital gain, or tax-exempt income when it was earned.

[1] Undistributed Income on the Contract

[a] Holder Is a Natural Person

The value of a deferred annuity contract may increase with time, just as an insurance contract does, due to the interest or dividend rate credited to the account (ordinary annuity) or the actual performance of the investments selected (variable annuity). The resulting income on the contract is not generally taxable on a current basis if the contract is held by a natural person. Therefore, if no distributions are made from the contract prior to commencement of the annuity, no income tax should be owed until that time.[14] This tax deferral represents the tax advantage of the investment.

---

[13] E.g., Tex. Ins. Code Ann. art. 21.22 (Vernon 1996). See Ch. 53.

[14] IRC §§ 72(a), 72(e)(1), 72(e)(2).

[b] Holder Is Not a Natural Person

Section 72(u)(1) provides that if a non-natural person[15] (i.e., an entity) holds a deferred annuity other than as an agent for a natural person,[16] the income on the contract each year will be taxable to the holder as ordinary income, unless the contract is acquired by the estate of a decedent because of the decedent's death or the contract is an immediate annuity.[17] This statutory language seems to indicate that normal family trusts cannot avail themselves of tax-deferred annuities. However, the legislative history states that the intent of this provision was to prevent businesses from using tax-deferred annuities as substitutes for qualified employee benefit plans.[18] There is no indication that the provision was targeting family trusts. At least two private letter rulings hold that, under certain facts, a private nongrantor trust owning a deferred annuity contract would be treated as a natural person for these purposes, and therefore would not recognize income before distribution.[19]

[2] Non-Annuity Distributions

The taxation of a NAD depends on whether it is made before or after the annuity starting date.

[a] Made Before Annuity Starting Date

A NAD made before the annuity starting date is taxable as ordinary income to the extent of income on the contract.[20] To the extent that such a NAD exceeds the income on the contract, it will be treated as a tax-free return of cost.[21] The allocation is reversed for income allocable to investment in a

---

[15] While a non-natural person is any entity, it should not include a revocable trust or other grantor trust since such trusts are deemed owned by the grantor for income tax purposes. However, if a grantor trust ceases to be a grantor trust during the grantor's lifetime, recognition of accrued income may occur. See Madorin v. Comm'r, 84 TC 667 (1985). Estates are excluded from the entity taxation rules. IRC § 72(s)(3)(A).

[16] See Priv. Ltr. Rul. 9639057 (June 24, 1996) for an example of a contract held by a trust as agent for a natural person.

[17] IRC §§ 72(u)(1), 72(u)(3). Income from certain employment-related annuity contracts and from contracts funding personal injury lawsuits is also excepted. IRC §§ 72(u)(1), 72(u)(3).

[18] HR Rep. No. 426, 99th Cong., 1st Sess., 703-04 (1985).

[19] Priv. Ltr. Rul. 9204014 (Oct. 24, 1991); Priv. Ltr. Rul. 9204010 (Oct. 10, 1991).

[20] IRC §§ 72(e)(1)(A)(ii), 72(e)(2)(B)(i), 72(e)(3)(A).

[21] IRC § 72(e)(2)(B)(ii).

contract before August 13, 1982.[22] For such "grandfathered" distributions, cost is recovered first, while the remaining distributions are taxed as income.[23]

[b] Made on or After Annuity Starting Date

A NAD made on or after the annuity starting date is taxable as ordinary income.[24] A refund of the consideration paid for the contract, and the proceeds of a complete surrender, however, are taxed under the rules described in ¶ 13.03[2][a] above.[25] A complete surrender will result in a deductible ordinary loss if the investment in the contract exceeds the surrender value,[26] unless the contract was purchased for personal, noninvestment reasons.[27]

[c] Effect on Investment in the Contract

A loan, assignment, or transfer of a contract for inadequate consideration that constitutes a NAD before the annuity starting date will increase the investment in the contract by the amount included in the holder's income.[28]

[d] Penalties for Early Distributions

Congress intended that tax-advantaged annuities be used for long-term investment, and not for short-term tax shelters.[29] Accordingly, rules have been enacted to discourage early withdrawals. The income-out-first rule described above is one. The penalty tax on premature distributions is another.

[i] Ten percent penalty tax—general rule. Generally speaking, any distribution made before the annuity starting date is subject to a ten percent penalty tax.[30]

[ii] Ten percent penalty tax—exceptions. Exceptions relevant to a commercial annuity purchased as an investment include distributions:

---

[22] IRC § 72(e)(5)(B); Rev. Rul. 85-159, 1985-2 CB 29.

[23] IRC § 72(e)(5)(A).

[24] IRC § 72(e)(2)(A).

[25] IRC § 72(e)(5)(E).

[26] Rev. Rul. 61-201, 1961-2 CB 46.

[27] IRC § 165; Early v. Atkinson, 175 F2d 118 (4th Cir. 1949).

[28] IRC §§ 72(e)(4)(A), 72(e)(4)(C)(iii).

[29] S. Rep. No. 494, 97th Cong., 2d Sess., pt. 2, at 350.

[30] IRC § 72(q).

- Made when the taxpayer is 59$\frac{1}{2}$ or older;[31]
- Made on or after the death of a holder who is a natural person;[32]
- Made on or after the death of the annuitant, if the holder is not a natural person;[33]
- Attributable to the taxpayer's disability;[34]
- Allocable to pre-August 14, 1982 investments in the contract, including earnings on those investments;[35]
- Made under an immediate annuity contract;[36] or
- Made as part of a series of substantially equal periodic payments payable at least annually for the life or life expectancy of the taxpayer or the joint lives or joint life expectancies of the taxpayer and his designated beneficiary.[37]

What if the holder and the annuitant are not the same person? For the above purposes, the "taxpayer" is presumably the holder (if the holder is a natural person) and the annuitant (if the holder is not a natural person).[38]

[3] Annuity Payments

Amounts received as an annuity are subject to Section 72. Each annuity payment is deemed to consist partly of nontaxable return of basis and partly of taxable income.[39] Subparagraphs [a] through [d] of this subsection discuss the income taxation rules applicable to ordinary (non-variable) annuities. Subparagraph [e] discusses the income tax rules applicable to variable annuities. Subparagraph [f] applies to both types of annuities.

---

[31] IRC § 72(q)(2)(A).

[32] IRC § 72(q)(2)(B).

[33] IRC § 72(q)(2)(B).

[34] IRC § 72(q)(2)(C).

[35] IRC § 72(q)(2)(F).

[36] IRC § 72(q)(2)(I). Can a taxpayer avoid the penalty on early distributions by exchanging a deferred annuity contract for an immediate annuity contract under IRC § 1035? Not according to the IRS, which has ruled that, when one annuity is exchanged for another, the date of purchase for purposes of determining whether payments begin within one year of purchase is deemed to be the date of purchase of the original annuity contract, so that payments under the new annuity do not qualify as an immediate annuity if the original annuity was purchased more than one year before payments are made under the new annuity. Rev. Rul. 92-95, 1992-2 CB 43.

[37] IRC § 72(q)(2)(D).

[38] Sen. Comm. Rep. on Pub. L. No. 98-369 (Deficit Reduction Act of 1984).

[39] Dividends received in addition to the annuity payment, however, are generally fully includable in income. IRC §§ 72(e)(1)(B), 72(e)(2).

[a] Exclusion Ratio

The "exclusion ratio" is the percentage of each annuity payment which is excluded from income. To compute the exclusion ratio, divide the investment in the contract by the expected return on the contract; then round the quotient to the nearest tenth of one percent.[40]

A new exclusion ratio will be determined under certain circumstances (for example, when the contract is sold, when certain withdrawals are made, or if payments drop below the excludable amount, in the case of certain variable annuity contracts).[41]

[b] Expected Return on the Contract

[i] **Payments for life.** The expected return of any annuity for a life or lives is the product of the life expectancy of the measuring life or lives (as determined by the IRS annuity tables published in the Section 72 regulations) and the amount of one year's annuity payment.[42] For purposes of determining life expectancies, the unisex tables are used for amounts attributable to investments in the contract made after June 30, 1986.[43] For other amounts, the gender-based tables are used.[44] This rule is subject to some elections under transitional rules.[45]

[ii] **Installment payments.** If payments do not depend on the life or life expectancy of any person, the expected return is the sum of the guaranteed payments.[46] Special rules apply to payments which may vary due to factors other than lives or life expectancies.[47]

[iii] **Combination payments.** Special factors apply if the annuity payments depend on the life or life expectancy of any person, plus a fixed payment feature (such as the longer of life or a term certain).[48]

---

[40] IRC § 72(b)(1); Treas. Reg. § 1.72-4(a)(2).

[41] Treas. Reg. §§ 1.72-4(b)(2), 1.72-4(d)(3), 1.72-11(e).

[42] IRC § 72(c)(3); Treas. Reg. §§ 1.72-5(a), 1.72-5(b).

[43] Treas. Reg. § 1.72-9.

[44] Treas. Reg. §§ 1.72-9, 1.72-5(g).

[45] Treas. Reg. § 1.72-5(g).

[46] IRC § 72(c)(3)(B); Treas. Reg. §§ 1.72-5(c), 1.72-5(d).

[47] Treas. Reg. § 1.72-5(d).

[48] Treas. Reg. §§ 1.72-5(e), 1.72-5(f).

[c] Taxation of Annuity Payments

Each payment received consists of a nontaxable portion and a taxable portion. The nontaxable portion is the exclusion ratio multiplied by the payment amount. The balance of the payment is taxable as ordinary income.

> EXAMPLE: Mom purchases an annuity contract measured by her life in 1996 and invests a total of $40,000 in the contract. The expected return on the contract (determined by the IRS tables) is $120,000. Mom's exclusion ratio is 40,000/120,000, or 1/3. If Mom receives annual payments of $3,000, she should include $2,000 in her gross income each year, in addition to including any dividends that are paid to her with respect to the contract.

If the investment in the contract is greater than or equal to the expected return, the exclusion ratio is 100 percent and no portion of the annuity payment will initially be taxable.[49]

Post-1986 annuities. For contracts with annuity starting dates after 1986, once the entire investment in the contract has been recovered, subsequent annuity payments will be fully includable in income.[50]

Pre-1987 annuities. The exclusion ratio is always applied to determine the nontaxable portion of the annuity payment, even though the entire investment in the contract has been recovered through prior annuity payments.

[d] Special Cases

Special rules detailed in the regulations under Section 72 apply to the computation of the taxable portion of: (1) annuities with refunding or period-certain features, (2) joint and survivor annuities, (3) annuities with investments in the contract made both before and after June 30, 1986, and (4) annuities with various combinations of these features.[51]

[e] Variable Annuity

The expected return of a variable annuity equals the investment in the contract. The excludable portion is determined by dividing the investment in the contract by the number of years it is anticipated that the annuity will be paid, using the IRS tables.[52] For annuities with pre-1987 starting dates, this percentage is excludable as long as the payments are received But, for annuities with starting dates after 1986, this percentage is excludable only until the

---

[49] IRC § 1.72-4(d)(2).

[50] IRC § 72(b)(2).

[51] Treas. Reg. §§ 1.72-5, 1.72-7.

[52] Treas. Reg. § 1.72-2(b)(3).

investment in the contract is recovered.[53] If payments drop below the excludable amount for any year, the annuitant can elect to redetermine the excludable amount in a succeeding year.[54]

[f] Payments to Annuitant Who Is Not the Holder

If the holder can change the annuitant, the income attributable to annuity payments should be taxable to the holder under the assignment of income doctrine. If the holder has no right to change the annuitant, the annuitant will be taxable on the annuity payments.

[4] Death of Holder/Annuitant

[a] Minimum Distribution Requirements

Certain minimum distribution requirements apply at the death of the holder. If a contract issued after April 22, 1987 is owned jointly, the distribution requirements are applied at the death of the first holder.[55] If a contract issued after April 22, 1987 is owned by an entity whose income is not directly taxed to an individual, the following distribution rules apply on the death of the primary annuitant or a change in the primary annuitant:[56]

- *Holder dies before annuity starting date.* Generally, the entire interest in the contract must be distributed within five years after the death of the holder.[57]
- *Holder dies on or after annuity starting date.* Generally, the remaining interest in the contract must be distributed at least as rapidly as under the method of distribution being used as of the date of death of the holder.[58]
- *Exception for payments to designated beneficiary.* Regardless of when the holder dies in relation to the annuity starting date, the interest may be paid out over the life or life expectancy of a designated beneficiary if distributions begin no later than one year after the holder's death.[59] If the surviving spouse is the designated beneficiary, the spouse will be

---

[53] IRC § 72(b)(2); Tax Reform Act of 1986, Pub. L. No. 99-514, §§ 1122(c)(2), 1122(h)(2)(B), 100 Stat. 2085 (1986).

[54] IRC § 1.72-4(d)(3).

[55] Tax Reform Act of 1986, Pub. L. No. 99-514, § 1826, 1986-3 CB 1.

[56] IRC §§ 72(s)(6), 72(s)(7).

[57] IRC § 72(s)(1)(B).

[58] IRC § 72(s)(1)(A).

[59] IRC § 72(s)(2).

treated as the holder for purposes of the minimum distribution rules.[60] "Designated beneficiary" means any individual designated as beneficiary by the holder.[61] If the annuity were payable under a qualified plan, individual beneficiaries of trusts named as beneficiaries could be designated beneficiaries under certain circumstances.[62] The qualified plan regulations do not by their terms apply to commercial annuities.

[b] Taxation of Beneficiary if Annuitant Dies Before Annuity Starting Date

If the annuitant dies before the annuity starting date, the beneficiary will be paid a death benefit—equal, for example, to the greater of the amount of premiums paid or the accumulation value of the contract. The beneficiary will realize gain taxed as ordinary income to the extent that the death benefit received exceeds the investment in the contract.[63]

[c] Taxation of Beneficiary if Annuitant Dies on or After Annuity Starting Date

Some contracts guarantee that an annuity will be paid for a certain term of years, or provide that if the annuitant dies before distributions totaling a certain guaranteed amount have been made, the beneficiary will receive a distribution in the nature of a "refund" of the difference between the guaranteed amount and the amount of payments actually made. The investment in the contract for such an arrangement is reduced by the present value of the refund feature for purposes of determining the tax on distributions.[64]

The beneficiary of an annuity with a refund feature receives all non-annuity distributions tax-free as a recovery of cost until the investment in the contract is recovered (including the excludable amounts received by the annuitant). Distributions exceeding that amount are taxed as ordinary income.[65]

If the beneficiary receives the benefits as annuity payments, he will be taxed under the annuity rules.[66]

If the annuity is a joint and survivor annuity, the survivor excludes from income the same percentage of each payment that was excludable before the first annuitant's death, until (for contracts with a post-December 31, 1986

---

[60] IRC § 72(s)(3).

[61] IRC § 72(s)(4).

[62] Prop. Reg. § 1.401(a)(9)-1, Q&A D-6.

[63] IRC §§ 72(e)(5)(E), 72(e)(5)(A).

[64] IRC § 72(c)(2).

[65] Treas. Reg. §§ 1.72-11(a), 1.72-11(c).

[66] IRC § 72(e)(5); Treas. Reg. §§ 1.72-11(c), 1.72-11(e).

starting date) the total exclusion by both annuitants equals the investment in the contract.

In the case of a contract with an annuity starting date after July 1, 1986, if the benefits received on the annuitant's death are less than the investment in the contract, the beneficiary may deduct the unrecovered investment in the contract for the taxable year in which the refund payments are received.[87]

[d] Termination of Life-Only Annuity Before Recovery of Investment

If the annuitant dies and payments terminate before the annuitant has received an amount which represents the recovery of the entire investment in the contract, is a loss deduction available? No loss is available if the annuity starting date was before July 2, 1986. However, if the starting date is after July 1, 1986, the amount of the unrecovered investment in the contract is a deductible loss by the annuitant in the annuitant's final tax year.[88] Moreover, if the annuity was purchased for business purposes, the deduction is considered a trade or business deduction for purposes of determining a net operating loss.[89]

[e] Income in Respect of a Decedent Considerations

Annuity payments received after the holder's death fit the definition of income in respect of a decedent (IRD).[70] Such payments are: (1) taxable income to the recipient, to the extent that the proceeds exceed the investment in the contract; (2) included in the gross estate of the holder; and (3) not generally eligible for a change in basis on the holder's death, to the extent of taxable income to the recipient.[71] If the taxable income portion of the annuity is subject to estate tax, the beneficiary should be entitled to the Section 691(c) IRD income tax deduction for the estate tax paid.[72] In this regard, however, the IRS has argued that payments pursuant to annuity contracts are not eligible for the IRD deduction unless they are described in Section 691(d),[73] which provides that an IRD deduction is available for a payment received

---

[87] IRC § 72(b)(3)(B); Pub. L. No. 99-514, § 1122(h)(2)(B).

[88] IRC § 72(b)(3)(A); Pub. L. No. 99-514, § 1122(h)(2)(B).

[89] IRC § 72(b)(3)(C).

[70] IRC § 691(a).

[71] IRC § 1014(b)(9)(A). There is a grandfathering rule for variable annuities purchased and completely paid for before October 21, 1979. Such contracts acquire a new basis at the holder's death before the annuity starting date. Rev. Rul. 79-335, 1979-2 CB 292.

[72] IRC §§ 691(c), 691(d).

[73] See William L. Raby, Tax Treatment of "Inherited" Variable Annuity Contracts, 55-60 Tax Notes 1235 (Dec. 6, 1993); Priv. Ltr. Rul. 8845002 (Nov. 10, 1988),

under a joint and survivor annuity contract after the annuity starting date and during the survivor's life expectancy period. The IRS's theory is that the language of Sections 1014(b)(9)(A) and 1014(c), and Sections 691(d) and 691(c), respectively, would be redundant if all annuity payments received after the holder's death were entitled to the IRD deduction.

Since annuities are not generally entitled to a step-up in basis at death, they are poor wealth transmission vehicles, even assuming that the Section 691(c) IRD deduction is available. An annuity may be subject to a 55 percent or 60 percent estate tax, as well as a 39.6 percent income tax.

> EXAMPLE: Dad dies, leaving an annuity payable to Child. The annuity is valued at $1,000,000, and the investment in the contract was $400,000. If the 55 percent estate tax is paid from the annuity, an immediate distribution of $550,000 will be required. Total income on the contract is $1,000,000 — $400,000, or $600,000. There should be a deduction from the income tax of the amount of estate tax payable on the income. Since 60 percent of the value of the contract consists of income on the contract, 60 percent of the $550,000 estate tax paid on the contract, or $330,000, was paid on the income. If a lump sum benefit of $1,000,000 is taken by Child, income of $600,000 will be realized, less the income in respect of a decedent deduction of $330,000. Net taxable income of $270,000 will result in an income tax of $106,920 (at 39.6 percent). Total tax is $550,000 estate tax plus $106,920 income tax, for a total of $656,920, leaving only 34.3 percent of the annuity value for Child (after payment of all taxes).

If there is no IRD deduction, then taxation of the benefit at the 55 percent estate tax and 39.6 percent income tax rates would result in a tax of 94.6 percent of the benefit.

If the holder's death appears imminent, it may be prudent to withdraw the annuity benefits to get the income tax out of the estate.

[f] Constructive Receipt Issues

What if the beneficiary after the annuitant's death has the option to receive the proceeds in a lump sum, but wants to elect an installment or life income method of payment? He can elect to have the proceeds taxed under the normal annuity rules (rather than as a lump sum) if the contract provides an annuity option and the beneficiary elects that form of payment within 60 days after the lump sum becomes payable. Otherwise, he will be in constructive receipt of all the proceeds he could have received in a lump sum.[74]

---

revoked by Priv. Ltr. Rul. 9245034 (Aug. 11, 1992) and replaced by Tech. Adv. Mem. 9346002 (Nov. 19, 1993).

[74] IRC § 72(h). Treas. Reg. § 1.72-12.

[g] Funding Bequests With Annuity Contracts

If an annuity contract is used to fund a pecuniary bequest, the funding will be treated as a sale by the estate or other "selling" entity, triggering the deferred income on the contract. If an annuity contract is used to fund a bequest (pecuniary or not) to a trust, the funding will result in recognition of income on the contract by the recipient trust in the year of receipt of the annuity contract.[75]

¶ 13.04 ESTATE TAXATION OF ANNUITIES

[1] Inclusion in Holder's Gross Estate

A commercial annuity contract entered into after March 3, 1931 will be wholly or partially included in the holder's estate if:

- The holder was receiving or possessed the right to receive (either alone or with others) payments that could not or did not end before his death and
- The contract provides that an annuity or other payment is payable to a beneficiary by reason of surviving the decedent.[76]

The amount included in the holder's estate under this rule is that part of the value of the beneficiary's interest that is proportionate to the amount contributed by the holder (rather than any co-holder) toward the purchase of the annuity contract.[77] For example, if one holder pays all the premiums, the entire value of the annuity or other payment will be included in that holder's estate. For purposes of these rules, the holder will be considered to have "possessed the right to receive payments" so long as, immediately before his death, he had an enforceable right to receive the payments either then or at some point in the future. Accordingly, whether the holder dies before or after the annuity starting date does not matter for these purposes.[78]

[2] Valuation of the Annuity

The estate tax value of a commercial annuity issued by a company regularly engaged in the sale of annuities is established by data regarding the sale of

---

[75] IRC § 72(u).

[76] IRC § 2039(a).

[77] IRC § 2039(b). Of course, if the holder's estate were the beneficiary, the entire amount payable would be included in the holder's estate under IRC § 2033. Also, if the holder transferred an annuity contract to another and the holder retained the power to alter or revoke the annuitant's interest, the value of the contract should be included in the holder's estate under IRC §§ 2036 or 2038, even though the holder had no interest in the annuity payments. See Wishard v. United States, 143 F2d 704 (7th Cir. 1944).

[78] Treas. Reg. § 20.2039-1(b)(2), example 3.

comparable contracts by the issuing company.[79] A letter with this information from the issuing company should be sufficient to substantiate the value.

State lotteries. For this purpose, payments made by state lotteries are apparently not considered commercial annuities. The IRS has ruled that lottery payments must be valued by the annuity tables issued under Section 7520.[80]

[3] Qualification for the Marital Deduction

[a] Methods of Payment Considerations

The proceeds of a commercial annuity included in the deceased spouse's estate and payable to the surviving spouse may qualify for the marital deduction in the following variety of ways.

- Lump sum payment to the surviving spouse.[81]
- Annuity payable to the surviving spouse for her life, and terminating at her death.[82]
- Annuity payable to the surviving spouse for life, with any refund or continued annuity payments passing to her estate.[83]
- Annuity payable only to the surviving spouse during her life, with refund or continued annuity payments passing to a third person after her death. The survivor's annuity will automatically be considered qualified terminable interest property (and therefore deductible), unless the executor of the deceased spouse's estate elects otherwise.[84]
- Proceeds (lump sum or annuity) paid to a QTIP trust, with all income from the proceeds payable to the surviving spouse at least annually, provided the executor properly makes the QTIP election.[85]

QUESTION: *Where the proceeds are paid in an annuity form to a QTIP trust, with all income from the proceeds payable to the surviving spouse at least annually, and the executor properly makes the QTIP election, how much of an annuity payment is considered income for this purpose?*

ANSWER: The IRS has ruled on a formula allocating income and principal in the case of lottery installment payments made to a unified credit trust and QTIP trusts after a decedent's death. In the ruling, the IRS determined that

---

[79] Treas. Reg. § 20.2031-8(a).

[80] Priv. Ltr. Rul. 9616004 (Dec. 29, 1995).

[81] IRC § 2056(a).

[82] This form of payment does not constitute a nondeductible terminable interest. Treas. Reg. §§ 20.2056(b)-1(a), 20.2056(b)-1(c), 20.2056(b)-1(g), example 3.

[83] Treas. Reg. § 20.2056(b)-1(g), example 3.

[84] IRC § 2056(b)(7)(C).

[85] IRC § 2056(b)(7).

the amount of each payment allocated to income was equal to the product of: (1) an assumed rate of return equal to the Section 7520 rate[86] for the month in which the payment was received and (2) the discounted present value of the entire unpaid balance of the lottery proceeds remaining to be paid (using the 7520 rate in effect at the time). The balance of the lottery payment was allocated to principal. The IRS also indicated that the formula would not disqualify the QTIP trusts for the marital deduction. The significance of the taxpayer's use of this method of qualification (rather than the method described in the foregoing bullets) is that the surviving spouse does not receive the entire amount of the installments paid during her life. Note, however, that the funding of a trust with an annuity contract will result in recognition of income on the contract.[87]

Proceeds retained by insurer. Though the proceeds are held by the insurer, they may qualify for the marital deduction if either installments of the proceeds or interest on the proceeds are paid to the surviving spouse at least annually for the surviving spouse's life (with refund or continued annuity payments passing to a third person after her death), provided that (1) the payments commence within 13 months after the deceased spouse's death, (2) the surviving spouse has the power alone and in all events to appoint the proceeds to herself or to her estate, and (3) no one has the power to appoint the proceeds to anyone other than the surviving spouse or her estate.[88] If all of the proceeds do not meet the above requirements, the marital deduction is still available for that portion (determined on a fractional or percentage basis) that does meet these requirements.[89] For example, if one-half of the proceeds meet the requirements, then one-half of the proceeds qualify.

[b] Annuity Payable Out of Larger Fund

If the surviving spouse receives an annuity of a specific dollar amount out of a larger fund (for example, if the spouse gets the first $15,000 per month of the proceeds), then the marital deduction is only available if the following transition rule applies.

Under the transition rule, if the decedent died before October 25, 1992, the deductible amount is the amount of proceeds required to earn income in the amount of the annuity, computed with reference to the 7520 rate in effect at the decedent's death. However, under a grandfather provision, this transition rule is also applicable for decedents dying after October 24, 1992, if (1) the annuity passes to the spouse under a will or revocable trust executed on or

---

[86] The "7520 rate" is 120 percent of the applicable federal midterm rate, rounded to the nearest 2/10ths of one percent. IRC § 7520(a)(2).

[87] IRC § 72(u).

[88] IRC § 2056(b)(6); Treas. Reg. § 20.2056(b)-6(a).

[89] Treas. Reg. § 20.2056(b)-6(b); IRC § 2056(b)(10).

before October 24, 1992; (2) the decedent died before October 24, 1995 or on October 24, 1992 was mentally incompetent and did not regain competence before his death; and (in either case) (3) the will or revocable trust did not change after October 24, 1992 so as to increase the amount of the marital deduction or alter the terms by which the interest passed to the surviving spouse.[90]

For all other decedents (that is, those decedents dying after October 24, 1992 who do not come within the terms of the grandfather provision), a gift of an annuity out of a specific fund (including the entire estate, the residuary estate, or the proceeds of the annuity contract) is not deductible if it consists of a specific dollar amount.[91]

> EXAMPLE: Husband, who was mentally competent, held an annuity contract when he died in 1996. Annuity contract proceeds are $2,000,000. Contract provides that payment is made in 10 annual installments of 1/10th of the principal and all interest earned for that year. Wife gets $150,000 per year, and Son gets remaining amount of each installment. The transition rule does not apply in this situation. Wife's annuity does not qualify for the marital deduction.

The IRS has announced its intention to provide further guidance on annuities and the marital deduction.[92]

[c] Post-Mortem Purchase of Annuity for Surviving Spouse

If the executor or trustee is directed to purchase an annuity for the surviving spouse, no marital deduction is available for the funds used to purchase the annuity, even if the annuity would have qualified for the marital deduction had it been left directly to the surviving spouse.[93]

[4] Community Property Issues

If the annuity contract is community property, but only one spouse is the holder, taxation of the contract upon a spouse's death depends on whether the holder or non-holder spouse dies first.

[a] Non-Holder Dies First

If the spouse of the holder of the contract dies first, one-half of the value of the contract will be included in the non-holder spouse's estate. If the

---

[90] Treas. Reg. § 20.2056(b)-5(c)(3).

[91] IRC § 2056(b)(10).

[92] Preamble to TD 8522, 59 Fed. Reg. 9642 (Mar. 1, 1994).

[93] Treas. Reg. §§ 20.2056(b)-1(f) and 20.2056(b)-1(g), example 7.

non-holder spouse's one-half interest passes to the surviving spouse, the marital deduction should be available.

[b] Holder Dies First and Beneficiary Is Not the Surviving Spouse

If the holder of the contract dies first, one-half of the value of the contract will be included in his estate. If the beneficiary of the contract is not the surviving spouse, the surviving spouse may be deemed to have made a gift of her interest in the contract if the holder's death causes the surviving spouse's transfer of her interest in the contract to another beneficiary to become irrevocable.[94] If so, she will recognize her one-half of the income on the contract on the transfer.

¶ 13.05 LIFETIME TRANSFERS OF ANNUITIES AND ANNUITY PAYMENTS

[1] Exchanges of an Annuity

The following annuity exchanges are nontaxable under Section 1035(a):

- The exchange of a life insurance policy for an annuity contract;
- The exchange of an endowment contract for an annuity contract; and
- The exchange of one annuity contract for another.

Variable annuity contracts are eligible for these tax-free exchanges.[95] If one annuity is exchanged for another, the benefits must be payable to the same person or persons.[96] An exchange can result in a new period in which surrender charges apply.

WARNING: If the annuity contract being exchanged is grandfathered under one of the numerous effective date provisions, the exchange can destroy the grandfathering.

---

[94] Cf. Treas. Reg. § 25.2511-1(h)(9).

[95] Rev. Rul. 72-358, 1972-2 CB 473; Rev. Rul. 68-235, 1968-1 CB 360.

[96] Treas. Reg. § 1.1035-1(c).

[2] Sale of an Annuity

Regardless of the manner in which it is held, if an annuity contract is sold, income on the contract is taxed to the seller as ordinary income.[97]

[3] Gift of an Annuity

[a] Post—April 22, 1987 Annuities

If an individual transfers an annuity contract issued after April 22, 1987 for less than full consideration, he will be treated as having received as an non-annuity distribution the amount by which the cash surrender value (as of the date of the gift) exceeds his investment in the contract.[98] The consequences are that the donor includes in his gross income in the year of transfer the amount deemed received.[99]

> EXAMPLE: Dad gives an annuity contract, newly issued in 1990, to Child. The cash surrender value of the annuity is $100,000, and Dad's investment in the contract is $40,000. Dad will recognize $60,000 of income on the gift. Child will take an investment in the contract of $100,000—$40,000 representing Dad's investment in the contract, plus $60,000 of income Dad recognized on the transfer.

[b] Pre—April 23, 1987 Annuities

When the donee surrenders a contract issued before April 23, 1987, the donor must report as taxable income in the year of surrender the excess (if any) of the cash surrender value over the donor's investment in the contract on the date of the gift.[100]

[4] Annuity Transfers Between Spouses and Former Spouses

[a] Gift Tax

Suppose Husband transfers an annuity contract to Wife. If Husband gives Wife the annuity contract outright, the transfer should qualify for the gift tax marital deduction. If Husband gives Wife an annuity payable out of a larger

---

[97] See, e.g., First Nat'l Bank of Kansas City v. Comm'r, 309 F2d 587 (8th Cir. 1962), aff'g Estate of Katz v. Comm'r, 1961 PH TC Memo. ¶ 61,270, 20 TCM (CCH) 1411 (1961).

[98] IRC § 72(e)(4)(C); Pub. L. No. 99-514, § 1826(b)(3). See interspousal transfer exception, described below.

[99] IRC § 72(e)(4)(C); Pub. L. No. 99-514, § 1826(b)(3).

[100] Rev. Rul. 69-102, 1969-1 CB 32.

fund, rules similar to the above rules governing the estate tax marital deduction apply to the gift tax marital deduction.[101]

[b] Income Tax

No income is recognized on the transfer, since it is a transfer between spouses.[102] Wife takes Husband's investment in the contract. The same income tax rules apply to a transfer by Husband to Ex-Wife, provided that Section 1041(a) applies to the transfer as a result of its being a transfer incident to a divorce.[103]

[5] Payments to Annuitant Who Is Not the Holder

If the holder of the contract and the annuitant are different people, and the holder retains rights to change the annuitant, then a gift is made by the holder to the annuitant each time an annuity payment is made. If the holder relinquishes his rights to change the annuitant, the holder will make a completed gift of the contract at that time and the above-discussed income tax consequences of making a transfer of the contract will ensue.

---

[101] IRC § 2523(f)(3).

[102] IRC § 72(e)(4)(C)(ii).

[103] IRC § 72(e)(4)(C)(ii).

CHAPTER **14**

Qualified Plan and IRA Benefits

¶ 14.01 INTRODUCTION

Many people accumulate significant benefits in qualified employee benefit plans[1] and individual retirement accounts (IRAs). These benefits are subject to a maze of tax rules. Both the participants and their beneficiaries need advice on the plethora of choices they face. This chapter focuses primarily on those features of qualified plans and IRAs that influence the estate planning process.

¶ 14.02 GENERAL BACKGROUND INFORMATION

[1] Qualified Plans

Qualified plans can offer income tax advantages on various levels.

[a] Treatment of Contributions to Plans

Employer contributions to a qualified plan are generally deductible by the employer when the contributions are made.[2] Employee contributions may or may not be permitted by the plan. If employee contributions are permitted, they may be made with pre-tax or after-tax dollars, depending on the type of plan and the terms of the plan. All contributions are subject to certain overall limits.[3]

[b] Accumulations of Plan Earnings

Qualified plan assets are generally kept in a qualified trust.[4] Some Section 401 plans are kept in custodial accounts that are treated as trusts for purposes of the taxation of the accounts.[5] Qualified plan trusts are not subject to income

---

[1] A "qualified plan" means a plan that meets the requirements of IRC § 401. For purposes of this chapter, it does not include plans of governments and other tax-exempt entities, which are subject to special rules. E.g., IRC §§ 403(b), 457. It also does not include nonqualified executive compensation plans. IRC § 402(b).

[2] IRC § 404. If the employer is a partnership, S corporation or other pass-through entity that has established a qualified plan, a participant who is a partner or shareholder will receive a deduction.

[3] IRC §§ 402(g), 404, 415.

[4] IRC § 501(e).

[5] IRC § 401(f). This provision is only applicable to certain plans; assets of plans that are subject to Title I of ERISA may be required to be held in trust. IRC § 403(a). "ERISA" refers to the Employee Retirement Income Security Act of 1974, Pub. L. No. 93-406, 93d Cong., 2d Sess. (1974), as amended. Some plans are also insured.

tax, except to the extent that they have unrelated business taxable income.[6] Thus, trust or account earnings can accumulate free of income tax until they are distributed.

[c] Types of Plans

Qualified plans fall into one of two general categories: defined contribution plans and defined benefit plans.

A defined contribution plan has a separate account for each participant.[7] The amount of the contributions that will or can be made to the plan determines what will or can be held in the account. The amount of distributions that the participant or beneficiary will receive depends on the amount which is in the participant's account. The investment performance of the account therefore has a significant effect on how much the benefits from this account will ultimately be.

Defined benefit plans include all other qualified plans.[8] A defined benefit plan promises each participant a specifically defined benefit. Contributions are targeted to fund the total benefits promised. Thus, the investment performance of the plan assets generally has no effect on how much the participant ultimately receives, except to the extent that the plan has insufficient funds to pay the promised benefit.

[2] Individual Retirement Accounts

[a] Treatment of Individual Contributions

Virtually any individual who receives compensation for personal services may establish his own IRA. All contributions must be made in cash.[9] The individual's employer can contribute to an individual's IRA under certain circumstances.[10]

---

[6] IRC §§ 501(a), 511.

[7] ERISA § 1002(34); IRC § 414(i).

[8] ERISA § 1002(35); IRC § 414(j).

[9] IRC § 408(a)(1).

[10] Through a simplified employee pension (SEP) or savings incentive match plan for employees of small employers (SIMPLE retirement account) arrangement. SEPs and SIM-PLEs are not further explained in this chapter because they will rarely constitute significant assets of the affluent. The applicable statutes are IRC §§ 408(k) and 408(p).

Earned income limits on contributions. Generally, a contributor to an IRA cannot contribute more than his/her earned income in that year.[11] However, under certain circumstances, a married individual with no or little earned income can still make contributions to an IRA, up to the annual limits described below.[12]

Dollar limits on contributions. Contributions are generally limited as follows, subject to the sunsetting of the Economic Growth and Tax Relief and Reconciliation Act of 2001 (EGTRRA).[13]

Year	Applicable Limit
2001	$2,000
2002–2004	$3,000
2005–2007	$4,000
2008	$5,000
2009 and thereafter	$5,000, indexed from 2007

Note, however, that an individual who has reached age 50 by the close of the year can contribute $500 more per year than the above numbers for tax years 2002 through 2005, and $1,000 more per year for tax years 2006 and thereafter.

Deductibility of contributions. Contributions are deductible, subject to certain limitations.

For instance, the amount of the deduction for contributions to IRAs is limited for IRA owners who are active participants in qualified plans or who are spouses of such active participants.[14] Specifically, the ability to claim a deduction for IRA contributions phases out around $60,000 of adjusted gross income (AGI) for single individuals who are active participants in a qualified retirement plan and at $100,000 of AGI for spouses filing jointly where either spouse is an active participant in a qualified retirement plan.[15] If a married couple files a joint return and only one spouse is a participant in an employer plan, however, the nonparticipant spouse may deduct his or her IRA contributions up to the applicable limit, provided that the couple's AGI does not exceed $150,000;[16] the amount of the deduction for the IRA contribution in such a case phases out completely at AGI of $160,000.

---

[11] IRC § 219(b)(1)(B). For this purpose, a non-earning spouse in a community property state does not have to count half of the earning spouse's income as her own earned income.

[12] IRC §§ 219(c), 219(g).

[13] IRC §§ 219(a)(1)(A), 219(b)(5).

[14] IRC § 219(g).

[15] IRC § 219(g)(3)(B); Senate Report.

[16] IRC § 219(g)(7); Senate Report.

Nondeductible contributions. Even if a taxpayer's contributions are not deductible, nondeductible IRA contributions are permitted up to the otherwise applicable limit for the year.[17]

IRAs are regularly found among the affluent, including IRAs established when deductible contributions could be made even with a higher income, IRAs established with nondeductible contributions, and rollover IRAs. Large IRA accounts have usually been the recipients of rollover contributions from qualified plans.

[b] Accumulations in IRA Accounts

An IRA is not generally subject to income tax on its earnings. Therefore, even if a contribution is not deductible, the earnings on that contribution will be tax-free as long as they remain in the IRA, except to the extent of the IRA's unrelated business taxable income.[18]

[c] Special Types of IRAs

Certain special types of IRAs are discussed in summary fashion because they are primarily useful vehicles only for low-income and middle-income taxpayers.

[i] Education IRAs (Coverdell education savings acounts). The limit on contributions to an education IRA is $2,000[19] per beneficiary per year, and contributions are not allowed if AGI exceeds $110,000 for single taxpayers and $220,000[20] for married taxpayers filing jointly, subject to the sunsetting of EGTRRA.[21]

[ii] Roth IRAs.

[A] *Contributions.* An individual can contribute up to $2,000 per year (less any contribution to a regular IRA for the year) to a Roth IRA.[22] Unlike regular IRAs, there is no age limit for making contributions.[23] Contributions, however, are not deductible.[24] Further, no contributions to a Roth IRA are al-

---

[17] IRC § 408(o)(2)(B)(i).

[18] IRC § 408(e).

[19] IRC § 530(b)(1)(A)(iii), subject to the sunsetting of EGTRRA. Limit was $500 for years before 2002.

[20] IRC § 530(c)(1). The limit was $160,000 for years beginning before 2002.

[21] IRC § 530(c)(1); Conference Report.

[22] IRC § 408A(c)(2).

[23] IRC § 408A(c)(4).

[24] IRC § 408A(c)(1).

lowed if AGI exceeds $110,000 for a single person or $160,000 for spouses filing jointly.[25] For purposes of determining this AGI limit, gross income from the rollover of a regular IRA into a Roth IRA is excluded, along with certain other distributions from IRAs.[26]

[B] _Distributions._ Distributions are not taxable if they are attributable to contributions held for at least five taxable years, and are made (1) at or after age 59½, (2) after the death or disability of the contributor, or (3) for "first-time homebuyer expenses."[27]

The five-year waiting period for nontaxable distributions does not begin again with an inherited Roth IRA. Instead, the decedent's holding period is tacked to that of the beneficiary. This is true for a surviving spouse-beneficiary even if she treats the Roth IRA as her own.

The five-year period for a beneficiary's own Roth IRAs is generally determined separately from that of an inherited Roth IRA, with an important spouse-friendly exception. If a surviving spouse treats an inherited Roth IRA as her own, the five-year period for _all_ of the surviving spouse's Roth IRAs ends on the earlier of the period for the inherited Roth IRA or the surviving spouse's own Roth IRAs.

[C] _Minimum required distributions._ Distributions during the lifetime of the participant are not required.[28] The following rules apply after the death of the participant.[29]

Non-spouse beneficiary. Where the surviving spouse is _not_ the sole beneficiary of the account, the entire remaining Roth IRA account balance is, at the deceased account owner's election (or if the deceased has not elected, at the election of the beneficiary or beneficiaries), distributed under either of the following methods: (1) by the end of the year containing the fifth anniversary of the account owner's death, or (2) over the life expectancy of the designated beneficiary (if there is one), starting no later than December 31 of the year following the year in which the account owner died.

Where distributions have not begun by December 31 of the year following the year in which the account owner died, the first distribution method applies. If the second distribution method is used, each year's minimum payment is determined by dividing the account balance as of December 31 of the preceding year by the designated beneficiary's life expectancy, using the beneficiary's attained age as of his birthday in the year distributions must commence and subtracting 1 for each passing year. Under the regular IRA rules, a desig-

---

[25] IRC § 408A(c); Conference Report.

[26] IRC § 408A(c)(3)(C)(i).

[27] IRC § 408A(d).

[28] IRC § 408A(c)(5).

[29] Treas. Reg. § 1.408A-6, Q&A 14(b).

nated beneficiary's life expectancy is found in Table V of Treasury Regulation § 1.72-9.

These rules are essentially the same as those that apply to regular IRA distributions to a nonspouse beneficiary where the account owner dies before his required beginning date.

Spouse beneficiary. If the surviving spouse is the sole beneficiary of the account, the spouse is treated as the account owner.[30] The surviving spouse beneficiary of a Roth IRA apparently does not have to make any withdrawals at all during her lifetime.

[D] *Estate planning advantages.* Roth IRAs are not addressed extensively in this treatise because persons with higher incomes cannot generally establish them. Estate planners should be aware, however, that if a Roth IRA is in the picture, it makes a nice asset for funding a bypass trust or a GSTT-exempt trust at the death of the owner. This is because the Roth IRA's assets can continue to grow tax-free for the permitted payout period. Additionally, no distributions need be made during a surviving spouse's lifetime if she is the sole beneficiary of the trust. (If the surviving spouse does not have the ability to withdraw the assets of the Roth IRA, non-marital deduction treatment can be arranged so that the Roth IRA does not have to be subjected to estate tax.)

A transfer of a Roth IRA by lifetime gift will be treated as an assignment resulting in a deemed distribution of all of the IRA's assets. After such a transfer, the assets will no longer be considered held in an IRA.[31]

General guidance on Roth IRAs is provided in the regulations.[32]

[iii] Scope of IRA discussions. Except as otherwise specifically noted, the discussion of IRAs in this chapter is intended to address only regular IRAs, and not Roth IRAs or other special types of IRAs.

[3] IRAs Versus Qualified Plans—Important Differences

There are significant differences between IRAs and qualified plans. These differences become a matter of particular concern when a participant is considering whether to roll over a qualified plan distribution into an IRA.[33] In addition to generally applicable legal differences discussed below, the particular plan's features should be reviewed carefully before deciding whether the plan is more or less desirable than an IRA.

---

[30] Treas. Reg. § 1.408A-2, Q&A 4.

[31] Treas. Reg. § 1.408A-6, Q&A 19.

[32] Treas. Reg. §§ 1.408A-0 et seq.

[33] See discussion at ¶¶ 14.02[3][g], 14.06[7] below.

[a] Spousal Rights

A nonparticipant spouse will have no federally mandated spousal benefits in the participant spouse's IRA.[34] In contrast, a nonparticipant spouse generally has a federally created right to survivorship benefits in certain qualified plans of the participant spouse, absent an effective waiver of that right.[35]

Certain community property laws are pre-empted by ERISA with respect to qualified plans.[36] In contrast, state community property laws are generally not pre-empted with respect to IRAs.[37]

[b] Borrowing From the IRA or Qualified Plan

Neither the participant nor any related party can borrow from the participant's IRA, use the IRA as security for a loan, or otherwise engage in certain self-dealing transactions with the IRA without causing the entire IRA to be deemed distributed.[38] A qualified plan may permit the participant to borrow from the plan, subject to certain limitations.[39] Certain dealings between the plan and the participant, however, may be prohibited transactions that can result in an excise tax.[40]

[c] Holding Life Insurance Policies

Life insurance cannot be held by an IRA.[41] A qualified plan may or may not be able to hold life insurance.[42]

[d] Plan Investments

A participant in an IRA can have extensive input regarding the investment of the IRA assets. In contrast, a participant in a qualified plan may have limited or no control over the investment of the plan assets, although many defined contribution plans allow participants to select from a range of investment

---

[34] ERISA §§ 201(6), 205; IRC § 408.

[35] IRC §§ 401(a)(13), 408(d)(6), 414(p).

[36] Boggs v. Boggs, 520 US 833 (1997).

[37] Priv. Ltr. Rul. 8040101 (July 15, 1980); see also Boggs v. Boggs, 520 US 833 (1997) (although IRA was involved in the case, it was rolled over from qualified plan after nonparticipant spouse's death; accordingly, qualified plan (not IRA) rules applied to determination of nonparticipant spouse's rights at her death).

[38] IRC §§ 408(e)(2), 408(e)(3), 4975(c)(1), 4975(d), 4975(e).

[39] IRC §§ 72(p), 4975(d)(i); Treas. Reg. § 1.72(p)-1; 29 CFR § 2550.408b-1.

[40] IRC § 4975.

[41] IRC § 408(a)(3).

[42] See ¶ 14.09 below.

options. Some qualified plans offer investments that are not generally available in IRAs, such as non-publicly traded employer securities or group insurance contracts.

[e] Investment in Collectibles

An IRA cannot invest in collectibles.[43] "Collectibles" means works of art, rugs, antiques, metals, gems, stamps, certain coins, alcoholic beverages, musical instruments, historical objects (documents, clothes, etc.), and any other tangible personal property deemed a "collectible" by the IRS.[44] A qualified plan can generally make these investments, except in a self-directed account. In the case of a self-directed account, an investment in collectibles is treated as a distribution.[45]

[f] Creditors' Rights

Federal law excepts qualified plans from most claims of creditors, other than certain governmental claims and claims for alimony and child support.[46] An IRA is not exempt from creditors, except to the extent that state law exempts it. Some states exempt IRAs to some extent.[47]

An IRA will be included in a participant's bankruptcy estate unless state law exempts it and the participant elects his state law exemptions.

[g] Defined Benefit Plans—Rollover to IRA versus Annuity Option

Participants who reach their required beginning dates are faced with a particularly difficult decision in the case of defined benefit plans that offer participants a choice between a lump sum option (which can be rolled over into an IRA) or various life annuity payment options. Many defined benefit plans offer little or no death benefit,[48] making a lump sum option attractive to a participant with serious health problems or other mortality concerns. In some plans, however, a participant who elects a lump sum may forfeit the value of early retirement subsidies[49] or future cost of living increases. Another consideration is the effect of the interest rate and other assumptions used by the plan to

---

[43] IRC § 408(m)(1).

[44] IRC §§ 408(m)(2), 408(m)(3); Prop. Reg. § 1.408-10.

[45] IRC §§ 408(m)(2), 408(m)(3); Prop. Reg. § 1.408-10.

[46] See Chapter 53 on asset protection for further discussion.

[47] E.g., Tex. Prop. Code § 42.0021 (exempting deductible and rollover contributions).

[48] Under IRC § 411(a)(3)(A), employer-provided benefits may be forfeited on death, except for any surviving-spouse annuities required under IRC § 401(a)(11).

[49] Treas. Reg. § 1.411(a)-11(a)(2).

calculate the lump sum. For example, a plan that uses a low discount rate will calculate a larger lump sum; in such a case, it may be more beneficial for the taxpayer to select the lump sum, which could then be invested in a rollover IRA that could generate larger returns than the annuity payments would provide.

[h] Flexibility of Distribution Options

Many IRAs will allow any distribution option permitted by law. In contrast, many qualified plans allow a limited menu of options.

[i] Mandatory Distributions

In a qualified plan, a participant owning less than five percent of the company does not have to start taking distributions until April 1 of the year following her actual retirement date, even if she is over age 70½.[50] In contrast, the owner of an IRA must begin receiving distributions by April 1 of the year after she attains age 70½.

¶ 14.03 ESTATE TAXATION OF INTERESTS IN PLANS AND IRAs

A participant's interest in his qualified plan or IRA is generally included in his estate for estate tax purposes.[51] This fact, combined with the fact that the participant's interest constitutes a right to income in respect of a decedent (IRD), makes qualified plans and IRAs[52] poor vehicles for passing wealth on to succeeding generations. Let's examine the treatment of benefits after the participant's death.

[1] Qualification for Marital Deduction

Benefits payable out of qualified plans and IRAs qualify for the marital deduction if they are payable in a qualified form.[53]

---

[50] IRC § 401(a)(9)(C).

[51] IRC §§ 2033, 2039. There are some grandfathered benefits that are not included in the estate. See ¶ 14.03[4] below.

[52] Except Roth IRAs, to the extent distributions are not subject to income tax.

[53] IRC § 2056. It is assumed in this chapter that the surviving spouse is a U.S. citizen. If the surviving spouse is not a U.S. citizen, benefits payable to her will have to be held in a qualified domestic trust to be eligible for the marital deduction. IRC

[a] Lump Sum Payable to Spouse

Qualified plan or IRA benefits that are payable outright to the surviving spouse in a lump sum will qualify for the marital deduction.[54]

If the surviving spouse can choose whether to take the benefits in a lump sum or otherwise, and elects to receive a lump sum or directly roll over the benefits to an IRA, the benefit should qualify for the marital deduction.[55]

What if a surviving spouse has the option to take the benefit in a lump sum, but irrevocably chooses a different form of payout? If the payout is a qualified survivor annuity, the marital deduction should be available.[56] Even if it is not a qualified survivor annuity, however, the marital deduction should be available. This is because the surviving spouse had the right to cause the entire benefit to be paid to her immediately, and therefore, she had a nonlapsing presently exercisable general power of appointment by deed.[57] Some experts have expressed disagreement on this point under the following theory: if the surviving spouse elects a different form of payout, and thus relinquishes her general power, the trust does not continue to meet the general power requirements.[58] However, this would seem incorrect—the spouse's release (or exercise) of her general power after her husband's death should not affect the initial qualification for the marital deduction. The release of the general power should also not be taxable as a gift unless a benefit is irrevocably conferred on another beneficiary.

Why would the surviving spouse not elect to receive a lump sum where possible? For the same reasons she might want to buy an annuity in general. She may wish to (1) leave the cash with the financial institution or pension plan to invest, (2) have a guarantee that she will receive a certain amount of income for her life or a term, or (3) defer the income tax on the benefits. It should be noted, however, that income tax deferral can usually be accomplished through a rollover. Therefore, if deferral is the surviving spouse's primary objective, she may wish to choose the lump sum and roll it over into her

---

§ 2056(d)(1). Planning for noncitizens through the use of qualified domestic trusts is discussed in Chapter 52 on international issues.

[54] IRC § 2056(a).

[55] Estate of Mackie v. Comm'r, 545 F2d 883 (4th Cir. 1976); see also Estate of Neugass v. Comm'r, 555 F2d 322 (2d Cir. 1977); Estate of Tompkins v. Comm'r, 68 TC 912 (1977), acq., 1982-1 CB 1; Rev. Rul. 82-184, 1982-2 CB 215.

[56] IRC § 2056(b)(7)(C), discussed at ¶ 14.03[1][b][i] below.

[57] See Treas. Reg. § 20.2056(b)-5(f)(6). This regulation says that the surviving spouse must have the right, exercisable in all events, to have the corpus distributed to her at any time during her life. The surviving spouse has such a power until the time she elects not to take the lump sum.

[58] See Treas. Reg. §§ 20.2056(b)-5(g)(1), 20.2056(b)-5(g)(3) (power must be fully exercisable in spouse's favor at any time during spouse's life or in favor of spouse's estate at any time during life or by will).

own IRA, which can also be structured to pay her an amount of income for her life or a term. If a rollover is undesirable in the particular circumstances, the marital deduction should nevertheless be available regardless of the spouse's actual choice of benefit provided that she could have chosen a lump sum.[59]

[b] Other Payments to Spouse

[i] **Qualifying annuity.** If an employer annuity is included in the gross estate under Section 2039, and only the surviving spouse has the right to receive payments before her death, the annuity will qualify for the marital deduction as qualified terminable interest property (QTIP).[60] Qualified joint and survivor annuities and qualified pre-retirement survivor annuities will qualify.[61] Annuities paid to a marital deduction trust can also qualify where the trustee must distribute each annuity payment to the surviving spouse.[62] It is unclear, however, whether a series of installment payments would constitute an annuity for this purpose.[63]

[ii] **Other forms of benefits.** If the beneficiary is the surviving spouse and benefits are not payable to her in the form of a lump sum or qualifying annuity, the plan or IRA itself must qualify for QTIP treatment to qualify for the marital deduction.[64]

Suppose a beneficiary designation provides that payments will be made to Wife for a ten-year period, or, if she dies within the ten-year period, the remaining payments will be made to Child. The status of this payment under Section 2056(b)(7)(C) is not clear.[65] To qualify for the marital deduction, either Wife must be entitled to all of the income from the participant's interest

---

[59] This conclusion is based on logic and the final sentence of Treas. Reg. § 20.2056(b)-5(f)(6).

[60] IRC § 2056(b)(7)(C).

[61] IRC §§ 2056(b)(7)(C), 2523(f)(6). See ¶ 14.06[1] below for a description of these annuities.

[62] Priv. Ltr. Rul. 9204017 (Oct. 25, 1991): Priv. Ltr. Rul. 9822031 (Feb. 25, 1998) (concerning nonqualified deferred compensation). The inclusion of such payments will not cause the rest of the property in the trust to be ineligible for the regular QTIP deduction.

[63] Generally, "amounts received as an annuity" are amounts that are payable at a regular interval over a period of more than one full year from the date on which they are deemed to begin, provided that the total of the amounts so payable or the period for which they are to be paid can be determined as of that date. See Treas. Reg. § 1.72-1(b). In the context of IRC § 7520, the Tax Court considered a series of 18 annual payments from lottery winnings to be an annuity, after an in-depth consideration of various possible meanings of the term. Estate of Gribauskas v. Comm'r, 116 TC No. 12 (2001).

[64] See Treas. Reg. § 20.2056(b)-7(h), Example 10.

[65] See note 63.

in the plan/IRA on an annual or more frequent basis[66] or all of the remaining benefit at Wife's death must go to her estate, rather than to Child.[67] If Wife could have withdrawn all of the funds, but elected to take the ten-year installment payout instead, the marital deduction should be available under Section 2056(b)(5) (because a lifetime general power of appointment is considered equivalent to meeting the marital deduction annual income payment requirements).[68]

[c] Benefits Payable in "Estate Trust" Format

If the spouse is the only beneficiary of the qualified plan or IRA during her lifetime and the plan or IRA assets must be paid to her estate when she dies, the marital deduction should be available.[69]

[d] Plan or IRA Benefits Payable to QTIP Trust

If benefits under an IRA or a qualified plan are paid to a QTIP trust in a lump sum, the benefits will qualify for the marital deduction. If the benefits are not paid in a lump sum, the benefits and the QTIP must be specially structured to enable the benefits to qualify for the marital deduction under Section 2056(b)(7).[70] Thorny issues can arise in this context. The following describes methods that have been used to qualify such payments for the marital deduction.

Practice Pointer: Of course, these methods will only work if they are permitted by the plan or IRA agreement. One issue with all of these methods is that they require the spouse or QTIP trustee to have a measure of control over the distributions from and/or investments made by the plan or IRA. Hence, the following methods may be more suitable for IRAs than qualified plans.

---

[i] Revenue Ruling 2000-2 method. The IRS has issued a revenue ruling that describes a method ensuring availability of the marital deduction.[71] In this

---

[66] IRC § 2056(b)(7)(B)(ii); Treas. Reg. § 20.2056(b)-7(h), Example 10.

[67] Treas. Reg. § 20.2056(c)-2(b)(1)(iii).

[68] Treas. Reg. § 20.2056(b)-5(f)(6); see also discussion at ¶ 14.03[1][a] above. See also Priv. Ltr. Rul. 199936052 (June 16, 1999), in which the IRS ruled that the continued right of the designated beneficiary and contingent beneficiary (the wife of the designated beneficiary) to withdraw the entire account balance would make the account balance eligible for the marital deduction at the designated beneficiary's death.

[69] Treas. Reg. § 20.2056(c)-2(b)(1).

[70] See, e.g., Priv. Ltr. Rul. 9320015 (Feb. 17, 1993).

[71] Rev. Rul. 2000-2, 2000-3 IRB 305.

ruling, a testamentary trust was named as the beneficiary of an IRA. The trust had the standard provisions that would enable it to qualify for QTIP treatment. In addition, the trust gave the surviving spouse the power, exercisable annually, to compel the trustee to withdraw (from the IRA) and distribute to the surviving spouse an amount equal to the income earned that year on IRA assets. The IRA did not limit withdrawals to the annual minimum required distribution. The IRS determined that the spouse's rights satisfied the standard of Treasury Regulation § 20.2056(b)-5(f)(8), and therefore, the QTIP election could be made for both the IRA and the trust. (The IRS indicated that the QTIP election must be made for the IRA as well as the trust because the trust is merely a conduit for income payments from the IRA to the surviving spouse.) The IRS volunteered that the ruling result would be the same if the QTIP trust required the QTIP trustee to withdraw from the IRA annually an amount equal to all income earned on IRA assets and pay that amount to the surviving spouse.

The revenue ruling does not purport to set forth the only way the marital deduction can be obtained—it simply describes a safe harbor method. As a practical matter, it may be difficult to duplicate with qualified plans, for reasons discussed in ¶ 14.03[1][d][iii].

[ii] Other methods. The following are other methods that may be used to qualify payments from a plan or IRA for the marital deduction:

- Provide in the beneficiary designation that the plan or IRA must pay out annually at least the greater of the minimum required distribution or all income of the account.[72] In addition, give the spouse the ability to (1) require that the plan or IRA trustee invest in income-producing property or (2) direct the QTIP trustee to require the plan or IRA trustee make such an investment at the spouse's request.[73]

- Require the QTIP trustee to elect the type of payout described in the previous method, direct the QTIP trustee to require the plan or IRA trustee to invest in income-producing property, and pass the income of the plan or IRA through the QTIP trust to the spouse.

- Require the QTIP trustee to demand that the IRA distribute all of its income for the year to the trust, and allow the spouse to compel the trustees to exercise this authority.[74] In the cited private letter ruling, the trustees were also required to treat distributions received from IRAs, to the extent of the income of the distributing IRAs, as income of the

---

[72] Priv. Ltr. Ruls. 9738010 (June 18, 1997), 9544038 (Aug. 9, 1995), 9537005 (June 13, 1995).

[73] Priv. Ltr. Rul. 199931033 (Aug. 6, 1999).

[74] Priv. Ltr. Rul. 9830004 (Apr. 10, 1998).

QTIP trust (in addition to any amounts otherwise required to be allocated to trust income).

- Include provisions in the QTIP trust that give the spouse the ability to have the QTIP trustee convert the plan or IRA interest to income-producing assets (if permitted by the plan), and, perhaps, also give the spouse the right to demand distributions as if the plan or IRA were earning reasonable income. Some rulings indicate that arrangements that do both will work.[75]

- Define QTIP trust income to include the income distributed from the plan or IRA, regardless of other provisions of law or the document. Of course, this alone will not guarantee that all income with respect to the participant's interest in the plan or IRA will in fact be distributed to the QTIP trust.

- Include provisions in the will or trust stating that trust income cannot be charged with expenses properly chargeable to principal.[76] Once again, other measures would also need to be taken to ensure that all income from the plan or IRA is distributed to the QTIP trust.

- Provide that all the assets in the QTIP trust (including the interest in the plan or IRA) must be paid to the spouse's estate on the death of the spouse.[77]

- Require the QTIP trustee to elect a distribution that is equal to the greater of the minimum distribution or all of the net income of the IRA or plan, and distribute it to the spouse in the year of receipt.[78]

[iii] Caution required if benefits under a qualified plan are involved.

[A] *Difficulty with determinations/payment of income.* One difficulty with methods that require the plan to distribute all of the income each year is determining the income with respect to the participant's interest in the

---

[75] Cf. Tech. Adv. Mem. 9220007 (Jan. 30, 1991). The spouse only had the right, in the event the trust did not produce a reasonable amount of income, to request that the trustee distribute property from principal equal to the income the spouse should have received if the property had produced income. The arrangement did not qualify for the marital deduction.

[76] A QTIP trust should never allow income to be charged with expenses that are only properly chargeable to principal. However, many expenses could properly be charged to either income or principal, and are subject to trustee discretion.

[77] Treas. Reg. § 20.2056(c)-2(b)(1).

[78] Priv. Ltr. Ruls. 9245033 (Aug. 11, 1992), 9348025 (Sept. 2, 1993); see also Rev. Rul. 89-89, 1989-2 CB 231; Priv. Ltr. Ruls. 9324024 (Mar. 22, 1993), 9322005 (Feb. 24, 1993), 9321059 (Feb. 26, 1993), 9321035 (Feb. 24, 1993), 9321032 (Feb. 24, 1993), 9320015 (Feb. 17, 1993), 9317025 (Jan. 29, 1993), 9738010 (June 18, 1997), 9704029 (Oct. 31, 1996), 9537005 (June 13, 1995), 9521015 (Sept. 21, 1995), 9442032 (July 21, 1994). Rev. Rul. 89-89 was declared obsolete by Rev. Rul. 2002-2, 2000-3 IRB 305.

plan—a number which may not be available to the plan beneficiaries on a timely basis, or at all. For example, in a defined benefit plan, the income attributable to a particular individual's interest may not be a meaningful number or may not be calculable at all. In a defined contribution plan, available information may include only increases or decreases in the value of the plan interest over the year, and not the fiduciary income, which is the relevant concept for a QTIP trust.

Even if income records will be available, how does one establish that fact as an initial matter? In one ruling regarding a QTIP trust that was the beneficiary of a profit-sharing plan, the IRS relied on the representations that the plan administrator's business records would reflect the exact source and character of income earned by the plan, and that these records would provide enough information that the plan administrator could compute the decedent's portion of the plan's fiduciary accounting income under state law. The ruling that the plan benefits qualified for the marital deduction was issued on the basis that the decedent's entire portion of the plan's fiduciary accounting income could thus be distributed, at least annually, to the QTIP trust, and could be characterized as fiduciary accounting income of the trust.[79]

[B] *Plan limitations.* When the benefit is payable from a qualified plan rather than an IRA, the flexibility required by the methods described above may not be permitted by the plan. If this is the case, one must be careful about paying the plan benefit to a QTIP trust. In order to ensure that a designation in favor of a QTIP trust will work, the plan documents must allow the QTIP trustee to obtain the required distributions from the qualified plan, and the plan trustees must have the ability and willingness to meet the needs of the QTIP trustee. If these measures are not permitted under the plan document and the participant is not in a position to require that the plan document be changed, designating a QTIP trust as beneficiary runs the risk that the plan benefits will not qualify for the estate tax marital deduction. As a consequence of these limitations, designation of a QTIP trust as beneficiary, as a practical matter, may only be possible with an IRA. Hence, if the participant is able to transfer the plan benefits to an IRA before his death, much more flexibility can be attained.

---

[79] Priv. Ltr. Rul. 9232036 (May 13, 1992).

Practice Pointer: Unless Mom and Dad have children from prior marriages and their interests in plans are major assets of their estates, it may be better to avoid naming a QTIP trust as beneficiary of plan benefits. Most of the other objectives in naming a QTIP trust as beneficiary can be achieved in other ways. For example, if Mom prefers to have a steady stream of payments for the rest of her life, she may be able to elect to take the benefits in the form of an annuity rather than a lump sum. Even if Mom must take a lump sum, she can roll it over into her own IRA,[80] and payouts can then be structured so that some benefits are left for the children upon her death. The one benefit that cannot be achieved if Mom is the beneficiary and has the right to a lump sum is Dad's ability to control the disposition of the property after his death.

[iv] **Avoiding deemed gifts.** Many of the above methods involve rights of the QTIP trustee or surviving spouse to withdraw income from an IRA. Some issues can arise if the trustee or spouse does not actually withdraw the income, and, thereafter, the right to withdraw it lapses. In general, there should be no income or estate tax consequences, because the IRA is not subject to constructive receipt rules and the IRA will be in the spouse's estate anyway. However, if the spouse does not have a power of appointment over the income and the right to withdraw lapses, the spouse may be viewed as making a gift that is artificially augmented under Section 2519 or Section 2702. *The solution:* Give the spouse a power of appointment or make the rights nonlapsing. (Another alternative that might avoid the spouse being considered the transferor would be to have any undistributed income of the IRA (not just the QTIP trust) paid to the spouse's estate following her death.)

[e] **Payment to Participant Spouse's Estate**

In Private Letter Ruling 9729015,[81] the IRS ruled that a trust would qualify for the marital deduction when (1) a participant's estate was the beneficiary of IRA proceeds, (2) the participant's executor planned to request a lump sum distribution of a portion of the IRA proceeds, and (3) the QTIP trust would be funded with the lump sum portion.

---

[80] A trust beneficiary is not generally eligible for a rollover. Priv. Ltr. Rul. 9303031 (Oct. 29, 1992). However, the IRS has ruled that if the trustee of a trust that receives the IRA proceeds has no discretion with respect to the allocation of the IRA proceeds or the payment of the IRA proceeds to the surviving spouse, the surviving spouse will be treated as acquiring the IRA proceeds from the decedent rather than the trust. Priv. Ltr. Rul. 9502042 (Oct. 21, 1994).

[81] Priv. Ltr. Rul. 9729015 (Apr. 16, 1997).

[2] Funding Bequests With Plan or IRA Benefits

If the right to receive plan benefits is used to fund a pecuniary bequest at the executor's discretion, the income tax will be accelerated (even if no amounts are actually distributed from the plan). In such a circumstance, the income portion of the value of the plan interest[82] will be taxed as income to the estate immediately (or, to the beneficiaries, to the extent a distribution deduction is available to the estate).[83]

Practice Pointer: In a situation where no federal estate tax will be payable on the first death, and federal estate tax is expected to be payable on the second death, it will normally be best to pay the plan and IRA benefits to the spouse or to a marital deduction trust, rather than to the unified credit trust. This is because the full marital deduction is available for the total amount of the benefits, even though the amount will be diminished by the income tax on the distributions. If the benefits are paid to the unified credit trust, the credit will be partly wasted.

EXAMPLE: Decedent with interest in qualified plan dies in 2003. Executor funds residuary unified credit trust with $1,000,000 of plan benefits. If the trust or beneficiaries are in a 40 percent income tax bracket, the trust or beneficiaries will only receive $600,000 after income tax—40 percent of the unified credit will have been used on money that will never go to the beneficiaries.

Moral: Do not fund unified credit and GSTT exemption bequests with income in respect of a decedent (IRD) items when estate taxes will ultimately be due and other alternatives are available.[84]

[3] Qualified Plans and IRAs as Wealth Transmission Vehicles

Qualified plans and IRAs can be wonderful for the lifetime of the participant and his spouse. However, they are not good vehicles for transmitting wealth to the rest of the family because of their status as a right to receive IRD.[85] An IRD item will be exposed to both income and estate tax.

---

[82] Defined below.

[83] Treas. Reg. § 1.661(a)-2(f)(1).

[84] See Chapter 8 for a further discussion.

[85] Income in respect of a decedent includes amounts meeting the following requirements: (1) the amount is received after a decedent's death; (2) the decedent had become entitled to receive the amount as of the time of his death; and (3) the amount would have been taxable income to the decedent if he had lived to receive it. A decedent's last paycheck is an example. See IRC § 691.

To illustrate, suppose a 90-year-old man's rollover IRA is worth $1,000,000. He dies in January, and designates his child as beneficiary. Here's what happens:[86]

VALUE OF IRA		$1,000,000
Less: Estate Tax—at 50%		
Computation:		
Total Account	$1,000,000	
× Estate Tax Rate	× 50%	
	500,000	$ 500,000
Less: Income Tax—at 40%		
Computation:		
Total Account	$1,000,000	
Less IRD Deduction for Estate Tax[87] Attributable to Account	500,000	
	$ 500,000	
× Income Tax Rate	× 40%	
	200,000	$ 200,000
BALANCE REMAINING FOR CHILD		$ 300,000

The $1,000,000 IRA is thus reduced to 30 percent of its original value, after the two taxes are paid.

Think that's bad? What if the participant's grandchild is the beneficiary?

VALUE OF IRA		$1,000,000
Less: Estate Tax—at 50%		
Computation:		
Total Account	$1,000,000	
× Estate Tax Rate	× 50%	
	500,000	$ 500,000
Less: GSTT—at 50% (on amount received by beneficiary)		
Computation:		
Total Account	$1,000,000	
Less Regular Estate Tax	500,000	
	500,000	

---

[86] Assuming an estate tax rate of 50 percent, a combined state and federal income tax rate of 40 percent and no estate tax deductions. Note that these examples do not take into account state death taxes, which are not deductible in determining IRD. Consequently, the actual income tax will be higher, with the precise difference depending on the amount of the state death tax in question.

[87] If an item of IRD is taxed in an estate, the recipient of the IRD is entitled to a deduction from his federal income tax for estate tax paid on the item. IRC § 691(c)(1). The deduction is not subject to the two percent floor on itemized deductions. IRC § 67(b)(7). The deduction is computed at the marginal rate—that is, one measures the amount of tax due, and subtracts the amount that would have been due if the IRD had not been included in the recipient's income. The deduction is limited to the federal estate tax; thus, no deduction is available for the amount of state death taxes—even the pickup tax. IRC § 691(c)(1)(C). A deduction is allowed, however, for the generation-skipping transfer tax (GSTT) on certain generation-skipping transfers. IRC § 691(c)(3).

Amount of GST transfer for a direct skip[87.1]	× .667	
Amount Passing to Grandchild	$ 333,333	
× GSTT Rate	× 50%	
	166,677	$ 166,677

Less Income Tax—at 40%		
Computation:		
Total Account	$1,000,000	
Less IRD Deduction for Estate Tax and GSTT Attributable to the Taxable Income in the Account ($500,000 + $166,677)	666,667	
	$ 333,333	
× Income Tax Rate	× 40%	
	133,333	$ 133,333
BALANCE REMAINING FOR GRANDCHILD		$ 200,000

After the three taxes are paid, the grandchild receives just 20 percent of the date of death value of the IRA.

For a wealthy person with no surviving spouse, a charity may make sense as the beneficiary of the plan or IRA. There will be no income tax, estate tax, or GSTT on the distribution to a charity, because the charity is not taxable.

QUESTION: *Does it make sense for a wealthy person to keep money destined for younger generations in qualified plans and IRAs?*

ANSWER: If the participant and his spouse do not need the money in the plan, it may not. The participant will accumulate benefits tax-free during life, just to have them slashed by the estate tax and possibly GSTT. The following may be more effective alternatives: (1) name a charitable beneficiary; (2) withdraw the benefits, pay the income tax, and contribute the net proceeds to an ILIT to buy a life insurance policy (because the proceeds will not be subject to further income tax or to estate tax); or (3) withdraw the benefits, pay the taxes, and give away the net proceeds at the gift tax rates. The gift tax rates are much lower than the estate tax rates.[88]

[4] Grandfathered Benefits

Certain grandfathered benefits are partially or fully exempt from estate tax. A $100,000 exclusion from estate tax is available for certain plan benefits if the participant was in pay status on December 31, 1984, and irrevocably elected the form of benefit before July 18, 1984.[89] An unlimited exclusion for certain

---

[87.1] See Chapter 5.

[88] See Chapters 1 and 8 for a discussion.

[89] Deficit Reduction Act of 1984, Pub. L. No. 98-369, § 525(b)(2), 98 Stat. 494 (1984) (DEFRA).

qualified plan benefits applies to the estate of a participant who was in pay status on December 31, 1982, and irrevocably elected the form of benefit before January 1, 1983.[90]

The exclusions described in the preceding paragraph are applicable to annuities and other payments received under qualified plans, except to the extent that those payments are attributable to nondeductible contributions by the participant. The exclusions also apply to certain annuities payable under IRAs, except to the extent the annuity payments are attributable to nondeductible contributions by the participant that are not rollover contributions. An excluded annuity payable under an IRA must be paid in substantially equal periodic payments to a beneficiary for his life or over a period extending for at least 36 months after the date of the decedent's death. However, neither exclusion is applicable if the executor of the participant's estate is named beneficiary of the plan.

A participant in a qualified plan who had not irrevocably elected a form of benefit and was not in pay status by the prescribed time, but who separated from service before 1983 (in the case of the full exclusion) or 1985 (in the case of the $100,000 exclusion), is subject to a special rule (the "1986 exception"). Under this rule, the participant is treated as if he satisfied all of the requirements for the exclusion if he does not change the form of benefit before his death.[91] Designating a new beneficiary is apparently not considered a change in the form of benefit for this purpose.[92] The 1986 exception apparently does not apply to IRAs.[93]

Practice Pointer: These exclusions should continue to be available for some time, so practitioners should be alert to their applicability. A participant who hopes to take advantage of the 1986 exception should not roll over plan benefits that will be excluded from his estate (into an IRA), as this may cause the benefits to become includable in his estate because they no longer will be payable from a qualified plan. Participants who can take advantage of the 1986 exception should also be careful not to change the form of benefit.[94]

---

[90] DEFRA § 525(b)(3); Tax Equity and Fiscal Responsibility Act of 1982, Pub. L. No. 97-248, 245(a)-245(a)(b), 96 Stat. 324 (1982) (TEFRA).

[91] Tax Reform Act of 1986 (TRA 1986), Pub. L. No. 99-514, § 1852(e)(3), 100 Stat. 2548 (1986).

[92] Priv. Ltr. Rul. 9221030 (Feb. 21, 1992).

[93] See Rev. Rul. 92-22, 1992-1 CB 313; see also S. Rep. No. 313, 99th Cong., 2d Sess. 1019 (1986).

[94] Rev. Rul. 92-22, 1992-1 CB 313.

[5] Qualification for Charitable Income Tax Deduction for Estate Beneficiary

The IRS has ruled privately that an estate will be eligible for a charitable income tax deduction with respect to deferred compensation and nonqualified stock options bequeathed to charitable organizations. The IRS further ruled that the estate would not be taxed on IRD generated by the deferred compensation and nonqualified stock options, concluding that such income was income of the charities.[95] The theory should also be applicable to qualified plans and IRAs.

¶ 14.04 MAXIMIZING INCOME TAX DEFERRAL

Income accumulates free of income tax in a qualified plan or IRA. Some participants and beneficiaries want to maintain benefits in the plan or IRA as long as possible in order to perpetuate this tax-free accumulation of assets.

[1] Is Maximum Deferral a Good Idea?

Not always. Why not? Of course, many beneficiaries want the plan benefits sooner rather than later for non-tax reasons. Additionally, from a tax perspective, maximum deferral may not make sense for a participant whose goal is to transmit wealth, rather than to provide retirement funds for himself and his spouse.[96] It may actually be more tax-efficient for a person in a high transfer tax bracket who is not depending on the plan for support to accelerate the income before he dies, so as to get the income tax out of his estate. Otherwise, the plan benefits will be subject to estate tax on money that is already headed to the IRS or state tax collector. The advantage provided by continued deferral of the income tax may not make up for having to pay estate tax on the deferred income tax. Withdrawing the assets also allows the participant to put the after-tax funds to use in further estate planning techniques.

Having said that, we'll exercise strategies for deferral. Note, however, that while deferral is a good thing in many situations, its desirability should not be automatically assumed.

---

[95] Priv. Ltr. Rul. 200002011 (Sept. 30, 1999); see also Priv. Ltr. Rul. 200012076 (Dec. 23, 1999).

[96] As discussed at ¶ 14.03[3] above.

[2] Designated Beneficiaries

To take advantage of many income tax deferral options, the participant must have a "designated beneficiary."

[a] Definition

A "designated beneficiary" includes any natural person who is designated as beneficiary either by the terms of the plan or, if the plan provides, by affirmative election by the participant (or the surviving spouse, if applicable).[97]

[b] Estate As Beneficiary

Consistent with both the 1987 and 2001 proposed regulations, the final regulations provide that an estate is not a designated beneficiary.[98] Under the similar 1987 proposed regulations, when an estate was named beneficiary but the surviving spouse was the sole executor of the estate and the sole beneficiary under the will, the IRS treated amounts received through the estate by the survivor as if the survivor had been the designated beneficiary.[99] The final regulations provide that the fact that the participant's plan will pass to a certain individual under a will does not make that individual a designated beneficiary; however, the regulations do not specifically address the situation described in the preceding sentence.[100]

[c] Trust As Beneficiary

A trust itself cannot be a designated beneficiary, because it is not a natural person. However, the trust beneficiaries may be eligible to be designated beneficiaries.

Practice Pointer: Not all qualified plans permit trusts to be named as beneficiaries.

---

[97] Treas. Reg. § 1.401(a)(9)-4, Q&A-1.

[98] Treas. Reg. § 1.401(a)(9)-4, Q&A-3.

[99] E.g., Priv. Ltr. Rul. 9450042 (Sept. 23, 1994); see also Priv. Ltr. Rul. 200032044 (May 15, 2000) (surviving spouse is the sole executor and beneficiary of one third of decedent's residuary estate).

[100] Treas. Reg. § 1.401(a)(9)-4, Q&A-1.

[d] Beneficiary of Trust As Designated Beneficiary

Individual beneficiaries of certain trust-beneficiaries of a plan or IRA can qualify as designated beneficiaries.[101] To qualify individual trust beneficiaries as designated beneficiaries, the trust must meet certain requirements.

[i] Valid trust. The trust must be a valid trust under state law, or the trust would be valid but for the fact that the trust has no principal.

[ii] Irrevocability requirements. The trust must either be presently irrevocable or must become irrevocable on the participant's death. A testamentary trust will meet this requirement.[102]

[iii] Identifiable beneficiaries. The trust beneficiaries must be identifiable from the trust instrument.[103] A trust beneficiary is generally any person or entity that can receive plan or IRA benefits under the trust at any time.

One concern for practitioners is whether a trust giving a beneficiary a power of appointment will meet this identifiability requirement. The members of a class of beneficiaries capable of expansion or contraction will be treated as identifiable if it is possible to identify the class member with the shortest life expectancy.[104] Hence, a power of appointment would apparently meet the requirement if the beneficiaries were sufficiently defined.

Another concern deals with allocation of estate expenses. The IRS has privately ruled that no designated beneficiary of a trust exists if an IRA can be charged with estate expenses, on the theory that payment of the expenses could benefit someone other than the putative designated beneficiary during that beneficiary's lifetime.[105] Query whether this is the correct rule if (1) the apportionment of expenses to the IRA is required by law, or (2) the particular beneficiary is charged with the expenses under the apportionment provisions of the trust and local law (so that payment of estate expenses from the IRA does not benefit anyone other than that beneficiary). In any case, however, state law will usually allow a will to apportion estate expenses away from plans and IRAs.

[iv] Documentation. One of the following two documentation alternatives is complied with after the participant's death:[106]

---

[101] Treas. Reg. § 1.401(a)(9)-4, Q&A-5.

[102] See Treas. Reg. § 1.401(a)(9)-5, Q&A-7(c)(3), Example 1.

[103] Treas. Reg. § 1.401(a)(9)-4, Q&A-5(b)(3).

[104] Treas. Reg. §§ 1.401(a)(9)-4, A-5(b)(3), A-1.

[105] Priv. Ltr. Ruls. 9805009, 9820021.

[106] Treas. Reg. § 1.401(a)(9)-4, Q&A-6(b). The documentation requirement will also apply during the participant's life if the surviving spouse is to be the designated beneficiary under the trust. Treas. Reg. § 1.401(a)(9)-4, Q&A-6(a).

1. *Trust instrument.* A copy of the trust instrument may be provided to the plan administrator.[107] If this method is used to provide documentation before the participant's death, the participant must agree that if the trust instrument is amended at any time in the future, the participant will, within a reasonable time, provide a copy of each amendment.[108]

2. *Certification.* A final certification as to the beneficiaries (including contingent and remainder beneficiaries) of the trust may be provided to the plan administrator by October 31 of the year following the calendar year of the participant's death.[109] The trustee must also certify that the other requirements for the trust beneficiaries to be treated as designated beneficiaries are satisfied and agree to provide a copy of the trust instrument to the plan administrator upon demand. This rule applies even if a copy of the trust instrument was provided to the plan administrator before the participant's death.[110] If this method is used to provide documentation before the participant's death, the participant must give the certification and agree to correct it to the extent any future amendment to the trust changes the information previously certified.[111]

A plan will not be disqualified merely because the terms of the actual trust instrument are inconsistent with the information in the certifications or trust instruments provided to the plan administrator if the plan administrator reasonably relies on the information provided.[112] However, the minimum required distributions for years after the year in which any discrepancy is discovered must be determined based on the actual terms of the trust instrument. For those years, the minimum required distribution will be determined by treating the employee's beneficiaries as having been changed in the year in which the discrepancy was discovered.[113]

[v] No entity beneficiary. All the trust beneficiaries must be natural persons. If any non-individual can ever be a beneficiary, then the trust has no designated beneficiaries.[114] For this purpose, an entity beneficiary is not

---

[107] Treas. Reg. § 1.401(a)(9)-4, Q&A-6(b)(2).

[108] Treas. Reg. § 1.401(a)(9)-4, Q&A-6(a)(1).

[109] Treas. Reg. § 1.401(a)(9)-4, Q&A-6(b)(1).

[110] Treas. Reg. § 1.401(a)(9)-4, Q&A-6(b)(2).

[111] Treas. Reg. § 1.401(a)(9)-4, Q&A-6(a)(2).

[112] Treas. Reg. § 1.401(a)(9)-4, Q&A-6(c).

[113] However, for purposes of determining the amount of the excise tax under Section 4974 (including application of a waiver, if any, for reasonable error under Section 4974), the minimum required distribution is determined for any year based on the actual terms of the trust in effect during the year. Treas. Reg. § 1.401(a)(9)-4, Q&A-6(c)(2).

[114] Treas. Reg. § 1.401(a)(9)-4, Q&A-3.

considered a beneficiary if its sole right under the trust is as a potential successor to the interest of a prior beneficiary.[115]

In this regard, the IRS ruled under the similar 1987 proposed regulations that charitable beneficiaries did not meet the above requirement when they were entitled to trust principal at the income beneficiary's death if (1) the principal was not distributed to the income beneficiary for health and medical needs, and (2) the income beneficiary did not appoint it under her general testamentary power of appointment to other beneficiaries.[116]

If the beneficiary of a trust is another trust, the beneficiaries of the second trust will be treated as the beneficiaries of the first trust (so that the existence of a trust beneficiary does not by itself preclude designated beneficiaries).[117]

[e] Time for Determination of Designated Beneficiary

In general, the identity of the designated beneficiary(ies) is not determined until September 30 of the year following the participant's date of death.[118] This is quite helpful because it allows time for planning and adjustment to circumstances.

EXAMPLE: Wife is the primary beneficiary and is alive on Husband's death in Year 1. Wife disclaims or dies before September 30 of Year 2. Child, the contingent beneficiary, will be considered the designated beneficiary.

[3] Minimum Distribution Rules

Assets cannot be held indefinitely in a qualified plan or IRA.[119] Certain distributions are required on or before specified dates or events. These requirements constitute the "minimum distribution rules."

---

[115] Treas. Reg. § 1.401(a)(9)-5, Q&A-7(c)(1).

[116] Priv. Ltr. Rul. 9820021 (Feb. 18, 1998). The IRS took the position in this ruling that the interest of the charities vested during the income beneficiary's lifetime, subject to the contingency of the property's use for the income beneficiary's health and medical needs, even though the charity's interest was subject to the beneficiary's general testamentary power of appointment over the trust.

[117] Treas. Reg. § 1.401(a)(9)-4, Q&A-5(d).

[118] Treas. Reg. § 1.401(a)(9)-4, Q&A-4(a). Exception: If the surviving spouse is the designated beneficiary as of the September 30 date but dies before distributions to her have begun, then the surviving spouse's designated beneficiary is determined as of September 30 of the calendar year following the year of the spouse's death. Treas. Reg. § 1.401(a)(9)-4, Q&A-4(b).

[119] They must be distributed on or before a specified date or event.

Final regulations on the minimum distribution rules were issued in April 2002.[120] They are generally effective for determining required distributions for calendar years beginning on or after January 1, 2003.[121]

The minimum distribution rules provide that (1) payment of benefits must begin by a certain date, and (2) the participant's entire interest must be distributed within certain specified periods.[122] Subsections [a] through [e], below, discuss distributions from individual accounts—generally, defined contribution accounts and IRAs. Subsection [f] discusses annuities from defined benefit plans and annuity contracts purchased from an insurance company with the assets of an individual account.

Minimum distributions complying with the regulations will generally satisfy the incidental benefit requirement of Section 401(a)(9)(G)[123] with respect to defined contribution plans.

Practice Pointer: If income tax deferral is important, examine the plan or IRA documents. Qualified plans and IRAs are not required to provide payout options that maximize deferral, and many qualified plans do not. If the plan or IRA agreement requires faster distribution than the law would have allowed, the agreement will govern.

---

[a] Required Beginning Date for Distributions During Lifetime

In most cases, the latest time at which distributions can begin is the "required beginning date" (RBD),[124] which is generally April 1 of the calendar year following the later of (1) the year in which the participant attains age 70½ or (2) if the plan allows, the calendar year in which the participant retires.[125]

However, the rule allowing deferral of distributions until the year of retirement (1) does not apply to IRAs,[126] and (2) does not apply to a participant

---

[120] TD 8987, 2002-19 IRB 852.

[121] Treas. Reg. § 1.401(a)(9)-1, Q&A-2. For determining required minimum distributions for calendar year 2002, taxpayers may rely on the final regulations, the 2001 proposed regulations, or the 1987 proposed regulations. See TD 8987, 2002-19 IRB 852, 859.

[122] IRC § 401(a)(9).

[123] Treas. Reg. § 1.401(a)(9)-5, Q&A-1(d).

[124] Treas. Reg. § 1.401(a)(9)-2, Q&A-2.

[125] IRC § 401(a)(9)(C)(i), Treas. Reg. § 1.401(a)(9)-2, Q&A-2(a), Q&A-2(e).

[126] Small Business Jobs Protection Act §§ 1404(a), 1404(b), effective for years beginning after Dec. 31, 1996; Treas. Reg. § 1.408-8, Q&A-3.

who is a five percent owner,[127] determined as of the plan year ending in the calendar year in which the participant attains age 70½.[128]

[b] Required Payout During Participant's Life

The minimum distribution period during the participant's lifetime is determined annually by consulting an IRS table—either the Uniform Life Table or the Joint and Last Survivor Table.[129] The tables are found in Treasury Regulation § 1.401(a)(9)-9, Q&A-4(a)(2).

The Uniform Life Table is used, except in one circumstance. If (1) the payout period is the joint life expectancy of the participant and his spouse; (2) the spouse is the sole beneficiary of the employee's entire interest at all times during the calendar year; *and* (3) the spouse is more than ten years younger than the participant, then the minimum distribution period for that year is the longer of the period under the Uniform Lifetime Table or the Joint and Last Survivor Table for the participant's and spouse's joint life expectancy.[130]

The Uniform Table contains two columns—one headed "Age of employee," and the other headed "Distribution period." To determine the minimum distribution for any year, the participant finds the distribution period applicable to her age, and then divides the account balance by the distribution period.[131] Recalculation of life expectancy(ies) is automatic each year.

The account balance for a qualified plan for distributions made in—say, Year Two—is the balance as of the last valuation date in Year One, adjusted for contributions, forfeitures and distributions made in Year One after the valuation date.[132] Additional rules apply in the case of rollovers and plan-to-plan transfers.[133]

---

[127] *Who is a five percent owner?* If the employer is a corporation, any person who owns (or is considered as owning, within the meaning of Section 318, with some adjustments) more than five percent of the outstanding stock of the corporation or stock possessing more than five percent of the total combined voting power of all stock in the corporation. IRC §§ 401(a)(9)(C)(ii)(I), 416(i)(1)(B)(i)(I).

If the employer is not a corporation, any person who owns more than five percent of the capital or profits interest in the employer (IRC §§ 401(a)(9)(C)(ii)(I), 416(i)(1)(B)(i)(II)), using attribution rules based on principles similar to those used for corporations. IRC § 416(i)(1)(B)(iii)(II).

[128] IRC § 401(a)(9)(C)(ii), Treas. Reg. § 1.401(a)(9)-2, Q&A-2(b).

[129] Treas. Reg. §§ 1.401(a)(9)-5, Q&A-1, 1.401(a)(9)-4(a).

[130] Treas. Reg. § 1.401(a)(9)-5, Q&A-4(b). The reason that the Uniform Lifetime Table is used if the spouse is not more than 10 years younger than the participant is that the table is based on a joint life expectancy of the participant and a beneficiary 10 years younger than the participant.

[131] Treas. Reg. § 1.401(a)(9)-5, Q&A-1.

[132] Treas. Reg. § 1.401(a)(9)-5, Q&A-3.

[133] Treas. Reg. § 1.401(a)(9)-5, Q&A-3(d).

For an IRA, the account balance in Year Two is the balance as of December 31 of Year One.[134] Adjustment is no longer made for the year containing the RBD.[135]

[c] Required Payout After Participant's Death

The life expectancy table utilized for determining distribution periods after the participant's death is the Uniform Life Table used for lifetime distributions.[136] The period depends on whether there is a designated beneficiary and, if so, who it is.

[i] No designated beneficiary.

[A] *Death before RBD.* The distribution period is the remaining life expectancy under the Uniform Life Table of someone the same age as the participant was or would have been on the participant's birthday occurring in the year of the participant's death.[137] For each subsequent calendar year, the distribution period is reduced by one for each calendar year elapsed since the year of death.[138]

> **EXAMPLE:** Lora turns 75 on January 1 and dies on January 2 with no designated beneficiary. The initial distribution period is determined by the life expectancy of a 75-year old, and the distribution period is reduced by 1 each subsequent year.

[B] *Death on or after RBD.* Distributions must commence by December 31 of the year following the participant's death, and the account must be distributed by the end of the calendar year containing the fifth anniversary of the participant's death.[139]

[ii] **Designated beneficiary other than spouse.** The minimum distribution period is determined under the Uniform Life Table. It is the longer of (1) the beneficiary's life expectancy as of the beneficiary's birthday occurring in the year after the participant's date of death, or (2) the remaining life expectancy of someone the same age as the participant was or would have been on

---

[134] Treas. Reg. § 1.408-8, Q&A-6.

[135] Treas. Reg. § 1.408-8, Q&A-6.

[136] It is found in Treas. Reg. §§ 1.401(a)(9)-9 (Q&A-1 and Q&A-2), 1.401(a)(9)-5, Q&A-5(a); Temp. Reg. § 1.401(a)(9)-6T.

[137] Treas. Reg. §§ 1.401(a)(9)-5, Q&A-5(a)(2), 1.401(a)(9)-5, Q&A-5(c)(3).

[138] Treas. Reg. § 1.401(a)(9)-5, Q&A-5(c)(3).

[139] IRC § 401(a)(9)(B)(ii), Treas. Reg. §§ 1.401(a)(9)-3, Q&A-2, 1.401(a)(9)-5, Q&A-5(b).

the participant's birthday occurring in the year of the participant's death.[140] For each subsequent calendar year, the distribution period is reduced by one for each calendar year elapsed since the year of death. This is true even if the designated beneficiary dies and another designated beneficiary steps in.[141]

> **EXAMPLE:** Lora is 50 on January 1 and dies on January 2 of Year One. The designated beneficiary turned 45 in Year One. The initial distribution period is the life expectancy of a 46-year-old.

If the participant dies before the RBD, distributions must commence by December 31 of the year following the participant's death.[142]

[iii] Surviving spouse is sole designated beneficiary.

[A] *Death after RBD.* The minimum distribution period each year is calculated under the Uniform Life Table using the spouse's life expectancy as determined on her birthday.[143]

In the year after the spouse's subsequent death, the minimum distribution period is determined by reference to the life expectancy of someone the same age as the spouse was or would have been on the spouse's birthday occurring in the year of her death. In each year thereafter, the distribution period is reduced by one year for each year elapsed since the spouse's death.[144]

[B] *Death before RBD.* The payout is determined under the same rules applicable to death after the RBD,[145] except that the spouse may elect to delay distributions until December 31st of the year in which the participant would have reached age 70½.[146]

If the surviving spouse dies before distributions to her commence,[147] then the other distribution rules are applied at her death as if the surviving spouse were the participant.[148] In that case, the date of death of the surviving spouse is substituted for the date of death of the employee.[149] However, the special rules

---

[140] Treas. Reg. §§ 1.401(a)(9)-5, Q&A-5(a)(1), 1.401(a)(9)-5, Q&A-5(c)(1), 1.401(a)(9)-5, Q&A-5(c)(3).

[141] Treas. Reg. § 1.401(a)(9)-5, Q&A-7(c)(2).

[142] Treas. Reg. § 1.401(a)(9)-3, Q&A-3(a).

[143] Treas. Reg. § 1.401(a)(9)-5, Q&A-5(a)(1), Q&A-5(c)(2).

[144] Treas. Reg. § 1.401(a)(9)-5, Q&A-5(c)(2).

[145] Treas. Reg. § 1.401(a)(9)-5, Q&A-5(b), Q&A-5(c)(2).

[146] Treas. Reg. § 1.401(a)(9)-3, Q&A-3(b).

[147] Distributions are considered to have begun on the required date, even if distribution is not actually made. Treas. Reg. § 1.401(a)(9)-3, Q&A-6.

[148] Treas. Reg. §§ 1.401(a)(9)-4, Q&A-4(b), 1.401(a)(9)-3, Q&A-5.

[149] Treas. Reg. §§ 1.401(a)(9)-4, Q&A-4(b), 1.401(a)(9)-3, Q&A-5.

for sole-beneficiary spouses will not be available to the spouse's surviving spouse.[150]

[iv] Elections. If the plan allows, a participant employee who has a designated beneficiary can elect to apply the five-year rule or the life expectancy rule to distributions after death.[151]

[d] Identity of Designated Beneficiary for Required Distribution Payout Purposes

[i] Sole beneficiary. If a person is the sole beneficiary of a trust during her lifetime, but she is not required to receive all amounts distributed to the trust from the plan or IRA during her lifetime, then the remainder beneficiaries are also considered beneficiaries for purposes of determining the beneficiary with the shortest lifetime.[152] However, if the person is entitled under the trust instrument to all amounts distributed to the trust from the plan or IRA during her lifetime, then she is considered the sole designated beneficiary. And, if such person is the surviving spouse, she is eligible for the special payout rules applying in such a case.[153]

[ii] Multiple beneficiaries—no separate accounts. If the deceased participant's plan or IRA has multiple designated beneficiaries, the distribution period is determined by reference to the life expectancy of the oldest designated beneficiary.[154] Contingent beneficiaries are counted for this purpose, unless the only contingency causing the beneficiary's entitlement is the death of another beneficiary.[155] If any of the counted beneficiaries is not an individual, the participant is treated as having no designated beneficiary.[156] Because the designated beneficiary is not determined until September 30 of the year fol-

---

[150] Treas. Reg. § 1.401(a)(9)-3, Q&A-5.

[151] Treas. Reg. § 1.401(a)(9)-3, Q&A-4(c).

[152] The IRS has ruled under similar proposed regulations that this was even when the life beneficiary had a general testamentary power of appointment. Priv. Ltr. Ruls. 9805009, 9820021.

[153] Treas. Reg. § 1.401(a)(9)-5, Q&A-7(c)(3), Example 2.

[154] Treas. Reg. § 1.401(a)(9)-5, Q&A-7(a)(1).

[155] Treas. Reg. §§ 1.401(a)(9)-5, Q&A-7(b), 1.401(a)(9)-5, Q&A-7(c)(1).

[156] Treas. Reg. §§ 1.401(a)(9)-5, Q&A-7(a)(2), 1.401(a)(9)-4, Q&A-3.

lowing the participant's death, a disclaimer or distribution may be used to eliminate this problem.[157]

[iii] Multiple beneficiaries—separate accounts. The separate account exception to the multiple-beneficiary rule permits the creation of separate accounts for each designated beneficiary. The life expectancy of each designated beneficiary is then used to determine the distribution period with respect to that person's share.[158] A separate account exists only if there is separate accounting for investment gains and losses and for other account attributes on a pro rata basis in a reasonable and consistent manner.[159]

If a trust with multiple beneficiaries is named as beneficiary, but the trust is divided into completely separate shares, each share will be treated as a separate account for purposes of the minimum distribution rules. In effect, each share will be treated for purposes of the MRD rules as a separate trust.

In a situation where the accountholder had been receiving distributions at the time of his death based on the joint life expectancy of himself and the oldest beneficiary of a trust, the IRS ruled that the division of an IRA and the trust that was the beneficiary of the IRA into four separate trusts and IRA subaccounts, each benefiting a different family group, would not result in a taxable distribution and could be distributed over the period not exceeding the life expectancy of the oldest designated beneficiary.[160]

Practice Pointer: Not all plans permit separate accounts to be created. The reason is that the plan designers may not want the plan administrators to have the administrative burden of determining several different payout periods for separate portions of the participant's interest in the plan.

---

[e] Spousal Rollover

[i] Qualified plans. Regardless of when the participant dies, if the designated beneficiary of a qualified plan is the surviving spouse, she can roll over most distributions to her own IRA and defer any distribution from that IRA until her own RBD.[161] If the surviving spouse wants to roll over the benefit to

---

[157] Treas. Reg. § 1.401(a)(9)-4, Q&A-4(a). To satisfy the requirements of IRC § 401(a)(9), any disclaimer must satisfy IRC § 2518.

[158] Treas. Reg. § 1.401(a)(9)-8, Q&A-2(a)(2).

[159] Treas. Reg. § 1.401(a)(9)-8, Q&A-3.

[160] Priv. Ltr. Rul. 200008044 (Dec. 3, 1999).

[161] IRC §§ 402(c)(9), 402(c)(4); Treas. Reg. §§ 1.408-8, Q&A-5, 1.408-8, Q&A-7.

her own IRA, she must do so within 60 days of the distribution of the benefit to her (not within 60 days of the participant's death).[162]

[ii] IRAs. Also, regardless of when the participant dies, if (1) the sole designated beneficiary of an IRA is the surviving spouse, and (2) she has an unlimited right of withdrawal over the account, she can elect to treat the IRA as her own, and defer any distribution from that IRA until her own RBD.[163]

The surviving spouse can make the election at any time after the IRA owner's death.[164] The election can be made by changing the account owner to the surviving spouse.[165] The election to use the surviving spouse's RBD is assumed if no distributions occur at the time they would otherwise occur.[166]

The surviving spouse is not considered the sole beneficiary for this purpose if a trust is the IRA beneficiary, even if she is the sole beneficiary of the trust.[167]

If the surviving spouse elects to do a standard rollover of an IRA in the year of the IRA owner's death, the spouse is required to take a minimum distribution for that year based on the deceased spouse's life expectancy (to the extent such a distribution was not made to the IRA owner before death).[168]

[f] Annuity Payouts

If Dad selects an annuity form of payout, how can he feel confident that his account or the plan will earn enough money to make the payments for his entire lifetime or whatever other period is chosen?

In a defined benefit plan, benefits do not depend on the account balance or plan earnings—the plan sponsor must contribute in accordance with the minimum funding rules applicable to such plans.[169] The Pension Benefit Guaranty Corporation usually guarantees benefits up to a limit. In a defined contribution plan, when an annuity payout is selected, the plan may purchase an annuity contract from an insurance company, so that the insurance company's assets stand behind the annuity.[170]

When an annuity payout is selected, the annuity (1) must be payable at least annually; (2) must be for a permitted period; (3) must generally provide

---

[162] IRC § 402(c)(3).

[163] IRC §§ 402(c)(9), 402(c)(4). Treas. Reg. §§ 1.408-8, Q&A-5, 1.408-8, Q&A-7.

[164] Treas. Reg. § 1.408-8, Q&A-5.

[165] Treas. Reg. § 1.408-8, Q&A-5(b).

[166] Treas. Reg. § 1.408-8, Q&A-5(b)(1).

[167] Treas. Reg. § 1.408-8, Q&A-5(a).

[168] Treas. Reg. § 1.408-8, Q&A-5(a).

[169] IRC § 412.

[170] Treas. Reg. § 1.401(a)(9)-5, Q&A-1(e).

for nonincreasing payments,[171] and (4) must begin payout no later than the RBD or the date of purchase.[172] Generally, if the spouse is a joint beneficiary, the spouse's annuity payments may equal the payments to the participant.[173] If the joint beneficiary is not the spouse and is more than ten years younger than the participant, the payment to the joint beneficiary cannot equal the benefit payable to the participant and is reduced by the applicable percentage set out in a table provided in the regulations.[174]

If the distribution form includes a life annuity and a period certain, the period certain is limited. The payout periods are similar to those for individual account distributions.[175]

Specific rules regarding annuity payouts are addressed in temporary regulations.[176]

¶ 14.05 SPOUSAL RIGHTS IN QUALIFIED PLANS AND IRAs

[1] REA Plans

The Retirement Equity Act of 1984[177] gave surviving spouses survivor annuity rights in certain retirement plans.[178] We'll call those "REA plans." These rules do not apply to IRAs.[179] They consist primarily of the right of the surviving spouse to receive a survivor annuity from certain plans.

As a practical matter, many defined contribution plans take advantage of an exception to the annuity rule. A defined contribution plan that is not subject to the funding standards of Section 412[180] is exempt from the spousal annuity requirement if:

---

[171] Exceptions include: cost-of-living adjustments, a change in joint beneficiary, refunds upon the participant's death of cash contributions, or increases in benefits under the plan. Temp. Reg. § 1.401(a)(9)-6T, Q&A-1(a).

[172] Temp. Reg. § 1.401(a)(9)-6T, Q&A-1(c).

[173] Temp. Reg. § 1.401(a)(9)-6T, Q&A-2(b).

[174] Temp. Reg. § 1.401(a)(9)-6T, Q&A-2(c).

[175] Temp. Reg. §§ 1.401(a)(9)-6T, Q&A-2, 1.401(a)(9)-6T, Q&A-3.

[176] Temp. Reg. § 1.401(a)(9)-6T.

[177] Pub. L. No. 98-397, 98th Cong., 2d Sess. (1984).

[178] They are (1) defined benefit plans; (2) defined contribution plans that are subject to the funding standards of IRC § 412; and (3) other defined contribution plans that are not subject to the exception described in the text. IRC § 401(a)(11)(B).

[179] See ERISA §§ 201(6), 205.

[180] Defined contribution plans that are subject to the funding standards are primarily money-purchase plans and target benefit plans.

- The plan provides that the entire benefit payable at death is payable (1) to the surviving spouse unless the surviving spouse consents otherwise, or (2) if the surviving spouse consents otherwise, to a designated beneficiary;
- The participant does not elect to receive payment of benefits in the form of a life annuity; and
- With respect to the participant, the plan is not a transferee of assets transferred after December 31, 1984, from a defined benefit plan or a defined contribution plan that was subject to the Section 412 funding standards.[181]

Most profit-sharing plans (including Section 401(k) plans) and employee stock ownership plans use this exception. One aspect of this exception is that the participant can usually exercise total control over withdrawals, distributions, and borrowings during his or her lifetime without the spouse's consent.[182]

The following discussion addresses REA plans that do not fit the above exception.

[a] Definitions

Generally, if the participant and spouse do not elect otherwise, and an exception is not available, the benefits of REA plans will be payable in the form of a qualified joint and survivor annuity (QJSA) or a qualified pre-retirement survivor annuity (QPSA).[183] This includes benefits attributable to the participant's after-tax contributions.[184]

A QJSA is an annuity for the participant's life, with a survivor annuity for the life of his spouse. The periodic amount payable to the spouse must (1) be at least 50 percent of (and no more than 100 percent of) the periodic amount payable during the joint lives of the participant and his spouse, and (2) meet other actuarial requirements, as well.[185] A QPSA is a lifetime annuity for the surviving spouse that meets certain actuarial requirements.[186] Certain defined contribution plans can be designed to require a QPSA for only 50 percent of a participant's account balance at date of death.[187]

---

[181] IRC § 401(a)(11)(B)(iii).

[182] Reg. § 1.401(a)-20, Q&A-24(a)(1) deals with loans.

[183] IRC §§ 401(a)(11), 417(a)(2); Treas. Reg. § 1.401(a)-20. For plans that are subject to Title I of ERISA, see ERISA § 205. These rights are enforceable by civil action, and are not merely tax qualification requirements.

[184] Treas. Reg. § 1.401(a)-20, Q&A 11.

[185] IRC § 417(b).

[186] IRC § 417(c).

[187] Treas. Reg. § 1.401(a)-20, Q&A 31(b)(3).

[b] Automatic Designated Beneficiary of Certain Qualified Plans

In REA plans, unless the participant and spouse both consent to other arrangements or an exception applies, the participant will be required to take a QJSA if he is married at the "annuity starting date." For purposes of the QJSA rules, the "annuity starting date" is the first day of the first period for which an amount is payable as an annuity (regardless of when or whether a payment is actually made) or, in the case of benefits not payable in annuity form, the date on which all events have occurred that entitle the participant to begin receiving the benefit.[188]

Thus—in the absence of an exception—and unless the spouse consents otherwise, the beneficiary of a REA plan must be the participant's spouse and the benefit must be payable as a qualified joint and survivor annuity.[189] A similar rule applies on the death of the participant before retirement, in which case the spouse must receive a QPSA if the required consents do not exist.

If the couple has been married less than one year on the earlier of the annuity starting date or the participant's death and the plan so provides, the above rules do not apply.[190]

[c] Waiver of Spousal Benefits

If the plan permits,[191] the participant (with his spouse's consent) may elect to waive a QPSA form of benefit during the period beginning on the first day of the plan year in which the participant attains age 35 and ending with the participant's death;[192] provided, however, when the participant separates from service, the period for waiving a QPSA with respect to benefits accrued prior to the separation from service can begin no later than the date of separation from service.[193] A participant (with his spouse's consent) can elect to waive

---

[188] IRC § 417(f); Treas. Reg. § 1.401(a)-20, Q&A 10(b)(2). An unmarried participant in such a plan is required to be able to choose a single life annuity; the plan may, but does not have to, offer another option.

[189] IRC §§ 401(a)(11), 417(a)(2). This means that a spouse must consent in order for the benefits to be paid to a QTIP trust.

[190] IRC § 417(d); Treas. Reg. § 1.401(a)-20, Q&A 25(b)(2). Note, however, that many plans do not incorporate this rule.

[191] The plan is not required to permit a waiver if it fully subsidizes the cost of the annuities and does not permit the participant to waive the benefit or designate another beneficiary. IRC § 417(a)(5). This provision typically applies to defined benefit plans.

[192] IRC § 417(a)(6)(B). Note that the regulations allow the waiver to be executed before age 35, but require it to be renewed after age 35. Treas. Reg. § 1.401(a)-20, Q&A 33(b).

[193] IRC §§ 417(a)(6), 417(a)(7).

the rights to a QJSA form of benefit no earlier than 90 days before the annuity starting date.[194]

For a participant's election to waive either a QPSA or QJSA to be effective, (1) the participant's spouse must consent to the election in writing; (2) the election must designate a beneficiary or form of benefit, which may not be changed without further spousal consent (or the spouse's consent must expressly permit further designations by the participant without further spousal consent); and (3) the spouse's consent must acknowledge the effect of the election and be witnessed by a plan representative or notary public. An improper or incomplete spousal consent may still leave an effective beneficiary designation for the portion of the benefits that exceed the amount payable to the spouse.[195]

A prenuptial agreement in and of itself is generally ineffective to waive spousal rights because it will not meet the requirements of a valid waiver.[196] Specifically, one of the requirements of a valid waiver is that it be made by the spouse—by definition, there is no spouse when a prenuptial agreement is executed. (However, a few courts have hinted that they might reach a different result if the only deficiency in the waiver by prenuptial agreement is that the agreement is executed before marriage.)[197] Likewise, an agreement by one prospective spouse to execute a waiver after the marriage is thought to be unenforceable under state law because of ERISA pre-emption.[198]

In any case, in order for the spousal consent to be valid, the spouse must receive an adequate explanation of the benefits she is waiving.[199] A prenuptial agreement may not be able to accomplish this.

---

[194] IRC § 417(a)(6)(A).

[195] Profit Sharing Plan for Employees of Republic Fin. Servs., Inc. v. MBank Dallas, N.A., 683 F. Supp. 592 (ND Tex. 1988); but see United Parcel Service, Inc. v. Riley, 532 NYS2d 473 (1988). Sample consents are contained in Notice 97-10, 1997-1 CB 370.

[196] Treas. Reg. § 1.401(a)-20, Q&A-28; Hurwitz v. Sher, 982 F2d 278 (2d Cir. 1992), cert. denied, 508 US 912 (1993); Nellis v. Boeing Co., 1992 WL 122,773, No. 91-1011-K, (D. Kan. 1992); Pedro Enters., Inc. v. Perdue, 998 F2d 491 (7th Cir. 1993). Callahan v. Hutsell, Callahan & Buchino, 813 F. Supp. 541 (WD Ky. 1992), vacated and remanded, 1993 US App. LEXIS 34005 (6th Cir. 1993) (unpublished opinion). Contra Estate of Hopkins, 214 Ill. App. 3d 427, 574 NE2d 230 (1991), appeal denied, 580 NE2d 115 (1991).

[197] Hurwitz v. Sher, 982 F2d 278 (2d Cir. 1992); Pedro Enters., Inc. v. Perdue, 998 F2d 491 (7th Cir. 1993); Callahan v. Hutsell, Callahan & Buchino, 813 F. Supp. 541 (WD Ky. 1992).

[198] Hurwitz v. Sher, 982 2d 278 (2d Cir. 1992); Zinn v. Donaldson Co., 799 F. Supp. 69 (D. Minn. 1992).

[199] See IRC § 417(a)(3)(A)(iii); Treas. Reg. §§ 1.417(e)-1(b)(2); 1.401(a)-20, Q&A 36; 1.401(a)-11(c)(3). If the spouse does not receive adequate explanation, her waiver may not be valid. Lasche v. George W. Lasche Basic Retirement Plan, 870 F. Supp. 336 (SD Fla. 1994), aff'd, 111 F3d 863 (11th Cir. 1997), holding Merrill Lynch form of spousal consent inadequate; Pedro Enters., Inc. v. Perdue, 998 F2d 491 (7th Cir. 1993), holding

It should be noted, however, that there appears to be nothing prohibiting a prenuptial agreement from reducing other benefits received by the spouse to account for retirement benefits the spouse takes in breach of the agreement.

[d] Plan Loans

Generally, a REA plan may not, after August 18, 1985, make a loan to the participant using benefits as security, without spousal consent.[200] However, certain defined contribution plans that are exempt from the spousal annuity requirements (see ¶ 14.06[1] above) are permitted to make loans without spousal consent.[201]

[e] IRAs

REA does not apply to IRAs. Hence, if the participant in an REA plan rolls his benefits over to an IRA, the REA rules will no longer apply to the benefits. Generally, in the absence of an exception, spousal consent will be required to obtain a distribution that can be rolled over from a REA plan, if the participant is married at the time.

[2] State Law Property Rights

[a] Preemption Issues

The issue of federal preemption of state property laws arises with respect to ERISA plans.

Divorce. In the event of divorce, federal law clearly defers to state law to a certain extent. The divorce court can award all or part of qualified plan benefits to the nonparticipant spouse or the children, depending on the particular state involved.[202] The plan benefits can be paid directly by the plan to those persons if a qualified domestic relations order (QDRO) is entered.[203] Generally speaking, the rights of former spouses are only respected by the plan to the ex-

---

that a prenuptial agreement waiving benefits did not constitute an informed waiver of rights in a plan which did not exist at the date of the agreement.

[200] IRC § 417(a)(1)(4); Treas. Reg. § 1.401(a)-20, Q&A 24.

[201] IRC § 401(a)(11)(B)(iii); Treas. Reg. § 1.401(a)-20, Q&A 24(a).

[202] See IRC § 414(p)(8) (alternate payee to whom payments may be made pursuant to a QDRO include spouses, former spouses, children, and other dependents to the extent provided in the QDRO).

[203] IRC §§ 401(a)(13)(B), 414(p).

tent provided by a QDRO.[204] (They may still be respected between the parties under state law.)[205]

Sometimes, a participant will name a spouse as beneficiary, get a divorce, and forget to change the beneficiary. Many state laws automatically revoke such a designation. Are those laws pre-empted?

The Supreme Court has held that such a statute was pre-empted, because the statute "directly conflicted with ERISA's requirements that plans be administered, and benefits be paid in accordance with plan documents."[206]

Practice Pointer: Be extra careful to change the beneficiary designation in an ERISA plan after a divorce, if the former spouse is not the desired beneficiary. Otherwise, the benefit may be paid to the employee's ex-spouse instead of his or her children—as happened in the above case.

---

[b] Community Property Issues—Non-ERISA Plans and IRAs

Boggs v. Boggs[207] held that a nonparticipant spouse holding a community property interest in a qualified plan has no devisable interest in the plan under ERISA. However, *Boggs* does not apply to non-ERISA plans (including IRAs). What happens in a non-ERISA plan if the nonparticipant spouse dies first? If the benefits were community property, the nonparticipant spouse's community property interest in the benefits may be taxable in her estate if she dies first.[208] However, all benefits (both his half and her half) pass to the named beneficiary. If the nonparticipant spouse is not the named beneficiary, the nonparticipant spouse may make a taxable gift of her community one-half interest in the benefits to the beneficiary on the death of the participant spouse.[209]

---

[204] IRC §§ 401(a)(13)(B), 414. According to the Fourth Circuit, surviving spouse benefits vest in a current spouse on the date a participant retires; hence, a former spouse cannot obtain a QDRO after the participant has remarried and retired. Hopkins v. AT&T Global Information Solutions Co., 105 F3d 153 (4th Cir. 1997).

[205] State law rights may include community property, equitable distribution, and other rights provided to a spouse on divorce.

[206] Egelhoff v. Egelhoff, 121 S. Ct. 1322 (2001).

[207] Boggs v. Boggs, 520 US 833 (1997).

[208] IRC §§ 2033, 2039. This could create a significant liquidity problem in her estate. Due to *Boggs*, this should not be a problem in an ERISA plan because either the nonparticipant spouse has nothing to transfer on her death, or, if she is transferring the interest to her spouse, the transfer should generally qualify for the martial deduction. Conversely, if the participant spouse dies first and the benefits are community property, only the participant's community property interest in the benefits should be taxable in his estate.

[209] Rev. Rul. 75-240, 1975-1 CB 240. But see Estate of Street v. Comm'r, 152 F3d 482 (5th Cir. 1998).

Practice Pointer: To avoid confusion, it may be wise for the nonparticipating spouse to bequeath any interest in the participant spouse's non-ERISA plans to the participant spouse.

Marital deduction. The nonparticipant spouse's community property interest in an annuity benefit in which she has a devisable interest will qualify for the marital deduction in certain circumstances. The marital deduction is available with respect a predeceasing spouse's community property interest in an annuity that is included in the predeceasing spouse's estate pursuant to Section 2033, provided that only the surviving spouse has the right to receive payments before the surviving spouse's death.[210] This provision, of course, applies to non-ERISA annuities, such as annuities payable from IRAs and commercial annuities.

Voluntary division of community property IRAs. A community property IRA may be able to be partitioned into equally owned separate property of the spouses without a distribution being deemed to occur in appropriate circumstances.[211]

Voluntary division of community property qualified plan benefits. May the spouses voluntarily divide qualified plan benefits, if they are not divorcing? Evidently not. A plan may not distribute, segregate, or otherwise recognize the attachment of any portion of a participant's benefits in favor of the participant's spouse, former spouse, or dependents unless such action is mandated by a QDRO.[212] The voluntary partition of a participant's vested account balance between his spouse and himself in a community property state has been held to be an invalid attempt to alienate benefits, possibly causing the plan funds to lose their tax-exempt status.[213]

---

[210] IRC § 2056(b)(7)(C).

[211] Priv. Ltr. Rul. 9439020 (July 7, 1994) corrected on other issues, Priv. Ltr. Rul. 9510069 (Dec. 14, 1994). Contra Priv. Ltr. Rul. 199937055 (June 24, 1999), in which the IRS ruled that if the spouse of an IRA owner transfers his or her community property interest in the IRA into a separate IRA established in the name of the spouse, the transfer will be taxable as a distribution of IRA proceeds.

[212] IRC §§ 401(a)(13)(A), 401(a)(13)(B), 414(p). Whether all the benefits could be partitioned to the participant (with the spouse, perhaps, receiving other community property) is another issue.

[213] Priv. Ltr. Rul. 8735032 (June 2, 1987). Merchant v. Kelly, Haglund, Garnsey & Kahn, 874 F. Supp. 300 (D. Colo. 1995). The idea that an invalid attempted alienation of benefits could cause the plan to lose its qualified status seems highly questionable. If the plan prohibits alienation, as it must, then the partition should be regarded merely as an invalid act of a plan beneficiary. In the cited Colorado case, the partition may have been recognized and acted upon as if it were valid by the plan administrator. In the usual case, if plans could be disqualified if a beneficiary attempted a void assignment, then plan disqualification could take place at any time for reasons outside the control or knowledge of

¶ 14.06 INCOME TAXATION OF DISTRIBUTIONS TO PARTICIPANT

[1] No Taxation of Undistributed Amounts

Amounts in qualified plans and IRAs are not generally taxable to the participant until and to the extent that distributions are made. This is true even if the participant is free to withdraw the entire account.[214] An exception applies in the case of IRAs that engage in prohibited transactions and plan loans that do not satisfy the requirements of Section 72(p).

[2] Extent and Character of Income

When amounts are distributed from the plan or IRA in excess of the employee's investment in the contract and are not rolled over, they are generally considered income.[215] The earnings on after-tax employee contributions are taxable. If both after-tax and other contributions are involved, each distribution is usually deemed to consist of a pro rata portion of each.[216]

The character of the distribution as income does not depend on the character of the income as it was earned in the plan or IRA. Thus, even if a plan invests in tax-exempt investments and distributes the income, or distributes principal, the distribution still constitutes taxable income to the participant.[217]

[3] Basis in a Plan or IRA

The participant's basis in a plan or IRA, if any, is recovered tax-free. Generally, a participant's basis in a plan or IRA is any amount in the plan or IRA on which he has already paid income tax (e.g., after-tax employee contributions and costs of life insurance protection which have been includable in in-

---

the plan administrator for actions which are invalid and which the plan administrator does not recognize.

[214] Technical translation: the constructive receipt doctrine does not apply. IRC §§ 402(a), 408(d)(1).

[215] Certain exceptions exist—e.g., certain life insurance on which economic benefit costs have been paid. IRC § 402(e).

[216] IRC §§ 72(e)(2)(B), 72(e)(8).

[217] IRC §§ 72, 402(a), 408(d)(1); see also D. Bennett et al., Taxation of Distributions From Qualified Plans ¶ 15.03[1] (1997). Note that tax-exempt securities would be an unusual investment for a plan, given that the plan itself is generally exempt from income tax.

come (for a common law participant only)[218] or loans that were taxed), *reduced by* any amounts previously distributed to the participant that were excludable from his gross income.[219]

[4] Pre-Retirement Distributions

Pre-retirement distributions (i.e., those received before the annuity starting date)[220] made to a participant who has a cost basis under a pension, profit-sharing, or stock bonus plan, or under an annuity contract purchased by any such plan, are taxed under a rule which provides that a pro rata portion of each distribution will be treated as recovery of basis.[221]

If a plan, on May 5, 1986 permitted in-service withdrawal of participant contributions, the pro rata recovery rules do not apply to investments in the contract prior to 1987.[222]

[5] Retirement Distributions

Any distribution (other than a grandfathered lump sum distribution)[223] is taxed under the annuity rules of Section 72.[224] In applying the annuity rules, this subsection will use the term "basis in the plan" rather than "investment in the contract."[225]

---

[218] An owner-participant cannot include the annual one-year term cost in his cost basis, even though the cost was not deductible. IRC § 72(m)(2); Treas. Reg. § 1.72-16(b)(4).

[219] IRC §§ 72(f), 402(d)(4)(D).

[220] The annuity starting date is the first day of the first period for which an amount is received as an annuity under the plan. IRC § 72(c)(4).

[221] IRC § 72(e)(8).

[222] IRC § 72(e)(8)(D).

[223] See ¶ 14.06[10].

[224] IRC § 402(a).

[225] The annuity rules are explained at length in Chapter 13. Generally, however, a participant's basis for his interest in a plan will equal the sum of: (1) any after-tax (nondeductible) contributions to the plan that were not previously withdrawn; (2) certain amounts included in the participant's taxable income that are attributable to life insurance protection; (3) employee contributions that were previously taxed; (4) the participant's principal payments on any loans to the employee that were treated as distributions; and (5) certain pre-1963 employer contributions attributable to foreign service by the employee.

[a] No Basis in Plan

If the participant has no cost basis for his interest in the plan, the full amount of each payment is taxable to him as ordinary income.[226]

[b] Basis in Plan

If the participant has a cost basis for his interest in the plan and his annuity starting date is after July 1, 1986, the regular annuity rules apply, subject to certain special rules for annuities from qualified plans.[227]

[i] Recovery of basis.

[A] *General rule.* Under the regular annuity rules, the participant recovers his cost basis as a pro rata percentage of each distribution. The excluded percentage is determined as of the annuity starting date.[228] Basically, the excluded percentage is determined by dividing the participant's cost basis by his expected distributions. In the case of a straight life annuity, the amount of expected distributions is determined by multiplying the total amount he will receive each year by the number of years he is expected to live (as determined pursuant to the actuarial tables contained in the regulations under Section 72). If the participant's annuity starting date is after 1986, the total amount that the participant can exclude during his lifetime is limited to his basis.[229] With respect to earlier starting dates, the excluded percentage continues to apply, even to amounts received in excess of the participant's basis.[230]

[B] *Qualified plans—annuities with starting dates before November 19, 1996.* If the annuity is paid from a qualified plan, the participant can elect a simplified safe harbor method of computing the tax if (1) the annuity payments depend on his life or the joint lives of himself and a beneficiary and (2) his annuity starting date is after July 1, 1986. If the participant is age 75 or older when the annuity payments commence, this method can be used only if fewer than five years of payments are guaranteed to be made.[231] Under this method, the participant's cost basis is divided by the total number of monthly annuity payments expected. This number is taken from an actuarial table (not the tables found in the regulations under Section 72) and is based on the participant's age at the annuity starting date. (Of course, if the annuity starting

---

[226] Treas. Reg. §§ 1.61-11(a), 1.72-4(d)(1); IRC §§ 72, 402(a), 403(a).

[227] IRC §§ 402(a), 403(a). A simplified safe harbor method of computing the tax may be available (see below).

[228] IRC § 72(b); Treas. Reg. § 1.72-4(a).

[229] IRC § 72(b)(2).

[230] TRA 1986, § 1122(h)(2)(B).

[231] Notice 88-118, 1988-2 CB 450.

date is after December 31, 1986, annuity payments received after the basis is recovered are fully includable in income.) If available, this method will usually be preferable from an income tax standpoint because a greater amount will be excluded from the participant's income until his basis is recovered.

[C] Qualified plans—annuities with starting dates beginning on or after November 19, 1996. If the annuity is payable from a qualified plan, the portion of each annuity payment that represents a return of basis equals the participant's total basis as of the annuity starting date, divided by the number of anticipated payments under the following table:[232]

Age	Number of Payments
55 or Younger	360
56–60	310
61–65	260
66–70	210
Older Than 70	160

Effective for annuities beginning after 1997, the above table applies only if there is one annuitant.[233] Where payments are made over the lives of more than one individual, the expected return is found by dividing the investment in the contract by the number of anticipated payments that varies with the combined ages of the annuitants on the annuity starting date, as follows.

- 110 and under, the number of payments is 410;
- 111 to 120, the number of payments is 360;
- 121 to 130, the number of payments is 310;
- 131 to 140, the number of payments is 260; and
- 141 and over, the number of payments is 210.[234]

Neither table applies if the primary annuitant is over age 75 and there are at least five years of guaranteed payments.[235] In that situation, the prior method for annuities with a starting date before November 19, 1996, applies.

If the annuity is a fixed number of payments, then the number of monthly annuity payments under the contract will be the denominator.[236] Adjustments are made if the payments are not made on a monthly basis.[237] This rule does not apply in any case where the primary annuitant has attained age 75 on the

---

[232] SBJPA § 1403(a), adding IRC §§ 72(d)(1)(B)(i)(II), 72(d)(1)(B)(iii).

[233] IRC § 72(d)(1)(B)(iii).

[234] IRC § 72(d)(1)(B)(iv).

[235] IRC § 72(d)(1)(E).

[236] IRC § 72(d)(1)(B)(i)(II).

[237] IRC § 72(d)(1)(F).

annuity starting date unless there are fewer than five years of guaranteed payments under the annuity.[238]

[ii] Annuity payment periods other than straight life. The regulations under Section 72 provide methods of computing the investment in the contract of various special types of annuities (e.g., annuities with a term certain or refunding feature, joint and survivor annuities, etc.). Where one of these types of annuities is paid from a qualified plan, the annuity rules as expressly applied to payments under that type of annuity will govern.

For annuities with starting dates on or after November 19, 1996, the investment in the contract is determined without regard to any refund feature.[239]

[iii] Annuity commencing in connection with lump sum payment. If the participant in a qualified plan receives a lump sum payment in connection with the commencement of annuity payments, the lump sum payment will be taxable as a payment received before the starting date, and the basis in the plan will be determined as if the payment had been so received, where the annuity starting date is after November 19, 1996.[240]

[iv] Unrecovered basis on death. If a participant dies prior to recovering his basis, the unrecovered basis will be allowed as a deduction on his final income tax return.[241] If payments are guaranteed or the plan has a refund feature so that the annuity continues after the participant's death, the beneficiary may deduct the remaining unrecovered investment in the contract in the year the guaranteed or refund payments are made.[242]

[v] Computation of tax-exempt portion. The IRS has explained how to calculate the tax-free portion of qualified plan annuity payments under the 1996 and 1997 changes.[243] Notice 98-2 explains which annuities are treated as single-life annuities and which are treated as joint and survivor annuities.

This Notice describes the computations applicable to (1) an annuity for the life of one annuitant with a term certain; (2) an annuity for the life of one annuitant with a temporary annuity payable to the annuitant's child until the child reaches an age specified in the plan (not more than age 25); (3) an annuity payable to a primary annuitant and more than one survivor annuitant; (4) an annuity payable to more than one survivor annuitant where there is no primary annuitant; (5) an annuity with any survivor annuitant whose entitlement to payments is contingent on an event other than the death of the primary an-

---

[238] IRC § 72(d)(1)(E).

[239] IRC § 72(d)(1)(C).

[240] IRC § 72(d)(1)(D).

[241] IRC § 72(b)(3)(A).

[242] IRC § 72(b)(3)(B).

[243] Notice 98-2, 1998-1 CB 266.

nuitant; (6) an annuity which does not depend in whole or in part on the life expectancy of one or more individuals; (7) an annuity where several annuitants receive payments at the same time; (8) an annuity which is not paid on a monthly basis; and (9) an annuity with a starting date after November 18, 1996, and before January 1, 1997.

[6] Ten Percent Penalty Tax on Early Distributions

In general, an early distribution or early withdrawal is a distribution before the participant reaches age 59½. A plan or IRA may or may not permit early withdrawals. Subject to certain exceptions, any early distribution is subject to a penalty tax of ten percent of the amount included in income.[244] The relevant exceptions include:

- A withdrawal made after the death of the participant;[245]
- A withdrawal attributable to the participant's disability;[246]
- A withdrawal that is part of a series of substantially equal periodic payments made at least annually for the life or life expectancy of the participant or the joint lives or joint life expectancies of the participant and his designated beneficiary after the participant has separated from service,[247] provided the annuity is not modified;[248]
- A withdrawal made after the participant has separated from service and attained age 55;[249]
- A withdrawal made to pay certain medical expenses;[250]
- A withdrawal made pursuant to a QDRO;[251]
- A withdrawal consisting of dividends paid on certain stock held in an ESOP;[252]
- A withdrawal made by certain unemployed persons to the extent of amounts paid during the year for health insurance;[253]
- A withdrawal to pay qualified higher education expenses;[254]

---

[244] IRC § 72(t)(1).

[245] IRC § 72(t)(2)(A)(ii).

[246] IRC § 72(t)(2)(A)(iii).

[247] IRC § 72(t)(3)(B).

[248] IRC § 72(t)(4).

[249] IRC § 72(t)(2)(A)(v) (this does not apply to IRAs).

[250] IRC § 72(t)(2)(B).

[251] IRC § 72(t)(2)(C) (this does not apply to IRAs).

[252] IRC § 72(t)(2)(A)(vi).

[253] IRC § 72(t)(2)(D) (applies only to IRAs).

[254] IRC § 72(t)(2)(E) (applied only to IRAs).

- A withdrawal made to pay certain first-time homebuyer's expenses;[255]
- A withdrawal made on account of a Section 6331 levy on the plan;[256]
- A withdrawal from a Roth IRA; and
- Certain withdrawals from education IRAs (called Coverdell education savings accounts as of mid-2001).[257]

[7] Rollovers

Most distributions[258] to a participant can be rolled over (in whole or in part) to an IRA or another qualified plan within 60 days of the participant's receiving the distribution.[259] No income tax will be due on the distribution. However, a distribution that is made to the participant before it is rolled over is usually subject to 20 percent withholding.[260]

[8] Direct Rollover Option

Many participants want to move their qualified plan accounts from one employer plan to another if they change jobs. Qualified plans are generally required to offer a "direct rollover" payment option.[261]

If the participant does not elect a direct plan-to-plan or plan-to-IRA rollover, the distribution will be subject to withholding.[262]

[9] Social Security Tax

Pre-tax amounts contributed to and amounts payable from a qualified plan under Section 401(a) for the benefit of a common law employee are generally not subject to FICA taxes.[263] Self-employment tax applies to all contributions

---

[255] IRC § 72(t)(2)(F) (applies only to IRAs).

[256] IRC § 72(t)(2)(A)(vii).

[257] IRC § 530.

[258] Other than minimum distributions required by IRC § 401(a)(9) and distributions that are not eligible for rollover under IRC § 402(c)(4) or Treas. Reg. §§ 1.402(c)-2, Q&A 3, 1.402(c)-2, Q&A-4.

[259] Temp. Reg. § 1.402(c)-2T, Q&A-9.

[260] Temp. Reg. § 1.402(c)-2T, Q&A-9.

[261] See IRC § 401(a)(31).

[262] IRC § 3405(c); Temp. Reg. § 1.401(a)(31)-1T, Q&A 1(b)(1).

[263] IRC § 3121(a)(5). *Exception:* certain employee pre-tax contributions made by a common law employee to a 401(k) plan. IRC § 3121(v)(1). A "common law employee" (as distinguished from a self-employed person) is a person whose relationship with the

by self-employed persons to qualified plans.[264] Hence, distributions (to the extent attributable to previously taxed contributions and investment income) should not be subject to the tax.

[10] Grandfathered Benefits—Lump Sum Distributions

Before 2000, a number of special rules applied to lump sum distributions from qualified plans and IRAs. Effective for tax years beginning after 1999, all of the former special tax treatment of lump sum distributions (including five-year averaging) for non-grandfathered benefits is repealed.[265]

However, the availability of ten-year averaging and of capital gains treatment for the capital gains portion of a distribution is continued for those who are eligible under the pre-SBJPA rules.[266] Hence, the following discussion describes grandfathered benefits only, and references are to Section 402(d) as it existed before repeal.

[a] Definition of Lump Sum Distribution

A distribution from a qualified plan is considered a "lump sum distribution" if it consists of the entire balance to the credit of the participant, and is payable:

- On account of the participant's death;
- After the participant attains age 59½;
- On account of the participant's separation from service (in the case of a common law participant only); or
- After the participant has become disabled (in the case of a self-employed person only).[267]

[b] Taxable Amount of a Lump Sum Distribution

The amount of the lump sum distribution (after reduction for basis) is the "total taxable amount."[268] An annuity contract distributed as all or part of a

---

person for whom he performs services is the legal relationship of employer and participant under the usual common law rules. This typically means that the participant is subject to the will and control of the employer not only as to what shall be done, but how it shall be done. Treas. Reg. § 31.3121(d)-1(c).

[264] Gale v. United States, 768 F. Supp. 1305 (ND Ill. 1991).

[265] SBJPA § 1401.

[266] SBJPA § 1401(c)(2).

[267] Former IRC § 402(d)(4)(A).

[268] Former IRC § 402(d)(4)(D).

lump sum distribution is part of the "total taxable amount," but the tax on the annuity contract will be deferred.[269]

[c] Special Tax on Long-Term Capital Gain Portion

A participant who was age 50 before January 1, 1986, may elect to have the portion of the distribution that is allocable to pre-1974 participation treated as long-term capital gain and taxed at a rate of 20 percent.[270] The capital gain portion is determined by dividing the number of calendar years of active participation in the plan before 1974 by the number of total calendar years of active plan participation. This election may be made only once with respect to any participant and the election applies to all lump sum distributions received in the year.[271]

[d] Ten-Year Averaging

[i] **Eligible participants.** A participant who attained age 50 before 1986 may elect ten-year averaging with respect to certain benefits. Such a participant who receives a lump sum distribution can elect to determine the tax on the "ordinary income portion" using a special ten-year averaging formula.[272] The election applies to all lump sum distributions received with respect to a participant during the tax year.[273] To be eligible to make the election, a participant must have[274] been a participant in the plan for at least five taxable years before the year in which the distribution is made.[275]

---

[269] Former IRC § 402(d)(2). See discussion at ¶ 14.06[10][e] below.

[270] TRA 1986, § 1122(h)(3).

[271] TAMRA § 1011A(b)(13); TRA 1986, § 1122(h)(3).

[272] Former IRC §§ 402(d)(1), 402(d)(4)(B)(iii).

[273] Former IRC § 402(d)(4)(B).

[274] Former IRC § 402(d)(4)(B)(i).

[275] Former IRC § 402(d)(4)(F).

Practice Pointer: Many participants who change jobs transfer their interest in a previous employer's plan to the new employer's plan. Participation in the previous employer's plan counts for purposes of eligibility for averaging if a trustee-to-trustee transfer occurred.[276] However, ability to average is destroyed if (1) the amount is rolled over from one plan to an IRA and from there to another qualified plan, or (2) if the amount goes through the participant's hands before being transferred to the new plan.[277]

One-time only election. The election to use ten-year averaging is made on the taxpayer's income tax return.[278] Only one ten-year averaging election may be made with respect to any participant.[279]

[ii] Tax computation. A tax is computed on one-tenth of the total taxable amount, after reduction by the minimum distribution allowance.[280] This tax is determined apart from the participant's other taxable income,[281] using the rate used by single persons,[282] without deductions and without regard to community property laws.[283] The tax is then multiplied by ten.[284]

> **EXAMPLE:** Mom receives a lump sum distribution of $500,000 and elects five-year averaging. The minimum distribution allowance is zero. The tax is computed on a base amount of $500,000 divided by five, or $100,000.

Election of averaging should be compared carefully with the alternative of rolling over the distribution and deferring tax. The latter may have the effect of preserving more principal for investment and maximizing assets after income tax. Averaging, however, may achieve the objective of getting the distribution out of the plan and income tax paid before death. Also, if the funds are

---

[276] Priv. Ltr. Ruls. 9002010 (Oct. 6, 1989), 8830086 (Apr. 22, 1988), 8535059 (June 5, 1985), 8535050 (June 4, 1985), 8934051 (May 31, 1989), 8902017 (Sept. 30, 1988). The fact that the transfer was at the participant's election apparently makes no difference.

[277] Priv. Ltr. Ruls. 8542069 (July 24, 1985), 8519061 (Feb. 14, 1985), 8441068 (July 13, 1984), 8246103 (Aug. 19, 1982).

[278] Temp. Reg. § 11.402(e)(4)(B)-1.

[279] Former IRC § 402(d)(4)(B); see also Priv. Ltr. Rul. 9003061 (Oct. 24, 1989).

[280] The "minimum distribution allowance" is defined in former IRC § 402(d)(1)(C). It will never be more than $10,000. It phases to zero for a total taxable amount of $70,000 or more. Former IRC § 402(d)(1)(B).

[281] Former IRC § 402(d)(1)(A).

[282] The tax rates used are those in Technical and Miscellaneous Revenue Act of 1988, Pub. L. No. 100-647, § 1011A(b)(15)(B), 102 Stat. 3342 (1988) (TAMRA); TRA 1986, § 1122(h)(5). These rates began at 11 percent and graduated to 50 percent of amounts over $85,790. Former IRC § 402(d)(1)(B).

[283] Former IRC § 402(d)(4)(E).

[284] Former IRC § 402(d)(1)(B).

distributed and not rolled over, they can be used for related party investments that would be prohibited under Section 4975 if the funds were in an IRA or qualified plan.

[e] Annuity Contracts

The tax on a lump sum distribution will be reduced by the portion of the tax attributable to annuity contracts that were distributed.[285] The actuarial value of an annuity contract on the date of distribution is the taxable amount of the contract.[286] The participant will not be taxed on this value unless and until he surrenders the contract. He will be taxed on the annuity payments as he receives them. Contracts issued after 1962 must be nontransferable to qualify for this tax-deferred treatment.[287]

¶ 14.07 INCOME TAXATION OF DISTRIBUTIONS WHEN PARTICIPANT DIES BEFORE RETIREMENT/RBD

The rules applicable to distributions to living participants generally apply, but with some additional considerations.

[1] Distribution Other Than Life Insurance Proceeds

[a] Beneficiary's Basis in Plan

The beneficiary's basis in the plan is generally determined in the same manner as the participant's basis.

[b] Distributions—General Rule

The beneficiary is taxed as the participant would have been taxed had he lived and received the distributions. However, the beneficiary's basis, rather than the participant's basis, is used. The regular annuity rules apply, using the beneficiary's basis as the investment in the contract.[288]

---

[285] Former IRC § 402(d)(2)(A).

[286] Former IRC § 402(d)(2)(C).

[287] IRC § 401(g); Treas. Reg. §§ 1.401-9, 1.402(a)-1(a)(2).

[288] For an explanation of the basic annuity rules and their application to various types of payments, see Chapter 13.

[c] Lump Sum Distributions to Beneficiary—Grandfathered Benefits

A law change in 2000 eliminated most special benefits for lump sum distributions.[289]

To the extent that the participant was eligible for special averaging with respect to grandfathered benefits, a deceased participant's beneficiary can elect special averaging whether or not the participant had been a participant for at least five years.[290] Each recipient can elect special averaging separately (except two or more trusts, which must all make the same election).[291] Where a beneficiary elects to use special averaging for grandfathered benefits, the IRD deduction reduces the "total taxable amount" of the lump sum distribution (except in calculating the minimum distribution allowance).[292]

[d] Multiple Beneficiaries

When more than one beneficiary is to receive payments under the plan, the cost basis is apportioned among them according to each one's share of the total death benefit payments.[293]

[2] Distribution of Life Insurance Proceeds

If the death benefit payments come from life insurance proceeds, the proceeds are divided into two parts: the "amount at risk" (proceeds in excess of the cash surrender value immediately before death) and the cash surrender value.[294]

[a] Amount at Risk

The part of the payments attributable to the "amount at risk" is taxable under Section 101(d) as life insurance proceeds settled under a life income or installment option, as the case may be. Generally, the "amount at risk" is prorated over the payment period (whether for a fixed number of years or for life), and the prorated amounts are excludable from the beneficiary's gross income as a return of principal.[295] The balance of this portion of the payments is

---

[289] See ¶ 14.06[10].

[290] Prop. Reg. § 1.402(e)-2(e)(3); Priv. Ltr. Rul. 7805054 (Nov. 7, 1977).

[291] IRC § 402(d)(2)(D).

[292] IRC § 691(c)(5).

[293] Treas. Reg. § 1.101-2(c)(1).

[294] Treas. Reg. § 1.72-16(c).

[295] Where payments are for life, the beneficiary's life expectancy is taken from IRS unisex annuity tables V and VI if the insured died after October 22, 1986. Temp. Reg. § 1.101-7T.

taxable as interest except to a surviving spouse of an insured who died before October 23, 1986. If the beneficiary is such a surviving spouse, the beneficiary may exclude up to $1,000 of such interest annually.[296]

[b] Cash Surrender Value

The part of the payments attributable to the cash surrender value is taxed in the same manner as any other distribution from a qualified plan to the beneficiary.

[3] Deduction For Income In Respect of a Decedent

The beneficiary is entitled to an income tax deduction for any estate tax attributable to the inclusion of the plan or IRA proceeds in the participant's estate.[297]

¶ 14.08 INCOME TAXATION OF DISTRIBUTIONS WHEN PARTICIPANT DIES AFTER RETIREMENT/RBD

[1] Basis

If the participant had no basis for his interest or had fully recovered his basis from payments received during his life, all amounts received by the beneficiary will be fully taxable.

[2] Section 691(c) Deduction

The beneficiary is entitled to an income tax deduction for any estate tax attributable to the participant's interest in the plan.[298]

[3] Joint and Survivor Annuity

The method of taxing the survivor annuity payments to the beneficiary will depend upon how the participant was taxed. If the participant was taxed on the

---

[296] Treas. Reg. § 1.101-4.

[297] IRC § 691(c).

[298] IRC § 691(c).

entire payment, the survivor annuitant will be similarly taxed.[299] If the participant was taxed under the regular annuity rules or under the safe harbor method, the survivor will continue with the same excluded percentage;[300] however, if the participant's annuity starting date was after December 31, 1986, no amount is excludable by the participant or the survivor after the cost basis has been recovered.[301]

[4] Beneficiary Under Life Annuity With Refund or Period-Certain Guarantee

If the participant had a cost basis for his interest in a plan with a refund provision, and had not recovered the full amount, the beneficiary can exclude the balance of the cost basis from his gross income. Otherwise, everything received by the beneficiary is taxable.[302]

If the beneficiary receives the refund in a grandfathered lump sum distribution, the lump sum distribution rules apply.[303] (However, if the beneficiary surrenders an annuity contract that was previously distributed to the participant, the payment does not qualify for lump sum treatment, because, according to the IRS, it is not a distribution from the plan but a payment in settlement of the insurer's liability to make future payments.)[304]

If the beneficiary receives the refund in installments, the taxable payments are ordinary income. If a participant whose annuity starting date was after July 1, 1986, did not fully recover his cost basis prior to his death, the participant's beneficiary may take a deduction for the remaining unrecovered amount in the year the payments are received.[305]

[5] Installment Payments

Where a participant had begun to receive payments for a fixed period or payments of a fixed amount (not involving a life contingency) before his death, the method of taxing the payments will depend upon how the participant was taxed. If the participant was taxed on everything, the beneficiary will be also.[306] If the participant was taxed under the regular annuity rules or under the

---

[299] Treas. Reg. § 1.72-4(d).

[300] Treas. Reg. §§ 1.72-4, 1.72-5.

[301] IRC § 72(b)(2).

[302] Treas. Reg. §§ 1.72-11, 1.72-13.

[303] See ¶ 14.06[10] above.

[304] Rev. Rul. 68-287, 1968-1 CB 174.

[305] IRC § 72(b)(3)(B).

[306] Treas. Reg. § 1.72-4(d).

safe harbor method, the beneficiary will continue to exclude the same portion of each payment from gross income.[307] If the annuity starting date was after December 31, 1986, the beneficiary can exclude amounts only until the investment in the contract has been fully recovered; thereafter, all amounts are included in income.[308]

If the beneficiary receives grandfathered benefits in a lump sum distribution, the lump sum payment is taxable under the lump sum distributions rules.

¶ 14.09 LIFE INSURANCE IN A QUALIFIED PLAN

The rules on life insurance in a qualified plan are complex and arcane. A benefit plan will not usually be the best place for insurance. However, because this alternative is occasionally suggested, and since there is sometimes no other source of funds, here is a very general set of rules that apply in this circumstance.

Warning: This particular section is included just to give an overview of the general rules. Most of these general rules are subject to specific requirements and numerous exceptions, exceptions to the exceptions, etc.

---

[1] Eligibility as a Plan Asset

[a] IRA

No part of an IRA can be invested in life insurance policies.[309]

[b] Eligibility of Qualified Plan to Hold Life Insurance

As noted above, the rules on eligibility of life insurance as a qualified plan investment are complex. The administrative requirements applicable to plans that hold life insurance are also cumbersome. Because of this, many plans either do not allow investments in life insurance or provide stricter limits than the law requires.

A qualified plan can hold life insurance policies on the participant payable to or for the benefit of the participant, his estate, or a named beneficiary

---

[307] Treas. Reg. § 1.72-4(a).

[308] IRC § 72(b)(2).

[309] IRC § 408(a)(3).

under certain circumstances. The general rule is that the death benefit provided through insurance held by a qualified plan must be "incidental" to the plan's primary retirement benefit.[310] These "incidental benefit" rules limit the percentage of employer contributions that can be used to purchase life insurance.

The IRS has ruled that a pension plan cannot provide insurance on the life of anyone (other than the employee) in whom the employee has an insurable interest.[311] It is not clear whether this rules out second-to-die policies.

Because life insurance purchased within a plan will be a plan asset, it must qualify as a prudent investment, within the context of the plan as a whole. In at least one case, the Department of Labor filed a civil complaint against the trustees of a pension plan (and other defendants) for allegedly imprudently investing a significant amount of plan assets in whole life policies.[312] If, however, the investment in life insurance is pursuant to an individual participant's direction in a self-directed account and all of the safe harbor rules for self-directed accounts are met, the plan trustees are not liable for the investment performance of the policies.[313]

[2] Income Taxation of Life Insurance in Plans

[a] Payment of Premiums

Depending on the source of the premium payments, life insurance held in a plan for the benefit of the participant's estate or his beneficiary may cause current income tax consequences to the participant. Specifically, the participant will have current taxable income if premiums are paid with (1) contributions that are deductible by the employer,[314] (2) income earned by the plan,[315] or (3) amounts attributable to deductible or pre-tax employee contributions (including net earnings allocable to them.[316] To the extent premiums are paid with after-

---

[310] Treas. Reg. § 1.401-1(b)(1); see also Rev. Rul. 74-307, 1974-2 CB 126; Rev. Rul. 61-164, 1961-2 CB 99; Rev. Rul. 60-83, 1960-1 CB 157; Rev. Rul. 66-143, 1966-1 CB 79; Rev. Rul. 54-51, 1954-1 CB 147 (regarding what constitutes "incidental" for purposes of life insurance held by qualified plans).

[311] Rev. Rul. 69-523, 1969-2 CB 90. This rule presumably does not apply to profit-sharing plans. See Priv. Ltr. Rul. 8445095 (Aug. 13, 1984); Treas. Reg. § 1.401-1(b)(1)(ii).

[312] Dole v. Framingham Union Hosp., Inc., 744 F. Supp. 29 (D. Mass. 1990). The case was settled by the fiduciary defendants, so the fiduciary issues were not heard in court.

[313] 29 CFR § 2550.404(c)-1(d)(2).

[314] IRC § 72(m)(3)(B); Treas. Reg. § 1.72-16(b).

[315] IRC § 72(m)(3)(B); Treas. Reg. § 1.72-16(b).

[316] IRC § 72(o)(3) It is unclear whether such amounts are subject to a premature distribution penalty; the IRS has specifically exempted P.S. 58 costs of life insurance protec-

tax employee contributions, however, they are not subject to current income tax.[317] Premiums paid by a contributory plan are considered to be paid first from deductible employer contributions or trust earnings unless the plan specifically provides that employee contributions are to be applied first.[318]

The amount includable in the participant's income, attributable to insurance purchased with deductible employer contributions or earnings of such contributions, will equal the cost of the life insurance protection. However, if life insurance is purchased with deductible employee contributions or earnings thereon, the amount used is the measure of income to the employee.

[b] Distribution of Policy

When a life insurance contract is distributed to a plan participant, the participant is taxed on the excess of the cash surrender value of the policy at that time over his basis (except to the extent that, within 60 days of the distribution, all or a portion of the policy value is irrevocably converted into an annuity contract that has no life insurance element).[319] If the participant wants to roll over assets to an IRA, he would have to sell or surrender the policy and roll over the proceeds because an IRA cannot hold a life insurance policy.[320]

[c] Distribution of Policy Proceeds

[i] Participant was taxed on or paid insurance costs. If the participant was subject to current income tax on the cost of insurance coverage of the policy (as described above) or paid those costs with after-tax contributions, then an amount equal to the cash surrender value of the policy immediately before the participant's death is part of the taxable amount of the distribution.[321] The taxable amount of the cash surrender value is reduced by the participant's basis in the insurance benefits, which is recovered tax-free. The excess of the

---

tion included in income from such a penalty. (The P.S. 58 costs are generally no longer allowed, however, the principle should apply to Table One or other permitted values. See Chapter 12).

[317] D. Bennett et al., Taxation of Distributions From Qualified Plans ¶ 10.2[2][a] (1997).

[318] Rev. Rul. 68-390, 1968-2 CB 175.

[319] Treas. Reg. § 1.402(a)-1(a)(2).

[320] Rev. Rul. 81-275, 1981-2 CB 92.

[321] Treas. Reg. § 1.72-16(c)(2)(ii).

proceeds payable over the cash surrender value is not subject to income tax, because it is exempt from income taxation as life insurance.[322]

[ii] Participant was not taxed on and did not pay insurance costs. If the total cost of the life insurance protection portion of the premiums was not paid with after-tax plan contributions or taxed to the participant, then all of the death proceeds payable under the policy held in the plan (less the insured's investment in the contract) would be subject to income tax when received by the beneficiary.[323]

[3] Estate Taxation

The insurance proceeds payable on the death of a participant are not included in the participant's estate under Section 2039 as part of the qualified plan.[324] However, the policy proceeds held in a qualified plan will generally be includable in the estate of the participant, due to the participant's incidents of ownership over the policy.[325] The anti-alienation rules applicable to qualified plans prevent the participant from assigning the policy while it is still in the plan. However, if the plan distributes the policy to the participant, and he or she transfers it (for example, to an irrevocable life insurance trust, or "ILIT") at least three years before death, the policy may be removed from the estate.[326]

[4] Getting Insurance out of the Plan

[a] Sale or Distribution to the Participant

The sale or exchange of an insurance policy between a qualified plan and a plan participant is permitted only under certain circumstances.[327] The participant can purchase the policy if (1) the purchase is not a prohibited transaction because of the position that the participant occupies with respect to the plan; (2) the plan would otherwise surrender the policy; and (3) the plan receives an

---

[322] IRC § 101(a); Treas. Reg. § 1.72-16(c)(2)(ii).

[323] Treas. Reg. § 1.72-16(c)(4).

[324] IRC § 2039(a).

[325] IRC § 2042(2). If the policy is on the life of another (e.g., a second-to-die policy where the participant is the first insured to die), the value included would presumably be the interpolated terminal reserve value (or other applicable estate tax value) of the policy. See Chapter 12 on life insurance.

[326] IRC §§ 2035, 2042(2).

[327] DOL Prohibited Transaction Class Exemption No. 92-5, 57 Fed. Reg. 5019 (Feb. 11, 1992); DOL Prohibited Transaction Class Exemption No. 92-6, 57 Fed. Reg. 5190 (Feb. 11, 1992).

amount sufficient to put the plan in the same position it would have been in had it simply surrendered the policy.[328] The plan could also distribute the policy to the participant, subject to the restrictions on premature and other distributions. Once the participant owns the policy, he could contribute it to his ILIT.

[b] Sale by the Plan to an ILIT

[i] **Prohibited transaction.** If the participant occupies certain positions with respect to the plan, such a transaction may be considered a "prohibited transaction," subject to penalties.[329]

[ii] **Income tax issues.** Ordinarily, a transfer of a policy for consideration will result in at least a portion of the proceeds of the policy being taxable income to the recipient.[330] This rule does not apply if the sale is to the insured.[331] If the ILIT[332] is structured as a grantor trust, so that the insured is treated for income tax purposes as the owner of the trust assets, will this "transfer for value" rule be avoided? The Eighth Circuit, affirming the Tax Court, thought so in *Swanson*.[333]

The IRS, which disagreed with *Swanson*,[334] declined to address this issue in a later private ruling in which the taxpayer specifically requested a ruling that the grantor trust rules excepted the transfer of the policy from the transfer for value rules.[335] The taxpayers in the ruling had retained the right to reacquire trust property by substituting property of equal value, but had retained no right that would cause the trust to be includable in their estates for estate tax purposes. The IRS, stating that this area of the law is under extensive study, refused to rule on whether the trust was a grantor trust or whether the transfer

---

[328] DOL Prohibited Transaction Class Exemption No. 92-5, 57 Fed. Reg. 5019 (Feb. 11, 1992); DOL Prohibited Transaction Class Exemption No. 92-6, 57 Fed. Reg. 5190 (Feb. 11, 1992).

[329] IRC §§ 4975(a), 4975(b), 4975(c)(1)(A), 4975(e)(2).

[330] IRC § 101(a)(2).

[331] IRC § 101(a)(2)(B).

[332] The income tax consequences of a sale of an insurance policy to an ILIT are described further in Chapter 12.

[333] Swanson v. Comm'r, 518 F2d 59 (8th Cir. 1975). Note that in this case, however, the insured retained such controls over the trust that the trust property would have been included in his estate had he died. The IRS registered its disapproval of this decision (AOD 1975-351 (July 23, 1975)), but declined to seek certiorari on the case since there was no circuit conflict on this issue.

[334] AOD 1975-351 (July 23, 1975).

[335] Priv. Ltr. Rul. 9413045 (Jan. 4, 1994).

of the policies to the trust qualified as an exception to the transfer-for-value rule because of the grantor trust rules.

[c] Sale by the Plan to Another

The plan could sell the policy to a relative who has an insurable interest in the insured (e.g., the insured's child).[336] In order to avoid the transfer-for-value rules, the person will need to fit one of its exceptions (e.g., a partner of the insured).

[5] Exclusion of Plan-Held Life Insurance From Estate

Excluding life insurance held by a nongrandfathered plan[337] from the insured's estate is an objective that has been the subject of some discussion but no authority. The goal is to maintain life insurance coverage in a qualified plan while providing for estate tax exclusion of the insurance. The concept calls for irrevocably designating a beneficiary, providing in the plan document that the insurance policy cannot be distributed to the participant, and, in certain situations, creating a subtrust in the plan document itself (or in a separate document structured in accordance with plan provisions allowing for such a trust). The subtrust would have an independent trustee to possess all incidents of ownership with respect to life insurance held in the plan. If the beneficiary named by the participant is an irrevocable trust, the trust agreement could specify the plan beneficiaries or give the trustee the ability to choose among a class of beneficiaries.

A discussion of the merits and demerits of such a plan is contained in various articles.[338] There is a serious issue about whether this subtrust plan is consistent with the qualified plan rules, which require the participant to have the right to designate the beneficiary of the plan proceeds (subject to REA spousal rules) and prevent alienation of the participant's rights.

The purchase of a second-to-die policy in the plan is another method of using plan benefits to keep assets out of a couple's estates. The success of this plan involves getting the policy out of the plan before the survivor dies.

---

[336] See Prohibited Transaction Exemption 92-6, a class exemption, holding that a plan can sell a policy it holds on a participant's life if, among other requirements, the sale is to the insured, a relative of the insured, or an employer whose employees are covered by the plan.

[337] See ¶ 14.06[10] above.

[338] E.g., Beverly R. Budin, 826 T.M., Life Ins. III. D. (1994); Falk, "Using Life Insurance in Qualified Retirement Plans," Est. Plan. 357 (Oct. 1996); Jansen, "Section 2042 From Soup to Nuts," ACTEC Notes 24 (1996).

[6] Spousal Issues

In a plan that is subject to the requirements of the Retirement Equity Act, spousal consent may be required to accomplish the appropriate planning.[339]

[7] Additional Reading

A more detailed discussion of the issues, along with some other ideas, is contained in Willms, "Using Qualified Plan Money to Purchase Life Insurance," Journal of the American Society of CLU and ChFc 54 (July 1996).

¶ 14.10 PLANNING WITH ESOPs

This is a very brief overview of employee stock ownership plans (ESOPs). ESOP transactions are quite complex and all parties need competent representation.

An ESOP may be established by a closely held corporation. An owner or family often establishes an ESOP to purchase all or a portion of the family's stock.[340] The family thereby achieves some liquidity, while maintaining control of the company or putting control in friendly hands. Often, this is done on a leveraged basis.

Such a transaction may work as follows. Family Corp. borrows money from a bank. Family Corp. lends this money to the ESOP. The ESOP uses the proceeds of the loan to fund its cash purchase of Family Corp. stock from Dad. Family Corp. will make contributions to the ESOP sufficient to repay the loan. What are the tax effects on each party?

Bank-grandfathered transactions. For loans made before August 21, 1996, under Section 133, the bank can exclude from its taxable income 50 percent of the interest income it earns on the bank loan (translating, normally, into the availability of a lower interest rate to Family Corp.), provided that (1) the terms of the bank loan mirror the terms of the ESOP loan; (2) the loan term does not exceed 15 years; (3) after the transaction, the ESOP owns over 50 percent of Family Corp.; (4) the plan provides for pass-through voting on allocated ESOP shares; and (5) certain other requirements are met.[341] Section 133

---

[339] See ¶ 14.05 above for a discussion.

[340] Note, however, that ESOP trustees can be held liable under ERISA for investing in employer stock when the value of the stock is declining and the employer's financial condition is deteriorating. Moench v. Robertson, 62 F3d 553 (3d Cir. 1995), cert. denied, 116 S. Ct. 917 (1996).

[341] IRC § 133.

has been repealed with respect to loans made after August 21, 1996.[342] Certain refinancings of loans in existence before August 21, 1996, are grandfathered.[343] A loan made pursuant to a binding written contract in effect before June 10, 1996, and at all times thereafter before the loan is made, is also grandfathered.[344]

Dad. If Dad sells enough stock to the ESOP to reduce his ownership to a minority interest, his remaining stock may be subject to minority discounts for gift and estate transfers. If the ESOP uses debt to finance its purchase of the stock, the debt will generally appear on the company's balance sheet, and will reduce the value of the company for purposes of future gifting.

On the income tax front, Dad may be able to report the gain on the sale as a capital gain from a sale or exchange. An ESOP sale may thus avoid the Section 302 dividend treatment that frequently results from a direct redemption of stock by Family Corp.[345]

Alternatively, Dad can elect to defer recognition of gain on the sale of Family Corp. stock if (1) the ESOP holds 30 percent or more of Family Corp.'s stock after the sale and (2) the proceeds of the sale are timely invested in qualified replacement property (generally, securities of domestic corporations other than Family Corp. stock, provided that no corporation had passive investment income for the preceding year that exceeded 25 percent of the corporation's gross receipts).[346]

When the qualified replacement securities are disposed of, gain will generally be recognized.[347] However, gain will not be recognized if the disposition is made as a result of certain reorganizations, Dad's death, Dad's gift of the securities, or another Section 1042 transaction.[348]

The Section 1042 disposition rules generally override other nonrecognition provisions in the Code.[349] For example, Dad's transfer of the replacement securities to a partnership in exchange for a partnership interest will cause recognition of the deferred gain notwithstanding Section 721, which generally exempts contributions to a partnership in return for partnership interests from gain or loss.[350] If ownership of the replacement securities by a partnership is

---

[342] SBJPA § 1602(c)(1).

[343] SBJPA § 1602(c)(2).

[344] SBJPA § 1602(c)(3).

[345] See Chapter 19 on C corporations for an explanation of redemptions. See also Rev. Proc. 87-22, 1987-1 CB 718, for the IRS's ruling guidelines in this area.

[346] IRC § 1042. The qualified replacement property can be transferred to a charitable remainder trust, if Dad wishes to further diversify on a tax-deferred or tax-free basis. The qualified replacement property will take the basis of the Family Corp. stock sold by Dad.

[347] IRC § 1042(e)(1).

[348] IRC § 1042(e).

[349] IRC § 1042(e)(1).

[350] Rev. Rul. 2000-18, 2000-1 CB 847.

desired, Dad should, if possible, first contribute his Family Corporation stock to the partnership, and the partnership may then sell the qualified securities to the ESOP and acquire replacement securities.[351]

If Dad holds the replacement securities until his death, they will receive a new basis at his death.[352] If the replacement securities have not been purchased by the time Dad dies, the estate may still purchase them and delay recognition of gain, but the replacement shares may not receive a new basis.

Participants. The employees of Family Corp. will receive annual allocations of employer stock as the ESOP loan is repaid. However, Dad and certain family members cannot receive allocations if Dad made the Section 1042 deferral election.[353]

ESOP trust. Voting rights on major corporate matters must be given to participants on allocated shares; the ESOP trustee (appointed by Family Corp.'s board) may vote the unallocated shares.[354] If, however, (1) the bank excludes interest income from its taxable income (as described above), or (2) Family Corp. has a class of securities required to be registered under Section 12 of the Securities and Exchange Act of 1934, or exempt from registration under Section 12(g)(2)(H) of that Act, passthrough voting on all matters (including routine board elections) is required.[355]

Family Corp. Family Corp. can (in effect) deduct its repayments of principal on the loan because the repayments will be treated as contributions to the plan.[356] In addition, Family Corp. can generally deduct annual contributions to the plan up to 25 percent of the aggregate participant compensation if the contributions are used by the ESOP to pay principal on the loan.[357] Contributions in excess of the 25 percent limit can be deducted to the extent they are used to pay interest on the loan if certain requirements are met.[358]

Family Corp. can also deduct cash dividends on ESOP stock paid: (1) to participants or their beneficiaries; (2) to the plan and distributed in cash to participants or their beneficiaries within 90 days of the end of the plan year; and (3) as principal or interest on the loan incurred by the ESOP to purchase the stock with respect to which the dividends are paid.[359] Amounts paid by Family

---

[351] Priv. Ltr. Rul. 9846005 (Aug. 6, 1998).

[352] See Priv. Ltr. Rul. 9109024 (Nov. 30, 1990).

[353] See IRC § 409(n).

[354] IRC § 409(e)(5); Rev. Rul. 95-57, 1995-35 IRB 5.

[355] IRC §§ 133(b)(7), 409(e)(2).

[356] IRC §§ 404(k), 415.

[357] IRC § 404(a)(9)(A).

[358] IRC § 404(a)(9)(B).

[359] IRC § 404(k).

Corp. to redeem stock of the participants generally will not constitute deductible dividends.[360]

What are the singular features of an ESOP that might affect a choice to engage in this plan? ESOPs must have certain provisions and features—

Feature #1. A participant who has reached age 55 and has ten years of participation may elect annually to diversify a portion of his account each year over six years (25 percent in the first five years; 50 percent in the sixth year).[361] This is done by offering at least three investment options other than employer stock or by distributing the account balance to be diversified.[362]

Feature #2. Distribution of ESOP benefits must begin (1) within one year after the end of the plan year in which the participant's death, retirement, or disability occurs, or (2) within one year after the end of the fifth plan year following the participant's separation from service, *unless* the participant elects otherwise, the participant resumes employment, or the distribution is attributable to employer stock acquired with the proceeds of an ESOP loan and the loan has not been repaid.[363]

Feature #3. The participant must have a right to demand distribution of benefits in the form of employer securities, unless the employer securities are subject to certain ownership restrictions.[364] If the distributed securities were acquired by the ESOP with the proceeds of an exempt loan and are not publicly traded, their sale by the participant may be subject to a right of first refusal in favor of the ESOP trust, the corporation, or both.[365] If the distributed securities are not readily tradable on an established market, the participant must have the right to require the corporation to repurchase the stock under a fair valuation formula determined by an independent appraiser.[366] If the participant's put right is at an undiscounted value, that factor can be taken into account in determining the value of Family Corp. stock sold to the ESOP.

Feature #4. The ESOP assets must be valued at least once a year.[367] If the assets are not readily tradable, the valuation must be made by an independent appraiser.[368] The ESOP cannot pay more than current fair market value for Family Corp. stock.

---

[360] Tech. Adv. Mem. 9612001 (Aug. 1, 1995); Priv. Ltr. Rul. 9304033 (Nov. 6, 1992).

[361] IRC § 401(a)(28)(B).

[362] IRC § 401(a)(28)(B)(ii).

[363] IRC § 409(o).

[364] IRC §§ 409(h)(1)(A), 409(h)(2).

[365] Treas. Reg. § 54.4975-7(b)(9).

[366] IRC §§ 401(a)(28)(C), 409(h)(1)(B).

[367] Rev. Rul. 80-155, 1980-1 CB 84.

[368] IRC § 401(a)(28)(C).

Practice Pointer: Occasionally, the family will want the ESOP to buy its stock at an undiscounted price, when the stock is being redeemed from other shareholders at a discounted price. While this is not specifically prohibited if the facts and circumstances warrant it, it does raise some questions. Very good documentation of the value should be obtained in such a case, as the penalties for engaging in a prohibited transaction[369] can be severe.[370]

---

[369] E.g., the purchase by the ESOP of stock from a party-in-interest for more than adequate consideration. See ERISA § 1108(e).

[370] IRC § 4975. Plan fiduciaries, such as trustees, can also be personally liable for losses caused to the plan or profits gained by the trustee in ESOP transactions where there is a fiduciary breach, such as a prohibited transaction. See ERISA § 1109(a).

PART IV

Family Business and Investment Entities

CHAPTER 15

Family Business and Investment Entities

¶ 15.01 INTRODUCTION

This chapter serves as an introduction to the part of this book that addresses family-owned entities. The family limited partnership is used as an example in discussing the benefits and drawbacks of family entities in general. The specific issues that must be considered in deciding whether to use a particular entity are found in the chapter devoted to that entity in particular. However, in considering a different entity, the partnership chapter should be consulted as well for its analysis of general benefits and issues applicable to all family-owned entities.

    In any case, the selection and use of a family entity is a significant decision. It must be made with knowledge of the tax and non-tax rules applicable to the entity chosen as well as alternative entities. Most estate planners are not specialists in the income tax laws applicable to business entities in the same sense that other tax lawyers might be. However, estate planners should have at least a nodding acquaintance with the income tax and other laws dealing with the organization of the entity, transfers of interests in the entity, the extraction of money and other assets from the entity, and the general year-to-year taxation of the ordinary activities of the entity. To assist in making a choice of entity, the following chapters briefly summarize these rules, as well as compare the different types of entities.

Some of the advantages of owning interests in common businesses and investments as a unit, rather than as fractional interests, are also listed below, along with a brief comment on other aspects of family entities.

¶ 15.02　ADVANTAGES OF ENTITIES

There are many advantages of owning property in an entity. The following subparagraphs describe these advantages, which are discussed in more detail in other chapters of this book.

[1]　Economies of Scale

Pooling family investments can allow the family members to benefit from economies of scale, such as access to investment advisors who require a minimum amount to invest; access to more expensive investments, if those are desired; lower management fees for larger investment accounts, and so forth.

[2]　Qualification for Special Tax Provisions

Interests in some businesses qualify for special estate tax benefits—for example, Section 6166 (dealing with deferred payout of estate taxes), Section 2032A (dealing with the valuation discounting of farm and ranch property), and Section 303 (dealing with the redemption of corporate stock to pay estate taxes). In appropriate circumstances, an entity can be helpful in qualifying for these benefits as an initial matter, and may be essential in managing the disposition of the property to ensure that unexpected adverse consequences (such as recapture, acceleration of deferred tax, or elimination of further benefits) do not occur after filing the estate tax return. This could happen, for example, if property qualifying for special treatment under Section 2032A or Section 6166 were sold.

[3]　Perpetuation of Family Business

Many entrepreneurs are keenly interested in having the businesses they have built remain in the family. Putting the business in entity format can go a long way toward meeting that goal.

[4] Asset Protection

Certain types of entities protect assets from creditors. Such entities can do this because (1) creditors of the entity may not be able to reach the assets of the entity's owners and (2) creditors of the entity owners may not be able to reach the assets of the entity.

[5] Discounted Values for Entity Interests

Interests in entities may have discounted values for transfer tax purposes.

[6] Unity of Management

Many businesses are difficult (or even impossible) to manage as fractional interests. Entities can centralize management of business assets and enable the people who are knowledgeable about the business to take charge.

Real estate and mineral interests can also be problematic to hold in undivided interests. For example, persons who hold real estate as tenants in common frequently all have the unlimited right to use the property and to rent it to other people, subject to the obligation to share the rent. As another example, oil companies often will not drill a property unless at least 95 percent (or another substantial percentage) of the owners have signed a lease. One ten percent owner could prevent the entire property from becoming productive.

[7] Probate Avoidance

An interest in real estate owned as a tenancy in common will usually require probate in the jurisdiction where the real estate is located when one of the owners dies. If the real estate is held inside an entity, however, the real estate itself will not normally be subject to probate. Of course, the owners' interests in the entity will be subject to probate in the jurisdictions where the owners are domiciled.

Personal property held inside an entity is also not subject to probate. Use of the entity will prevent the necessity of listing the individual assets and debts held inside the entity in the probate records pertaining to an owner. Since probate records are generally available for public inspection, use of an entity can satisfy some privacy concerns.

[8] Coping With Divorce

Jointly owned assets may be subject to division on divorce. Assets held inside an entity will usually not be subject to being awarded to a divorcing spouse unless the assets were conveyed to the entity in violation of the divorcing spouse's marital property rights. The ownership interest in the entity may be subject to division, but the governing documents of the entity can usually be drafted to permit the other owners to buy an ex-spouse out.

¶ 15.03 AVOIDING THE TRAPS

[1] Formalities Must Be Respected

The family should take the entity seriously and administer it in accordance with the requirements of the entity's governing documents and applicable local law. If the family members do not respect the formalities of the entity, do not keep proper books, or if they treat the entity assets as if they were privately owned by the individual entity owners, the entity may afford them little advantage. Such behavior could even serve as the basis of an action for fraud by third parties as well as the IRS. Accordingly, the family must be committed to properly administering a family entity before the entity is formed.

[2] Difficulties With Dynasties

Estate planning often involves putting properties into long-lasting entities. The longer an entity lasts, the more likely it is that a conflict will arise among the family members. Although most experienced estate planners are painfully familiar with this, it is an unusual entrepreneur who is willing to accept the reality of such impending conflicts and plan for their avoidance or resolution. Keeping a family business intact when many people are involved or when the owners do not agree is difficult. In particular, a family business is ripe for conflicts if it is owned by both family members in its employ and others who are not.

Family members who are employed by the business are more likely to want to plow the earnings back into the business rather than make distributions to the owners, pay themselves high salaries and bonuses, establish generous employee benefits programs, and so forth. Even where implementing these decisions is good for the business entity, at some point the nonemployed owners will likely become less than enthusiastic about those choices.

> EXAMPLE: The employed son defends his large bonus on the grounds that the business has been unusually profitable that year due to his personal efforts and that the bonus will be deductible for corporate income tax purposes. His arguments may not sit well with his sister, who owns part of the business but is employed elsewhere. She believes that the increased profitability of the business is due to the fact that previous years' earnings, which she feels should have been distributed to the owners, were left in the entity.

Typically, nonemployed owners want to realize the value of their family business interests, either through distributions of entity earnings or through the sale of such interests. Some, in the effort to realize this value, may mortgage their interests to secure personal loans. And, if they default on their obligations under such loans, lenders may foreclose on their interests, bringing outsiders into the picture. Also, if the business is a pass-through entity for income tax purposes, owners who are paying taxes on entity earnings and not getting distributions may be angry about owning interests which result in negative cash flow to them.

Finally, it must be noted that once the entity passes beyond the brother-sister generation, and on to cousins or more distant collaterals, the familial bond becomes attenuated and these problems can become enormous.

PRACTICE POINTER: If the business owner is willing to think about it, arrangements should be considered (or at least the flexibility should be allowed) to put the business in the hands of the participating family members, and give other family members a chance to realize their equity for a fair value, if they so desire. How is this done? If there are enough other assets to make it possible, the business owner can give or bequeath the business to the involved family members and other assets to the uninvolved members. If there are not enough other assets to do that at the outset, a buy-sell agreement might be implemented so that the uninvolved members can elect to sell or redeem their interests, and/or the involved members can elect to buy out the uninvolved members at a fair price. In order to avoid putting undue pressures on the entity, a sale of a family member's interest to outsiders might be subject to a right of first refusal by the entity and the entity might be permitted to pay for the interest in whole or in part with a note bearing a market rate of interest and payable over a period of years.[1]

[3] Limitations on Transfers

If a family entity is used, estate planning will ultimately involve transfers of interests in the entity and/or distributions from the entity. Before wheeling and dealing with the entity, the planner must be aware of potential limitations.

Restrictions on transfers of interests and/or distributions may exist outside of the entity's governing documents and local law. For example, the entity's loan agreements may prohibit changes in capital structure of a business or may prohibit distributions. This can be especially important if the owner needs distributions to pay tax on his share of a pass-through entity's income.

A transfer can also cause other types of difficulties. For example, a transfer of S corporation stock to a transferee who is an ineligible shareholder can

---

[1] See Ch. 45 on extracting money from entities and Ch. 27 on IRC § 2703 for an analysis of some of the tax issues involved in entering into such an agreement.

terminate the S election. A sale or exchange of over 50 percent of an interest in a partnership can terminate the partnership (a gift, however, will not). Distributions may give rise to taxable income which would not have resulted if the property were held outright. If a business involves licensed professionals, a transferee may be required to be licensed. A change in ownership of a regulated business (e.g., changes in control of a bank, changes in ownership of television stations, changes in ownership of businesses with liquor or gaming licenses) may require permission of a governmental agency.

[4] Equity Recharacterization Issues

Quite different tax results will usually ensue, depending on whether an interest in an entity is characterized as debt or equity. The Internal Revenue Code sets out guidelines for determining when a note or other debt will be recharacterized as equity.[2] Other interests (leases and employment contracts, for example) can also be recharacterized as equity in appropriate circumstances.

¶ 15.04 ADDITIONAL READING

Jerome Manning, Nontax Aspects of Planning for a Family Business, Est. Plan. 345 (Nov./Dec. 1995).

---

[2] IRC § 385.

CHAPTER **16**

Limited Partnerships

¶ 16.01 INTRODUCTION

The family limited partnership is a popular entity used by families to hold their business and investment assets. The family limited partnership is often used by parents and grandparents as a vehicle to transfer assets to younger generations during the older generations' lifetimes and at their deaths. This chapter will elaborate on the tax issues pertaining to family limited partnerships.

There are numerous reasons to establish a partnership to manage family assets as they pass through succeeding generations. These may include:

- Provision of asset management for family members who need/want it;
- Preventing interests in family property from passing to outsiders as a result of death, divorce, or other disposition;
- Protection of family assets from individual creditors of a partner;
- Access to investment managers with minimum account requirements;
- The possibility of negotiating reduced fees with investment managers of large accounts;
- Access to the talents of business managers who want to manage a large business;
- Avoiding the difficulties associated with ownership of fractional interests in property;
- Controlling distributions to preserve wealth for the benefit of the family;
- Changing the nature of real property to personal property and perhaps taking advantage of more favorable state laws (e.g., converting Louisiana real property to personal property of an out-of-state resident to allow dispositions not permitted in Louisiana wills);

- Providing accounting and fund management to the family;
- Centralizing management;
- Avoiding veto power by small owners;
- Facilitating gifts; and
- Providing a vehicle to minimize potential disputes.

To understand the ramifications of a family partnership, it is critical to understand the nature of a partnership interest, and what happens on transfer of a partnership interest. A partnership interest represents two types of rights: economic rights and management rights. Its "economic rights" include the partner's right to be allocated his share of the income, gain, losses, deductions, and credits of a partnership, to receive distributions when they are made, and to receive his share of partnership assets on liquidation. Its "management rights" include the partner's right to vote on issues affecting the partnership as provided in the agreement or under state law and (in the case of a general partner) to operate the partnership business.

Generally, a partner cannot transfer the management rights incident to his partnership interest without the consent of his partners. He usually can, however, transfer the economic rights in the interest—such as, the right to receive distributions from the partnership when and if it makes distributions. The recipient of the economic rights without management rights is an "assignee" of the partnership interest. When a partner transfers a partnership interest which turns into an assignee interest in the hands of the recipient, the transferor-partner may or may not retain the management rights incident to the interest, depending on state law and the partnership agreement. If he transfers his entire economic interest, the management rights, incident to the interest may lapse, or part or all of the remaining partners may be able to terminate the transferor's status as a partner.[1] When the transfer of an interest in a partnership occurs as a result of a partner's death, his interest generally turns into an assignee interest in the hands of his estate. A partner's executor will usually be deemed to hold an assignee interest, although the executor may have whatever powers the partner would have had, so far as necessary to administer the partnership interest.[2]

---

[1] RULPA § 702. For purposes of this chapter, RULPA is the Revised Uniform Limited Partnership Act (1976), 6A ULA 1 (Amended 1985), and UPA is the Uniform Partnership Act, 6 ULA 125 (1914), each of which has been adopted in a large number of states. There are a few states which have not adopted RULPA and UPA, and some states have adopted the 1994 version of the Uniform Partnership Act (6 ULA 1 (1994) (Supp. 1997)). Even those states that have adopted RULPA and UPA have often substantially modified the provisions of the Uniform Acts. Hence, practitioners should always check the partnership law of the applicable state.

[2] RULPA § 705; Texas Revised Uniform Limited Partnership Act (TRULPA) § 7.05 (limited partner's executor). Note that this is a difference between a partnership interest held outright and a partnership interest held by a revocable trust. If the interest is held by a revocable trust, the partner's death does not have a consequence per se in

In this chapter, the transfer of a *partnership* interest refers to a situation in which the transferee becomes a substituted partner with respect to the transferred interest, and the transfer of an *assignee* interest refers to a situation in which the transferee is only an assignee.

This chapter first discusses considerations in designing a partnership, and then explains some important tax ramifications of family partnerships.

¶ 16.02 STRUCTURE OF THE FAMILY LIMITED PARTNERSHIP

If Mom is structuring a family limited partnership, one of the first decisions she must make is who the partners will be.

[1] General Partner(s)

The general partners are responsible for managing the day-to-day affairs of the partnership's business.

[a] Number of General Partners

Should there be more than one general partner? There is no right or wrong answer to this in most cases. Some of the pros and cons of each choice are listed below.

[i] Pros and cons: one general partner. A sole general partner will be the only partner who is legally empowered to manage the partnership's assets. This is an advantage for those who want to maintain control in one person. Any general partner can legally bind the partnership without the consent of the other partners on most matters.[3] This may be true even if the general partner is acting in contravention of the partnership agreement, since a general partner will normally have apparent authority to conduct business on behalf of the partnership. The more general partners a partnership has, the more partners there are who can act on behalf of the partnership in a way contrary to what the other partners would have preferred. However, using only one general partner will avoid management by committee, and thus eliminate daily disagreements among authorized managers over how partnership affairs are conducted.

---

the partnership ownership structure, and the revocable trust will continue as the partner.

[3] RULPA § 403(a); UPA § 9.

Use of a sole general partner can result in a taxable lapse of rights when the general partner ceases to serve, as discussed in ¶ 16.03[3][d] below.

[ii] Pros and cons: more than one general partner. Multiple general partners may be desirable for nontax reasons. If one of the general partners becomes incapacitated, continuity in managing the partnership can be ensured if another general partner is in place to continue the business. In addition, family members may prefer for personal reasons to have more than one general partner. For example, a husband and wife may both wish to act as general partner. Psychological, as well as business, considerations can enter into the decision. Thus, in a case where it is desirable for a junior family member to serve as general partner, parents may want to name both of their children as general partners, rather than seeming to favor one over the other. On one hand, when one junior member of the family acts as general partner, resentment and even conflict can arise when other junior family members who are limited partners do not agree with his decisions. Even if their disagreement with actual decisions is not an issue, the very fact that Dad names Child One as general partner and not Child Two may be hard for Child Two to accept. This can be true regardless of whether both children are actively involved in the business, neither child is actively involved, or one is and one isn't. On the other hand, one child may be in a better position to make good decisions for the business than another.

There may also be tax and stability reasons to select more than one general partner, especially in the case of an individual general partner who will eventually die. On a sole general partner's death, the entity dissolves and will have to be liquidated unless all or, if provided in the partnership agreement, a specified percentage of the limited partners vote to continue the enterprise. Using more than one general partner can help avoid this situation, since the remaining general partners can continue the business without additional limited partner approval, provided that the partnership agreement and state law so allow. Along this line, a partnership interest may be valued at an artificially high value for estate tax purposes if the deceased partner had the right to cause the entity to liquidate.[4] Use of more than one general partner with the right to continue the business can avoid this result.[5]

If there is more than one general partner, the partnership agreement should name one of the general partners as the tax matters partner, who is the partner responsible for communicating with the IRS.[6] Additionally, the partnership agreement may designate one of the general partners as a managing

---

[4] IRC § 2704(a).

[5] See discussion at ¶ 16.03[3][d] below.

[6] See IRC §§ 6223(g), 6231(a)(7); Treas. Reg. § 301.6231(a)(7)-1.

general partner, and delegate certain responsibilities to her alone. Such a designation should be effective as between two parties, but it may not be effective against third parties in the event that a non-managing general partner conducts partnership business in contravention of the agreement without the third party's knowledge.[7]

[b] Powers and Duties of General Partner

How much power can the general partner have? State law usually imposes few restrictions on a general partner's ability to manage the partnership.[8] Many partnership agreements also give broad powers to the general partner, allowing him wide discretion to decide when to make distributions and how to invest the partnership assets. Additionally, the partnership agreement sometimes provides the general partner with additional powers that are not granted by statute.

How much power should the general partner have? From a non-tax point of view, it is important that the general partner be given sufficient breadth of authority to permit him to conduct the partnership business in an efficient manner, but that his authority be restricted with respect to important issues to the extent this makes the limited partners more comfortable. Moreover, the grant of extremely broad powers to general partners may reduce the value of limited partnership interests.[9]

Giving a general partner overly broad powers, however, may have adverse tax implications, particularly where the general partner is making gifts of limited partnership interests.[10] The fiduciary duty owed and carried out by a general partner to a limited partner should prevent gifted limited partnership interests from being brought back into the general partner's estate upon his death.[11] However, if a general partner retains too much control over the partnership and the limited partnership interests, the limited partners may not be respected as such for federal income tax purposes, causing the general partner to be taxed on the limited partners' actual shares of partnership income.[12] Finally, where a general partner is given more control over family partnership matters than would be given to a general partner of a partnership between unrelated parties, any unusual authority or restrictive powers granted

---

[7] UPA § 9(1); see also RULPA § 1105 (providing that UPA governs where RULPA is silent).

[8] RULPA § 403(a); UPA §§ 9–10.

[9] See ¶ 16.03[1] below.

[10] See ¶¶ 16.03[3][c], 16.03[4] and 16.04[7][a].

[11] See IRC §§ 2036(a)(2), 2038(a)(1) and discussion at ¶ 16.03[4] below.

[12] See Treas. Reg. § 1.704-1(e)(2) and discussion at ¶ 16.04[7][a] below.

to the general partner may be ignored in valuing gifted limited partnership interests for transfer tax purposes.[13]

A general partner has duties as well as powers. For example, a general partner acts in a fiduciary capacity with respect to the limited partners.[14] One of her fiduciary duties is the duty of loyalty.[15] Generally speaking, even if the partnership agreement gives the general partner broad discretion regarding management and distributions, she should have a legitimate business reason for her decisions.[16] If the general partner withholds distributions from some partners while making distributions to other partners, or if the general partner withholds all distributions for reasons not related to the partnership business, the general partner may be in breach of her fiduciary duty.[17] If the family attempts to provide in the agreement that the general partner owes no fiduciary duty to the limited partners, the provision may not be respected under state law. It may also cause transfer tax problems when limited partnership interests are being transferred.[18]

[c] Extent of General Partner's Interest

A partner can be both a general partner and limited partner in the same partnership. What percentage of the partnership should the general partner hold as general partner (in addition to any interest he has as limited partner)? In pre-"check-the-box" days, in order to get a ruling that an entity qualified as a partnership, the general partner or partners at all times had to have in the aggregate at least one percent of the interests (including limited partnership

---

[13] See IRC §§ 2703(a)(2), 2703(b) and discussion at ¶ 16.03[3][c] above.

[14] LSP Inv. Partnership v. Bennett (In re Bennett), 989 F2d 779, 787, 790 (5th Cir. 1992), opinion amended per curiam on reh'g, No. 91-1059, 1993 US App. LEXIS 19366 (5th Cir. 1993), cert. denied, 114 S. Ct. 601 (1993); Palmer v. Fuqua, 641 F2d 1146, 1155 (5th Cir. 1981); Fleck v. Cablevision VII, Inc., 763 F. Supp. 622, 627 (DDC 1991); Ayerslee Corp., N.V. v. Overlook Sponsor Corp., 618 F. Supp. 1398, 1403 (SDNY 1985), aff'd, 800 F2d 1127 (2d Cir. 1986); Crenshaw v. Swenson, 611 SW2d 886, 890 (Tex. Civ. App.—Austin 1980, writ ref'd n.r.e.); see also Huffington v. Upchurch, 532 SW2d 576, 579 (Tex. 1976) (managing partner of general partnership owes co-partners one of highest fiduciary duties recognized in the law).

[15] I Alan R. Bromberg & Larry E. Ribstein, Partnership (1988).

[16] See, e.g., Moore v. Tristar Oil & Gas Corp., 528 F. Supp. 296, 312–314 (SDNY 1981); Wyler v. Feuer, 149 Cal. Rptr. 626, 632-33 (Cal. Ct. App. 1978).

[17] See Washington Medical Ctr., Inc. v. Holle, 573 A2d 1269, 1274–1276 (DC 1990) (managing partner's use of proceeds of sale of partnership asset to satisfy its own creditors, thereby making distributions to himself while not paying partner his distributive share, was breach of fiduciary duty).

[18] See discussion at ¶¶ 16.03[3][c] and 16.03[4] below.

interests held by the general partners) in each item of partnership income, gain, loss, deduction or credit.[19]

[d] Who Should Be (or Control) the General Partner

Should Mom be or control the general partner of the family partnership? Or is she better off being just a limited partner? If Mom is contributing a significant portion of the partnership property, she may prefer to be the general partner, both to simplify administration and to give her control over partnership assets. Similarly, if Mom and Dad are contributing a family business that they manage, one or both of them may want to act as general partner so that they can remain the decision makers with respect to the business.

If Mom and Dad are getting on in years, they may wish to form a family limited partnership without retaining the sole responsibility of managing the partnership. In such an instance, they might ask a junior family member to act as a co-general partner, while the older family members are still there to show her the ropes, or as the sole general partner, if the junior person already knows the ropes. This arrangement can be helpful in passing management of the family business or investments to younger family members, helping the partnership operate smoothly during its initial years, and avoiding certain transfer tax pitfalls if and when partnership interests are transferred by Mom and Dad.[20] As mentioned above, Mom and Dad might want to think about the family dynamics in deciding which junior members would make good general partners.

If Mom is concerned with asset protection, the most conservative strategy suggests that neither she nor Dad should be a general partner or the owner of an entity general partner.[21] In such a case, another family member, a corporation owned by other family members, or a trust could act as general partner. A trusted unrelated individual could also be selected (or a corporation wholly owned by that individual if he wishes to limit the extent of his liability). A corporate general partner can then hire one of the family members as president, although this may entail certain risks (depending on the other features of the partnership and the corporation) if asset protection is an objective.[22]

There also can be certain estate tax ramifications where an individual owns both a general partnership interest and a limited partnership interest.[23]

---

[19] Rev. Proc. 89-12, 1989-1 CB 798. It is not clear to what extent this sort of provision would still apply after the check-the-box rules. We'll assume it is still relevant for purposes of this chapter.

[20] See discussion at ¶ 16.03[3][d] below.

[21] See discussion at Ch. 53.

[22] See discussion at Ch. 53.

[23] See discussion at ¶ 16.03[3][d] below.

If the family members decide to use a corporate general partner, they must next decide who will own the corporation. One option is for the corporate general partner to be wholly owned by the individual who would otherwise have acted as general partner had a corporation not been selected. If there are any transfer tax problems with the individual's holding the general partnership interest, however, the interposition of her wholly owned corporation as general partner may not help matters.[24]

[e] Individual or Entity General Partner

Should the general partner be an individual or an entity? There are advantages and disadvantages to each approach, as well as special rules to consider.

[i] **Individual as general partner.** The general partner, in contrast with the limited partners, is personally liable for partnership debts.[25] Depending on the nature of the partnership business, this can affect whether an individual or entity would be the best choice as general partner.

Having an individual as general partner may not be a problem if the partnership will hold only passive investments and is expected to incur only minimal debt. However, if the partnership is expected to have sizable recourse debt or if the partnership property is such that tort liabilities could be a problem, an individual may not want to be the general partner. Also, where the partnership is actively involved in a business, an individual will probably not want to act as general partner if the business might create unforeseen partnership liabilities down the road. In such a case, selecting a corporation or other limited liability entity as general partner may be a good option.

EXAMPLE: Mom wants to contribute a sole proprietorship that manufactures baby strollers to limited partnership A. Mom feels that the nature of the business leaves it open to a personal injury suit. Hence, she may want to use a corporate or limited liability company general partner of partnership A. If partnership B is expected to hold only marketable securities, Mom might feel comfortable acting as a general partner of partnership B herself.

[ii] **Corporation as general partner.** Assuming the formalities of the corporate entity are respected, using only a corporate general partner eliminates automatic general liability of any individual for partnership obligations. Part-

---

[24] See, e.g., Treas. Reg. § 25.2701-6 (generally providing that for purposes of valuing certain transfers of property between family members, an individual who has an interest in a corporation, partnership, estate or trust will be treated as directly holding property owned by such entity); see also discussion at ¶ 16.03[4] below.

[25] RULPA § 403(b); UPA § 15.

nership creditors who pursue the corporate partner should generally be limited to the corporate general partner's assets and, unless its shareholders have disregarded the corporate form, should not generally be able to reach the assets of the shareholders.

Using a corporate general partner can also help simplify the transition of partnership management. An individual may die while acting as general partner. If no successor general partner is named in the agreement, the limited partners will have to formally agree to continue the partnership and choose a new general partner.[26] In contrast, a corporate general partner can continue perpetually. On the death of a stockholder, the corporation will continue to act as general partner. Although there are other circumstances (e.g., bankruptcy) in which a corporation may cease to be general partner, many of these circumstances apply to individual general partners as well.[27]

Tax and nontax consequences of choosing an individual or a corporate general partner can sometimes conflict, making the choice difficult. A sole individual general partner's death will terminate the management rights attributable to his interest, so that his potential successors will not automatically be able to step into his shoes.[28] A lapse of his management rights can result in a taxable transfer.[29] As a corporate general partner's management rights do not necessarily lapse on the death of a stockholder, no lapse that could create a deemed taxable transfer should occur. However, if the corporate general partner could cause the liquidation of the entity, then the estate tax valuation of the stock will reflect that fact. Also, the persons who succeed to the deceased stockholder's interest (e.g., his wife and children) will control the corporate general partner (and the partnership, if the corporation is the sole general partner) unless the partnership agreement provides that a change in the stock ownership of the general partner is deemed a withdrawal (which may result in a lapse).

Using a corporate general partner can have asset protection ramifications as well. An individual general partner's creditors will not usually be able to exercise the management rights of the partner and will often be limited to obtaining a charging order. In contrast, if an individual stockholder's creditors seize her corporate stock, they will assume the partnership management rights associated with ownership of the stock, unless the partnership agreement prohibits this with a change-of-ownership clause. A corporate general partner that is controlled by one family member therefore may actually be worse for asset protection purposes than if the individual herself were a general partner.

Finally, if the same person owns all of the stock or otherwise controls the corporate general partner as well as limited partnership interests, this could

---

[26] RULPA § 801(4).

[27] See discussion at ¶ 16.02[1][f][i] below.

[28] RULPA § 402(6)(i).

[29] See IRC § 2704(a) and discussion at ¶ 16.03[3][d][i] below.

affect whether the partnership is considered a partnership for certain state tax purposes and whether the limited partners are respected as such for federal income tax purposes.[30]

A corporate general partner may need to be substantially capitalized for its partnership to be classified as a partnership for certain state tax purposes, particularly if the partnership agreement does not prohibit partners from transferring their interests.[31] Moreover, capitalization is also desirable from a liability standpoint, in that creditors may find it easier to "pierce the corporate veil" of a shell corporation to reach the assets of the shareholders.

[iii] Limited liability company general partner. Using a limited liability company (LLC) as general partner can offer some of the same advantages as a corporate general partner (e.g., no single individual should be liable for partnership obligations). However, smooth transition of partnership management, an advantage with a corporate general partner, may not be quite as smooth with an LLC general partner. Like general partnerships, LLCs typically dissolve on the death or other withdrawal of a member, unless the other members agree to continue the business of the LLC.[32] Where family members own the LLC, a dissolution without continuation of the LLC may result in an unexpected taxable transfer due to a deemed lapse of the general partner's management rights.[33] Using an LLC as general partner will necessitate deciding who will be members of the LLC, as well as whether the LLC will be member-managed or manager-managed. An LLC will ordinarily not be taxed as a corporation for federal income tax purposes.[34]

[iv] Trust general partner. Another alternative is having a trust for the benefit of family members act as general partner. Use of a trust general partner (like a corporate general partner) can help limit the liability of individual family members for partnership debts.

If family trusts funded with other assets will be limited partners, it may be preferable to use a different trust as general partner. This will insulate large trusts containing other assets from liability for partnership debts and, in states with the old federal tax classification system, help ensure that the partnership

---

[30] See discussion at 16.04[7][a] below.

[31] See discussion at ¶ 16.04[2] below.

[32] See, e.g., Texas Limited Liability Company Act, Tex. Rev. Civ. Stat. Ann. art. 1528n, art. 6.01 (West Supp. 1996). Some states allow the members to agree in advance that the LLC will not dissolve on the death or withdrawal of a member. Such an agreement can be an issue in a state which does not use the federal check-the-box system for classification of entities, and may be ignored under IRC §§ 2703 or 2704. See Chs. 26 and 27 on the latter two points.

[33] See IRC § 2704(a) and discussion at ¶ 16.03[3][d][i] below.

[34] See Ch. 17 on LLCs for a more detailed discussion of the ins and outs of LLCs.

will be respected as such.[35] If asset protection is a goal of one of the family members, it is better if neither the person seeking asset protection nor his spouse is the trustee of the trust general partner.[36]

Like a corporation, a trust general partner can offer better continuity of partnership management than an individual general partner. The death or resignation of the trustee does not generally cause the partnership to dissolve.[37]

PRACTICE POINTER: If a trustee distributes a general partnership interest to a trust beneficiary, the distribution constitutes an assignment of the partnership interest.[38] The trust beneficiary will consequently be an assignee rather than a general partner, although he could be admitted as a general or limited partner with the consent of the other partners or if permitted by the agreement.[39] This aspect of partnership law is easy to miss. In a situation where a goal is to keep the interests of two different branches of the family equal, and trusts are being used, the trustee and the family should think about the consequences of distributing a partnership interest. If Brother's Trust and Sister's Trust each own 50 percent of the partnership and Brother's Trust terminates, Brother will have an assignee interest and Sister's Trust will keep all the management rights. The family members could consider providing in the partnership agreement that a distributee from a trust have (at a minimum) the right to be admitted as a limited partner (not leaving Brother, for example, in assignee status).

[f] Withdrawal and Assignment Provisions

[1] Event of withdrawal

[A] *General partner's voluntary withdrawal and assignment.* A general partner may withdraw from the partnership at any time by giving written notice to the other partners.[40] Even if the partnership agreement prohibits a general partner from withdrawing, a general partner still has the power to

---

[35] See discussion at ¶ 16.04[2] below.

[36] See discussion at Ch. 53.

[37] RULPA § 402(7).

[38] In addition, if a trust is a general partner, the termination of the trust (but not the substitution of a new trustee) will constitute a withdrawal of the trust general partner and trigger a dissolution of the partnership, unless one of the exceptions to dissolution is met. See RULPA §§ 402(2), 402(7), 702, 801(4) and discussion at ¶ 16.02[1][f][ii] below; cf. RULPA § 402(10) (providing that where an estate is general partner, the distribution of the estate's entire interest in the partnership will be considered a withdrawal unless the other partners consent otherwise at the time).

[39] RULPA §§ 702, 704.

[40] RULPA § 602.

withdraw in contravention of the agreement. In such a case, the partnership may recover damages from the withdrawing general partner for breach of the partnership agreement and offset these damages against the amount otherwise distributable to the general partner.[41]

RULPA allows a general partner to assign his interest in profits and his right to distributions, but not his management rights.[42] A general partner who assigns only part of his economic interest will retain his management powers, and thus continue to act as general partner,[43] unless the partnership agreement provides otherwise. A general partner who assigns all of his economic interest will cease to be a partner, and will be treated as having withdrawn, unless all remaining partners specifically consent otherwise.[44]

The assignee of the general partner will not automatically become a general partner, but will take an assignee interest. He can become a general or limited partner only if all of the other partners consent or if the partnership agreement permits the assignor to make the assignee a limited partner (and the assignor does so).[45] However, the assignee will not be entitled to exercise the assigning general partner's management powers even if the assignee is admitted as a limited partner.

[B] *General partner's involuntary withdrawal.* Unless the partnership agreement provides otherwise or the other partners consent in writing, a general partner will be deemed to have withdrawn as general partner if (1) the general partner: makes an assignment for the benefit of creditors; files a bankruptcy petition; is declared bankrupt or insolvent; seeks reorganization, arrangement, composition, readjustment, liquidation, dissolution or similar relief; files a pleading in one of the above-described proceedings which fails to contest the material allegations of the petition; or seeks, consents to, or acquiesces in the appointment, of a trustee, receiver, or liquidator of the general partner or of all or any substantial part of his properties; or (2) a proceeding described in (1) above has not been dismissed, vacated or stayed within a specified period of time.[46]

The partnership agreement can also provide that the general partner will be removed on the occurrence of certain other events unless the other partners

---

[41] RULPA § 602; J. Gallison, Partnership Law and Practice § 19.05 (McGraw-Hill, Inc. 1994).

[42] See RULPA §§ 101(10), 702.

[43] See RULPA §§ 402(2), 702.

[44] RULPA §§ 402(2), 702. Some state laws provide that the assignor partner will remain a partner unless the other partners terminate his status.

[45] RULPA §§ 702, 704.

[46] RULPA §§ 402(4), 402(5).

consent to his remaining as general partner.[47] One such event that families may want to provide for is divorce. For example, if the general partner is the spouse of a family member and the two become divorced, the other family members may not want the former spouse to continue to act as general partner. This and similar concerns can be addressed in an agreement that has been tailored to suit the family's needs.

Unless the partnership agreement provides otherwise, an individual general partner who dies or is declared incompetent will generally be treated as withdrawing unless the other partners consent otherwise at the time.[48] Also, unless otherwise agreed in the partnership agreement or by consent of all partners, a trust general partner will be deemed to have withdrawn on termination of the trust (but not substitution of a successor trustee).[49] As mentioned above, the beneficiaries of the trust will not automatically become general partners in place of the trustee. A corporate general partner is deemed to have withdrawn when the corporation dissolves or its charter is revoked, unless the other partners consent otherwise in the agreement or at the time of withdrawal.[50]

What happens in the above situations if the other partners consent so that a particular event is not considered a withdrawal? Interestingly, there is not always a very clear answer to this question. For example, in the case of a general partner's incompetency, does such a consent cause his personal representative to become the general partner? Or does it mean that the incompetent person remains a general partner, with no legal ability to exercise his rights? These are interesting conundrums. But, all can be avoided if the partners clearly express their intent in their consent or agreement.

[ii] Effects of General Partner's Withdrawal.

[A] *Rights of general partner.* Except as otherwise provided under local law, a withdrawing general partner is entitled to receive any distribution to which she is entitled under the partnership agreement.[51] In addition, unless the partnership agreement provides otherwise, the withdrawing general partner is entitled to receive (within a reasonable time after withdrawal) the fair value of her interest in the partnership as of the date of withdrawal based upon her right to share in distributions.[52] These amounts may be reduced by dam-

---

[47] RULPA § 402(3).

[48] RULPA § 402(6).

[49] RULPA § 402(7).

[50] RULPA § 402(9).

[51] RULPA § 604.

[52] RULPA § 604. Where the partnership business is continued, some states give the other partners the option to convert the withdrawing general partner's interest into

ages payable to the partnership if the withdrawal constitutes a breach of the partnership agreement.[53] These amounts may also be reduced where partnership liabilities are sufficient to warrant this.[54]

[B] *Dissolution and winding up.* The withdrawal of a general partner will cause the partnership to dissolve and its affairs to be wound up unless: (1) there is at least one other general partner, the partnership agreement permits the business of the partnership to be continued by the other general partner, and she does so, or (2) within 90 days of the withdrawal, all partners (or a lesser percentage of partners, if provided by the agreement) agree in writing to continue the business of the partnership and to appoint one or more new general partners, if necessary or desired.[55]

PRACTICE POINTER: A decision point in each partnership is what percentage of partners is required to continue the business of the partnership after a general partner's withdrawal, and (if relevant) what percentage of votes it takes to convert the interest of a withdrawing general partner to that of a limited partner. The percentage should be at least 51 percent of the limited partners for purposes of helping ensure that the partnership is classified as a partnership for state tax purposes, if state tax which depends on the pre-check-the-box rules for entity classification is an issue.[56] A percentage which is less than that specified in the default rule under state law may be ignored for transfer tax purposes under Section 2704(b).

Where a general partner withdraws and neither of the above exceptions applies, then, except as otherwise provided in the partnership agreement, the general partners (other than those who have wrongfully caused the partnership to dissolve) or the limited partners (if there are no general partners except those who have wrongfully caused dissolution) may wind up the partnership's affairs.[57] Alternatively, a court of competent jurisdiction may wind up a dissolved partnership's affairs upon application of any partner or his legal representative or an assignee under certain circumstances.[58]

---

a limited partnership interest rather than paying him the fair value of his interest. See, e.g., Texas Revised Limited Partnership Act, Tex. Rev. Civ. Stat. Ann. art. 6132a-1, § 6.02(b)(1) (West Supp. 1996).

[53] RULPA § 602.

[54] RULPA § 607.

[55] RULPA § 801(4).

[56] Rev. Proc. 89-12, 1989-1 CB 798.

[57] RULPA § 803.

[58] RULPA § 803.

[2] Limited Partners

Deciding who should be a limited partner is also very important.

[a] Rights and Duties of Limited Partners

Limited partners will have whatever rights are given to them under the partnership agreement. Such rights vary from agreement to agreement, and typically consist of the right to vote on certain important partnership matters.[59] For example, an agreement might provide that a certain percentage of the limited partners must consent to the selection of a new general partner, to the sale of substantially all of the partnership assets, or to the partnership's borrowing funds in excess of a certain percentage of the value of the partnership's assets.[60] The nature of the rights given to the limited partners will depend on the family's circumstances and the goals the family has in mind in entering into the partnership. If the limited partners have too many rights, however, they may lose their limited liability.[61] On the other hand, if they have too few rights, the partnership itself may come under attack as not being reflective of third-party agreements, and the limited partners' interests may be valued for transfer tax purposes as if they have more rights than they actually have.[62]

PRACTICE POINTER: In deciding what rights should be given to the limited partners of a family partnership, a good plan is to start with the applicable state partnership law, and to make changes (i.e., add, modify, or delete provisions) only if such changes are important enough in the particular situation to outweigh the possibility that they may be ignored for certain tax purposes, and other possible disadvantages.

Limited partners are entitled to inspect and copy partnership records and, upon reasonable demand to the general partners, to obtain true and full information regarding the state of the business and the financial condition of the partnership, a copy of the partnership's income tax returns promptly after they are available, and whatever other information regarding the affairs of the partnership that is just and reasonable for them to have.[63]

A limited partner has the right to seek judicial dissolution from a court of competent jurisdiction if it is not reasonably practicable to carry on the partnership business in conformity with the partnership agreement.[64]

---

[59] See RULPA § 302.

[60] Cf. RULPA § 303(b)(6).

[61] See RULPA § 303(a).

[62] See IRC § 2703 and discussion at ¶ 16.03[3][c] below.

[63] RULPA § 305.

[64] RULPA § 802 (this authority is also given to a general partner).

[b] Liability of Limited Partners for Entity Debts

Limited partners are called "limited" because their liability for partnership debts is usually limited to their interest in the partnership.[65] This rule does not apply where a limited partner is also acting as a general partner.[66] If a limited partner participates in the control of the partnership business, he may be treated as a general partner and thus lose his limited liability.[67]

Rights given to the limited partners under state law, however, will not jeopardize the limited partners' limited liability. Also, if it is desirable for the limited partners to have other types of powers or greater involvement in the partnership business than they might otherwise have, the general partner can employ them on behalf of the partnership without causing the limited partners to lose their limited liability.[68]

[c] Extent of Limited Partners' Interest

The limited partners will own whatever interest in the partnership is not owned by the general partners (and assignees of partnership interests, if any). In a case where the family wants the general partner(s) to have the minimum interest, the limited partners in the aggregate will usually own 99 percent of the partnership, and the general partner(s) will own one percent.[69]

[d] Identity of Limited Partners

Often, senior family members will be the initial limited partners of a family limited partnership (and possibly, the general partners, as well). The senior family members can then make gifts of limited partnership interests to junior family members or to trusts for the benefit of junior family members. Alternatively, junior family members or their trusts may be limited partners from the partnership's inception. Other relatives, in-laws, charities, friends, business associates, and trusts may also be limited partners.

Should the limited partners be individuals or trusts? Let's consider this question in the following subsections.

[i] Using individuals as limited partners. Making transfers of limited

---

[65] RULPA § 303(a).

[66] RULPA § 303(a).

[67] RULPA § 303(a).

[68] See RULPA § 303(b)(1).

[69] Rev. Proc. 89-12, 1989-1 CB 798. The one percent was required to obtain a ruling under pre-check-the-box law; the requirement may still be relevant, since the revenue procedures dealing with classification issues were only obsoleted insofar as they related to application of the old four-factor test. We'll assume here that it is.

partnership interests to individuals rather than trusts has the advantage of simplicity, and may be attractive for families who are averse to the use of trusts or who wish to limit the number of separate entities involved in the partnership. In addition, there may be business reasons for certain individuals to hold limited partnership interests directly. For example, where a family business that is a franchise has been transferred to the partnership, the franchisor may require that certain persons employed by the business have direct ownership interests in the partnership.

Gifts to individuals may also be made where families do not want to bother with establishing trusts for such persons, believing that they have no management rights. Giving outright gifts of limited partnership interests can be problematic, however, for reasons such as the following:

- A limited partner may have the right under the partnership agreement to vote on certain partnership issues and, depending on the partnership agreement, may effectively have a veto power over major partnership actions.

- It is easy to lose contact with unrelated individual partners over the years.

- An individual limited partner could become incompetent, lose interest, adopt an incompatible view with the other partners, become insolvent, or die.

- If the limited partner is a business associate of the general partner, he and the general partner may have a subsequent falling out or part ways for other reasons.

- If the limited partner is a spouse or in-law of a family member, a divorce can be detrimental to the operation of the partnership.

- If the general partner requests additional capital contributions from the partners to pay partnership liabilities, and the partnership agreement obligates limited partners to either make such contributions or forfeit their interests (a provision which may be desirable where a family business has been transferred to the partnership), this kind of obligation may become troublesome for certain individual limited partners.

- In certain situations, it may be desirable to make distributions to some partners and not others. Making a selective distribution among the partners raises a number of issues.[70] If the partners were trusts rather than individuals, the distributions could be made to all partners, but

---

[70] A non-pro rata distribution may constitute a breach of the partnership agreement, or of the general partner's fiduciary duty. Even if it is permitted, a non-pro rata

the money would not necessarily have to be distributed from the trust to the individual beneficiary.

- Interests of minors can cause court involvement.

EXAMPLE: Mom forms a partnership with her children and transfers the family business to the partnership. Mom gives a 10 percent limited partnership interest to each of her grandchildren, some of whom are minors. Unrelated Party offers to buy the business, which is the partnership's only asset. The partnership agreement provides that the limited partners must consent to a sale of substantially all of the partnership assets. Depending on the particular state law governing the partnership, Mom may have to go to court to have a guardian appointed for her minor grandchildren so that they may effectively consent to the sale.

PRACTICE POINTER: Of course, there can also be good reasons to involve individual partners directly; the issues simply need to be considered, and they often are not, under the erroneous assumption that a limited partner has no management rights. In many cases, trusts or other controlled interests for those persons will be appropriate. If it is best to have unrelated parties own interests directly, then a buy-sell agreement, including rights of first refusal, mandatory redemptions and call options, may be desirable. In structuring such an agreement, the effects of Section 2703, which provides special rules governing transfers that are subject to buy-sell agreements, should be considered.[71] In addition, providing a right of first refusal can impact whether the partnership is treated as such for certain state tax purposes.[72]

[ii] Using trusts as limited partners. Trusts offer many advantages over individual donees, although they also add complexity to the plan. A trust limited partner is a suitable vehicle for managing the limited partnership interests themselves. Mom can be trustee of limited partner trusts for the benefit of her descendants.[73]

---

distribution will reduce the donee partner's capital account disproportionately, thus lowering the donee's share in certain partnership items.

[71] See discussion at ¶ 16.03[3][c] below.

[72] See ¶ 16.04[2] below.

[73] Of course, if Mom acts as trustee, the trust should be structured so that its assets will not be included in Mom's estate and possibly so that its income will not be taxable to Mom. See IRC §§ 671-679, 2036.

PRACTICE POINTER: To help ensure that the partnership is treated as a partnership if asset protection and other non-tax issues arise, and that the trust partners are treated as the "real" owners of their interests for income tax purposes, it is preferable that the same person does not act as both general partner and trustee of the limited partner trusts.[74] If Mom wants to be general partner, she may want to ask a trusted friend or advisor to serve as trustee of limited partner trusts. If Mom prefers to act as trustee, she might use a general partner other than herself or an entity she controls.

Trusts can provide other benefits, as well. Gifts to trusts, and in particular dynastic trusts, can offer greater transfer tax savings than outright gifts. In addition, if Mom would like her family and friends to share in the partnership without actually making them limited partners, a discretionary trust for the benefit of such persons can be useful. If such a trust is desirable, Mom may want to select an independent person to act as the trustee in control of discretionary distributions if she does not want to be taxed on the trust's income under the grantor trust rules.[75] Finally, if Mom has young children, children who are not able to handle money well, or children with special needs (or grandchildren or other descendants who fall into any of these categories), a trust may be preferred, particularly where those limited partners have substantial voting rights or are expected to receive regular distributions of profits from the partnership.

[e] Withdrawal and Assignment Provisions

[i] Limited partner's withdrawal or assignment. A limited partner may withdraw from the partnership upon the occurrence of events specified in the partnership agreement and in accordance with the terms of the agreement.[76] If the partnership agreement does not specify a time or event after which a limited partner may withdraw or a definite time for the dissolution and winding up of the partnership, a limited partner may withdraw upon six months' notice to each general partner.[77] To prevent a limited partner from being able to withdraw upon six months' notice, many family limited partnership agreements provide that the partnership will automatically dissolve after a certain period of time

---

[74] See IRC § 704(e)(1); Treas. Reg. § 1.704-1(e)(2)(vii); Ginsberg v. Comm'r, 502 F2d 965 (6th Cir. 1974); Krause v. Comm'r, 497 F2d 1109 (6th Cir. 1974), cert. denied, 419 US 1108 (1975); Reddig v. Comm'r, 30 TC 1382, 1394-1395 (1958); Offord v. Comm'r, 1961 PH TC Memo. ¶ 61,159, 20 TCM (CCH) 797, 802-803 (1961); see also discussion at ¶¶ 16.04[2] and 16.04[7][a] below.

[75] IRC §§ 671, 674(c).

[76] RULPA § 603.

[77] RULPA § 603. Some states do not provide a withdrawal right.

(e.g., 40 years). Some have speculated that such a provision may cause transfer tax problems under Section 2704(b), and some have speculated that it helps avoid such problems.[78] The IRS has taken the position that such a provision would be ignored under Section 2704.[79]

State law generally allows a limited partner to assign the economic rights incident to her interests. The assignee, however, will generally become a substitute limited partner only if the assignor grants the assignee the management rights incident to the assigned interest and the partnership agreement allows this or all partners consent.[80] Note that this means that where an estate or trust holds a limited partnership interest and the fiduciary distributes that interest to a beneficiary, the beneficiary will not automatically become a limited partner. It may therefore be desirable to provide in the partnership agreement that on certain types of transfers of partnership interests (such as trust distributions), the transferor can designate that the transferee will automatically become a limited partner.[81]

Family limited partnership agreements often further restrict a limited partner's ability to transfer her interest. This may be done to ensure that the partnership will be treated as such for certain state tax purposes (by avoiding the corporate characteristic of free transferability of interests),[82] for creditor protection reasons, to prevent non-family members from participating in the partnership, as well as for other reasons.

A partnership agreement may (1) prohibit transfers of limited partnership interests (subject to the validity under local law of restraints on alienation), (2) permit transfers only to family members or trusts for family members, (3) require the consent of the general partners or the other partners to transfer an interest, (4) treat an attempt to transfer a partnership interest as an event of default (and thereby subject the transferor to a redemption of her interest), (5) provide the other partners with a right of first refusal when one partner proposes to transfer her interest, or (6) any combination of the above. When structuring the partnership and restricting a limited partner's ability to transfer her interest or withdraw, it is important to keep in mind both the enforceability of such restrictions under local law and the transfer tax effects of Chapter 14 of the Internal Revenue Code.[83] In addition, restrictions on transferability of a partner's interest may cause her not to be considered a

---

[78] See discussions at ¶ 16.03[3][d] below and Ch. 26.

[79] E.g., Tech. Adv. Mem. 9723009 (Feb. 24, 1997), Tech. Adv. Mem. 9725002 (Mar. 3, 1997).

[80] RULPA § 704(a).

[81] Such a provision may impact whether the partnership is treated as such for certain state tax purposes. See ¶ 16.04[2] below.

[82] See discussion at ¶ 16.04[2] below.

[83] See discussion at ¶¶ 16.03[3][c] and 16.03[3][d] below.

partner for federal income tax purposes[84] or prevent gifts of partnership interests from qualifying for the gift tax annual exclusion.[85]

[ii] Effects of limited partner's withdrawal.

[A] *Rights of limited partner.* Except as otherwise provided by state law, a withdrawing limited partner is entitled to receive any distribution to which he is entitled under the partnership agreement and, except as otherwise provided in the agreement, is entitled to receive, within a reasonable time after withdrawal, the fair value of his interest in the partnership as of the date of withdrawal.[86] However, a partner may not receive a distribution to the extent that the distribution will cause partnership liabilities to exceed the fair value of partnership assets.[87] Moreover, under certain circumstances, a partner may be compelled to return distributions representing a return of his contribution if necessary to discharge any liability the partnership incurred while the contribution was held by the partnership.[88]

[B] *Dissolution.* A limited partner's withdrawal does not ordinarily cause the partnership to dissolve. As mentioned above, however, a limited partner may seek judicial dissolution where the partnership business cannot be carried out[89] or where the general partner has breached her fiduciary duty.

[3] Funding

What assets should be used to fund a family limited partnership? Under most state laws, a limited partnership must carry on a business for profit.[90] The Internal Revenue Code provides a similar rule.[91] Business and investment assets are therefore generally the best choice. Marketable securities and other

---

[84] See discussion at ¶ 16.04[7][a] below.

[85] See IRC § 2503(b); Treas. Reg. § 25.2503-3.

[86] RULPA § 604.

[87] RULPA § 607.

[88] RULPA § 608.

[89] RULPA § 802.

[90] UPA § 6. "Business," for state law purposes, should include investments for profit and, indeed, investment partnerships are commonplace.

[91] IRC § 7701(a)(2) (partnership must carry on a business, financial operation, or venture).

liquid assets should be fine. Special income tax rules relating to in-kind contributions must be kept in mind.[92]

Funding a family limited partnership with non-business assets which are used frequently for personal purposes is not recommended. Use of such personal assets, when combined with other factors, may result in the partnership being disregarded in whole or in part.[93]

Where asset protection is desired, contribution of personal assets that the contributor continues to use may also be a problem. For example, certain personal assets held by an individual might be exempt from creditors under state law. Transfer of such assets (such as, a partner's homestead) to a partnership may result in the loss of this exemption. In addition, the transfer of non-exempt assets may be viewed as a fraudulent transfer; where the contributor continues to use the assets, this may invoke the continuing concealment doctrine.[94]

If a partner or other person does make personal use of any of the partnership assets, some of the above problems may be avoided if the partnership is fully compensated for their use.

¶ 16.03 TRANSFER TAXATION OF INTERESTS IN FAMILY PARTNERSHIPS

Making gifts of limited partnership interests can be a good way to utilize a client's unified credit,[95] generation-skipping transfer tax exemption,[96] and annual exclusion.[97] Taxable gifts of limited partnership interests may also be attractive for wealthier clients who have used their unified credits and generation-skipping transfer tax exemptions, particularly where the interests are expected to grow in value.[98]

Transfers of limited partnership interests are frequently valued at a discount for gift, estate, and generation-skipping transfer tax purposes. If Mom gives Child a limited partnership interest, the value of the interest for transfer

---

[92] See discussions at ¶¶ 16.04[3] and 16.04[4] below.

[93] See Treas. Reg. §§ 1.701-2(b)(1), 1.701-2(c)(6).

[94] The continuing concealment doctrine may apply when a debtor transfers legal title to his property to another, continues to use and enjoy the property and does not report this "de facto" interest to creditors and/or the bankruptcy court. The combination of the transfer of legal title, the continued use, and the failure to report the "interest" is sometimes considered a continuing concealment of a de facto equitable interest of the debtor in the property and can result in a denial of discharge in bankruptcy. See Ch. 53 on asset protection for a more detailed discussion of this doctrine.

[95] Described in Ch. 10.

[96] Described in Ch. 5.

[97] Described in Ch. 10.

[98] See discussion at Ch. 8.

tax purposes is the price at which the interest would change hands between a willing buyer and a willing seller, neither being under any compulsion to buy or to sell, and both having reasonable knowledge of relevant facts.[99] The IRS is not entitled to assume that the hypothetical buyer would be a relative,[100] and the IRS is not entitled to aggregate the transferred interest with other interests held by the donor or donee.[101] The IRS has conceded these issues.[102]

What do we mean by transferring an interest at a "discount"? Suppose Mom transfers a five percent limited partnership interest. If a willing buyer would pay more for five percent of the assets outright than for a five percent limited partnership interest, we will say that the value of the partnership interest is "discounted" from the value of the pro rata share of underlying assets.

> EXAMPLE: Mom transfers a five percent limited partnership interest to Son. Five percent of the partnership assets is worth $5,000. The 5 percent limited partnership interest, however, is worth $3,000. Mom has made a gift of $3,000.

Is the above example an outrage, resulting in Mom effectively transferring $5,000 of underlying assets at a gift tax value of $3,000? No, the reason it worked out this way is that the interest she actually transferred is not worth much. If Son takes his limited partnership interest and tries to buy a Lamborghini with it, or even a cup of coffee, he'll be quick to discover how little trading value his interest has. Although large discounts may be resisted by the IRS, in the real world, these interests are relatively worthless when the test is their sale value in the open market. As a practical matter, interests in family limited partnerships are likely to be virtually unmarketable outside the family group.

The following example illustrates the power of making gifts subject to discounts.

> EXAMPLE: In 1996, Dad forms a family limited partnership, transferring assets valued at $6,000,000 to the partnership. Dad is initially a one percent general partner and a 99 percent limited partner. Shortly after the formation of the partnership, Dad gives a 25 percent limited partnership interest to each of two trusts for his two children, for a total transfer of 50 percent of the partnership. The value of the gift is discounted 33 1/3 percent for lack of marketability and lack of control, so the total transfer

---

[99] Treas. Reg. §§ 20.2031-1(b), 20.2031-3, 25.2512-1, 25.2512-3.

[100] E.g., Estate of Bright v. United States, 658 F2d 999, 1005-1006 (5th Cir. 1981); Estate of Andrews v. Comm'r, 79 TC 938, 952, 954-956 (1982).

[101] E.g., Propstra v. United States, 680 F2d 1248, 1251, 52 (9th Cir. 1982); Estate of Bright v. United States, 658 F2d 999, 1001-1005 (5th Cir. 1981).

[102] See Rev. Rul. 93-12, 1993-1 CB 202 and discussion of aggregation in Ch. 25; but see discussion at ¶ 16.03[2][b] below regarding interests that carry swing votes.

to the trusts is valued not at $3,000,000, but at $2,000,000 (i.e., 66 2/3 percent of 50 percent of $6,000,000), for federal gift tax purposes.

In 1997, Dad reports the gift on his 1996 gift tax return, and Mom splits the gift. Mom and Dad, who have never made taxable gifts, each pay gift tax of $153,000 after using their unified credits. Mom and Dad also allocate their generation-skipping transfer tax exemptions to the trusts.

In each of years 1996 through 2000, Dad also makes gifts of a 1/4 percent limited partnership interest to each of four trusts for his grandchildren. The trusts meet the requirements of the gift tax and generation-skipping transfer tax annual exclusions. The value of the partnership assets does not change during this period, and the value of each annual exclusion gift is discounted 33 1/3 percent. The gifts are within the limits of the gift and generation-skipping tax annual exclusions (66 2/3 percent of 1/4 percent of $6,000,000 equals $10,000).[103]

Dad dies in 2004, at which time the partnership assets have appreciated to $8,000,000. Even assuming Dad's remaining partnership interests are not eligible for any estate tax valuation discount, he has effectively removed $4,400,000 (the undiscounted value of Dad's gifts and the appreciation on them prior to his death) from his estate at a tax cost to him and Mom of $306,000 (and use of their unified credits).

Had Dad not formed the family limited partnership or made gifts, his estate would have paid estate tax of $2,420,000 (55 percent of $4,400,000) with respect to the gifted property, assuming the marital, charitable and other deductions did not apply. (For an apples-to-apples comparison, Dad's estate would have owed $1,868,000 and used his unified credit if the $4,400,000 were the only asset in his estate.)

In addition, each 25 percent limited partnership interest held by one of the exempt trusts for Dad's descendants can continue to grow in value and should not be subject to transfer tax as long as the interest (or, if the partnership dissolves and is wound up, the trust's share of partnership assets) remains in trust and the trust legally continues to exist under state law (often up to 100 years). (Although the partnership interests held in the grandchildren's annual exclusion trusts will also grow, they will be included in the grandchildren's estates.)

PRACTICE POINTER: If the family limited partnership is used as a gifting vehicle, proper order of transfers is important. If Dad wants to give Daughter $100,000 to be held in the family limited partnership, he could give Daughter the $100,000 and she could contribute it to the partnership. Or, Dad could put the $100,000 in the partnership and give a partnership interest to Daughter. These are two distinctly different transactions, each leading to a variety of different tax consequences. Usually, the second alternative will be desirable.

---

[103] Of course, Dad could give twice as much if Mom splits the gift.

[1] Details on Discounts

Family limited partnership interests are subject to discounts for lack of control and lack of marketability, as well as other reasons.

[a] Lack of Control

A transfer of a minority interest in a closely held corporation will often be valued at a discount. This is called a "minority discount." "Minority discount" is a bit of a misnomer, as the critical factor is the lack of control the transferor enjoys over the entity.[104] Transfers of partnership interests are also eligible for discounts for lack of control.[105] A transfer of a limited partnership interest that constitutes a majority of the partnership interests may still be eligible for a valuation discount for lack of control.

For instance, if Mom transfers a 99 percent limited partnership interest in a family limited partnership, the interest may be subject to a discount for lack of control. A discount for a limited partnership interest is appropriate because the general partner has so much control over the management of the partnership. The limited partner typically has little voice in partnership operations, cannot obtain his pro rata share of partnership assets by compelling the partnership to liquidate, cannot (until the partnership dissolves) obtain the value of his interest in a term partnership by redeeming it, cannot transfer his management rights in the partnership without the consent of the other partners, cannot compel distributions in most cases, and must pay taxes on his allocable share of the income of the entity whether or not it is distributed to him. This lack of control over so many aspects of the partnership may make the limited partner's interest worth considerably less than his pro rata share of the partnership assets.

The rights a limited partner has in the particular entity may affect the amount of discount for lack of control. For example, if a partnership agreement gives 50 percent of the limited partners the right to vote to liquidate the partnership, Mom transfers a 50 percent limited partnership interest to Son, and Son becomes a substitute limited partner, then the valuation of the 50 percent interest Mom gives to Son will take into account Son's right to liquidate the entity.

Transfers of general partnership interests may also receive discounts for lack of control where the transferee becomes either an assignee or a limited

---

[104] E.g., Estate of Luton v. Comm'r, 1994 RIA TC Memo. ¶ 94,539, 68 TCM (CCH) 1044, 1053 (1994), supp. op., 1996 RIA TC Memo. ¶ 96,181, 71 TCM 2772 (1996); Moore v. Comm'r, 62 TCM (CCH) 1128, 1133 (1991); see also Estate of Jung v. Comm'r, 101 TC 412, 442 (1993); Estate of Newhouse v. Comm'r, 94 TC 193, 249, 251-52 (1990), nonacq., 1991-2 CB 1.

[105] E.g., Harwood v. Comm'r, 82 TC 239, 267-268 (1984), aff'd, 786 F2d 1174 (9th Cir.), cert. denied, 479 US 1007 (1986).

partner,[106] or the interest does not carry control of the entity. However, under certain circumstances, the discount may be offset in whole or in part by a deemed gift resulting from the lapse of the former general partner's voting rights.[107]

The discount may be even greater if the interest transferred is only an assignee interest. If the transferor remains a general partner, however, a risk may exist that the assignee interest ends up back in the general partner's estate to the extent the transferor retained too many powers over the interest and/or did not owe sufficient fiduciary duties to the assignee.[108]

[b] Lack of Marketability

Transfers of limited partnership interests are also subject to valuation discounts for lack of marketability.[109] The discount for lack of marketability is based on the fact that few unrelated parties would be inclined to purchase an interest in a family limited partnership without receiving a substantial discount from its pro rata share of the entity's total value. Restrictions, in addition to those imposed by state law, on a partner's ability to turn his interest into cash by selling or redeeming his interest tend to make the interest even less marketable and therefore may call for a higher discount. Placing too many restrictions on a partner's ability to use his interest, however, may cause him not to be recognized as a partner for federal income tax purposes.[110] Additionally, the restrictions may be ignored pursuant to Chapter 14 of the Internal Revenue Code, so the use of restrictions should be carefully considered.[111]

[c] Amount of Discount

While the discounts for lack of control and lack of marketability are conceptually separate, they do overlap to a certain extent. After all, one reason that a limited partnership interest lacks marketability is that, as a general rule, a limited partner is relatively powerless with regard to controlling the partnership's day-to-day activities and he cannot readily extract himself from the

---

[106] See RULPA § 704(a).

[107] See discussion at ¶ 16.03[3][d] below.

[108] See discussion at ¶ 16.02[1][b] above and ¶ 16.03[4] below.

[109] E.g., Estate of Andrews v. Comm'r, 79 TC 938, 953 (1982); Estate of Luton v. Comm'r, 1994 RIA TC Memo. ¶ 94,539, 68 TCM (CCH) 1044, 1055 (1994); Estate of Bennett v. Comm'r, 1993 RIA TC Memo. ¶ 93,034, 65 TCM (CCH) 1816, 1826–1827 (1993).

[110] See Treas. Reg. § 1.704-1(e)(2) and discussion at ¶ 16.04[7][a] below.

[111] See discussion at ¶¶ 16.03[3][c] and 16.03[3][d] below.

partnership.[112] As a consequence, the courts often do not separate the two discounts.[113] The combined discount frequently ranges between 25 percent and 35 percent, and discounts of 50 percent or more have been upheld in reported cases involving partnerships.[114] Although most of the cases on valuation discounts involve transfers of interests in closely held corporations, much of the reasoning is equally applicable to transfers of interests in family limited partnerships.

[d] Other Discounts

Other valuation discounts may be appropriate. For example, where a family limited partnership conducts a business and one partner is instrumental to the success of that business, a "key person" discount may be warranted. This discount reflects the fact that a business whose value depends on the efforts of a single person may be a riskier investment than other businesses of its type. Numerous other discounts may apply, depending on the circumstances.[115]

[2] Valuation Premiums

Certain transfers of partnership interests may attract a valuation premium, rather than (or in addition to) a valuation discount.

[a] Control Premium

A transfer of a general partnership interest may be subject to a control premium where the transferee is entitled to become a general partner and the agreement permits him to control the family limited partnership. However, factors that might tend to offset such a premium include (1) a grant of broader

---

[112] See Estate of Andrews v. Comm'r, 79 TC 938, 952 (1982).

[113] See, e.g., Harwood v. Comm'r, 82 TC 239, 268 (1984), aff'd, 786 F2d 1174 (9th Cir.), cert. denied, 479 US 1007 (1986) (allowing a 50 percent discount based on lack of control, lack of marketability and restrictions on transferability); Knott v. Comm'r, 1988 PH TC Memo. ¶ 88,120, 55 TCM (CCH) 424, 432 (1988) (allowing a 30 percent discount to reflect illiquidity and lack of control after applying discount based on present value of partners' right to receive net underlying asset value of partnership in ten years); see also Estate of Andrews v. Comm'r, 79 TC 938, 957 (1982).

[114] Harwood v. Comm'r, 82 TC 239 (1984), aff'd, 786 F2d 1174 (9th Cir.), cert. denied, 479 US 1007 (1986); Estate of McLendon v. Comm'r, 77 F3d 477 (5th Cir. 1995), on remand, 1996 RIA TC Memo. ¶ 96,307, 72 TCM 42 (1996); see also Gallun v. Comm'r, 1974 PH TC Memo. ¶ 74,284, 33 TCM (CCH) 1316, 1321 (1974); acd. AOD 1975-008 (Jan. 17, 1975) (discounting net asset value of an investment portfolio held by a corporation by 55 percent).

[115] See Ch. 25 for a more extended discussion.

powers to the limited partners, (2) the fiduciary responsibility of the general partner which inhibits her right to deal with the partnership in a way that specifically benefits her own interests to the detriment of the other partners, and (3) the unlimited exposure of the general partner with respect to partnership debt and other liabilities. Where both a general partnership interest and a limited partnership interest are transferred at death, a control premium may apply for purposes of valuing the limited partnership interest as well as the general partnership interest.[116]

[b] "Swing Vote" Premium

The IRS has taken the position that gifts of interests in closely held corporations may be valued at a premium where circumstances would permit a donee either to join with another shareholder to form a majority or to refrain from joining with another shareholder and effectively veto an action.[117] For example, where Mom owns 51 percent of a corporation and Dad owns 49 percent and Mom transfers two percent to Child, the IRS's position may be that Child's two percent should be valued at a premium.

Taken to its logical conclusion, this position would seem to indicate that all shareholders in a three-shareholder corporation where no one shareholder has a majority position will have swing vote premiums. For example, if Mom owns 100 percent of a corporation and she transfers one-third of the stock to Son and one-third to Daughter, the IRS apparently may take the position that each one-third has a swing vote, subject to valuation at a premium, since each owner can join with one other owner to control the partnership. This situation is known as a "swing vote" scenario. The theory that a premium should be applied in valuing a "swing vote" interest appears to have found some support in the courts.[118] Although a swing vote scenario is much more likely to occur in a corporate context, it could also occur in a family limited partnership context where there are multiple general partners or where the limited partners are given sufficiently substantial voting rights. If the IRS position is followed, the effect of transferring a partnership interest that has a swing vote is that part or all of any valuation discount allowed for lack of control may be offset by a swing vote premium.

---

[116] See IRC § 2704 and ¶ 16.03[3][d] below.

[117] Tech. Adv. Mem. 9436005 (May 26, 1994).

[118] E.g., Estate of Winkler v. Comm'r, 1989 PH TC Memo. ¶ 89,231, 57 TCM (CCH) 373, 381-383 (1989); see also Estate of Bright v. United States, 658 F2d 999, 1007, 1009 n.9 (5th Cir. 1981).

[3] Chapter 14—Special Valuation Rules

In 1990, Chapter 14 of the Internal Revenue Code[119] was adopted. In certain circumstances, Chapter 14 will alter the valuation rules from the Chapter 11 and Chapter 12 rules that would otherwise apply.

[a] Section 2701—Preferred Interests

Section 2701 contains special rules for valuing transfers of interests in closely held businesses from senior family members to junior family members. More specifically, Section 2701 provides that if Mom transfers a junior equity interest to Son and retains a preferred equity interest herself, she may be deemed to have made a gift, even though the transfer might not be a gift under normal rules.

Section 2701 will not apply to Mom's transfer of a partnership interest to Son if she does not have any kind of preferred interest in the partnership. Whether an interest is preferred typically depends on the distribution, liquidation, and conversion rights associated with it. This means that general partnership interests may or may not be junior interests and limited partnership interests may or may not be preferred interests (and vice versa). While most plain vanilla family limited partnerships do not have actual preferred equity interests, "hidden" preferred interests may result as a consequence of collateral contractual arrangements such as loans and leases, if they operate in practical effect as disguised equity interests.

The rules of Section 2701 are very complex, and can result in adverse tax consequences that are both unexpected and severe.[120]

[b] Section 2702—Grantor Retained Annuity Trusts as Partners

Section 2702, which provides special valuation rules for intrafamily transfers of interests in trusts, does not directly apply to interests in family limited partnerships. It does, however, offer an estate planning technique called the grantor retained annuity trust (GRAT)[121] that can be a very effective means of saving transfer taxes when used in conjunction with a family limited partnership.

Summarizing briefly, a GRAT is similar in structure to a charitable lead annuity trust. The grantor of a GRAT transfers property to the trust, retaining an annuity payable for a term of years that the grantor is expected to outlive, or the shorter of his life or such a term of years. At the end of the term,

---

[119] IRC §§ 2701-2704.

[120] They are explained in more detail in Ch. 31.

[121] The GRAT is discussed in detail in Ch. 22.

the trust property will remain in trust for, or be distributed to, the beneficiaries selected by the grantor when the GRAT was established.

The grantor's gift of the remainder interest in the trust is valued using the 7520 rate.[122] Generally, GRATs are advantageous from a transfer tax standpoint when interest rates are low, and when the property to be transferred to the GRAT is expected to grow at a greater rate than the 7520 rate. Where a limited partnership interest in a family limited partnership is used to fund the GRAT, however, valuation discounts can make it easier to earn more than the 7520 rate, since the annuity payable to the grantor is valued as a percentage of the discounted value of the partnership interest. Use of family limited partnership interests thus can make a GRAT feasible even when interest rates are relatively high.

> EXAMPLE: Dad is a partner in a family limited partnership with a total value of $5,000,000. The partnership assets typically grow at an annual rate of $7^1/_2$ percent.
>
> In January of Year One, when the 7520 rate is 9.6 percent, Dad transfers a 60 percent limited partnership interest to a GRAT with an annuity term of 10 years and an annuity rate of 8 percent. The partnership interest Dad transfers to the GRAT is valued for gift tax purposes at $2,000,000 after a 33 1/3 percent discount for lack of control and lack of marketability is applied. The discount means that rather than receiving a $240,000 annuity each year (8 percent of $3,000,000), Dad will receive a $160,000 annuity (8 percent of $2,000,000). In addition, Dad has made a taxable gift of $999,744 ($2,000,000 less the value of Dad's retained interest, $1,000,256), rather than a gift of $1,499,616 ($3,000,000 less the value of Dad's retained interest, $1,500,384) that he would have made had no discounts been applicable, for a gift tax savings of over $275,000 (assuming the maximum rate of 55 percent applies).
>
> In this case, had no discounts been applicable, the payment of Dad's annuity would have required dipping into the part of the GRAT that was treated as a gift at the time of the transfer, because the rate of growth of the partnership assets ($7^1/_2$ percent) is less than the 7520 rate (9.6 percent). The fact that the annuity rate (8 percent) is also higher than the rate of growth of partnership assets ($7^1/_2$ percent) means that payment of the annuity would also require invading capital from a state law accounting point of view. With the discounts, Dad receives an annuity of 8 percent, which is effectively an annuity of $5^1/_3$ percent of the undiscounted value of what he transferred to the GRAT. Moreover, a growth rate of $7^1/_2$ percent of the undiscounted value of the partnership ends up being a growth rate of $11^1/_4$ percent of the discounted value, well above the 7520 rate.

---

[122] The 7520 rate is equal to 120 percent of the midterm applicable federal rate published by the IRS, rounded to the nearest 2/10 of one percent. IRC § 7520. See Ch. 11 for a discussion of the 7520 rate and its effect on actuarial estate planning techniques.

Making a GRAT a partner in a family limited partnership should not cause the grantor to be viewed as holding a preferred interest in the partnership for purposes of Section 2701 by virtue of his right to receive the annuity. Although the grantor will be treated as the direct owner of the pro rata partnership interest held by the GRAT for purposes of Section 2701,[123] it is the GRAT itself, not the partnership, which has the obligation to make the annuity payments. The trustee of the GRAT could sell the partnership interest to a third party and would still have the obligation to pay the annuity to the grantor from the sales proceeds.

[c] Section 2703—Buy-Sell Agreements and Excessive Restrictions

Under Section 2703, certain rights possessed by, and restrictions imposed on, partners are ignored in determining the transfer tax value of a partnership interest.[124] The legislative history of Section 2703 indicates that it was intended to allow the IRS to disregard the value of an interest in a business where the value is established pursuant to a buy-sell agreement that permits members of the seller's family to buy the business interest at less than fair market value. It also permits the IRS, when determining the transfer tax value of property, to disregard other restrictions on the right to sell or use property that are not comparable to those contained in third-party agreements.[125]

Let's say that Mom has entered into a partnership with members of her family. The partnership agreement gives the partners the right to purchase, under certain circumstances, another partner's interest for less than its fair market value, and contains restrictions on the partners' ability to transfer or otherwise use their partnership interests. Will these rights and restrictions be taken into account in valuing Mom's interest? Under Section 2703, a right or restriction will be respected if it meets the following three tests:

- First, the right or restriction must be a bona fide business arrangement.[126]
- Second, the right or restriction cannot be a device to transfer Mom's property to family members for less than adequate consideration.[127]
- Finally, the right or restriction's terms must be comparable to similar arrangements entered into by persons in an arm's length transaction.[128]

---

[123] See Treas. Reg. § 25.2701-6(a)(4).

[124] IRC § 2703(a).

[125] IRC § 2703 is discussed in detail in Ch. 27.

[126] IRC § 2703(b)(1).

[127] IRC § 2703(b)(2).

[128] IRC § 2703(b)(3).

These three tests will be deemed to be met if more than 50 percent of the partnership is owned by persons other than members of Mom's family and natural objects of her bounty.[129]

The last test imposed by Section 2703 raises certain evidentiary issues. The regulations indicate that a right or restriction will be considered comparable to similar arrangements if the right or restriction could have been achieved in a fair bargain among unrelated parties in the same business. A right or restriction will be considered achievable in a fair bargain if it conforms with the general business practice of unrelated parties in the same business.[130] Actual examples of other agreements may be difficult to obtain due to confidentiality considerations. Expert witness testimony may be helpful. Tracking state law in the partnership agreement should also be effective, since state law represents the legislature's determination of the terms of an appropriate agreement.

The easiest course for most families entering into family limited partnerships may be to try to avoid application of Section 2703 altogether. To do this, they could first provide that any right of first refusal, mandatory redemption, or similar type of buy-sell provision, commonly found in a partnership agreement, will provide for a fair market value purchase price. This should be relatively easy to do. However, it may not be what the family really wants, because it may entail the time, trouble and expense of hiring an independent appraiser each time a buy-sell trigger event occurs. Second, they could provide only for restrictions that are comparable to restrictions entered into by third parties dealing at arm's length. This is easy to say, but is it that easy to do?

Many family limited partnership agreements allow limited partners to withdraw their capital only when the partnership is dissolved and restrict the transferability of partnership interests. There are generally nontax reasons for such restrictions (asset protection and a desire to keep family assets within the family, to name two). Consequently, most families are likely to want either or both of these restrictions in their family partnership agreements. These restrictions also typically depress the value of limited partnership interests by increasing applicable lack of control and lack of marketability.[131]

The IRS has been unhappy with valuation discounts in family transfer situations.[132] As mentioned above, the IRS has had little success in attacking discounts by trying to apply family attribution principles.[133] The IRS has

---

[129] Treas. Reg. § 25.2703-1(b)(3).

[130] Treas. Reg. § 25.2703-1(b)(4).

[131] See discussion at ¶ 16.03[1] above.

[132] The IRS nevertheless does apply such discounts to marital and charitable transfers. E.g., Tech. Adv. Mem. 9403005 (Oct. 14, 1993) (applying minority discount to transfer of part of decedent's interest in entity to marital deduction trust); Ahmanson Foundation v. United States, 674 F2d 761, 771-772 (9th Cir. 1981), appeal after remand, 733 F2d 623 (1984) (applying discount to interest passing to charity).

[133] See discussion at ¶ 16.03[1] above.

therefore been attacking the restrictions imposed in family limited partnership agreements under Section 2703. In essence, the IRS has expressed a view that third parties would not enter into an agreement with no exit strategy. In other words, the IRS's apparent position, at least in certain circumstances, has been that unrelated parties negotiating at arm's length would not enter into a partnership unless they could sell their interests freely or redeem them after a short time.[134] If the IRS position is ultimately upheld, many interests in family limited partnerships could be subject to valuation under Section 2703, which would probably result in a valuation that ignores certain partnership restrictions.

Apart from the correctness or incorrectness of the IRS position, the consequences of ignoring restrictions on a partner's ability to transfer his interests may not be very impressive. Suppose that a partnership agreement prohibits the sale of a partnership interest without the general partner's consent. State law rules prohibiting restraints on alienation and/or the partnership agreement itself may allow a limited partner to assign the economic component of his interest, despite the provision prohibiting sale of the interest without the general partner's consent. This would mean that, at most, the partnership agreement prevents a partner from transferring the management rights associated with his interest. Ignoring that restriction pursuant to Section 2703 should make no difference, because state law typically prevents the transfer of management rights in any case.[135]

Ignoring a restriction on a partner's right to withdraw could prove more troubling. State law provides that a partner in a partnership for a term of years may not withdraw from the partnership except as provided in the partnership agreement.[136] By arguing that a prohibition on withdrawal is a restriction to be ignored under Section 2703, the IRS is essentially arguing that state law should be ignored. Having gone that far, the IRS might as well argue (and, in fact, has argued) that assets held in a partnership should be valued as if no partnership existed, due to the restrictive nature of the entity. Disregarding restrictions inherent in the nature of a partnership as defined by state law would be an extreme reading of Section 2703, and appears to go far beyond anything contemplated by Congress. Nevertheless, the IRS has taken that position in several technical advice memoranda.[137]

---

[134] See, e.g., Tech. Adv. Mem. 9723009 (Feb. 24, 1997), Tech. Adv. Mem. 9725002 (Mar. 3, 1997). Note, however, that there are many types of arrangements between third parties (for example, hedge funds, venture capital pools, and syndicated investments) where an investor's ability to withdraw or transfer his interest is also severely restricted.

[135] See RULPA § 702.

[136] See RULPA § 603.

[137] E.g., Tech. Adv. Mem. 9723009 (Feb. 24, 1997), Tech. Adv. Mem. 9719006 (Jan. 14, 1997). Tech. Adv. Mem. 9725002 (Mar. 3, 1997).

Section 2703 has one final twist to it that can trip up family members who have formed a family limited partnership. Specifically, although Section 2703 does not apply to partnership agreements created on or before October 8, 1990, it does apply to such agreements with regard to rights or restrictions that are substantially modified after that time.[138] Families that have grandfathered partnerships should therefore carefully consider the possible effects of Section 2703 before amending or modifying the partnership agreements or entering into further agreements.[139]

[d] Section 2704(a): The Taxing of Lapsing Rights

Section 2704(a) has some impact on family limited partnerships.[140]

[i] General rule. If Mom has a "voting right" or "liquidation right" in the family limited partnership, and either right "lapses," the lapse is treated as a taxable transfer by Mom, if she and members of her family control the partnership both before and after the lapse.[141]

A lapse will not necessarily occur on the transfer of an interest. This is because, when a partnership interest is transferred, in many cases, the transferor retains the management rights associated with the interest.[142] A lapse will also not occur if the transferee succeeds to the rights incident to the interest. So—the lapse is limited to the situation where rights disappear altogether as a result of a transfer. Because of this, we will refer to the lapse of a right by its more commonly applicable absolute meaning—the "disappearance" of a right. Hence, a lapse will generally occur, if at all, on an event that constitutes a withdrawal of a partner—that is, death, incompetency, certain transfers of a partner's interest, bankruptcy, etc. In such a case, the transferee's or personal representative's interest will be an assignee interest, which will not possess voting or liquidation rights (since we are assuming that the transferee or estate is not admitted as a limited partner). Generally, the measure of the gift or estate tax value of the disappearance of rights is the value of all of the transferor's interests immediately before the rights disappeared less the value of those interests immediately after the rights disappeared, measured as

---

[138] Treas. Reg. § 25.2703-2.

[139] See Ch. 27 for a fuller discussion of IRC § 2703 and what actions can constitute a "substantial modification."

[140] IRC § 2704 is generally explained in Ch. 26. This chapter contains a specific discussion of its application to partnerships.

[141] IRC § 2704(a)(1).

[142] Cf. RULPA § 702; UPA 27(1).

if the interests were all held by the same person.[143] A deemed transfer by lapse can result in an increase in the partner's taxable gifts (even where the transfer was pursuant to a sale rather than a gift), an increase in the partner's estate, or in no increase in the transferor's taxable gifts or estate. The measure of the transfer depends on whether the value of the total interests before the lapse was more valuable than it was after the lapse, disregarding any split in the interests among different persons.

NOTE: The discussion in the remainder of ¶ 16.03[d] will assume that, on a particular transfer, the transferor has not retained the management rights incident to the transferred interest, and the transferee has not become a substitute partner or otherwise been assigned those rights. That is, we are assuming that the management rights have disappeared.

[A] *Disappearance of voting rights.* Both general and limited partners have voting rights in a limited partnership. The limited partners' voting rights are usually limited to major decisions. An assignee of a partnership interest, however, usually does not have the right to vote, even on extraordinary matters.[144] Thus, it appears that any transfer of a partnership interest under our assumptions may cause a disappearance of the interest's voting rights. In addition, other events (e.g., bankruptcy or incompetency) may result in the disappearance of a partnership interest's voting rights.[145]

If voting rights disappear on a transfer because the transferee is not admitted as a substitute partner and the withdrawing partner does not retain the rights, then a disappearance of those rights occurs. The value attributable to the disappearance (and thus the deemed taxable transfer) will depend on how much the voting rights added to the value of the interest.

[B] *Disappearance of liquidation rights.* A "liquidation right" is the right or ability to compel the partnership to acquire all or part of the partner's interest in the partnership, regardless of whether the exercise of that right would result in the liquidation of the partnership itself.[146] That is, it is actually a right to cause a redemption of one's interest. Due to the fact that Section 2704(b) speaks of a "right to liquidate," which refers to a different concept than a "liquidation right" under Section 2704(a), the statute is confusing.

---

[143] See Ch. 26 for an explanation of such adjustments. Adjustment is made for consideration received on the transfer. We'll assume for purposes of further discussion that no consideration is received. Additionally, adjustments are made for changes in the value of the interest not caused by the lapse.

[144] RULPA § 702.

[145] RULPA §§ 402, 705.

[146] Treas. Reg. § 25.2704-1(a)(2)(v).

Hence, we will refer to a "liquidation right" under Section 2704(a) by a more specific term—a "redemption right." A lapse of a redemption right occurs when a presently exercisable redemption right is restricted or eliminated. A transfer that results in the disappearance of a redemption right is not generally subject to Section 2704(a) if the rights associated with the transferred interest itself are not restricted or eliminated—that is, if they can still be exercised by the transferee.[147]

> EXAMPLE: Mom owns a 70 percent limited partnership interest and no general partnership interest in a partnership. The partnership agreement allows the owners of 70 percent of the limited partnership interests to liquidate the partnership. If Mom transfers her limited partnership interest, her ability to liquidate the partnership (and therefore turn her interest into cash) lapses. If, however, the transferee becomes a substituted limited partner retaining the same rights, the right does not disappear and the transfer should not be subject to tax under Section 2704(a).

When does a partner have a redemption right, under state law? And, if a partner does have a redemption right, what events cause it to disappear? The analysis usually depends on whether the partner is: a general partner, but not a limited partner; a limited partner, but not a general partner; or both a general partner and a limited partner.

[ii] Disappearance of general partner's redemption right, where general partner is not a limited partner. Under RULPA, where a general partner who is not also a limited partner transfers her general partnership interest (whether by gift or at death), if her management rights disappear, there will be a disappearance of her redemption right (consisting of her right to withdraw and receive the fair value of her interest). A general partner can withdraw at any time and receive the fair value of her interest in the partnership (less damages if withdrawal is prohibited by the partnership agreement).[148] This right is arguably a redemption right. If a general partner transfers her interest, by gift or at death, the transferee does not become a general partner unless all of the other partners consent or the agreement provides for admission in some other manner.[149] If the general partner retains the management rights, then a disappearance should not occur, since the transferor and the transferee together still own the pre-transfer value of the interest. Conversely, if the transferee is admitted as a general partner, no disappearance should occur. However, if the management rights attributable to the general partnership interest disappear altogether on the transfer, then the transferee, even if admitted as a

---

[147] Treas. Reg. § 25.2704-1(c)(1).

[148] See RULPA §§ 602, 604.

[149] RULPA § 401.

limited partner, will probably not have the ability to withdraw and receive the fair value of his interest, unless the partnership has no specific term; that is, the transferee does not succeed to the withdrawing partner's redemption rights.[150] Hence, on a withdrawal of the general partner, the general partner's redemption right will ordinarily disappear. However, the disappearance may have no effect on value (and hence not be taxable under Section 2704(a)) if the amount for which she could have redeemed her interest is no greater than the value she could have obtained on a sale of her interest to a third-party buyer.

Some state laws do not give the general partner a right to receive the fair value of his interest on withdrawal. For example, under Texas partnership law, a general partner who attempts to withdraw can be compelled by a majority of the limited partners to become a limited partner.[151] Thus, under Texas law, a general partner who does not own a majority of the limited partnership interests cannot compel the partnership to redeem her interest, and a transfer of her general partnership interest should not result in a disappearance of a redemption right.

[iii] **Disappearance of limited partner's redemption right, when limited partner is not a general partner.** Suppose a limited partner who is not also a general partner transfers a limited partnership interest. Has a disappearance of a redemption right occurred? It depends on the circumstances and the terms of the partnership agreement.

> EXAMPLE: Dad is a 60 percent limited partner in a partnership with no term (sometimes referred to as a partnership at will). Under state law, Dad is entitled to withdraw his capital upon six months' notice to the general partner. This right of withdrawal is a redemption right for purposes of Section 2704(a). Dad transfers a 30 percent limited partnership interest to Son, and Son becomes a 30 percent limited partner. As Son has the same right to withdraw from the partnership that Dad had, there should be no disappearance of a redemption right.

Where a limited partner transfers his partnership interest, does not retain the management rights, and the assignee is not admitted as a new partner, it appears that there will be a disappearance of both voting and redemption rights (to the extent the limited partners have such rights).

> EXAMPLE: Assume the same facts as the preceding example, except that Dad dies and Son does not become a limited partner. As Son is an assignee with no right to redeem his interest, there has been a disappearance of the redemption right incident to Dad's interest.

---

[150] RULPA § 603.

[151] See Tex. Rev. Limited Partnership Act, Tex. Rev. Civ. Stat. Ann. art. 6132a-1, § 6.02(b)(1) (West Supp. 1996).

[iv] Disappearance of redemption right if the partner is both a general and limited partner. The analysis becomes more complicated where the transferor is both a general and a limited partner.

> EXAMPLE: Dad is a 60 percent limited partner in a term partnership. Dad is also the sole general partner of the partnership. Dad transfers a 30 percent limited partnership interest to Son. State law requires that the partnership wind up if the general partner withdraws, unless the limited partners (except those who are withdrawing as general partners in breach of the agreement) unanimously consent to continue the partnership.
>
> To begin with, does Dad have a redemption right that can disappear as a result of Dad's transfer to Son? He can withdraw as general partner, and receive the value of his general partnership interest under state law. So, he has a redemption right over his general partnership interest. But, more importantly in this case, does Dad have a redemption right over his limited partnership interest? As limited partner, he cannot withdraw, so the only redemption right he could be theorized to have is in a capacity to liquidate the entire entity as general partner, and thus receive the value of his limited partnership interest. Let's analyze. If Dad withdrew as general partner, there would be no general partner. If Dad (as general partner) withdrew in breach of the agreement, he could not compel liquidation of the entity. Hence, if his withdrawal would be a breach, he might not have a redemption right. If he withdrew and his withdrawal did not constitute a breach, he could effectively compel liquidation of the entity, before the assignment to Son, because he could vote his limited partnership interest to veto continuation of the business. Thus, if his withdrawal would not be a breach, he might have a redemption right over not only his general partnership interest, but also his limited partnership interest.

> EXAMPLE: Mom is both general partner and a limited partner in a partnership. Under this partnership agreement, Mom can compel liquidation of the partnership by withdrawing as general partner and vetoing any attempt by the other limited partners to continue the business. A transfer of Mom's general partnership interest where the transferee does not become a general partner (and Mom loses her general partnership management rights) may result in a taxable disappearance of a redemption right, not only with respect to the general partnership interest, but also with respect to the retained limited partnership interest.[152]

The above example illustrates the principle that a transfer that results in the elimination of a general partner's ability to compel the redemption of her limited partnership interest may also be a disappearance of a redemption right with respect to the limited partnership interest.[153]

---

[152] See Treas. Reg. § 25.2704-1(f), example 5.

[153] Treas. Reg. § 25.2704-(c)(1). The transfer of the limited partnership interest alone would not result in a taxable disappearance, discussed below. However, on the

A limited partnership interest held in conjunction with a general partnership interest poses other special issues. For example, if the general partner can cause the limited partnership to be liquidated, the limited partnership interest may be considered to have a greater value in conjunction with a general partnership interest than it would have if it were held alone.[184]

Suppose that under a particular agreement Dad has a redemption right over both his general and limited partnership interests. Suppose that Dad transfers a 30 percent limited partnership interest to Son. Even though Son cannot redeem the interest, the value of any Chapter 14 portion of the transfer is zero. The value of Dad's interests before the transfer is the liquidation value of both classes of interest. The value of those interests in one person's hands after the transfer is the same as before—if he were holding both the general partnership interest and the limited partnership interest, the total interest would still be valued at liquidation value (assuming that going concern value would be less). Interestingly enough, the Chapter 12 value of the 30 percent interest Dad transferred to Son will most likely be discounted, but there should be no additional gift as a result of Chapter 14.

A transfer of a limited partnership interest alone may result in an additional gift under Section 2704(a), if it results in the general partner's losing her power to liquidate the entity.

> EXAMPLE: Dad is a 60 percent limited partner in a term partnership. Dad is also the sole general partner of the partnership. Suppose that Dad transfers an assignee interest in his entire limited partnership interest to Son and does not retain the management rights. This may cause Dad to lose his power to liquidate the entity, because if he withdraws as a general partner, he no longer can vote that limited partnership interest to veto the continuation of the partnership. The value of a general partnership interest plus the 60 percent assignee interest may be different from the liquidation value of the general partnership interest and a 60 percent limited partnership interest.[185]

Using two general partners can help avoid this particular sort of lapse.

> EXAMPLE: Mom is a 1 percent general partner and a 60 percent limited partner in a partnership. She can compel the partnership to liquidate during her lifetime by withdrawing and voting her limited partnership

---

disappearance of the general partner's redemption right, the measure of the resulting taxable transfer is the change in value between all interests (both general and limited partnership interests) held by the general partner before the transfer, and the same interests (now, limited partnership and/or assignee interests) after the transfer as if they were held by one person—so the disappearance of the general partner's redemption rights will also take into account the disappearance of his right to cause the redemption of the limited partnership interest.

[184] Treas. Reg. § 25.2704-1(f), example 5; RULPA §§ 602, 801.

[185] See Treas. Reg. § 25.2704-1(f), examples 5, 6; but see Treas. Reg. § 25.2704-1(f), examples 4, 7.

interest to veto the continuation of the partnership. The liquidation value of the partnership is $1,000,000. The liquidation value of Mom's partnership interests is $10,000 for her general partnership interest and $600,000 for her limited partnership interest. Assume that the fair market values of the partnership interests are $8,000 for her general partnership interest and $400,000 for her limited partnership interest. As seen in the preceding example, if Mom is the sole general partner and she dies, her estate loses her right to liquidate the partnership that her combination of interests gave her during life. Under Section 2704, her partnership interests may have a combined estate tax value of $610,000 even though their actual value is probably less than $408,000 (assuming her interests became assignee interests upon her death).

Suppose, however, that Dad is also a general partner. If Mom withdrew during her lifetime, unanimous consent of the limited partners to continue the partnership would not be needed because Dad would be available to continue the partnership.[156] Mom has no ability to obtain the liquidation value of her partnership interests. If Mom dies, no disappearance of redemption rights should occur.[157]

[v] **Exceptions to rule.** A disappearance of a redemption right will not result in the application of Section 2704(a) if the disappearance occurs solely by reason of a change in state law or, to the extent necessary to avoid double taxation, if the redemption right was previously valued under Section 2701.[158] In addition, Section 2704(a) will not apply to a disappearance of Mom's redemption right if Mom, Mom's estate, and members of her family cannot, immediately after the disappearance, redeem Mom's partnership interest.[159]

EXAMPLE: Dad is a 60 percent limited partner, and an unrelated party is general partner of a partnership. The partnership agreement gives Dad the right to redeem his interest in three months' notice. Dad dies. His successor is not admitted to the partnership as a substitute limited partner. No taxable disappearance of redemption rights should occur because Dad's family cannot redeem Dad's interest.

Whether a partnership interest can be redeemed by a family immediately after the disappearance of a partner's redemption right is determined by the state law generally applicable to the partnership, as modified by the partnership agreement.[160] However, any restriction that is disregarded pursuant to

---

[156] See RULPA § 801(4).

[157] There may, of course, be a disappearance of voting rights on Mom's death.

[158] Treas. Reg. § 25.2704-1(c)(2)(ii)–25.2704-1(c)(2)(iii).

[159] Treas. Reg. § 25.2704-1(c)(2)(i)(A).

[160] Treas. Reg. § 25.2704-1(c)(2)(i)(B).

Section 2704(b) (discussed below) will also be disregarded for purposes of Section 2704(a).[161]

> EXAMPLE: Mom is a sole general partner of a family limited partnership. Mom owns 98 percent and Mom's children own one percent of the limited partnership interests. An unrelated party owns the remaining one percent limited partnership interest. The partnership agreement gives Mom, in her individual capacity, the right to liquidate the partnership. This right disappears on her death. Mom dies. State law provides that if a general partner dies, the business will be liquidated unless the surviving limited partners vote unanimously to continue the business, so that under state law, Mom's children could cause the partnership to be liquidated. The partnership agreement, however, provides that if Mom dies, the business will be continued unless the surviving limited partners vote unanimously to liquidate it, so that Mom's family cannot liquidate the partnership or redeem her limited partnership interest. Mom's death will result in a taxable disappearance of a redemption right with respect to her limited partnership interest, because if the agreement had not provided otherwise, state law would have enabled Mom's family to redeem that interest after her death.[162]

[vi] Section 2704(a)—technical summary. The following is a quick technical summary of the effects of Section 2704(a), depending on what Mom owns and how she transfers it. The summary assumes that the applicable state law is RULPA, that Mom retains no rights incident to an interest when she transfers that interest, and that the transferee of Mom's interest remains an assignee. If Mom's transferee becomes a substituted partner with all of Mom's rights or if Mom retains the management rights incident to the transferred interest, then no disappearance of rights will occur on the transfer. The summary posits results of Mom's death on lifetime gifts in the following scenarios:

- If Mom dies while acting only as a limited partner of a partnership that lasts for a term of years, the only taxable disappearance of rights under Section 2704(a) should be a disappearance of her voting rights, which should be relatively small in value, as she is a limited partner.[163] If Mom gives away part or all of her partnership interest during her lifetime, there may be a disappearance of Mom's voting rights, but no disappearance of her non-existent redemption rights.

- If Mom dies while acting only as limited partner of a partnership at will, her death will result in a taxable disappearance of her right to

---

[161] Treas. Reg. § 25.2704-1(c)(2)(i)(B).

[162] See Treas. Reg. § 25.2704-1(f), examples 5, 6.

[163] But see Tech. Adv. Mem. 9723009 (Feb. 24, 1997), Tech. Adv. Mem. 9725002 (Mar. 3, 1997), holding that a disappearance of a deemed right to withdraw the value of her interest on six months' notice occurs.

withdraw the value of her interest on six months' notice. Similarly, if Mom gives away all or part of her limited partnership interest, there will be a taxable disappearance of that redemption right. If the value that she could have withdrawn is the fair market value of her interest, rather than the liquidation value, the disappearance of that right should add no taxable value to her Chapter 12 gift tax value.

- If Mom dies while acting only as general partner of a partnership, there will be a taxable disappearance of rights under Section 2704(a) with respect to her general partnership interest. If Mom gives away an individually owned general partnership interest, there will be a taxable disappearance of her management rights, and of her right to withdraw and receive the fair value of her interest. The disappearance of the withdrawal right may add no value to the Chapter 12 gift tax value. If an entity controlled by Mom owns the general partnership interest, and Mom dies or gives the entity away, no disappearance of rights will occur in the absence of special drafting.

- If Mom dies while she is both a limited partner and the sole general partner, there will be a taxable disappearance of rights under Section 2704(a) with respect to both her general and limited partnership interests, if she could have withdrawn and caused the liquidation of the partnership during her life. If Mom transfers her general partnership interest during her lifetime, the same result would occur. If she holds her partnership interests indirectly through an entity, there will be no disappearance of rights, but the normal chapter 11 and 12 rules will value the interests taking into account any continuing ability to liquidate the partnership.

- If Mom is acting as sole general partner and as a limited partner and she gives away part or all of her limited partnership interest, the only disappearance of rights that should occur would be a disappearance of the voting rights given to a limited partner, unless: Mom could have redeemed her limited partnership interest before the transfer using her combined interests, and she could not after the transfer, even if she held the transferred interest in addition to her general partnership interest.

- If Mom is acting as one of two or more general partners and as a limited partner, and she dies or gives away her general partnership interest, any disappearance of rights should be limited to those rights incident to her general partnership interest, at least if the other partner(s) can continue the partnership after Mom's withdrawal, because Mom cannot compel redemption of her limited partnership interest before her death or gift.

[e] Section 2704(b): Ignoring Restrictions on Partnership Liquidation

Section 2704(b) also has some impact on family limited partnerships.[164] Section 2704(b) disregards restrictions on liquidation of an entity for transfer tax purposes under certain circumstances.[165] If Mom transfers a partnership interest to or for the benefit of a member of her family, and if she and members of her family control the partnership immediately before the transfer, certain restrictions limiting the partnership's ability to liquidate ("applicable restrictions") will be disregarded in valuing the transferred partnership interest for transfer tax purposes.[166]

A restriction on liquidation is an applicable restriction only when (1) the restriction lapses, in whole or in part, after the transfer of the partnership interest or (2) Mom or any member of her family, either alone or collectively, has the right to remove the restriction, in whole or in part, after the transfer of the partnership interest.[167] However, restrictions that are commercially reasonable and arise through a financing arrangement between the partnership and an unrelated party, as well as restrictions imposed by federal or state law, will not be considered applicable restrictions.[168]

> EXAMPLE: Mom is a general partner and limited partner of a family limited partnership. The partnership agreement provides that the partnership will not liquidate after Mom's death if 51 percent of the limited partners vote to continue. State law is RULPA, which provides for liquidation unless 100 percent of the limited partners vote to continue. Mom dies. The requirement that the partnership cannot liquidate if 51 percent of the limited partners vote to continue is an applicable restriction that will be disregarded in valuing Mom's partnership interests for estate tax purposes. Mom's partnership interests will be valued as if 100 percent of the limited partners must vote to continue.

As mentioned above, Section 2704(b) refers to restrictions on "liquidation." RULPA, however, uses the terms "dissolution" and "winding up." Under RULPA, a limited partnership will not necessarily be wound up (and thus liquidated) after dissolution. Thus, unless a general partner can cause both the dissolution and the winding up of the partnership, the general partner does not have the ability to liquidate the partnership. Where an individual is

---

[164] IRC § 2704 is generally explained in Ch. 26. This chapter contains a specific discussion of its application to partnerships.

[165] Note that under RULPA, a terminating partnership is "dissolved" and then "wound up." In contrast, IRC § 2704 speaks only of "liquidation," a term not used in RULPA, making it confusing to interpret references to state law provisions for liquidation that are made in that section.

[166] IRC § 2704(b)(1).

[167] IRC § 2704(b)(2).

[168] IRC § 2704(b)(3).

both a general partner and a limited partner, and the withdrawal from the partnership is not a breach, then, provided that no other general partner has the right to continue the partnership, the individual may be able to compel the partnership to dissolve and wind up by withdrawing (as general partner) and refusing (as limited partner) to agree to continue the partnership business.[169] Under such circumstances, the IRS may take the position that additional restrictions on a general partner's ability to dissolve the partnership are effectively restrictions on his ability to liquidate the partnership and are therefore governed by Section 2704(b).

Note that Section 2704(b) appears to apply to liquidation of the partnership itself, unlike Section 2704(a), which applies to liquidation of a partner's interest in the partnership. The regulations under Section 2704(b) refer to a restriction on the ability to liquidate the entity in whole or in part.[170] Should a limited partner's ability to withdraw on six months' notice to the general partners, under the state law applicable in the absence of agreement to the contrary, be considered an ability to partially liquidate the partnership, thereby causing any more restrictive limitation in the partnership agreement to be disregarded for transfer tax purposes pursuant to Section 2704(b)? This interpretation of Section 2704(b) appears without merit when one considers the fact that the term "liquidation right," specifically defined in the regulations under Section 2704(a) to include a partner's right to compel a partnership to acquire her interest, is not similarly defined in the regulations under Section 2704(b).[171] Additionally, the term "partial liquidation," in other contexts, generally refers to the discontinuance of a line of business or a geographical place of business or a similar discrete assignment of the business and distribution of that business or the proceeds of its sale (e.g., Section 355). It is not interpreted as including the redemption of an owner's interests. The IRS has nevertheless taken the position that a limited partner's right to withdraw is an ability to partially liquidate the partnership, and that a restriction on such a right to withdraw is therefore an applicable restriction.[172] Notwithstanding the IRS position, a provision that a partnership will terminate at the end of a term of years which therefore prohibits a limited partner from liquidating his interest by withdrawing under state law, should not be considered an applicable restriction. This is because applicable restrictions do not include restrictions conferred by state law. State law provides for two types of partnership: a partnership at will, which enables the limited partner to withdraw on six months' notice to the general partners, and a partnership for a term of

---

[169] See RULPA § 801(4).

[170] Treas. Reg. § 25.2704-2(b).

[171] Compare Treas. Reg. § 25.2704-1(a)(2)(v) with Treas. Reg. § 25.2704-2.

[172] Priv. Ltr. Rul. 9723009 (Feb. 24, 1997); Tech. Adv. Mem. 9725002 (Mar. 3, 1997).

years, which permits a limited partner to withdraw only to the extent provided in the partnership agreement.[173]

[f] Section 2704: Practice Tips

Minimizing effects of Section 2704(a). The primary risk of Section 2704(a) is that partnership interests will be valued for transfer tax purposes at more than they are really worth. Under the theory that Mom will own only one percent as general partner, and that limited partnership interests by themselves will not carry redemption rights, the practical consequence of a disappearance of rights incident to a general partnership interest alone or a limited partnership interest alone are unlikely to be disastrous. If this is so, the real problem could occur if a person with a redemption right over a general partnership interest is also deemed to have a redemption right over the limited partnership interest, and that redemption right disappears. There are several ways to minimize this risk.

First, for example, Mom could try to give away her entire limited partnership interest during her lifetime, so that the tax consequences of a disappearance of her remaining rights at her death are limited to the consequences of a lapse of rights incident to a small general partnership interest. Or, second, Mom might hold her general partnership interest in an entity such as a revocable trust or a wholly owned corporation. This plan should avoid any disappearance of rights incident to general partnership interests at Mom's death (since, at Mom's death, the trust or corporation will continue as general partner). Of course, the owners of that entity will exercise general partner rights after Mom's death. In addition, the valuation of her limited partnership interest will take into account the corporation's ability to liquidate the partnership, if that right exists.

Third, the partnership could have more than one general partner, with the other general partner(s) authorized to continue the business after Mom's death. In this way, Mom does not have a redemption right with respect to her limited partnership interest, so, if Mom dies, any taxable disappearance of rights should be limited to those incident to her general partnership interest.

Fourth, when Mom makes a transfer of her limited partnership interest during life or at death, the transferees could be admitted as substitute partners, so that a disappearance of rights is avoided.

---

[173] In fact, choosing a term partnership provides an additional means for the partnership to liquidate—reaching the end of the term—that is not available with a partnership at will. See RULPA § 801. Consequently, the decision to choose a term partnership (thereby eliminating a limited partner's right to liquidate her interest) should not be viewed as an applicable restriction for purposes of IRC § 2704(b), because the restrictions on liquidating the partnership itself are fewer.

PRACTICE POINTER: If it is harder to liquidate the partnership under the partnership agreement than it would be under state law, partnership interests will be valued as if state law applies. A partnership organized according to state law rules should not produce applicable restrictions.[174]

[4] Other Transfer Tax Consequences

As mentioned above, the transfer of family partnership interests can trigger other transfer tax traps. A prime concern, in this regard, is to ensure that transferred partnership interests are not included in the transferor's estate.

> **EXAMPLE:** Mom is general partner and a limited partner of a partnership which she has funded with her own property. Mom transfers her limited partnership interest to her children, but retains authority as general partner to decide when to make distributions to them. Mom dies while serving as general partner. Do Section 2036(a)(2) and Section 2038(a)(1) require inclusion in Mom's estate of the limited partnership interests Mom gave away during her lifetime? No—only her general partnership interest should be included in her estate.

Why? As a general partner, Mom owes a fiduciary duty to the limited partners. The IRS has frequently ruled that this fiduciary duty is sufficient to keep the gifted partnership interests out of Mom's estate.[175] These rulings follow the reasoning of the *Byrum* case,[176] which held that stock gifted by a shareholder who retained a majority of the corporation's stock at his death was not includable in his estate because he owed a fiduciary duty to the minority shareholders. Although *Byrum* was legislatively overruled with respect to certain corporations with the enactment of Section 2036(b), the rule has not been changed for partnerships.

For this as well as non-tax reasons, a family partnership agreement should not eliminate the general partner's fiduciary duty to the limited partners. A provision eliminating such fiduciary duty is occasionally inserted in an attempt to reduce the value of gifted limited partnership interests for transfer tax purposes. Such a restriction would be unlikely to be respected under

---

[174] As discussed above, notwithstanding the IRS's contrary view, it is submitted that a partnership for a term of years should not be treated as a partnership at will.

[175] Priv. Ltr. Rul. 9546007 (Aug. 17, 1995); Priv. Ltr. Rul. 9546006 (Aug. 14, 1995); Priv. Ltr. Rul. 9415007 (Jan. 12, 1994); Priv. Ltr. Rul. 9332006 (Aug. 20, 1992); Priv. Ltr. Rul. 9310039 (Dec. 16, 1992); Priv. Ltr. Rul. 9131006 (Apr. 30, 1991); Priv. Ltr. Rul. 8611004 (Nov. 15, 1985). This analysis assumes that the partnership is respected. If the partnership formalities are ignored, the gifted interest may be included in the estate. Estate of Schauerhamer v. Comm'r, 73 TCM (CCH) 2855 (1997) (gifted limited partnerships included in donor's estate under IRC § 2036(a)(1) when partnership income deposited directly in donor partner's personal bank account and used to pay her personal expenses).

[176] United States v. Byrum, 408 US 125 (1972).

Section 2703. But even if Section 2703 were not a problem, it accomplishes little to give away highly discounted partnership interests if they are brought back into the donor's estate under Sections 2036(a)(2) and 2038(a)(1).

Similarly, if Mom transfers a partnership interest to Child and Child is intentionally not admitted as a substitute partner in an effort to get a lower value for the assignee interest, could problems arise? A number of courts have held that a partner owes no fiduciary duty, solely by virtue of the assignment, to the holder of an assignee interest in the partnership who is not admitted as a substitute partner.[177] This is because, where a partner has transferred an assignee interest, the assignee is not admitted as a partner. In such an instance, the assignor partner generally has control over the interest, either as general partner or as assignor with retained management rights. Accordingly, under these circumstances, might the IRS take the position that the assignor partner's lack of fiduciary duty to the assignee will cause the assignee interest to be included in the assignor's estate? Of course, the assignor might have fiduciary duties to other partners, if not to the particular assignee, which would render all of his conduct subject to fiduciary standards. Or, if the transferor is a limited, rather than a general, partner his fiduciary duties to the other partners would have been much less than those of a general partner, in any case. Finally, if all the interests besides the general partner's are assignee interests, could the IRS assert that no partnership exists any longer? It seems that Revenue Ruling 77-137, holding that an assignee is taxed as a partner, would prevent this.[178]

PRACTICE POINTER: If Dad wants to make annual exclusion gifts of limited partnership interests, the partnership agreement should provide that limited partners may transfer their interests (subject to a right of first refusal in the other partners if desired), rather than prohibiting transfer altogether or permitting transfer only with the general partner's consent. This is because, where limited partners have no right to sell or redeem their interests and no control over or right to distributions, the IRS may take the position that the limited partners have no ability to obtain any current value, and hence that gifts of the limited partnership interests are gifts of future interests that do not qualify for the gift tax annual exclusion.[179] The IRS could also argue, under these circumstances, that the limited partners are

---

[177] Griffin v. Box, 910 F2d 255, 261 (5th Cir. 1990); Bynum v. Frisby, 311 P2d 972, 975 (Nev. 1957); Kellis v. Ring, 155 Cal. Rptr. 297, 299-300 (Cal. Ct. App. 1979); accord 7547 Corp. v. Parker & Parsley Dev. Partners, L.P., 38 F3d 211, 216-220 (5th Cir. 1994) (highlighting distinction between assignees and limited partners in denying assignees standing to sue derivatively on behalf of partnership). According to J. Gallison, Partnership Law and Practice § 21.15 (McGraw-Hill, Inc. 1994), there is a question about what fiduciary duty, if any, is due to assignees. He points out that, even if an assignee cannot bring a derivative suit for breach of duty, the assignee is entitled to share in the recovery if the actual limited partners bring such a suit.

[178] See RULPA § 101(7).

[179] See Ch. 10.

not truly partners for income tax purposes.[180]

[5] Limited Partnership Interests Received in Non-Gift Transactions

In some cases, it may be desirable for junior family members or trusts for junior family members to invest their own assets in the family limited partnership in exchange for partnership interests. Junior family members may do this because they have sizable estates of their own and might be enthusiastic about making current or future gifts of their own limited partnership interests. In addition, where a family business is transferred to the partnership, some of the business assets may already be owned by junior family members. In such a case, the junior family members would receive a partnership interest on account of their ownership of these business assets.

Junior family members or trusts can also purchase limited partnership interests after the partnership is formed. This may be recommended where the senior family members do not wish to make gifts. The junior family members or trusts might purchase the partnership interests for cash, with an installment note (with interest payable at the applicable federal rate),[181] or by paying an annuity to the senior family member, depending on which is more favorable under the circumstances. Valuation of these partnership interests should be determined in a similar manner as gifted interests.

Of course, there will be income tax consequences associated with the sale of a partnership interest. Income tax consequences can also occur on a contribution to a partnership in exchange for a partnership interest.[182]

¶ 16.04 INCOME TAXATION OF FAMILY PARTNERSHIPS

[1] Basic Rules

A partnership is not a taxable entity.[183] Rather, the partnership passes through its tax items to the partners. As a consequence, partners report items of partnership income, gain, loss, deduction, and credit on their own return.[184] The rules of partnership taxation are far beyond the scope of this book. However, a few highly simplified basics of particular relevance to estate planning are included.

---

[180] See regulations under IRC § 704(e) and discussion at ¶ 16.04[7][a] below.

[181] See Ch. 11 for a description of the applicable federal rate.

[182] See discussion at ¶ 16.04[3] below.

[183] IRC § 701.

[184] IRC § 701.

[a] Partnership Classification—Federal Income Tax

Merely calling an entity a partnership does not mean that it will be considered a partnership for federal income tax purposes. Some partnerships are considered associations that are taxable as corporations for income tax purposes. That result is usually unacceptable. Partnerships, which are treated as partnerships for federal income tax purposes are pass-through entities, with income being taxed and deductions being taken at the partner level rather than the partnership level. In contrast, corporate income (other than certain income of S corporations) is subject to a double tax—that is, the corporation pays tax on its income and the shareholders then pay tax on the corporate distributions they receive. A partnership that is treated as an association taxable as a corporation will not be an S corporation, since it will not have made an S election.[185] It is therefore important that the partnership be structured so that it is not taxed as a C corporation.

A domestic partnership will generally be classified as a partnership if there are at least two partners.[186] In the past, a special four-factor test, determining whether the partnership lacked the corporate characteristics of centralized management, limited liability, free transferability of interests, and continuity of life, had to be passed for an entity to be classified as a partnership for federal income tax purposes. At present, however, the check-the-box system has replaced this four-factor test.[187]

[b] Anti-Abuse Regulations

The family partnership should be structured not only so that it constitutes a valid partnership for federal tax purposes, but also so that transactions involving partnership property and interests in the partnership will be respected. The anti-abuse regulations under subchapter K (the federal partnership income tax provisions) provide that certain transactions involving partnerships, or even the partnerships themselves, may be disregarded where a principal purpose of the transaction is to substantially reduce the present value of the partners' aggregate federal tax liability in a manner inconsistent with the intent of subchapter K.[188]

According to the anti-abuse regulations, the intent of subchapter K should be satisfied if the partnership meets the following three tests:

- First, the partnership must be bona fide and each partnership trans-

---

[185] Note, however, that it appears that a partnership that is taxable as an association is eligible to make an S election (assuming it otherwise meets the requirements of an S corporation). See IRC §§ 1361(b), 7701(a)(3); Treas. Reg. § 1.1361-1(c).

[186] Treas. Reg. §§ 301.7701-3(b)(1), 301.7701-3(b)(3).

[187] See ¶ 16.04[2] below.

[188] Treas. Reg. § 1.701-2(b).

action (or series of transactions) must be entered into for a substantial business purpose.

- Second, the form of partnership transactions should reflect the substance of what is taking place.
- Third, the income tax consequences to each partner of partnership operations, and of transactions between that partner and the partnership, should reflect the partners' economic agreement and that partner's income.[189]

If the partnership does not satisfy these requirements, the income tax consequences of the partnership or the partners' activities may be recharacterized by the IRS. The regulations describe a number of forms that such recharacterization may take, and give examples of specific situations where recharacterization may occur in cases where the partnership does not comply with the intent of subchapter K and the partners' aggregate tax liability is reduced.[190]

Although the anti-abuse regulations only apply for income tax, and not transfer tax purposes,[191] general principles of law may permit the courts to disregard partnerships and partnership transactions which are abusive and inconsistent with Congressional intent. As it is not always clear precisely how such principles would apply, and as the IRS has indicated that it may issue separate transfer tax anti-abuse rules designed to address family partnerships, it is important that the intent of both partnership income and transfer tax laws be considered in the design and operation of the family partnership.

[c] Capital Accounts

Each partner has a capital account. A partner's capital account is generally credited with the amount of his contributions and his share of income of the partnership and is debited by his share of losses and by distributions to him.[192] Certain events cause the capital accounts to be "booked up," which means adjusted to reflect the fair market value of the partners' respective shares of partnership property. Many of the complexities of partnership income tax and accounting rules center around what happens when losses or distributions would make a partner's capital account negative.

[d] Limitations on Losses

The ability of a partner to deduct his share of partnership losses may be limited by several rules.

---

[189] Treas. Reg. § 1.701-2(a).

[190] Treas. Reg. §§ 1.701-2(b)–1.701-2(d).

[191] See IRS Announcement 95-8, 1995-7 IRB 56.

[192] Treas. Reg. § 1.704-1(b)(2)(iv).

Section 704(d) basis limitation. A partner cannot take losses in excess of his basis in his partnership interest. To the extent that he acquired his partnership interest other than through making contributions to the partnership in exchange for his interest, his basis is determined according to normal basis rules applicable to any property.[193] For example, if he purchases a partnership interest from another partner for $100, his basis in his partnership interest is initially $100. Thereafter, his partnership basis is (1) increased by the tax basis of his contributions to the partnership, his share of partnership taxable and tax-exempt income, his share of the excess of depletion deductions over the basis of the depleting partnership property, and his share of partnership liabilities, and (2) decreased by his share of partnership losses, his share of the partnership's nondeductible expenses which are not properly chargeable to capital account, certain depletion deductions, and the value of any partnership distributions to him.[194]

Here, it pays to mention one significant difference between partnerships and S corporations—that is, while both partners and S corporation shareholders are subject to a similar basis restriction on the deduction of entity losses, a partner gets to include entity liabilities in his basis for purposes of this limitation, but an S corporation shareholder cannot.

A partner's share of a partnership liability depends on whether the debt is recourse or nonrecourse. If the debt is recourse to the partnership, or to any partner, the partners share the liability to the extent of their economic risk of loss.[195] This generally means that limited partners cannot take losses for recourse debt, once their capital accounts are exhausted. If the debt is nonrecourse, all of the partners can share in basis attributable to that debt, even if the losses allocated to them on account of the debt exceed their capital accounts, provided the partnership agreement contains certain so-called "gain chargeback" provisions.[196]

Section 469 passive loss limitation. A partner cannot deduct losses attributable to a passive activity of the partnership, except to the extent of passive income. The rules on passive losses are very complicated. An activity is generally considered passive rather than active with respect to an owner if the owner does not "materially participate" in the activity. An interest held by a limited partner is generally treated as an interest with respect to which the limited partner does not materially participate.[197] Hence, putting an active trade or business into a limited partnership can limit the ability of the limited partners to take losses with respect to that activity.

Section 465 at-risk limitation. A partner's ability to deduct losses may be limited by the at-risk rules, which generally provide that a partner cannot take

---

[193] IRC § 742.

[194] IRC § 705(a).

[195] Treas. Reg. § 1.752-3.

[196] Treas. Reg. § 1.752-3.

[197] IRC § 469(h)(2).

a tax loss with respect to certain activities unless he actually bears the risk of economic loss. Hence, the at-risk rules will generally prevent a limited partner from taking losses on those activities conducted by the partnership, except to the extent of actual money contributed by him plus his obligation (if any) to contribute additional capital.[198]

Section 707(b)(1) related party loss disallowance rule. No deduction is allowed in respect of a loss from a sale or exchange of property (other than an interest in the partnership), directly or indirectly (1) between a partnership and a person who owns, directly or indirectly, more than 50 percent of the capital interest or the profits interest in the partnership or (2) between two partnerships in which the same persons own, directly or indirectly, more than 50 percent of the capital interests or profits interests.[199]

Losses which cannot be deducted currently because of the above rules may be suspended. Certain events can enable the partner or a transferee to take the suspended losses at a later time, or the losses can end up being added to the basis of property, or might be lost altogether. The rules are complex.

[e] Taxable Year and Partner's Death

A partnership is generally required to use the taxable year of its major partners, unless the IRS gives permission to use a different year based on a business purpose.[200] Family partnerships are often on calendar years. Suppose Partner and Partnership are both on a calendar year. Partner dies. Partnership continues its business, so the partnership year does not close.[201] Since the taxable year does not close, none of the partnership income for the taxable year in which Partner's death occurs will be included in Partner's last return, and Partner's entire distributive share for the year will be taxable to his estate or to his designated successor in interest.[202] This will be true even if Partner's estate does not actually receive any of the income attributable to the period before his death.

However, the partnership year will close if a sale or exchange of the partner's interest occurs on the date of death, pursuant to an agreement existing at the date of death.[203]

---

[198] IRC § 465.

[199] IRC § 707(b)(1).

[200] IRC § 706(b)(1).

[201] IRC § 706(c).

[202] Treas. Reg. § 1.706-1(c)(3)(iii).

[203] Treas. Reg. § 1.706-1(c)(3)(iv).

[2] Partnership Classification—Certain State Taxes

To determine whether a partnership will be treated as a partnership or a corporation for state tax regimes that use the old pre-check-the-box federal tests, the entity will be examined to see if it resembles a corporation.

NOTE: The old federal rules will be explained here, but they are only generally applicable for such state tax purposes. The check-the-box rules have made the rules obsolete for federal income tax purposes.

Four features that are characteristic of both partnerships and corporations are: centralization of management, limited liability, continuity of life, and free transferability of interests. Under the old federal test, if an entity had more corporate than non-corporate characteristics, the entity would be taxable as a corporation.[204] For example, if a partnership had centralized management and free transferability of interests but lacked continuity of life and limited liability, and if it had no other characteristics which were significant in determining its classification, it would not be classified as an association taxable as a corporation.[205] Three leading cases on partnership classification were *Morrissey v. Commissioner,*[206] *Zuckman v. United States,*[207] and *Larson v. Commissioner.*[208]

[a] Centralization of Management

Many family limited partnerships will have the corporate characteristic of centralization of management. An entity has centralized management if any person (or any group of persons which does not include all of the members) has continuing exclusive authority to make management decisions necessary to the conduct of the entity's business.[209] This regulatory provision did not equate centralized management with the concentration of authority in less than all the members of a group—for example, in the general partner of a limited partnership. Rather, the regulation provided that a limited partnership subject to a statute corresponding to the Uniform Limited Partnership Act or RULPA generally would not have centralized management unless substantially all of the interests in the partnership were owned by the limited part-

---

[204] Former Treas. Reg. § 301.7701-2(a)(3).

[205] Former Treas. Reg. § 301.7701-2(a)(3).

[206] 296 US 344 (1935).

[207] 524 F2d 729 (Ct. Cl. 1975).

[208] 66 TC 159 (1976), acq., 1979-1 CB 1.

[209] Former Treas. Reg. § 301.7701-2(c)(1).

ners.[210] The theory appeared to be that the general partners will be acting as representatives of the limited partners (comparable to a board of directors) where the limited partners own substantially all of the interests in the partnership, but will be acting for their own benefit if they have a substantial interest. Thus, when a family limited partnership is initially formed, it may lack centralized management where Son has a one percent limited partnership interest, and Mom is the one percent general partner and a 98 percent limited partner. Once she gives away her limited partnership interests, however, Mom will have only a one percent interest as general partner, and thus the partnership will be considered to have centralized management.

How much is "substantially all" of the partnership interests? It is not a bright-line test. The former regulations contained an example in which centralized management was found to exist when the general partners owned in the aggregate 5.66 percent of the interest in the limited partnership.[211] Under pre-check-the-box law, the IRS would rule that a partnership lacked centralized management if limited partnership interests (excluding those held by general partners) constituted less than 80 percent of the total interests in the partnership.[212]

Even if the general partner owned 20 percent or more of the total interests in the partnership, the regulations also provided that the right of all, or a specified group, of the limited partners to remove a general partner might affect whether the partnership has centralized management, depending on the facts and circumstances.[213] Thus, if the limited partners can remove the general partner for any reason, the partnership should have centralized management. Conversely, if the limited partners may only remove the general partner under substantially restricted circumstances (e.g., the general partner's gross negligence, self-dealing, or embezzlement), this should not in and of itself cause the partnership to have centralized management.[214]

Should the limited partners have the authority to remove the general partner? Most family limited partnerships will lack at least two out of three of the other corporate characteristics, as discussed below. Consequently, it should not be necessary to avoid giving the limited partners this authority just to ensure that the partnership will lack centralized management. However, both practical and tax considerations may make granting such authority less than desirable. Mom may want to surrender control of the family business at a time of her own choosing, and not whenever her children think they are

---

[210] Former Treas. Reg. § 301.7701-2(c)(4). All references in Treas. Reg. § 301.7701-2 to the Uniform Limited Partnership Act (6 ULA 561 (1976) (ULPA) are also deemed to be references to RULPA. Treas. Reg. § 301.7701-2(a)(5).

[211] Former Treas. Reg. § 301.7701-3(b)(2), example 1.

[212] Rev. Proc. 89-12, 1989-1 CB 798.

[213] Former Treas. Reg. § 301.7701-2(c)(4).

[214] Former Treas. Reg. § 301.7701-2(c)(4).

ready to take over. From a state tax viewpoint, allowing the limited partners to remove the general partner can affect whether the partnership lacks some of the other corporate characteristics, as discussed below. For federal tax purposes, such a provision may increase the value of limited partnership interests that are given away.[215]

[b] Limited Liability

A limited partnership will possess the corporate characteristic of limited liability if the general partner has no substantial assets (other than his interest in the partnership) and is merely a dummy of the limited partners.[216]

[i] "Dummy" test. Many family limited partnerships cannot be assured of a favorable outcome when the dummy test is applied. A dummy general partner is generally defined as a partner who is under the control of the limited partners. If a corporate general partner is owned by the limited partners (or persons related to the limited partners), it may be considered a dummy of the limited partners, especially if there is a pattern of subservience to the limited partners' wishes.[217]

[ii] "Substantial capitalization" test. Under the old rules, the IRS had issued revenue procedures that provided safe harbors for determining whether an individual or corporate general partner would be considered to have substantial assets, thus ensuring that the partnership lacked limited liability. If the safe harbor was not met, the issue of whether the general partner had substantial assets would be decided on a facts-and-circumstances basis.

Under pre-check-the-box rules, to obtain a ruling that a corporate general partner was substantially capitalized, the net worth of the corporate general partner (excluding its interest in the partnership) must have equaled at least ten percent of the total contributions to the limited partnership and must have been expected to continue to meet or exceed that level throughout the life of the partnership.[218] If there was more than one corporate general partner, this requirement could be met on a collective basis.[219] A special rule applied to a

---

[215] See discussion at ¶ 16.03[1] above.

[216] Former Treas. Reg. § 301.7701-2(d)(2) (emphasis added).

[217] But see Zuckman v. United States, 524 F2d 729, 740–741 (Ct. Cl. 1975), which held that if the general partner were a dummy, the limited partners would be personally liable under state law, and therefore the partnership would lack the corporate characteristic of limited liability.

[218] Rev. Proc. 89-12, 1989-1 CB 798, amplified, Rev. Proc. 91-13, 1991 CB 477, modified, Rev. Proc. 92-88, 1992-2 CB 496.

[219] Rev. Proc. 92-88, 1992-2 CB 496.

corporation that was a general partner in more than one limited partnership.[220] In addition, the IRS had indicated that for purposes of meeting the safe harbor, a corporate general partner could be capitalized with a shareholder note if the note was a negotiable demand note that accrued interest (compounded, if not paid) at a reasonable market rate.[221] Furthermore, the shareholder(s) had to have sufficient assets, reachable by creditors, to satisfy the note.[222] The requirements for obtaining a favorable ruling were not substantive requirements to be used for audit purposes. Each case was decided on its own facts.[223]

If the sole general partner of the partnership was an individual, the IRS had stated that the partnership would lack the corporate characteristic of limited liability if the general partner's net worth (excluding his or her interest in the partnership) equaled or exceeded the lesser of ten percent of the total contributions to the partnership or $1,000,000.[224] If there was more than one individual general partner, this requirement could be met on a collective basis.[225]

If the general partners of a partnership included both corporations and individuals, in order to receive a favorable ruling under the pre-check-the-box rules, either the corporate and individual general partners had to meet the corporate net worth requirement on a collective basis, or the individual general partner(s) in the aggregate had to meet the individual net worth requirement.[226]

[iii] Limited liability issues for family partnerships. There is no history of applying the dummy/substantial capitalization test to a trust general partner.

Should a corporate general partner be substantially capitalized or can the family rely on the general partner not being considered a dummy? The dummy test is relatively subjective and unpredictable. For example, while the corporate general partner may not seem to be under the control of the limited partners at the beginning, in later years this may change. Moreover, if Mom decides not to own the corporate general partner in the first place, or to give her stock to her children later, this may affect the outcome of the dummy test. It may therefore be desirable to transfer some assets to the corporation in

---

[220] GCM 39798 (Nov. 6, 1989).

[221] GCM 39798 (Nov. 6, 1989).

[222] GCM 39798 (Nov. 6, 1989).

[223] Rev. Proc. 89-12, § 1.03.

[224] Rev. Proc. 92-88, 1992-2 CB 496. The test may exclude assets which are exempt from creditors. See Rev. Proc. 89-12, § 4.07.

[225] Rev. Proc. 92-88, 1992-2 CB 496.

[226] Rev. Proc. 92-88, 1992-2 CB 496.

addition to the partnership interest.[227] In particular, the general partner may need to be substantially capitalized where the partnership agreement does not prohibit partners from transferring their interests. There may also be nontax reasons for substantially capitalizing the corporate general partner. Practically speaking, partnership creditors may find it easier to "pierce the corporate veil" of a shell corporation rather than a corporation with some assets, particularly where some informality exists in the operation of the corporation.[228]

Does an individual general partner have to have substantial assets? The old revenue procedure listing the requirements for obtaining a ruling on classification required a representation that the individual had substantial assets.[229] However, the former regulations only referred to corporations.

[c] Continuity of Life

Family limited partnerships will often lack the corporate characteristic of continuity of life. An organization lacks continuity of life if any member has the power under local law to dissolve (not liquidate) the organization. A limited partnership subject to a statute corresponding to ULPA or RULPA automatically lacks continuity of life because the withdrawal of a general partner causes the dissolution of the partnership.[230]

Often a family limited partnership agreement will permit a certain percentage in interest of the partners to continue the partnership after all the general partners have withdrawn. Before the check-the-box rules, if the partnership agreement permitted less than a majority in interest of the limited partners to elect a new general partner to continue the partnership, the IRS would not rule that the partnership lacked continuity of life.[231] If, however, under local law and the partnership agreement, the bankruptcy or removal of a general partner of a limited partnership caused a dissolution of the partnership unless the remaining general partners or at least a majority in interest of all remaining partners agreed to continue the partnership, the IRS would not take the position that the limited partnership had continuity of life.[232] The "majority in interest" requirement would be deemed to be satisfied if remaining partners owning a majority of the profits interests and a majority of the

---

[227] Where the corporate general partner is substantially capitalized, it may be advisable to elect S corporation treatment to avoid a double tax on its income.

[228] 1 James D. Cox, Thomas Lee Hagen, & F. Hodge O'Neal, Corporations § 7.11 (1995); Robert Clark, Corporate Law 74 (1986).

[229] Rev. Proc. 92-88, 1992-2 CB 496.

[230] Former Treas. Reg. §§ 301.7701-2(a)(5), 301.7701-2(b)(1), 301.7701-2(b)(3).

[231] Rev. Proc. 89-12, 1989-1 CB 798.

[232] Rev. Proc. 92-35, 1992-1 CB 790.

capital interests agreed to continue the partnership.[233] For purposes of this safe harbor, profits were determined and allocated based on any reasonable estimate of profits from the date of the dissolution event to the projected termination of the partnership, taking into account present and future allocations of profits under the partnership agreement. Capital was determined as of the date of the dissolution event. If capital accounts were determined and maintained in accordance with Treasury Regulation § 1.704-1(b)(2)(iv), capital determined as of the date of the dissolution event represented the capital account balances on that date.[234]

[d] Free Transferability of Interests

Family limited partnerships will often need to be structured so that they lack the corporate characteristic of free transferability of interests, particularly where the partnership may have the corporate characteristic of limited liability because the general partner is not substantially capitalized. Free transferability exists if members "owning substantially all of the interests in the organization have the power, without the consent of other members, to substitute for themselves in the same organization a person who is not a member of the organization."[235] Consequently, if the general partner's consent is required for an assignee to be admitted to the partnership as a substitute limited partner, free transferability should not exist. The Tax Court has nevertheless held that free transferability will exist if the general partner's consent may not be unreasonably withheld under the partnership agreement.[236] Thus, many family limited partnership agreements formerly provided that a partner could transfer his interest only with the general partner's consent, which might be given (or not given) in the general partner's sole and absolute discretion. Note, however, that if the corporate general partner is owned by the limited partners or persons related to the limited partners, the view could be taken that the general partner will consent to whatever the limited partners want, thereby making a consent provision meaningless. Moreover, such a requirement may increase the risk that gifted interests will be included in the general partner's estate under Section 2036(a)(2) or Section 2038(a)(1), if fiduciary requirements are eliminated.[237] This requirement may also raise issues under Section 2703.[238] Finally, the presence of a requirement that the general partner con-

---

[233] Rev. Proc. 94-46, 1994-2 CB 688.

[234] Rev. Proc. 94-46, 1994-2 CB 688.

[235] Former Treas. Reg. § 301.7701-2(e)(1).

[236] Larson v. Comm'r, 66 TC 159, 163 (1976), acq., 1979-1 CB 1.

[237] See discussion at ¶ 16.03[4] above.

[238] See discussion at ¶ 16.03[3][c] above.

sent to a transfer may result in certain partners not being recognized as partners for federal income tax purposes.[239]

If a family wants to better ensure that the partnership lacks free transferability of interests, this may generally be accomplished by providing in the partnership agreement that no partner may transfer his management interests in the partnership.[240] Under the old rules, the IRS had indicated that a partnership would lack "free transferability" if the partnership agreement prohibited the transfer of an interest or provided for the partnership's dissolution upon the transfer of an interest.[241] This was true even if the affected partners had the power to amend the partnership agreement to allow transfers. The IRS also took the position that a partnership would lack free transferability of interests if, throughout the life of the partnership, the partnership agreement expressly restricted[242] the transferability of partnership interests representing more than 20 percent of all interests in partnership capital, income, gain, loss, deduction, and credit.[243] Note once again, however, that either such provision may affect whether all of the partners are recognized as such for federal income tax purposes.[244] In addition, prohibiting partners from transferring their interests may not be a good idea if family members wish to make annual exclusion gifts to other family members, and it may cause problems under Section 2703.[245]

[e] Structuring the Partnership

If, for state tax purposes, it is necessary to qualify as a partnership under the old federal rules, families have some choice in deciding which corporate characteristics to avoid, but this choice will be influenced by the other decisions they make in structuring the partnership. Most family limited partnerships will have centralization of management and will not have continuity of life. In a family limited partnership, the fact that the parties are closely related raises the issue of whether the general partner is amenable to the will of the limited partners. If the general partner is so viewed, where the general partner is not substantially capitalized, the limited liability requirement may not be met on the theory that the general partner is a "dummy." In addition, where the partnership agreement allows the partners to transfer their interests with the general partner's consent, rather than prohibiting transfers of the man-

---

[239] See discussion at ¶ 16.04[7][a] below.

[240] Former Treas. Reg. § 301.7701-2(e)(1).

[241] Rev. Rul. 93-4, 1993-1 CB 225.

[242] Within the meaning of former Treas. Reg. § 301.7701-2(e)(1).

[243] Rev. Proc. 92-33, 1992-1 CB 782.

[244] See discussion at ¶ 16.04[7][a] below.

[245] See discussion at ¶¶ 16.02[2][e] and 16.03[3][c] above.

agement rights associated with partnership interests, the free transferability requirement may not be met on the theory that the requirement of the general partner's consent to a transfer is meaningless.

The family will therefore need to make a decision. Specifically, where the family decides not to substantially capitalize the general partner, it is best if the partnership agreement prohibits all partners from transferring the management rights with respect to their interests. Where the family decides to substantially capitalize the general partner, the partnership agreement may restrict, or refrain from restricting, the partners' ability to transfer their interests as necessary to best achieve the family's wishes and objectives. Either choice will require consideration of the effect any restrictions on transferability may have on whether all partners will be respected as such for federal income tax purposes[246] and on valuation for transfer tax purposes.[247]

[3] Tax Consequences of In-kind Contributions to Partnership

[a] General Rule

Generally, neither the partnership nor any of its partners will recognize gain or loss as a result of transferring appreciated or depreciated property to the partnership in exchange for a partnership interest.[248] When the partnership ultimately sells the property, the partners will generally share the gain or loss in a manner that takes into account any variations between the fair market value of the property when it was contributed and the partnership's basis in the property.[249] In essence, this means that where a partner contributes property to a partnership that would if sold result in a gain (built-in gain property) or loss (built-in loss property), he (as opposed to the other partners) will typically recognize the gain (or loss) when the partnership later disposes of the property, to the extent of the built-in gain or loss existing at the time such property was contributed to the partnership. If a partner gives away partnership interests, presumably the donees who accede to the donor partner's basis would also accede to these Section 704(c) built-in gain/built-in loss consequences attributable to that interest.

[b] Taxable Contributions

There are a number of situations where a partner who contributes appreciated property will recognize gain.

---

[246] See discussion at ¶ 16.04[7] below.

[247] See discussion at ¶¶ 16.03[3][c] and 16.04 above.

[248] IRC § 721(a).

[249] IRC § 704(c)(1)(A).

[i] **Contributor's liabilities assumed.** Gain may be recognized on the contribution of property if a partner's liabilities are assumed by the partnership or if the partnership takes property subject to the partner's liabilities, and those liabilities exceed the partner's basis in the partnership (as increased for her allocable share of those liabilities).[250] The portion of the partner's liability assumed by the partnership allocated to other partners is, in substance, treated as a cash distribution to the contributor.[251] This distribution decreases the contributor's basis in his partnership interest (but not below zero), and any distribution in excess of basis generates taxable gain to the contributor.[252]

> EXAMPLE: Mom contributes a commercial building valued at $1,000,000 to a partnership in exchange for a 20 percent limited partnership interest. Mom's basis in the building is $340,000 at the time of the contribution. The building is subject to a nonrecourse debt of $800,000. Upon the contribution, Mom's allocable share of the debt is $160,000 (20 percent of $800,000), and her basis in her partnership interest is $500,000 ($340,000 basis in the building + $160,000 Mom's 20 percent share of the liability after it was assumed by the partnership). Immediately thereafter, Mom will be treated as having received a cash distribution of $640,000 (the amount of her debt that is allocable to the other partners). Mom's $500,000 basis in her partnership interest will be reduced to zero as a result of the deemed distribution and she will recognize $140,000 ($640,000 deemed distribution − $500,000 basis) of taxable capital gain.

[ii] **Investment partnerships.** Nonrecognition treatment does not apply to contributions to partnership "investment companies."[253] A partnership is an "investment company" for this purpose if, after the relevant contribution, more than 80 percent of the value of its assets (excluding cash and nonconvertible debt obligations) consists of readily marketable stocks or securities (or interests in regulated investment companies or real estate investment trusts) held for investment.[254] Thus, where Mom and Son each contribute different marketable stocks to a partnership in exchange for partnership interests, Mom and Son may each recognize gain (but not loss) with respect to the stock she or he contributed.

There is an important exception to these Section 721(b) recognition requirements that applies if the contribution does not result in diversification of the transferor's interests.[255] In this regard, the transfer of assets to an entity

---

[250] IRC §§ 752, 731(a)(1).

[251] IRC § 752(b).

[252] IRC §§ 731(a)(1), 741.

[253] IRC § 721(b); S. Rep. No. 938, 94th Cong., 2d Sess., pt. 2, at 43 (1976).

[254] IRC § 721(b); Treas. Reg. § 1.351-1(c)(1)(ii)(c).

[255] See S. Rep. No. 938, 94th Cong., 2d Sess., pt. 2, at 43–44. See Priv. Ltr. Rul. 9538023 (June 26, 1995), Priv. Ltr. Rul. 9550023 (Sept. 15, 1995), and Priv. Ltr. Rul.

will not result in diversification of the transferor's interest if each transferor transfers an already diversified portfolio of stocks and securities to the partnership.[256]

If family members desire to contribute diverse investments to a partnership, Section 721(b) should be examined carefully, as the intent of Section 721(b) is to prevent use of the nonrecognition rule of Section 721(a) to achieve tax-free diversification of investments. If Section 721(b) would otherwise be applicable, some practitioners recommend providing for special allocations of income, gain, and loss from specific property to the contributing partner and requiring that a partner receive the property she contributed upon withdrawal.[257] Where such allocations are used, however, it may call into question whether a partnership with respect to that property truly exists. In addition, providing for this type of special allocation may result in unexpected and adverse gift tax consequences under the special valuation rules of Chapter 14 of the Internal Revenue Code.[258] Consequently, rather than incorporating special arrangements designed to avoid the investment company gain recognition rules into the partnership agreement, it is often preferable to adjust the property used to fund the partnership and thus avoid the investment company rules altogether.

[iii] **Disguised sales.** Nonrecognition treatment is not provided to contributions that are "disguised sales." A contribution of property by a partner to a partnership may be recharacterized as a "disguised sale" if before or after such contribution, the partnership distributes to the contributing partner cash or other property that is, in substance, consideration for the contribution.[259] Any contribution by and distribution to a partner within a two-year period will be presumed to be a sale.[260] For example, if within a two-year period Mom transfers property to the partnership and the partnership transfers money or other consideration to Mom, Mom's transfer of property to the partnership is presumed to be a sale of the property by Mom to the partnership, unless the facts and circumstances clearly establish that the transfer is not a sale.[261]

[iv] **Distribution of contributed property to another partner.** If a partner contributes property to the partnership, and the partnership distributes the

---

9544012 (Aug. 1, 1995) for examples of situations which did not result in diversification.

[256] Treas. Reg. § 1.351-1(c); IRC § 721(b).

[257] See S. Rep. No. 938, 94th Cong., 2d Sess., pt. 2, at 44.

[258] See discussion at ¶ 16.03[3][a] above.

[259] IRC § 707(a)(2).

[260] Treas. Reg. § 1.707-3(c).

[261] Treas. Reg. § 1.707-3(c)(1).

contributed property to another partner within five years, the contributing partner generally must recognize the precontribution built-in gain or loss from the "sale" of such property, to the extent that she would have realized it if the property had been sold by the partnership at its fair market value at the time of the distribution.[262] The Section 704 regulations contain anti-abuse provisions designed to ensure that this rule is not circumvented.[263]

[v] Distribution of other property to contributing partner. In the case of an in-kind distribution to a partner who has previously made in-kind contributions, the distributee partner must recognize gain equal to the lesser of: (1) the excess of the fair market value of the distributed property over the adjusted basis of the distributee partner's partnership interest or (2) the net precontribution gain of the distributee partner.[264] The net precontribution gain is the gain that would have been recognized by the distributee partner under Section 704(c)(1)(B) if all relevant property had been sold for its fair market value on the date of distribution. Relevant property is property that was contributed to the partnership by the distributee partner within five years of the distribution and was held by the partnership immediately before the distribution.

> EXAMPLE: Mom contributes Blackacre to Partnership. Blackacre has a basis of 10 and a value of 15, so Mom's net precontribution gain is 5. Suppose Mom receives Whiteacre (valued at 7) as a partnership distribution a year later. Mom will recognize gain, as if Blackacre had been sold on the date she received Whiteacre, up to a maximum gain of 5.

[4] Taxation of Distributions Received From Partnership

With certain exceptions, a partner does not recognize gain or loss on receiving a distribution from the partnership.[265] Where money is distributed, however, the partner will recognize gain to the extent the money distributed exceeds the adjusted basis of the partner's interest in the partnership immediately before the distribution.[266] In addition, in certain cases, a partner may recognize loss upon distributions in liquidation of a partner's partnership interest.[267]

A reduction in a partner's share of liabilities is considered a distribution of money.[268] Also, for purposes of gain recognition, marketable securities are

---

[262] IRC § 704(c)(1)(B)(i); Treas. Reg. § 1.704-4(a).

[263] See Treas. Reg. § 1.704-4(f).

[264] IRC § 737.

[265] IRC § 731(a).

[266] IRC § 731(a).

[267] IRC § 731(a)(2).

[268] IRC § 752(b).

generally considered money when distributed.[269] An exception applies, however, where the partner to whom the marketable security is distributed is the person who originally contributed the security to the partnership.[270] An additional exception provides that a distribution of marketable securities from an "investment partnership" to an "eligible partner" will not result in gain recognition.[271] An "investment partnership" is a partnership that has never engaged in a trade or business and whose assets consist of money, stocks, bonds and other indebtedness, futures and certain other contracts and foreign currency (e.g., a partnership formed solely for the purpose of holding marketable securities for investment or sale to customers).[272] An "eligible partner" is a partner who (1) has not contributed assets to the partnership other than those described in the preceding sentence, and (2) did not receive his partnership interest in a transaction in which gain was not recognized from a person who was not an eligible partner.[273] Partnership tiers are looked through for purposes of applying the investment partnership exception; thus, a partnership that purchases an interest in another partnership that does engage in a trade or business will not qualify for the exception.[274]

Final regulations were issued under Section 731(c) on December 24, 1996.[275] The regulations apply to partnership distributions of marketable securities occurring after December 25, 1996.

Property distributions. In-kind distributions raise a host of issues, and a partnership tax lawyer should be consulted if these are made, whether in liquidation of the partnership or otherwise.

Redemption of a partnership interest. A few special rules apply to payments in redemption of a partner's interest.[276] Generally, those payments are treated under the normal distribution rules, if their amounts depend on the income of the partnership, and as guaranteed payments if they don't.

Guaranteed payments. A payment made to a partner to compensate him for his services to the partnership or for the partnership's use of his capital will be treated as a guaranteed payment (and not a partnership distribution), provided that the amount of such payment is not determined with respect to

---

[269] IRC § 731(c).

[270] IRC § 731(c)(3)(A)(i). Except to the extent that the value of the security is attributable to the fact that direct or indirect contributions have been made to the entity to which the distributed security relates.

[271] IRC § 731(c)(3)(A)(iii).

[272] IRC § 731(c)(3)(C)(i).

[273] IRC § 731(c)(3)(C)(iii).

[274] IRC § 731(c)(3)(C)(iv).

[275] Treas. Reg. § 1.731-2.

[276] IRC § 736.

the partnership's income. A guaranteed payment for such purposes is treated the same as a payment made to a non-partner for such purposes.[277] If the amount of a payment to a partner for services or the use of capital is determined with respect to the partnership's income, the payment will generally be treated as a distribution to the partner.

[5] Termination of Partnership

One thing that practitioners must be aware of is that certain events can terminate the partnership for income tax purposes. In particular, the sale or exchange of 50 percent or more of the total interest in partnership capital or profits within a 12-month period will terminate the partnership.[278] A transfer by gift, bequest, or inheritance does not constitute a sale or exchange, and therefore will not terminate the partnership. However, although a distribution from an estate or trust should not be considered a sale or exchange if it is not treated as such for trust or estate income tax purposes, an issue exists as to such distributions, according to McKee, Nelson & Whitmire, Federal Taxation of Partnerships and Partners, ¶ 12.03[1][3]. On the death of one partner in a two-member partnership, the partnership will not terminate if the estate or other successor in interest of the deceased partner continues to share in the profits and losses of the partnership business.[279]

The consequence of a termination formerly was that the partnership was deemed to have liquidated and distributed its property to the partners, and the remaining partners were deemed immediately thereafter to have contributed the properties to a new partnership. New regulations were issued in May 1997.[280] These regulations say that, instead of the above rule, the partnership will be deemed to transfer all of its assets and liabilities to a new partnership, with the terminated partnership distributing interests in the new partnership to the partners in liquidation. The regulations apply to constructive terminations of partnerships occurring after May 8, 1997, and may be applied to terminations occurring after May 8, 1996, if the partnership and its partners apply the rules to the termination in a consistent manner. The consequence of terminations can be surprising. For example, the tax year of the partnership closes on the termination, and the elections of the terminated partnership are not valid for the new partnership. A partnership tax specialist should be consulted if the requisite percentage interest will be sold or exchanged.

---

[277] IRC § 707(c).

[278] IRC § 708(b)(1)(B).

[279] Treas. Reg. § 1.708-1(b)(1)(i)(a).

[280] Treas. Reg. § 1.708-1(b)(1)(iv).

[6] Section 754 Election to Adjust Basis in Partnership Property

A partnership is entitled to elect to adjust the basis of partnership assets under certain circumstances. The election, if made, may only be revoked with the approval of the district director.[281] Specifically, if appreciated or depreciated assets are distributed to a partner, the partnership may elect to adjust the basis of its remaining assets.[282] In addition, where a partnership interest has been transferred to a new partner, the partnership may adjust the basis of assets with respect to the new partner's interest.[283]

The election can be useful when a partner dies, and the basis in her partnership interest is increased to fair market value pursuant to Section 1014. The partnership can elect to increase its basis in its assets with respect to the transfer by a similar amount, thus increasing the inside basis of the deceased partner to reflect the increase in the outside basis. The basis increase will only affect the tax treatment of the partner with respect to whom it is made. The inside basis of each of the other partners is unaffected by the election.

Non-family partnerships frequently either will not agree to make Section 754 elections at all or will charge the affected partner for the extra bookkeeping expense.

[7] Tax Allocation of Income Among Family Members—Section 704(e)

If the partnership interests of family members are created by gift or by purchase from other family members, the family partnership rules of Section 704(e) must be considered. These rules affect both whether a partner will be recognized as such for income tax purposes and the allocation of partnership income for federal income tax purposes.

[a] Recognition of Donee/Purchaser as a Partner

The test of whether a donee or purchaser of a partnership interest will be recognized as a partner for federal income tax purposes varies depending on whether the partnership uses capital or services to produce its income, whether the donee/purchaser has a capital interest in the partnership, and whether the donee/purchaser is the "real" owner of his interest.

[i] Capital interest owner in non-services partnership.

Nature of partnership and donee/purchaser's interest. Regardless of whether the partnership interest is derived by purchase or gift from any other

---

[281] Treas. Reg. § 1.754-1(c).

[282] IRC § 734.

[283] IRC §§ 743, 754.

person, Section 704(e)(1) provides that the donee/purchaser will be respected as a partner for federal income tax purposes if he owns a capital interest in a partnership in which capital is a material income-producing factor.[284] A person owns a capital interest if he has an interest in partnership assets that will be distributable to him upon withdrawal or liquidation.[285] Thus, a donee-purchaser who has only a profits interest in the partnership will not meet the requirements of the Section 704(e)(1) safe harbor.[286]

Whether capital will be considered a material income-producing factor is determined by reference to the particular facts and circumstances. Generally, capital is a material income-producing factor where a substantial portion of the partnership's income is attributable to use of capital in the partnership business or where the operation of the partnership business requires substantial inventories or a substantial investment in plant, machinery, or other equipment. Capital will not generally be a material income-producing factor where the partnership's income consists principally of fees, commissions, or other compensation for personal services performed by partners or partnership employees.[287] This may often be the case in a professional partnership (e.g., a partnership among several doctors). Family partnerships where the partnership business consists of investments or the manufacture of a product should generally be considered partnerships in which capital is a material income-producing factor, as partnership capital will typically be responsible for generating partnership revenues.

Donor's retained control over donee/purchaser's interest. Assuming that capital is a material income-producing factor in a particular partnership, the remaining question is whether the donee/purchaser is the "real owner" of his partnership interest (i.e., whether he (or the trustee or personal representative acting for his benefit) has dominion and control over the interest, or whether the donor/seller has effectively retained control over the interest).[288] Transactions between family members are closely scrutinized by the IRS to determine whether the ownership of each partnership interest is bona fide.[289]

Whether a donee/purchaser is the "real owner" depends on all of the facts and circumstances of the particular case.[290] Some of the factors that will be taken into account in determining whether the donor/seller has retained excessive control include: (1) the execution of documents legally sufficient to irrevocably transfer the partnership interest; (2) the conduct of the parties

---

[284] See also Treas. Reg. § 1.704-1(e)(1)(ii).

[285] Treas. Reg. § 1.704-1(e)(1)(v).

[286] Treas. Reg. § 1.704-1(e)(1)(v).

[287] Treas. Reg. § 1.704-1(e)(1)(iv).

[288] See Treas. Reg. § 1.704-1(e)(1)(ii).

[289] See Treas. Reg. § 1.704-1(e)(1)(ii).

[290] Treas. Reg. § 1.704-1(e)(2).

with respect to the gift/sale; (3) retention of direct controls by the donor/seller (including retention of control over distributions, retention of control of partnership assets essential to the business and retention of unusual management powers); (4) retention of indirect controls by the donor/seller; (5) participation by the donee/purchaser in management of the partnership business; (6) distributions of income to the donee/purchaser; (7) the conduct of the partnership business; (8) the conduct of trustees as partners; (9) the treatment of interests of minor children; and (10) whether tax-avoidance is a motive.[291]

Any limitation imposed by the donor/seller on the donee/purchaser's rights to liquidate or sell his interest in the partnership without financial detriment may be viewed as a negative factor in determining whether the donee/purchaser is a partner, especially if there is no compelling business reason for the limitation.[292] For this reason, it is preferable that the donor/seller not retain excessive control over the gifted/sold interest. If considerable restrictions are placed on the donee/purchaser's rights with respect to her partnership interest, in addition to those imposed by state law, it may be wise for someone other than the donor/seller or an entity controlled by him to act as general partner. Where the donor/seller is the general partner and there are too many restrictions, the donor/seller, rather than the donee/purchaser, may be taxed on what should be the donee/purchaser's share of partnership income. While this may not necessarily be a bad thing, the restrictions could also conceivably have adverse gift and estate tax consequences.

If a trust created for the benefit of the general partner's children is to be a limited partner, it is preferable if the trustee is unrelated to and independent of the grantor, as such a trustee will normally be recognized as the owner of the partnership interest held in the trust.[293] If the grantor or a person amenable to the grantor's will is trustee, the terms of the trust agreement and the partnership agreement and the conduct of the parties will be considered in deciding whether the trustee is the real owner of the partnership interest.[294]

[ii] Other situations. Section 704(e)(1) and the regulations under that section are silent regarding when a donee/purchaser will be treated as a partner for federal income tax purposes if capital is not a material income-producing factor or if the donee/purchaser does not own a capital interest. A donee/purchaser finding herself in this situation will therefore need to satisfy the common law requirements for being considered a partner for tax purposes.

---

[291] Treas. Reg. § 1.704-1(e)(2).

[292] See Treas. Reg. §§ 1.704-1(e)(2)(ii)(b), 1.704-1(e)(2)(ii)(d); see also discussion at ¶ 16.02[2][d] above.

[293] Treas. Reg. § 1.704-1(e)(2)(vii).

[294] Treas. Reg. § 1.704-1(e)(2)(vii).

These requirements are set forth in *Commissioner v. Culbertson*.[295] The Supreme Court in *Culbertson* held that the real question is not whether the partner's contribution of services was sufficient to satisfy an objective standard. Rather, the test is a subjective test: whether, after considering all the facts, the parties in good faith and acting with a business purpose intended to join together in the present conduct of the enterprise.[296]

The Supreme Court additionally held that a person's intent to provide services to the partnership in the future would not be sufficient for the person to be treated as a partner for federal income tax purposes. Thus, an individual, to be considered a partner, must actually contribute (in his capacity as partner, not as an employee, a partner's spouse, or otherwise) services or some other valuable item to the partnership. Later cases have agreed.[297] A partner who provides advice and contacts to the partnership may be recognized as a partner.[298] In addition, a partner without a capital interest in the partnership who puts his separate assets at risk or otherwise assumes risk on behalf of the partnership may be considered a partner.[299]

[b] Allocation of Income

Section 704(e)(2) sets forth rules for determining a donee/purchaser's distributive share of income for federal income tax purposes when gifts or purchases from family members are involved. The donor/seller must be allocated income sufficient to compensate him for services rendered to the partnership. The donee/purchaser may be allocated enough income to compensate him for services as well. After that, income must be allocated for federal income tax purposes in proportion to retained and donated capital.[300]

> EXAMPLE: Dad contributes $90,000 to the partnership and makes a gift of $10,000 to Son, which Son in turn contributes to the partnership. Dad receives a salary from the partnership (apart from his distributive share)

---

[295] 337 US 733 (1949).

[296] Culbertson, 337 US at 742.

[297] E.g., Hornback v. United States, 298 F. Supp. 977 (WD Mo. 1969) (no partnership between husband and wife; wife's services in assisting husband in business were intended to accommodate husband, not make her a partner); Miranda v. Comm'r, 1965 TC Memo. ¶ 65,220, 24 TCM (CCH) 1126 (1965) (no partnership between cousins; one cousin performed no real services and did not have genuine capital account).

[298] See, e.g., Blalock v. Allen, 100 F. Supp. 869 (MD Ga. 1951); Pucci v. Comm'r, 10 TCM (CCH) 529 (1951).

[299] See, e.g., Dyer v. Comm'r, 211 F2d 500 (2d Cir. 1954), appeal after remand, 233 F2d 175 (1956); Staunchfield v. Comm'r, 191 F2d 826 (8th Cir. 1951); Maxwell v. Comm'r, 1970 PH TC Memo. ¶ 70,293, 29 TCM (CCH) 1356 (1970).

[300] IRC § 704(e)(2).

to compensate him for his services. Son renders no services to the partnership. At least nine-tenths of the remaining income of the partnership will be allocated to Dad for federal income tax purposes and at most one-tenth to Son, even if the partnership agreement provides for more income to be allocated to Son.

Note that in the preceding example, if the agreement provides for more than nine-tenths of the remaining income to be allocated to Dad, this allocation should be respected for federal income tax purposes, although it may not be desirable for transfer tax reasons.[301] Section 704(e) overrides Section 704(b), which otherwise requires that income allocations have substantial economic effect in order to be recognized.[302] Many families find it simplest to allocate income in accordance with each partner's percentage interest in the partnership, once any compensation for services to the partnership has been paid.

[8] Additional Reading

There are many other income tax issues affecting partners and partnerships. For a good general discussion of the income tax issues affecting partnerships, see McKee, Nelson, and Whitmire, Federal Taxation of Partnerships and Partners (Warren, Gorham & Lamont 3d ed. 1997) and Willis, Pennell, and Postlewaite, Partnership Taxation (Warren, Gorham & Lamont 6th ed. 1997).

¶ 16.05 THOUGHTS ON THE IRS ANTI-FAMILY PARTNERSHIP MISSION

When you get down to the nitty gritty, the reason that some folks at the IRS are unhappy with the discounts which can result on transfers of partnership interest is that they, in essence, do not like the rules of valuation which assign a value to each gift, as an individual interest without regard to any other interest, and which assign a value to both gifts and transfers at death without regard to family relationships or other holdings of the transferee. In some cases, these rules will reflect the true value of a transferred interest to the transferor or the transferee. In other cases, they will not. A gift of a minority interest may have a value to a particular transferee which is in excess of the value it would have to a hypothetical willing buyer holding no other interest in the entity. This is a consequence of using a test which does not consider all factors relating to a particular situation. Such rules are often used in tax matters. For example, the actuarial tables produce values for large groups of

---

[301] See discussion at ¶ 16.03[3][a] above.
[302] Treas. Reg. § 1.704-1(b)(1)(iii).

people, and provide an easy, inexpensive determiantion of value, but are often inaccurate as applied to particular individuals. Similarly, the hypothetical "willing buyer-willing seller" rule is a workable and accurate rule in many situations. However, there are cases in which it will not reflect the specific value of a transfer to a particular transferee. The rule that family attribution does not apply in the valuation context is an accurate rule in many cases, and prevents the courts from having to spend valuable resources delving into individual situations; however, in a family or non-family situation where the other partners are in fact willing to allow a minority owner to have his way, the interest will be worth more in that interest owner's hands than it would to a hypothetical stranger. Similarly the use of a valuation standard related to the possible sale of a property, as opposed to some other standard related to holding value, may produce a tax valuation unrelated to the agenda of a person who never sells the property.

Where do these thoughts point us? The IRS is approaching its family partnership issues by applying the normal rules to selected extreme fact situations and making moral outrage arguments, as well as by applying somewhat strained interpretations of Sections 2703 and 2704. Of course, the IRS has always had the power to attack sham transactions and truly abusive schemes. However, in other situations, their real problem is that they are upset about the normal valuation rules, as they apply to these transfers. Their direct approach to relief is to convince the appropriate rulemakers to change the transfer tax valuation rules that they consider inappropriate.

CHAPTER **17**

Limited Liability Companies

¶ 17.01 INTRODUCTION

Limited liability companies (LLCs) offer an alternative to limited partnerships. The LLC has lately come into vogue in estate planning, as family limited partnerships have become more popular.

The LLC law of each state is different. A uniform statute was approved and recommended for enactment in January of 1995.[1]

When to consider an LLC. If a person wants to use a family limited partnership, an LLC will often be an alternative. That pretty much says it all. The LLC's primary attraction is that it can be taxed like a partnership for income tax purposes, even though the members (including managing members) are not generally liable for LLC debts; unlike a partnership, no member needs to be liable for the entity's debts. There are numerous other ramifications of the LLC format, however. The pros and cons of one form versus the other should be considered in each situation.

¶ 17.02 STATE LAW RULES

[1] Brief Description

The owners of the LLC are called "members." Generally, any individual or legal entity is allowed to be a member of an LLC.[2] No member of an LLC has personal liability for entity debts solely as a result of being a member.[3] The governing instruments can, but (unlike partnership agreements) do not have to, designate persons with management authority. If they do, those persons are called "managers." Managers may or may not be members of the LLC, depending on the requirements of the governing instruments and local law.[4] If

---

[1] Unif. Ltd. Liability Co. Act, 6A ULA 429 (1995) (ULLCA).

[2] E.g., Texas Limited Liability Company Act, Tex. Rev. Civ. Stat. Ann. art. 1528n, arts. 1.02A(4), 4.01C (West Supp. 1996) (Texas LLC Act).

[3] This is a major difference between LLCs and limited partnerships, where the general partner has personal liability.

[4] For example, Texas law does not require managers to be members. See Texas LLC Act art. 2.12; see also ULLCA § 101(10).

no managers are designated, the authority to operate the company is vested in the members.

[2]　State Laws

The limited liability company is a creature of statute. All 50 states and the District of Columbia have limited liability company statutes.

The state statutes vary considerably, and the consequences of the LLC form of organization will vary depending on which state statute is used. Therefore, this chapter must speak generally. Rather than quoting from random statutes, this chapter will use the Uniform Act and the Texas statute as a model and discuss certain variations that appear in other states. Anyone establishing an LLC must carefully examine the applicable state statute.

Some states do not allow certain businesses (e.g., professional service firms, banks, insurance companies, or building and loan associations) to operate in LLC form. This type of limitation may be found either in the state's LLC statute or in the statutes regulating the particular business.

The state statute may also list what kinds of property are permitted to be contributed to an LLC.[5]

[3]　Required Documentation

The documentation of an LLC in many ways resembles that of a corporation. Documents corresponding to corporate articles of incorporation and bylaws are the "articles of organization" and "operating agreement," known in some states as the "regulations."[6] The formation of an LLC will entail filing articles of organization with the Secretary of State or other state authority.[7] Other documents which generally have to be filed for corporations may also have to be filed for LLCs, such as an amendment of articles, change of registered office, change of registered agent for service of process or change of agent's address, and so forth.[8]

State law may also require that certain detailed information be kept available and shown to any member or assignee of a membership interest on

---

[5] ULLCA § 401 (members may contribute tangible or intangible property or other benefits to the company, including money, promissory notes, services performed, or other agreements to contribute cash or property, or contracts for services to be performed); Texas LLC Act art. 5.01A (members may contribute cash, property, services, or a note or other obligations to pay cash or transfer property).

[6] See, e.g., Texas LLC Act art. 2.09.

[7] ULLCA § 202; Texas LLC Act art. 3.01.

[8] ULLCA §§ 108, 109, 204; Texas LLC Act arts. 2.06, 2.07, 3.07.

request.[9] This may be more information than a partnership would have to provide to an assignee of a partnership interest.

[a] Articles of Organization

The articles of organization will usually include provisions similar to corporate articles, such as the name of the entity, which must indicate its limited liability nature; registered office and agent; period of duration, etc.[10] The LLC's existence as an LLC may not be recognized until the articles have been filed and the appropriate state authority has issued a certificate of organization recognizing that the LLC requirements have been met.[11] Failure to file the articles and obtain a certificate presumably could cause the LLC to be treated as an unincorporated association or general partnership. This would prevent the company from taking advantage of the limited liability provisions offered by the LLC statute.

[b] Operating Agreement

The members of an LLC may have an agreement regarding its affairs, the conduct of its business, and the relationships between members. This document, which is not generally required, is comparable to corporate bylaws or a partnership agreement. In the absence of an operating agreement, or if the operating agreement is silent on a point, the state law default rules will control. Interestingly, the operating agreement is allowed to be oral in some states, leaving some potential problems in establishing just what the agreement is and whether the oral agreement or the state law default rules will govern.

---

[9] E.g., Texas LLC Act art. 2.22. This information may include: the name and mailing address of each member; the percentage or other interest in the LLC owned by each member; the names of the members who are members of specified classes or groups having certain rights, powers, and duties, including voting rights, if applicable; copies of the federal, state, and local information or income tax returns for each of the LLC's six most recent tax years; a copy of the articles of organization and regulations, with all amendments or restatements; executed copies of any powers of attorney; copies of any document that creates classes or groups of members; a written statement of the amount of the cash contribution and a description and statement of the agreed value of any contribution made by each member; a description and statement of the agreed value of any contribution that the member has agreed to make in the future as an additional contribution; the times at which additional contributions are to be made or the events requiring additional contributions to be made, and the events requiring the LLC to be dissolved and its affairs wound up; the date on which each member in the LLC became a member; correct and complete books and records of account of the LLC; and the street address of its principal U.S. office in which the records are required to be maintained or will be made available.

[10] ULLCA § 203; Texas LLC Act art. 3.02.

[11] E.g., Texas LLC Act art. 3.04.

[4] Rights of the Members

State limited partnership acts and corporation acts will usually give certain rights to the partners or the shareholders unless the entity documents provide otherwise (or sometimes even if they do). Similarly, when entity documents are silent, LLC acts provide default rules defining the rights of members. A certain number or percentage of the members will generally have to consent to certain actions that can have a significant effect on the operations and members of the LLC.[12]

[5] Classes of LLC Membership

Many states permit the organizational documents to establish more than one class of membership.[13] Note, however, that if the LLC does this and is classified for income tax purposes as an association taxable as a corporation rather than a partnership, the LLC will not be able to elect S status. However, in the absence of an affirmative election to be taxed as a corporation, the check-the-box regulations will generally result in the entity's being treated as a partnership (in the case of more than one member) or as a sole proprietorship (in the case of one member).[14]

[6] Management of the LLC

The articles of organization can provide that the management of the LLC will reside in certain designated "managers."[15] Unless the articles of organization or the operating agreement provides otherwise, a manager need not be a member.[16] Unless the operating agreement reserves this right to specific members, the members will generally have the right to elect and remove managers

---

[12] Such actions can include amending the articles of organization or operating agreement; changing the LLC from a member-managed LLC to a manager-managed LLC, or vice versa; issuing additional membership interests; approving any merger, consolidation, share or interest exchange, or similar transactions; voluntarily dissolving the LLC; authorizing any transaction, agreement, or action that is unrelated to the purpose of the LLC or that contravenes its operating agreement; authorizing any act that would make it impossible to carry on the ordinary business of the LLC; and (where management of the LLC is vested in the members) taking any action that is not apparently for the carrying on of the business of the LLC in the usual way. Texas LLC Act art. 2.23D, 2.23E; see also ULLCA § 404(c) (listing matters of a member or manager-managed company's business that require the consent of all members).

[13] E.g., Texas LLC Act art. 4.02A.

[14] IRC § 1361(b)(1)(D).

[15] ULLCA § 404; Texas LLC Act arts. 2.12, 3.02A(5).

[16] ULLCA § 101(10); Texas LLC Act art. 2.12.

or to fill manager vacancies.[17] State law may permit several classes of managers to be established by the operating agreement.[18]

If management is not delegated to managers, it resides in the members, who can vote in accordance with their interests in the LLC or in whatever other proportions the particular statute or organizational documents permit.[19]

[7] Apparent Authority of Members

As far as third parties are concerned, the following persons generally have apparent authority to act on behalf of the LLC: (1) any one or more officers or other agents who are vested with actual or apparent authority; (2) each manager, to the extent that management is vested in that manager; and (3) each member, to the extent that management of the LLC has been reserved to that member.[20]

Any act for the purpose of apparently carrying on the business of the LLC in the usual way by any of these persons binds the LLC even if the person so acting lacks the authority to act for the LLC, unless the third party with whom the acting person was dealing knew that the acting person did not have authority.[21] Third parties may request evidence of each member's or manager's authority to act, as shown by the organizational or other documents which vest management rights in the member or manager. Disclosing this information will prevent third parties from later claiming to have relied on statements or actions by a member or manager with no actual authority.

[8] Limited Liability

[a] General Rule

The members and managers of an LLC are not liable for debts or other obligations of the LLC unless they are liable by other rules of law.[22]

[b] Exception—Liability Outside of Member Status

Under what circumstances might a member be liable under other rules of law? A member who guaranteed an LLC note would be personally liable for

---

[17] Texas LLC Act arts. 2.13, 2.15; see also ULLCA § 404(b)(3) (manager must be elected or removed by a majority of the members).

[18] E.g., Texas LLC Act art. 2.14A.

[19] Texas LLC Act arts. 2.12, 2.23A; but see ULLCA § 404(a)(2) (requiring consent of majority except where statute provides otherwise).

[20] Texas LLC Act art. 2.21C; see also ULLCA § 301.

[21] ULLCA § 301; Texas LLC Act art. 2.21D.

[22] ULLCA § 303; Texas LLC Act art. 4.03A.

payment of the note. A member who personally committed a tort while conducting LLC business would not be limited in his liability by the fact that the LLC existed. A manager might be liable for environmental contamination occurring on LLC property during his watch. These examples would also apply to owners of interests in other limited liability entities, such as corporations and limited partnerships. However, unlike limited partners, LLC members can participate in management of an LLC without becoming personally liable for the debts of the entity.[23]

[c] Exception—"Piercing the Corporate Veil"

The limited liability of the shareholders of a corporation can be lost if the corporate formalities are not respected (for example, minutes are not prepared, meetings are not held, etc.). Reaching the shareholders' assets is called "piercing the corporate veil." This doctrine may be applicable to LLCs as well, either under common law or by statute.[24] If the LLC format requires fewer formalities than a corporation does in the applicable state, it may be correspondingly more difficult to pierce its veil. An analogy would be corporations operating under close corporation statutes, which allow electing corporations to operate with minimal formalities.

[9] Distributions in Kind

Unless the organizational documents provide to the contrary, state law usually provides that a member does not have a right to demand distributions in kind, and does not have to accept distributions in kind.[25] Some states have an exception if all partners are receiving undivided interests in an in-kind distribution of property.

[10] Member's Withdrawal

Many states provide that in the absence of a contrary provision in the LLC's organizational documents a member has the right to withdraw on a predetermined amount of written notice.[26] If these organizational documents prohibit

---

[23] Compare Texas LLC Act arts. 2.12A, 4.03A with Tex. Rev. Limited Partnership Act, Tex. Rev. Civ. Stat. art. 6132a-1, § 3.03 (West Supp. 1996).

[24] For a discussion of this, see Note, Piercing the Veil of Limited Liability Companies, 62 Geo. Wash. L. Rev. 1143 (1994).

[25] ULLCA § 405(b); Texas LLC Act art. 5.07A. Distributions in kind are distributions of assets other than cash.

[26] E.g., La. R.S. 12 :1325B (1997) (Withdrawal on 30 days' written notice; but see ULLCA § 602(a) (member may withdraw at any time unless otherwise provided in the

withdrawal, the withdrawing member may still be able to withdraw. However, the withdrawing member may be liable for damages to the extent provided in the organizational documents.[27] Some states provide that where the LLC is for a term of years or a specific undertaking, a member may not withdraw from the LLC before the expiration of that term or undertaking.[28]

When a member withdraws, depending on the state statute and the terms of the organizational documents, he may be (1) entitled to a return of his contribution,[29] (2) treated as an assignee of his interest where the withdrawal causes dissolution of the LLC,[30] or (3) entitled to the fair value of his interest within a reasonable time after withdrawal.[31]

[11] Transfers of Interests

A member's interest in an LLC is assignable, absent a contrary provision in the operating agreement.[32] An assignment does not dissolve the LLC or entitle the assignee to become a member or exercise any management rights.[33] To the extent provided in the applicable state law, the assignee receives the rights that an assignee of a partnership interest would have—that is, primarily (1) the rights to be allocated his share of income, gain, loss, deduction, credit, and similar items; (2) to receive his share of distributions from the LLC, as and when they are made; and (3) for any proper purpose, to require reasonable information or account of transactions of the LLC and to make reasonable inspection of the LLC's books and records.[34] The assignee would not, however, have the right to participate in entity affairs, unless the other members consented.

Until the assignee becomes a member, the assignor member continues to be a member and therefore exercises all rights and powers of a member, except

---

operating agreement); Texas LLC Act. art. 5.05A (providing that a member may withdraw or be expelled as provided in the regulations).

[27] ULLCA § 602(c); Texas LLC Act art. 5.06A.

[28] E.g., Ark. Code Ann. § 4-32-802 (Michie 1997).

[29] See, e.g., Colo. Rev. Stat. § 7-80-603 (1996) (withdrawing member entitled to receive his share of profits or other income and a return of his contribution).

[30] E.g., Ariz. Rev. Stat. Ann. § 29.707 (1997).

[31] E.g., Texas LLC Act art. 5.06A.

[32] Texas LLC Act art. 4.05A(1); see also ULLCA § 501(c) (interest transferable to the extent provided in the operating agreement).

[33] ULLCA § 502; Texas LLC Act art. 4.05A(2).

[34] E.g., Texas LLC Act art. 4.05A(3); see also ULLCA § 503(e) (detailing rights of an assignee who does not become a member).

to the extent those rights and powers are permissibly assigned.[35] This provision can pose difficulties, as illustrated in the following example.

> EXAMPLE: Suppose Mom assigns her entire membership interest in an LLC to Son. The LLC's organizational documents impose no restrictions on transfers. Son acquires Mom's economic rights in the entity. Unless the other members consent, Son would not become a member, and his rights would be limited to receiving distributions whenever they are made and receiving enough information to account for his rights. Mom would retain the management and voting rights attributable to the interest. Section 2036(b) provides that if a shareholder in a family corporation transfers voting stock and retains the voting right, the stock is included in that person's estate.
>
> Could this rule be applied in the LLC context to a donor like Mom, who gives away her interest and retains the voting rights? The answer should be no. However, if a member assigns her LLC interest, caution would indicate that she should not retain the management rights incident to that interest if the retention of rights is not necessary.

An assignee only becomes a member if the organizational documents so allow or all members consent.[36] The transfer rules are very much like the rules that apply to transfers of partnership interests.

[12] Conversion of Existing Entity Into LLC Format

Many families would like to convert their existing C corporations, S corporations, or partnerships to the LLC format. It should be noted that, after conversion, a general partner of a converting partnership is still generally liable for pre-conversion liabilities.[37] The conversion of a corporation into an LLC will involve liquidating the corporation, a move that can cause major tax consequences in some cases.

[13] Dissolution of an LLC

Dissolution of an LLC occurs, generally, on any of the following: (1) a time or event specified in the organizational documents; (2) the consent of a majority or other designated percentage of the members; (3) the death, withdrawal, resignation, expulsion, bankruptcy, or dissolution of a member, or

---

[35] ULLCA §§ 502–03; Texas LLC Act art. 4.05A(4).

[36] ULLCA § 503(a); Texas LLC Act art. 4.07A.

[37] See, e.g., Tex. Rev. Partnership Act, Tex. Rev. Civ. Stat. art. 6132b-3.04, -9.01(d) (West Supp. 1996) (addressing conversion to limited partnership).

other event that terminates a member's membership; or (4) the entry of a judicial decree dissolving the entity.[38]

An assignment of a member's interest may not itself dissolve the entity because the assignor does not withdraw by assigning his interest.[39] When the assignor's membership interest terminates, however, the entity dissolves. One of the critical distinctions between LLCs and family limited partnerships is that the death of a limited partner does not cause a dissolution of the entity, whereas in some states the death of an LLC member causes the dissolution of an LLC.

[14] Liquidation of an LLC

Dissolution is not the same as liquidation. On dissolution, certain events may be triggered, which may or may not include liquidation. The statutes generally provide that, on dissolution, the LLC's business will be wound up and liquidated, unless there is at least one remaining member and the business is continued by the vote of the members (or class of members) as set forth in the organizational documents or, if such documents are silent, by a vote of all remaining members.[40] Unless the organizational documents provide otherwise, state law may require that the election to continue must be made within 90 days of the dissolution event.[41] If the entity dissolves and the business is continued, a withdrawing member is usually entitled to the fair value of his interest, assuming the entity documents do not provide otherwise.[42]

[15] LLC's Operation in Other Jurisdictions

If the LLC's operations or activities are conducted in a jurisdiction other than the one in which it was formed, the following questions arise:

What if an LLC conducts operations in a jurisdiction other than its domiciliary jurisdiction? Among other things, the LLC may be required to obtain a certificate of authority from the foreign jurisdiction to do business there.[43] And, depending on the applicable state law, the LLC may be prohibited from conducting certain businesses in the target state.[44]

---

[38] ULLCA § 801(b) (company also dissolves on occurrence of unlawful event that is not cured within 90 days); Texas LLC Act arts. 2.23D(5), 6.01A.

[39] ULLCA § 801(b); Texas LLC Act art. 4.05A(2), (4).

[40] Texas LLC Act art. 6.01B; see also ULLCA § 801(b)(3).

[41] E.g., Texas LLC Act art. 6.01B.

[42] ULLCA § 701; Texas LLC Act art. 5.06A.

[43] ULLCA § 1002; Texas LLC Act art. 7.01A.

[44] E.g., Texas LLC Act art. 7.01A.

What if the target jurisdiction does not have an LLC statute or does not permit the LLC form to be used for the LLC's particular business?

If the LLC conducts business in that jurisdiction, are the members and managers still protected from liability for entity debts? One of the primary concerns of an entity holding an active business which transacts business in other jurisdictions is whether the limited liability nature of the entity will be respected in that jurisdiction's courts should the entity happen to be sued there under long-arm statutes or otherwise.

PRACTICE POINTER: An LLC may not be considered to have transacted business in another jurisdiction unless its activities rise to the level of carrying on a business in that jurisdiction.[45] There is little authority yet as to whether a jurisdiction that would not recognize the LLC if it were a domiciliary entity will recognize the limited liability of the members.

Some LLC statutes apply the laws of the jurisdiction of an LLC's organization as to matters of member liability. Some LLC statutes do not address the matter at all. Thus, there is no assurance that a different jurisdiction will apply the home state organizational rules limiting liability. The full faith and credit clause of the federal constitution does not appear to mandate that the forum state adopt the limited liability provisions of the LLC's state of organization. Moreover, a judgment rendered by a court in the target jurisdiction against a member or manager might be entitled to full faith and credit in the state of organization.

An interesting case relating to this is *Means v. Limpia Royalties,*[46] in which an Oklahoma business trust conducted business in Texas. Although the business trust granted limited liability to its owners under Oklahoma law, the Texas court noted that Texas law did not recognize business trusts and treated the owners as general partners.

The bottom line is that numerous arguments exist on this issue, but, in essence, there is always potential risk involved if an LLC is sued in a jurisdiction which does not recognize LLCs or has different rules on limited liability than the home state.

International LLCs. What if the LLC has contacts with a jurisdiction that is outside of the United States? If a member or manager has personal assets located in the foreign jurisdiction in which a suit is brought, the member or manager might consider those assets to be at risk if the LLC is not recognized there. If the members and managers have no personal assets located in the foreign jurisdiction, and the LLC creditors come to a state in which the LLC is recognized in order to sue the members or managers individually, the

---

[45] See, e.g., ULLCA § 1003; Texas LLC Act art. 7.01B.

[46] 115 SW2d 468 (Tex. Civ. App.—Fort Worth 1938), writ dismissed.

creditors will probably have a hard time getting a judgment against the individual, in the absence of additional facts.

PRACTICE POINTER: If it is necessary to conduct business in a foreign jurisdiction that does not have an LLC statute, and a member/manager wants to keep significant assets there, consider a different type of entity for that jurisdiction.

[16] Asset Protection

If a creditor of a member attacks by attachment or otherwise that member's interest in the LLC, what can he reach? Generally, a judgment creditor can obtain a charging order and will receive distributions to which the member is entitled as, if, and when they are made, until the debt is satisfied.[47] In addition, he may have the rights of an assignee until the debt is satisfied.[48] A court may also order a foreclosure of a lien on the interest subject to the charging order.[49]

If the member files for bankruptcy, state law (in the absence of contrary provisions in the organizational documents) may cause the LLC to dissolve.[50] This, in turn, will cause the entity to be liquidated unless the requisite percentage of remaining members elect to continue the business.[51] If they do continue the business, the bankruptcy trustee may be entitled to the fair value of the estate's interest.[52] The bankruptcy trustee may also try to assert that the dissolution provision/statute is unenforceable under federal bankruptcy law. If the dissolution is not enforceable, the bankruptcy trustee would succeed to whatever rights the debtor-member had in the LLC, and may be able to exercise whatever rights the member could have exercised.[53]

[17] Securities Laws

A membership interest in an LLC may be a security for federal securities law purposes, at least for the nonmanaging members, since it may be an investment contract. Under the securities laws, an investment contract exists if a

---

[47] ULLCA § 504; Texas LLC Act art. 4.06A.

[48] ULLCA § 504(b); Texas LLC Act art. 4.06A.

[49] ULLCA § 504(b).

[50] Texas LLC Act art. 6.01A(5); see also ULLCA § 601(7) (no option to provide otherwise in organizational documents).

[51] ULLCA § 801(b)(3); Texas LLC Act art. 6.01B.

[52] E.g., Texas LLC Act art. 5.06A.

[53] See Ch. 53 on asset protection.

person invests money or other property in a common enterprise with the expectation of profits derived solely from the efforts of others.[54]

A limited partnership interest is presumed to be a security, and a general partnership interest is presumed not to be a security.[55] Each of these presumptions can be overcome. If these same tests are applied to LLCs and an LLC is managed by managers, the presumption will be that a nonmanaging interest is a security. If this is the case, the issuance and any transfer of an interest will need to fall under one of the exemptions from securities law or otherwise comply with the applicable requirements of the securities acts and regulations.

[18] State Taxation of LLCs

State law may tax LLCs in a different manner than other entities. For example, in Texas, the state franchise tax applies to LLCs and corporations but not to partnerships.

¶ 17.03 INCOME TAXATION OF LLCS

[1] Classification as Partnership or C Corporation

[a] Federal Income Tax Classification

An LLC with more than one member may be taxed as a partnership or as an association taxable as a C corporation.[56] For federal income tax purposes, the classification will be determined under the check-the-box rules.[57]

In all cases, the persons who are organizing a multi-member LLC should want the LLC to be taxed as a partnership, and not as a corporation. If the founders want an entity taxable as a corporation, they should form a corporation. An LLC that is taxed as a corporation has no advantages over an actual corporation, and has certain disadvantages. The LLC format does, however, have some advantages over the partnership form.

---

[54] SEC v. W. J. Howey Co., 328 US 293 (1946).

[55] SEC v. Murphy, 626 F2d 633, 640 (9th Cir. 1980); Goodman v. Epstein, 582 F2d 388, 406 (7th Cir. 1978), cert. denied, 440 US 939 (1979).

[56] Although an association may elect to be taxed as an S corporation to the extent it qualifies, it probably will not have made the election if it expects to be taxed as a partnership. See IRC §§ 1361(b), 7701(a)(3); Reg. § 1.1361-1(c). Although there is no formal procedure for making a protective S election, the LLC might attempt to do so by filing Form 2553 with the words "Protective S Election" at the top.

[57] These rules are discussed at length in Ch. 20 of this book.

[b] State Tax Classification

Classification for state tax purposes will, of course, depend on each state law. Many state statutes piggyback federal law, and thus automatically follow the classification status of the LLC for federal tax purposes (now determined under the check-the-box rules). However, some states do not automatically track the federal tax laws. In many of those states, the old four-factor federal classification system that was in effect before 1997 is followed.

How readily an LLC will be classified as a partnership under the old four-factor test will depend on the provisions of the applicable state statute and the terms of the LLC's organizational documents. Some state statutes are drafted so as to cause all LLCs to be taxed as partnerships. Other states have enacted LLC statutes that enable an LLC to be taxed as a corporation or as a partnership, depending on the terms of the LLC's organizational documents.

In Revenue Procedure 95-10,[58] the IRS provided guidelines for LLCs with regard to the four primary characteristics (discussed below) that were analyzed in determining whether an entity would be taxed as a corporation or a partnership under pre-check-the-box rules. The IRS had also issued revenue rulings on many state statutes. These rulings officially announced how LLCs organized under particular statutes would be classified by the IRS before adoption of the check-the-box rules. It is a good idea to check the revenue ruling with respect to a particular state before organizing an LLC there, if the state tax depends on the pre-check-the-box tests.[59]

Under pre-check-the-box rules, in order to be taxed as a partnership, the LLC had to have at least two members. Once this bridge has been crossed in states with flexible statutes, the state taxation of the LLC as a partnership or as an association taxable as a corporation under the old federal rules depends on whether it has more coporate than noncorporate characteristics.[60] Generally speaking, the objective will be not to have more than two of the following four features which are characteristic of a corporation.

[i] Continuity of life. An LLC will avoid continuity of life if the withdrawal of a member will cause the dissolution (not necessarily the liquidation) of the entity.[61] Some state statutes provide that the withdrawal of a member will dissolve the entity.[62] The IRS has taken the position, where LLC members have designated one or more members to act as manager, that the LLC will be deemed to lack continuity of life if the LLC will dissolve without further action on the withdrawal of any one of the member-managers, unless the

---

[58] 1995-1 CB 501.

[59] Reg. § 301.7701-3(a)(2).

[60] Reg. § 301.7701-2.

[61] Reg. § 301.7701-2(b)(1).

[62] E.g., Texas LLC Act art. 6.01A(5).

business of the LLC can be continued after the withdrawal by less than a majority in interest of the remaining members.[63] Thus, if the operating agreement or articles provide that the business will automatically be continued after withdrawal of a member, the entity may have continuity of life. In the case of an LLC that is managed by all of its members or a non-member manager, the IRS' position was that the LLC would lack continuity of life only if the LLC would dissolve without further action upon the withdrawal of any one of the members.[64]

Can the members agree in advance that they will vote to continue the business after the withdrawal of a member? In the partnership context, the prior regulations provided that such an agreement would not result in continuity of life if the partner retained the power to dissolve the entity under local law—that is, if the contract to continue only rendered him liable for damages for breach and was not specifically enforceable.[65] The LLC situation may be different if a member does not have the power to withdraw in contravention of the agreement.

Revenue Procedure 95-10 referred to dissolution triggered by the death, insanity, bankruptcy, retirement, resignation or expulsion of a member-manager or member. These events will not necessarily be considered events of withdrawal under all LLC acts, and some state laws may permit the LLC (through its articles or operating agreement) to vary the events that will cause dissolution. This should not cause a problem as long as the events of withdrawal apply in the same manner to all member-managers or members and there remains a meaningful possibility of dissolution.[66]

Conclusion. A reasonable provision on withdrawal might provide that the withdrawal causes a dissolution, but that a majority in interest of the remaining members can elect to continue the business. Such a provision should allow the LLC to avoid continuity of life even if voluntary withdrawal is prohibited.

[ii] Centralization of management. An entity may have centralized management if fewer than all of the members are vested with authority to make business decisions for the entity.[67] To determine how this test might be applied to LLCs, we must consult its application to partnerships.

A general partnership does not have centralized management even if the partners have agreed that fewer than all partners will be the managing part-

---

[63] Rev. Proc. 95-10, 1995-1 CB 501, § 5.01(1).

[64] Rev. Proc. 95-10, 1995-1 CB 501, § 5.01(2).

[65] Reg. § 301.7701-2(b).

[66] See Rev. Proc. 95-10, 1995-1 CB 501, § 5.01(4).

[67] Reg. § 301.7701-2(c)(1).

ners because, as a matter of state law, each partner has the authority to act in the partnership's behalf.[68]

A limited partnership will have centralized management only if the limited partners own substantially all the interests in the partnership or have an unfettered right to remove the general partner.[69]

In order for an LLC that has designated one or more members to act as managers to obtain a ruling that it lacks centralization of management, the member-managers must own at least 20 percent of the total interests in the LLC. Even where this requirement is met, the IRS formerly considered other relevant facts and circumstances (including member control of the managers) in determining whether the LLC lacked centralized management. If the member-managers were subject to periodic elections by the non-managing members or the non-managing members had a substantially unrestricted power to remove the member-managers, the IRS would not rule that the LLC lacked centralized management.[70]

If, pursuant to the governing law or the operating agreement as provided in the governing law, the LLC was managed by the members exclusively in their capacity as members, the IRS would generally rule that the LLC lacked centralized management.[71]

So far, the IRS had determined that an LLC has centralized management merely because it is run by managers.[72] However, the LLC may not have centralized management where all of the members retain both the power to bind the LLC and the right to participate in its management and they appoint one member to run the LLC's day-to-day operations.[73]

Revenue Procedure 95-10 was conspicuously silent on the subject of LLCs that are managed by a non-member manager. However, it seems likely that such an LLC will be deemed to have centralized management, just as a limited partnership in which substantially all of the interests are held by the limited partners is viewed as having centralized management.[74]

Conclusion. Does an LLC have centralized management under the old IRS test? If the LLC is managed by a nonmember, or the non-managing

---

[68] Reg. § 301.7701-2(c)(4).

[69] Reg. § 301.7701-2(c)(4).

[70] Rev. Proc. 95-10, 1995-1 CB 501, § 5.03(2).

[71] Rev. Proc. 95-10, 1995-1 CB 501, § 5.03(1).

[72] Rev. Rul. 94-5, 1994-1 CB 337; Rev. Rul. 93-92, 1993-2 CB 318; Rev. Rul. 93-81, 1993-2 CB 314; Rev. Rul. 93-49, 1993-2 CB 308; Rev. Rul. 93-38, 1993-1 CB 233, Situation 2; Rev. Rul. 93-30, 1993-1 CB 231; Rev. Rul. 93-5, 1993-1 CB 227; Rev. Rul. 88-76, 1988-2 CB 260.

[73] See Priv. Ltr. Rul. 9325048 (Mar. 30, 1993); Priv. Ltr. Rul. 9321070 (Mar. 3, 1993); Priv. Ltr. Rul. 9320045 (Feb. 24, 1993); Priv. Ltr. Rul. 9320019 (Feb. 18, 1993).

[74] Reg. § 301.7701-2(c)(4).

members own more than 80 percent of the entity: yes. In other situations: perhaps no.

[iii] Limited liability. An LLC will avoid limited liability if any member is personally liable for all of the debts of or claims against the entity.[75] The IRS generally would not rule that an LLC lacked limited liability unless at least one member assumed personal liability for all obligations of the LLC pursuant to express authority granted in the governing law.[76] In some states, one or more members can waive limited liability if they like.[77]

Even if a member assumes personal liability for the LLC's obligations, limited liability may still be present if the assuming member is a "dummy" of the other members and does not have substantial assets other than LLC and partnership interests. The IRS ruling created a safe harbor for substantially capitalized members comparable to that applicable to partnerships.[78]

The trouble of establishing and capitalizing an S corporation to be the general partner of a limited partnership is eliminated if an LLC is used. However, if the particular LLC is relying on a waiver of limited liability to fail the limited liability test, the member who has waived limited liability may need to be substantially capitalized.

Conclusion. One of the reasons to choose the LLC format is to avoid general liability for all members. Hence, the LLC will usually have the corporate characteristic of limited liability.

[iv] Free transferability of interests. An entity has free transferability of interests if those members owning substantially all (i.e., 80 percent or more) of the entity's interests are entitled to confer all attributes of their interests on a nonmember without the consent of the other members.[79]

Under the LLC laws, a member typically cannot assign the management rights in his interest without the consent of all of the members, or some lesser percentage stated in the documents. The IRS had ruled that if the assignee's exercise of management and other membership rights was conditioned on the approval of a majority of members other than the assignor (or, in the case of an LLC managed by designated members, a majority in interest of the managers other than the assignor), the LLC will lack free transferability.[80] However, the IRS would not rule that an LLC lacked free transferability of interests if the ability to withhold consent to a transfer was not a meaningful

---

[75] Reg. § 301.7701-2(d)(1).

[76] Rev. Proc. 95-10, 1995-1 CB 501, § 5.04.

[77] E.g., Texas LLC Act art. 4.03A.

[78] See Rev. Proc. 95-10, 1995-1 CB 501, § 5.04, and discussion in Ch. 19.

[79] Reg. § 301.7701-2(e).

[80] Rev. Proc. 95-10, 1995-1 CB 501, §§ 5.02(1)-5.02(2).

restriction on the transfer (for example, if such consent could not be unreasonably withheld).[81] If the members have an agreement that they will consent to transferees becoming substituted members, and the agreement is enforceable, the LLC may possess free transferability.

The IRS would rule that a partnership lacked free transferability of interests if the agreement restricted the transferability of more than 20 percent in interest of the partners.[82] The IRS had ruled similiarly in the case of LLCs.[83] The IRS had also ruled that an LLC would lack free transferability of interests if the operating agreement prohibited transfer of a member's interest or provided that a transfer would cause the LLC to dissolve.[84]

Conclusion. If the entity documents provide that more than 20 percent in interest of the members cannot transfer the management rights in their interests without the consent of members other than the assignor, the LLC should lack free transferability.

PRACTICE POINTER: A typical manager-managed LLC with two members or more will lack continuity of life and free transferability, and may possess centralized management (certainly if the nonmanaging members own substantially all of the LLC) and limited liability. Customization of the organizational documents within state law limits should suffice. Under pre-check-the-box law, if the LLC in fact possessed three out of the four characteristics, it was taxed as a corporation. If it possessed two or fewer, it was taxed as a partnership.

[v] **Check-the-box.** The IRS has issued regulations which adopt a check-the-box classification system and thereby eliminate the above tests.[85] Under the regulations, a domestic LLC that is not specifically classified as a corporation under Reg. § 301.7701-2(b) and that has two or more members will automatically be considered a partnership unless it elects otherwise.[86]

[2] **Allocation of Income and Loss and Other Income Tax Issues**

An LLC that is taxable as a partnership is usually permitted to make non-pro rata distributions of its cash and property. Also, like a partnership, an LLC

---

[81] Rev. Proc. 95-10, 1995-1 CB 501, § 5.02(4).

[82] Rev. Proc. 92-33, 1992-1 CB 782.

[83] Rev. Proc. 95-10, 1995-1 CB 501, § 5.02(1).

[84] Priv. Ltr. Rul. 9510037 (Dec. 9, 1994); Priv. Ltr. Rul. 9507004 (Nov. 8, 1994).

[85] Reg. § 301.7701-3; see also IRS Notice 95-14, 1995-1 CB 297, and discussion in Ch. 20.

[86] Reg. § 301.7701-3(a), 301.7701-3(b)(1). See Ch. 20 for a further discussion.

that is taxable as a partnership is usually permitted to allocate profits and losses in ways that differ from the members' current interests in the entity, provided that the allocations have substantial economic effect under the rules applicable to partnerships. In absence of a valid allocation or distribution provision to the contrary, the default rule provides generally that distributions will be made and profits and losses allocated in proportion to the members' contributions.[87] It should also be noted that the family partnership rules regarding reallocation of income in certain fact patterns will apply to an LLC that is taxable as a partnership.[88]

In general, the tax rules applicable to partnerships apply with equal force to LLCs, including those rules for determining the basis of a member's interest, the distinction between redemptions and sales of a member's interest, the difference between capital contributions and sales of member property to the LLC, etc.[89] Also, the members of the LLC, like partners of a partnership, must be the real owners of their interests in order to be recognized as such for tax purposes.[90] However, an important exception applies in the case of entity liabilities. Specifically, unless a member has guaranteed an LLC debt, all members of an LLC will generally share in the tax basis generated by liabilities—unlike a limited partnership, where the general, but not the limited, partners share partnership recourse liabilities after the limited partners' capital accounts are exhausted.

[3] LLC's Method of Accounting

In general, most partnerships are allowed to choose an accounting method other than the accrual method. However, there has been some discussion about whether an LLC is a tax shelter, and thus must use the accrual method of accounting.[91] For this purpose, the term "tax shelter" includes a syndicate (as defined in Section 1256(e)(3)(B)) and a tax shelter(as defined in Section 6662).[92] A syndicate includes an entity in which more than 35 percent of the losses are allocated to certain limited entrepreneurs.

---

[87] Texas LLC Act arts. 5.02-1A (profits and losses allocated in accordance with percentage interests), 5.03A (distributions allocated in proportion to contributions).

[88] See Ch. 16 for discussion.

[89] See Ch. 16 for a discussion of these rules.

[90] See discussion in Ch. 16.

[91] See IRC § 461(i)(1).

[92] A partnership or other entity is a tax shelter if its principal purpose is the avoidance or evasion of federal income tax. IRC §§ 461(i)(3)(B), 461(i)(3)(C), 6662(d)(2)(C)(iii).

The IRS has, however, ruled in particular cases that LLCs were permitted to use the cash method of accounting.[93] But, these rulings were based on the active involvement of all the members or the consistent practice of the entity of reporting income rather than a loss.

[4] Self-Employment Tax

Is a member's share of income from a trade or business subject to self-employment tax? The IRS has issued proposed regulations on the application of the self-employment tax to members of an LLC and partners of a partnership.[94] The proposed regulations would subject a member's distributive share to self-employment tax only if the member is liable for LLC debt as a result of his membership status, or has authority to contract on behalf of the LLC, or spends more than 500 hours per year on the trade or business of the LLC, or spends more than a de minimis amount of time on an LLC trade or business which consists of the rendering of personal services. Even in cases where these conditions apply, distributions attributable to a class of LLC income will not be subject to tax if that class represents the interest of capital members, as opposed to service members.

[5] Conversion of LLC Into a Partnership or Corporation

A conversion of a general or limited partnership to an LLC should be treated as a nontaxable event, except to the extent a member recognizes income as a result of a reduction in the member's share of the entity's liabilities.[95]

A conversion of a C corporation or S corporation to an LLC will involve a taxable liquidation of the corporation and contribution of the assets to the LLC.

¶ 17.04　TRANSFER TAXATION

[1] Gift and Estate Tax

Gifts and sales of LLC interests should be eligible for discounts, similar to those available with respect to transfers of limited partnership interests or minority interests in corporations. Transfers at death may also be eligible for valuation discounts, particularly for a non-managing member.

---

[93] E.g., Priv. Ltr. Rul. 9535036 (June 1, 1995); Priv. Ltr. Rul. 9422034 (Mar. 3, 1994); Priv. Ltr. Rul. 9412030 (Dec. 22, 1993); Priv. Ltr. Rul. 9407030 (Nov. 24, 1993); Priv. Ltr. Rul. 9350013 (Sept. 15, 1993); Priv. Ltr. Rul. 9321047 (Feb. 25, 1993).

[94] Prop. Reg. § 1.1402(a)-18(a).

[95] See Rev. Rul. 84-52, 1984-1 CB 157 (dealing with limited partnerships).

[2] Preferred Interests—Section 2701

Section 2701, dealing with the special valuation rules applicable to entities with preferred equity interests, should not apply unless there is more than one class of member interest or a member has another arrangement with the LLC which is in effect a preferred equity interest.

[3] Lapses of Rights

A lapse of a member's voting rights or liquidation rights can trigger the applicability of Section 2704(a), which will result in the member's interest being valued, in general, as if it had not lapsed. A member will not necessarily have the right to liquidate his interest under state law. Even if the member can withdraw and the withdrawal would cause a dissolution, the other members could agree to continue the LLC, and therefore the withdrawing member would not be able to extract anything but the fair value of his interest. Hence, even if a member could liquidate his interest, he could not obtain more than its fair value (which may not be its liquidation value). Members will usually have voting rights, however. If a member dies or transfers his interest, and the voting rights incident to his interest disappear, Section 2704(a) will apply, and the transferred interest will be valued for transfer tax purposes as if it still carried the voting rights.[96] Presumably, a managing member would be treated as a general partner and a nonmanaging member as a limited partner for purposes of Section 2704(a), which speaks in terms of partnership interests.

In a normal case where a member does not have the ability to obtain the liquidation value of his interest, the application of Section 2704(a) should not have much impact.

[4] Disregard of Applicable Restrictions

In valuing an LLC interest, restrictions on the ability of a family entity to liquidate which are more restrictive than state law will generally be disregarded.[97] For example, if after the death of a member, state law provides that all of the members must consent to continue the business, a contrary provision in the operating agreement that allowed a majority of the members to consent would be ignored for purposes of valuing an interest in the LLC.[98]

---

[96] The rules under IRC § 2704(a) are more fully explained in Ch. 16 on limited partnerships and Ch. 26 on IRC § 2704.

[97] IRC § 2704(b).

[98] More comprehensive discussions of IRC § 2704(b) are contained in Ch. 16 and Ch. 26.

CHAPTER **18**

S Corporations

¶ 18.01 INTRODUCTION

This chapter examines those aspects of S corporations that are of most interest to estate planners.[1]

An S corporation, generally speaking, is a pass-through entity for income tax purposes, like a partnership. That is, with certain exceptions, the S corporation's items of income, gain, loss, deduction, and credit (i.e., its "income tax items") are reported directly by its shareholders on their own income tax returns, and are thus not generally taxable to the corporation. However, S corporations that were once C corporations may be subject to certain taxes at the corporate level. And, unlike a partnership, an S corporation will recognize gain on the distribution of appreciated property. An S corporation, instead of a noncorporate entity, is used as an estate planning tool if the corporate format is desirable for nontax reasons. For instance, the corporate format may be desirable because it has the advantage of stability. Unlike a partnership or limited liability company, a corporate entity does not dissolve on withdrawal of certain owners.

If it is determined that the corporate format is appropriate, the next planning choice that needs to be made concerns the type of corporation to be formed. The Internal Revenue Code contains two systems of income taxation of a corporation and its shareholders—subchapter C and subchapter S. Subchapter S will often be preferable for family corporations, due to the pass-through income taxation it provides. A subchapter C corporation may be a less desirable format in many situations because it results in two levels of tax, once at the corporate level on corporate earnings and again at the shareholder level when those earnings are distributed as dividends.

¶ 18.02 ELIGIBILITY FOR S STATUS

To be eligible to elect S corporation status, a corporation must meet certain tests. Final regulations regarding such eligibility matters were issued on July 20, 1995. These regulations apply to taxable years of a corporation beginning after July 21, 1995.[2] Moreover, the Small Business Jobs Protection Act of 1996 also revised the eligibility requirements, generally for taxable years beginning in 1997 and later. For prior years, different rules govern.

[1] Shareholders

The number and type of eligible shareholders for an S corporation are limited.

---

[1] For further reading on other aspects of S corporations, see James S. Eustice & Joel D. Kuntz, Federal Income Taxation of S Corporations (WG&L 3d. ed. 1992).

[2] Treas. Reg. § 1.1361-1(k)(2)(i). This chapter assumes these final regulations are applicable except where otherwise noted.

[a] Numerical Shareholder Requirement

There must be no more than 75 shareholders;[3] for taxable years beginning before 1997, however, the maximum number of shareholders was limited to 35. For purposes of determining the number of shareholders, a husband and wife, as well as their estates, are treated as a single shareholder.[4]

Ordinarily, a trust is counted as a single shareholder. However, in the case of an electing small business trust (ESBT),[5] any potential current beneficiary of the ESBT is considered a shareholder.[6] For this purpose, a potential current beneficiary is any person who is currently entitled to, or at the discretion of any person may receive, a distribution from the trust, except a person who first becomes a potential current beneficiary during the 60-day period ending with the trust's disposition of all of its stock in the S corporation.[7]

PRACTICE POINTER: Be careful with powers of appointment in ESBTs. If the assets of an ESBT may be appointed to a group of beneficiaries containing more than 75 people, the trust may not be a qualified S shareholder.

A tax-exempt entity that is a shareholder counts as one shareholder.[8]

[b] Qualitative Shareholder Requirements

The only permissible S corporation shareholders are (1) certain individuals who are US citizens or residents,[9] (2) certain estates (for a limited time period), (3) certain types of trusts,[10] and (4) in certain cases, another S corporation.[11]

PRACTICE POINTER: Practitioners should consider drafting S corporation shareholder agreements to provide that a shareholder will take no action, without the corporation's or other shareholders' consent, that will cause the shareholder to cease being an eligible shareholder and thereby result in the corporation's loss of S corporation status.

---

[3] IRC § 1361(b)(1)(A); Treas. Reg. § 1.1361-1(e)(2).

[4] IRC § 1361(c)(1).

[5] ESBTs are discussed at ¶ 18.05 below.

[6] IRC § 1361(c)(2)(B)(v).

[7] IRC § 1361(e)(2).

[8] Comm. Rep., Small Business Jobs Protection Act of 1996.

[9] IRC § 1361(b)(1)(C).

[10] IRC §§ 1361(b)(1)(B)—1361(b)(1)(C).

[11] Other entities are permitted to hold stock as nominees for qualified stockholders, but may not have beneficial ownership in the stock. Treas. Reg. § 1.1361-1(e)(1).

[i] **Estates of deceased shareholders.** An estate can be a shareholder as long as the estate is legitimately being administered,[12] and is a United States estate.[13] The continuation of an estate beyond the period of administration solely for the purposes of making installment payments under Section 6166, however, will not cause it to cease being an eligible shareholder.[14]

[ii] **Bankruptcy estates.** The bankruptcy estate of an otherwise qualified individual is an eligible S corporation shareholder.[15]

[iii] **Holders of life estates.** The IRS has expressed its intention to deliver guidance at some future occasion on S stock that is held in a life estate or usufruct form.[16]

[iv] **Trusts.** Certain trusts are eligible shareholders.[17]

[v] **S corporation holding stock of a qualified subchapter S subsidiary.** For taxable years beginning after 1996, an S corporation can be the shareholder of a qualified subchapter S subsidiary (QSSS).[18] Only a wholly owned domestic corporation that would be eligible to be an S corporation if its stock were held directly by the shareholders of its S corporation parent is eligible to be a QSSS.[19] The parent must elect QSSS treatment.[20] The QSSS is not treated as a separate corporation for income tax purposes.[21] Its tax items are reported directly by the parent S corporation.[22] Instructions for making the QSSS election have been issued.[23]

---

[12] IRC § 1361(b)(1)(B).

[13] Treas. Reg. § 1.1361-1(e)(2).

[14] Rev. Rul. 76-23, 1976-1 CB 264.

[15] IRC § 1361(c)(3).

[16] Preamble to TD 8600, 1995-33 IRB 10. The usufruct is a Louisiana form of life estate.

[17] They are discussed at ¶ 18.03.

[18] IRC § 1361(b)(3); Small Business Jobs Protection Act § 1317(a).

[19] IRC § 1361(b)(3)(B).

[20] IRC § 1361(b)(3)(B)(ii).

[21] IRC § 1361(b)(3)(A)(i).

[22] IRC § 1361(b)(3)(A)(ii).

[23] Notice 97-4, 1997-2 IRB 24 (Jan. 13, 1997).

[vi] Tax-exempt entities. In taxable years beginning after 1997, "qualified tax-exempt organizations" can be S shareholders.[24] A qualified tax-exempt organization is an entity which is described in Section 401(a) or Section 501(c)(3) and is exempt under Section 501(a). That is, qualified employee plan trusts and tax-exempt charitable entities will qualify as shareholders.[25] Pension trusts will rarely make good S corporation shareholders, because the S income will be taxed at the trust level as unrelated business taxable income (UBTI), and then it will be taxed again to the beneficiary when distributions are made.

PRACTICE POINTER: Charitable remainder trusts are not qualified tax-exempt organizations, since they are tax-exempt under Section 664, and not Section 501(a). Individual retirement accounts are described in Section 408, rather than Section 401(a), and are also not qualified tax-exempt organizations.

[c] Other Concerns

S corporation income as unrelated business taxable income. Items of income or loss of an S corporation will flow through to qualified tax-exempt shareholders as UBTI, regardless of the source or nature of the income.[26] Gain or loss on the sale or disposition of S stock will be treated as UBTI.[27]

ESOP as an S corporation shareholder. An ESOP can be a qualified tax-exempt S shareholder. However, certain tax rules relating to ESOPs will not apply with respect to an S corporation held by the ESOP. No deduction is allowed for a contribution to an ESOP by an S corporation[28] or for a dividend paid by an S corporation to an ESOP.[29] And, an individual shareholder cannot obtain tax-free rollover treatment for sales of S corporation stock to an ESOP.[30]

Distribution of subchapter C earnings. If a qualified tax-exempt shareholder purchases stock of an S corporation, any dividends it receives which are distributions of subchapter C earnings and profits will reduce the qualified tax-exempt shareholder's basis in the stock, except to the extent provided in regulations.[31]

---

[24] IRC § 1361(b)(1)(B), 1361(c)(7); Small Business Jobs Protection Act § 1316(f).

[25] IRC § 1361(c)(7).

[26] IRC § 512(e)(1)(B)(i).

[27] IRC § 512(e)(1)(B)(ii).

[28] IRC § 404(a)(9)(C).

[29] IRC § 404(k)(1).

[30] IRC § 1042(c)(1)(A).

[31] IRC § 512(e)(2).

Charitable contributions of S stock. Where a taxpayer contributes S corporation stock to a charity, the reductions in the income tax deduction which occur under Section 170(e) are determined by looking through to the assets of the S corporation, except that the look-through rule does not apply to tangible personal property held by the corporation.[32]

[2] Corporations Ineligible to Make S Elections

The following types of corporations cannot be S corporations:[33]

- *Foreign corporations.* A foreign corporation cannot be an S corporation.[34]
- *Other ineligible corporations.* Generally speaking, financial institutions which use the bad debt reserve method of accounting for bad debts under Section 585 (generally, small banks which do not use the specific charge-off method of accounting for bad debts), life insurance companies, companies electing the Puerto Rico and possession tax credit, and former domestic international sales corporations are ineligible.[35]
- *Former S corporations.* Generally, if an S corporation terminates its S status, it is not eligible to re-elect S status for five years, unless the IRS consents.[36] However, any S corporation that terminated its S election within the five-year period before August 21, 1996 may re-elect S status without the consent of the IRS.[37]

---

[32] IRC §§ 170(e)(1), 751.

[33] IRC §§ 1361(b)(1), 1361(b)(2). For taxable years beginning before 1997, an S corporation could not be a member of an affiliated group, as defined in IRC § 1504, and without regard to the exceptions described therein. IRC § 1361(b)(2)(A). Generally, this meant that an S corporation could not have a subsidiary. A corporation had a subsidiary for this purpose if it possessed at least 80 percent of the total voting power of the stock of another corporation and at least 80 percent of the total value of the other corporation. IRC § 1504(a)(2). An exception existed for a shell subsidiary which had not begun business at any time on or before the close of the period in question, and did not have gross income for the period. IRC § 1361(c)(6). Although an S corporation can now have a subsidiary, it still cannot file a consolidated return. IRC §§ 1501, 1504(a)(1), 1504(b)(8).

[34] IRC § 1361(b)(1).

[35] IRC § 1361(b)(2)(B)—1361(b)(2)(E). For taxable years beginning before 1997, no financial institutions were eligible S shareholders.

[36] IRC § 1362(g).

[37] IRC § 1362(g).

[3] Single Class of Stock Rule

[a] General Rule

An S corporation cannot have more than one class of stock.[38] In determining whether there is more than one class of stock, it is the economic rights, and not the voting rights, that a class of stock carries that is important. Thus, if there are two classes of stock, but the only difference between them is with respect to voting rights, then there is only one class of stock for purposes of the single class of stock requirement.[39] Hence, Dad can keep voting stock, and give nonvoting stock to the kids, as long as the economic rights associated with both classes are the same.

[b] Recharacterization of Interest as Additional Class of Stock

One of the major issues in dealing with S corporations is whether and when differing rights of shareholders with respect to the corporation will be recharacterized as additional classes of stock. A classic example is the recharacterization of debt as equity.

[i] **Debt as equity.** *Recharacterization as equity.* If one of the shareholders of the corporation lends money to the corporation, and the corporate debt to the shareholder is recharacterized as equity, the corporation will be deemed to have two classes of stock.

Safe harbor for straight debt. There is a statutory safe harbor from reclassification for "straight debt."[40] Straight debt has the following characteristics:

- The S corporation has executed a written unconditional promise to pay.[41]
- The debt is payable on demand or on a specified due date or dates.[42]
- The amount of the debt is a sum certain in money.[43]
- The interest rate and interest payment dates are not contingent on profits, the borrower's discretion, or similar factors.[44]
- The debt is not convertible directly or indirectly into stock.[45]

---

[38] IRC § 1361(b)(1)(D).

[39] IRC § 1361(c)(4).

[40] IRC § 1361(c)(5).

[41] IRC § 1361(c)(5)(B).

[42] IRC § 1361(c)(5)(B).

[43] IRC § 1361(c)(5)(B).

[44] IRC § 1361(c)(5)(B)(i).

[45] IRC § 1361(c)(5)(B)(ii).

- The creditor is an individual citizen or resident of the United States, an estate, a trust which is qualified to be an S shareholder, or an entity which is actively and regularly engaged in the business of lending money.[46]

[ii] Life insurance. Some S corporations buy life insurance on certain shareholders and pay for it via the split-dollar method.[47] In such a program, the shareholder generally gets to name the beneficiary or make an assignment of the risk portion of the policy. Questions have arisen as to whether that practice will constitute the establishment of a second class of stock. The theory is that the shareholders are receiving interest-free loans from the corporation if the corporation is paying the cost of the shareholder's (or other third party's) portion of the policy. The IRS has privately ruled that use of the split-dollar method to purchase life insurance on a shareholder will not constitute the establishment of a second class of stock, as long as the shareholder has to reimburse the corporation on a current basis for the economic benefit of the life insurance coverage.[48] The economic benefit is, at the taxpayer's option, either the P.S. 58 cost (or the cost as computed under U. S. Life Table 38 for a joint and survivor policy) or the actual cost of one year of term insurance for a standard risk person of the shareholder's age.

The IRS has also privately ruled, in the context of an employer-pay-all split-dollar policy, with no reimbursement, that a split-dollar arrangement for an employee-shareholder did not constitute a second class of stock.[49] The theory was that the agreement was a fringe benefit, and not a vehicle for the circumvention of the single-class-of-stock requirement. The life insurance agreement was analogized to payment of accident and health insurance premiums by an S corporation on behalf of "2 percent + shareholder-employees." The IRS has held, in a public ruling, that payment of such premiums would be disregarded for purposes of the one-class-of-stock requirement.[50]

If the split-dollar arrangement is not structured in accordance with the fact pattern in Revenue Ruling 64-328 (i.e., the corporation is entitled to receive the greater of the premiums paid or the cash surrender value of the policy on termination of the arrangement by death, or the cash surrender

---

[46] IRC § 1361(c)(5)(B)(iii). For taxable years beginning before 1997, the creditor could not be an entity other than an estate or eligible trust.

[47] See Ch. 12 on life insurance for a description of the split-dollar method of purchasing life insurance.

[48] Priv. Ltr. Rul. 9331009 (May 5, 1993); Priv. Ltr. Rul. 9318007 (Jan. 29, 1993); Priv. Ltr. Rul. 9235020 (May 28, 1992).

[49] Priv. Ltr. Rul. 9413023 (Dec. 23, 1993), Priv. Ltr. Rul. 9248019 (Aug. 31, 1992).

[50] Rev. Rul. 91-26, 1991-1 CB 185.

value on other termination), the shareholder may be deemed to receive a benefit in excess of the economic benefit, as defined above.[51] In such a case, the IRS might take the position that the shareholder benefiting from the arrangement has a second class of stock.

PRACTICE POINTER: S corporations should be cautious about establishing split-dollar arrangements which are outside the fact pattern of Revenue Ruling 64-328. Alternatively, include a provision in the split-dollar agreement to the effect that, if additional income is ultimately deemed received by the shareholder in any year in excess of the economic benefit, the shareholder will reimburse the corporation to that extent.

    [iii] Redemption agreements. Can an agreement by the S corporation to purchase a shareholder's stock in the S corporation constitute a right incident to the stock which will cause the stock to be characterized as a second class? Yes, if a principal purpose of the agreement is to circumvent the single-class-of-stock requirement, and the agreement establishes a purchase price that, at the time of the agreement, is significantly more or less than the stock's fair market value.[52] The theory in support of this rule is that a redemption of stock is treated as a dividend under certain circumstances.[53] If the stock subject to the agreement is deemed to give a right to special dividends, the stock may in fact be a second class of stock. However, a bona fide agreement to purchase stock at the death, divorce, disability, or termination of employment of a shareholder will not ordinarily cause the stock subject to the agreement to constitute a second class of stock.[54]

[4] S Election

A corporation must file an initial election in order to be taxed under the subchapter S rules.[55] All of the shareholders who own stock on the date the election is made must consent to the election.[56] The election can be made for any year at any time during the year preceding the first S year, or on or before the fifteenth day of the third month of the first S year.[57]

    EXAMPLE: If a corporation wants to be an S corporation in Year Two, it

---

[51] See Tech. Adv. Mem. 9604001 (Sept. 8, 1995).

[52] Treas. Reg. § 1.1361-1(l)(2)(iii)(A).

[53] See Ch. 19 for a discussion of the taxation of corporate redemptions.

[54] Treas. Reg. § 1.1361-1(l)(2)(iii)(B).

[55] IRC § 1362(a)(1).

[56] IRC § 1362(a)(2).

[57] IRC § 1362(b)(1).

may make its election at any time during Year One or at any time on or before the fifteenth day of the third month of Year Two. If the election is made later in Year Two, it will be treated as an election for Year Three.[58] An election is effective for all years during and after its effective date[59] until it is terminated.

The IRS can waive an invalid election due to an inadvertent failure to qualify as an S corporation or to obtain required shareholder consents.[60] Additionally, the IRS can treat a late S election as timely if reasonable cause for failure to make a timely election exists.[61]

An entity which is classified as an association taxable as a corporation can elect S corporation treatment if it otherwise qualifies.[62]

[5] Termination of S Election

[a] Termination Triggers

There are three ways for an S election to terminate:

- *Revocation.* More than one-half of the shareholders (in interest) can revoke the election.[63]
- *Ineligibility.* The corporation or any of its shareholders can cease to meet the S corporation or S shareholder requirements.[64]
- *Excess passive income.* An S corporation which was formerly a C corporation can have too much passive investment income.[65]

[b] Effects of Termination

A termination of S status will generally cause the corporation to be taxed as a regular corporation under subchapter C after the termination. However, if the termination was inadvertent, and certain other requirements are met, the IRS has the power to grant relief.[66] Many relief rulings have been issued.

In the year of termination, the portion of the year before the termination day will be treated as a short S year, and the rest of the year will be treated as

---

[58] IRC § 1362(b)(3).

[59] IRC § 1362(c).

[60] IRC § 1362(f).

[61] IRC § 1362(b)(5).

[62] Treas. Reg. §§ 1.1361-1(c), 1.1361-1(h), 1.1361-1(j).

[63] IRC § 1362(d)(1)(B).

[64] IRC § 1362(d)(2).

[65] IRC § 1362(d)(3). See ¶ 18.09[2][a] below.

[66] IRC § 1362(f).

a short C year. The income for the entire year of termination is allocated pursuant to statutory rules.[67]

¶ 18.03 TRUST SHAREHOLDERS

Eligible small business trusts (ESBTs), eligible testamentary trusts, and eligible grantor trusts which become nongrantor trusts after the death of the shareholder constitute a category of eligible trusts in which the income attributable to the S corporation is taxed to the trust under rules set out in subchapter J. We will call the other category of eligible trusts "pass-through trusts," because the trust income attributable to the S corporation will pass through to a deemed shareholder.

[1] Deemed Shareholders

An eligible trust (other than an ESBT) will have at least one "deemed shareholder." The identity of the deemed shareholders depends on the type of trust, and will be discussed in the following section on eligible trusts.

[a] Deemed Qualification Shareholder

Even if an eligible trust (other than an ESBT) is the actual holder of shares in an S corporation, there will always be a different "deemed shareholder" of those shares for qualification purposes.[68] The identity of the deemed shareholder is determined by the rules discussed below. We'll call that person the "deemed qualification shareholder." Both the deemed qualification shareholder and the trust must be eligible shareholders.[69]

[b] Deemed Income Tax Shareholder

Additionally, an eligible pass-through trust will have a different deemed shareholder for purposes of reporting the income tax items of the S corporation. The "deemed income tax shareholder" is the person who will be treated for income tax purposes as the owner of the S stock which is actually owned by the trust, and that person will directly report the trust's share of the S corporation's income tax items.

---

[67] IRC § 1362(e).

[68] Treas. Reg. § 1.1361-1(h)(3).

[69] Treas. Reg. § 1.1361-1(h)(3).

[2] Eligible Trusts

A foreign trust cannot be an S shareholder.[70] Hence, for purposes of the following discussion of trust shareholders, it will be assumed in all cases that the trust is a US trust.

[a] Grantor Trust During Deemed Owner's Life[71]

A trust that is treated as wholly owned by an individual who is a US citizen or resident is eligible.[72] Ordinarily, the trust must be treated as owned by only one person. However, a grantor trust with husband and wife as the sole grantors is an eligible shareholder.[73] The deemed owner(s) of the trust for income tax purposes will be considered both the deemed qualification shareholder(s) and the deemed income tax shareholder(s).[74]

Examples of trusts which might qualify under this category are revocable trusts, defective grantor trusts,[75] and GRITs and GRATs during the grantor's term.[76]

[b] Grantor Trust After Deemed Owner's Death

A trust which was treated for income tax purposes as owned by an individual citizen or resident of the United States immediately before his death is eligible to hold S stock for two years after the deemed owner's death.[77] The estate of the deemed owner will be the deemed qualification shareholder,[78] and the trust will report its share of the S corporation's income tax items (i.e., there will be no deemed income tax shareholder for the trust's qualifying period).[79]

---

[70] IRC § 1361(c)(2)(A). This is true even if the trust is a grantor trust and US citizens are the grantors. Treas. Reg. § 1.1361-1(h)(2).

[71] A grantor trust is a type of trust which is transparent for income tax purposes. The grantor or deemed grantor reports the trust's income tax items directly. IRC §§ 671-679. See Ch. 6 for a full explanation.

[72] IRC § 1361(c)(2)(A)(i).

[73] Treas. Reg. § 1.1361-1(e)(2).

[74] IRC § 1361(c)(2)(B)(i).

[75] A "defective" grantor trust is an irrevocable trust for the benefit of beneficiaries other than the settlor which is intentionally designed so that the income will be taxable to the grantor.

[76] These trusts are discussed in Ch. 7 (revocable trusts), Ch. 6 (defective grantor trusts), Ch. 24 (GRITs), and Ch. 22 (GRATs).

[77] IRC § 1361(c)(2)(A)(ii). For taxable years beginning before 1997, some such trusts were eligible shareholders for only 60 days.

[78] IRC § 1361(c)(2)(B)(ii); Treas. Reg. § 1.1361-1(h)(3)(i)(B).

[79] Treas. Reg. § 1.1361-1(h)(3)(ii)(A).

If husband and wife were both grantors of the trust when they were both living, will the trust qualify for two years after one grantor's death? Regulations issued under the pre-1997 rules provided that, for the purpose of determining whether the entire trust was includable in the estate of the deceased owner and therefore qualified for the two-year holding period, the decedent's spouse's interest is disregarded if the decedent's spouse was treated as owner under the grantor trust rules immediately before the decedent's death.[80] The rule should be the same under the new law, which was a liberalizing provision that dropped the requirement that a trust had to have been entirely included in the deceased owner's estate to qualify for the two-year eligibility. If the trust consisted of community property, and the decedent's community property interest in the trust is includable in the decedent's gross estate, then the entire trust will be deemed includable in the decedent's gross estate.

> **EXAMPLE:** Husband and Wife are grantor-beneficiaries of a grantor trust. The assets of the trust are all community property. Husband dies. As long as the trust owns the stock, Husband's estate will be treated as a qualified shareholder and owner of one-half of the trust for qualification and income tax purposes for up to two years after Husband's death. Wife will continue to be treated as grantor of the other one-half of the trust. If the trust had also included separate property of Husband, his estate would be considered the owner of that property, too.[81]

PRACTICE POINTER: An estate can hold S stock for its entire period of administration. However, a revocable trust that becomes irrevocable on the grantor's death can only hold S stock for two years after the grantor's death.

[c] Testamentary Trust

A testamentary trust can hold S stock for two years after it receives the stock.[82] This means two years after the trust is actually funded—not two years after the death of the testator. The testator's estate will be the deemed qualification shareholder for the two-year period,[83] but the trust will report the S corporation's income tax items—i.e., there will be no separate deemed income tax shareholder for the two-year period.[84]

---

[80] Treas. Reg. § 1.1361-1(h)(1)(ii).

[81] Treas. Reg. § 1.1361-1(h)(3)(i)(B).

[82] IRC § 1361(c)(2)(A)(iii). For taxable years beginning before 1997, the maximum period was 60 days.

[83] IRC § 1361(c)(2)(B)(iii); Treas. Reg. § 1.1361-1(h)(3)(i)(D).

[84] Treas. Reg. § 1.1361-1(h)(3)(ii)(B).

[d] Voting Trust

A voting trust is an eligible S corporation shareholder, if the beneficiaries are all treated as the owners of their respective portions of the trust for income tax purposes, and the trust was created pursuant to a written agreement containing provisions listed in the regulations.[85] The trust beneficiaries will be both the deemed qualification shareholders and the deemed income tax shareholders.[86]

[e] Qualified Subchapter S Trust and Eligible Small Business Trust

Qualified subchapter S trusts and eligible small business trusts are special types of trusts that can be S corporation shareholders; they are discussed below at ¶ 18.04 and ¶ 18.05.

¶ 18.04 QUALIFIED SUBCHAPTER S TRUSTS

A qualified subchapter S trust (QSST) is an eligible shareholder of an S corporation.[87] A QSST must meet certain requirements. For illustration, let's assume that Kelly is the income beneficiary of a QSST.

[1] Special Rule for Husband and Wife QSST Beneficiaries

If (1) Kelly (income beneficiary of QSST) is married and both she and her husband are income beneficiaries of the same QSST, (2) the spouses file a joint return, and (3) each is a United States citizen or resident, then the spouses will be treated as one beneficiary for all QSST purposes.[88] Among other things, this means that both spouses must sign the QSST election (described below), and that the requirements below must continue to be met with respect to both of them for the entire QSST period.[89]

[2] Only One Current Income Beneficiary

Subject to the spousal rule described at [1] above, the trust instrument must provide that, during Kelly's life, she is the only income beneficiary.[90] How-

---

[85] IRC § 1361(c)(2)(A)(iv); Treas. Reg. § 1.1361-1(h)(1)(v).

[86] IRC § 1361(c)(2)(B)(iv).

[87] IRC § 1361(d)(1).

[88] Treas. Reg. § 1.1361-1(j)(2)(i).

[89] Treas. Reg. § 1.1361-1(j)(2)(i).

[90] IRC § 1361(d)(3)(A)(i).

ever, if state law permits a third person, such as a creditor, to obtain access to Kelly's trust interest by a court order, the trust will qualify as a QSST until such a person actually obtains such access.[91] Similarly, if Kelly's interest in the trust is assignable, the trust will still qualify, unless and until she assigns the interest in a manner that causes the interest to fail the QSST test.[92]

[3] Corpus Distributions Only to the Then Current Income Beneficiary

Subject to the spousal rule described at subparagraph [1] above, the trust instrument must provide that, during Kelly's life, principal can be distributed only to her.[93] Among other things, this means that Kelly cannot have a limited power of appointment over a QSST during her lifetime.[94] The trust, however, is not required to have a spendthrift clause. If it does not, Kelly can assign her interest in the trust. In such instance, the trust will still be treated as a QSST. However, if Kelly does assign her interest, the assignee will then be treated as the income beneficiary, and the trust will have to satisfy the QSST requirements after the assignment to retain its status as a QSST.[95] For example, if Kelly is named as income beneficiary for life, and she assigns her interest to her brother, Louis, the trust will no longer qualify as a QSST, since Louis's interest will terminate on Kelly's death rather than on Louis's death.[96]

Subject to the spousal rule described at subparagraph [1] above, the trust instrument must provide that Kelly's income interest must terminate at the earlier of the current income beneficiary's (here, Kelly's) death or the termination of the trust.[97]

[4] Termination Distribution of All Trust Assets to the Current Income Beneficiary

Subject to the spousal rule described at subparagraph [1] above, the trust instrument must provide that, if the trust terminates during Kelly's life, the trust must distribute all of its assets to her.[98]

---

[91] Treas. Reg. § 1.1361-1(j)(1)(v).

[92] Treas. Reg. § 1.1361-1(j)(iv), 1.1361-1(k), example 5.

[93] IRC § 1361(d)(3)(A)(ii).

[94] Treas. Reg. § 1.1361-1(j)(2)(iii).

[95] Treas. Reg. §§ 1.1361-1(j)(2)(iv), 1.1361-1(k), example 5.

[96] Treas. Reg. §§ 1.1361-1(j)(2)(iv), 1.1361-1(k), example 5.

[97] IRC § 1361(d)(3)(A)(iii).

[98] IRC § 1361(d)(3)(A)(iv).

[5] Mandatory Current Distribution of All Trust Income to the Current Income Beneficiary

Subject to the spousal rules described at subparagraph [1] above, all of the trust's income (determined according to fiduciary accounting principles) must in fact be distributed currently to Kelly.[99] This requirement does not have to be set forth in the trust instrument as long as it is actually met.

A special sixty-five day rule applies to prevent the current income distribution requirement from being violated by income distributions occurring within the first 65 days of the year following the year in which the trust earned the income distributed, provided that the Section 663(b) election is made. For example, suppose the trustee distributes income earned in Year One during the first 65 days of Year Two, and makes an election under Section 663(b) to treat the distribution as having been made in Year One. Distributions of Year One income during the 65-day period will satisfy the income distribution requirement for Year One.[100]

If the income beneficiary is a minor, the distribution can be made to a custodian for the minor under the Uniform Gifts to Minors Act or Uniform Transfers to Minors Act, or to the child's legal guardian.[101]

PRACTICE POINTER: If a lawyer or accountant is asked to give an opinion that a trust has been a QSST from a certain date forward, this requirement will usually be the hardest one to tie down. It requires making sure all of the trust's receipts and disbursements have been properly allocated between income and principal, and that the income has been timely distributed.

[6] Separate Shares Treated as Separate QSSTs

For purposes of QSST qualification, a substantially separate and independent share of a trust will be treated as a separate trust.[102]

[7] Current Income Beneficiary Must Be a U.S. Citizen or Resident

Kelly must be a citizen or resident of the United States.[103] And, if Kelly's husband is a nonresident alien and holds a current ownership in the stock held

---

[99] IRC § 1361(d)(3)(B).

[100] Treas. Reg. § 1.1361-1(j)(1)(i).

[101] Priv. Ltr. Rul. 9506011 (Nov. 3, 1994); Priv. Ltr. Rul. 9410035 (Dec. 13, 1993); Priv. Ltr. Rul. 8435153 (June 1, 1984).

[102] IRC § 1361(d)(3).

[103] IRC § 1361(d)(3)(B).

in the trust (for example, through a community property interest in the trust), the trust will not qualify.[104]

[8] Current Income Beneficiary's Election to Treat Trust as QSST

An election to treat the trust as a QSST and to treat the income beneficiary as the owner of the trust's S stock must be made by the income beneficiary (not the trustee) within two months and 16 days after the trust's receipt of the S stock.[105]

Many inadvertent failures and terminations of S elections occur because the election is signed by the QSST trustee, rather than the income beneficiary; such a defective election results in an ineligible shareholder. In fact, an election signed by the trustee is such a common mistake that the IRS has an automatic correction procedure. If the error is corrected within two years, and certain other tests are met, S corporation status will be automatically and retroactively restored to the corporation.[106]

If the income beneficiary is treated as the owner of all or part of the trust for income tax purposes under the grantor trust rules, she can make a protective QSST election.[107]

An election can be made on behalf of a child or other person under a legal disability by the person's guardian or other legal representative, or if there is none, by the person's natural or adoptive parent.[108]

The requirements of the election are set forth in the regulations.[109] The QSST election is irrevocable[110] and is treated as having been made by any successor income beneficiaries, unless such a beneficiary affirmatively refuses to consent to the election.[111]

If a successor income beneficiary wants to refuse consent, he must file the refusal to consent with the IRS within 15 days and two months after the date

---

[104] Treas. Reg. § 1.1361-1(g).

[105] IRC § 1361(d)(1). The deadline is two months and 16 days after the termination of the grantor trust status of the trust, if a grantor trust is converting to a QSST. Treas. Reg. § 1.1361-1(j)(6)(iii)(C). The deadline is two months and 16 days after the estate ceases to be treated as the shareholder, in the case of a trust which terminated its grantor trust status due to the death of the deceased owner. Treas. Reg. § 1.1361-1(j)(6)(iii)(C).

[106] Rev. Proc. 94-23, 1994-1 CB 609.

[107] Treas. Reg. § 1.1361-1(j)(6)(iv).

[108] Treas. Reg. § 1.1361-1(j)(6).

[109] Treas. Reg. § 1.1361-1(j)(6).

[110] IRC § 1361(d)(2)(C).

[111] IRC § 1361(d)(2)(B)(ii).

on which the successor income beneficiary became the income beneficiary.[112] The refusal will be effective as of the date the successor income beneficiary became the current income beneficiary.

[9] Current Income Beneficiary Taxed on Trust's Share of S Corporation Items

The QSST's income beneficiary is treated as the S shareholder for most income tax purposes.[113] This means that the trust's share of the S corporation's income tax items will be reported directly by the income beneficiary, regardless of whether she gets any distributions or not. The QSST itself will report its other income tax items, just as any trust would. Since the QSST is required to distribute all of its income currently, the income beneficiary will be taxable on the fiduciary income of the trust (up to the trust's distributable net income).[114] The QSST will, however, be taxed on items of taxable income that constitute principal for fiduciary accounting purposes.[115]

The QSST will be treated as the shareholder for purposes of the income tax treatment of the sale of the S stock held by the QSST.[116] The practical effect of this rule is that the QSST, rather than the income beneficiary, will report and pay the capital gains tax on the sale of the stock, and that the QSST is eligible to sell S stock on the installment sale basis.[117]

A transition rule exists which allows a QSST that disposed of S stock before July 22, 1995, to treat the sale as a taxable transaction for the QSST or the income beneficiary in certain circumstances.[118]

---

[112] Treas. Reg. § 1.1361-1(j)(10).

[113] IRC § 1361(d)(1)(B).

[114] See Ch. 6 on Income Taxation of Trusts and Beneficiaries for a discussion of distributable net income and the income taxation of trusts.

[115] For example, capital gains.

[116] Treas. Reg. § 1.1361-1(j)(8).

[117] For a description of the previous controversy over this issue, see William R. Culp, Jr. & Jonathan E. Gopman, Ruling on Qualified Sub S Trusts Raises Phantom Gain and Installment Problems, 78 J. Tax'n 282 (1993).

[118] Treas. Reg. § 1.1361-1(k)(2)(ii).

PRACTICE POINTER: A QSST can be used to make tax-free transfers to the trust beneficiaries, similar to defective grantor trust planning. For example, suppose Grandpa establishes QSST with Dad (who is wealthy) as the income beneficiary and Son (who is poor) as the remainder beneficiary. The S corporation held by the QSST earns income but never pays a dividend. Dad pays the income tax on the S corporation income, which ultimately passes to Son on Dad's death. This opportunity for Dad to make a tax-free transfer in the amount of the income tax exists because the income beneficiary is taxable on the QSST's share of taxable income of the S corporation, but is only required to take distributions of the QSST's accounting income.

[10] QSST Distributions Satisfying the Grantor's Support Obligation

Any distribution to the income beneficiary that satisfies a legal support obligation owed by the grantor to the income beneficiary will cause the trust to cease to qualify as a QSST.[119] A prohibition in the trust instrument might be in order.

[11] QSST Requirements Must Be Permanent

All of the governing instrument requirements must apply from the date of the QSST election throughout the term of the trust.[120] Accordingly, the trust instrument cannot provide that the QSST-required provisions apply only during the period that the trust holds S stock.

> **EXAMPLE:** Income beneficiary of Trust A has a lifetime limited power of appointment, except during any period that the trust holds S stock. Trust A will not qualify as a QSST. Once the trust becomes a QSST, the required provisions must apply for the remaining life of the trust. In this case, the income beneficiary could never again have a lifetime power of appointment, once the trust became a QSST.

[12] QSST Is Not a Grantor Trust to the Grantor

A QSST election cannot be made for a trust that is actually treated as owned by the grantor for income tax purposes. However, the trust may be a grantor trust as to an income beneficiary treated as the grantor under Section 678.[121]

---

[119] Treas. Reg. § 1.1361-1(j)(2)(ii)(B).

[120] Treas. Reg. § 1.1361-1(j)(5).

[121] Treas. Reg. § 1.1361-1(j)(6)(iv).

[13] QTIP Trust as a QSST

A QTIP trust created after the death of the first spouse to die should always qualify as a QSST, if the election is made, unless the surviving spouse is a nonresident alien. However, a QTIP trust established during the lifetime of the grantor spouse will never qualify as a QSST as long as the spouses are still married to each other. This is because the grantor spouse will be treated as the owner of the trust under the grantor trust rules.[122] However, the trust will still be an eligible S shareholder if it is totally a grantor trust.[123]

[14] Death of Income Beneficiary

If, after the death of the income beneficiary, the trust continues in existence and continues to hold S stock, but is no longer a QSST and is not a grantor trust, then the income beneficiary's estate will be treated as the deemed quali-fication shareholder for the period permitted to estate shareholders.[124] During that period, the trust will be the deemed income tax shareholder.[125]

[15] Avoid Excessive Current Income Distribution Burden: Separate QSST From Other Trusts

QSSTs are problematic from a number of standpoints. However, one of the principal reasons is that all of the QSST's income must be distributed cur-rently. For this reason, it is a good idea to provide in wills and trusts that if S stock is held by a trustee, it will immediately be transferred to a separate trust that qualifies for QSST status and holds only S stock. That way, the income from all of the trust assets will not have to be paid to the income beneficiary due to a holding of S stock in the trust. If transferring an item from another trust to the QSST changes the rights of the beneficiaries, and the trustee(s) is a beneficiary or is related or subordinate to the grantor, the trustee's powers to invest the trust assets in S corporation stock must be considered from an estate and income tax point of view.

[16] Using a QSST to Capture an Unusable Trust or Estate Loss

A QSST can be used to free up an otherwise trapped trust or estate loss. For example, suppose that Trust A has shares of publicly traded stock that have a

---

[122] IRC § 677.

[123] See Treas. Reg. § 1.1361-1(k)(1), example 10.

[124] See ¶ 18.02[1][b][i] above.

[125] Treas. Reg. § 1.1361-1(j)(7)(ii).

value less than basis. If Trust *A* sells the stock, it will have a capital loss. If it has no likelihood of capital gains equal to the loss, it cannot use the loss, and it cannot allow the trust beneficiaries to take advantage of the loss until the trust terminates. Trust *A* can transfer the shares to a drop-down QSST, which can then transfer the loss assets to an S corporation in a Section 351 transfer. Then, the S corporation can sell the low-basis shares, passing through the capital loss to the income beneficiary.

¶ 18.05 ELECTING SMALL BUSINESS TRUSTS

[1] Qualification of Trust

[a] All Beneficiaries Must Be Qualified

All beneficiaries of an electing small business trust (ESBT) must be individuals, estates, or certain charitable organizations.[126] However, for taxable years beginning in 1997, charitable organizations may only hold contingent interests and may not be potential current beneficiaries.[127]

PRACTICE POINTER: According to the legislative history and the Bluebook, individual beneficiaries must be eligible to be S shareholders, and therefore, nonresident aliens cannot be beneficiaries.[128] If a US beneficiary has a broad inter vivos limited power of appointment which could include nonresident aliens, will the trust be disqualified? The answer is not clear.

[b] No Trust Interest Can Be Purchased

No interest in the trust may be acquired by purchase.[129] "Purchase," for this purpose, means an acquisition of an interest in which the basis of the interest is determined under Section 1012 (i.e., at cost).[130] Acquisitions of interests in the trust by gift, bequest, etc., are therefore okay.

---

[126] IRC § 1361(e)(1)(A)(i). A question has been raised about whether a trust which continues in further trust with a different configuration of beneficiaries after the death of a particular beneficiary or other event will be considered to have a trust beneficiary and thus not qualify as an ESBT.

[127] Small Business Jobs Protection Act of 1996 § 1316(f).

[128] Conference Report to HR 3448, HR Rep. No. 737, 104th Cong., 2d Sess. (1996), and Joint Committee on Taxation, General Explanation (Bluebook) of Tax Legislation Enacted in 104th Congress (JCS-12-96), at 113.

[129] IRC § 1361(e)(1)(A)(ii).

[130] IRC § 1361(e)(1)(C).

[c] Trust Elects ESBT Status

A trust must elect to be treated as an ESBT.[181] The election applies to the tax year in which it is made, and later years, unless it is revoked with IRS consent or the trust ceases to qualify as an ESBT.[182] The mechanics of making the election are spelled out in Notice 97-12.[183]

[d] Trusts Which Cannot Be ESBTs

[i] In general. A QSST or tax-exempt trust cannot be an ESBT.[184] A grantor trust is ignored for income tax purposes, and therefore cannot be an ESBT. What if the trustee of an existing QSST wants to make an ESBT election? We know he cannot do it directly. If he engineers a disqualification of the QSST, the corporation's S qualification will ordinarily be lost, if even for an instant, and then the S election cannot be made again for five years. The Bluebook has indicated congressional intent that the Treasury provide guidance on this issue.

[ii] Charitable remainder trusts. A charitable remainder trust is apparently not an ESBT, even after 1997, because it is a tax-exempt trust. There is an argument that, if the CRT has unrelated business income, it is not tax-exempt, and therefore could be an ESBT after 1997. A member of the staff of the Joint Committee on Taxation has announced that a technical corrections bill will be introduced to clarify the intent that a CRT not be an ESBT.[185] In addition, the Bluebook states that a CRT will not qualify as an ESBT, and that a technical correction may be necessary to make that clear.[186]

[iii] Individual retirement accounts. Does the same theory applicable to CRTs apply to IRAs? No, because IRAs are tax-exempt, except *to the extent that* they have UBTI, whereas charitable remainder trusts are tax-exempt *unless* they have UBTI. Hence, an IRA cannot be an ESBT.

[iv] Charitable lead trusts. A charitable lead trust should be able to be an

---

[181] IRC § 1361(e)(1)(A)(iii), (e)(3).

[182] IRC § 1361(e)(3).

[183] 1997-3 IRB 1.

[184] IRC § 1361(e)(1)(B).

[185] Comment of Joseph M. Mikrut at meeting of the ABA Section of Taxation's S Corporation committee, January 10, 1997, as reported in Tax Notes Today, Jan. 27, 1997.

[186] Joint Committee on Taxation, General Explanation (Bluebook) of Tax Legislation Enacted in 104th Congress (JCS-12-96), at 114, fn. 117.

ESBT after 1997. However, the S income will apparently be taxable to the ESBT at the maximum rates, even if the income is in fact distributed to a charity. Thus, an ESBT election for a charitable lead trust would not normally be advantageous.

[2] Taxation of ESBT

[a] S Corporation Portion

The portion of the trust that consists of stock in an S corporation is treated as a separate trust for income tax purposes.[137] This deemed separate trust is taxed as follows.

[i] **Applicable tax rate.** The deemed separate trust is taxed on its taxable income at the highest individual rate applicable to income of trusts (currently 39.6 percent of ordinary income and 28 percent of net capital gain).[138] Further, the trust's alternative minimum tax exemption amount under Section 55(d) is zero.[139]

[ii] **ESBT's taxable income.** Taxable income of the deemed separate trust includes the following "deemed separate trust items":

- Tax items allocated to it as an S corporation shareholder under the S corporation rules;
- Gain or loss from the sale of the S corporation stock; and
- To the extent provided in regulations, state and local income taxes and administrative expenses of the trust properly allocable to the S corporation stock.[140]

Otherwise allowable capital losses are allowed only to the extent of capital gains.[141]

[iii] **Distributable net income.** The deemed separate trust items are not included in distributable net income of the trust.[142] Hence, no deduction is

---

[137] IRC § 641(d)(1).

[138] IRC §§ 641(d)(2)(A), 641(e), 641(h).

[139] IRC § 641(d)(2)(B).

[140] IRC § 641(d)(2)(C).

[141] IRC § 641(d)(2)(D).

[142] IRC § 641(d)(3).

available for distributions to beneficiaries, and no amount is includable by the beneficiaries or can be apportioned to the beneficiaries.[143]

[iv] Loss carryovers and excess Section 642(h) deductions. On the termination of all or any part of the separate portion of the ESBT, any loss carryovers or excess deductions under Section 642(h) are taken into account by the entire trust, subject to the usual rules.[144]

[b] Other Property in ESBT

The other property in the ESBT is taxed as follows.

[i] Cessation of separate trust treatment. The deemed separate trust items are disregarded. Distributions from the entire trust are deductible from the income of this portion of the trust, but distributable net income does not include income attributable to the deemed separate trust.[145]

> EXAMPLE: In Year One, Trust A, an ESBT, has $100 of S corporation ordinary income and $75 of other distributable net income. Trust A distributes $80 in Year One. After taking into account the distribution deduction of $75, Trust A will have taxable income of $100 in Year One. All of the S corporation income is taxable to Trust A. The other $75 of distributable net income is taxable to the beneficiary because it was distributed. This is true even if the $80 distributed consisted of dividends of the S corporation.

[ii] Termination of the ESBT. Where the trust terminates before the end of the S corporation's taxable year, the trust takes into account its pro rata share of S corporation items for its final year.[146]

[c] Pros and Cons of ESBTs

The ESBT can accumulate income and spray distributions. However, all of the trust's income attributable to the S corporation will be taxable at the maximum rate, and that result cannot be minimized by distributions to the beneficiaries. In this respect, it is not clear, when distributions are made, whether they will be considered distributions of the S income or the non-S income. In order for this question to arise, however, the S corporation would presumably have to declare a dividend or redeem the trust's stock; otherwise,

---

[143] IRC § 641(d)(2)(C).

[144] IRC § 641(d)(4).

[145] IRC § 641(d)(3).

[146] IRC § 1366(a)(1).

there would not be a way under state law to get the S corporation income from the S corporation to the trust, and thence to the beneficiaries.

¶ 18.06 TRANSFERS OF S CORPORATION STOCK

There are some traps for the unwary here which an estate planner needs to keep in mind.

[1] Effect of Pro Rata Income Sharing

In general,[147] the S corporation is a pass-through entity, with items of S corporation income and loss being passed through to the shareholders. Unlike partnerships, however, S corporations must allocate income pro rata to the shareholders, in accordance with their percentage of stock ownership in the corporation.[148]

[a] General Rule for Mid-Year Changes in S Corporation Stock Ownership

If there is a change in ownership of the S corporation stock during the year, each shareholder's share of income is generally determined for the portion of the year in which he held his stock, as if all income for the year was earned in an equal amount each day of the year.[149]

EXAMPLE: Louis and Martina each own 50 percent of S corporation on January 1. On July 1, each of them sells one-half of his/her shares to Phil, resulting in a $1/3$-$1/3$-$1/3$ ownership for the second half of the year. Shares of the S corporation's income for the year will be allocated according to each shareholder's percentage ownership of the stock for each fraction of the year. Louis and Martina will each be allocated $(1/2 \times 1/2) + (1/3 \times 1/2)$, or $5/12$ths of the year's income. Phil will be allocated $1/3 \times 1/2$, or $1/6$th of the year's income.

This formula allocation will not be fair if the S corporation's income is not in fact earned equally throughout the year.

EXAMPLE: In the above example, say the corporation is worth $150 on July 1, and that $30 of that amount consists of income earned during the first one-half of the year. Phil pays $50 to buy one-third of the corporation. The corporation earns no income during the rest of the year. Phil will be entitled to one-third of the income earned during the entire year

---

[147] With the exceptions noted at ¶ 18.09 below.

[148] IRC § 1377(a)(1).

[149] IRC § 1377(a)(1).

(including the $30 income earned during the first one-half of the year, one-third of which he purchased). However, he will be taxed on only one-sixth of the year's income. Fairness may require an adjustment in the price he pays for the stock, taking into account the tax that Louis and Martina will have to pay on income that Phil receives. (The amount of income that Phil receives cannot be adjusted, short of distributing the income before Phil buys his shares, because no variations among shareholders' rights to income can exist.)

[b] Exceptions

[i] **Complete termination of S shareholder's stock interest.** If a shareholder completely terminates his interest in the S corporation, then all affected shareholders can consent to have the taxable year consist of two taxable years for the purpose of allocating taxable income.[160] If they do, then each shareholder will be allocated a pro rata amount of the income actually earned in each taxable year in which he was a shareholder.[151] "Affected shareholders" are shareholders whose interests have terminated and all shareholders to whom the shareholder has transferred shares during the year.[152] If a shareholder transferred shares to the corporation, affected shareholders include all persons who were shareholders during the year.[153]

Death of a shareholder. According to the regulations, the death of a shareholder is a complete termination of his interest for this purpose.[154] This is important, because the general rule can pose a problem in the year of death.

> **EXAMPLE:** S corporation has a calendar taxable year. Joe, who holds 100 percent of stock in the S corporation in joint tenancy with right of survivorship with his son, dies on November 30. The S corporation realizes a large capital gain in December. If the books are not closed, the estate will be taxable on 11/12ths of the gain from the S stock, even though neither Joe nor his estate receives any of the money attributable to the gain.

[ii] **Shareholder's substantial disposition of S corporation stock.** The regulations provide that if any shareholder disposes of 20 percent or more of the corporation's issued stock in a 30-day period, the corporation and all

---

[160] For taxable years beginning before 1997, all shareholders had to consent.

[151] IRC § 1377(a)(2)(A).

[152] IRC § 1377(a)(2)(B).

[153] IRC § 1377(a)(2)(B).

[154] Treas. Reg. § 1.1377-1(b)(4).

shareholders can consent to an election to close the books on the disposition.[155]

[iii] Shareholder's redemption treated as exchange. If any shareholder surrenders at least 20 percent of the S corporation's outstanding stock in a transaction treated as an exchange under Section 302(a) or Section 303(a) during any 30-day period within the S corporation's tax year, the S corporation and all shareholders can consent to an election to close the books on the redemption.[156]

[iv] Issuance of new S corporation stock. If the S corporation issues new stock to one or more shareholders during any 30-day period during the S corporation's tax year, the corporation and shareholders can consent to an election to close the books on the issuance.[157]

[v] "All shareholders" defined. For purposes of paragraphs [ii], [iii], and [iv] above, "all shareholders" apparently means each shareholder who held stock at any time during the tax year (without regard to the split).[158]

[c] Deferral and Bunching of S Corporation Income and Loss

In some cases, deferral opportunities (and bunching dangers) can be created if the S corporation and a shareholder do not have the same taxable year.[159]

[2] Real Owners of Stock

A transfer of ownership of S corporation stock only occurs when real ownership of the stock changes. An S shareholder's stock will be treated as owned by him for income tax purposes, as long as he is the "real owner" of the interest. The same factors as discussed in Chapter 16 on partnerships apply in determining the real stockholder for S corporation purposes.[160]

---

[155] Treas. Reg. § 1.1368-1(g)(1).

[156] Treas. Reg. § 1.1368-1(g)(2)(i)(B).

[157] Treas. Reg. § 1.1368-1(g)(2)(i)(C).

[158] Treas. Reg. § 1.1368-1(g)(2)(iii).

[159] See Ch. 50 on post-mortem elections for an analysis with respect to estates.

[160] See, e.g., Speca v. Comm'r, 1979 PH TC Memo. ¶ 79, 120, 38 TCM (CCH) 544 (1979), aff'd, 630 F2d 554 (7th Cir. 1980).

¶ 18.07 S CORPORATION DISTRIBUTIONS TO SHAREHOLDERS—INCOME TAX EFFECTS

Estate planners often need to know the income tax consequences of distributions from entities, as various shareholders may have reasons to extract money or property from an entity as part of an estate plan.

A distribution to a shareholder with respect to stock in an S corporation is not a taxable event unless (1) the S corporation has earnings and profits or (2) the amount of the distribution exceeds the shareholder's basis in the stock. In general, an S corporation cannot have earnings and profits unless it was once a C corporation or has engaged in certain capital transactions causing it to take all or part of another corporation's earnings and profits.[161] Accordingly, it is rare that a distribution from an S corporation which was never a C corporation will be a taxable dividend of corporate earnings to a shareholder. On the other hand, as discussed below, it is not so unlikely that a distribution from any S corporation will be taxable to a shareholder because it exceeds his stock basis.

For purposes of this explanation, it will be assumed that the S corporation does not have any amounts treated as previously taxed income (which is undistributed taxed income earned by an S corporation in taxable years starting before 1983).

Distributions with respect to stock of corporations are classified for income tax purposes as dividends or capital transactions. Capital transactions are redemptions that are not classified as dividends. Rights to dividend distributions from S corporations must always be pro rata among the shareholders, since S corporations cannot have variations in the economic rights of shareholders without violating the single-class-of-stock requirement. The same pro rata requirement applies to deemed dividends, unless an exception applies to the single-class-of-stock requirements.

[1] Dividend Distributions

[a] S Corporations With No C Corporation Earnings and Profits

If an S corporation does not have earnings and profits, a distribution is not taxable to the shareholder unless it exceeds the shareholder's basis in her stock. If it does, then the excess of the distributed amount over the adjusted basis of the stock is treated as capital gain.[162]

---

[161] IRC § 1371(c)(1).

[162] IRC § 1368(b).

[b] S Corporations With Earnings and Profits

[i] The accumulated adjustments account. An S corporation which has earnings and profits is required to maintain an accumulated adjustments account (usually referred to as the "AAA"—pronounced "triple A"—account). Generally, the AAA account is an account containing the S corporation's undistributed earnings for the most recent continuous period during which the corporation has been an S corporation, starting with years beginning on or after January 1, 1983.[163] The earnings in the AAA account have generally already been subject to tax at the shareholder level. The rules, which provide that the AAA account is deemed to be distributed before earnings and profits, allow an S corporation to distribute its already-taxed S earnings before distributing earnings that would generate ordinary income to the shareholders. Hence, the S corporation can generally distribute the amount of the AAA account with no further income tax (as long as appreciated property is not distributed, of course).[164]

PRACTICE POINTER: Sometimes, when an owner wants to lower the value of S stock before gifting it, she will withdraw her share of the AAA account. In such a case, if there is more than one shareholder, pro rata distributions of the AAA account should generally be made to all shareholders if the withdrawal is not made pursuant to a redemption. Non-pro-rata distributions will not necessarily result in more than one class of stock; however, other tax consequences can result.[165]

[ii] General rule for dividend distributions. If the corporation makes a dividend distribution to a shareholder, the distribution will be treated as follows:

- First, as a nontaxable distribution of the shareholder's portion of the AAA account, up to the amount of basis of the stock;
- Second, as capital gain, to the extent, if any, that the AAA account exceeds the shareholder's basis;
- Third, as a dividend to the extent of earnings and profits;[166]
- Fourth, as a reduction in the shareholder's remaining basis; and
- Fifth, as capital gain.[167]

---

[163] IRC § 1368(e). Some special adjustments apply.

[164] See ¶ 18.07[3] below for a discussion of the consequences of a distribution of appreciated property. Also, if a shareholder's portion of the AAA account exceeds his basis in the stock, a capital gain will result.

[165] Treas. Reg. § 1.1361-1(l)(2).

[166] IRC § 1368(c)(2).

[167] IRC §§ 1368(c)(1)-1368(c)(3); Treas. Reg. § 1.1368-3.

[iii] Election to treat distribution as coming first from earnings and profits. The shareholders can elect, by unanimous consent, to have the S corporation's earnings and profits treated as having been distributed first.[168]

[2] Redemptions

The tax consequences of a redemption of C corporation stock will often vary considerably, depending on whether the redemption is characterized as a dividend or as a capital transaction.[169] The same, however, is not usually true of a redemption of S stock. If a redemption is classified as a dividend, the redemption is treated under the rules discussed above in ¶ 18.07[1]. However, treatment as a dividend from an S corporation may not be important to an S corporation shareholder, unless there are earnings and profits, because the shareholders will have already paid tax on prior years' earnings from the S corporation's operations.

Does a redemption treated as a dividend violate the single-class-of-stock requirement, under the theory that some shareholders are receiving dividends and others are receiving an increased ownership interest in the corporation? Not usually. Redemption agreements are disregarded in determining whether more than one class of stock exists, unless certain abusive facts exist.[170]

A redemption that is not treated as a dividend would result in a capital gain to the extent of the amount received by the shareholder less her basis in her stock. If there are earnings and profits, the redeeming shareholder may receive them without paying ordinary income tax at the shareholder level. The same result occurs in the case of a C corporation with earnings and profits when a redeeming shareholder receives exchange treatment on a redemption.

[3] Distributions of Appreciated Property

From the point of view of the S corporation, a distribution of appreciated property to a shareholder (whether a dividend or redemption distribution to the shareholder) is treated as a sale by the S corporation to the shareholder, and will result in taxable gain to the S corporation.[171] As a pass-through item,

---

[168] IRC § 1368(e)(3).

[169] See Ch. 19 on C corporations for an explanation.

[170] Treas. Reg. § 1.1361-1(1)(2)(iii); see also Priv. Ltr. Rul. 9404020 (Oct. 28, 1993). See ¶ 18.02[3][b][iii] above for further information.

[171] IRC §§ 311, 1371(a).

the gain will be included in the income of the shareholders, according to their proportionate ownership of the S corporation.

[4] Distributions After Death of a Shareholder

A shareholder's S stock receives a new basis on the shareholder's death. This fact, of course, can change the tax consequences of a distribution to the beneficiary receiving the shareholder's stock.

[a] Income in Respect of a Decedent Considerations

The basis of a deceased shareholder's S stock is not adjusted to the extent that the value of the stock is attributable to items constituting income in respect of a decedent,[172] effective for estates of decedents dying after August 21, 1996. In this regard, items of S corporation income are not treated as income in respect of a decedent just because the shareholder died before the last day of the year. His share of those items will be reported on his final return. Rather, it includes items which have been earned at date of death but are not properly reported on a return for periods during life (e.g., amounts of gain at date of death on an installment note receivable by the S corporation).

[b] Disparity Between Outside Basis and Inside Basis

For S corporations, there is no provision similar to the partnership Section 754 election.[173] Hence, if an S corporation holds appreciated property at the death of a shareholder, even if a shareholder's estate gets a stepped-up basis for his S stock on his death, the S corporation's basis in the appreciated property retains the same "inside" basis. The shareholder's step-up in basis can, however, be utilized in such a case on liquidation of the corporation. If the S corporation liquidates, and either distributes its assets to its shareholders or sells its assets and distributes the proceeds, the deceased shareholder's estate will recognize a gain on the distribution, an increase in its basis in the stock for the amount of gain recognized, and a corresponding loss on the liquidation of the shareholder's interest.

> EXAMPLE: Barbara owns 100 percent of an S corporation. Her stock has a basis of $10. She dies. No items of income in respect of a decedent are owned by the corporation. The stock gets a step-up in basis in her estate

---

[172] IRC § 1367(b)(4).

[173] An IRC § 754 election, in this context, would be an election to step up the basis of a deceased shareholder's share of the corporation's assets to reflect the stepped-up basis of his stock to its estate tax value. See Ch. 16 for more details on IRC § 754 elections.

to its market value of $100. The S corporation holds real estate with a value of $110 and a basis of zero. The S corporation liquidates. Upon the distribution of the real property to the estate, the S corporation will recognize a gain (passed through to the estate) of $110. This will increase the estate's basis in the stock by $110, resulting in a total basis of $210. On the liquidation of the estate's interest in the stock immediately thereafter, the estate will incur a loss of $100 ($210 basis of stock − $110 distribution). Therefore, her estate will have both a pass-through gain of $110 and a loss on liquidation of $100, resulting in the utilization of her estate's stepped-up basis in the stock as an offset against the value of property received in liquidation.

In the following cases, this offsetting of a recognized gain with a liquidation loss will not ideally occur. For example, if the distribution to Barbara's estate and the liquidation of the corporation do not occur in the same year, her estate will have gain in one year and a loss in another year. Also, if the gain on distribution of appreciated property consists partly of ordinary income, it cannot be offset by the capital loss on liquidation, except to the extent of $3,000 per year.[174] And, finally, if the estate is not the only shareholder of a liquidating S corporation, and other shareholders have appreciated stock, they will not have an offsetting loss for their share of the gain on distribution.

¶ 18.08   CONTRIBUTIONS TO AN S CORPORATION

The tax treatment of contributions to S corporations is governed by the general rules applicable to C corporations.[175]

¶ 18.09   INCOME TAXATION OF S CORPORATIONS AND SHAREHOLDERS (GENERAL OPERATIONS)

The taxable income or loss resulting from the general operations of an S corporation is calculated similarly to the taxable income or loss of an individual, with some exceptions.[176]

[1] General Rules

An S corporation is a hybrid entity, generally subject to pass-through treatment. This means that its income, gain, loss, deduction, and credit are generally reported directly by the shareholders in proportion to their percentage

---

[174] IRC § 1211(b)(1). The limit is $1,500 in the case of a married individual filing a separate return.

[175] See Ch. 19 for a discussion.

[176] IRC § 1363(b).

interests in the entity.[177] However, unlike other entities, no special (i.e., disproportionate) allocations of S corporation items to its shareholders are permitted.[178]

[a] Basis Limitations on Losses and Deductions

A shareholder's share of S corporation losses and deductions cannot be deducted by a shareholder to the extent that the aggregate of such losses and deductions exceed the shareholder's basis in the S corporation's stock and any debt of the corporation to that shareholder.[179]

There is an indefinite carryover of losses and deductions that are disallowed due to basis limitations.[180] The suspended losses can be taken whenever the shareholder acquires enough basis to use them. However, the carryover expires on the termination of the shareholder's interest by any means, including the S shareholder's death.[181]

[b] Determination of Shareholder's Basis

The S corporation shareholder's basis for her shares is initially determined under the normal rules dealing with the basis of any other property. Thereafter, it is *increased* by her share of the S corporation's income, her capital contributions to the S corporation, her outstanding loans to the S corporation, and certain other items, and is *decreased* by her share of the S corporation's losses, distributions from the S corporation to her, payment on any debt to her and certain other items.[182]

Inclusion of debt in shareholder's basis. A shareholder-creditor will have basis in a direct loan by her to the S corporation.[183] Unlike a partner, however, an S shareholder does not generally include entity-level debt in her basis, except as described in the preceding sentence.

[c] Family Service and Capital Providers

If a member of the family of one or more S shareholders renders services to the S corporation or furnishes capital to it without reasonable compensa-

---

[177] IRC §§ 1361(b)(1)(D), 1366(a)(1).

[178] IRC §§ 1361(b)(1)(D), 1366(a)(1).

[179] IRC § 1366(d)(1).

[180] IRC § 1366(d)(2).

[181] IRC § 1366(d)(2) specifically limits the carryover of a shareholder's losses and deductions to "that shareholder." Such losses and deductions would not seem to be available to a deceased shareholder's estate, because it is not "that shareholder."

[182] IRC § 1367.

[183] Treas. Reg. § 1.1367-2.

tion, the IRS may adjust the income of the S corporation and the individual to reflect the value of the services or capital.[184] The adjustments apply only for income tax purposes, and not for transfer tax purposes.

[d] Fringe Benefits Paid to Shareholder-Employees

For purposes of taxation of fringe benefits, the S corporation is treated as a partnership, and any "2 percent plus shareholder" is treated as a partner.[185] Fringe benefits include items such as group term life insurance and death and medical benefits.[186] A "2 percent plus shareholder" is any person who owns (or is deemed to own within the meaning of Section 318) more than two percent of the outstanding stock or more than two percent of the total combined voting power of the corporation on any day of the taxable year.[187]

The effect of this rule is to include the value of certain fringe benefits in a "2 percent plus shareholder's" income, to the same extent that the fringe benefits would be includable in a partner's income.

[e] S Corporation With Foreign Income and Activities

For purposes of taxation of income from foreign sources, an S corporation is treated as a partnership, and the shareholders are treated as partners.[188] For purposes of Section 904(f), relating to recapture of foreign losses that effectively reduced US tax, the making or termination of an S election is considered a disposition of the corporation's business (potentially resulting in the recognition of gain on corporate property used predominantly outside the United States in a trade or business).[189]

[f] S Corporation's Taxable Year

An S corporation must generally use a calendar year, unless it receives a determination from the IRS that a different year is appropriate based on a business purpose other than deferral of income.[190] An S corporation can make an election under Section 448 to have a different taxable year, provided that

---

[184] IRC § 1366(e).

[185] IRC § 1372(a).

[186] See IRC §§ 79 (regarding group term life insurance), 101(b) (regarding death benefits), 105, 106 (regarding medical benefits).

[187] IRC § 1372(b).

[188] IRC § 1373(a).

[189] IRC § 1373(b).

[190] IRC § 1378.

the period of deferral does not exceed three months and payments are made pursuant to Section 7519.[191]

[g] S Corporation Alternative Minimum Tax Items

An alternative minimum tax (AMT) is imposed on corporations.[192] This tax should not apply to S corporations.[193] Corporations are subject to certain minimum tax adjustments that individuals are not.[194] The most commonly applicable adjustment is an adjustment for items of income for book purposes that are not income for tax purposes.[195] This adjustment does not apply to an S corporation, and so will not pass through to its shareholders.[196] Other AMT items of an S corporation should pass through to the shareholders and enter into their own AMT calculations.

[h] Shareholder Self-Employment Tax Considerations

Income that passes through from an S corporation is apparently not subject to self-employment tax.[197] Dividends from the S corporation, however, can be recharacterized as wages if they actually constitute payment for services.[198]

[i] S Corporation Employee Plans

Pass-through income of an S corporation is not treated as net earnings from self-employment, and therefore is not includable income for purposes of computing Keogh plan contributions.[199]

[2] Special Considerations for S Corporations That Were Formerly C Corporations

Special tax provisions apply to S corporations that were once C corporations. These provisions need to be carefully considered in making a decision whether

---

[191] IRC § 444.

[192] IRC § 55.

[193] IRC § 1363(a).

[194] IRC § 56(c).

[195] IRC § 56(c)(1).

[196] IRC § 56(g)(6).

[197] Rev. Rul. 59-221, 1959-1 CB 225 (issued under prior law, but with no subsequent law changes relating to this issue).

[198] Rev. Rul. 74-44, 1974-1 CB 287; Radtke v. United States, 895 F2d 1196 (7th Cir. 1990).

[199] Durando v. United States, 70 F3d 548 (9th Cir. 1995).

to convert a C corporation to S corporation status. Each of these provisions is quite complicated. The following discussion is a simplified summary intended to alert the estate planner to issues requiring further examination on conversion of a C corporation to S corporation status, on the S corporation's sale of its assets, on the S corporation's purchase of appreciated assets from a C corporation, and on the S corporation's investment of a former C corporation's funds in assets which produce passive income.

[a] Penalties for Excess Net Passive Investment Income

An S corporation with C corporation earnings and profits is subject to extra income tax in any year if more than 25 percent of its gross receipts for that year consist of passive investment income. If this situation occurs for three consecutive years, the S election will terminate.

[i] **Tax on excess net passive investment income.** If an S corporation has C corporation earnings and profits at the close of a taxable year, and if more than 25 percent of its gross receipts for the year consist of "passive investment income," a corporate tax will be imposed on its "excess net passive investment income" at the highest corporate rate.[200] No credit is allowable against this tax, except a credit for certain uses of gasoline and special fuels.[201] For purposes of passing through income to the shareholders, the corporate tax on excess net passive investment income is subtracted from total passive investment income[202] —that is, it is treated as a deduction for purposes of income reported by the shareholders. The effect is that excess net passive income is treated like C corporation earnings—the corporate level tax reduces the amount of earnings which is taxed to the shareholders. For this purpose, "passive investment income" generally means receipts from royalties, rents, dividends, annuities, and net gains from sales or exchanges of stock or securities.[203] There are certain adjustments to this definition.[204] "Net passive investment income" generally means passive investment income, reduced by deductions directly attributable to the production of the income.[205] Recognized built-in gain or loss is not included.[206]

Dividends received by an S corporation from a subsidiary C corporation are not treated as passive investment income to the extent the dividends are

---

[200] IRC § 1375(a), 1375(b)(4).

[201] IRC §§ 34, 1375(c).

[202] IRC § 1366(f)(3).

[203] IRC §§ 1362(d)(3)(D), 1375(b)(3).

[204] IRC § 1362(d)(3)(D).

[205] IRC § 1375(b)(2).

[206] IRC § 1375(b)(4). See ¶ 18.09[3] below.

attributable to the earnings and profits of the C corporation which are derived from the active conduct of a trade or business.[207] However, tax-exempt interest from municipal bonds is considered passive investment income, even though it is generally excludable from gross income.[208]

[ii] **Excess net passive investment income for any year.** "Excess net passive investment income" is determined in the following manner:

Step 1. Determine the amount by which passive investment income exceeds 25 percent of the gross receipts for the taxable year.

Step 2. Divide the number reached by the passive investment income for the year.

Step 3. Multiply that number by the net passive investment income of the year.

The result, with certain adjustments,[209] is excess net passive investment income. Excess net passive investment income is further limited by the taxable income of the corporation, with certain adjustments.[210]

EXAMPLE: S Corporation has $100 of gross receipts, $80 of passive investment income, and $75 of net passive investment income for the year. Excess net passive investment income is $60.94 (i.e., (($80 − 25 percent of $100) ÷ $80) × $75 = $60.94).

[iii] **Excess net passive investment income for three consecutive years.** If an S corporation has earnings and profits from its C corporation days, and over 25 percent of its gross receipts consist of passive investment income for three consecutive taxable years, the S election will terminate as of the first day of the following year.[211]

[b] **LIFO[212] Recapture**

If the S corporation was formerly a C corporation, and the C corporation inventoried goods under the LIFO method, the LIFO recapture amount must be included in the C corporation's income for its last taxable year as a C

---

[207] IRC § 1362(d)(3)(F).

[208] Treas. Reg. §§ 1.1362-2(c), 1.1375-1(f), example 2.

[209] IRC § 1375(b).

[210] IRC § 1375(b)(1)(B).

[211] IRC § 1362(d)(3)(A).

[212] "LIFO" is the last-in, first-out method of accounting for sales of inventory. "FIFO" is the first-in, first-out method.

corporation.[213] The LIFO recapture amount is the excess of the inventory value under FIFO over the inventory value under LIFO, determined at the end of the taxable year.[214]

[c] Carryovers and Carrybacks

Generally, no loss carryover or carryback can take place between C corporation years and S corporation years.[215] However, exceptions exist for computing the tax on built-in gains.[216]

[3] Tax on Built-in Gains

This tax applies to a former C corporation which converted to S corporation status after 1986, and which had appreciated property[217] on the date of conversion. The tax also applies to any S corporation that acquires appreciated property from a C corporation in a nonrecognition transaction. Generally, the S corporation is subject to a separate tax at the corporate level if it sells the property within ten years of the conversion or acquisition.

[a] Tax on Former C Corporations

Under Section 1374, if an S corporation has a net recognized built-in gain for any taxable year beginning in the recognition period there is a tax imposed on that net recognized built-in gain equal to the highest corporate rate specified in Section 11(b).

For this purpose, the "built-in gain" of any asset is its fair market value on date of conversion to S status, less its basis on that conversion date. The "recognition period" is the 10-year period beginning with the conversion date.[218] If the S corporation has had nonconsecutive S corporation periods, the recognition period begins with the last one.[219] The "net unrealized built-in gain" is the value of the S corporation's assets as of the conversion date, less the total bases of its assets at that time.[220] If assets with built-in gain are disposed of during the recognition period, gain or loss recognized is "net recognized built-in gain." Similar concepts to the above definitions relating to

---

[213] IRC § 1363(d)(1).

[214] IRC § 1363(d)(3).

[215] IRC § 1371(b).

[216] IRC § 1374(b).

[217] Appreciated property is property which has value in excess of its basis.

[218] IRC § 1374(b)(7).

[219] IRC § 1374(d)(9).

[220] IRC § 1374(d)(1).

gain also apply to loss. The "net unrecognized built-in gain" in any year is the net unrealized built-in gain, reduced by net recognized built-in gain for prior taxable years beginning in the recognition period, and further offset by net recognized built-in loss for the year.[221]

EXAMPLE: S corporation owns two assets on its conversion date, January 1, 1997—a chair with a basis of zero and a value of $100, and a desk with a basis of zero and a value of $500. On the conversion date, the built-in gain of the chair is $100, and the built-in gain of the desk is $500. The recognition period is the period beginning January 1, 1997, and ending December 31, 2006. The corporation's net unrealized built-in gain is $600. If the desk is sold in 1998 for $300, the corporation has net recognized built-in gain for that year of $300 (sale price of $300 less basis of zero). The corporation's net unrecognized built-in gain for 1999 is $300 (net unrealized built-in gain of $600 less net recognized gain in 1998 of $300).

As stated above, if any appreciated property held by the S corporation on the date of conversion from C status is sold by the S corporation during the recognition period, the S corporation will be subject to a tax on any gain, limited by (1) the built-in gain on that asset, (2) the S corporation's net unrecognized built-in gain, and (3) the taxable income of the S corporation for the year, with certain adjustments.[222] Certain carryovers of gain that was not recognized due to income limitations in prior years are available.[223] The tax will be imposed at the highest corporate rate.[224] For purposes of computing this tax only, a net operating loss carryforward from a C corporation year can be used against the recognized gain.[225] Limited credits and credit carryforwards are also allowed.[226]

For purposes of the pass-through of S corporation items to the shareholders, the amount of the corporate tax on built-in gains is treated as a loss.[227]

EXAMPLE: S corporation recognizes built-in gains of $90, and pays a corporate tax on those gains of $31.50. The $31.50 will be treated as a loss to the S corporation for purposes of passing income through to the shareholders. If the S corporation's taxable income were $90, all attributable to built-in gains, the shareholders collectively would report gains of $90 under the pass-through of gains and an offsetting loss of $31.50, for a net gain of $58.50.

---

[221] IRC § 1374(d)(2).

[222] IRC §§ 1374(a), 1374(c).

[223] IRC § 1374(d)(2)(B).

[224] IRC § 1374(b)(1).

[225] IRC § 1374(b)(2).

[226] IRC § 1374(b)(3).

[227] IRC § 1366(f)(2).

[b] Assets Acquired From C Corporations in a Nonrecognition Transaction

The built-in gain rule also applies if an S corporation acquires an asset, and its basis in the asset is determined in whole or in part by reference to the basis of the asset in the hands of a C corporation—that is, in a nonrecognition transaction such as a tax-free merger.[228] In such a case, the recognition period begins on the day on which the asset was acquired by the S corporation.[229]

[c] Avoiding the Built-in Gains Tax

The built-in gains tax can be avoided by retaining the appreciated property for ten years after the date of conversion (or acquisition, if applicable), or by limiting taxable income during the recognition period. The technique of "stuffing" the corporation with loss property before the conversion or acquisition as a means of avoiding the built-in gains tax is disallowed by a special anti-stuffing rule.[230]

¶ 18.10　FINAL THOUGHTS: WHEN IS AN S CORPORATION USEFUL?

Because of the inflexible tax requirements applicable to S corporations, the recognition of gain on distribution of appreciated property, and the extra entity-level taxes on certain corporations, an S corporation will rarely be the entity of choice if a partnership, or a limited liability company (LLC) which is taxable as a partnership, is a viable alternative.

An S corporation does not receive the complete pass-through treatment that partnerships and LLCs do. Moreover, an S corporation will recognize gain on the distribution of appreciated property. This means that the entity cannot be liquidated without the recognition of gain, if it owns appreciated property. A partnership or LLC can be liquidated without gain in many circumstances. Also, if a family already has an S corporation, which is being taxed as such, and the family would like to convert to status as a partnership or other entity, gain on liquidation will have to be recognized if appreciated property is held by the entity. Additionally, for S corporations which were once C corporations, taxes on built-in gains can be a problem, and passive investment income can be subject to a corporate tax or even terminate the S election.

Further, shareholders ordinarily receive no basis increase for entity debt, while partners and LLC members do. Income and losses of S corporations

---

[228] IRC § 1374(d)(8).

[229] IRC § 1374(d)(8).

[230] Treas. Reg. § 1.1374-9.

cannot be specially allocated, as in the case of partnerships. And, trust shareholders can cause difficulties if income is taxed to persons who do not receive it.

Where do we see S corporations being used today? We see them often as the one percent general partners of family partnerships. We may also see an S election made if the shareholders of a C corporation want to convert to a pass-through entity and find it uneconomical to liquidate and form a partnership or LLC.

An S corporation may, however, be a favorable choice if a C corporation is the only other real alternative. This will often be the case for new entities if business considerations dictate use of the corporate form.

CHAPTER **19**

C Corporations

¶ 19.01 INTRODUCTION

This chapter is not an exhaustive treatment of the taxation of C corporations. Rather, it examines those aspects of C corporations that are of most interest to estate planners.

Accordingly, this chapter gives a brief overview of how a C corporation and its shareholders are taxed. It also discusses those aspects of C corporation taxation that are particularly apt to be encountered in family contexts, including ways to extract money from the entity through redemptions and other distributions and how to avoid certain asset/income configurations which can result in the more punitive income tax consequences.

A C corporation (unlike a partnership, limited liability company, or S corporation) is not a pass-through entity. Consequently, it pays tax on its own income at the entity level. In addition, when the C corporation pays dividends, the shareholders pay ordinary income tax on the dividends, to the extent that the corporation has earnings and profits.[1] Hence, the C corporation is an entity whose income is potentially subject to double taxation—once at the corporate level, and once at the shareholder level, when corporate earnings are distributed as dividends to shareholders. For this and other reasons, C corporations are often not the most desirable entities for conducting family businesses and family investment companies where pass-through entities will serve.

Some family businesses are nevertheless conducted successfully in C corporation form, usually because they hold businesses which make operation in the corporate form attractive for non-tax reasons, and either (1) cannot operate as S corporations for some reason—for example, because they have too many shareholders or ineligible shareholders (e.g., nonqualifying trusts or

---

[1] IRC § 301(a).

nonresident aliens); (2) S status is undesirable for some reason; (3) conversion to S status would have unacceptable tax costs; or (4) the shareholders consider it important to be able to use special provisions applicable only to C shareholders.[2]

Estate planners usually cross paths with the subchapter C rules in determining how to extract money from a C corporation at minimum tax cost, advising on potential transfers of shares, and assisting clients in avoiding the punitive income tax treatment applicable to certain types of C corporations.

¶ 19.02 DISTRIBUTIONS FROM A C CORPORATION—CAPITAL TRANSACTION OR DIVIDEND

A distribution from a C corporation can be treated as a dividend or as a capital transaction.

[1] General Rule

Distributions from a C corporation, which are not related to redemptions or complete liquidations, are normally taxed as dividends—first, as ordinary income to the extent of the earnings and profits of the corporation, thereafter, as an offset of basis of the stock, and finally, as capital gain.[3]

[2] Redemptions Treated as Capital Transactions

A stock redemption which qualifies as a capital transaction is treated as a sale, and therefore results in capital gain to the extent the amount received by the redeeming shareholder exceeds the shareholder's basis in the stock, and as a return of basis to the extent of the shareholder's basis.[4] Any other stock redemption is treated as a dividend to the extent of earnings and profits of the corporation.[5] So if the corporation has earnings and profits, it will usually be important to avoid having the proceeds of a stock redemption taxed as a dividend.

---

[2] E.g., IRC §§ 1202, 1244.

[3] IRC § 301(a), 301(c). "Earnings and profits" is defined in IRC § 312.

[4] IRC § 302(a).

[5] IRC § 302(c)(1).

The theoretical underpinning of the rules governing redemptions is that a redemption should be treated as a capital transaction only if the shareholder's percentage of stock is "meaningfully reduced" as a result of the transaction. If, after the redemption, the shareholder still has essentially the same percentage ownership that he had before (counting the stock of related parties as his own), the proceeds should be treated as a dividend—the theory is that the shareholder should not be able to withdraw earnings and profits of the company (i.e., the function of a dividend) at capital gains rates through the guise of a redemption.

The consequence of treating a distribution as a dividend, rather than as a capital transaction, is twofold: first, the dividend will be taxed at ordinary income rates instead of capital gain rates and, second, to the extent of earnings and profits, the stockholder's basis in the stock cannot be offset against the distribution.

These rules often work in unexpected ways in the context of a family corporation because of the family stock attribution rules, which treat one family member as owning the stock actually owned by other family members. Thus, even if a shareholder's actual stock interest is meaningfully reduced in a redemption, or terminated altogether, these attribution rules deem that he still owns all stock owned by related parties. After the attribution rules are applied, the redeeming shareholder's deemed interest in the corporation may not be "meaningfully reduced," and therefore he may be considered to receive a dividend. Let's examine this further.

[a] Attribution Rules

[i] **Primary attribution.** For purposes of determining whether a distribution qualifies as a redemption rather than a dividend, the attribution rules of Section 318 generally apply.[8] These rules attribute stock ownership of related individuals, trusts, and estates to any stockholder whose stock is being redeemed. Ownership can also be attributed to entities and reattributed to other individuals and entities for this purpose. Accordingly, the attribution rules make the capital transaction tests hard to meet in a family context.

Suppose Dad is the stockholder who wants to get some money out of the company in exchange for stock. Due to the attribution rules, Dad is considered to own all stock owned by or for his wife, children, grandchildren, and parents.[7]

In addition, Dad will be considered to own stock owned by or for a trust in proportion to his actuarial interest in the trust, and all stock owned by a

---

[7] IRC § 318(a)(1).

grantor trust of which he is treated as the owner.[8] Dad's actuarial interest in a trust is determined in accordance with the estate tax regulations governing the valuation of partial interests in a trust.[9] Where distributions from a trust are wholly discretionary, so that the amount of the beneficiaries' interests in the trust cannot be actuarially computed, the IRS has applied a "facts and circumstances" method to determine each beneficiary's interest in the trust, taking into account factors such as patterns of past distributions, mortality assumptions, the fiduciary duty of the trustee, and the relationship of the trustee to the beneficiaries.[10]

Thus, if Dad owns at least 50 percent of a corporation, he will be deemed to own stock owned by or for the corporation in proportion to his stock interest in the corporation.[11] If he has an interest in a partnership or an estate that owns stock, he will be considered to own the amount of stock that is proportional to his interest in the partnership or estate.[12] And, if he has an option to acquire stock, he will be deemed to own that stock.[13]

The attribution rules also work in reverse. Stock owned by or for a partner of a partnership or beneficiary of an estate will be considered owned by the entity.[14] Stock owned by or for a trust beneficiary will be treated as owned by the trust unless the beneficiary has only a remote contingent interest.[15] Stock owned by the grantor of a grantor trust is considered owned by the grantor trust.[16] If 50 percent or more in value of the stock of a corporation is held by one person, the corporation will be considered to own stock held directly or indirectly by that person.[17]

[ii] Reattribution of stock. Generally, stock which is constructively owned by Dad will be considered actually owned by him (so that Dad's

---

[8] IRC § 318(a)(2)(B).

[9] Treas. Reg. § 1.318-3(b); Rev. Rul. 62-155, 1962-2 CB 132.

[10] See Priv. Ltr. Rul. 9024076 (Mar. 21, 1990).

[11] IRC § 318(a)(2)(C).

[12] IRC § 318(a)(2)(A).

[13] IRC § 318(a)(4).

[14] IRC § 318(a)(3)(A).

[15] IRC § 318(a)(3)(B)(i). If, assuming the trustee exercises maximum discretion in favor of a beneficiary, the beneficiary's actuarial interest in the trust is 5 percent or less of the value of the trust, the beneficiary's contingent interest will be considered remote. It is significant that the maximum exercise of discretion must be in the trustee's fiduciary capacity. Otherwise, the existence of a broad limited power of appointment in a trust would result in the trust's being considered to own stock of everyone in the world.

[16] IRC § 318(a)(3)(B)(ii).

[17] IRC § 318(a)(3)(C).

constructively owned stock can be attributed to yet another taxpayer),[18] subject to the following four rules:

Rule One. Stock which is attributed to Dad because of a family relationship will not be reattributed to another taxpayer under the family member rules.[19]

> EXAMPLE: Dad owns 50 percent of Corporation *A*. The other 50 percent is owned by Son-In-Law. Under the attribution rules, Daughter would be deemed to own 100 percent of Corporation *A*. However, Dad and Son-In-Law will each be deemed to own only 50 percent (i.e., Daughter's attributed ownership is not reattributed to them).

Rule Two. Stock constructively owned by an entity will not be reattributed to another taxpayer by the rules dealing with attribution from entities.[20]

> EXAMPLE: Dad and Third Person are equal partners of Partnership *A*. Dad owns 100 shares of Corporation B. Partnership A is deemed to own 50 shares of Corporation *B*.[21] The 50 shares constructively owned by Partnership A are not reattributed to Third Person.

Rule Three. If stock is constructively owned by Dad by reason of both the family and the option rules, it will be considered owned by him by reason of the option rules (and thus, could be reattributed to another family member).[22]

Rule Four. An S corporation and its shareholders will be treated as a partnership and its partners, except for attributing ownership of stock of the S corporation.[23]

[b] Exception: Distribution Not Equivalent to a Dividend

This exception means that the distribution is not made on a substantially pro rata basis to the stockholders, after taking the attribution rules into account.[24]

> EXAMPLE: Mom and Son each own 50 percent of a C corporation. Mom receives a distribution of 40 percent of the assets of the corporation in exchange for 40 percent of the stock, leaving Son with five-sixths of the remaining outstanding stock. This seems like a non-pro rata distribution. However, after application of the attribution rules, Mom is deemed to have owned 100 percent of the stock both before and after the distribu-

---

[18] IRC § 318(a)(5)(A).

[19] IRC § 318(a)(5)(B).

[20] IRC § 318(a)(5)(C).

[21] IRC § 318(a)(3)(A).

[22] IRC § 318(a)(5)(D).

[23] IRC § 318(a)(5)(E).

[24] IRC § 302(b)(1).

tion. Since she received 100 percent of the distribution, it is deemed to have been made pro rata.

If this transaction had involved Mom and an unrelated third party, Mom's redemption would have qualified as a redemption under this test.

Because of the attribution rules, the "not essentially equivalent to a dividend" test will usually not be helpful in a family corporation. However, occasionally, it will—for example, in a corporation owned by several siblings.

[c] Exception: Substantially Disproportionate Distribution

A distribution will meet this test if (1) the percentage of stock owned by the redeeming shareholder after the redemption is less than 80 percent of the percentage he owned before the redemption and (2) immediately after the redemption, the shareholder owns less than 50 percent of the total combined voting power of all classes of stock entitled to vote.[25] The attribution rules apply.[26]

> EXAMPLE: In the example above, Mom actually owned one-half of the stock before the redemption, and one-sixth of the stock after the redemption. If Mom and Son were not related, this would qualify as a capital transaction under the substantially disproportionate distribution test. However, since they are related, Mom is considered to own 100 percent of the stock before and after the redemption, and the redemption will not meet the test.

[d] Exception: Termination of Shareholder's Interest

If the redemption entirely eliminates Mom's interest in the corporation, it is taxable as a capital transaction, and not as a dividend.[27] The attribution rules apply, in determining whether her actual and deemed interest in the corporation is terminated, unless: (1) Mom stays uninvolved with the corporation for ten years after the redemption, (2) Mom did not acquire stock from a related person within the ten years before the redemption for an income tax avoidance purpose, and (3) no related party acquired stock from Mom during the ten-year period before the date of redemption for an income tax avoidance purpose.[28]

---

[25] IRC § 302(b)(2).
[26] IRC § 302(c)(1).
[27] IRC § 302(b)(3).
[28] IRC § 302(c)(2).

[i] Ten-year suspension of redeeming shareholder's involvement. The attribution rules do not apply to Mom only if the following tests are met:[29]

- Immediately after the distribution, Mom has no interest in the corporation (including an interest as officer, director, or employee) other than an interest as a creditor.[30]
- Mom does not acquire any interest in the corporation or become an officer, director, or employee of the corporation within ten years from the date of the distribution.[31] It is okay, however, if Mom acquires stock by bequest or inheritance during the 10-year period.[32]
- Mom files an agreement to notify the IRS of any acquisition of stock (other than by bequest or inheritance) within the 10-year period and to retain necessary records.[33]
- The "bad intent" provisions described in subparagraphs [ii] and [iii] below do not apply.

If Mom does acquire an interest in the corporation (including an interest as an officer, director, or employee) within 10 years after the distribution (other than the acquisition of stock by bequest or inheritance), and the redemption is treated as a dividend, additional income tax will be imposed retroactively. The statute of limitations is tolled for this purpose.[34]

[ii] Pre-redemption acquisition with bad intent. The attribution rules will apply in determining whether Mom's interest is terminated if Mom acquired any portion of the redeemed stock, directly or indirectly:

- Within the ten-year period preceding the date of distribution;
- From a person whose stock is constructively owned by Mom under the attribution rules;
- With a principal purpose of avoiding federal income tax.[35]

[iii] Pre-redemption disposition with bad intent. The attribution rules will also apply in determining whether Mom's interest is terminated if:

- Any person owns (at the time of the distribution) stock which is constructively owned by Mom; and

---

[29] IRC § 302(c)(2)(A).

[30] IRC § 302(c)(2)(A)(i).

[31] IRC § 302(c)(2)(A)(ii).

[32] IRC § 302(c)(2)(A)(ii).

[33] IRC § 302(c)(2)(A)(iii).

[34] IRC § 302(c)(2).

[35] IRC § 302(c)(2)(B)(i).

- That person directly or indirectly acquired any stock in the corporation from Mom within the 10-year period preceding the date of the distribution (unless that stock is redeemed in the same transaction); and
- One of the principal purposes of Mom's pre-redemption disposition of the stock was avoiding federal income tax.[36]

EXAMPLE: Suppose, in the above example, that Mom had given Son his stock five years before the redemption. In order for Mom to be able to treat her stock redemption as a capital transaction, Son's stock would also have to be redeemed, unless the gift to him was not made for the purpose of avoiding federal income tax. (The purpose of avoiding gift and estate tax is apparently okay.) Note that the redemption of Son's stock will not be a practical solution here, unless another shareholder is brought in, since the redemption of both Mom's and Son's stock would leave no stockholder; as a result, the corporation will be deemed to have liquidated.

[iv] **Relief through waiver by entities.** The attribution rules also apply in determining whether an entity meets the termination of interest test, unless (1) the entity and each related person meet the requirements described in ¶ 19.02[2][d] above and (2) each related person agrees to be jointly and severally liable for any deficiency (including interest and additions to tax) resulting from an acquisition within the ten-year period.[37]

As a practical matter, this means that an estate cannot qualify under the termination of interest exception if any of its beneficiaries still own stock in the corporation.[38]

[e] Exception: Distributions to Pay Death Taxes

A distribution in redemption of certain stock which is included in a decedent's taxable estate is taxable as a capital transaction, to the extent that the distribution does not exceed the estate, inheritance, legacy, and succession taxes imposed because of the decedent's death (including interest), certain generation-skipping transfer taxes, and the amount of funeral and adminis-

---

[36] IRC § 302(c)(2)(B)(ii).

[37] IRC § 302(c)(2)(C)(i). For this purpose, a related person is any person to whom ownership of stock in the corporation is attributable under the family attribution rules if that stock is further attributable to the corporation under the attribution to entity rules. IRC § 302(c)(2)(C)(ii)(II). For example, if Dad owns 70 percent of the stock of Corporation A and Dad's shares are attributed to Daughter by the family attribution rules, Daughter's attributed stock would be further attributed to Corporation A under the attribution to entity rules; so Daughter is a related person.

[38] Further discussion of redemptions by an estate can be found in Ch. 45.

trative expenses allowable as deductions to the estate under Section 2053 or Section 2106.[39] Certain conditions, however, must be met.[40]

[f] Exception: Partial Liquidation

A distribution to a noncorporate shareholder in partial liquidation of the corporation will be treated as a capital transaction, even if the distribution is made on a pro rata basis, unless the corporation is a collapsible corporation.[41]

A distribution is made in partial liquidation if (1) it is not essentially equivalent to a dividend (determined at the corporate rather than the shareholder level); (2) it is subject to a plan of partial liquidation, and (3) it occurs within the year the plan is adopted or the following year.[42]

What does the first test mean? It means that the distribution will be considered "not essentially equivalent to a dividend" at the corporate level, provided that the corporation ceases to conduct a qualified trade or business, makes a distribution to shareholders of the business assets or other property as a result, and is still actively engaged in a "qualified trade or business" immediately after the distribution.[43] A qualified trade or business is one that was actively conducted throughout the five-year period ending on the date of redemption, and was not acquired by the corporation during the five-year period in a transaction in which gain or loss was recognized.[44]

> EXAMPLE: Corporation A has two active businesses—a barber shop and a beauty salon. Corporation A decides to go out of the barbering business. The first test is met if the barber shop is distributed to the shareholders in redemption and Corporation A remains actively engaged in the beauty salon business. The beauty salon must have been in active operation for the five years preceding the redemption, and Corporation A cannot have bought the beauty salon during those five years in a taxable transaction.

[g] Exception: Distributions With Respect to Preferred Stock

Certain distributions in redemption of preferred stock, called "306 stock," are taxable as dividends.[45]

---

[39] IRC §§ 303(a), 303(d).

[40] The rules governing this type of redemption are contained in IRC § 303. Redemptions qualifying under IRC § 303 are discussed in Ch. 45.

[41] Collapsible corporations are discussed at ¶ 19.03[2]. IRC §§ 302(b)(4), 302(e)(4).

[42] IRC § 302(e)(1).

[43] IRC § 302(e)(2).

[44] IRC § 302(e)(3).

[45] IRC § 306(a)(2). The rules are contained in IRC § 306 and are discussed in ¶ 19.03[3][b].

[h] Special Rule: Distributions From Collapsible Corporations

Certain distributions from collapsible corporations will be treated as ordinary income, rather than capital gain,[46] even if they would qualify as capital transactions in a non-collapsible corporation.[47]

[3] Distributions in Complete Liquidation of Corporation

A distribution to a shareholder in complete liquidation of a corporation will not be treated as a dividend,[48] unless (1) the corporation is a collapsible corporation[49] or (2) the distribution is in liquidation of a personal holding company and certain other requirements are met.[50]

[4] Stock Dividends—Actual and Constructive

Special rules apply to actual and constructive stock dividends.[51] When a distribution is taxable under these special rules, the distribution will be treated as a dividend distribution—that is, taxable as ordinary income to the extent of the corporation's earnings and profits.

[a] Actual Stock Dividends

Actual stock dividends are normally not taxable.[52] Again, as in most cases, certain exceptions apply.

[i] Dividend treatment for distributions in lieu of money. If the shareholder can choose whether to receive stock or money, the distribution will be taxable, whichever he chooses.[53]

---

[46] IRC § 341(a).

[47] The collapsible corporation rules are discussed in ¶ 19.03[2] below.

[48] IRC § 331.

[49] IRC § 341(e).

[50] IRC §§ 331(b), 316(b)(2)(B).

[51] IRC § 305. A stock dividend is a distribution of additional stock to shareholders.

[52] IRC § 305(a).

[53] IRC § 305(b)(1).

[ii] Dividend treatment for certain non-pro rata distributions to shareholders. If a distribution (or a series of distributions)[54] results in the receipt of property by some shareholders, and an increase in the proportionate interest of other shareholders in the assets or earnings and profits of the corporation, the distribution will be taxable. Both the shareholders receiving property and the shareholders receiving an increased interest will be treated as receiving a distribution.

[iii] Dividend treatment for non-pro rata distribution of common and preferred stock. If the distribution (or a series of distributions) results in the receipt of preferred stock by some common shareholders and the receipt of common stock by others, the distribution will be taxable to all shareholders.[55]

[iv] Dividend treatment for distributions on preferred stock. Distributions with respect to preferred stock are generally taxable.[56]

[v] Dividend treatment for distributions of convertible preferred stock. Distributions of convertible preferred stock are taxable, unless the IRS agrees that the distribution will not result in the receipt of property by some shareholders and an increased interest in the corporation by others.[57]

[b] Constructive Stock Dividends

Certain transactions are treated as distributions for purposes of the above rules relating to stock dividends.[58] The following corporate events can be treated as constructive stock dividends in the manner provided under the regulations: (1) a change in conversion ratio, (2) a change in redemption price, (3) a difference between redemption price and issue price, (4) a redemption which is treated as a dividend, or (5) a recapitalization or any other transac-

---

[54] IRC § 305(b)(2). A series of distributions for purposes of this rule and the rule in ¶ 19.02[4][a][iii] need not be made pursuant to a plan as long as the result addressed in these rules is ultimately achieved. Treas. Reg. § 1.305-3(c)(2). However, if 36 months elapse between the receipt of cash or other property by some shareholders and the receipt of stock by other shareholders (or, in the case of the rule in ¶ 19.02[4][a][iii], between the receipt of preferred stock by some shareholders and the receipt of common stock by others), the rule requiring that the distribution is taxable will not apply unless the distributions are made pursuant to a plan. Treas. Reg. § 1.305-3(c)(4).

[55] IRC § 305(b)(3).

[56] IRC § 305(b)(4). There is an exception for an increase in the ratio of convertible preferred stock made solely to take account of a stock dividend or split with respect to the stock into which the convertible preferred is convertible.

[57] IRC § 305(b)(5).

[58] IRC § 305(c).

tion which results in any shareholder's proportionate interest in the earnings and profits or assets of the corporation being increased.

Under this rule, a distribution will be deemed made to the shareholder whose interest has increased. The regulations also prescribe certain rules where a redemption premium exists as a result of a redemption requirement or a put option,[59] and providing that the issuance of preferred stock which bears a redemption premium will be treated as a distribution or series of distributions to the preferred shareholder.[60]

[c] Isolated Transaction Exception

An isolated transaction is an exception to the above rules.[61]

EXAMPLE: Jean and Austin are shareholders. Jean redeems her shares for cash. Austin's interest in the corporation increases as a result. If this is an isolated transaction, Austin's increased interest in the corporation should not be treated as a distribution to Austin.

The Section 305 rules are quite complicated, but this summary should give an idea when a proposed distribution should be further examined for taxability.

¶ 19.03 SALES AND EXCHANGES OF SHARES

[1] General Rule

If a sale or exchange of shares is a taxable transaction, the transaction will ordinarily result in capital gain or loss. There are a few exceptions, involving exchanges of shares that qualify as nontaxable reorganizations.[62]

[2] Collapsible Corporation

The collapsible corporation rules are highly complex. Generally speaking, if (1) a corporation manufactures, constructs or produces property, or purchases certain assets referred to as "section 341 assets" and (2) its stock is sold or exchanged (or the corporation makes a distribution in complete liquidation, partial liquidation or as a non-capital transaction) before the corporation realizes two-thirds of the taxable income attributable to that property, then

---

[59] IRC § 305(c).

[60] Treas. Reg. § 1.305-5.

[61] Treas. Reg. § 1.305-3(e), example 12.

[62] See IRC § 368.

gain realized on the disposition will be considered ordinary income.[63] "Section 341 assets" means property which is held by the corporation for less than three years and which is either inventory, property held for sale to customers in the ordinary course of business, unrealized receivables or fees, or certain other property used in a trade or business.[64]

> EXAMPLE: A classic example of a collapsible corporation is the old movie shelter. A film producer would create a corporation for the purpose of producing a movie. Just after the movie's release, the corporation would be liquidated or sold.[65] The producer would report the difference between the amount of the liquidating distribution and his basis in the stock as long-term capital gain, rather than ordinary income. If the corporation had, instead, leased the movie or had the project been conducted in noncorporate form, the proceeds from the release would have been ordinary income. Under the pre-collapsible corporation rules, the producer succeeded in transforming ordinary income into capital gain.

> EXAMPLE: Mom, as part of her estate planning, wants to sell stock of Corporation to Child. If Corporation is a collapsible corporation, the proceeds of the sale will constitute ordinary income.

A corporation is presumed to be a collapsible corporation if at the time of the sale, exchange, or distribution of the stock, the fair market value of its section 341 assets is equal to (1) 50 percent or more of the fair market value of its total assets and (2) 120 percent or more of the adjusted basis of the section 341 assets.[66] For purposes of the above sentence, the fair market value of the assets is determined without regard to the corporation's cash, capital assets, and stock in other corporations.[67]

Numerous limitations, exceptions, and other conditions apply. The above should illustrate the "evil" that the collapsible corporation doctrine was designed to correct, so that we can watch for its applicability.

As a practical matter, the repeal of the *General Utilities*[68] doctrine has decreased the importance of the collapsible corporation rules, as far as liquidations are concerned. In the shelter days, distributions of property made in liquidation of a corporation were not taxed at the corporate level. Now, all distributions of appreciated property, whether in liquidation or otherwise, are

---

[63] IRC § 341(b)(1).

[64] IRC § 341(b)(3).

[65] Under the applicable laws in the shelter days, the corporation did not recognize gain as a result of the liquidating distribution.

[66] IRC § 341(c)(1).

[67] IRC § 341(c)(2).

[68] General Utilities & Operating Co. v. Helvering, 296 US 200 (1935).

treated as sales to the distributee shareholder, and will be taxed as ordinary income if they consist of ordinary income property.[69]

Although the collapsible corporation rules are not as relevant to distributions and liquidations any more, they still have some bite on the sale of stock. Basically, they can increase the tax on the gain by 11.6 percent (from 28 percent to 39.6 percent).

[3] Disposition of Preferred Stock

The thrust of Section 306 is to prohibit the preferred stock bailout. This type of transaction has a history. Formerly, a corporation would provide cash to its shareholders at capital gains rates by arranging a "preferred stock bailout." The corporation would recapitalize and issue a nontaxable preferred stock dividend to its shareholders. The shareholders would "bail out" corporate earnings and profits by selling that preferred stock to another individual or entity, and recognize capital gains on the sale. Then, the corporation would redeem the preferred stock from the purchaser. The net result was that the same shareholders still held all the stock and had received property on a pro rata basis without dividend treatment.

If preferred stock is being disposed of for consideration, such as Mom's preferred stock in Mom Corp., Section 306 should be examined.

[a] General Rule

As a general rule, the amount received by Mom as a result of certain transfers and redemptions of her preferred stock (in Mom Corp.) will be treated as a dividend.

[i] Disposition of Section 306 stock other than in a redemption. If Mom sells or otherwise disposes of "section 306 stock," and the disposition is not a redemption, the amount realized is treated as ordinary income, except to the extent that it exceeds the stock's ratable share of the corporation's earnings and profits at the date of distribution.[70] Any excess is treated as an offset of basis, then as capital gain.[71] No loss is recognized, even if basis is not fully recovered.[72]

[ii] Disposition of Section 306 stock in a redemption. If the transaction is a redemption, then the amount received for the Section 306 stock is treated

---

[69] IRC § 311(b).

[70] IRC § 306(a)(1)(A).

[71] IRC § 306(a)(1)(B).

[72] IRC § 306(a)(1)(C).

as a dividend to the extent of the redeeming corporation's earnings and profits, then as an offset of basis, and then as capital gain.[73]

[b] "Section 306 Stock" Defined

Is Mom's stock "306 stock"? Stock which is described in one of the following four paragraphs is "306 stock—"

Stock received as a stock dividend. Section 306 stock includes stock (other than a distribution of common stock issued as a dividend to a holder of common stock) which was distributed to Mom, if, by reason of Section 305(a), any part of the distribution was not includable in her gross income.[74] For example, if Mom wants to redeem preferred stock she received as a dividend on common stock, the stock will be 306 stock, and the proceeds of the redemption will be considered ordinary income to the extent of earnings and profits.

Stock received in a corporate reorganization or separation. Non-common stock received by Mom in a reorganization or exchange in which gain was not recognized is Section 306 stock, under certain circumstances.[75]

Stock having transferred or substituted basis. If the basis of the stock in Mom's hands is determined by reference to the basis of 306 stock, it will be 306 stock.[76] For example, if Grandpa owned 306 stock and gave it to Mom, Mom took his basis, so the stock is 306 stock in her hands, too.

Stock acquired in Section 351 exchange. Section 306 stock includes preferred stock acquired in an exchange to which Section 351 applied, if receipt of money would have been treated as a dividend.[77] Thus, if Mom contributes $100,000 to a corporation (with earnings and profits of $150,000 on the date of contribution) and receives preferred stock, Mom's preferred stock is 306 stock.

NOTE: Stock received in a transaction in which the stock takes a new basis (e.g., a purchase or inheritance) is not 306 stock because it is not determined with reference to the transferor's basis.[78] Thus, if Mom dies owning 306 stock, the stock is no longer 306 stock in the hands of the person who receives the stock as a result of Mom's death.

---

[73] IRC § 306(a)(2).

[74] IRC § 306(c)(1)(A). Section 305(a) contains the general rule that stock dividends are not taxable.

[75] IRC § 306(c)(1)(B).

[76] IRC § 306(c)(1)(C).

[77] IRC § 306(c)(3).

[78] Treas. Reg. § 1.306-3(e).

[c] When Section 306 Does Not Apply

Sale of entire interest to independent party. Section 306 does not apply if the disposition is not a redemption, the transferee is not a person whose stock is attributed to the selling shareholder, and the disposition terminates the shareholder's entire stock interest in the corporation, after taking the attribution rules into account.[79]

Redemption in complete termination of interest or partial liquidation. Section 306 does not apply to the proceeds of a redemption that is not treated as a dividend due to its being a complete termination of the shareholder's interest or a partial liquidation.[80]

Complete liquidation of corporation. Section 306 does not apply to a complete liquidation of the corporation.[81]

Nonrecognition transaction. Section 306 does not apply if gain or loss is not recognized on the disposition.[82]

IRS-approved nonavoidance transaction. Section 306 does not apply to the proceeds of a disposition or redemption if the IRS agrees that the disposition or redemption is not in pursuance of a plan having as one of its principal purposes the avoidance of federal income tax.[83]

Distribution by corporation with no earnings and profits. Section 306 stock does not include stock distributed to a shareholder if there would have been no dividend treatment of the distribution even if money had been distributed.[84]

[4] Ordinary Loss on Stock Sale—Section 1244

If an individual or partnership owns Section 1244 stock, losses on the stock are treated as ordinary losses, even though gains from the sale of the stock will qualify for capital gain treatment.[85] The amount that can be treated as an ordinary loss under this section is limited to $50,000 per year ($100,000 for spouses filing a joint return). The corporation must derive over 50 percent of its gross receipts from non-portfolio sources[86] and the aggregate contributions to capital must not exceed $1,000,000.[87] Although the amounts involved in Section 1244 are relatively small, it can be a useful provision in the right circumstances. One situation that does not fall within the right set of circum-

---

[79] IRC § 306(b)(1)(A).

[80] IRC § 306(b)(1)(B). See ¶¶ 19.02[2][d] and 19.02[2][f] above.

[81] IRC § 306(b)(2).

[82] IRC § 306(b)(3).

[83] IRC § 306(b)(4).

[84] IRC § 306(c)(2).

[85] IRC § 1244(a).

[86] IRC § 1244(c)(1)(C).

[87] IRC § 1244(c)(3).

stances occurs where an S corporation owns the Section 1244 stock. The IRS has ruled that shareholders of an S corporation cannot take advantage of Section 1244 on the S corporation's sale of stock in an Section 1244 corporation.[88]

[5] Exclusion of Gain on Small Business Stock—Section 1202

A taxpayer other than a corporation can exclude from income 50 percent of the gain on the sale of qualified small business stock held for more than five years.[89] The rules contain elaborate requirements. The following is a brief summary.

[a] Definition of "Qualified Small Business Stock"

"Qualified small business stock" is C corporation stock which is originally issued after August 10, 1993, if the corporation is a qualified small business at date of issuance of the stock and the stock is acquired in exchange for money or other property (not including stock) or as compensation for services provided to the corporation (other than underwriting).[90] It also includes stock acquired by gift, at death, or from a partnership to a partner if the transferor acquired it in a qualifying manner.[91]

[b] Definition of "Qualified Small Business"

A qualified small business is any domestic C corporation if the aggregate gross assets of the corporation or any predecessor at all times after August 10, 1993 and before the relevant stock issuance did not exceed $50,000,000, and the amounts received by the corporation in the issuance do not increase its assets above $50,000,000.[92] The measure of the assets is their aggregate bases, or with respect to property contributed to the corporation or with a basis determined with respect to property so contributed, the fair market value at date of contribution.[93] All corporations that are members of the same parent-subsidiary group are treated as one corporation.[94]

---

[88] Tech. Adv. Mem. 9130003 (Mar. 25, 1991).

[89] IRC § 1202(a).

[90] IRC § 1202(c)(1).

[91] IRC §§ 1202(h)(1), 1202(h)(2).

[92] IRC § 1202(d)(1).

[93] IRC § 1202(d)(2).

[94] IRC § 1202(d)(3).

[c] "Active Business" Requirement

During substantially all of the taxpayer's holding period, the corporation must meet certain active business requirements.[95] The active business requirement is met for any period if during that period at least 80 percent in value of the assets are used in the active conduct of one or more qualified trades or businesses.[96]

A qualified trade or business is any trade or business other than: (1) a business involving the performance of services in the fields of health, law, engineering, architecture, accounting, actuarial science, performing arts, consulting, athletics, financial services, brokerage services, or any trade or business where the principal asset of such trade or business is the reputation or skill of one or more of its employees; (2) any banking, insurance, financing, leasing, investing, or similar business; (3) any farming business; (4) any business involving the production or extraction of products for which a depletion deduction is allowed; or (5) any business of operating a hotel, motel, restaurant or similar business.[97]

A corporation does not meet the active business test for any period during which more than ten percent of the value of its net assets consists of stock or securities in other corporations which are not the corporation's subsidiaries.[98] However, stock or securities in non-subsidiaries are not counted if they are (1) held as a part of the reasonably required working capital needs of a qualified trade or business of the corporation or (2) held for investment and are reasonably expected to be used within two years to finance research and experimentation in a qualified trade or business or increases in working capital needs of a qualified trade or business.[99] After the corporation has been in existence for at least two years, no more than 50 percent of the assets can qualify as active business assets under this exception.[100] There are also certain limitations on real estate holdings not used in the active conduct of the business.[101]

[d] Ineligible Corporations

A qualifying corporation cannot be a (1) domestic international sales corporation (DISC) or former DISC, (2) a corporation with respect to which an election under Section 936 is in effect or which has a direct or indirect

---

[95] IRC § 1202(c)(2).

[96] IRC § 1202(e)(1).

[97] IRC § 1202(e)(3).

[98] IRC § 1202(e)(5).

[99] IRC § 1202(e)(6).

[100] IRC § 1202(e)(6).

[101] IRC § 1202(e)(7).

subsidiary with respect to which such an election is in effect, (3) a regulated investment company, (4) REIT, (5) REMIC, (6) FASIT, or (7) cooperative.[102]

[e] Amount of Excludable Gain

The maximum gain which can be excluded in any year is the greater of (1) $5,000,000 ($2,500,000 in the case of a married person filing separately) *less* gain previously excluded or (2) ten times the aggregate adjusted bases of qualified small business stock issued by the corporation and disposed of by the taxpayer during the year, determined without regard to any addition to basis after the date of original issuance.[103]

[f] Excludable Gain Recognized by a Pass-Through Entity

Gain which is included in an individual's income due to the sale of qualified small business stock by a partnership, S corporation, regulated investment company, or common trust fund in which the individual has an interest is excludable under certain conditions.[104]

¶ 19.04 CONTRIBUTIONS TO A C CORPORATION

[1] Recognition of Gain on the Contribution

[a] General Rule

Technically, a transfer to a corporation in exchange for stock is a sale. Consequently, if appreciated property is transferred to a corporation in exchange for stock, gain will be recognized unless an exception applies.

[b] Section 351 Transfers

A contribution to a C corporation solely in exchange for stock does not result in taxable gain to the contributor if, immediately after the contribution, the contributors have at least 80 percent of the total combined voting power of all classes of stock entitled to vote and at least 80 percent of the total number of shares of all nonvoting classes of stock of the corporation.[105] If property other than stock is received on the contribution (i.e., "boot"), then gain on the transaction will be recognized to the extent of the amount of

---

[102] IRC § 1202(e)(4).

[103] IRC § 1202(b).

[104] IRC § 1202(g).

[105] IRC §§ 351(a), 368(c).

money and other property received.[106] No loss is, however, recognized under such circumstances.[107]

If a contribution otherwise qualifies for nonrecognition of gain under the above rule and the corporation assumes a liability of the contributor (or acquires property from the contributor subject to a liability), the liability will not disqualify the transaction and will not be treated as money or other property,[108] unless the principal purpose of the contribution with respect to the assumption or acquisition was the avoidance of federal income tax or some other non-bona fide business purpose.[109] Notwithstanding the above, if the liability exceeds the basis of the property, then the excess will generally be subject to tax as a capital gain or as income, as the case may be.[110]

[c] Transfer to Investment Company

Notwithstanding the rules discussed in subparagraph [b] above, gain is recognized on transfer of appreciated assets to an "investment company."[111] In general, a transfer is considered to be made to an investment company if both: (1) the transfer directly or indirectly results in diversification of the transferor's interests and (2) 80 percent or more of the corporation's assets are readily marketable stocks and securities held for investment.[112] For these purposes, stock and securities in a subsidiary are disregarded and the parent corporation is deemed to own its ratable share of the subsidiary's assets.[113] Cash, cash items, and government securities are excluded in determining total assets.[114]

Regulations issued in 1996 provide a special rule prescribing that a transfer of stocks and securities will not result in diversification if each transferor contributes a diversified portfolio of stocks and securities. This test is met if (1) not more than 25 percent of the total assets transferred by each transferor consists of stock and securities of a single issuer and (2) not more than 50 percent of the value of the total assets contributed by each transferor consists of stock and securities of five or fewer issuers. For purposes of these tests,

---

[106] IRC § 351(b)(1).

[107] IRC § 351(b)(2).

[108] IRC § 357(a).

[109] IRC § 357(b)(1).

[110] IRC § 357(c).

[111] IRC § 351(e)(1).

[112] Treas. Reg. § 1.351-1(c)(1).

[113] Treas. Reg. § 1.351-1(c)(4). A corporation will be considered a subsidiary if the parent owns 50 percent or more of the combined voting power of all classes of stock entitled to vote, or 50 percent or more of the total value of shares of all classes of stock outstanding. Id.

[114] IRC §§ 351(a), 351(e)(1), 368(a)(1), 368(a)(1)(F)(iii).

government securities are included in the denominators of the fractions, but are not treated as securities for purposes of the numerators.[115]

[2] Basis of C Corporation Stock

A shareholder's basis in C corporation stock is generally determined under normal rules dealing with property in general. If the contribution of property qualifies for nonrecognition under Section 351, or the stock was acquired in certain other types of corporate nonrecognition transactions, the basis of the holder's stock is the basis of the property exchanged for the stock, *decreased by* the value of any money or other property received in the exchange and the amount of loss recognized on the exchange, and *increased by* any amount received in the exchange that was treated as a dividend as well as the amount of other gain recognized by the taxpayer on the exchange.[116]

¶ 19.05 INCOME TAXATION OF C CORPORATIONS

A C corporation is a separate taxable entity. Its income taxation differs from the income taxation of individuals in various respects.

[1] C Corporation Tax Rates and Penalty Taxes

A corporation's income tax rates depend on whether the corporation is subject to special rules. The top corporate income tax rate is slightly lower than the top rate for individuals. Not so long ago, the top corporate rate was much lower than the top individual rate. At that time, a common strategy was to incorporate businesses and investments, so that their income would be taxable at the lower corporate rate. The earnings and assets would be left in corporate solution until an individual owner needed them. At that time, the corporation would pay a deductible salary or bonus to the individual in the amount of the needed funds. We'll call this technique the "corporate shelter strategy." Is this still a good strategy today? Let's examine.

[a] General Rule

Generally, a corporation's income is taxed at the rates described below.

[i] Rates on corporate ordinary income. Ordinary income is income other than capital gains. The rates are: 15 percent of taxable income of $50,000

---

[115] Treas. Reg. § 1.351-1(c)(6).

[116] IRC § 358(a)(1).

or less; 25 percent of taxable income that exceeds $50,000 but does not exceed $75,000; 34 percent of taxable income that exceeds $75,000 but does not exceed $10,000,000; and 35 percent of taxable income that exceeds $10,000,000.[117]

[ii] Surtaxes on corporate income. If a C corporation has taxable income over $100,000, the amount of tax computed above is increased by the lesser of $11,750 or five percent of the amount of taxable income in excess of $100,000.[118] If a corporation has taxable income exceeding $15,000,000, the tax will be increased by the lesser of $100,000 or three percent of the amount of taxable income in excess of $15,000,000.[119] The effect of the surtaxes is to phase out the lower tax rate brackets. Thus, a C corporation with taxable income of more than $335,000 pays tax on all of its income at an effective rate of 34 percent, and a corporation with taxable income of more than $18,333,333 pays tax on all of its income at an effective rate of 35 percent.

[iii] Rate for corporate capital gains. The capital gains of a corporation, unlike the gains of an individual, are not subject to special rates, except that if the tax computed under Section 11 (without regard to the three percent surtax) would exceed 35 percent, the maximum rate applicable to capital gains will be 35 percent.[120] That is, the surtax on income exceeding $15,000,000 does not apply to capital gains. As the maximum rate under Section 11 currently is 35 percent (even when the surtax is applied), this provision should only apply if the regular corporate income tax rate is increased.

PRACTICE POINTER: Incorporating investment assets can result in capital gains tax on the sale of the investments increasing from 28 percent at the highest individual level to 35 percent at the highest corporate level.

[iv] Corporate alternative minimum tax. The corporate alternative minimum tax (AMT) applies when the tax on a corporation's taxable income, determined after certain adjustments have been made and certain otherwise allowable exclusions and deductions have been disregarded, exceeds the regularly computed corporate income tax.[121] The corporate AMT is imposed at a rate of 20 percent. The purpose of the AMT is to ensure that taxpayers with

---

[117] IRC § 11(b)(1). Unlike the rate brackets for individuals, the rate brackets for corporations are not adjusted for inflation.

[118] IRC § 11(b)(1).

[119] IRC § 11(b)(1).

[120] IRC § 1201(a).

[121] See generally IRC §§ 55–58.

substantial income pay at least some tax by limiting the benefit such taxpayers might otherwise receive from exclusions, deductions, credits, and other tax incentives. The corporate AMT was enacted in 1986 and constituted a significant change to the way corporations are taxed. Although a discussion of the alternative minimum tax is beyond the scope of this book, practitioners should be aware of its potential application.[122]

[v] **Corporate shelter strategy analysis.** The corporate shelter strategy (as described above) is counterproductive with respect to capital gains. On the other hand, ordinary income of a corporation can be taxed at a rate somewhat lower than individual rates, unless the corporation is one of the following types: personal service corporation, personal holding company, or a corporation subject to accumulated earnings tax.

[b] **Qualified Personal Service Corporations**

Can Dad incorporate his dental practice and pay less income tax due to the rate differential between the prevailing tax rates for individuals and corporations?

At one point the answer may have been yes. In days past, dentists, doctors, and other professionals would incorporate their practices, pay themselves salaries, and keep any excess income in the corporation, which was taxable at lower rates than they were. Now, however, the advent of the tax on personal service corporations has emasculated this technique. Thereunder, the income of a "qualified personal service corporation" is taxed at a flat rate of 35 percent.[123] The 35 percent rate applies to all taxable income, not just the corporation's personal service income.

A "qualified personal service corporation" is a corporation in which substantially all activities involve the performance of services in the fields of health, law, engineering, architecture, accounting, actuarial sciences, performing arts, or consulting and substantially all of the stock (by value) is directly or indirectly held by (1) employees performing the personal services, (2) retired employees who formerly performed the services, (3) the estate of any such employee or retired employee, or (4) for a two-year period after the death, persons who acquired stock by reason of the death of such an employee or retired employee.[124] For purposes of this test, community property laws are

---

[122] A corporation that is not subject to the alternative minimum tax may nevertheless have to compute its income for alternative minimum tax purposes in order to compute its environmental tax for certain taxable years beginning after 1986 and before 1996. See IRC § 59A.

[123] IRC § 11(b)(2).

[124] IRC § 448(d)(2).

disregarded and stock held in a qualified retirement plan is treated as if it were held by an employee performing the personal services.[125]

Corporate shelter strategy analysis. If earnings are retained in a qualified personal service corporation, a very slight benefit for high-bracket individuals (4.6 percent for individuals at the top bracket) is available for ordinary income on account of the corporate form, and the corporate form is counterproductive with respect to capital gains.

[c] Personal Holding Company

Can Mom incorporate her stocks and bonds, and pay less income tax? At one time, the answer was yes. However, the personal holding company rules were enacted to counteract perceived abuses in the days when the corporate tax rate was much less than the individual tax rate. Before enactment of the personal holding company rules, people incorporated their investments and kept them in corporate solution as long as possible, so that they could take advantage of the lower corporate income tax rates. Now, however, such a "personal holding company" is generally taxed on its investment income at the highest rate applicable to individuals.

Now that the corporate rates are more comparable to the individual rates, even without considering the double tax, most knowledgeable people would not put a family investment company into C corporation form. It is nevertheless possible for families to inadvertently stumble into the personal holding company rules and be unpleasantly surprised by the results. For example, a C corporation that sells its assets, invests the proceeds, and does not immediately liquidate could turn into a personal holding company. It is therefore a good idea to have a basic understanding of when these rules may apply.

As a general rule, the personal holding company rules should be examined in any case where there is closely held ownership of a C corporation and that corporation has a high percentage of investment income. Family investment companies will often fall into this category. Where the personal holding company rules apply, the corporation will pay a special tax unless it distributes its investment income.

[i] Personal holding company tax rate. A personal holding company is subject to an extra tax of 39.6 percent on its undistributed personal holding company income.[126]

[ii] Definition of a personal holding company. Simply stated, a corpora-

---

[125] IRC § 448(d)(4).

[126] IRC § 541. The extra tax represents the tax that would have been imposed on an individual in the highest bracket if the corporation had declared a dividend and distributed the dividend to individuals in the highest bracket.

tion is a "personal holding company" if at least 60 percent of its "adjusted ordinary gross income" is derived from passive investments, and if five or fewer shareholders (after attribution rules are applied) hold a majority of its stock. Family investment companies will therefore usually be personal holding companies.

[A] *Personal holding company income test.* The first test is whether 60 percent or more of the corporation's "adjusted ordinary gross income" for the year is "personal holding company income."[127] Generally, personal holding company income refers to passive income—dividends, interest, royalties, annuities, etc.—and certain personal service income.[128] The actual definition is quite complex, and many exceptions and elaborations apply.[129] "Ordinary gross income" means gross income, excluding capital gains, other gains from the sale of certain property used in business, and certain types of income where the corporation is a foreign corporation.[130] "Adjusted ordinary gross income" is ordinary gross income, less certain deductions for expenses incurred with respect to the production of personal holding company income.[131]

[B] *Five or fewer shareholders test.* A corporation that meets the income test will be considered a personal holding company in a given year if more than 50 percent in value of the corporation's outstanding stock is owned, directly or indirectly, by or for the benefit of not more than five individuals at any point during the last half of the year.[132] For this purpose, a pension trust, charitable organization, or charitable trust is considered an individual.[133] Numerous attribution rules apply.[134]

[iii] **Income subject to the personal holding company tax rate.** A personal holding company is subject to the extra tax on its undistributed personal holding company income.[135] If the personal holding company income, as adjusted, is not distributed on or before the fifteenth day of the third month

---

[127] IRC § 542(a)(1).

[128] IRC § 543(a).

[129] IRC § 543.

[130] IRC § 543(b)(1).

[131] IRC § 543(b)(2).

[132] IRC § 542(a)(2).

[133] IRC § 542(a)(2).

[134] IRC § 544.

[135] IRC § 545. For the technically minded, "undistributed personal holding company income" means taxable income: reduced by certain taxes, charitable contributions (without regard to the deduction limitations), net after-tax capital gains, and certain capital gains and losses of foreign corporations; increased by certain corporate deduc-

following the close of the corporation's taxable year, then the 39.6 percent penalty tax applies for that year.[136]

Corporate shelter strategy analysis. There is no income tax benefit for investment income of a personal holding company, and there is potential for a higher tax than would have been imposed if the investments had been held in unincorporated form.

[d] Imposition of the Accumulated Earnings Tax

Can Family keep all of the earnings of its incorporated business undistributed inside the corporation, and pay lower taxes? Under the accumulated earnings tax, a C corporation is taxable on its accumulated taxable income at a rate of 39.6 percent if the corporation accumulated the income for the purpose of avoiding income tax with respect to its shareholders or the shareholders of another corporation.[137] Like the personal holding company tax, the accumulated earnings tax is a penalty tax that applies in addition to the regular corporate income tax.[138] However, unlike the personal holding company tax, which is determined by a mathematical formula and automatically applies, the accumulated earnings tax is not automatic, but depends on subjective judgments by the IRS (or a court) regarding the corporation's intentions concerning the retention of its earnings.

[i] Bad purpose for accumulation of corporate earnings. The corporation will be deemed to have had the purpose of avoiding shareholder tax if it accumulates earnings and profits beyond the "reasonable needs of the business," unless it can demonstrate a proper non-tax motivation.[139] The purpose of avoiding shareholder tax need not be the primary purpose for the accumulation—the mere fact that it was *a* purpose is sufficient.[140]

For this purpose, the reasonable needs of the business include—

---

tions related to net operating losses, and certain deductions from property that are in excess of the income from the property; and then reduced by any dividends paid.

[136] IRC § 563(b). A corporation which is liable for this tax may under certain circumstances make a distribution to its shareholders which will be taken into account retroactively for purposes of the tax, thereby entitling the corporation to a full or partial refund. IRC § 547.

[137] IRC §§ 531, 532.

[138] The extra tax represents the tax that would be imposed if the corporation had distributed the accumulated earnings, and the shareholders were all in the maximum individual bracket.

[139] IRC § 533(a).

[140] United States v. Donruss Co., 393 US 297 (1969).

Reasonably anticipated needs of the business. Reasonable needs include all reasonably anticipated needs of the business.[141] Product liability loss reserves are okay if product liability losses are reasonably anticipated.[142]

Section 303 redemption needs. Reasonable needs include the corporation's need to accumulate funds to buy a deceased shareholder's interest pursuant to Section 303.[143] The Section 303 redemption needs may be considered only in the taxable year of the death of the shareholder whose stock is to be redeemed and subsequent years.[144]

Excess business holding redemption needs. Reasonable needs include the corporation's need to accumulate funds to buy certain holdings of a private foundation which are in excess of permissible limits.[145] Excess business holding redemption needs should rarely be encountered, since the exception relates generally to property held by the foundation on May 26, 1969, or receivable by the foundation pursuant to a will or irrevocable trust in effect on that date.[146]

Finally, the fact that a corporation is a mere holding or investment company is prima facie evidence of the purpose to avoid income tax with respect to shareholders.[147] A "holding company" is a corporation having practically no activities except holding property and collecting and investing the income. A corporation is an "investment company" if substantially all of its activities consist of holding company activities and/or buying and selling investment property. Property is investment property if income from the property is derived from investment yields (such as dividends) and market fluctuations.[148]

[ii] Automatic accumulated earnings credit. Corporations that are potentially subject to the accumulated earnings tax in a given year are entitled to an automatic lifetime credit amount, which is calculated in different ways, depending on the corporation and its history of accumulation.[149] In essence,

---

[141] IRC § 537(a)(1).

[142] IRC § 537(b)(4).

[143] IRC §§ 537(a)(2), 537(b)(1). See Ch. 45 for a discussion of IRC § 303 redemptions.

[144] IRC § 537(b)(1).

[145] IRC § 537(a)(3), 537(b)(2).

[146] IRC § 537(b)(2).

[147] IRC § 533(b).

[148] Treas. Reg. § 1.533-1(c).

[149] If the corporation is not a holding or investment company, it will be allowed a lifetime accumulated earnings credit of $250,000. The minimum lifetime credit is $150,000 in the case of a corporation which principally performs services in the field

the credit amount is a safe harbor that will be deemed to be accumulated for the reasonable needs of the business.

[iii] Income subject to the tax. Accumulated taxable income means taxable income *less* certain taxes, charitable contributions in excess of deductible limits (computed without regard to certain capital gains and losses and with certain other adjustments), *less* dividends paid and the accumulated earnings credit.[150]

[iv] Corporations exempt from the accumulated earnings tax. The accumulated earnings tax does not apply to personal holding companies, foreign personal holding companies, exempt charities, and passive foreign investment companies.[151]

Corporate shelter strategy analysis. There is no tax advantage to accumulating earnings in excess of the business needs beyond the automatic credit, and there is potential for higher taxation on accumulated earnings than would have resulted if the assets had been held in unincorporated form.

[e] General Comment on Using Corporate Shelter Strategies

There is no entity available which generally allows the sheltering of a significant amount of money at rates substantially lower than individual rates. Substantial tax penalties can apply if various types of C corporations are attempted to be used for this purpose. Accordingly, the C corporation will generally not be a tax shelter for family businesses and investments.

[2] C Corporation's Deduction of Employee Compensation

Family businesses held in C corporation form frequently have family employees to whom salaries and other compensation are paid. Sometimes the compensation is high enough that its deduction will offset the corporation's taxable income. In order to be deductible, however, compensation for personal services must be reasonable.[152] When family members are employed, the corporation should be prepared to justify any compensation paid as equivalent to that which would be paid to a non-family member to do the same job.

Some corporations zero out their income by paying deductible expenses, such as salaries and employee benefits, and thus eliminate the double tax.

---

of health, law, engineering, architecture, accounting, actuarial science, performing arts, or consulting. IRC §§ 535(c)(2)(A), 535(c)(2)(B).

[150] IRC § 535(a), 535(b).

[151] IRC § 532(b).

[152] IRC § 162(a)(1).

Since the top individual income tax bracket is higher than the top corporate income tax bracket, is it a good idea from a tax perspective to pay reasonable salaries to avoid the double tax? As the following examples illustrate, it depends.

> EXAMPLE: Corp pays Dad a salary of $100,000. If Corp is in the 34 percent bracket, and pays a $100,000 salary to Dad, who is in the top bracket, Dad will pay an immediate tax of 39.6 percent plus Medicare tax of 2.9 percent, or $42,500, resulting in an immediate additional tax burden of $8,500,[153] compared to the $34,000 Corp would have paid if it had retained the $100,000.[154]

> EXAMPLE: Instead of paying Dad a salary, Corp pays tax on the $100,000 and retains the after-tax amount of $66,000. Corp owes $34,000 in that year, and adds $66,000 to its earnings and profits.

> EXAMPLE: Instead of paying Dad a salary, Corp pays a 34 percent tax on the $100,000, and pays a dividend to Dad of the after-tax amount of $66,000. Dad would owe tax of $26,136 ($66,000 × 39.6 percent tax rate), for a total tax of $34,000 on Corp and $26,136 on Dad, or $60,136, which is still a bad deal compared to the $42,500 payable under the first example above. If Dad has available deductions, however, so that he is not in the top bracket, or if Corp is in a lower bracket or does not have earnings and profits, the result could change.

[3] C Corporation's Distribution of Appreciated Property

A C corporation is taxed on the distribution of appreciated property[155] to its shareholders. The distribution is deemed to be a sale of the property to the shareholder at the property's fair market value, and is taxed to the corporation as capital gain or ordinary income, as the case may be.[156] The corporation's earnings and profits will be increased by the deemed sale, and then decreased on account of the distribution.[157]

A major exception here is that a corporation never recognizes gain on the distribution, or the acquisition, of its own stock.[158]

If property is distributed to a shareholder, and gain or loss is recognized to the corporation on the distribution, the shareholder will take a fair market value basis in the property. Otherwise, the shareholder will take the corporation's basis.

---

[153] Assuming that Dad has already maxed out on FICA tax.

[154] Assuming that no special taxes apply. See ¶ 19.06[1] above.

[155] Appreciated property is property with a fair market value in excess of its basis.

[156] IRC § 311.

[157] IRC § 312(b).

[158] IRC § 1032(a).

Choice of Entity

¶ 20.01 INTRODUCTION

This chapter outlines some of the tax differences between C corporations, S
corporations, partnerships, limited liability companies (LLCs), and trusts. Its
purpose is to help a family, considering whether to hold business or other
assets in an entity, determine which entity will best suit the family's needs.
Although there are other entities that can hold property,[1] most are more
specialized than families doing estate planning generally want to use, and are
therefore not discussed in this chapter.

This chapter is organized in terms of the characteristics of the entities,
and compares each entity on the basis of each characteristic. Most of the

---

[1] E.g., REITs, RICs, REMICs, business trusts, land trusts, and settlement trusts.

characteristics are discussed in more detail in the specific chapters discussing each entity. For this reason, the specific chapters should be consulted regarding the ramifications of these various characteristics.

NOTE: Since it will generally be desirable to have a limited liability company (LLC) taxed as a partnership rather than an association, this chapter will assume that the LLCs discussed in this chapter are classified as partnerships for income tax purposes. Furthermore, unless otherwise specified, the trust descriptions in this chapter assume that a trust is not a charitable trust, a charitable remainder trust, a grantor trust, an electing small business trust, a qualified subchapter S trust, or a foreign trust.[2] Income with respect to property held in a grantor trust would be directly taxed to the grantor or beneficiary.[3]

¶ 20.02 TAXABLE ENTITY OR PASS-THROUGH ENTITY

Various entity types are available for use in connection with the holding of a family business or other assets—

C corporation. A C corporation is a separate taxable entity. It pays income tax on its own earnings. The rates are graduated, and are generally equal to or less than individual rates for most levels of income. The maximum rate is 35 percent,[4] except for personal service corporations and personal holding companies. When a C corporation distributes its earnings in the form of dividends, the shareholders are then taxable on the dividends. This is what is meant by a double tax on corporate earnings.

S corporation. An S corporation is primarily a pass-through entity.[5] However, it may incur a corporate tax if: (1) it was formerly a C corporation, it has C corporation earnings and profits, and more than 25 percent of its gross receipts in any year consist of passive investment income; (2) it was formerly a C corporation and sells property which was appreciated when the S corporation conversion was made, where the sale occurs during the 10-year period after the conversion;[6] or (3) it sells property fewer than ten years after acquiring it from a C corporation in a transaction in which all or part of the gain

---

[2] Charitable trusts are discussed in Chs. 37 and 38. Charitable remainder trusts are discussed in Ch. 33. Electing small business trusts and qualified subchapter S trusts are discussed in Ch. 18. Foreign trusts are discussed in Ch. 52.

[3] IRC §§ 671–679. A grantor trust is a trust of which a settlor or beneficiary is treated as the owner for income tax purposes. See Ch. 6 for an explanation of grantor trusts.

[4] IRC § 11(b)(4).

[5] IRC § 1366.

[6] IRC § 1374.

or loss was not recognized, if the property was appreciated at the date of acquisition.[7]

Partnership and LLC. Partnerships and LLCs are truly pass-through entities, and do not incur any entity-level income tax.

Trust. A trust is a separate taxable entity, except to the extent that it is a grantor trust. However, it generally does not present the same double tax problem as a corporation because the trust receives a deduction for certain distributions to beneficiaries, which are then taxable to the beneficiaries.[8] In addition, like a partnership (and unlike a corporation), the character and source of such distributions flow through to the beneficiaries from the trust. To the extent a trust is taxed on its income, it pays income tax at the highest individual rate for income in excess of $8,100 (in 1997), as indexed for inflation.

¶ 20.03   WHO REPORTS THE ENTITY'S INCOME TAX ITEMS

For some entities, the entity and/or its owners pay income tax on income recognized by the entity; for others only the owners pay tax on this income—

C corporation. A C corporation reports its own items of income, deduction, gain, loss and credit ("income tax items").

S corporation. An S corporation's income tax items pass through to its shareholders, resulting in a corresponding upward (income) or downward (loss) adjustment to the basis of their stock.[9] When an eligible trust shareholder is involved, some other party (not the trust) may be a deemed shareholder for income tax purposes. In such a case, the income tax items generally pass through to that party, rather than being reported by the trust.[10] While Chapter 18 discusses in detail the deemed income tax shareholders who report their shares of the S corporation's income tax items, the following is a short summary of these rules:

- If a grantor trust with a living deemed owner holds the shares, the deemed owner of the trust under the grantor trust rules is the deemed income tax shareholder.
- In the case of a former grantor trust whose grantor is deceased (and which does not qualify as a qualifying subchapter S trust or an electing small business trust), the trust reports the income tax items.
- If a testamentary trust (not qualifying as a qualifying subchapter S trust or an electing small business trust) is the owner, the trust reports

---

[7] IRC § 1374.

[8] IRC §§ 651, 661.

[9] IRC §§ 1366, 1367.

[10] IRC § 1361(c)(2); Treas. Reg. §§ 1.1361-1(h)(3), 1.1361-1(j)(7).

the income tax items (or the beneficiaries who receive distributions, under the usual rules of subchapter J).

- If a voting trust is the owner, the voting trust beneficiaries report the income tax items.
- If a qualifying subchapter S trust is the owner, the income beneficiary reports the income tax items, except for gains and losses on disposition of the S corporation stock.
- If an electing small business trust is the owner, the trust reports the income tax items and cannot pass them through to the beneficiaries by making distributions. The electing small business trust's share of the S corporation's income tax items is taxed at the highest individual rate.

Partnership and LLC. Partnership and LLC income tax items pass through to the partners and members. The owners receive a basis adjustment for their interests in the entity reflecting certain partnership or LLC income, gain, deduction, or loss reported by them.

Trust. A trust reports all income and losses with respect to trust property. To the extent that distributions carrying out distributable net income are made from the trust, the beneficiaries report such income, and the trust receives a distribution deduction.[11] Beneficiaries generally cannot be distributed losses except in the trust's final year.[12]

¶ 20.04 SPECIAL ALLOCATIONS OF INCOME AND LOSS AMONG OWNERS

Certain entities can assign disproportionate shares of entity income or loss among their owners—

C corporation. Income and losses may only be specially allocated if the corporation has multiple classes of stock.

S corporation. No special allocations of income and loss are permitted.[13]

Partnership and LLC. Special allocations of income and loss may be made by agreement, subject to the requirement that the allocations have substantial economic effect.[14]

Trust. Special allocations of income and loss may be made in the trust agreement, subject to the requirement that the allocations have substantial economic effect.[15]

---

[11] IRC §§ 651, 652, 661, 662.

[12] IRC § 643(a)(3); Treas. Reg. § 1.643(a)-3(d), example 4.

[13] IRC § 1361(b)(1)(D).

[14] Treas. Reg. §§ 1.704-1(b)(1)(i), 1.704-1(b)(2).

[15] Treas. Reg. § 1.643(b)-1.

¶ 20.05   CLASSES OF EQUITY INTERESTS

In the case of some entities, different classes of ownership interests, which carry with them different types of economic and other rights, are allowed—

C corporation. A C corporation may have different classes of ownership interests.

S corporation. An S corporation can have classes of stock, if the only difference between classes is in voting rights.[16]

Partnership and LLC. Partnerships and LLCs may have different classes of equity interests.

Trust. Although trust beneficiaries may not truly have an "equity interest" in a trust, the trust can be structured so as to give the beneficiaries differing rights in the trust comparable to classes of equity interests.

¶ 20.06   DISTRIBUTIONS NOT MADE IN REDEMPTION OF OWNERSHIP INTEREST

Among the various types of entities, current (non-liquidating) distributions are treated differently—

C corporation. Distributions that are not in redemption of a shareholder's interest are taxed as dividends.[17] Dividend distributions are treated as ordinary income to the extent of the corporation's earnings and profits, then as a nontaxable return of basis in the stock, and then as capital gain.[18]

S corporation. Dividend distributions first reduce the AAA account, then reduce old C corporation earnings and profits, and then offset the shareholder's remaining stock basis. Any remaining amount is treated as capital gain.[19]

Partnership and LLC. Distributions do not result in taxable income unless: (1) the distribution is of money[20] and exceeds the partner's[21] basis in the partnership interest;[22] (2) the share of a partner's liabilities decreases as a result of the distribution and the decrease exceeds the partner's basis in the partnership interest;[23] (3) a partner contributes appreciated property and within two years receives a distribution, unless he can establish that the trans-

---

[16] IRC §§ 1361(b)(1)(D), 1361(c)(4).

[17] IRC § 301.

[18] IRC § 301(c).

[19] IRC § 1368.

[20] Under certain circumstances, "money" includes marketable securities. IRC §§ 731(c)(1), 731(c)(3).

[21] In this paragraph, "partner" also refers to "member," if an LLC is involved, and "partnership" refers to the LLC.

[22] IRC § 731(a)(1).

[23] IRC §§ 731(a)(1), 752(b).

action was not a disguised sale;[24] (4) a partner contributes appreciated property which is distributed to another partner within five years;[25] (5) under certain circumstances, a partner contributes appreciated property, and the partnership makes a distribution of other property to the contributing partner within five years after the contribution while it is still holding the contributed property;[26] or (6) the distribution is a guaranteed payment.[27]

Trust. Distributions of current or accumulated income can have tax effects to the distributee.[28]

¶ 20.07 ENTITY GAIN ON DISTRIBUTION OF APPRECIATED PROPERTY

Depending upon the entity involved, a distribution can have varying tax consequences to the entity—

C corporation. A distribution of appreciated property is treated as a sale of the property to the distributee, and any gain thereon will be taxed to the corporation.[29]

S corporation. A distribution of appreciated property is treated as a sale of the property to the distributee, and any gain thereon will be taxed to the shareholders (or deemed income tax shareholders, in certain circumstances).

Partnership and LLC. A distribution of appreciated property by the partnership or LLC does not ordinarily result in recognition of gain to the entity unless the distribution is in satisfaction of a dollar amount owed to the partner or member. However, in certain circumstances, a distribution of appreciated marketable securities having a value in excess of the distributee's basis in his entity interest is taxed as a sale by the entity to the distributee.[30]

Trust. Gain will be recognized upon a distribution if the distribution is in satisfaction of a dollar amount owed to the beneficiary or if the trust elects to recognize gain.[31]

¶ 20.08 LENGTH OF ENTITY'S LIFE

The nature of the term of life of an entity also varies in accordance with its type—

---

[24] IRC § 707(a)(2)(B).

[25] IRC § 704(c)(1)(B).

[26] IRC § 737.

[27] IRC § 707(c).

[28] IRC §§ 652, 662, 667.

[29] IRC § 311.

[30] IRC §§ 731, 737.

[31] IRC § 643(e).

C corporation. The existence of a C corporation can be perpetual.

S corporation. The existence of an S corporation can be perpetual.

Partnership. A partnership does not exist in perpetuity. It dissolves on the withdrawal of any general partner, and such dissolution will cause a winding up of the partnership business unless the remaining general partner(s), or some percentage of the remaining limited partners, choose to continue the business pursuant to a right permitted in the agreement. The withdrawal of a limited partner does not dissolve the partnership. The sale or exchange of 50 percent or more of the total interest in partnership capital and profits will cause a termination for income tax purposes of the partnership under Section 708(b)(1)(B).

PRACTICE POINTER: After adoption of the check-the-box regulations, the dissolution provisions of a partnership agreement are no longer driven by federal income tax requirements, but are matters of state law, state tax, and general non-tax considerations. The withdrawing partner's interest must be accounted for, or, if state law permits, the remaining partners can elect to convert the withdrawing partner's interest to a limited partnership.

LLC. The withdrawal of any member dissolves a limited liability company under some state laws and, on dissolution, the business will be wound up unless some percentage of the remaining members (100 percent in some states) vote to continue the business. This is a major difference between LLCs and limited partnerships.

Trust. A trust can last for the applicable rule against perpetuities, or perpetually, if no rule against perpetuities applies under state law.

¶ 20.09   ELIGIBLE ENTITY OWNERS

While some entity's interests can be owned by all persons, for other entities, ownership is restricted—

C corporation, partnership, and LLC. There are no restrictions on the type of entity that may own an interest in a C corporation, partnership, or LLC, except to the extent provided by state law, federal law specific to a regulated industry, or other non-tax law.

S corporation. Only U.S. citizen or resident individuals, U.S. estates, certain types of trusts, certain tax-exempt entities, and, in certain cases, another

S corporation can be shareholders of an S corporation.[32] The maximum number of shareholders is 75, counting a husband and wife as one shareholder.[33]

Trust. There are no restrictions on eligible beneficiaries of a trust.

¶ 20.10 RIGHTS OF CREDITORS OF AN OWNER TO ENTITY ASSETS/MANAGEMENT

Creditor's rights with respect to the entity and its owners also vary significantly depending on the type of entity involved—

C corporation. Generally, a creditor or bankruptcy trustee of a stockholder can seize stock. The creditor's rights will then depend on what rights the stock carries and what restrictions and agreements govern the stock. In certain cases, shareholders' agreements may provide some protection.

S corporation. A creditor or bankruptcy trustee of an S corporation shareholder can seize the shareholder's stock, just as he could if the entity were a C corporation. However, the creditor may have additional leverage in the S corporation context, if he can terminate the S election by assigning the stock to an ineligible shareholder, or if he himself is an ineligible shareholder. Limitations on assignments in the articles, bylaws, and contractual agreements may help the owners of the S corporation to control this to some extent.

Partnership. The creditor or bankruptcy trustee of a partner in a general partnership may be entitled to require the partnership to wind up, or at least account for the partner's interest.[34] The creditor or bankruptcy trustee of a general partner in a limited partnership may be able to require the partnership to wind up or may be able to step in and exercise the general partner's rights. The creditor or bankruptcy trustee of a limited partner may obtain a charging order. If the charging order is not likely to satisfy the creditor's claims within a reasonable time, a court may have the ability to grant other relief.

LLC. Although there is little authority, the creditor or bankruptcy trustee of a member should have rights similar to a creditor or bankruptcy trustee of a partner in a limited partnership. A bankruptcy trustee may be able to step into the member's shoes.

Trust. Spendthrift trust provisions are valid against many creditors. Discretionary provisions for distributing trust income and principal are valid against most or all creditors.[35]

---

[32] IRC § 1361(b). Tax-exempt entities are only eligible for taxable years beginning after 1997.

[33] IRC §§ 1361(b)(1), 1361(c)(1) (for taxable years beginning after December 31, 1996).

[34] See Ch. 53 on asset protection.

[35] See Ch. 53 on asset protection.

¶ 20.11 LARGE PROPORTION OF PASSIVE INVESTMENT INCOME

The tax consequences of an entity's retention of passive income varies according to the type of entity involved.

C corporation. If the corporation has too much passive income, the personal holding company tax[36] may be imposed. In other cases, if the corporation retains earnings and profits in excess of the reasonable needs of its business, the accumulated earnings tax may be imposed.[37]

S corporation. Passive income can be a problem for an S corporation with C corporation earnings and profits (accrued before the corporation's election of S corporation status). In such a case, (a) net passive investment income is subject to corporate tax to the extent that it exceeds 25 percent of the S corporation's gross receipts in any year and (b) the S election is terminated if net passive investment income exceeds 25 percent of gross receipts for three consecutive years.

Partnership, LLC, and trust. The general system of taxation of partnerships, LLCs, and trusts is not affected by the existence of passive income.

¶ 20.12 FAMILY ENTITY'S OWNERSHIP OF CORPORATE STOCK

[1] Ownership of a Subsidiary

In certain cases, the amount of stock an entity can own in a corporation is limited—

C corporation, partnership, LLC, and trust. There is no limitation on the amount of stock that these entities can own in a corporation or the extent to which they can control a corporation.

S corporation. Prior to 1997, there was a limit on the amount of stock an S corporation could hold in another corporation. Now, however, for taxable years beginning after 1996, there is no such limitation, subject to special rules relating to taxation of the S corporation shareholder.[38]

[2] Ownership of S Corporation Stock

In certain cases, an entity's ownership of S corporation stock is prohibited or limited—

---

[36] IRC § 541 et seq.

[37] IRC § 531 et seq.

[38] IRC § 1361(b)(2)(A).

C corporation, partnership, and LLC. C corporations, partnerships, and LLCs are not eligible to be shareholders in an S corporation, except as nominees for eligible shareholders.[39]

S corporation. An S corporation is generally not eligible to own stock in another S corporation. However, for taxable years beginning after 1996, an S corporation can have a wholly owned subsidiary S corporation. In such a case, the subsidiary S corporation is not treated as a separate taxable entity.

Trust. Certain trusts can own S stock.[40]

¶ 20.13 PASSIVE LOSS LIMITATIONS

Section 469 limits certain taxpayers' ability to take losses derived from trades or businesses in which they do not materially participate. Its rules, as applied to the various entities discussed in this chapter, are as follows—

C corporation. Except for certain personal service corporations and certain closely held corporations, the passive loss limitations do not apply to C corporations. In those instances where the passive loss rules apply, a closely held C corporation or personal service corporation will be treated as materially participating in an activity only if stockholders owning more than 50 percent in value of the stock materially participate, or, in the case of a closely held C corporation which is not a personal service corporation, certain other requirements are met.[41]

S corporation. A shareholder who materially participates in the activities of an S corporation (other than rental real estate activities or working interests in oil and gas properties) can avoid the passive loss limitations.[42] The IRS has taken the position that a closely held C corporation's passive activity losses cannot be used by its successor S corporation.[43]

Limited partnership. A limited partner who is not also a general partner will generally be subject to passive loss limitations if the partnership has passive losses.[44] However, a limited partner who meets one of three material participation tests may escape passive loss treatment.[45]

LLC. Although the passive loss rules do not specifically address LLCs, the passive loss rules should apply at the member level, rather than the entity level. Presumably, then, in one of the three ways provided in the regulations, a member with limited liability who materially participates in the LLC busi-

---

[39] IRC § 1361(b)(1)(B).

[40] IRC §§ 1361(b)(1)(B), 1361(c), 1361(d), 1361(e). See Ch. 18.

[41] IRC § 469(h)(4).

[42] Temp. Reg. § 1.469-1T(e)(1).

[43] Tech. Adv. Mem. 9628002 (Oct. 10, 1995).

[44] IRC §§ 469(h), 469(h)(2); Temp. Reg. § 1.469-5T.

[45] Temp. Reg. §§ 1.469-5T(a)(1), 1.469-5T(a)(5), 1.469-5T(a)(6), 1.469-5T(e)(2).

ness should be able to avoid the passive loss limitations.[46] If the member is treated as a general partner, he should be able to demonstrate material participation in various other ways as well.[47]

Trust. Passive loss limitations apply if the trustee does not materially participate in the activity in his fiduciary capacity.[48] Material participation by a beneficiary who is not also a trustee is apparently not considered.[49]

¶ 20.14 APPLICATION OF SELF-EMPLOYMENT TAX TO PASSIVE OWNERS

The application of the rules concerning imposition of self-employment tax to income received by owners of an entity (in their capacity as owners, not as service providers) vary according to the type of entity involved—

C corporation and S corporation. The self-employment tax does not apply to the earnings of stockholders in a C or an S corporation.

Partnership. Distributions to limited partners are not subject to self-employment tax, except to the extent that a distribution is a guaranteed payment made in return for services. According to proposed regulations, a person will be treated as a limited partner unless the person has certain attributes of (1) a general partner (personal liability for partnership debts, authority to contract on behalf of the partnership) or (2) a service partner (participation in the partnership's trade or business for more than 500 hours in the year or provision of more than a de minimis amount of services in a part of a service partnership's business). If the person has those attributes, the member is subject to self-employment tax, subject to certain exceptions.[50]

LLC. The application of the self-employment tax to non-managing members is uncertain. However, the proposed regulations discussed above would apply to all entities classified as partnerships for federal income tax purposes, regardless of their classification under state law.

Trust. Distributions from trusts are not subject to self-employment tax in the hands of beneficiaries.

¶ 20.15 INCOME TAXATION OF CONTRIBUTIONS TO ENTITY

The transferor's tax treatment on contributions to an entity varies in accordance with the type of entity involved—

---

[46] See Temp. Reg. §§ 1.469-5T(a)(1), 1.469-5T(a)(5), 1.469-5T(a)(6), 1.469-5T(e)(2).

[47] Temp. Reg. §§ 1.469-5T(a)(2), 1.469-5T(a)(3), 1.469-5T(a)(4), 1.469-5T(a)(7).

[48] S. Rep. No. 313, 99th Cong., 2d Sess. 735 (1986).

[49] S. Rep. No. 313, 99th Cong., 2d Sess. 735 (1986).

[50] Prop. Reg. § 1.1402(a)-18(a).

C corporation and S corporation. Subject to limited exceptions, contributions to a corporation do not give rise to tax if the contributing shareholder group owns at least 80 percent of the corporation. Contribution of property subject to a liability exceeding its basis is, however, taxable. Contribution to an investment company resulting in the diversification of the shareholders' investment portfolios is treated as a sale by the contributing shareholders to the corporation.[51]

Partnership and LLC. Contributions to a partnership or LLC are nontaxable except in the following limited situations: (1) contributions to an investment partnership resulting in the diversification of the partners' investment portfolios; (2) contributions of assets that are subject to liability in excess of basis; (3) contributions of assets in exchange for an assumption of a liability of the contributor which exceeds the basis of the contributed assets; or (4) contributions that are recharacterized as disguised sales.

Trust. Contributions to a trust are not subject to income tax in most situations.

¶ 20.16 STABILITY OF TAX STATUS

In some cases, the tax status of an entity can be affected by the action or inaction of its owners—

C corporation. The tax status of a C corporation is not generally affected by acts of shareholders in their capacity as individuals not acting on behalf of the entity.

S corporation. The shareholders of an S corporation must file an S corporation election. Qualifying subchapter S trust elections must be filed by the income beneficiaries of qualifying subchapter S trusts, and electing small business trust elections must be filed by the trustees of electing small business trusts. S corporation shareholders are restricted to certain types and numbers of individuals and entities. Thus, S corporation status can be terminated by acts of the shareholders.

Partnership and LLC. No federal elections are required to establish an entity's status as a partnership or LLC; a domestic partnership or LLC with more than one owner will be taxed as a partnership under federal law unless the owners elect otherwise pursuant to the check-the-box rules. Partners and members may be able to dissolve the entity by withdrawing. Such dissolution may affect the tax status of the entity.

Trust. The tax status of a trust is relatively stable, and is generally not affected by the status of the beneficiaries (except for special types of trusts such as QSSTs). Eventually, the trust must terminate if required by the terms set forth in the trust instrument or local law.

---

[51] IRC § 351(e)(1).

¶ 20.17 ENTITY DEBTS INCLUDED IN OWNER'S BASIS

It is desirable to have a pass-through entity's debts included in an owner's basis if the entity generates losses, since entity losses are generally deductible by the owner only to the extent of her basis in her entity interest. However, not all entities permit their owners to include entity debt in the basis of their ownership interests—

C corporation. Corporate debts are not included in a shareholder's stock basis. However, losses are taken by the entity, and not the shareholder.

S corporation. Corporate debts are not included in the basis of a shareholder's stock, except to the extent that the corporation's debt is owed to that particular shareholder.[52]

Partnership and LLC. Partnership and LLC debts are included in the owners' bases in their interests, subject to limitations relating to debt for which the partner/member is not personally liable. In an LLC, unlike a partnership, all debts should be considered nonrecourse to the members, unless a member has agreed to be personally liable. Hence, it should be easier for members of an LLC to receive an allocation of basis for entity-level debts than for limited partners, because the recourse liabilities of a limited partnership may have to be allocated to the general partner(s) after the limited partners' capital accounts have been exhausted.

Trust. Trust debt is not included in a beneficiary's basis in his/her trust interest. However, entity losses are taken by the trust or passed through to beneficiaries in the year of termination. When taken by a beneficiary, such losses are not generally limited to a beneficiary's basis.

¶ 20.18 ELECTION TO ADJUST THE BASIS OF ENTITY ASSETS

Upon the occurrence of certain events, a Section 754 election requires a partnership to adjust its basis in certain partnership assets. This type of adjustment will, of course, also result in the adjustment of a partner's share of the partnership's basis in its assets (that is, the partner's inside basis).

C corporation and S corporation. Neither a Section 754 nor similar election is available for a C or an S corporation.

Partnership and LLC. The Section 754 election is available for partnerships and LLCs classified as partnerships for tax purposes.

Trust. Neither the Section 754 election nor a similar election is permitted to trusts. However, a basis adjustment similar to the adjustments triggered by a Section 754 election occurs in the case of trusts if the trust is included in a person's taxable estate because the assets of the trust in such a case will generally receive a new basis under Section 1014.

---

[52] Rev. Rul. 70-50, 1970-1 CB 178.

¶ 20.19 STATE TAXES AND FEES

Entities may be treated differently for state tax purposes than for federal income tax purposes, depending on the laws of the state. Filing requirements (including fees) for different entities may also vary from state to state.

¶ 20.20 LOSSES ON SECTION 1244 STOCK

Section 1244 permits a taxpayer to treat certain losses from his interest in a worthless entity as ordinary losses rather than as capital losses. Can entity owners take advantage of Section 1244 if the following entities become worthless?

C corporation. Yes, Section 1244 losses are available for C corporation shareholders if the C corporation becomes worthless, provided that Section 1244's requirements are met.

S corporation. As a practical matter, Section 1244 losses are not available unless the loss results from a decline in value of the assets, rather than from operations. Ordinary losses resulting from operations are passed through to the shareholders currently to the extent of their basis.[53] Moreover, shareholders of an S corporation apparently cannot take advantage of Section 1244, with respect to corporate stock owned by the S corporation.[54]

Partnership and LLC. No ordinary loss is available to partners on the worthlessness of a partnership. However, ordinary losses resulting from operations are passed through to owners currently to the extent of their basis.

Trust. Equivalent treatment allowed, to some extent (i.e., in the case of net operating loss carryovers, capital loss carryovers, and deductions in excess of income available to beneficiaries in final year of trust). If a trust owns small business stock that becomes worthless, it is not entitled to the benefits of Section 1244.[55]

¶ 20.21 USE OF CASH METHOD OF ACCOUNTING

The availability of the cash basis method of accounting varies according to the type of entity involved—

C corporation. C corporation may not use the cash method of accounting.

S corporation, partnership, and LLC. These entities may use the cash method of accounting, unless the entity has a C corporation as an owner, or

---

[53] See Williams & Gyles, "Lost in the Maze: The Subchapter S/Section 1244 Potential Tax Trap," Prac. Tax Law. (Winter 1997).

[54] Priv. Ltr. Rul. 9130003 (Mar. 25, 1991).

[55] Treas. Reg. § 1.1244(a)-1(b)(2).

is a tax shelter, as defined by Section 461(i)(3),[56] and does not meet any of the exceptions. An important exception is that the cash method is available for any year if, for all prior taxable years beginning with 1986, the entity's three-year moving average of gross receipts has never exceeded $5,000,000.[57]

Trust. Trust may use the cash method of accounting.

¶ 20.22   ITEMS OF INCOME IN RESPECT OF A DECEDENT IN THE ENTITY—BASIS ADJUSTMENT AT DEATH OF OWNER

The impact of the rules concerning income in respect of a decedent (IRD) items is not the same for deceased owners of the various types of entities discussed in this chapter—

C corporation. Items of IRD held by a corporation have no effect on the adjustment in the shareholder's basis of his stock in the corporation upon his death.

S corporation, partnership, and LLC. No basis adjustment is available for an interest in the entity to the extent that the value of the interest consists of a pro rata share of IRD.[58]

Trust. If the trust is included in the decedent's estate, assets owned by the trust will receive a new basis, except for IRD. A beneficiary's trust interest will also receive a new basis if the trust is included in the estate. If a trust is not included in an individual's estate, or in a transfer subject to generation-skipping transfer tax (GSTT), no basis adjustment occurs on the death of the individual.

¶ 20.23   SECTION 1237—PRESUMPTION OF CAPITAL TREATMENT ON SALE OF LOTS OR PARCELS OF LAND

Section 1237 creates a presumption that the sale of lots or parcels of land owned by certain entities is the sale of property that is a capital asset. Accordingly, if Section 1237 applies, a qualifying entity's gain on the sale of such property would give rise to capital gain, and not ordinary income, not all entities qualify for Section 1237 benefits—

---

[56] IRC § 448(d)(3).

[57] IRC § 448(c).

[58] IRC § 1014(c); Treas. Reg. § 1.742-1; see also Woodhall v. Comm'r, 454 F2d 226 (9th Cir. 1972); Rev. Rul 66-325, 1966-2 CB 249. Applies to S corporations with respect to decedents dying after August 20, 1996.

C corporation. C corporations do not qualify for the Section 1237 presumption, Therefore, there is no presumption that a sale of part of a tract of land by a C corporation will result in capital gain treatment.

S corporation, partnership, LLC, and trust. A sale of part of a tract of land by the entity is presumed to give rise to capital gain under certain circumstances.[59]

¶ 20.24 ALTERNATIVE MINIMUM TAX

In certain cases, an entity's or its owners' liability for alternative minimum tax resulting from the entity's activities poses serious considerations—

C corporation. A C corporation is subject to a 20 percent tax on its alternative minimum taxable income, less its exemption amount.[60] The exemption amount is $40,000,[61] reduced by 25 percent of the amount by which alternative minimum taxable income exceeds $150,000.[62] Among other adjustments, a special adjustment applicable to C corporations, but not other entities, is an increase to alternative minimum taxable income for a percentage of the value of certain items considered income for book purposes, but not for tax purposes.[63] One example of this is life insurance payable to the corporation.

S corporation. S corporations and their shareholders are subject to the alternative minimum tax. However, the adjustments for book income in excess of taxable income do not apply to an S corporation or its shareholders.[64]

Partnership and LLC. The alternative minimum tax does not apply to partnerships or LLCs. It does, however, apply to entity income in the hands of partners and members.

Trust. A trust is subject to alternative minimum tax of 26 percent or 28 percent on its alternative minimum taxable income.[65]

¶ 20.25 INCOME TAXED TO PERSON OTHER THAN EQUITY OWNER

In certain cases, which can differ for different types of entities, entity income can be taxed directly to a non-owner of the entity—

---

[59] IRC § 1237(a). This rule is applicable to S corporations in taxable years beginning after 1996.

[60] IRC § 55(b)(1)(B).

[61] IRC § 55(d)(2).

[62] IRC § 55(d)(3)(A).

[63] IRC §§ 56(c), 56(g)(4)(B).

[64] IRC § 56(g)(6).

[65] IRC § 55(b)(1)(A)(i).

C corporation. In the case of C corporations, entity income will not generally be taxed to a non-stock owner, unless the IRS uses Section 385 or Section 482 to reallocate income among related parties.

S corporation. Income passed through to certain trust shareholders is taxed to a party other than the trust. Under various tax rules set forth in the regulations or adopted by the courts, income can be reallocated to "real owners" or to service or capital providers.

Partnership and LLC. In addition to generally applicable tax rules (e.g., the assignment of income doctrine) that can cause entity income to be taxed to a non-owner, the family partnership rules may apply to reallocate partnership income. Under the family partnership rules, income may be reallocated to the donor/seller in the case of entity interests which have been directly or indirectly gifted or sold by one family member to another. They may also apply to reallocate income if the "real owner" is different from the nominal owner. In addition, precontribution gain and loss with respect to assets held in a partnership are allocated to the contributing partner/member.

Trust. Income earned by property held in a grantor trust is taxable to the grantor or beneficiary rather than the trust.

¶ 20.26 CHOICE OF TAXABLE YEAR

The options for the election of a taxable year are different depending on the type of entity involved—

C corporation. A C corporation (which is not a professional service corporation) can generally elect, without limitation, either a calendar year or any fiscal year as its taxable year.

S corporation, partnership, and LLC. These entities must use a calendar year, with limited exceptions.[66]

Trust. A trust must use a taxable year which is a calendar year.[67]

¶ 20.27 CLASSIFICATION-ORIENTED TAX TREATMENT

The tax scheme set forth under the Internal Revenue Code varies according to the type of entity involved—

C corporation. C corporations are taxed as corporations, and are taxed under subchapter C.

S corporation. S corporations are taxed under the subchapter S rules, unless the requirements of subchapter S are not met, in which case they are taxed as C corporations.

---

[66] IRC §§ 444, 706.

[67] IRC § 645(a).

Partnership and LLC. Care must be taken to ensure that partnerships and LLCs are taxed as partnerships under the rules of subchapter K. Regulations have been issued which allow certain noncorporate entities to be taxed as partnerships by making the so-called "check-the-box" election on the partnership tax return.[68] Certain default rules (in absence of the election) also apply under which multiple-member domestic partnerships and LLCs are automatically taxed as partnerships, provided that they make no contrary election. Also, under these default rules, single-member LLCs are automatically taxed as sole proprietorships or branches of non-entity owners unless they elect to be taxed as corporations.

Trust. Trusts are generally taxed as trusts under the subchapter J rules. However, they will be treated as associations taxable as corporations if they have associates and an objective of engaging in business for a profit.

¶ 20.28 SECTION 1202 CAPITAL GAIN EXCLUSION FOR QUALIFIED SMALL BUSINESS STOCK

Section 1202 provides that 50 percent of any gain from the sale or exchange of "qualified small business stock" will be excluded from gross income. Only a C corporation can qualify as a "qualified small business."[69] And, not all entities holding qualified small business stock get the benefit of the capital gain exclusion—

C corporation and S corporation. A corporate owner of qualified small business stock is not eligible for the gain exclusion.[70]

Other entities. If a noncorporate entity owns qualified small business stock, that entity (or its pass-through owners) is eligible for the gain exclusion.[71]

¶ 20.29 FRINGE BENEFITS TO OWNER-EMPLOYEES

Special rules, which vary according to the type of entity involved, apply to the tax treatment of owner-employees who receive fringe benefits—

C corporation. Shareholder-employees of a C corporation can receive certain fringe benefits, such as health insurance, tax-free, even though payments for those benefits are deductible by the C corporation.

Other entities. Entity owners holding more than two percent of a part-

---

[68] Treas. Reg. §§ 301.7701-1, 301.7701-2, 301.7701-3.

[69] IRC § 1202(c)(1).

[70] IRC § 1202(a).

[71] IRC § 1202(a).

nership, LLC, or S corporation are generally taxed on payments of fringe benefits by the entity.[72]

¶ 20.30   EFFECT OF DONOR'S RETENTION OF RIGHT TO VOTE GIFTED ENTITY INTEREST

Special rules apply to determine the consequences of the donor's retention of the right to vote the gifted interest in the entity—

C corporation and S corporation. If the donor's family owns at least 20 percent of the corporation, the donor cannot retain voting rights in gifted stock without adverse tax consequences.

Partnership and LLC. Section 2036(b), which triggers estate tax inclusion in the case of C and S corporations, does not apply to the retention of voting rights with regard to gifted interests in these entities.

¶ 20.31   APPLICATION OF AT-RISK RULES

The deduction of losses of certain entities are limited by the at-risk rules—

C corporation. At-risk rules do not apply, except to certain closely held corporations.

Other entities. The at-risk rules apply to losses generated by S corporations, partnerships, and LLCs, as well as trusts.[73]

¶ 20.32   LIABILITY OF OWNERS FOR ENTITY OBLIGATIONS

The nature of an entity owner's liability with respect to debts incurred by the entity varies according to the type of entity involved—

C corporation and S corporation. Limited liability exists for all shareholders if corporate formalities are respected.

Limited partnership. Limited partners are not liable for a limited partnership recourse debt. However, at least one partner (an individual or another entity) must have general liability for such obligations. And, a limited partner may lose his limited liability if he participates in management, unless he participates in management of the partnership as an employee of an entity general partner.

LLC. All members can have limited liability. However, this limited liability may not be respected in non-U.S. jurisdictions.

---

[72] IRC §§ 1372(a)(2), 1372(b).

[73] IRC §§ 465(a)(1)(A), 641(b).

Trust. As a general rule, neither the trustee(s) nor the beneficiary(ies) is individually liable for trust obligations.

¶ 20.33 AVAILABILITY OF DIVIDENDS RECEIVED DEDUCTION AND THE FILING OF CONSOLIDATED RETURNS

Noncorporate entities are not entitled to exclude dividends received from corporations nor file consolidated returns with corporations (although partnership or LLC income will be taxed directly to a corporate owner).

C corporation. A C corporation can exclude 70 percent of qualifying dividends from income (80 percent if the investor corporation holds 20 percent or more of the stock).[74] A C corporation can file a consolidated return, if it is a member of the affiliated group.

S corporation. An S corporation is not entitled to the dividends received deduction,[75] nor may it file a consolidated return with any other entity.[76] However, the income of certain wholly owned subsidiaries can be treated as directly owned by a parent S corporation.[77]

¶ 20.34 DEDUCTIBILITY OF INTEREST ON DEBT-FINANCED EQUITY

The rules for deducting the interest paid on a loan used to finance the purchase of an interest differ depending on the type of entity involved—

C corporation. Interest on money borrowed by a shareholder to purchase stock may be deductible as investment interest. Deduction as business interest has been denied when the corporation, rather than the stockholder, owned the business.[78]

S corporation, partnership, and LLC. Interest on debt incurred to acquire an ownership interest in a pass-through entity is investment interest only to the extent allocated to the portion of the corporate assets comprised of portfolio or other investment assets. However, a business interest deduction will be allowed for interest on money borrowed to purchase an ownership interest if the purchaser materially participates in the activity's trade or business, but only to the extent that the entity's assets produce active trade or business income. For example, if an S corporation shareholder materially participates

---

[74] IRC § 243.

[75] IRC § 1363(b); HR Comm. Rep. on IRC § 1371, enacted by Small Business Jobs Protection Act of 1996.

[76] IRC § 1504(b)(8).

[77] IRC § 1361(b)(3)(A).

[78] Russon v. Comm'r, 107 TC No. 15 (1996).

in the S corporation's business, the shareholder will be allowed a business deduction for interest incurred to purchase his shares. However, if the entity owns nonoperating assets of a trade or business, such as a rental property, a portion of the interest will have to be allocated to passive activities and that portion cannot be deducted as a business interest. On the other hand, if the shareholder does not materially participate in the S corporation's activities, the interest expense allocated to the trade or business assets is reported as a passive activity and either decreases passive activity income or increases passive activity loss on the shareholder's return.[79]

Trust. Because interests in trusts are usually not purchased, the interest deduction issues discussed with respect to other entities rarely arise.

¶ 20.35   ENTITY OWNER'S ABILITY TO BORROW FROM ENTITY'S QUALIFIED PLANS

An entity's ability to borrow from an entity's qualified plan varies according to the type of entity involved—

C corporation. A shareholder's degree of ownership of stock does not affect his ability to borrow from the corporation's qualified plan, if the loan provisions of the plan are properly structured.[80]

S corporation. A shareholder who owns more than 5 percent of the corporation cannot borrow from the corporation's qualified plan.[81] Furthermore, when an S election is contemplated by a C corporation, there may be a problem if shareholders of a C corporation have borrowed from the corporation's qualified retirement plan. The prohibited transaction rules of Section 4975 apply to loans to five percent-or-more S corporation shareholder-employees, but not to C corporation shareholder-employees. Thus, any existing loans on conversion from C to S corporation status become prohibited transactions.

Partnership and LLC. An individual cannot borrow from the entity's qualified plan if the individual owns ten percent or more of either the capital interest or the profits interest in the partnership.[82]

Trust. A trust does not normally carry on a trade or business in sole proprietorship form, and thus will not normally have a qualified plan.

---

[79] See Temp. Reg. § 1.163-8T.

[80] IRC § 4975(d)(1).

[81] IRC § 4975(d).

[82] IRC §§ 401(c)(3), 4975(d).

¶ 20.36 CONTRIBUTIONS TO QUALIFIED PLAN—PAYROLL TAXES

The payroll tax treatment of contributions to an entity's qualified plan depends on the type of entity involved—

C corporation. Contributions to a qualified plan under Section 401(a) on behalf of a common law employee are not subject to Social Security and Medicare tax.

Other entities. Contributions to such qualified plan on behalf of a self-employed person or an employee other than a common law employee (such as a partner) are subject to Social Security and Medicare tax.

¶ 20.37 CONTRIBUTIONS TO KEOGH PLAN—PASS-THROUGH INCOME

The ability to make individual Keogh plan contributions based on a share of entity income varies according to the type of entity involved—

C corporation and trust. Keogh plan contributions cannot be based on dividends or trust distributions.

S corporation. Pass-through income from S corporations has been held not to constitute includable income for purposes of calculating permissible Keogh plan contributions.

Partnership and LLC. Keogh plan deductions can be based on pass-through income, if personal services of the member/partner are a material income-producing factor.

¶ 20.38 ENTITY CLASSIFICATION (CHECK-THE-BOX RULES)

Under prior law, a great deal of attention was devoted to structuring an entity so as to avoid its classification as an association taxable as a corporation. The "check-the-box" regulations issued on December 17, 1996, have substantially changed the law on entity classification and minimized this burden. These rules are effective as of January 1, 1997.[83]

The new classification system follows a decision-tree format.

[1] Decision-Tree Analysis

The answers to the following questions will guide the practitioner through application of the check-the-box rules.

---

[83] Treas. Reg. §§ 301.7701-1(f), 301.7701-2(e), 301.7701-3(f).

Is there a separate taxable entity or not? The first step in the classification process is to determine whether there is a separate entity for federal income tax purposes. For example, an expense-sharing venture does not normally create a separate taxable entity, if no revenues are shared.[84]

If there is a separate entity, is it a trust, business entity, or specially treated entity? An organization that is recognized as a separate entity for federal tax purposes is either a trust or a business entity, unless the Internal Revenue Code expressly provides for special treatment (e.g., as a qualified settlement fund or a real estate mortgage investment conduit).[85] Trusts generally do not have associates or an objective to carry on business for profit.[86] The distinctions between trusts and business entities are not changed by these regulations.

If the separate entity is a business entity, is it a corporation or an eligible entity? Business entities that are automatically classified as corporations for federal tax purposes include entities organized as corporations under applicable non-tax law, as well as associations, joint-stock companies, insurance companies, organizations that conduct certain banking activities, organizations wholly owned by a state or political subdivision, organizations that are taxable as corporations under a provision of the Internal Revenue Code other than Section 7701(a)(3), and certain organizations formed under the laws of a foreign jurisdiction (including a U.S. possession, territory, or commonwealth).[87] All other business entities are entities eligible to make the check-the-box election (i.e., "eligible entities").[88]

If the business entity involved is an eligible entity, does it make an election or do the default rules apply? Any business entity that is not required to be treated as a corporation for federal tax purposes (referred to in the regulation as an eligible entity) may choose its classification. An eligible entity with at least two members can be classified as either a partnership or an association, and an eligible entity with a single member can be classified as an association or can be disregarded as an entity separate from its owner.[89] However, if an eligible entity does not make an election regarding its classification, it will be classified according to certain default rules. For domestic[90] entities, a newly formed eligible entity will be classified as a partnership if it has at least two members, and will be disregarded as an entity separate from its owner if it has

---

[84] The rules determining whether a venture is a separate taxable entity are contained in Treas. Reg. § 301.7701-1(a).

[85] Treas. Reg. § 301.7701-1(b).

[86] Treas. Reg. § 301.7701-4.

[87] Treas. Reg. § 301.7701-2(b).

[88] Treas. Reg. § 301.7701-3(a).

[89] Treas. Reg. § 301.7701-3(a).

[90] A domestic entity is one which is created or organized in the United States or under the laws of the United States or of any state. Treas. Reg. § 301.7701-1(d). A foreign entity is any other entity. Id.

a single owner.[91] The default classification for an entity existing on January 1, 1997 is the classification that the entity claimed on December 31, 1996.[92] An entity's default classification continues until the entity elects to change its classification by means of an affirmative election.[93]

[2] Tax Consequences of a Change in Classification Under the Check-The-Box Election

A change in classification, no matter how achieved, will have certain tax consequences that must be reported. An entity can change its classification only once during any 60-month period.[94] The IRS can waive the application of the 60-month limitation by letter ruling if there has been more than a 50 percent ownership change[95] since the last change of election was filed.

[3] Mechanics of Election

An eligible entity may affirmatively elect its classification on Form 8832, Entity Classification Election.[96] The regulations require that the election be signed by each member of the entity or any officer, manager, or member of the entity who is authorized to make the election and who represents to having such authorization under penalties of perjury.[97] A retroactive election must also be signed by each owner who was an owner during the effective period and who is no longer an owner when the election is filed.[98]

Taxpayers can specify the date on which an election will be effective, provided that date is not more than 75 days before or 12 months after the date the election is filed.[99] If a taxpayer specifies an effective date more than 75 days prior to the date on which the election is filed, the election will be effective 75 days prior to the date on which the election was filed.[100] If a taxpayer specifies an effective date more than 12 months from the filing date, the election will be effective 12 months after the date the election was filed.[101]

---

[91] Treas. Reg. § 301.7701-3(b)(1).

[92] Treas. Reg. § 301.7701-3(b)(3)(i).

[93] Treas. Reg. § 301.7701-3(a).

[94] Treas. Reg. § 301.7701-3(c)(iv).

[95] Treas. Reg. § 301.7701-3(c)(iv).

[96] Treas. Reg. § 301.7701-3(c)(1)(i).

[97] Treas. Reg. § 301.7701-3(c)(2).

[98] Treas. Reg. § 301.7701-3(c)(2)(ii).

[99] Treas. Reg. § 301.7701-3(c)(iii).

[100] Treas. Reg. § 301.7701-3(c)(iii).

[101] Treas. Reg. § 301.7701-3(c)(iii).

Where there is uncertainty about an entity's status as a business entity, protective elections are not prohibited under the regulations.[102]

[4] Grandfather Rules for Pre-1977 Entities

The IRS will not challenge the prior classification of an eligible entity in existence on December 31, 1996 if (1) the entity had a reasonable basis (within the meaning of Section 6662) for its claimed classification; (2) the entity and all members of the entity recognized the federal tax consequences of any change in the entity's classification within the 60 months prior to January 1, 1997; and (3) neither the entity nor any member had been notified in writing on or before May 8, 1996, that the classification of the entity was under examination (in which case the entity's classification will be determined in the examination).[103]

[5] Special Rule for Entity Claiming or Determined to Be Tax-Exempt Entity

An eligible entity that has been determined to be, or claims to be, exempt from taxation under Section 501(a) is treated as having made an election to be classified as an association.[104] The deemed election will be effective as of the first day for which exemption is claimed or determined to apply, regardless of when the claim or determination is made. And, such election will remain in effect unless a different election is made after the date the claim for exempt status is withdrawn or rejected or the date the determination of exempt status is revoked.[105] Note the effect of this rule. An exempt organization which is organized and properly classified as a trust is still taxed as a trust, since trusts are not eligible entities. Non-trust exempt organizations will automatically be taxed as corporations.

[6] Election's Impact on State Tax Classification

One difficulty with utilization of the check-the-box regulations is that state tax laws may not parallel the new federal treatment. For example, a single-member LLC may be taxed as a corporation for state income tax purposes.

---

[102] Preamble to Regulations, Part C.

[103] Treas. Reg. § 301.7701-3(f)(2).

[104] Treas. Reg. § 301.7701-3(c)(v)(A).

[105] Treas. Reg. § 301.7701-3(c)(v)(A).

PART V

Non-Charitable Actuarial Techniques

CHAPTER 21

Qualified Personal Residence Trusts

¶ 21.01   INTRODUCTION

The "qualified personal residence trust" (QPRT)[1] is one of the best transfer tax savings techniques around. It allows a person to give away one or more personal residences at a fraction of the transfer tax cost that would be incurred on an ordinary gift or estate transfer. However, it involves a gamble, since the untimely death of the donor will cause the house to be brought back into his estate.

---

[1] The qualified personal residence trust is described in IRC § 2702 and regulations.

[1] How a QPRT Works

The technique involves the transfer of a personal residence to a trust. The contributor to the trust is the "donor." The donor, as the termholder, retains the right to live in the house for a fixed number of years. We'll call that period the "term." After the term, the property passes to other beneficiaries. If the donor dies within the term, the house reverts to the donor's estate. A number of specific provisions are required in the QPRT instrument.[2]

> EXAMPLE: Dad gives his house to a QPRT. Dad retains the right to live in the house for 20 years or until his earlier death. When his right to live in the house expires after 20 years, the house will pass to, or continue to be held in trust for the benefit of, his children.

[2] Reward

As discussed above, the principal risk is that the donor dies during the term of the QPRT. In this instance, the trust will be included in his estate.[3] On the other hand, if the donor outlives the term of years, substantial transfer tax savings can result. Specifically, on the date that the donor transfers the house to the trust, the donor makes a gift of the value of the remainder interest in the house (the right to own the house after the term). This will be a fraction of the house's fair market value. The fraction is ordinarily determined by reference to the Treasury's actuarial tables.[4] The factors which determine the fraction are the length of the term, the age of the donor (since a smart estate planner will put in a contingent reversion taking effect if the donor dies during the term),[5] and the 7520 rate[6] at the date of the gift. If the donor outlives the term, the remainder beneficiaries take the house at no further estate or gift tax cost to the donor or the donor's estate.

> EXAMPLE: Elaborating on the previous example, suppose Dad is 52 years old, and the personal residence is worth $5,000,000. When the 7520 rate is nine percent, he gives the residence to a QPRT that lasts for 20 years or until his earlier death. If he is alive at the end of the 20-year term, the QPRT terminates in favor of trusts for his children. If he dies during the 20-year term, the house reverts to his estate.

---

[2] Treas. Reg. § 25.2702-5(c).

[3] IRC § 2036(a)(1).

[4] Found in Publication 1457, Alpha Volume, and Publication 1458, Beta Volume.

[5] Discussed at ¶ 21.02[3] below.

[6] The "7520 rate" is 120 percent of the applicable federal midterm rate, rounded to the nearest 2/10ths of one percent. IRC § 7520. The 7520 rate and its ramifications are discussed more fully in Ch. 11.

The interest transferred to the children's trusts (the right to receive the house in 20 years if Dad is still alive) is valued by the tables at only 12.6265 percent of the value of the house. That means Dad would make a gift of $631,325 on the transfer of the house to the trust. The gift tax would be $347,229 (at a 55 percent rate).

If Dad survives the 20-year term, the house will pass to the children's trusts at no further estate or gift tax cost. If the house is worth $10,000,000 at that time, Dad will have given a $10,000,000 house to his children's trusts at a transfer tax cost of only $347,229. If Dad continues to live in the house after the term, Dad will pay rent to his children's trusts, further reducing his estate at no gift tax cost. If, however, Dad dies during the 20-year term, the house will be included in his estate, and his estate will receive a credit for the gift taxes paid on the initial gift. If the house is worth $10,000,000 at his death, the estate tax on that asset would be $5,500,000 (at 55 percent), so after the credit of $347,229, the estate would owe an additional $5,152,771 in tax, for a total transfer tax cost of $5,500,000.

PRACTICE POINTER: If the donor is a hedger of bets, he might consider purchasing a term insurance policy (in an irrevocable life insurance trust, of course), to protect his estate from the possibility of his death within the term.

EXAMPLE: In the above example, if an Irrevocable Life Insurance Trust purchases insurance on Dad's life in the amount of $5,153,000, then on Dad's death within the term, the trust would receive enough cash to pay the estate tax. It could buy part of the house or other assets from the estate, or lend money to the estate, to get the cash in the estate's hands.[7]

[3] What Makes This Technique So Effective?

In most cases, the actuarial tables are used to value the gift of the remainder interest. The donor's taxable gift is reduced by the actuarial value of his retained right to income. However, the expectation is that he will actually receive no income (which would increase the value of his estate), since the property is not income-producing. Since the taxable gift is reduced by an income interest, a QPRT will be a better tax-minimizing device when interest rates are higher (because the actuarial tables will attribute more value to the retained income interest, and less value to the gifted remainder interest).

---

[7] For a general discussion of Irrevocable Life Insurance Trusts, see Ch. 12.

¶ 21.02 STRUCTURING THE TRANSACTION

[1] Choosing a Term

It is important to choose a term that the donor is expected to outlive. The longer the term is, the less the amount of the gift will be. However, it should be remembered that the risk that the donor will die within the term increases with a longer term. As a matter of choosing the optional term, most of the reduction in value of the gift occurs in the early years of the term. This will be truer, the higher the 7520 rate is.

[2] Managing the Gift Tax

The amount of gift tax can be chosen by selecting a term for the QPRT that results in an acceptable amount of gift tax. In the previous example, if 52-year-old Dad is in the 55 percent gift tax bracket and the 7520 rate is nine percent, he would pay $347,229 of gift tax upon the transfer of his $5,000,000 house to a 20-year QPRT. As the following table demonstrates, adjusting the term would result in different amounts of gift tax.

Trust Term	Percent of Transfer Treated as Gift	Amount of Gift	Gift Tax at 55%
5 years	62.3280%	$3,116,400.00	$1,714,020.00
10 years	38.0105%	$1,900,525.00	$1,045,288.00
15 years	22.4260%	$1,121,300.00	$ 616,715.00
25 years	6.6191%	$ 330,955.00	$ 182,025.00

It should be noted that the IRS has indicated that the gift tax incurred on the creation of a QPRT may be further reduced to the extent that a remainder beneficiary of the trust purchases his remainder interest from the transferor.[8]

EXAMPLE: Under Dad's set of facts, suppose that, instead of giving the house to the trust, he contributes it in exchange for Son's payment of $631,325 for the remainder interest in the trust. Dad's gift will be zero. (He will, however, include the payment of $631,325 received from Son, along with the earnings from the payment, in his estate if he dies and has not consumed these items. And, he will recognize gain on the sale, if the house is appreciated and no exception to recognition applies.)

Finally, it should be noted that a gift to a QPRT will not qualify for the annual exclusion, since the remainder interest is not a present interest.

---

[8] Priv. Ltr. Rul. 9315010 (Jan. 13, 1993). The joint purchase rules of IRC § 2702 do not affect the transfer because IRC § 2702 does not apply to the transfer of an interest in trust that meets the requirements of a QPRT or personal residence trust. (Personal residence trusts, which are similar to QPRTs, are discussed at ¶ 21.04 below.)

[3] Contingent Reversion

The trust should contain a provision that the house will return to the donor's estate or be subject to a general power of appointment if he dies during the trust term. This provision will reduce the value of the gift.[9] Since the entire house will be included in the donor's gross estate in any case on his death during the term,[10] no additional estate tax consequences result from the contingent reversion.

[4] Donor as Trustee

The donor can be the trustee, as long as he retains no prohibited powers or interests after the initial term.[11]

[5] Payment of Residence Expenses

Who bears the costs associated with the house during the term? During the term, the donor bears the expenses normally allocated to a life tenant—that is, ordinary maintenance, property taxes, and insurance. The remainder beneficiaries bear the costs of improvements and major repairs. If the donor pays for those items that are the responsibility of the remainder beneficiaries, the payment will constitute either a loan or a gift to the trust, depending on the terms of the arrangement. Since the QPRT is a grantor trust, the donor should be able to deduct property taxes paid by him or the trust to the extent that the deduction would be available to him as an individual.

[6] Choosing the Property

[a] Personal Residence—Used Primarily for Residential Purposes

A residence is a personal residence only if its primary use is as a residence of the term holder when occupied by the term holder. Certain business uses of the term holder's principal residence are okay, however, as long as they are secondary to the house's residential use. A residence is not used primarily as a residence if it is used to provide transient lodging and substantial services are provided in connection with the provision of that lodging (e.g., a hotel or a bed and breakfast). Moreover, a residence is not a personal residence if, during any

---

[9] This can be sensed intuitively. The value of (1) the right to receive property after 20 years will always be greater than the value of (2) the right to receive property after 20 years only if the donor is still alive.

[10] IRC § 2036(a).

[11] See Ch. 9 for a discussion of prohibited powers and interests.

period not occupied by the term holder, its primary use is other than as a residence.[12] On the other hand, the principal residence can have a home office or a separately rented area, such as a garage apartment (provided no substantial hotel-like services come with the rental and the house is not primarily used as a place of business).[13] In this vein, a vacation home can have such subsidiary uses if it is used primarily as a residence when the term holder is there and is used primarily as a residence (or is vacant) when the term holder is not there—i.e., it cannot be used primarily for business when the term holder is not there.

[b] Use of Personal Residence by Donor

A trust is a qualified personal residence trust only so long as the residence is used or held for use as a personal residence of the donor.[14]

[i] **Meaning of "used by donor."** A personal residence is used as a personal residence if it is (1) the donor's principal residence;[15] (2) one other residence of the donor (so long as the donor uses the residence for personal purposes during each year for the greater of 14 days or 10 percent of the number of days the property is rented at fair rental);[16] or (3) an undivided fractional interest in either.[17] Use by the donor, for this purpose, generally requires that he is physically occupying the premises—storing his skis in the garage is not a sufficient use.[18]

So, assuming the vacation house is not rented and not used for any nonresidential purpose, it will be eligible if the donor physically resides in it at least 14 days of each year.

[ii] **Meaning of "held for use by donor."** What happens when the donor does not actually occupy the residence for the required period during a year (for example, he lives in a nursing home or doesn't go to his Aspen home one year)? In such a case, the residence will still be considered held for use as a personal residence of the donor, so long as the residence (1) is not occupied by

---

[12] Treas. Reg. §§ 25.2702-5(b)(2)(iii), 25.2702-5(c)(2)(iii).

[13] Priv. Ltr. Rul. 9609015 (Nov. 22, 1995).

[14] Treas. Reg. § 25.2702-5(c)(7)(i).

[15] As defined by IRC § 1034.

[16] The number of days the property is used for personal purposes is determined by IRC § 280A(d)(1), without regard to IRC § 280A(d)(2). What this means is that the donor himself must actually use the house for personal purposes for this period of time; use by relatives does not count.

[17] Treas. Reg. § 25.2702-5(b)(2)(i).

[18] See Prop. Reg. § 1.280A-1(e).

any person other than the donor, the donor's spouse, or the donor's dependents and (2) is available at all times for use by the donor as a personal residence.[19]

Suppose Dad spends all his time in the nursing home and Mom still occupies the main house. If the house is available for use by Dad at all times as his personal residence and Dad, Mom, and Dad's dependents are the only occupants, the house will still be "held for use by Dad." Mom's occupancy of the main house is clearly within the rules—but what if Mom's mother stays over for a month or the grown children or grandchildren come to visit for a summer? And what about the couple's vacation home? Suppose Dad and the family don't make it to Aspen all year, but they let some friends use the house for a few weeks?

The IRS has privately ruled that the presence of occasional house guests was okay when the house guests occupied the house only with the permission of the donor, paid no consideration for their occupancy, acquired no rights in the house, and could stay only so long as the donor's permission was not withdrawn.[20]

What if Mom has live-in help at the main house? And a caretaker lives in the garage apartment at the Aspen cottage? Perhaps logic similar to that applied in the above rulings would be applied to allow for the presence of domestic servants in a QPRT residence that is "held for use" as a residence, even though such persons are not included in the permitted class described in the regulations.[21] The distinction between this situation and the house guests is that the servants provide services in exchange for their occupancy of the house. This fact should not make a difference, since their occupancy of the house is for the convenience of the employer.

Suppose Mom dies and Son (who is not a dependent of Dad's) rents out the Aspen house on Dad's behalf. If the rental is full-time, the house is no longer Dad's personal residence. If it is rented for 330 days, and Son takes Dad to stay in the house for 33 days during that year, the house should still qualify as actually used by Dad. The house should also still qualify as used by Dad if Son rents the house out only during ski season and takes Dad to the house for at least 14 days in the year. If Dad does not occupy the house for enough days to qualify as actually using the house, the house cannot be rented out at all, since the house would not then qualify as being held for use by Dad at all times.

---

[19] Treas. Reg. § 5.2702-5(c)(7)(i).

[20] Priv. Ltr. Rul. 9448035 (Sept. 2, 1994); Priv. Ltr. Rul. 9249014 (Sept. 4, 1992).

[21] Treas. Reg. § 25.2702-5(c)(7)(i).

[c] Transfer of Cooperative Apartment to a QPRT

The fact that the form of ownership of the transferred residence is gained through a combination of a lease and of stock ownership in a cooperative housing corporation does not preclude qualification of the property as a personal residence.[22] However, many co-ops will not permit a transfer of title of shares to a QPRT. To accommodate this type of limitation, the IRS has ruled that a transfer of beneficial title to the shares to the QPRT, with the donor retaining legal title as nominee for the trust, was okay.[23]

[d] Additional Property as Part of the Residence

A personal residence may include appurtenant structures used by the term holder for residential purposes and adjacent land which is reasonably appropriate for residential purposes (taking into account the residence's size and location).[24] However, the term personal residence does not include any personal property (e.g., household furnishings).[25]

Under certain circumstances, real property consisting of more than one residence may qualify as a single personal residence, at least where one of the residences is the primary residence and the use of the adjacent residences effectively links them to the main residence (for example, where adjacent residences are guest houses or servants' quarters).[26]

The IRS has privately ruled that the use of a house adjacent to the donors' vacation house as a guest house for friends and family members of the donors did not cause the real property transferred to the trust to fail to qualify as a personal residence used by the transferors. The IRS indicated, however, that this ruling was contingent on the fact that the persons occupying the guest house did so only at the sufferance of the transferors, did not pay rent or other consideration, and did not otherwise establish any rights of continuing occupancy.[27] As the value of the adjacent house was only 3.7 percent of the value of the entire property transferred to the trust, the IRS apparently considered the guest house to be an appurtenant structure within the meaning of Treasury Regulation § 25.2702-5(c)(2)(ii).

A personal residence does not include any structure that is used for nonresidential purposes when it is not occupied by the donor.[28] For example,

---

[22] Priv. Ltr. Rul. 9151046 (Sept. 26, 1991).

[23] Priv. Ltr. Rul. 9249014 (Sept. 4, 1992).

[24] See, e.g., Priv. Ltr. Rul. 9544018 (Aug. 2, 1995) (18-acre site with swampland and stream), Priv. Ltr. Rul. 9442019 (July 19, 1994) (10 acres of land on three separate lots), Priv. Ltr. Rul. 9639064 (June 27, 1996) (43 acres with swimming pool, pool house, greenhouse, tool shed, barn, corral, and quarters for caretaker and housekeeper).

[25] Treas. Reg. §§ 25.2702-5(b)(2)(ii), 25.2702-5(c)(2)(ii).

[26] See Priv. Ltr. Rul. 9328040 (Apr. 21, 1993).

[27] Priv. Ltr. Rul. 9328040 (Apr. 21, 1993).

[28] Treas. Reg. § 25.2702-5(b)(2)(iii). However, nonresidential structures "appurtenant" to a residence are apparently okay. See, e.g., Priv. Ltr. Rul. 9606003 (Nov. 7,

a guest house which is used as a leasing office when the term holder is not there is not a personal residence.

[e] Multiple Homes in QPRTs

A married couple can put up to three properties in QPRTs—their principal residence and one vacation home each, provided that each spouse owns one vacation home as separate property.[29] If the husband and wife each had separate principal residences, then it would be possible for the couple to have four QPRTs. The regulation limiting the use of the QPRT technique to two houses per person, and providing that one must be the principal residence, is not included in the statute, which has no such limitations.

[f] Interests of Spouses in the Same Residence

If spouses hold interests in the same residence (including community property interests), the spouses may transfer their interests in the residence (or a fractional portion of their interests in the residence) to the same personal residence trust or qualified personal residence trust, provided that the governing instrument prohibits any person other than one of the spouses from holding a term interest in the trust concurrently with the other spouse.[30] Further, a discount may apply if fractional interests in a house are transferred. Care must be taken not to make a completed gift to the spouse, as the gift will not qualify for the gift tax marital deduction due to the fact that it will terminate during the spouse's life. Retention of a contingent reversion in case of the donor's death during the term should do the trick.

PRACTICE POINTER: The problems in drafting a joint QPRT are formidable. Hence, many drafters give each spouse's fractional interest in the house to a separate trust. Care should be taken that the reciprocal trusts doctrine is not called into play after the respective terms.[31] Also, in drafting the QPRT, if both spouses are grantors and/or beneficiaries, consider addressing the possibility of a divorce or the death of one spouse during the term.

1995) (separate garage used to store inventory of grantors' business and garage apartment considered part of residential property).

[29] Treas. Reg. §§ 25.2702-5(b)(2), 25.2702-5(c)(2).

[30] Treas. Reg. §§ 25.2702-5(b)(2)(iv), 25.2702-5(c)(2)(iv).

[31] See Ch. 2 for an explanation of that doctrine. An example of a joint QPRT which was approved by the IRS is contained in Priv. Ltr. Rul. 9626041 (Apr. 2, 1996).

[g] Transfer of Mortgaged Property to a QPRT

The fact that a residence is subject to a mortgage does not affect its status as a personal residence.[32] If the house is transferred to the QPRT subject to the mortgage, and the donor continues to pay the mortgage, each payment of principal will be considered an additional gift (or loan, depending on the arrangement between the donor and the trust). The donor's payment of interest, however, should not be an additional gift, since the interest payment would usually be chargeable to the life tenant.

Use of mortgaged property would generally result in an initial gift equal to the net value of the residence, followed by gifts of increasing portions of the principal payments as the term decreases. Thus, use of the mortgaged property is inefficient. An alternate way to structure the transaction may be to structure the initial transfer so that the donor promises to pay the mortgage.[33]

WARNING: Regardless of the manner in which the transfer of encumbered property is structured, the donor must check with the bank before hauling off and deeding mortgaged property to the QPRT. Under most mortgages, transfer of the collateral will usually accelerate the payments under the note.

[7] What Happens if House Ceases to Be Donor's Personal Residence

If the house is sold or destroyed during the term, or the donor ceases to use it as a personal residence, it can be replaced with another personal residence within two years. If the house is not replaced, then the house (or the proceeds of its disposition) must be either (1) given back to the donor or (2) converted to a grantor retained annuity trust (GRAT).[34]

[a] House Is Sold

If the house is sold during the term, and the trust does not acquire another personal residence of the donor within two years after the sale, the transfer to the donor or the GRAT conversion must occur within 30 days after the second anniversary of the sale.[35] However, since all income of the QPRT

---

[32] Treas. Reg. §§ 25.2702-5(b)(2)(ii), 25.2702-5(c)(2)(ii).

[33] McCaffrey, "GRATs and QPRTs, Split Interest Transfers: An Estate Planner's Panacea?" 20 ACTEC Notes 70 (1994).

[34] Treas. Reg. § 25.2702-5(c)(8)(i). For a discussion of GRATs, see Ch. 22.

[35] Treas. Reg. §§ 25.2702-5(c)(7)(ii), 25.2702-5(c)(8)(i). Presumably, if the donor's term will terminate in less than two years, the reversion/conversion provisions would not be triggered if the house were never replaced.

during the donor's term is taxable to the donor,[36] the sale of the house should qualify for tax-free rollover of gain under Section 1033 or Section 1034, and the Section 121 exclusion of up to $125,000 of gain for taxpayers 55 and over, if those sections would otherwise be applicable to the grantor.[37]

[b] House Is Damaged or Destroyed

If, during the donor's term interest in the trust, the house is damaged or destroyed so that it is unusable as a residence, the trust has two years to repair or replace the house.[38] If the house is not repaired or replaced within two years after the damage or destruction, the transfer to the donor or the GRAT conversion must occur within 30 days after the second anniversary of the damage or destruction.[39]

[c] Donor Otherwise Ceases to Use House as a Personal Residence

If, during the donor's term interest in the trust, the donor ceases to use the house as a personal residence for reasons other than sale of, damage to, or destruction of the residence, the transfer to the donor or GRAT conversion must occur within 30 days after the cessation of use.[40]

[d] Consequences if House Is Not Replaced

The trust must provide for a disposition of the proceeds of the house if it is sold, damaged, or destroyed during the donor's term, or the donor ceases to use it as a personal residence, and the house is not replaced within two years. The most flexible alternative is to provide that the proceeds will be returned to the donor or converted to a GRAT, in an independent trustee's discretion. This choice should not be made by the donor, since he would have the power to reacquire the trust property for no consideration by moving out and electing to distribute to himself. This power could cause the initial transfer to the trust to be an incomplete gift, and the expiration of the donor's term to constitute a completed gift of the house at its full value.

Usually, choosing to give the property back to the donor will not be attractive, since that will return the house to the donor's taxable estate at its

---

[36] IRC § 677.

[37] See Rev. Rul. 66-161, 1966-1 CB 164; Rev. Rul. 85-45, 1985-1 CB 183; Priv. Ltr. Rul. 9026036 (Mar. 28, 1990). These provisions are discussed in Ch. 4.

[38] Treas. Reg. § 25.2702-5(c)(7)(iii).

[39] Treas. Reg. §§ 25.2702-5(c)(7)(iii), 25.2702-5(c)(8)(i). Presumably, if the term will end in less than two years, the reversion/conversion provisions would not be triggered if the house were never replaced.

[40] Treas. Reg. §§ 25.2702-5(c)(7), 25.2702-5(c)(8)(i).

full value. A GRAT is better than a reversion to the grantor; however, a GRAT is not as effective a tax-saver as the QPRT. This is because, with a QPRT, the donor gets a reduction of his gift for the value of the income interest for the term, when no income will actually be distributed to him. In a GRAT, the annuity actually has to be distributed to the donor, thus returning funds to the donor that will increase his estate.

[8] Will the Donor Be Homeless at the End of the Term?

At the end of the term, the house will pass to the remainder beneficiary(ies). The usual plan is for the donor to lease the house from the beneficiary, if both parties are willing and can agree on terms. Many people are concerned about whether they will be evicted from their houses by the new owner. This issue may be addressed in the following ways.

[a] Spousal Trust as Remainder Beneficiary

The remainder beneficiary can be a non-marital deduction trust for the benefit of the donor's spouse.[41] The trustee can let the spouse live there rent-free, and the spouse just possibly may allow the donor to live there too on the same basis. With this option, the donor counts on (1) no divorce or separation occurring, (2) predeceasing the spouse, unless the trust contains a contingency plan for his surviving her, and (3) not being thrown out by the trustee. The donor can be the trustee of this trust, as long as he does not retain powers or interests that would result in estate inclusion.[42]

[b] Descendants' Trust as Remainder Beneficiary

The remainder beneficiary can be a trust for the benefit of the donor's descendants (or for anyone else). The donor can rent the house from the trust after the term. The donor can be the trustee of this trust, as long as he does not retain powers or interests that would result in estate inclusion.[43] Thus, as trustee, the donor is in control of whether or not he or she will lease the house, and of the rental amounts payable, subject to fiduciary obligations to the beneficiaries and the requirement that the rental be for fair consideration. Fair

---

[41] Note that naming the surviving spouse or a marital deduction trust as the remainder beneficiary after the initial term is not a good tax-planning idea. If the donor outlives the initial term, the residence will be fully includable in the surviving spouse's estate; the donor might as well just leave the house to the spouse in his will—the leveraging advantages of the QPRT will be lost.

[42] These powers and interests are described in Chs. 2 and 9.

[43] These powers and interests are described in Chs. 2 and 9.

rent is important—fiduciary liability and estate tax inclusion can occur if the rent is too low, and gifts can occur if the rent is too high.

[c] Execution of a Sale/Lease Agreement

The IRS has privately ruled that a QPRT would be qualified even if the donor contracted with the trustee at the inception of the trust to allow the donor to purchase the property at the expiration of the term for its then fair market value[44] or allow the donor to lease the property after the expiration of the term at fair market value.[45] Meanwhile, the IRS has issued proposed regulations that would prohibit the donor's purchase of the house from the QPRT, as described in ¶ 21.02[8][d] below.[46]

[d] Purchase of House Before End of Donor's Term

One disadvantage of using a QPRT is that an appreciated house will not receive a stepped-up basis at the donor's death. As a solution to this problem, it has been suggested that the donor purchase the house from the trust before the trust's term ends. Since the QPRT is a grantor trust during the term, and the IRS does not recognize transactions between an individual and his grantor trust, the idea is that there will be no gain on the sale,[47] and therefore the house will receive a new basis when it is included in the donor's estate.[48] An equal amount of value will have been removed from the donor's estate.

But . . . in April 1996, the IRS proposed a regulation which says that the trust instrument must prohibit the trustee from selling or transferring the residence, directly or indirectly, to the grantor, the grantor's spouse, another grantor trust of which the grantor or the grantor's spouse is a deemed owner, or any entity controlled by the grantor or the grantor's spouse.[49] The prohibition must apply both during the term and at any time after the term.[50]

The regulation is proposed to be effective for trusts created after May 16, 1996.[51] However, the IRS has announced that if it finds a pre-effective date trust inconsistent with the purposes of the statute or regulations, it may treat the trust as not qualifying as a QPRT by using established legal doctrines,

---

[44] Priv. Ltr. Rul. 9441039 (July 15, 1994).

[45] Priv. Ltr. Rul. 9433016 (May 18, 1994); Priv. Ltr. Rul. 9425028 (Mar. 28, 1994); Priv. Ltr. Rul. 9249014 (Sept. 4, 1992); Priv. Ltr. Rul. 9714025 (Jan. 6, 1997).

[46] Prop. Reg. §§ 25.2702-5(b)(1), 25.2702-5(c)(9).

[47] IRC § 677(a)(1); Rev. Rul. 85-13, 1985-1 CB 184.

[48] IRC § 1014.

[49] Prop. Reg. §§ 25.2702-5(b)(1), 25.2702-5(c)(9).

[50] Prop. Reg. §§ 25.2702-5(b)(1), 25.2702-5(c)(9).

[51] Prop. Reg. § 25.2702-7.

such as the substance-over-form doctrine. For example, if the grantor actually purchases the residence from the trust pursuant to a right or option to purchase that is stated in the trust instrument or a collateral document, the IRS may not treat the trust as a qualified personal residence trust.[52] What is the consequence of the trust not being treated as a QPRT? No one knows, but presumably the IRS would try to treat the transfer of the house as a gift of the entire corpus for transfer purposes, valuing the grantor's retained interest at zero, pursuant to Section 2702, either as of the initial transfer to the trust, or as of the date of the disqualifying event. The trust would it seems, still be a grantor trust.

[9] Rent Paid by the Donor After the Trust Term

The rent paid to the owner at the end of the term further reduces the donor's estate. It is, of course, taxable income to the lessor/owner. The lessor/owner should also be able to offset all or part of the rent with depreciation, subject to the limits of Section 280A (limiting deductions on rental of homes to relatives) and Section 469 (limiting deductions on passive activities).

[10] Donor's Death During the Term

If the donor dies during the term, the QPRT's assets will be included in the donor's estate at date-of-death value. The donor can, of course, leave the assets in a marital deduction-qualifying form, if he is married at death. If the donor and his spouse split the initial gift and the non-donor spouse survives, the non-donor spouse's use of her unified credit and run-up the brackets will not be restored for gift tax purposes, and will only be restored for estate tax purposes if the donor dies within the first three years of the term.[53]

[11] Generation-Skipping Transfer Tax

Exemption cannot be effectively allocated to the trust until the donor's interest expires.[54]

¶ 21.03 DRAFTING THE QPRT PROVISIONS

A qualified personal residence trust instrument must contain certain provisions and may contain others.

---

[52] Preamble to Proposed Regulations, 61 Fed. Reg. 16,623 (1996).

[53] See Ch. 8 for an explanation.

[54] IRC § 2642(f).

[1] Income Distributions to Term Holder (Required Provision)

Any income of the trust must be distributed to the term holder at least once a year.[55] Practically speaking, the trust is unlikely to have income, unless the house is rented or sold, or insurance proceeds are received.

The IRS has taken the view with respect to GRATs that the trust instrument must contain a provision requiring the trustee to reimburse the grantor for income taxes paid on amounts in excess of the grantor's annuity payment. Such a provision should not be necessary in a QPRT (except, perhaps, for the back-up GRAT), since the grantor will be entitled to all the fiduciary income during the term and will have a contingent reversion in taxable income which is allocable to principal.

[2] Principal Distributions (Required Provision)

Prior to the expiration of the trust's term, distributions of principal to any beneficiary other than the transferor must be prohibited.[56]

[3] Permissible Trust Assets

[a] Residence and Cash (Required Provision)

Except for any cash, sales proceeds, or insurance proceeds described below, during the entire term of the trust, the trust must not hold any asset other than one residence to be used or held for use as a personal residence of the term holder.[57]

[b] Additions of Cash to the Trust (Optional Provision)

[i] Additions. If additions of cash are permitted under the trust instrument, they must be held in a separate account. The total amount of cash held in the account must not exceed the amount required:

- For the trust's payment of expenses (including mortgage payments) already incurred or reasonably expected to be paid by the trust within six months from the date the addition is made;

---

[55] Treas. Reg. § 25.2702-5(c)(3).

[56] Treas. Reg. § 25.2702-5(c)(4). This regulation should read "term holder" rather than "transferor" to be consistent with the other regulations.

[57] Treas. Reg. § 25.2702-5(c)(5)(i). The regulation actually prohibits the trust from holding any assets other than one residence and certain assets associated with the residence for the entire term of the trust. This seems inconsistent with the statute. These requirements should only apply for the duration of the term interest.

- For improvements to the residence to be paid by the trust within six months from the date the addition is made;
- For the trust's purchase of the initial residence within three months of the date the trust is created, but only if the trustee has previously entered into a contract to purchase that residence; and
- For the trust's purchase of a replacement residence within three months of the date the addition of cash is made, but only if the trustee has previously entered into a contract to purchase that residence.[58]

[ii] **Mandatory distributions of excess cash.** If additions of cash are allowed, the trustee must determine, at least once a quarter, whether the trust holds cash in excess of the amounts permitted above for payment of expenses. If so, the trustee must immediately distribute the excess cash to the term holder. In addition, upon termination of the term holder's interest in the trust, any cash held by the trust that is not in fact used to pay trust expenses due and payable on the date of termination (including expenses directly related to the termination) must be distributed outright to the term holder within 30 days of termination.[59]

[c] **Addition of Improvements to the Trust (Optional Provision)**

Improvements to the residence may be added to the trust, provided that the residence, as improved, meets the requirements of a personal residence.[60]

[d] **Sales Proceeds Held by the Trust (Optional Provision)**

The trustee can sell the house and hold the sale proceeds in a separate account.[61]

QUESTION: *Is interest earned on the sales proceeds permitted to be held as well?*

ANSWER: Presumably yes, until the required annual payment of income to the donor.

[e] **Insurance and Insurance Proceeds Held by the Trust (Optional Provision)**

The trust can hold policies of insurance on the residence. If the residence is damaged or destroyed, the trust can hold insurance proceeds in a separate

---

[58] Treas. Reg. § 25.2702-5(c)(5)(ii)(A)(1).

[59] Treas. Reg. § 25.2702-5(c)(5)(ii)(A)(2).

[60] Treas. Reg. § 25.2702-5(c)(5)(ii)(B).

[61] Treas. Reg. § 25.2702-5(c)(5)(ii)(C).

account. If the residence is involuntarily converted,[62] the proceeds of the conversion are treated as proceeds of insurance.[63]

QUESTION: *Is interest earned on the insurance proceeds permitted to be held in the trust as well?*

ANSWER: Presumably yes, until the required annual payment of income to the donor.

[4] No Prepayment of the Term Holder's Interest (Required Provision)

Commutation (prepayment) of the term holder's interest is prohibited.[64]

> EXAMPLE: Dad establishes QPRT, retaining a term interest for ten years, with remainder to Daughter. Five years into the term, Dad develops a terminal illness, and is no longer expected to survive the ten-year term. At that date, suppose Dad's actuarial interest in the trust is one-third of the trust value. However, on his death within the term, the entire value of the house will be included in his estate. Trustee cannot change this result by terminating the trust and paying Dad one-third of the value of the assets.

It may be possible to achieve the same result as sought by terminating the trust and paying Dad (the termholder) the current value of his interest by reforming the trust in accordance with state law procedures. Or, perhaps, Dad can sell his interest in the trust for its actuarial value. In order to accomplish this, the QPRT could not be a spendthrift trust with respect to Dad, and Dad must have at least a 50 percent chance of living for a year after the date of sale (so that the actuarial tables can be used to value his interest). It should be noted, however, that the IRS might view these techniques as "bait and switch" techniques, similar to its view of the grantor's purchase of the house.[65]

---

[62] Within the meaning of IRC § 1033. Condemnation of the house would be an example of an involuntary conversion.

[63] Treas. Reg. § 25.2702-5(c)(5)(ii)(D).

[64] Treas. Reg. § 25.2702-5(c)(6).

[65] Preamble to Proposed Reg. § 25.2702-5, 96 TNT 75-9 (Apr. 16, 1996).

[5] Cessation of Use as a Personal Residence (Required Provision)

[a] General Rule

A trust ceases to be a QPRT if the residence ceases to be used or held for use as a personal residence of the term holder.[66] This rule, taken from the Treasury Regulations, must actually mean that the cessation of use as a residence occurs for reasons other than sale of, or damage to or destruction of, the house. Otherwise, the next two rules would not make sense.

[b] Special Rule for Sale of the Personal Residence (Required Provision)

The trust ceases to be a QPRT upon sale of the residence if the trust instrument does not permit the trust to hold proceeds of sale of the residence in a separate account, as described above. If the trust instrument permits the trust to hold proceeds of sale as described, the trust must cease to be a QPRT with respect to all proceeds of sale held by the trust by the earliest of: (1) two years after the date of sale; (2) the termination of the term holder's interest in the trust; or (3) the acquisition of another residence by the trust.[67]

[c] Special Rule for Damage to or Destruction of Personal Residence (Required)

[i] In general. If damage or destruction renders the residence unusable as a residence, the trust ceases to be a QPRT two years after the date of damage or destruction (or the date of termination of the term holder's interest in the trust, if earlier) unless, before that date: (1) replacement of or repairs to the residence are completed or (2) a new residence is acquired by the trust.[68]

[ii] Mandatory insurance proceeds provision. If the trust instrument permits the trust to hold proceeds of insurance received as a result of damage to or destruction of the residence, as described above, the trust must cease to be a QPRT with respect to all the insurance proceeds held by the trust by the earliest of: (1) two years after the date of the damage or destruction; (2) the termination of the term holder's interest in the trust; or (3) the acquisition of another residence by the trust.[69]

---

[66] Treas. Reg. § 25.2702-5(c)(7)(i).

[67] Treas. Reg. § 25.2702-5(c)(7)(ii).

[68] Treas. Reg. § 25.2702-5(c)(7)(iii)(A).

[69] Treas. Reg. § 25.2702-5(c)(7)(iii)(B).

[6] Disposition of Trust Assets on Cessation as QPRT (Required Provision)

Within 30 days after the trust has ceased to be a QPRT with respect to any assets, either: (1) those assets must be distributed outright to the term holder; (2) those assets must be converted to and held for the balance of the term in a separate share of the trust meeting the requirements of a GRAT;[70] or (3) the trustee can be given discretion to comply with either (1) or (2).[71]

QUERY: Suppose the QPRT's term is 10 years. Nine years into the term, the personal residence is sold. One year later, at the end of the original term, trustee still has the proceeds. If he elects to convert to a qualified annuity trust for the balance of the term, there is no balance of the term. Must he pay the proceeds to the term holder? Or must he run them through the annuity trust, even though there is no term left? Or can he pay the proceeds directly to (or continue to hold them for) the remainder beneficiaries at that point? Logically, he should do the latter, although the regulations are not clear on this issue.

Donor-trustee with power to distribute sales proceeds to himself or convert interest. If the donor to the trust is also the trustee, he should not have the power to sell the property and distribute the proceeds to himself. This power will render the transfer to the QPRT an incomplete gift from the first. If the trustee-donor has the power to sell the property and convert his interest to a qualified annuity interest, his retained interest should be valued at the higher of the value of a retained income interest or a retained annuity interest, since the remainder beneficiaries are assured of getting only the remainder after the greater of those two interests.

The most flexible provision is to have an independent trustee decide whether to sell the residence and whether to distribute the proceeds or convert them to a qualified annuity interest.

[7] Requirements for Conversion to a Qualified Annuity Interest

If the donor's interest in the trust can be converted to a qualified annuity interest, the trust instrument must contain the following provisions.[72]

[a] Effective Date of Annuity

Under the governing instrument, the right of the term holder to receive the annuity amount must begin on the date of sale of the residence, the date

---

[70] See Ch. 22 for a description of GRATs.

[71] Treas. Reg. § 25.2702-5(c)(8)(i).

[72] Treas. Reg. § 25.2702-5(c)(8)(ii)(A).

of damage to or destruction of the residence, or the date on which the residence ceases to be used or held for use as a personal residence, as the case may be ("the cessation date").

However, the trust instrument may provide that the trustee may defer payment of any annuity amount otherwise payable after the cessation date until 30 days after the conversion of the assets to a qualified annuity interest ("the conversion date"); but, any deferred payment must bear interest from the cessation date at a rate not less than the 7520 rate in effect on the cessation date. The trust instrument may permit the trustee to reduce aggregate deferred annuity payments by the amount of income actually distributed by the trust to the term holder during the deferral period.[73]

It should be noted that Treasury Regulation § 25.2702-5(d), example 6 is inconsistent with Treasury Regulation § 25.2702-5(c)(8)(ii)(B). The example says that payment may be deferred until 30 days after the new residence is purchased. Treasury Regulation § 25.2702-5(c)(8)(ii)(B), on the other hand, allows the trustee to convert the trust to a qualified annuity trust within 30 days after the date a new residence is purchased.[74] Then, it allows a further 30 days for payment of the deferred annuity.[75]

[b] Determination of Annuity Amount

Under the governing instrument, the annuity amount must be at least the amount determined in the following paragraphs.[76]

[i] Entire trust ceases to be a QPRT. If, on the conversion date, the trust does not hold a qualifying residence, the annuity must be computed as follows:

First: Determine the lesser of the value of: (1) all interests retained by the term holder, as of the date of the original transfer or transfers or (2) the value of all the trust assets, as of the conversion date.

Next: Divide that number by an annuity factor determined: (1) for the original term of the term holder's interest and (2) at the 7520 rate at the time of the original transfer.[77]

EXAMPLE: QPRT is established with a term of 10 years. The 7520 rate is 8 percent. The term holder, who is 50 years old, retains a contingent reversion. The value of the residence is $1,000,000. Based on these facts, the value of all interests retained by the term holder on the original date of transfer is $576,280.63. No further transfers to the trust are made.

---

[73] Treas. Reg. § 25.2702-5(c)(8)(ii)(B).

[74] Treas. Reg. §§ 25.2702-5(c)(7)(ii)(C), 25.2702-5(c)(8)(i).

[75] Treas. Reg. § 25.2702-5(c)(8)(ii)(B).

[76] Treas. Reg. § 25.2702-5(c)(8)(ii)(C)(1).

[77] Treas. Reg. § 25.2702-5(c)(8)(ii)(C)(2).

During the term, the residence held by the trust is sold, and no new residence is purchased. Two years later, the assets of the trust are worth $1,200,000. What annuity should be paid to the term holder upon conversion of the trust assets to a qualified annuity interest? This is determined by dividing the lesser of $576,280.63 or $1,200,000 by an annuity factor determined for 10 years at a rate of 8 percent. According to the actuarial tables, the trust should pay the term holder an annuity for the period from the sale of the residence through the end of the term of $88,733.64 (or $85,882.57, if the annuity factor does not take into account the contingent reversion).

Multiple transfer issues. The regulations require that the annuity factor to be used on conversion be determined with reference to the 7520 rate at the time of the original transfer, despite the fact that the regulations contemplate the possibility of more than one transfer to the trust. Is the 7520 rate in effect at the time of each transfer to be used to calculate the annuity to be paid with respect to the portion of the trust associated with that transfer? Is the fair market value of the term holder's entire interest to be redetermined with each addition? This would make the calculation considerably more complicated where more than one transfer to the trust takes place.

Gift on conversion problem. There has been some speculation that, if the house has appreciated at the time of conversion to a GRAT, or if the 7520 rate has increased between the trust's inception and the date of conversion, the conversion formula in the regulations may produce a gift on the date of conversion, unless a provision is added measuring the annuity amount by the value of the trust assets and the 7520 rate as of the conversion date in such a case.[78] This is because a higher 7520 rate or an increase in the value of the trust will produce a larger annuity payment. For example, if use of the 7520 rate as of the conversion date were required, and the 7520 rate at the date of conversion were 9 percent, the amount of the annuity payable to the term holder in the above example would increase from $88,733.64 to $92,718.19.

[ii] Only a portion of trust ceases to be a QPRT. If, on the conversion date, the trust holds a qualifying residence, the annuity must be at least the amount determined in subparagraph [i] above, multiplied by a fraction. The numerator of the fraction is the excess of the fair market value of the trust assets on the conversion date over the fair market value of the assets which the trust can continue to hold in a qualified personal residence trust. The denominator of the fraction is the fair market value of the trust assets on the conversion date.

EXAMPLE: In the above example, suppose that the trust had purchased a $400,000 replacement residence. The remaining $800,000 proceeds from

---

[78] See Priv. Ltr. Rul. 9448035 (Sept. 2, 1994).

the sale of the original residence is converted to a qualified annuity interest. The annuity amount is computed as follows: $88,733.64 \times$ ($1,200,000 − $400,000) / $1,200,000 = $59,155.76$

[8] Cure Through Reformation of Imperfect Trust Instrument

Proposed regulations provide that if a trust instrument fails to contain the required provisions, it will still be treated as complying if the trust is modified by judicial reformation (or nonjudicial reformation if that is effective under state law).[79]

The reformation must be commenced within 90 days after the due date (including extensions) of the gift tax return reporting the transfer of the residence to the trust. It must be completed within a reasonable time after its commencement. If the reformation is not completed by the due date (including extensions) of the gift tax return, the grantor or grantor's spouse must attach a statement to the gift tax return stating that the reformation has been commenced or will be commenced within the 90-day period.[80]

PRACTICE POINTER: It would be wise to include in the trust instrument a provision allowing the trust to be reformed or modified to meet the QPRT requirements.

The effective date of the proposed reformation regulation would be January 18, 1992.[81]

[9] Assignment of Termholder's QPRT Interest

What happens if the termholder-donor assigns his interest in the trust? The IRS has privately ruled that a donor may transfer his retained income interest in a QPRT to another trust (provided the donor retains certain types of rights in the trust) without causing the QPRT to cease to qualify.[82] It is unclear from the ruling whether the trust to which the retained interest was transferred required all income to be paid annually to the transferor.

¶ 21.04 PERSONAL RESIDENCE TRUSTS

The regulations offer the option of "personal residence trusts," in addition to QPRTs. A "personal residence trust" cannot hold anything other than the

---

[79] Prop. Reg. § 25.2702-5(a)(2).

[80] Prop. Reg. § 25.2702-5(a)(2).

[81] Prop. Reg. § 25.2702-7.

[82] Priv. Ltr. Rul. 9315010 (Jan. 13, 1993).

personal residence, and insurance proceeds for a two-year period, during the term of the trust.[83] It is thought that this option was included to avoid the potential invalidation of the QPRT regulations, due to the existence of numerous QPRT requirements and restrictions that are not included in the statute. Like the QPRT, however, the creator of a personal residence trust is also subject to the two-residence limitation,[84] and the rules on use or holding for use as a personal residence.[85]

The trust instrument must prohibit the trust from holding, during the term, any asset other than one residence to be used or held for use as a personal residence of the term holder and "qualified proceeds."[86] "Qualified proceeds" are insurance proceeds payable as a result of damage to, or destruction or involuntary conversion[87] of, the residence held by the trust, provided that the trust instrument requires that the proceeds (including any income thereon) be reinvested in a personal residence within two years from the date of receipt.[88]

A trust is not a personal residence trust if, during the term, the residence may be sold or otherwise transferred by the trust or may be used for a purpose other than as a personal residence of the term holder. Expenses of the trust, whether or not attributable to trust principal, may be paid directly by the term holder of the trust.[89] If they are attributable to principal, they may be gifts or loans.

The reformation provisions applicable to QPRTs also apply to personal residence trusts.[90]

---

[83] Treas. Reg. § 25.2702-5(b).

[84] Treas. Reg. § 25.2702-5(a).

[85] Treas. Reg. § 25.2702-5(b)(2)(iii).

[86] Treas. Reg. § 25.2702-5(b)(1).

[87] Within the meaning of IRC § 1033.

[88] Treas. Reg. § 25.2702-5(b)(3).

[89] Treas. Reg. § 25.2702-5(b)(1).

[90] See ¶ 21.03[8] above.

CHAPTER 22

Grantor Retained Annuity Trusts

¶ 22.01   INTRODUCTION

A grantor retained annuity trust (GRAT) is an estate freezing technique which is specifically authorized by statute and can be a dramatic tax-saver in the right circumstances.[1] The structure of a GRAT is similar to that of a charitable lead annuity trust (CLAT).[2] This chapter discusses how a GRAT works and its advantages, when to use a GRAT and how to structure one in specific situations.

¶ 22.02   OVERVIEW

[1] How a GRAT Works

For our purposes, we'll call the contributor to the GRAT the "grantor." The grantor of a GRAT transfers property to the trust and retains an annuity payable for a term of years or for the shorter of the grantor's life or a term of years.[3] The period for which the grantor retains the annuity is referred to as the "term." This term should be shorter than the grantor's life expectancy. At the end of the term, the trust property will remain in trust for, or pass directly to, the remainder beneficiaries provided in the trust instrument.

---

[1] IRC §§ 2702(a)(2)(B), 2702(b).

[2] Charitable lead trusts are discussed in Ch. 35.

[3] The grantor can also retain an annuity payable for her life; however, since this will never be a good idea, we will not discuss that alternative.

EXAMPLE: Teresa establishes a GRAT with a term of ten years. She contributes a bond with a coupon of 12 percent. The bond's face amount is $1,000,000. She reserves an annuity of 7 percent. Teresa (or her estate, if she dies within the term) will receive $70,000 per year over the 10-year term. At the end of the term, the trust assets will pass to her beneficiary(ies), who could be her children, trusts for her husband or children, any combination of the above, or, indeed, anyone else in the world.

On the initial transfer of the bond to the GRAT, Teresa makes a taxable gift of the value of the remainder interest after the term. The amount of the gift is ordinarily determined under actuarial tables published by the Department of Treasury, and depends on the length of the term (ten years), the amount of the retained annuity (7 percent), and the 7520 rate[4] at the date of transfer. Whether Teresa's age will affect the amount of the gift is an unresolved issue.[5] During the term, the trust will be a grantor trust.[6] Accordingly, Teresa will report the trust's items of income, deduction, gain, loss, and credit on her own income tax return. She is not taxed directly on the annuity that she receives—rather, she is taxable as if she owned the trust assets.

At the end of the 10-year term, the property will pass to the remainder beneficiaries without any further transfer tax (unless they are skip persons, in which case there will be a generation-skipping transfer at the time).

[2] Risk Involved

If Teresa dies during the 10-year term, part or all of the trust property may be includable in her gross estate. If this occurs, she has lost the opportunity to do other estate planning that might have been successful in removing the trust property from her estate.

[3] Reward to Be Gained

Teresa makes a taxable gift of the remainder interest. The gift will ordinarily be valued pursuant to the actuarial tables. The opportunity in the table valuation is that Teresa can transfer to the remainder beneficiaries, free of gift tax, an amount equal to—

---

[4] The "7520 rate" is 120 percent of the applicable federal midterm rate determined under IRC § 7520, rounded to the nearest 2/10ths of one percent. It changes monthly. The applicable federal rate is a function of Treasury obligations. See Chapter 11 for a further discussion.

[5] See ¶ 22.05[2] below.

[6] IRC §§ 673, 677. The IRS may be considering whether Teresa's payment of income tax in excess of the annuity she receives is an impermissible additional contribution to the GRAT if she is not reimbursed by the trust. See discussion at ¶ 22.03[10] below.

- Any excess of the value they actually receive at the end of the term *less*
- The amount they would have received at the end of the term if the trust property had earned the 7520 rate which applied at the time of transfer.

So, the zing in the GRAT is the opportunity to make a tax-free gift of an amount greater than the amount the actuarial tables say is being transferred. That is, the GRAT offers a chance to transfer all of the appreciation in the transferred property in excess of a fixed amount at no or minimal gift tax. Benefits can be spectacular with rapidly appreciating property.

> **EXAMPLE:** Mom owns Private Company stock worth $1,000,000. She transfers the stock to a two-year GRAT with a 60 percent annuity. According to the actuarial tables in effect at the date of transfer, Mom makes no gift. Three months after the transfer, Private Company stock goes public and doubles in value (remaining at that value until the end of the term). At the end of the day, Mom gets back $1,200,000, and her kids get $800,000—all for zero gift tax and no use of unified credit. What if, instead, the stock does not go public or increase in value at all? Mom gets the stock back, and the only thing lost (from a transfer tax perspective) is the opportunity to have used a different technique.

¶ 22.03 STRUCTURE OF TRUST

[1] GRAT or GRUT

The statute allows the trust to be structured as either a GRAT or a grantor retained unitrust (GRUT). In a GRUT, the grantor's unitrust interest would not be a fixed amount, as in the case of an annuity under a GRAT. Rather, it would be a percentage of the value of the trust each year, so that the amount of the grantor's annual payment would float with the value of the trust.

As a practical matter, an individual establishes an estate-freezing trust to transfer as much as possible to the remainder beneficiaries for a given amount of gift tax. Assets that are expected to earn a great deal of income and/or appreciate substantially are chosen to fund the trust, in the hope that as much as possible of that income/appreciation can pass to the remainder beneficiaries. Accordingly, in such a situation it would be counterproductive to do a GRUT, which would increase the grantor's interest with each increase in the value of the trust assets. GRUTs are consequently not discussed further in this chapter.[7]

---

[7] A transferor who needed a stream of cash flow from the property could conceivably do a GRUT if no better estate freezing opportunity were available. The rules applicable to GRUTs are found in Treas. Reg. §§ 25.2702-3(c), 25.2702-3(d).

[2] Payment of Annuity

The annuity must be structured as a "qualified annuity interest," which is an irrevocable right to receive a fixed amount.[8]

[a] Time of Payment

The annuity must be payable to (or for the benefit of) the holder of the annuity interest at least once a year for each taxable year of the term.[9] The annuity payment may be made after the close of the taxable year, provided that it is made by the due date of the trust's federal income tax return for the taxable year (without regard to extensions).[10] This will usually mean that the annuity payment for Year One must be made by April 15 of Year Two.[11] If the annuity is paid more frequently than annually, an adjustment factor must be used in calculating the gift of the remainder interest. The gift will be smaller if the installments are paid more frequently.

[b] Fixed Amount

A "fixed amount" means a stated dollar amount or a fixed fraction or percentage of the initial fair market value of the property transferred to the trust (as finally determined for federal tax purposes). In either case, the amount payable in any year cannot exceed 120 percent of the amount payable in the preceding year.[12]

[c] Graduated Annuity

The regulations permit the annuity to increase by up to 20 percent per year.[13] And, a graduated annuity may be advantageous from a tax perspective, since the trust will have more time in the early years to accumulate funds to pay the later years' annuities and leave a return for the remainder beneficiaries. The tradeoff is that a higher gift tax will be payable with a graduated

---

[8] Treas. Reg. § 25.2702-3(b)(1)(i).

[9] Treas. Reg. § 25.2702-3(b)(1)(i). The holder of the initial annuity interest will always be the grantor or his spouse, since a transfer of both the annuity interest and the remainder interest in property to others results in a gift of the entire property (not actuarially valued); such a transfer does not offer the leveraging opportunities afforded by the retention of an interest which is likely to be worth less than its actuarially determined value.

[10] Treas. Reg. § 25.2702-3(b)(1)(i).

[11] IRC §§ 645(a), 6072(a). It is not clear what the consequences are if an annuity payment is made late. However, why find out?

[12] Treas. Reg. § 25.2702-3(b)(1)(ii).

[13] Treas. Reg. § 25.2702-3(b)(1)(ii).

annuity than with a level annuity of the same total dollars. In such an instance, the value of the gift can be computed as follows:

- *Step 1.* Determine the amounts payable at the end of each year in the term.
- *Step 2.* Determine the present values of the remainder interests after each amount determined in Step 1.
- *Step 3.* Total the amounts determined in Step 2.
- *Step 4.* Subtract the amount determined in Step 3 from the total value transferred to the GRAT.[14]

[d] Income in Excess of the Annuity Amount

A qualified annuity trust may permit income in excess of the annuity to be paid to or for the benefit of the holder of the annuity interest. However, the right to receive the excess income is not a qualified interest, will not increase the value of the grantor's retained annuity interest, and, hence, will not decrease the gift made at the outset.[15]

Since the point of a GRAT is to transfer the maximum amount to the remainder beneficiaries for the minimum gift tax cost, payment of excess income to the grantor will not generally be a desirable provision in a GRAT. Note, however, that the IRS may take the position that paying additional amounts to the grantor in excess of the annuity amount may be necessary for the trust to qualify as a GRAT in certain circumstances.[16]

[e] Incorrect Valuations of Trust Property

If the annuity is stated in terms of a fraction or percentage of the initial fair market value of the trust property, the trust instrument must contain adjustments to the annuity payments for any initially incorrect determination of the fair market value of the property in the trust.[17]

---

[14] Another method for computing the gift is to: (1) determine the annuity factors for a series of increasing annuities payable for a series of increasing terms; (2) discount the annuity factors and add them together; (3) multiply the sum by the amount of the initial annuity; and (4) subtract this amount from the total value transferred to the GRAT. See Ch. 11 for an explanation of how to determine the annuity factor.

[15] Treas. Reg. § 25.2702-3(b)(1)(iii).

[16] See discussion at ¶ 22.03[10] below.

[17] Treas. Reg. § 25.2702-3(b)(2). The required provisions are similar to those described in Treas. Reg. § 1.664-2(a)(1)(iii) for charitable remainder trusts.

[f] Proration of Annuity in Short Year

The trust instrument must prorate the annuity amount in short taxable years (often the first taxable year, and usually the last taxable year, of the term).[18]

[g] Form of Payment

[i] Withdrawal rights. A right of withdrawal, whether or not cumulative, is not a qualified annuity interest.[19]

[ii] Note to grantor/payment with funds borrowed from grantor. Some commentators have suggested that payment of the annuity amount with a note is acceptable. But, where stock contributed to a trust was not income-producing and the annuity was paid with money borrowed from the grantor, the IRS ruled that the trust did not qualify as a GRAT because the annuity was in substance paid with a note. Later, the IRS ruled that a GRAT's foreseeable payment of the annuity amount with a promissory note disqualified the GRAT from its inception.[20] The IRS stated that the trust's note was merely a promise to pay, and not an actual payment of, the annuity. Consequently, according to the IRS, the grantor's interest could not be characterized as a right to receive a fixed amount at least annually, and therefore delivery of the note violated the requirement that the annuity be payable at least once a year.[21]

Could the result be different if the note were negotiable, so that the annuitant received a readily saleable note that could be sold to a bank or unrelated third party in a bona fide and arm's-length transaction? There is no primary authority on this.[22] Some experts think payment with a note may be

---

[18] Treas. Reg. § 25.2702-3(b)(3). The required provision is similar to that described in Treas. Reg. § 1.664-2(a)(1)(iv) for charitable remainder trusts.

[19] Treas. Reg. § 25.2702-3(b)(1)(i).

[20] Tech. Adv. Mem. 9604005 (Oct. 17, 1995); Tech. Adv. Mem. 9717008 (Apr. 25, 1997).

[21] Tech. Adv. Mem. 9604005 (Oct. 17, 1995); Tech. Adv. Mem. 9717008 (Apr. 25, 1997).

[22] But compare Priv. Ltr. Rul. 9515039 (Jan. 17, 1995), involving joint purchases of an annuity and remainder interest (note issued by a trust) remainder owner in satisfaction of the annuity payment would not disqualify the annuity as a qualified interest, where note was payable on demand, interest-bearing, and guaranteed by the remainder owner with full recourse to her own assets, and she, the individual beneficiary of the trust possessed sufficient independent wealth to assure payment; note issued by trust remainder owner alone not permissible because trust held no assets except purchased remainder interest).

all right if the note is negotiable, bears a market rate of interest (which is at least the 7520 rate), is payable on demand, and is secured by the trust assets.[23]

[iii] Payment in kind. The annuity can be payable in kind. If property is delivered in satisfaction of the annuity, a sale has technically taken place; however, no gain or loss should be recognized by the trust, since the IRS does not recognize transactions between a grantor and his grantor trust for income tax purposes.[24]

[3] Additional Contributions Prohibited

The GRAT instrument must prohibit additional contributions to the trust.[25] This requirement should not present a problem unless there is some sort of inadvertent constructive additional contribution, since smart planning will usually entail a one-asset GRAT, anyway.[26]

An example of a constructive additional contribution was contained in Technical Advice Memorandum 9604005.[27] In this GRAT, the payments were in substance funded with a note to the grantor which did not bear interest until the GRAT ceased to be a grantor trust. The IRS characterized the forgone interest each year as additional contributions, which violated the requirement that no additional contributions can be made. The bottom-line is: If a person wants to make another gift to a GRAT, he needs to do another GRAT.

PRACTICE POINTER: To avoid inadvertent contributions, it might be advisable to include a provision that if any additional property is deemed to be contributed to the GRAT, such property will automatically be held in a separate trust.

---

[23] E.g., Blattmachr & Slade, 836 T.M., Partial Interests—GRATs, GRUTs, QPRTs (Section 2702).

[24] Rev. Rul. 85-13, 1985-1 CB 184; Treas. Reg. § 1.1001-2(c), example 5; see also Madorin v. Comm'r, 84 TC 667, 680 (1985); but see Rothstein v. United States, 735 F2d 704 (2d Cir. 1984) (allowing grantor to deduct interest with respect to installment note payable to grantor trust for grantor's purchase of stock originally contributed by grantor, allowing grantor a new basis in stock equal to the purchase price, and allowing trust to elect installment sales treatment on gain).

[25] Treas. Reg. § 25.2702-3(b)(4). This requirement does not apply to GRUTs.

[26] See discussion at ¶ 22.08[3] below. The IRS may take the position that a grantor's unreimbursed payment of income tax on income in excess of his annuity is an impermissible additional contribution to the GRAT. See discussion at ¶ 22.03[10] below.

[27] Oct. 17, 1995.

[4] Amounts Payable to Other Persons

The trust instrument must prohibit distributions to or for the benefit of any person other than the holder of the qualified annuity interest during the term.[28]

[5] Term of the Annuity Interest

The trust instrument must fix the term of the annuity interest. The term must be for (1) the life of the term holder, (2) a specified term of years, or (3) the shorter of these periods.[29] Successive term interests for the benefit of the same individual are treated as the same term interest.[30]

The period chosen should always be a term of years that the grantor is expected to outlive. If the life of the grantor is chosen, part or all of the trust property may inevitably be included in his estate. The longer the term is, the less the value of the remainder beneficiaries' interest will be, meaning that a smaller gift will be made. Conversely, a longer term will increase the likelihood of the grantor's death within the term, therefore increasing the possibility of estate tax inclusion of all or part of the trust property.

In choosing the term, the grantor may want to keep in mind that, actuarially speaking, most of the reduction in value of the remainder interest occurs during the early years of the term (particularly when interest rates are high).

[6] Prohibition of Commutation

The trust instrument must prohibit commutation (prepayment) of the interest of the term holder.[31]

> EXAMPLE: Dad establishes GRAT, retaining a term interest for ten years, with remainder to Daughter. Five years into the term, Dad develops a terminal illness, and is no longer expected to survive the ten-year term. At that date, suppose Dad's actuarial interest in the trust is one-third of the trust value. However, on his death within the term, more than one-third of the GRAT may be included in his estate. Trustee cannot change this result by terminating the trust and paying Dad one-third of the value of the assets. However, it might be possible to reform the trust to provide the same result, with or without court approval, as determined by state law.

---

[28] Treas. Reg. § 25.2702-3(d)(2).

[29] Treas. Reg. § 25.2702-3(d)(3).

[30] Treas. Reg. § 25.2702-3(d)(3).

[31] Treas. Reg. § 25.2702-3(d)(4).

Alternatively, perhaps Dad can sell his interest in the trust to Daughter (or for that matter, to another person) for its actuarial value. Of course, the consideration received for the interest would be includable in Dad's estate, but that would be only one-third of the trust value, rather than the entire value. In order to accomplish this, the GRAT could not be a valid spendthrift trust with respect to Dad, and Dad must have at least a 50 percent chance of living for a year after the date of sale (so that the actuarial tables can be used to value his interest).

[7] Provisions Concerning Grantor's Death During the Term

[a] Contingent Reversion

Retention of a contingent reversion if the grantor dies within the fixed term is permissible, but the contingent reversion will be valued at zero, and will therefore not reduce the initial gift.[32] One must be careful about automatically tossing in contingent reversions, as they will force inclusion of the entire trust in the grantor's estate if he dies during the term. If the grantor does not retain a contingent reversion and dies during the term, only a part of the trust may be included in his gross estate. That part may not be known until his death.[33] Hence, a contingent reversion in the entire trust property may unnecessarily increase the amount included in the grantor's gross estate. A formula limiting the contingent reversion to the amount which would otherwise be included in the grantor's estate, however, should be permissible.

Since a reversion will not reduce the gift made at the outset, and may increase the amount included in the grantor's gross estate if the grantor dies during the term, why would a contingent reversion ever be desirable? A partial contingent reversion may be desirable to give the grantor's estate funds to pay any estate tax imposed as a result of the inclusion of GRAT property in the grantor's estate. Some planners also use a contingent reversion where the GRAT will hold S stock and they want to be sure that the GRAT will be treated as a grantor trust, and therefore a qualified S corporation shareholder.[34] A reversion should not be necessary for that purpose, since a GRAT should be a grantor trust because of the fact that all of the assets theoretically could return to the grantor to make the annuity payments.[35]

[b] Apportionment

The GRAT should be permitted to provide that, if the grantor dies during the term, and thus all or part of the interest is includable in his gross

---

[32] Treas. Reg. § 25.2702-3(e), example 1.

[33] See ¶ 22.06 below.

[34] See ¶ 22.04 below.

[35] IRC § 677.

estate, estate taxes allocable to the trust assets can be paid from the part of the trust which is includable. Such a provision should be permitted because it is a form of contingent reversion, which is clearly permitted.[36] The value of the initial gift to the remainder beneficiaries will not be reduced by such a provision.[37]

[c] Marital Deduction

The trust should be permitted to provide that if the grantor dies during the term, the amount included in the grantor's gross estate passes to the surviving spouse in a form that qualifies for the marital deduction. This provision will not reduce the initial gift.[38]

[8] Trustee

The grantor may act as trustee of the GRAT during the term. After the term, he may continue to act as trustee of a continuing trust for the remainder beneficiaries, in the absence of any state law restriction. Of course, the usual rules with respect to taxation of the assets in the grantor's estate and the income to the grantor (if the grantor-trustee has powers causing such taxation) would apply.[39]

[9] Revocable Spousal Interest

Can the retention of a revocable spousal interest be advantageous in a GRAT? It seems so, although the IRS doesn't agree in all cases.

Suppose Husband retains an interest for the shorter of five years or his life, and the trust provides that if he dies during the five-year term, Wife will

---

[36] Of course, the remainder beneficiaries will usually be members of the grantor's family (i.e., the grantor's spouse, an ancestor or descendant of the grantor or his spouse, a sibling of the grantor or a sibling's spouse). See Treas. Reg. § 25.2702-2(a)(1). If the grantor wanted a charity to be the remainder beneficiary, he would set up a charitable remainder trust instead, and thereby ensure the availability of the charitable deduction. In addition, if the grantor wanted an individual who is not a member of his family to be the remainder beneficiary, IRC § 2702 would not apply, and the intricate rules of the GRAT would not need to be followed. Treas. Reg. § 25.2702-1(a).

[37] See Treas. Reg. § 25.2702-(3)(e), example 1.

[38] Only retained interests can reduce the amount of gift made on creating a GRAT, and a retained interest must be a qualified interest or it will generally be valued at zero. Treas. Reg. § 25.2702-1(b). Providing that any amount included in the grantor's estate will pass, for example, to a QTIP trust for the grantor's spouse does not cnstitute the retention of an interest; the spousal contingent interest would not be a qualified interest in any case. See ¶ 22.03[9] below for a discussion of revocable spousal interests.

[39] These powers and rules are discussed in Ch. 2.

receive the annuity for the remaining part of the five-year period, or for her life, if shorter. However, Husband retains the right to revoke her interest by will. How is this beneficial? If Wife's contingent annuity interest were irrevocable, her interest would be a taxable gift that does not qualify for the marital deduction[40] —definitely a bad result, since this will not decrease the gift made by Husband at the outset and could result in additional property being included in Wife's estate, even though no marital deduction was available for the initial transfer. If Husband, however, retains the right to revoke Wife's qualified interest, he may be treated as having retained her interest,[41] pursuant to an exception to the general rule that revocable interests are valued at zero for purposes of Section 2702. Here, if Wife's revocable interest should be valued according to the actuarial tables for gift tax purposes, it thus would reduce the initial gift to that extent.[42] Giving Wife an interest subject to revocation would result in a smaller gift to the remainder beneficiaries than if the remainder merely took effect on Husband's death within the term, since the existence of Wife's interest will lower the chance that the remainder beneficiary will receive the property before the term expires.

If Husband dies during the term, part or all of the trust assets will be includable in his estate. If the amount includable is to qualify for the marital deduction, Husband must revoke Wife's annuity interest, and either his will (if he retains a contingent reversion) or the GRAT (if he doesn't) must provide a disposition which qualifies for the marital deduction (for example, a QTIP trust to hold any GRAT assets included in Husband's estate). (If Husband does not revoke Wife's interest, the interest will not qualify for the marital deduction since the trust assets will pass to a third party during Wife's life if she outlives the term.)

If Husband outlives the term, the trust assets may have been transferred at a lower gift tax cost than if Husband had been the sole term holder.[43]

If the GRAT term does not end on Husband's death, remaining payments go to Husband's estate if he dies during the term, and Example 5 (discussed below) is correctly determined to be wrong, a spousal provision should not make any difference in the amount of the gift. However, if the IRS successfully maintains its position that the value of Husband's retained inter-

---

[40] This assumes that the gift consisted of Husband's separate property. Of course, a different rule would apply if Wife were also a grantor—for example, on a transfer of community property to a GRAT.

[41] Treas. Reg. § 25.2702-2(a)(5).

[42] See Treas. Reg. § 25.2702-2(d)(1), example 7. This example deals with a non-contingent revocable interest in the spouse—that is, one which does not depend on the grantor's dying.

[43] See, e.g., Priv. Ltr. Rul. 9451056 (Sept. 26, 1994) (three GRATs created; in each case, the value of a right to receive annuity for a term of years or until the prior death of the last to die of two persons constituted over 98 percent of the initial value of the trust principal).

est is always limited to the value of a retained interest for the shorter of the term or his life[44] regardless of whether Husband's estate receives the remaining payments, then a revocable spousal interest may be helpful even with a term not related to Husband's life.

However, the IRS's viewpoint is that Wife's revocable interest will be valued at zero if Wife's interest is contingent on Husband's death within his term.[45] The concern is apparently that the interest, which is contingent rather than fixed, does not exactly fit Example 7 of Treasury Regulation § 25.2702-2(d), and is like a contingent interest in Husband's estate, which would not be given value under Treasury Regulation § 25.2702-3(c), Example 5 (which itself is probably wrong, as discussed at ¶ 22.05[2] below). The IRS's position is that the spousal interest will not reduce the initial gift by Husband, and not that it will disqualify the GRAT.[46]

[10] Payment of Income Taxes on Income in Excess of Annuity

It is understood that the IRS may not rule on the qualification of a GRAT unless the trust instrument provides that the trust will reimburse the grantor for income tax paid on trust taxable income in excess of the annuity amount or the grantor is entitled to the greater of the trust income or the annuity amount. The theory is that the grantor's payment of the tax is an additional contribution, and that (as explained above) additional contributions to a GRAT are prohibited. Many estate planners consider the IRS position unjustified.[47] And, there are signs that the IRS may be reconsidering its position.[48]

¶ 22.04 INCOME TAX CONSEQUENCES OF GRATS

[1] Identity of Taxpayer

The trust's items of income, deduction, gain, loss, and credit should be taxed to the grantor during the term.[49] Section 677 provides that the grantor will be treated as the owner of a trust, if without the approval of any adverse party,

---

[44] See ¶ 22.05[2] below.

[45] Tech. Adv. Mem. 9707001 (Oct. 25, 1996).

[46] Covey, "Practical Drafting" 4432 (U.S. Trust Co. July 1996).

[47] For more on this topic, see Ch. 6 on grantor trusts.

[48] See Priv. Ltr. Rul. 9543049 (Aug. 3, 1995) (modifying Priv. Ltr. Rul. 9444033 (Aug. 5, 1994) by deleting paragraph stating that a provision for reimbursement would be necessary to prevent additional gifts from being made by grantor on paying income tax with respect to income that would otherwise be taxed to the trust).

[49] IRC §§ 673(a), 677(a).

trust income may be distributed to the grantor (or his spouse) or held or accumulated for future distribution to the grantor (or his spouse). Moreover, the Tax Court has held that where the grantor of a trust retains an annuity, the grantor is taxable on the entire income of the trust (including income attributable to corpus, such as capital gains) under circumstances where the entire corpus of the trust could return to the grantor.[50] It is always theoretically possible that all of the assets of a GRAT may return to the grantor during the term, since the value of the assets may decline to an amount less than or equal to that required to make the remaining annuity payments. Hence, a GRAT should always be a grantor trust during the term under Section 677. The IRS has ruled on the grantor trust status of GRATs based solely on Section 677 in a number of circumstances.[51]

A contingent reversion or general power of appointment valued at greater than five percent of the trust can also be used to ensure that a trust will qualify as a grantor trust during the initial term.[52] Using a contingent reversion, however, may have some unwarranted estate tax consequences.[53]

[2] GRAT Holding S Corporation Stock

[a] During the Term

A GRAT can hold S corporation stock, as long as it is a grantor trust.[54] A GRAT will not be a qualified S trust ("QSST") during the term, since the corpus of the trust can be paid to someone other than the term holder during

---

[50] Weigl v. Comm'r, 84 TC 1192, 1228 (1985); Stern v. Comm'r, 77 TC 614, 648 (1981), rev'd on other grounds, 747 F2d 555 (9th Cir. 1984).

[51] Priv. Ltr. Rul. 9444033 (Aug. 5, 1994); Priv. Ltr. Rul. 9448018 (Aug. 12, 1994); Priv. Ltr. Rul. 9451056 (Sept. 26, 1994); Priv. Ltr. Rul. 9449012 (Sept. 9, 1994); Priv. Ltr. Rul. 9449013 (Sept. 9, 1994); Priv. Ltr. Rul. 9504021 (Oct. 28, 1994).

[52] See, e.g., Priv. Ltr. Rul. 9625021 (June 21, 1996) (grantor's wife could pay him income in excess of the annuity amount and grantor had general power of appointment by will over principal during his term); Priv. Ltr. Rul. 9551018 (Sept. 21, 1995); Priv. Ltr. Rul. 9519029 (Feb. 10, 1995) (grantor was entitled to greater of income or annuity amount and had retained contingent reversion); Priv. Ltr. Rul. 9152034 (Sept. 30, 1991) (settlor retained contingent reversion in qualified annuity trust; trust treated as grantor trust under IRC § 673 and therefore qualified as a permitted S corporation shareholder); Tech. Adv. Mem. 9707005 (grantors retained testamentary general power of appointment over trust income during the term of their interest).

[53] See ¶ 22.06 below.

[54] IRC § 1361(c)(2)(A).

the term holder's life.[55] Hence, the GRAT must be a grantor trust to be an eligible shareholder.[56]

[b] After the Term

When a GRAT ceases to be a grantor trust at the end of the term, the S corporation will lose its S status if the GRAT does not turn into a QSST or ESBT at that point. The trust can, however, be drafted so that it will automatically qualify for QSST or ESBT treatment at the end of the term.[57] It is, of course, also possible for a GRAT to continue to qualify as a grantor trust even after the term interest has ceased, under the normal grantor trust rules.[58]

[c] Amendment Powers

Trustees are often given the power or direction to amend trusts designed to qualify as S corporation shareholders, if an amendment is necessary to comply with applicable S corporation rules. Similarly, a trustee of a GRAT may be given the power or direction to amend the trust as necessary to comply with the GRAT rules, although in particular cases (e.g., Private Letter Ruling 9717008 (April 25, 1997)) the amendment may not be respected by the IRS. If such amendment powers are to be given, however, the creator of a GRAT that will hold S corporation stock must decide which amendment power should take precedence in the event that the S corporation and GRAT provisions conflict.[59]

[3] Recognition of Gain or Loss

Since a GRAT is a grantor trust, neither the grantor nor the trust should recognize any gain or loss as a result of (1) the grantor's transfer of property to the trust, (2) the trust's transfer of the property to the grantor in satisfaction

---

[55] IRC § 1361(d)(3)(A)(ii).

[56] A GRAT does not appear to qualify as an ESBT, since all or part of a GRAT is treated as owned by the grantor, rather than the trust.

[57] QSST and ESBT requirements are discussed in Ch. 18.

[58] These rules are discussed in Ch. 6.

[59] See Priv. Ltr. Rul. 9152034 (Sept. 30, 1991) (Trust contained provision directing trustees to amend or reform trust to comply with IRC § 1361(c)(2)(A)(i), and directed trustee to amend or reform trust to comply with IRC § 2702, if this did not conflict with compliance under IRC § 1361(c)(2)(A)(i). IRS indicated that its ruling that trust was a qualified GRAT would no longer apply if trust was reformed or amended and no longer complied with GRAT requirements).

of annuity payments, or (3) the grantor's exchange of cash or other property for stock held by the trust.[60]

¶ 22.05 GIFT TAX CONSEQUENCES OF ESTABLISHING A GRAT

[1] General Rule for Determining Amount of Gift

The grantor's gift of the remainder interest in the trust is ordinarily valued according to the Treasury's actuarial tables in Publication 1457.[61] The gift's value is partly a function of the 7520 rate on the date of the gift. A low 7520 rate at the date of gift will result in a smaller gift than a high 7520 rate would, all other factors being equal.[62] It should be noted that the gift will not qualify for the annual exclusion, since the remainder interest is a future interest.

[2] Annuity Not Terminated by Grantor's Death

The Treasury Regulations are not clear on what value will be placed on the grantor's retained interest if, on the grantor's death during the annuity term, the trust continues making annuity payments to the grantor's estate. The much-discussed *Example 5*,[63] which limits the valuation of such a retained interest to the lesser of the term of years or the grantor's life, is generally thought to be wrong.[64] Why is this?

> EXAMPLE: Dad transfers property to a GRAT, retaining an interest for ten years. The GRAT provides that if Dad dies within the 10-year period, the remainder vests in his children. The retained interest is valued as the right to receive the annuity for the shorter of ten years or Dad's remaining life. This result is unsurprising. However, if (on Dad's death), the remaining payments are to be paid to his estate, one would expect that Dad's interest would be valued as a 10-year term interest. However, according to *Example 5*, the retained interest is still valued as the lesser of a right to receive a qualified annuity until the earlier of the expiration of ten years or Dad's death.[65]

---

[60] E.g., Priv. Ltr. Rul. 9239015 (June 25, 1992).

[61] Table B in the case of a GRAT for a term of years, (assuming Example 5, described below, is wrong), and Table H in the case of a GRAT for the shorter of a term of years or the grantor's life.

[62] See Ch. 11 on the actuarial tables for an explanation of the effect of the 7520 rate on actuarial gifts.

[63] Treas. Reg. § 25.2702-3(c), example 5.

[64] See, e.g., Jerry Kasner, Has the IRS Been Playing Fast and Loose With the Annuity Tables? 62 Tax Notes 1033 (Feb. 21, 1994).

[65] Treas. Reg. § 25.2702-3(e), example 5. A comment on this result, in chess notation: ??.

The IRS takes the position that the estate's right to receive payments after Dad's death is a contingent interest which is valued at zero.[66] According to an IRS ruling, the estate's right is contingent, not fixed and ascertainable, and is not different in substance from a contingent reversion retained by Dad, which would be valued at zero. However, providing that Dad's estate will receive the annuity if Dad dies during the term does not create a contingent reversion in Dad. Rather, it creates a vested right in Dad to receive the annuity in all events during the term. Moreover, other examples in the regulations suggest that this retained interest will be valued as a qualified annuity interest for the entire ten years, leaving the law in a state of complete murkiness.[67] Further clouding the issue, if Dad retains a right to an annuity for ten years, remainder to children, and does not specifically state what happens on his death before the end of the 10-year term, then pursuant to most state laws, the annuity amount will continue to be paid to his estate if he dies during the term.

How much difference does it make anyway? The following charts set out the gifts made for various terms if the valuation is based on the right to receive payments (1) for the entire term and (2) for the term or until the term holder's prior death. The charts assume that the term holder is 60 years old and that the 7520 rate is eight percent.

AMOUNT OF GIFTED REMAINDER INTEREST
AS A PERCENTAGE OF PROPERTY VALUE

Annuity Trust Pays 5 Percent Annually:

Length of Term	Valuation Based on Term of Years	Valuation Based on Shorter of Term of Years or Life
5 years	80.0365	80.7345
10 years	66.4496	68.8655
15 years	57.2027	61.8994
20 years	50.9093	58.0980

Annuity Trust Pays 8 Percent Annually:

Length of Term	Valuation Based on Term of Years	Valuation Based on Shorter of Term of Years or Life
5 years	68.0583	69.1751
10 years	46.3193	50.1848
15 years	31.5242	39.0390
20 years	21.4548	32.9568

---

[66] Tech. Adv. Mem. 9707001 (Oct. 25, 1996).

[67] Treas. Reg. § 25.2702-3(e), examples 2, 3.

Annuity Trust Pays 10 Percent Annually:

Length of Term	Valuation Based on Term of Years	Valuation Based on Shorter of Term of Years or Life
5 years	60.0729	61.4689
10 years	32.8991	37.7310
15 years	14.4053	23.7987
20 years	1.8185	16.1960

[3] Zero-Gift GRAT

The zero-gift GRAT involves the *Example 5* issue. Under this popular technique, property is transferred to a GRAT, but gift tax is not incurred because the annuity is set so that the present value of the grantor's annuity interest is equal to the fair market value of the property transferred. The IRS has ruled that the chance that the grantor might die before the term ends makes it impossible to create a "zeroed-out" GRAT by using that number.[68] If the amount necessary to zero out the gift, determined as if the term were the shorter of the term of years or the grantor's remaining life, must be used, it will take a larger annuity to zero out the GRAT.[69]

> **EXAMPLE:** Hank, who is 55 years old, creates a GRAT with a term of 10 years, at a time when the 7520 rate is 7.8 percent. If the table amount for a 10-year interest is used, Hank may zero out the gift to the GRAT by retaining an annuity of 14.76887 percent. If Hank's retained interest must be valued as a right to receive an annuity for 10 years or until his prior death, Hank must retain an annuity of 15.52173 percent to zero out the gift.

It appears that, if the shorter of the term of years or life is the correct measure, the gifted amount in such a situation would be determined in accordance with the following steps:

- *Step 1.* Determine the number of years it would take for the annuity to

---

[68] Priv. Ltr. Rul. 9239015 (June 25, 1992). Note, however, that the GRAT addressed in this private letter ruling provided the grantor with a right to receive an annuity for a term of years or until the grantor's earlier death; therefore, the valuation rules would in any event have required that the possibility of the grantor's early death be taken into account. See also Rev. Rul. 77-454, 1977-2 CB 351; Treas. Reg. § 25.2702-3(e), examples 1, 5.

[69] This assumes that the use of the actuarial tables to compute the gift is appropriate, as described at ¶ 22.05[4] below.

exhaust the trust assets, assuming that the fund earns income or otherwise grows at the 7520 rate.

- *Step 2.* Determine the annuity factor for an annuity for the shorter of the number of years determined in Step 1 or the remaining lifetime of a person of the grantor's age.
- *Step 3.* Multiply the annuity factor Step 2 by the amount of the retained annuity.
- *Step 4.* Subtract the number determined in Step 3 from the value of the trust—the result is the amount of the gift.[70]

Some have suggested that the IRS's position is that it is impossible to zero out the gift even with the larger annuity number discussed above, which would ordinarily result in a zero gift if the term were the lesser of a term of years or the grantor's life. The theory apparently is that, even with an annuity amount large enough to zero out the gift under the actuarial tables, there is always a chance that the grantor will die during the term, and hence always a chance that he, as a living individual, would not receive the entire value of the trust. Further, so the theory goes, only the amount that the grantor personally receives while he is alive will be given value; ergo, the value of the grantor's interest can never equal the entire trust. Alternatively, the idea is that the estate's interest is contingent, not fixed and ascertainable, and therefore is not a qualified payment (e.g., Technical Advice Memorandum 9707001). Whether or not it is impossible to zero out a GRAT under either of these curious theories, it should be possible to structure a GRAT with a very small initial gift.

If *Example 5*[71] is in fact incorrect, one should be able to use the table values for a 10-year term where annuity payments will continue to be made to the grantor's estate for the balance of the term if the grantor dies during the term.

[4] Limitations on Use of Actuarial Tables

The actuarial tables cannot be used for GRATs under the following circumstances:

Terminally ill measuring life. In certain cases where the term depends on a person's life, and the person has an abbreviated life expectancy as a result of a terminal illness, the tables cannot be used to value the term interest.[72]

---

[70] See Ch. 11 for a discussion of the actuarial tables. This computational approach was blessed in Estate of Shapiro v. Comm'r, 1993 RIA TC Memo. ¶ 93,483, 67 TCM 1067 (1993).

[71] Treas. Reg. § 25.2702-3(e), example 5.

[72] Treas. Reg. §§ 20.7520-3(b)(3)(i), 25.7520-3(b)(3). See Ch. 11 for a discussion.

Annuity rate greater than 7520 rate. Also, if the annuity amount (as a percentage of the initial value of the property) is greater than the 7520 rate at the inception of the trust, the principal will be assumed to gradually exhaust. If the trust, under that assumption, would not be able to pay all of the annuity payments, a special computation must be used.[73]

Annuity for years. Subparagraph [3] above also discusses a debatable regulatory position that a grantor who retains the right to receive an annuity for a term of years is treated as retaining the right to receive the annuity for the lesser of a term of years or life.

Nonconforming trust provisions. The actuarial tables cannot be used unless the effect of the administrative and dispositive provisions of the trust is to assure that the property will be adequately preserved and protected (e.g., from erosion, invasion, depletion, or damage) until the remainder or reversionary interest takes effect in possession and enjoyment.[74]

Before the Section 7520 regulations were promulgated, the IRS had ruled that unusual investment discretion granted to the trustee (e.g., the power to invest in highly speculative assets without regard to the preservation of principal) might substantially increase the risk of loss to the trust. Accordingly, the trust was deemed to be inadequately funded to make the payments for the entire term of the trust, and the actuarial tables were unavailable to value the interests.[75] The regulations (which, for this purpose, were effective for transfers made after December 13, 1995) did not expressly incorporate this requirement with respect to annuity interests, although there is some protective language regarding income and remainder interests.[76]

[5] Gift-Splitting

If the grantor and his spouse split a gift to the GRAT, and all or part of the GRAT is included in the grantor's estate, the spouse's unified credit and run-up the brackets will not be restored for gift tax purposes. Moreover, they will only be restored for estate tax purposes if the property is included in the grantor's estate under Section 2035.[77]

---

[73] See Treas. Reg. §§ 20.7520-3(b)(2)(i), 25.7520-3(b)(2)(i), 25.7520-3(b)(2)(v), example 5. See also Estate of Shapiro v. Comm'r, 1993 RIA TC Memo. ¶ 93,483, 67 TCM 1067 (1993), and Rev. Rul. 77-454, 1977-2 CB 351.

[74] Treas. Reg. §§ 1.7520-3(b)(2)(iii), 20.7520-3(b)(2)(iii), 25.7520-3(b)(2)(iii).

[75] See Priv. Ltr. Rul. 9543049 (Aug. 5, 1994); Priv. Ltr. Rul. 9444033 (Aug. 5, 1994); Priv. Ltr. Rul. 9248016 (Aug. 31, 1992).

[76] Treas. Reg. §§ 1.7520-3(b)(2)(i)-(iii), 20.7520-3(b)(2)(i)-(iii), 25.7520-3(b)(2)(i)-(iii).

[77] See Ch. 8 for a discussion. In this regard, IRC § 2035 brings in certain transfers which are or would have been included in the decedent's estate if he had retained them under IRC §§ 2036, 2037, 2038, or 2042 (not § 2039). IRC § 2035(d)(2).

[6] Payment of Income Tax as Gift

As noted above, a GRAT should be a grantor trust during the term. The IRS took the view in a private ruling that the grantor's payment of income tax on trust income in excess of the annuity amount in the year in question constitutes a gift to the trust if the grantor does not retain a right to be reimbursed by the trust.[78] The paragraph espousing this view was, however, subsequently withdrawn from the ruling.[79]

[7] Annual Exclusion

A gift of the remainder interest in a GRAT will not qualify for the gift tax annual exclusion, since it will not be a present interest.[80]

¶ 22.06 ESTATE TAX CONSEQUENCES

If the grantor dies within the term, some, all, or none of the trust assets may be included in his gross estate. Intriguingly, there is authority for all three positions.

[1] None of the Trust Is Included (Except Under Section 2033)

The Seventh Circuit, reversing the Tax Court, has held that no part of a trust was includable in the estate of a grantor who retained an annuity for life.[81] The Seventh Circuit's theory was that the retention of an annuity is not the equivalent of the retention of an income interest under Section 2036.

The GRAT may give rights to the remaining annuity to the grantor's estate if he dies within the term. Even if none of the trust is included in the grantor's estate under Section 2036, the present value of any payments the estate is actually entitled to receive from the GRAT would be included in the grantor's gross estate under Section 2033.

[2] Part of the Trust Is Included

Support for this position may be found in authority concerning charitable remainder trusts. The IRS has an official position, stated in Revenue Ruling

---

[78] Priv. Ltr. Rul. 9444033 (Aug. 5, 1994).

[79] Priv. Ltr. Rul. 9543049 (Aug. 3, 1995).

[80] IRC § 2503.

[81] Estate of Maria Becklenberg v. Comm'r, 273 F2d 297, 301 (7th Cir. 1959), rev'g 31 TC 402.

82-105,[82] on the amount includable in the grantor's estate when the deceased grantor of a charitable remainder annuity trust retained an annuity for life. The amount includable in his gross estate under Section 2036(a)(1) is that portion of the trust property that would generate the income necessary to produce the annuity for the lifetime of a person of the grantor's age immediately before his death, using the discount rate in effect at the grantor's death.[83]

The formula to determine that portion of the property is:

$$\frac{\text{annuity rate (as a percentage of date of death trust value)}}{\text{7520 rate at date of death}} \times \text{value of trust at date of death} = \text{amount includable in the gross estate under Section 2036}$$

Under this formula, the amount includable in the estate is determined by the 7520 rate existing at the grantor's death, rather than at the date the contribution to the trust was made. As a result, less than full inclusion will occur when the payout rate at the date of the grantor's death (as a percentage of the value of the trust on that date) is less than the 7520 rate then in effect.

> EXAMPLE: In Year One, Dad transfers $1,000,000 to a charitable remainder annuity trust which pays him eight percent of the initial fair market value of the trust, or $80,000, for life. At the time, the 7520 rate is nine percent. Six years later, Dad dies. At that time the property in the trust is worth $1,600,000, and the annuity ($80,000) is therefore five percent of the estate tax value of the trust. The 7520 rate at that time is eight percent. Only five-eighths of the trust, or $1,000,000, will be includable in Dad's estate (5 percent ÷ 8 percent).

The same rule was also applied by the IRS in a private letter ruling dealing with the establishment of a settlement trust providing a life annuity to the grantor.[84]

Although the above formula could result in a fraction greater than one, the maximum amount of estate inclusion, of course, is the value of the trust at the date of grantor's death, or alternate valuation date, if applicable.

Revenue Ruling 82-105 addresses the amount includable if the grantor retains an annuity for life. A GRAT will typically not have a life annuity, but a term of years. Does it make any difference if the grantor retains an annuity for a term of years and dies within the term? The Tax Court has ruled on at least one occasion that the portion of trust property required to yield retained annuity payments for the remainder of the transferor's life expectancy imme-

---

[82] 1982-1 CB 133.

[83] Rev. Rul. 82-105, 1982-1 CB 133.

[84] Priv. Ltr. Rul. 9638036 (June 24, 1996).

diately before his death was includable in the grantor's estate, even though the right to the annuity was limited to a term of years.[85]

> EXAMPLE: *A* establishes a GRAT, retaining an annuity of $10,000 for 20 years. Nineteen years have passed when *A* dies. The 7520 rate is 6 percent on *A*'s death. If the *Pardee* case is correct, the amount includable in *A*'s estate would be the lesser of $10,000/6 percent (i.e., $166,667) or the value of the trust property, and not the remaining amount that *A*'s estate actually has the right to receive, namely, $10,000 after one year has elapsed.

[3] Entire Trust Is Includable

The IRS position is apparently that the entire amount of a GRAT is includable in the estate of the grantor who dies within the term under Section 2039.[86] Section 2039 includes the value of any annuity or other payment receivable by any beneficiary by reason of surviving the decedent, if, under the agreement, an annuity or other payment was payable to the decedent. The IRS position may not be supportable for a GRAT for a term of years which provides that the grantor's estate receives the balance of the payments if the grantor dies within the term, since, in that case, no trust beneficiary receives payments as a result of surviving the decedent.

¶ 22.07 GENERATION-SKIPPING TRANSFER TAX CONSEQUENCES

The grantor cannot effectively allocate his generation-skipping transfer tax exemption to a trust until the trust would no longer be includable in his estate or his spouse's estate if either of them died, except pursuant to Section 2035 (the three-year rule).[87] Since the amount that will be includable in the estate of the grantor as a result of establishing a GRAT may be unknown until the earlier of the end of the term or the grantor's death, it is unclear how this concept applies to a GRAT.

If the remainder interest passes to the grantor's grandchildren (or any other skip person), the ultimate transfer to the skip persons at the end of the term will be a taxable termination rather than a direct skip.[88] If the remainder passes to them as a result of the grantor's death during the term, then the

---

[85] Estate of Pardee v. Comm'r, 49 TC 140, 150 (1967), acq., 1973-2 CB 3.

[86] Priv. Ltr. Rul. 9451056 (Sept. 26, 1994); Priv. Ltr. Rul. 9345035 (Aug. 13, 1993).

[87] IRC § 2642(f).

[88] IRC § 2612.

transfer will be a direct skip to the extent that the property is included in the grantor's estate.[89]

¶ 22.08 FINAL THOUGHTS AND POINTERS ON THE USE OF GRATS

[1] GRAT or Outright Gift of Value of Remainder Interest?

If the gifted property has a lower rate of return than the 7520 rate, an immediate gift of an amount equal to the value of the remainder interest will be more advantageous than a GRAT, using consistent assumptions.

> EXAMPLE: Jeff, who is 85 years old, owns a family business that generally earns five percent annually. Jeff is considering transferring a 20 percent interest in the business, valued at approximately $250,000, to a GRAT in January of Year One, when the 7520 rate is 9.6 percent. The GRAT will pay an annuity of five percent for five years. Jeff's gift to the remainder beneficiaries would be $202,127.50. If the assets actually grew at 9.6 percent per year, and paid the five percent annuity to Jeff, Jeff would receive a total of $62,500 and the beneficiaries would have $319,651.69 at the end of the term.
>
> If Jeff transfers the 20 percent interest to the GRAT, and the business continues to earn five percent per year, he will still make an initial gift of $202,127.50. He will still receive a total of $62,500 during the term. At the end of the five-year term, however, the amount passing to the remainder beneficiaries will be $250,000.
>
> On the other hand, if Jeff instead immediately transfers outright an amount equal to the value of the remainder interest, he will make a gift of $202,127.50, and pay the same amount of gift tax. He will receive no annuity, and at the end of five years the amount which has passed to the remainder beneficiaries will be $257,971.60 ($202,127.50 + 5 percent of $202,127.50 compounded for 5 years).

Where trust assets generate a return below the 7520 rate, the outright gift of an amount equal to the value of the remainder interest will always be a better option (just considering taxes), because part of the portion of the GRAT that comprises the taxable gift will end up being used to pay the grantor's annuity. The reverse is true if the assets earn more than the 7520 rate.

> EXAMPLE: Assume the same facts as the preceding example, except that Jeff's business generally earns 15 percent annually. Jeff's transfer to the GRAT will still result in a gift of $202,127.50. However, at the end of the 5-year term, the remainder beneficiaries will have $418,559.53. If Jeff had given the beneficiaries $202,127.50 at the outset, then, after five years, they would have only $406,550.60—less than they would have had after

---

[89] Treas. Reg. § 26.2632-1(c)(4).

the GRAT term. This difference comes about because the remainder interest is valued for gift tax purposes at less than its real value.

Intuitively, one can see that a grantor's gift will be correctly valued (in the sense that he will pay gift tax on exactly the amount the beneficiaries receive) if the property earns exactly the 7520 rate. If the property actually earns more than the 7520 rate, there will be more for the remainder beneficiaries, and the grantor will not pay gift tax on that additional value. If the property actually earns less than the 7520 rate, part of the earnings, or even principal, which was supposed to go to the remainder beneficiaries according to the gift tax computations, will be returned to the grantor.

[2] Short-Term GRATs

An advantageous approach is the establishment of a two-year zeroed-out GRAT. A two-year zeroed-out (or almost zeroed-out) GRAT will have a high annuity payment. If the grantor likes, he can use the annuity payments received from each GRAT to create successive two-year zeroed-out GRATs for as long as desired. The short-term GRAT approach reduces the risk of adverse estate tax consequences due to the grantor's death during the term, and reduces the risk of income and appreciation from high-performance years having to subsidize the annuity in low-performance years. It is understood that the IRS will not issue a ruling on a short-term GRAT.

[3] One-Investment GRATs

Use of one investment per GRAT is wise, as the effect of an investment which does not earn as much as expected can be limited to the single GRAT that holds it, and high-performing investments in the other GRATs will not be required to compensate for the poor performers.

[4] Discounts and GRATs

GRATs may be extremely effective when the grantor's interest in a business is transferred and valuation discounts are applicable.

EXAMPLE: Wayne is a partner in a limited partnership with a total value of $5 million. The partnership assets typically grow at an annual rate of $7^1/_2$ percent. In Year One, when the 7520 rate is 9.6 percent, Wayne transfers a 60 percent limited partnership interest to a GRAT with an annuity term of ten years and an annuity rate of 8 percent. The transferred interest is valued for gift tax purposes at $2 million, after a $33^1/_3$ percent discount for lack of control and lack of marketability is applied. The discount means that rather than receiving a $240,000 annuity each year, Wayne will receive a $160,000 annuity. In addition, Wayne has made a taxable gift of $999,746, rather than the gift of $1,499,619 that he would have made had no discounts been applicable, for a gift tax savings of nearly $500,000.

The partnership was a sensible step from a transfer tax perspective. Had no discounts been applicable, part of Wayne's annuity would have had to be paid from the part of the GRAT that was treated as a gift at the time of the transfer, because the 7520 rate is higher than the rate of growth of the undiscounted value of the partnership assets. The fact that the annuity rate is also higher than the rate of growth of the undiscounted value of the partnership assets exacerbates this problem. With the discounts, Wayne receives an annuity of 8 percent, which is effectively an annuity of $5^1/_3$ percent of the undiscounted value of what he transferred to the GRAT. Moreover, a growth rate of $7^1/_2$ percent of the undiscounted value of the partnership ends up being a growth rate of $11^1/_4$ percent of the discounted value—well above the 7520 rate.

In a 1997 private letter ruling,[90] involving transfers of nonpublicly traded limited partnership to GRATs, it appears that a representation was required that the partnership interests gift tax value was determined without regard to discounts for lack of control.

---

[90] Priv. Ltr. Rul. 970727.

Private Annuities

¶ 23.01 INTRODUCTION

A private annuity is a transaction in which one individual sells another individual[1] an item of property in exchange for an annuity, often measured by the seller's lifetime.

The annuity must be unsecured to avoid immediate taxation of gain arising from the sale.[2] The seller can retain no interest in the transferred property, nor should payment of the annuity be tied to income from the property.[3]

Additionally, whether the sale is to an individual or a trust, the annuity should be payable with full recourse to the obligor's independent assets. If the annuity is only payable out of the transferred property, there is too much danger that the annuity will be recharacterized as an interest in the transferred property. Thus, the purchaser should be liable for payment of the annuity even if the transferred property is exhausted in paying the annuity, and he should be in a financial position to be able to pay the annuity.[4]

The following global example will be used throughout this chapter to explain the effects of a private annuity.

GLOBAL EXAMPLE

Mom sells Blackacre to Son in exchange for Son's promise to pay her $100,000 per year for her remaining life. At the time of the sale, Mom is 51 years old, and the 7520 rate[5] is 8.2 percent.

---

[1] A private annuity can also be transacted with an entity. Such a transaction is subject to special rules and is discussed at ¶ 23.07 below. An annuity can also be paid in reurn for cash.

[2] If the annuity payments are secured, the transaction will be treated as a commercial annuity, subject to immediate tax on the gain on the property sold. Bell v. Comm'r, 60 TC 469 (1973).

[3] IRC § 2036; see also Ray v. United States, 762 F2d 1361 (9th Cir. 1985); Lazarus v. Comm'r, 513 F2d 824 (9th Cir. 1975), aff'g 58 TC 854 (1972), acq., 1973-2 CB 2.

[4] Estate of Mitchell v. Comm'r, 1982 PH TC Memo. ¶ 82,185, 43 TCM (CCH) 1034 (1982).

[5] The "7520 rate" is 120 percent of the applicable federal midterm rate, rounded to the nearest 2/10 of one percent. IRC § 7520. The 7520 rate and its ramifications are discussed more fully in Ch. 11.

[1] Overview of Transfer Tax Consequences

If the value of Son's promise (according to the tables issued under Section 7520) equals the value of Blackacre, Mom does not make a gift. When Mom dies, nothing is included in her estate.

GLOBAL EXAMPLE

According to the tables, the actuarial value of Mom's annuity is $999,450. If the fair market value of Blackacre is $999,450, Mom should not be deemed to have made a gift and Blackacre should not be included in Mom's estate.

---

[2] Benefits

The actuarial tables[8] are key in deciding whether to use a private annuity. When are private annuities likely to be a good deal? Primarily, in the following circumstances—

When assets perform better than 7520 rate. If the transferred asset is expected to outperform the 7520 rate at the date of the sale, a private annuity will be expected to be a successful estate freeze.

GLOBAL EXAMPLE

Blackacre's value is increasing by 10 percent each year. If Blackacre is worth $999,450 at the time the private annuity transaction is entered into, and Mom lives for 5 years, she will have excluded property worth $1,609,624 from her estate at the cost of including $589,004 in her estate (assuming Mom reinvested each of her $100,000 annuity payments and earned the 7520 rate (8.2 percent)).

When the annuitant has a shorter life expectancy than indicated in the actuarial tables. The other situation that calls for consideration of a private annuity is one in which a person is not expected to live for his full life

---

[8] The tables are found in Publications 1457 (Alpha Volume) and 1458 (Beta Volume).

expectancy, but whose life expectancy may still be valued under the actuarial tables.[7]

A determination of whether Mom has made a gift on the initial sale will depend partly on her life expectancy at the time. For instance, suppose, in the Global Example, that Blackacre is worth $3,997,800 and Mom sells it to Son in exchange for an annuity of $400,000/year for Mom's life. Mom's life expectancy according to the tables is thirty years, but she has an advanced case of diabetes and is actually expected to live for five years. Mom is still eligible to use the tables. However, the probability is that only five payments will be made. If, in fact, Mom dies after receiving only five payments, Mom will have made a transfer-tax-free gift of $1,997,800 ($3,997,800 less $2,000,000)—a stunning estate planning result.

There does reach a point at which an unhealthy seller cannot use the actuarial tables. According to the regulations, the actuarial tables cannot be used if there is at least a 50 percent chance that the taxpayer will die within a year, due to his affliction with a terminal illness or condition.[8] Hence, the private annuity is not a deathbed technique. Rather, it should be considered in situations in which the seller's life expectancy is shorter than normal, but more than one year.

When the annuitant needs income. A third situation could exist if, for personal financial reasons, the seller cannot surrender the property sold without receiving an income. In such a situation, the private annuity would need to be compared to similar techniques that can provide an income stream to the seller.

¶ 23.02 GIFT TAX CONSEQUENCES

Does Mom make a gift when she sells property in exchange for a private annuity? Here's how we tell: we compare the present value of all payments expected to be made under the annuity contract with the fair market value of Blackacre. The actuarial tables issued under Section 7520 are used in ordinary circumstances. Adjustments are provided if the annuity is payable at the beginning of a period, or if payments are made more frequently than annually.[9] Annuities with bells and whistles (indexing, refund features, e.g.) are valued according to their actual fair market values based on the facts and circumstances.[10] If Blackacre is worth $4,000,000, and the present value of the

---

[7] See Ch. 11 for a discussion of when the tables cannot be used due to a person's poor health. This chapter assumes that the tables can be used unless specifically noted otherwise.

[8] Treas. Reg. §§ 20.7520-3(b)(i), 25.7520-3(b)(3). See Ch. 11 on the actuarial tables for an extensive discussion.

[9] Table K, Publication 1457 (Alpha Volume).

[10] Treas. Reg. §§ 20.7520-3(b)(1)(iii), 25.7520-3(b)(1)(iii).

expected payments is also $4,000,000, there is no gift. If there is a gift element, it will be the excess of Blackacre's value over the present value of the annuity.

In order for no gift to occur, annual payments will need to be higher than they would have been under an installment sale for a term exactly equaling Mom's life expectancy. This is so because we must account for the possibility that Mom will die during the term and for the fact that the annuity is discounted at the Section 7520 rate, whereas with an installment note, we can use the applicable federal rate. (Generally, 120 percent of the federal mid-term rate will be greater than 100 percent of the short-term or long-term rates.)

¶ 23.03 ESTATE TAX CONSEQUENCES FOR ANNUITANT-SELLER

If no gift is made at the outset, and the annuity terminates on Mom's death, the original property that Mom sold in exchange for the annuity will not be includable in Mom's estate at her death, since her interest vanishes at that time. However, any annuity payments (and income or appreciation) which Mom has received but not consumed will be includable in her estate. If the private annuity agreement contemplates payments to a beneficiary who survives Mom, the value of the remaining payments due to the beneficiary will be includable in Mom's estate.[11]

If there was a gift element in the transaction, and Mom dies within three years of the sale, the value of any gift tax payable with respect to the gifted portion of property will be included in the value of Mom's gross estate.[12] The gifted property should not be included in Mom's estate unless she is deemed to have retained an annuity or income interest in the property itself.[13]

¶ 23.04 INCOME TAX CONSEQUENCES TO THE SELLER

The income tax consequences of a private annuity are complicated and somewhat unfavorable to the person responsible for paying the annuity (the buyer). The income tax consequences for the seller are determined by reference to the actuarial tables issued under Section 72, which are different from the Section 7520 tables.[14]

---

[11] IRC § 2039.

[12] IRC § 2035(c).

[13] Of course, the property could also be included in Mom's estate if the annuity were a sham. See, e.g., Horstmier v. Comm'r, 1983 PH TC Memo. ¶ 83,409, 46 TCM (CCH) 738, 756 (1983), aff'd, 776 F2d 1052 (9th Cir. 1985).

[14] IRC § 72; Rev. Rul. 69-74, 1969-1 CB 43; see also Treas. Reg. §§ 20.7520-3(a)(2), 25.7520-3(a)(2).

A private annuity contract is not generally subject to the original issue discount rules.[15] The IRS has issued proposed regulations addressing the subject.[16] An annuity contract under which payments are wholly contingent on the continued life of an individual generally is not a debt instrument for federal income tax purposes.[17] Even if the payments are not wholly contingent on an individual's life, an annuity contract qualifies for the exception from the definition of a debt instrument if all payments under the contract are periodic payments that (1) are made at least annually for the life or lives of one or more individuals, (2) do not increase at any time during the term of the contract, and (3) are part of a series of payments that begins within one year of the date of the initial investment in the contract.

Under the rules of Section 72, Mom will recognize income as she receives annuity payments. A formula is used to determine how much of each payment is principal, capital gain, and income.[18] After Mom has received enough principal to recover her basis in the property, the remaining payments are taxable as income.[19]

[1] Formula Determining Income Tax Consequences to Seller

The income tax consequences to Mom are set out in Revenue Ruling 69-74[20] and Section 72. Each payment is divided into three elements: recovery of basis, gain, and interest (called the annuity element).

[2] Basis Recovery Element

[a] Revenue Ruling 69-74

Revenue Ruling 69-74 provides that the portion of each payment which will be treated as a nontaxable recovery of basis (the "excluded portion") is the "investment in the contract" divided by the "expected return on the contract." Under the ruling, the "investment in the contract" is the adjusted basis of the property sold (or the present value of the annuity, if less than the basis).[21] The "expected return" is obtained from the annuity tables under

---

[15] IRC § 1275(a)(1)(B)(i).

[16] Prop. Reg. § 1.1275-1(d)(2), to be effective for annuity contracts bought after April 6, 1995 and held on or after the date 30 days after final regulations are published in the Federal Register.

[17] Preamble to Proposed Reg. § 1.1275-1(d)(2) (Apr. 7, 1995).

[18] IRC § 72. See Ch. 13 on income taxation of annuities.

[19] IRC § 72(b)(2).

[20] 1969-1 CB 43.

[21] LaFargue v. Comm'r, 800 F2d 936 (9th Cir. 1986), aff'g 1985 PH Memo. ¶ 85,090 (1985).

Section 72 by multiplying one year's annuity payments by the life expectancy multiple provided in Table V under Treasury Regulation § 1.72-9 (or Table I for annuities entered into before July 1986). If the annuity starting date is in 1987 or later, the excluded portion is excluded from each annuity payment until the investment in the contract is recovered. Then, the portion formerly excludable is included as ordinary income.[22]

GLOBAL EXAMPLE

Suppose that, under the facts of the Global Example, the investment in the contract is $600,000. The expected return is $3,220,000. According to the formula, $600,000/$3,220,000, or about 18.634 percent of each $100,000 payment (i.e., $18,634) is treated as a recovery of basis until the total basis has been recovered. After that point, that 18.634 percent will be treated as income.

---

[b] Case Law

In *Bell v. Commissioner*,[23] the Tax Court said that the investment in the contract was the fair market value of the property sold (not the basis), unless there was a gift. In the *Bell* case, there was a gift, and the court held that the investment in the contract was therefore the present value of the annuity received in exchange for the property. The court found that the principles of Revenue Ruling 69-74[24] did not apply because the annuity in *Bell* was secured.

The case of *212 Corp. v. Commissioner*[25] also involved a secured private annuity, so that Revenue Ruling 69-74 was not strictly tested. There was no gift element in the transaction, and the Tax Court held that the investment in the contract was therefore the fair market value of the property. In both *Bell* and *212 Corp.*, the gain was recognized in the year of transfer.

The Court of Claims and Federal Circuit have upheld Revenue Ruling 69-74 in a case involving an unsecured annuity.[26]

---

[22] IRC § 72(b)(2).

[23] 60 TC 469 (1973).

[24] 1969-1 CB 43.

[25] 70 TC 788 (1978).

[26] Garvey, Inc. v. United States, 726 F2d 1569 (Fed. Cir. 1984), cert. denied, 469 US 823 (1984), aff'g 1 Cl. Ct. 108 (1983).

[3] Gain Element

Continuing with the formula in Revenue Ruling 69-74,[27] the capital gain portion of a payment is the amount of gain divided by the annuitant's life expectancy on the date of the sale. The amount of gain is the excess of the present value of the annuity over the adjusted basis of the property. The present value of the annuity is determined by the estate and gift tax tables.[28] The life expectancy of the annuitant is obtained from Table I or Table V of the income tax annuity tables.[29] This portion is reportable as capital gain until the total amount of gain has been received, which will be at the expiration of the annuitant's life expectancy at the date of transfer. Thereafter, the gain portion is taxed as ordinary income.

GLOBAL EXAMPLE

In Mom's case, the present value of an annuity of $100,000 for Mom's life is $999,450. The adjusted basis of the transferred property is $600,000. The gain is $999,450 less $600,000, or $399,450. Mom's life expectancy is 32.2 years. So, the gain reported each year is $399,450/32.2, or $12,405, until the $399,450 is recovered (32.2 years). Then, this portion of the payment will be reported as income.

---

[4] Interest Element

The remaining portion of each payment is treated as ordinary income from the start to the finish.

[5] Gift Element

If there is a gift element in the annuity, the gift will be considered made on the date of sale. The gift will reduce the gain element thereafter present in each payment, as the present value of the annuity will be less than it would have been if no gift had been made (in which case the present value of the annuity would have equaled the fair market value of the property). Since Mom will take the whole value of the expected return into account in determining her

---

[27] 1969-1 CB 43.

[28] Rev. Rul. 69-74, 1969-1 CB 43. These are the tables issued under IRC § 7520 for annuities entered into after April 30, 1989.

[29] Treas. Reg. § 1.72-9.

recovery of basis, her ordinary income will be relatively larger and her gain will be relatively smaller than it would have been if the transaction had been made at fair market value.

> **EXAMPLE:** Assume Blackacre is worth $999,450, Mom's adjusted basis in Blackacre is $600,000, Mom is 51 years old and the 7520 rate is 8.2 percent. If Mom sells Blackacre to Son in return for an annuity of $100,000 per year for the rest of Mom's life, so that no gift is deemed to have been made, each annuity payment (before basis is fully recovered) would consist of: $18,634 in recovery of basis;[30] $12,405 in gain;[31] and $68,961 in ordinary income. On the other hand, if Mom sells Blackacre to Son in return for an annuity of $75,000 per year for the rest of Mom's life, so that a gift is deemed to have been made, each annuity payment (before basis is fully recovered) would consist of: $18,634 in recovery of basis;[32] $4,646 in gain;[33] and $51,720 in ordinary income.

[6] Recognition of Losses on Annuity Sales

[a] Sale of Depreciated Property

If the property Mom sells to Son is depreciated (i.e., its basis exceeds its value) and the value of the annuity is equal to or less than the basis of the property, she realizes an immediate loss. Since Son is a related party, she cannot recognize the loss.[34] Son can use the loss later if he sells the property for an amount greater than the fair market value of the property on date of sale.[35]

[b] Additional Loss for Failure to Recover Investment in Contract

If Mom dies before recovering her investment in the contract, a loss can be taken on her final income tax return.[36]

---

[30] [Mom's $600,000 adjusted basis divided by the total expected return [32.2 (i.e., Mom's life expectancy under Table V times $100,000)], times the annuity payment ($100,000).

[31] [The present value of Mom's annuity ($999,450), less Mom's adjusted basis ($600,000), with the difference divided by Mom's life expectancy (32.2)], times the annuity payment ($100,000).

[32] [Mom's adjusted basis ($600,000) divided by the total expected return (32.2 times $75,000)], times the annuity payment ($75,000).

[33] The present value of Mom's annuity ($749,587.50) less Mom's adjusted basis ($600,000), with the difference divided by Mom's life expectancy (32.2).

[34] IRC § 267(b).

[35] IRC § 267(d).

[36] IRC § 72(b)(3).

[c] Loss on Nonpayment of Annuity

What if Son becomes unable to make the annuity payments? Two courts have held that a capital loss to Mom results.[37]

¶ 23.05 INCOME TAX CONSEQUENCES TO THE BUYER

[1] While Seller and Buyer Are Alive

As mentioned above, the tax consequences of a private annuity are not favorable to the buyer. The first of these adverse consequences concerns the buyer's basis in the purchased property. For example, in a sale by Mom to Son in exchange for a private annuity, Son does not receive a new basis in the purchased property immediately, as the buyer in an installment sale does. Rather, his basis at any time is the amount of the payments he has actually made.[38] Another adverse tax effect is that the element taxed to Mom as interest is not deductible as interest by Son. No portion of Son's payments are deductible, as the payments are considered a capital expenditure by him.[39] However, because no portion of the annuity payment is treated as interest as to Son, Son does not have to withhold tax on annuity payments to Mom, unless Mom is a non-resident alien.[40]

[2] Death of Seller

When Mom dies, and the annuity terminates, Son's basis in the property is limited to the payments that he actually made, adjusted, of course, for depreciation or similar deductions taken by Son.

---

[37] McIngvale v. Comm'r, 936 F2d 833 (5th Cir. 1991), aff'g 1990 PH TC Memo. ¶ 90,340, 60 TCM (CCH) 53 (1990).

[38] Determining Son's basis when Son has not yet disposed of the property is primarily important if the property is depreciable, depletable, or amortizable and Son wishes to take deductions.

[39] E.g., Dix v. Comm'r, 392 F2d 313 (4th Cir. 1968); Rye v. United States, 25 Cl. Ct. 592 (1992); Garvey, Inc. v. United States, 1 Cl. Ct. 108 (1983), aff'd 726 F2d 1569 (Fed. Cir.), cert. denied, 469 US 823 (1984) and cases cited therein; Bell v. Comm'r, 76 TC 232 (1981), aff'd per curiam, 668 F2d 448 (8th Cir. 1982); but see Moore Corp. v. Comm'r, 15 BTA 1140 (1929), aff'd, 42 F3d 186 (2d Cir. 1930) (allowing deduction of imputed interest; held to have been repudiated as stated in *Garvey*).

[40] IRC § 1441.

PRACTICE POINTER: If estate tax is saved by Son's not having to make all the payments predicted by the actuarial tables, the estate tax savings will be offset by any income tax later incurred by Son on the sale of the property (or incurred in the year of Mom's death, if Son has sold the property during Mom's life).[41]

[3] Death of Buyer During Seller's Life

If the buyer dies before the seller-annuitant, the buyer's estate steps into the buyer's shoes. The estate can deduct the actuarial value of the debt under Section 2053. In such an instance, there is a potential trap if there is not enough property subject to claims[42] in buyer's estate to take advantage of the deduction. In that case, an estate tax deduction for the buyer's debts is allowed for payments made from property not subject to claims (exempt probate property and many nonprobate assets) to the extent that the debts are paid before the due date for filing the estate tax return.[43] To the extent that the annuity payments last longer than that, there may be no debt deduction allowed for them. On the other hand, they may not actually have to be paid, to the extent that there is insufficient property subject to claims to pay them.

If the buyer did not have sufficient property subject to claims to pay the debt, this could also create a problem for an obligor who is jointly and severally liable for the annuity payments, or for the seller-annuitant (Mom), if she was counting on the annuity payments. It could also create tax problems, if the debt is satisfied anyway out of property not subject to claims, since no estate tax deduction will be available for the amounts paid after the due date of the return. Similarly, the payor might be making a taxable gift if he pays the debt even though it is not enforceable and he is not personally liable.

If the property is sold after the buyer's death, gain or loss is determined with respect to the property's basis as determined by its value for estate tax purposes. Further payments on the annuity should not affect the basis.

[4] Sale of the Property During the Annuitant's Life

The IRS's official guidance on tax consequences to the obligor is stated in Revenue Ruling 55-119.[44]

---

[41] See ¶ 23.05[4] below for consequences when Son sells the property during Mom's life.

[42] "Property subject to claims" is property includable in the gross estate if the property, or the proceeds of the property, would bear the burden of the payments of the claims in the final adjustment and settlement of the decedent's estate. IRC § 2053(c)(2).

[43] IRC § 2053(c)(2).

[44] 1955-1 CB 352.

[a] Gain or Loss on Sale

If buyer sells the property during the seller-annuitant's life, his basis for determining gain is the total amount of payments he has actually made, plus the actuarial value of future annuity payments to be made. The buyer's basis for determining loss is the total amount of payments actually made. If the sales price is greater than the total amount of payments made but less than that amount plus the actuarial value of future payments, no gain or loss is recognized. The character of the gain or loss will be ordinary or capital, and long-term or short-term, depending on how long the buyer held the property and what kind of property it is.[46]

[b] Payment of Annuity After Sale

What happens when the buyer continues to make post-sale annuity payments? The answer depends on the sale's tax consequences to the buyer.

[i] **Buyer recognized gain on the sale.** If the buyer recognized gain on the sale, nothing happens until the total payments exceed the actuarial value used to compute the gain. Thereafter, the buyer can treat each payment as a loss. The character of this later loss is the character it would have been assigned had the buyer realized it on the sale. If the seller-annuitant dies before the buyer's annuity payments equal the actuarial value used to compute the gain, the buyer will have income in the year of the seller-annuitant's death equal to the difference between that actuarial value and the payments the buyer actually made.

[ii] **Buyer recognized loss on sale.** If the buyer recognized a loss on the sale, each additional annuity payment to the seller-annuitant results in a further loss with the same character as the original loss.

[iii] **Buyer did not recognize gain or loss on sale.** If the buyer did not recognize a gain or loss, he can treat each payment as a loss only after all annuity payments actually made equal the amount realized from the sale. When the seller-annuitant dies, if the amount of the buyer's annuity payments (less any depreciation or similar deductions claimed by the buyer) is less than the amount realized on the sale, the buyer will have taxable income in the year of the seller-annuitant's death.

[iv] **Buyer's basis in a part-gift transaction.** It appears that the usual rules for computing basis in part-sale/part-gift transactions would now apply

---

[46] See Arrowsmith v. Comm'r, 344 US 6 (1952).

(instead of the rules listed in Revenue Ruling 55-119) where property is sold in exchange for an annuity at a bargain price. Thus, if Mom made a partial gift to Son when she sold him property in exchange for an annuity, Son's basis in the property for purposes of computing gain or depreciation should be the greater of (1) the amount Son paid for the property or (2) Mom's basis in the property plus any increase in basis for gift tax paid by Mom.[46] For purposes of computing loss, however, Son's basis may not exceed the fair market value of the property at the time Mom transferred it to Son.[47] Revenue Ruling 55-119 suggests that the buyer (Son) would have two separate bases—one for the gifted portion of the property and one for the sold portion—which would be added together to determine his total basis. Treasury Regulation § 1.1015-4, which was promulgated in 1957, seems to have superseded Revenue Ruling 55-119 in this context, however.

¶ 23.06 VARIATIONS ON ANNUITY-TRANSACTION STRUCTURE

[1] Stock Redemption for Private Annuity

If Mom is interested in conveying her remaining interest in a family corporation to Son, who is the only other owner, she might consider redeeming her stock in exchange for an annuity. If Mom's entire interest is redeemed and she resigns any position she holds in the corporation, and complies with the other requirements of the Section 302 termination of interest provisions, so that the family attribution rules of Section 318 may be waived,[48] the redemption may qualify for capital gain treatment rather than dividend treatment.[49] However, because the right to receive a long-term annuity from a corporation may be likened to an equity interest, if Mom is expected to live more than 15 years, the IRS may take the position that her interest in the corporation has not completely terminated and therefore, dividend treatment should apply.[50] If this is a concern, the annuity term might have to be for the shorter of Mom's

---

[46] Treas. Reg. § 1.1015-4.

[47] Treas. Reg. § 1.1015-4.

[48] It is very important that the proper waiver be filed. See Fehrs Fin. Co. v. Comm'r, 58 TC 174 (1972), aff'd, 487 F2d 184 (8th Cir. 1973), cert. denied, 416 US 938 (1974).

[49] See Priv. Ltr. Rul. 7802013 (Oct. 11, 1977).

[50] See e.g., Priv. Ltr. Rul. 8503058 (Oct. 24, 1984) (IRS required representation that last annuity payment would be made no more than 15 years after date of redemption); Priv. Ltr. Rul. 8313073 (Dec. 28, 1982) (similarly); Priv. Ltr. Rul. 8301036 (Sept. 30, 1982) (similarly); see also Rev. Proc. 97-3, 1997-1 IRB 85 (the IRS will not issue rulings on the redemption of stock in exchange for a note of more than 15 years' duration); see Ch. 19 on C corporations for a discussion of redemptions.

life or 15 years. Generally, one of the disadvantages of a private annuity is that the basis of the property will be reduced if Mom dies before payments equal to the property's fair market value have been made. However, if a family corporation buys stock from Mom for a private annuity, it doesn't matter if the corporation takes less than a fair market value basis in the stock, since it will never recognize gain or loss on sale of its own stock.[51]

[2] Private Annuity Subject to a Limit

A private annuity can be subject to a limitation, either to a certain number of years or to a certain dollar amount.

A straight annuity for life will be treated as a private annuity for income tax purposes, and not as an installment sale. If, however, the private annuity has a limitation, either of a dollar amount or a term, then the transaction will be treated as an installment sale with contingent payments, if the seller's life expectancy is more than the maximum period over which the annuity will be paid.[52]

> EXAMPLE: Mom sells Blackacre to Son for payments of $100,000 per year for ten years or the life of Mom, whichever is shorter. If Mom's life expectancy is longer than ten years, the transaction will be treated as an installment sale.[53]

[3] Private Annuity With Bells and Whistles

The IRS has ruled that a transaction would be taxed for income tax purposes as a private annuity even when (1) a cost-of-living adjustment applied to the annuity payments, (2) a minimum payment clause was inserted, so that if the annuitant died during the term, a minimum amount would be paid to her estate, and (3) the annuitant had the power to elect to accelerate the payments and receive the lump sum amount remaining.[54] However, the tables may not be available to value an annuity with non-standard terms.[55]

---

[51] IRC § 1032(a).

[52] Gen. Couns. Mem. 39503 (May 7, 1986); see also Rev. Rul. 86-72, 1986-1 CB 253.

[53] Gen. Couns. Mem. 39503 (May 7, 1986).

[54] Priv. Ltr. Rul. 9009064 (Dec. 8, 1989).

[55] Treas. Reg. §§ 20.7520-3(b)(1)(iii), 25.7520-3(b)(1)(iii).

[4] Sale for Annuity Issued by Insurance Company

A sale of property for an annuity issued by an insurance company is not governed by the private annuity rules.[56] Instead, the transaction is treated as closed and gain, if any, must be recognized immediately. Thereafter, the annuity payments are taxed under the commercial annuity rules described in Chapter 13.

¶ 23.07 ANNUITY TRANSACTION WITH AN ENTITY

[1] Retained Interest Problem

[a] Section 2036(a)—Retained Life Estate

If a transfer in exchange for a private annuity is successfully characterized as a transfer with a retained interest in the property, all or part of the property transferred will be included in Mom's estate. This issue could be encountered if Mom, for example, sells Blackacre to a trust, and the only source of payment is Blackacre.[57] However, a properly structured transaction with a trust should be workable.[58]

> EXAMPLE: Suppose Mom wants to sell Whiteacre to Grandchildren's Trust in exchange for an annuity. If Son's Trust has other assets that can be expected to pay the annuity for the purchase of Whiteacre, Mom should not be deemed to have retained an interest in Whiteacre. If the trust does not have substantial other assets, perhaps a guarantee by Son will solve the problem. A private annuity with an individual obligor is not generally considered to create retained interest issues if the individual has unlimited liability to pay the annuity. What if Son is penniless, and will, as a practical matter, have no source of repayment but the property and its income, as distributed to him? That could cause Mom to be deemed to have retained an interest in Whiteacre.[59]

The Tax Court has listed six factors it will consider in evaluating whether a private annuity is a transfer with a retained interest. In structuring a private annuity transaction with a trust, it is desirable that the following factors weigh in favor of a legitimate annuity/sale rather than a retention of an interest in the trust:

---

[56] Rev. Rul. 84-162, 1984 CB 200; see also IRC § 7520(a).

[57] LaFargue v. Comm'r, 800 F2d 936 (9th Cir. 1986); Benson v. Comm'r, 80 TC 789 (1983).

[58] See Estate of Fabric v. Comm'r, 83 TC 50 (1984); Stern v. Comm'r, 747 F2d 555 (9th Cir. 1984), rev'g 77 TC 614 (1981).

[59] See Estate of Mitchell v. Comm'r, 1982 PH TC Memo. ¶ 82,185, 43 TCM (CCH) 1034 (1982).

- The relationship between the creation of the trust and the transfer of assets to the trust in exchange for an annuity;
- The tie-in between the income generated by the transferred property and the annuity payment;
- The degree of control over the transferred properties exercisable by the annuitant;
- The nature and extent of the annuitant's continuing interest in the transferred properties;
- The source of the annuity payment; and
- The arm's-length nature of the annuity/sale transaction.[60]

[b] Annuity Transaction With Section 2702 Ramifications

If the private annuity is transacted with a trust as the obligor and the annuity is successfully recharacterized as a retained interest, the transaction may be affected by Section 2702. This statute provides that if a donor transfers property to a trust and retains an annuity, the annuity must be a "qualified annuity" in order to avoid punitive gift tax consequences. A qualified annuity is an irrevocable right to receive a fixed amount for a definite period. If Mom "retains" any rights in the property other than a qualified annuity, those rights will be valued at zero for gift tax purposes. If Mom retains a qualified annuity interest in the property, the transaction will be treated as a transfer to a grantor retained annuity trust.[61]

[c] Trust Assets Subject to Power of Appointment

If the trust assets are subject to a power of appointment in a beneficiary, the IRS position is that the right to receive the annuity is valueless, because the holder of the power could remove the only source of funding.[62]

[2] Availability of Actuarial Tables to Value Annuity

If payment of the annuity is restricted to a certain fund, such as a trust, the trust must be expected to support the annuity in order for the annuity tables to be used. The calculation[63] is as follows.

---

[60] Weigl v. Comm'r, 84 TC 1192 (1985).

[61] See Ch. 22 for a discussion of qualified annuities and grantor retained annuity trusts.

[62] Rev. Rul. 76-491, 1976-2 CB 301. This position seems questionable because (1) the appointees would be liable for the debt, at least to the extent of what they received, and (2) the same situation would exist if the trustee had discretion to make distributions pursuant to the terms of the instrument.

[63] Treas. Reg. §§ 20.7520-3(b)(2)(i), 25.7520-3(b)(2)(v), example 5.

Determine the rate of the annuity as a percentage of the fund on the date of transfer. Determine the 7520 rate on the date of transfer. If the annuity rate is equal to or less than the 7520 rate, there is no problem. However, if the annuity rate is greater than the 7520 rate, it will be assumed that payment of the annuity will gradually deplete principal. If the principal is expected to be depleted before Mom's life ends, the annuity tables cannot be used. For this purpose, Mom will be assumed to die at age 110.[64]

> EXAMPLE: Suppose Whiteacre is worth $1,000,000. The annuity rate is 10 percent. The 7520 rate is 8.2 percent. The valuation method assumes that Mom will live until 110. If Mom is 51 years old at the date of transfer, the annuity will be expected to deplete the property between the 21st and 22d year. Accordingly, the life interest tables cannot be used.[65] Note that the regulation imposing this rule, if upheld as applicable in the private annuity context, will make it difficult to convey property in exchange for a lifetime private annuity without making a gift, where annuity payments exceed the 7520 rate and are to be made from a trust or other limited fund. This is because each annual payment of the annuity will be deemed to exhaust principal, and the annuity payments will be deemed to continue (and exhaust principal) for many years after any reasonable life expectancy.

[3] Income Tax Consequences

If the transaction is respected as an annuity, and the property sold is depreciable by the buyer, any gain is treated as ordinary income if the sale is to a controlled entity (certain corporations, partnerships, and trusts of which Mom or her husband is a beneficiary).[66]

If the transaction with a trust is recharacterized as a retained interest, then, whether or not the transaction is treated as a transfer to a grantor retained annuity trust, the trust will be treated as a grantor trust. No capital gain will be recognized on the transfer to the trust, and the income of the trust will be taxed directly to Mom.[67]

---

[64] Treas. Reg. §§ 20.7520-3(b)(2)(i), 25.7520-3(b)(2)(i).

[65] However, Treas. Reg. § 25.7520-3(b)(2)(v), example 5 provides a method for computing the value of the annuity. See Ch. 11 for an explanation of special factors used in such a situation.

[66] IRC § 1239.

[67] Rev. Rul. 68-183, 1968-1 CB 308.

CHAPTER 24

Other Actuarial Techniques

¶ 24.01 INTRODUCTION

In the seventies and eighties, it became fashionable to plan with actuarial interests. Transfers to trusts with retained income interests, sales of remainder interests, and joint purchases of actuarial interests in property proliferated. Congress was ultimately convinced that some of these techniques were loopholes and, in 1990, enacted Section 2702, which restricts non-charitable actuarial planning to certain techniques and heavily penalizes attempts to use proscribed techniques.

Generally, if (1) the grantor "transfers" property to a trust, (2) any trust beneficiary is a "member of the grantor's family," and (3) the grantor (or any "applicable family member") retains an "interest in the trust," then the value of the retained interest will be disregarded for gift tax purposes (resulting in the entire value of the property transferred to the trust being treated as a gift). Exceptions to this rule, however, include the retention of a qualified annuity interest,[1] the retention of an income interest in certain nondepreciable tangible property, and other retained interests listed below. We'll call the excepted interests "qualified interests," and other interests "nonqualified interests."

---

[1] See Ch. 22 on grantor retained annuity trusts (GRATs).

¶ 24.02 HOW SECTION 2702 WORKS

[1] Consequences of Retaining a Nonqualified Interest

If the grantor's or applicable family member's retained interest is not structured as a qualified interest, then, for purposes of determining whether the
grantor's "transfer" to the trust is a gift (and the amount of the gift), the
nonqualified "interest in trust" retained by the grantor or any applicable
family member is valued at zero[2] if the other beneficiaries are "members of the
family" of the grantor. For example, if Joe transfers $1,000,000 to a trust for
members of his family, and retains a nonqualified interest, he makes a taxable
gift of $1,000,000, regardless of the actual value of his retained interest.

[2] Transfer

Treasury Regulations provide that a transfer in trust includes a transfer to a
new or existing trust and an assignment of an interest in an existing trust.[3]
Thus, Section 2702 can apply to situations that do not involve actuarial planning at all—e.g., a lapse of a withdrawal right in excess of a "five-or-five"
power appears to be a transfer under the regulations.[4]

[3] Applicable Family Member

A grantor's applicable family members are the grantor's spouse, ancestors of
the grantor or the grantor's spouse, and the spouses of their ancestors.[5]

[4] Interest in Trust

[a] Definition

An "interest in trust" can include a power with respect to a trust if the
existence of the power would cause any portion of a transfer to be treated as
an incomplete gift under the gift tax rules.[6] For example, if X transfers property to a trust, and retains the power to appoint the income among his descendants for ten years, X will be considered to have retained an interest in the

---

[2] IRC § 2702(a)(1)-(2)(A).

[3] Treas. Reg. § 25.2702-2(a)(2).

[4] Treas. Reg. § 25.2702-2(a)(2)(i). This appears to be true despite the fact that the
preamble to the regulations states that a recommended exception for lapses of "Crummey" powers was adopted. Crummey powers and five-or-five powers are discussed in
Ch. 10 on tax-free transfers and Ch. 2 on property included in the gross estate.

[5] IRC §§ 2701(e)(2), 2702(a).

[6] Treas. Reg. § 25.2702-2(a)(4).

trust. Apparently, this arrangement will be treated as if the grantor had retained the right to the income and paid it to the beneficiaries after receiving it.

[b] Recharacterization of Interests

If Grantor sells property to a trust, and takes back a note, is her right to receive payment pursuant to the note a retained interest in the trust? The regulations do not specifically address the issue, but they suggest that rights held as a creditor are not interests in trust, provided that the debt is bona fide.

What if the note from the trust is nonrecourse, is payable only if and when the property securing the note is sold by the trust, and bears interest defined as a percentage of gain from the sale of the property? Whether a right to receive payments pursuant to a note, lease, employment contract, etc., is a retained interest may depend on whether the arrangement is a true debt, lease, employment contract, etc. If such an agreement is characterized as a retained interest, it may be a qualified interest[7] if it meets the requirements.

[5] Member of the Family

The special rules only apply if a trust beneficiary is a member of the grantor's family. A "member of the family" of an individual means: (1) the individual's spouse, (2) any ancestor or lineal descendant of the individual or the individual's spouse, (3) any brother or sister of the individual, and (4) any spouse of any individual described in (2) or (3).[8]

[6] Value of Gift

[a] Use of the Subtraction Method

The subtraction method apparently applies. The regulations provide that the value of the gift is determined by subtracting the value of any portion of the gift that is a qualified interest from the value of the entire transferred property.[9]

[b] Application to Other Taxes

The preamble to the first set of proposed regulations stated that Section 2702 does not change the value of the transferred property for tax purposes

---

[7] Discussed at ¶ 24.02[7][a] below.

[8] IRC §§ 2702(e), 2704(c)(2); Treas. Reg. § 25.2702-2(a)(1).

[9] Treas. Reg. § 25.2702-1(b).

other than the gift tax. Thus, for example, Section 2702 would not apply for generation-skipping transfer tax purposes.[10]

[7] Exceptions to Rule

[a] List of Exceptions

The only exceptions to this rule are the following types of retained interests:

- A qualified annuity or unitrust interest;[11]
- A qualified income interest in certain personal residences;[12]
- A term income interest in certain tangible property;[13]
- A noncontingent remainder interest after a qualified annuity or unitrust interest;[14]
- An interest in a charitable remainder trust;[15]
- An interest in a pooled income fund;[16]
- An interest in a charitable lead trust;[17]
- An interest as a permissible recipient of distributions of income, in the sole discretion of an independent trustee;[18]
- An interest retained by a spouse in a trust he establishes for the other spouse, if the transfer is deemed to be for full and adequate consideration by reason of Section 2516 (relating to certain property settlements);[19]

---

[10] Notice of Prop. Rulemaking, 1991-1 CB 999. The proposed regulations were revised and adopted as final regulations by TD 8395, 1992-1 CB 316.

[11] See Chs. 22, 33, and 35 on GRATs, charitable remainder trusts, and charitable lead trusts, respectively.

[12] See Ch. 21 on qualified personal residence trusts (QPRTs).

[13] Discussed below at ¶ 24.04.

[14] Treas. Reg. § 25.2702-2(b)(2).

[15] Treas. Reg. § 25.2702-1(c)(3). This exception is necessary because not all charitable remainder trusts involve only annuity or unitrust amounts. See IRC § 664(d)(3). Proposed Regulation § 25.2702-1(c)(3) would apply IRC § 2702 to certain charitable remainder trusts. See ¶ 33.02[i][e].

[16] Treas. Reg. § 25.2702-1(c)(4). Pooled income funds are defined in IRC § 642(c)(5).

[17] Treas. Reg. § 25.2702-1(c)(5).

[18] As defined in IRC § 674(c) (referring to powers exercisable by a trustee or trustees, none of whom is the grantor or the grantor's spouse, and no more than half of whom are related or subordinate parties subservient to the grantor's wishes). Treas. Reg. § 25.2702-1(c)(6).

[19] Treas. Reg. § 25.2702-1(c)(7).

- Interests retained after an incomplete gift;[20] and
- Interests retained by a spouse after certain transfers to a qualified domestic trust.[21]

[b] Rules for Incomplete Gifts

The special valuation rules will not apply if the transfer would not be considered a gift, whether or not consideration is received for the transfer.[22] Thus, for example, if Barbara transfers property to a revocable trust, the transfer is excepted from Section 2702. However, a transfer that is wholly incomplete as to an undivided fractional share of the property transferred (without regard to any consideration received by the transferor) is only treated as incomplete as to that share.[23] For example, if Barbara transfers property to an irrevocable trust for the benefit of herself and family members, and retains a special power of appointment over one-half of the property, one-half of the transfer is not subject to Section 2702.

The regulations treat a gift which is partially incomplete due to a retained special power of appointment as if it were a wholly completed gift.

> EXAMPLE: Barbara transfers property to an irrevocable trust for the benefit of herself and family members, but retains a special power of appointment over the income for ten years. The current statute provides that the 10-year interest is not subject to valuation under Section 2702. However, the regulations provide that Section 2702 shall apply to the entire gift.

[8] Qualified Domestic Trust

If a noncitizen surviving spouse receives property included in the deceased spouse's gross estate, and then assigns this property to a qualified domestic trust to qualify for the marital deduction, the value of the property will not be subject to Section 2702. This is so even if the surviving spouse retains only an income interest, and the remainder interest passes to her family members.[24]

[9] Nonqualified Interests

In some circumstances, it may be desirable to intentionally retain a nonqualified interest. The special rules only cause a larger gift on transfer, and do not

---

[20] Discussed at ¶ 24.02[7][b] below.

[21] Discussed at ¶ 24.02[8] below.

[22] IRC §§ 2702(a)(3)(A)(i), 2702(a)(3)(B).

[23] Treas. Reg. § 25.2702-1(c)(1).

[24] Treas. Reg. §§ 25.2702-1(c)(8), 20.2056A-4(b)(5), 20.2056A-4(d), example 5.

cause the trust assets to be includable in the transferor's estate. Hence, an estate freeze can still be accomplished if the assets are not included in the estate for other reasons. However, beware of the adjustment provisions, which may not compensate for the gift.

[10] Adjustment in Tax for Subsequent Transfers of Specially Valued Property

[a] Inter Vivos Transfer of Donor's Retained Interest

If an individual holds an interest which is specially valued[25] in his hands, and the individual subsequently transfers that interest by gift, the individual is entitled to a reduction in his aggregate taxable gifts. "Aggregate taxable gifts" means the individual's taxable gifts for the calendar year determined under the normal rules.[26]

> EXAMPLE: *A* transfers property to an irrevocable trust in 1997, retaining a life interest specially valued at zero. In 1998, *A* transfers his retained interest by gift. *A* is entitled to reduce his taxable gifts for the calendar year 1998, as discussed in subparagraph [c] below.[27]

[b] Effect of Testamentary Transfers

An individual's estate is entitled to a reduction in the individual's adjusted taxable gifts in computing his federal estate tax, if either (1) a term interest in trust is included in the individual's gross estate solely by reason of Section 2033 or (2) a remainder interest in trust is included in the individual's gross estate, and the term or remainder interest was previously specially valued in that individual's hands.[28]

[c] Amount of Reduction

[i] **In general.** The amount of the reduction in aggregate taxable gifts (or adjusted taxable gifts) is the lesser of: (1) the increase in the individual's taxable gifts resulting from the interest being specially valued at the time of the initial transfer or (2) the increase in the individual's taxable gifts (or gross estate) resulting from the subsequent transfer of the interest.[29]

---

[25] For purposes of this chapter, "specially valued" means valued under Treas. Reg. §§ 25.2702-2(b)(1) or 25.2702-2(c).

[26] Treas. Reg. § 25.2702-6(a)(1).

[27] Treas. Reg. § 25.2702-6(a)(1).

[28] Treas. Reg. § 25.2702-6(a)(2).

[29] Treas. Reg. § 25.2702-6(b)(1).

EXAMPLE: In 1997, A transfers property worth $1,000,000 to a trust and retains an income interest. A has made no prior taxable gifts. He pays gift tax of $153,000. His interest in the income is valued at $400,000, so if it had not been for Section 2702, he would have paid no gift tax. In 1998, A transfers his retained income interest, which is then valued according to the tables at $350,000, for no consideration. He makes no other gift in that year. A's aggregate taxable gifts before reduction for 1998 are $350,000. He is entitled to reduce the amount of these gifts by the lesser of $400,000 (the increase in his taxable gifts for 1997 occasioned by Section 2702) or $350,000 (the increase in his taxable gifts resulting from the 1998 transfer).

EXAMPLE: In 1997, A transfers property worth $1,000,000 to a trust and retains a nonqualified remainder interest. He pays gift tax of $153,000. His nonqualified remainder interest is valued at $400,000, so if it had not been for Section 2702, he would have paid no gift tax. In 1998, A dies. The remainder interest is then valued at $350,000, and is included in A's estate. A's estate would receive a reduction in his adjusted taxable gifts of $350,000 (the lesser of $400,000 or the value of the remainder interest on the date of his death).

[ii] Treatment of annual exclusion. For purposes of determining the increase in an individual's taxable gifts or gross estate resulting from a subsequent transfer of a specially valued interest, the gift tax annual exclusion applies first to transfers in the year of subsequent transfer other than the transfer of the interest previously specially valued.[90]

EXAMPLE: In 1997, A transfers property worth $1,000,000 to a trust and retains an income interest. A has made no prior taxable gifts. He pays gift tax of $153,000. His interest in the income is valued at $400,000, so if it had not been for Section 2702, he would have paid no gift tax. In 1998, A transfers his retained income interest, which is then valued according to the tables at $350,000, for no consideration to a person who also received another $10,000 gift from A in that year. Both 1998 gifts qualified for the annual exclusion. The increase in taxable gifts for 1998 would be calculated without any subtraction for the annual exclusion.

[iii] Overlap with Section 2001. Notwithstanding the above rules, the reduction does not apply to the extent Section 2001 otherwise applies to reduce the amount of an individual's adjusted taxable gifts.[31] Hence, the Section 2702 adjustment only applies to the extent a Section 2001 adjustment would not apply with respect to the interest.

---

[90] Treas. Reg. § 25.2702-6(b)(2).

[31] Treas. Reg. § 25.2702-6(b)(3).

[d] Gift-Splitting

If an individual who is entitled to a reduction in aggregate taxable gifts (or adjusted taxable gifts) subsequently transfers the interest in a gift which is split with the individual's spouse, the individual may assign one-half of the amount of the reduction to the consenting spouse. The assignment must be attached to the Form 709 on which the consenting spouse reports the split gift.[32]

> EXAMPLE: In 1997, *H* gives property worth $1,000,000 to a trust for his daughter, retaining an income interest. In 1998, he transfers his retained income interest to his daughter. His wife agrees to split the 1998 gift. One-half of *H*'s allowable reduction may be assigned to his wife. The assignment must be attached to the Form 709 on which the wife reports the split gift.

[e] Retained Powers of Appointment

The regulations provide that if *A* transfers property to a trust and retains no interest, but retains the power to determine the distributees of the income for a period of time, *A* will be treated for purposes of Section 2702 as if he had retained an income interest valued at zero.[33] If the income is later distributed, example 7 of Treasury Regulation § 25.2702-6(c) says that no adjustment will be made in *A*'s aggregate taxable gifts. However, Treasury Regulation § 25.2702-6(c), example 8 says that an adjustment will be made if all of the property subject to the retained power is transferred.

[f] Situations in Which No Adjustment Is Allowed

First, no adjustment applies if an applicable family member who owned an interest that was subject to special valuation makes a subsequent transfer of that interest.

> EXAMPLE: Grandmother established a trust in 1996, retaining an income interest and giving Mother a remainder interest. In 1997, Mother transfers her remainder interest in the trust to Daughter. Grandmother's retained income interest in the trust is valued at zero under Section 2702. Mother's gift is $200,000, taking into account Grandmother's interest. When Grandmother dies, the trust is included in her estate under Section 2036(a). There is no adjustment for the gift tax previously paid by Mother on the value of Grandmother's interest, because Grandmother never made a taxable gift of any of her interest. When Mother dies, none of the trust is included in her estate, so her estate receives no adjustment, even

---

[32] Treas. Reg. § 25.2702-6(a)(3).

[33] Treas. Reg. § 25.2702-6(c), examples 6, 7.

though she paid a gift tax on her interest.

Second, in order for any adjustment to be made, the retained interest must be includable in the transferor's estate. Double taxation can result if the interest has been sold or naturally terminated.

EXAMPLE: If Mother transfers property to a trust for her child and retains an income interest for five years, the income interest will be valued at zero for purposes of the gift tax. If Mother dies seven years later, the trust will not be included in her estate, and there will be no adjustment. However, all of the income attributable to the retained interest will be includable in her estate.

EXAMPLE: If A retains an income interest for ten years and gives the interest away after nine years, A will have accrued nine years of income and the trust will be depleted because of it. The adjustment will be limited by the value of the interest at the date of gift, despite the fact that it has been depleted by income payments which will increase A's estate.

The above items illustrate the fact that the adjustment does not always fully compensate for the double taxation of transfers valued under Section 2702.

[11] Statute of Limitations Considerations

The statute of limitations does not begin to run on a gift which is valued under Section 2702 unless the gift is "adequately shown" on a gift tax return.[34] "Adequately shown" is defined in Treasury Regulation § 25.2701-4.

An amended return may not operate to start the statute of limitations running, although a late return should.[35] Thus, a person who files a gift tax return without disclosure of the "gift" may be in a worse position than the person who does not file a timely gift tax return at all.

Last, it should be noted that the statute of limitations does not run even with respect to (1) a gift for which a return is not required to be filed due to the annual exclusion or (2) a transfer for adequate consideration under the normal rules, as long as it is a gift under the special rules.

¶ 24.03 GRANTOR RETAINED INCOME TRUSTS

[1] Background

Prior to the enactment of Section 2702, grantor retained income trusts (GRITs) were popular estate planning devices. A typical plan was to put a

---

[34] Treas. Reg. § 301.6501(c)-1(e)(1).

[35] IRC §§ 6501(a), 6501(c)(9). See Badaracco v. Comm'r, 464 US 386, 401 (1984).

non-income-producing asset into a trust, retain an income interest for a term of years, and make a gift of the remainder interest. When the term of years ended, the property passed to the remainder beneficiaries tax-free. Although the income interest retained by the grantor reduced the value of the remainder interest for transfer tax purposes, it did not reduce the value of the property or add to the amount in the grantor's estate, because the property was non-income-producing.

> EXAMPLE: Horace gave $1,000,000 in growth stock to a GRIT. He retained an income interest for ten years and a contingent reversion, so that the stock would revert to his estate if he died during the 10-year term. Assume the remainder interest was worth $600,000. Horace made a taxable gift of $600,000. The growth stock never paid dividends and therefore never produced any income. When the 10-year period was over, the stock was worth $1,300,000. There was no gift tax at that time. The effect was that Horace's gift was valued for gift tax purposes by subtracting the value of his income interest, when he never received any value from his income interest; therefore, he transferred the present value of $1,300,000 for the transfer tax cost of a $600,000 gift.

In 1990, Congress passed Section 2702, which effectively rendered the common law GRIT unavailable for members of the grantor's family. For non-family members, the GRIT is still an excellent tax-saving device. For example, Horace from the preceding example could establish a GRIT for the benefit of his nieces and nephews.

A GRIT will generally be better from a transfer tax perspective than a GRAT. With a GRIT, the initial gift will be computed on the assumption that the property earns (and thus returns to the grantor) the 7520 rate;[36] however, the property can be invested in growth assets, so that the grantor does not actually receive as much income as the gift computation assumes he will. With a GRAT, the grantor will actually receive the annuity used in the computation of the gift, and the annuity payments will be included in the grantor's estate to the extent they are not consumed.

[2] How a GRIT Works

[a] The Gift

The grantor transfers property to a trust and retains an income interest for a number of years; at the end of the term, the interest passes to other

---

[36] The 7520 rate is 120 percent of the applicable federal midterm rate, rounded to the nearest 2/10ths of one percent. IRC § 7520.

beneficiaries. On the contribution to the trust, the grantor makes a gift, ordinarily valued according to the Treasury's actuarial tables.[37]

[b] The Contingent Reversion

The grantor retains a contingent reversion if he dies within the term. The reversion will reduce the gift tax value and will not increase the estate tax, because the trust will be includable in the grantor's estate if he dies within the term anyway. The following tables illustrate the gift tax effects of retaining a contingent reversion for different term interests. The tables assume a $1,000,000 transfer by a 50-year old grantor when the 7520 rate is eight percent.

Years in Term	Value of Retained Interest Without Contingent Reversion	Value of Gift (Remainder Interest)	Gift Tax (at 55% Rate)
5	$343,048	$656,952	$361,323.60
10	$576,281	$423,719	$233,045.45
15	$734,422	$265,578	$146,067.90

Years in Term	Value of Retained Interest With Contingent Reversion	Value of Gift (Remainder Interest)	Gift Tax (at 55% Rate)
5	$371,538	$628,462	$345,654.10
10	$633,001	$366,999	$201,849.45
15	$818,671	$181,329	$ 99,730.95

Years in Term	Gift Tax Savings Due to Contingent Reversion
5	$15,669.50
10	$31,196.00
15	$46,336.95

[c] Funding the Trust With Non-Income-Producing Property

The actuarial tables are not available unless the GRIT term holder has rights similar to the beneficiary of a QTIP trust.[38] This means that the term holder must have the right to require the trustee to make the trust assets

---

[37] IRC § 7520. The actuarial tables are published pursuant to IRC § 7520, and are found in Publication 1457 (Alpha Volume) and Publication 1458 (Beta Volume).

[38] Treas. Reg. § 25.7520-3(b)(2)(ii).

productive of income.[38] The trust will meet the test if the term holder has the right to cause the assets to be productive as a matter of state law, even if the rate of return contained in state law is less than the 7520 rate.[40] If the property in the GRIT does not earn at least that much, and the term holder does not require the trustee to convert the property to income-producing property, the term holder may be deemed to make a transfer to the trust each year she does not exercise her right to make the property productive of income.[41]

[3] Limitation to Non-Family Members

Because of Sections 2702 and 2704, a GRIT is not an effective tool if a trust beneficiary is: the grantor's spouse; an ancestor or descendant of the grantor or his spouse; the grantor's sibling; or a spouse of any of the previously described persons.[42] Therefore, a GRIT might be established, for example, for the benefit of nieces, nephews, friends, children of a significant other, a significant other who is not a member of the family, etc.

[4] Income Tax Consequences of a GRIT

The trust will be a grantor trust during the term.[43] Hence, all items of income, deduction, gain, loss and credit will be reported directly on the grantor's return.

¶ 24.04 TRANSFER WITH A RETAINED TERM INTEREST IN TANGIBLE PROPERTY

[1] How It Works

Generally, if one person gives property to a family member while retaining an income interest in the transferred property, the donor will be treated as having given away the entire property.[44]

Section 2702 excepts from this general rule a transfer of an income interest in tangible property if the property is not depletable or depreciable and is not subject to actual decline in value as a result of use (e.g., art,

---

[38] Treas. Reg. § 25.7520-3(b)(2)(v), example 2.

[40] Treas. Reg. § 25.7520-3(b)(2)(v), example 2.

[41] Priv. Ltr. Rul. 9045047 (Aug. 15, 1990); Priv. Ltr. Rul. 9035029 (May 31, 1990); Priv. Ltr. Rul. 9035022 (May 31, 1990); Priv. Ltr. Rul. 8923007 (Mar. 2, 1989); all of these rulings precede the Section 7250 Regulations.

[42] IRC §§ 2702(a), 2702(e), 2704(c)(2).

[43] IRC §§ 673, 677.

[44] IRC § 2702.

unimproved real estate).[45] However, depletable or depreciable property can be included in the transfer if (1) it consists of improvements to transferred property which is non-depletable or non-depreciable and (2) its value does not exceed five percent of the amount of the transferred property (e.g., fences and pens on grazing lands).[46]

The difference between this technique and the GRIT is that, if family members are beneficiaries, the donor's retained interest in the tangible property is not valued using the actuarial tables.[47] Instead, it is valued at fair market value—that is, at the amount which the donor can establish as the amount a willing buyer would pay a willing seller for the retained interest, each having knowledge of the relevant facts and neither being under any compulsion to buy or sell.[48] The best evidence of value, in such an instance, is actual sales or rentals that are comparable both as to the nature and character of the property and the duration of the term interest.[49] However, little weight will be accorded to appraisals in the absence of this evidence, and amounts determined under the actuarial tables are not evidence at all.[50] If the grantor cannot reasonably establish the value of the term interest, the interest is valued at zero.[51]

As a practical matter, it may be quite difficult to establish the value of retained interests in tangible property. Some term interests, such as a ten-year term interest in a tapestry, are too uncommon to be valued using a comparable transaction method. On the other hand, real estate is often rented for periods of time, and thus may be readily valued. Items such as works of art are also sometimes rented for periods of time. However, even if a rental market for art works for a one-year period can be established, the value of a ten-year interest in the artwork will not necessarily be ten times the value of a one-year interest.[52]

> EXAMPLE: *A* sells his child a remainder interest in a painting. Whether *A* exercises his rights to use the painting or not does not have a substantial effect on the valuation of the remainder interest in the painting, because its value depends mostly on appreciation potential. (Apparently, it is assumed that both *A* and any other holder will take good care of the painting.)[53] If *A* used or rented out the painting, that would not decrease

---

[45] Treas. Reg. § 25.2702-2(c)(2)(i).

[46] Treas. Reg. § 25.2702-2(c)(2)(ii).

[47] Treas. Reg. § 25.2702-2(c)(1).

[48] Treas. Reg. § 25.2702-2(c)(1).

[49] Treas. Reg. § 25.2702-2(c)(3).

[50] Treas. Reg. § 25.2702-2(c)(3).

[51] Treas. Reg. § 25.2702-2(c)(1).

[52] Treas. Reg. § 25.2702-2(d)(2), example 9.

[53] See Treas. Reg. § 25.2702-2(d)(2), example 8.

the value of the remainder interest. In this case, the value of the income interest in the painting for purposes of determining the gift tax will be the value at which the income interest could be sold to an unrelated third party (not the values determined under the tax tables).

EXAMPLE: A sells his child a remainder interest in an oil well. A's life interest would be treated as having a value of zero, because A's exercise of his rights under his life estate to extract oil from the well will decrease the value of the remainder interest. The regulations reflect this by providing that depletable property is ineligible for the tangible property exemption.

[2] Effect of Additions or Improvements to Property

[a] Additions or Improvements Substantially Affecting the Nature of Property

The entire qualified property is deemed to convert into ineligible property as of the date an addition or improvement to the qualified property is commenced if the addition or improvement affects the nature of the property to such an extent that the property would have been ineligible property[84] if it had included the addition or improvement at the time it was transferred. In such an instance, the now ineligible property will be treated as described below in ¶ 24.04[4].[85]

EXAMPLE: Mom gives the remainder in a piece of real estate to Son, retaining a life estate. A hotel is subsequently constructed on the property. Since the value of the hotel exceeds 5 percent of the fair market value of the entire property at the time of the original transfer, the real property is deemed to be converted as of the date the hotel construction commenced.

[b] Other Additions or Improvements

If an addition or improvement is made to qualified tangible property, and the qualified tangible property would have been eligible property even if it had included the addition or improvement at the time it was transferred, the addition or improvement is treated as an additional transfer (effective as of the date the addition or improvement commenced), subject to the rules of Treasury Regulation § 25.2702-2(b)(1).[86]

---

[84] "Ineligible property" is our term for any property, if a term interest in the property would not qualify for the tangible property exception.

[85] Treas. Reg. § 25.2702-2(c)(5)(i).

[86] Treas. Reg. § 25.2702-2(c)(5)(ii).

EXAMPLE: Mom transfers the remainder interest in a ranch to Son. If Mom then adds a fence which would have constituted less than 5 percent of the value of the ranch at the date of original transfer, the fencing will be treated as a gift, as of the date construction of the fence begins. Mom's retained interest in the gift will be valued at zero as provided in Treasury Regulation § 25.2702-2(b)(1), unless she can show the fair market value of an interest in a fence for the remaining term (or, even if she can show such value, the fact that the fence is depreciable may render it ineligible when considered as a separate gift).

If the grantor improves the property, then, depending on the arrangements, a gift under Chapter 12 may be made to the remainder beneficiaries, either immediately (in the amount of the value of the remainder interest) or when they take the property at the end of the term.

[3] Income Tax Deductions Attributable to the Property

If the property is not held in trust, the life tenant will take any depreciation and depletion deductions that are available with respect to the property.[57]

[4] Conversion of Qualified Property Into Ineligible Property

[a] In General

Except as described below, if the property is converted into ineligible property during the term, the conversion is treated as a gift of the value of the unexpired portion of the term interest.[58]

EXAMPLE: Mom gives Son a remainder interest in her Renoir, retaining an interest for ten years. After three years, Mom and Son sell the Renoir and retain their respective interests in the cash proceeds. Mom is treated as making a gift of the remaining seven-year income interest in the cash on the date of sale, even though she will still continue to receive interest payments.

[b] Value of Gift on Conversion to Ineligible Property

The regulations provide the following formula for valuing the gift of the unexpired portion of the term interest when property is converted into ineligible property:[59]

---

[57] IRC §§ 167(d), 611(b)(2).

[58] Treas. Reg. § 25.2702-2(c)(4)(i).

[59] Treas. Reg. § 25.2702-2(c)(4)(ii).

Value of unexpired portion of term interest = (A/B) × C, where:
where

- "A"—the value of the term interest as of the date of the original transfer, determined under the tangible property exception rules; and

- "B"—the value of the term interest as of the date of the original transfer, actuarially determined pursuant to Section 7520; and

- "C"—the value of the term interest as of the date of conversion, actuarially determined pursuant to Section 7520, using the 7520 rate in effect on the date of the original transfer and the fair market value of the property as of the date of the original transfer.

It is unclear whether the value of the term interest as of the date of conversion is calculated based on the value of a term interest equal to the number of years remaining in the original term or on the value of the original term interest less the value of a term interest equal to the number of years already expired in the original term. It makes a difference, because the income interests for each year in the term don't have equal values. The interests in the earlier years have a greater actuarial value than those in the later years.

EXAMPLE: Dad transfers a remainder interest in a painting to Son and retains a 10-year interest in the painting. The painting is worth $1,000,000. Dad's 10-year interest is worth $300,000 (determined by comparables), so Dad makes a gift of $700,000. The rate under Section 7520 at the time of the transfer is 8 percent; the actuarial value of Dad's 10-year interest under Section 7520 is $536,807. Four years later, the painting is sold for $2,000,000. The value of a 6-year interest in a painting worth $1,000,000 when the 7520 rate is 8 percent is $369,831. If this is the correct value, then the value of the unexpired portion of the term interest, and hence the gift, would be $206,683.78, calculated by multiplying the value of the six-year interest using the 7520 rate ($369,831) by a fraction, the numerator of which is the value of Dad's 10-year interest ($300,000) as determined by comparables and the denominator of which is the value of Dad's interest using the 7520 rate ($536,807). If, on the other hand, the value of the remaining 6-year term interest is calculated by subtracting the value of a 4-year term from the value of a 10-year term, the resulting gift would be different. The value of a 10-year interest less a 4-year interest is $271,837. If this is the measure, the value of the gift would be $151,918.85, calculated by multiplying the difference between the values of the 10-year interest and the 4-year interest ($271,837) by the same fraction as above. This second computation seems theoretically appropriate, since it better reflects the facts.

[c] Conversion to Qualified Annuity Interest

The conversion into ineligible property will not be treated as a gift if the income interest is converted to a qualified annuity interest. For instance, if in the above example, Dad converts the cash from the sale of the painting to a GRAT, he will not be treated as making a gift on the conversion.[60]

The rules for converting the property held in a QPRT to a qualified annuity interest[61] apply for purposes of determining the amount of the annuity payment and the determination of whether the interest meets the requirements of a qualified annuity interest.[62] The following formula is used to determine the minimum annuity amount:

- *Step 1.* Determine the lesser of the value of all interests retained by the termholder (as of the date of the original transfer) and the value of all of the gifted assets (as of the conversion date).
- *Step 2.* Determine an annuity factor for the original term of the term-holder's interest at the 7520 rate used in valuing the retained interest at the time of the original transfer.
- *Step 3.* Divide the number determined in Step 1 by the number determined in Step 2.[63]

¶ 24.05 SALE OF REMAINDER INTEREST OR JOINT PURCHASE OF ACTUARIAL INTERESTS

Before the enactment of Section 2702 in 1990, a popular estate planning technique was for Mom to sell Son a remainder interest in property for fair market value, actuarially determined. Since Mom had not made a transfer for less than adequate consideration, the property would not be included in Mom's estate on her death, even if she died soon after the transfer. Particularly if the property were not actually income-producing, Mom had made a transfer of the entire property for the cost of a capital gains tax on the sale of the remainder interest, if the property transferred was appreciated.

A variation on this technique was for Mom and Son to jointly purchase a piece of property from a third party. Mom would buy the life interest and Son would buy the remainder interest. Each would pay the percentage of the purchase price that corresponded to his or her share of the property, com-

---

[60] See Ch. 21 on QPRTs for an example computing the amount of the converted annuity interest.

[61] Treas. Reg. § 25.2702-5(c)(8) (including governing instrument requirements).

[62] Treas. Reg. § 25.2702-2(c)(4)(iii). See Ch. 22 for a discussion of GRATs.

[63] Treas. Reg. § 25.2702-5(c)(8)(ii)(C)(2). See Ch. 21 on QPRTs for a discussion of the possibility of a gift on conversion, using this formula and an example computing the amount of the annuity.

puted according to the Treasury actuarial tables. When Mom died, the property would not be included in her estate.

In 1990, Section 2702 was enacted and put an end to this technique with respect to members of the same family. The technique is still available for those who are not family members.

[1] Sale of Remainder Interest

For purposes of Section 2702, the transfer of an interest in property with respect to which there are one or more term interests shall be treated as a transfer of an interest in a trust.[64]

> EXAMPLE: Mom sells Child a remainder interest (worth $40) in property and retains a life estate (worth $60). Child pays $40. Mom will be treated as having transferred the entire property to Child, thereby making a gift of $60.[65] On Mom's death, will the entire property be included in her estate under Section 2036(a), due to the failure of Child to pay $100 for the remainder interest? Presumably, the statutory answer is no, since the preamble to the first set of proposed regulations indicated that Section 2702 only applies for purposes of the gift tax.[66]

If, instead of an income interest, parent sells child a remainder interest and retains an annuity, what is the result? Parent should be held to retain a qualified interest if the governing instrument includes all the requirements of a qualified annuity interest.

[2] Term Interests Determined

[a] In General

A term interest is one of a series of successive (as contrasted with concurrent) interests. Thus, a life interest in property or an interest in property for a term of years is a term interest. However, a term interest does not include

---

[64] IRC § 2702(c)(1); Treas. Reg. § 25.2702-4(a).

[65] See Treas. Reg. § 25.2702-4(d), example 2.

[66] Notice of Proposed Rulemaking, 1991-1 CB 999. The proposed regulations were revised and adopted as final regulations by TD 8395, 1992-1 CB 316. See also IRC § 2702(a). However, in addition to the statutory construction question, the issue raised in Gradow v. United States, 897 F2d 516 (Fed. Cir. 1990) and its progeny still exists. This case says that adequate consideration for the remainder interest after a life income interest must be the entire value of the property, in order to keep the property from being included in the estate. Contra Estate of D'Ambrosio v. Comm'r, 78 AFTR2d 96-5602 (3d Cir. 1996). See Ch. 4 for a discussion of this issue.

a fee interest in property merely because it is held as a tenant in common, a tenant by the entirety or a joint tenant with right of survivorship.[67]

[b] Leases

A leasehold interest in property is not a term interest to the extent that the lease is for full and adequate consideration (without regard to Section 2702). A lease will be considered made for full and adequate consideration if, under all the facts and circumstances as of the time the lease is entered into or extended, a good faith effort is made to determine the fair rental value of the property and the terms of the lease conform to the value so determined.[68]

[3] Joint Purchases

If two or more members of the same family acquire interests in any property in the same transaction (or a series of related transactions), and at least one interest is a term interest, the person (or persons) acquiring the term interests will be deemed, under Section 2702, to have acquired the entire property and then transferred the remainder interests to the other persons involved in the transaction (or series of transactions). The deemed transfer shall be treated as made in exchange for the consideration (if any) provided by the other persons for the acquisition of their interests in such property.[69]

This rule applies solely for purposes of Section 2702.[70]

EXAMPLE: Candy store is worth $100. Father purchases life estate (worth $60) and Son purchases remainder interest (worth $40) in the store. Father will be treated as if he had purchased the entire property and transferred the remainder interest to Son for $40, resulting in a taxable gift of $60 (since Father's retained life estate will be given a value of zero for gift tax purposes).

An example of a joint purchase of interests in a family partnership that was approved by the IRS is contained in Private Letter Ruling 9515039.[71]

---

[67] Treas. Reg. § 25.2702-4(a).

[68] Treas. Reg. § 25.2702-4(b).

[69] IRC § 2702(c)(2).

[70] Treas. Reg. § 25.2702-4(c).

[71] Jan. 17, 1995.

[4] Limitation on Deemed Transfer

The amount of an individual's gift will not exceed the amount of consideration furnished by that individual for all interests in the property.[72]

> EXAMPLE: In the above example, if Father purchased his interest for $50, his deemed gift will be limited to $50.

> EXAMPLE: Parent establishes a trust, which gives the income interest to Child and the remainder interest to Grandchild. Have Child and Grandchild "acquired" term interests in property, subjecting them to this rule? Perhaps.[73] If so, Child's "gift" to Grandchild should be limited to the consideration, if any, that Child paid to Parent. In the case of a transfer to Child by Parent for no consideration—a routine gift by Parent of income to Child, remainder to Grandchild—Child's "gift" should be zero.

[5] Remainder After Annuity

Parent and Child jointly acquire property. Parent acquires a qualified annuity interest and Child acquires the remainder. How is this treated? It should be treated as if Parent acquired the entire property, retained a qualified annuity interest, and transferred a qualified remainder interest to Child, provided that the governing instrument contains the required provisions.

It is not specifically stated how the joint purchase rules interrelate with the rules governing personal residences in trust.[74] If there is a joint purchase of a personal residence, the personal residence is treated as having been acquired by the term holder and transferred in trust. If the personal residence rules apply, the document governing the rights of the term holder and remainder beneficiary would presumably have to meet the requirements of a personal residence trust or qualified personal residence trust in order to come within the personal residence exception.

---

[72] Treas. Reg. § 25.2702-4(c).

[73] See Treas. Reg. § 25.2702-4(d), example 4.

[74] See Ch. 21 for a discussion of QPRTS.

PART VI

Valuation Planning

CHAPTER 25

Valuation Issues

¶ 25.01 VALUATION DEPRESSORS—GENERAL

Estate planning may involve ownership structures that are subject to valuation discounts when the assets are transferred by gift or at death. What does this mean?

First, assets are generally valued at their true fair market value for transfer tax purposes. The term "discount" is therefore somewhat of a misnomer. That is, to the extent that the term "discount" implies that the value of any asset for transfer tax purposes is less than its true fair market value, the term is misleading. However, for transfer tax purposes, the term "discount" is commonly used to indicate that the fair market value of an asset is less than its apparent face value or, in the case of a discount for a partial interest in property, less than its pro rata share of the value of the whole. In most instances, a characteristic, feature, action, or event[1] that depresses the value of an asset for transfer tax purposes also reduces the "real" value of the asset, in the sense that a willing buyer would pay less to a willing seller because of it.[2]

For reporting purposes, the federal gift tax return requires the taxpayer to check a box if the valuation of a reported gift reflects a discount for lack of marketability, a minority interest, a fractional interest in real estate, blockage, market absorption, or any other reason. An explanation of the factual basis for the discount and the amount of the discount is also required.

This chapter discusses some reasons that assets might be worth more in one structure than another.

¶ 25.02 INTERESTS IN ENTITIES

An interest in an entity may be valued at less than its pro rata share of the value of the entity as a whole. This might be true for a variety of reasons. The interest may have limited or no voting rights or it may be a voting but noncontrolling interest. Other characteristics of the interest (e.g., restrictions on its sale) or the entity (e.g., the identity of the other owners) can also affect the interest's appeal in the marketplace.

---

[1] An example of an event which reduces the value of an asset would be a transfer of a partnership interest which becomes an assignee interest on transfer.

[2] An exception to this rule is the action of qualifying for IRC § 2032A, which provides an artificially low valuation for certain agricultural property. This section is discussed in Ch. 48.

EXAMPLE: Corporation X is worth $100,000. Dad owns 100 percent of Corporation X. He transfers 20 percent of the stock to Son. The 20 percent interest transferred to Son is probably not worth $20,000.

EXAMPLE: Dad and two adult sons form a new corporation, each transferring $100,000 to it. Each one-third interest received would normally be worth less than $100,000 because each is a minority interest and most likely unmarketable.

Consider the last example, and assume that neither Dad nor the sons have any intention of making a gift to each other. Why would each family member transfer assets to a business when the absolute value of what he holds may be immediately reduced as a result of the transfer? For the same reason he might form this business with two unrelated parties, which would have the same result. In fact, transactions such as those described in this example occur frequently among unrelated parties. The discounted value of each minority interest reflects the fact that the value of a business entity as a whole is often greater than the value of the sum of the parts. This synergy is in fact the reason many people invest together—the investors hope to eventually earn more together than they could individually.[3] The example illustrates the absurdity of the position that a gift takes place just because the value of property contributed to an entity does not immediately match the value of the stock or other ownership interest received in return.[4]

---

[3] The concept that the sum of the parts does not equal the whole is the reason that the subtraction method (which values one interest by subtracting the value of all other interests in the entity from the value of the entity as a whole) is not proper in the real world, and is only used where it is mandated, as in IRC §§ 2701 and 2702. See, e.g., Estate of Newhouse v. Comm'r, 94 TC 193 (1990), nonacq., 1991-2 CB 1.

[4] One case which seemed to present an opposing view was Trenchard v. Comm'r, 1995 RIA TC Memo. ¶ 95,232, 69 TCM (CCH) 2164 (1995). In this case, the Tax Court appeared to hold that a taxpayer's contribution of property to a corporation was a gift, where the value of the contribution exceeded the value of the preferred stock and debentures received in exchange. The court did specifically note that it was not dealing with a situation where all shareholders made proportional contributions and received proportional interests, so it did not have to decide whether all shareholders would be deemed to make reciprocal gifts in such a situation.

For an example of the general reluctance to characterize contributions to family partnerships as gifts based on the inequality of value contributed and value received, see the following line of cases, which developed the rule that constructive gifts were not made by existing partners to new partners who contributed value in exchange for their partnership interests, unless the value contributed was less than the value received *and* the earnings of the entity came from "special capital" (unique property), not from services of the other partners, managerial skill of the partners, or income from "ordinary capital." Gross v. Comm'r, 7 TC 837 (1946), acq., 1946-2 CB 2; Rothrock v. Comm'r, 7 TC 848 (1946), acq., 1946-2 CB 4; Fischer v. Comm'r, 8 TC 732 (1947), acq., 1947-1 CB 2; Friedman v. Comm'r, 10 TC 1145 (1948), acq., 1948-2 CB 2;

The courts and the IRS[5] have recognized several types of discounts that normally apply to interests in entities.

[1] Lack of Control ("Minority") Discount

A minority discount is appropriate in valuing an interest which does not enable its owner to control the management of the entity or to compel distributions from the entity. In fact, the term "minority discount" is misleading, since an interest does not actually have to be a minority interest to be subject to the discount;[6] the discount should properly be called (and sometimes is called) a "lack of control" discount.[7] For example, a gift of a 75 percent limited partnership interest might receive a "minority" discount, despite the fact that it is not truly a minority interest, because a limited partner has no actual control over day-to-day partnership management. Limited partnership interests, nonvoting stock, and minority interests in corporations are frequently eligible for minority discounts simply because these interests will carry little (if any) control of the operation of the entity.

Appraisers can find empirical support for values of illiquid minority/"no control" interests by reviewing sales of interests in real estate investment trusts, closed-end mutual funds, and secondary limited partnership markets.[8]

However, lack of control does not always mean lack of *complete* control. Even a majority owner often will not have control over all aspects of decision-making. Control comes in various levels. For example, control may be mea-

---

Lippert v. Comm'r, 11 TC 783 (1948), remanded to vacate decision pursuant to stipulation of parties, 184 F2d 672 (8th Cir. 1950).

[5] Rev. Rul. 59-60, 1959-1 CB 237.

[6] Estate of Wheeler v. United States, 96-1 USTC ¶ 60,226 (WD Tex. 1996), adopting order recommended at 77 AFTR2d 1405 (1995), rev'd on other issues, 97-2 USTC ¶ 60,278 (5th Cir. 1997) (IRS unsuccessfully attempted to deny a minority discount for a 50 percent interest in a corporation on the basis that 50 percent is not a minority interest).

[7] Estate of Frank v. Comm'r, 1995 RIA TC Memo. ¶ 95,132, 69 TCM (CCH) 2255, 2262 (1995) (holding that a minority discount is appropriate if the interest does not enjoy the rights associated with control); see also Estate of Jung v. Comm'r, 101 TC 412, 442 (1993); Estate of Newhouse v. Comm'r, 94 TC 193, 249, 251-52 (1990), nonacq., 1991-2 CB 1; Estate of Chenoweth v. Comm'r, 88 TC 1577, 1582 (1987); Harwood v. Comm'r, 82 TC 239, 267 (1984), aff'd without published opinion, 786 F2d 1174 (9th Cir.), cert. denied, 479 US 1007 (1986); Estate of Andrews v. Comm'r, 79 TC 938, 957 (1982).

[8] Empirical data is important in proof of valuation. Several cases have held that a list of discounts in unrelated cases was not sufficient by itself to support a discount. Estate of Pauline E. Dattel v. Comm'r, 37 AFTR2d, 76-1525, 76-1 USTC 13,119 (1975); Wildman v. Comm'r, 1995 RIA TC Memo. ¶ 89,667, 58 TCM 2006 (1988); Estate of Pillsbury v. Comm'r, 1992 RIA TC Memo. ¶ 92,425, 64 TCM 284 (1992).

sured in relation to one of the following standards required to effect a particular entity act:

Unanimous consent. A particular entity action may require the affirmative consent of all owners. Accordingly, with respect to such acts, anything short of a 100 percent ownership in a single person indicates a lack of control.

Supermajority. In any particular case, the entity documents and/or state law may provide that a certain percentage (greater than 51 percent) is necessary to approve extraordinary measures, such as a sale or liquidation of substantially all of the entity's assets. In such cases, control (or the lack thereof) will depend on the percentage of approval required for the measure.

Majority ownership. Majority ownership of the voting/managing interests is usually enough to enable the majority owner to control day-to-day operating decisions. In such cases, ownership of 50 percent or less voting interest constitutes a lack of control.

PRACTICE POINTER: Any time there is a noncontrolling owner, a controlling owner may owe fiduciary duties to the noncontrolling owner.

[a] Gift and Estate Tax Valuation Differences

Minority discounts tend to be available more often in valuing gifts than estate transfers. Why? For gift tax purposes, each interest gifted to a particular donee is generally valued standing alone, without regard to other interests held by the donor or donee. In contrast, all interests that were owned by a decedent at his death (and perhaps even all interests that are otherwise included in his gross estate)[9] are valued as an aggregate for purposes of determining the value of the estate, regardless of how many beneficiaries take the property. Thus, a majority shareholder can make a gift of a minority interest that may have a discounted value for gift tax purposes. However, the same discount would not be available in the majority shareholder's estate if he died.

[b] Gift Tax Valuation

Revenue Ruling 93-12[10] was a landmark ruling in the valuation arena. It reflects the IRS's decision to throw in the towel after losing numerous cases on the valuation of gifts of minority interests in family-owned entities. The fact situation in the ruling involved a parent who controlled a corporation and gave each of his children 20 percent of the stock. The IRS stated that each child's gift would be valued without regard to the family relationship of the parties, even though the transferred interests (when aggregated with other

---

[9] See ¶ 25.02[1][c][ii] below.

[10] 1993-1 CB 202.

interests held by family members) would constitute a controlling interest in the entity. Hence, if Dad gave 20 percent of a corporation to each of his five children, each 20 percent gift should be valued as a minority interest. This is in contrast to the estate tax valuation that would result if the same disposition were made at Dad's death.

[c] Estate Tax Valuation—Determining Gross Estate

If Dad dies owning 100 percent of a corporation and he leaves 20 percent of the stock to each of five beneficiaries, the entire value of the corporation, undiscounted for fractional interests, will be included in Dad's estate.[11]

A minority discount may be appropriate in valuing an interest for estate tax purposes when the estate includes only a noncontrolling interest. For example, if Dad had owned 100 percent of an entity but transferred 51 percent of it during his life, his estate may then be allowed a minority discount for the remaining 49 percent. Can Dad effectively reduce his interest just before he dies?

[i] Deathbed transfers. If Dad waits until he is on his deathbed to reduce his holdings to a noncontrolling interest, his estate may not receive the discount. The *Murphy*[12] case involved such a situation. Mrs. Murphy owned 51.41 percent of a family entity. She transferred 0.88 percent of it to each of her two children 18 days before her death, reducing her interest to 49.65 percent. The Tax Court found that the sole purpose of the transfer was to obtain a minority discount in Mrs. Murphy's estate.

The evidentiary basis for this finding was contained in a nonprivileged letter from the family accountant urging that the transfer be made before Mrs. Murphy's death for the purpose of obtaining a discount. The court disallowed any minority discount, based on alternate theories. One was that Mrs. Murphy's transfers of control to her children by the gifts and testamentary gifts in trust for their benefit on her death 18 days later were collapsed under the step transaction doctrine. The other was a theory that a "deduction" (apparently for a minority discount) will not be allowed if a transfer has little effect on the taxpayer's beneficial interest except to reduce transfer taxes.

Both of the court's stated legal theories are questionable. (For example, the first theory would deny the annual exclusion for annual exclusion gifts made shortly before death. The second theory, if "deduction" means "exclusion," would deny the annual exclusion for any annual exclusion gift, regard-

---

[11] IRC § 2033; see also Tech. Adv. Mem. 9449001 (Mar. 11, 1994).

[12] Estate of Murphy v. Comm'r, 1990 RIA TC Memo. ¶ 90,472, 60 TCM (CCH) 645 (1990).

less of when made, if the annual exclusion gift did not appreciably affect the transferor's holdings.[13]) The Tax Court was apparently offended by the facts.

A subsequent case in the same court was decided differently.[14] In this case, Mr. Frank was terminally ill, and his death appeared imminent. Mr. Frank's revocable trust owned a 50.3 percent interest in a family corporation. Mr. Frank's child, acting pursuant to a durable power of attorney, withdrew 18.2 percent of the stock from the trust and gave it to Mrs. Frank, who was also terminally ill. This transfer resulted in Mr. Frank's revocable trust owning 32.1 percent of the corporation, and Mrs. Frank owning 18.2 percent of the corporation. Mr. Frank in fact died two days later, and Mrs. Frank died 15 days after his death. The Tax Court held that both spouses' estates were entitled to minority interest valuations. In addressing the IRS's argument that the transfer to Mrs. Frank should be ignored because it was made solely for tax reasons, the court deemed the motive for the transfer irrelevant, but commented that, if tax avoidance had been the sole motive, a substantially smaller number of shares could have been transferred (since a transfer of 0.4 percent would have changed his majority interest to a minority interest).[15]

[ii] **Aggregation of interests included in gross estate under separate estate tax provisions.** The IRS has taken the position that all interests which are included in one individual's gross estate are aggregated, even when they were actually held by different owners. This situation usually arises when interests in the same property were held by a combination of the decedent, a QTIP trust for the decedent's benefit, and/or other people, in the case of other property included in the decedent's gross estate, but not owned by him.[16]

In this regard, suppose Dad owns a 100 percent interest in property. If Dad transfers a 20 percent undivided interest in the property, and the interest is brought back into his estate under one of Sections 2035-2038, it may be proper to value the property in Dad's estate as a 100 percent interest, rather

---

[13] For an actual example of an attack on annual exclusion gifts based on an aggregation theory, see Driver v. United States, 38 AFTR2d 76-6315, 76-2 USTC ¶ 13,155, at 85, 699 (WD Wis. 1976). The Court aggregated certain gifts, including annual exclusion gifts, for valuation purposes (thus denying a minority discount for each gift when in the aggregate, a controlling interest was transferred) because the gifts were made two days apart—on December 31 of one year and January 2 of the next.

[14] Estate of Frank v. Comm'r, 1995 RIA TC Memo. ¶ 95,132, 69 TCM (CCH) 2255 (1995).

[15] Estate of Frank v. Comm'r, 1995 RIA TC Memo. ¶ 95,132, 69 69 TCM (CCH) 2255, 2259 (1995).

[16] E.g., Tech. Adv. Mem. 9608001 (Aug. 18, 1995) (interests includable in decedent's estate under IRC §§ 2038 and 2044 aggregated for purpose of valuation in decedent's estate); Tech. Adv. Mem. 9550002 (Aug. 31, 1995) (similarly, with respect to interests included under IRC §§ 2033 and 2044); Tech. Adv. Mem. 9140002 (June 18, 1991) (same).

than as an 80 percent and a 20 percent interest.[17] This analysis does not necessarily apply in case of inclusion of a directly owned interest and a QTIP interest, which was not included in Dad's estate as a result of a transfer made by Dad.[18]

[d] Estate Tax Valuation—Determining Marital and Charitable Deductions

The valuation of property may not be the same for determining the amount of the gross estate and for determining the amount of the marital and charitable deductions. This concept is a real trap for the unwary. The dichotomy can exist because the value of property in a person's estate is based on the estate's entire interest in the property. The marital and charitable deductions are measured by the amount passing to the spouse or charity.[19] Hence, splitting an estate asset into minority interests can have adverse tax consequences, whether the split is accomplished by the dispositive instruments or by funding decisions.

Valuation reductions caused by dispositive instruments. This kind of problem can be caused by the nature of the dispositions made by the decedent. Suppose Dad bequeaths 20 percent of an entity to each of five beneficiaries. No minority discount is available for purposes of valuing Dad's interest in the entity which is includable in his gross estate (i.e., 100 percent of the entity). However, if any of Dad's five beneficiaries is a charity or his wife, then that beneficiary's 20 percent interest may be discounted in determining the amount passing to the charity/wife when calculating the estate's charitable/marital deduction.[20] This set of circumstances can also trigger the inclusion of phan-

---

[17] See Rev. Rul. 79-7, 1979-1 CB 294, treating a transferred asset which is includable in the transferor's gross estate under IRC § 2035(a) as if no transfer had been made.

[18] Estate of Bonner v. United States, 84 F3d 196 (5th Cir. 1996) (en banc) (no aggregation of individually held interest and interest held by QTIP trust which merged into 100 percent fee ownership by decedent's estate at his death) (tenancies in common in real and personal property). The Fifth Circuit noted that, at the time of decedent's death, his estate did not have control over the QTIP assets such that it could act as a hypothetical seller negotiating with willing buyers free of the handicaps associated with fractional undivided interests. Query whether the result would have differed if that fact had been different. Compare Tech. Adv. Mem. 9608001 (Aug. 18, 1995) (holding that partnership interests in such circumstances should be aggregated).

[19] IRC §§ 2056(a), 2055(a).

[20] Ahmanson Foundation v. United States, 674 F2d 761 (9th Cir. 1981); Estate of Chenoweth v. Comm'r, 88 TC 1577 (1987). Priv. Ltr. Rul. 9403005 (Oct. 14, 1993). Compare Provident Nat'l Bank v. United States, 581 F2d 1081 (3d Cir. 1978), on remand, 502 F. Supp. 908 (ED Pa. 1980), holding that stock bequeathed to a marital deduction trust must be given the same value for purposes of IRC §§ 2031 and 2056.

tom amounts in Dad's estate.[21]

> EXAMPLE: Dad's estate consists of a 100 percent interest in a corporation. Dad left one-half of the stock to his wife and the other one-half to a charity. If each beneficiary's interest is discounted for lack of control, Dad will have a taxable estate, even though his entire estate passes to a charity and the surviving spouse.

Valuation reductions caused by funding decisions. What if the valuation reduction is caused by funding of the bequests, rather than by the decedent's testamentary direction? Suppose Dad held a 100 percent interest in a corporation. The disposition of Dad's estate is governed by a formula will with a bypass trust and a QTIP trust. The corporation is valued in Dad's estate at $1,000,000. The executor duly distributes 60 percent of the corporation to the bypass trust and 40 percent to the QTIP trust. What happens? —

- If the 40 percent interest passing to the QTIP trust is discounted 25 percent, will only $300,000 in value be deemed to have passed to the QTIP trust? If so, will this cause an estate tax?
- Or, will the executor be liable to the QTIP trust for reducing the value of its bequest by funding in kind instead of selling the entire corporation and distributing $400,000 to the QTIP trust?
- Or, does the will's funding formula require putting more than 40 percent of the corporation in the QTIP trust? For example, a pecuniary marital deduction bequest, to be satisfied at date-of-distribution values, may require putting enough of the stock in the trust to actually equal $400,000 of value. This would in turn reduce the amount passing to the bypass trust.
- Or, if the funding formula is a fractional share, or a bypass trust funded at date-of-distribution values, can the division of an entity be used as a planning technique, enabling the executor to reduce the value of the marital deduction trust by funding it with a fractional interest worth less than its pro rata share of the entity without reducing the marital deduction?

[e] More Aggregation Theories

[i] No aggregation of transferred interest with recipient's interests. From a valuation standpoint, it does not matter if a gift or bequest of a minority interest gives the recipient a controlling interest when it is aggregated

---

[21] Phantom amounts are values includable in the gross estate which do not actually exist in reality, or which are not actually receivable by a beneficiary or creditor of the estate.

with the interest already owned by the recipient.[22] In addition to court cases, the IRS itself has privately ruled that the value of a minority interest may be discounted even if the transfer will make the transferee the 100 percent owner.[23] The decedent whose estate was the subject of the ruling owned a minority interest in a corporation and bequeathed the interest to the only other shareholder. The IRS stated that neither the relationship of the decedent to the legatee nor the number of legatees to whom shares in the corporation passed was relevant in valuing the shares includable in the estate.

[ii] Sleight-of-hand transactions. The IRS may attack a plan which is implemented by a number of separate simultaneous transactions that together result in the actual transfer of a controlling interest to a particular person. For example, in one case, a shareholder owned 52 percent of a corporation and his son owned 48 percent. One day, he gave one percent of the company to his daughter-in-law and one percent each to his two grandchildren. Pursuant to a long pattern of behavior, the daughter-in-law immediately transferred her stock to the son, and the grandchildren's interest was never reflected on the books of the corporation or respected in reality. On the same day, the corporation redeemed Dad's remaining 49 percent interest, leaving the son with all of the stock, as reflected on the company books. Dad claimed a minority valuation of the 1 percent gifts, and redeemed his 49 percent interest for a price reflecting a minority discount without reporting the redemption as a gift. The Tax Court gave a thumbs-down to this plan, holding that the entire transaction constituted a gift of a controlling interest to the son. The gifts to the son's wife and children were treated as gifts directly to the son since the transfers to them lacked any reality. When viewed as a whole, the separation of the gifts and redemption transaction was held to be a device for obtaining a minority discount on the actual gift of a 52 percent interest.[24]

[f] Interest with a Swing Vote

The IRS has taken the position that a "swing vote" premium may be appropriate for a transfer of a noncontrolling interest which can achieve control by aggregating with another interest.[25] Such a premium would tend to

---

[22] Estate of Andrews v. Comm'r, 79 TC 938 (1982); Estate of Lee v. Comm'r, 69 TC 860 (1978), nonacq., 1980-2 CB 2, withdrawn and acq., Rev. Rul. 93-12, 1993-1 CB 202; Estate of Pillsbury v. Comm'r, 1992 RIA TC Memo. ¶ 92,425, 64 TCM 284 (1992) (undivided interests held by marital trust and bypass trust not aggregated on surviving spouse's death, despite the fact that the assets of the marital trust passed to the bypass trust).

[23] Tech. Adv. Mem. 9432001 (Mar. 28, 1994).

[24] Estate of Cidulka v. Comm'r, 1996 RIA TC Memo. ¶ 96,149, 71 TCM (CCH) 2555 (1996).

[25] Tech. Adv. Mem. 9436005 (May 26, 1994).

offset the effect of any otherwise allowable minority discount.[26] The theory is that a hypothetical willing buyer, who has knowledge of relevant facts, would be willing to pay more for such an interest than for an interest that did not offer this opportunity. An example would be a gift of a two percent interest, if the remaining two shareholders owned 49 percent each. Taken to its logical extreme, this theory would also appear to apply to a transfer of a one-third interest, if two other shareholders each owned one-third.[27]

In the case of a transfer of a "swing" interest, what if one of the swing shareholders is the transferee?

EXAMPLE: Dad, Daughter and Mom each own one-third of a corporation. Dad gives his one-third to Daughter. Does the swing vote theory, which requires consideration of the ownership of the nongifted shares, mandate that the interest be valued as a controlling interest, due to Daughter's ability to combine the votes attributable to that one-third with her own pre-existing one-third interest? No. The gifted interest is treated as if it were bought by a hypothetical third party buyer. The IRS's position is that the gifted interest would be given a higher value than it might otherwise be given, however, due to the hypothetical buyer's ability to combine with either Mother or Daughter and thereby achieve control.

Another way of understanding the swing vote theory is to think of it as a veto power. In a company owned equally by three unrelated parties, each owner effectively has a veto over actions to be taken by either one of the other owners acting alone. In the previous example, although the hypothetical buyer receiving the gifted interest would in theory have the same veto power, in reality, a third party buyer might anticipate that Mom and Daughter would tend to vote with each other (rather than with the third party buyer) anyway, and might value the interest less for that reason. Revenue Ruling 93-12,[28] however, requires that family attribution not be considered.

A variation of the swing vote argument is occasionally made—that is, if a minority interest would be enough to give control to a single buyer, who

---

[26] E.g., in Estate of Winkler v. Comm'r, 1989 PH TC Memo. ¶ 89,231, 57 TCM (CCH) 373 (1989), the Tax Court recognized a 10 percent swing vote premium offsetting a minority discount for a 10 percent interest in a corporation when remaining stock was held 40 percent by decedent's family and 50 percent by another family. There was some controversy over whether it was appropriate to consider swing vote characteristics if the 50 percent block was owned by members of a family rather than by one individual. The Tax Court held that, if that fact was important, the decedent's estate had not submitted evidence on the ownership of the stock, and had thus failed to carry its burden of proof that the block was not held by a single individual.

[27] Or any other ownership pattern, if no one shareholder has control, but the transferred interest is enough by itself for the transferee shareholder to join with another shareholder and exercise joint control.

[28] 1993-1 CB 202.

already owns an interest, the existence of that potential buyer would be enough to increase the value of the minority interest.

[g] Interaction With Section 2032A Special Use Valuation

If a minority interest in property is specially valued under Section 2032A, how does the reduction in value for special use property interrelate with the minority discount? The Tenth Circuit has held that the reduction in value of a minority interest in property due to Section 2032A is subtracted from the true fair market value of the minority interest, after applying the minority discount.[29] This case reversed the Tax Court, which had held that a minority discount is not available for an entity containing Section 2032A property.[30]

[2] Discount for Lack of Marketability

Interests in family entities often suffer a depressed value, due to lack of marketability. The marketability discount reflects the facts that a ready market for an interest in a family business often does not exist and that a willing third-party buyer to purchase an interest in such a business is hard to find. Even controlling interests in such businesses can be subject to a marketability discount.[31] This is because even a controlling interest in a family business can be hard to sell.

[a] Wholly Owned Entities

In fact, a marketability discount has been allowed in cases where the decedent owned 100 percent of the entity.[32] How could this be? The discount is said to reflect the fact that even an entire closely held business entity is difficult to market, due to limited interest, potential liabilities, etc. Those opposing a discount in such a situation would value the entity at a floor of its

---

[29] Estate of Hoover v. Comm'r, 69 F3d 1044 (10th Cir. 1995).

[30] 102 TC 777 (1994), rev'd, Estate of Hoover v. Comm'r, 69 F3d 1044 (10th Cir. 1995).

[31] But not always. See O'Connell v. Comm'r, 1978 PH TC Memo. ¶ 78,191, 37 TCM (CCH) 1138 (1978), aff'd in part and rev'd in part, 640 F2d 249 (9th Cir. 1981) (denying marketability discount for ranch company, partly because decedent held a controlling interest).

[32] Estate of Dougherty v. Comm'r, 1990 PH TC Memo. ¶ 90,274, 59 TCM (CCH) 772 (1990); Estate of Bennett v. Comm'r, 1989 PH TC Memo. ¶ 86,425, 65 TCM (CCH) 1816 (1993). Contra, Estate of Jephson v. Comm'r, 87 TC 297 (1986). See also Estate of Cloutier v. Comm'r, 1996 RIA TC Memo. ¶ 96,049, 71 TCM (CCH) 2001 (1996) (dictum that such a discount could apply in some cases, although a marketability discount was inappropriate in this case, where the stock was not valued with reference to listed stock).

liquidation value, arguing that the shareholder could always liquidate the entity and realize the value of the assets. Would they be correct? Not necessarily.

PRACTICE POINTER: We can't jump to the conclusion that a sole owner can always liquidate a wholly-owned entity. A sole owner's ability to liquidate a business entity is often restricted by contractual agreements with third parties. Covenants not to liquidate are frequently found, for example, in loan agreements and leases.

Even if a sole owner can liquidate the entity, liquidation value, of course, is often not the highest value of a business. Many times, a business is more valuable as a going concern than as a collection of individual assets.[33] In such a case, should a marketability discount from going concern value be applied to an interest owned by a sole shareholder, who could sell the whole entity? Yes, in appropriate circumstances.

EXAMPLE: The sole shareholder cannot sell without the consent of a third party, such as a lender. Even if the lender consented, the consent would likely be predicated on the purchaser's becoming subject to the same requirement, so the depressant effect on value would still exist.

EXAMPLE: Prospective purchasers often do not want to buy the stock of a going concern, due to unknown liabilities. They may prefer to buy the particular assets that they need.

[b] Factors in Determining Marketability Discount

The Tax Court has set forth a detailed discussion of factors it considered in determining marketability discount applicable to stock of a corporation.[34] They included:

- Private versus public sales of stock;
- Financial statement analysis;
- Dividend policy;
- Company's nature, history, industry position, and economic outlook;
- Company's management;
- Amount of control in transferred shares;
- Restrictions on transferability of stock;

---

[33] Generally accepted accounting principles require valuation of a business as a going concern, unless there is reason to believe that the entity is in danger of demise or that it actually intends to liquidate.

[34] Mandelbaum v. Comm'r, 1995 RIA TC Memo. ¶ 95,255, 69 TCM 2852 (1995), aff'd, 91 F3d 124 (3d Cir. 1996).

- Holding period expected to enable investor to reap a reasonable profit;
- Company's redemption policy (if any); and
- Costs associated with public offering.

General evidentiary support for marketability discounts for interests in closely held entities tends to be found in such places as: public secondary markets for limited partnership interests; closed-end mutual funds; REITs; court cases with similar facts; restricted stock studies; and pre-IPO studies. For instance, a secondary market exists for many syndicated limited partnership interests offered in the 1970's and 1980's. Pricing tends to demonstrate deep discounts from partnership net asset value, and frequently no buyer can be found at any price.[35] Factors driving deeper discounts include: low cash distributions; low underlying cash flow; low frequency of sales of interests; low number of investors; long time horizon until liquidation; small pool of potentially interested buyers; securities restrictions on resale; rights of first refusal; unpopular types of assets; low information flow to limited partners; single-property entity; general partner who has a bad or no reputation or who is incompetent, dishonest, or uncooperative; and high debt. Similarly, pre-IPO studies have found that a significant discount from the IPO price is usually experienced.[36]

[3] Overlap of Minority and Marketability Discounts

Although the courts generally refer to both minority and marketability discounts, their opinions often do not measure the discounts separately—rather, one overall discount figure may be used. The two types of discounts tend to overlap as a theoretical matter, since part of the reason an interest is difficult to market may be its lack of control.

[4] Inherent Decline in Value of Interest on Transfer

Sometimes, the value of an interest will partially disappear if the interest is transferred. A good example is a partnership interest, if the interest is transformed into an assignee interest on transfer. The value of the transferred interest may be reduced by the fact that the donee receives an assignee interest

---

[35] See annual reports by The Partnership Spectrum.

[36] The Tax Court recognized this in Eyler v. Comm'r, 1995 RIA TC Memo. ¶ 95,123, 69 TCM (CCH) 2200 (1995), aff'd, F3d 445 (7th Cir. 1996), where it imposed a fine respecting a transaction in which an ESOP purchased shares for an excessive price, using a value based on a proposed offering price for an IPO which was abandoned several months before the purchase.

rather than a partnership interest, and therefore does not acquire the management participation rights of a partner.[37]

A donor's dream gift is often a gift of property that he continues to control after the transfer. Hence, a donor will often transfer assets to a family limited partnership, retain a general partnership interest, and make gifts of limited partnership interests. What if the donor-general partner then dies or gives away his general partnership interest? The value of the interest will typically be worth less after its transformation to an assignee interest than it was worth in the general partner's hands.

Section 2704 disallows some (but not all) discounts due to disappearing value. It does so by characterizing the amount of the vanished value as a taxable transfer.[38]

[5] Discount for Restrictive Contractual Provisions

Partnership agreements and other contractual agreements entered into by entities or their owners will often contain provisions that limit the owners' rights. Common restrictions include limitations on the ability to transfer an interest and limitations on the ability to withdraw capital from the entity. Also, loan agreements may preclude distributions, further borrowing, or changes in capital structure. Such restrictions similarly tend to reduce value.

[6] Discount for Securities Restrictions

Securities law restrictions on transfers can affect the value of securities, particularly in a volatile market.[39] Discounts can be substantial for publicly traded stock which cannot be sold for a period of time, since the stock will necessarily be subject to the vagaries of the market for that period.[40]

---

[37] Estate of McLendon v. Comm'r, 77 F3d 477 (5th Cir. 1995), unpublished opinion rev'g and remanding 1993 RIA TC Memo. ¶ 93,459, 66 TCM (CCH) 946 (1993). However, see Ch. 16 on limited partnerships and Ch. 27 on Section 2704 for discussions of situations in which disappearing value can be problematic.

[38] See Ch. 16 on family partnerships and Ch. 27 on Section 2704 for an explanation.

[39] See Ch. 51 on taxation of persons owning interests in publicly traded companies for a discussion of securities restrictions.

[40] E.g., Estate of Sullivan v. Comm'r, 1983 PH TC Memo. ¶ 83,185, 45 TCM (CCH) 1199 (1983) (applying 15 percent discount based on securities law restrictions); Estate of Stratton v. Comm'r, 1982 PH TC Memo. ¶ 82,744, 45 TCM (CCH) 432 (1982) (applying 25 percent discount to unregistered stock that could only be sold by private placement); Estate of Brownell v. Comm'r, 1982 PH TC Memo. ¶ 82,632, 44 TCM (CCH) 1550 (1982) (applying 33 percent discount to unregistered stock that could only be sold by private placement); Estate of Little v. Comm'r, 1982 PH TC

[7] Discount for Large Interest in Publicly Traded Company (Blockage)

Owning a large interest in a public company is not a guarantee of owning a more valuable interest, share for share, than a smaller holding. Even a large block of publicly held stock may be valued at a discount, if the market will not absorb the stock in a reasonable time.[41] If it will take an extended time to liquidate property in an orderly manner, the holdings will be subject to the volatility of the market for a longer period.

Separate lifetime gifts of stock to different individuals generally are not aggregated for purposes of determining whether a blockage discount applies.[42] However, an exception may apply where gifts are made to an individual and to a trust for that individual.[43]

Courts have often combined discounts based on blockage and securities law restrictions. These are conceptually distinct types of discounts, but the factors in determining each can overlap.[44] Some of the factors to be considered in determining whether a blockage discount is appropriate are: the size of the block (as a percentage of the publicly held shares of the stock); the amount of stock normally traded in the market each day; the absolute dollar value of the shares in the block; the price per share of the stock; and the practically available methods of disposal of the shares.

The holder of a large block of stock may have several alternatives available for disposition of his shares. The availability, expense, and practicality of each of the following alternatives can affect the valuation of the block:

- *Dump holder's block in the open market.* In doing so, the holder risks depressing the price, or even causing it to go into a market free-fall.

Memo. ¶ 82,206, 43 TCM (CCH) 319 (1982) (applying 60 percent total discount for securities restrictions, blockage, and other factors); Bolles v. Comm'r, 69 TC 342 (1977) (applying discounts for restricted securities); Rev. Rul. 77-287, 1977-2 CB 319. See also Estate of McClatchy v. Comm'r, 106 TC 206 (1996) (stock valued at its full fair market value when Rule 144 restrictions on a decedent's stock ceased to apply on his death). Valuation of restricted stock is further discussed in Ch. 51.

[41] Treas. Reg. §§ 20.2031-2(e), 25.2512-2(e); see also United States v. Helvering, 301 US 540 (1937) (blockage discount of over 38 percent applied); Bull v. Smith, 119 F2d 490 (2d Cir. 1941); Estate of Kopperman v. Comm'r, 1978 PH TC Memo. ¶ 78,475, 37 TCM (CCH) 1849 (1978).

[42] Treas. Reg. § 25.2512-2(e); Maytag v. Comm'r, 187 F2d 962 (10th Cir. 1951); see also Rushton v. Comm'r, 60 TC 272 (1973), aff'd, 498 F2d 88 (5th Cir. 1974); Avery v. Comm'r, 3 TC 963 (1944).

[43] Cf. Priv. Ltr. Rul. 8049015 (Aug. 29, 1980) (addressing similar question with respect to applicability of discount for securities law restrictions).

[44] E.g., Estate of Little v. Comm'r, 1982 PH TC Memo. ¶ 82,632, 43 TCM (CCH) 319 (1982).

- *Dribble out shares over a period of time.* Here, the holder's hope will be that he can sell the stock in small enough batches that the sales will not depress the price. The longer the expected time it will take to dispose of the stock in this fashion, the higher the discount should be.
- *Sell the shares in a secondary offering.* Public offerings are generally expensive and time-consuming. Additionally, if the block holder is an officer or director, the sale may be viewed as a negative sign by analysts. Secondary offerings can result in both large discounts and large premiums to per-share value. Valuation based on a possible secondary offering tends to be speculative.
- *Privately place the block with a large buyer.* There are traders who specialize in buying and selling large blocks of stock. They are called, appropriately enough, block traders.
- *Sell the stock short to protect against value loss.* A discount for having to leave the shares exposed to the vagaries of the public market may be countered by the argument that the holder could sell the stock short to protect against a decline in value.[45] This may not be easily done with a large block, since it may not be possible to obtain short buyers for a large amount of stock at a price equal to the current price. Additionally, short sales do have significant transaction fees, and the market implications of shorting large blocks can be negative.

[8] Liquidation Value and the Right to Dissolve

The IRS has unsuccessfully argued in partnership cases that a general partnership interest should be valued at its liquidation value if the general partner had the right to dissolve the partnership by withdrawing.[46] The right to dissolve does not necessarily convey the right to liquidate.[47]

For example, in the *Scanlon* case, the Tax Court valued a minority general partnership interest at a discount, holding that owners of minority general partnership interests in the partnership in question held little meaningful ability to participate in management and that the legal ability of a general partner to dissolve the partnership had little impact. The court al-

---

[45] See description of "short-against-the-box" transactions in Ch. 30.

[46] Moore v. Comm'r, 1991 PH TC Memo. ¶ 91,601, 62 TCM 1128 (1991); McCormick v. Comm'r, 1995 PH TC Memo. ¶ 95,371, 70 TCM (CCH) 318 (1995); Estate of Watts v. Comm'r, 823 F2d 483 (11th Cir. 1987), aff'g 51 TCM 60. See also Estate of Barudin v. Comm'r, 1996 RIA TC Memo. ¶ 96,395, 72 TCM (CCH) 488 (1996), where IRS unsuccessfully argued that a minority general partner could meaningfully participate in management and court sua sponte brought up the right to dissolve, holding that it had little effect on value.

[47] See Ch. 16 on family partnerships for an explanation.

lowed a discount of 45 percent (19 percent for lack of control and 26 percent for lack of marketability).[48]

Even if the general partner does have the right to liquidate the partnership, the value of his interest is not necessarily his pro rata portion of the partnership assets. In *McCormick*,[49] the taxpayer conceded that a general partner in the particular partnership had the ability to cause the partnership to be liquidated. However, the Tax Court recognized that the general partner's declaration of dissolution of the partnership would not result in the general partner's immediate receipt of a check. It would only cause the partnership to begin winding up. Additional time and expense would be required to liquidate the partnership assets.

[9] Discount for Corporate-Level Tax on Unrealized Capital Gains

It seems rational that a discount would in fact apply to a corporation that had high unrealized capital gains on appreciated property. In *Estate of Luton v. Commissioner*,[50] the Tax Court stated that it has been its consistent position that a discount for potential capital gains tax at the corporate level is unwarranted where there is no evidence that a liquidation of the corporation was planned or that the liquidation could not have been accomplished without incurring a corporate level tax. Although the court denied a direct value reduction for the eventual capital gains tax, it did consider the tax as a factor in determining a marketability discount. Let's consider the two conditions—

Intent to liquidate. The court in *Luton* stated that costs of sale or liquidation of corporate property (including any capital gains tax incurred on such a sale or liquidation) are not proper deductions in arriving at estate tax value where the sale or liquidation is speculative. The IRS has also taken the position that the unrealized tax on appreciated assets has no effect on valuation if the liquidation of the underlying assets is speculative.[51]

---

[48] Estate of Scanlon v. Comm'r, 1996 RIA TC Memo. ¶ 96,331, 72 TCM (CCH) 160 (1996).

[49] 1995 RIA TC Memo. ¶ 95,371, 70 TCM 318 (1995).

[50] 1994 RIA TC Memo. ¶ 96,539, 68 TCM 1044 (1994), supplemental op., 1996 RIA TC Memo. ¶ 96,181, 71 TCM 2772 (1996).

[51] Tech. Adv. Mem. 9150001 (Aug. 20, 1991); Estate of Bennett v. Comm'r, 65 TCM 1816 (1993). Compare Clark, Jr. v. United States, 36 AFTR2d 75-6417 (EDNC 1975) (disallowing separate deduction of hypothetical tax liability from sale of assets of corporation, but allowing the tax liability as a factor to consider in determining value); Estate of Newhouse v. Comm'r, 94 TC 193 (1990), nonacq., 1991-2 CB 1. Precedents which antedate the repeal of the *General Utilities* doctrine in 1986 may no longer be applicable, despite Tech. Adv. Mem. 9150001 to the contrary.

Tax-free liquidation. The Tax Court's second condition in *Luton* was predicated on the fact that, under a transition rule, the S corporations involved could liquidate without paying capital gains tax 14 months after the date of death. Therefore, it is not clear that this reasoning would apply to a C corporation. After the Tax Reform Act of 1986, C corporations can no longer liquidate without paying capital gains tax on appreciated property. A C corporation might be able to avoid capital gains tax on liquidation by electing S status and waiting ten years before liquidating or disposing of appreciated assets. However, not all corporations can elect S status and, in any case, this seems an extreme price to pay for tax-free treatment—in the same vein as the position that a capital gains tax can be avoided if the corporation holds its assets forever (or at least until they decline in value) and does not liquidate.

[10] Reduction for Selling Expenses

It has been said that a reduction in value for expenses which would be incurred if property were sold is generally not allowed unless the property is actually sold or is being actively marketed at the time the valuation is being made.[52] However, the Tax Court has explained, in setting a marketability discount, that it took into account the fact that a buyer might have to incur a subsequent expense to register the stock for public sale.[53]

¶ 25.03 BUSINESS FACTORS AFFECTING VALUE

[1] Dependence on Key Person

If Dad is the key person in the business and he dies, an estate tax discount is proper—recognizing the fact that the value of the business is depressed without its key person. If another equally capable person is not found quickly to replace Dad, the value of the business may plummet irreparably. An example might be a professional practice or other type of business that is dependent to a large degree on a particular person.

---

[52] Estate of Koss v. Comm'r, 1994 RIA TC Memo. ¶ 94,599, 68 TCM (CCH) 1356 (1994). But see Estate of Newhouse v. Comm'r, 94 TC 193 (1990), nonacq., 1991-2 CB 1, which held that the most reasonable manner of selling an estate's shares of a company was through an underwritten public offering, and allowed an estate tax valuation reduction for selling expenses that would be incurred in connection with such an offering, even though no such offering was contemplated.

[53] Estate of Scanlon v. Comm'r, 1996 RIA TC Memo. ¶ 96,331, 72 TCM (CCH) 160 (1996). In Estate of Freeman v. Comm'r, 1996 RIA TC Memo. ¶ 96,372, 72 TCM (CCH) 373 (1996), the Tax Court held that failure to take into account the possibility of an IPO, which actually occurred after death and was being considered before death, was erroneous, noting that "we assume that venture capital investors invest with the hope, if not the expectation, that a public offering will not be too far off."

A valuation discount for transfers of interests in such a business is realistic even while the key person is still with the business. Other factors being equal, any business that is heavily dependent on the efforts of one, or a small number of, hard-to-replace individual(s) is worth less than an equivalent business with more depth of personnel.

Similarly, a discount may be appropriate for a business that is dependent on one or a few major clients.

[2] Excessive Debt

Excessive debt weakens the balance sheet of an entity. Many businesses cannot survive under a heavy debt burden. Moreover, even if an entity with a great deal of debt can and does meet its payment obligations, the value of the entity may vary substantially with changes in interest rates.

> EXAMPLE: Company A has heavy debt at a 10 percent interest rate. If the debt cannot be refinanced, an investment in Company A will be less desirable than an investment in a company which can borrow at a lower rate, other things being equal. Even if the debt can be refinanced, the company will be more valuable in periods when interest rates are less than 10 percent, and it would cost less to re-borrow the money, than it will in a higher-interest environment.

[3] Passive Investments

The IRS has taken the position that no discount will be allowed if the entity holdings consist of liquid or passive assets. This position has not received support in the courts.[54]

---

[54] See Estate of Luton v. Comm'r, 1994 RIA TC Memo. ¶ 94,539, 68 TCM 1044 (1994), supplemental op. 1996 RIA TC Memo. ¶ 96,181, 71 TCM (CCH) 2772 (1996) (20 percent discount applied to 78 percent interest in passive real estate corporation; 35 percent discount applied to 33 percent interest in corporation that owned a duck hunting preserve; 10 percent discount applied to interest in IRC § 337 liquidating trust which was required to distribute the proceeds of its only asset, a note paying 10 percent from a creditworthy corporation, 30 days after receiving the cash proceeds); Estate of S. C. Simpson v. Comm'r, 1994 RIA TC Memo. ¶ 94,207, 67 TCM 2938 (1994) (30 percent discount applied to 100 percent interest in investment holding company); Dougherty v. Comm'r, 1990 PH TC Memo. ¶ 90,274, 59 TCM 772 (1990) (35 percent discount applied to 100 percent of the stock of a personal holding corporation with assets consisting of notes receivable, marketable securities, and passive real estate partnership interests); Estate of Gillet v. Comm'r, 1985 PH TC Memo. ¶ 85,394, 50 TCM 636 (1985) (20 percent minority interest discount and 15 percent marketability discount applied to 26.4 percent interest in stock of a corporation with assets consisting largely of passive investments); Estate of Mundy v. Comm'r, 1976 PH TC Memo. ¶ 76,395, 35 TCM 1778 (1976) (40 percent discount applied to interest in personal holding corporation which had only stocks, bonds, and treasury securities); Estate of

[4] Environmental Factors

Real estate in general can be subject to discounts due to potential liability for contamination. However, such a discount is not automatic.[55]

¶ 25.04 VALUING JOINTLY HELD PROPERTY

Some interests are not held in any formal entity. Instead, two or more people or entities may co-own property as tenants in common or other joint ownership form. Fractional interests are typically difficult to sell or otherwise deal with, as the consent of all owners may be required to make decisions. The more owners there are, the more unwieldy this becomes. However, as a matter of state law, co-tenants of real property are usually entitled to sue for a partition.[56] Co-tenants of personal property may enjoy the same right. In a partition suit, the court will divide the property in kind among the co-tenants or, if that is not practicable, will order the property sold at a judicial sale and divide the net proceeds among the former co-tenants. The IRS has contended that the discount for tenancies in common in real estate should be limited to the cost of partition.[57] This view has been supported in at least one case.[58] A traditional joint interest discount has been applied in other cases.[59] Factors increasing the discount have tended to include the

---

Thalheimer v. Comm'r, 1974 PH TC Memo. ¶ 74,203, 33 TCM 877 (1974) (34 percent discount and 37 percent discount applied to voting and nonvoting stock of corporation which owned substantial common stock investments).

[55] See Estate of Pillsbury v. Comm'r, 1992 RIA TC Memo. ¶ 92,425, 64 TCM 284 (1992), where no discount was applied even where leakage of underground gas storage tanks had occurred, where no evidence existed that a buyer would pay less on that account. The lessee of the tanks had primary liability for the cleanup costs, and the estate-lessor never investigated the effect of the contamination on value of the property until its preparation for the Tax Court trial, causing the Tax Court to doubt its importance.

[56] Restatement of Property § 51 (1936).

[57] Priv. Ltr. Rul. 9336002 (May 28, 1993).

[58] Estate of Cervin v. Comm'r, 1994 RIA TC Memo. ¶ 94,550, 68 TCM (CCH) 1115 (1994), rev'd and remanded on other issues, 111 F3d 1252 (5th Cir. 1997).

[59] Estate of Youle, 1989 PH TC Memo. ¶ 89,138, 56 TCM (CCH) 1594 (1989) (applying 12.5 percent discount to tenancy in common interest); Estate of LeFrak v. Comm'r, 66 TCM 1297 (1993) (applying 20 percent discount to tenancy in common interest); Estate of Baggett v. Comm'r, 1991 PH TC Memo. ¶ 91,362 (1991) (applying a 35 percent minority interest discount to a partial interest in mineral rights).

difficulty or impossibility of borrowing money secured by a fractional interest, the lack of a market for fractional interests, and any limits on control of the management of the joint asset.

Whether or not the IRS position is correct, it still can allow a significant discount. The costs of partition (surveys, appraisals, legal fees, court costs, delay, etc.) can be very substantial, particularly in a contested matter.[60]

Planning with undivided interests. What if Grandma owns a 90 percent interest in her home, after having given a 10 percent interest to Child? Will Grandma's interest be valued at less than 90 percent of the value of the entire house at her death? It should be, assuming that Grandma and Child treat the co-ownership as arm's-length parties would. If Child's interest was not respected during Grandma's lifetime, however, Section 2036 may apply to bring the gifted interest back into Grandma's estate, as a transfer with an implied agreement that she could enjoy the entire property without paying consideration. In this case, for example, Grandma should pay rent if she continues to live in the house,[61] and Child should pay his share of the insurance, taxes, and mortgage.

WARNING: Speaking of the mortgage, no transfer of an interest in mortgaged property should be made without checking to see if the transfer will accelerate the due date of the note.

¶ 25.05 THE DISCOUNTED VALUE OF ASSETS HELD OUTRIGHT

Many assets not held in entity or co-owned form are subject to similar discounts as those available to entities. For example, Georgia O'Keeffe's estate was entitled to a blockage discount for her paintings, since the art market could not absorb a large number of her works except over a long period of time.[62] For the same reason, a portfolio of diverse business or real property assets may sell at a greater discount than a single property.

---

[60] E.g., Estate of Cervin v. Comm'r, 1994 RIA TC Memo. ¶ 94,550, 68 TCM (CCH) 1115 (1994) (applying 20 percent discount), rev'd and remanded on other issues, 111 F3d 1252 (5th Cir. 1997).

[61] Under most state laws, co-tenants have equal rights to occupy the co-owned property, so that rent might not be necessary under state law. However, unless Child is occupying the property 10 percent of the time, a cautious approach is for Grandma to pay (presumably) 10 percent of the fair market rental of the house to Child each year to compensate him in order to avoid a retained interest argument.

[62] Estate of O'Keeffe v. Comm'r, 1992 RIA TC Memo. ¶ 92,210, 63 TCM (CCH) 2699 (1992) (applying 25 percent blockage discount for certain paintings and 75 per-

A procedure exists for obtaining a determination of value of certain art works before filing the return reporting the relevant transaction.[63] This procedure may not be of much practical benefit in lifetime gift situations, since it cannot be initiated until after the gift is made. The donor is required to attach the statement of value to the return, whether or not the donor agrees with it. Hence, there is some risk involved in asking for the determination of value.

¶ 25.06 INTENTIONAL USE OF VALUATION DEPRESSORS

There are many actions a person could take which reduce the value of an asset. For example, if Dad owns a piece of real estate, he could encumber it with complicated restrictions, easements, and boundary lines (if legally permissible under local law), or he could subject it to a long-term enforceable lease to his children. Or, he could erect a hideous structure on it and contaminate it with noxious chemicals. The possibilities are limited only by the boundaries of his imagination. But let's get a sense of perspective. Even if these tricks work as value-reducers, the tax saved by the beneficiaries may not be worth the long-term headache.

A technique like a long-term lease may cause few additional troubles. However, if there was no purpose for the lease other than estate tax reduction, it may be ignored for tax purposes. Or, if the lease is characterized as an equity interest, the transaction may be subject to the dreaded Chapter 14, which may disregard the lease in valuing the property.[64] Or, if the lease is real and has a business purpose, but the rent is below market, entering into the lease may result in a taxable gift at the outset.

Of course, if the formalities of any transaction reducing value are not respected, the IRS may successfully assert that the whole transaction should be ignored as a sham. Similarly, if there is no purpose for such a transaction other than tax avoidance, or if tax avoidance is the primary reason for the transaction, the IRS may attempt to ignore it. While it is not a foregone conclusion that a transaction entered into with the purpose of reducing taxes will be ignored by a court, a good independent purpose can't hurt.

---

cent blockage discount for others); see also Jack D. Carr v. Comm'r, 1985 PH TC Memo. ¶ 85,019, 49 TCM 507 (1985), allowing a market absorption discount for undeveloped land held in a corporation which was involved in a real estate development.

[63] Rev. Proc. 96-15, IRB 1996-3.

[64] IRC § 2701, if the property is owned by a corporation or partnership, or IRC § 2702, if the property is owned by a trust.

¶ 25.07   THE THORN ON THE ROSE

The reason that the values of certain interests are discounted is that such interests are really and truly less valuable than equivalent interests which are not encumbered by discounting characteristics. In considering measures that reduce the value of property, one must be aware that there is a definite tradeoff. The reduction in transfer taxes is a benefit. The detriment is that the beneficiary/donee receives an interest that may not be salable except for pennies on the dollar, may not generate predictable income distributions, may create ongoing income tax liabilities, and may result in negative cash flow problems. In addition, the property can become much more complicated to administer as a result of the measures taken to reduce its value.

Finally, aggressive discounting may backfire and result in worse transfer tax consequences than a more conservative approach would have.

> **EXAMPLE:** Dad is a general and limited partner in a partnership. He gives Daughter an assignee interest in a limited partnership interest. If the partnership agreement is written so as to give Dad, as general partner, unlimited power to distribute or withhold, refuse to consent to transfers, etc., with no fiduciary liability to Daughter, the IRS may try to include Daughter's partnership interest in Dad's estate under Section 2036(a)(2) or disregard the restrictions for gift tax purposes under Section 2703.

Moral. A cost/benefit analysis of each value-reducer should be done. The game is not always worth the candle.

CHAPTER **26**

Section 2704: Rights That Lapse and Restrictions on Liquidation

¶ 26.01 INTRODUCTION

The rules for valuing interests in family-owned entities were complicated by the enactment of Section 2704 in 1990. This section of the Internal Revenue Code contains special rules relating to both the lapse of certain rights with respect to an entity and certain restrictions on the liquidation of entities.

Section 2704 applies to all types of business entities. However, as a practical matter, its primary application is to partnerships and limited liability companies (LLCs). There is a substantial and fairly nontechnical explanation of Section 2704 in Chapter 16 on family partnerships. This Chapter 26 covers the application of Section 2704 to other entities and discusses the specifics of the section on a more technical level. Because of the section's relatively recent emergence on the estate planning scene, and its complex and mysterious nature, we will examine it on three levels—a low-tech overview, a semi-technical explanation, and then a high-tech analysis.

¶ 26.02 LOW-TECH OVERVIEW OF SECTION 2704

Section 2704 treats lapses of certain rights with respect to an entity as taxable transfers and disregards certain restrictions on liquidating an entity for transfer tax valuation purposes.

[1] Lapse of Voting or Liquidation Right as Taxable Transfer—Section 2704(a)

If an individual has voting rights in a family entity[1] or the right to liquidate his interest in the entity, and such voting rights or liquidation rights lapse, this lapse may be considered a taxable transfer by the individual.[2] If the individual transfers an interest in the entity during his life or at death, and the lapse occurs as a result of the transfer, the value of the transferred interest for transfer tax purposes will be its—

- Normal transfer tax value, plus
- An amount equal to the value of all interests in the entity held by the individual before the transfer reduced by the value of all of the same interests after the transfer, as if all of those interests were held by one person.

If the interest transferred is sold, there may be a gift of the special amount even if no gift is made for regular gift tax purposes.

> EXAMPLE: Dad owns 80 percent of a corporation. His 80 percent interest is worth $700,000. He transfers 30 percent of the corporation to Daughter. The 30 percent interest is actually worth $200,000. What addition to value, if any, does Section 2704(a) require, assuming that a lapse of rights has occurred? Before the transfer, all interests held by Dad were worth $700,000. After the transfer, the 50 percent Dad retained and the 30 percent Daughter received would still be worth $700,000 if they were held by one person. Therefore, the special amount added to the gift under Section 2704(a) is zero.[3] Thus, the gift tax value is the actual value of the

---

[1] A "family entity" is controlled by the transferor and/or members of his family. IRC §§ 2704(a)(1)(B)–2704(C). "Members of the family" are the transferor's spouse, ancestors, descendants, spouse's ancestors, spouse's descendants, siblings, and the spouses of the foregoing individuals. IRC § 2704(c)(2).

[2] IRC § 2704(a).

[3] $700,000 (value of interest held by Dad before the transfer) less $700,000 (value of that same interest if it were held by one person after the transfer).

stock—$200,000.

EXAMPLE: Dad is a general partner of a partnership. His interest is worth $500,000. He assigns his general partnership interest to Daughter. The transfer causes a lapse of the management rights incident to that general partnership interest under state law, reducing the value of the interest to $300,000. The special amount under Section 2704(a) is $200,000.[4] So, the taxable gift will be the actual value of the interest ($300,000) plus the Section 2704(a) special amount ($200,000)—that is, a total gift of $500,000.

Why does the partnership transfer example result in a different answer than the corporate transfer example? Because Dad's partnership interest permanently declined in value as a result of its transformation into an assignee interest. Any decrease in value of the interest solely due to its fractionalization is not an addition to value under Section 2704(a) in either the partnership or corporate case.

Stated another way, the special Section 2704(a) tax is imposed in addition to the regular gift tax. The special Section 2704(a) tax will be zero, unless the transferor's interests held just before the transfer decrease in value as a result of the transfer, without regard to the fact that the interests have been divided among several owners.

The tax applies to decreases in value resulting from the lapse of voting rights and liquidation rights. The liquidation right with which Section 2704(a) is concerned is a right or ability to liquidate the owner's interest in the entity, and not a right to liquidate the entity itself. If the owner does not have the right or ability to liquidate his interest, then the rules on the lapse of a liquidation right will not generally apply.

[2] Disregarded Restrictions—Section 2704(b)

If an interest in a family entity is transferred, certain restrictions on the entity's ability to liquidate are disregarded in valuing the transferred interest for transfer tax purposes.[5]

EXAMPLE: Under state law, the holder of 51 percent of the stock in a corporation can compel the corporation to liquidate. The shareholders agree that a 100 percent vote is required to liquidate the corporation. If the stockholders are family members, the restriction will be disregarded for purposes of valuing transfers of the stock. If an unrelated party holds stock, the restriction may be respected if the unrelated party's interest is substantial and bona fide.

---

[4] $500,000 (value of interest held by Dad before the transfer) less $300,000 (value of same interest after transfer, valued as held by one person after the transfer).

[5] IRC § 2704(b).

[3] Bottom Line

Section 2704 usually only comes into play with partnerships and LLCs, since these entities inherently involve ownership interests with rights that lapse on certain events as a matter of law, and can be liquidated by means other than the vote of a majority in interest of the owners. However, even these entities are often structured for business reasons so that, as a matter of state law, a partner or member cannot unilaterally cause the entity to liquidate.

As a general matter, Section 2704 should be considered in designing the structure of an entity. If an entity is properly structured, and the law is applied in accordance with Congress's statement of its intent in enacting the law, Section 2704 should have little effect on valuation. However, the law on the subject is unsettled and complex, and it is hazardous to count on predicting its development with complete accuracy.[6]

¶ 26.03 SEMI-TECHNICAL EXPLANATION (GOOD ENOUGH FOR MOST REASONABLE PEOPLE)

Special valuation rules apply to transfers of certain interests in family entities. The rules, contained in Section 2704, were enacted in 1990.

[1] Lapsing Rights—Section 2704(a)

Section 2704(a) treats lapses of certain rights to vote and to compel the liquidation of an owner's interest in an entity as taxable transfers.

[a] Statutory Intent

The rules are difficult to understand without knowing their historical context. Hence, the following short history lesson . . .

In 1979, Mr. Harrison was dying. His sons, acting under a power of attorney, transferred some of his assets to a family partnership, designating Mr. Harrison as a one percent general partner and 77.8 percent limited partner, and each of themselves as 10.6 percent general partners. The partnership agreement granted each general partner the right to dissolve the partnership. If he exercised that right, the partnership would liquidate, subject to the election by the other general partners within 90 days to continue the partnership. On the general partner's exercise of his right, he would, as a contractual matter, receive his pro rata share of the partnership assets, including those

---

[6] For example, see Tech. Adv. Mem. 9725002 (Mar. 25, 1997), taking the position that a limited partner's interest would be valued as if the limited partner could withdraw on six months' notice if state law would accord that right to a limited partner in a partnership at will.

attributable to his limited partnership share (regardless of whether the partnership actually liquidated or the other general partners agreed to continue the partnership).

Mr. Harrison died a few months later. The general partnership interest was subject to a buy-sell agreement, and was valued accordingly at $757,116. The controversy arose as to the value of the limited partnership interest. The IRS argued that since Mr. Harrison, as general partner, had the right to liquidate his entire interest in the partnership and obtain a pro rata share of the assets, his limited partnership interest should be valued at its liquidation value. The liquidation value of the limited partnership interest was stipulated to be $59,555,020. The value of the interest without regard to liquidation rights was stipulated to be $33,000,000.

The estate successfully argued that, under state law, the general partner's ability to liquidate the partnership lapsed on his death and, consequently, the limited partnership interest should not be valued as if the owner's power to liquidate it still existed.[7] After this result became generally known, lapsing liquidation rights were recommended in speeches and articles nationwide. The IRS was outraged, and persuaded Congress to pass the anti-lapse provisions of Section 2704.

Importance of history. Section 2704 is an extremely confusing section. When one is deep into its befuddling details, it helps to step out of the trees and get a view of the forest by remembering what the primary purpose of the statute was—to statutorily overrule the Tax Court's decision in *Harrison.*[8] That is, the statute was enacted to provide that if a partner's partnership interest carries the power to compel the partnership to liquidate and distribute to the partner the value of the partner's pro rata share of the partnership assets, and this power disappears at the partner's death regardless of who holds the interest, then the partnership interest will be valued for estate tax purposes as if the power to liquidate the interest still existed. Presumably, a similar result was intended to apply in the gift tax context.

[b] How Section 2704(a) Works

Essentially, Section 2704(a) provides that: (1) if A has the right to liquidate his interest in a family entity, (2) as a result of his transfer of an interest in that entity, the interest's liquidation right lapses, and (3) the total value of the transferred interest, plus the value of any interest retained by A, measured as if the same person held both interests, would be less than the total value of those interests before the transfer, the decrease in value will be treated as an additional gift. Note that even if A sells the transferred interest for its fair market value, under Section 2704, the decrease in value can still be treated as

---

[7] Estate of Harrison v. Comm'r, 52 TCM (CCH) 1306 (1987).

[8] HR Rep. No. 964, 101st Cong., 2d Sess. 1130, 1137 (1990).

a gift. Additionally, a lapse is treated as a transfer if no transfer otherwise occurs.

Confused? Maybe some examples will help—

EXAMPLE: Dad owns 100 percent of a corporation. His stock is worth $1,000,000. He gives 60 percent of the corporation to Daughter. After the transfer, the original 100 percent interest would still be worth $1,000,000 if it were held by one person. The value of the gift of the 60 percent is its normal gift tax value.

EXAMPLE: Dad owns 40 percent of the corporation. His 40 percent interest is worth $500,000. He and the other stockholders have agreed that he can put his stock to the company in exchange for his pro rata share of the corporation's value. The right is personal to him, and therefore lapses when he dies. As a result, the 40 percent interest is worth only $300,000 on his death. Section 2704 will deem the estate tax value of the stock to be $200,000[9] plus $300,000 (the interest's normal estate tax value), or $500,000.

PRACTICE POINTER: The obvious moral of this story is not to create voting and liquidation rights that lapse as a contractual matter without a clear understanding of the consequences.

Rights which lapse as a matter of state law present a more difficult question. These are largely encountered in partnerships and limited liability companies.[10]

[c] Voting Rights

Voting rights which lapse as a matter of state law are common in partnerships and LLCs. We'll use partnerships to illustrate, but members of an LLC will often be subject to similar rules. Generally speaking, when a partner dies or transfers his interest, the transferee becomes an assignee of the partnership interest. This means that the transferee is entitled to his share of distributions from the partnership, when and if they are made. He is not entitled to exercise voting or other management rights, unless he is admitted as a partner.

Hence, voting rights will always lapse on a transfer of a partnership interest to an assignee. This is true even of transfers of limited partnership interests, since limited partners can usually vote on certain important matters.

---

[9] The value of the interest before the transfer—$500,000, less the value of the interest after the transfer as held by one person—$300,000.

[10] Although this chapter generally discusses the application of IRC § 2704 in the context of a partnership, similar rules often apply to interests in limited liability companies.

[d] Liquidation Rights

What about liquidation rights? If a partner has liquidation rights which lapse on a transfer, Section 2704(a) comes into play. The regulations have interpreted "liquidation right" to mean a right to liquidate the partner's interest in the partnership—not the right to liquidate the entire partnership.[11]

[i] The crucial difference between liquidation and dissolution. Dissolution and liquidation are not the same thing. The statute and regulations speak in terms of "liquidating" an interest. In contrast, state law governing partnerships generally refers to "dissolution" and "winding up." A dissolution of a partnership as a result of a general partner's withdrawal may or may not give the withdrawing partner a right to compel the partnership to buy his interest or wind up.

State law. Generally speaking, if a general partner withdraws, the partnership is dissolved as a legal matter. It will then be wound up and liquidated unless there is a remaining general partner(s) who can continue the partnership or all of the limited partners elect to continue the business and, in doing so, elect a new general partner.[12] What if the partnership continues? In some states, the limited partners can convert the former general partnership interest to a limited partnership interest.[13] In other states (and in all states, if his interest is not converted to a limited partnership interest), the partnership must pay the general partner the fair value of his general partnership interest,[14] less damages if his withdrawal constituted a breach of the agreement. The fair market value is not necessarily the liquidation value of the partnership interest.[15]

[ii] Rights of a general partner. A general partner will normally have the power under state law to dissolve the partnership by withdrawing, even if he has contractually promised not to do so. The consequences of this power in the case of a general partner who is not also a limited partner are not necessarily

---

[11] Treas. Reg. § 25.2704-1(a)(2)(v).

[12] Revised Uniform Limited Partnership Act § 801(4), 6A ULA 1 1976 (Amended 1985) (RULPA).

[13] E.g., Tex. Rev. Limited Partnership Act, Tex. Rev. Civ. Stat. Ann. art. 6132a-1, § 6.02(b) (West Supp. 1996).

[14] RULPA § 604.

[15] Cf. Vanderplow v. Fredricks, 32 NW2d 718 (Mich. 1948) (holding that to cash out other partners, plaintiff should have offered to pay them one-third of the net worth of the firm, including their entire equity in the real estate at its appreciated value; court's decision indicates that goodwill and other factors may be taken into account under certain circumstances in determining value to be paid to other partners); see also Rev. Unif. Partnership Act § 701, 6 ULA 328 (Supp. 1997) (buyout price of a dissociated partner's interest is greater of liquidation value or going concern value).

that bad. If the general partner cannot force a liquidation by withdrawing, then the value of his liquidation right is usually limited to the right to compel the partnership to pay him the fair value of the general partnership interest. In addition, a general partner will usually have only a one percent general partnership interest, so that even if the one percent interest had to be valued at its pro rata share of the entity value, it would not be a serious problem.

[iii] Rights of a limited partner. State law usually gives a limited partner the right to withdraw and receive the fair value of his interest upon six months' notice, unless the partnership has a fixed term.[16] Where, however, the partnership has a fixed term, the limited partner has no ability to compel the liquidation of his interest until the term of the partnership has expired or other events occur (such as the death or withdrawal of the last general partner) which give him the right to vote on whether the partnership should continue.[17] Further, even if the limited partner is also a general partner, he cannot use his status as general partner to unilaterally liquidate his limited partnership interest as a matter of state law, unless (1) there is no other general partner, (2) the vote of his limited partnership interest is required to continue the partnership, and (3) his interest is entitled to a vote.[18]

Accordingly, a limited partner will not usually have a right to liquidate his interest in a partnership for a fixed term. A general partner who is also a limited partner may or may not have the power to unilaterally liquidate his limited partnership interest, depending on how the partnership is structured and applicable state law. If a general partner who is also a limited partner does not have the unilateral power to liquidate his limited partnership interest, Section 2704 should not be a problem with respect to the limited interest, unless a right to liquidate his interest is contractually granted. But the IRS does not agree with this interpretation of the rules applicable to term partnerships.

Term partnerships. Contractual restrictions on a partner's ability to liquidate his interest will be ignored for purposes of valuing a transferred interest under Section 2704. Restrictions imposed by state law should be respected.[19] Since a limited partner of a term partnership cannot liquidate his interest, he should not be considered to have a liquidation right. However, the IRS has taken the position that a limited partner will be treated, for purposes of Section 2704(b), as having the ability to liquidate his interest on six months'

---

[16] RULPA §§ 603, 604.

[17] RULPA §§ 603, 801.

[18] It might not be entitled to a vote, for example, if he were withdrawing in breach of the agreement and state law provided that only the nonbreaching partners were entitled to vote on continuation.

[19] Treas. Reg. §§ 25.2704-1(c)(2)(i)(B), 25.2704-2(b).

notice, even if the partnership has a longer term, under the theory that state law would allow such a withdrawal in a partnership without a term and the decision to choose a term is not imposed by state law.[20]

The idea underlying this IRS position is that the partners are not required by state law to enter into a term partnership, so the state law ramifications of selecting a term partnership will be ignored. This seems a bit on the audacious side. One might as well say that the state law ramifications of being a limited partner will be ignored because the partners could have chosen to form a general partnership or that the state law ramifications of being a partner will be ignored because the partners could have chosen to do business in a form other than a partnership. (And, as discussed in Chapter 27, the IRS has, in fact, said exactly that.)

[iv] **Future treatment of valuation discounts.** The IRS has grown very concerned about the recognition of valuation discounts in the context of family entities. Although the Section 2704 arguments should not succeed in a proper case, the IRS can probably be expected to continue to fight the discounts in the courts and to lobby Congress for legislation that would eliminate the recognition of discounts as we know them.

[2] Restrictions on Liquidation—Section 2704(b)

[a] How the Rules Work

For purposes of transfer tax valuation, Section 2704(b) ignores voluntarily imposed restrictions on the ability to liquidate a family entity. For example, if Family Corp requires a unanimous vote to liquidate and a smaller percentage would be required under state law, the unanimous vote requirement will be ignored in valuing the stock.

Unlike the test in Section 2704(a), the test in Section 2704(b) is the ability to liquidate the entity, not an interest in the entity.[21] Nevertheless, the IRS has interpreted Section 2704(b) as applying to a restriction on a right to liquidate an interest in the entity. This interpretation is based on the theory that Section 2704(b) applies to a restriction on the right to liquidate an entity in whole or in part, and the liquidation of an interest in the entity constitutes a partial liquidation of the entity.[22]

---

[20] Tech. Adv. Mem. 9725002 (Mar. 25, 1997). The Technical Advice Memorandum does not address the valuation of the limited partner's interest, which presumably would be whatever he could receive under state law (not necessarily a pro rata portion of the assets).

[21] IRC § 2704(b)(2)(A).

[22] Tech. Adv. Mem. 9725002 (Mar. 25, 1997).

[b] Use of a Non-Family Owner to Avoid Section 2704(b)

The statute only applies if family members can liquidate the entity.[23] Some families try to avoid the application of Section 2704(b) by making a nonfamily member a small owner and by requiring the consent of all owners to liquidate. In such a case, Section 2704(b) does not on its face apply.

Some advertisements that are being circulated regarding this technique suggest giving a charity a .001 percent interest and requiring the charity's consent to liquidate the entity. A de minimis interest such as this may be disregarded as a sham or as having no purpose other than tax avoidance. Additionally, the existence of this arrangement may make the partnership easier to attack under Section 2703, if an arm's-length partnership would not require the consent of the holder of an infinitesimal interest to liquidate.[24]

Additionally, if substantially all of the assets of the entity can be distributed to the partners without the charity's consent, leaving a shell entity, the IRS may take the position that the family has the de facto ability to liquidate the entity.

[c] Effect of Ignoring a Restriction

In some cases, ignoring a restriction will not necessarily increase the value of the entity. For example, if a restricted interest is essentially unmarketable even without a restriction or transfer, ignoring the restriction will not especially matter.

[d] Bottom Line

It is risky to make conclusions about Section 2704, as the law is largely undeveloped. Having said that, let's rush in where angels fear to tread.

Section 2704 is primarily an anti-*Harrison* statute. As long as an owner does not have the right (such as Mr. Harrison had) to liquidate his interest and receive a value higher than the transfer tax value of the interest without that right, and as long as the owner cannot cause the actual or virtual liquidation of the entity, Section 2704 should not be a serious problem if the partnership structure is properly designed.

This is not to say that the issues posed by Section 2704 are going away. The IRS has taken the position that a limited partnership interest in a partnership for years will be valued as if the limited partner could withdraw the fair value of his interest on six months' notice, in a state which would allow such a withdrawal in a partnership at will.[25] How much of a problem is this?

---

[23] IRC § 2704(b)(2)(B)(ii).

[24] See Ch. 27 for a discussion of IRC § 2703.

[25] Tech. Adv. Mem. 9725002 (Mar. 25, 1997).

If the fair value that the limited partner could withdraw on six months' notice is no more than what he could have sold his interest for, no additional value exists, so no problem results. In any case, establishment of the partnership and conduct of its business in a state that does not provide its limited partners with such a right should eliminate that particular issue. However, as family entities become more common, recognition of the discounted value of interests in those entities may be restricted or eliminated. It will probably take legislation to fully accomplish that.

¶ 26.04 HIGH-TECH ANALYSIS FOR DIEHARDS

[1] Lapse Treated as Transfer—Section 2704(a)

[a] General Rule

For purposes of the gift, estate, and generation-skipping transfer taxes, if (1) there is a lapse of any voting or liquidation right in a corporation or partnership and (2) the individual directly or indirectly holding such right immediately before the lapse (the "holder") and members of the holder's family, both before and after the lapse, control the entity, the lapse is either treated as a gift by the holder or a transfer which is includable in the holder's gross estate, whichever is applicable.[26]

[b] Legislative History

As discussed above,[27] this rule is designed to legislatively overrule the case of *Estate of Harrison v. Commissioner*.[28] It is not designed to affect minority discounts or other discounts available under current law.[29]

[c] Definitions

[i] Control. "Control" generally means ownership of: (A) 50 percent of the voting power or total fair market value of the equity interests in a corporation; or (B) 50 percent of either the capital interest or the profits interest in a partnership; or (C) any equity interest as a general partner of a limited partnership. Thus, limited partners and nonvoting shareholders can be deemed to control an entity for purposes of Section 2704(a).[30]

---

[26] IRC § 2704(a)(1); Treas. Reg. § 25.2704-1(a).

[27] See ¶ 26.03[1][a] above.

[28] 1987 PH TC Memo. ¶ 87,008, 52 TCM (CCH) 1306 (1987).

[29] HR Rep. No. 964, 101st Cong., 2d Sess. 1137 (1990).

[30] Treas. Reg. §§ 25.2701-2(b)(5), 25.2704-1(a)(2)(i).

[ii] Member of the family. A member of the holder's family means his spouse, ancestor, lineal descendant, spouse's ancestor, spouse's lineal descendant, brother, sister, and any spouse of the above.[31]

[iii] Holdings of an individual.

Indirect holdings. An individual will be treated as holding an interest in an entity that is owned by a corporation, partnership, trust or estate, to the extent that the individual has an interest in the owner entity.[32] *Holdings not otherwise includable in estate.* An interest is directly or indirectly held by a person only to the extent that the value of the interest would have been includable in his gross estate if he had died immediately prior to the lapse.[33]

> EXAMPLE: Dad is the beneficiary of a trust which is not includable in his estate. He will not be deemed to hold an interest which is actually held by the trust.

[iv] Voting right. A voting right means a right to vote with respect to any matter of the entity. A general partner's right to participate in partnership management is a voting right. The right to compel the entity to acquire all or part of the holder's equity interest in the entity by reason of voting power is considered a liquidation right and is not treated as a voting right.[34]

In most states, nonvoting shareholders have the right to vote on certain extraordinary matters. Similarly, limited partners usually have the right to vote on extraordinary matters. Unless these extraordinary voting rights can be and are eliminated by the applicable entity documents, it appears that even holders of nonvoting shares and limited partnership interests will be considered to have voting rights.

An assignee of a partnership interest usually does not have the right to vote, even on extraordinary matters.[35] Thus, it appears that any transfer of a partnership interest may cause a lapse of the transferor's voting rights, unless the transferee is admitted to the partnership and has at least the same voting rights as the transferor (e.g., the transferee is admitted as a general partner where the transferor was a general partner). In addition, other events may result in the lapse of voting rights in a partnership (e.g., the bankruptcy or incompetency of a general partner).[36]

---

[31] Treas. Reg. §§ 25.2702-2(a)(1), 25.2704-1(a)(2)(ii).

[32] IRC §§ 2701(e)(3), 2704(c)(3).

[33] Treas. Reg. § 25.2704-1(a)(2)(iii).

[34] Treas. Reg. § 25.2704-1(a)(2)(iv).

[35] RULPA § 702; Uniform Limited Partnership Act §§ 9, 19, 6 ULA 586, 603 (1916) (ULPA); Uniform Partnership Act § 27, 6 ULA 353 (1914) (UPA).

[36] RULPA §§ 402, 705.

It does not appear that all of the voting rights attributable to an interest must lapse in order for Section 2704(a) to apply. A lapse of the right to vote on any matter will apparently trigger its application. In the case of a limited partner, at least, the decrease in value resulting from the lapse may be relatively small, if the limited partner's participation rights were sufficiently limited. The decrease in value with respect to a general partner's voting rights, however, may be more significant. If the general partner also owns a limited partnership interest, the lapse of the general partner's voting rights may result in a substantial decrease in value, since the decrease in value of all the interests owned by the former holder of the lapsed rights would be the measure of transferred value. And, the limited partnership interests might decrease in value if they are not held in conjunction with a general partnership interest.

[v] **Liquidation right.** A liquidation right is the ability to compel the entity to acquire any of the holder's equity interest.[37] For example, if Father has a power to cause corporation to redeem all of his stock and this power lapses upon his death or the transfer of his interest, the death or transfer will result in the lapse of a liquidation right. Similarly, if Father owns a general partnership interest and a limited partnership interest, and the partnership agreement gives Father, as general partner, the power to liquidate both of his interests in the entity, Father has a liquidation right with respect to his general and his limited partnership interests.[38]

Future liquidation rights. A future right to liquidate may apparently be treated as a liquidation right.

EXAMPLE: Dad's ownership of a majority of stock in a corporation gives him the right to liquidate the corporation, but he has agreed with the other shareholders not to liquidate for two years. The restriction for the 2-year period is disregarded under Section 2704(b).[39] Restrictions that are disregarded under Section 2704(b) are also disregarded under Section 2704(a) for purposes of determining whether Dad and his family can liquidate the entity.[40] Since Dad will be deemed to have the right to liquidate the corporation, and therefore his own interest, immediately, he is deemed to have a liquidation right for purposes of Section 2704(a), and his stock is valued accordingly, even if he could not liquidate his interest under the state law applicable in the absence of an agreement.

It is unclear how a future right to liquidate will be viewed where the right is merely to liquidate the holder's interest, and not the entity.

---

[37] Treas. Reg. § 25.2704-1(a)(2)(v).

[38] See Treas. Reg. §§ 25.2704-1(a)(2)(v), 25.2704-1(f), examples 5, 6.

[39] See Treas. Reg. § 25.2704-2(d), example 2.

[40] Treas. Reg. § 25.2704-1(c)(i)(B).

[d] Lapses

[i] Lapse of a voting right. A lapse of a voting right occurs at the time a presently exercisable voting right is restricted or eliminated.[41]

> EXAMPLE: A partner transfers his partnership interest. The transferee becomes an assignee; the voting rights incident to the partnership interest are thus eliminated.

> EXAMPLE: Dad owns 70 percent of a corporation. He transfers 30 percent of the corporation to Daughter. The transfer does not result in a lapse of voting rights, even though the transfer results in Dad's loss of voting control.[42] No voting rights incident to the stock have been restricted or eliminated.

Exception for no real change. No voting right will be deemed to have been restricted or eliminated where the holder of each share of stock will have relatively the same voting rights after the transaction as he did before. The same rule applies in the case of liquidation rights.[43]

> EXAMPLE: State corporation law imposes a franchise tax on corporations, based on the number of authorized shares. Corporation X has 2,500,000 authorized shares of $10 par preferred stock, with 400,000 shares outstanding, and 1,500,000 authorized shares of $1 par common stock, with 2,000 shares outstanding. Each outstanding share of preferred or common stock is entitled to one vote. The stockholders of X decide to implement a reverse split recapitalization of X by (1) reducing the number of preferred shares to 25,000 and increasing the par value of preferred stock to $1000 per share and (2) reducing the number of common shares to 15,000 and increasing the par value to $100 per share. No voting or liquidation right will lapse as a result of the recapitalization for purposes of Section 2704.[44]

A transfer of a partnership interest will always result in a lapse of voting rights if the transfer will, as a matter of state law, cause the voting rights with respect to the interest to be restricted or eliminated. Most state laws provide that the assignee of a partnership interest will not have voting rights.[45] If the assignee is admitted as a substitute partner with the same voting rights, however, no lapse of voting rights should occur.

Limited to right eliminated or restricted in transferee's hands. A lapse of a liquidation right occurs at the time a presently exercisable liquidation right

---

[41] Treas. Reg. § 25.2704-1(b).

[42] Treas. Reg. § 25.2704-1(f), example 4.

[43] Priv. Ltr. Rul. 9309018 (Dec. 3, 1992).

[44] Priv. Ltr. Rul. 9309018 (Dec. 3, 1992).

[45] RULPA § 702; ULPA §§ 9, 19; UPA § 27.

is restricted or eliminated, but generally only if the rights with respect to the transferred interest are restricted or eliminated in the transferee's hands.

> EXAMPLE: Father owns a general partnership interest and a limited partnership interest in Partnership X. The partnership agreement gives Father the right, as a general partner, to withdraw the value of his entire general and limited partnership interests in the partnership. If Father transfers his limited partnership interest and the transferee becomes a limited partner, no rights have been restricted or eliminated in the transferee's hands. If Father transfers his general partnership interest, however, this apparently causes a lapse of the right to liquidate his limited partnership interest.[46] This lapse will be a taxable gift which will have a positive value, unless the transferee is given the same right.

Transfer of senior interest can eliminate a liquidation right over subordinate interest. A transfer of a senior interest (i.e., a transfer that eliminates the transferor's ability to compel the entity to acquire a subordinate interest retained by him) is a lapse of his right to liquidate the subordinate interest.[47] For Section 2704 purposes, a senior equity interest is an equity interest which carries a right to distributions of income or capital that is preferred in comparison with a "subordinate" interest.[48]

> EXAMPLE: All preferred stock of Corporation A is redeemable at the option of the holder. Father transfers his preferred stock to Son. This transfer is not a lapse because Son now has the right to redeem the stock.

> EXAMPLE: The holder of a majority interest in preferred stock may compel the corporation to liquidate. Father owns some nonvoting common stock and a majority interest in preferred stock. Father transfers his preferred stock to Son. The transfer results in a lapse of Father's ability to compel the corporation to liquidate his common stock.

> EXAMPLE: Father owns 70 percent of the voting stock and 100 percent of the nonvoting stock of an S corporation. He transfers his voting stock to his son. His transfer results in the elimination of his right to compel liquidation of his 100 percent nonvoting stock interest. The transfer is not a lapse with respect to the voting stock, since that stock's rights are not eliminated. The transfer is also not a lapse of the right to liquidate his nonvoting stock, since the nonvoting stock is not a subordinate interest with respect to the voting stock.[49]

A preferred interest is not always labeled as such, and transactions that are seemingly unrelated to Section 2704(a) can cause a preferred interest to exist.

---

[46] See Treas. Reg. § 25.2704-1(f), example 5.

[47] Treas. Reg. § 25.2704-1(c)(1).

[48] Treas. Reg. §§ 25.2701-3(a)(2)(ii)–25.2701-3(a)(2)(iii), 25.2704-1(a)(2)(vi).

[49] See Treas. Reg. § 25.2704-1(f), example 7.

EXAMPLE: Stockholder has employment agreement with Corporation which guarantees him a salary and benefits while he remains employed by Corporation. The salary is in excess of what would reasonably be paid to a person performing the work he is performing. The employment agreement plus stock can be viewed together as a preferred equity interest.[50]

[ii] Exception for lapse of a liquidation right where family cannot obtain liquidation value. Section 2704(a) does not apply to the lapse of a liquidation right to the extent the holder (or the holder's estate) and the holder's family cannot, immediately after the lapse, liquidate the holder's former interest.[51]

EXAMPLE: Father and third party each own 50 percent of a corporation. Father has the right to put his stock to the corporation. On his death, the right lapses. The lapse is not treated as a transfer under Section 2704, because Father's family cannot acquire the liquidation value of his interest.

Can an interest be liquidated by the holder's family immediately after the lapse? This question is determined under state law, as modified by the governing instruments of the entity, but without regard to any restriction described in Section 2704(b). Thus, if (after any restriction described in Section 2704(b) is disregarded) the requirements for liquidation under the governing instruments are equally as restrictive as, or less restrictive than, the otherwise applicable state law, the ability to liquidate is determined by reference to the governing instruments.[52]

EXAMPLE: Father has the contractual right to put his stock to a corporation. A third party owns 49 percent of the corporation. Father owns 51 percent of the corporation, which would be enough to liquidate the corporation under state law; however, the shareholders' agreement requires unanimous consent to liquidate the corporation. Father dies, and his right to put his stock to the corporation lapses, as a contractual matter. The determination of whether Father's family can liquidate his interest after his death is made under applicable state law, as modified by the governing instruments, without regard to the unanimous consent restriction on the ability to liquidate.[53] Therefore, the lapse of Father's redemption right will be taxable, and will not be covered by the exception dealing with the inability of the family to liquidate the corporation.

---

[50] Tech. Adv. Mem. 9352001 (Sept. 3, 1993).

[51] Treas. Reg. § 25.2704-1(c)(2)(i)(A).

[52] Treas. Reg. § 25.2704-1(c)(2)(i)(B).

[53] What about the rule saying that a transfer does not result in a lapse if the rights incident to the interest pass to the transferee? That rule does not prevent the lapse of the put right from being treated as a transfer under IRC § 2704, since the right to redeem the interest (as opposed to the deemed right to liquidate the corporation) lapses and does not pass to the transferee.

This rule could be particularly important in the case of partnership interests. Often, under state law, any general partner can liquidate his interest by withdrawing and receiving its fair value. Under many state laws, limited partners can liquidate their interests by withdrawing and receiving the fair value of their interests on a certain amount of notice to the partnership if the partnership does not have a term.[54] Some partnership agreements prohibit any partner from withdrawing his interest, even if state law would otherwise allow the withdrawal. The determination of whether a partner and his family can liquidate his interest may be made without regard to such a restriction in appropriate cases.

[iii] **Lapse of a liquidation right previously valued under Section 2701.** Section 2704(a) does not apply to the lapse of a liquidation right previously valued under Section 2701 to the extent necessary to prevent double taxation (taking into account any adjustment available under Treasury Regulation § 25.2701-5).[55]

EXAMPLE: Father owns common and preferred stock in a corporation, and has the right to put his preferred stock to the corporation. When Father transfers his common stock to daughter, the put right is valued at zero pursuant to Section 2701. If Father's put right lapses on his death, the lapse should not be treated as a transfer pursuant to Section 2704.

The above exception only applies while the stock is in the hands of the person in whose hands it was valued under Section 2701.[56]

EXAMPLE: Grandfather has a right to put his preferred stock to the corporation. Father transfers his common stock to Daughter. Grandfather's put right is valued at zero pursuant to Section 2701, presumably increasing the amount of Father's gift. If Grandfather's put right lapses on his death, the exception appears to apply, since the right was valued under Section 2701 in the hands of Grandfather, even though its valuation did not affect his own taxable gifts.

[iv] **Lapse of a liquidation right due to changes in state law.** Section 2704(a) does not apply to the lapse of a liquidation right that occurs solely by reason of a change in state law. For this purpose, a change in the governing instrument of an entity is not a change in state law.[57]

---

[54] RULPA §§ 602–604; ULPA § 16; UPA § 42.

[55] Treas. Reg. § 25.2704-1(c)(2)(ii).

[56] Treas. Reg. § 25.2704-1(f), example 8.

[57] Treas. Reg. § 25.2704-1(c)(2)(iii).

[v] **Grandfathered lapse provisions.** If a transaction results in a lapse of a voting or liquidation right where the lapse was imposed by agreement entered into before October 9, 1990 (the effective date of Section 2704(a)), the lapse should not be taxable.[58]

[vi] **Temporary lapses.** If a right that has temporarily lapsed may be restored only upon a future event outside the control of the holder or the holder's family, the lapse is recognized at the time it becomes permanent (by a transfer of the interest or otherwise).[59]

EXAMPLE: Dad is a general partner. His voting rights have lapsed on his incompetency, but will be restored if he ever regains competency. Since the recovery of his competency is not within anyone's control, his voting rights will not be considered to lapse until the earlier to occur of a transfer of his interest or a permanent lapse of his rights.[60] It is unclear whether a determination by a doctor that Dad is permanently incompetent would be considered a permanent lapse.

QUERY: What if the lapsed right can be restored on the occurrence of an event that is within the control of the holder's family? For example, suppose Father has a right to put his stock to the corporation. This is a liquidation right. Father and Son (the other shareholder) agree that the right shall no longer be exercisable. Presumably, this agreement would result in a taxable lapse, even though Father and Son could always get together and agree to restore the put right. If so, can Father and Son defer the taxation of the lapse by providing that the put right shall not be exercisable for the next twenty years?[61]

[vii] **Source of right or lapse.** A voting right or a liquidation right may be conferred by and may lapse by reason of a state law, the corporate charter or bylaws, an agreement, or other means.[62]

[e] **Amount of Transfer**

The statute provides that the amount of the deemed transfer occurring by reason of a lapse in liquidation or voting rights is the excess (if any) of:

---

[58] See Priv. Ltr. Rul. 9229028 (Apr. 21, 1992) and ¶ 26.04[3] below.

[59] Treas. Reg. § 25.2704-1(a)(3).

[60] Treas. Reg. § 25.2704-1(f), example 9.

[61] This should not be an applicable restriction ignored under IRC § 2704(b), if it is not a restriction on the right to liquidate the entity in whole or in part.

[62] Treas. Reg. § 25.2704-1(a)(4).

- The value of all interests in the entity held by the holder immediately before the lapse (determined as if the voting and liquidation rights were nonlapsing), *over*
- The value of such interests immediately after the lapse.[63]

The regulations have a slightly different calculation. They state that the amount of the transfer is the excess, if any, of:

- The value of all interests in the entity owned by the holder immediately before the lapse (determined immediately after the lapse as if the lapsed right was nonlapsing), *over*
- The value of the interests described in the preceding paragraph immediately after the lapse (determined as if all such interests were held by one individual).[64]

[i] Measuring "interests before lapse" against "interests after lapse." Presumably, the phrase "the value of the interests described in the preceding paragraph" refers to the value of all of the interests owned by the holder before the lapse, and to those same interests after the lapse, although the regulation could be clearer.[65]

EXAMPLE: Father has the right to put his stock to a corporation. This right lapses on any transfer. Father gives his stock to Son. Father's stock immediately before the transfer was worth $100. The value of the stock immediately after the gift is $75. Father is treated as having transferred $100, even though Son only receives $75 of value. Calculation: Father gives $75 pursuant to Chapter 12 and $25 pursuant to Chapter 14.

EXAMPLE: Wife has a 60 percent general partnership interest. The value of her interest is $1,000. Wife's parents have the other 40 percent general partnership interest. Wife dies, leaving her interest to Husband. On Wife's death, her estate becomes an assignee and loses the right to vote. An assignee's interest is worth only $800, because of loss of control. For estate tax purposes, the value of the interest is $1,000 ($800 pursuant to Chapter 12 and $200 pursuant to Chapter 14). Is the $200 Section 2704(a) "transfer" treated as a bequest to Husband (thus qualifying for the marital deduction), even though Husband does not receive that value? Or is it treated as a bequest to Wife's parents? Or is it treated as a phantom amount, passing to no one? The answer is not clear from Section 2704(a) and the regulations, but is obviously important.

---

[63] IRC § 2704(a)(2).

[64] Treas. Reg. § 25.2704-1(d).

[65] The last sentence of Treas. Reg. § 25.2704-1(f), example 5, is a little ambiguous, as well; it is open to the interpretation that the phrase refers to the value of any interests still held by the original holder after the lapse.

[ii] Value lost by reasons other than lapse of rights. The parenthetical phrase in the regulation—"determined immediately after the lapse as if the lapsed right was nonlapsing"—is difficult to understand. The preamble to the Section 2704 regulations, as originally proposed, indicated that the reference is intended to avoid treating reductions in value which are not attributable to the lapse as part of the value of the lapsed rights.

> **EXAMPLE:** Father has the right to put his stock to a corporation for $100. This right lapses on any transfer. Father gives his stock to Son and concurrently retires. The value of the stock immediately after the transfer is $60. The appraiser tells Father that the value of the stock has decreased by $25 due to the lapse of Father's put right and by $15 due to the business' loss of its key person, Father. The amount transferred for gift tax purposes would be $100 minus $15, or $85 ($60 pursuant to Chapter 12 and $25 pursuant to Chapter 14).

[iii] Valuation lost due to fractionalization of interest. The language "as if all interests were held by one individual" operates so as to ignore value which disappears solely as a result of the division of rights among several individuals.

> **EXAMPLE:** Father owns 60 percent of the voting stock of a corporation. He has a put right which lapses on transfer of the stock. Father gives the stock to his three children. The value of the stock in the hands of Father was $100. The value of Father's 60 percent interest before the transfer was $100; the value of the same 60 percent interest after the transfer, as if one person held it (i.e., the value without the put right) is $70. The actual value of each 20 percent interest in the hands of each child is $20—specifically, $33¹/₃, decreased by $10 due to the lapse of the liquidation right and $3¹/₃ due to a minority discount. The taxable value of Father's gift will be $90 ($60 pursuant to Chapter 12 and $30 pursuant to Chapter 14). The $10 decrease due to the change of a majority interest into a minority interest is not taxed.

[iv] Distinctions that make a difference. Section 2704 does not cause problems in some transfers of corporate stock where value seems to disappear.

> **EXAMPLE:** Father owns 70 percent of the voting stock of Corporation X and 100 percent of the nonvoting stock. He transfers the voting stock to Child. Values are: voting stock—$70; nonvoting stock—$100; value of both interests held together—$200. No lapse occurs. The Chapter 14 transfer is zero, and the Chapter 12 transfer is $70.

The answer may be different in a partnership context—

> **EXAMPLE:** Father has a 70 percent general partnership interest, and a 100 percent limited partnership interest. He transfers his general partnership interest to Daughter as assignee. Values are: general

partnership interest—$70; limited partnership interest—$100; value of general partnership and limited partnership interests together—$200; general partnership interest without its management rights—$50. Father's Chapter 14 transfer would be: $200 (value of his interests before transfer) minus $150 (value of those interests as held by one person after the transfer), or $50, and the Chapter 12 transfer would be $50, for a total gift of $100. This amount reflects the decrease in value of Father's general and limited partnership interests as a result of the lapse of the management rights.

EXAMPLE: What if, in the immediately preceding example, Father transfers his limited partnership interest to his daughter in Year One, retains his general partnership interest, and dies unexpectedly in Year Two? The Year One transfer is only taxable under Chapter 14 to the extent that the value of a general partnership interest held with a limited partnership interest exceeds the value of a general partnership interest held with an assignee interest. Assuming that this amount is zero, the Year One transfer is $100 (assuming that an assignee interest were equal in value to a limited partnership interest) and the amount included in Father's estate at death is $70.

EXAMPLE: Dad owns 70 percent of the voting common stock and 100 percent of the nonvoting preferred stock of a corporation. The voting common stock is worth $700. The nonvoting preferred stock is worth $100, and the value of both classes of stock when they are held together is $1,000. Dad gives his voting common stock to his daughter and his nonvoting preferred stock to his son. If a Chapter 14 transfer is deemed to have taken place with respect to the lapse of Dad's right to liquidate the nonvoting preferred stock, what is its value? The daughter actually receives voting common stock worth $700, and the son actually receives nonvoting preferred stock worth $100. The Chapter 14 transfer is the excess of the value of the voting common stock and nonvoting preferred stock owned by A immediately before the gift ($1,000) over the value of all of the stock immediately after the gift, determined as if both classes of stock were held by one individual ($1,000), or zero.

[f] Double Taxation

There may be no adjustment for tax imposed on a lapse that has been the subject of a previously taxed transaction.

EXAMPLE: Father and Son establish a corporation. Father takes stock with voting rights which will lapse on Father's death. Son contributes fair market value for his stock, which will be at a premium, taking into consideration the lapsing voting rights of Father's stock. Father dies. The value attributable to the lapsed rights on Father's death is included in Father's estate, with no adjustment for the fact that Son has already paid for the value attributable to the lapsing rights.

[g] Similar Rights

By regulations, the Secretary may apply the rule of Section 2704(a) to rights similar to voting and liquidation rights.[66]

[2] Transfer of Property Subject to Restrictions—Section 2704(b)

For transfer tax purposes, if there is a transfer of an interest in a corporation or partnership to (or for the benefit of) a member of the transferor's family, and the transferor and members of the transferor's family hold, immediately before the transfer, control of the entity, then any "applicable restriction" is disregarded in determining the value of the transferred interest.[67]

[a] What is an Applicable Restriction?

An "applicable restriction" is a limitation on the ability to liquidate the entity (in whole or in part) that is more restrictive than the limitations that would generally apply under state law to the entity in the absence of the restriction. A restriction is an applicable restriction, however, only to the extent that either (1) the restriction by its terms will lapse at any time after the transfer or (2) the transferor (or the transferor's estate) and any members of the transferor's family can remove the restriction immediately after the transfer.[68]

> EXAMPLE: X owns 75 percent of Corporation A, which would be enough to liquidate under state law. The articles of incorporation provide that 100 percent of the stockholders must vote to approve liquidation. On X's death, the 100 percent voting requirement will be an applicable restriction if the 100 percent requirement will lapse by its terms at any time after X's death, or if X's estate and any member(s) of X's family (alone or collectively) can remove the restriction immediately after X's death.

Ability to remove restrictions. The regulations take the position that the ability to remove the restriction is determined by reference to the state law that would apply but for a more restrictive rule in the governing instruments of the entity.[69] This concept does not appear in the statute.

> EXAMPLE: Suppose, in the above example, that the restriction does not lapse by its terms. X's estate owns 75 percent of the stock, and an unrelated party owns 25 percent. Even though X's estate cannot in fact liq-

---

[66] IRC § 2704(a)(3); Treas. Reg. § 25.2704-1(e) (reserved).

[67] IRC § 2704(b)(1); Treas. Reg. § 25.2704-2(a).

[68] Treas. Reg. § 25.2704-2(b).

[69] Treas. Reg. § 25.2704-2(b).

uidate the entity, the restriction will be disregarded in valuing X's interest for estate tax purposes, since state law would allow X's estate to liquidate in the absence of the restriction. This result seems outrageous.

[i] Exception for restrictions arising from financings. "Applicable restriction" does not include any commercially reasonable restriction arising as part of any financing (for trade or business operations) by the corporation or partnership with a person who is not related to the transferor or transferee, or a member of the family of either.[70] For example, if Bank lends Family Corporation money for working capital, and the loan agreement between Family Corporation and Bank prohibits Family Corporation from liquidating while a loan is outstanding, this restriction will be respected in valuing an interest in Family Corporation.

For trade or business operations only. The regulations impose an additional requirement that the financing must be provided to the entity for trade or business operations, whether in the form of debt or equity.[71] Does this regulation mean that restrictions on liquidation imposed by third-party lenders for appropriate corporate purposes other than operations (e.g., debt refinancing, funds for raising capital) will not be respected? Hopefully, "operations" can be read in a broad sense.

Unrelated person requirement. An unrelated person is any person whose relationship to the transferor, the transferee or any member of the family of either is not described in Section 267(b), provided that for this purpose the term "fiduciary of a trust" as used in Section 267(b) does not include a bank as defined in Section 581.[72]

[ii] Exception for restriction imposed by federal or state law. "Applicable restriction" does not include any restriction imposed, or required to be imposed, by any federal or state law.[73] For example, state law may impose a fiduciary duty on a majority shareholder not to liquidate the corporation if liquidation would negatively affect the minority shareholders. This fiduciary limitation can be taken into account in valuing the majority shareholder's interest for transfer tax purposes. Similarly, if state law provides that a limited partner has no right to dissolve a partnership, that limitation should be considered in determining the transfer tax value of a limited partnership interest.[74]

---

[70] IRC § 2704(b)(3)(A).

[71] Treas. Reg. § 25.2704-2(b).

[72] Treas. Reg. § 25.2704-2(b).

[73] IRC § 2704(b)(3)(B); Treas. Reg. § 25.2704-2(b).

[74] See, however, Tech. Adv. Mem. 9725002 (Mar. 25, 1997), in which the IRS took the position that a limited partner's lack of rights to withdraw from a term partnership will be ignored.

[iii] **Exception for rights subject to Section 2703.** "Applicable restriction" does not include an option, right to use property, or agreement that is subject to Section 2703.[75] The meaning of "subject to Section 2703" is not altogether clear.

QUERY: *A and B are shareholders of Corporation X. A buy-sell agreement provides that neither A nor B can transfer his stock without offering it to the other for a formula value. The agreement meets the commercially reasonable exception of Section 2703(b). A dies. Is the estate tax valuation determined by Section 2703, rather than Section 2704? Or does the fact that the agreement is excepted from the general valuation rules of Section 2703(a) mean that it is not subject to Section 2703, and consequently is subject to Section 2704?*

[b] Exceptions for Other Restrictions

The Treasury is authorized to issue additional regulations providing that other restrictions will be disregarded in determining the value of the transfer of any interest in a corporation or partnership to a member of the transferor's family if a restriction reduces the value of the transferred interest for gift, estate or generation-skipping transfer tax purposes but does not ultimately reduce the value of the interest to the transferee.[76]

[c] Effect of Disregarding Restriction

If an applicable restriction is disregarded for purposes of Section 2704, the transferred interest subject to the restriction is valued as if the restriction does not exist and as if the rights of the transferor are determined under the state law that would apply but for the restriction.[77]

EXAMPLE: Dad owns 51 percent of a corporation. Child owns 49 percent. Under state law, Dad could liquidate the corporation. The shareholders' agreement requires the consent of 100 percent of the shareholders to liquidate the corporation. Dad gives his stock to Grandchild. Even though Dad cannot in fact liquidate the corporation, his stock is valued for gift tax purposes as though he could.[78]

When state law offers choices in structuring an entity that result in different types of restrictions on liquidation, the choice of a particular structure should not be regarded as an applicable restriction. For example, most state partnership laws allow the partners to create a partnership for a term of

---

[75] Treas. Reg. § 25.2704-2(b). See Ch. 27 for an analysis of IRC § 2703.

[76] IRC § 2704(b)(4).

[77] Treas. Reg. § 25.2704-2(c).

[78] See Treas. Reg. § 25.2704-2(d), example 1.

years or a partnership at will. Generally, a partnership for a term of years offers an additional event of dissolution (the end of the term) than a partnership at will, and therefore is less restrictive in terms of liquidating the entity as a whole. On the other hand, a partnership at will typically permits a limited partner to withdraw and receive the fair value of his interest on six months' notice, while a partnership for a term of years only permits a limited partner to withdraw before the term expires if the agreement so provides. Thus, a partnership at will is less restrictive in terms of liquidating a particular limited partner's interest. Because both choices are offered under state law, neither choice should be viewed as an applicable restriction for purposes of Section 2704(b).

However, it appears, as further discussed in Chapter 16 on limited partnerships, that the IRS might view the choice of either structure as an applicable restriction, depending on the circumstances. For example, the IRS has taken the view in a technical advice memorandum that a restriction on withdrawal applicable to a partnership for years would be treated as an applicable restriction to be ignored under Section 2704(b), when state law provided that limited partners in partnerships at will could withdraw their interests on six months' notice.[79] If the value that the limited partner could withdraw is the fair value that he could get if the interest were sold, no additional value should be deemed transferred. If the value is considered the limited partner's pro rata share of the partnership assets, and if that value is more than a sale of the interest would bring, then an interest in a family partnership will be valued at more than the same interest in a partnership among unrelated parties. Some states do not allow limited partners in partnerships at will to withdraw. In such states, the restriction or withdrawal incident to a term partnership would presumably not be an applicable restriction.

[d] Permissive "Restrictions"

If the restrictions are less restrictive than state law, they will not be disregarded. Thus, if an agreement permits a ten percent shareholder to liquidate the corporation, that agreement will be considered in determining the value of the shareholder's interest, even if state law would require more than ten percent in the absence of an agreement.[80]

[e] Interaction with Section 2701

An applicable restriction will be disregarded when valuations under Section 2701 are made.[81]

---

[79] Tech. Adv. Mem. 9725002 (Mar. 25, 1997).

[80] Treas. Reg. § 25.2704-2(d), example 3.

[81] Treas. Reg. §§ 25.2704-2(c), 25.2704-2(d), example 5. See Ch. 31 on preferred equity interests for a discussion of IRC § 2701.

EXAMPLE: Dad owns all of the preferred stock and all of the common stock of Corporation X. He transfers the common stock to Son in 1996. The preferred stock has a right of redemption after the year 2000. The restriction on Dad's ability to liquidate the preferred stock before the year 2000 will be disregarded for Section 2704 purposes. This apparently means that Dad will be deemed to have an immediate right to liquidate, which is more than the preferred stock has under the agreement or would have had if state law applied. The Section 2701 treatment would be either to value the liquidation right at zero or, if the preferred stock is treated as conferring a qualified payment right, to value the preferred stock at the lower of its liquidation value or the value of the qualified payment right.

[3] Effective Date

The rules described in Section 2704 apply to restrictions, rights, and limitations on rights created after October 8, 1990.[82]

The Section 2704 regulations apply to lapses occurring after January 28, 1992 of rights created after October 8, 1990 and to transfers occurring after January 28, 1992 of property subject to applicable restrictions created after October 8, 1990. In determining whether a voting right or liquidation right has lapsed prior to January 29, 1992, and for purposes of determining whether the lapse is subject to Section 2704(a), taxpayers may rely on any reasonable interpretations of the statutory provisions. For transfers of interests occurring before January 28, 1992, taxpayers may rely on any reasonable interpretation of the statutory provisions in determining whether a restriction is an applicable restriction that must be disregarded in determining the value of the transferred interest. For these purposes, the provisions of the previously proposed regulations are considered a reasonable interpretation of the statutory provisions.[83]

In addition, a restructuring or recapitalization of an entity that does not result in substantive changes to the owners' rights should not cause future lapses imposed under otherwise grandfathered agreements to become taxable.[84]

[4] Fundamental and (Incredibly) Unanswered Questions

Who is the transferee of a Section 2704 transfer? A lapse of a voting right, for example, will not necessarily increase the value of any other interest holder's interest. In such a case, who is the transferee of the "transfer"?

---

[82] Omnibus Budget Reconciliation Act of 1990, Pub. L. No. 101-508, § 11602(e)(1)(A)(iii), 104 Stat. 1383 (1990).

[83] Treas. Reg. § 25.2704-3.

[84] E.g., Priv. Ltr. Rul. 9451050 (Sept. 22, 1994); Priv. Ltr. Rul. 9352012 (Sept. 29, 1993).

Is Section 2704 constitutional? If the lapse of a right results in no increase in the value of any other interest holder's interest, there appears to be no transfer of property in reality. Is it constitutional to apply transfer tax when no transfer in fact occurs?[85]

---

[85] See Stacy Eastland's various articles raising this point.

CHAPTER 27

Section 2703: Buy-Sell Agreements, Options, and Noncommercial Restrictions

¶ 27.01　INTRODUCTION

Buy-sell agreements have long been used which fix transfer tax values (and actual values) of interests in entities at levels which are arguably more or less than the value that such interests would have if the agreement were not in place. Restrictions on certain rights normally associated with ownership of an equity interest are often imposed on business interests for nontax reasons; they may also result in lowering the transfer tax value of the interest. Section 2703, which was enacted in 1990, provides rules affecting the transfer tax value of property subject to buy-sell agreements, options, and restrictions on its sale or use.

　　Section 2703 can be obscure, so this chapter will include both a low-tech overview and a high-tech analysis of this section.

¶ 27.02　LOW-TECH OVERVIEW OF SECTION 2703

[1] Buy-Sell Agreements

There is a body of case law on buy-sell agreements. Let's examine that before jumping into the statute. We'll do this by analyzing the following global example.

GLOBAL EXAMPLE

Dad and Child own 80 percent and 20 percent, respectively, of a corporation. They enter into an agreement providing that, if either of them dies, the survivor has the right to buy the stock of the decedent's estate at book value. Dad dies first. On Dad's death, his 80 percent is worth $800,000 without regard to the agreement, and it has a book value of $500,000. What is the result?

Whether or not the agreement is subject to Section 2703, the tests listed in subparagraphs [a], [b], and [c] below must be met in order to fix the value of Dad's 80 percent interest at $500,000.[1] If Section 2703 applies, the test described in subparagraph [d] below must also be met.

[a] General Case Law Requirements

[i] **Obligation to sell.** Dad's estate must be obligated to sell the interest if Child wants to buy.[2] If the estate is not compelled to sell, the stock's book value or other agreed upon value cannot be used.[3]

In the Global Example, assume Dad's agreement meets this requirement.

[ii] **Determinable price.** The agreement must contain a method for determining the price, which must be fixed or determinable pursuant to a formula.[4]

In the Global Example, the stock's book value is a determinable number, so Dad's agreement should meet this requirement.

[iii] **Binding during life.** The agreement must provide that Dad cannot

---

[1] See S. Budget Comm., 101st Cong., 2d Sess., Informal Report on S. 3209, 136 Cong. Rec. S15,629, S15,683 (Oct. 18, 1990) (indicating that the new statute would not otherwise alter requirements for a buy-sell agreement, such as the requirement that it have lifetime restrictions in order to be binding on death); see also Treas. Reg. § 20.2031-2(h); Dorn v. United States, 828 F2d 177 (3d Cir. 1987); St. Louis County Bank v. United States, 674 F2d 1207 (8th Cir. 1982); Estate of Lauder v. Comm'r, 1992 RIA TC Memo. ¶ 92,736, 64 TCM (CCH) 1643 (1992).

[2] E.g., Lomb v. Sugden, 82 F2d 166 (2d Cir. 1936); Wilson v. Bowers, 57 F2d 682 (2d Cir. 1932); Estate of Salt v. Comm'r, 17 TC 92 (1951), acq., 1952-1 CB 4.

[3] See, e.g., Baltimore Nat'l Bank v. United States, 136 F. Supp. 642 (D. Md. 1955).

[4] See, e.g., Estate of Bischoff v. Comm'r, 69 TC 32 (1977); Estate of Weil v. Comm'r, 22 TC 1267 (1954), acq., 1955-2 CB 10; Estate of Salt v. Comm'r, 17 TC 92 (1951), acq., 1952-1 CB 4; see also Rev. Rul. 53-157, 1953-2 CB 255.

dispose of his interest during his life without first offering it to Child for no more than the contract price.[5]

In the Global Example, we do not know from the assumed facts whether the agreement contained such a provision.

[iv] **Fair price.** The price must be fair when the agreement is made.[6]

An agreement to fix the estate tax value of the business at book value is unlikely to meet the test, unless the business (1) holds only publicly traded securities, which are marked to market on a daily basis or (2) has some other characteristic that will cause book value to approximate the true value of the assets. In the Global Example, it is doubtful that the agreement will meet this test.

[b] Bona Fide Business Arrangement

The agreement must have a bona fide business purpose.[7] An arrangement to keep the business in the family will satisfy this requirement.[8]

In the Global Example, Dad's agreement probably meets this requirement.

[c] No Testamentary Device

The agreement must not be a device to transfer the property to the natural objects of Dad's bounty for less than adequate consideration.[9] Thus, if

---

[5] Treas. Reg. § 20.2031-2(h); see also Estate of Weil v. Comm'r, 22 TC 1267 (1954), acq., 1955-2 CB 10; Estate of Salt v. Comm'r, 17 TC 92 (1951), acq., 1952-1 CB 4. Thus, if an owner of stock provides in his will that a certain person has a right to purchase the stock at a certain price, this provision will not fix the estate tax value of the stock, as the provision is not binding during his lifetime. Ahmanson Foundation v. United States, 674 F2d 761, 768 (9th Cir. 1981), appeal after remand, 733 F2d 623 (9th Cir. 1984); Priv. Ltr. Rul. 9550002 (Aug. 31, 1995).

[6] E.g., Estate of Carpenter v. Comm'r, 1992 RIA TC Memo. ¶ 92,653, 64 TCM (CCH) 1274 (1992).

[7] Treas. Reg. §§ 20.2031-2(h), 25.2703-1(b)(1); Rev. Rul. 59-60, § 8, 1959-1 CB 237. Dorn v. United States, 828 F2d 177 (3d Cir. 1987); St. Louis County Bank v. United States, 674 F2d 1207 (8th Cir. 1982); Estate of Lauder v. Comm'r, 1992 RIA TC Memo. ¶ 92,736, 64 TCM (CCH) 1643 (1992).

[8] E.g., Estate of Bischoff v. Comm'r, 69 TC 32 (1977); Estate of Reynolds v. Comm'r, 55 TC 172 (1970); Estate of Littick v. Comm'r, 31 TC 181 (1958), acq., 1959-2 CB 5, acq. withdrawn in part, acq. in result in part, 1984-2 CB 1; Baltimore Nat'l Bank v. United States, 136 F. Supp. 642 (D. Md. 1955).

[9] Treas. Reg. §§ 20.2031-2(h), 25.2703-1(b)(1); see also Dorn v. United States, 828 F2d 177 (3d Cir. 1987) (finding decedent's children and grandchildren to be natural objects of her bounty); St. Louis County Bank v. United States, 674 F2d 1207 (8th Cir. 1982) (decedent's daughter and granddaughter were natural objects of his

Dad agreed that his estate would sell its interest to Child for $1, this rule would surely be violated.

The statute uses the phrase "members of the decedent's family," rather than "natural objects of the transferor's bounty." The regulations, in what may be an unwarranted extension of the statutory language, incorporate the term "natural objects of a transferor's bounty." The term, which is very subjective, is not defined in the regulations. The preamble to the Section 2703 Regulations indicates that the term cannot be reduced to a specific formula or specific classes of relationship, and is not necessarily limited to persons related by blood or marriage.[10] Logically, it would include Dad's descendants and other closely related members of his family (for example, his wife). Unlike the objective group consisting of Dad's family, natural objects of Dad's bounty may exclude an estranged child, but may include a close friend or collateral relative (particularly if Dad has no living descendants).

[d] Comparable to Other Agreements

Section 2703 adds another requirement for agreements entered into or substantially modified after October 8, 1990. The agreement must have terms comparable to similar agreements entered into by persons in an arms' length transaction.[11] Controversy has dogged this requirement, since many practitioners deem it too hard to meet as a purely practical matter. In particular, evidence of comparable arrangements may be difficult to obtain. The IRS has indicated that it will not necessarily require evidence of comparable agreements in all cases.[12] Moreover, the IRS National Office has informally indicated that it does not intend to use this evidentiary requirement as a back-door means to eliminate the recognition of values pursuant to buy-sell agreements as establishing value for transfer tax purposes. However, some IRS offices are requiring evidence of similar agreements on audits.

[2] Evaluating the Effect of Stock Restrictions

Section 2703(a)(2) also applies the tests described in ¶ 27.02[1][b], [c], and [d] above to determine whether restrictions on the right to sell or use property should be respected for transfer tax purposes. Such restrictions might include

---

bounty); Estate of Lauder v. Comm'r, 1992 RIA TC Memo. ¶ 92,736, 64 TCM (CCH) 1643 (1992) (decedent's sons and their children were natural objects of his bounty).

[10] TD 8395, 57 Fed. Reg. 4250 (Feb. 4, 1992).

[11] Treas. Reg. § 25.2703-1(b)(1).

[12] Cf. Priv. Ltr. Rul. 9350016 (Sept. 16, 1993) (no discussion of whether evidence of comparable arrangements was required in ruling that requirements to avoid application of IRC § 2703 were met).

prohibitions against pledging one's interest in an entity or transferring one's interest to another person without the consent of the other owners.

The IRS has begun using Section 2703 to attack family partnerships and other arrangements. Some agents have been requiring taxpayers to come up with specific evidence that restrictions do not vary from those imposed by standard commercial agreements between unrelated parties.

PRACTICE POINTER: If the IRS interprets and uses this provision in accordance with its evident intent, we could probably expect something like the following. If an agreement has reasonable and relatively common provisions, Section 2703(a)(2) should not create a problem. In this regard, if the provisions of the applicable state uniform limited partnership act are used, the IRS would seem to have a difficult time saying that the provisions are not comparable to third-party arrangements. After all, the applicable state legislature (along with 49 other state legislatures) thought those provisions constituted the appropriate agreement, in default of other agreements. If the agreement contains unusual provisions, if unusual circumstances exist, or if the IRS takes a very strict approach with this section, the taxpayer might have to come up with evidence that third parties would normally agree to those provisions.

It should also be noted that the IRS has issued several technical advice memoranda holding that Section 2703 can be used to disregard an entire partnership agreement, if the partnership itself is a device designed to avoid transfer tax.[13]

[3] Effective Date

Agreements entered into or restrictions imposed before October 9, 1990 are not subject to the comparability test unless they are substantially modified after October 8, 1990. Substantial modifications include modifications (1) that are not required by the agreement, (2) that do not bring the price set in the agreement closer to fair market value, and (3) that result in more than a minimal change to the quality, value, or timing of the rights of any party with respect to property subject to the agreement.[14] Numerous private letter rulings have been issued on whether a change to an agreement would result in a substantial modification.

---

[13] E.g., Tech. Adv. Mem. 9725002 (Mar. 25, 1997); Tech. Adv. Mem. 9723009 (Feb. 24, 1997).

[14] Treas. Reg. § 25.2703-1(c).

[4] Consequences of Having an Agreement Which Does Not Fix Transfer Tax Value

If an agreement is enforceable, but does not fix estate tax values, some thorny problems can occur.

In the Global Example, assume that the agreement does not fix the value for estate tax purposes. Child can buy the interest for $500,000, but the estate will pay estate tax on $800,000. Who is apportioned the estate tax on the phantom $300,000 value? Also, suppose Dad's will provides that his entire estate passes to his wife, and that the probate estate bears all taxes. Wife will receive an interest that is worth $500,000. There would appear to be no marital deduction available for the phantom $300,000, since it does not pass to the wife.[15] If the marital deduction is not available for the phantom value, the estate will have to pay estate tax on that value, thus further reducing the marital deduction and pushing the estate tax computation into a spiral This will result in the wife effectively paying estate tax of $366,000 (122 percent of $300,000) on the phantom value (assuming the estate is in the 55 percent bracket).

Can the tax be apportioned to Child, since she got the benefit of paying the low price? Most state laws would not apportion the tax to her, since she is not actually a beneficiary of the estate. Special drafting in the will and the agreement might accomplish it.

¶ 27.03 HIGH-TECH ANALYSIS OF SECTION 2703

[1] General Rule

For purposes of the estate, gift, and generation-skipping transfer taxes, the value of any property shall be determined without regard to:

- Any option, agreement, or other right to acquire or use the property at a price less than the fair market value of the property (without regard to such option, agreement, or right); or
- Any restriction on the right to sell or use such property.[16]

---

[15] A marital deduction is available for the amount that actually passes to Wife. Restrictions on the transferability of stock should not disqualify the stock from qualifying for the marital deduction, as long as the spouse receives full value. E.g., Priv. Ltr. Rul. 9606008 (Nov. 9, 1995).

[16] IRC § 2703(a).

[2] "Rights" and "Restrictions"

[a] Defined

The options, agreements, rights and restrictions above referenced are referred to in the regulations as "rights or restrictions."[17] A right or restriction may be contained in a partnership agreement, articles of incorporation, corporate bylaws, a shareholders' agreement, or any other agreement, or may be implicit in the capital structure of an entity.[18] Rights and restrictions usually go hand in hand. A restriction imposed on one owner may give rights to the other owners.[19]

Various types of provisions can constitute rights or restrictions—

- *Right of first refusal.* A right of first refusal is a right or restriction.[20]
- *Conservation easement.* A perpetual restriction on the use of real property that qualified for a charitable deduction under either Section 2522(d) or Section 2055(f) (both relating to conservation easements) is not treated as a right or restriction.[21]
- *Entire partnership agreement?* The IRS has taken the view that Section 2703 allows it to disregard an entire partnership agreement on the grounds that the restricted property consists of the assets transferred to the partnership and the restrictions include all of the restrictions imposed by a partnership.[22] Many planners believe this view is wrong.

[b] Time for Determining Whether Price Is Below Fair Market Value

The determination of whether the rights or restrictions are below fair market value is apparently made at the date of a taxable transfer. For example, if a five-year lease at $10/acre was fair when entered into, and three years later at the lessor's death, the going rate is $15/acre, the lease will be disregarded for estate tax valuation purposes, unless the standard commercial exception applied when the lease was signed.

---

[17] Treas. Reg. § 25.2703-1(a)(2).

[18] Treas. Reg. § 25.2703-1(a)(3).

[19] For example, a provision in a trust giving a particular person the right to buy stock held by the trust at the death of the income beneficiary is considered a restriction on the trust's right to sell or use the stock under IRC § 2703(a)(2). Tech. Adv. Mem. 9550002 (Aug. 31, 1995).

[20] Moreover, if the right of first refusal is silent regarding the purchase price, the right may be disregarded if it does not fall within the standard commercial exception. E.g., Tech. Adv. Mem. 9550002 (Aug. 31, 1995). The "standard commercial exception" is what we'll call the exception described below which relates to agreements which are consistent with similar agreements between parties dealing at arm's length.

[21] Treas. Reg. § 25.2703-1(a)(4).

[22] Tech. Adv. Mem. 9725002 (Mar. 25, 1997); Tech. Adv. Mem. 9723009 (Feb. 24, 1997).

[3] Consequences of Disregarding a Right or Restriction

This disregarding of rights or restrictions means that property may be subject to estate tax at a high value even though it has low true value. This can cause serious problems for the estate.

[a] Marital Deduction Issues

Phantom asset value amounts (created under Section 2703) will presumably not qualify for the marital deduction. Additional tax payable out of marital deduction assets can cause a spiraling tax effect, subsuming a large portion of the marital deduction bequest.

EXAMPLE: Husband owns stock that is subject to an agreement requiring his estate to sell his stock to the other shareholders (his siblings) for $100. The value of the stock determined without regard to the agreement is $200. Husband bequeaths the stock to his wife. The estate tax value is $200, but the value actually passing to the wife and qualifying for the marital deduction is $100. If the marital bequest bears the estate tax, then, at the maximum rate, the additional estate tax caused by the phantom amount will be $122.

[b] Drafting Tip: Apportionment of Tax on Phantom Value

If the estate tax value of property subject to a disregarded right or restriction exceeds the amount to be received for the property by the estate under the agreement, the will drafter may want to provide for apportionment of the payment of the tax on the phantom value. If the individual benefiting from the right or restriction is chosen to pay the tax, and that individual is not a beneficiary of the probate estate, the agreement signed by the individual and containing the right or restriction could presumably be drafted to give the estate a right of recovery of the tax.

[c] Multiple Restrictions

If an agreement has one restriction which is ignored (e.g., the right to purchase real estate at book value on the death of a partner), will the other rights and restrictions in the agreement be respected? The answer depends on whether the rights and restrictions are considered separate or integral parts of the same right or restriction. If two restrictions are separate, the failure of one restriction will not necessarily cause the others to be disregarded. On the other hand, if the two restrictions are integral parts of a single restriction, they will apparently be respected or ignored as a group.[23] The IRS has, in fact, taken the

---

[23] Treas. Reg. § 25.2703-1(b)(5).

position that an entire partnership agreement can be ignored under Section 2703.[24]

[d] Tax on Value Passing to Unrelated Party

Even though an unrelated party is the principal beneficiary of a right or restriction, it seems that no adjustment is made to the value of the property as determined under Section 2703.

> **EXAMPLE:** Corporation *A* is owned 40 percent by Mother, ten percent by Child, and 50 percent by Unrelated Third Party. A buy-sell agreement provides that stock of a deceased shareholder is to be purchased by Corporation *A* at book value. The buy-sell agreement therefore contains a restriction. At Mother's death, the book value of Mother's stock is $100. Without regard to the agreement, the value of the stock is $150. It appears that the estate tax value of the stock is $150 even though Unrelated Third Party gets most of the benefit of the agreement, unless the requirements of the standard commercial exception are met.

[e] Pre-Existing Restrictions

In the example above, what if Child had purchased or been given his interest several years after the restrictions were already in place (i.e., the initial agreement was between Mother and Unrelated Third Party)? For example, suppose Mother and Unrelated Third Party each owned 50 percent of A when the agreement was entered into in 1991. Mother assigns 30 percent of A to Child in 1996, subject to the agreement. It appears that the gauntlet of Section 2703 would have to be run for the price under the agreement to be respected for estate tax purposes upon Mother's death. If the agreement was entered into for genuine non-tax-avoidance reasons between unrelated parties, that should presumably be evidence that the restrictions met the standard commercial exemption, described below.

[4] Exceptions

[a] Standard Commercial Exception

A right or restriction will be respected under the standard commercial exception if all of the following three conditions exist:[25]

---

[24] Tech. Adv. Mem. 9725002 (Mar. 25, 1997); Tech. Adv. Mem. 9723009 (Feb. 24, 1997).

[25] IRC § 2703(b). Note, however, that a buy-sell agreement would also still have to meet the requirements listed at ¶ 27.02[1][a] above, which are considered elements of the following tests:

- The right or restriction results from a bona fide business arrangement;
- The right or restriction is not a device to permit the transferor to make non-arm's length property transfers to the transferor's family; and
- The terms of the right or restriction are comparable to rights or restrictions included in arm's-length transactions between unrelated parties.

These three conditions are deemed satisfied if the "unrelated party rule," discussed below in subparagraph [b], is applicable.

[i] **Bona fide business arrangement.** The right or restriction must be a bona fide business arrangement.[26] Case law makes clear that this requirement will be satisfied by a desire to maintain family control.[27] The IRS has privately ruled that where a restriction on stock was not binding on all shareholders or applicable to all outstanding stock and was imposed by a testamentary instrument after the stock was issued, the restriction did not represent a bona fide business arrangement.[28]

[ii] **No device.** The right or restriction cannot be a device to transfer the property to members of the decedent's family for less than full and adequate consideration in money or money's worth.[29]

Legislative history note. The legislative history indicates that Congress adopted the reasoning of *Saint Louis County Bank v. United States*,[30] namely, that the above tests are two separate tests. Congress clearly rejected the suggestion of other cases that the objective of maintenance of family control standing alone assures the absence of a device to transfer wealth.[31]

Guidelines for purchase price should be provided. The IRS has privately ruled that where a right of first refusal does not specify a purchase price or provide guidelines for determining a purchase price, the right may not satisfy the "no device" requirement if the terms of the purchase may be more favorable than those which the potential purchaser could otherwise obtain.[32]

---

[26] IRC § 2703(b)(1).

[27] Estate of Bischoff v. Comm'r, 69 TC 32 (1977); Estate of Reynolds v. Comm'r, 55 TC 172 (1970); Estate of Littick v. Comm'r, 31 TC 181 (1958); Baltimore Nat'l Bank v. United States, 136 F. Supp. 642 (D. Md. 1955).

[28] Tech. Adv. Mem. 9550002 (Aug. 31, 1995).

[29] IRC § 2703(b)(2).

[30] 674 F2d 1207 (8th Cir. 1982).

[31] See S. Budget Comm., 101st Cong., 2d Sess., Informal Report in S. 3209, 136 Cong. Rec. S15,629, S15,683 (Oct. 18, 1990); see also Treas. Reg. § 25.2703-1(b)(2).

[32] Tech. Adv. Mem. 9550002 (Aug. 31, 1995) (five-year installment contract with interest at the prime rate on date of sale).

WARNING: "Member of the decedent's family" is undefined in the statute. It is curious that members of the family are limited to decedents' families, rather than also including the donors' families. The regulations adopt the definition in Section 2701. Additionally, the regulations substitute "natural objects of the bounty of the transferor" for "members of the decedent's family" in the "no device" requirement.[33] The preamble to the regulations indicates that the term is not limited to relatives by blood or marriage. To the extent that the regulations interpret "members of the family" to include persons who are not related by blood, marriage, or adoption, they are exceeding the terms of the statute.

[iii] **Marketplace agreement.** The terms of the right or restriction must be comparable to similar arrangements entered into by persons in an arm's-length transaction.[34] This test applies at the time the right or restriction is created.[35]

General rule. A right or restriction is treated as comparable to similar arrangements entered into by persons in an arm's-length transaction if the right or restriction is one that could have been obtained in a fair bargain among unrelated parties in the same business dealing with each other at arm's length. A right or restriction is considered a fair bargain among unrelated parties in the same business if it conforms with the general practice of unrelated parties under negotiated agreements in the same business. This determination generally will entail consideration of such factors as the expected term of the agreement, the current fair market value of the property, anticipated changes in value during the term of the arrangement, and the adequacy of any consideration given in exchange for the rights granted.[36] The failure to be specific regarding the right or restriction (for example, a buy-sell agreement which contains no purchase price or method for setting a purchase price), as mentioned above, may cause the operative effect of the right or restriction to be unclear, which in turn may be viewed as not typical of arm's length transactions.[37]

Evidence of general business practice. The regulations say that evidence of general business practice is not met by showing isolated comparables. If more than one valuation method is commonly used in a business, a right or restriction does not fail to evidence general business practice merely because it uses only one of the recognized methods. It is not necessary that the terms of a right or restriction parallel the terms of any particular agreement. If compa-

---

[33] Treas. Reg. § 25.2703-1(b)(1)(ii); see also discussion at ¶ 27.03[5] below.

[34] IRC § 2703(b)(3).

[35] Treas. Reg. § 25.2703-1(b)(1)(iii).

[36] Treas. Reg. § 25.2703-1(b)(4)(i).

[37] E.g., Tech. Adv. Mem. 9550002 (Aug. 31, 1995).

rables are difficult to find because the business is unique, comparables from similar businesses may be used.[38]

While the method of demonstrating significant comparables is a safe harbor valuation method, it appears that fairness can be established in other ways. This is important, since comparables may be difficult to obtain for privacy reasons.

In the case of a partnership agreement, provisions that track the applicable state statute should be considered to be consistent with general business practice; however, it should be noted that, in Technical Advice Memorandum 9725002 (March 25, 1997) and other recent rulings, partnership agreements tracking state RULPA provisions were disregarded under Section 2703.

[iv] **No device.** Each of the requirements described in subparagraphs [i], [ii], and [iii] above must be independently satisfied for a right or restriction to meet the standard commercial exception.[39]

Legislative history note. The Senate Report provides that current law is continued for other requirements necessary to fix values.[40] If this is true, then, in order for a buy-sell agreement to fix the estate tax value of stock, it will be necessary, in addition to the foregoing requirements, that the price be fixed or determinable, the estate be obligated to sell, and that a lifetime restriction on the transfer of the affected interest exist.[41]

[b] Exception for Right or Restriction Among Unrelated Parties

A right or restriction is considered to meet each of the three requirements described above if more than 50 percent by value of the property subject to the right or restriction is owned directly or indirectly[42] by individuals who are not members of the transferor's family.[43] In order to meet this exception, the property owned by those individuals must be subject to the right or restriction to the same extent as the property owned by the transferor.[44]

---

[38] Treas. Reg. § 25.2703-1(b)(4)(ii).

[39] Treas. Reg. § 25.2703-1(b)(2).

[40] See S. Budget Comm., 101st Cong., 2d Sess., Informal Report on S. 3209, 136 Cong. Rec. S15,629, S15,683 (Oct. 18, 1990).

[41] See ¶ 27.02[1][a] above for an explanation of these requirements.

[42] Direct or indirect ownership is determined in accordance with Treas. Reg. § 25.2701-6, which contains rules for attributing an equity interest held by a corporation, partnership, estate, or trust to the owners of the corporation or partnership and the beneficiaries of the estate or trust.

[43] See, e.g., Priv. Ltr. Rul. 9616035 (Jan. 23, 1996).

[44] Treas. Reg. § 25.2703-1(b)(3).

[5] Members of the Transferor's Family

The regulations define members of the transferor's family to include the transferor's spouse, any ancestor of the transferor or his spouse, the spouse of any such ancestor, the lineal descendants of the parents of the transferor or the transferor's spouse, and any other individual who is a natural object of the transferor's bounty.[45] Any property held by a member of the transferor's family under the indirect ownership rules of Treasury Regulation § 25.2701-6 (without regard to the multiple attribution rules under that regulation) is treated as held only by a member of the transferor's family.[46]

Note that the last sentence of this exception presumably means that any property treated as indirectly owned by a member of the transferor's family pursuant to Treasury Regulation § 25.2701-6 (without applying the multiple attribution rules) will not be reattributed to a party unrelated to the transferor.

Finally, it is doubtful whether Congress intended the term "members of the [transferor's] family" to be as broadly construed as it is in the regulations. The IRS has ruled that nephews constitute members of a transferor's family for purposes of Section 2703.[47]

[6] Relation to Other Taxes

[a] Section 2701

It is unclear how Section 2703 interrelates with the requirement of Section 2701 that certain liquidation, put, call, and conversion rights are to be valued at zero for gift tax purposes.

[b] Income Tax

The value determined under Section 2703 applies for all transfer tax purposes. It does not appear to apply for income tax purposes.

[7] Effective Date

Effective date of Section 2703. The rules described in Section 2703 apply to agreements, options, rights, or restrictions which are entered into or

---

[45] Treas. Reg. §§ 25.2703-1(b)(3), 25.2701-2(b)(5). To the extent that unrelated parties are included as "natural objects of the transferor's bounty," the regulations appear to exceed the limits of the statute.

[46] Treas. Reg. §§ 25.2701-2(b)(5), 25.2703-1(b)(3).

[47] Priv. Ltr. Rul. 9222043 (Feb. 28, 1992).

granted after October 8, 1990, or, though entered into or granted before October 9, 1990, are substantially modified after October 8, 1990.[48]

Effective date of the Section 2703 regulations. The regulations apply to any right or restriction created or substantially modified after October 8, 1990, and are effective as of January 28, 1992. With respect to transfers occurring prior to January 28, 1992, and for purposes of determining whether an event occurring prior to January 28, 1992, constitutes a substantial modification, taxpayers may rely on any reasonable interpretation of the statutory provisions. For these purposes, the provisions of the proposed regulations and the final regulations are considered a reasonable interpretation of the statutory provisions.[49]

A right or restriction imposed by a will entered into before October 9, 1990 will generally be subject to Section 2703 where the testator died after October 8, 1990.[50] Query: Would the testator's incapacity on and after October 8, 1990, make any difference?

[a] Definition of Substantial Modification

A right or restriction that is substantially modified is treated as a right or restriction created on the date of the modification.[51] Any discretionary modification of a right or restriction, whether or not authorized by the terms of the agreement, that results in other than a de minimis change to the quality, value, or timing of the rights of any party with respect to property that is subject to the right or restriction is a substantial modification.[52] If the terms of the right or restriction require periodic updating, the failure to update is presumed to substantially modify the right or restriction unless it can be shown that updating would not have resulted in a substantial modification.[53]

Addition of a family member. The addition of any family member as a party to a right or restriction (including by reason of a transfer of property that subjects the transferee family member to a right or restriction with respect to the transferred property) is considered a substantial modification unless the addition is mandatory under the terms of the right or restriction or the added family member is assigned to a generation[54] no lower than the

---

[48] Omnibus Budget Reconciliation Act of 1990, Pub. L. No. 101-508, § 11602(e)(1)(A)(ii), 104 Stat. 1383 (1990).

[49] Treas. Reg. § 25.2703-2.

[50] Tech. Adv. Mem. 9550002 (Aug. 31, 1995).

[51] Treas. Reg. § 25.2703-1(c)(1).

[52] Treas. Reg. § 25.2703-1(c)(1).

[53] Treas. Reg. § 25.2703-1(c)(1).

[54] Determined under the rules of IRC § 2651.

lowest generation occupied by individuals already party to the right or restriction.[55]

EXAMPLE: In 1997, Parent gives Child stock in *X* Corporation. A buy-sell agreement executed in 1982 requires that transferees of stock be or become parties to the agreement, so the agreement is amended to add Child as a party. The IRS has taken the position that the amendment is a substantial modification because the agreement did not require that parties transfer stock to non-parties.[56]

This position would make it unlikely that any agreement would remain grandfathered where new parties are added, even where the original agreement contemplated and required the addition of new parties, and required that new transferees be parties.

[b] Non-Substantial Modifications

A substantial modification does not include:

- A modification required by the terms of a right or restriction;[57]
- A discretionary modification of an agreement conferring a right or restriction if the modification does not change the right or restriction;[58]
- A modification of a capitalization rate used with respect to a right or restriction if the rate is modified in a manner that bears a fixed relationship to a specified market interest rate;[59] and
- A modification that results in an option price that more closely approximates fair market value.[60]

EXAMPLE: A 1982 agreement provides that on the death of a shareholder, his shares will be redeemed in exchange for a ten-year note bearing interest at ten percent per year. The shareholders in 1996 decide to amend the agreement to provide that the note will be a 15-year note bearing interest at a rate 2 percent higher than the prime rate, adjusted semi-annually. The IRS has ruled that if the modification will cause the proceeds of the redemption to approximate fair market value more closely and provide a reasonable rate of interest, the extension of the term will be a de minimis change and the amendment will not be a substantial modification of the original agreement.[61]

---

[55] Treas. Reg. § 25.2703-1(c)(1).

[56] Priv. Ltr. Rul. 9324018 (Mar. 19, 1993).

[57] Treas. Reg. § 25.2703-1(c)(2)(i).

[58] Treas. Reg. § 25.2703-1(c)(2)(ii).

[59] Treas. Reg. § 25.2703-1(c)(2)(iii).

[60] Treas. Reg. § 25.2703-1(c)(2)(iv).

[61] Priv. Ltr. Rul. 9322035 (Mar. 10, 1993).

IRS Rulings. The IRS has issued many other rulings regarding what constitutes a substantial modification, focusing on whether the modification affects the quality, value or timing of any rights of parties to the agreement.[62] Interestingly, the IRS has ruled that many amendments to shareholder agreements which actually result in significant changes do not constitute substantial modifications. For example, the IRS has ruled that an amendment allowing holders of voting common stock to convert their shares to non-voting stock was not a substantial modification because neither the quality, value nor timing of the rights of the parties to the agreement being amended would be substantially modified. In addition, an amendment instituting a minimum dividend for preferred stock did not constitute a substantial modification.[63]

QUERY: If an otherwise grandfathered agreement is substantially modified, and the parties want to meet the requirements of the standard commercial exception, does the third requirement of that exception that an agreement must be comparable to similar arrangements found in arm's length transactions[64] have to be met with respect to all terms of the agreement, or only the modified terms?

[8] Conclusion

Under the current tax regime, it is probably well-advised to do buy-sell agreements at fair market value. Fair market value may legitimately reflect minority and marketability discounts. In addition, it is wise to structure other rights and restrictions in agreement in a standard and reasonable fashion, and to

---

[62] See, e.g., Priv. Ltr. Rul. 9620017 (Feb. 15, 1996) (transfer of stock subject to restrictive agreement that removes significant transfer restrictions on stock that is transferred would cause agreement to lose grandfathered status because it would be more than a de minimis change; however, issuance of additional stock to non-family members in consideration for services rendered and subsequent repurchase of such stock on termination of shareholder's employment was not substantial modification); Priv. Ltr. Rul. 9507028 (Nov. 18, 1994) (numerous minor amendments to partnership agreement are not substantial modification); Priv. Ltr. Rul. 9451050 (Sept. 22, 1994) (restructuring of partnership into three partnerships with substantially identical provisions is not substantial modification); Priv. Ltr. Rul. 9449017 (Sept. 13, 1994) (revising buy-sell agreement to give other shareholders option to purchase decedent's stock at same price provided for mandatory corporate redemption already provided for in agreement is not substantial modification). See also Priv. Ltr. Rul. 9432017 (May 16, 1994); Priv. Ltr. Rul. 9417007 (Jan. 13, 1994); Priv. Ltr. Rul. 9241014 (July 8, 1992); Priv. Ltr. Rul. 9226063 (Mar. 31, 1992); Priv. Ltr. Rul. 9226051 (Mar. 30, 1992); Priv. Ltr. Rul. 9218074 (Jan. 31, 1992); Priv. Ltr. Rul. 9152031 (Sept. 30, 1991); Priv. Ltr. Rul. 9141043 (July 16, 1991).

[63] Priv. Ltr. Rul. 9324019 (Mar. 19, 1993).

[64] IRC § 2703(b)(3).

consider the amount and nature of rights and restrictions used by unrelated parties in their dealings.

¶ 27.04 STRUCTURING BUY-SELL AGREEMENTS FUNDED WITH INSURANCE

Buy-sell agreements are often funded with insurance. These buy-sell agreements are generally structured either as cross-purchase or redemption agreements. Various considerations arise in choosing a structure.

GLOBAL EXAMPLE

Dan owns a 50 percent share in a C corporation. The other shareholder is John. On the death of either shareholder, the company, or if it fails to exercise its option, the surviving shareholder, has an option to buy the stock of the deceased shareholder for fair market value. Dan and John are interested in funding the buyout with life insurance. They have asked what the advantages and disadvantages of the various ways to structure this are.

---

[1] Cross-Purchase Arrangement

Under a cross-purchase agreement, Dan purchases a policy on John's life, and John purchases one on Dan's life. If Dan dies, John decides whether or not to buy Dan's estate out with his share of the proceeds, and vice versa.

There are various aspects that need to be considered in the context of a cross-purchase arrangement. They are as follows—

Payment of premiums by corporation. If, in the Global Example, the corporation pays Dan and John the money to pay for the premiums, that will be treated as compensation or a dividend, depending on the facts. If it is compensation, it may be deductible to the company. Either way, it would be taxable to Dan and John.

Capital gain on sale by estate. On Dan's death, if John buys Dan's interest from Dan's estate, there will be no capital gain to Dan's estate, except to the extent that the purchase price exceeds the fair market value of Dan's stock for estate tax purposes.[65]

Payment of premiums by individuals. Payments made by Dan and John for premiums on the policies would not be deductible by them personally. Therefore, they will be paid at their after-tax individual rates.

---

[65] IRC § 1014.

Termination of agreement. Ordinarily, the buy-sell agreement would give each shareholder the right to purchase the unmatured policy on his life from the other shareholder in case of termination of the agreement.

Transfer for value. The policies must be newly purchased (i.e., the shareholders cannot exchange existing policies on each other's lives) in order to avoid the policy proceeds being taxable as income.[66]

Exclusion of proceeds from insured's estate. The policy proceeds will not be included in the deceased shareholder's estate, as long as the policy and agreement gave the deceased shareholder no incidents of ownership in the policy.[67]

Creditors. The proceeds of any insurance received by the surviving shareholder are not subject to claims of the corporation's creditors except to the extent that the stockholder is individually liable for corporate obligations.

Basis of purchased stock. The surviving shareholder will receive a cost basis for shares purchased.

No income tax. The surviving shareholder receives the proceeds tax-free.

Differences in premiums. To the extent that underwriting costs differ, one policy may cost more than the other, resulting in an unequal burden on the two shareholders.

[2] Redemption Arrangement

The company would purchase the insurance on both lives. On a death, the company would decide whether or not to redeem the stock from the decedent's estate.

There are various aspects that need to be considered in the context of a redemption arrangement. They are as follows—

Dividend to estate on redemption. The redemption of shares will not be treated as a dividend to the deceased shareholder's estate if either (1) all of the stock is redeemed and no related party continues to have an interest in the corporation in any capacity other than a creditor or (2) Section 302's capital transaction requirements are otherwise met.[68]

Capital gain to estate on redemption. The redemption of the stock in the corporation should not result in a capital gain to the deceased shareholder's estate, except to the extent that the purchase price exceeds the value of the stock for estate tax purposes.[69]

Dividend to survivor on redemption. The survivor will not be treated as having received a constructive dividend as a result of the redemption unless

---

[66] IRC § 101(a).

[67] IRC § 2042.

[68] IRC § 302.

[69] IRC § 1014.

the redemption satisfied his own primary, unconditional obligation to buy the stock.

Premium payments. The corporation cannot deduct premium payments. Therefore, it will pay for the policies at the after-tax corporate rate.

No regular income tax on proceeds. The death proceeds are free of regular income tax.[70]

No basis increase on redemption. The value of the stock owned by the survivor will be increased by his share of the difference between the death proceeds and the cash surrender value prior to death. The cost basis of the survivor's stock will not be increased. Therefore, the increase in value due to the insurance may result in additional gain to the survivor if he sells his stock during his lifetime.

Earnings and profits. Earnings and profits of the corporation are increased by the excess of the insurance proceeds over the aggregate premiums paid.

Accumulated earnings tax. The use of corporate earnings to purchase life insurance could subject a corporation to the accumulated earnings tax unless the insurance serves a valid business need. The purchase of life insurance to compensate the corporation for loss of a key person's services through early death should be a reasonable business need.

Alternative minimum tax. Life insurance proceeds received by a C corporation can be taxable under the corporate alternative minimum tax. This is because the corporate alternative minimum tax taxes certain items which increase a corporation's book earnings, but are not considered taxable income.

Exclusion of proceeds from insured's estate. The proceeds are not directly includable in the value of the deceased shareholder's estate as long as the corporation is the beneficiary. However, the value of the deceased shareholder's stock is includable in his estate. In valuing his stock, his share of the insurance proceeds will be included unless the purchase price under the terms of the agreement is determined without regard to the receipt of the insurance proceeds, and the agreement is effective in fixing the value of the business interest for estate tax purposes. In the example, the proceeds are not excluded from the purchase price under the terms of the agreement, and Dan and John may not want them to be.

Creditors. Policies and proceeds may be subject to corporate creditors.

Limitations on redemptions. The agreement must comply with local law regarding the corporation's right to redeem its shares.

[3] Individually Owned Life Insurance as an Alternative

In the global example, Dan could own a policy on Dan's life, and John could own a policy on John's life. Each would name the other as beneficiary. This,

---

[70] IRC § 101.

however, is not a good alternative, because the proceeds of the policy would be included in the deceased shareholder's gross estate, and may be subject to income tax in the survivor's hands if the contractual cross-beneficiary arrangement were considered a transfer for value.

[4] General Thoughts

As long as the agreement is funded by life insurance, Dan and John should give some thought to making the purchase or redemption mandatory instead of optional on the part of the survivor or the company.

There is no bright-line answer as to which way to go. The answer depends on the particular circumstances.

[5] Buy-Sell Arrangements Involving Entities Other Than C Corporations

If the entity were an S corporation, a partnership, or a limited liability company, some of the answers above would change accordingly, but the issues to be analyzed would remain the same.

Estate Freezing Techniques

CHAPTER 28

Loans

¶ 28.01 INTRODUCTION

This chapter focuses on the use of loans which are not made in the context of a sale or exchange of property as an estate planning technique; seller-financed dispositions of property are discussed in Chapter 30.

A low-interest loan is usually a good estate freezing technique, provided that the borrower can invest the proceeds and earn more than the interest rate on the loan.

> EXAMPLE: Mom lends Son money at a 6 percent interest rate. Son invests the money in an asset that earns 11 percent. Son gets all of the appreciation and income of the asset in excess of 6 percent.

QUERY: While this technique is clearly available with cash, there is little authority on its use with other property. For example, what would be the result if Mom charged Son a bargain rent for use of her vacation home, and then Son sublet the home at a fair market rent? Or, what if Mom allowed Son to use her securities as collateral for a loan that could not otherwise be obtained without the use of such collateral?[1]

A number of rules apply to this technique. One set of rules discussed in this chapter is contained in Section 7872, which imputes interest on certain below-market loans for both income and gift tax purposes. Other rules require that original issue discount be amortized as income in certain loans on which interest accrues but is not yet payable.[2] Estate tax discounting of low-interest loans receivable is also possible, but is limited by certain gift and income tax considerations.

---

[1] See generally Priv. Ltr. Rul. 9113009 (Dec. 21, 1990) (modified on other issues, Priv. Ltr. Rul. 9409018 (Dec. 1, 1993)), in which the IRS ruled that the value of the economic benefit conferred by a guarantee constitutes a gift, if appropriate consideration is not paid.

[2] IRC §§ 1272, 1273, 1275.

¶ 28.02   SECTION 7872: IMPUTED INTEREST ON BELOW-MARKET LOANS

The interest-free loan was a very popular estate freezing technique before *Dickman v. Commissioner*[3] was decided by the Supreme Court in 1984. *Dickman* involved no-interest demand loans. The Supreme Court held that the interest forgone by the lender was a gift to the borrower.

Congress responded to *Dickman* by enacting Section 7872, which governs the tax treatment of certain interest-free and low-interest loans of cash. Generally, when Section 7872 applies, it imputes interest on certain below-market loans at the applicable federal rate (AFR), and deems that a transfer of the "forgone interest" by the lender to the borrower is made.[4]

The AFR is the average rate on Treasury obligations for the period concerned. There are three AFRs—short-term (obligations of three years or less), midterm (more than three years, but less than nine years), and long-term (nine years or more).[5] The AFR is published monthly in the Internal Revenue Bulletin. A blended annual rate is published in July of each year.[6]

The "forgone interest" on any loan for any year is the excess of the interest which would have been payable if interest had accrued at the AFR for the period of the loan and such interest was payable annually on the last day of the calendar year over any interest actually payable on the loan properly allocable to that year.[7]

Assuming that the loan is the type of a loan to which Section 7872 applies (discussed in ¶ 28.03 below), the type of effect Section 7872 will have depends on whether the loan is a demand loan or a term loan.

[1] Demand Loans

[a] Definition

A "demand loan" includes: (1) any loan payable in full at any time on the demand of the lender, (2) any loan with an indefinite maturity, and (3) any loan conditioned on the future performance of substantial services by an individual if the interest benefits are not transferable.[8]

> EXAMPLE: Sue lends money to her employee, with a due date of five years. The loan is due in full if the employee quits during the five-year

---

[3] 465 US 330 (1984).

[4] IRC §§ 7872(a), 7872(e)(2).

[5] IRC § 1274(d).

[6] Rev. Rul. 96-34, 1996-28 IRB 4.

[7] IRC § 7872(e)(2).

[8] IRC § 7872(e)(5).

period, and the employee is not free to assign her obligations or rights under the agreement. Interest will be imputed according to the rules for a demand loan.

[b] Below-Market Demand Loan

If interest is payable on a demand loan for any period for which it is outstanding at a rate less than the short-term AFR, compounded semiannually, a demand loan is a below-market loan for that period.[9]

[c] Tax Treatment of Below-Market Demand Loan

Under Section 7872, the lender is treated as making a gift to the borrower of cash equal to the forgone interest for that year and then receiving the forgone interest from the borrower as an interest payment on the demand loan. This treatment results in the lender being deemed to have received taxable interest income and then made a gift[10] for the year. The borrower is deemed to have paid interest to the lender.[11]

> EXAMPLE: On January 1, Mom lends Son $100,000 at no interest and takes a demand note. The AFR is 8 percent for the year. At the end of the year, payment has not been demanded. Assuming that no exception to the general rules applies, Mom will be treated for tax purposes as if she received $8,160[12] of interest income from Son on the last day of the year[13] and then made a gift of $8,160 to Son on that day. Son is treated as having paid interest to Mom of $8,160. He can deduct it to the extent that it would otherwise be deductible.[14]

[2] Term Loans

A term loan is a below-market loan if the amount loaned exceeds the present value of all payments due under the loan.[15] The present value of the payments

---

[9] IRC §§ 7872(a)(1), 7872(e), 7872(f)(2)(B).

[10] Or other transfer, if the characterization of the low-interest feature is not a gift (e.g., if it is compensation).

[11] IRC § 7872(a)(1).

[12] Interest payable on $100,000 for one year at 8 percent, compounded semiannually.

[13] IRC § 7872(a)(2).

[14] See Ch. 29 for a summary of the rules on deductibility of interest for income tax purposes.

[15] IRC § 7872(e)(1)(B).

is determined using a discount rate equal to the AFR for the term of the note, compounded semiannually.[16]

Unlike the demand loan, the tax consequences of a below-market term loan depend on whether the loan is a gift loan or not.

[a] Gift Loan

A gift loan is a loan in which the low-interest feature is in the nature of a gift. If a below-market term loan is a gift loan, the forgone interest each year is treated as transferred from the lender to the borrower as a gift and then re-transferred by the borrower to the lender as a payment of interest on the last day of the year.[17]

> EXAMPLE: Mom lends Son $1,000,000 for five years at no interest. The midterm AFR on the date of the advance is 8 percent. For Year One, forgone interest is 8 percent, compounded semi-annually. If the advance were made on July 1, the forgone interest would be $40,000. Assuming that no exception to the general rules applies, Mom will be treated as making a $40,000 gift to Son on December 31 and receiving a $40,000 interest payment from him on that same day. Son will also be treated as paying interest of $40,000 to Mom on December 31. These rules will apply during each year of the loan.

[b] Non-Gift Loan

If a non-gift, below-market term loan is made, the lender is treated as having transferred to the borrower on the date of the advance an amount equal to the money lent, less the present value of all payments due under the loan.[18] The present value is determined at the date of the advance, using a discount rate equal to the AFR for the term of the loan.[19] The treatment of the lump sum amount deemed transferred to the borrower is determined by the deemed characterization of the transfer—compensation, dividend, etc.

The loan will be considered to have original issue discount (OID) equal to the excess of the money lent over the present value of the payments due on the loan.[20] The lender will accrue interest income ratably in each year of the loan. The treatment of the imputed interest to the borrower depends on whether he can deduct the interest under the general rules; in any case, if he can deduct it, it must be deducted ratably over the period of the loan.

---

[16] IRC §§ 7872(f)(1), 7872(f)(2)(A).

[17] IRC § 7872(a).

[18] IRC §§ 7872(b)(1), 7872(d)(2).

[19] IRC § 7872(f)(1).

[20] IRC § 7872(b)(2)(A). This amount of OID is in addition to any OID that the note would otherwise carry. IRC § 7872(b)(2)(B).

EXAMPLE: Mom makes a $100,000 loan to Son in his capacity as her employee, at no interest. Mom takes a three-year note from Son. The present value of the payments due under the note, discounted at the short-term AFR, is $80,000. Assuming that no exception to the general rules applies, Mom is treated as paying compensation of $20,000 to Son on the date the loan is made. The $20,000 of OID will be reported by Mom ratably over the three-year period, and deducted by Son ratably over the period, to the extent that it is otherwise deductible.

¶ 28.03 LOANS SUBJECT TO THE SECTION 7872 IMPUTED INTEREST RULES

[1] General Rules

Generally, the imputed interest rules apply to the following loans:

- A loan where the forgone interest is in the nature of a gift.[21]
- A loan directly or indirectly between an employer and his employee, or an independent contractor and the person receiving the contractor's services.[22]
- A loan directly or indirectly between a corporation and its shareholder.[23]
- A loan that has a principal purpose of avoiding any federal tax.[24]
- Other loans that have interest arrangements that significantly affect any federal tax liability of the lender or the borrower, to the extent provided in regulations.[25]
- Any loan to any qualified continuing care facility pursuant to a continuing care contract.[26]

[2] Exceptions

Certain below-market loans, though described in one of the above categories, are excepted from Section 7872's imputed interest rules.

[a] De Minimis Loan Exception for Certain Loans of $10,000 or Less

[i] Loans between individuals. If a gift loan is made directly between individuals, the imputed interest rules do not apply on any day on which the

---

[21] IRC §§ 7872(c)(1)(A), 7872(f)(3).

[22] IRC § 7872(c)(1)(B).

[23] IRC § 7872(c)(1)(C).

[24] IRC § 7872(c)(1)(D).

[25] IRC § 7872(c)(1)(E).

[26] IRC § 7272(c)(1)(F).

aggregate outstanding loans between the individuals is $10,000 or less, except to the extent that such a loan is attributable to the purchase or carrying of income-producing assets.[27]

[ii] Loans made to the lender's employee, independent contractor, or shareholder. Loans to the lender's employee, independent contractor, or shareholder are not subject to the imputed interest rules on any day on which the aggregate amount of such loans is $10,000 or less, unless a principal purpose of the low-interest arrangement is the avoidance of any federal tax.[28]

[iii] Special term loan exception-to-exception. In the case of term loans, if the aggregate loans described above exceed the above limitations on any day, Section 7872 will continue to apply for the remainder of the loan term, notwithstanding the small loan exceptions described above.[29] In the case of a term gift loan, the imputed interest rules will only apply for purposes of the gift tax.[30] In other words, if aggregate non-gift term loans ever exceed the de minimis limitations, Section 7872 will continue to apply, even after enough principal has been repaid by the borrower so that the aggregate loans outstanding are less than $10,000. Section 7872 ceases to apply for income tax purposes to aggregate gift loans once the aggregate amount outstanding is less than $10,000.

> EXAMPLE: On January 1 of Year One, Mom makes an interest-free gift loan to Son of $20,000, payable in two equal installments, on December 31 of Years One and Two. Assuming no other exceptions apply, in Year One, she will be deemed to make a gift of the forgone interest and have imputed income, and Son will have imputed interest expense. After Son makes his actual $10,000 payment at the end of Year One, the amount outstanding between Mom and Son (assuming no other loans exist) is $10,000. In Year Two, no interest is imputed for income tax purposes, due to the de minimis exception; however, Mom will still be deemed to make a gift of the forgone interest.

[b] Exception for Loans to Continuing Care Facilities

An exception for loans to certain nursing homes exists.[31] This exception permits a senior citizen to make below-market loans, which in the aggregate do not exceed $90,000 plus an adjustment for inflation, to "qualified continu-

---

[27] IRC § 7872(c)(2).

[28] IRC § 7872(c)(3).

[29] IRC § 7872(f)(10).

[30] IRC § 7872(f)(10).

[31] IRC § 7872(g).

ing care facilities," provided that such loans are made pursuant to "continuing care contracts."

[c] Not-So-De-Minimis Rule for Loans of $100,000 or Less

Special rules apply to gift loans directly between individuals where the aggregate of any loans made by a lender[32] to the borrower on that day is more than $10,000 but less than or equal to $100,000.[33] These special rules apply only if the gift loan did not have as one of its principal purposes the avoidance of any federal tax.[34]

Under these rules, the amount of "forgone interest" which is deemed paid by the borrower to the lender each year in such a case is limited to the borrower's net investment income for the year.[35] And, if the borrower's net investment income is $1,000 or less, the net investment income will be considered to be zero.[36]

EXAMPLE: On January 1, Mom lends Son $100,000 for no interest on a demand basis. The AFR is 8 percent. Son has $1,500 of net investment income for the year. Mom is deemed to have made a gift to Son of $8,160 on December 31.[37] For income tax purposes, however, she will be deemed to have received $1,500 of interest income for the year, and Son would be deemed to have paid her $1,500 of interest for the year.

[d] Seller-Financed Obligation Exception: Debt to Which Section 483 or Section 1274 Applies

The Section 7872 rules do not apply to any loan to which Section 483 or Section 1274 applies.[38] Generally, this means that Section 7872 only applies to loans, and not to installment sales or other deferred payment sales of property.

[e] Exception for Certain Loans From Foreign Trusts

Section 7872 does not apply to a direct or indirect loan of cash or marketable securities from a foreign trust to a U.S. grantor or beneficiary (or

---

[32] For purposes of determining the amount of loans outstanding by or to any individual, a husband and wife are considered one person. IRC § 7872(f)(7).

[33] IRC §§ 7872(d)(1)(A), 7872(d)(1)(B), 7872(d)(1)(D).

[34] IRC §§ 7872(d)(1)(A), 7872(d)(1)(B), 7872(d)(1)(D).

[35] IRC § 7872(d)(1)(A).

[36] IRC § 7872(d)(1)(E)(ii). Net investment income is defined in IRC § 163(d)(4). IRC §§ 7872(d)(1)(A), 7872(d)(1)(E)(i).

[37] $100,000 at 8 percent for one year, compounded semiannually.

[38] IRC § 7872(f)(8).

persons related to such grantor or beneficiary) if Section 643(i) treats the loan as a distribution.[39]

[f] Exception for Employee Relocation Loans

There are special rules for employee relocation loans, which are certain term loans made by an employer to an employee and used to purchase a principal residence in connection with the employee's commencement of employment or change in principal workplace.[40]

¶ 28.04 MARKET-RATE LOANS WITH OID (ACCRUED BUT UNPAID INTEREST)

Balloon notes, on which interest accrues currently but is payable on a deferred basis, are not unusual in a family context. In such instances, Section 7872 can be avoided by providing an interest rate equal to or exceeding the AFR, or qualifying for an exception from its application. However, that is not the end of the story. With respect to balloon notes, the original issue discount (OID) rules must also be examined.

[1] General Rules

If the interest accrues, but is not actually payable, the OID rules will apply.[41] This means that the OID will be amortized ratably for income tax purposes.

> EXAMPLE: Mom lends Junior $1,000,000. The note provides that interest at the AFR accrues during the term of the loan and a balloon payment of principal plus all accrued interest is due at the end of the term. If this arrangement is bona fide, it should successfully avoid the application of the gift tax. However, for income tax purposes, the interest which is accrued but not paid will constitute OID.[42] Assuming that no exception to the general rules applies, Mom will have to report interest income during the term of the loan, even though she is not getting paid. Junior will get to deduct the imputed interest paid, even if he is not actually paying it, if the interest is of a character that would otherwise be deductible by him.

---

[39] IRC § 7872(f)(8).

[40] IRC § 7872(f)(11).

[41] IRC §§ 1272, 1273.

[42] IRC § 1272(a).

[2] Exceptions

[a] Small Loan Exception

OID does not apply to loans between natural persons if the loan is not made in the course of a trade or business of the lender, and the amount of all outstanding loans from the lender to the borrower is $10,000 or less.[43] This exception will not apply, however, if a principal purpose of the loan was the avoidance of any federal tax.[44] A husband and wife who lived together during any part of the year are treated as one person.[45]

[b] Exception for Loan of Personal Use Property

If the debt is incurred in connection with the acquisition or carrying of personal use property and the obligor uses the cash method, the OID is deductible by the obligor only when it is paid.[46] For this purpose, "personal use property" is all property except property which is wholly or almost wholly used in connection with a trade or business of the obligor or for the production of income, determined as of the date of issuance of the debt instrument.[47]

> EXAMPLE: Mom lends Junior $1,000,000. The note provides that interest at the AFR accrues during the term of the loan and a balloon payment of principal plus all accrued interest is due at the end of the term. Junior used the $1,000,000 as a down payment on a loan for a vacation home. For income tax purposes, the interest which is accrued but not paid will constitute OID. Assuming that no exception to the general rules applies, Mom will have to report interest income during the term of the loan, even though she is not getting paid. Junior will get to deduct the OID when he actually pays it, and not as it accrues over the term of the loan.

¶ 28.05 COMMON LENDING TECHNIQUES

[1] Prepayments and Renewals

If a loan can be automatically renewed at the borrower's option, the initial term of the loan is considered to include all such renewal periods.[48] If the loan was not automatically renewable, but in fact is renewed, a new AFR will be determined as of the renewal date. When interest rates decline, it appears that

---

[43] IRC § 1272(a)(2)(E)(i).

[44] IRC § 1272(a)(2)(E)(ii).

[45] IRC § 1272(a)(2)(E)(iii).

[46] IRC § 1275(b)(2).

[47] IRC § 1275(b)(3).

[48] IRC §§ 1274(d)(3), 7872(f)(2)(A).

the borrower can prepay the principal of a high interest loan and re-borrow the money at a lower rate or, as a shortcut, simply cancel the old note and renew at a lower rate. There is no reason that this should be prohibited in the appropriate economic circumstances when transactions between unrelated parties commonly do not include prepayment penalties.

[2] Forgiveness

The forgiveness of a loan results in cancellation of indebtedness income unless the forgiveness is intended to effect a gift. The forgiveness of a family loan will often be a gift.

[a] Periodic Forgiveness

A number of people make loans and then forgive them at the rate of $10,000 per year, to qualify for the gift tax annual exclusion. The IRS has a long history of attacking this sort of transaction. The theory is that the loan was never intended to be repaid, and that a gift of the entire loan amount was intended at the outset.

The IRS has not done well with this approach,[49] and there are reasons for this. Even if the lender actually intends to gradually forgive the entire loan, (1) he is free to change his mind at any time, (2) his interest in the note can be seized by a creditor or bankruptcy trustee, who will surely enforce it, and (3) if the lender dies, his executor will be under a duty to collect the note. Therefore, if the loan is documented and administered properly, this technique should work, even if there is a periodic forgiveness plan, since the intent to make a gift in the future is not the same as making a gift in the present. However, if the conduct of the parties negates the existence of an actual bona fide debtor-creditor relationship at all, the entire loan may be recharacterized as a gift made at the time the loan was made[50] or the property lent may be

---

[49] See Estate of Kelley v. Comm'r, 63 TC 321 (1974), nonacq. 1977-2 CB 2; Haygood v. Comm'r, 42 TC 936 (1964), nonacq. 1977-2 CB 2.

[50] E.g., Miller v. Comm'r, 1996 RIA TC Memo. ¶ 96,003, 71 TCM 1674 (1996), aff'd, 1997 US App. LEXIS 11426 (9th Cir. 1997) (no interest charged, note unsecured, fixed maturity date ignored, only one partial repayment made, underlying records of loan inconsistent, tax treatment of transaction inconsistent from year to year and inconsistent with documentation of parties); Crane v. United States (Estate of Musgrove), 33 Fed. Cl. 657 (1995) (amount loaned to decedent's son included in decedent's estate—note was interest-free, unsecured, cancelable on decedent's death; decedent never made a demand and restricted the use of the money loaned to payment of his deceased daughter's estate taxes; son was sole beneficiary of decedent's estate; no repayment schedule prepared, no payments made, son did not know if or when he could repay the loan, and decedent was seriously ill at date of loan). See also, McGinnis v. Comm'r, 1993 RIA TC Memo. ¶ 93,045, 665 TCM (CCH) 1870 (1993) (holding that

included in the lender's estate, depending on whether the lender or the borrower is considered to "really" own the property.

[b] Insolvent Obligor

If the borrower is insolvent (or otherwise clearly will not be able to pay the debt) when the loan is made, the lender may be treated as making a gift at the outset. If the borrower could pay the debt at the loan origination, but the borrower's financial position subsequently declines, the lender's failure to exercise his rights with respect to the borrower, resulting in the loan becoming worthless, may be treated as a gift at the time the loan becomes uncollectible.

However, if the obligor is insolvent when the loan is forgiven, and has no further prospect of repaying the loan, the forgiveness may not be a gift, but rather a reflection of economic reality. In such circumstances, the lender may be able to take a bad debt deduction for the year in which the loan becomes worthless.

[c] Equalization Clauses

If Mom lends money to Son and forgives the debt, she has made a transfer to Son that she has not made to his siblings. Mom may want to have an equalization clause in her will to treat the forgiven loan as an advance against Son's share of her estate.

[3] Loan of Tangible Items

No-interest loans (or rent-free use) of tangible property are sometimes made in families. For example, Mom might, on an undocumented basis, let Son live in her garage apartment rent-free. There is no authority that requires Mom to treat that rent-free use of the apartment as a gift. What if Son in turn leased the garage apartment to a renter and Mom allowed Son to keep the rent? This would probably be a gift by Mom, since she could probably evict the renter or, in any case, insist on Son's turning over the rent from her own property. What if she had a no-rent written lease with Son that did not prohibit subletting? Food for thought.

---

grantor would be treated as owner of trusts established for his children and funded with demand notes, on the theory that his power to demand repayment gave him power of disposition over the beneficial enjoyment of the trusts' assets).

¶ 28.06 ESTATE TAX REPORTING OF LOANS RECEIVABLE

[1] Loans with Imputed Interest and/or OID

The estate tax is supposed to take term loans into account in a manner consistent with the income tax rules, as provided in Treasury regulations.[51]

[2] Estate Tax Valuation of Loan Receivable

What value is used to report a loan receivable in the lender's estate? The regulations provide that there is a presumption that a note is included at face value, plus accrued interest.[52] If the note is reported to have an estate tax value that is less than face value plus accrued interest, satisfactory proof must exist that the note is worth less than its face amount due to a low interest rate, an extended term, or other cause. Additionally, a reduced value may also be reported if there is satisfactory proof that the note is not wholly collectible due to either the insolvency of the obligor, the insufficiency of the security, or other similar cause.[53] The IRS Estate Tax Examiner's Handbook advises agents that the reporting of a note from a related party at less than its face amount raises strong evidence that a gift was made at the date of issuance of the note.[54]

If a discount in valuation of a note is allowed for estate tax purposes, the note will take a new basis equal to the discounted estate tax value. Therefore, the holder of the note will recognize ordinary income when payments are made, to the extent that the payments exceed the discounted value of the note used for estate tax purposes.

> EXAMPLE: Mom lends Son $1,000,000 at the then AFR of 7 percent. When she dies, the value of the note is $750,000, for whatever reason, even though $1,000,000 is still outstanding. If the note's value for estate tax purposes is $750,000, then when the $1,000,000 is paid, the recipient will have ordinary income of $250,000. If the note is distributed to Son, he will have cancellation of indebtedness income of $250,000 on the distribution.

---

[51] IRC § 7872(h)(2).

[52] Treas. Reg. § 20.2031-4.

[53] Treas. Reg. § 20.2031-4. See Smith v. United States, 923 F. Supp. 896 (SD Miss. 1996), supplemental opinion Smith v. United States, 1996 US Dist. LEXIS 9274 (SD Miss. May 17, 1996), for an example of allowance of a discount for a note from a Fortune 500 company, based on an interest rate less than market at date of death, and on the fact that decedent held a two-thirds undivided interest in the note.

[54] Internal Revenue Manual ch. 800, § 842.

WARNING: The above rules do not apply to notes received in an installment sale.[55]

¶ 28.07 GUARANTEES AS GIFTS

What if Dad guarantees Son's loan? The IRS has issued a private ruling that the value of the economic benefit conferred on Son by the guarantee constitutes a gift, if appropriate consideration is not paid.[56] Assuming arguendo that this theory is correct, the value of the gift would presumably be measured by the fee which would be charged by a bank for a similar guarantee. If Son does not repay the loan, and Dad has to pay it, Dad will be subrogated to the creditor's rights against Son. If Dad does not collect from Son, and Son could have paid, Dad will be viewed as making a gift of the amount paid to the creditor.

---

[55] The rules for installment sale notes are discussed in Ch. 30 on installment sales.

[56] Priv. Ltr. Rul. 9113009 (Dec. 21, 1990), modified on other issues, Priv. Ltr. Rul. 9409018 (Dec. 1, 1993).

Leases and Leasebacks

¶ 29.01 INTRODUCTION

Suppose Dad owns appreciating real estate, and wants to "freeze" his interest in the property (i.e., keep the appreciation with respect to the property out of his estate). A sale-leaseback or gift-leaseback of the appreciating property to a younger family member or trust for the benefit of a younger family member can be a useful estate freezing technique in the right circumstances.

¶ 29.02 HOW A LEASEBACK WORKS

Dad has appreciating real property, which he wants to continue using. He gives or sells the property to Junior, and then rents the property from Junior. Junior receives rental income. If Junior buys the property, his basis in the property will be its cost, and he may take depreciation deductions with respect to the property if it is depreciable. If the transfer to Junior is a sale for deferred payments, Junior can deduct the interest he pays. Dad can deduct the rent if the property is used in a trade or business or for investment. In any particular case, Dad's and Junior's deductions may be limited by the passive loss rules,[1] the at-risk rules,[2] limitations on deductibility of interest,[3] the limitations on deductions related to personal residences,[4] and other applicable rules.

In the case of a sale-leaseback, if the property appreciates more than the net cash inflow to Dad from the transaction, the sale and leaseback has been a successful freezing technique. Of course, Dad may recognize gain from the sale.

In the case of a gift-leaseback, Dad generally enjoys the advantages incident to making lifetime gifts[5] and also gets the rent payments out of his gross estate.

¶ 29.03 SALE-LEASEBACK OF PERSONAL RESIDENCE

One plan that is suggested from time to time is for Dad to sell the family house to Daughter for an installment note. Dad then rents his house from Daughter. Is this a good idea? Let's see.

¶ 29.04 THE PLAN TO SELL AND LEASEBACK A PERSONAL RESIDENCE

One purpose of this plan is to generate deductions within the family—as long as Dad owns the house, he cannot deduct expenses related to the house other than interest and real property taxes, since it is a personal residence.

To address this problem, the sale-leaseback plan may be promoted in this manner. Under the sale-leaseback transaction, Daughter takes a new basis in an appreciated asset. Daughter is then able to claim large non-cash depreciation deductions against her other income. The amount of the rent is set to

---

[1] IRC § 469.

[2] IRC § 465.

[3] IRC § 163.

[4] IRC § 280A.

[5] See Ch. 8 for a discussion.

offset her note payment (so that Daughter has no actual cash inflow or outflow) or, alternatively, the rent is set at an amount equal to the interest on the note (so that rental income and deductible interest payments are a wash). As the rental income and note or interest payment offset each other, the net tax consequences to Daughter are deductions for taxes and depreciation. Eventually, as depreciation deductions are used up, and she pays the note down, she will begin to develop a positive taxable income stream. And, as the property appreciates, the increase in value will accrue to Daughter free of transfer tax because the appreciation occurs while she is the owner of the property.

Is this a good plan? While it has some merits, changes in the law limit this technique as an income tax shelter. Nevertheless, it still works as an estate freezing technique, if the property's increase in value is greater than the interest Daughter pays on the note. However, one cost is that the plan requires recognition of nonexcludable gain, if any, on an asset which would otherwise get a stepped-up basis in Dad's estate.

> **EXAMPLE:** Dad sells his personal residence to Daughter for a $1,000,000 note. The note is payable at $5,000/month. Dad will recognize capital gain (if any) on the sale, to the extent that the gain exceeds the available exclusion for gain on the sale of a principal residence. However, Dad will recognize no loss for income tax purposes, if the property was his principal residence.[6] Even if the house was a vacation home, Dad will not be able to recognize a loss, since he is selling to a related party;[7] however, in this case, Daughter can take advantage of the unrecognized loss later, if she sells the property for more than the value of the house on the date she purchased it.[8]

Illustration of effects. Each month, Dad will receive a note payment consisting of: interest income; capital gain, if any; and return of basis. Each month, Dad will also pay rent to Daughter. Dad cannot deduct the rent payment, since it is a personal expense. Daughter receives taxable income in the amount of the rent. She will have a cost basis in the house. Daughter can receive deductions for taxes, interest, maintenance, insurance, casualty losses, and depreciation, subject to the limits of Sections 280A and 469.

As indicated in the example, note payments from Daughter to Dad are $5,000/month. In month one, assume that the note payment consists of $200 in return of basis, $300 in capital gain, and $4,500 in interest. For month one, the rental payment from Dad to Daughter is $4,000, real property taxes are $1,000, and depreciation is $3,000.

---

[6] IRC § 165(c).

[7] IRC § 267(b).

[8] IRC § 267(d). For further explanation, see Ch. 8.

Summary of components of the monthly payments:

	Dad	Daughter
	$200 basis recovery	($500 principal payment)
	$300 capital gain	($4,500 interest payment)
	$4,500 interest income	($1,000 real estate taxes)
	($4,000 rent payment)	($3,000 depreciation) (non-cash)
		$4,000 rental income
Net pre-tax cash flow	$1,000	($2,000)
Income taxes[a]	$1,866[b]	($1,782)[c]

---

[a]Assuming maximum tax rates and no limitations on deductions.

[b]($4,500 × .396) + ($300 × .28).

[c]($4,000 × .396) − (($4,500 × .396) + ($1,000 × .396) + ($3,000 × .396)).

Note, however, that Daughter's deductions for interest may be limited by the investment interest rules,[9] and her depreciation deductions may be limited by Sections 280A and 469.

[1] Special Rules Limiting Deductions Attributable to a Personal Residence

Section 280A is a complex provision that limits the deductions attributable to property used as a residence by the taxpayer or related parties to those deductions that would be available if the house were a personal-use item (that is, generally, real estate taxes, casualty losses and interest on the mortgage, subject to limitations for large notes on vacation homes).[10]

However, if the residence is rented on a fair market value basis to a lessee who is a family member and it is the lessee's principal residence, then the owner's deductions will not be disallowed by Section 280A.[11] On the other hand, if the residence is used personally by the owner herself or is not the lessee's principal residence, the owner's deductions will be limited to the income the owner receives with respect to the property. And, therefore, such deductions will not be allowed to shelter other income.[12] Deductions that are

---

[9] IRC § 163(d).

[10] IRC §§ 280A(a), 280A(b), 280A(d)(2).

[11] IRC §§ 280A(a), 280A(d)(3)(A). However, IRC § 183 (disallowing certain deductions attributable to an activity that is not engaged in for profit) may apply.

[12] IRC §§ 280A(a), 280A(c)(3), 280A(c)(5). Note that in applying the gross income limitations of IRC § 280A(c)(5), items such as interest and taxes that would be deductible in any case are counted against income before other deductions. Prop. Reg. § 1.280A-3(d)(3).

disallowed by virtue of this gross income limitation may be carried forward to the next year.[13]

In our example, if, after the sale-leaseback, the house is Dad's principal residence, Daughter does not use the house herself, and the rental arrangement is on a fair market value basis, Daughter's depreciation deductions will not be limited by Section 280A. If the house were a vacation home, then the deductions would be limited to her income from the property.[14]

So, if the lease is not affected by Section 280A because it is the principal residence of the lessee who pays a fair rental, is that the end of the inquiry? No, there is the possibility that otherwise allowable deductions will be limited under the passive activity loss rules.[15]

[2] Limitations on Artificial Rental Payments

Setting the rent equal to either the amount of the note payment or the interest on the note payment will only work as a technique if it coincidentally happens to match fair market value rent. If, however, the rental is not at fair market value, then the exceptions to the limitations imposed by Section 280A will not be available. In that instance, Daughter's depreciation deductions will at best equal the rental income, and gifts (if the rent is too high) or estate inclusion (if the rent is too low) may occur.

Application of Section 183's "not-for-profit" loss limitation. Although Section 280A generally trumps Section 183 (disallowing certain deductions attributable to an activity that is not engaged in for profit), Section 183 may apply where Section 280A's definitional requirements are not met (for example, where the owner does not use the residence herself and rents it to a family member who uses the home as his principal residence).

¶ 29.05 SALE-LEASEBACK OF INVESTMENT PROPERTY

This kind of sale-leaseback is fairly straightforward. Dad sells Daughter some rental real estate for an installment note, and leases it back from her. Dad recognizes gain and interest income and recovers his basis in the real estate on the installment basis. If Dad has a loss on the sale, he cannot recognize it, but Daughter can use it later, if she sells the property for an amount greater than the value of the property at the date of the sale.[16] Dad can deduct the rent he pays to Daughter, to the extent permitted by other sections of the Internal Revenue Code (primarily Section 469, which limits losses on passive invest-

---

[13] IRC § 280A(c)(5)(B).

[14] IRC § 280A(c)(5).

[15] Discussed at ¶ 29.08 below.

[16] IRC §§ 267(b), 267(d). See Ch. 8.

ment activities). Dad will also continue to receive the rent from the third-party subtenant of the property. Dad may have more or less taxable income than he had before the sale of the property (depending on the deductions he had as owner), the gain and interest from the sale, and the rent he pays as lessee.

Daughter will have rental income, and will be able to deduct the interest portion of her note payments, subject to applicable limitations.[17] If the note between Dad and Daughter does not have stated interest equal to at least the applicable federal rate, interest equal to 110 percent of the applicable federal rate, compounded semi-annually, will be imputed.[18]

¶ 29.06　GIFT-LEASEBACK

In a gift-leaseback, including a sale-leaseback for less than fair consideration, the property can be included in the transferor's estate if the transferor retained a right to enjoy the property for less than fair consideration.[19] Hence, on gift-leasebacks, it will be especially important to be sure that the donor is paying enough rent. Sale-leasebacks where Dad makes annual exclusion gifts by forgiving part of the installment note principal each year may also cause the property to be included in Dad's estate.[20]

The Fourth and Fifth Circuit Courts of Appeal require a business purpose for the entire gift-leaseback transaction, holding that the lessor cannot deduct the rent if the test is not satisfied.[21] The Tax Court, as well as other circuits that have addressed the issue, apply the business purpose test only to the leaseback portion of the transaction.[22] Because the gift portion of the

---

[17] Limitations on deductions of interest and passive activity losses are discussed at ¶¶ 29.08 and 29.09 below.

[18] IRC § 1274(e).

[19] IRC § 2036(a).

[20] See Maxwell v. Comm'r, 98 TC 594 (1992), aff'd, 3 F3d 591 (2d Cir. 1993).

[21] Van Zandt v. Comm'r, 341 F2d 440 (5th Cir. 1965), cert. denied, 382 US 814 (1965); Mathews v. Comm'r, 520 F2d 323 (5th Cir. 1975), rev'g 61 TC 12 (1973); Perry v. United States, 520 F2d 235 (4th Cir. 1975), cert. denied, 428 US 1052 (1976).

[22] E.g., Skemp v. Comm'r, 168 TC 598 (7th Cir. 1948); Brown v. Comm'r, 180 F2d 926 (3d Cir.), cert. denied, 340 US 814 (1950); Rosenfeld v. Comm'r, 706 F2d 1277 (2d Cir. 1983); Quinlivan v. Comm'r, 599 F2d 269 (8th Cir. 1979); Brooke v. United States, 468 F2d 1155 (9th Cir. 1972); May v. Comm'r, 723 F2d 1434 (9th Cir. 1984); Mathews v. Comm'r, 61 TC 12 (1973), rev'd, 520 F2d 343 (5th Cir. 1975). The *Mathews* case developed certain criteria for the recognition of gift-leasebacks, which the Tax Court has applied in cases outside the Fourth and Fifth Circuits. These criteria are: the lessee cannot retain substantially the same control over the property before and after the gift; the lease should be in writing and must require reasonable rent; the lease must have a business purpose; and the lessee must not possess a disqualifying equity in the property within the meaning of IRC § 162(c)(3).

gift-leaseback transaction will generally not have a business purpose, the effective use of a gift-leaseback in the Fourth and Fifth Circuits is uncertain.

Even in the Fourth and Fifth Circuits, a three-party gift-leaseback may work. This is because the IRS has said it will not challenge gift-leasebacks if the lessee is a separate taxable entity from the donor.[23] For example, if Dad gives property to Daughter, and Daughter leases the property to Dad's C corporation, the situation should fit within the IRS no-challenge area. However, if the lessee is a pass-through entity, such as a partnership or S corporation, the IRS no-litigation position does not apply, according to Revised Action on Decision CC-1984-038.

If the gift is made to a corporation, partnership, limited liability company, or trust, and the leaseback is characterized as an equity interest or a retained right to use the property for less than fair consideration, the punitive provisions of Sections 2701, 2702, and 2703 can come into play.[24]

¶ 29.07 TRUE LEASE

For a lease to be recognized as such, it must evidence a true lease arrangement, and not a disguised sale or financing arrangement or a sham. Factors that tend to indicate a true lease arrangement include: (1) the legal owner, and not the lessee, bears the burdens and enjoys the benefits of ownership; (2) the lessee has no equity in the property; (3) the lease payments represent a fair rental; and (4) the lessee does not automatically acquire title to the property after a given period and does not have the option to do so for a nominal sum.[25]

If a purported lease is considered to effect a sale, and is not a true lease, then the lessee's rent payments will be treated as installments of the purchase price payable to the lessor and any gain on the "sale" will be recognized by the lessor. This gain will be reported in accordance with the installment sale rules, if they apply, or the non-installment sale rules, if they don't. In either case, if the property is depreciable, the lessee, rather than the legal owner (i.e., the lessor), will be entitled to depreciation deductions.

If a transaction constitutes a sale instead of a lease, it will be because too much ownership resides in the lessee-purchaser. What if, instead, too much ownership interest is retained by the donor-seller? In such a case, the payments for the purchase price may be considered gifts, and the gifted/sold property may be included in the donor-seller's estate. To minimize the chances

---

[23] Rev. AOD CC-1984-038, 1984-2 CB 1.

[24] These sections are discussed in Chs. 31, 24, and 27, respectively.

[25] See IRS Examination Tax Shelters Handbook, IRM 4236, ch. 800, at 852, 872-873, Equipment Leasing Tax Shelters; see also, Frank Lyon Co. v. United States, 435 US 561 (1978), rev'g 536 F2d 746 (8th Cir. 1976) (Supreme Court cited numerous factors in determining whether the lessor held enough attributes of the traditional lessor to support deductions).

of this, a fee simple interest in the property should be transferred to the donee-purchaser, the donor-seller should not retain control over the property (except as a lessee), and the formalities of the transaction should be well documented and respected.

¶ 29.08   PASSIVE ACTIVITY LOSS LIMITATIONS

The buyer in the sale-leaseback or the donee in a gift-leaseback may find, even if deductions are otherwise allowable with respect to the property received, that Section 469's passive activity loss limitation provisions apply to restrict or defer such deductions.

Generally speaking, any trade, business, or investment activity in which the taxpayer does not materially participate is considered a passive activity.[26] Losses and other deductions with respect to a passive activity are allowable only to the extent of income from passive activities. Such losses and deductions cannot shelter portfolio income or trade or business income.[27]

[1] Rules for Rental Activities

Unless the taxpayer meets certain tests for being involved at least 750 hours per year in the real estate business[28] or the taxpayer meets the "active participation" test,[29] income from any rental activity is treated as a passive activity[30] even if the owner materially participates in the activity.[31] "Active participation" means active participation in management decisions respecting the property.[32] If the taxpayer actively participates in management of the rental property, he or his spouse can shelter up to $25,000 of non-passive income.[33] The $25,000 exception is reduced by one-half of the amount by which the taxpayer's adjusted gross income (subject to certain adjustments) exceeds $100,000. Accordingly, the $25,000 exception is phased out altogether for a taxpayer with an adjusted gross income of $150,000 or more.[34]

EXAMPLE: Dad sells his principal residence to Daughter, leasing it back

---

[26] IRC §§ 469(c)(1), 469(c)(6).

[27] IRC § 469.

[28] IRC § 469(c)(7).

[29] IRC § 469(i).

[30] IRC § 469(c)(2).

[31] IRC § 469(c)(4).

[32] S. Rep. No. 313, 99th Cong., 2d Sess. 737-738 (1986).

[33] IRC §§ 469(i)(6), 469(i)(2).

[34] IRC § 469(i)(3).

at a fair rental, so that Section 280A does not apply. Daughter will be able to take deductions equaling her income from passive activities, plus $25,000 of other income, if she meets the active participation test, and does not exceed the income limitations.

[2] The Fate of Disallowed Losses

Passive losses that are disallowed can be carried over and/or used against other passive income when it later arises.[35]

In addition, disallowed losses can be used when the property is disposed of, in accordance with the following rules:

- When the investment is disposed of by sale or taxable exchange to an unrelated party, the suspended losses that are in excess of passive income can be taken against other income in the year of disposition;[36] if the taxpayer sells the investment through an installment sale, the suspended losses are allowed pro rata over the term of payment.[37]
- If the sale or taxable exchange is to a related party, the loss in excess of passive income will be suspended until the year in which the interest is acquired by an unrelated party in a transaction in which gain or loss is recognized.[38]
- If the taxpayer dies before the losses are used, any suspended losses in excess of passive income can be taken on the taxpayer's final return to the extent that the suspended losses are greater than the increase in basis the investment receives in the taxpayer's estate.[39]
- If the investment is disposed of by gift, the basis of the investment will be increased by the suspended losses, and the losses will not be available as a deduction to the donor for any year.[40]
- If an estate or trust distributes passive activity property, suspended losses are added to the basis of the property at that time and are no longer allowable as deductions.[41]

Any suspended losses that cannot be used when the investment is disposed of are lost forever. Subject to that limitation, passive loss carryovers last for the taxpayer's lifetime.

---

[35] IRC § 469(b).

[36] IRC § 469(g)(1).

[37] IRC § 469(g)(3).

[38] IRC § 469(g)(1)(B).

[39] IRC § 469(g)(2).

[40] IRC § 469(j)(6).

[41] IRC § 469(j)(2).

¶ 29.09   LIMITATIONS ON INTEREST DEDUCTIONS RELATED TO PURCHASE OF REAL ESTATE

If the buyer in a sale-leaseback transaction incurs any debt in connection with the acquisition of the property, he may find that interest paid on the debt is not deductible. Specifically, interest payments are not deductible unless the interest is (1) trade or business interest, (2) investment interest, (3) interest incurred in a passive activity, (4) qualified residence interest, or (5) interest incident to certain deferred payments of estate taxes. Any other interest is considered "personal interest," and is not deductible.[42] However, most interest on real estate debt should not constitute personal interest,[43] even if the real estate is just used for picnics, since real estate will almost always be considered an investment.

[1] Special Rule for Qualified Residence Interest

A building used as a personal residence by the taxpayer is generally personal use property. However, interest may still be deductible if it is "qualified residence interest."

Qualified residence interest is interest payable with respect to "acquisition indebtedness" or "home equity indebtedness." Acquisition indebtedness is indebtedness which is secured by the home and was incurred to acquire, construct, or substantially improve the home. Interest on such indebtedness is deductible.[44] Refinancing of acquisition indebtedness is also acquisition indebtedness, but only to the extent the total indebtedness resulting from the refinancing does not exceed that portion of the original indebtedness that was refinanced.[45] Acquisition indebtedness cannot exceed $1,000,000.[46]

The interest on any other debt which is secured by the home is deductible as "home equity indebtedness." The deduction of such interest is limited to the lesser of the home's fair market value (less its acquisition indebtedness) or $100,000 ($50,000 for an individual who is married filing separately).[47] Special rules apply to indebtedness incurred on or before October 13, 1987.[48]

---

[42] IRC § 163(h).

[43] Except for certain debts related to houses used by the taxpayer as personal residences. IRC § 163(h)(5)(A)(i).

[44] IRC § 163(h)(3)(B)(i).

[45] IRC § 163(h)(3)(B)(i).

[46] IRC § 163(h)(3)(B)(ii).

[47] IRC § 163(h)(3)(C).

[48] IRC § 163(h)(3)(D). Generally, such indebtedness will be treated as acquisition indebtedness, and the $1,000,000 limitation will not apply. IRC § 163(h)(3)(D)(i). However, the $1,000,000 ceiling with respect to indebtedness incurred after October 13, 1987 is reduced by outstanding indebtedness incurred on or before that date. IRC

In all cases, only interest with respect to the taxpayer's principal residence and one other residence used by the taxpayer as a residence is eligible for deduction as qualified residence interest.[49] In the case of a married couple filing separately, no more than two residences can be counted by the two of them.[50] If the taxpayer does not rent the residence on any day of the year, he can treat it as a residence.[51] Otherwise, he must use the residence for personal purposes for the greater of 14 days or 10 percent of the days during which it is rented for fair market value.[52]

Also, in all cases, interest on indebtedness secured by the home is not disqualified as deductible interest just because the security interest is unenforceable under a state or local homestead law in existence on August 16, 1986.[53]

Interest on indebtedness secured by a residence held by an estate or trust is qualified residence interest of the estate or trust, provided that the residence is the qualified residence of a beneficiary who has a present interest in the estate or trust or an interest in the residue of the estate or trust.[54]

[2] Investment Interest Limitation

Investment interest is only deductible to the extent of the taxpayer's net investment income.[55] Any disallowed investment interest can be carried forward as long as the taxpayer lives.[56] Investment interest is interest accrued on indebtedness allocable to investment property, but does not include qualified residence interest or interest incurred in a passive activity.[57] Investment property includes property producing interest, dividends, annuities, or royalties, and any interest in an activity involving the conduct of a trade or business

---

§ 163(h)(3)(D)(ii). Debt incurred before October 13, 1987 and secured by the residence on that date and all dates thereafter during the term of the loan that is refinanced is still considered as incurred on or before October 13, 1987, to the extent the principal amount of the indebtedness was not increased. IRC § 163(h)(3)(D)(iii). Refinanced debt will not be included in this category of indebtedness beyond the expiration of the term of the original debt, or if the original debt was not amortized over its term, the expiration of the first refinancing, or 30 years after the date of the first refinancing, if earlier. IRC § 163(h)(3)(D)(iv).

[49] IRC § 163(h)(4)(A).

[50] IRC § 163(h)(4)(A)(ii).

[51] IRC § 163(h)(4)(A)(iii).

[52] IRC §§ 163(h)(4)(A)(i)(II), 280A(d)(1).

[53] IRC § 163(h)(4)(C).

[54] IRC § 163(h)(4)(D).

[55] IRC § 163(d).

[56] IRC § 163(d)(2).

[57] IRC § 163(d)(3).

which is not a passive activity and with respect to which the taxpayer does not materially participate.[58] If the investment property is rental real estate, it will be considered a passive activity, and the limitations on investment interest will not apply.[59]

[3] Passive Activity Interest

Passive activity losses are computed without regard to qualified residence interest[60] or any deduction, income, gain, or loss allocable to a dwelling unit to which Section 280A(c)(5) applies for the year.[61] Section 280A(c)(5) limits deductions with respect to certain residences partially used for business to the gross income from the business use of the residence less certain deductions.

¶ 29.10 DEDUCTION OR CAPITALIZATION OF TAXES

The buyer in the sale-leaseback or the donee in a gift-leaseback may find that the deductibility of taxes incurred with respect to the property acquired is subject to special rules. As a general rule, the following taxes are deductible, regardless of whether or not they are incurred in a profit-making venture: state, local, and foreign real estate taxes; state and local personal property taxes; state, local, and foreign income, war profits, and excess profits taxes; generation-skipping transfer tax on income distributions; and the environmental tax formerly imposed on corporations by Section 59A.[62] However, other state, local, and foreign taxes are deductible only if they are paid in carrying on a trade or business or activity for the production of income. Even though such taxes are nondeductible if paid in connection with the acquisition or disposition of property, they are treated as a cost of the property's acquisition or will reduce the amount realized on the property's subsequent disposition.[63]

---

[58] IRC § 163(d)(5).

[59] IRC § 163(d)(3)(B)(ii).

[60] IRC § 469(k)(7).

[61] IRC § 469(k)(10).

[62] IRC § 164(a).

[63] IRC § 164(a).

CHAPTER **30**

Deferred Payment Sales

¶ 30.01 INTRODUCTION

A sale of an appreciating or income-producing asset to a family member is a commonly used estate freezing method. Especially common is a sale for deferred payments. This method basically works as follows. Mom sells Asset to Son in exchange for a note. Under the installment sale rules, gain on the sale (if any) is recognized as the note is paid. If the yield on Asset exceeds the interest paid, Mom's estate will be successfully frozen.

Under the installment method, the gain Mom recognizes for any taxable year is a proportion of the payments she receives in that year. The proportion is the gross profit which will be realized when payment is completed, divided by the total contract price. So, for example, if the gross profit is 20 percent of the total contract price, Mom will treat 20 percent of each principal payment as gain from the sale. Son's note is ordinarily not considered a payment, even if the note is guaranteed by another person. That does not, however, mean that his note will never be deemed a payment. For instance, if the note is payable on demand or meets certain other requirements not ordinarily present in a family transaction, the face amount of the note or its value may be deemed a current payment.[1]

The steps for determining taxability of amounts received in an installment sale are:

- *First*, determine what amount is interest under the rules discussed below.
- *Next*, recapture any depreciation as ordinary income in the year of sale.
- *Then*, determine the profit percentage, which is (1) the total gain after depreciation recapture, divided by (2) the total selling price (exclusive of interest).
- The profit percentage of each annual principal payment must be reported as capital gain or ordinary income, depending on the character of the asset sold.

TERMINOLOGY: In this Chapter, the word "note" includes any deferred payment obligation.

¶ 30.02 INELIGIBILITY FOR INSTALLMENT SALE TREATMENT

Not all transactions are eligible for installment sale treatment. Ineligible sales include the following.

---

[1] IRC §§ 453(f)(3), 453(f)(4).

[1] Sales in Which Full Payment Is Made in Year of Sale

To qualify for installment sale treatment, at least some part of the payment must be made after the close of the taxable year in which the sale occurs.[2]

[2] Sales of Depreciable Property to a Related Person

All or part of the payments received pursuant to a sale of depreciable property to a related person may be ineligible for installment sale treatment.

[a] Installment Method Unavailable for Entire Sale

The installment method is not generally available for a sale of depreciable property to a "related person."[3] Rather, all noncontingent deferred amounts are treated as paid immediately. In the case of contingent payments, the seller may recover basis ratably as payments are received. However, the buyer cannot increase his basis in the property by any contingent amount until the amount is includable in the seller's income.[4]

If the taxpayer establishes to the satisfaction of the IRS that a transaction does not have the avoidance of federal income tax as a principal purpose, the IRS can grant installment sale treatment to a sale of depreciable property between related persons.[5] In the Senate Report addressing this provision, the IRS is directed to treat the taxpayer and his family equitably in light of all the facts and circumstances of each case, in a manner consistent with the remedial intent of the provision.[6] The taxpayer can apparently make the effort to convince the IRS in an explanation on the income tax return reporting the sale.[7]

Assuming Mom is the seller, "related persons," for purposes of this rule, would include the following:[8]

- Mom and a corporation, if more than 50 percent of the value of the outstanding stock is owned directly or indirectly by or for Mom;[9]

---

[2] IRC § 453(b)(1).

[3] IRC § 453(g)(1).

[4] IRC § 453(g)(1).

[5] IRC § 453(g)(2).

[6] S. Rep. No. 1000, 96th Cong., 2d Sess. (1980), 1980-2 CB 494, 503.

[7] See Instructions to Form 6252, Part III.

[8] IRC § 453(g)(3). Related persons now also include Mom and any estate of which she is a beneficiary, except in the case of a sale or exchange in satisfaction of a pecuniary bequest. This is true for taxable years beginning after August 5, 1997. IRC §§ 267(b)(13), 1239(b)(3); TRA § 1308(c).

[9] IRC §§ 1239(b)(1), 1239(c)(1)(A).

- Mom and a partnership, if more than 50 percent of the capital *or* profits interests is owned directly or indirectly by or for Mom;[10]
- Two partnerships, if the same persons own, directly or indirectly, more than 50 percent of the capital *or* profits interests;[11]
- Two corporations that are members of the same controlled group;[12]
- A corporation and a partnership, if the same persons own more than 50 percent in value of the outstanding stock of the corporation, and more than 50 percent of the capital or profits interests in the partnership;[13]
- An S corporation and another S corporation, if the same persons own more than 50 percent in value of the outstanding stock of each corporation;[14]
- An S corporation and a C corporation, if the same persons own more than 50 percent in value of the outstanding stock of each corporation;[15]
- Mom and any trust in which Mom or her husband is a beneficiary, unless the beneficial interest in the trust is remote and contingent within the meaning of Section 318(a)(3)(B)(i);[16] this means that, assuming the trustee exercises the maximum amount of discretion in favor of the beneficiary, the actuarial value of the beneficiary's interest is five percent or less of the value of the trust property.[17]

[b] Installment Method Unavailable for Recapture Portion of Purchase Price

Even if installment sale treatment applies, any recapture income must be recognized in the year of sale.[18] Recapture income means the amount that would be treated as ordinary income for the year of disposition, assuming all payments were received in the year of disposition, under (1) Section 1245 or Section 1250 (concerning the recapture of depreciation and amortization deductions claimed with respect to the property described in those sections), or (2) Section 751 (to the extent that the amount realized from the sale of a part-

---

[10] IRC §§ 1239(b)(1), 1239(c)(1)(A).

[11] IRC § 707(b)(1)(B).

[12] IRC §§ 1239(b)(1), 1239(c)(1)(C), 267(b)(3).

[13] IRC §§ 1239(b)(1), 1239(c)(1)(C), 267(b)(10).

[14] IRC §§ 1239(b)(1), 1239(c)(1)(C), 267(b)(11).

[15] IRC §§ 1239(b)(1), 1239(c)(1)(C), 267(b)(12).

[16] IRC § 1239(b)(2).

[17] IRC § 318(a)(3)(B)(i).

[18] IRC § 453(i).

nership interest is attributable to partnership Section 1245 or Section 1250 property).[19]

[3] Sales of Dealer Property/Inventory

An installment sale does not include dispositions by dealers or dispositions of inventory.[20] For example, if Dad is a developer of real property, his sale of subdivided lots is not eligible for installment sale treatment.

[4] Sale of Marketable Securities

Securities that are traded on an established securities market cannot be sold under the installment sale method.[21] The IRS has ruled that stock that cannot be sold on an established securities market except under Rule 144 is not a marketable security for this purpose and can be sold on the installment sale basis.[22] If Mom wants to sell marketable securities on an installment basis, she can put the securities into an entity and sell an interest in the entity instead.

[5] Sales for Which the Seller Elects out of Installment Sale Treatment

If a person does not want to be taxed under the installment sale method, he can elect out.[23] The election must be made on a timely filed income tax return for the taxable year in which the disposition occurs.[24] A late election is permitted only when the IRS concludes that the taxpayer had good cause for failing to make a timely election.[25] Recharacterizing a transaction as a sale in a tax year subsequent to the year of the transaction is not good cause.[26] Also, no

---

[19] IRC § 453(i)(2).

[20] IRC § 453(b)(2).

[21] IRC § 453(k)(2)(A). The section containing this rule is difficult to spot on a browse through the Internal Revenue Code, as its section heading is "Current Inclusion in Case of Revolving Credit Plans, Etc."

[22] Priv. Ltr. Ruls. 9803009 (Oct. 14, 1997), 9803021 (Oct. 20, 1997), 9803022 (Oct. 20, 1997).

[23] IRC § 453(d).

[24] IRC § 453(d)(2); Temp. Reg. § 15A.453-1(d)(3)(i).

[25] Temp. Reg. § 15A.453-(1)(d)(3)(ii).

[26] Temp. Reg. § 15A.453-(1)(d)(3)(ii).

conditional elections are permitted.[27] The election is irrevocable, unless the IRS consents to a revocation.[28]

[6] Liquidations Involving Installment Notes

Special rules apply to receipt of installment notes in corporate liquidations.[29]

¶ 30.03 DISPOSITION OF PROPERTY BY RELATED PURCHASER WITHIN TWO YEARS OF SALE

Special provisions apply if the seller and purchaser are related[30] and the purchaser disposes of the purchased property within two years. The two-year rule is Congress's reaction to a formerly used technique in which Mom sold property to Son on the installment basis, and Son immediately sold the property to a third party for cash. Mom had no immediate gain because she had not been paid. Son had no gain because the amount of Son's note to Mom was included in his basis in the property on the sale. Thus, Mom deferred gain on the sale, even though the family had received the cash tax-free.

Under current law, if Son disposes of the purchased asset (1) before making all of his payments to Mom and (2) within two years of Mom's sale to Son, then the amount realized by Son on his disposition will be treated as being received by Mom on the date of Son's sale.[31]

> **EXAMPLE:** Mom owns Blackacre, which has a basis of $600,000 and a value of $2 million. Mom sells Blackacre to Son in exchange for a 20-year note, and reports her gain on the installment sale basis. One year later, before making any payments, Son sells Blackacre for $2 million. Mom is treated as receiving $2 million, even if Son does not pay her.

This can cause a cash flow problem for Mom because she will have gain to report and may not have received anything from Son.

---

[27] Temp. Reg. § 15A.453-(1)(d)(3)(ii).

[28] IRC § 453(d)(3).

[29] IRC § 453(h).

[30] Under IRC § 453(f)(1), "related person" means any person whose stock would be attributed to Mom under IRC §§ 318(a)(1)–318(a)(3), or a person who bears a relationship to Mom that is described in IRC § 267(b).

[31] IRC § 453(e)(1). The statute of limitations is extended in accordance with the relevant periods. IRC § 453(e)(8).

Practice Pointer: In drafting the note from Son to Mom, consider inserting a covenant that Son will pay Mom at least enough to cover her accelerated income tax, if he disposes of the property within the two-year period; or, have Son agree not to dispose of the property within two years.

---

[1] Ceiling on Amount Deemed Received in First Disposition

If Mom sells Blackacre to Son, and he disposes of it during the two-year period, a limitation exists on the amount that Mom will be deemed to receive. To calculate this limit:[32]

Step 1: Determine the lesser of (i) the total amount realized by Son before the close of the taxable year of his disposition or (ii) the total contract price for Mom's sale to Son.

Step 2: Add (i) the aggregate amount of payments actually received by Mom before the close of the year of Son's disposition and (ii) the aggregate amount treated as received by Mom for prior years by reason of Son's disposition.

Step 3: Subtract the "Step 2 amount" from the "Step 1 amount." The difference is the ceiling on the amount treated as received by Mom as a result of Son's disposition.

For example, if Son received $3 million on his sale of Blackacre, and he had already paid Mom $500,000, then Mom would be deemed to have received $1,500,000, that is, $2 million (lower of amount realized by Son, or contract price for Mom's sale), less $500,000 (previous payments).

[2] Seller Recognizes Income Even if Purchaser Does Not

The measure of accelerated income to Mom is the "amount realized" by Son.[33]

[a] Sale or Exchange by Son

The "amount realized" by Son is not the same as "payment," which is defined to exclude most notes and property received in a like-kind exchange under Section 1031.[34] So, if Son sells Blackacre for a note, the receipt of the

---

[32] IRC § 453(e)(3).

[33] IRC § 453(e)(1).

[34] IRC §§ 453(f)(3), 453(f)(6).

note will not be treated as the receipt of payment by Son for purposes of his own installment sale treatment, but will be included in Mom's income as an amount realized by Son.[35] Similarly, if Son trades Blackacre in a like-kind exchange, Son will not recognize gain, but Mom will apparently be taxed at that time because Son realized an amount equal to the value of the property received in the trade.[36]

[b] Other Disposition

What if Son's disposition is not a sale or exchange? For example, what if Son gives the property to his child? In such an instance, the fair market value of Blackacre is considered the amount realized in applying the above rules.[37]

[3] Effect of Actual Payments Received After Deemed Payment

If Mom recognizes gain as a result of Son's disposition of Blackacre, and he continues to pay her under the terms of his note, Mom will not be treated as receiving payments to the extent that she was deemed to receive payments as a result of Son's disposition.[38]

[4] Exceptions to Second Disposition Rules

Under the following circumstances, a disposition by Son within two years of his purchase from Mom will not result in a deemed payment to Mom:

- *Involuntary conversions.* Blackacre is involuntarily converted[39] in Son's hands, and Mom's sale occurred before the threat or imminence of the conversion.[40]
- *Death of Mom or Son.* Blackacre is disposed of after Mom's death, or after Son's death.[41]

---

[35] IRC § 453(e)(1).

[36] IRC § 453(f)(6) definition of "payment" does not appear to result in exclusion of like-kind property from inclusion in Mom's income pursuant to IRC §§ 453(e)(1) and 1001(b).

[37] IRC § 453(e)(4).

[38] IRC § 453(e)(5).

[39] Within the meaning of IRC § 1033.

[40] IRC § 453(e)(6)(B).

[41] IRC § 453(e)(6)(C).

- *Nontax avoidance purposes.* Mom or Son satisfies the IRS that neither Mom's sale nor Son's disposition had as one of its principal purposes the avoidance of federal income tax.[42]

[5] Suspension of Two-Year Period

The two-year period is suspended for any period during which Son's risk of loss is substantially diminished by (1) the holding of a put option with respect to Blackacre or similar property, (2) the holding by another person of a right to acquire Blackacre, or (3) a short sale or any other transaction.[43] These provisions would be unusual in a family contract. But, Mom must be cautioned if she contractually protects Son during the interim from suffering the economic loss of any decline in value of Blackacre.

¶ 30.04 INTEREST CHARGE ON LARGE DEFERRED TAX LIABILITY

In the case of certain installment sales, a tax in the nature of an interest charge is imposed on the "applicable percentage" of the "deferred tax liability."[44]

GLOBAL EXAMPLE

Mom sells Whiteacre (long-term capital gain property) to Son for a $12 million, 20-year note. Principal is payable in a balloon at the end of the term. Mom's basis in Whiteacre was $3 million.

---

[1] Deferred Tax Liability

The "deferred tax liability" with respect to a taxable year is the amount of gain that has not been recognized at the close of the year, multiplied by the maximum income tax rate for that year.[45] The maximum rate on capital gains is

---

[42] IRC § 453(e)(7). The taxpayer can explain the transactions to the IRS on Form 6252. See Instructions to Form 6252, Part III.

[43] IRC § 453(e)(2)(B).

[44] IRC § 453A(c)(1).

[45] IRC § 453A(c)(3).

used for any portion of the deferred tax liability that is long-term capital gain.[46]

> **EXAMPLE:** Based on the Global Example's facts, Mom's deferred tax liability at the end of Year One is $9 million × .15, or $1,350,000.

[2] Applicable Percentage

The "applicable percentage" of the deferred tax liability for the year, with respect to obligations arising in a taxable year, is (x) the aggregate face amount of those obligations outstanding as of the close of such year in excess of five million dollars,[47] divided by (y) the aggregate face amount of those obligations outstanding as of the close of the year.

> **EXAMPLE:** At the end of Year One, in the Global Example, Son's $12 million installment note to Mom is outstanding. The applicable percentage of the installment obligation is $7 million/$12 million, or seven-twelfths. If her deferred tax liability at the end of the year is $1,350,000, then seven-twelfths of it, or $787,500, is subject to the interest charge.

[3] Amount and Deductibility of Interest Charge

The applicable percentage of the deferred tax liability, multiplied by the underpayment rate on tax deficiencies in effect under Section 6621(a)(2) for the month in which Mom's taxable year ends, is the interest charge for that year.[48]

> **EXAMPLE:** If, in the Global Example, the underpayment rate on tax deficiencies at the end of the Year One is 9 percent, then Mom's interest charge for the year is $787,500 × .09, or $70,875.

The tax payment will be treated as interest for purposes of computing the taxpayer's deduction for interest paid during the tax year.[49]

---

[46] IRC § 453A(c)(3).

[47] IRC § 453A(c)(4). For purposes of determining whether applicable installment obligations exceed $5 million, certain entities that are under common control are treated as one person. IRC § 453A(b)(2).

[48] IRC § 453A(c)(2).

[49] IRC § 453A(c)(5).

[4] Applicable Installment Obligations

The interest charge only applies to certain obligations. Generally, it applies to installments received in dispositions of property in which the sales price of the property exceeds $150,000.[50] For this purpose, all sales or exchanges that are part of the same transaction or series of transactions are treated as one sale or exchange.[51]

Exception for personal use property. The interest charge does not apply to an installment obligation arising from the disposition of personal use property.[52] "Personal use property" is any property, unless substantially all of its use by the taxpayer is in connection with the taxpayer's trade or business or in the production of income.[53] The determination of use is made as of date of the sale.[54] Thus, if Mom sells her home to Son for an installment note, the interest charge does not apply to Son's note, and Son's note will not be counted in determining whether $5 million of installment obligations receivable from Son to Mom are outstanding.

Exception for farm property. The interest charge does not apply to a note received from the sale of any property used or produced in the trade or business of farming.[55]

¶ 30.05 PLEDGE OF INSTALLMENT OBLIGATION

In the case of any obligation that is subject to the interest charge discussed in ¶ 30.04 above, certain rules apply with respect to a seller's pledge of the installment obligation.[56] Generally, if such an obligation is used as collateral or security for a new loan to the seller, the net proceeds of the new borrowing are treated as a payment on the installment obligation to the extent of the unpaid balance of the purchase price on the installment obligation.[57] The "payment" resulting from this new borrowing is deemed made on the later of the date the new borrowing is secured by the installment obligations or the date

---

[50] IRC § 453A(b)(1).

[51] IRC § 453A(b)(5).

[52] IRC § 453A(b)(3)(A).

[53] IRC §§ 453A(b)(3)(A), 1275(b)(3).

[54] IRC §§ 453A(b)(3)(A), 1275(b)(3).

[55] IRC § 453A(b)(3)(B). Farming is defined with reference to IRC §§ 2032A(e)(4) and 2032A(e)(5), and generally includes any business involving the raising of agricultural or horticultural commodities, including animals and trees.

[56] IRC § 453A(a)(2).

[57] IRC §§ 453A(d)(1), 453A(d)(2).

the net proceeds of the borrowing are received by the taxpayer. Appropriate adjustments are made for later payments.[58]

> **EXAMPLE:** Mom sells Whiteacre to Son for a note. She then pledges Son's note to secure a new loan. All or a portion of the loan proceeds will be treated as a payment of Son's note. This will trigger accelerated recognition of gain, taxable in the same manner as a prepayment of the note.

¶ 30.06 DISPOSITION OF INSTALLMENT OBLIGATION

If an installment note is satisfied at less than face value, or the holder in any way disposes of the note, then the holder will recognize gain or loss on the difference between her basis in the obligation and either the amount realized (in the case of satisfaction at other than face value or a sale or exchange) or the fair market value of the obligation at the time of disposition (in the case of any other transaction).[59] The gain or loss will be of the same character as the original sale.[60]

> **EXAMPLE:** Using the facts of the Global Example, if Mom gives Son's installment note to Grandchild in Year Two, she will recognize gain of $9 million.

[1] Basis of the Obligation

The basis of an installment obligation is the excess of the face value of the obligation over the amount of income that would be recognized if the obligation were paid in full.[61] Income, for this purpose, does not include interest.[62]

> **EXAMPLE:** The basis of Mom's note in the Global Example is $3 million.

---

[58] IRC § 453A(d)(3).
[59] IRC § 453B(a).
[60] IRC § 453B(a).
[61] IRC § 453B(b).
[62] See Treas. Reg. § 1.453-9(b).

[2] Death of Owner of Obligation

In the Global Example, Mom's death will not trigger a gain unless the obligation becomes unenforceable.[63] However, the note will not receive a new basis at Mom's death, so the gain will be considered income in respect of a decedent, and will be taxed to the owner of the note under the applicable rules.

[3] Obligation Is Canceled or Becomes Unenforceable

If an installment obligation is canceled or otherwise becomes unenforceable, the obligation is considered disposed of in a transaction other than a sale or exchange.[64] If the obligor and obligee are related persons, the fair market value of the obligation is treated as no less than its face amount.[65]

> **EXAMPLE:** Dad sells Blackacre to Daughter for a 10-year note. The principal amount of the note is $500,000. If Dad cancels the note during his life, or if he dies and the note is distributed to Daughter or otherwise canceled, gain will be recognized on the difference between $500,000 and Dad's basis in the note. Daughter will receive cancellation of indebtedness income, or a gift/bequest, as the case may be.

In the case of cancellation or unenforceability on the seller's death, who recognizes the gain? The IRS's position is that the gain is income in respect of a decedent, taxable to the seller's estate.[66] The Tax Court has held that the gain is taxable on the decedent's final return.[67] The Tax Court's position is more favorable to the taxpayer because the income tax will not be included in the estate, as it would under the IRS approach. The Eighth Circuit has agreed with the IRS in the case of a self-canceling installment note.[68]

[4] Transfer Between Spouses or Former Spouses

A direct transfer of an installment note between spouses (or, if incident to a divorce, former spouses) is not considered a disposition of the installment note, and thus does not trigger a gain, provided that the transferee spouse or

---

[63] IRC §§ 453B(c), 453B(f).

[64] IRC § 453B(f)(1).

[65] IRC § 453B(f)(2).

[66] Rev. Rul. 86-72, 1986-1 CB 253; GCM 39503 (May 7, 1986) (both applying to SCINs).

[67] Estate of Frane v. Comm'r, 98 TC 341 (1992) (dealing with cancellation under SCINs), rev'd, 998 F2d 567 (8th Cir. 1993).

[68] Estate of Frane v. Comm'r, 998 F2d 567 (8th Cir. 1993).

former spouse is a United States citizen or resident alien.[69] However, a transfer by a spouse to a trust for the other spouse does not come within this exception.[70]

Section 1041, which applies to gain and loss, does not shield the accrued interest payable on the transferred installment note from taxation as an assignment of income by the transferor spouse.

[5] Dispositions Which Do Not Trigger Gain

Certain dispositions do not trigger recognition of gain. They include the following:

- *Contribution of note to controlled corporation.* Section 351 overrides Section 453.[71]
- *Contribution of note to partnership.* A contribution to a new or existing partnership, whether or not in exchange for a partnership interest, does not trigger gain.[72]
- *Distribution of note from partnership to partner.*[73]
- *Transfer of note at death.*[74]

¶ 30.07 SELF-CANCELING INSTALLMENT NOTES (SCINs)

The SCIN is a technique that is sometimes used to avoid the inclusion of a note receivable in the holder's estate.[75]

> EXAMPLE: Dad sells Blackacre to Daughter for a note. Daughter's note is for a period of ten years or Dad's life, whichever is shorter. If Dad dies before the note is fully paid, the note is not technically canceled—rather, it has been satisfied, because all payments required pursuant to its terms have been made. Therefore, there is nothing to include in Dad's estate. However, in order for Dad not to have made a gift to Daughter at the outset, the consideration for Blackacre would have had to be more than

---

[69] IRC § 453B(g).

[70] IRC § 453B(g).

[71] Reg. § 1.453-9(c)(2), issued under former IRC § 453(d), which had same substantive provisions.

[72] Reg. § 1.721-1(a).

[73] Reg. § 1.453-9(c)(2); IRC §§ 731(b), 731(c).

[74] IRC § 453B(c).

[75] See IRC § 453B(f); ¶ 30.06[2].

Dad would have received under a straight 10-year note, to reflect the fact that Daughter would not have had to pay the whole price if Dad died during the period. In addition, in a case where Dad's life expectancy is less than the term of the note, the IRS has taken the position that the transaction will be taxed for income tax purposes as a private annuity.

A SCIN is an installment obligation that terminates on the occurrence of a certain event (often the seller's death) before it is otherwise due.

Gift taxation. The buyer must pay a premium for the property to be sure that the original sale is not a partial gift.[76] The design of the premium is problematic.[77]

Estate taxation. A SCIN is not generally includable in the seller's estate.[78]

Of course, if the SCIN were recharacterized as a retained interest in the property, the property would be included in the seller's estate. This is generally an issue in installment sales to trusts or other entities.

Additionally, if the original value of the SCIN is less than the value of the assets purchased, and the SCIN is still outstanding when the seller dies, the assets will be included in the seller's estate at their date-of-death value, subject to reduction for the actual consideration paid.[79]

In a case where certain formalities were not followed, the Tax Court held that assets sold in exchange for a SCIN were included in the decedent's estate because there was no bona fide transaction for full and adequate consideration. The Tax Court focused on the parties' failure to follow the terms of the agreement as evidence that the transaction was not made at arm's length or for adequate consideration. The Sixth Circuit reversed, holding that the discrepancies were adequately explained, and that the parties could not have known that the decedent would die during the note term. More importantly, the Sixth Circuit specifically rejected an argument by the IRS that would invalidate all SCINs— namely, that a sale in exchange for a SCIN is not bona fide because the only reason to enter into such a transaction is the expectation that the decedent will die during the term of the note. The court also rejected the taxpayer's argument that the fair market value of the SCIN was established by the presumption that the value of a note between family members is the amount of unpaid principal, plus interest accrued to the date of death, and remanded the case to

---

[76] IRC § 7872.

[77] See Rapkin, "Freezing Estates with Private Annuities and Self-Canceling Installment Notes," 12 J. Tax'n Inv. 33, 41 (1994). It has been suggested that the increase could be determined with reference to Table 80 CNSMT. R. Covey, Practical Drafting, 2921–2922 (July 1992).

[78] Estate of Moss v. Comm'r, 74 TC 1239 (1980), acq. in result, 1981-1 CB 2; GCM 39503 (May 7, 1986).

[79] IRC § 2036.

consider the IRS's alternative argument that the transaction was a bargain sale under Section 2512.[80]

Income taxation during seller's life. The SCIN may be treated as a private annuity or an installment sale. If there is a stated maximum payment that will be made within the seller's life expectancy, based on Table V of Treasury Regulation § 1.72-9, the transaction will be treated as an installment sale.[81] If not, the IRS may tax the transaction as a private annuity.[82]

Income taxation after seller's death. If the seller dies before the note is paid and the note/property is not included in his estate, the purchaser's basis will be adjusted to reflect the unpaid amount of the note, or, if the purchased asset has been disposed of, deferred gain will be recognized.[83]

The IRS's position is that the seller's unrecognized gain on date of death is taxable to the seller's estate as income in respect of a decedent. This position has been litigated, however.[84] It may be possible to avoid this problem area by disposing of the note before the seller's death and thereby accelerating the gain (thus getting the income tax out of the estate) if death during the term appears likely, although the other consequences of the disposition (e.g., a taxable gift of an asset which would not be included in the estate) must always be considered.

¶ 30.08 IMPUTED INTEREST ON DEFERRED PAYMENT OBLIGATIONS

The stated principal and interest on a note issued for property will not necessarily be taxed as such. Nor will the timing of taxation necessarily be determined using the cash basis of accounting. Rather, certain sections of the Code, primarily Sections 1274 and 483, can impute a higher interest rate than the stated rate, and require recognition of interest income and deductions at different times than the interest payments are actually made.

Applicable federal rate. Interest is usually imputed using the applicable federal rate (AFR) or some percentage of the AFR.

---

[80] Estate of Costanza v. Comm'r, TCM 2001-128, 81 TCM (CCH) 1693 (2001), rev'd and remanded, 320 F3d 595 (6th Cir. 2003).

[81] GCM 39503 (June 28, 1985).

[82] GCM 39503 (June 28, 1985). See Chapter 23 for discussion of private annuities.

[83] GCM 39503 (June 28, 1985).

[84] Frane v. Comm'r, 998 F2d 567 (8th Cir. 1993) (holding that gain was IRD), rev'g 98 TC 341 (1992) (gain taxable on decedent's final return). The Tax Court holding is more favorable for the taxpayer because the income tax is removed from the taxpayer's estate.

The AFR is a federally determined rate. It is published monthly, and a different rate is determined for short-term (three years or less), mid-term (more than three years but not more than nine years), and long-term (more than nine years) obligations.[85]

These rates are based on the average market yield, during any one-month period ending in the calendar month in which the determination is made, on outstanding marketable obligations of the United States with remaining periods of maturity of three years or less (for short-term obligations), and corresponding periods for mid- and long-term obligations.[86] Options to renew or extend are taken into account in determining the length of the term.[87]

The AFR is determined based on semiannual compounding, and rates are published each month which convert the AFR to interest rates which are compounded at different time periods.

[1] Original Issue Discount on Deferred Payment Obligations— Section 1274

Section 1274 imputes interest in the case of deferred payments in exchange for property. It provides that the original issue discount rules will apply to transactions within its scope. Its scope includes all such payments not specifically excepted.

An exception exists for certain notes if (1) the principal does not exceed $3,057,700[88] and (2) the taxpayers elect to report on the cash method.[89] This exception will make Section 1274 inapplicable to many family transactions.

However, let's proceed to analyze its effect on those transactions that it does cover.

The general rule is that, if an applicable obligation[90] does not carry "adequate stated interest," then the obligation will be considered to carry original issue discount (OID), and the OID must be amortized by both the purchaser and the seller over the term of the note.[91] This will be true, even though the cash payments will not match the income and deductions reported.

---

[85] IRC § 1274(d)(1).

[86] IRC § 1274(d)(1)(C).

[87] IRC § 1274(d)(3).

[88] Rev. Rul. 2002-79, 2002-48 IRB 908. The above amount, which is updated annually, applies for 2003. This number is indexed for inflation. For current amount, see Appendix ¶ A.01, Table of Indexed Amounts, in supplement.

[89] IRC § 1274A. See discussion at ¶ 30.08[3] below.

[90] See ¶ 3.08[1][b] for description of obligations not subject to IRC § 1274.

[91] IRC §§ 1272(a)(1), 1274(a)(1).

EXAMPLE: Dad sells Blackacre to Daughter for a ten-year note with a principal amount of $10 million and no stated interest. Original issue discount exists, and is computed on the basis of the lowest AFR for the month of the sale and the preceding two months.[92] Dad will report interest income in the amount of the OID ratably during the term of the note, and Daughter will report an equal interest deduction, if the interest is otherwise deductible.

[a] Calculation of OID

The difference between the principal amount of the note and the "stated redemption price at maturity" is considered OID.[93]

To calculate OID—

Step 1. Calculate the "stated redemption price at maturity." The "stated redemption price at maturity" includes all payments to be received under the agreement, except interest based on a fixed rate and payable unconditionally at fixed periodic intervals of one year or less during the entire term of the debt instrument.[94] Thus, in the Example, the stated redemption price at maturity is $10 million. If the note is issued in exchange for certain property that is publicly traded, then the amount of OID is the stated redemption price at maturity, less the fair market value of the property.[95] If it isn't, the calculation continues with the following steps.

Step 2. Compute the "imputed principal amount." Generally, the "imputed principal amount" is the sum of the present values of all payments due under the contract (including interest payments).[96] The present values are computed using the lowest AFR for the month of the sale and the two preceding months, compounded semiannually.[97] Thus, in the above Example, if the lowest AFR is 3 percent, the imputed principal amount would be $7,424,704. However, in a "potentially abusive situation," the "imputed principal amount" is the fair market value of the property sold.[98] A "potentially abusive situation" includes a "tax shelter" or any other situation that, by reason of recent sales transactions, nonrecourse financing, financing with a term in excess of the economic life of the property, or other circumstances is of a type which the regu-

---

[92] IRC § 1274(d)(2).

[93] IRC §§ 1273(a)(1), 1274(a)(2).

[94] IRC § 1273(a)(2).

[95] IRC §§ 1274(c)(3)(D), 1273(b)(3); Reg. §§ 1.1274-1(b)(2)(ii)(C), 1.1273-2(c). Note that Section 1273, rather than Section 1274, applies in such a case.

[96] IRC § 1274(b)(1).

[97] IRC §§ 1274(b), 1274(d)(2).

[98] IRC § 1274(b)(3)(A).

lations specify as having potential for tax avoidance.[99] A "tax shelter" is an entity or plan or arrangement the principal purpose of which is to avoid or evade federal income tax.[100]

Step 3. See if "adequate stated interest" exists. If the stated principal amount is less than or equal to the imputed principal amount, then the obligation carries adequate stated interest. If not, it doesn't. Thus, in the above Example, the stated principal amount ($10 million) exceeds the imputed principal amount ($7,424,704), so the loan does not have adequate stated interest.

Step 4. Determine the amount of OID.[101] If the note does not carry adequate stated interest, the amount of OID will be the stated redemption price at maturity, less the imputed principal amount.[102] Thus in the above Example, the amount of OID would be $2,575,306. If the note does carry adequate stated interest, the amount of original issue discount, if any, is the stated redemption price at maturity, less the stated principal amount.[103] If the OID is less than one fourth of one percent of the stated redemption price at maturity, multiplied by the number of complete years to maturity, then the OID is deemed to be zero.[104]

> **EXAMPLE:** Mom sells Blackacre to Daughter for a note with a principal amount of $10 million and interest payable at the AFR. The principal and interest are all payable in a balloon payment at the end of the ten-year term. The stated principal amount ($10 million) is the same as the imputed principal amount ($10 million), so the note has adequate stated interest, and no additional interest will be imputed. However, because the stated redemption price at maturity ($10 million, plus the balloon interest payments) is greater than the stated principal amount ($10 million), Section 1274 will effectively put the taxpayers on an accrual basis for tax purposes with respect to the interest.

[b] Exceptions to the OID rules

Section 1274 does not apply, or applies with exceptions, to certain obligations. Exceptions normally applicable in a family situation include the following types of transactions—

---

[99] IRC § 1274(b)(3)(B).

[100] IRC § 6662(d)(2)(C)(iii).

[101] IRC § 1274(c)(2).

[102] IRC § 1274(c)(1)(A)(ii).

[103] IRC § 1274(c)(1)(A)(i).

[104] IRC § 1273(a)(3).

- *Short-term obligation.*[105] Any note for which payments are due less than six months from date of sale.
- *Old obligation.* A note issued pursuant to a sale made before 1985.[106]
- *Sale of small farm or business.* Any note arising from the sale or exchange of a farm by an individual, estate, testamentary trust, small business corporation,[107] or partnership meeting requirements similar to those of a small business corporation, if the sales price cannot exceed $1 million, considering related transactions to be one sale.[108]
- *Sale of principal residence.* Any note arising from the sale or exchange by an individual of his principal residence.[109]
- *Small transaction.* Any note arising from the sale or exchange of property if the aggregate amounts of all payments under the contract (both principal and interest) and all other consideration received and to be received for the sale or exchange cannot exceed $250,000. Related transactions may be aggregated.[110]
- *Sale of land to family member.* A note to which Section 483(e) applies.[111]
- *Sale for annuity.* Sale of property in exchange for a private annuity, if Section 72 applies and the terms of the contract depend in whole or in substantial part on the life expectancy of one or more persons.[112]
- *Sale for cash method debt instrument, if the taxpayers elect.*[113] Applies to certain notes where the stated principal amount does not exceed $3,057,700.[114]
- *Sale of publicly traded property.* Any publicly traded note or note issued in exchange for certain publicly traded property.[115]

---

[105] IRC § 1274(c)(1)(B).

[106] P.L. 98-369, § 41(a).

[107] As defined in IRC § 1244(c)(3).

[108] IRC § 1274(c)(3)(A). A "farm" includes stock, dairy, poultry, fruit, fur-bearing animals, truck farms, plantations, ranches, nurseries, ranges, greenhouses, or other similar structures used primarily for the raising of agricultural or horticultural commodities, and orchards. IRC §§ 1274(c)(3)(A)(i), 6420(c)(2).

[109] IRC § 1274(c)(3)(B).

[110] IRC § 1274(c)(3)(C).

[111] IRC § 1274(c)(3)(F); generally, a note arising from sales of land to a family member in a calendar year for and aggregate amount of $500,000 or less.

[112] IRC § 1275(a)(1)(B).

[113] See discussion infra ¶ 30.08[3].

[114] The above amount, which is updated annually, applies for 2003. This number is indexed for inflation. For current amount, see Appendix A.01, Table of Indexed Amounts, in supplement.

[115] IRC §§ 1274(c)(3)(D), 1273(b)(3); Reg. §§ 1.1274-1(b)(2)(ii)(C), 1.1273-2(c). Note that Section 1273, rather than Section 1274, applies in such a case.

- *Certain sales of patents.*[116]
- *Transactions between husband and wife.* A note issued by one spouse to the other or one former spouse to the other if the transfer is incident to divorce.[117]

[2] Imputed Interest Under Section 483

Section 483 generally applies to obligations issued in exchange for property that are not covered by Section 1274. Unlike Section 1274, Section 483 does not alter the timing of recognition of income or deductions. However, like Section 1274, it imputes interest on obligations that do not have a sufficient stated interest rate.

For purposes of the income and transfer taxes, in the case of any "applicable payment" under any contract for the sale or exchange of any property, that portion of the "total unstated interest" is allocable to the payment will be treated as interest.[118]

[a] Applicable Payments

The imputed interest rule generally applies to any payment on account of the sale or exchange of property that is (1) part or all of the sales price and (2) due more than six months after the date of sale, if some or all of the payments under the contract are due more than one year after the date of the sale.[119] A note from the purchaser is not generally considered payment; rather, payments pursuant to the note are the payments to which the imputed interest rule applies.[120] In other words, if any payment is due more than one year after the sale, and the stated interest rate is less than the AFR or other applicable discount rate, Section 483 will increase the portion of each payment that will be considered interest for federal tax purposes.

[b] Total Unstated Interest

"Total unstated interest" on a contract for the sale or exchange of property is the excess of the payments due under the contract (including interest

---

[116] IRC § 1274(c)(3)(E).

[117] Reg. § 1.1274-1(b)(3)(iii).

[118] IRC § 483(a).

[119] IRC § 483(c)(1).

[120] IRC § 483(c)(2). In a particular case, however, the constructive receipt doctrine could apply, such as the case of a demand note.

payments) over the sum of the present values of the payments.[121] The present value of any payment is determined using a discount rate equal to the AFR for the transaction.[122] The lowest AFR in effect for the month of sale and the two preceding months will be the AFR for the transaction.[123]

> **EXAMPLE:** Dad sells Blackacre to Daughter for a $2 million 10-year balloon note with no stated interest. If the AFR is 3 percent, the "total unstated interest" is $693,710. If more than one payment were made, the amount of interest allocable to each payment would be equal to the sum of the daily portions of the total unstated interest for each day during the taxable year on which Dad held the note.[124]

[c] Exceptions to Section 483's Imputed Interest Rules

Exceptions to the imputed interest rule of Section 483 apply to obligations arising in the following types of sale transactions:

- *Sale of publicly traded property.* The rules do not apply to a publicly traded debt instrument or a note issued in exchange for certain publicly traded property.[125]
- *Sale subject to Section 1274.* The rules do not apply to any debt instrument governed by Section 1274.[126]
- *De minimis sale.* If the sales price cannot exceed $3,000, the rules do not apply.[127]
- *Sale of personal property providing for carrying charges in lieu of interest.* If Mom sells Son personal property pursuant to a contract which provides for carrying charges, but not interest, a 6 percent interest rate will be imputed under Section 163(b), and Section 483 will not apply.[128] Carrying charges include finance charges, service charges, and the like.[129]
- *Sale of land to family member.* If Mom sells land to or exchanges land with a member of her family, then Section 483 applies, but the discount rate for determining the total imputed interest shall not exceed six per-

---

[121] IRC § 483(b).

[122] IRC § 483(b).

[123] IRC § 1274(d)(2).

[124] IRC §§ 483(a), 1272(a).

[125] IRC §§ 483(d)(1), 1273(b)(3).

[126] IRC § 483(d)(1). See ¶ 30.08[1].

[127] IRC § 483(d)(2).

[128] IRC §§ 163(b), 483(d)(3).

[129] Treas. Reg. § 1.163-2.

cent, compounded semiannually.[130] However, the six percent limit does not apply, and the general rules do apply, to the extent that the total sales price for the sale and all prior such sales made during the year exceeds $500,000.[131] If either Mom or the family member is a nonresident alien, the six percent limit does not apply at all.[132] A family member includes only Mom's brothers and sisters, husband, ancestors, and lineal descendants.[133]

- *Sale for annuity.* Section 72, rather than Section 483, applies to a sale for a private annuity which is treated as such for income tax purposes if the terms of the contract depend in whole or in substantial part on the life expectancy of one or more persons.[134]
- *Sale between spouses or between former spouses incident to divorce.*[135] Section 483 does not apply to any transfer of property subject to Section 1041.
- *Short term obligation.*[136] Section 483 does not apply to a note having a fixed maturity date of one year or less.
- *Sale made before 1985.*[137]

[3] Special Rules for Certain Obligations

[a] Qualified Debt Instruments—Notes Which Are Not Huge

A qualified debt instrument is any debt instrument given in exchange for property (other than new Section 38 property), if the stated principal amount of the note does not exceed $4,280,800.[138] "New Section 38 property" is property defined as such under Section 48(b) as it was in effect the day before the

---

[130] IRC §§ 483(e)(1), 483(e)(2).

[131] IRC § 483(e)(3).

[132] IRC § 483(e)(4).

[133] IRC §§ 267(c)(4), 483(e)(2).

[134] Reg. § 1.483-1(c)(3)(iv).

[135] Reg. § 1.483-1(c)(3)(i).

[136] IRC § 483(c)(1)(A).

[137] Pub. L. No. 98-369, § 41(b).

[138] This number applies for 2003, and is indexed for inflation. For current amount, see Appendix ¶ A.01, Table of Indexed Amounts, in supplement.

enactment of the Revenue Reconciliation Act of 1990, and is generally property which was eligible for the old investment tax credit.[139]

[i] Nine percent interest ceiling. The discount rate applied to a qualified debt instrument under Section 483 or Section 1274 will not exceed 9 percent, compounded semiannually.[140]

[ii] Election to use cash method. In the case of a qualified debt instrument that is a "cash method debt instrument," the taxpayers can elect that Section 1274[141] will not apply, and interest will be taken into account by both the lender and the borrower under the cash receipts and disbursements method of accounting.[142] This means that Section 483 will apply.[143]

A "cash method debt instrument" means any qualified debt instrument if (1) the stated principal amount does not exceed $3,057,700;[144] (2) the lender does not use an accrual method of accounting and is not a dealer in the property sold; (3) Section 1274 would have applied to the instrument but for the election; and (4) the election is jointly made by the borrower and the lender.[145] Any successor to the borrower or the lender is bound by this election unless the lender or a successor to the lender transfers it to a taxpayer who uses an accrual method of accounting. In that case, apparently the borrower could still use the cash method.[146]

Practice Pointer: As a practical matter, this provision will take many family transactions out of the application of Section 1274. Remember to make the election to report on the cash basis.

[iii] Aggregation of sales. For purposes of the special rules applicable to qualified debt instruments, all sales or exchanges that are part of the same transaction or a series of related transactions will be treated as one sale, and all debt instruments arising from the same transaction or a series of related transactions will be treated as one debt instrument.[147]

---

[139] IRC §§ 1274A(b), 1274A(d).

[140] IRC § 1274A(a).

[141] IRC §§ 1274A(b), 1274A(d).

[142] IRC § 1274A(c)(1).

[143] IRC § 483(d).

[144] The above amount, which is updated annually, applies for 2003. This number is indexed for inflation. For current amount, see Appendix ¶ A.01, Table of Indexed Amounts, in supplement.

[145] IRC § 1274A(c)(2).

[146] IRC § 1274A(c)(3).

[147] IRC § 1274A(d)(1).

[b] Sale-Leasebacks

In the case of any sale to which Section 1274 or Section 483 applies, if the seller or any related person leases the property after the sale pursuant to a plan, the discount rate will be 110 percent of the AFR.[148] A note issued in connection with such a transaction is not eligible for the "cash method debt instruments" exception to Section 1274 for cash method debt instruments.[149]

[c] Sale of Personal Use Property

If Mom sells Blackacre to Son for a note, and Blackacre is personal use property in the hands of Son, Sections 1274 and 483 will not apply to Son.[150] They will apply to Mom, however. This means that Son may not get interest deductions in the same amount as, or at the same time as, Mom recognizes interest income.

Property is personal use property unless substantially all of its use is in connection with Son's trade or business or in connection with the production of income. Whether property is personal use property is determined at the time of the sale.[151]

[4] Path to Determine Taxation of Deferred Payment Obligations

The rules on deferred payment obligations can seem a trackless jungle. Here is a trail to follow to determine what rules apply to a particular obligation. Where dollar limitations apply, related transactions may be aggregated.

[a] Transactions for Which Obligations Are Not Subject to Either Section 1274 or Section 483

The obligations arising in the following transactions are not subject to either Section 1274 or Section 483:

- Sale for $3,000 or less.[152]
- Sale of personal property where carrying charges are stated separately, but interest is not ascertainable.[153] Section 163(b) applies, and imputes interest at 6 percent.

---

[148] IRC § 1274(e).

[149] Reg. § 1.1274A-1(b)(1).

[150] IRC § 1275(b)(1).

[151] IRC § 1275(b)(1).

[152] IRC § 483(d)(2).

[153] IRC §§ 163(b), 483(d)(3).

- Sale between spouses or between former spouses incident to divorce.[154]
- Sale for an annuity governed by Section 72 and determined by human life expectancy.[155]
- Sale for short term obligation.[156]

[b] Obligations Subject to Section 483

Section 483 imputes interest at lowest of three-month AFRs, except as specifically noted below. Section 483 affects the allocation of a payment between principal and interest. It does not impute interest income at a time other than actual payment dates for a cash method taxpayer. It governs deferred payment arrangements under the following transactions, other than those excepted under subsection ¶ 3.08[4][a] above:

- Sale of a farm or small business for $1 million or less by an individual, estate, testamentary trust, or certain entities.[157]
- Sale of principal residence.[158]
- Sale of any property where all payments under the contract (including principal and interest) and other consideration total $250,000 or less.[159]
- Sale made before 1985.[160]
- Sale for obligation in which the stated principal amount is $3,057,700[161] or less, certain other requirements are met, and the borrower and lender jointly elect.[162]
- Sale of land between related parties. Maximum interest rate imputed is six percent. Applies to sale of land between family members, to the extent that the sale price of all such sales made in the year does not exceed $500,000.[163]
- Sale for note bearing stated interest at the applicable discount rate, compounded or paid at least annually.[164]

---

[154] Reg. § 1.483-1(c)(3)(iii).

[155] Reg. § 1.483-1(c)(3)(iv).

[156] IRC §§ 483(c)(1)(A), 1274(c)(1)(B).

[157] IRC § 1274(c)(3)(A).

[158] IRC § 1274(c)(3)(B).

[159] IRC § 1274(c)(3)(C).

[160] Pub. L. No. 98-369 § 41(b).

[161] Rev. Rul. 2002-79, 2002-48 IRB 908. The above amount, which is updated annually, applies for 2003. For current amount, see Appendix ¶ A.01, Table of Indexed Amounts, this supplement.

[162] IRC § 1274A.

[163] IRC §§ 483(e), 1274(c)(3)(F).

[164] Reg. § 1.483-1(a)(1).

- Transfers between husband and wife or between ex-spouses incident to divorce.[165]

Special interest rates. In addition to the above exclusion, certain special interest rates apply. First, if stated principal amount of obligation is $4,280,800[166] or less, and the property is not new Section 38 property (as specially defined), the maximum imputed interest/discount rate is nine percent, compounded semiannually.[167] Second, if a note is issued in connection with a sale-leaseback, interest is imputed at 110 percent of the AFR.

[c] Obligations Subject to Section 1274

Section 1274 applies to any obligation other than those described in ¶ 3.08[4][a] or ¶ 3.08[4][b] above. It imputes interest at lowest of three-month AFRs and effectively puts the taxpayers on the accrual basis with respect to interest on the obligation. The following special rules apply:

- *Sale of personal use property.* Section 1274 applies to lender only.[168]
- *Smaller obligations.* If stated principal amount of obligation is $4,280,800[169] or less, and the property is not new Section 38 property (as specially defined), the maximum imputed interest/discount rate is nine percent, compounded semiannually.[170]
- *Sale-leasebacks.* If a note is issued in connection with a sale-leaseback with a related party, interest is imputed at 110 percent of the AFR.

¶ 30.09 GIFT TAX ASPECTS OF SALES FOR DEFERRED PAYMENTS

For purposes of determining whether a sale for deferred payments constitutes a gift, the value of the payments to be received is compared to the value of the property sold. If the property is worth more than the value of the payments, a gift ordinarily occurs.

---

[165] Reg. § 1.483-1(c)(2).

[166] The above amount, which is updated annually, applies for 2003. For current amount, see Appendix ¶ A.01, Table of Indexed Amounts, this supplement.

[167] IRC § 1274A.

[168] IRC § 1275(b)(1).

[169] For indexed amounts for 2002 and thereafter, see Appendix ¶ A.01, Table of Indexed Amounts, this supplement.

[170] IRC § 1274A.

Does the fact that a below-fair-market value interest rate is adequate to meet a safe harbor from imputed interest for income tax purposes mean that the rate is adequate to protect it from resulting in a gift for gift tax purposes? Most courts that have addressed the issue have said "no."[171] So, for purposes of determining the present value of the payments for transfer tax purposes, does an actual fair market value discount rate (rather than the AFR) have to be used? Many practitioners believe that the AFR (or other applicable discount rate) is sufficient, and the IRS has taken that position at least twice.[172] The AFR would be sufficient to avoid gift tax treatment (at least as a result of the interest rate) in the case of a note that is not issued in exchange for property.[173] However, unlike Section 7872, Sections 1274 and 483 have no direct application to valuation of notes for gift tax purposes, other than to characterize what amounts constitute principal and interest.

Proposed regulations on the subject of related party transactions where the value of the property and the value of the note are not the same were issued in 1986.[174] However, these did not apply in a part-gift/part-sale context.[175]

¶ 30.10 SALE TO INTENTIONALLY DEFECTIVE GRANTOR TRUST

An intentionally defective grantor trust (IDGT) is a trust that is treated as owned by the grantor for income tax purposes, but not for gift or estate tax purposes. Sales to IDGTs have a number of uses in estate planning.

[1] Estate Freezing

A sale of property to an IDGT for a note is a very popular estate freezing device. Here's how it works.

---

[171] Schusterman v. United States, 63 F3d 986 (10th Cir. 1995), cert. denied, 517 US 1208 (1996), aff'g 1994 US Dist. LEXIS 2773 (ND Okla. 1994); Krabbenhoft v. Comm'r, 939 F2d 529 (8th Cir. 1991), cert. denied, 112 S. Ct. 967 (1992); Frazee v. Comm'r, 98 TC 554 (1992). Contra Ballard v. Comm'r, 854 F2d 185 (7th Cir. 1988), rev'g 1987 PH TC Memo. ¶ 87,128, 53 TCM (CCH) 323 (1987).

[172] Frazee v. Comm'r, 98 TC 554 (1992); Priv. Ltr. Rul. 9535026 (May 31, 1995).

[173] IRC §§ 7872, 7820.

[174] Prop. Reg. § 1.1012-2.

[175] Prop. Reg. § 1.1012-2(a).

Dad sells property to an IDGT for a note. Because the IDGT is a grantor trust, Dad realizes no gain on the sale or income from the interest payments.[176] Dad does continue to pay income tax directly on the income of the trust. The appreciation on and income from[177] the assets from date of sale are removed from Dad's estate.

> **EXAMPLE:** Dad transfers ownership of Redacre (which is worth $1 million and has a zero basis) to a partnership, which has a corporate entity as the one percent general partner and himself as the 99 percent limited partner. He also gives $75,000 to a grantor trust for his grandchildren, and then sells the trust his 99 percent limited partnership interests for a note. The purchase price is $750,000 (the appraised value of the limited partnership interests, after discounting). Principal and interest are payable in a balloon at the end of nine years. Interest is payable at the mid-term AFR. Dad allocates $75,000 of his generation-skipping transfer tax exemption to the trust.
>
> Nine years later, Redacre is worth $3 million. The partnership either sells Redacre or borrows against it and distributes $1 million principal plus accrued interest on the note to the trust. (For simplicity, assume that Redacre earned exactly enough income to pay Dad's interest on the note.)
>
> After the trust pays off Dad's note, it owns a partnership interest worth approximately $1,500,000 (at the same discount that was applied originally), with underlying assets worth $2 million. Dad pays income tax on the gain from the sale of Redacre, or gets a deduction for the interest incurred on its mortgage, since the trust is a grantor trust. Redacre has a carryover basis of zero for the same reason. The OID rules, which might ordinarily apply in this situation to impute interest on a current basis, do not apply because the trust is a grantor trust. The only transfer tax that has been paid is the gift tax, if any, on the seed gift of $75,000.

Why a grantor trust? Of course, any installment sale can be useful as an estate freeze. The beneficial features that the grantor trust adds are that it (1) avoids gain on the intra-family sale and income tax on the interest and (2) allows Dad to pay income tax on the trust's income without gift tax consequences.

Why the seed gift of $75,000 in the above EXAMPLE? Many practitioners like to see at least a 10 percent cushion in the trust, to help avoid characterization of the note as a retained interest in the trust. Many practitioners also like to see interest payments made annually for the same reason. If the note is characterized as a retained interest, then the rules of Section 2702 will apply. Those rules will treat the entire loan as a gift, unless the note is structured as a

---

[176] Rev. Rul. 85-13, 1985-1 CB 184; but see Rothstein v. United States, 735 F2d 704 (2d Cir. 1984).

[177] To the extent that the grantor does not retain a reimbursement right for income tax paid on income that he did not receive.

qualified annuity, in which case the GRAT rules will apply. Additionally, if Dad dies within the term of the note, the assets transferred in exchange for the note may be included in his estate under Section 2036. Hence, care needs to be taken that the note constitutes real debt, and not a retained interest.[178]

What if Dad dies during the term of the note? Unless the note is a SCIN, it will be included in Dad's estate at fair market value, which is presumed to be the face amount plus accrued interest.[179] Because the trust assets are not included in Dad's estate, the basis of the partnership interests held by the trust will not change to fair market value at Dad's death.

The continuing income tax consequences are unclear. When the trust ceases to be a grantor trust at Dad's death, it may be treated for income tax purposes as if Dad had transferred the partnership interests to the trust at that point.[180] Thus, prospective treatment of the remaining transaction as an installment sale may be appropriate.

Some think that the installment note receives no basis step-up in Dad's estate, because it is a right to receive income in respect of a decedent. If so, the remaining payments will be treated as capital gain and interest income to Dad's estate as they are received, and the trust will probably receive a cost basis in the partnership interests when Dad dies equal to its remaining principal obligations (in this case $750,000).

Others believe that, because the note is not recognized as having existed before Dad's death for income tax purposes, the note should not be characterized for income tax purposes as an installment note owned by Dad, and, therefore, the basis of the note should change to date-of-death value and should be treated as originally acquired by the estate on the date of death. Assuming that date-of-death value is the face amount of the note plus interest, the consequence would be that neither Dad nor his estate would recognize income as a result of the sale, except to the extent of interest earned after Dad's death. Additionally, the trust may receive a cost basis in the assets, presumably in the amount of principal remaining on the note.

Other opinions exist, however. No one knows for sure what the answers will be, and it may be prudent, if practicable, to pay the note off before Dad's death.

---

[178] A discussion of when a receivable from a trust constitutes a retained interest rather than debt is contained in Chapter 23 on private annuities.

[179] Treas. Reg. § 20.2031-4.

[180] Rev. Rul. 77-402, 1977-2 CB 222; Madorin v. Comm'r, 84 TC 667 (1985).

[2] Tax-Free Liquidity for Grantor

The cash and other readily marketable assets received by Dad as a result of sale to an IDGT constitute tax-free liquidity for Dad. He has frozen the value of the assets for estate tax purposes and received cash or other liquid assets without paying capital gains tax. Of course, if the trust sells the underlying assets, the gain will be recognized directly by Dad.

[3] Tax-Free Basis Step-Up for Appreciated Property Held in Trust

What if Dad plans to leave his estate to charity or in an otherwise nontaxable manner, and the IDGT holds appreciated property? Because the IDGT is not includable in the grantor's estate, the trust assets would not normally receive a step-up in basis on Dad's death. However, if the trust sells the property to Dad for cash, no gain will be recognized, but the appreciated assets will receive a new basis in Dad's estate. So, a step-up in basis is achieved with no income tax consequences.

[4] Comparison Between Sale to IDGT and GRAT

The GRAT[181] and the sale to an IDGT are both popular estate freezing devices. A comparison of their features follows.

[a] Estate Tax

GRAT. If the transferor survives the retained interest term, the transferred property is out of the estate. If the transferor dies during the term, all or part of the property may be included. Property returned to the transferor as an annuity is includable in the transferor's estate if he still has it when he dies.

Sale to IDGT. Transferred property is out of the estate immediately. If the transferor dies before the note is paid, the note is includable in the transferor's estate. Payments made pursuant to the note while the transferor is alive are included in the transferor's estate, if he still has them.

---

[181] See Chapter 22 for discussion of GRATs.

[b] Gift Tax

GRAT. No gift (or almost no gift) if the annuity is high enough.[182]

Sale to IDGT. No gift is made if the sale is for fair market value and interest is payable at (at least) the AFR. An initial seed gift to the trust may be desirable, however.

[c] Income Tax

GRAT. No sale takes place. Transferor is taxable on entire income of trust during the term. After the GRAT term, beneficiaries take a carryover basis in the assets (unless the transaction is deemed a sale as described below). If the transferor dies during the term, beneficiaries take an estate-tax-value basis in the assets. If mortgaged property exists in the GRAT at the end of the GRAT term, the IRS will treat the termination of the GRAT as a sale for the amount of the remaining unpaid balance of the mortgage debt.[183]

Sale to IDGT. No sale is recognized as long as the trust remains a grantor trust. If the seller dies before the note is paid, the income tax consequences are not altogether certain. The worst possibility is probably that the trust takes a cost basis in the assets in the amount of the outstanding principal at date of death and the seller's estate recognizes gain (if any) on the remaining payments.

[d] Generation-Skipping Transfer Tax

GRAT. The exemption cannot be allocated until the end of the estate tax inclusion period (ordinarily the GRAT term).

Sale to IDGT. The exemption can be allocated immediately.

[e] Actuarial Values Used for Discounting

GRAT. The annuity is discounted at the Section 7520 rate.

Sale to IDGT. The installment note payments are discounted at the AFR for the note term. This will be a more favorable rate than the Section 7520 rate unless the note is for more than nine years and the long-term AFR is more than 120 percent of the mid-term AFR.

---

[182] The IRS will not rule on a GRAT if (1) the amount of the annuity is more than 50 percent of the initial fair market value of the property transferred to the trust or (2) the present value of the remainder interest is less than 10 percent of the initial net fair market value. Rev. Proc. 2002-3, 2002-1 IRB 117, § 4.01(51).

[183] Tech. Adv. Mem. 200010010 (Nov. 23, 1999); Priv. Ltr. Rul. 200011005 (Mar. 17, 2000).

[f] Payment to Transferor in Kind

GRAT. The annuity payment can be made with appreciated property with no income tax consequences.

Sale to IDGT. The note payments can be made with appreciated property with no consequences as long as the trust is a grantor trust. If the seller dies before the note is paid, further payments in kind with appreciated property will generate gain to the trust. The trust's basis in the assets will be a carryover basis while the trust is a grantor trust; thereafter, basis will probably be related to its post-grantor-trust cost.

[g] Backloading Payments

GRAT. The annual payment can only increase at the rate of 20 percent per year.

Sale to IDGT. Payments of principal and interest can be backloaded.

[h] Flexibility in Distributions

GRAT. The only permissible distributee during the GRAT term is the owner of the retained interest.

Sale to IDGT. Distributions can be made to all permitted beneficiaries under the trust instrument.

[i] Valuation Adjustment Clause

If the property transferred to the GRAT or IDGT is not susceptible of precise valuation, its value as finally determined for transfer tax purposes may ultimately be different from the value returned. To what extent can the transferor protect against an additional gift as a result of a revaluation?

GRAT. A GRAT can have a valuation adjustment clause. Thus, if the annuity is determined as a percentage of value of the property contributed, the annuity can (and indeed must) be adjusted to reflect the revaluation, thus increasing the annuity, but leaving the amount of gift the same.

Sale to IDGT. The tax effect of a formula designed to reflect a purchase price adjusted to reflect value as finally determined for transfer tax purposes is not clear. Thus, the possibility that a court would determine an increased gift on revaluation exists.

[j] General Thoughts on GRAT vs. IDGT

If the note is paid before the seller dies, the sale to the IDGT can generally produce results superior to the GRAT. However, if the seller dies before the trust assets have had a chance to appreciate, and the note does not receive a step-up in basis, the sale to the IDGT can actually be worse than doing nothing because the value of the assets at date of sale is included in the seller's estate (via the value of the note or payments), but gain (measured by the seller's basis) may still be recognized.

> **EXAMPLE:** Mom owns Asset worth $100, with a basis of zero. Mom dies in 2003. She has estate tax of $49 on Asset, and Asset takes a new basis of $100. If her executor sells the assets the day after she dies, there is no capital gains tax. If, however, Mom sells Asset for $100 cash the day before she dies, she has capital gains tax of $15 and still has estate tax of $42 (that is, 49% of ($100-$15)) on the after-tax cash. Generally, if the note does not receive a stepped-up basis, the Asset must increase in value or earn after-tax income before the transferor's death by an amount equal to the capital gains tax that would have been imposed if the property had been sold in a taxable transaction on date of sale (adjusted for estate tax benefit of deducting the capital gains tax from the estate) to the IDGT in order for the sale to the IDGT to be better than doing nothing.

What are the chances of the whole transaction cratering in either case? In a properly drafted GRAT, the chances should be small because the GRAT is a technique expressly permitted by statute and regulations. The sale to the IDGT, however, rests on the application of general rules. A sale to an IDGT has not been tested in court, except in the *Rothstein*[184] case (involving a purchase by a grantor from his grantor trust), in which the Second Circuit held that an installment sale between a grantor and a grantor trust should be recognized for purposes of determining the grantor's cost basis in the assets he purchased from the grantor trust, and his interest deduction for interest on the installment payments made to the trust. The sale-to-IDGT technique largely relies on the IRS's own determination that transactions between a grantor and grantor trust will not be recognized. The IRS should be bound by its own published ruling; however, because (unlike the GRAT) there is no specific authority regarding the taxation of the transaction as a whole, there is always a chance that an unexpected interpretation of the rules will prevail.

Additionally, if the IRS withdraws its ruling,[185] then the *Rothstein*[186] case would support a position that the income tax items of both the trust and the seller would be reported on the seller's return. Then, the seller would recognize gain, and the interest income/deduction items of the seller and the trust may or may not offset each other, depending on other facts in the seller's income tax picture.

---

[184] Rothstein v. United States, 735 F2d 704 (2d Cir. 1984), rev'g 574 F. Supp. 19 (D. Conn. 1983).

[185] Rev. Rul. 85-13, 1985-1 CB 184.

[186] Rothstein v. United States, 735 F2d 704 (2d Cir. 1984).

¶ 30.11 RECHARACTERIZATION OF SALE OR NOTE

If a sale is not entered into on normal third-party terms, the IRS may attempt to recharacterize it.[187]

A successful sale to an entity depends on the proper characterization of the note as a debt. If the note from the entity is recharacterized as a retained interest, then the assets (rather than the note) will be included in the seller's estate, and a gift pursuant to Section 2702 will be made unless the note is structured as a qualified annuity.

¶ 30.12 REFINANCE OF NOTE

As the AFR decreases, it is common to refinance installment notes to reflect the lower rate. Such a transaction should be supported by consideration where consideration is required under state law to make the contract enforceable. Additionally, consideration may be useful to counter any argument by the IRS that the refinance constitutes a gift. Consideration supporting a refinance at a lower rate might include shortening the term of the note. Generally speaking, refinances at a fair market rate do not constitute gifts if prepayment is allowed, under the theory that the borrower could go out and borrow the money at a lower rate to prepay the current lender. It may be that the refinance will not constitute a gift as long as the new interest rate is at least the new AFR. On the other hand, the refinance might be deemed a gift if the value of the new rate is less than the value of the old rate and the borrower could not, in actuality, have borrowed the money from an outside source and repaid the note?

In any case, the exchange of one note for another is a taxable exchange under Section 1001.

---

[187] See, for example, Estate of Brown v. Comm'r, TC Memo. 1997-195, in which the IRS tried to recharacterize an installment sale as a transfer with a retained interest, causing estate tax inclusion under IRC § 2036. Decedent had sold shares of stock to an unrelated shareholder for a note payable at the end of ten years. The purchaser granted Decedent's sons the right to purchase the stock at the end of the year for a fixed price (which was less than the price paid by purchaser to Decedent), reduced by any outstanding balance of principal and interest on the note. Decedent and his sons took a security interest in the stock. Decedent retained the right to vote the shares for the entire ten-year period. The Tax Court first held that the purchase of the Decedent's stock was for adequate and full consideration. It also refused to characterize the interest of the sons under the option agreement as a retained interest retained by the Decedent. The IRS argued that the sons were certain to exercise the option, given its fixed, and low, purchase price, but the court said that the option price would be lower than the stock's value at the end of the ten-year period. The Tax Court added, sua sponte, that since the IRS did not contend that the Decedent made a constructive gift to his sons in 1993 by virtue of the purchaser's grant of the purchase option, the court did not need to decide that issue.

¶ 30.13 EXTENSION OF NOTE

Sometimes, a principal (or interest) payment comes due, and it is inconvenient to pay it. In such a case, the parties may extend the due date. If an installment note is to be extended, the extension should occur before the note is due. If the note is extended after the payment is due and the obligor could have made arrangements to pay the amount due, the obligee may be in constructive receipt of the amount due.[188]

---

[188] Boccardo v. Comm'r, 164 F3d 629, 82 AFTR2d 98-6794 (9th Cir. 1998) (unpublished opinion).

CHAPTER **31**

Preferred Equity Interests

A. General

¶ 31.01 INTRODUCTION

In the 1970s and 1980s, estate freezing with preferred equity interests was fashionable. The technique involved structuring family-owned entities so that senior family members owned preferred equity interests that were frozen in value and younger members owned growth interests. The technique can still be used in some circumstances.

> **EXAMPLE:** Dad owns preferred stock. The stock has a preferred dividend of three percent per year, and a liquidation preference. Dad owns none of the common stock. Structuring the ownership in this manner will result in the value of Dad's interest increasing very little or not at all as the business increases in value. If the business doubles in value, Dad's interest will not double. If the children own the common stock, they will receive the bulk of the increase in the value of the corporation.

Preferred equity interests were formerly such a popular estate planning technique that in 1990, Congress passed Section 2701, which drastically limited the utility of preferred equity interests as estate freezing devices. Although the preferred equity interest will still successfully freeze the value of the preferred interest for estate tax purposes, the new law imposes severe gift taxes along the way.

¶ 31.02 NONTECHNICAL EXPLANATION—SECTION 2701

Let's examine the once-common recapitalization technique.

GLOBAL EXAMPLE

Dad owns all of the stock of a corporation. Under prior law, he could recapitalize the corporation into preferred stock and common stock. He would retain the preferred stock himself and give the common stock to Junior or sell it to Junior for fair market value. The preferred stock would carry various rights that Dad never intended to exercise,[1] thus inflating the value of Dad's preferred interest and reducing the value of the common stock transferred to Junior to a small amount, or even to zero. The recapitalization was done because the company was expected to grow in value. The purpose was that all of the growth would be reflected in the increased value of Junior's common stock, with the value of Dad's stock changing little, if at all.

---

[1] For example, the right to liquidate the entity for the value of his stock, the right to receive noncumulative preferred dividends, the right to control the entity if a dividend was not declared, the right to sell ("put") his stock to the company for its par value, and the right to convert his preferred stock to common stock.

Under the Internal Revenue Code's gift tax provisions, the transfer of common stock could be held to be a gift, but only to the extent that there was actual value transferred to Junior in excess of any consideration paid.[2] How will this technique now work under Section 2701? Section 2701 primarily affects the valuation of the common stock transferred to Junior. It applies special rules for valuing Dad's preferred stock, which in turn affects the value of the common stock Junior receives.

[1] Rights Valued at Zero

Under Section 2701, certain rights retained by Dad (in the Global Example)—liquidation, put, call, and conversion rights, as well as certain rights to dividends—are generally valued at zero, and therefore will not reduce the value of the common stock transferred to Junior for gift tax purposes.[3]

[2] Qualified Payment Rights

Section 2701 provides that Dad's dividend rights (in the Global Example) will only be given value if they are "qualified payment rights," meaning that they entitle Dad to receive a fixed amount on a periodic basis.[4] For example, if Dad owned stock which entitled him to receive an annual, cumulative dividend of eight percent and the stock had certain other features, Dad's right to receive the dividend would be a qualified payment right, and would be valued at its fair market value in determining the total value of Dad's preferred stock and Junior's common stock.

[3] Hybrid Interests

If qualified payment rights are held in conjunction with liquidation, put, call, or conversion rights, the qualified payment rights are not necessarily given fair market value. Rather, Junior's common stock will be valued as if the liquidation, put, call, or conversion rights were exercised in the manner giving the lowest value for Dad's preferred stock.[5]

If Dad has a right to liquidate the company, that right will not be considered in valuing the common stock transferred to Junior. If Dad has a

---

[2] Estate of Trenchard v. Comm'r, 1995 RIA TC Memo. ¶ 95,121, 69 TCM (CCH) 2164 (1995).

[3] IRC §§ 2701(a)(1), 2701(a)(3), 2701(b)(1).

[4] IRC §§ 2701(a)(3)(A), 2701(c)(3)(A).

[5] IRC § 2701(a)(3)(B).

right to noncumulative dividends of $10/share, this right will be treated as valueless for purposes of determining what Junior's interest is worth.[6] If Dad has a right to cumulative dividends payable at least annually, and his preferred stock carries certain other rights protecting its value, the value of the right to receive those dividends will be recognized.[7] What if Dad has a right to receive cumulative dividends and the right to sell his stock to the company at any time for $100? Dad's stock will be valued at the lesser of $100 or the value of his cumulative dividend right.

Note that the hybrid interest rule could apply where the family owners collectively have the ability to compel the entity to liquidate, even where no family member alone has a right to compel liquidation of his interest.[8]

[4] Elections

If, in the Global Example, Dad has dividend rights that are not qualified, he may elect to have them treated as qualified payment rights, so they will be given value. Similarly, Dad may elect to treat qualified payment rights as if they were not qualified.[9] This may be desirable if there are doubts as to whether the company will be able to pay dividends as scheduled.

[5] Qualified Payments Which Are Not Made

Where qualified payment rights exist and the payments are not made, Section 2701 generally provides that after a four-year grace period, accumulated unpaid dividends will be deemed to have been paid to Dad and reinvested by him at the 7520 rate.[10] Moreover, the value of the compounded unpaid dividends will be added to the value of the transfer when a gift or bequest of the interest is subsequently made.[11] The consequences of this can be severe.

EXAMPLE: Mom owns 1,000 shares of $1.00 par value preferred stock, which carries a right to receive an annual cumulative dividend of 10 percent. Mom transfers common stock to Daughter and allows her preferred dividend right to be treated as qualified by not making an election to the contrary. The 7520 rate at the time of the transfer is 8 percent. Five years later, Mom dies. None of Mom's dividends have been paid. Mom's

---

[6] Unless Dad makes the special election described in ¶ 31.10[3][d][ii] below.

[7] Unless Dad elects otherwise.

[8] See Treas. Reg. § 25.2701-2(d), examples 3, 4. HR Rep., Small Business Jobs Protection Act of 1996, saying that Treasury Regulations may so provide.

[9] IRC § 2701(c)(3)(C).

[10] The "7520 rate" is 120 percent of the applicable federal midterm rate, rounded to the nearest 2/10 ths of one percent. IRC § 7520.

[11] IRC § 2701(d).

stock will be valued in her estate at its actual value, plus $634 (the amount that Mom would have had if the dividends had been paid on time and reinvested for an 8 percent yield).

[6] Subtraction Method

Section 2701 requires use of the subtraction method in valuing the common stock transferred to Junior.[12] In the Global Example, this method requires subtraction of the value of Dad's preferred stock from the value of the entity as a whole and treatment of the remaining value of the entity as the value of the common stock.

Suppose the value of the entire company owned is $1,000. Dad's preferred stock is specially valued for purposes of Section 2701 at $400 and the common stock is actually worth $300. In this case, the value of the whole is more than the sum of the parts. The normal method of valuing interests in entities for transfer tax purposes, which includes valuation discounts,[13] recognizes this. Under the subtraction method required by Section 2701, if Dad transfers all of the common stock to Junior, the common stock cannot be valued at its actual $300 value. Rather, the value of the entire entity ($1,000) is determined, the special value of Dad's preferred stock ($400) is subtracted, and the stock transferred to Junior is valued at $600 (twice its real value).

Note that the mandatory use of the subtraction method is enough to make preferred equity freezing techniques undesirable in most family situations.

[7] When Are Preferred Equity Freezes Appropriate?

Preferred equity interests are rarely a great idea, if an alternative is available. Aside from the problems with compounding on unpaid distributions, the applicable federal rate is not available as a safe harbor interest rate in valuing qualified payments,[14] and the subtraction method, which will usually give an unrealistically high value to transferred property, appears to be mandatory.[15]

If no alternative is reasonably available, traditional freezes may still be viable. However, because Section 2701 requires that most aspects giving value to preferred interests be ignored, the preferred interest must carry a relatively

---

[12] Treas. Reg. §§ 25.2701-1(a)(2), 25.2701-3(a)(1).

[13] Discussed in Ch. 25.

[14] See Priv. Ltr. Rul. 9324018 (Mar. 19, 1993) (holding that in determining the value of a dividend stream in perpetuity, use of a discount factor based on the 7520 rate is rarely valid when a corporation is closely held).

[15] Treas. Reg. §§ 25.2701-1(a)(2), 25.2701-3(a)(1).

high yield to avoid making a gift altogether.[16] The following guidelines are helpful in assessing the efficacy of a traditional freeze:

- If the preferred interest can carry a market dividend rate, the freeze can be accomplished with no gift.

  EXAMPLE: Father owns 100 shares of common stock and 1,000 shares of preferred stock in Corporation. Corporation is worth $10,000. Father's preferred stock is non-voting and carries a qualified payment right to receive a 10 percent dividend annually, which Corporation is able to pay. The preferred stock carries no liquidation preference, put, or conversion rights. Father transfers his common stock to Daughter at a time when the appropriate market discount rate is 10 percent. Father's transfer of common stock to Daughter may not result in a gift.

- If the preferred interest carries a below-market dividend rate, a freeze can still be accomplished. The gift tax value of the common interest will be increased, but future appreciation will be excluded from the transferor's estate.

  EXAMPLE: Assume the same facts as the preceding example, except that the preferred stock pays only an 8 percent dividend. Father's transfer of common stock to Daughter will be a gift. However, Daughter will enjoy the benefit of future appreciation in the stock.

- If the preferred interest does not carry a qualified payment right or if the transferor elects out of qualified payment treatment, the rules regarding unpaid distributions and compounding can be avoided. This structure might be ideal for a start-up entity, when the value of the entire entity may be very low.

  EXAMPLE: Father transfers $10,000 to Newco, retaining preferred stock which is valued at zero under Section 2701 and transferring common stock to Daughter. Father has made a $10,000 gift to Daughter; however, future appreciation of Newco should not be in Father's estate.

[8] Conclusion

Section 2701 does away with the usefulness of the preferred equity freeze in most instances. Consequently, the nontechnical explanation of this technique will not go into more detail. The technical explanation at ¶ 31.07, et seq. can be consulted for further details.

---

[16] Although voting rights with respect to preferred stock, where given, will undoubtedly have some value, transfers of common stock are still likely to result in some gift where the other rights with respect to the preferred stock are ignored.

¶ 31.03 REVERSE FREEZES

Reverse freezes have potential. The reverse freeze is like the old, pre-Section 2701 freezing technique, except that Dad owns the common stock and Junior owns the preferred. The preferred interest will have a high dividend rate, to reflect the fact that few people would pay for it, at any price. The common stock would have all of the bells and whistles that were given to preferred stock in the old days.[17] Section 2701 will not apply, since no one in the older generation will retain a preferred interest.

In a reverse freeze situation, Dad, who owns all of the stock of the corporation, causes the corporate stock to be recapitalized into preferred and common. Dad retains the common stock, which carries a right to liquidate the corporation for its then current value. He gives the preferred stock to Junior. The preferred has a 15 percent dividend rate. If Dad liquidated the corporation today, Junior would get nothing, so arguably the gift to him is valued at zero, or some very low number. As Junior's stock earns 15 percent per year, growth/income is transferred to Junior free of additional gift tax. If the company's value grows 15 percent per year, on Dad's death, his common stock will be frozen at its original value.

NOTE: To accomplish a reverse freeze in the corporate context, a C corporation is required. This is because an S corporation cannot have more than one class of stock.

Partnership reverse freezes. If the entity is a partnership, and Dad receives a share of income from the partnership which is less than his proportionate share of capital, after taking into account compensation for services rendered to the entity by both partners, Dad will nevertheless be taxed for income tax purposes on the income attributable to his proportionate share of capital.[18] The effect of this is similar to the establishment of a defective grantor trust—Dad will pay tax on income that goes to Junior. As long as this does not cause Dad a cash problem, Dad will make gift-tax-free payments that benefit Junior each year.

EXAMPLE: Dad owns a 50 percent capital interest in Partnership (value of $500,000) and Junior owns the other 50 percent interest ($500,000). Partnership earns $150,000. Junior is allocated all of the income, due to his 15 percent preferred interest. However, Dad will pay income tax on one-half of the income, or $75,000.

Note that the reverse freeze is an interesting idea, although it seems to be discussed much more than it is actually done.

---

[17] See n. 1 above.

[18] IRC § 704(e)(2).

¶ 31.04 USE OF GRANDFATHERED ENTITIES

Transfers that took place before October 9, 1990, are exempt from the application of Section 2701.[19] Subsequent transfers of interests in entities which existed on October 9, 1990 or were created thereafter, are subject to Section 2701; recapitalizations, capital contributions, and redemptions with respect to an equity interest may be deemed transfers for this purpose.[20]

Certain opportunities to use grandfathered entities for freezing nevertheless continue to exist. If Dad has an appreciating asset, for example, he might sell his interest in the asset for fair market value to a previously "frozen" entity for fair consideration. Then, the asset could continue to appreciate in the frozen entity with Junior, as the common stock owner, enjoying most of the benefit of that appreciation.

With respect to property transferred before October 9, 1990, a failure to exercise a right of conversion, pay a dividend, or exercise other rights specified in regulations is not treated as a subsequent transfer subject to Section 2701.[21] This implies that where a post-effective date transfer is made, the failure to exercise rights that were given value in determining any gift may be treated as a taxable transfer, for purposes of Section 2701, if not for normal gift tax purposes.

¶ 31.05 NON-EXERCISE OF RIGHTS: DEEMED GIFT?

One issue that arises with freeze-style entities is the consequence of the non-exercise of a right. For example, if Dad, the noncumulative preferred shareholder, is in control of the corporation, and does not declare a dividend, has he made a gift to the common shareholder in the amount that he could have taken out of the corporation?[22] If Dad could convert his preferred shares to common, and does not, has he made a gift?[23]

---

[19] Omnibus Budget Reconciliation Act of 1990, Pub. L. No. 101-508, § 11602(e)(1), 104 Stat. 1383 (1990) (OBRA).

[20] IRC § 2701(e)(5).

[21] OBRA 11602(e)(1)(B).

[22] See Tech. Adv. Mem. 8723007 (Feb. 18, 1987) (citing Dickman v. Comm'r, 465 US 330 (1984), in support); see also Tech. Adv. Mem. 9301001 (June 30, 1992).

[23] See Snyder v. Comm'r, 93 TC 529 (1989); see also Tech. Adv. Mem. 9420001 (Dec. 15, 1993) (failure of common stockholder to prevent preferred stockholders from converting their shares was gift); Tech. Adv. Mem. 9301001 (June 30, 1992); Daniels v. Comm'r, 1994 RIA TC Memo. ¶ 94,591, 68 TCM (CCH) 1310 (1994) (failure of controlling shareholder to declare dividends on his preferred stock was not a constructive gift by the preferred shareholder or a constructive dividend to the common shareholders where corporation needed the funds for business purposes and did actually use the funds to meet its business needs).

¶ 31.06 FIXED PAYMENT OBLIGATIONS

Leases, employment contracts, installment sales, private annuities, regular notes, and self-canceling installment notes are not covered by Section 2701, as long as they are what they purport to be.[24] If they are actually disguised preferred equity interests, then creation of such rights may cause a transfer to be subject to Section 2701.

B. Technical Explanation

¶ 31.07 IN GENERAL

Section 2701 was added to the Internal Revenue Code in 1990; at the same time, old Section 2036(c) was repealed.[25] Final regulations were adopted effective as of January 28, 1992.[26] Additional regulations were adopted effective as of May 4, 1994.[27]

Under Section 2701, special valuation rules are applied to determine whether a gift arose on the transfer of an interest in a corporation or partnership to or for the benefit of a "member of the transferor's family," as well as the value of the transfer. In particular, the value of any "applicable retained interest" held by the transferor or any "applicable family member" immediately after the transfer is specially determined.[28]

¶ 31.08 SECTION 2701 CONCEPTS AND TERMS DEFINED

[1] Member of the Transferor's Family

For purposes of Section 2701, the term "member of the family" means, with respect to any transferor: the transferor's spouse, a lineal descendant of the transferor or the transferor's spouse, and, the spouse of any such descendant.[29] It is not clear why the transferor's spouse is included in this definition nor what effect the inclusion has for purposes of intramarital transfers.

---

[24] See discussion at ¶ 31.08[2][a] below.
[25] OBRA § 11602.
[26] Treas. Reg. §§ 25.2701-1 -25.2701-4, 25.2701-6 - 25.2701-8.
[27] Treas. Reg. § 25.2701-5.
[28] IRC § 2701(a).
[29] IRC § 2701(e)(1); Treas. Reg. § 25.2701-1(d)(1).

In determining who is a member of a transferor's family, a relationship by legal adoption is treated as a relationship by blood.[30]

[2] Applicable Retained Interest

The term "applicable retained interest" means any equity interest in a corporation or partnership with respect to which there is either (1) a "distribution right," in the case of a "controlled entity;" or (2) an "extraordinary payment right" in any entity.[31]

[a] Distribution Right

The term "distribution right" means a right to a shareholder's distributions from a corporation with respect to his stock and a partner's right to distributions from a partnership with respect to his partnership interest.[32]

QUERY: Does a right to payments other than in one's capacity as an equity owner[33] constitute a distribution right? The term "applicable retained interest" refers only to equity interests.[34] Presumably, the general debt-equity tests would apply to determine whether an interest constitutes an equity interest.

It appears that transfers of options will not be subject to Section 2701 if the options carry no rights traditionally associated with equity interests (e.g., the right to vote or receive dividends) until they are exercised.[35] Similarly, a transfer of property to an entity in exchange for a note should not result in the application of Section 2701 if the note represents true debt.[36]

EXAMPLE: Father transfers common stock in X Corporation to Son and retains a note from X. If the note is considered equity under general

---

[30] IRC § 2701(e)(4); Treas. Reg. § 25.2701-1(d)(3).

[31] Treas. Reg. § 25.2701-2(b)(1).

[32] IRC § 2701(c)(1)(A).

[33] For example, under a note, lease, or employment contract.

[34] Treas. Reg. §§ 25.2701-2(b)(1), 25.2701-2(b)(3).

[35] E.g., Priv. Ltr. Rul. 9616035 (Jan. 23, 1996); Priv. Ltr. Rul. 9350016 (Sept. 16, 1993).

[36] E.g., Priv. Ltr. Rul. 9535026 (May 31, 1995) (20-year balloon note with adequate interest under IRC § 7872 (dealing with below-market loans), secured by stock, repayable in cash or in kind but not with a note, is not applicable retained interest and therefore IRC § 2701 does not apply); Priv. Ltr. Rul. 9436006 (Mar. 14, 1994) (sale of partnership interest to trust in return for note was not subject to IRC § 2701; note provided for 25-year term, balloon payment, and quarterly interest payments at long-term applicable federal rate).

income tax principles, the note may be characterized as a distribution right subject to special valuation under Section 2701.

However, a distribution right does not include (1) any right to receive distributions with respect to an interest that is of the same class as, or a class that is subordinate to, the transferred interest, (2) any extraordinary payment right (as defined below), or (3) certain rights that are neither distribution rights nor extraordinary payment rights.[37]

EXAMPLE: Dad owns preferred stock and common stock. He transfers common stock to Junior. Dad's right to receive dividends on common stock is not a distribution right.

EXAMPLE: *B* owns Class A preferred stock, which is entitled to the first $100 of dividends each year. *B* also owns Class B preferred stock, which is entitled to the second $100 of dividends, and all of the common stock. *B* transfers the Class A preferred stock to his child. The retained Class B preferred stock is not specially valued in determining the value of the transferred Class A preferred stock.[38]

[b] Extraordinary Payment Right

The term "extraordinary payment right" means any put, call, or conversion right, any right to compel liquidation, or any similar right, if the exercise or nonexercise of the right affects the value of the transferred interest.[39] Thus, if *X* has the right to put his stock to a corporation at any time for the higher of the stock's fair market value or its cost to *X*, the put. This is an extraordinary payment right.

[i] Call. A call includes any warrant, option, or other right to acquire one or more equity interests.[40]

[ii] Conversion right. Presumably, a conversion right only includes discretionary changes in interests, not automatic changes, such as interests in partnerships in which the allocations to partners flip.

[iii] Exception for rights not affecting value of transferred interest. If the exercise or nonexercise of a put, call, or conversion right, right to compel

---

[37] Treas. Reg. § 25.2701-2(b)(3). Rights which are neither distribution rights nor extraordinary payment rights are discussed at ¶ 31.08[2][c] below.

[38] IRC § 2701(c)(1)(B)(i). Treas. Reg. § 25.2701-2(b)(3)(i).

[39] Treas. Reg. § 25.2701-2(b)(2).

[40] Treas. Reg. § 25.2701-2(b)(2).

liquidation, or similar right would not affect the value of a transferred interest, the right is not an extraordinary payment right with respect to that transfer.

> EXAMPLE: Dad gives one class of preferred stock to Junior. Mom, the holder of a subordinate class of preferred stock, has the right to convert her shares to nonvoting common stock. Mom's right to convert her junior preferred stock into another interest that is junior to the transferred senior preferred stock will not affect the value of the transferred senior preferred stock. Mom's conversion right will not constitute an extraordinary payment right, at least with respect to the transfer of the senior preferred stock.[41]

[iv] **Right to participate in distribution upon liquidation.** Suppose Dad owns 75 percent of the voting stock of a corporation, which is enough to cause the corporation to be liquidated. Will his right to participate in the corporation's liquidation proceeds be classified as an extraordinary payment right, a distribution right, or a right which is neither an extraordinary payment right nor a distribution right?

Treasury Regulation § 25.2701-2(b)(4)(ii) provides that a liquidation participation right is neither an extraordinary payment right nor a distribution right (translation: it is valued under normal rules). However, other portions of the regulation indicate that if a transferor, members of the transferor's family, and applicable family members hold sufficient voting power to compel liquidation of a corporation, their rights to participate in liquidation are extraordinary payment rights (meaning the rights would be given no value).[42] This latter interpretation seems unreasonable, since a majority stockholder may have fiduciary obligations to a minority shareholder in deciding whether to liquidate a corporation. In addition, this interpretation undercuts the statement in the legislative history that the valuation of voting rights was not intended to be affected by Section 2701.

[c] **Excluded Rights**

The following rights are neither distribution rights nor extraordinary payment rights: mandatory payment rights, liquidation participation rights, rights to guaranteed payments of a fixed amount under Section 707(c), and nonlapsing conversion rights.[43] Excluded rights are valued under normal rules.

---

[41] Priv. Ltr. Rul. 9204016 (Oct. 24, 1991).

[42] Treas. Reg. § 25.2701-2(d), examples 3, 4; see also Priv. Ltr. Rul. 9417024 (Jan. 27, 1994) (holding that right of owner who could compel liquidation to participate in liquidation was extraordinary payment right). For a discussion of the conflict within the regulations, see ¶ 31.08[2][c][ii] below.

[43] Treas. Reg. § 25.2701-2(b)(4).

[i] Mandatory payment right. An extraordinary payment right does not include any right which must be exercised at a specific time and at a specific amount.[44] The right to receive a specific amount on the death of the holder is a mandatory payment right.[45] Thus, if X has the right to put his common stock to corporation Z on December 31, 1997 for $100, the put is not an extraordinary payment right.

Regulations' different view. The statute reads differently from the regulations, which provide that a mandatory payment right is a right to receive a payment required to be made at a specific time for a specific amount.[46] Read literally, this could apply to dividends on preferred stock (e.g., the right to receive $X per share on December 31 of each year). The statement in the regulations is accompanied by an example providing that a right to require that preferred stock be redeemed at its fixed par value on a date certain is a mandatory payment right, and therefore not an extraordinary payment right or a distribution right.[47] Presumably, the legislative intent was to define a mandatory payment right as a discretionary right held by the transferor (or an applicable family member) and exercisable in a limited fashion, rather than as a nondiscretionary right to receive payments (which would be treated as a distribution right), as the regulations could be read to suggest.

[ii] Liquidation participation right. The right to participate in a liquidating distribution is neither a distribution right nor an extraordinary payment right.[48] If, however, the transferor and members of the transferor's family (or applicable family members) have the ability to compel liquidation, the liquidation participation right is valued as if the ability to compel liquidation either did not exist or, if the "lower of" rule[49] applies, is exercised in a manner that is consistent with that rule.[50]

To illustrate, assume Dad and his children own stock in X Corporation. If Dad's stock does not confer a qualified payment right, Dad's right to participate in liquidation proceeds will be given its normal value, except that the value will be determined as if Dad and his children could not compel liquidation, regardless of their actual ability to compel liquidation. Even if

---

[44] IRC § 2701(c)(2)(B).

[45] Treas. Reg. § 25.2701-2(b)(4)(i).

[46] Treas. Reg. § 25.2701-2(b)(4)(i).

[47] Treas. Reg. § 25.2701-2(b)(4)(i). Note, however, that if the time for redemption can be extended, the right will not be deemed to be mandatory and may therefore be viewed as an extraordinary payment right. See Tech. Adv. Mem. 9447004 (July 29, 1994).

[48] Treas. Reg. § 25.2701-2(b)(4)(ii).

[49] The "lower of" rule deals with the valuation of extraordinary payment rights held in conjunction with qualified payment rights. It is discussed at ¶ 31.10[4] below.

[50] Treas. Reg. § 25.2701-2(b)(4)(ii).

Dad's stock in X does confer a qualified payment right, Dad's right to participate in liquidation distributions will still be given its normal value, provided that Dad and members of his family cannot compel X to liquidate. In both instances, the "normal value" would be the right to participate in distributions upon liquidation at some undetermined time in the future.

If Dad's stock confers a qualified payment right, and Dad and members of his family do have the ability to compel X to liquidate, the "lower of" rule will apply. Assuming the right to compel liquidation of X is valued at $100 and the qualified payment right is valued at $200, the value of the combination of these rights under the "lower of" rule will be $100. In contrast, if the value of the right to compel liquidation of X is $200 and the value of the qualified payment right is $100, under the "lower of" rule, the X stock will also be valued at $100 (plus the value of voting rights and any other rights that are not valued under Section 2701), and the ability of Dad and his children to liquidate X will be ignored.

NOTE: Treasury Regulation § 25.2701-2(d), example 3, indicates that a right to participate in liquidation will be considered an extraordinary payment right if a transferor and applicable family members have the ability to compel liquidation.[51] This seems inconsistent with Treasury Regulation § 25.2701-2(b)(4)(ii), which would only value a liquidation participation right at zero (thereby treating it as if it were an extraordinary payment right) only if this were necessary to be consistent with application of the "lower of" rule.

[iii] **Right to payment under Section 707(c).** The right to a guaranteed payment of a fixed amount under Section 707(c) is neither a distribution right nor an extraordinary payment right. In order to be excluded, the right must consist of the right to receive a guaranteed payment.[52] The amount of the guaranteed payment must be determined at a fixed rate (including a rate that bears a fixed relationship to a specified market interest rate). A payment that is contingent as to time or amount is not a guaranteed payment of a fixed amount.[53]

[iv] **Nonlapsing conversion right.**

As to interests in corporations. A "nonlapsing conversion right" is a right which is (1) a right to convert into a fixed number (or a fixed percentage) of shares of the same class of stock in a corporation as the transferred stock in such corporation (or stock which would be of the same class but for nonlaps-

---

[51] See also Treas. Reg. § 25.2701-2(d), example 4; Priv. Ltr. Rul. 9417024 (Jan. 27, 1994).

[52] Within the meaning of IRC § 707(c).

[53] Treas. Reg. § 25.2701-2(b)(4)(iii).

ing differences in voting power), (2) is nonlapsing, (3) is subject to proportionate adjustments for splits, combinations, reclassifications, and similar changes in the capital stock, and (4) is subject to adjustments similar to the adjustments under Section 2701(d)[54] for accumulated but unpaid distributions.[55] The proportionate adjustments test is met if the equity interest is protected from dilution resulting from changes in the corporate structure.[56] Note that the regulations use the term "equity interest" rather than stock.

As to interests in partnerships. A nonlapsing conversion right, in the case of a partnership, is a right which: (1) is a right to convert an equity interest in a partnership into a specified interest (other than an interest represented by a fixed dollar amount) of the same class as the transferred interest (or into an interest that would be of the same class but for nonlapsing differences in management rights or limitations on liability), (2) is nonlapsing, (3) is subject to proportionate adjustments for changes in the equity ownership of the partnership, and (4) is subject to adjustments similar to those provided in Section 2701(d) for unpaid payments.[57] The proportionate adjustments test is met if the equity interest is protected from dilution resulting from changes in the partnership structure.[58]

Adjustments for unpaid corporate or partnership distributions. For either a corporation or a partnership, an equity interest is subject to adjustments similar to those provided in Section 2701(d) if it provides for: (1) cumulative payments, (2) compounding of any unpaid payment at the rate specified in Treasury Regulation § 25.2701-4(c)(2), and (3) adjustment of the number or percentage of shares or the size of the interest into which it is convertible to take account of accumulated but unpaid payments.[59] Convertible preferred equity interests do not ordinarily provide for this type of adjustment mechanism to account for unpaid distributions.[60]

Theory supporting this exclusion. The theory underlying the nonlapsing conversion right exception is that such a right does not freeze the holder's interest.

EXAMPLE: A right to convert 100 shares of preferred stock into 100

---

[54] Discussed at ¶ 31.12 below.

[55] IRC § 2701(c)(2)(C); Treas. Reg. § 25.2701-2(b)(4)(iv)(A).

[56] Treas. Reg. § 25.2701-2(b)(4)(iv)(C).

[57] Treas. Reg. § 25.2701-2(b)(4)(iv)(B).

[58] Treas. Reg. § 25.2701-2(b)(4)(iv)(C).

[59] Treas. Reg. § 25.2701-2(b)(4)(iv)(D).

[60] But see Priv. Ltr. Rul. 9451051 (Sept. 23, 1994) in which a holder of convertible preferred stock was found to have a nonlapsing conversion right which, together with the other rights associated with the stock, caused the preferred stock to be considered to be in the same class as the non-preferred stock, thereby escaping valuation under IRC § 2701.

shares of common stock is a nonlapsing conversion right, if the other requirements are met. On the other hand, a right to convert 100 shares of preferred stock into shares of common stock equal to the fixed dollar value of the preferred stock at date of conversion is not a nonlapsing conversion right, and will be considered an extraordinary payment right (since it freezes the preferred stock at a certain dollar value).

[d] Applicable Family Member

"Applicable family member" means: (1) the transferor's spouse, (2) an ancestor of the transferor or the transferor's spouse, and (3) the spouse of any such ancestor.[81] A relationship by legal adoption is treated as a relationship by blood.[82]

[e] Controlled Entity

A "controlled entity" is a corporation or partnership "controlled," immediately before a transfer, by the transferor, the transferor's applicable family members, and any lineal descendants of the parents of the transferor or the transferor's spouse.[83]

[i] Corporations.

"Control" means the holding of at least 50 percent of the total voting power or total fair market value of the equity interests in the corporation.[84]

Extraordinary voting rights. Equity interests that carry no right to vote other than on liquidation, merger, or a similar event are not considered to have voting rights for purposes of the control test.[85]

Joint voting rights. A voting right is considered held by an individual to the extent that the individual, either alone or in conjunction with any other person, is entitled to exercise (or direct the exercise of) the right.[86]

Fiduciary voting rights. If an equity interest carrying voting rights is held in a fiduciary capacity, the voting rights are not considered held by the fiduciary, but instead are considered held by each beneficial owner of the interest

---

[81] IRC § 2701(e)(2); Treas. Reg. § 25.2701-1(d)(2).

[82] IRC § 2701(e)(4); Treas. Reg. § 25.2701-1(d)(3).

[83] Treas. Reg. § 25.2701-2(b)(5)(i); IRC §§ 2701(b)(1)(A), 2701(b)(2)(C), 2701(e)(3). See discussion of the rule requiring the attribution of interests between family members at ¶ 31.08[2][e][iii] below.

[84] Treas. Reg. § 25.2701-2(b)(5)(ii)(A).

[85] Treas. Reg. § 25.2701-2(b)(5)(ii)(B).

[86] Treas. Reg. § 25.2701-2(b)(5)(ii)(B).

and by each individual who is a permissible recipient of the income from the interest.[67]

> EXAMPLE: If A owns 10 percent of the stock of X Corporation individually and 90 percent as trustee of a trust for the sole benefit of Unrelated Party, A effectively controls X. However, Unrelated Party is considered to own the equity interest. So, for purposes of determining whether X is a controlled entity, Unrelated Party will be treated as controlling X even though he has no actual control over X.[68]

Contingent voting rights. A voting right does not include a right to vote that is subject to a contingency that has not occurred, other than a contingency that is within the control of the individual holding the right.[69]

[ii] **Partnerships.** "Control" means: (1) the holding of at least 50 percent of the capital or profits interest in the partnership or (2) in the case of a limited partnership, the holding of any interest as a general partner.[70]

QUERY: In the case of a limited partnership, is this an "and/or" test? That is, suppose X holds a 60 percent limited partnership interest, and Unrelated Third Party owns a 40 percent general partnership interest. Each of X and Unrelated Third Party is apparently deemed to control the partnership under the regulations,[71] even though X is a limited partner and as such, has no control.

Impact of indirect ownership. In the last example, addressing ownership of an interest as a fiduciary, suppose the entity is a general partnership rather than a corporation. Who controls the partnership? Under the trust attribution rules, Unrelated Party is deemed to own a 90 percent interest in the partnership, and therefore to control the partnership.[72] If the interest is held by an executor instead of a trustee, are the answers the same?[73]

How is the amount of a partnership interest determined? In a partnership with special allocation provisions, it is unclear how the profits interest is determined. It is also unclear what a partner's capital interest is—his

---

[67] Treas. Reg. § 25.2701-2(b)(5)(ii)(B).

[68] Treas. Reg. § 25.2701-6(a)(4).

[69] Treas. Reg. § 25.2701-2(b)(5)(ii)(B).

[70] IRC § 2701(b)(2)(B); Treas. Reg. § 25.2701-2(b)(5)(iii).

[71] Treas. Reg. § 25.2701-2(b)(5)(iii).

[72] Treas. Reg. § 25.2701-6(a)(4).

[73] See the discussion of attribution from trusts and estates at ¶ 31.09[3][b][iii] below.

capital account? Or the amount he would receive if the partnership liquidated?

Guaranteed payments. Any right to a guaranteed payment under Section 707(c) of a fixed amount is disregarded in determining whether a person holds 50 percent of the capital or profits interest in a partnership.[74]

[iii] **Control by family members: indirect holding rules.** For purposes of determining "control" of both corporations and partnerships, the regulations provide that the indirect holding rules of Treasury Regulation § 25.2701-6 apply.[75]

¶ 31.09 TRANSFERS

[1] In General

The word "transfer" is not defined in the statute or regulations. However, the regulations provide that Section 2701 determines the existence and amount of any gift, regardless of whether the transfer would otherwise be a taxable gift under Chapter 12, the normal federal gift tax provisions. This means that Section 2701 applies to transfers that would not otherwise be gifts under Chapter 12, such as transfers for full and adequate consideration.[76]

QUERY: The statute on its face applies to a transfer of an interest in an entity. Suppose Mom makes an outright gift of cash to Daughter, who immediately invests the cash in stock of a corporation owned by Mom. Has Mom transferred an interest in the corporation?

[2] Transactions Which Are Not Transfers Subject to Section 2701

[a] Disclaimers

A transfer does not include a shift of rights occurring upon the execution of a qualified disclaimer described in Section 2518.[77]

---

[74] Treas. Reg. § 25.2701-2(b)(5)(iii).

[75] See Treas. Reg. § 25.2701-2(b)(5)(i) and discussion at ¶¶ 31.08[2][e][i] and 31.08[2][e][ii] above.

[76] Treas. Reg. § 25.2701-1(b)(1).

[77] Treas. Reg. § 25.2701-1(b)(3)(ii).

[b] Exercise of Limited Powers of Appointment

A transfer does not include a shift of rights occurring upon the release, exercise or lapse of a limited power of appointment, except to the extent that the release, exercise or lapse would otherwise be a transfer under Chapter 12.[78]

[3] Deemed Transfers

[a] Indirect Transfers

If an individual is treated as holding an interest pursuant to the indirect holding rules,[79] any transfer which causes that interest to be treated as no longer held by such individual is treated as a transfer of such interest.[80]

EXAMPLE: Suppose Brother owns 20 percent of C Corporation, and Sister owns 80 percent. C corporation owns 50 percent of Subsidiary. As described below, Brother is treated as holding a 10 percent interest in S. C sells its Subsidiary stock to Brother's son; therefore, Brother is no longer treated as indirectly holding the Subsidiary stock. For purposes of Section 2701, Brother has made an indirect transfer of an interest in a controlled corporation to his son, regardless of whether Brother had any actual control over this transaction.

Regulations' different view. The regulations both expand and limit the statutory rule. They provide that a transfer includes the termination of an indirect holding in an entity if the property is held in a trust as to which the indirect holder is treated as the owner under the grantor trust rules.[81] Additionally, the termination is treated as a transfer to the extent that the value of the indirectly held interest would have been included in the value of the indirect holder's gross estate for federal estate tax purposes if the indirect holder had died immediately prior to the termination.[82] The regulations also provide that a contribution to capital by an entity is treated as a transfer under the above circumstances to the extent an individual indirectly holds an interest in the entity.

---

[78] Treas. Reg. § 25.2701-1(b)(3)(iii). See Ch. 3 for an analysis of taxation of releases, exercises, and lapses of limited powers of appointment.

[79] Discussed at ¶ 31.09[3][b] below.

[80] IRC § 2701(e)(3)(A).

[81] Part E, Subchapter J of chapter 1 of the Internal Revenue Code contains the grantor trust rules.

[82] Treas. Reg. § 25.2701-1(b)(2)(C).

[b] Indirect Holdings

An individual is treated as holding any interest to the extent such interest is held indirectly by such individual through a corporation, partnership, trust, or other entity.[83]

[i] Attribution to individuals from corporations.

A person is considered to hold an equity interest held by or for a corporation in the proportion that the fair market value of the stock the person holds bears to the fair market value of all the stock in the corporation (determined as if each class of stock were held separately by one individual).[84] This rule applies to any entity classified as a corporation or as an association taxable as a corporation for federal income tax purposes.[85] Thus, if Corporation *A* owns stock in Corporation *B* and Joe owns 25 percent of the stock in Corporation *A*, then 25 percent of Corporation *A's* stock in Corporation *B* will be attributed to Joe.

Treatment of treasury stock. Treasury stock owned by a corporation will be attributed to the shareholders unless the corporation holds the stock as fiduciary or agent for other beneficial owners.[86]

[ii] Attribution to individuals from partnerships.

A person is considered to hold an equity interest held by or for a partnership in the proportion that (1) the fair market value of the larger of the person's profits interest or capital interest in the partnership bears to (2) the total fair market value of the corresponding profits interests or capital interests in the partnership, as the case may be (determined as if each class were held by one individual). This rule applies to any entity classified as a partnership for federal income tax purposes, and so would also apply to a limited liability company taxed as a partnership.[87]

> EXAMPLE: A partnership has a preferred interest worth $500,000 and a common interest worth $1,000,000. Dad owns 50 percent of the preferred interest. Presumably, Dad would be attributed one-sixth ($1/2 \times$ $500,000/($500,000 + $1,000,000)) of the equity interests held by the partnership.

Special allocations. In a partnership with complex special allocations, the partner's profits interest may not be easily determinable.

---

[83] IRC § 2701(e)(3)(A).

[84] Treas. Reg. § 25.2701-6(a)(2).

[85] Treas. Reg. § 25.2701-6(a)(2).

[86] Treas. Reg. § 25.2701-6(b), example 2.

[87] Treas. Reg. § 25.2701-6(a)(3).

[iii] Attribution to individuals from other entities.

Extent of attribution. A person is deemed to hold an equity interest that is held by or for an estate or trust to the extent such person's beneficial interest in the estate or trust may be satisfied by either (1) the equity interest held by the estate or trust or (2) the income or proceeds from the disposition thereof. In making this determination it is assumed, where discretion is a factor in determining what the person may receive, that the maximum exercise of discretion in favor of the person occurs. Thus, if income of Trust can be distributed to either *A* or *B*, in the trustee's discretion, both *A* and *B* will be attributed all of the equity interests held by Trust, subject to application of the multiple attribution rules discussed below.

A beneficiary of an estate or trust who cannot receive any distribution with respect to an equity interest held by the estate or trust, including the income therefrom or the proceeds from the disposition thereof, is not considered the holder of the equity interests held by the estate or trust. The rules set out in this paragraph, apply to any entity that is not classified as a corporation, an association taxable as a corporation, or a partnership for federal income tax purposes.[88]

> EXAMPLE: Stock held by a decedent's estate has been specifically bequeathed to *A*. The residue of the estate has been bequeathed to *B*. The stock is considered held only by *A*, since *B* cannot receive any of the stock.[89]

When property is held by an estate. Property is considered held by a decedent's estate for this purpose if the property is subject to claims against the estate and expenses of administration.[90] Thus, nonprobate property is generally excluded, even if it is included in the gross estate.

When a person holds a beneficial interest. A person holds a beneficial interest in a trust or an estate so long as the person may receive distributions from the trust or the estate (other than payments for full and adequate consideration).[91] Such a person is considered a beneficiary even if the person can only receive distributions in the future.[92]

> EXAMPLE: Trust provides that Dad will receive distributions of income for his life, with the remainder passing to Child on Dad's death. Both Dad and Child can be attributed ownership of equity interests held by Trust.

> EXAMPLE: Trustee has discretion to distribute all of the income of a trust

---

[88] Treas. Reg. § 25.2701-6(a)(4)(i).

[89] Treas. Reg. § 25.2701-6(a)(4)(i).

[90] Treas. Reg. § 25.2701-6(a)(4)(ii)(A).

[91] Treas. Reg. § 25.2701-6(a)(4)(ii)(B).

[92] Treas. Reg. § 25.2701-6(b), examples 3, 4, 5.

to either of two beneficiaries. Both beneficiaries are deemed to own all of the equity interest held by the trust, even if the equity interest itself can never be distributed to either of them.[93]

ESOP participants. A participant in an ESOP may be deemed to indirectly own shares held by the ESOP.

EXAMPLE: Dad transfers an interest in Corporation to its ESOP in exchange for cash. Dad retains preferred stock in Corporation. If Dad's child is a participant in the ESOP, the exchange may be subject to Section 2701.[94]

Interests held by grantor trusts. An individual is deemed to hold an equity interest held by or for a trust if the individual is considered an owner of the trust under the grantor trust rules.[95] If an individual is treated as the owner of only a fractional share of a grantor trust because there are multiple grantors, the individual is deemed to hold each equity interest held by the trust, except to the extent that the fair market value of the equity interest exceeds the fair market value of the individual's fractional share.[96] Thus, if a grantor trust containing $1,000,000 in assets is treated as owned equally by Husband and Wife, and the trust owns stock worth $600,000, Husband and Wife are each treated as owning $500,000 of the stock.

[iv] **Attribution from one entity to another.** An equity interest held by a lower-tier entity is attributed to higher-tier entities in accordance with the foregoing rules. For example, if an individual is deemed to own 50 percent of the property of a trust that holds 50 percent of the preferred stock of a corporation, 25 percent of the preferred stock is considered held by the individual.[97]

[v] **Interest held in multiple capacities.** If an equity interest is treated as held by a particular individual in more than one capacity, the interest is treated as held by the individual in the manner that attributes the largest total ownership of the equity interest.[98]

[vi] **Multiple attribution.** The multiple attribution rules are used to sort

---

[93] Treas. Reg. § 25.2701-6(a)(4)(i).

[94] Priv. Ltr. Rul. 9253018 (Sept. 30, 1992).

[95] IRC §§ 671–679.

[96] Treas. Reg. § 25.2701-6(a)(4)(ii)(C).

[97] Treas. Reg. § 25.2701-6(a)(1).

[98] Treas. Reg. § 25.2701-6(a)(1).

out who is the attributed owner when more than one person could be so considered.

Applicable retained interests. If an applicable retained interest is attributed to more than one individual in a class consisting of the transferor and one or more applicable family members, the interest is attributed within that class in the following order: if the interest is held in a grantor trust, to the individual treated as the owner thereof; next, to the transferor; then, to the transferor's spouse; and, last, to each applicable family member on a pro rata basis.[99]

Subordinate equity interests. Although the indirect holding rules do not define the term "subordinate equity interest," the valuation rules do. A subordinate equity interest is an equity interest as to which an applicable retained interest is a senior equity interest. A senior equity interest is an equity interest that carries a right to distributions of income or capital that is preferred as to the rights of the transferred interest.[100]

If a subordinate equity interest is attributed to more than one individual in a class consisting of the transferor, applicable family members, and members of the transferor's family, the interest is attributed within that class in the following order: first, to the transferee; next, to each member of the transferor's family on a pro rata basis; then, if the interest is held in a grantor trust, to the individual treated as the owner thereof; then, to the transferor; then, to the transferor's spouse; and, last, to each applicable family member on a pro rata basis.[101]

The attribution to the transferor's spouse in the next to last category above may be redundant, since the spouse will already have been allocated an interest as a member of the transferor's family.

Rules on multiple attribution. Generally, applicable retained interests are attributed to upper generations and subordinate equity interests are attributed to lower generations.

QUERY: When an equity interest is attributed on a "pro rata basis," what does that mean?

QUERY: H dies leaving a will which establishes a testamentary trust for the benefit of H's wife and children. The trust is funded with common stock of Corporation X. Ownership of the common stock is attributable to H's wife and children on a pro rata basis. What is such a basis?

---

[99] Treas. Reg. § 25.2701-6(a)(5)(i).

[100] Treas. Reg. §§ 25.2701-3(a)(2)(ii), 25.2701-3(a)(2)(iii).

[101] Treas. Reg. § 25.2701-6(a)(5)(ii).

QUERY: Common stock held by a decedent's estate is not specifically bequeathed to any beneficiary of the estate. The decedent's will provides for a pecuniary credit shelter trust permitting discretionary income payments to the surviving spouse and children and a residuary marital trust providing for mandatory income payments to the spouse. During the estate administration, the surviving spouse and the decedent's children will be treated as holding the stock, in accordance with the multiple attribution rules, on a pro rata basis. How are the multiple attribution rules applied where the executor of the decedent's estate has discretion to fund either trust (or even a bequest to an unrelated party of an amount of property equal to a pecuniary amount) with the stock?

QUERY: A deemed transfer as a result of the termination of an indirect ownership in a trust raises other problems as well. Who is liable for the gift tax resulting from the application of Section 2701?

QUERY: A QTIP trust for the benefit of Wife holds preferred stock and common stock in Corporation. The trust sells common stock to Son for its actual fair market value. Because of the special valuation rules, Section 2701 does not attribute full value to the preferred stock, and a gift tax results. Who pays it? There does not appear to be an answer to this question.

The multiple attribution rules can cause a transaction that might otherwise appear to escape the valuation rules of Section 2701 to be subject to them.

EXAMPLE: Parent is the income beneficiary and Child is the remainder beneficiary of QTIP Trust. Parent, Child, and QTIP Trust own all of the common stock in X corporation. They decide to recapitalize X, with each share of common stock being redeemed for one share of common stock and one share of preferred stock. At first glance, it appears that the recapitalization will not be a transfer for purposes of Section 2701, because each shareholder will hold the same interest in X's equity after the recapitalization as before. However, the multiple attribution rules cause the common stock held by QTIP Trust to be treated as held by Child and all the preferred stock to be treated as held by Parent, and thus Section 2701 will apply to the recapitalization.[102]

[c] Multiple Attribution in the Case of an Indirect Transfer

A transfer can be deemed to result from the termination of an indirect holding in an entity or from a contribution to capital by an entity to the extent an individual indirectly holds an interest in the entity. If the transfer of such an indirect holding in property is treated as a transfer with respect to more than one indirect holder, the transfer is attributed in the following order: first,

---

[102] See Priv. Ltr. Rul. 9321046 (Feb. 25, 1993).

to the indirect holder(s) who transferred the interest to the entity (without regard to Section 2513); next, to the indirect holder(s) possessing a presently exercisable power to designate the person who shall possess or enjoy the property; then, to the indirect holder(s) presently entitled to receive the income from the interest; then, to the indirect holder(s) specifically entitled to receive the interest at a future date; and, last, to any other indirect holder(s) proportionally.[103]

> EXAMPLE: In the last example, the Section 2701 transfer would apparently be deemed to be made by Parent, making Parent liable for the gift tax. Parent may not have sufficient funds to pay the gift tax with respect to the deemed transfer.

[4] Contributions to Capital

[a] In General

Except as provided in regulations, a contribution to the capital of a corporation or partnership is treated as a transfer of an interest in such entity to which Section 2701 applies if the taxpayer (or an applicable family member) receives an applicable retained interest in the entity pursuant to the contribution to capital or, under regulations, otherwise holds, immediately after the transfer, an applicable retained interest in such entity.[104]

[b] Regulatory Rule

The regulations word this rule slightly differently, providing that any contribution to the capital of a new or existing entity is considered a transfer for purposes of Section 2701.[105]

> EXAMPLE: If Father owns all of the preferred stock in X Corporation and Daughter owns all of X's common stock, a contribution to capital by Father might be treated as a gift if the preferred stock would be valued at less than its fair market value under the special valuation rules. The addition of capital to an existing corporation or partnership should result in the application of these rules only to the extent of the contribution.[106]

> EXAMPLE: Mother and Daughter form a new corporation. Mother con-

---

[103] Treas. Reg. § 25.2701-1(b)(2)(ii).

[104] IRC § 2701(e)(5).

[105] Treas. Reg. § 25.2701-1(b)(2)(i)(A).

[106] Conf. Rep. at 1137. The "Conf. Rep." refers to HR Rep. No. 964, 101st Cong., 2d Sess. 1130 (1990), published by the House-Senate Conference Committee on October 27, 1990. "S. Rep." refers to Sen. Budget Comm., 101st Cong. 2d Sess., Informal Report on S. 3209, 136 Cong. Rec. S15,629 (Oct. 18, 1990).

tributes $1 million in exchange for preferred stock worth $1 million, and Daughter contributes $1 million in exchange for common stock worth $1 million. Mom's contribution is deemed to be a transfer which must be specially valued under Section 2701. What if Mother and Daughter each purchases her interest in the entity from an unrelated third party?

[5] Capital Structure Transactions

[a] General Rule

Except as provided in regulations, a redemption, recapitalization, or other change in the capital structure of a corporation or partnership (a "capital structure transaction") is treated as a transfer of an interest in such entity to which Section 2701 applies if the taxpayer or an applicable family member receives an applicable retained interest in the entity pursuant to such capital structure transaction or, under regulations, otherwise holds, immediately after the transfer, an applicable retained interest in the entity.[107]

[b] Regulatory Rule

The regulations provide that such transactions will result in a transfer for purposes of Section 2701 in the following circumstances:

[i] **Receipt of applicable retained interest in a capital structure transaction.** A transfer includes a capital structure transaction, if the transferor (or an applicable family member) receives an applicable retained interest in the capital structure transaction.[108]

> EXAMPLE: Father owns 50 percent of the common stock of X Corporation. Son owns the other 50 percent. X is recapitalized. Son takes all of the common stock. Father takes all of a new class of preferred stock. This is considered a transfer of Father's 50 percent of common stock in exchange for an applicable retained interest (preferred stock).

[ii] **Receipt of property by holder of applicable retained interest.** A transfer includes a capital structure transaction, if the transferor (or an applicable family member) holding an applicable retained interest before the capital structure transaction both surrenders a subordinate interest (that is, an equity interest that is junior to the applicable retained interest) and receives property other than an applicable retained interest.[109]

---

[107] IRC § 2701(e)(5).

[108] Treas. Reg. § 25.2701-1(b)(2)(i)(B)(1).

[109] Treas. Reg. § 25.2701-1(b)(2)(i)(B)(2).

EXAMPLE: Father holds 100 percent of the preferred stock and 50 percent of the common stock of a corporation. The other 50 percent of the common stock is held by Son. The corporation redeems Father's common stock for cash. The transfer will be treated as a transfer by Father of his 50 percent of the common stock to Son in exchange for cash.

[iii] **Change in fair market value of applicable retained interest.** A transfer includes a capital structure transaction, if the transferor (or an applicable family member) holding an applicable retained interest before the capital structure transaction surrenders an equity interest in the entity (other than a subordinate interest) and the fair market value of the applicable retained interest is increased.[110]

[c] Exceptions

The above general rule regarding capital structure transactions will not apply to any such transaction if the interests in the entity held by the transferor, applicable family members, and members of the transferor's family before and after the transaction are substantially identical.[111] Thus, a change in corporate name would not effect a transfer.[112]

Regulatory interpretation. The regulations provide that for this exception to apply to a capital structure transaction, the transferor, each applicable family member, and each member of the transferor's family must hold substantially the same interest after the transaction as that individual held before the transaction. For this purpose, common stock with nonlapsing voting rights and nonvoting common stock are interests that are substantially the same.[113]

EXAMPLE: Mother owns all of the preferred stock and Daughter owns all of the common stock of *X* Corporation. Mother's stock is exchanged for non-voting preferred stock. This should not be considered a transfer for Section 2701 purposes, even if the fair market value of the common stock is thereby increased.

EXAMPLE: A recapitalization for the purpose of reducing the corporation's franchise tax will not be a transfer subject to Section 2701 where the transferor, each applicable family member and each member of the transferor's family hold substantially the same in-

---

[110] Treas. Reg. § 25.2701-1(b)(2)(i)(B)(3).

[111] IRC § 2701(e)(5); see also Priv. Ltr. Rul. 9638016 (June 14, 1996) (redemption in exchange for pro rata share of remainder interest in lease); Priv. Ltr. Rul. 9511028 (Dec. 16, 1994); Priv. Ltr. Rul. 9451050 (Sept. 22, 1994); Priv. Ltr. Rul. 9352012 (Sept. 29, 1993).

[112] Conf. Rep. at 1137.

[113] Treas. Reg. § 25.2701-1(b)(3)(i); see also Priv. Ltr. Rul. 9414013 (Dec. 28, 1993); Priv. Ltr. Rul. 9414012 (Dec. 28, 1993).

terests after the transaction as before.[114]

¶ 31.10 SPECIAL VALUATION RULES

Solely for purposes of determining whether a transfer of an interest in a corporation or partnership to (or for the benefit of) a member of the transferor's family is a gift (and determining the amount of the gift), the value of any right with respect to an interest retained by the transferor (or an applicable family member) is determined as provided in the special rules below.[115] Certain transfers by their nature are, however, exempted from valuation under the special rules of Section 2701.[116]

NOTE: The preamble to the first set of proposed regulations provided that Section 2701 does not change the value of the transferred property for any tax purpose other than the gift tax.[117] Thus, transferred property would be valued under chapters 11 and 13 for estate and generation-skipping transfer tax purposes.

[1] Rights Valued at Zero

The general rule is that certain rights with respect to all applicable retained interests are valued at zero.[118] Specifically, all extraordinary payment rights and all distribution rights (other than qualified payment rights) in controlled entities are valued at zero.[119]

> EXAMPLE: Father conveys common stock to Son for $100, retaining preferred stock. The value of the retained preferred stock, which pays noncumulative dividends, is $200. Aggregate value of all family-held interests (as defined below) in the company is $300. Assume that the value of rights not generally valued under Section 2701 (e.g., voting rights, the right to participate in liquidation) is zero.[120] Father is treated as having made a gift of $200 (the value of the family-held interests less the consideration furnished by son), unless he elects to treat the preferred stock as conferring a right to receive qualified payments.[121]

---

[114] Priv. Ltr. Rul. 9309018 (Dec. 3, 1992).

[115] IRC § 2701(a)(1).

[116] See ¶ 31.10[6] below.

[117] 56 Fed. Treas. Reg. 14,321 (1991).

[118] IRC § 2701(a)(3)(A).

[119] Treas. Reg. §§ 25.2701-2(a)(1), 25.2701-2(a)(2).

[120] Note that this assumption is generally made in each example in this chapter unless the example specifically states otherwise.

[121] Qualified payment rights are discussed at ¶ 31.10[3] below.

A liquidation, put, call, or conversion right can increase the value of an interest for estate tax purposes. Thus, if A retains a right to put his stock to a corporation at any time for $10 per share, for gift tax purposes, the Section 2701 value of the put is zero. However, for estate tax purposes, the $10 per share will constitute a floor on the value of A's stock (as long as the corporation is financially and legally able to honor the put).

[2] Specially Valued Rights

A right (other than an extraordinary payment right, a distribution right that does not constitute a qualified payment right, or a hybrid interest)[122] is valued as if any "zero-valued" right did not exist and as if any right valued under the "lower of" rule (applicable in valuing hybrid interests) is exercised in a manner consistent with the assumptions of that rule, but otherwise without regard to Section 2701.[123] It should be noted that valuing a right as if it were exercised in a manner consistent with the "lower of" rule may result in the right being valued at zero or at less than its value determined without regard to Section 2701.[124]

[3] Qualified Payment Rights

[a] Definition

A qualified payment is any dividend payable on a periodic basis under any cumulative preferred stock (or a comparable payment under any partnership interest) to the extent that such dividend (or comparable payment) is determined at a fixed rate.[125] A comparable payment evidently includes any cumulative distribution payable on a periodic basis with respect to an equity interest, to the extent determined at a fixed rate or as a fixed amount.[126] The periodic payments must be made at least annually.[127] A payment is considered determined at a fixed rate if the payment rate bears a fixed relationship to a specified market interest rate.[128] Also, the Senate Report at S15,681 provides that a qualified payment must have a preference on liquidation. This requirement, however, does not appear in the statute or the regulations.

---

[122] Discussed at ¶ 31.10[4] below.

[123] Treas. Reg. § 25.2701-2(a)(4).

[124] See discussion at ¶ 31.08[2][c][ii] above regarding valuing liquidation participation rights.

[125] IRC § 2701(c)(3)(A).

[126] Treas. Reg. § 25.2701-2(b)(6)(i)(B).

[127] Treas. Reg. §§ 25.2701-2(b)(6)(A), 25.2701-2(b)(6)(B).

[128] IRC § 2701(c)(3)(B); Treas. Reg. § 25.2701-2(b)(6)(ii).

[b] Valuation of Qualified Payment Rights—In General

Except in the case of hybrid interests,[129] qualified payment rights are subject to the rule governing the valuation of other interests.[130] The Section 2701 value of an applicable retained interest, which carries a qualified payment right but is not a hybrid interest, should be its fair market value.[131]

Fair market value of a qualified payment right. Presumably, in the absence of comparables, a right to qualified payments conveyed by an applicable retained interest in a corporation or partnership would be valued by determining the value of the income stream, using appropriate market discount rates and considering the entity's probable ability to make the payment. For example, if preferred stock with a par value of $1,000 carried an eight percent cumulative dividend, and eight percent were the appropriate market rate, the value of the stock (assuming only distribution rights have value) would be approximately $1,000 (its par value). On the other hand, if the stock carried a four percent dividend rate, but the appropriate market rate were eight percent, the value of the stock (assuming only distribution rights have value) would be less than par value.

The formula for valuing a perpetual annuity is:

$$\frac{\text{annuity amount}}{\text{interest rate}}$$

Thus, if preferred stock has a par value of $1,000,000, and a dividend rate of nine percent, and the market interest rate is ten percent, the value of the preferred stock as a perpetual annuity (assuming only distribution rights have value) would be $900,000 (that is, $90,000 annuity amount ÷ 10 percent interest rate).

Impact of the transferor's control. Senate Report at S15,681 provides that the determination of whether the payment can reasonably be expected to be timely paid is made without regard to the transferor's control.

Interest rate used for discounting. There is no safe harbor interest rate, such as the applicable federal rate. Thus, what will constitute an appropriate market rate is likely to be subject to debate. The IRS has indicated that, in determining the value of preferred stock based on the present value of a perpetual dividend stream, the use of a discount factor based on the Section 7520 rate (120 percent of the applicable federal midterm rate rounded to the

---

[129] Discussed at ¶ 31.10[4] below.

[130] Discussed at ¶ 31.10[2] above.

[131] See Treas. Reg. §§ 25.2701-2(a)(4), 25.2701-2(d), example 4. IRC § 2701(a)(3)(C).

nearest 2/10 of one percent) will rarely be valid when the corporation is closely held.[132]

[c] Minimum Value of Junior Equity Interests

[i] **In general.** If a junior equity interest (as defined below) in a corporation or partnership is transferred and an applicable retained interest is held by the transferor (or an applicable family member), the value of the transferred junior equity interest cannot be less than its proportionate share of ten percent of the sum of: (1) the total value of all of the equity interests in such entity, plus (2) the total amount of indebtedness of such entity to the transferor (or an applicable family member).[133] This rule overrides the regulatory provision that the value of a non-hybrid preferred interest conferring a right to qualified payments is its fair market value.

> EXAMPLE: Corporation *A* has two classes of stock, preferred and common. Rights under the preferred stock qualify as rights to receive qualified payments. Father owns 100 percent of both classes. He transfers all of the common stock to his son. The corporation is worth $1000, and it owes $500 to Father. The qualified payment valuation rules cannot operate so as to reduce the value of the common stock below $150. The gift tax value of the common stock will be at least $150, even if its actual worth is zero.

As the following example indicates, it can be better to time family loans after family transfers.

> EXAMPLE: In the example above, assume that the corporation owes nothing to Father, but plans to borrow $500 from him. If the corporation borrows the $500 before the transfer, the minimum value of the common stock will be $150. If it borrows after the transfer, the minimum value at date of transfer will be $100.

[ii] **"Junior equity interest defined".** "Junior equity interest" means common stock or, in the case of a partnership, any partnership interest under which the rights as to income and capital (or, to the extent provided in regulations, either income or capital) are junior to the rights of all other classes of equity interests.[134] "Equity interest," for this purpose, means stock or any interest as a partner, as the case may be.[135] Common stock means the

---

[132] Priv. Ltr. Rul. 9324018 (Mar. 19, 1993).

[133] IRC § 2701(a)(4)(A); Treas. Reg. § 25.2701-3(c)(1).

[134] IRC § 2701(a)(4)(B)(i); Treas. Reg. § 25.2701-3(c)(2).

[135] IRC § 2701(a)(4)(B)(ii).

class or classes of stock that, under the facts and circumstances, are entitled to share in the reasonably anticipated residual growth in the entity.[136]

Additionally, Section 2701 does not apply to a transfer of preferred stock where common stock is retained, and thus does not affect a reverse freeze.[137]

QUERY: Section 2701(a)(4)(B)(i) defines "junior equity interest" in the case of a partnership as an interest under which the rights to income and capital are junior to the rights of all other classes of equity interests.[138] If Father has a preferred interest in a partnership, gives daughter a junior interest, and gives a third person a nominal amount of an even more junior interest, are the rules regarding the minimum value of junior equity interests as to partnerships avoided? The answer will depend on the regulations.

[iii] **Indebtedness.** What does "indebtedness" owed to the transferor or an applicable family member mean? Does it include amounts payable to the transferor for services, rent, etc.? The regulations supply some of the answers—

First, for purposes of the rule regarding the minimum value of junior equity interests, indebtedness owed to the transferor or an applicable family member does not include—

- Short-term indebtedness incurred with respect to the current conduct of a trade or business (such as amounts payable for current services);
- Indebtedness owed to a third party solely because it is guaranteed by the transferor or an applicable family member; or
- Amounts permanently set aside in a qualified deferred compensation arrangement, to the extent the amounts are unavailable for use by the entity.[139]

QUERY: Where entity indebtedness is guaranteed by the transferor or an applicable family member, should it make a difference if the transferor or applicable family member has had to pay the lender?

Lease vs. loan. A lease of property is not indebtedness, without regard to the length of the lease term, if the lease payments represent full and adequate consideration for use of the property. Lease payments are considered to be made for full and adequate consideration if a good faith effort is made to

---

[136] Treas. Reg. § 25.2701-3(c)(2).

[137] For example, where the transferor retains common stock and transfers preferred stock.

[138] See also Treas. Reg. § 25.2701-3(c)(2).

[139] Treas. Reg. § 25.2701-3(c)(3)(i).

determine the fair rental value under the lease and the terms of the lease conform to the value so determined. However, arrearages with respect to a lease are indebtedness.[140]

[d] Elections

[i] **To treat qualified payments as non-qualified payments.** A transferor (or applicable family member) may elect to treat a right to receive payments under any interest specified in such election as a non-qualified payment right.[141] This election prevents unpaid distributions from being subject to the punitive compounding rule.[142] Such an election cannot be revoked,[143] except with the consent of the IRS.[144]

Regulatory rule. The regulations provide that a transferor holding an interest that confers a qualified payment right may elect to treat all interests held by the transferor of the same class as interests conferring rights that are not qualified payment rights. A partial election is permitted, but must be exercised with respect to a consistent portion of each payment right in the class as to which the election has been made.[145]

Qualified payments held by applicable family members. The holding of qualified payments by applicable family members can present a problem. The applicable family members may have adverse tax consequences as a result of unpaid distributions with respect to qualified payments. The statute and regulations address this problem by providing that no interest held by an applicable family member will be treated as a qualified payment right unless the applicable family member affirmatively elects[146] to treat it as a qualified payment right. Any partial election must be exercised with respect to a consistent portion of each payment right in the class as to which the election has been made.[147]

[ii] **To treat non-qualified payments as qualified payments.** A transferor (or applicable family member) may elect to treat any distribution right as a right to receive qualified payments (to be paid in the amounts and at the times specified in such election), to the extent the amounts and times so specified are

---

[140] Treas. Reg. § 25.2701-3(c)(3)(ii).

[141] IRC § 2701(c)(3)(C)(i).

[142] Discussed at ¶ 31.12 below.

[143] IRC § 2701(c)(3)(C)(iii).

[144] Treas. Reg. § 25.2701-2(c)(3).

[145] Treas. Reg. § 25.2701-2(c)(1).

[146] As described in ¶ 31.10[3][d][ii] below. IRC § 2701(c)(3)(C)(i).

[147] Treas. Reg. § 25.2701-2(c)(4).

consistent with the underlying legal instrument giving rise to such right.[148] Such an election is irrevocable,[149] except with the consent of the IRS.[150]

Regulatory rule. The regulations specify that any individual may make this election, but only with respect to a distribution right with respect to an interest held by that individual in a controlled entity. A partial election is permitted, provided that the election is exercised with respect to a consistent portion of each payment right in the class as to which the election has been made. The election is effective only to the extent specified in the election and then only to the extent that the payments so elected are both permissible under the instrument giving rise to the right and consistent with the legal right of the entity to make the payment.[151]

[iii] **Manner of making elections.** Either election described above is made by attaching a statement to the transferor's gift tax return on which the transfer is reported. An election filed after the time of filing the gift tax return reporting the transfer is not a valid election.[152] The contents of the elections are specified in the regulations.[153] In the case of an election by an applicable family member, the regulations require that a statement be attached to another person's gift tax return (namely, the transferor's).

[iv] **Maximum value of elected qualified payment.** The value attributed to an applicable retained interest as a result of electing to treat a distribution right as a qualified payment right cannot exceed the fair market value of the interest determined without regard to Section 2701.[154]

[4] Treatment of Hybrid Interests

If any applicable retained interest confers a distribution right that consists of the right to a qualified payment, and there are one or more liquidation, put, call, or conversion rights with respect to such interest, then the value of all such rights is determined as if each liquidation, put, call, or conversion right were exercised in the manner resulting in the lowest value being determined

---

[148] IRC § 2701(c)(3)(C)(ii).

[149] IRC § 2701(c)(3)(C)(iii).

[150] Treas. Reg. § 25.2701-2(c)(3).

[151] Treas. Reg. § 25.2701-2(c)(2).

[152] An election filed as of March 28, 1992 (60 days after the effective date of the regulation) was effective for prior transfers. Treas. Reg. § 25.2701-2(c)(5).

[153] Treas. Reg. § 25.2701-2(c)(5).

[154] Treas. Reg. § 25.2701-2(c)(2).

for all such rights.[155] This rule is known as the "lower of" valuation rule. The determination of value must use a consistent set of assumptions and give due regard to the entity's net worth, prospective earning power and other relevant factors.[156]

The Conference Report indicates that the values to be compared for purposes of the "lower of" rule are the value of the interest assuming the extraordinary payment is exercised and the value assuming that the extraordinary payment right is not exercised and therefore, the cumulative dividend is paid every year in perpetuity.

> EXAMPLE: Father transfers common stock to son and retains cumulative preferred stock with a dividend of $100 per year. Father also retains a right to put his preferred stock to the corporation at any time for $1,000. The combined distribution and put rights in the preferred stock will be valued at the lower of $1,000 or the present value of $100 paid every year in perpetuity.[157]

The IRS has implied that this interpretation of the valuation rule is too simplistic. In Private Letter Ruling 9324018 (Mar. 19, 1993), the IRS indicated that there are "many factors" to be considered in valuing hybrid interest preferred stock, two of which are the liquidation preference accorded the preferred stock and the yield of the preferred stock. Citing Revenue Ruling 83-120,[158] the IRS discussed the need to determine the adequacy of the dividend rate of the hybrid interest stock by comparing it with that of high-grade, publicly traded preferred stock. In addition, the IRS discussed how to measure the risk that the corporation cannot pay the stated dividends on time or that it will be unable to pay the full liquidation preference at liquidation. The IRS indicated that, ultimately, the appropriate analysis would compare the value of the stock, considering all factors other than the liquidation preference, with the value of the liquidation preference.[159]

> EXAMPLE: Father transfers common stock to Son and retains cumulative preferred stock with a dividend of $100 per year. Father also retains the right to put his preferred stock to the corporation at any time for $1000. The corporation is in good financial health and is expected to be able to pay its dividends on time and to pay the full amount should Father decide to put his stock. However, high-grade, publicly traded preferred stock similar to Father's generally pays a dividend of $90 per year. For purposes of Section 2701, Father's preferred stock will be valued at the lower

---

[155] IRC § 2701(a)(3)(B).

[156] Such as those described in Treas. Reg. §§ 20.2031-2(f), 20.2031-3 and Treas. Reg. § 25.2701-2(a)(3).

[157] See Conf. Rep. at 1134.

[158] 1983-2 CB 170.

[159] See also Priv. Ltr. Rul. 9417024 (Jan. 27, 1994).

of $1000 or the value of the stock, considering all factors other than the put right. In determining the value of the stock, the fact that Father's preferred stock pays a higher dividend than comparable preferred stock, and is therefore worth more, should be taken into account. However, this factor will have no impact on the value of Father's preferred stock unless the other factors involved in computing the value of such stock would cause the value to be less than $1000.

Legislative history. The "lower of" rule is, according to the Conference Report, intended to give greater recognition to the value of liquidation, put, call, or conversion rights than a zero value would.[160] Actually, the only effect is to lower the value of the accompanying qualified payment, and not to increase the value of an extraordinary payment right. If an extraordinary payment right had a zero value, such a right would have no effect on the value of a retained qualified payment. Under the enacted rule, an extraordinary payment right can only reduce the value of the qualified payment, since the valuation will be the lower of the value of the qualified payment under normal rules or the value of the extraordinary payment right under normal rules.

Valuation of hybrid interest. A hybrid interest may be valued even lower than one otherwise might expect as a result of the "lower of" rule. For example, suppose the value of the liquidation right is lower than the value of the hybrid interest after considering all factors other than the liquidation right. The interest may be valued lower than its liquidation right if the net assets of the entity would be unable to support the full liquidation right.[161]

> EXAMPLE: In the previous example, suppose that the corporation is not in good financial health and the likelihood is only 50 percent that it will be able to pay the full amount owed should Father put his stock. In addition, suppose the value of Father's put, without considering the corporation's ability to pay ($1000), is less than (or even equal to) the value of the perpetual dividend stream. For purposes of Section 2701, the value of Father's preferred stock will not be $1000, but will be further discounted to reflect the risk that the corporation will be unable to pay if Father exercises his put right.

It should be noted that Treasury Regulation § 25.2701-2(d), example 4 implies that any time the transferor, members of the transferor's family, and applicable family members have sufficient ownership to compel liquidation of an entity, and the transferor or applicable family members retain a right to a qualified payment, a hybrid interest will exist.[162] The value of the interest, then, would be the lower of the qualified payment under normal valuation

---

[160] Conf. Rep. at 1134.

[161] Priv. Ltr. Rul. 9324018 (Mar. 19, 1993).

[162] Note, however, that this example appears inconsistent with Treas. Reg. § 25.2701-2(b)(4), as discussed at ¶ 31.08[2][c][ii] above.

rules and the value of the right to compel and participate in liquidation under normal rules. This situation may represent the majority of cases subject to Section 2701.

PRACTICE POINTER: Care should be taken in giving extraordinary payment rights in conjunction with qualified payment rights (even though, in actuality, extraordinary payment rights add value). Such rights will not just be ignored—they can actually lower the Section 2701 value of the accompanying qualified payment right.

[5] Splitting of Applicable Retained Interest

Regulations may treat an applicable retained interest as two or more separate interests.[163] The regulations provide for such treatment by regulation, revenue ruling, notice, or other document of general application.[164] This would allow, for example, value to be accorded to the participating feature of a participating preferred interest pursuant to the exception for retained interests that are of the same class as the transferred interest.[165] In addition, the IRS may, by ruling issued to a taxpayer upon request, treat any applicable retained interest as two or more separate interests as may be necessary and appropriate to carry out the purposes of Section 2701.[166]

> **EXAMPLE:** Mother owns all of the stock in a corporation. One class of stock is entitled to the first $100 in dividends each year plus half the dividends paid in excess of $100 that year; the second class is entitled to one half of the dividends paid above $100. The preferred right under the first class is cumulative. Mother retains the first class and gives the second class to child. According to the Conference Report, Treasury regulations may treat an interest of the first class as two interests under the provision: one, an interest bearing a preferred right to dividends of $100; the other, an interest bearing the right to half the annual dividends in excess of $100, which would fall within the exception for retained interests of the same class as the transferred interest.[167]

It should be noted that the last sentence of Treasury Regulation § 25.2701-7 implies that, in the absence of a regulation or other document of general application, a taxpayer may not merely elect to treat an applicable retained interest as two or more separate interests, but must obtain a ruling.

---

[163] IRC § 2701(e)(7).

[164] Treas. Reg. § 25.2701-7.

[165] Conf. Rep. at 1135.

[166] Treas. Reg. § 25.2701-7.

[167] Conf. Rep. at 1135.

The Conference Report appears to encourage the issuance of regulations to that effect.

EXAMPLE: Father and Daughter enter into a partnership agreement under which Father is to receive the first $1,000,000 in net cash receipts and is thereafter to share equally in distributions with Daughter. Under the Conference Report, Treasury regulations may treat Father's retained interests as consisting of two interests: (1) a distribution right to $1,000,000 and (2) a 50 percent partnership interest. The Conference Report states that Father may elect to treat the first interest as a right to receive qualified payments at specified amounts and times. The second interest would then fall within the exception for retained interests of the same class as the transferred interest.[168] Hence, neither interest has to be valued at zero.

[6] Exceptions to Applicability of Section 2701

[a] Marketable Securities

The special valuation rules do not apply to applicable retained interests or transferred interests for which market quotations are readily available as of the date of transfer on an established securities market.[169]

[b] Same Class Interests

Section 2701 does not apply if the applicable retained interest is of the same class of equity as the transferred interest or is of a class that is proportionally the same as the class of the transferred interest.[170]

[i] Significance of difference in voting rights. A class is the same class as (or is proportional to the class of) the transferred interest if the rights are identical (or proportional) to the rights of the transferred interest, except for nonlapsing differences in voting rights (or, for a partnership, nonlapsing differences with respect to management and limitations on liability).[171]

EXAMPLE: Mother transfers 50 percent of the common stock in Corporation to her son and retains 50 percent of the common stock. The retained 50 percent is valued without regard to the special valuation rules.

---

[168] Conf. Rep. at 1135.

[169] IRC §§ 2701(a)(1), 2701(a)(2)(A); Treas. Reg. §§ 25.2701-1(c)(1), 25.2701-1(c)(2).

[170] IRC §§ 2701(a)(2)(B), 2701(a)(2)(C); Treas. Reg. § 25.2701-1(c)(3). See also Priv. Ltr. Rul. 9451050 (Sept. 22, 1994); Priv. Ltr. Rul. 9352012 (Sept. 29, 1993).

[171] Treas. Reg. § 25.2701-1(c)(3).

EXAMPLE: In the above example, the result is the same even if there are two classes of common stock, if their only difference is in voting rights.

EXAMPLE: A transfers Class A common stock and retains Class B common stock. The classes are identical, except that Class A stock receives distributions on a two-to-one basis with Class B stock. A's retained Class B stock is subject to normal valuation rules.

[ii] **Retained interests.** The statute applies this exception to applicable retained interests.[172] The regulations take the position that this exception applies to retained interests even if they are not applicable retained interests.[173]

[iii] **Partnership allocation requirements.** For purposes of this exception, nonlapsing provisions needed to comply with partnership allocation requirements of the Internal Revenue Code[174] are nonlapsing differences with respect to limitations on liability.[175] Such required nonlapsing provisions are therefore ignored when determining whether a retained interest in a partnership has rights identical (or proportional) to the rights of the transferred interest. An interest in a partnership is not an interest in the same class as the transferred interest if the transferor (or applicable family members) have the right to alter the liability of the transferee of the transferred property.[176]

EXAMPLE: Mom transfers a general partnership interest to Daughter and retains a limited partnership interest. The only differences in the interests are with respect to management and limitations on liability. This transfer should fall within the exception. The difference in liability between a general partner and a limited partner necessarily involves differences in the allocations of partnership income and loss between them. For example, once the capital account of the limited partner is reduced to zero, any further losses of the partnership must be allocated to the general partner.

It is not clear what the last sentence of Treasury Regulation § 25.2701-1(c)(3) (dealing with the right to alter the liability of the transferee of a partnership interest) is intended to address.

[iv] **Lapses by reason of law.** Except as provided by the Secretary of the Treasury, any difference (between interests which are proportionally the same) which lapses by reason of federal or state law is treated as a nonlapsing

---

[172] IRC § 2701(a)(2).

[173] Treas. Reg. § 25.2701-1(c)(3).

[174] E.g., IRC § 704(b).

[175] Treas. Reg. § 25.2701-1(c)(3).

[176] IRC § 2701(a)(2); Treas. Reg. § 25.2701-1(c)(3).

difference.[177] In this regard, the regulations provide for such treatment unless "the Secretary determines, by regulation or by published revenue ruling, that it is necessary to treat such a right as a lapsing right to accomplish the purposes of section 2701."[178]

> EXAMPLE: Dad is a general partner and a limited partner of a partnership. He transfers his limited partnership interest to Son. Dad's rights as general partner are the same as those of the limited partners, except for his management and liability rights. At his death, his management rights will lapse by reason of state law. Unless the Secretary has provided otherwise, the transfer of the limited partnership interest to Son will not be governed by the valuation rules of Section 2701. However, if the partnership agreement provides that Dad's management rights will lapse upon the occurrence of certain events which would not cause a lapse under state law, the exception will not apply. And, the value of the transfer will therefore be governed by Section 2701.

[v] **Legislative history.** The legislative history provides that regulations may give zero value to rights which lapse by reason of laws which effectively transfer wealth that would not pass in the absence of a specific agreement. Such regulations could, for example, give zero value to a management right that lapses, under the Uniform Partnership Act as adopted in a state, by reason of the death of a partner if the decedent had waived in the partnership agreement the right to have his interest redeemed at fair market value under that Act.[179] The statute does not provide for such regulations.

[c] Proportionate Transfers

Section 2701 does not apply to an individual's transfer of equity interests to a member of the individual's family to the extent that such transfer results in a proportionate reduction of each class of equity interest held by the individual and all applicable family members in the aggregate immediately before the transfer.[180] The preamble to the proposed regulations referred to this as excluding a transfer of a "vertical slice" of interests in the entity.

> EXAMPLE: Suppose Father owns 100 percent of the preferred stock and 100 percent of the common stock of X Corporation. He transfers 10 percent of the preferred stock and 10 percent of the common stock to

---

[177] IRC § 2701(a)(2).

[178] Treas. Reg. § 25.2701-1(c)(3). Permitting revenue rulings to establish exceptions seems wrong, since the IRS, rather than the Secretary, issues revenue rulings, and revenue rulings do not have the safeguards provided by the public notice and comment required to promulgate regulations.

[179] Conf. Rep. at 1136.

[180] Treas. Reg. § 25.2701-1(c)(4).

Son. This transfer should come under the exception. Similarly, if all parties have the same proportionate shares in an entity after recapitalization that they did before recapitalization, Section 2701 should not apply.[181]

EXAMPLE: Assume the same facts as the preceding example, except that Father initially owned only 50 percent of the preferred stock, and Grandfather owned the other 50 percent. Section 2701 still does not apply to the transfer, even though Father's interest in the preferred stock is reduced by 20 percent, and his interest in the common stock is reduced by 10 percent. This outcome appears to result from the application of the indirect holding rules.[182]

¶ 31.11　COMPUTATION OF AMOUNT OF TRANSFER

[1] Possible Methodologies

Neither the statute nor the legislative history indicates how to compute the value of the gift in many common situations.

Hint offered in the Senate Report. The Senate Report provides that the value of a residual interest in a corporation or partnership is determined by subtracting the value of the preferred interest (as specially valued) from the value of all interests in the corporation or partnership, with an adjustment to reflect the actual fragmented ownership.[183] The Senate Report purports to base this valuation method on the law in existence at the time of enactment, despite the fact that there was contrary authority.[184] Minority discounts and control premiums would not be affected, according to the Senate Report.[185]

Other approaches. The regulatory method is discussed in the following subparagraphs. Other methods of valuation can be postulated.[186]

---

[181] See Priv. Ltr. Rul. 9241014 (July 8, 1992).

[182] Treas. Reg. § 25.2701-1(c)(4); see also Priv. Ltr. Rul. 9226063 (Mar. 31, 1992). The indirect holding rules are discussed at ¶ 31.09[3][b] above.

[183] S. Rep. at S15,679, S15,681; see also Tech. Adv. Mem. 9447004 (July 29, 1994) (holding that subtraction method should be used to value gift under IRC § 2701).

[184] Estate of Newhouse v. Comm'r, 94 TC 193 (1990), 244–245, nonacq., 1991-2 CB 1.

[185] S. Rep. at S15,681.

[186] See letter from Lloyd L. Plaine, et al. to Kenneth W. Gideon, et al., 91 Tax Notes Today 28-33, (Feb. 5, 1991).

[2] Valuation Method Adopted by Treasury Regulations

The regulations take the position that the gift computation is based on the subtraction approach discussed in the legislative history.[187] More specifically, the regulations provide that the amount of the Section 2701 transfer is determined by subtracting the values of all family-held senior equity interests from the fair market value of all family-held interests in the entity determined immediately before the transfer. The values of the senior equity interests held by the transferor and applicable family members generally are determined under Section 2701, while other family-held senior equity interests are valued at their fair market value. The balance is then appropriately allocated among the transferred interests and other family-held subordinate equity interests. Finally, certain discounts and other appropriate reductions are provided, but only to the extent permitted by the regulations.[188]

Definitions. "Family-held" means held (directly or indirectly) by the transferor, applicable family members, and any lineal descendants of the parents of the transferor or the transferor's spouse. "Senior equity interest" means an equity interest in the entity that carries a right to distributions of income or capital that is preferred as to the rights of the transferred interest. "Subordinate equity interest" means an equity interest in the entity as to which an applicable retained interest is a senior equity interest.[189]

The following fact pattern is used to illustrate the steps of the regulations' valuation method, discussed in the following subparagraphs.

ILLUSTRATION 1: In a corporation worth $2,000,000, suppose Father owns 100 percent of the common stock, valued at $1,000,000, and 60 percent of the preferred stock, which does not confer a right to qualified payments, valued at $600,000. Third Party owns 40 percent of the preferred stock, valued at $400,000. Father gives 40 percent of the common stock to Son. What is the value of the transfer under Section 2701?

[a] Step 1: Value Family-Held Interests

Determine the fair market value of all family-held equity interests in the entity immediately after the transfer. The fair market value is determined by assuming that the interests are held by one individual, using a consistent set of assumptions.[190] Thus, using the facts of Illustration 1, the value after Step 1 would be $1,600,000.

---

[187] Treas. Reg. §§ 25.2701-1(a)(2), 25.2701-3(a)(1).

[188] Treas. Reg. § 2701-3(a)(1); see also Tech. Adv. Mem. 9447004 (July 29, 1994), which goes through an actual calculation under the subtraction method.

[189] Treas. Reg. §§ 25.2701-2(b)(5)(i), 25.2701-3(a)(2).

[190] Treas. Reg. § 25.2701-3(b)(1)(i).

[b] Step 2: Subtract the Value of Senior Equity Interests

From the value determined in Step 1, subtract the following:

- An amount equal to the sum of the fair market value of all family-held senior equity interests (other than applicable retained interests held by the transferor or applicable family members) and the fair market value of any family-held equity interests of the same class as or a subordinate class to the transferred interests held by persons other than the transferor, members of the transferor's family, and applicable family members of the transferor; and
- The value of all applicable retained interests held by the transferor or applicable family members (other than an interest received as consideration for the transfer), determined under the special valuation rules and taking into account the adjustment described in ¶ 31.11[2][f] below.[191]

Fair market value defined. For purposes of the first part of Step 2, the fair market value of an interest is its pro rata share of the fair market value of all family-held senior equity interests of the same class (determined, immediately after the transfer, as if all family-held senior equity interests were held by one individual).[192]

Thus, applying the facts set forth in Illustration 1, the value after the first part of Step 2 would be $1,600,000, because all of the family-held preferred stock is held by Father (the transferor), and all of the family-held common stock is held by Father and Son (the transferor and a member of the transferor's family). The value after the second part of Step 2 would be $1,600,000, if the preferred stock held by Father is specially valued at zero.

[c] Step 3: Allocate the Remaining Value Among the Transferred Interests and Other Family-Held Subordinate Equity Interests

The value of the transfer remaining after Step 2 is allocated among the transferred interests and other subordinate equity interests held by the transferor, applicable family members, and members of the transferor's family. If more than one class of family-held subordinate equity interests exists, the value remaining after Step 2 is allocated, beginning with the most senior class of subordinate equity interest, in a manner that would most fairly approximate their value if rights valued under Section 2701 at zero did not exist (or would be exercised in a manner consistent with the assumptions of the rule for valuing rights other than extraordinary payment rights or distribution rights (other than qualified payment rights)). If there is no clearly appropriate

---

[191] Treas. Reg. § 25.2701-3(b)(2)(i).

[192] Treas. Reg. § 25.2701-3(b)(2)(i)(A).

method of allocating the remaining value pursuant to the preceding sentence, the remaining value (or the portion remaining after any partial allocation pursuant to the preceding sentence) is allocated to the interests in proportion to their fair market values determined without regard to Section 2701.[193]

Therefore, using the facts of Illustration 1, the value allocated to the transferred interest pursuant to Step 3 would be 40 percent of $1,600,000, or $640,000.

[d] Step 4: Determine the Amount of the Gift

The amount allocated to the transferred interests in Step 3 is reduced by the amounts determined below.

[i] Reduction for minority or similar discounts. Except as provided under the "minimum value rule" (described below), if the value of the transferred interest (determined without regard to Section 2701) would be reduced on account of a minority or similar discount with respect to the transferred interest, the amount of the Section 2701 gift is reduced by the excess, if any, of—

- A pro rata portion of the fair market value of the family-held interests of the same class (determined as if all voting rights conferred by family-held equity interests were held by one person who had no interest in the entity other than the family-held interests of the same class, but otherwise without regard to Section 2701), over
- The value of the transferred interest (without regard to Section 2701).[194]

Thus, if, in Illustration 1, minority and lack of marketability discounts totaling 25 percent would have been applicable in the absence of valuation under Section 2701, the value after Step 3 would be reduced by $100,000 (25 percent × $400,000, the value without regard to Section 2701 of the common stock Father gave to Son), for a total gift of $540,000.

[ii] Adjustment for transfers with a retained interest. If the value of the transferor's gift (determined without regard to Section 2701) would be reduced under Section 2702 to reflect the value of a retained interest, the Section 2701 value is reduced by the same amount.[195]

[iii] Reduction for consideration received by the transferor. The amount

---

[193] Treas. Reg. § 25.2701-3(b)(3).

[194] Treas. Reg. § 25.2701-3(b)(4)(ii).

[195] Treas. Reg. § 25.2701-3(b)(4)(iii).

of the transfer (determined under Section 2701) is reduced by the amount of consideration in money or money's worth received by the transferor, but not in excess of the amount of the gift (determined without regard to Section 2701). The value of consideration received by the transferor in the form of an applicable retained interest in the entity is determined under Section 2701.[196]

[e] Section 2701 Transfers Resulting From Contributions to Capital

The regulations provide for a slightly different valuation methodology where a Section 2701 transfer results from a contribution to the capital of an entity. The following are the steps of this alternate valuation methodology:

- First, determine the fair market value of the contribution to capital.[197]
- Next, subtract the value of any applicable retained interest received in exchange for the contribution to capital determined under the special valuation rules.[198]
- Last, apply the Steps 3 and 4 described above (at ¶¶ 31.11[2][c] and 31.11[2][d]), except that where consideration received by the transferor is in exchange for a contribution to capital in the form of an applicable retained interest in the entity, the Step 4 value of the applicable retained interest is zero.[199]

[f] Valuation Adjustment

[i] **In general.** For purposes of Step 2 of the valuation process, if the percentage of any class of applicable retained interest held by the transferor and by applicable family members (including any interest received as consideration for the transfer) exceeds the family interest percentage, the excess is treated as a family-held interest that is not held by the transferor or an applicable family member.[200]

[ii] **Family interest percentage.** The family interest percentage is the highest ownership percentage (determined on the basis of relative fair market values) of family-held interests in any class of subordinate equity interest or all subordinate equity interests, valued in the aggregate.[201]

In Illustration 1, the adjustment to Step 2 does not apply, since the transferor and family own 100 percent of the common stock. However, in-

---

[196] Treas. Reg. § 25.2701-3(b)(4)(iv).
[197] Treas. Reg. § 25.2701-3(b)(1)(ii).
[198] Treas. Reg. § 25.2701-3(b)(2)(ii).
[199] Treas. Reg. § 25.2701-3(b)(4)(iv).
[200] Treas. Reg. § 25.2701-3(b)(5)(i).
[201] Treas. Reg. § 25.2701-3(b)(5)(ii).

stead, suppose that Father owns 60 percent of the common stock and 80 percent of the preferred stock, while the remaining 40 percent of the common stock is held by Unrelated Third Party and the remaining 20 percent of the preferred stock is family-held but is not held by applicable family members (that is, it is held by junior family members). The family interest percentage is the percentage of family-held interest in the common stock, i.e., 60 percent. The preferred stock does not confer a right to qualified payments. Father transfers 20 percent of the common stock to Son. Here, 60 percent of the preferred stock is valued at zero (unless the transferor elects to treat the preferred stock as if it conferred a right to qualified payments). The remaining 20 percent would be valued at 20 percent of the fair market value of all of the preferred stock.

QUERY: Suppose *P* owns 100 percent of preferred stock, worth $1,000,000, and 100 percent of common stock, worth $1,000,000. Child and unrelated third party buy the common stock for $1,000,000. Child buys five percent and third party buys 95 percent. Is all of the preferred stock specially valued, or only five percent? The above rule does not provide an answer, since it is not clear whether the valuation adjustment is applied before or after the transfer. The parenthetical in Treasury Regulation § 25.2701-3(b)(5)(i), providing that the percentage of any class of applicable retained interest held by the transferor and applicable family members includes any interest received as consideration for the transfer, suggests that the valuation adjustment is applied after the transfer, meaning that only 5 percent of the preferred stock will be specially valued. This seems to be the correct result, given the realities of the transaction.

[g] Minimum Value Rule

The value determined under the above method is adjusted to allow for the rule regarding minimum value of junior equity interests.[202] Thus, in Illustration 1, the minimum value of the common stock is ten percent of $2,000,000, or $200,000. Suppose the corporation borrows $20,000,000 from Father. Then, the minimum value of the common would be ten percent of $22,000,000 (i.e., $2,200,000), and the value of the transfer would be $880,000. This is because the debt to Father would be considered equity for this purpose.

¶ 31.12 TREATMENT OF UNPAID DISTRIBUTIONS

If a taxable event occurs with respect to any applicable retained interest that confers a qualified payment right (a "qualified payment interest"), certain consequences with respect to unpaid distributions ensue.

---

[202] Treas. Reg. § 25.2701-3(b)(4)(ii). The rule for determining the minimum value of a junior equity interest is discussed at ¶ 31.10[3][c] above.

[1] What is a Taxable Event?

[a] Statutory Rule

A "taxable event" is one of the three following occurrences:

- *Death of transferor.* The death of the lifetime transferor is a taxable event if the qualified payment interest is includable in the estate of the transferor.[203]
- *Lifetime transfer of interest.* The lifetime transfer of a qualified payment interest is a taxable event.[204]
- *Late payment.* At the election of the taxpayer, the payment of any qualified payment more than four years after its due date is a taxable event, but only with respect to the period ending on the date of such payment.[205]

[b] Regulatory Rule

[i] In general. A taxable event means the transfer of a qualified payment interest, either during life or at death, by the individual in whose hands the interest was originally valued under Section 2701 (the "interest holder") or by any individual treated in the same manner as the interest holder, as described below.[206]

[ii] Termination of rights. Unless specifically excepted, any termination of an individual's rights with respect to a qualified payment interest is a taxable event. Thus, if an individual is treated as indirectly holding a qualified payment interest held by a trust, a taxable event occurs on the earlier of: (1) the termination of the individual's interest in the trust (whether by death or otherwise) or (2) the termination of the trust's interest in the qualified payment interest (whether by disposition or otherwise).[207]

Exception. If, at the time of a termination of an individual's rights with respect to a qualified payment interest, the value of the property would be includable in the individual's gross estate for federal estate tax purposes if the individual died immediately after the termination, a taxable transfer does not occur until the earlier of: (1) the time the property would no longer be in-

---

[203] IRC § 2701(d)(3)(A)(i).

[204] IRC § 2701(d)(3)(A)(ii).

[205] IRC § 2701(d)(3)(A)(iii).

[206] In certain circumstances, discussed at ¶¶ 31.12[5] and 31.12[6] below, the person with respect to whom a taxable event occurs is not the original interest holder who made the IRC § 2701 transfer. The regulations provide adjusting language for computing the increase in taxable transfers when a taxable event occurs with respect to a person treated as the interest holder. Treas. Reg. § 25.2701-4(b)(1).

[207] Treas. Reg. § 25.2701-4(b)(1).

cludable in the individual's gross estate (other than by reason of Section 2035) or (2) the death of the individual.[208]

[2] Consequences of Taxable Event

[a] Taxable Event: Death of Transferor

The taxable estate of the transferor will be increased in the case of a taxable event occurring at the transferor's death by the amount described in ¶ 31.12[3] below.[209] Note that the regulations refer to an increase in the taxable estate of the individual holding the interest, rather than the transferor.[210]

[b] Taxable Event: Lifetime Transfer or Late Payment

In the case of any other taxable event, the transferor's taxable gifts for the calendar year in which the taxable event occurs are increased by the amount described in ¶ 31.12[3] below.[211] Note that the regulations refer to an increase in the taxable gifts of the individual holding the interest, rather than the transferor.[212]

Phantom amounts. There is no indication of the identity of the deemed recipient of these increases in cases where the increase includes a phantom amount (i.e., one that no one will ever actually receive). And, in the case of phantom amounts, Sections 1014 and 1015 may not allow any basis increase, since there is no property actually transferred to which a basis increase would normally attach. Similar problems exist under Sections 2013, 2056, and 2503.

[3] Amount of Increase

[a] General Rule

The amount of the increase is the excess, if any, of—

- The value of the qualified payments payable during the period beginning on the date of the specially valued transfer (or, in the case of an individual treated as the interest holder, on the date the interest of the prior interest holder terminated) and ending on the date of the taxable event, determined as if all such payments were paid on the due dates, and all such payments were reinvested as of the date of payment at a

---

[208] Treas. Reg. § 25.2701-4(b)(2).

[209] IRC § 2701(d)(1)(A).

[210] Treas. Reg. § 25.2701-4(a).

[211] IRC § 2701(d)(1)(B).

[212] Treas. Reg. § 25.2701-4(a).

yield equal to the discount rate used in specially valuing the applicable retained interest, OVER

- The value of such payments paid during the above period computed above on the basis of the time when such payments were actually paid, plus to the extent required to prevent double inclusion, an amount equal to the sum of: (1) the portion of the fair market value of the qualified payment interest solely attributable to any legal right to receive unpaid qualified payments determined as of the date of the taxable event; (2) the fair market value of any equity interest in the entity received by the individual in lieu of qualified payments and held by the individual at the taxable event; and (3) the amount by which the individual's aggregate taxable gifts were increased by reason of the failure of the individual to enforce the right to receive qualified payments.[213]

The regulations address the fact that, absent the above provision, double taxation could result to the extent that the retained distribution right that will itself be in the transfer tax base already includes in its value a cumulative or compounding feature.

[b] Payments

[i] Payments made on dates other than their due dates. Any payment made (or treated as made) during the four-year period beginning on its due date is treated as having been made on such due date.[214] The regulations provide the same treatment for payments made before such four-year period, provided the payments are made before the date of the taxable event. In addition, the regulations provide that the transfer of a debt obligation bearing compound interest from the due date of the payment at a rate not less than the appropriate discount rate is a qualified payment if the term of the obligation (including extensions) does not exceed four years from the date issued. A payment in the form of an equity interest in the entity is not a qualified payment.[215] The appropriate discount rate is the discount rate that was applied in determining the value of the qualified payment right at the time of the specially valued transfer.[216]

Treasury Regulation § 25.2701-4(c)(5) provides that a payment in the form of an equity interest in the entity is not a qualified payment, although Treasury Regulation § 25.2701-4(c)(1) takes the fair market value of any

---

[213] IRC § 2701(d)(2)(A); Treas. Reg. § 25.2701-4(c)(1).

[214] IRC § 2701(d)(2)(C).

[215] Treas. Reg. § 25.2701-4(c)(5).

[216] Treas. Reg. § 25.2701-4(c)(3).

equity interest received in lieu of qualified payments into account in determining the increase to an interest holder's taxable estate or taxable gifts.

[ii] **Application of payments.** Any payment of an unpaid qualified payment is applied in satisfaction of unpaid qualified payments beginning with the earliest unpaid qualified payment. Any payment in excess of the total of all unpaid qualified payments is treated as a prepayment of future qualified payments.[217]

[iii] **"Due date" defined.** With respect to any qualified payment, the "due date" is that date specified in the governing instrument as the date on which payment is to be made. If no date is specified in the governing instrument, the due date is the last day of each calendar year.[218]

> EXAMPLE: Suppose that in 1991, A transfers common stock, retaining an applicable retained interest which consists of a right to receive $100 per year of dividends on preferred stock. The dividend is discounted at 10 percent for purposes of valuation. As of 1995, no dividends have been paid. In 1996, all back payments are made. With no election to treat the late payment as a taxable event, A will eventually pay gift or estate tax (subject to the value limitations discussed below) on the excess of the value of the unpaid dividends, based on the assumption that the dividends were paid on time and invested at 10 percent until A's eventual transfer of the preferred stock, over their value on the assumption that the dividends were paid at their actual payment date and reinvested at 10 percent until such transfer.

Numerous questions still remain about the application of the rules computing the amount of increase. These are examined using the facts of the following illustration.

> ILLUSTRATION 2: X owns preferred stock which gives him a right to receive qualified payments of $100 on December 31 of each year. In November 1991, X transfers common stock to his daughter, retaining the qualified payment preferred stock. The market dividend rate is 10 percent. The preferred stock dividend is passed in 1991. In 1992, X transfers his preferred stock to a third party.

In Illustration 2, what happens when the second transfer is made before the four-year grace period expires? The qualified payment could be deemed to be paid, the grace period could terminate on the transfer, or a tax could be assessed on the unpaid dividends at the date of transfer. If the last alternative

---

[217] Treas. Reg. § 25.2701-4(c)(4).
[218] Treas. Reg. § 25.2701-4(c)(2).

applies, X will be treated as having made a gift in 1992, equal to $100, plus interest of 10 percent from December 31, 1991.

What happens in Illustration 2 if the 1991 dividend is paid in 1992 to the then holder of the stock? Is X entitled to a refund of his gift taxes?

In Illustration 2, suppose that X's daughter owns 50 percent of the common stock and an unrelated third party owns the other half. The failure to make the payment benefits the third party as well as the Daughter, since the third party's interest includes 50 percent of the retained earnings. On the taxable event, is there a gift of $50 plus interest to Daughter and $50 plus interest to third party?

NOTE: A gratuitous transfer to a corporation is deemed to be a gift to the shareholders.[219] Such a gift has been held not to qualify for the annual exclusion.[220]

What if, in Illustration 2, instead of X transferring his preferred stock in 1992, X's daughter sells her common stock to an unrelated third party? There is no provision stopping the continued compounding of unpaid dividends, even though all family members have ceased to own any of the common stock.

Further, in Illustration 2, suppose that the qualified payment preferred stock was valued at 60 percent of face, due to possible inability of the company to pay the dividends, and that the 60 percent valuation of the preferred stock increases X's taxable gift to his daughter. If X is treated as making an additional gift of $100 in 1992, he will have paid additional gift tax on the original transfer of the common stock to his daughter in 1991, due to the corporation's probable inability to pay the preferred stock's dividend, and in 1992, will again pay gift tax on the nonpayment. No adjustment is made for this double tax.

Will constructive dividends under the Internal Revenue Code count as payments?

Failure to pay or enforce right to be paid dividends. If a *Dickman* analysis[221] applies to a failure to pay dividends, resulting in a taxable gift in the years of failure to pay, the Chapter 14 gift on the ultimate taxable event is reduced by the amount by which the interest holder's aggregate taxable gifts were increased due to his or her failure to enforce the right to receive qualified payments.[222] Also, the IRS has taken the position that not only may the failure to enforce the right to receive qualified payments result in a taxable gift, but the failure of an individual who controls a corporation either to cause the

---

[219] Treas. Reg. § 25.2511-1(h)(1).

[220] E.g., Chanin v. United States, 393 F2d 972, 975-976 (Ct. Cl. 1968); Georgia L. Ketteman Hollingsworth Trust v. Comm'r, 86 TC 91, 107-108 (1986); Rev. Rul. 71-443, 1971-2 CB 337, 338.

[221] From Dickman v. Comm'r, 465 US 330 (1984).

[222] Treas. Reg. § 25.2701-4(c)(1)(ii)(C)(3).

corporation to increase dividends to a level commensurate with the dividend rate in the prevailing market or to liquidate the corporation may also give rise to a taxable gift.[223] Although the IRS cites *Snyder v. Commissioner*[224] in support of its position, the holding in the technical advice memorandum appears to be at the least an extension of *Snyder*, and perhaps inconsistent with the Tax Court's determination that the failure to exercise a put option does not give rise to a taxable gift.[225]

PRACTICE POINTER: Will drafters should be careful to take the additional tax into account in drafting the tax apportionment clause in the will or other dispositive instrument. There is no automatic right of apportionment provided under federal law. Consideration should be given to the fact that the identity of the recipient of the deemed transfer is not at all clear under the statute and the tax increase may be imposed on additional value which does not actually exist.

[c] Limitation on Increase

[i] General rule. The increase in an individual's taxable estate or taxable gifts cannot exceed the applicable percentage (as defined below) of the excess, if any, of—

- The sum of (1) the fair market value of all outstanding equity interests in the entity that are subordinate to the applicable retained interest, determined as of the date of the taxable event without regard to any accrued liability attributable to unpaid qualified payments, and (2) any amounts expended by the entity to redeem or otherwise acquire any such subordinate interest during the period beginning on the date of the specially valued transfer (or, in the case of an individual treated as an interest holder, on the date the interest of the prior interest holder terminated) and ending on the date of the taxable event (reduced by any amounts received on the resale or issuance of any such subordinate interest during the same period), OVER
- The fair market value of such subordinate interests, determined as of the date of the transfer which was specially valued (or, in the case of an individual treated as an interest holder, on the date the interest of the prior interest holder terminated).[226]

EXAMPLE: *X* owns 100 percent of the stock of Corporation. He transfers all of the common stock to child, retaining the preferred stock, which

---

[223] Tech. Adv. Mem. 9301001 (June 30, 1992).

[224] 93 TC 529 (1989).

[225] See Snyder, 93 TC at 546-547.

[226] IRC § 2701(d)(2)(B)(i); Treas. Reg. § 25.2701-4(c)(6)(i).

confers a qualified payment right. The common stock is worth $1,000 on the date of transfer. The entity has $400 of unpaid preferred stock dividends when X dies. The value of the common stock at the date of X's death, without any reduction on account of the $400 of unpaid preferred stock dividends, is $1200. Corporation spent $100 to redeem part of the common stock three months before X's death. The increase in X's taxable estate is limited to $300.

[ii] **Special rule.** For purposes of computing the limitation on the increase to an individual's taxable estate or taxable gifts, the aggregate fair market value of the subordinate interests in the entity is determined without regard to the rule concerning the minimum value of junior equity interests.[227]

EXAMPLE: X owns 100 percent of the stock of Corporation. He transfers all of the common stock to child, retaining the preferred stock, which confers a qualified payment right. Due to the application of the minimum value rule, the common stock is worth $1,000 on the date of transfer, but its real value was zero. The entity has $400 of unpaid preferred stock dividends when X dies. The value of the common stock at the date of X's death, without any reduction on account of the $400 of unpaid preferred stock dividends, is $1200. Corporation spent $100 to redeem part of the common stock three months before X's death. The increase in X's taxable estate is limited to $1,300.

[iii] **Applicable percentage.** The "applicable percentage" is the percentage determined by dividing—

- The number of shares or units of the applicable retained interest held by the interest holder (or an individual treated as the interest holder) on the date of the taxable event, by
- The total number of such shares or units outstanding on the same date.[228]

EXAMPLE: X owns 100 percent of the stock of Corporation. He transfers all of the common stock to child, retaining the 60 percent of the corporation's preferred stock, which confers a qualified payment right. The common stock is worth $1,000 on the date of transfer. The entity has $400 of unpaid preferred stock dividends when X dies. The value of the common stock at the date of X's death, without any reduction on account of the $400 of unpaid preferred stock dividends, is $1200. Corporation spent $100 to redeem part of the common stock three months before X's death. The increase in X's taxable estate is limited to $180.

---

[227] Treas. Reg. § 25.2701-4(c)(6)(ii).
[228] Treas. Reg. § 25.2701-4(c)(6)(iii).

If an individual holds applicable retained interests in two or more classes of interests, the applicable percentage is equal to the largest applicable percentage determined with respect to any class.[229] Thus, if X owns 75 percent of Class A preferred stock and 80 percent of Class B preferred stock, the limitation on increase is 80 percent of the increase in value of the common stock, as adjusted above.

It should be noted that the formula increases the transfer base, even when transfers benefit unrelated third parties.

> EXAMPLE: Suppose P owns 100 percent of the cumulative preferred stock of X Corporation, worth $1,000,000. P and Third Party each own one--half of the common stock, worth $500,000 each. P transfers 10 percent of the common stock to Child. No dividends have been paid on the preferred stock when P dies ten years later. The value of the common stock, without regard to the unpaid dividends, is then $1,500,000. The cap in value of the increase in P's estate is $500,000, notwithstanding that 50 percent of the benefit of P's not receiving dividends accrues to an unrelated party and 40 percent of this benefit accrues to P himself, and is included in his estate.[230]

[4] Special Rule for Elected Taxable Events

An interest holder (or an individual treated as an interest holder) may elect to treat the making of a late payment as a taxable event.[231] This election will stop the compounding of interest on the late payment. Once made, the election may not be revoked without the consent of the IRS.[232]

[a] Time and Manner of Election

[i] Timely filed return. The election may be made by attaching a statement to the qualified payment recipient's timely filed federal gift tax return for the year in which the qualified payment is received. Once the election is filed, the taxable event is deemed to occur on the date the qualified payment is received.[233] The regulations detail the requirements of the statement.[234]

---

[229] Treas. Reg. § 25.2701-4(c)(6)(iii).

[230] Note, however, that Treas. Reg. § 25.2701-4(c)(1)(ii)(C)(1) appears to provide an adjustment for the inclusion of P's right to receive unpaid qualified payments in P's estate.

[231] Treas. Reg. § 25.2701-4(d)(1).

[232] Treas. Reg. § 25.2701-4(d)(1).

[233] Treas. Reg. § 25.2701-4(d)(3)(i).

[234] Treas. Reg. § 25.2701-4(d)(3)(iii).

[ii] **Late return.** The election may also be made by attaching a statement to a late federal gift tax return by the qualified payment recipient for the year in which the qualified payment is received. In that case, the taxable event is deemed to occur on the first day of the month immediately preceding the month in which the late return is filed. Moreover, if an election, other than an election on a timely return, is made after the death of the interest holder, the taxable event with respect to the decedent is deemed to occur on the later of (1) the date of the recipient's death or (2) the first day of the month immediately preceding the month in which the return is filed.[235]

[b] Payments to Which Election Applies

If an election is made to treat a late payment as a taxable event, the increase in the interest holder's taxable estate or taxable gifts is determined only with respect to the elected payment.[236]

EXAMPLE: *A* holds a qualified payment interest that he retained when he made a transfer in 1991. No dividends were paid in 1992 through 1996. In 1997, *A* received a late qualified payment. No election was made to treat that payment as a taxable event. In 1998, *A* received another late qualified payment. *A* elects to treat the payment in 1998 as a taxable event. The election increases *A*'s taxable gifts in 1998. The regulations treat the election as applying to the payments made in both 1997 and 1998, but these were written before the amendment of Section 2701(d)(3)(A)(iii) in 1996.[237]

[c] Computation of Transfers for Future Taxable Events

Payments for which an election applies are treated as having been paid on their due dates for purposes of subsequent taxable events.[238]

EXAMPLE: *A* holds a qualified payment interest that he retained when he made a transfer in 1991. No dividends were paid in 1992 through 1996. In 1997, A received a late qualified payment. No election was made to treat that payment as a taxable event. In 1998, *A* received another late qualified payment. *A* elects to treat the payment in 1998 as a taxable event. If the due date of the late payments was in 1991, *A* will be able to treat them as having been paid and reinvested in 1991, for purposes of computing the tax on future transfers or late payments.

---

[235] Treas. Reg. § 25.2701-4(d)(3)(ii).

[236] IRC § 2701(d)(3)(A)(iii).

[237] Treas. Reg. § 25.2701-4(d)(1).

[238] Treas. Reg. § 25.2701-4(d)(1).

[d] No Limitation on Increase

While the regulations provide that the limitation on the increase in value (described at ¶ 31.12[3][c] above) does not apply if a taxpayer elects to treat a late payment as a taxable event,[239] this is inconsistent with the statute. The preamble to the proposed regulations stated that, absent this rule, a taxpayer could manipulate the timing of payments and elections to take advantage of temporary fluctuations in the value of the entity.[240] Thus, in the absence of this rule, a qualified payment interest holder would want to make an election when the value of the company is low enough to result in little or no gift tax being paid.

[e] Unpaid Arrearages

Unfortunately, no election is available to treat unpaid arrearages as a taxable gift.

[5] Marital Exceptions

[a] Transfers to Spouses at Death

[i] **Transfers qualifying for marital deduction.** The rule that the death of a transferor will result in a taxable event giving rise to an increase in the transferor's taxable estate does not apply to any interest includable in the transferor's gross estate if a marital deduction is allowable with respect to such interest under Section 2056 or Section 2106(a)(3).[241]

[ii] **Regulatory interpretation.** The regulations state this exception somewhat differently, providing that if an interest holder (or an individual treated as the interest holder) transfers a qualified payment interest, the transfer is not a taxable event (and thus does not give rise to an increase in the interest holder's taxable estate) to the extent that a marital deduction is allowed with respect to the transfer under Section 2056 or Section 2106(a)(3).[242]

[iii] **Special rule for discretionary funding of marital bequests.** If the selection of property with which a marital bequest is funded is discretionary, a transfer of a qualified payment interest will not be considered a transfer to the surviving spouse unless—

---

[239] Treas. Reg. § 25.2701-4(d)(2).

[240] 56 Fed. Reg. 14,321 (1991).

[241] IRC § 2701(d)(3)(B)(i).

[242] Treas. Reg. § 25.2701-4(b)(3)(ii)(A).

- The marital bequest is funded with the qualified payment interest before the due date for filing the decedent's federal estate tax return (including extensions actually granted) (the "due date"), or
- The executor: (1) files a statement with the return indicating the extent to which the marital bequest will be funded with the qualified payment interest and (2) before the date that is one year prior to the expiration of the period of limitations on assessment of the federal estate tax, notifies the IRS district director of the extent to which the bequest was funded with the qualified payment interest (or the extent to which the qualified payment interest has been permanently set aside for that purpose).[243]

Under the circumstances, it may be advisable for an interest holder to recommend in his will that his executor or administrator consider using qualified payment interests held by the estate to fund the marital bequest, if the interest holder wants the transfer of the qualified payment interest to qualify for the marital deduction.

[iv] Purchase of qualified payment interest by surviving spouse. The regulations provide that if the surviving spouse or a QTIP trust purchases, before the due date, a qualified payment interest held (directly or indirectly) by the decedent immediately before death, the purchase is considered a transfer with respect to which the marital deduction is allowable, but only to the extent that the marital deduction is allowed to the estate.[244]

EXAMPLE: A bequeaths $100,000 to his wife in his will. A's wife then purchases a qualified payment interest from A's estate for $200,000, its fair market value. One-half of the qualified payment interest is considered a transfer for which a marital deduction is allowable. The economic effect of the transaction is the equivalent of a bequest from A to his wife of the qualified payment interest, with one-half of the bequest qualifying for the marital deduction.[245]

Time of purchase. If the purchase is not made before the due date of the decedent's estate tax return, the purchase of the qualified payment interest will not be considered a bequest for which a marital deduction is allowed unless the executor—

- Files a statement with the return indicating the qualified payment interests to be purchased by the surviving spouse or a QTIP trust, and
- Before the date that is one year prior to the expiration of the period of limitations on assessment of the federal estate tax, notifies the district

---

[243] Treas. Reg. § 25.2701-4(b)(3)(ii)(B).
[244] Treas. Reg. § 25.2701-4(b)(3)(ii)(C).
[245] Treas. Reg. § 25.2701-4(b)(3)(ii)(C).

director that the purchase of the qualified payment interest has been made (or that the funds necessary to purchase the qualified payment interest have been permanently set aside for that purpose).[246]

Availability of marital deduction. If the taxable estate of an individual is increased by the amount of compounded unpaid distributions, this amount may not qualify for the marital deduction. For example, if X's estate is increased by an amount which represents $100,000 of unpaid qualified payments, and $36,000 of compounding, does all (or any) of this amount pass to the surviving spouse, as required to qualify for the marital deduction? Because the surviving spouse may not be entitled under state law to the unpaid dividends and will rarely be entitled to the compounded interest payment, no amount (or an amount less than $136,000) may actually pass to the surviving spouse.

[b] Lifetime Transfers

A transfer to the transferor's spouse will not result in a taxable event (thereby giving rise to an increase in the transferor's taxable gifts) if the transfer does not result in a taxable gift because of the applicability of the marital deduction or the annual exclusion, or because consideration for the transfer was provided by the spouse.[247] In this regard, it should be noted that no gift tax marital deduction is available if the transferee-spouse is a not a U.S. citizen.[248]

[c] Spousal Treatment

[i] In general. If a transfer is not treated as a taxable event by reason of the above rules, the spouse is treated in the same manner as the transferor in applying the rules relating to unpaid distributions with respect to the interest involved.[249] Among other things, this means that the transferee-spouse will be subject to gift or estate tax for unpaid distributions, with compounding, relating from the date of the original specially valued transfer.

[ii] Regulatory interpretation. The regulations provide that the transferee-spouse will be treated as if he or she were the holder of the interest from the date the transferor spouse acquired the interest.[250] However, it is

---

[246] Treas. Reg. § 25.2701-4(b)(3)(ii)(C).

[247] IRC § 2701(d)(3)(B)(ii).

[248] IRC § 2523(i)(1).

[249] IRC § 2701(d)(3)(B)(iii).

[250] Treas. Reg. § 25.2701-4(b)(3)(ii)(A).

unclear why the IRS's position is that the transferee spouse is to be treated as the holder of the interest from the date the transferor spouse acquired the interest, rather than from the later to occur of this date or the date of the original specially valued transfer.

[iii] **Charitable remainder trusts.** If the deduction for a transfer to a spouse is allowable under Section 2056(b)(8) or Section 2523(g) (relating to charitable remainder trusts), the transferee spouse is treated as the holder of the entire interest passing to the trust.[251] Presumably this treatment only applies for purposes of the rule regarding the compounding of unpaid distributions.

QUERY: Where a qualified payment interest is transferred to a QTIP trust, is the surviving spouse liable for the extra gift or estate tax on the late or unpaid dividends which are supposed to be paid to the trust? If the spouse is liable, a will drafter could provide for extra distributions to the spouse during the spouse's life, and for payment of the estate tax, out of a QTIP trust. But what about a charitable remainder trust with the spouse as beneficiary?

[6] Special Rules for "Applicable Family Members"

[a] Family Member Treated as Transferor

An applicable family member is treated in the same manner as the transferor with respect to any distribution right retained by such family member that was specially valued under Section 2701.[252]

EXAMPLE: A's mother owns all the preferred stock of X Corporation. A owns all the common stock. A transfers all the common stock to his daughter. If the preferred stock qualifies as a qualified payment interest, and A's mother does not elect out or is not treated as having elected out under the regulations, A's gift will be reduced by the value of the preferred stock, but A's mother will be subject to the compounding rules and the additional gift and estate taxes on any unpaid dividends.

[b] Transfer to Applicable Family Member

In the case of a lifetime transfer of an applicable retained interest to an applicable family member (other than the transferor's spouse), the applicable family member is treated in the same manner as the transferor under the rules

---

[251] Treas. Reg. § 25.2701-4(b)(3)(ii)(A).

[252] IRC § 2701(d)(4)(A).

regarding unpaid distributions to distributions accumulating with respect to such interest after such transfer.[253] The regulations provide that, if a taxable event involves the transfer of a qualified payment interest by the interest holder (or an individual treated as the interest holder) to an applicable family member of the individual who originally made the specially valued transfer (other than the spouse of the individual transferring the qualified payment interest), the transferee applicable family member is treated in the same manner as the interest holder with respect to late or unpaid qualified payments first due after the taxable event.[254]

The original transferor will be liable for the tax on unpaid distributions that have accumulated up to the date of transfer. The transfer to the applicable family member will be a taxable event causing an increase in the transferor's taxable gifts. The transferee is treated thereafter in the same manner as the interest holder with respect to late or unpaid qualified payments first due after the taxable event.[255] Hence, one cannot avoid the tax on future unpaid distributions by a transfer to an applicable family member (unless it is a transfer by death). The regulations do not limit this treatment to lifetime transfers, although that is clearly called for by the statute.[256]

Accordingly, it appears that, in the case of a transfer to one's spouse which does not qualify for the marital deduction, the spouse will not be liable with respect to unpaid qualified payments first due after the transfer.

¶ 31.13   ADJUSTMENTS

Under regulations, if there is any subsequent transfer or inclusion in the gross estate of any applicable retained interest which was specially valued under Section 2701, appropriate adjustments are made for purposes of the gift, estate, or generation-skipping transfer tax (1) to reflect the increase in the amount of any prior taxable gift made by the transferor or decedent by reason of such valuation or (2) to reflect the inclusion of unpaid amounts with respect to a qualified payment.[257]

The original proposed regulations applied an estate tax credit system of adjustment. The final regulations provide for a reduction in the decedent's adjusted taxable gifts.

---

[253] IRC § 2701(d)(4)(B).

[254] Treas. Reg. § 25.2701-4(b)(3)(i).

[255] Treas. Reg. § 25.2701-4(b)(3)(i).

[256] Treas. Reg. § 25.2701-4(b)(3)(i).

[257] IRC § 2701(e)(6).

[1] Reduction in Adjusted Taxable Gifts

[a] In General

Except as provided in ¶ 31.13[1][b] below, in determining the federal gift or estate tax with respect to an individual (the "initial transferor") who previously made a transfer subject to Section 2701 (the "initial transfer"): (1) the initial transferor may reduce the base on which his tentative gift tax is computed, where a Section 2701 interest (as defined below) has been transferred to someone other than himself (or an applicable family member) or (2) the initial transferor's executor may reduce the decedent's adjusted taxable gifts[258] by the amount determined in ¶ 31.13[2] below (the "reduction").[259] Special rules apply where the initial transfer is split pursuant to Section 2513.[260]

[b] "Section 2701 Interest" Defined

"Section 2701 interest" means an applicable retained interest that was valued using the special valuation rules of Section 2701 at the time of the initial transfer. An interest will not be considered a Section 2701 interest except to the extent that the transfer of the interest effectively reduces the aggregate ownership of that class of interest by the initial transferor and applicable family members below what their ownership had been at the time of the initial transfer (or the remaining portion thereof).[261]

[2] Amount of Reduction

[a] In General

The amount of the reduction is the lesser of (1) the amount by which the transferor's taxable gifts were increased as a result of the application of Section 2701 to the initial transfer or (2) the amount[262] duplicated in the transfer tax base at the time of the transfer of the Section 2701 interest (the "duplicated amount").[263]

---

[258] Under IRC § 2001(b).

[259] Treas. Reg. § 25.2701-5(a).

[260] Treas. Reg. § 25.2701-5(e).

[261] Treas. Reg. § 25.2701-5(a)(4).

[262] Determined under ¶ 31.13[2][b] below.

[263] Treas. Reg. § 25.2701-5(b).

[b] Duplicated Amount

[i] In general. The duplicated amount is the amount by which the Section 2701 interest's transfer tax value[264] at the time of the subsequent transfer exceeds the Section 2701 value of the interest at the time of the initial transfer. If, however, the amount allocated to the transferred interest under Step 3 of the procedure used in valuing the initial transfer[265] is less than the entire amount then available for allocation, then the duplicated amount (as determined in the preceding sentence) is multiplied by a fraction, the numerator of which is the amount allocated to the transferred interest at the time of the initial transfer pursuant to Step 3, and the denominator of which is the amount determined after application of Step 2 of the valuation procedure.[266]

[ii] Transfer tax value. The transfer tax value is the value of the Section 2701 interest as finally determined for federal estate or gift tax purposes, reduced by any deductions allowed with respect to the Section 2701 interest to the extent the deductions would not have been allowed if the Section 2701 interest had not been included in the initial transferor's gifts or estate.[267]

[iii] Special rules affecting transfer tax value.

Transfers for consideration. Except where a transfer is made in a nonrecognition transaction (discussed below), if a Section 2701 interest is transferred for consideration (or in a transfer that is deemed to be for consideration) during the initial transferor's lifetime to (or for the benefit of) an individual other than the initial transferor (or an applicable family member), the transfer of the Section 2701 interest is deemed to take place at the death of the initial transferor. Under these circumstances, the estate of the initial transferor receives a reduction in adjusted taxable gifts as if the estate included a Section 2701 interest with an estate tax value equal to the consideration received (determined as of the time of the exchange).[268]

Interests held by applicable family members. If a Section 2701 interest is held by an applicable family member (rather than the initial transferor) at the time of the initial transferor's death, the Section 2701 interest is deemed to have been transferred at that death to someone other than the initial transferor or an applicable family member. The transfer tax value in such a case is the value that the executor of the initial transferor's estate can demonstrate would

---

[264] As defined below.

[265] Discussed at ¶ 31.11[2] above.

[266] Treas. Reg. § 25.2701-5(c)(1).

[267] Treas. Reg. § 25.2701-5(c)(2). Rules similar to those found in IRC § 691(c)(2) are applicable in determining whether a deduction would not be allowed.

[268] Treas. Reg. § 25.2701-5(c)(3)(i).

be determined for gift tax purposes had the interest been transferred immediately prior to the initial transferor's death.[269]

Non-recognition transactions. To the extent the transferor exchanged a Section 2701 interest in a transaction in which gain or loss was not recognized, the exchange is not treated as a transfer of a Section 2701 interest, and the transfer tax value of the Section 2701 interest is determined as if the new interest were the Section 2701 interest.[270]

Other rules. If a subsequent transfer is made of less than the entire Section 2701 interest, the amount of the reduction is reduced proportionately.[271] If more than one class of Section 2701 interest exists, the reduction is determined separately with respect to each class.[272] The reduction in the case of an initial transferor who has made more than one initial transfer is the sum of the reductions computed with respect to each initial transfer.[273]

[3] "Double Taxation Otherwise Avoided" Rule

Notwithstanding any other provision of the rules governing the reduction of a transferor's adjusted taxable gifts, no reduction is available to the extent that (1) double taxation is otherwise avoided in the computation of the estate tax under Section 2001 (or Section 2101) or (2) a reduction was previously taken with respect to the same Section 2701 interest and the same initial transfer.[274]

¶ 31.14　EFFECTIVE DATE

The rules described in Section 2701 only apply to transfers after October 8, 1990.[275] Note, however, that a transfer after October 8, 1990 of common stock by a holder of grandfathered preferred stock would be subject to Chapter 14.

With respect to property transferred before October 9, 1990, (1) any failure to exercise a right of conversion, (2) any failure to pay dividends, and (3) any failure to exercise other rights specified in regulations, is not treated as a subsequent transfer.[276] This provision shelters such a transaction from Chap-

---

[269] Treas. Reg. § 25.2701-5(c)(3)(ii).

[270] Treas. Reg. § 25.2701-5(c)(3)(iii).

[271] Treas. Reg. § 25.2701-5(c)(3)(iv).

[272] Treas. Reg. § 25.2701-5(c)(3)(v).

[273] Treas. Reg. § 25.2701-5(c)(3)(vi).

[274] Treas. Reg. § 25.2701-5(g).

[275] OBRA § 11602(e)(1)(A)(i).

[276] OBRA § 11602(e)(1)(B).

ter 14 consequences, but apparently does not prevent the taxation of such a transaction as a taxable gift under Chapter 12.[277]

QUERY What if a pre–October 9, 1990 partnership agreement requires additional capital contributions? Will capital contributions made after October 8, 1990 be grandfathered?

The final Section 2701 regulations are effective as of January 28, 1992, except for Treasury Regulation § 25.2701-5, which is effective May 4, 1994. For transfers made prior to the effective date of the regulations, taxpayers may rely on any reasonable interpretation of the statutory provisions. For these purposes, the provisions of the proposed regulations and the final regulations are considered a reasonable interpretation of the statutory provisions.[278]

---

[277] See S. Rep. at S15,679-80.
[278] Treas. Reg. § 25.2701-8.

PART **VIII**

Charitable Planning

Outright Charitable Gifts

¶ 32.01 INTRODUCTION

Charitable gifts often play a much bigger part in planning for large estates than they do for smaller ones. This chapter discusses some federal income, estate, gift, and generation-skipping transfer tax considerations individuals should keep in mind in deciding whether and how to make charitable gifts.

¶ 32.02 INCOME TAX DEDUCTION FOR CHARITABLE GIFTS—GENERAL

In many instances, contributions to charities will generate an income tax deduction. Various rules apply, as discussed below.

[1] Advantages of Lifetime Gifts to Charity

Other things being equal, it is usually better for the donor to make a charitable gift during life than at death, because the gift can generate an income tax charitable deduction for the donor.[1] There is also an income tax charitable deduction for estates and irrevocable trusts, including a revocable trust which

---

[1] IRC § 170(a).

has become irrevocable due to a death.[2] However, the deduction is only available to the extent that the entity's income (a) is permitted by the governing instrument or applicable law to be paid to charity and (b) actually is paid to charity (estates and trusts) or set aside for charity (estates only) during the taxable year. That is, no income tax charitable deduction is allowed for disposition of the estate or trust assets existing at the donor's death—only for disposition of the estate's or trust's income to charity.

> **EXAMPLE:** Charles has income of $100,000. He makes a $50,000 gift to the Red Cross. He receives an income tax charitable deduction of $50,000,[3] even if the $50,000 donation did not consist of income he earned in that year.

> **EXAMPLE:** Charles dies, leaving a $50,000 specific bequest to the Red Cross, residue to his children. His estate has $100,000 income in Year One. The estate cannot claim an income tax charitable deduction for the payment or set-aside of the bequest itself. It can only claim an income tax charitable deduction for amounts of estate income which the charity is entitled to receive as a result of the bequest. If, for instance, the residuary estate were entitled to all of the estate's income, no income tax charitable deduction would be available on account of the bequest. If, however, the Red Cross's bequest entitled it to a share of the estate's income, then that share would be eligible for a deduction by the estate on its payment or set-aside.

[2] Limitations Applicable to Charitable Income Tax Deduction for Contributions During Lifetime of Donor

Certain limits apply to the income tax charitable deduction. The limits may depend on the type of donee charity. The two general types of categories are "50 percent charities" and "30 percent charities," as explained below. Additional factors which may limit the deduction include—

- The amount of the donor's contribution base (defined below);
- Whether the contributed property is ordinary income property, capital gain property, or neither;
- Whether the property will be used to further the charity's exempt purpose; and
- Other factors, as discussed below.

The two charts below can be used to determine the above limitations on the deductibility of non-split-interest outright gifts to charity. Apply Charts A and B. The lowest amount deductible applies. The deduction can be further

---

[2] IRC § 642(c).

[3] Subject to other applicable limitations, of course, as discussed below.

reduced if the rules on mixed gifts (discussed below) apply or if other special rules (also discussed below) apply.

Contribution Base Limits

Type of Gift	Percentage of Contribution Base Deductible
Gift to 50 percent charity (except long-term capital gain property)	50 percent
Gift of long-term capital gain property to 50 percent charity	30 percent, or 50 percent if deduction is limited to basis
Gift to 30 percent charity (except long-term capital gain property)	30 percent
Gift of long-term capital gain property to 30 percent charity	20 percent

Property For Which Deduction is Limited To Basis

- Gift to 50 percent charity, if the donor has elected to limit the deduction of long-term capital gain property to basis, as a tradeoff for the 50 percent-of-contribution-base limit.
- Property which would generate short-term capital gain or ordinary income if it were sold.
- Gift of tangible personal property to 50 percent charity, if the charity will not use the property in its exempt purpose.
- Any gift to a 30 percent charity, except gift of qualified appreciated stock made in certain years before 1995 or during the period July 1, 1996, through May 31, 1997.

¶ 32.03   INCOME TAX DEDUCTION—GIFTS TO 50 PERCENT CHARITIES

Favorable deduction rules apply to certain types of charities, which we'll call "50 percent charities."

[1] Definition of "50 percent Charity"

The three types of 50 percent charities[4] are public charities, governments, and certain private charities.

---

[4] Defined in IRC § 170(b)(1)(A).

[a] Public Charities

"Public charities" include all charities which are not private foundations.

[b] Governments

"Governments" include only domestic (federal and state) governments and their divisions, agencies, etc. Foreign governments and their divisions or agencies cannot qualify as 50 percent charities.

[c] Certain Private Charities

Three special types of private charities qualify: the "private operating foundation," the "private pass-through foundation," and the "private investment fund." These three types of private charities must meet certain "qualifying distribution" requirements in order to qualify as 50 percent charities.

General rule. A qualifying distribution is any amount (including reasonable and necessary administrative expenses) paid directly to accomplish charitable purposes or any amount paid to acquire an asset used directly in carrying out a charitable purpose.[5]

Exception. However, a qualifying distribution does not include any distribution which is made to either: (1) an organization that is controlled, directly or indirectly, by the private charity or by one or more disqualified persons[6] as to such charity or (2) a private foundation which is not a private operating foundation (defined below).[7]

Exception to the exception. A distribution not qualifying as a qualifying distribution under the above exception will nevertheless be a qualifying distribution if: (1) by the end of the taxable year following the year of the contribution, the donee organization itself distributes an amount equal to the contribution in a qualifying distribution that is treated as made out of principal[8] and (2) the donor organization obtains adequate records or other evidence from the donee organization showing that the qualifying distribution was made.[9]

EXAMPLE: Charity *A* makes a grant of $10,000 to Private Foundation *X*

---

[5] IRC § 4942(g)(1). Assets paid or used directly to accomplish charitable purposes do not include grants to other charities or investment assets. See Treas. Reg. § 53.4942(b)-1(b)(1).

[6] Disqualified persons are defined in IRC § 4946, and are further discussed in Ch. 37 on private foundations.

[7] IRC § 4942(g)(1)(A).

[8] That is, the qualifying distribution is not part of the donee organization's undistributed income for the year of the contribution and the next year.

[9] IRC § 4942(g)(3).

in Year One. Charity A's grant is a qualifying distribution if (1) Foundation X itself makes a qualifying distribution of $10,000 out of principal by the end of Year Two and (2) Charity A obtains sufficient evidence from Foundation X of its distribution.

[i] Private operating foundation. A "private operating foundation," generally speaking, is a private foundation which:[10] (1) makes qualifying distributions directly for the active conduct of its charitable purpose equal to substantially all (at least 85 percent)[11] of its adjusted net income[12] or its minimum investment return,[13] whichever is less, and (2) meets either the direct conduct of charitable activities test, the extra distributions test, or the public support test, as follows:[14]

- To meet the "direct conduct of charitable activities test," substantially more than one-half (at least 65 percent)[15] of the foundation's assets must be devoted directly to exempt activities or functionally related businesses, or to a subsidiary which is wholly devoted to those activities.[16]

- To meet the "extra distributions test," the foundation must normally make distributions directly for its exempt purpose at least equal to two-thirds of its minimum investment return.[17]

- To meet the "public support test," the foundation: (1) must receive substantially all of its support from the general public and from five or more exempt organizations which are unrelated to each other or the recipient foundation,[18] (2) must normally receive no more than one-fourth of its support (exclusive of gross investment income) from any one such exempt organization, and (3) must receive 50 percent or less of its support from gross investment income.[19]

---

[10] IRC § 4942(j)(3).

[11] Treas. Reg. § 53.4942(b)-1(c).

[12] Adjusted net income is a modified version of taxable income. It is defined in IRC § 4942(f).

[13] The minimum investment return is five percent of the fair market value of all assets which are not used (or held for use) directly for the charity's exempt purpose, less the acquisition indebtedness with respect to those assets (without regard to the taxable year in which the indebtedness was incurred). IRC § 4942(e). These concepts are discussed more fully in Ch. 37 on private foundations.

[14] IRC § 4942(j)(3)(A).

[15] Treas. Reg. § 53.4942(b)-2(a).

[16] IRC § 4942(j)(3)(B)(i).

[17] IRC § 4942(j)(3)(B)(ii).

[18] Within the meaning of IRC § 4946(a)(1)(H).

[19] IRC § 4942(j)(3)(B)(iii).

An example of a private operating foundation might be a private foundation which operates a library or museum.

[ii] **Private pass-through foundation.** A private foundation is a "private pass-through" foundation if: (1) the foundation is required to and does make qualifying distributions to public charities or private operating foundations which are not controlled, directly or indirectly, by the foundation or any disqualified person;[20] (2) these distributions (a) are treated as made out of principal, (b) are made in an amount equal to 100 percent of contributions received in a taxable year, and (c) are made by the fifteenth day of the third month after the end of the taxable year of receipt; and (3) the foundation provides the donors with adequate records or other sufficient evidence that it made those distributions.[21]

EXAMPLE: Pass-through foundation receives $1,000 in contributions in Calendar Year One. It must (1) make qualifying distributions of $1,000 plus its undistributed income by March 15 of Year Two and (2) give the donors evidence of its distributions.

[iii] **Private investment funds.** "Private investment funds" can be found with various investment firms. The brokerage house sets up the fund. People do not generally retain a lawyer to advise them on individual contributions.

All of the contributions to a private investment fund must be pooled in a common fund. The fund must meet the qualifications of a Section 509(a)(3) support organization,[22] except that a donor or his spouse: (1) can annually designate the charitable recipients of the income attributable to the donor's contribution and (2) can direct payment[23] to such charities of fund principal attributable to the donor's contribution.

All of the charitable recipients must be described in Section 509(a)(1)—that is, they must either be governmental units or public charities.

All of the fund's income must be distributed to such charities by the fifteenth day of the third month after the close of the year in which the fund realizes the income. All of the principal attributable to any donor's contribution must be distributed to such charities within one year after the donor's death or, if the spouse has the right to designate the recipients, within one year after the surviving spouse's death.[24]

---

[20] "Disqualified person" is defined in IRC § 4946 and discussed in Ch. 37 on private foundations.

[21] IRC § 170(b)(1)(E)(ii).

[22] An IRC § 509(a)(3) support organization is discussed in Ch. 38 on designer charities.

[23] During life or by will.

[24] IRC § 170(b)(1)(E)(iii).

[2] Limitations on Income Tax Charitable Deduction for Gifts to 50 Percent Charities

[a] Contribution Base

Many limitations relate to a donor's "contribution base" for a particular year. For this purpose, the donor's contribution base is his adjusted gross income, without regard to any net operating loss carryback to the year.[25]

[b] Limitations Based on Percentage of Contribution Base

Contributions to 50 percent charities are, in most instances, deductible up to a total of 50 percent of the donor's contribution base for the year of the contributions.[26] As further discussed below, the limit is 30 percent of the contribution base if the contribution consists of long-term capital gain property.[27] In either case, there is a five-year carryover of the disallowed portion of the deduction.[28]

> EXAMPLE: Marie contributes $1,000 cash to the Red Cross. This contribution is wholly deductible if her contribution base is $2,000 or more. To the extent that the $1,000 contribution exceeds one-half of her contribution base, she will get a carryover for the next five years.

[c] Long-Term Capital Gain Property

[i] Gifts of long-term capital gain property—advantages. Despite the 30 percent limitation mentioned above on the deduction of gifts of long-term capital gain property,[29] long-term capital gain property can be an attractive candidate for funding a charitable gift. This is because the donor receives a charitable deduction based on 100 percent of the fair market value, and does not have to recognize the unrealized capital gain inherent in the value of the asset.

> EXAMPLE: Donor owns Security A, which has a zero basis and a value of $100. Donor is in the maximum income tax bracket of 39.6 percent, and his contribution base is $1,000. Since 30 percent of Donor's contribution base exceeds $100, the 30 percent limitation does not reduce the deduction available as a result of a charitable donation of Security A. The

---

[25] IRC § 170(b)(1)(F).

[26] IRC § 170(b)(1)(A).

[27] IRC § 170(b)(1)(C).

[28] IRC §§ 170(b)(1)(c)(ii), 170(d)(1).

[29] IRC § 170(b)(1)(C)(i). For this purpose, long-term capital gain property is property which would generate a long-term capital gain if it were sold by the donor for its fair market value on the date of the contribution. IRC § 170(b)(1)(C)(iv).

donation will cost Donor $61.40 after Donor's income taxes are reduced by the charitable deduction of $39.60 (.396×$100).

If, instead, Donor sold Security *A* before making the gift, Donor would pay $28 of capital gains tax. The charity would receive the $72 of after-tax proceeds, and Donor's charitable deduction would reduce his income tax by $28.51 (.396× $72). The gift would cost Donor $71.49, after the income tax reduction of $28.51.

[ii] Election to have 50 percent limit apply to deduction for gift of long-term capital gain property. As stated above, gifts of long-term capital gain property are generally deductible up to 30 percent of the donor's contribution base.[30] Any disallowed portion of the deduction may be carried forward for five years.[31] A donor can avoid this 30 percent limitation, and instead have the 50 percent limitation apply, if the donor elects to limit her deduction to the amount of the long-term capital gain property's income tax basis.[32] This might be a useful election if, for example, the property had only a small amount of unrealized gain.

The election must be made for all long-term capital gain property contributed by the donor during the year.[33] It cannot be made on an asset-by-asset basis, other than through timing of contributions (i.e., making contributions of property for which the election is desirable and property for which the election is not desirable in different years). If the election is made, then any 30 percent limit carryovers from prior years must be recalculated as if the election had been made in the years in which the carryovers arose.[34]

[d] Short-Term Capital Gain Property and Ordinary Income Property

In addition to other limitations, the deduction for charitable contributions of either short-term capital gain property or ordinary income property is limited to the tax basis of such property.[35] For this purpose, short-term capital gain property or ordinary income property is appreciated property which would generate long-term capital gain or ordinary income if sold by the donor for fair market value on the date of contribution.[36]

---

[30] IRC § 170(b)(1)(C)(i). If the long-term capital gain property is tangible property, the deduction may be limited to basis, as discussed below. In such a case, the 50 percent limitation will apply. IRC § 170(b)(1)(C)(iv).

[31] IRC § 170(b)(1)(C)(ii).

[32] IRC § 170(b)(1)(C)(iii).

[33] IRC § 170(b)(1)(C)(iii).

[34] Treas. Reg. § 1.170A-8(d)(2)(i)(b).

[35] IRC § 170(e)(1)(A).

[36] IRC § 170(e)(1)(A).

[e] Tangible Personal Property

A donation of tangible personal property which is not directly used by the charity in furtherance of its exempt purpose is deductible only to the extent of the property's tax basis.[37] The donor can establish proof of use by (1) giving evidence of actual use or (2) establishing that, at the date of contribution, it is reasonable to anticipate that the property will not be put to an unrelated use by the donee.[38]

QUESTION: *What if Donor has a valuable appreciated painting that he would like to give to a museum?*

ANSWER: In the case of a contribution to a museum, if the object donated is of a general type normally retained by museums for museum purposes, it will be deemed reasonable for Donor to anticipate that the object will be put to a related use by the museum, whether or not the museum later sells or exchanges the object, unless Donor had actual knowledge that the museum was not going to put the object to a related use.[39]

QUESTION: *What if Donor gives the painting to (for example) a hospital, which plans to hang the painting in a waiting room? Does this constitute use in the charity's exempt purpose?*

ANSWER: It should.[40] However, since a painting may not be an item which would normally be retained by a hospital, Donor should obtain evidence of actual use by the hospital.

PRACTICE POINTER: If it is important to the donor to get the fair market value deduction for a gift of appreciated tangible personal property, he should get a written commitment from the charity that it will actually use the property in its exempt purpose. It is not clear how long the charity's period of use must be.

¶ 32.04 LIMITATIONS ON INCOME TAX DEDUCTION—GIFTS TO 30 PERCENT CHARITIES

Gifts to 30 percent charities are subject to more severe limitations than gifts to 50 percent charities.

---

[37] IRC § 170(e)(1)(B)(i).

[38] Treas. Reg. § 1.170A-4(b)(3)(ii).

[39] Treas. Reg. § 1.170A-4(b)(3)(ii)(b).

[40] See Treas. Reg. § 1.170A-4(b)(3)(i); Priv. Ltr. Rul. 8301056 (Oct. 4, 1982); Priv. Ltr. Rul. 8143029 (July 29, 1981).

[1] Definition of "30 percent Charities"

The term "30 percent charities" refers to all charities which are private foundations not qualifying as 50 percent charities.[41] Gifts to 30 percent charities are deductible up to 30 percent of the donor's contribution base.[42] A five-year carryover is available for unused deductions.[43]

[2] Deduction for Gifts of Appreciated Property to 30 percent Charities

In the case of gifts of long-term capital gain property[44] to 30 percent charities, the fair market value of long-term capital gain property is only deductible up to 20 percent of the donor's contribution base.[45] Moreover, for gifts made after 1994, the deduction for any contribution to a 30 percent charity is limited to the basis of the contributed property, subject to the exception described below for qualified appreciated stock.[46] There is a five-year carryover of any unused portion of the deduction.[47]

[3] Qualified Appreciated Stock

For certain years before 1995 and for the period from July 1, 1996 through May 31, 1997, the fair market value of gifts to 30 percent charities of "qualified appreciated stock" is deductible up to 20 percent of the donor's contribution base.[48] Qualified appreciated stock is stock that: (1) is readily tradable on an established securities market as of the date of the contribution and (2) is long-term capital gain property.[49] The IRS has taken the position that stock which is subject to restrictions on sale is not "readily tradable."[50]

---

[41] Although all 30 percent charities are private foundations, not all private foundations are 30 percent charities. See ¶ 32.03[1][c] above.

[42] IRC § 170(b)(1)(B). Contribution base is defined at ¶ 32.03[2][a] above.

[43] See n. 42.

[44] For this purpose, long-term capital gain property is property which would generate a long-term capital gain if it were sold by the donor for its fair market value on the date of contribution. IRC § 170(b)(1)(C)(iv).

[45] IRC § 170(b)(1)(D).

[46] IRC §§ 170(e)(1)(A), 170(e)(1)(B)(ii).

[47] IRC § 170(b)(1)(D)(ii).

[48] IRC § 170(e)(5).

[49] IRC § 170(e)(5)(B).

[50] For example, the IRS has privately ruled that Rule 144 stock which is subject to restrictions on sale in the donee charity's hands does not constitute qualified appreciated stock because the restrictions prevent the stock from being easily and pre-

However, if stock would otherwise be qualified appreciated stock, but is not long-term capital gain property (e.g., securities with a holding period of less than one year, or securities held by a dealer), the stock is deductible only to the extent of its basis.[51]

¶ 32.05 INCOME TAX DEDUCTION—SPECIAL RULES

[1] Special Limitations Applicable to Mixed Gifts

The following subparagraphs on "mixed gifts" (that is, gifts to two different types of charities or gifts of two different classes of property) discuss ordering rules for determining which gifts receive a deduction when the total gifts exceed the applicable limits.

PRACTICE POINTER: These rules are very important and often overlooked. In a situation where the percentage-of-contribution-base limitations are likely to be relevant, mixed gifts should be carefully planned. In some cases, it will be advantageous to make different kinds of gifts in different years.

[a] Gifts to 50 percent Charities and 30 percent Charities in Same Year

If a donor makes gifts to 50 percent charities and to 30 percent charities in the same year, the deduction for the gifts to 30 percent charities is limited to the lower of: (1) 30 percent of the donor's contribution base or (2) 50 percent of the donor's contribution base, as reduced by current-year gifts to 50 percent charities.[52]

EXAMPLE: Donor's contribution base is $1,000,000 in Year One. He gives cash gifts of $300,000 to a 50 percent charity and $300,000 to his private

---

cisely valued by reference to an established market. Priv. Ltr. Rul. 9320016 (Feb. 17, 1993), *supplementing* Priv. Ltr. Rul. 9247018 (Aug. 24, 1992). Conversely, the IRS has also ruled that restricted stock which is transferred to a charity pursuant to an exemption available under Rule 144 and which may be freely resold by the charity constitutes qualified appreciated stock. Priv. Ltr. Rul. 9441032 (July 13, 1994); Priv. Ltr. Rul. 9440034 (July 12, 1994); Priv. Ltr. Rul. 9435007 (June 1, 1994).

What if the donee charity's shares will be aggregated with the donor's shares for purposes of determining how many shares can be freely resold by the charity? In such a circumstance, one private letter ruling has stated that the stock would be qualified appreciated stock if the donor contracted with the charity that he would not sell any of his own shares in any fashion which would reduce the free salability of the donee charity's shares. Priv. Ltr. Rul. 9441032 (July 13, 1994).

[51] IRC § 170(e)(1).

[52] IRC § 170(b)(1)(B).

foundation. The gift to the public charity will first use up 30 percent of Donor's contribution base. Hence, Donor will receive a deduction of $300,000 for the gift to the public charity. The deduction for the gift to the private foundation is then limited to the lower of: (1) $300,000 (30 percent of the contribution base) or (2) $200,000 [50 percent of the contribution base ($500,000) – gifts to 50 percent charities ($300,000)]. A five-year carryover will be available for the unused $100,000 of deductions.[53]

[b] Gifts of Long-Term Capital Gain Property and Other Gifts in Same Year

Gifts of long-term capital gain property use up the contribution base last.[54] Therefore, by the time the deduction limit for gifts of such property must be determined, the contribution base may be reduced to zero. Deductions for gifts of such property, to the extent limited in this manner, can be carried forward for five years.

EXAMPLE: Donor has $1,000,000 contribution base. In one year, he gives $300,000 cash to a 50 percent charity and $300,000 property with a zero basis to another 50 percent charity. The cash gift uses up the contribution base first. Hence, the deduction for the gift of appreciated property will be limited to $200,000. A carryover will be available.

[c] Gifts of Long-Term Capital Gain Property to 50 percent and 30 percent Charities in Same Year

Gifts of long-term capital gain property to 50 percent charities use up the contribution base first.[55]

EXAMPLE: Donor has contribution base of $1,000,000 in Year One. Donor gives Appreciated Property A with value of $250,000 and zero basis to 50 percent charity. Donor also gives Appreciated Property B with value of $100,000 and zero basis to 30 percent charity. The gift to the 50 percent charity uses up the contribution base first. Hence, there will be a $50,000 deduction for the contribution to the 30 percent charity, with a carryover for the remaining $50,000.

[2] Limitations Applied to "Excess Charitable Gift" Carryovers

As described above, current-year charitable gifts in excess of the 50 percent or 30 percent contribution base limitations (i.e., "excess charitable gifts") may be

---

[53] IRC § 170(b)(1)(B).

[54] IRC § 170(b)(1)(C)(i).

[55] IRC § 170(b)(1)(C)(i).

deducted by the individual in later years (subject to a five-year carryover period). Gifts carried over during the five-year carryover period are taken into account as charitable gifts in the current tax year only after the available deductions for all charitable contributions actually made during the current year are allowed.[56] Since charitable gifts made in the current year are considered first in determining the allowable current-year charitable deduction, charitable deductions for excess charitable gifts can (without proper planning) be lost, as illustrated in the following example.

> EXAMPLE: In Year One, Donor has contribution base of $1,000,000 and a $500,000 carryover which will expire in Year One. If Donor makes $500,000 of allowable deductible contributions in Year One, his carryover will expire unused. He cannot use the expiring carryover in Year One and carry over the deduction for Year One contributions to Year Two.

Additionally, the deduction for an excess charitable gift carried forward to the current tax year is subject to the same limitations that applied in the year of contribution. Thus, if a prior year gift was the type of gift subject to the 30 percent contribution base limitation in the year the gift was made, the excess charitable gift carryover will also be limited to 30 percent of the donor's contribution base for the carryover year.

WARNING: If the donor dies with a charitable contribution carryover, it will be lost, unless the donor's surviving spouse can use it in the final joint return for the year of the donor's death.[57]

[3] Ceiling Limitation for Gifts of Depreciated Property

Under Treasury Regulation § 1.170A-1(c), the amount of deduction for a charitable contribution of property is the property's fair market value at the time of contribution, as reduced under the rules set forth in Sections 170(e)(1) and (3). Implicit in this rule is the notion that gifts of property can never generate a deduction in an amount greater than the fair market value of such property even if the individual's basis in the property is greater than the property's value. Accordingly, the amount of the deduction for charitable gifts of depreciated (or loss) property,[58] before any other limitations are applied, is limited to the property's fair market value.

---

[56] IRC §§ 170(d)(1), 170(b)(1)(B), 170(b)(1)(C)(ii), 170(b)(1)(D)(ii).

[57] Treas. Reg. § 1.170A-10(d)(4)(iii).

[58] "Depreciated property" is property with a fair market value less than its tax basis.

[4] Additional Limitations on Itemized Deductions

Charitable contributions by individuals are itemized deductions, and, as such, fall within the general limitations imposed on itemized deductions.

[a] Section 68—Reduction of Certain Itemized Deductions

Under Section 68, certain itemized deductions (including the deduction for charitable gifts) are reduced by 3 percent of the taxpayer's adjusted gross income in excess of $121,200 ($60,600 for married couples filing separately).[59]

EXAMPLE: Donor has $1,000,000 of income from stocks and bonds. His only deduction is a $100,000 gift of cash to a charity. His deduction is limited by this rule to $73,636, determined as follows: (1) $1,000,000 adjusted gross income less $121,200 floor, equals $878,800; (2) $878,800 times the 3 percent limitation, equals $26,364 reduction amount; and (3) $100,000 contribution less $26,364 reduction amount, equals $73,636 deductible amount. Note that the $26,364 excess deduction cannot be carried forward, unlike excess charitable deductions created by application of the 50 percent and 30 percent contribution base limitations.

[b] Section 212—Expenses of Making a Charitable Gift

A donor's expenses incurred in effectuating a charitable gift are deductible pursuant to Section 212.[60] However, the donor's total Section 212 expenses, including those associated with charitable gifts, are deductible only to the extent they exceed 2 percent of the donor's adjusted gross income.[61]

[5] No Deduction for Contribution of Services

A deduction is not allowed for services rendered by an individual to charity.[62] But, the donor's out-of-pocket costs incurred in rendering services to charity may be deducted if they are otherwise deductible under the rules for deduction of charitable gifts.[63]

---

[59] IRC § 68. This number applies for the year 1997, and is indexed annually. Note that the reduction is actually the lesser of the amount described in the text or 80 percent of the itemized deductions otherwise allowable; however, in many cases, the latter figure will be larger and hence will not apply.

[60] See Rev. Rul. 67-461, 1967-2 CB 125; Neely v. Comm'r, 85 TC 934 (1985); Temp. Reg. § 1.67-1T(a)(1)(iii).

[61] IRC § 67(a).

[62] Treas. Reg. § 1.170A-1(g).

[63] Treas. Reg. § 1.170A-1(g).

PRACTICE POINTER: Some charities have programs which recognize a donor's contributions for hard-to-value items based on the income tax deduction allowed for the contribution, without regard to limitations particular to the donor's tax situation. Suppose Charity A has such a program. If a lawyer performs legal work worth $5,000 for Charity A, and does not bill the charity, no deduction is available. However, suppose the lawyer bills the charity $5,000, and then makes a cash contribution to the charity of $5,000. When the charity pays his bill, he has income of $5,000, and a charitable deduction of $5,000 (assuming no limitations apply). The cash flow consequences in this scenario are a wash, but the cash gift will qualify the donor for recognition of donations.

[6] Alternative Minimum Tax Considerations

The alternative minimum tax generally disallows certain deductions for purposes of its computation. The charitable deduction is not disallowed or limited by the alternative minimum tax. However, the alternative minimum tax must be considered in determining how much tax benefit a deduction will achieve for the donor.

[7] Substantiation Requirements

A charitable contribution which is not properly substantiated will be wholly or partially nondeductible. Charitable contributions must be substantiated in specific ways:

- First, a deduction for a contribution of $250 or more requires a written receipt from the charity executed by the date that the gift tax return for the year of gift is filed (or due, if earlier).[64]
- Second, in quid pro quo transactions, where the amount received by the charity is more than $75, the charity must provide the donor with a written receipt estimating what amount is attributable to goods and services received by the donor in exchange for his gift.[65]
- Last, deductions for amounts in excess of $5,000 require a qualified appraisal and appraisal summary, unless the donated property is cash or publicly traded securities.[66]

---

[64] IRC § 170(f)(8). Final regulations were issued regarding substantiation in December 1996.

[65] IRC § 6115. Final regulations were issued regarding substantiation in December 1996.

[66] The requirements of a qualified appraisal are described in Treas. Reg. § 1.170A-13(c)(1).

[8] Gift of Stock Followed by Redemption

Suppose a donor gives appreciated stock of his closely held corporation to a charity. And, suppose further that the charity subsequently redeems the stock, thereby converting its interest to cash and increasing the donor's remaining interest in the corporation.

For many years, the IRS took the position, largely unsuccessfully, that the donor would be treated as if he had redeemed the stock and then given the proceeds to the charity. This recharacterization would result in capital gain or ordinary income to the donor, depending on how a distribution to him in redemption of his stock would have been taxed.[67]

However, in a throw-in-the-towel ruling, the IRS announced that, in this type of situation, the transaction will be respected as a donation of stock by the donor and separate redemption of stock by the charity, unless the charity is legally bound or can be compelled by the corporation to surrender the shares for redemption.[68] An agreement which precludes the charity from transferring shares of the corporation without first offering them to the corporation may not qualify for the ruling's protection. The charity's redemption of the stock will reduce corporate earnings and profits for the year of redemption.[69]

PRACTICE POINTER: The theory espoused in this ruling should also be applicable to interests in other types of property.[70]

[9] Charitable Gifts of Partial Interests

Ordinarily, there is no charitable income tax deduction for the contribution of a partial interest in property.[71] Exceptions are contributions made in the following form:

---

[67] See Ch. 19 for a discussion of taxation of redemptions from C corporations.

[68] Rev. Rul. 78-197, 1978-1 CB 83.

[69] Rev. Rul. 79-376, 1979-2 CB 133.

[70] But see Blake v. Comm'r, 697 F2d 473 (2d Cir. 1982). In this case, the taxpayer donated publicly traded securities worth approximately $687,000, with a basis of $98, to charity. The charity sold the stock for approximately $702,000, and used $675,000 of the proceeds to buy a yacht worth $250,000 from the taxpayer. The charity netted $27,000 cash ($702,000–$685,000) plus a yacht worth $250,000. The court determined that the entire arrangement was pre-planned. It held that the taxpayer would be deemed to have sold the stock to the charity (making him taxable on the gain) and to have contributed the yacht to the charity (entitling him to a charitable deduction for its value).

[71] IRC §§ 170(f)(2)(A), 170(f)(2)(B), 170(f)(2)(3)(A).

- Charitable remainder trust;[72]
- Charitable lead trust;[73]
- Pooled income fund;[74]
- Charitable gift annuity;[75]
- Taxpayer's entire interest in property, unless the taxpayer's entire interest was the result of a division of interests done to avoid the split-interest rule;[76]
- Undivided portion of the taxpayer's entire interest in property;[77]
- Remainder interest in personal residence or farm;[78]
- Conservation contribution.[79]

Split-interest gifts are discussed in Chapter 33 (on charitable remainder trusts), Chapter 34 (on charitable gift annuities) and Chapter 35 (on charitable lead trusts).

[10] Bargain Sale to a Charity

[a] Part Sale–Part Gift Treatment

If appreciated property is sold to a charity for less than its fair market value, the transaction will be divided into a sale portion and a gift portion. The basis of the property will be allocated between the two portions as follows:

- Sale Price
  Fair Market Value
  x Total Basis = Basis Allocated to the Sale
- Basis Allocated to the Charitable Gift = Total Basis less Basis Allocated to the Sale

EXAMPLE: Property has a value of $100 and a basis of $40. If property is sold to charity for $20, what happens? One-fifth of the transaction is deemed a sale, and four-fifths is a charitable gift. The basis allocable to the sale portion is $20/$100×$40, or $8. Hence, gain of $12 ($20 sales price less $8 allocated basis) will be recognized by the donor.[80]

---

[72] IRC § 170(f)(2)(A).

[73] IRC § 170(f)(2)(B).

[74] IRC § 170(f)(2)(A).

[75] IRC § 170(f)(2)(B); Treas. Reg. § 1.170A-(7)(b)(2).

[76] Treas. Reg. § 1.170A-7(a)(2)(i).

[77] IRC § 170(f)(3)(B)(ii).

[78] IRC § 170(f)(3)(B)(i).

[79] IRC § 170(f)(3)(B)(iii).

[80] IRC § 1011(b).

[b] Gift of Encumbered Property

The transfer of property subject to a mortgage is considered a bargain sale if the amount paid by the charity (including the amount of the liability) is less than the property's fair value.[81] The amount of the liability is still counted as an amount paid by the charity even if the donor remains liable on the mortgage. However, the amount of the liability is not included as part of the amount paid by the charity if the donor formally undertakes to pay the debt as it comes due.[82]

EXAMPLE: Gross value of property is $100. Property has a basis of $70, and is subject to a mortgage of $40. Donor contributes Property to a charity, subject to the mortgage. This is treated as a sale of the property to the charity for $40, even if the donor remains liable on the mortgage. The sale portion is 40 percent, so 40 percent of the deemed proceeds and 40 percent of the basis are taken into account in the taxable part of the transaction. Gain recognized is $12, which equals the $40 deemed sales price less $28 basis allocable to the sale portion of gift. The charitable contribution portion is $60; if basis is an applicable limitation on deductibility, $42 is the charitable portion of the basis.

However, if the donor undertakes in writing, when he makes the gift, to pay the mortgage as it comes due, then the amount of the charitable contribution will be $100. If he actually does not pay, he may then have to recapture the charitable deduction of $40, in accordance with the tax benefit rule.

[c] Charity's Default on Mortgage After Contribution of Encumbered Property

If, after a gift of encumbered property, the charity defaults on the mortgage, and the donor has to pay it, he will have a loss if the charity cannot reimburse him, or an additional charitable gift if the charity could pay him, but he does not require it.

[11] Estate's and Trust's Income Tax Charitable Deduction for Income Attributable to Gifts Made at Death

A decedent's estate can claim a charitable income tax deduction. However, the deduction is available only for estate income (not principal) which is actually paid to or set aside for the benefit of charity pursuant to the terms of the will.[83]

---

[81] Treas. Reg. § 1.1011-2(a)(3); Rev. Rul. 75-194, 1975-1 CB 80. The Tax Court has held that the amount of a nonrecourse mortgage is included in the amount realized. Brown v. Comm'r, 1996 RIA TC Memo. ¶ 96,325, 72 TCM 139 (1996).

[82] Priv. Ltr. Rul. 8526015 (Mar. 28, 1985).

[83] IRC § 642(c)(1)(2).

EXAMPLE: Will leaves entire residuary estate to charity. If the charity is entitled, under state law, to the income from the residuary estate during administration, the income will be deductible. If the estate has any income which does not go to the residuary beneficiary, such income cannot be offset by a charitable deduction for principal passing to charity.

A deduction is similarly allowed to irrevocable trusts for income actually paid to charity pursuant to the trust instrument.

PRACTICE POINTER: If a revocable trust is the dispositive instrument, rather than a will, be aware that there is no charitable set-aside deduction for revocable trusts that become irrevocable at death, as there is for estates.[84]

The charitable income tax deduction for irrevocable trusts and estates is unlimited.[85] However, in the case of a charitable trust, the trust's charitable deduction may be limited if the trust has unrelated business taxable income (UBTI)[86] (as determined under Section 512 for charitable trusts and charitable split-interest trusts). The deduction for charitable gifts made out of the trust's UBTI is subject to the same limitations applicable to individuals.[87]

EXAMPLE: Charitable trust's only income is unrelated business taxable income of $100,000, which it pays to a 50 percent charity. The deduction for the charitable payment is limited to that percentage of the income which applies to individuals—here, 50 percent of $100,000, or $50,000, with a five-year carryover.

¶ 32.06 ESTATE AND GIFT TAX CHARITABLE DEDUCTION

Gift and estate tax deductions are available for property passing outright to charity.[88] The deduction for such gifts is unlimited.[89]

Unlike the income tax charitable deduction, the amount of the allowable gift and estate tax charitable deductions does not vary with the identity of the charity, as long as it is a qualified charity. Moreover, unlike the income tax

---

[84] IRC § 642(c)(2) (grandfathering exists for certain trusts established under instruments in effect on or before October 9, 1969).

[85] IRC §§ 642(c)(1)-642(c)(2).

[86] UBTI includes (i) income from a trade or business which is unrelated to the direct performance of the organization's exempt function, with certain modifications, and (ii) certain debt-financed income. IRC §§ 511, 512, 514.

[87] IRC § 681; Treas. Reg. § 1.681(a)-2.

[88] IRC §§ 2055, 2522.

[89] IRC §§ 2055, 2522.

deduction, the gift and estate tax deductions are available for gifts to foreign charities.[90]

WARNING: It should be noted that a foreign charity may not have a determination letter that it qualifies as a Section 501(c)(3) organization. While such a letter is a prerequisite for a deduction for most domestic charities,[91] the letter is not required to support a charitable deduction for gifts to foreign charities. However, the estate or donor may be called upon to give evidence that a gift to the foreign charity entitled the donor (or estate) to the deduction.[92]

The limitations on deductibility of partial interests for estate and gift tax purposes are similar to those for the income tax charitable deduction.[93] If a split-interest trust does not qualify, however, a post-death reformation is available under certain circumstances to cure the defect preventing the deduction.[94]

If a residuary gift to charity is combined with a noncharitable pecuniary gift which can be satisfied in cash or in kind, the pecuniary gift may require funding language, similar to that detailed in Revenue Procedure 64-19[95] applicable to marital deduction bequests, to be deductible.[96]

¶ 32.07 GENERATION-SKIPPING TRANSFER TAX

There is no charitable deduction per se from the GSTT. However, charities are assigned to the grantor's generation,[97] so gifts and bequests to charities will not generate a GSTT.

¶ 32.08 RECOMMENDED READING

An excellent desk reference is Tax Economics of Charitable Giving (Byrle Abbin, et al., eds. 12th ed. 1995) (Arthur Andersen). Coverage can also be found in James W. Colliton, Charitable Gifts (WG&L 2d ed. 1996).

---

[90] Treas. Reg. §§ 20.2055-1(a), 25.2522(a)-1(a).

[91] IRC § 508(a).

[92] Treas. Reg. §§ 20.2055-1(c), 25.2522(a)-1(c).

[93] Deductible partial interests in property for estate and gift taxes include: undivided portion of the taxpayer's entire interest; remainder interest in a personal residence or farm; conservation contribution; charitable remainder trust; pooled income fund; charitable lead trust; and guaranteed annuity interest or unitrust interest. Treas. Reg. §§ 20.2055-2(e)(2), 25.2522(c)-3(c)(2).

[94] IRC § 2055(e)(3).

[95] 1964-1 CB 682.

[96] See, e.g., Rev. Rul. 81-20, 1981-1 CB 471.

[97] IRC § 2651(e)(3).

CHAPTER 33

Charitable Remainder Trusts

¶ 33.01 INTRODUCTION

How does a charitable remainder trust (CRT) work? The donor transfers property to a trust, and then one or more noncharitable beneficiaries receive a specified amount each year from the trust for a term. At the end of the term, the charity gets the remaining trust assets.

The advantages of a CRT include (1) an income tax charitable deduction on transfer of property to the trust; (2) tax-free sale of appreciated property by the trust; (3) tax-free accumulation of income inside the trust; and (4) deferral of income taxation to the individual beneficiary until the income or gain is actually received by the beneficiary.

Disadvantages include (1) tying up the property transferred to the trust; (2) application of certain private foundation rules to the trust; and (3) primarily, permanent loss of the property to the family (except to the extent of the annuity or unitrust payments).

¶ 33.02 TYPES OF CHARITABLE REMAINDER TRUSTS

[1] Charitable Remainder Annuity Trusts

A charitable remainder annuity trust (CRAT) pays the noncharitable beneficiary an annuity of a specific dollar amount, which may be stated in the trust's governing instrument as such or as a percentage of the initial value of the trust.[1]

[2] Charitable Remainder Unitrusts

All charitable remainder unitrusts (CRUTs) require an annual payout to the noncharitable beneficiary, which is wholly or partially based on a percentage of the value of the trust determined annually (i.e., the Noncharitable Percentage).[2]

[a] Fixed Percentage CRUT

A fixed percentage charitable remainder unitrust (CRUT) pays the individual beneficiary an annual amount equal to the Noncharitable Percentage.

---

[1] Treas. Reg. §§ 1.664-2(a)(1)(ii), 1.664-2(a)(1)(iii).

[2] Treas. Reg. § 1.664-3(a)(1)(i)(a).

[b] Income Exception Trusts

[i] NIOCRUT: Net income only CRUT. A net income only charitable remainder unitrust (NIOCRUT) provides that the unitrust amount payable to the individual beneficiary in any year will be limited to the lesser of: (1) the Noncharitable Percentage or (2) the net income of the trust in the year, as determined for trust accounting (not federal tax) purposes.[3]

[ii] NIMCRUT: Net income with makeup CRUT. If the trust contains the NIOCRUT definition of the unitrust amount, but also contains a provision saying that a shortfall in the Noncharitable Percentage amount in any year can be made up from income earned in excess of the Noncharitable Percentage amount in a subsequent year, it is known as a net income with make up charitable remainder unitrust (NIMCRUT).[4]

[iii] Illustrations of Payouts from Types of CRTs. Suppose a CRT has an initial value of $100,000, and 5 percent is the percentage chosen, the following amount is payable each year from each type of trust:

- CRAT—Annuity amount is $5,000 per year or 5 percent of the initial value of the trust.
- CRUT—Unitrust amount is 5 percent of the value of the trust, as annually determined.
- NIOCRUT—Unitrust amount is 5 percent of the value of the trust, as annually determined, or the trust accounting income for the year, whichever is less.
- NIMCRUT—Unitrust amount is 5 percent of the value of the trust for any particular year or the trust accounting income for the year, whichever is less. If the trust earns income exceeding 5 percent of its value in any year, the excess can be used to make up for years in which the income was less than 5 percent.

[c] FLIPCRUT: Flip Unitrust

A "flip unitrust" (FLIPCRUT) is a unitrust that begins as a NIMCRUT or NIOCRUT and, after a trigger event, flips to a fixed-percentage CRUT.[5]

The governing instrument of a FLIPCRUT provides that, on a permissible triggering event, the FLIPCRUT will convert to the fixed percentage method

---

[3] Treas. Reg. § 1.664-3(a)(1)(i)(b)(1).

[4] Treas. Reg. § 1.664-3(a)(1)(i)(b).

[5] Treas. Reg. § 1.664-3(a)(1)(i)(c). Final regulations on flip unitrusts were issued in December 1998.

for calculating the unitrust amount.[6] The regulations include examples of permissible and impermissible triggering events.[7] For example, permissible triggering events with respect to any individual include marriage, divorce, death, or birth of a child.[8] The CRT's sale of an unmarketable asset, such as real estate, is also a permissible triggering event.[9] Examples of impermissible triggering events include the sale of marketable assets and a request from the unitrust recipient or the unitrust recipient's financial advisor that the trust convert to the fixed percentage method.[10]

"Unmarketable assets" are assets other than cash, cash equivalents, or assets that can be readily sold or exchanged for cash or cash equivalents.[11] For example, "unmarketable assets" include real property, closely held stock, and unregistered securities for which there is no available exemption permitting public sale.[12]

The conversion to the fixed percentage method must occur at the beginning of the taxable year that immediately follows the taxable year in which the triggering date or event occurs.[13] Any make-up amount in a NIMCRUT is forfeited when the trust converts to the fixed percentage method.[14]

The only type of permissible conversion is from an income-exception CRUT to a fixed-percentage CRUT.[15] Thus, a CRAT cannot convert to a CRUT without losing its status as a CRT. Similarly, a CRUT using the fixed percentage method cannot convert to an income exception method without losing its status as a CRT.

The rules allowing FLIPCRUTs were effective for NIMCRUTs and NIOCRUTs created on or after December 10, 1998.[16]

---

[6] Treas. Reg. § 1.664-3(a)(1)(*i*)(*c*).

[7] Treas. Reg. § 1.664-3(a)(1)(*i*)(*e*).

[8] Treas. Reg. § 1.664-3(a)(1)(*i*)(*d*).

[9] Treas. Reg. § 1.664-3(a)(1)(*i*)(*d*).

[10] Treas. Reg. §§ 1.664-3(a)(1)(*i*)(*e*), Examples 3; 1.1664-3(a)(1)(*i*)(*e*), Example 9.

[11] Treas. Reg. § 1.664-3(a)(7)(ii).

[12] Treas. Reg. § 1.664-3(a)(7)(ii).

[13] Treas. Reg. § 1.664-3(a)(1)(i)(*c*)(*2*).

[14] Treas. Reg. § 1.664-3(a)(1)(i)(*c*)(*3*).

[15] Treas. Reg. § 1.664-3(a)(1)(i)(*e*), Example 10.

[16] The regulations allowed pre-effective date, income exception CRUTs to be reformed to add provisions allowing a conversion to the fixed percentage method, provided the triggering event did not occur before the year in which the court issued the order reforming the trust. The addition of conversion provisions did not cause the CRUT to fail to function exclusively as a CRT, and was not an act of self-dealing under IRC § 4941 if the trustee initiated legal proceedings to judicially reform the trust by June 30, 2000, or completed a nonjudicial reformation by June 30, 2000. Notice 99-31, 1999-1 CB 1185.

Practice Pointer: FLIPCRUTS are most useful when a need to convert the trust into a cash-flowing entity will exist at some predictable future time or event. A flip provision will allow the trustee to (1) invest for growth purposes before the trigger and (2) distribute more cash after the trigger, without having to convert the growth assets into income-producing assets at an inopportune time. Common triggers might be:

- Sale of an unmarketable asset;
- A child's graduation from high school (to provide distributions for college money);
- The donor's death (to provide funds for a surviving spouse); or
- The donor's 65th birthday (to provide distributions for retirement); note that the donor's actual retirement date cannot be used as the trigger because it is within the donor's control.[17]

Practice Pointer: Where the purpose of the FLIPCRUT is to preserve assets for greater distributions after the flip and the FLIPCRUT allocates post-contribution gains to income, capital gains incurred before the flip will have to be distributed as they are incurred if the net income part of the formula applies in a particular year.

---

[3] CRAT vs. CRUT

What's the best choice? If a CRT is funded with property that is expected to earn income or appreciate (including appreciation resulting from inflation), a CRUT with a certain noncharitable percentage is expected to provide more dollars to the noncharitable beneficiary than a CRAT with the same annuity percentage. On the other hand, in tough economic times, the CRAT's level payments may deliver more dollars to the noncharitable beneficiary than the CRUT.

¶ 33.03 STRUCTURE AND OPERATION OF TRUST

Certain documentary and operational requirements and choices apply.

---

[17] Treas. Reg. § 1.664-3(a)(1)(i)(a)(*1*).

[1] Governing Instrument

The trust instrument is required to contain some provisions, permitted to contain others, and prohibited from containing still others. Detailed requirements and rules for CRTs exist under the Section 664 Regulations.

[a] Annual Payout

Permissible payments from CRTs are described in ¶ 33.02. In all cases, the annuity amount payable from a CRAT must be at least 5 percent and not more than 50 percent of the initial value of the trust assets, and the noncharitable percentage of a CRUT must be at least 5 percent of the annual value of the trust assets.[18] The annuity must be set so that the charitable interest is at least 10 percent of the value of the trust at its inception.[19] As a practical matter, these requirements mean that a CRT cannot be established for the life of a young person.

[b] Trust term

The trust term can be (1) a term of years (not exceeding 20 years); (2) a term measured by the life or lives of the designated recipients (who must be in being at the creation of the trust); or (3) a term defined as the shorter of a term of years (not exceeding 20 years) or the life or lives of the designated recipients.[20] At the end of the term, the CRT's remaining assets pass to charity or continue in trust for charity.[21]

[c] Noncharitable Beneficiaries

Generally, any noncharitable beneficiary of a trust with a noncharitable term that could last more than 20 years must generally be an individual. However, in the case of a legally incompetent beneficiary, the IRS has allowed payment of the amount due to a certain type of trust for the benefit of the beneficiary. Any noncharitable trust can be the recipient of the annuity or unitrust amount if the term does not exceed 20 years.[22] The donor can retain the power to terminate or revoke a noncharitable beneficiary's interest at the donor's death.[23]

---

[18] IRC §§ 664(d)(1)(A), 664(d)(2)(A).

[19] IRC §§ 664(a)(1)(D), 664(d)(2)(D).

[20] Treas. Reg. §§ 1.664-2(a)(5)(i), 1.664-3(a)(5)(i).

[21] IRC §§ 664(d)(1), 664(d)(2); Treas. Reg. § 1.664-1(a)(1)(i).

[22] Priv. Ltr. Rul. 9821029 (Feb. 18, 1998).

[23] Treas. Reg. §§ 1.664-2(a)(4), 1.664-3(a)(4). See discussion at ¶ 33.08 below.

[d] Charitable Beneficiaries

If the income tax charitable deduction available to 50 percent charities is desired, the charitable beneficiaries must be limited to Section 170(b)(1)(A) charities.[24] The donor can retain the power to change the charitable beneficiary(ies) at any time.

[e] No Grantor Trust

A CRT cannot be structured as a grantor trust.[25] The retention of the right to the annual payment is ignored in determining whether the trust is a grantor trust.[26]

[f] Donor As Trustee

The donor can be the trustee of the CRT, as long as he does not retain powers that would cause the trust to be a grantor trust.

[g] Warning on Sample IRS Forms

Sample forms for CRTs have been issued by the IRS in several revenue procedures.[27] However, these forms are over 10 years old and do not take into account statutory and regulatory amendments since 1989.[28] The IRS has announced a plan to revise its forms.[29]

[2] Operational Requirements

[a] Valuation of Unmarketable Assets

For purposes of determining the noncharitable payment, if (1) a CRT has assets other than cash, cash equivalents, or marketable securities; and (2) the trustee is the grantor, a noncharitable beneficiary, or a related or subordinate

---

[24] See discussion at ¶ 33.04[2][a] below.

[25] Grantor trusts are discussed in Chapter 6.

[26] Treas. Reg. § 1.664-1(a)(4).

[27] E.g., Rev. Proc. 89-20, 89-1 CB 841; Rev. Proc. 89-21, 89-1 CB 842; Rev. Proc. 90-30, 90-1 CB 534; Rev. Proc. 90-31, 90-1 CB 539; Rev. Proc. 90-32, 90-1 CB 546; and Rev. Proc. 90-33, 90-1 CB 551.

[28] Notice 2000-37, 2000-2 CB 118.

[29] Notice 2000-37, 2000-2 CB 118.

party to the grantor or a noncharitable beneficiary,[30] *then* the trustee must use a qualified appraisal[31] from a qualified appraiser[32] to value the assets[33] or the trust's unmarketable assets must be valued by an independent trustee or co-trustee.[34] An "independent trustee" is a person who is not the grantor (or a related or subordinate party to the grantor)[35] or a noncharitable beneficiary.[36]

Unmarketable assets are assets other than cash, cash equivalents, or assets that can be readily sold or exchanged for cash or cash equivalents.[37] For example, "unmarketable assets" include real property, closely held stock, and unregistered securities for which there is no available exemption permitting public sale.

[b] Due Date of Payments of Noncharitable Amounts

[i] Income exception CRUTS. An income exception unitrust must pay the noncharitable beneficiary within a reasonable time after the close of the taxable year.[38]

[ii] CRATS and fixed-percentage CRUTs. For CRATs and fixed percentage CRUTs, the annuity or unitrust amount must generally be paid on the last day of the taxable year. However, it may be paid within a reasonable time after the close of the year for which it is due in the situations described below. A reasonable time ordinarily will not extend beyond the due date (including extensions) of the Form 5227.[39]

Assume that a CRAT or fixed percentage CRUT provides that its annuity or unitrust amount is payable on December 31, which is the last day of Year One. When must the trustee actually pay the annuity or unitrust amount for Year One?

1. The payment can be made within a reasonable time after December 31 if:

---

[30] Within the meaning of Section 672(c).

[31] Defined in Treas. Reg. § 1.170A-13(c)(3).

[32] Defined in Treas. Reg. § 1.170A-13(c)(5).

[33] Treas. Reg. § 1.664-1(a)(7)(a).

[34] Treas. Reg. § 1.664-1(A)(7)(b). The rules for valuing unmarketable assets are effective for trusts created on or after December 10, 1998.

[35] Within the meaning of Section 672(c) and the applicable regulations.

[36] Treas. Reg. § 1.664-1(a)(7)(b)(iii).

[37] Treas. Reg. § 1.664-1(a)(7)(b)(iii).

[38] Treas. Reg. § 1.664-3(a)(1)(i)(j).

[39] Treas. Reg. §§ 1.664-2(a)(1)(c), 1.664-3(a)(1)(k).

- The payment is treated as ordinary income, capital gains, or tax-exempt income to the recipient;[40] or
- An in-kind payment consists of property that the trustee owned on December 31, and the trustee elects to treat any portion of the distribution in Year Two as distributed in Year One;[41] or
- The payment consists of cash that was contributed to the trust in a deductible contribution[42]; or
- The payment consists of cash proceeds from the sale in Year One of an asset contributed to the trust in a deductible contribution[43], and the cash is a return of basis; or
- The CRT was created before December 10, 1998, and the annuity or unitrust amount is 15 percent or less.[44]

> 2. In all other cases, the annuity or unitrust amount must be paid by December 31 of Year One.

¶ 33.04 INCOME TAX DEDUCTION TO DONOR

[1] Amount of Deduction

If the donor transfers real property or intangible personal property (e.g., stocks, bonds, cash, etc.) to a CRT, the donor is entitled to an income tax charitable deduction in the year of transfer equal to the actuarially determined value of the charity's remainder interest in the trust.[45] If tangible personal property is donated to a CRT, the charitable deduction is allowed when the property is sold to an unrelated party[46] or the noncharitable period ends, whichever comes first.[47]

---

[40] Treas. Reg. § 1.664-3(a)(1)(i)(*g*).

[41] Treas. Reg. § 1.664-3(a)(1)(i)(*g*)(*1*).

[42] Treas. Reg. § 1.664-3(a)(1)(i)(*g*)(2). That is, a contribution for which the remainder interest was deductible.

[43] Treas. Reg. § 1.664-3(a)(1)(i)(*g*)(*3*).

[44] Treas. Reg. § 1.664-2(a)(1)(i)(*b*)

[45] Treas. Reg. §§ 1.664-2(d), 1.664-3(d).

[46] That is, a party who is not a related person within the meaning of IRC § 267(b) or IRC § 707(b). A CRT cannot sell property to a disqualified person described in IRC § 4946, on pain of prohibitive penalties. IRC § 4941.

[47] IRC § 170(a)(3).

The amount of the income tax deduction is ordinarily determined using the actuarial tables in the regulations.[48] The factors determining the amount of the charitable deduction will generally be: (1) the length of the noncharitable term; (2) the amount of the noncharitable payment; and (3) the applicable Section 7520 rate.[49] However, with respect to the amount of the noncharitable payment, the value of the charitable remainder of a NIMCRUT and NIOCRUT is calculated in the same manner as that of a CRUT.[50] Accordingly, the donor's income tax deduction for a contribution to a CRUT, NIOCRUT, or NIMCRUT is the same.

The donor can choose from among three different Section 7520 rates— the Section 7520 rate for the month of the transfer to the trust or the Section 7520 rate from either of the two months preceding the transfer.

Which rate should the donor choose? The value of an annuity varies inversely with interest rates, so a high Section 7520 rate will mean that a relatively low value will be attributed to the noncharitable annuity and a correspondingly higher deduction will be available for the value of the charity's remainder interest. Consequently, the donor should choose the highest of the three interest rates available when creating an annuity trust, as this will give the maximum charitable deduction. The same is true of a unitrust, but the importance of the choice is diminished. This is because the income tax charitable deduction for a unitrust does not vary as a function of interest rates (except for slight interest-rate-sensitive adjustments for frequency and timing of payment of the noncharitable amount), and the donor and the charity will share the consequences of increases and decreases in value.[51]

[2] Limitations on Ability to Take Deduction

[a] Percentage of Donor's Contribution Base

As discussed in Chapter 32, a donor's income tax charitable deduction is limited to a certain percentage of the donor's contribution base.[52] A gift to a CRT will be considered a gift to a 50 percent charity, and contributions can be

---

[48] Treas. Reg. §§ 1.664-2(c), 1.664-4, 1.7520-1(a)(1). More complete versions of the actuarial tables are found in Publication 1457, Book Aleph, and Publication 1458, Book Beth. For a CRT with more than two measuring lives, the IRS will furnish a factor. See Priv. Ltr. Rul. 200150019 (Sept. 13, 2001).

[49] The 7520 rate is 120 percent of the applicable federal midterm rate, rounded to the nearest two tenths of one percent. IRC § 7520.

[50] Treas. Reg. § 1.664-4.

[51] The tables for unitrusts are contained at Treas. Reg. § 1.664-4(e)(6).

[52] The contribution base is adjusted gross income, without regard to net operating loss carrybacks. IRC § 170(b)(1)(F). See Chapter 32.

deducted up to 50 percent of the donor's contribution base, if (1) the CRT's charitable beneficiaries are limited to 50 percent charities or there is only a negligible possibility that the CRT's remainder will go to a 30 percent charity,[53] and (2) the charitable remainder interest goes to the charity outright at the end of the noncharitable term.

Gifts to the CRT will be restricted to the contribution base percentage limitations for gifts to 30 percent charities if (1) a charitable remainder beneficiary can be a 30 percent charity,[54] or (2) the charity's interest remains in trust after the noncharitable term.[55]

Practice Pointer: The IRS sample forms allow distribution to any charity qualified under Section 170(c), which will result in limitations to private foundation-type deductions. The potential charitable beneficiaries must be limited to Section 170(b)(1)(A) charities in order to qualify gifts to the CRT as gifts to a 50 percent charity.

---

[b] Property Contributions—Basis and Timing

The rules limiting a charitable deduction to the basis of certain donated property[56] apply to deductions for gifts to CRTs. In the case of tangible personal property contributions, the charitable deduction is deferred until the property is sold to an unrelated party or the noncharitable term ends.[57] The deduction at that time is limited to the tax basis in the contributed property or, if lower, the property's fair market value. For this determination, the property's basis and value at the time the deduction becomes allowable are determinative—not the basis and value on the date on which the property was transferred to the CRT.[58]

[c] Chart Illustrating Deduction Limitations

The chart below summarizes the limitations on deductions for a contribution to a CRT. Additional rules apply if mixed gifts are made in one year.[59]

---

[53] See Rev. Rul. 80-38, 1980-1 CB 56; cf. Rev. Rul. 79-368, 1979-2 CB 109 (50 percent limitation denied when charitable beneficiary could be changed to an organization subject to the private foundation limitations). Fifty percent charities and 30 percent charities are defined in Chapter 32.

[54] Rev. Rul. 79-368, 1979-2 CB 109.

[55] Treas. Reg. § 1.170A-8(a)(2).

[56] Discussed in Chapter 32.

[57] IRC § 170(a)(3)

[58] IRC § 170(a)(3).

[59] See Chapter 32.

TYPE OF GIFT	LIMITATIONS ON INCOME TAX DEDUCTION AS A PERCENTAGE OF CONTRIBUTION BASE
To CRT which can only benefit 50% charities:	
Long-term capital gain property	30%; or, 50%, if donor elects to deduct basis only (or fair market value, if lower)
Other property	50%
To CRT which can benefit 30% charities:	
Long-term capital gain property	20%
Other property	30%; or, 50%, if donor elects to deduct basis only (or fair market value, if lower)

SPECIFIC TYPES OF GIFTS TO CRT	DEDUCTION LIMITED TO:
Short term capital gain and ordinary income property	Lower of basis or fair market value
Tangible personal property	Zero, until property is sold to unrelated party or noncharitable term ends; at the first of these to occur, deduction is lower of basis or fair market value of property
Any other gift to CRT which can benefit nonpublic charity	Lower of basis or fair market value, except that fair market value is allowed for gift of qualified appreciated securities, as defined in Section 170(e)(5)(B).[60]

[3] Contribution of Encumbered Property or Options to Purchase Such Property

The gift of an option to purchase property has been used to avoid application of the bargain sale rules to charitable gifts of mortgaged property. Doubt was thrown on this technique by the IRS in Technical Advice Memorandum 9501004,[61] in which the IRS took the position that the transfer of an option to purchase encumbered property to a CRUT will cause the trust to cease to qualify as a CRUT. This ruling was based on the IRS's position, taken in an earlier ruling, that a contribution of mortgaged property to a unitrust disqualified the trust as a CRUT, where the donor was personally liable.[62]

---

[60] See ¶ 32.04[3] for a description of qualified appreciated securities.
[61] Tech. Adv. Mem. 9501004 (Sept. 29, 1994).
[62] Priv. Ltr. Rul. 9015049 (Jan. 16, 1990).

¶ 33.05 INCOME TAXATION OF THE NONCHARITABLE BENEFICIARY

[1] Taxability of Distributions

Distributions to the noncharitable beneficiaries may be taxable to those beneficiaries, depending on the characterization of the distributions. Distributions take on the same tax characteristics (applying a flow-through analysis) as those amounts had at the trust level. Each dollar distributed is not, however, deemed to come pro rata from each class of income earned by the trust. Instead, distributions are deemed made from different classes of income in the following order: ordinary income; capital gain; and tax-exempt income. After all these categories of receipts have been distributed, distributions are deemed to come from trust principal.[63]

> **EXAMPLE:** Trust has $100 of ordinary income and $1,000 of capital gain in Year One. In that year, Trust makes distribution of $150 to the individual beneficiary. The individual beneficiary will be treated as receiving $100 of ordinary income and $50 of capital gain.

> Short-term capital gains are deemed to be distributed before long-term capital gains.[64]

> No amount of long-term capital gain distributed from a CRT will be considered 28 percent gain, regardless of when the gain was recognized, except for dispositions of collectibles and small business stock.[65]

> The regulations,[66] in an example, explain the operation of the ordering rules when the unitrust amount is computed under an income exception method.

[2] CRT With Unrelated Business Taxable Income

If a CRT has even $1 of UBTI (including debt-financed income) in any year, the entire income of the trust that year is subject to the normal subchapter J rules on income taxation of complex trusts.[67] Thus, if a CRT contemplates receiving or investing in assets that will generate UBTI, alarm bells should go off in someone's (preferably the trustee's) head.

---

[63] IRC § 664(b).

[64] Notice 98-20, 1998-1 CB 776, modified by Notice 99-17, 1999-1 CB 871.

[65] Pub. L. No. 105-277, §§ 4002(i)(3), 4003(B) (Oct. 21, 1998).

[66] Treas. Reg. § 1.664-1(d).

[67] Treas. Reg. § 1.664-1(c). The trust will not be treated as a grantor trust, even if the donor or his spouse is the noncharitable beneficiary. Id.

Suppose a CRT sells its appreciated assets for a gain of $20,000 during a year in which it has no UBTI, and then invests the proceeds in tax-exempt securities, which earn $99 of tax-exempt income and $1 of UBTI in each of the following years. Its annual payout is $100. The distribution for the first year will consist of $100 of capital gain. Can the trustee then use the normal ordinary rules of complex trusts to carry out the one percent ordinary income and 99 percent tax-exempt distributable net income in the following years, and thereby avoid recognition of the capital gains? In other words, can the sourcing rules for distributions be avoided by not earning UBTI in years when tax-exempt treatment of the CRT is desirable and earning UBTI in years when the complex trust rules would be desirable?

The answer: Apparently not. Neither the grantor trust rules nor the rules dealing with the character of amounts distributed to beneficiaries of complex trusts apply to a CRT, regardless of whether it is exempt.[68] The IRS takes the position that the ordering rules apply each year, regardless of whether the trust has UBTI in any year.[69]

[3] CRT Which Borrows Money

Certain types of borrowings will result in debt-financed income characterized as UBTI.[70] Even in cases where borrowed money does not result in UBTI, the use of borrowed money cannot avoid the noncharitable beneficiary's recognition of capital gains.[71]

> **EXAMPLE:** On January 1 of Year One, Derry contributed assets worth $1,000,000 with a zero basis to a CRT, with a term ending January 31 of Year Three. The annuity amount of $450,000 was due at the end of each calendar year. The trustee borrowed money to obtain the cash necessary to pay the required amounts to Derry. Because borrowing funds would not result in income to the trust, the trustee characterized the $900,000 cash distributions to Derry as a return of principal under Section 664(b)(4). In January of the year of termination, the trustee sold the appreciated asset for $1,000,000, repaid the bank $900,000 plus interest, paid Derry $37,500 (one twelfth of his normal annual amount), and distributed the remaining cash to the charitable beneficiary. Thus, Derry received almost the entire value of the asset in cash. Has Derry limited his recognition of capital gains on the sale to the extent of the amount received in January of the last year? *The answer:* No.

---

[68] Treas. Reg. § 1.664-1(d)(1)(ii).

[69] Priv. Ltr. Rul. 9633017 (May 13, 1996).

[70] IRC § 512.

[71] Treas. Reg. § 1.643(a)-8.

The regulations address the above situation by applying the following two-step analysis:

- Was any part of an annuity or unitrust amount paid characterized as a return of principal under the usual ordering rules?[72]
- If so, did all or any part of that amount exceed the amount of previously undistributed (1) basis in any assets sold by the trust, or (2) cash contributed to the trust for which a deduction was allowable under Section 170, Section 2055, Section 2106, or Section 2522?[73]

If both questions are answered "yes" with respect to any property, the trust will be treated as having sold a pro rata portion of the trust assets in the year for which the distribution was due.[74] Further, the regulations provide that any transaction that has the purpose or effect of circumventing the regulation will be disregarded.[75]

Thus, in the above Example, the trust would be deemed to have sold a portion of the asset as the annual payments were due, and Derry would be deemed to have realized capital gain on receipt of the payments.

The above regulations apply to trust distributions made after October 18, 1999.[76] However, pre-effective date transactions are not protected.[77]

¶ 33.06 INCOME TAXATION OF CRT

A CRT is exempt from income tax unless it has any unrelated business taxable income (UBTI) in any year. If it does, all of the CRT's income for that year is fully taxed under the complex trust rules, except that the CRT rules still apply to the characterization of trust distributions.[78]

[1] Tax-Free Income Accumulation

A CRT (without UBTI) allows tax-free accumulation of income in the trust, to the extent distributions are not required.

---

[72] Treas. Reg. § 1.643(a)-8(b)(2).

[73] Treas. Reg. § 1.643(a)-8(b)(1).

[74] Treas. Reg. § 1.643(a)-8.

[75] Treas. Reg. § 1.643(a)-8(b)(2).

[76] Treas. Reg. § 1.643(a)-8(d).

[77] Treas. Reg. § 1.643(a)-8(b).

[78] IRC § 664(c). Leila G. Newhall Unitrust v. Comm'r, 105 F3d 482 (9th Cir. 1997), aff'g 104 TC 236 (1995).

[2] Deferral or Avoidance of Capital Gains Tax on Sale of Appreciated Property

A classic time to consider a transfer of property to a CRT is when the prospective donor is contemplating a sale of highly appreciated property. In lieu of selling the property and paying tax on the gain recognized, the donor can transfer the property to a CRT and let the CRT sell it.

[a] Taxation of Sale to Donor

In order for the donor to avoid being taxed on the property's appreciation when the sale occurs, the transfer to the CRT must occur before the donor, as a practical matter, acquires a right to the income from a specific sale of the property.[79]

The IRS has adopted the position that, if property is transferred to a charity and the charity is legally bound to sell it to a third party, the sale will be attributed to the donor and the donor will be taxed on the gain recognized from this sale. This ruling would also apply to a sale by a CRT.[80]

In this regard, the IRS has ruled that the sale or redemption of contributed stock by a CRT would not be attributed to the donor in a situation where: (1) the donor was the sole trustee and (2) the CRT could not sell its stock without offering the stock to a corporation under a right of first refusal agreement.[81] The IRS determined that, under these circumstances, there was no prearranged sale contract whereby the trust was legally bound to sell the stock after its contribution by the donor.

[b] Taxation of Sale to CRT

Assuming that the sale is not attributed to the donor, the donor can make the transfer to the CRT, the CRT can then sell the property, and the CRT will realize the gain attributable to the property's appreciation. This sale does not generate a tax for the donor or other noncharitable beneficiary, nor does it generate a tax for the CRT, because the CRT (assuming it is without UBTI) is tax-exempt.

Taxable gain from the sale of the property will be recognized by the noncharitable beneficiary as that beneficiary receives trust distributions of the gain during the noncharitable term.[82] However, if the invested proceeds of the sale earn ordinary income of at least the amount of the trust distributions during the

---

[79] See, e.g., Ankeny v. Comm'r, 1987 PH TC Memo. ¶ 87,247, 53 TCM (CCH) 827 (1987); Ferguson v. Comm'r, 108 TC 244 (1997), aff'd, 174 F3d 997 (9th Cir. 1999).

[80] Rev. Rul. 78-197, 1978-1 CB 83.

[81] Priv. Ltr. Rul. 9452020 (Sept. 28, 1994).

[82] IRC § 664(b).

noncharitable term, no tax will ever be paid on the gain realized by the CRT on the sale of the appreciated property. This is because, as explained below, under the trust distribution sourcing rules, the capital gains will never be deemed paid (and will never in fact be paid) to the noncharitable beneficiary (who will have received all distributions out of the trust's ordinary income).

> **EXAMPLE:** Donor has a signed contract of sale regarding Blackacre. If he donates Blackacre to a CRT and the CRT makes the sale, the gain on the sale is taxable to Donor if he could have enforced the sale of Blackacre himself. If Donor does not have a put or other right to the income from the sale of the property when he donates it to the CRT, the CRT will realize the capital gain on the sale, but will not be taxed on the capital gain. Instead, the capital gain will be taxed to Donor (assuming Donor is the noncharitable beneficiary) as the gain is distributed by the CRT to Donor. However, if the trust has ordinary income as well as capital gains, the distribution to Donor is taxed as ordinary income before any portion of the distribution is taxed as capital gain.

[3] Multiple Donors/Noncharitable Beneficiaries

The IRS has taken the position that a CRT with multiple donors and noncharitable beneficiaries did not qualify as a CRT because it would be taxed as an association rather than as a trust.[83] The IRS has not applied this theory where a husband and wife were the donor-beneficiaries.[84] Use of multiple CRTs joining in an investment partnership, rather than a multiple-contributor CRT, appears to avoid the association problem in a case where CRT beneficiaries want to make mutual investments.[85]

¶ 33.07 USE OF NIMCRUT AS RETIREMENT PLAN

A NIMCRUT is sometimes used as a substitute for a retirement plan. The idea is that the trustee invests in growth-producing assets during the donor's working years, makes few or no distributions, and accumulates gains tax-free. Then, when the donor retires, the trustee will invest in income-producing properties

---

[83] Priv. Ltr. Rul. 9547004 (Aug. 9, 1995).

[84] See Priv. Ltr. Rul. 200109006 (Nov. 20, 2000) (division of CRT in which husband and wife were donor-beneficiaries into two CRTs as part of divorce does not affect pre-existing qualification of either trust as a CRT).

[85] See Priv. Ltr. Ruls. 9626007 (Mar. 25, 1996) through 9626018 (Mar. 25, 1996), 9705013 (Oct. 31, 1996).

to fund the donor's retirement, and will use the makeup provision to make larger distributions than would have been possible with a fixed-percentage CRUT. (A FLIPCRUT cannot serve this purpose as well, because makeup amounts are forfeited on the flip.)

> **EXAMPLE:** Donor transfers low basis land to NIMCRUT with 8 percent payout. Trustee sells land and invests proceeds in growth stocks that pay low or no dividends. Donor retires at age 65. Trustee sells stocks and re-invests in high-yielding bonds. Donor begins receiving 8 percent annual payout. He can also receive any excess trust income to make up for the previous years in which he did not receive his full 8 percent payout.

One practical difficulty with using a NIMCRUT as a retirement plan is that it does not work well unless the trust's investments meet certain perform-ance expectations. For example, in the above situation, the market for the CRT's stocks may be down when the owner is 65 years old, and liquidating the stocks at that time might be the equivalent of a fire sale. In order to ad-dress this issue, various plans have evolved to fund the NIMCRUT with assets that by their nature, grow in value for a while and then start generating trust accounting income.[86] The IRS and Treasury are studying whether investing the assets of a NIOCRUT or NIMCRUT to take advantage of the timing differ-ence between the receipt of trust accounting income and federal tax income causes the trust to fail to qualify as a CRT.[87] The IRS has described its view of potentially abusive CRTs in "Charitable Remainder Trusts: The Income Deferral Abuse and Other Issues," which is contained in its Fiscal Year 1997 Exempt Organizations CPE text.

[1] Strategies for Assuring Suitable Retirement Investments at the Proper Time

These strategies involve specific definitions of "trust accounting income." The IRS takes the position, with respect to NIOCRUTs and NIMCRUTs, that a definition of income in the trust instrument that departs fundamentally from concepts of local law as to what is income and what is principal will be disre-garded.[88] This is an overlay to the following descriptions.

---

[86] For example, deferred annuities and zero coupon bonds.
[87] Rev. Proc. 97-23, 97-1 CB 354.
[88] Priv. Ltr. Rul. 9609009 (Nov. 20, 1995); Treas. Reg. § 1.643(b)-1.

[a] Investment in Deferred Annuities

How does an investment in deferred annuities accomplish the objective of deferring recognition of trust accounting income until the date such income is needed, and then providing the income?

A deferred annuity earns money for a time, and begins to make payments to the annuitant after the deferral period.[89] The NIMCRUT is drafted to provide that the inside buildup of the annuity value is treated as trust accounting income only when annuity payments are made to the CRT;[90] in order to be effective, such a provision must be valid under state law. Normally, a deferred annuity's inside buildup would be taxable on an annual basis to a trust owner.[91] However, the income inside the annuity contract held by a NIMCRUT builds up tax-free, despite Section 72(u), because the NIMCRUT itself is not taxable.[92] The theory, then, is that the NIMCRUT does not have to distribute anything to the individual beneficiary until the trustee actually takes distributions from the annuity, as there will be no trust accounting income until then. When the donor retires, the NIMCRUT can make withdrawals from the annuity and distribute them to the donor.

There is little specific authority or local law with respect to characterization of increases in the value of an annuity contract.

The argument has been made that a NIMCRUT, with a grantor-trustee who has the power to invest in deferred annuities and the discretion to withdraw funds for purposes of generating net income to be distributed, could run afoul of the grantor trust rules (specifically, Section 674(a)), resulting in its disqualification as a CRT.[93] This argument seems to prove too much because it is essentially based on the assumption that a grantor-trustee of a trust that could invest in assets earning a higher rate of fiduciary income than the assets are actually earning has a prohibited power which violates the grantor trust rules. However, for the conservative NIMCRUT designer, this issue should be avoidable through the use of an independent special trustee to exercise the questioned power.

---

[89] See Chapter 13 for a discussion of annuities.

[90] This is similar to the standard rule that earnings inside a corporation are not considered income until dividends are paid.

[91] IRC § 72(u).

[92] In Priv. Ltr. Rul. 9009047 (Dec. 5, 1989), a CRUT that held a deferred annuity was held by the IRS to be a qualified CRT that did not hold the annuity as an agent for a natural person under IRC § 72(u)(1) (and so would not incur a penalty for withdrawing funds before the donor reached age 59½). The IRS declined to rule on whether earnings accumulating inside the annuity were income for trust accounting purposes, saying that this was an issue of local law.

[93] Treas. Reg. § 1.664-1(a)(4) provides that a trust that is a grantor trust for any reason other than the return of the noncharitable amount to the grantor or his spouse (IRC §§ 673, 677(a)) is not a CRT.

Another issue is whether annuities designed to, or resulting in, the charities' actual remainder interest being zero or unduly small will violate the CRT rules. This could occur, for example, if the CRT invests in an annuity contract with a "life-only" annuity option for the life of the noncharitable beneficiary and distributes all the annuity payments to the noncharitable beneficiary. In that case, either the noncharitable beneficiary or the insurance company (in the case of the noncharitable beneficiary's early death) might receive a large sum, and the charity would receive nothing. The correct answer would seem to be that a general power to invest in annuities should be permissible, as long as (1) the trustee is subject to fiduciary liability for making investments from which it is predictable that the charitable beneficiaries will receive too little, and (2) the trustee does not in fact abuse the power so as to deprive charity of its remainder interest.

The IRS will not issue private letter rulings on whether a NIOCRUT or NIMCRUT qualifies as a CRT if a grantor, trustee, beneficiary, or person related or subordinate to a grantor, trustee, or beneficiary can control the timing of the trust's receipt of income from a deferred annuity contract.[94] On October 29, 1997, the IRS issued a memorandum involving a CRT with the grantor's nephew as trustee. The IRS determined that (1) the CRT's purchase of deferred annuity policies when the annuitants were disqualified persons would not constitute acts of self-dealing; (2) the purchase of the annuity policies would not jeopardize the trust's CRUT status; and (3) the annuity withdrawal provision would not result in income to the CRUT, if nothing was actually withdrawn.[95]

Practice Pointer: If deferred annuity policies are purchased by a CRT, the CRT should be the owner and beneficiary under the policies. The CRT agreement should define fiduciary accounting income to exclude cash buildup within the policy. The decision to invest in, and retain or sell, a policy should be made by an independent trustee.

All these technical issues aside, the fact remains that an individual on his own can, of course, purchase an annuity contract and achieve deferral of the inside buildup.[96] He doesn't need a CRT to accomplish that.

QUESTION: *So . . . what does a CRT holding a deferred annuity contract accomplish for the donor that he couldn't accomplish if he just bought the annuity himself and left any amounts payable on his death to charity in his will?*

---

[94] Rev. Proc. 2003-3, 2002-1 IRB 117, § 4.01(39); Priv. Ltr. Rul. 199901023 (Oct. 8, 1998).

[95] Tech. Adv. Mem. 9825001 (Oct. 29, 1997).

[96] See Chapter 13 on annuities.

ANSWER: The CRT (1) gives the donor an income tax charitable deduction on its establishment; (2) may allow withdrawal of funds from the annuity contract before the donor reaches age 59½ without the 10 percent penalty;[97] and (3) allows the deferral of income taxation on amounts that are withdrawn by the trustee from the annuity contract and not immediately distributed to the donor.

[b] Investment in Zero-Coupon Bonds

It has also often been suggested that NIMCRUTs invest in zero-coupon bonds. The idea underlying this advice is similar to the theory regarding deferred annuities. That is, during the donor's pre-retirement years, the bonds accumulate interest tax-free, and the bond discount is not generally considered trust accounting income until the bond matures.[98] When the bond matures during the donor's retirement, the proceeds then can be used to make larger distributions, making up for the lack of distributions in earlier years.

[c] Investment in Partnership Interests

NIMCRUT investment in partnership interests has been suggested as a good tax strategy, because a partnership allows the partners to time the receipt of trust accounting income from the partnership. However, careful attention must be paid to the rules prohibiting self-dealing.[99] The IRS will not issue a ruling on whether a NIOCRUT or NIMCRUT that holds certain partnership interests will qualify as a CRT.[100]

[d] Investment in Life Insurance

It is possible to use life insurance on the life of the noncharitable beneficiary as a CRT asset, if the CRT has an insurable interest.[101] This is usually done in a NIMCRUT. The idea is that the inside buildup in cash surrender value does not constitute trust accounting income—either at all, or until it is

---

[97] Since the ten percent penalty is computed by reference to the tax paid by the taxpayer, and no tax is paid by a CRT, the ten percent penalty would appear to be inapplicable. IRC § 72(q). Priv. Ltr. Rul. 9009047 (Dec. 5, 1989).

[98] See Priv. Ltr. Ruls. 9018015 (Jan. 31, 1990) and 8604027 (Sept. 24, 1985), which held that bond discount did not constitute trust accounting income until the bond was redeemed or sold.

[99] See Chapter 37 for a discussion.

[100] Rev. Proc. 2002-3, 2002-1 IRB 117, § 4.01(39); Priv. Ltr. Rul. 199901023 (Oct. 8, 1998).

[101] GCM 37105 (Apr. 29, 1977); Priv. Ltr. Rul. 8745013 (Aug. 7, 1987).

withdrawn. The trustee of the NIMCRUT could withdraw the cash surrender value on the noncharitable beneficiary's retirement and distribute the portion, which is allocable to income, to the noncharitable beneficiary in his retirement years. However, the IRS indicated that it is currently studying the issue of whether investing the assets of a NIOCRUT or NIMCRUT to take advantage of the timing difference between the receipt of trust accounting income and federal taxable income causes the trust to fail to qualify as a CRT.[102]

The IRS has ruled that a transfer of a life insurance policy on the grantor's spouse to a NIMCRUT will not disqualify the trust as a CRT for federal income tax purposes.[103]

[e] Allocation of Capital Gain to Income

May the trust instrument of a NIMCRUT allocate capital gains to income so as to increase the amount that can be paid to the donor at retirement (or for that matter, before retirement)?

The answer: To some extent. The proceeds from the sale of an income exception CRUT's assets, at least to the extent of the fair market value of the assets when contributed to the trust, must be allocated to trust principal of an income exception CRUT.[104] However, the governing instrument, if permitted under applicable local law, may allow the allocation of capital gains attributable to post-contribution appreciation to trust income.

The IRS has issued proposed regulations that would recognize new definitions of income contained in local laws. For example, the proposed regulations would generally respect provisions requiring an equitable apportionment of capital gains to income, and, in some cases, unitrust amounts as measures of income.[105] However, for NIOCRUTS and NIMCRUTS, (1) trust income would be determined by reference to a fixed percentage of the annual fair market value of the trust corpus, and (2) any allocation of post-contribution capital gains to income would be allowed if permitted by local law and the governing instrument, but could not be discretionary with the trustee.[106] (Existing regulations already prohibit allocation of pre-contribution gain to income.)[107] The proposed regulations are not effective until they are published as final regulations.[108]

---

[102] Rev. Proc. 97-23, 97-1 CB 354.

[103] Priv. Ltr. Rul. 199915045 (Jan. 19, 1999).

[104] Treas. Reg. § 1.664-3(a)(1)(i)(b)(4), applicable to sales and exchanges occurring after April 18, 1997.

[105] Prop. Reg. § 1.643(b)-1.

[106] Prop. Reg. § 1.664-3(a)(1)(i)(b)(3).

[107] Treas. Reg. § 1.664-3(a)(1)(i)(b)(4).

[108] 66 Fed. Reg. 10,396.

¶ 33.08 GIFT AND ESTATE TAX RULES

[1] Gift Tax

If the noncharitable beneficiary is anyone other than the donor and/or his U.S. citizen spouse, the creation of the CRT will normally result in a taxable gift of the value of the noncharitable beneficiary's interest. However, retention of a testamentary power to revoke the interest will avoid a completed gift to the beneficiary whose interest is subject to revocation until the right to revoke expires, or, if earlier, the noncharitable beneficiary receives payment from the trust.[109]

Additionally, if the donor or any applicable family member[110] retains a unitrust interest in an income exception CRUT (including a flip trust), that unitrust interest will be valued at zero when a noncharitable beneficiary of the trust is someone other than (1) the donor, (2) the donor's U.S. citizen spouse, or (3) both the donor and the donor's U.S. citizen spouse.

This means that a transfer to an income-exception CRUT with noncharitable beneficiaries other than the donor or donor's U.S. spouse will generally result in taxable gifts on transfer of the value of the *entire* noncharitable interest, except to the extent the donor can revoke the beneficiaries' interests.

Section 2702 will not apply, however, when there are only two consecutive noncharitable beneficial interests and the donor holds the second of the two interests.[111]

[2] Estate Tax

On the donor's death, any noncharitable beneficiary's interest (to the extent that it extends beyond the donor's life) will be included in the donor's estate pursuant to the usual rules on revocable or amendable interests.[112]

The CRT has an interesting role as a possible marital deduction trust. Suppose that a couple is doing a testamentary plan. After the first death, they want a stream of cash flow to be available for the surviving spouse for life and the remaining assets at the spouse's death to go to charity. There are two common ways to accomplish this. First, a CRT with the surviving spouse as the sole noncharitable beneficiary for her life can qualify for the marital deduction.[113] Second, a QTIP trust that pays all income to the surviving spouse for

---

[109] Rev. Rul. 79-243, 1979-2 CB 343.

[110] Defined at IRC §§ 2702(e), 2704(c)(2).

[111] Treas. Reg. § 25.2702-1(c)(3).

[112] IRC §§ 2036, 2038.

[113] IRC § 2056(b)(8).

her lifetime, with the remainder after the survivor's death passing to charity, can also qualify.[114]

What differences are there between the CRT and the QTIP? First, in a CRT, the amount payable to the spouse is the annuity or unitrust amount, rather than the income (as in a QTIP trust). Second, in a CRT, the spouse (subject to general fiduciary law) is not required to have the right to make the trust assets productive of income (as she must in a QTIP trust), even if her payout is affected by the amount of income earned by the trust. Third, there is no income tax on amounts earned by the CRT, as long as the amounts remain in the CRT, whereas a QTIP trust is subject to the income tax rules applicable to simple or complex trusts, as the case may be. Fourth, an income tax charitable deduction may be available for part of the estate income passing to the CRT, whereas none would be available for amounts passing to the QTIP. Fifth, income tax to the spouse on distributions is determined by the CRT rules, instead of the private trust rules, in most instances. Last, self-dealing is not permitted by a CRT.

¶ 33.09 ASSET REPLACEMENT PLAN

A fairly standard twist to a plan involving a CRT is as follows. Establish a CRT, claim the available income tax charitable deduction, and use the income tax savings to purchase life insurance in an irrevocable life insurance trust for the benefit of the family, thus replacing part or all of the assets passing to charity from the CRT. If the CRT qualifies for the marital deduction or if the CRT terminates at the donor's death, zero estate tax will be paid with respect to the life insurance or the CRT assets. (However, estate tax will be paid on unconsumed distributions from the CRT.)

Under certain circumstances, the family comes out better than it would have if the CRT had not been established and the life insurance had not been bought. This is a concept most easily illustrated by the following extreme example.

> **EXAMPLE:** Donor has assets of $1,000,000. He dies. Estate tax is $500,000. His children receive the after-tax amount of $500,000. Suppose, instead, that Donor establishes a CRT, transfers the $1,000,000 to it, claims an income tax charitable deduction, and uses the income tax savings to fund an irrevocable life insurance trust, which purchases a $1,000,000 life insurance policy on Donor. He dies the next day. Charity will receive $1,000,000, and children will receive $1,000,000.

---

[114] IRC § 2056(b)(7).

One sidelight on this sort of projection is that, if one assumes a purchase of life insurance, the family may be even better off if it receives both the insurance proceeds and the after-tax estate, instead of establishing the CRT. For instance, in the above example, the family would receive $1,500,000 on Donor's death, less the cost of the life insurance (because, under this scenario, the life insurance is not funded by the income tax deduction).

¶ 33.10 APPLICATION OF THE PRIVATE FOUNDATION RULES

A CRT is subject to the private foundation prohibitions on self-dealing and taxable expenditures.[115] The major import of this is that a CRT is subject to the same prohibitions on dealings with disqualified persons as private foundations.

On this score, at the end of the noncharitable term, it is permissible for a CRT to either terminate (and pay its assets to other charities) or continue as a charitable trust. If it continues as a charitable trust, the continuing charitable trust will avoid the private foundation rules only if it qualifies as a 50 percent charity. If the CRT does continue as a charitable trust, it must file a Form 1023 and obtain a determination letter regarding its exempt status at the end of the noncharitable term.[116]

If, instead, the CRT terminates, then the terminating CRT, during the winding-up period, remains subject to the prohibitions on self-dealing and taxable expenditures under Sections 4941 and 4945. However, the terminating CRT has a reasonable period of time to wind up its affairs before any of the other previously inapplicable private foundation rules begin to apply.[117]

Can a CRT that continues as a charitable trust after the noncharitable term avoid the private foundation rules by not claiming exempt status? For example, assume a CRT, that is not subject to the private foundation excess business holdings rules (under Section 4943), owns all of the stock of an active business. Can the trust continue to hold the stock indefinitely as a nonexempt trust without regard to the excess business holding rules? Or, when the noncharitable term terminates, can the trustees individually buy the stock from the CRT and continue the trust as a nonexempt trust without liability for self-dealing?

The answer: No. If the trust was eligible for a charitable deduction initially, then, after the noncharitable term, unless it qualifies as a public charity, it will continue to be subject to the penalties on self-dealing and taxable ex-

---

[115] IRC § 4947(a)(2). See Chapter 37.

[116] Treas. Reg. §§ 1.508-1(a)(2)(i), 1.508-1(a)(2)(iii), 53.4947-1(b)(2)(iv).

[117] These rules are in IRC §§ 4940, 4942, 4943, and 4944.

penditures, and will be subject to the other private foundation rules after a reasonable time, whether it claims exempt organization status or not.[118]

¶ 33.11 RETIREMENT BENEFITS (OR OTHER IRD) PAYABLE TO A CHARITABLE REMAINDER TRUST

In some cases, a participant in a retirement plan or IRA may designate a CRT to receive plan benefits on the participant's death. If the only noncharitable beneficiary is the surviving spouse, and if the spouse's interest lasts for her life, the CRT will qualify for the marital deduction.[119] Amounts of taxable income paid to the CRT in excess of the spouse's payout will escape all income and estate taxation.

There are a few issues here.

[1] Satisfaction of Pecuniary Bequest With Retirement Assets

If the executor in his discretion uses the right to receive retirement assets to fund a pecuniary bequest to the CRT, the transfer to the CRT of the right to receive those assets will be treated as a sale made by the estate.[120] The deemed sale will accelerate recognition of the income in respect of a decedent (IRD) under Section 691,[121] causing the income to be recognized by the estate rather than the CRT itself. The estate will however, be entitled to a set-aside deduction to the extent that the IRD is irrevocably set aside for charity.

[2] Set-Aside Deduction

The estate will be entitled to a set-aside deduction for any amounts that cannot possibly be distributed to the noncharitable beneficiary. Thus, if (1) plan benefits are used by an estate to fund a bequest to an income exception CRUT; (2) the bequest is considered principal; and (3) there is no possibility that the plan benefits can be invaded to pay the unitrust amount, *then* the estate can receive a 100 percent income tax set-aside deduction under Section 642(c), even

---

[118] IRC § 4947.

[119] IRC § 2056(b)(8).

[120] Treas. Reg. § 1.1014-4(a)(3). If the executor selects retirement assets already received by the estate, the income will have been taxed to the estate, subject to any available set-aside deduction.

[121] See Chapter 14 for a discussion of the income in respect of decedent issues in regard to retirement plans.

though the estate tax deduction is limited to part of the value of the benefits passing to the CRT.[122]

What if the above transaction is implemented by a revocable trust, rather than an estate?

A revocable trust receives a charitable deduction only when amounts are actually paid to the CRT; it is not allowed the deduction merely by setting aside amounts for a charitable purpose.[123] However, under certain circumstances, a revocable trust can elect to be treated as part of the deceased grantor's estate for income tax purposes.[124] Such an election would enable the revocable trust to get a set-aside deduction.

[3] Specific Bequest of Plan Benefits

If a specific bequest of plan benefits to the CRT is made, the benefits paid to the CRT are not taxable to it,[125] because a CRT is tax-exempt. As distributions are made to the individual beneficiary, however, the individual beneficiary will recognize the income as ordinary income, which may or may not be eligible for the IRD deduction.

[4] IRD Deduction

Is the noncharitable beneficiary of a CRT entitled to an IRD deduction for any estate tax paid on the distribution of the plan assets? Treasury Regulation § 1.691(c)-2(a)(3) provides that, if a trust receives IRD in one year and distributes it in a subsequent year, the beneficiary will not be entitled to an IRD deduction in the subsequent year, because the trust would have been eligible for one in the first year. This regulation, of course, contemplates a taxable trust.

The IRS has analyzed the application of the regulation to distributions from a CRT.[126] The IRS's position is that (1) the IRD is included in the CRT's income for the year the distribution is received by the CRT; (2) the CRT is not taxable on its income for that year unless it has unrelated business taxable income; and (3) the IRD deduction reduces the amount that the CRT includes in its first tier ordinary income. Therefore, under the IRS's analysis, even though the deduction is not directly available to the noncharitable beneficiary, it can benefit the noncharitable beneficiary by eventually decreasing the portion of each distribution that is characterized as ordinary income.

---

[122] Treas. Reg. § 1.642(c)-2(d).

[123] IRC §§ 642(c)(1), 642(c)(2).

[124] IRC § 646(a).

[125] Priv. Ltr. Rul. 9237020 (June 12, 1992).

[126] Priv. Ltr. Rul. 199901023 (Oct. 8, 1998).

EXAMPLE: Suppose IRD worth $1,000,000 is paid to a CRAT in Year One, and that constitutes the sole income of the CRAT in Year One, and suppose the IRD deduction is $500,000. Then, under the IRS's analysis, the CRAT is considered to have ordinary income of $500,000 in Year One. So, if Beneficiary receives $50,000 per year, this $500,000 will be carried out as taxable income to the Beneficiary for ten years. If the CRT has had no other ordinary income or capital gains during this time, Beneficiary will begin to receive the benefit of the IRD deduction at that point, i.e., the point at which the remaining $500,000 of IRD is considered paid from principal. Thus, distributions of the remaining $500,000 would be tax-free returns of principal, except to the extent that the CRT has other ordinary income or capital gains.

It is not at all certain that the IRS's position is correct. In the above example, if the IRD deduction were directly available to the beneficiary and the life expectancy of beneficiary were twenty years, the beneficiary would receive $50,000 each year and the IRD deduction of $50,000 per year would be immediately available to deduct against the income, so that only $25,000 of each year's $50,000 payment would be taxable.

[5] Minimum Distribution Rules

Can a CRT or its individual beneficiaries qualify as "designated beneficiaries" of retirement benefits? No.[127] Hence, if the plan benefits are payable to a CRT, required distributions from the plan may be accelerated. However, this will normally be the desired result because the early distribution will enable an annuity or unitrust amount based on the entire retirement benefit to be available for the noncharitable beneficiary.[128]

¶ 33.12 S CORPORATION STOCK

A CRT cannot hold S stock.[129] This is because:

- A CRT cannot be a grantor trust or a QSST.

---

[127] See discussion of designated beneficiaries in Chapter 14.

[128] See Prop. Reg. §§ 1.401(a)(9)-1, Q&A D-5; 1.401(a)(9)-1, Q&A E-5(e)(1); 1.401(a)(9)-1, Q&A E-5(e)(6). New proposed regulations were issued for retirement plans in 2001, and both the prior proposed regulations and the new regulations apply until final regulations are issued. Under the 2001 proposed regulations, see Prop. Reg. §§ 1.401(a)(9)-4, Q&A A-1; 1.401(a)(9)-4, Q&A A-5. See Chapter 14 for a more complete discussion.

[129] IRC §§ 1361(b)(1)(B), 1361(c)(2)(A).

- A CRT cannot qualify as an electing small business trust because a trust that is exempt from income tax cannot be an electing small business trust.[130] The trust will not qualify under the laws permitting certain exempt organizations to be S shareholders, because the CRT is exempt under Section 664, not Section 501(a).[131]

¶ 33.13 ACCELERATION OR COMMUTATION OF CHARITABLE INTEREST

It is clearly permissible to provide for termination of the noncharitable interest in a CRT on a specified event (e.g., remarriage of surviving spouse).[132] This does not mean that the noncharitable beneficiary's interest will be commuted—it means that payments to her will cease altogether. The charitable deduction on the contribution to the CRT will, however, not take into account the contingency of that event occurring.[133] Additionally, such a provision would prevent a surviving spouse's interest from qualifying for the marital deduction.

The IRS has ruled that the partition of a charitable remainder unitrust into two trusts, in order to accelerate a portion of the gift to charity, is permissible, and will generate income tax and gift tax charitable deductions for the assignment of the life interest.[134] In the ruling, one CRUT was split into two CRUTs. The life tenant then assigned his income interest in one of the trusts to the charity. Under state law, this resulted in merger of the charity's interests in that trust's assets. The trust's assets were then distributed to the charity. The IRS said the remaining trust continued as a valid CRUT.

It is also permissible for the trust agreement to give the term interest holder the power to terminate the holder's term interest by assigning the trust principal to one or more of the charitable beneficiaries.[135]

The IRS has approved the termination of a CRT and commutation of interest pursuant to an agreement among the trustee, charitable beneficiary, and

---

[130] IRC § 1361(e)(1)(B)(ii). A CRT that is taxable due to the earning of UBTI in a particular year still will not be able to hold S stock.

[131] IRC § 1361(c)(7)(B).

[132] IRC § 664(f).

[133] IRC § 664(f)(2).

[134] Priv. Ltr. Rul. 200140027 (June 29, 2001).

[135] Priv. Ltr. Rul. 200124010 (Mar. 14, 2001).

non-charitable beneficiary.[136] Each party's interest was determined by its actuarial value, and, according to the IRS, the non-charitable beneficiary's term interest would be characterized as a capital asset with a zero basis. Thus, the non-charitable beneficiary would have capital gain to the full extent of the amount realized on termination.

¶ 33.14 REFORMATION

Section 2055(e)(3) permits reformation of defective testamentary charitable remainder trusts under certain circumstances. The IRS has taken the position that equivalent reformations of inter vivos trusts are also allowed.[137]

¶ 33.15 MISTAKES IN ADMINISTRATION

Failure to follow the administrative requirements of the trust may cause the trust to fail as a CRT, regardless of whether the terms contained in the agreement meet the requirements of a CRT. For example, the Tax Court denied an estate tax charitable deduction for the value of an inter vivos CRT where the CRT had never made the required payments to the individual beneficiary.[138]

¶ 33.16 ECONOMICS OF A CHARITABLE REMAINDER TRUST FOR A NONCHARITABLY MOTIVATED DONOR

Does a CRT make sense for a person who is not charitably minded? Assume that the donor transfers low-basis, highly appreciated property to a CRT, which immediately sells the property. One way to analyze this is to compare

---

[136] Priv. Ltr. Rul. 200127023 (Apr. 4, 2001) (payment of an actuarial amount to the non-charitable beneficiary upon termination was not self-dealing because it was in exchange for the individual's right to income).

[137] Tech. Adv. Mem. 9845001 (July 13, 1998). See also Priv. Ltr. Rul. 199923013 (Mar. 4, 1999), holding that the reformation of a trust's governing instrument to allow the trust to qualify as a CRT did not adversely affect the qualification of the CRT, even where the court's reformation was made retroactive to the date of the execution of the trust instrument; see also Priv. Ltr. Rul. 200002029 (Oct. 14, 1999), holding that a reformation of a trust to convert the trust from a NIMCRUT to a fixed percentage CRUT will not jeopardize the trust's qualification as a CRT.

[138] Atkinson v. Comm'r, 115 TC 26 (2000).

(1) the present value of the future payments made by the CRT to the noncharitable beneficiaries to (2) the present value of the future income earned by the after-tax proceeds of a sale of the property by the taxpayer, plus the present value of the principal at the date on which the CRT would terminate. If (1) is greater than (2), the CRT is expected to be better than doing nothing. Comparable analysis could be done with donations not involving a sale. The computations should include the effect of income taxes on distributions and earnings and the effect of estate taxes on any unconsumed distributions or on the principal at the date on which the CRT would terminate.

This analysis will indicate a number of years that the donor must live in order for the transaction to produce a greater return to the family than keeping the sale proceeds.

CHAPTER 34

Charitable Gift Annuities

¶ 34.01 CHARITABLE GIFT ANNUITY: WHAT IT IS AND HOW IT WORKS

The "charitable gift annuity" is something like a small-scale version of a charitable remainder trust, and is a viable planning alternative to consider with a creditworthy charity.

In a charitable gift annuity, the donor makes a gift to charity in return for the charity's promise to pay the donor or the donor's spouse (or other annuitant) an annuity, usually for the donor's lifetime or for the lifetimes of the donor and spouse (the term selected may be referred to as the noncharitable term). The value of the property donated, less the value of the annuity, is a charitable gift eligible for an income tax charitable deduction[1] and a gift or estate tax charitable deduction. The value of the annuity is ordinarily determined by reference to the IRS tables for annuities.[2] Factors determining the value of the gift, and thus the amount of the deduction are: (1) the length of

---

[1] Treas. Reg. § 1.170A-1(d).

[2] Reg. §§ 1.7520-1, 20.7520-1, 25.7520-1. The tables are found in IRS Publication 1457, Actuarial Values—Alpha Volume. See Ch. 11 for a discussion of circumstances in which the tables cannot be used.

the noncharitable term, (2) the amount of the annuity, (3) the 7520 rate,[3] (4) when the annuity begins, and (5) how often the annuity is payable.[4]

With regard to the 7520 rate, the donor can elect the 7520 rate for the month of transfer or the 7520 rate for either of the two months preceding the transfer.[5] The donor will want to choose the highest of those rates to maximize his charitable deduction because the highest 7520 rate will result in the lowest value of the retained annuity, and therefore, the highest value of the charitable gift and largest charitable deduction.

PRACTICE POINTER: Charitable gift annuities are usually done with relatively small gifts (perhaps $5,000 to $50,000) to a charity which has an established gift annuity program, or wants to start one. These tend to be charities which receive large numbers of smaller donations.

¶ 34.02 STRUCTURE OF ANNUITY

Unless the charity complies with certain specific requirements, the income from the transferred property will be characterized as unrelated debt-financed income, and will be taxable to the charity under the unrelated business income tax (UBIT).[6] Hence, charitable gift annuities are usually structured to fit the following requirements:[7]

- The annuity must be the sole consideration for the transferred property (other than certain pre-existing mortgages).[8]
- The present value of the annuity on the date of the transaction must be less than 90 percent of the donor's equity in the property.[9]
- The annuity must be payable over the lives of one or two living individuals.[10]
- The contract must not guarantee a minimum number of payments or specify a maximum number of payments.[11]
- The contract must not provide for adjustments to the amount of the

---

[3] The "7520 rate" is 120 percent of the federal mid-term rate, rounded to the nearest 2/10 of one percent. IRC § 7520.

[4] Treas. Reg. §§ 1.7520-1, 20.7520-1, 25.7520-1(b).

[5] IRC § 7520(a).

[6] IRC §§ 511(b)(1), 514.

[7] IRC § 514(c)(5).

[8] Treas. Reg. § 1.514(c)-1(e)(1)(i).

[9] Treas. Reg. § 1.514(c)-1(e)(1)(ii).

[10] Treas. Reg. § 1.514(c)-1(e)(1)(iii).

[11] Treas. Reg. § 1.514(c)-1(e)(1)(iv)(a).

annuity based on income earned by the transferred property or any other property.[12]

¶ 34.03 GIFT OF APPRECIATED PROPERTY IN EXCHANGE FOR A CHARITABLE ANNUITY

The contribution of property to the charity in exchange for an annuity will be treated as a bargain sale to the charity. Accordingly, as described in Chapter 32, the donor's basis will be allocated between the gift element and the sale element of the transaction to determine both gain and the amount of the donor's gift.[13] The gain on the sale element will be recognized and taxed to the donor. Gain recognized by the donor may be reported ratably over the period that the annuity payments are expected to be received if: (1) the annuity is non-assignable or assignable only to the charity and (2) the donor and a designated surviving annuitant or annuitants are the only annuitants.[14] If any other circumstances apply, all of the gain will be recognized in the year the sale transaction closes.

> EXAMPLE: Mom owns Blackacre, which has a basis of $60 and a fair market value of $100. She gives the property to charity, in return for an annuity which has a value of $80. The sale portion is $80/100, so 80 percent of $60, or $48, is the amount of basis allocated to the sale. Accordingly, the sale proceeds of $80 (amount realized) less $48 (allocable portion of basis), result in $32 of gain to Mom. The transaction also has a charitable contribution component. The charitable contribution is the fair market value of Blackacre ($100), less the value of the annuity received in return ($80), or $20. Depending on the facts, Mom will recognize the $32 of gain in the year of sale or ratably over the annuity term.

¶ 34.04 TAXATION OF ANNUITANT ON ANNUITY PAYMENTS RECEIVED

The general rules on taxation of annuities apply to the annuity received by the annuitant under a charitable annuity.[15] Accordingly, each annuity payment will be treated as part return of principal, part interest, and part capital gain (assuming the donor realized a gain on the transfer of property to the charity).[16]

The return of principal portion of each payment is determined by multiplying each payment by the applicable "exclusion ratio." The exclusion ratio is

---

[12] Treas. Reg. § 1.514(c)-1(e)(1)(iv)(b).

[13] Treas. Reg. § 1.1011-2(a)(4).

[14] Treas. Reg. §§ 1.1011-2(a)(4)(i)–1.1011-2(a)(4)(ii).

[15] IRC § 72. See Ch. 13 for a complete discussion of the taxation of annuities.

[16] See n. 15.

calculated by dividing the annuitant's investment in the annuity contract by the expected return on the contract. The investment in the contract is the non-gift element of the contribution (i.e., the purchase price of the annuity). The expected return is ordinarily determined by multiplying (1) the amount of the total annuity payments expected to be received annually by the annuitant by (2) the annuitant's actuarially determined life expectancy according to the IRS income tax actuarial tables.[17]

If the transfer was treated as a bargain sale, and gain on the sale is not required to be recognized immediately by the donor, then a portion of each annuity payment allocable to principal will also be treated as capital gain until all of the gain has been recognized.[18]

After the entire investment in the contract has been recovered (along with any gain recognized on the transaction), the remaining annuity payments constitute ordinary income to the annuitant.[19]

If cash is contributed to a charity in exchange for an annuity, a portion of each annuity payment will be a nontaxable return of principal (until the entire cash investment in the contract is recovered), and a portion will be taxable interest. Thereafter, all annuity payments received by the annuitant will be taxed in their entirety as ordinary income. This latter (mortality gain) situation will occur only if the annuitant lives longer than the life expectancy assigned under the actuarial tables used to determine the expected return on the annuity contract.

¶ 34.05 ESTATE AND GIFT TAX ISSUES

If the donor is the only annuitant, and the annuity is for the donor's lifetime, the transfer will neither be subject to gift tax at the time of the transfer nor to estate tax at the donor's death. The donor will, however, be treated as having made a gift if a person other than the donor is a current annuitant or a successor annuitant (unless the donor retains a power to revoke the non-donor annuitant's interest). In this event, the amount of the gift will equal the value of the non-donor annuitant's interest. If there is a successor individual annuitant after the donor-annuitant's death, the value of the annuity will be included in the donor's estate.[20]

In any of these cases, if the non-donor successor annuitant after the donor-annuitant's life is the donor's spouse, the annuity should qualify for the estate tax marital deduction if the surviving spouse is the only person who has the right to receive payments before her death.[21] The gift to the non-donor spouse will qualify

---

[17] Treas. Reg. § 1.72-4(a)(1).

[18] Treas. Reg. § 1.1011-2(c), example 8.

[19] IRC § 72(b)(2).

[20] IRC § 2039.

[21] IRC § 2056(b)(7)(c).

for the gift tax marital deduction if it is structured as a joint and survivor annuity.[22]

¶ 34.06 COMPARISON WITH CHARITABLE REMAINDER TRUST

The following table compares the characteristics of a charitable gift through a CRT with the characteristics of a charitable gift annuity:

CHARACTERISTIC	CHARITABLE ANNUITY	CRT
Structure	No structure; annuitant is simply general creditor of charity.	Trust is used to hold gift.
Charitable Deduction	The size of the charitable gift is based on the difference between the amount of property transferred and the value of the annuity;[a] a deduction for contributions of tangible personal property is allowed on date of transfer, subject to general limitations on deductions.	Value of remainder is deductible; valuation of the remainder depends on the type of CRT; no deduction for tangible personal property until the property is sold to an unrelated party or all private interests terminate.[b]
Security for Annuity Payment	The donor has no interest in any particular assets of the charity.	The annuitant (i.e., the noncharitable beneficiary of the trust) has an interest in trust assets.
Customized Design of Gift	No complexities allowed. No CRUT- type annuity is allowed, because the annuitant has no interest in assets to value each year; however, deferred annuities are allowed. In the case of a deferred annuity, a charitable deduction in the year of contribution is allowed; a higher annuity rate is usually payable for a deferred annuity.	Extensive customizing of the trust is permissible.

---

[22] IRC § 2523(f)(6).

Private Foundation	Private foundation rules are not applicable.	Prohibitions on self-dealing and taxable expenditures exist.[c25]
Appreciated Property	If appreciated property is transferred, the transaction will be treated as a bargain sale, and gain will be recognized, either immediately or over the expected term of the annuity.	A transfer of appreciated property to a CRT is not taxable; gain on the sale of appreciated property by a CRT can be deferred, and perhaps never taxed.
Income Taxation of Annuity Payments	The annuity receipts are taxed under § 72 (general rules on taxation of annuities); each annuity payment is treated as partly interest income, partly capital gain (if applicable), and partly return of principal.	Under § 664, the annuity amount is treated as having the same character it had in the CRT's hands—ordered as ordinary income, capital gain, tax-exempt income, and principal;[d] however, if the CRT has any unrelated business taxable income for a year, subchapter J rules applicable to complex trusts govern for that year.[e]
Charitable Beneficiary	Only one charity per gift annuity is available, and no change of charity is allowed.	Any number of charities can benefit, and the donor can reserve the right to change the charitable beneficiaries.

---

[a]Treas. Reg. §§ 1.170A-1(d)(1), 1.664-2(c).

[b]Treas. Reg. § 1.664-2(d), 1.664-3(d).

[c]IRC §§ 4941, 4945.

[d]IRC § 664(b).

[e]Reg. § 1.664-1(c).

Finally, aside from the above differences, it should be noted that a charity may like the gift annuity better than a charitable remainder trust, because the charity gets the money or property at the date of the gift, not later.

¶ 34.07 LAWSUIT CASTING SHADOW ON GIFT ANNUITIES

Some charities use annuity rates recommended by the American Council on Gift Annuities. This is an organization of charities, headquartered in Dallas, Texas, which suggests annuity rates from time to time. The suggested annuity rates are lower than those which could be obtained from commercial annuities, since a charitable element is intended.

The American Council on Gift Annuities and its member charities were recently sued for antitrust (price-fixing) and securities violations.[28] The case casts a shadow over all gift annuity programs, since most marketing, as well as the consummation, of these transactions is not normally conducted in accordance with the antitrust and securities laws generally applicable to sales of commercial annuities.

In December 1995, President Clinton signed legislation designed to address this case; the new statutes retroactively clarified that charitable gift annuities were exempt from many generally applicable antitrust and securities rules.[29] The defendants filed a motion to dismiss, based on the new federal legislation. In 1996, the court denied the motion to dismiss, holding that factual issues existed regarding qualification for the exemption. In April 1997, the Fifth Circuit upheld the district court's refusal to dismiss. Meanwhile, the plaintiffs had dropped their securities law claims, leaving the antitrust action and claim under Texas law as the remaining causes of action. The charitable community is following this case intently.

---

[28] See Ozee v. American Council on Gift Annuities, 888 F. Supp. 1318 (ND Tex. 1995).

[29] Philanthropy Protection Act of 1995, Pub. L. No. 104-62; Charitable Gift Annuity Antitrust Relief Act of 1995, Pub. L. No. 104-63.

Charitable Lead Trusts

¶ 35.01 INTRODUCTION

Use of a "charitable lead trust" (CLT) as a planning tool is uniquely suited for the wealthy—only they can usually afford the economic costs of such a technique.

[1] How Does the Charitable Lead Trust Work?

The CLT pays an annuity or unitrust interest to a named charity for a certain number of years (the charitable term) and then pays the remainder to designated noncharitable beneficiaries.[1] The donor gets a gift or estate tax charitable deduction and, in some cases, an income tax deduction for the value of the interest received by the charity. The value of the noncharitable beneficiaries' remainder interest is a taxable inter vivos gift by the donor or subject to estate tax as part of his gross estate.

A "charitable lead annuity trust" (CLAT) is a CLT paying a fixed percentage of the initial value of the trust assets to charity for the charitable term. A "charitable lead unitrust" (CLUT) is a CLT paying a percentage of the value of its assets, determined annually, to charity for the charitable term.

[2] When Should a Charitable Lead Trust Be Considered?

A CLT is a particularly good technique in any of the following four scenarios:

Scenario 1: The asset to be transferred to the CLT is expected to perform better than the 7520 rate;[2] here, the actuarial tables will value the taxable gift (i.e., the remainder interest) at less than the actual value that the gifted property will eventually have if it performs as expected.

Scenario 2: The ultimate value of the taxable gift is greater than the value of the taxable gift for gift tax purposes (as determined under the actuarial tables) because the charitable term is measured by the lifetime of a person who is not expected to live as long as the actuarial tables indicate.

Scenario 3: The donor has reached his limits on charitable income tax deductions,[3] and therefore wants to move income, which will go to charity, out of his income tax base and into the tax base of another (e.g., the CLT).

Scenario 4: The donor wants an income tax benefit for contributions to foreign charities.

---

[1] IRC §§ 170(f)(2)(B), 2055(e)(2)(B), 2522(c)(2)(B).

[2] The 7520 rate is 120 percent of the federal midterm rate, rounded to the nearest 2/10 of one percent. IRC § 7520. See Ch. 11 for a discussion of the 7520 rate.

[3] See Ch. 32 for a discussion of the limitations on charitable income tax deductions.

[a] Scenario 1: Property Expected to Outperform 7520 Rate

The gift and estate tax charitable deductions with respect to actuarial split-interest trusts like a CLT are ordinarily determined by reference to the actuarial tables published by the IRS.[4] If the transferred property increases in value at a rate greater than the 7520 rate, a larger gift will in fact be made to the noncharitable beneficiaries than the value of the gift as initially determined under the IRS actuarial tables.[5]

EXAMPLE: Mom gives $1,000,000 in cash to a CLT. Both the annuity payment to charity and the 7520 rate are 8 percent. The taxable gift will be the present value of $1,000,000 at the end of the charitable term. If the property actually earns the 7520 rate, the noncharitable beneficiaries will have $1,000,000 at the end of the term. If, instead, the property actually earns 12 percent, the family will have more than $1,000,000 left at the end of the term, for the same gift tax cost.

[b] Scenario 2: Anticipated Charitable Term Shorter Than Actuarially Determined Life Expectancy of Measuring Life

The CLT offers an opportunity to take advantage of the actuarial tables in the right circumstances.

Suppose Dad has a statistical life expectancy of 15 years and an actual life expectancy of four years. If Dad transfers money to a CLT, and the charitable term is measured by his lifetime, he will receive a gift tax charitable deduction for the value of the anticipated 15 payments to charity, when in fact the CLT is expected to actually make only four payments to charity. As illustrated in the following example this situation permits (albeit sadly) some stunning estate planning.

EXAMPLE: Dad (who has a statistical life expectancy of 15 years but an actual life expectancy of four years) transfers $10,000,000 in cash to CLT. The annuity rate and the 7520 rate are both eight percent. For gift tax purposes, the taxable portion of the gift will be the present value of $10,000,000 at the end of 15 years. If Dad lives four years, the actual gift will be the present value of $10,000,000 after these four years.

It has been suggested that the life of an unrelated person whose health is poor, but who is expected to live longer than a year, could also be chosen as the measuring life of the charitable term. In the above example, suppose Dad is fit as a fiddle. However, he knows a person who suffers from a mortal illness, but whose life expectancy still exceeds one year. The regulations, applied

---

[4] IRC § 7520. These tables are found in Publication 1457, Alpha Volume, and Publication 1458, Beta Volume. See Ch. 11 for a discussion of situations in which the tables cannot be used.

[5] See Ch. 11 for a discussion of this concept.

literally, would allow the use of this person's lifetime in calculating the deduction. There is no judicial authority on the issue.

[c] Scenario 3: Donor has Reached Charitable Deduction Limit

A CLT can be used to obtain the equivalent of an income tax charitable deduction, when the donor's deduction limits have been reached.

EXAMPLE: Donor has income-producing property worth $1,000,000. He would like to give another $100,000/year to charity, but he has reached his limit on available contribution deductions. If he gives away another $100,000, he will receive no income tax benefit. On the other hand, if he transfers property which produces $100,000 of income per year to a CLT (which is not structured as a grantor trust) and the CLT pays the $100,000 to a charity, that $100,000 of income will be excluded from the donor's taxable income (since it is realized by the CLT) and will benefit charity.

[d] Scenario 4: Support of Foreign Charities

Unlike an estate or trust, which gets an income tax charitable deduction for distributions to foreign charities (provided that evidence that the foreign charities qualify under Section 501(c)(3) can be obtained),[6] an individual donor cannot receive an income tax charitable deduction for gifts to foreign charities.[7] Nevertheless, if the donor contributes property to a CLT which is not a grantor trust, the income earned by the property will be excluded from the donor's income (because the income is realized by the CLT), and the CLT will receive a deduction for its income distributions to charity.

[3] Other Factors to Consider

[a] Effect of Interest Rates

CLATs are desirable when interest rates are low. The value of an annuity varies inversely with interest rates, so a lower interest rate will produce a higher charitable deduction, all other factors being equal.

EXAMPLE: Dad gives $1,000,000 to a CLAT with a charitable term of 20 years and an annuity rate of 6 percent. If the 7520 rate is 8 percent, the charitable deduction will be 58.9086 percent of the principal. If the 7520 rate is 10 percent, the charitable deduction will be 51.0816 percent of the principal. If the 7520 rate is 12 percent, the charitable deduction will be 44.8164 percent of the principal.

---

[6] IRC § 642(c).

[7] IRC § 170(c).

When a low interest rate is combined with rapidly appreciating property,[8] the estate planning benefits can be spectacular,[9] as illustrated in the following example.

EXAMPLE: Dad gives $1,000,000 to a CLAT. The 7520 rate and the annuity rate are 6 percent, and the charitable term is 20 years. The property actually earns 15 percent per year. The charitable deduction is $688,195, so the gift tax paid is $171,493, if Dad is in the 55 percent bracket. If the property actually earns 15 percent per year, the noncharitable beneficiaries will receive $10,219,922 at the end of the term. The donor will pass $10,219,922 to his noncharitable beneficiaries at the end of the 20-year term for a gift tax cost of $171,493.

CLUTS, unlike CLATs, are unaffected by fluctuations in interest rates,[10] so this kind of planning is not effective with a CLUT.

[b] Need for Surplusage of Family Funds and Assets

A CLT should only be considered when it is feasible to have family assets tied up for the years constituting the charitable term of the trust, at the end of which the assets pass to family members.

[c] S Corporation as a Trust Investment

For taxable years beginning before 1998, a CLT cannot be an S shareholder unless it is structured as a grantor trust. For taxable years beginning after 1997, a CLT that is not a grantor trust can apparently qualify as an electing small business trust and hold S corporation stock.[11] However, qualification as an electing small business trust is generally not desirable, since the income tax treatment of a CLT, which is an electing small business trust, is frequently prohibitive. That is, the CLT's share of the S corporation income is taxed at the highest rates applicable to trusts and estates, and apparently no offsetting deduction for charitable distributions is available.[12]

---

[8] As described in ¶ 35.01[1] above.

[9] However, where the annuity rate is higher than the 7520 rate, the IRS may take the position that the charitable deduction should be reduced to reflect the possibility that the trust may be exhausted prior to the end of the charitable term. See Treas. Reg. §§ 20.7520-3(b)(2)(i), 25.7520-3(b)(2)(i), 25.7520-3(b)(2)(v), example (5).

[10] Except where the unitrust payment must be adjusted based on frequency and timing of payments, as adjustment factors used are interest-sensitive. Whatever difference these adjustment factors make tend to be minor, although they become more significant the longer the charitable term.

[11] IRC § 1361(c)(2)(B)(v), 1361(e), Small Business Jobs Protection Act of 1996, §§ 1317(a), 1302(c), 1316(e).

[12] IRC § 641(d)(2)(C).

¶ 35.02 TERMS OF A CHARITABLE LEAD TRUST

A CLT instrument must provide that a certain amount (i.e., the "charitable amount") is payable to charity each year for a period of time (i.e., the "charitable term"). At the expiration of this charitable term, the remaining trust principal passes to noncharitable beneficiaries.

[1] Charitable Amount Defined

[a] In General

[i] **Annuity trust charitable amount.** In a CLAT, the charity must have the right to receive a guaranteed annuity.[13] A guaranteed annuity is an arrangement under which a certain amount is paid at least annually for the charitable term. Also, in a CLAT, the amount payable to the charity will often be expressed as a percentage of the initial net fair market value of the assets of the trust.

[ii] **Unitrust charitable amount.** In a CLUT, the charity must have a right to receive, not less often than annually, a fixed percentage of the net fair market value of the assets of the trust (as determined annually).[14] Unlike the rules governing a charitable remainder unitrust (CRUT), a provision requiring payment to charity of the lesser of either trust income or the unitrust amount is not acceptable for a CLUT.[15]

PRACTICE POINTER: In an inflationary economy, the annuity trust will usually be more desirable if the goal is to maximize the amount passing to the remainder beneficiaries at the end of the charitable term.

[b] No Minimum Payout Percentage

There is no minimum percentage which must be paid out during the initial term, as there is with charitable remainder trusts.[16]

---

[13] IRC §§ 170(f)(2), 2055(e)(2)(B), 2522(c)(2)(B).

[14] IRC §§ 170(f)(2), 2055(e)(2)(B), 2522(c)(2)(B).

[15] Treas. Reg. §§ 1.170A-6(c)(2)(i)(B), 1.170A-6(c)(2)(ii)(B), 20.2055-2(e)(2)(vi)(a), 20.2055-2(e)(2)(iii)(a); 25.2522(c)- 3(c)(2)(vi)(a), 25.2522(c)-3(c)(2)(vii)(a).

[16] Priv. Ltr. Rul. 9415009 (Jan. 12, 1994), which conditioned a ruling on a valid charitable lead trust that the charitable payout be at least 5 percent, was clarified by Priv. Ltr. Rul. 9431051 (May 16, 1994), which affirmed that there is no minimum payout requirement.

[c] Annuity Payment With Note or in Kind

Can the charitable annuity payments be paid with notes from the trust? While the IRS has not yet taken a clear position, it is possible that the IRS would answer "No," based on a 1995 letter ruling and 1997 technical advice memorandum[17] concerning grantor retained annuity trusts (the noncharitable analogue of a CRAT). In this ruling, the IRS determined that where the annuity is payable in the form of a note from the trust, the annuity interest does not constitute a qualified annuity interest. To constitute a qualified annuity interest, the fixed amount must be payable no less frequently than annually. According to the IRS, the use of notes to satisfy the annuity payment can effectively defer the payee's actual receipt of payment (as well as the trust's actual payment) in violation of this annual payment requirement.

The annuity payment can be made in kind, however. If the property used to pay the annuity is appreciated, a gain will be recognized by the trust. However, the trust will be able to claim an offsetting charitable deduction for the gain distributed to charity.[18]

[2] Charitable Term Defined

[a] Allowable Term

The charitable term can be—

- For a specified number of years;
- For the life or lives of an individual or individuals, each of whom is living at the date of the gift and can be ascertained at such date;[19] or
- For the life of a living person plus a term of years.[20]

[b] Rule Against Perpetuities Limitation

The CLT's term cannot be longer than the maximum valid trust term under the applicable rule against perpetuities.

[c] Prepayment of the Charity's Interest

It may be desirable at some point to terminate the CLT by prepaying the charity's interest. The IRS has, however, ruled that a trust is not a qualified

---

[17] Priv. Ltr. Rul. 9604005 (Oct. 17, 1995); Tech. Adv. Mem. 9717008 (Apr. 25, 1997).

[18] Rev. Rul. 83-75, 1983-1 CB 114; Priv. Ltr. Rul. 9112009 (Dec. 20, 1990).

[19] Treas. Reg. §§ 1.170A-6(c)(2)(i)(A), 1.170A-6(c)(2)(ii)(A); 20.2055-2(e)(2)(vi)(a), 20.2055-2(e)(2)(vii)(a); 25.2522(c)-3(c)(2)(vi)(a), 25.2522(c)-3(c)(2)(vii)(a).

[20] Treas. Reg. §§ 1.170A-6(c)(2)(i)(A), 1.170A-6(c)(2)(ii)(A); 20.2055-2(e)(2)(vi)(a), 20.2055-2(e)(2)(vii)(a); 25.2522(c)-3(c)(2)(vi)(a), 25.2522(c)-3(c)(2)(vii)(a).

CLT if the trustee is allowed to prepay the charitable entity at a discounted value to reflect current payment.[21] However, if the face amount of the charity's remaining payments is paid, rather than their discounted value, the IRS or the courts may take a different view.

[3] Other Aspects of Charitable Lead Trusts

[a] Additional Trust Contributions

[i] Additional contributions to the annuity trust. A CLAT should prohibit additional contributions. This is because the amount of the guaranteed annuity payment must be determinable at the trust's inception.[22]

[ii] Additional contributions to the unitrust. Additional contributions can be made to a CLUT.

[iii] Additional contributions as a result of death. In a charitable remainder annuity trust, all contributions made as a result of the grantor's death are considered one contribution.[23] The same should be true of a CLT.

[b] Selection of Charitable Beneficiaries

[i] Permissible charitable beneficiaries. The trust's charitable beneficiaries must be organizations which qualify for a gift or estate tax charitable deduction. Provision should be in the trust instrument ensuring that any recipient of an annuity or unitrust amount will be such an organization.

[ii] Selection by trustee. The trustee of a CLT is allowed to select the charitable recipients, provided that such power is granted by the trust instrument.[24] However, if the donor is a trustee or otherwise retains this right, the CLT will be included in the donor's estate if he dies within the charitable term.[25] Hence, the donor should not retain this power.

---

[21] Rev. Rul. 88-27, 1988-1 CB 331.

[22] Treas. Reg. §§ 1.170A-6(c)(2)(i), 20.2055-2(e)(2)(vi)(a), 25.2522(c)-3(c)(2)(vi)(a).

[23] Treas. Reg. § 1.664-2(b).

[24] Rev. Rul. 78-101, 1978-1 CB 301; Priv. Ltr. Rul. 9532007 (May 4, 1995); Priv. Ltr. Rul. 9331015 (May 6, 1993).

[25] IRC § 2036(a)(2).

[c] Payments for Private Purposes During Charitable Term

[i] In general. No payments for private purposes can be made by the trust during the charitable term other than amounts in payment of a (1) guaranteed annuity interest (in an annuity trust) or (2) unitrust interest (in a unitrust), unless the amount paid for a private purpose is paid from a separate, noncharitable portion of the trust.[26] Payment of the private annuity interest or unitrust interest must not be preferred to payment of the charitable interest.[27] Finally, it should be noted that payments made for full and adequate consideration (e.g., reasonable trustee fees) are not payments for a private purpose.[28]

[ii] Trusts with concurrent private interests. Trusts which provide for private interests during the charitable term are rare. In general, this chapter discusses trusts from which no payments can be made for private purposes during the charitable term. It should be noted, however, that a few of the rules discussed in this chapter vary somewhat if a private interest co-exists with the charitable interest. Care should be taken in determining whether these different rules apply if the decision is made to use this technique.

[iii] Trusts with consecutive interests. The regulations indicate that a charitable annuity or unitrust interest may not be preceded in time by a private annuity or unitrust interest.[29] However, the Tax Court has held these regulations invalid in the case of a CLUT, and the IRS has acquiesced in that decision.[30] Accordingly, at least in the case of a CLUT, an annuity or unitrust interest may be paid to a noncharitable beneficiary before the charity's interest becomes a present interest in the trust.

[iv] Payment of taxes. A charitable remainder trust is disqualified if it is required to pay estate taxes, generation-skipping transfer taxes, or private foundation excise taxes.[31] Presumably, payment of these taxes would also disqualify a CLT because such payment would be for a private purpose, although this is not altogether clear.

---

[26] Treas. Reg. §§ 25.2522(c)-3(c)(2)(vi)(f), 25.2522(c)-3(c)(2)(vii)(f), 20.2055-2(e)(2)(vi)(f), 20.2055-2(e)(2)(vii)(e).

[27] Treas. Reg. §§ 25.2522(c)-3(c)(2)(vi)(f), 25.2522(c)-3(c)(2)(vii)(f), 20.2055-2(e)(2)(vi)(f), 20.2055-2(e)(2)(vii)(e).

[28] Treas. Reg. §§ 25.2522(c)-3(c)(2)(vi)(f), 25.2522(c)-3(c)(2)(vii)(f), 20.2055-2(e)(2)(vi)(f), 20.2055-2(e)(2)(vii)(e).

[29] Treas. Reg. §§ 1.170A-6(c)(2)(i)(E), 1.170A-6(c)(2)(ii)(D), 20.2055-2(e)(2)(vi)(f), 20.2055-2(e)(2)(vii)(e), 25.2522(c)-3(c)(2)(vi)(f), 25.2522(c)-3(c)(2)(vii)(e).

[30] Estate of Boeshore v. Comm'r, 78 TC 523 (1982), acq., 1987-1 CB 1.

[31] Treas. Reg. § 1.664-1(a)(6), example 3.

¶ 35.03 INCOME TAX CHARITABLE DEDUCTION

[1] Tax Treatment of the Donor

[a] Trusts Which Provide Income Tax Charitable Deduction to Donor

The donor (also known as the grantor) receives no current income tax charitable deduction for a transfer to a CLT unless the trust is structured as a grantor trust—that is, in such a way that the donor reports, during the charitable term, all of the trust's taxable income, deductions, loss, gain, and credits directly on the donor's own individual income tax return.[32]

If the trust is structured as a grantor trust, the donor (grantor) gets an income tax charitable deduction for transfers to the trust. This deduction, however, will be limited to the charitable deduction available for gifts to 30 percent charities,[33] since a gift to a CLT is deemed to be a gift *for the use of a charity.*[34] The extent to which the donor can carry over an excess charitable deduction for the transfer to the CLT is uncertain. In an apparently erroneous private ruling, the IRS determined that no carryover was available for an excess charitable deduction if the beneficiary of the CLT was the donor's (grantor's) private foundation.[35]

It should also be noted that the donor will get no additional charitable deductions for amounts paid by the trust to charity during the term of the trust.

Finally, death or other termination of grantor trust status during the charitable term will trigger recapture of the original income tax charitable deduction, less the discounted value of trust income already paid to charity.[36]

PRACTICE POINTER: A grantor CLT must limit its charitable beneficiaries to United States charities in order for the donor to take an income tax deduction.[37]

PRACTICE POINTER: If the grantor CLT invests in non-income-producing properties or tax-exempt properties during the charitable term, the grantor trust rules, requiring inclusion of the trust's tax items on the donor's tax return, may not result in any additional tax liability for the grantor.

---

[32] IRC § 170(f)(2)(B); Treas. Reg. § 1.170A-6(c)(1). See Ch. 6 for a discussion of structuring a trust as a grantor trust.

[33] See Ch. 32 for a discussion of gifts to 30 percent charities.

[34] Treas. Reg. § 1.170A-8(a)(2).

[35] Priv. Ltr. Rul. 8824039 (Mar. 21, 1988). The ruling appeared to apply pre-Tax Reform Act of 1984 law to a proposed 1987 transaction.

[36] IRC § 170(f)(2)(B).

[37] IRC § 170(c).

QUESTION: *When would a grantor CLT be a good idea?*

ANSWER: A grantor CLT is a good idea when a person wants a large charitable deduction in a particular year (for example, in a year when she is receiving an unusually large amount of income, or if her tax rate will decrease substantially in following years). For example, the technique has been used when income tax rates were about to be lowered, so as to allow (for example) a deduction in Year One when maximum tax rates are 50 percent, followed by 28 percent to 39.6 percent taxation in the following years.

[b] Trusts Which Do Not Provide an Income Tax Charitable Deduction to Donor

As indicated above, if the CLT is not a grantor trust, the donor does not receive an income tax deduction on the initial gift. On the other hand, income earned by the nongrantor trust will not be included in the grantor's income.

[2] Tax Treatment of the Donor's Estate or Revocable Trust—Trust Established at Death

[a] Requirements for Charitable Payments From Charitable Lead Trust Established at Death

Even if payment of the annuity or unitrust amount is required to commence as of the date of the grantor's death, the actual payments probably need not be made until the trust is funded (by analogy to the charitable remainder trust rules).

[b] No Set-Aside Deduction

The estate may not be entitled to a charitable set-aside deduction for income accumulated for the benefit of the CLT, because the CLT is a taxable trust whose assets are not held exclusively for charitable purposes.[38] However, if it could be shown that the income accumulated could not possibly be used for a noncharitable purpose (i.e., was certain to be paid as part of the charitable annuity or unitrust payment), a set-aside deduction might be allowed. Of course, a revocable trust which becomes irrevocable at death is not entitled to a set-aside deduction at all.[39]

---

[38] See Treas. Reg. § 1.642(c)-2(d).

[39] IRC § 642(c).

[c] Deduction for Amounts Currently Paid Out

[i] Amounts paid to a CLT. The estate (or formerly revocable trust) should be entitled to a distribution deduction for income actually paid to a CLT under the governing instrument.[40] The CLT can then take a charitable deduction for amounts it pays to charity.[41] Therefore, in a deathtime transfer to a CLT, it will often be advantageous to fund the CLT with estate (or formerly revocable trust) income as that income is earned by that estate (or trust), and to begin payment of the charitable payout from the CLT immediately.

[ii] Amounts paid to beneficiaries of a CLT. Under Section 642, a charitable income tax deduction may be allowed to the estate (or formerly revocable trust) if the fiduciary pays, pursuant to authority granted in the governing instrument, the charitable amount directly to the trust's charitable beneficiaries out of income to which the CLT is entitled.[42]

[3] Tax Treatment of the Charitable Lead Trust

[a] Income Taxation of Charitable Lead Trusts—In General

A nongrantor CLT is a taxable entity and, therefore, is subject to the usual rules governing the income taxation of trusts and beneficiaries.

[b] Charitable Lead Trust's Charitable Deduction—In General

Subject to the exceptions described below, a CLT receives an unlimited charitable deduction for amounts distributed to charity during the year.[43] There is, however, no set-aside deduction for trusts established after October 9, 1969.[44]

The trustee may elect to treat any amount paid to the charitable beneficiary during the current year as paid during the previous year.[45] Note that this election applies only for purposes of determining the amount of the income tax charitable deduction.

---

[40] IRC § 661(a)(2).

[41] IRC § 642(c)(1).

[42] IRC § 642(c)(1).

[43] IRC § 642(c)(1).

[44] IRC § 642(c)(2).

[45] IRC § 642(c)(1).

The election may not be made for the purpose of meeting the requirement that a certain percentage of the value of the trust assets must be paid to charity each taxable year.

[c] Charitable Deduction Exceptions

[i] **Capital gains exception.** The charitable deduction is reduced by the amount of any deduction for net capital gains.

[ii] **Tax-exempt income exception.** No charitable deduction is allowed for amounts which were excluded from the trust's gross income.

[iii] **Unrelated business income exception.** The Internal Revenue Code does not allow the Section 642(c) unlimited charitable deduction for any portion of the amount paid to a charity to the extent that such portion is allocable to the trust's "unrelated business income" for the year.[46] Instead, to the extent that the trust's charitable contribution is allocable to the trust's unrelated business income, the charitable deduction for such contribution is allowed only to the extent that a charitable deduction would be allowed to an individual.

The trust's "unrelated business income" is the amount of trust income which would be computed as unrelated business taxable income under Section 512 if the trust were an exempt organization.[47] Generally speaking, unrelated business income includes income derived from an active business unrelated to an organization's exempt functions, debt-financed income, and certain interest, annuities, royalties, and rents derived from controlled organizations, less a specific deduction of $1,000.

> EXAMPLE: If a trust had unrelated business income of $101,000, its unrelated business taxable income would be $100,000 (that is, $101,000 less the $1,000 Section 512(b)(12) deduction). If the whole $101,000 were paid to a charity, the trust would be entitled to an unlimited charitable deduction for $1,000 of the amount paid to the charity (i.e., the specific deduction amount). Assuming that the charity is a charitable organization described in Section 170(b)(1)(A) (i.e., a 50 percent charity), a charitable deduction for the trust's $100,000 of unrelated business taxable income paid to the charity will be allowed, before limitations. However, this deduction is subject to the same limitations applied to contributions by individuals. Accordingly, in this instance, the trust's total allowable

---

[46] IRC § 681(a).

[47] IRC § 681(a); see also Treas. Reg. § 1.681(a)-2 for rules on allocating the deduction to unrelated business income.

charitable deduction for the year would be limited to $51,000. It is not clear whether a carryover of the $50,000 excess charitable deduction is available.

[d] Sourcing of Trust Distributions

It would be most tax-efficient, particularly in the case of a CLT which earns income in excess of the charitable payment, to provide in the trust instrument that trust distributions are sourced to specific classes of income, or first to certain classes of income and then to others. Without such a direction in the trust instrument, distributions will be considered made pro rata out of all types of income.[48]

The IRS has announced that it will not honor a priority or sourcing provision for distributions set forth in the trust instrument unless the sourcing: (1) is accomplished independent of tax consequences and (2) has substantial economic effect.[49] For example, in an ordinary complex trust, a requirement that all business income be paid to charity and all dividend income be paid to John should be recognized.[50] However, in a CLAT or straight CLUT, the charity will receive the same annuity amount, regardless of the sourcing of the distributions, so the IRS has taken the position that it does not recognize such a sourcing provision, on the basis of the above two requirements.[51] For example, the IRS may not respect a sourcing provision which provides that charitable payments are deemed to be first made from income other than unrelated business taxable income, given the Section 681 ramifications of the charitable deduction for contributions of such income.

[e] Distributions of Accumulated Income

If income is accumulated, an income tax charitable deduction will generally be allowed when the accumulated income is actually paid to charity.[52] There seems to be no literal prohibition on the availability of the unlimited charitable deduction for payments of accumulated unrelated business income. However, in view of Private Letter Ruling 8332049 (May 6, 1983), it seems the IRS does not necessarily agree that such a deduction is allowed to the extent it would have been disallowed in the year of accumulation if it had been distributed in that year.

---

[48] Treas. Reg. §§ 1.643(a)-5(b), 1.662(b)-2; Rev. Rul. 71-285, 1971-1 CB 248.

[49] Priv. Ltr. Rul. 8727072 (Apr. 8, 1987); GCM 39161 (Sept. 30, 1983).

[50] Reg. § 1.681(a)-2(c)(1) example (3).

[51] Priv. Ltr. Rul. 9233038 (May 20, 1992).

[52] Treas. Reg. § 1.642(c)-1(a)(1).

At the end of the charitable term, distributions of accumulated income to the noncharitable beneficiaries are potentially subject to the throwback tax.[53] In addition, the amount of any previously accumulated income which was subsequently distributed to charity will be considered distributed to the private beneficiaries, for purposes of the throwback tax.[54] To avoid application of the throwback tax, it may be desirable to pay any excess current income to charity in each trust year. While no additional income tax or other deduction will be allowed to the donor on account of those payments,[55] an additional income tax deduction at the CLT level should be available for these additional payments.[56]

[f] Depletion and Depreciation Reserves

The trust should establish reserves for depletion and depreciation in the amount of the trust's allowable depletion and depreciation deductions. In the absence of a reserve, part of the trust's deduction will be allocable to the charitable beneficiary and thus will be lost.

PRACTICE POINTER: State law may automatically provide for a depreciation or depletion reserve in all trust instruments. Such a reserve requirement is effective unless the instrument expressly provides to the contrary.[57]

[g] Sale of Appreciated Property Within Two Years of Contribution

If appreciated property is transferred to the CLT and sold within two years, the trust will pay tax on this gain equal to the tax the donor would have paid on such gain had the donor sold the property instead of contributing it

---

[53] See Ch. 6 for a discussion of the throwback tax.

[54] *Technical Explanation:* A payout of accumulated income to charity will not be an accumulation distribution, and thus will not reduce the throwback tax, if any, ultimately payable when the trust is finally distributed to noncharitable beneficiaries. Treas. Reg. § 1.642(c)-1(a)(1). (Charitable distributions do not reduce undistributed net income, so any distribution in excess of DNI will be treated as a distribution of undistributed net income when the charitable term has expired.) Treas. Reg. § 1.665(b)-1A(c)(2).

[55] Treas. Reg. §§ 1.170A-6(c)(2)(i)(C), 1.170A-6(c)(2)(ii)(C).

[56] Treas. Reg. § 1.170A-6(d)(2)(ii). Cf. Tech. Adv. Mem. 8745002 (July 15, 1987); Rebecca K. Crown Income Charitable Fund v. Comm'r, 98 TC 327 (1992), aff'd, 8 F3d 571 (7th Cir. 1993) (extra payments made in violation of trust agreement).

[57] For example, if no provision is made for the disposition of the proceeds from the sale, lease, or development of natural resources, the Texas Trust Code establishes a reserve for depletion in the amount of 27.5 percent of gross proceeds, not to exceed 50 percent of the net. Tex. Prop. Code Ann. § 113.107(d) (Vernon 1995).

to the trust.[58] This rule applies only to unrealized gain (i.e., built-in gain) which was existing on the date of transfer to the CLT.[59] This rule ceases to apply once the donor dies.[60]

[4] Grantor or Nongrantor Charitable Lead Trust?

Generally, a nongrantor CLT (which, as discussed above, does not permit the grantor to claim an income tax charitable deduction for transfers to the trust) will be used unless there is a particular reason to use a grantor CLT. This is because (1) a nongrantor CLT's income passing to charity does not enter the grantor's contribution base and thereby affect the deductibility of charitable contributions made directly by the grantor and (2) the nongrantor status of the trust avoids the mismatching of taxable income and cash flow inherent in a grantor trust situation.

QUERY: If the grantor trust format is used, can the grantor increase the amount that passes to the noncharitable beneficiaries free of transfer tax by paying the trust's taxes on income in excess of the charitable payment (the amount paid to charity being deductible anyway)? Or, will the IRS consider these payments of tax to be additional contributions to the trust?[61]

¶ 35.04   GIFT AND ESTATE TAX CHARITABLE DEDUCTIONS

In the usual case, the benefit of a CLT is found in its use as a tool to reduce estate and gift taxes through generating a gift or estate tax charitable deduction, rather than to reduce the grantor's income tax.

The amount of the estate or gift tax charitable deduction is ordinarily determined by the IRS tables.[62] The major factors entering into the determination of the deduction for a contribution to a CLAT are the length of the charitable term, the amount payable to charity, and the 7520 rate at the date of transfer to the trust. The amount of the charitable deduction for a contribution to a CLUT will not generally depend on interest rates. The donor to a CLAT will have a choice of three 7520 rates—the rate in effect for the month the gift is made, or the rate in effect for either of the two preceding months.[63]

---

[58] IRC § 644.

[59] IRC § 644(b).

[60] IRC § 644(e)(4).

[61] See Ch. 22 for a discussion of a similar issue on GRATs.

[62] See Ch. 11 for a discussion of the situations in which the tables cannot be used.

[63] IRC § 7520(a)(2).

The donor should elect the lowest interest rate of the three in order to obtain the maximum charitable deduction. If the annuity rate for a CLAT is high enough, the charitable deduction may equal 100 percent of the value of the property contributed.[64]

Annuity payout rates (as a percentage of the initial value of the donated property) that will result in a 100 percent charitable deduction for a gift to a CLAT if the 7520 rate is 10 percent (before the adjustment described below) are:

- 26.38 percent for 5 years
- 16.28 percent for 10 years
- 13.15 percent for 15 years
- 11.75 percent for 20 years

The Regulations under Section 7520 provide that, in cases (like the above) where the payout rate exceeds the 7520 rate, the principal will be assumed to gradually exhaust. Under this theory, it appears that the annuity factor necessary to zero out the gift to the CLT can be computed precisely where the annuity is payable for a term of years. The regulations provide that an adjustment need only be made if the product of the annuity factor provided in the tables and the annuity payout rate exceeds the amount transferred to the trust.[65] For example, the annuity factor for 10 years, given a 10 percent 7520 rate, is 6.1446. If Dad wants to transfer about $1,000,000 to a 10-year CLAT at no gift tax cost, multiply 6.1446 times $162,800 (the "zero-out" annuity payment). The result is $1,000,340.88, which is what Dad should transfer to the CLT for a zero taxable gift.

DRAFTING TIP:: The trust may provide that income in excess of the annuity amount is paid to charity yearly; however, no additional estate or gift tax deduction will be allowed.[66]

¶ 35.05 INCLUSION OF CHARITABLE LEAD TRUST IN GRANTOR'S GROSS ESTATE

If the CLT is established during the grantor/donor's lifetime, care must be exercised to avoid inclusion of the trust property in the grantor/donor's estate.[67] If, for example, a deceased donor retained powers over the trust which

---

[64] But see Treas. Reg. §§ 20.7520-3(b)(2)(i), 25.7520-3(b)(2)(i), 25.7520-3(b)(2)(v), example 5, which provide that where the annuity rate is higher than the 7520 rate, the charitable deduction may be reduced to reflect the possibility that the trust may be exhausted prior to the end of the charitable term.

[65] Treas. Reg. §§ 20.7520-3(b)(2)(i), 25.7520-3(b)(2)(i).

[66] Treas. Reg. §§ 20.2055-2(e)(2)(vi)(d), 25.2522(c)-3(c)(2)(vi)(d).

[67] See Ch. 2 for a discussion of trusts which are included in the donor's estate.

rendered the trust property includable in his estate, the 100 percent estate tax charitable deduction would not be available on the donor's death to offset this inclusion.

[1] Donor as Trustee

The donor can be trustee of the CLT, but his powers must only be those which avoid inclusion of trust property in his gross estate. For example, while the donor-trustee can select the trust's charitable beneficiaries from year to year without adverse *income* tax consequences,[68] this power (to designate the persons who enjoy trust income) will cause inclusion of the trust in his gross estate.[69]

[2] Private Foundation as Beneficiary

If a charitable annuitant is the grantor's private foundation, and the donor is a director or trustee of the private foundation-annuitant, this also may cause inclusion of the CLT property in the donor's estate.[70] In this instance, however, it may be possible to avoid estate tax inclusion by providing in the foundation's bylaws or other governing documents that the donor will not participate in decisions regarding the disposition of distributions from the foundation.[71] Or, alternatively, the donor could be changed to an advisory director of the foundation to avoid the potential for inclusion of trust property in the grantor's gross estate.

¶ 35.06 PENALTY TAXES ON FORBIDDEN ACTIVITIES

A CLT is treated as a private foundation for purposes of the foundation penalty taxes imposed by Section 4941 (self-dealing), Section 4943 (excess business holdings), Section 4944 (jeopardy investments), and Section 4945 (taxable expenditures).[72] However, the CLT will not be subject to Section 4943 or Section 4944 penalty excise taxes if the charitable gift or estate tax deduc-

---

[68] IRC § 674(b)(4); Priv. Ltr. Rul. 9331015 (May 6, 1993).

[69] IRC § 2036(a)(2); cf. Priv. Ltr. Rul. 9219025 (Feb. 7, 1992) (grantor's ability to select alternate charity, if primary charity fails to remain a qualified charity, did not cause estate inclusion).

[70] Estate of Rifkind v. United States, 5 Cl. Ct. 362 (1984).

[71] See Ch. 47 for a similar rule regarding disclaimers of property in favor of disclaimant's private foundation.

[72] IRC § 4947(a)(2). See Ch. 37 on private foundations for a discussion of these concepts.

tion is 60 percent or less of the value of the transferred property.[73] The penalty taxes are so high as to be prohibitive.

PRACTICE POINTER: As discussed further below, private foundation treatment of the CLT can present a problem: (1) if the CLT holds an interest in an active business in which the trust and disqualified persons[74] own more than 20 percent; (2) if the CLT enters into transactions with disqualified persons; or (3) if a private foundation is a recipient of charitable distributions from the CLT.

[1] Tax on Excess Business Holdings

The excess business holdings rules[75] apply to a CLT for which the estate or gift tax charitable deduction exceeds 60 percent of the value of the property transferred to the trust.[76] Generally, a CLT cannot hold a voting interest in excess of two percent of any active business, except to the extent that the holdings of the CLT and all disqualified persons in the business constitute 20 percent or less of the entire ownership of the business.[77]

> EXAMPLE: If Dad, a disqualified person, owns 17 percent of Corporation *X* and is the only disqualified person to have an ownership interest in Corporation *X*, the CLT can own up to three percent of the voting stock in Corporation *X*.

If the stock which would be an excess business holding is transferred to a CLT by gift or bequest, the CLT has five years to dispose of it before it becomes subject to the excess business holdings penalty excise tax.[78] However, the CLT cannot dispose of the stock by selling or otherwise transferring it to a disqualified person.[79]

PRACTICE POINTER: Hence, if a business interest which would constitute an excess business holding is to be transferred to the CLT, and the charitable term is more than five years, it may be desirable to limit the charitable interest to 60 percent of the value of the entire property transferred to the CLT.

---

[73] IRC § 4947(b)(3)(A).

[74] See Ch. 37 for a discussion of disqualified persons.

[75] Ch. 37 discusses excess business holdings in detail.

[76] IRC § 4947(a)(2), (b)(3).

[77] IRC § 4943.

[78] IRC § 4943(c)(6).

[79] IRC § 4941.

Annuity amounts that will result in a 60 percent charitable deduction for a CLAT if the 7520 rate is 10 percent are:

- 15.83 percent for 5 years;
- 9.77 percent for 10 years;
- 7.89 percent for 15 years; and
- 7.05 percent for 20 years.

[2] Tax on Self-Dealing

The private foundation self-dealing rules apply to all CLTs.[80] Accordingly, a CLT cannot engage in any transaction with a disqualified person, unless the transaction falls within an exception to the self-dealing rules.[81] The two most common exceptions are: (1) disqualified persons can furnish goods, services, etc. to the CLT for use in its charitable purposes for no charge,[82] and (2) the CLT can pay reasonable compensation for services to a disqualified person other than a government official.[83]

[3] Tax on "Taxable Expenditures"

The rules on taxable expenditures by private foundations apply to all CLTs.[84] From a practical standpoint, the risk of being subjected to this penalty tax is most easily nullified by insuring that the CLT avoids making distributions to private foundations. If a private foundation is a recipient of a CLT distribution, the CLT must then exercise expenditure responsibility to ensure that the foundation is properly administering the grant.[85]

¶ 35.07　GENERATION-SKIPPING TRANSFER TAX CONSIDERATIONS

Does a CLT make sense as a generation-skipping vehicle? Except for amounts to which the generation-skipping transfer tax (GSTT) exemption applies, the CLT will be subject to GSTT at the end of the charitable term if any amounts

---

[80] IRC § 4947(a)(2).

[81] IRC § 4941.

[82] IRC § 4941(d)(2)(C).

[83] IRC § 4941(d)(2)(E). See Ch. 37 for a discussion of self-dealing.

[84] IRC § 4947(a)(2).

[85] IRC § 4945(h). See Ch. 37 for a discussion of the mechanics of exercising expenditure responsibility.

are distributed to skip persons or held for their benefit.[86] Said another way, the gift/estate tax charitable deduction available on establishing the CLT is not an available deduction for purposes of the GSTT, which itself becomes applicable only when the charitable term expires. Therefore, if Grandma transfers property to a CLT and gets a 100 percent gift tax deduction, she does not get a similar GSTT deduction. Instead, the amount of any GSTT will be determined after the charitable term has expired.[87]

EXAMPLE: Grandma transfers $1,000,000 to a nonexempt CLAT, at its origination. The CLT earns and pays out exactly the annuity amount during the charitable term. At the end of the charitable term, $1,000,000 is left. If the $1,000,000 passes to her grandchildren, or continues to be held for their benefit, a taxable distribution/termination would take place, and $550,000 of GSTT would be due.

[1] GSTT Exemption Allocation: CLATs and CLUTs

QUERY: Can Grandma put $1,000,000 into a CLT, apply her GSTT exemption, and get that much to her family beneficiaries free of GSTT?

[a] Complete Exemption for CLATs

The $1,000,000 GSTT exemption cannot be allocated so as to guarantee that a CLAT will be completely exempt from GSTT. Why not? To determine what fraction of a CLAT is exempt, the following computation is done:

- *Step 1.* Determine the amount of GSTT actually allocated to the CLAT and when it was allocated.
- *Step 2.* Compound the actually allocated exemption annually at the 7520 rate in effect at the time of the initial gift (or the date of exemption allocation, if a late allocation is made), for the charitable term (or the remaining charitable term, in case of a late allocation).
- *Step 3.* Divide the number determined in Step 2 by the value of all property in the trust at the end of the term—the result is the exempt portion of the trust at the end of the charitable term.[88]

EXAMPLE: Grandma transfers $1,000,000 to a CLAT paying a 10 percent annuity for 10 years. At the time, the 7520 rate is 10 percent. According

---

[86] Technically speaking, the end of the charitable term and continuation of the trust for the benefit of a skip person, or termination in favor of a skip person, constitutes a taxable distribution or taxable termination under the normal generation-skipping transfer tax rules, since most charitable organizations are assigned to the transferor's generation for GSTT purposes. IRC § 2651(e)(3).

[87] IRC §§ 2601, 2611, 2612.

[88] IRC § 2642(e); Treas. Reg. § 26.2642-3.

to the tables, the value of the annuity is $614,460; the value of the taxable portion of the transfer is $1,000,000 - $614,460, or $385,540. Assume Grandma allocates the GSTT exemption of $385,540 to the CLAT on a timely filed gift tax return. The exemption amount at the end of the charitable term is thus $999,991.47 ($385,540 compounded annually at 10 percent for 10 years).[89] The applicable fraction (i.e., exempt portion of the trust) will be $1,000,000 divided by the value of the trust at the end of the term.

We can rely on a rule of thumb to predict how much of the trust will be exempt at the end of the charitable term, if we can predict an actual rate of return for the CLAT's assets. The exempt portion will, however, depend on the CLAT's earnings for the charitable term. We can illustrate the rule by looking at the above facts in the following three scenarios:

Scenario 1: The CLAT earns exactly the charitable payout rate (exemption exactly matches amount passing to skip persons). The CLAT earns exactly 10 percent for 10 years. This means that it will always distribute exactly the amount of its earnings each year of the charitable term, as its 10 percent annuity. At the expiration of the charitable term, the exempt percentage of the trust is 999,991.47/1,000,000, so that only $8.53 of the trust would be subjected to GSTT.

Scenario 2: The CLAT earns less than the charitable payout rate (too much exemption was allocated, resulting in wasted exemption). The trust earns only 8 percent for the 10-year term. Therefore, its 10 percent annuity must be paid partly from principal. At the expiration of the term, the exempt percentage would be 999,991.47/710,268.75 or 100 percent (the maximum GSTT exemption). The trust would be fully exempt from GSTT, but $289,731.25 of Grandma's exemption would have been wasted. According to the regulations, the portion of Grandma's GSTT exemption in excess of the amount needed to fully exempt the trust from GSTT will not be restored to Grandma or her estate.[90]

Scenario 3: The CLAT earns more than the charitable payout rate (results in partially exempt trust). Assume the CLAT earns 12 percent for the 10-year term. It will accumulate earnings in excess of the charitable annuity. At the expiration of the charitable term, the exempt percentage would be 999,991.47/1,350,974.70. Twenty-six percent of the trust would be exposed to GSTT.

[b] Complete Exemption for CLUTs

The $1,000,000 GSTT exemption can be effectively allocated at the date of transfer to a CLUT. If it is, then whatever value is left at the end of the

---

[89] This number is not $1,000,000 due to rounding in the table annuity factors.
[90] Treas. Reg. § 26.2642-3(b).

charitable term will be transferred to the beneficiaries free of GSTT, provided that the value of the remainder interest in the property contributed to the CLUT as of the date of transfer is no more than the amount of exemption allocated to the CLUT.

> **EXAMPLE:** Grandpa gives $2,302,089.00 to a CLUT that is structured so that no interest-rate-sensitive adjustments apply. The charitable term is ten years, and the annuity amount is 8 percent of the value of the CLUT each year. The charitable deduction is $1,302,089, and the taxable gift is $1,000,000. If $1,000,000 of GSTT exemption is allocated to the trust, then the trust will be exempt from GSTT at the end of the charitable term, regardless of how much money is left.

A CLUT will never be completely exempt without allocating the GSTT exemption, as the charitable deduction will never be 100 percent. The exemption will be wasted in a CLUT if the amount left in the CLUT at the end of the charitable term is less than the amount of exemption allocated to the CLUT.

To the extent that the GSTT exemption is not available to be allocated to a CLAT or CLUT, any transfers to grandchildren or other skip persons at the termination of the charitable term will be considered taxable terminations or taxable distributions, as the case may be. This is because most charitable organizations are assigned to the transferor's generation for GSTT purposes, as described above.[91]

[2] Estate Tax Inclusion Period

As discussed above, a donor to a CLT should not have powers which will cause the CLT to be included in the donor's gross estate. The same is true for the donor's spouse. In summary, if the donor or the donor's spouse has powers that would make the CLT includable in either's estate, the GSTT exemption cannot be allocated effectively until the end of the estate tax inclusion period (ETIP) (a concept which is explained in detail in Chapter 5). The end of the ETIP is the earliest of: (1) the time that the property would no longer be included in the donor's/spouse's estate if he/she died, (2) the donor's/spouse's actual death, or (3) the occurrence of a generation-skipping transfer with respect to the trust. If property goes directly to grandchildren (or other skip persons) at the end of the ETIP, the transfer will be considered a direct skip instead of a taxable termination or taxable distribution.[92]

---

[91] IRC § 2651(e)(3).

[92] IRC § 2642(f)(1).

¶ 35.08 CLAT OR CLUT—WHICH IS BETTER?

If the CLT property is expected to appreciate, a CLAT is usually the better choice, since the annuity remains fixed and more property can go to the family beneficiaries. If the CLT is being used for GSTT planning, a CLUT may be preferable because of the ability to allocate the exemption at the date of transfer to the trust. Note, however, that a trust making distributions to nonskip persons (here, the charities) is not the most efficient vehicle for allocating the GSTT exemption.

The following table compares the various features of CLATs[93] and CLUTs.

FEATURE	CLAT	CLUT
If GSTT exemption allocated, GSTT exempt portion of trust will be known:	At end of charitable term, or end of ETIP, if later.	At transfer of property to CLUT (or end of ETIP, if applicable).
Amount of GSTT exemption:	Allocated amount, compounded at the 7520 rate at date of transfer (or allocation, if later).	Allocated amount.
Which generates a higher charitable deduction, if same term and annuity amount (i.e., if both trusts pay 10 percent for 10 years):	CLAT's charitable deduction will be higher than deduction available for CLUT if annuity amount is greater than 7520 rate, because use of principal will be assumed to be required to make CLAT annuity payments.	CLUT's charitable deduction will be higher than deduction available for CLAT if annuity amount is less than 7520 rate, since it is assumed that CLAT charitable payment will not require use of principal.
Which leaves more (without regard to GSTT) for family at end of charitable term (i.e., if both trusts pay 10 percent for 10 years):	Amount passing will be higher than if CLUT were used if actual earnings exceed annuity amount, since principal will not be required to make charitable payments.	Amount passing will be higher than if CLUT were used if actual earnings exceed annuity amount, since principal will not be required to make charitable payments.

------

[93] See discussion at ¶ 35.07[1][a] above regarding allocation of exemption to a CLAT.

¶ 35.09 CHARITABLE LEAD TRUSTS FOR THE NONCHARITABLY INCLINED

If the donor is not actually charitably inclined, but is simply interested in transferring property to his descendants in the least costly way, a comparison can be made between the amount the family beneficiaries would have as remainder beneficiaries of the CLT and the amount they would have as recipients of an outright gift of the initial value of the remainder interest in the CLT. Under this comparative analysis, the CLT gets more money to the beneficiaries if the property actually earns more than the 7520 rate, and vice versa.[94]

> EXAMPLE: Dad transfers $1,000,000 in property to a CLAT with a ten year charitable term and an eight percent payout rate. The property earns ten percent (after-tax) yearly, and the 7520 rate at the time of the transfer is eight percent. The remainder interest is valued at $463,192 at the time of the transfer. At the end of the charitable term, the value transferred to Dad's children is $1,318,748.49. Had Dad initially made a gift of property worth $463,192 rather than creating the CLAT, the gifted property would be worth $1,201,400.76 at the end of ten years, assuming it grew at ten percent (after-tax) each year.

Finally, as discussed above, the CLT can also be more effective than an outright gift of the remainder interest if the charitable term (determined actuarially) is longer than the actual charitable term.

[94] See Zoe M. Hicks, Charitable Remainder and Lead Trusts: Special Applications and Problems, Presentation to Dallas Estate Planning Council (1995).

Other Charitable Split-Interest Gifts

¶ 36.01 INTRODUCTION

No gift, estate, or income tax charitable deduction is generally allowable for a donation of a partial interest in property (i.e., a split-interest gift).[1] There are, however, some exceptions to this rule. For example, split-interest trusts[2]

---

[1] IRC §§ 170(f), 2055(e), 2522(c).

[2] Discussed in Chs. 33 and 35.

may be used to make a contribution of a partial gift to charity. Other exceptions to this general rule, each of which may become important in particular situations, are described in this chapter.

¶ 36.02 POOLED INCOME FUND

[1] In General

A contribution to a pooled income fund, described in Section 642(c)(5), is a form of split-interest gift. In a pooled income fund, several donors make contributions to a single trust formed for the benefit of a public charity. The fund must be maintained by the charity which is the remainder beneficiary.[3] Deductions are available for the donors' contributions to the pooled income fund.[4]

Many charities maintain pooled income funds. We'll be brief in our description here, as large gifts are rarely made to pooled income funds. The typical donor who will find a pooled income fund attractive is someone who:

- Does not have sufficient investable assets to make seeking investment advice by a top advisor worthwhile;
- Wants to make a relatively small charitable gift (usually in the $1,000 to $50,000 range); and
- Possibly plans to convert an appreciated asset into a stream of income without incurring capital gains tax.

QUESTION: *How does the pooled income fund work in these circumstances?*

ANSWER: The donor transfers money or property to a trust maintained by the public charity, in exchange for a life income interest in the fund.[5] The donor receives an income tax charitable deduction on the transfer for the value of the charity's remainder interest in the property transferred to the fund. The amount of the donor's life interest, as a percentage of the fund's annual income, is based on the transferred property's fair market value, as compared to the fair market value of the total fund assets on the date of transfer.[6] To properly account for the donor's continuing interest in the fund, taking into account subsequent contributions to the fund and terminations of interests in the fund, the percentage of the transferred property's value as compared to the aggregate value of all fund assets is adjusted from time to time.

---

[3] IRC § 642(c)(5)(E).

[4] IRC §§ 170(f)(2)(A), 2055(e)(2)(A), 2522(c)(2)(A).

[5] IRC § 642(c)(5). For this purpose, a public charity is described in IRC §§ 170(b)(1)(A)(i)–170(b)(1)(A)(vi).

[6] Treas. Reg. § 1.642(c)-5(c)(2)(i).

The Treasury's actuarial tables are not used to value the charity's interest in the pooled income fund.[7] Instead, the value of the charity's remainder interest in the fund is discounted on the basis of the highest rate of return earned by the fund for any of the three taxable years immediately preceding the date of the donor's contribution to the fund.[8] If the fund has been in existence less than three taxable years before the date of transfer, the deemed rate of return is that rate (rounded to the nearest 0.2%) which is 1% less than the highest annual average of the monthly 7520 rates for the three calendar years immediately preceding the year in which the transfer to the pooled income fund is made.[9]

Further, only one charity can be named as a beneficiary of the fund.[10] Alternate charities can, however, be named if the first charity ceases to be qualified, but only one charity at a time may have a vested interest in the fund.[11] If the donor wants to maintain some flexibility as to the identity of the ultimate charitable beneficiary, he can contribute to a fund maintained by a community foundation.[12]

Drafting requirements for a pooled income fund are set forth in Revenue Rulings 82-38 and 85-57.[13] Revenue Procedure 88-53 contains sample pooled income fund documents.[14] The charity (not the donor) prepares these documents.

[2] Timing of the Donor's Charitable Deduction

The type of property contributed to the fund can affect the timing of the donor's charitable deduction. Upon a transfer of real estate or intangible personal property to the pooled income fund, the donor receives a charitable deduction for the year in which the gift is made.[15] However, upon a gift of tangible personal property, there is no deduction until the earlier of: (1) the termination of all intervening life interests held by the donor and related persons or (2) the sale of the property by the fund to an unrelated party.[16]

It is permissible for the charitable remainder beneficiary to buy the income beneficiary's interest (using its other assets) and thereby terminate the

---

[7] Reg. §§ 1.642(c)-6, 1.7520-3(b)(2)(iv), 25.7520-3(b)(2)(iv), 20.7520-3(b)(2)(iv).

[8] IRC § 642(c)(5).

[9] IRC § 642(c)(5); Treas. Reg. § 1.642(c)-6(e)(3).

[10] Treas. Reg. § 1.642(c)-5(b).

[11] Priv. Ltr. Rul. 8130070 (Apr. 29, 1981).

[12] Rev. Rul. 96-38, IRB 1996-33 (Aug. 12, 1996).

[13] Rev. Rul. 82-38, 1982-1 CB 96, as amplified in Rev. Rul. 85-57, 1985-1 CB 182.

[14] Rev. Proc. 88-53, 1988-2 CB 712.

[15] IRC § 170(a), (f)(2)(A).

[16] IRC § 170(a)(3); Treas. Reg. § 1.642(c)-5(a)(6)(ii).

income interest.[17] In that case, a suspended deduction for a gift of tangible personal property may then be claimed.

[3] Taxation of the Pooled Income Fund and Noncharitable Beneficiaries

The fund itself is a taxable trust and is taxed in accordance with generally applicable rules governing the taxation of trusts and their beneficiaries.[18] However, since the trust is required to distribute all of its trust accounting income each year,[19] it will get a distribution deduction for all trust income distributed, and therefore should be taxed only on trust income which is allocated to principal under state law. The fund's governing instrument may, but is not required to, provide for allocation of short-term capital gains to income and distribution of those capital gains to the life beneficiaries.[20] If such gains are distributed, they are taxable to the life beneficiaries as part of the fund's distributable net income. If not, such gains are taxable to the fund. A set-aside deduction is available for long-term capital gains, which cannot be distributed to a life beneficiary.[21]

When the life income beneficiary receives distributions, the distributions will be characterized as ordinary income and/or short-term capital gain in accordance with the trust taxation rules. However, long-term capital gains and other income allocated to principal cannot be distributed to the life income beneficiaries.

[4] Special Restrictions on Pooled Income Funds

Special restrictions apply to the activities of a pooled income fund. The fund cannot invest in tax-exempt securities.[22] A donor cannot be a trustee.[23] No life beneficiary can be a trustee.[24] The private foundation rules of Sections 4941

---

[17] Priv. Ltr. Rul. 8321162 (Feb. 28, 1983).

[18] Treas. Reg. § 1.642(c)-5(a)(2).

[19] IRC § 642(c)(5)(F).

[20] Priv. Ltr. Rul. 8404039 (Oct. 24, 1983).

[21] IRC § 642(c)(3); Treas. Reg. § 1.642(c)-5(b)(7).

[22] IRC § 642(c)(5)(C).

[23] IRC § 642(c)(5)(E).

[24] IRC § 642(c)(5)(E).

and 4945 apply, generally prohibiting self-dealing and expenditures for certain specified purposes.[25]

There are also limitations on the property that may be contributed to a pooled income fund. For example, there is some question about whether a fund will qualify if mortgaged property is contributed to it.[26]

¶ 36.03 CONTRIBUTION OF REMAINDER INTEREST IN PERSONAL RESIDENCE OR FARM

The donor can receive a charitable deduction for giving a charity a remainder interest in either a house used by him for residential purposes or a farm.[27] The house need not be the donor's principal residence.[28] Even a yacht can qualify if it is used as a residence.[29] A farm can be a farm, orchard, dairy, ranch, or other land used for the production of crops, fruit, agricultural products, or livestock.[30]

The donor's retained interest must be a legal life estate, and apparently cannot be held in trust.[31] One ramification of this restriction is that the sale of the residence or farm during the donor's lifetime will require the consent of both the donor and the charity. And after any such sale, the donor and charity would have, respectively, a life estate and remainder interest in the proceeds. Can the donor require, as a condition of the initial gift, that the charity agree to a sale if the life tenant ever wants to sell? No, according to the IRS.[32]

The donor's charitable deduction for donating a remainder interest in a personal residence or a farm is ordinarily computed in accordance with the IRS's actuarial tables, after taking into account a special depreciation and depletion factor.[33]

If the donor improves the property after donating the remainder interest, an additional charitable deduction for the remainder interest in the improve-

---

[25] IRC §§ 4947(a)(2), 4947(b)(3)(B); Treas. Reg. § 1.642(c)-5(a)(6). See discussion in Ch. 37 on private foundations for a discussion of these provisions.

[26] Cf. Priv. Ltr. Rul. 9015049 (Jun. 16, 1990).

[27] IRC § 170(f)(3)(D)(i).

[28] Treas. Reg. § 1.170A-7(b)(3).

[29] Priv. Ltr. Rul. 8015017 (Jan. 18, 1980).

[30] Treas. Reg. § 1.170A-7(b)(4).

[31] Ellis First Nat'l Bank of Bradenton v. United States, 550 F2d 9 (Ct. Cl. 1977); Estate of Cassidy v. Comm'r, 1985 PH TC Memo. ¶ 85,037, 49 TCM (CCH) 580 (1985); Rev. Rul. 76-357, 1976-2 CB 285; Priv. Ltr. Rul. 8110016 (Nov. 26, 1980).

[32] Rev. Rul. 77-305, 1977-2 CB 72.

[33] IRC § 170(f)(4); Treas. Reg. § 1.170A-12(b)(2).

ment is allowable, provided the improvement legally becomes part of the real estate.[34]

¶ 36.04 GIFT OF AN UNDIVIDED INTEREST

A charitable deduction is available for an undivided interest in property—e.g., a gift of 80% of Blackacre to charity.[35] Timesharing gifts of property as a tenant in common with the donor are also permissible—e.g., the right to possession and control of a painting or condominium for a period of months each year conforming to a percentage interest in the property.[36]

> EXAMPLE: A gives Charity a one-fourth interest in an oil painting. A deduction is available if Charity has the right to use the painting for three months of the year, and to sell its one-fourth interest.

Reversing a previous ruling to the contrary, the IRS now claims that overriding royalties and net profits interests carved out of working interests are not undivided interests within the meaning of Section 170, but are instead nondeductible partial interests.[37] However, a gift of a royalty which is not carved out of a working interest should be deductible as a charitable gift of an undivided interest because a royalty is generally a fractional share of the oil, gas, or other minerals in place (or the gross proceeds from the sale of such share of the oil, gas, or other minerals in place).

¶ 36.05 CONSERVATION CONTRIBUTIONS

A deduction is allowed for a gift of a qualified conservation contribution.[38] Such a gift must be: (1) a gift of qualified real property, (2) made to a qualified organization, and (3) used exclusively for conservation purposes.[39]

Rules on conservation contributions are extremely complicated, and should be thoroughly understood before such a gift is made. The statute and regulations are found in Section 170(h) and Treasury Regulation § 1.170A-14.

---

[34] Priv. Ltr. Rul. 8529014 (Apr. 16, 1985).

[35] IRC §§ 170(f)(3)(B)(ii), 2055(e)(2), 2522(c)(2).

[36] Treas. Reg. § 1.170A-7(b)(1)(i); Priv. Ltr. Rul. 8204220 (Oct. 30, 1981).

[37] Rev. Rul. 88-37, 1988-1 CB 97, overruling Priv. Ltr. Rul. 8417058 (Jan. 24, 1984).

[38] IRC §§ 170(f)(3)(B)(iii), 2055(e)(2), 2522(c)(2).

[39] IRC § 170(h)(1); Treas. Reg. § 1.170A-14(a).

[1] Qualified Real Property Defined

Qualified real property is real property which is described in one of the following three categories:[40]

- A remainder interest in real property.[41]
- A perpetual restriction on use of the property.[42]
- The donor's entire interest in property—the donor's entire interest in the real property must be donated, except that the donor can retain a qualified mineral interest,[43] which is the right to subsurface minerals and the right of access to the minerals, provided that no surface mining is permitted.[44]

[2] Qualified Organization Defined

The donee charity must be a governmental unit or certain type of public charity.[45]

[3] Meaning of "Used Exclusively for Conservation Purposes"

The purpose of the contribution must be for conservation. Conservation includes preservation of land for public recreation, public education, protection of natural ecosystems, preservation of certain open spaces, or preservation of historical sites.[46]

[4] Amount Deductible

In the case of a contribution of a remainder interest in property, the deduction is equal to the value of the remainder interest, taking into account depreciation and depletion of the property and any pre-existing or contemporaneously

---

[40] IRC § 170(h)(2).

[41] IRC § 170(h)(2)(B).

[42] IRC § 170(h)(2)(C).

[43] IRC § 170(h)(2)(A).

[44] IRC §§ 170(h)(6), 170(h)(5)(B)(i).

[45] IRC § 170(h)(3). Such organizations are organizations described in IRC §§ 170(b)(1)(A)(v)-170(b)(1)(A)(vi), or IRC § 501(c)(3) organizations which are qualified under IRC §§ 509(a)(2) or 509(a)(3) and are controlled by an IRC § 170(b)(1)(A)(v) organization or an IRC § 170(b)(1)(A)(vi) organization, or an IRC § 509(a)(2) organization.

[46] IRC § 170(h)(4).

recorded rights limiting (for conservation purposes) the uses to which the subject property may be put.[47]

In the case of perpetual restrictions (including easements), the deduction is equal to the fair market value of the easement, based on the sale of comparable easements. If, however, there are no comparables, the general rule is that the value equals the difference between the fair market value of the property before granting the easement or restriction and the fair market value of the property after granting the easement or restriction.[48]

The value of the charitable deduction for a conservation contribution of the donor's entire interest, where the donor has reserved a qualified mineral interest, is the fair market value of the surface rights contributed.[49]

¶ 36.06   GIFT OF WORK OF ART WITHOUT COPYRIGHT

The donation of a work of art, without its copyright, is deductible for gift and estate tax purposes only if:

- The work is tangible personal property with an existing federal copyright,
- The charity is a public charity or private operating foundation, and
- The charity uses the work in its exempt function.[50]

The measure of the deduction is the fair market value of the donated work of art. There are no parallel provisions in the rules providing for an income tax charitable deduction.

¶ 36.07   GIFT OF DONOR'S ENTIRE "PARTIAL" INTEREST

A charitable deduction is allowed for a contribution of the donor's entire interest in property, even if the interest would be a nondeductible partial interest if the donor held a complete interest in the property at the time of the contribution. This rule does not apply, however, if interests in the property were separated by the donor prior to the transfer in order to circumvent the partial interest rules.[51]

EXAMPLE: Mom leaves daughter a life estate in Blackacre. Daughter has no other interest in Blackacre. Daughter can donate her life estate to

---

[47] Treas. Reg. § 1.170A-14(h)(2).

[48] Treas. Reg. § 1.170A-14(h)(3)(i).

[49] Treas. Reg. § 1.170A-14(h)(1).

[50] IRC §§ 2055(e)(4), 2522(c)(4).

[51] Treas. Reg. § 1.170A-7(a)(2)(i).

charity and take an income tax deduction, if one is otherwise available.

¶ 36.08 GIFT OF FUTURE INTERESTS IN TANGIBLE PERSONAL PROPERTY

For purposes of the income tax charitable deduction, a gift of a future interest in tangible personal property, whether in trust or not, is treated as made only when all noncharitable interests in, and rights to possession of, the property have either expired or are held by persons other than the taxpayer or a related party.[52]

¶ 36.09 DONOR RETAINS ONLY INSUBSTANTIAL INTERESTS IN PROPERTY

Retained rights with regard to the donated property which are insubstantial will not convert the donated property into a non-deductible partial interest. Such insubstantial rights have been determined to include the right to hunt on donated land,[53] as well as the right to store property in a donated vacation home.[54]

Examples of gifts with retained rights deemed to be substantial, thereby rendering the contribution a nondeductible gift of a partial interest, include: (1) a gift of stock with retained voting rights[55] and (2) a gift of land with retained mineral interests, where the value of the mineral interests are not insubstantial.[56]

¶ 36.10 CHARITABLE INCOME TRUSTS

The charitable income trust, like the charitable lead trust, can be used to generate an income tax benefit for a person whose percentage limitations have been exceeded for a particular type of gift (e.g., gifts to a private foundation).

EXAMPLE: Donor gives property to a trust. The income of the trust is payable to charity annually, as the donor directs. On the donor's death, all of the undistributed income is payable to charity. The remainder is paid to family beneficiaries. During the term of the trust, the income it

---

[52] IRC § 170(a)(3).
[53] Priv. Ltr. Rul. 8110141 (Dec. 12, 1980).
[54] Rev. Rul. 75-420, 1975-2 CB 78.
[55] Rev. Rul. 81-282, 1981-2 CB 78.
[56] Rev. Rul. 76-331, 1976-2 CB 52.

earns will be excluded from the donor's income,[57] and will thus not be subject to the percentage limits. The trust will receive an unlimited deduction for distributions to charity. On the donor's death, the trust will be included in his estate.[58] The undistributed income will be eligible for a charitable estate tax deduction.[59]

One problem with this technique is that Treasury Regulation §§ 25.2702-2(b) and 25.2702-2(a)(4) appear to indicate that the donor's power of appointment over the charitable interest would render it an interest valued at zero, and therefore the entire value of the trust would be taxable as a gift at the outset. To avoid this, the donor could also retain a testamentary limited power of appointment over the principal, thus rendering the entire transfer to the trust an incomplete gift, which would not be subject to Section 2702.[60]

---

[57] IRC § 674(b)(4) provides that the power of the grantor to allocate among charitable beneficiaries will not cause the trust to be treated as a grantor trust.

[58] IRC § 2036(a).

[59] IRC § 2055(a).

[60] Reg. § 25.2702-1(c)(1); IRC § 674(b)(3) will prevent this provision from causing the trust to be a grantor trust.

CHAPTER 37

Private Foundations

¶ 37.01 INTRODUCTION

For various reasons, some donors will want to have a charitable foundation which they or their families control. Subject to certain limitations,[1] the gifts to such foundations are generally eligible for the income tax charitable deduction,[2] as well as an unlimited estate and gift tax charitable deduction.[3]

Private foundations[4] are suitable for many situations, and are generally governed by some of the same rules that govern public charities. However, the activities of private foundations are also subject to certain requirements and restrictions which, if violated, can result in the imposition of harsh penalty taxes. Careful attention must therefore be paid to a private foundation's conduct and operations so that these penalties are not triggered. This chapter will focus on the restrictions and requirements applicable to private foundations.

¶ 37.02 DISQUALIFIED PERSONS

A key player under the special rules governing private foundations is the "disqualified person." The question of "who is a disqualified person?" can be a complex and difficult query.

---

[1] See Ch. 32 for a discussion of the limitations.

[2] IRC § 170(a).

[3] IRC § 2055(a)(2).

[4] A private foundation is any IRC § 501(c)(3) organization which is not described in IRC §§ 509(a)(2), 170(b)(1)(A)(i), 170(b)(1)(A)(vi), or 509(a)(3). IRC § 509.

[1] "Disqualified Person" Defined

[a] Working Definition

Because of the extreme importance of the "disqualified person" concept, practitioners need a "rule of thumb" to identify a potential "disqualified person" problem, as well as the lengthy technical definition in ¶ 37.02[1][b].

As a rule of thumb, practitioners should assume, in the first instance, that a person is a disqualified person if the person in question is either: (1) a natural person or entity which is, or is related to, a "substantial contributor" or "foundation manager," or (2) an entity in which a substantial contributor, a foundation manager, or related parties have a substantial interest.

[b] Technical Definition

[i] **Section 4946(a)(1).** The technical statutory definition of a disqualified person with respect to a private foundation is as follows:

A disqualified person with respect to a private foundation includes:

(a) A substantial contributor to the foundation;

(b) A foundation manager;

(c) An owner of more than 20 percent of (1) the total combined voting power of a corporation, (2) the profits interest of a partnership, or (3) the beneficial interest of a trust or unincorporated enterprise, which is a substantial contributor to the foundation;

(d) A spouse, ancestor, child, grandchild, or great-grandchild of any person in (a), (b), or (c) above, and the spouse of a child, grandchild, or great-grandchild of such a person (referred to as the "members of the family" of a person);

(e) A corporation in which persons described in (a), (b), (c), or (d) above own more than 35 percent of the total combined voting power;

(f) A partnership in which persons described in (a), (b), (c), or (d) above own more than 35 percent of the profits interest;

(g) A trust or estate in which persons described in (a), (b), (c), or (d) above hold more than 35 percent of the beneficial interest;

(h) Only for purposes of determining whether the foundation has excess business holdings, a private foundation (1) which is effectively controlled (directly or indirectly) by the same persons who control the private foundation in question, or (2) substantially all contributions to which were made (directly or indirectly) by the same persons described in (a), (b), or (c), or members of their families, who made (directly or indirectly) substantially all of the contributions to the private foundation in question;

(i) Only for purposes of the restrictions on self-dealing, a government official.[5]

[ii] Attribution rules. In making the above determinations, certain attribution rules apply.[6] Specifically, for purposes of determining the total combined voting power in a corporation, the Section 267(c) constructive stock ownership rules apply, except that individuals who are members of a person's "family" (as described above) are treated as the members of the person's family for purposes of applying Section 267(c). (In other words, the term "members of the family" normally has a different definition under Section 267(c). The definition in Section 267(c) is disregarded in applying the constructive ownership rules to determine who is a disqualified person with respect to a private foundation.) Section 267(c) provides that: (1) stock directly or indirectly owned by or for a corporation, partnership, estate, or trust is considered owned proportionately by or for the shareholders, partners, or beneficiaries; (2) an individual is treated as owning any stock owned directly or indirectly by or for a member of his family; and (3) an individual who owns (other than through attribution from a family member) stock in a corporation is considered to own stock owned directly or indirectly by or for the individual's partner. Similarly, for purposes of determining whether the profits interest in a partnership or beneficial interest in a trust or estate meets the thresholds listed above, the concepts of Section 267(c) also apply (except for the rule attributing ownership of stock owned by a partner), with the term "members of the family" once again having the meaning given above rather than the meaning given in Section 267(c).

[2] "Substantial Contributor" Defined

A "substantial contributor" means any person (including an estate) who has contributed or bequeathed an aggregate amount of more than $5,000 to the foundation, provided that this aggregate amount was more than 2 percent of the total contributions and bequests ever received by the foundation from October 9, 1969 to the end of the year in which the person made the contribution or bequest.[7] It also means the creator of a charitable trust which is a private foundation.[8] For this purpose, an individual is treated as making all

---

[5] IRC § 4946(a)(1).
[6] IRC §§ 4946(a)(3), 4946(a)(4).
[7] IRC §§ 4946(a)(2), 507(d)(2)(A).
[8] IRC §§ 4946(a)(2), 507(d)(2)(A).

contributions and bequests made by his spouse during the marriage, even after one spouse dies or the couple is divorced.[9]

[3] Termination of "Substantial Contributor" Status

Generally, once a person achieves substantial contributor status, he remains a substantial contributor forever.[10] At times, it is quite inconvenient for a particular party to be categorized as a substantial contributor in perpetuity.

> EXAMPLE: Corporation A contributed $6,000 to Foundation ten years ago, at the request of a member of the family, and the contribution was more than 2 percent of all contributions ever received by Foundation up to that point. Except for that contribution, Corporation A has had no relationship with Foundation or any of its other disqualified persons. Foundation has since grown to $10,000,000. Now, Foundation would like to lease office space from Corporation A. The transaction is prohibited because Corporation A is a disqualified person.

A person can only shed substantial contributor status by qualifying for and going through a specific IRS procedure.[11] What if Corporation A, in the above example, wants to do this? Under the IRS procedure, it can, if:

- Neither Corporation A nor any related person has made any contribution to the foundation in the last ten years;[12]
- Neither Corporation A nor any related person was a foundation manager during the past ten years; and[13]
- The aggregate contributions made by Corporation A and related persons are determined by the IRS to be insignificant when compared to the contributions made by one other person.[14]

Applying this test to the facts of the example, a "related person" means any person who would be a disqualified person with respect to the Foundation by reason of his relationship with Corporation A.[15] In the case of a corporation, the term includes its officers and directors.[16] Finally, for purposes of making

---

[9] IRC § 507(d)(2)(B)(iii); Treas. Reg. § 1.507-6(c)(3).

[10] IRC § 507(d)(2)(B)(iv).

[11] IRC § 507(d)(2)(C).

[12] IRC § 507(d)(2)(C)(i)(I).

[13] IRC § 507(d)(2)(C)(i)(II).

[14] IRC § 507(d)(2)(C)(i)(III).

[15] IRC § 507(d)(2)(C)(ii).

[16] IRC § 507(d)(2)(C)(ii).

this determination, appreciation on contributions made to Foundation is taken into account for purposes of the third prong of this test.[17]

[4] "Foundation Manager" Defined

A foundation manager is anyone who has the ability to participate in a decision with respect to the transaction in question. The term includes officers, directors, and trustees of the foundation, as well as employees who have authority or responsibility with respect to the transaction.[18] Hence, an employee may be a foundation manager with respect to some transactions and not others.

[5] Termination of "Disqualified Person" Status

In contrast to the continuous and generally permanent status of substantial contributors, the status of a disqualified person is determined on a transaction-by-transaction basis at the time of a transaction in question.

> EXAMPLE: John is foundation manager in Year One. In Year Two, he is not. He is a disqualified person in Year One, and not in Year Two, provided he has no other relation to the foundation.

Further, if a person is a disqualified person solely because of the attribution rules, that person's status as a disqualified person may cease if the relationship causing the attribution terminates. Thus, John may cease to be a disqualified person as a result of (1) a divorce from or death of a person who caused John to be a disqualified person or (2) ceasing to hold certain interests or powers in entities.

> EXAMPLE: John's wife is a foundation manager. John is therefore a disqualified person. If John gets a divorce, he will no longer be a disqualified person, assuming that he has no other relation to the foundation.

¶ 37.03 CAN THE FOUNDATION HOLD THE FAMILY BUSINESS?

The donor may want to leave his closely held business to the foundation. If so, he must be aware of Section 4943, which generally prohibits private foundations from holding substantial interests in active businesses. The rules are known as the "excess business holdings" rules.

---

[17] IRC § 507(d)(2)(C)(i).

[18] IRC § 4946(b).

[1] Permitted Holdings in the Family Business

Subject to a 2 percent de minimis rule, a private foundation is prohibited from holding more than 20 percent (less the amount held by disqualified persons) of the voting stock in any corporation holding an active business.[19] In the case of a partnership or joint venture, "profits interest" is substituted for "voting stock."[20] In any other case, "beneficial interest" is substituted for "voting stock."[21] Any holdings over this limit are called "excess business holdings."[22] The 20 percent limit is raised to 35 percent, if the IRS agrees that effective control of the business is in one or more persons who are not disqualified persons.[23]

The following are *permitted* holdings for a private foundation:

- Up to two percent of any business.[24]
- Up to 20 percent (less any interest held by a disqualified person) of the voting interest (or profits interest or beneficial interest, if applicable) of an active business.[25]
- Up to 35 percent (less any interest held by a disqualified person) of the voting interest (or profits interest or beneficial interest, if applicable) of an active business, if the IRS has agreed that effective control of the business is in a nondisqualified person.[26]
- Nonvoting stock (or capital interest, in the case of a partnership or joint venture) if all disqualified persons together own 20 percent or less of the voting stock (profits interest or beneficial interest, if applicable) of a business enterprise.[27]
- Nonvoting stock (or capital interest, in the case of a partnership or joint venture) if all disqualified persons together own 35 percent or less of the voting stock (profits interest or beneficial interest, if applicable)

---

[19] IRC § 4943(c)(2)(A), 4943(c)(2)(C).

[20] IRC § 4943(c)(3)(A).

[21] IRC § 4943(c)(3)(C).

[22] IRC § 4943(c)(1).

[23] IRC § 4943(c)(2)(B).

[24] IRC § 4943(c)(2)(C). For this purpose, holdings of other private foundations controlled by the same persons as the foundation in question, or to which substantially all contributions were made by the same persons as the foundation in question, are attributed to the foundation.

[25] IRC § 4943(c)(2)(A).

[26] IRC § 4943(c)(2)(B).

[27] IRC § 4943(c)(2)(A) (flush language). Note that it appears that a limited partnership interest, which is typically comparable to nonvoting stock, is not generally treated differently than a general partnership interest for purposes of the excess business holdings rules. See Treas. Reg. § 53.4943-3(c)(2). Limited partner status should be relevant, however, in determining whether effective control is in other hands.

of a business enterprise, if the IRS has agreed that effective control of the business is in a nondisqualified person.[28]

- Any interest in a non-active or functionally related business.[29]

Non-active business defined. A business is not an active business if 95 percent or more of its gross receipts consist of passive items (e.g., dividends, interest, rents and royalties, if not tied to the profitability of the property).[30]

Functionally related business defined. A business is a functionally related business if it is not an unrelated trade or business within the meaning of Section 513, or if its activity is carried on within a larger group of activities or endeavors related to the foundation's exempt purposes.[31]

[2] Grace Period for Dispositions of Excess Business Holdings

As a general rule, once a private foundation has excess business holdings, the law imposes the penalty tax. However, depending on how the excess business holdings arose, the law may allow the foundation a period of time in which it can dispose of the excess business holdings without incurring the penalty tax.

[a] Acquisition by Gift or Bequest

If excess business holdings are acquired by a private foundation other than by purchase (e.g., by gift or inheritance), the foundation has until five years after receipt of the excess business holdings to dispose of them.[32] If the holdings were part of a decedent's probate estate, or part of a revocable trust that became irrevocable on the decedent's death, the five-year period does not begin to run until the holdings are actually distributed to the foundation or, if earlier, the date that the estate or trust is deemed terminated for income tax purposes[33] (i.e., when the administration of the estate or trust is complete).[34]

In the case of an unusually large gift or bequest of diverse holdings or holdings with complex corporate structures, the IRS, in its discretion, may extend the initial five-year period for up to another five years.[35] To gain the benefit of this extension, the foundation must establish that it made diligent efforts to dispose of the holdings within the initial five-year period, and that it

---

[28] IRC § 4943(c)(2)(B).

[29] IRC § 4943(d)(3).

[30] IRC § 4943(d)(3)(B); Treas. Reg. § 53.4943-10(c).

[31] IRC § 4942(j)(4).

[32] IRC § 4943(c)(6).

[33] Treas. Reg. § 53.4943-5(b)(1), 53.4943-6(b)(1).

[34] Treas. Reg. § 1.641(b)-3.

[35] IRC § 4943(c)(7).

was impossible to dispose of the holdings within such period (except at a price substantially below fair market value) by reason of the size and complexity or diversity of the holdings.[36] Furthermore, before the close of the initial five-year period, the foundation must submit to the IRS and the Attorney General of its state a plan for disposition of the holdings. Finally, the IRS must determine that it is reasonable to expect that this plan can be carried out by the foundation before the end of the extension period.[37]

[b] Acquisition Through Purchase by Foundation

There is no grace period for dispositions of excess business holdings purchased by the foundation. Accordingly, excess business holdings acquired by purchase immediately subject the foundation to penalty taxes.

[c] Excess Business Holdings Triggered Through Acquisition by Disqualified Person or Other Event

If a private foundation's permitted holdings turn into excess business holdings due to an acquisition of a business interest by a disqualified person or the occurrence of some event (other than a purchase by the foundation or gift or bequest to the foundation), the private foundation must dispose of its excess business holdings within 90 days of the date it knows or has reason to know of the event which caused the foundation to have excess business holdings.[38] The period can be extended to cover any period in which federal or state securities laws prevent the foundation from disposing of its excess business holdings.[39] The foundation cannot dispose of the excess business holdings to a disqualified person,[40] and material restrictions with respect to the business holdings so disposed of may not be imposed on the transferee.[41]

[3] Penalties

After any permitted holding (i.e., grace) period has expired without the disposition of the foundation's excess business holdings, there is an annual penalty tax imposed on the private foundation equal to 5 percent of the value of

---

[36] IRC § 4943(c)(7)(A).

[37] IRC § 4943(c)(7)(B)–4943(c)(7)(C).

[38] Treas. Reg. § 53.4943-2(a)(1)(ii).

[39] Treas. Reg. § 53.4943-2(a)(1)(iii).

[40] IRC § 4941.

[41] Treas. Reg. § 53.4943-2(a)(1)(iv).

the foundation's excess business holdings (not disposed of within the grace period, if any).[42]

A penalty of 200 percent of the value of the foundation's excess business holdings will be imposed if the five percent tax is imposed and the foundation's excess business holdings position is not timely corrected.[43] "Timely" means by the earlier of (1) the date a deficiency notice is mailed with respect to the five percent tax or (2) the date on which the five percent tax is assessed.[44]

[4] Should We Leave the Family Business to the Private Foundation?

If excess business holdings are bequeathed to the foundation, the foundation will have whatever time is required to administer the estate plus five years (or ten, in the IRS's discretion) to sell the excess holdings.[45] So, a fair amount of time will be available to sell the business and keep the proceeds in the foundation. However, if long-term holding of the business by the charitable entity is desired, and there is no viable strategy to deal with the holding issue, a private foundation is not the appropriate vehicle to hold the business.

PRACTICE POINTER: Certain complex strategies may be employed to minimize an excess business holdings problem. These may include (1) recapitalizing an entity into voting and nonvoting interests, (2) interposing holding companies between the foundation and an active business, and (3) extracting passive assets from active business entities.

¶ 37.04 SELF-DEALING

If the donor contemplates that any dealings between the foundation and disqualified persons will occur after the foundation is funded, other than (1) the payment of reasonable compensation for services and (2) the furnishing of goods and services to the foundation without charge, a private foundation will be an unsuitable vehicle for the donor's needs.[46]

---

[42] IRC § 4943(a)(1).

[43] IRC § 4943(b).

[44] IRC §§ 4943(b), 4943(d)(2).

[45] The permitted holding period begins on the date the holdings are *distributed* to the foundation (or the estate or revocable trust is terminated for income tax purposes, if earlier). Treas. Reg. § 53.4943-5(b)(1), 53.4943-6(b)(1).

[46] IRC § 4941.

[1] Penalties for Acts of Self-Dealing

Disqualified persons who engage in acts of "self-dealing" can find themselves in deep trouble. Any disqualified person who participates in a self-dealing transaction must pay a tax of 5 percent of the amount involved for each year that the transaction remains uncorrected.[47] In addition, a foundation manager who knows the transaction is prohibited, but participates in it anyway, must pay a tax of 2.5 percent of the amount involved for each year that the transaction remains in place (up to a limit of $10,000 for any one act of self-dealing).[48]

A penalty of 200 percent of the amount involved is also imposed on the disqualified person engaging in the self-dealing if the initial five percent tax was assessed and the transaction is not timely corrected. The foundation manager who does not correct the transaction must also pay a tax of 50 percent of the amount involved (up to a limit of $10,000 for any one act of self-dealing).[49] "Timely" means the earlier of (1) the date a deficiency notice is mailed with respect to the initial tax and (2) the date on which the initial tax is assessed.[50]

[2] Examples of Self-Dealing

Generally, self-dealing occurs when:

- A disqualified person and the private foundation enter into a transaction with each other (e.g., selling, exchanging or leasing property; lending money; or furnishing goods, services, or facilities);[51]
- The private foundation compensates or pays the expenses of a disqualified person;[52]
- The private foundation's income or assets are used by or for the benefit of a disqualified person;[53] or
- Payments are made from the private foundation to a government official.[54]

Self-dealing can also occur in seemingly innocuous situations as illustrated in the following example.

---

[47] IRC § 4941(a)(1).

[48] IRC § 4941(a)(2).

[49] IRC § 4941(b).

[50] IRC § 4941(b), 4941(e)(1).

[51] IRC §§ 4941(d)(1)(A), 4941(d)(1)(B), 4941(d)(1)(C).

[52] IRC § 4941(d)(1)(D).

[53] IRC § 4941(d)(1)(E).

[54] IRC § 4941(d)(1)(F).

EXAMPLE: Foundation, which owns art work, allows a disqualified person to display the art work at his home in exchange for the disqualified person's agreement to bear the costs of properly maintaining the art. This is self-dealing.[55]

Some other examples follow.

[a] Lease to Disqualified Person

Family Foundation owns Office Building *X*. Family members cannot lease space from Foundation for any price, no matter how advantageous to Foundation. Family must find a different place to office, regardless of the inconvenience.

[b] Buy-Sell Rights Between Foundation and Disqualified Person

Father, Mother, and Son, who are partners in a family business, enter into a buy-sell agreement, whereby each partner agrees to buy out his/her share of the interest of a deceased partner. Father dies, leaving his estate to Foundation. Foundation's bequest is funded with the partnership interest, and Father's estate is closed.

Mother and Son want to consummate the purchase of the Foundation's partnership interest, in accordance with the agreement. Neither Foundation nor Mother and Son can comply with the agreement without engaging in prohibited self-dealing.

WARNING: This is a trap for the unwary, since the partnership interests could have been sold to Mother and Son while the estate was in administration, if certain conditions were met.[56]

A year later, Mother dies and leaves her estate to Son. Son wants to complete his and Foundation's purchase of Mother's estate's interest in the partnership, pursuant to the agreement. Again, Foundation cannot fulfill its contractual obligation to buy Mother's interest. This situation is not just a trap for the unwary—even though Mother's estate is in administration, this situation does not come under the estate administration exception. The estate administration exception deals with transactions between the estate and third parties which affect the foundation's expectancy in estate assets—it does not allow the foundation itself to deal with the estate or with disqualified persons.

---

[55] Rev. Rul. 74-600, 1974-2 CB 385.

[56] See discussion at ¶ 37.04[2][e][iv] below regarding estate administration exception.

[c] Joint Ownership by Foundation and Disqualified Person

Generally speaking, even holding an asset with disqualified persons as tenants in common can be characterized as self-dealing.[57] The IRS has, however, issued a ruling that a co-investment by a partnership which was a disqualified person with a private foundation would not be self-dealing if the disqualified person did not benefit as a result of the co-investment and the foundation could withdraw on short notice.[58]

[d] Indirect Self-Dealing

"Indirect self-dealing" is an important concept, as many transactions are prohibited even when the foundation itself is not a party.

A transaction between the private foundation and a disqualified person is generally prohibited.[59] A transaction between two disqualified persons is not prohibited, unless (1) the foundation controls one of the disqualified persons or (2) the foundation's expectancy, or interest in property, is the subject of the transaction. "Control" means the power to cause the disqualified person to enter into the transaction, or to prevent the transaction.[60] For this purpose, control includes veto power (as in the case of ownership of 50 percent of a corporation), as well as control as a practical matter (even if control is not established by the entity documents).[61]

---

[57] See Priv. Ltr. Rul. 9127052 (Apr. 10, 1991) (marital trust, of which remainder beneficiary was private foundation, and residual trust were joint owners of income-producing property; marital trust's failure to divest itself of interest in property prior to distributing property to foundation would result in continuous acts of self-dealing between foundation and residual trust, a disqualified person); see also Priv. Ltr. Rul. 9438045 (June 30, 1994) (relying on estate administration exception in finding that holding and administering properties as tenants in common was not direct or indirect self-dealing); cf. Priv. Ltr. Rul. 9307026 (Nov. 24, 1992) (although joint ownership existed, no use by or for the benefit of disqualified persons would take place, and so no self-dealing would occur) and Priv. Ltr. Rul. 9651037 (Sept. 20, 1996) (tenancy in common formed with disqualified person in investment assets was not self-dealing).

[58] Priv. Ltr. Rul. 9448048 (Sept. 9, 1994). See, however, Priv. Ltr Rul. 9705013 (Oct. 31, 1996), holding that charitable remainder trust's participation in the formation and operation of investment partnership did not constitute self-dealing, but that capital contributions made by the trust after its initial capital contribution in exchange for a larger partnership interest would be self-dealing if the partnership were a disqualified person.

[59] IRC § 4941.

[60] Treas. Reg. § 53.4941(d)-1(b)(5).

[61] Treas. Reg. § 53.4941(d)-1(b)(5). But see Shearn Moody, Jr. v. Comm'r, 1995 RIA TC Memo. P95, 195, 69 TCM 2517 (1995), holding that 50 percent ownership of a corporation by a foundation constituted lack of control as a matter of law for purposes of determining whether a transaction with a disqualified person was self-dealing.

EXAMPLE: *A* Corporation is wholly owned by private foundation. *B* Corporation is owned 50 percent by private foundation and 50 percent by disqualified person. *B* Corporation cannot deal with *A* Corporation.

[e] "Permissible" Self-Dealing

There are some exceptions to the self-dealing prohibitions. A few of the most commonly applicable exceptions are listed below.

[i] **Reasonable compensation.** A private foundation can pay reasonable compensation to a disqualified person. Hence, Child can work for Dad's foundation, if the work is appropriate and the compensation is reasonable.[62] Compensation arrangements which are also transactions with a foundation manager may not be excepted. The IRS has held that providing a split-dollar insurance agreement for a foundation manager did not constitute self-dealing,[63] but that a low-interest loan by the foundation to a foundation manager as part of a compensation package was self-dealing, even if total compensation was reasonable.[64]

Can a foundation properly provide indemnities and insurance against liability to its foundation managers for their acts? Regulations address the issue—what sorts of arrangements will be considered compensation and what will be considered self-dealing.[65]

[ii] **Retail transactions.** If the private foundation actually sells goods, services, or facilities to the general public, a disqualified person may buy items available for sale to the public. However, to avoid classification of the sale as an act of self-dealing, the goods, services, or facilities must be available for purchase by the general public on at least as favorable a basis as the sale to the disqualified person.[66]

This rule is not always as simple as it seems. Suppose private foundation owns an electric company. Disqualified person, a large consumer of electricity, wants to buy electricity from the company. A customer of the size of disqualified person would normally receive a discount for volume purchases. What price does disqualified person have to pay?

[iii] **Corporate restructuring affecting a foundation's stock holdings.** A

---

[62] IRC § 4941(d)(2)(E).

[63] Priv. Ltr. Rul. 9539016 (June 29, 1995).

[64] Priv. Ltr. Rul. 9530032 (May 3, 1995), revoking Priv. Ltr. Rul. 9343033 (Aug. 2, 1993).

[65] Treas. Reg. §§ 53.4941(d)-2(f)(3)-53.4941(d)-2(f)(7).

[66] IRC § 4941(d)(2)(D); Treas. Reg. § 53.4941(d)-3(b).

corporate disqualified person can redeem stock held by a private foundation without engaging in an act of self-dealing if all other holders of the same class of stock have the same opportunity to redeem their stock and the terms of the redemption offer provide that the foundation will receive no less than fair market value.[67] Room may exist for creative planning using different classes of stock. The corporation should have sufficient funds to redeem the stock of all shareholders of the class in question, or the redemption offer may not be viewed as having been made on a uniform basis. Alternatively, imposing a dollar cap on the amount to be redeemed may be permissible, provided that all shareholders who want to redeem their stock can get a pro rata portion of their stock redeemed.[68] The transaction may also not be permitted where the private foundation receives property and other interest holders receive cash, or vice versa.[69]

[iv] Transactions during estate administration. Any transaction which involves the interest of a private foundation may be considered indirect self-dealing. For example, if the assets of an estate pass to a private foundation, the executor's sale of an asset of the estate to a disqualified person is indirect self-dealing, unless it falls within the estate administration exception.

The estate administration exception is a critical exception to the self-dealing rules. Self-dealing is permitted while the estate[70] is legitimately in administration,[71] provided that: (1) the executor is permitted to enter into the transaction pursuant to state law, (2) the private foundation will receive an interest at least as liquid as that which it would otherwise have taken, and (3) the transaction is approved by a court of competent jurisdiction.[72]

The estate administration exception is highly useful in dealing with closely held businesses, and in remedying future self-dealing problems that could arise after the estate administration has terminated.

> EXAMPLE: Estate owns a business. Decedent's son would like to buy the business. The estate assets will pass to a private foundation. Once the assets are distributed to the private foundation, the foundation cannot sell the business to the son at any price, because sales

---

[67] Treas. Reg. § 53.4941(d)-3(d)(1).

[68] Priv. Ltr. Rul. 9040064 (July 12, 1990) (redemption offer was subject to a cap, although this fact is not stated in the ruling).

[69] Priv. Ltr. Rul. 9040064 (July 12, 1990).

[70] A similar exception exists for a revocable trust which becomes irrevocable on the settlor's death. Treas. Reg. § 53.4941(d)-1(b)(3).

[71] See Treas. Reg. § 1.641(b)-3 for a discussion of when an estate administration is deemed to have terminated.

[72] Treas. Reg. §§ 53.4941(d)-1(b)(3)(i)-53.4941(d)-1(b)(3)(iv).

to disqualified persons are not allowed.[73]

The sale can take place during the estate administration, if the business has not been distributed to the foundation, and the other requirements listed above are met.

QUESTION: *Can the estate sell the business to the son for a note and distribute the note to the foundation?*

ANSWER: The receipt and holding of the note are permitted,[74] so long as the transaction qualifies under the estate administration exception described above.[75] The private foundation's subsequent exercise of any rights granted it under the note and any deed of trust, security agreement, or similar instrument that secures payment of the note should not constitute an act of self-dealing.[76] However, the private foundation's failure to enforce payment of the note will be an act of self-dealing if the son could pay.

PRACTICE POINTER: It is very easy to trip up on the self-dealing rules. Get rid of problem items in the estate. Do not be in a rush to distribute estate assets to the private foundation before self-dealing issues are resolved; once the property is in the foundation, the options for dealing with related persons are suddenly very limited.

WARNING: A private foundation is not a suitable long-term entity to hold a family business. Even during the initial five-year permitted holding period applicable under the excess business holding rules, opportunities for inadvertent self-dealing are plentiful. Consider a different type of recipient for a business.

¶ 37.05 OTHER ISSUES

[1] Investment Income Taxes

A private foundation is subject to a one percent or two percent tax on its investment income, depending on the level of its distributions.[77]

---

[73] The five-year or ten-year disposition period referenced in ¶ 37.03[2] above on family businesses buys extra time after the estate administration for disposition of excess business holdings, but *not* for self-dealing.

[74] Treas. Reg. § 53.4941(d)-2(c)(1).

[75] See, e.g., Priv. Ltr. Rul. 9434032 (June 3, 1994); Priv. Ltr. Rul. 9501038 (Oct. 6, 1994).

[76] See Priv. Ltr. Rul. 9042030 (July 23, 1990).

[77] IRC § 4940.

[2] Minimum Distribution Requirements

Generally, a private foundation must distribute at least 5 percent of the value of its assets each year to qualified charities.[78] The distribution for any year must be made by the end of the following year.[79]

Failure to timely distribute will attract a penalty tax of 15 percent of the undistributed amount.[80] An additional tax of 100 percent of the undistributed amount will be imposed if the initial tax is assessed and the distribution is not timely made.[81] "Timely" means the earlier of the date of mailing a deficiency with respect to the initial tax or the date the initial tax is assessed.[82] The minimum distribution rules necessitate periodic valuation of the private foundation's assets.[83] Specific rules are provided in the Code and Regulations regarding valuation of assets.[84]

[3] Jeopardizing Investments

The private foundation cannot invest in a manner which would jeopardize the charitable purpose of the foundation without incurring penalty taxes.[85] No investment is per se a jeopardizing investment, but certain types of investments will be closely scrutinized (e.g., puts, calls, working interests, etc.).[86] Whether an investment is a jeopardizing investment depends on the facts and circumstances—like obscenity, the fact finders will know it when they see it.[87]

[4] Taxable Expenditures

A private foundation generally cannot: (1) make grants to individuals for travel, study, or similar purposes without advance IRS approval; (2) try to influence legislation or the outcome of any specific public election; (3) carry on a voter registration drive; (4) make a grant to an organization which is not a

---

[78] IRC § 4942.

[79] IRC § 4942(a).

[80] IRC § 4942(a).

[81] IRC § 4942(b).

[82] IRC §§ 4942(b), 4942(j)(1).

[83] IRC § 4942.

[84] E.g., IRC § 4942(e)(2).

[85] IRC § 4944.

[86] Treas. Reg. § 53.4944-1(a)(2).

[87] Jacobellis v. Ohio, 378 US 184, 196 (1964) (comment by Stewart, J., concurring that he cannot define hard porn, but knows it when he sees it).

public charity unless it exercises expenditure responsibility; or (5) make any distribution for a noncharitable purpose.[88]

These expenditures are known as taxable expenditures. A foundation that makes a taxable expenditure will be taxed on 10 percent of the amount of the expenditure, and the foundation manager who agrees to a payment knowing it is a taxable expenditure will incur a tax equal to 2.5 percent of the amount of the expenditure.[89] Failure to timely correct the taxable expenditure will result in the imposition of a penalty tax on the foundation of 100 percent of the amount of the expenditure and a penalty tax of 50 percent of the amount of the expenditure on a foundation manager who refused to agree to part or all of the correction.[90] "Timely" means the earlier of the date of mailing a deficiency with respect to the initial tax or the date the initial tax is assessed.[91]

[a] Gifts to Individuals for Travel, Study, or Similar Purposes

A payment to an individual for travel, study, or similar purposes requires advance approval from the IRS.[92] Gaining such approval involves submitting a description of the scholarship program to the IRS. The program must meet certain requirements. Determination of the recipients must be made on the basis of merit, need, or both. Disqualified persons must not be eligible to receive such grants, and the application must identify disqualified persons. The student must report periodically on his progress. Procedures must be identified to investigate and pursue reimbursement of any misused funds.

If a payment is made directly to a school to establish or continue a scholarship program, and the school determines the identity of the recipients, the payment is not considered a gift to an individual, and does not require compliance with the above procedures.

Once the request for approval is made to the IRS, what happens? If the IRS does not respond with an objection within 45 days, the foundation can assume that scholarships granted pursuant to the procedure are permitted expenditures until it receives notice to the contrary.

[b] Gifts to Fund Work of Specific Individuals

May a private foundation fund a chair at a university, with a particular professor in mind, or make a gift to a medical school to fund a particular doctor's research? The foundation can recommend the professor or doctor, so

---

[88] IRC § 4945.

[89] IRC § 4945(a).

[90] IRC § 4945(b).

[91] IRC § 4945(i)(2).

[92] The approval procedure is described at Treas. Reg. § 53.4945-4.

long as the gift is actually made to a public charity and the public charity has the right to make the final determination as to who receives the benefits.[93]

[c] Scholarship Programs

[i] What if a private foundation wants to give a scholarship to a particular student? Grants to individuals for scholarships, fellowships, travel, study, and similar purposes are subject to the advance approval requirements described above. Available alternatives are:

- *Direct Gift to School.* As stated in ¶ 37.05[4][a] above, the foundation can give the scholarship funds to a school and recommend (but not designate) the student to the school as an appropriate scholarship recipient.[94]
- *Scholarship Program.* If the scholarship program is designed to pay the funds directly to the student, or directly to the school on behalf of a designated student, the scholarship program will have to receive advance approval from the IRS.[95]
- *Scholarship Program for Employees and Their Families.* If the private foundation (usually one established by a corporation or other employer to conduct its charitable activities) is used to fund scholarships for employees or family members of employees of a particular employer, strict requirements must be met.[96]

Chiefly, the applicable IRS revenue procedures, dealing with employee scholarship programs require that: (1) the persons determining the identity of the recipients must be independent of the foundation and employer; (2) the scholarships must be based on need or merit or both; (3) a scholarship must not terminate due to the employee's termination of employment; and (4) certain guidelines regarding the percentage of the eligible class who can actually receive benefits must be met (or if not met, the program must be determined to qualify based on its particular facts and circumstances).[97]

WARNING: Disqualified persons cannot receive scholarships from a private foundation.[98] A grant to a disqualified person would be an act of self-dealing.[99]

---

[93] Treas. Reg. § 53.4945-2(a)(5).

[94] Treas. Reg. § 53.4945-4(a)(4).

[95] IRC § 4945(g); Treas. Reg. § 53.4945-4(c).

[96] These are laid out in Rev. Proc. 76-47, 1976-2 CB 670 (for grants) and Rev. Proc. 80-39, 1980-2 CB 772 (for loans).

[97] Rev. Proc. 76-47, § 4; Rev. Proc. 80-39, § 4.

[98] IRC § 4942(g)(1).

[ii] **Charitable class rule.** Any scholarship fund must be for the benefit of a charitable class. This means that the group of eligible recipients must be sufficiently broad so that the giving of grants to members of the group would be considered to fulfill a religious, charitable, scientific, educational or literary purpose.[100]

> EXAMPLE: A class consisting of all high school seniors residing in New York City is okay. A class consisting of all high school seniors who are members of a certain family is not.

[d] Awards

An award for past performance is not subject to the program approval requirement, if there is no restriction on the recipient's use of the funds.

> EXAMPLE: A foundation could award $500 to the valedictorian of the local senior class each year without advance approval if the recipient could use it for any purpose she liked. The key is whether or not there is any attempt to control the recipient's use of the funds. In this example, the foundation would need advance approval if the recipient had to use the $500 for college.

[5] Taxable Expenditures—Gifts to Private Foundations

[a] In General

If a private foundation makes a grant to another private foundation, it must exercise "expenditure responsibility" over the grant.[101] This involves monitoring the donee to be sure that the funds are properly spent, and reporting to the IRS.[102]

WARNING: There is an important pitfall in this area. If a private foundation makes a large enough grant to an organization which has qualified under Section 509(a)(2) or Section 170(b)(1)(A)(vi) as a publicly supported organization, the gift may turn the recipient organization into a private foundation. If this happens, the donor-private foundation must exercise expenditure responsibility with respect to the grant, and its distributions to the recipient organization will not count toward satisfying the donor-private foundation's minimum distribution requirements, unless special tests are met.[103]

---

[99] IRC § 4941(d)(1)(E).

[100] Treas. Reg. § 53.4945-4(b)(2).

[101] IRC § 4945(d)(4)(B).

[102] IRC § 4945(h).

[103] See discussion of qualifying distributions in Ch. 32.

If the exemption letter reflects an advance ruling, the donor is entitled to rely on the organization's public charity status until notice of change of the organization's status is made public, unless (1) the donor actually has knowledge that the status is being revoked or (2) the organization is controlled by the donor.[104]

If the exemption letter reflects a final ruling, the donor *cannot* rely on the determination letter if: (1) the donor has knowledge of the revocation of the determination letter or (2) the donor is in part responsible for, or aware of, the act, failure to act, or change which causes the revocation of the determination letter.[105]

[b] Gift Causes Public Charity Donee to Be a Private Foundation

If, as mentioned above, the donor-foundation's gift is large enough to cause the donee Section 509(a)(2) or Section 170(b)(1)(A)(vi) organization to fail the public support tests, the organization will lose its public charity status and the donor will be treated as having made the gift to a private foundation. This will require the donor-private foundation to exercise expenditure responsibility and prevent the gift to the donee ex-public charity from counting toward the donor-foundation's minimum distribution requirements (unless certain additional requirements are met).

In light of these potential adverse consequences, a donor-foundation's safest course of action is to obtain a letter from the recipient public charity that the donor-foundation's grant will not result in a loss of the organization's classification as an organization which is not a private foundation, pursuant to Sections 170(b)(1)(a)(vi) or 509(a)(2). Such a letter will generally protect the donor-foundation from being considered responsible for or aware of any such change, provided it contains adequate data.[106] Alternatively, the donor-foundation can exercise expenditure responsibility and impose the qualifying distribution requirements on a protective basis, or be prepared to show that its grant qualifies as an "unusual grant" which, by definition, cannot change the recipient organization's status.[107]

[6] Grants to Noncharitable Organizations

Interestingly, there is no requirement that the actual recipient of the private foundation's funds be a charity at all. It should therefore be permissible to

---

[104] Treas. Reg. § 1.509(a)-3(e)(3); see also IRS guidelines issued March 13, 1989.

[105] Treas. Reg. § 1.509(a)-7.

[106] Treas. Reg. § 1.170A-9(e)(4)(v)(c), with respect to organizations qualifying under IRC § 170(b)(1)(A)(vi), and Treas. Reg. § 1.509(a)-3(c)(1)(iii)(b), with respect to organizations qualifying under IRC § 509(a)(2).

[107] See Treas. Reg. § 1.170A-9(e)(6)(ii).

make grants to a noncharitable organization if that organization agrees to use it for a charitable purpose.[108] However, the private foundation will need to exercise expenditure responsibility with respect to any such grants.[109]

¶ 37.06 PRIVATE OPERATING FOUNDATIONS

A "private operating foundation," in concept, is one which conducts its charitable activities directly (e.g., it operates a museum or a library), rather than simply contributing funds to other charitable organizations. (Most private foundations are grant-making foundations, rather than operating foundations.) Such a foundation must meet a number of tests regarding its level of distributions, the amount of its assets that are held for direct conduct of charitable activities, and its sources of support.[110]

 A private operating foundation is not subject to the tax on investment income (if the foundation meets certain other requirements),[111] is not subject to the minimum distribution requirements,[112] and is treated as a public charity for purposes of the income tax charitable deduction.[113]

¶ 37.07 SPLIT-INTEREST AND OTHER CHARITABLE TRUSTS

Many of the rules governing private foundations also apply to charitable remainder trusts and charitable lead trusts. Specifically, the self-dealing rules[114] and the taxable expenditure rules[115] generally apply to split-interest trusts.[116] The excess business holdings rules[117] and the jeopardizing investment rules[118] generally do not apply to charitable remainder trusts, and only apply to charitable lead trusts if the charitable deduction allowed on the creation of the trust exceeded 60 percent of the value of the trust assets.[119]

---

[108] IRC § 4945(d)(4).

[109] IRC § 4945(d)(4)(B).

[110] IRC § 4942(j)(3).

[111] IRC § 4940(d).

[112] IRC § 4942(a)(1).

[113] IRC §§ 170(b)(1)(A)(vii), (b)(1)(E)(i), (e)(1)(B)(ii). See Ch. 32 for elaboration of these tests.

[114] IRC § 4941.

[115] IRC § 4945.

[116] IRC § 4947(a)(2).

[117] IRC § 4943.

[118] IRC § 4944.

[119] IRC § 4947(b)(3).

The private foundation rules also apply to a charitable trust which has not obtained an exemption under Section 501(a), if an income, gift, or estate tax charitable deduction was allowed for any contribution to the trust.[120]

---

[120] IRC § 4947(a)(1).

CHAPTER **38**

Designer Charities

¶ 38.01　INTRODUCTION

A private foundation may work well as a charitable vehicle for holding a portfolio of stocks and bonds. However, it is the wrong format through which to perpetuate the family business. Moreover, it is also subject to many more statutory restrictions on the holding of business interests than a public charity. For example, unlike a private foundation, a public charity:

- Is not subject to prohibitions against self-dealing at fair market value;
- Is not subject to an excise tax on investment income;
- Is allowed to hold interests in active businesses;[1]
- Does not have to distribute 5 percent of its assets each year (although it must conduct charitable activities at a level commensurate with its size);
- Can hold nontraditional investments (subject to fiduciary standards); and
- Can make gifts to individuals without advance approval from the IRS.

Hence, if substantial family business interests are involved, a private foundation will generally not be an appropriate entity. In such instance, it may be a good idea to design a public charity for the particular family involved. Public charities come in four stripes—organizations described in Sections 170(b)(1)(A)(i)-(v) (automatic public charities), 170(b)(1)(A)(vi) (type of publicly supported charity), 509(a)(2) (type of publicly supported charity), and 509(a)(3) (support foundations).

¶ 38.02　AUTOMATIC PUBLIC CHARITIES—SECTIONS 170(b)(1)(A)(i) THROUGH 170(b)(1)(A)(v)

If an organization described in Sections 170(b)(1)(A)(i) through 170(b)(1)(A)(v) is a Section 501(c)(3) organization,[2] it will not be a private

---

[1] Provided that the primary activity of the charity does not generate unrelated business taxable income (UBTI). If it does, that may be solved by holding the business in a corporation.

[2] An organization qualifies under Section 501(c)(3) if: (a) it operates exclusively for religious, charitable, scientific, testing for public safety, literacy or educational purposes, or to further national or international amateur sports competition, or for the preservation of cruelty to animals, (b) no part of its earnings inure to the benefit of any private individual, and (c) it meets certain other requirements. IRC § 501(c)(3).

foundation, regardless of who supports or controls it.[3] Any of the following five types of organizations comes under this rule:

- A church or association of churches;[4]
- A school which normally maintains a regular faculty and curriculum and a regularly enrolled body of students;[5]
- A hospital or medical research organization which meets certain requirements;
- An organization which supports a state college or university as its sole activity, if it meets certain source-of-support requirements;[6] and
- A domestic governmental unit.[7]

PRACTICE POINTER: Due to the very specific nature of the requirements for these organizations, a donor will not typically be establishing an automatic public charity unless he has that specific purpose in mind.

¶ 38.03 CHARITIES RECEIVING PUBLIC SUPPORT OR EXEMPT FUNCTION REVENUES—SECTION 509(a)(2) AND SECTION 170(b)(1)(A)(vi)

If a person establishing a charity contemplates fund-raising activities or directly conducting charitable functions (as opposed to grantmaking),[8] he might organize a Section 509(a)(2) organization or Section 170(b)(1)(A)(vi) organization. Either of these types of charities can be controlled by disqualified persons.[9]

[1] Organization Receiving Exempt Function Revenues—Section 509(a)(2)

A Section 509(a)(2) organization must generally meet two tests. First, after ignoring (1) large donations, (2) donations from related parties, and (3) large receipts resulting from its charitable function that are received from any one person, the charity must receive over one-third of its total support from the

---

[3] IRC § 509(a)(1).

[4] IRC § 170(b)(1)(A)(i).

[5] IRC § 170(b)(1)(A)(ii).

[6] IRC § 170(b)(1)(A)(iv).

[7] IRC § 170(b)(1)(A)(v).

[8] The term "grantmaking" foundation will be used to describe a foundation whose charitable function consists primarily of making grants, rather than directly performing charitable activities (i.e., its major activity is not running a library, a soup kitchen, etc.).

[9] See Ch. 37 on private foundations for the definition of disqualified persons.

general public or receipts from its charitable function. Additionally, it must receive no more than one-third of its support from all sources (including all donations) from investment income and after-tax unrelated business taxable income (UBTI).

Let's examine these tests more closely.

[a] Support from General Public and Exempt Function Revenues

This type of entity must normally receive each year more than one-third of its support from (1) gifts, grants, contributions, membership fees, and/or (2) certain gross receipts from admissions, sales of merchandise, performance of services, or furnishing of facilities in activities which are not unrelated trades or businesses (i.e., "function revenues").[10] The function revenues described in (2) do not include amounts received from any one person or entity in excess of the greater of $5,000 or one percent of the charity's support for the year.[11] Examples of function revenues might be sales of products manufactured by the handicapped or receipts from ticket sales of a chamber music group. This one-third of total support must be received from persons (other than disqualified persons), governmental entities, and/or the automatic public charities discussed above.[12]

> EXAMPLE: Museum's total gross receipts for the year are a $100,000 grant from Disqualified Person, and gifts of $1,000 each from 100 other persons who are all unrelated to the museum. Total support is $200,000. Total support from non-disqualified persons is $100,000. The test fraction is $100,000 (gifts from general public)/$200,000 (total support). The one-third test is met, since Museum receives more than one-third of its support from the general public.

> EXAMPLE: In addition to the contributions described in the above example, Museum has investment income of $100,000. The test fraction will be $100,000 (gifts from general public)/$300,000 (total support). This fraction is one-third; since the test requires more than one-third, the test is not met and Museum does not qualify.

> EXAMPLE: Museum was established and is controlled by Family. However, it receives its entire support from admission tickets. No one person or entity spends more than $5,000 a year on admissions, and no admissions revenue was received from disqualified persons. The test fraction is receipts from admissions/total support. Since receipts from admissions equal Museum's total support, the fraction will be one, and the test is met.

---

[10] IRC § 509(a)(2)(A).

[11] IRC § 509(a)(2)(A)(ii).

[12] IRC § 509(a)(2)(A).

[b] Support from Investment Income

A Section 509(a)(2) organization must also normally receive no more than one-third of its support from the sum of its gross investment income plus after-tax UBTI.[13] This test generally prevents heavily endowed organizations from qualifying.

> **EXAMPLE:** Museum's total gross receipts for the year are a $100,000 grant from Disqualified Person, and gifts of $1,000 each from 100 other persons who are all unrelated to the museum. In addition to these contributions, Museum has investment income of $100,000. Total support from non-disqualified persons is $100,000. The test fraction would be $100,000 (investment income)/$300,000 (total support). This fraction is one-third, so Museum meets this test.

PRACTICE POINTER: If after-tax UBTI is a problem, it can generally be eliminated by incorporating the business generating the UBTI.

[2] Organization Receiving Public Support—Section 170(b)(1)(A)(vi)

This is a type of organization similar to the Section 509(a)(2) organization. A Section 170(b)(1)(A)(vi) organization must normally receive a substantial part of its support (excluding income received in performing direct charitable activities) from public contributions and/or grants from governments.[14]

Qualification for this public support test may be met in one of the following two ways:

- One-third of the organization's support is received from public contributions or governmental grants.
- One-tenth of the organization's support is received from the general public or through governmental grants and the organization can prove to the IRS that it is organized and operated to attract new and additional public and governmental support.

[a] One-Third Public Support

The organization will be considered "publicly supported" if it normally receives at least 33–1/3 percent (or one-third) of its total support (exclusive of

---

[13] IRC § 509(a)(2)(B).

[14] IRC § 170(b)(1)(A)(vi). "Government" means any federal, state, or local government, and any governmental agency. IRC § 170(c)(1).

function revenues) from public contributions and governmental grants.[15] If a contributor (other than certain public charities or a government) contributes more than two percent of an organization's total support, his contributions in excess of that two percent will not be taken into account for purposes of calculating the numerator of the organization's total fraction of public support.[16] Function revenues are not taken into account in either the numerator or the denominator of the fraction, unless almost all of the organization's support consists of exempt function revenues.[17]

> EXAMPLE: Museum's total gross receipts for the year are a $100,000 grant from Disqualified Person, and gifts of $1,000 each from 100 other persons who are all unrelated to the museum. Total support is $200,000. Total support from non-disqualified persons is $100,000. The test fraction = ($100,000 gifts from general public + $4,000 Disqualified Person's gift as limited by two percent of total support) over $200,000 total support. Accordingly, the public support fraction is 52 percent, and Museum qualifies.

> EXAMPLE: Museum was established and is controlled by Family. However, it receives its entire support of $100,000 from admission tickets. Museum does not qualify since all of its income is function revenues.

> Say Museum, in addition to ticket prices, earned $800 of interest income and $200 from donations from the general public. Then, the ordinary test fraction would be $200/$1,000, or 20 percent, so the Museum would not qualify under this test. Even if the donations from the general public were $333 or more, the Museum would probably not qualify, since that amount would probably be deemed insignificant compared to the Museum's total support, including function revenues.

[b] Ten Percent Support

An organization that does not meet the 33 1/3 percent support test will be considered "publicly supported" if (1) it normally receives ten percent or more of its support, exclusive of exempt function revenues (subject to the same calculation adjustments as the 33 1/3 percent test) from public contributions and governmental grants and (2) it can convince the IRS that it is organized and operated so as to attract new and additional public and governmental

---

[15] Treas. Reg. § 1.170A-9(e)(2). An organization will be considered as "normally" meeting the 33-1/3 percent support test for its current taxable year and the preceding year if for the four taxable years immediately preceding the current taxable year, the organization meets the 33 1/3 percent support test on an aggregate basis. Treas. Reg. § 1.170A-9(e)(4).

[16] Treas. Reg. § 1.170A-9(e)(6)(i).

[17] Treas. Reg. § 1.170A-9(e)(7). In such a case, the organization will not meet either the 33 1/3 percent test or the 10 percent test, if its support from governmental units and the general public is insignificant.

support on a continuous basis.[18] The IRS looks to many factors in determining whether this "facts and circumstances" test is met; included among these factors are the nature and extent of the organization's fund-raising activities, the relative percentage of financial support from the public and government (ten percent is the minimum, but the more, the better), support from a representative number of persons, the extent to which the organization's governing body represents the broad interests of the public, the accessibility of the organization's facilities and availability of its services to the public, and the extent to which the public participates in the conduct of the organization's programs and the formation of its policies.[19]

[3] Determination Letters and Advance Rulings

It can be difficult for an organization to raise funds without an IRS determination letter saying that the organization is a public charity. To obtain an advance ruling under Section 509(a)(2) or Section 170(b)(1)(A)(vi), Form 1023 (in which the charity founders describe their plan for achieving the desired level of public support) must be submitted to the IRS.[20] If the foundation appears to qualify, the IRS may give an advance ruling for a two-, three-, five- or six-year period that it does qualify.[21] At the end of the period, the foundation must submit additional information (on Form 8734) to enable the IRS to determine whether the foundation has actually met the requirements. The advance ruling period will be extended until the IRS is able to make a final determination, and issue a final ruling.[22]

[4] Reliance on Rulings—Large Grants to Section 509(a)(2) or Section 170(b)(1)(A)(vi) Organizations

If Dad is contemplating making a substantial contribution to a Section 509(a)(2) or Section 170(b)(1)(A)(vi) organization, and if it makes a difference (e.g., deduction limitations) whether he is making the contribution to a private foundation or a public charity, he should review the organization's exemption letter.[23]

---

[18] Treas. Reg. § 1.170A-9(e)(3).

[19] Treas. Reg. § 1.170A-9(e)(3).

[20] Treas. Reg. §§ 1.170A-9(e)(5)(i), 1.509(a)-3(d)(1).

[21] Treas. Reg. §§ 1.170A-9(e)(5)(i), 1.170A-9(e)(5)(iv), 1.509(a)-3(d)(1), 1.509(a)-3(d)(4).

[22] Treas. Reg. §§ 1.170A-9(e)(5)(iii)(a), 1.509(a)-3(e)(2).

[23] This is the determination letter from the IRS stating that the charity is tax-exempt and whether it is a private foundation.

[a] Reliance on Advance Ruling

If the exemption letter reflects an advance ruling, the donor is entitled to rely on the organization's public charity status until notice of change of the organization's status is made public, unless (1) the donor actually has knowledge that the status has been or is being revoked or (2) the organization is controlled by the donor.[24]

[b] Reliance on Definitive Ruling

If the exemption letter reflects a final ruling, the donor cannot rely on the determination letter if (1) the donor has knowledge of the revocation of the determination letter or (2) the donor is in part responsible for, or aware of, the act, failure to act, or change which causes the revocation of the determination letter.[25]

Interestingly, if a donor's gift is large enough to cause the organization to fail the support tests, the organization will lose its public charity status. In this case, the donor will be treated as having made the gift to a private foundation in the first instance, thereby subjecting an individual donor to greater limitations on his income tax charitable deduction or requiring a private foundation donor to exercise expenditure responsibility and impacting its qualifying distributions.

PRACTICE POINTER: Unless the donor is relying on an advance ruling, ask for evidence that a donor's large contribution to a Section 170(b)(1)(A)(vi) or Section 509(a)(2) organization will not cause the recipient organization to fail its support tests. A letter from the donee organization representing that the grant or contribution will not result in a loss of the donee's public charity status will generally protect a donor foundation from being subject to the Section 4945 penalty excise tax, if the letter contains adequate supporting data.[26]

[5] What Situations Call for Which Type of Charity?

The following is a tabular summary of differences between a Section 509(a)(2) organization and a Section 170(b)(1)(A)(vi) organization.

---

[24] Treas. Reg. § 1.509(a)-3(e)(3); see also IRS guidelines issued March 13, 1989.

[25] Treas. Reg. § 1.509(a)-7.

[26] Treas. Reg. §§ 1.170A-9(e)(4)(v)(c), 1.509(a)-3(c)(1)(iii)(b).

Feature	Section 509(a)(2) Charity	Section 170(b)(1)(A)(vi) Charity
Minimum Required Contributions From General Public:	Zero, if charitable function receipts are high enough.	1/3 of support, excluding charitable function receipts—automatic qualification; or 1/10 of support, excluding charitable function receipts—if facts and circumstances test is met.
"Public Support" Definition:	-includes gifts and charitable function receipts.	-includes gifts only.
	-excludes receipts from disqualified persons from numerator of public support test fraction.	-excludes receipts from any disqualified person in excess of 2 percent of total support from numerator of public support test fraction.
	-includes receipts from charitable function from any one person in numerator of public support test fraction up to $5,000 or 1 percent of support.	-excludes receipts from charitable function activities from numerator or denominator of public support test fraction; however, if virtually all income is from charitable function activities, the organization will not qualify unless governmental support and/or contributions from general public are significant.
Investment Income and After-Tax UBTI:	-limited to 1/3 of total support (counting all sources).	-limited to 2/3 of support, with above adjustments, if 1/3 automatic test is met; could be as much as 90 percent, with above adjustments, if facts and circumstances test is met.

Many organizations will meet both of the above tests. Neither exemption type is "better" than the other. Both types receive the same tax treatment, both at the entity and contributor levels. Accordingly, the choice will hinge on which qualifications will be easier for the particular entity to meet. Generally, if the charity's primary support is exempt function revenue, Section 509(a)(2) charity status will be the more likely choice. If an organization will have no contributions from the general public,[27] Section 509(a)(2) charity status will be the only choice, as Section 170(b)(1)(A)(vi) will require at least some public support. An organization which relies heavily on investment income and UBTI may choose charity status under Section 170(b)(1)(A)(vi), since the limitations are much less restrictive. If the foundation is a grantmaking foundation, then Section 509(a)(2) charity status will require that one-third of the contributions (exclusive of disqualified persons' contributions) come from the public. If the foundation will not receive contributions from the public and will not have exempt function receipts, it will not be possible to meet the Section 509(a)(2) and the Section 170(b)(1)(A)(vi) tests.

It is not necessary to know at the outset which charity status will be applicable. Form 1023 requires a designation of category, but a box can be checked to apply under either category. In applying for the definitive ruling, an exemption will be granted if the entity met either of the two tests during its advance ruling period, even if the test met by the organization was not the test it expected to satisfy at the outset.

PRACTICE POINTER: There is no need to fret about which of the two exemption categories to check at the outset. What is important is to meet one of them by the end of the advance ruling period. Of course, the same qualifications with respect to a particular exemption status must be met consistently—that is, the organization cannot use one exemption status in years 5, 7, and 9 and the other in years 6, 8, and 10.

¶ 38.04 SUPPORT ORGANIZATIONS—SECTION 509(a)(3)

If a donor contemplates forming a grantmaking charity, she might want to consider a Section 509(a)(3) support organization. A Section 509(a)(3) support organization is attractive to many donors for whom private foundations are, for some reason, not workable.[28]

A "support organization" can be structured in one of three ways, but one often chosen by families is a support organization that is "operated in connection with" a public charity.[29] Requirements for such an organization are detailed in Treasury Regulation § 1.509(a)-4(i), and reviewed below.

---

[27] The general public, for this purpose, includes governmental units, and certain other public charities. IRC § 170(b)(1)(A)(vi).

[28] E.g., too many business holdings, need for joint ownership between related parties and the charity, too many other private foundation difficulties.

[29] The other two are a support organization which is "operated, supervised, or controlled by" the beneficiary organization(s), Treas. Reg. § 1.509(a)-4(g), and a sup-

[1] Charitable Activity Requirement

The support organization must be tax-exempt under Section 501(c)(3).[30] And, after its qualification for tax-exempt status under Section 501(c)(3), the organization must conduct a charitable program commensurate with its size and resources to maintain its exempt status under Section 501(c)(3).[31] Hence, some reasonable amount of charitable activity must take place.

[2] Limitation on Beneficiaries

[a] Permissible Beneficiaries

The only permissible beneficiaries of a support organization[32] are (1) public charities described in Section 170(b)(1)(A)(i)-(vi) and (2) Section 509(a)(2) organizations.

A support organization can make distributions to individuals or organizations other than the specified publicly supported organizations only if:[33]

- The payment constitutes a grant to an individual who is a member of a charitable class benefited by the specified publicly supported organization; such a payment can be made through an unrelated organization, provided it constitutes a grant to the individual rather than a grant to the organization receiving it.[34]
- The payment is made to a Section 501(c)(3) organization which is not a private foundation and which is (1) operated, supervised, or controlled by, (2) supervised or controlled in connection with, or (3) operated in connection with the publicly supported organization; or

---

port organization which is "supervised or controlled in connection with" the beneficiary organization(s). Treas. Reg. § 1.509(a)-4(h).

[30] IRC § 509(a).

[31] Rev. Rul. 64-182, 1964-1 CB (Part 1) 186.

[32] IRC § 509(a)(3). Certain other organizations are also permissible beneficiaries, but will rarely be beneficiaries of a family support foundation. They are: (1) organizations described in Section 501(c)(4) (civic leagues, organizations operated exclusively for the promotion of social welfare, and certain local associations of employees which are devoted exclusively to charitable, educational, or recreational purposes), (2) Section 501(c)(5) organizations (labor, agricultural, or horticultural organizations), and (3) Section 501(c)(6) organizations (business leagues, chambers of commerce, real estate boards, boards of trade, professional football leagues not operated for profit or inuring to the benefit of any private individual).

Any beneficiary described in this footnote must be able to qualify as a Section 509(a)(2) organization, except that it does not have to qualify as a Section 501(c)(3) organization established for charitable purposes.

[33] Treas. Reg. § 1.509(a)-4(e)(1).

[34] Applicable rules are set forth in Treas. Reg. § 53.4945-4(a)(4).

● In certain circumstances, the payment is made to a college or university that is a governmental agency or instrumentality.

In certain cases, support organizations with "operated in connection with" structures have (over IRS objections) successfully established independent scholarship programs for students of particular schools, even though the programs were not operated by the supported schools.[35]

[b] Beneficiaries Specified by Name

The charitable beneficiaries must be listed by name in the support organization's governing instrument.[36] The support organization can vary the contributions among the named beneficiaries, and does not have to distribute to every named beneficiary.[37] However, beneficiary substitutions are not allowed, except under circumstances beyond the control of the support organization.[38]

PRACTICE POINTER: The number of named beneficiaries must be reasonably limited. Does this mean that a support organization cannot make distributions to whatever eligible charities it chooses, as a private foundation could? Theoretically, yes. But —

: Including a community foundation as a specified beneficiary is a simple means to allow for additional beneficiaries in a support organization "operated in connection with" its charitable beneficiaries. The support organization may make distributions to an advise and consult fund within the community foundation, recommending the charitable entities which should receive distributions from the fund. Of course, the community foundation must make the final determination of recipients.

---

[35] Warren M. Goodspeed Scholarship Fund v. Comm'r, 70 TC 515 (1978); Nellie Callahan Scholarship Fund v. Comm'r, 73 TC 626 (1980); Cockerline Memorial Fund v. Comm'r, 86 TC 53 (1986). See GCM 36043 (Oct. 9, 1974) and Rev. Rul. 75-437, 1975-2 CB 218, for statements of the IRS position.

[36] Treas. Reg. § 1.509(a)-4(d)(4). An exception applies if there has been an historic and continuing relationship between the supporting and supported organization so that there is a substantial identity of interests between them. Treas. Reg. § 1.509(a)-4(d)(2)(iv).

[37] Treas. Reg. § 1.509(a)-4(d)(4)(i)(c).

[38] For example, if a named beneficiary ceases to exist or loses its tax exemption. Treas. Reg. § 1.509(a)-4(d)(4)(i)(a).

[3] Requirements Concerning Organizational Documents

The organizational documents of the support organization (1) must limit the organization's purposes to exempt purposes, (2) cannot expressly empower the organization to engage in activities which do not further its exempt purposes, (3) must specify the publicly supported entities on whose behalf the organization is to be operated, and (4) cannot expressly empower the organization to support any organization other than the specified organizations.[39]

[4] Responsiveness Test

The support organization must meet the test of being responsive to one or more of its charitable beneficiaries.[40] This test is met in one of the following ways:

If the support organization is a corporation, the responsiveness test is met if:

- The support organization has a board member appointed by a beneficiary, a board member of a beneficiary occupies an important office of the support organization, or the governing bodies of the support organization and a beneficiary maintain a close and continuous working relationship, *and*
- By virtue of the above, a beneficiary is actively involved in the financial and charitable affairs of the support organization.[41]

If the support organization is a trust, the responsiveness test is met if:

- The support organization is a charitable trust under state law;
- The specified charitable beneficiaries are named in the trust agreement; *and*
- The beneficiaries can compel an accounting and enforce the trust under state law.[42]

PRACTICE POINTER: If the donor really wants to keep the charities out of management of the entity, the trust format allows that.

---

[39] Treas. Reg. § 1.509(a)-4(c)(1).

[40] Treas. Reg. § 1.509(a)-4(i)(1).

[41] Treas. Reg. § 1.509(a)-4(i)(2)(ii).

[42] Treas. Reg. § 1.509(a)-4(i)(2)(iii).

[5] Integral Part Test

The foundation must constitute an integral part of a beneficiary's activities.[43] This test may be met in one of two ways.

[a] "But For" Test

The "but for" test is met if the support organization's activities perform the functions of, or carry out the purposes of, the beneficiary organization, and but for the performance of these activities by the support organization, the beneficiary would normally perform these activities.[44] This test will usually not be met by a grantmaking organization.

[b] "Sufficiency" Test

[i] Income payout requirement. To meet the "sufficiency" test's income payout requirement, the support organization must pay out substantially all of its income to the beneficiaries each year.[45] The payout of 85 percent of income has been construed to meet the "substantially all" requirement.[46] The organization has at least until the end of the year following the year in which the income is earned to complete making its payments to the beneficiaries.[47] In addition, a support organization may use large distributions from the prior five years to reduce current required distributions.[48] A substantial amount of the total support provided by the support organization must go to the charitable beneficiaries who satisfy the "attentiveness" requirement described below.[49] The IRS has concluded that a "substantial amount" means at least 33 1/3 percent.[50]

[ii] "Attentiveness" requirement. The amount of support received by one or more of the beneficiary organizations must be sufficient to insure the attentiveness of these organizations to the operations of the support organization.[51] This requirement may be satisfied in one of three ways.

---

[43] Treas. Reg. § 1.509(a)-4(i)(3).

[44] Treas. Reg. § 1.509(a)-4(i)(3)(ii).

[45] Treas. Reg. § 1.509(a)-4(i)(3)(iii)(a).

[46] See Treas. Reg. § 53.4942(b)-1(c); Rev. Rul. 76-208, 1976-1 CB 161; Priv. Ltr. Rul. 9021060 (Feb. 28, 1990).

[47] Priv. Ltr. Rul. 9021060 (Feb. 28, 1990); GCM 36,523 (Dec. 18, 1975).

[48] Priv. Ltr. Rul. 9021060 (Feb. 28, 1990).

[49] Treas. Reg. § 1.509(a)-4(i)(3)(iii)(a).

[50] GCM 36,326 (June 30, 1975).

[51] Treas. Reg. § 1.509(a)-4(i)(3)(iii)(a).

Large grants test. The grants to the beneficiary are large enough to cause the beneficiary to be attentive. If payments are made to a particular department or school of a university, hospital or church, the payments need only be large enough to insure that such department or school will be attentive, rather than the entire institution.[52] The "large grants" test can be met by either of two means:

- The grants constitute a substantial percentage of the beneficiary's total support. The IRS has taken the position that less than 10 percent of the beneficiary's support is not generally considered enough to satisfy this test.[53] (This does not mean that 10 percent is enough — just that less than 10 percent is not enough.)

- The grants are large enough in absolute dollars to cause the beneficiary to be attentive. The IRS has taken the position that $200,000-$400,000 per year was a large enough dollar amount to cause a beneficiary to be attentive, even though that amount constituted less than 10 percent of the beneficiary's total support.[54]

"Particular activity" test. The support organization will satisfy the attentiveness requirement if it funds a particular substantial function or activity of the beneficiary, and this activity would not be funded, or would be interrupted, without the support organization's support.[55] For example, a support organization would likely satisfy the attentiveness requirement if it funded a chair at a university, or a series of concerts by a symphony.

Evidence of attentiveness. Actual evidence of attentiveness may allow the support organization to satisfy the attentiveness requirement, even if the tests set out above are not met.[56] For example, one factor indicating evidence of attentiveness would exist if the beneficiary requires the support organization to furnish it annual reports of the support organization's investment performance and assets, as well as information indicating that it has not engaged in actions which would constitute self-dealing, excess business holdings, jeopardizing investments, or taxable expenditures if the support organization were a private foundation.[57]

---

[52] Treas. Reg. § 1.509(a)-4(i)(3)(iii)(a).

[53] GCM 36379 (Aug. 15, 1975).

[54] GCM 36379 (Aug. 15, 1975).

[55] Treas. Reg. § 1.509(a)-4(i)(3)(iii)(b).

[56] Treas. Reg. § 1.509(a)-4(i)(3)(iii)(d).

[57] Treas. Reg. § 1.509(a)-4(i)(3)(iii)(d).

[6] Independent Control Requirement

A support organization cannot be controlled by persons who would be disqualified persons if the entity were a private foundation, other than foundation managers acting in their capacity as such.[58]

[a] What is Control?

The test refers to factual control, rather than a simple percentage interest test, and includes the power to veto any substantial transaction.[59]

> EXAMPLE: Son of founder is one of three directors. The other two directors are not disqualified persons. The articles require a unanimous vote of all directors for foundation actions. Foundation is controlled by son for these purposes, because he can prevent the foundation from acting on any issue.

> EXAMPLE: Same facts as above, except that the majority rules. Son is the only class A director, and no action can be taken without the approval of a majority of the class A directors. Son controls the foundation for these purposes.

[b] Employees of Disqualified Person

The IRS has taken the position that employees of a disqualified person may be considered disqualified persons for purposes of determining whether the support organization is controlled by disqualified persons, even though Section 4946 does not define them as disqualified persons.[60]

> EXAMPLE: Board of foundation consists of three members of donor's family and four of donor's employees. The employees are not included in the statutory definition of disqualified persons. The IRS would take the position that disqualified persons control this foundation.

[c] Outside Directors

A typical way to structure a support organization is to include three classes of directors—disqualified persons, friendly outsiders, and beneficiaries. No class, by itself, has control, but any two classes together can control. For the reasons discussed above, the disqualified person class cannot, by itself, have control or veto power.

> EXAMPLE: Foundation has three disqualified person directors, four out-

---

[58] Treas. Reg. § 1.509(a)-4(j)(1).

[59] Treas. Reg. § 1.509(a)-4(j)(1).

[60] Rev. Rul. 80-207, 1980-2 CB 193.

side directors, and three beneficiary directors. Majority rule governs. Foundation is not controlled by disqualified persons, in the absence of additional facts that would indicate otherwise.

EXAMPLE: Same facts, except the entity is a trust, and there are no beneficiary trustees. Trust is not controlled by disqualified persons, absent other facts.

[7] Pros and Cons of Support Organizations

[a] Pros

A support organization is not affected by the private foundation rules. Subject to the rules applicable to any exempt charitable organization, it can hold business interests, it can enter into transactions with related parties at fair market value, and it is exempt from any investment income tax.

[b] Cons

Control by disqualified persons is surrendered. Beneficiaries must be named (in an "operated in connection with" structure), have enforceable rights (as a group), and be involved with the foundation.

¶ 38.05 FORM OF ENTITY—TRUST OR CORPORATION

Whether a private foundation or a public charity is used, it must be decided whether to structure the entity as a trust or a corporation. Here is a comparison chart.

Trust	Corporation
• Cannot be easily changed (although certain amendments to trust instrument without court approval may be allowed to meet charitable or tax requirements).	• Can be easily changed by a vote of the directors; supermajorities may be allowed in certain instances.
• UBTI taxed at trust rates.	• UBTI taxed at corporate rates.
• Standard of conduct for trustees—generally, a "prudent person" rule, etc., although (subject to public policy considerations) standards may be changed in the trust instrument.	• Standard of conduct for directors—generally, reasonable business judgment.
• Beneficiary involvement in governance not required for a Section 509(a)(3) "operated in connection with" organization.	• Beneficiary involvement in governance required for a Section 509(a)(3) "operated in connection with" organization.

- Trust is accountable to court and beneficiaries.

- Corporation not required to formally account to court or beneficiaries; although it may be wise to report to the beneficiaries, if relying on the "evidence of attentiveness" test.

¶ 38.06   COMMUNITY FOUNDATION

A donor's alternative to any of the above is to make a gift to a "community foundation," typically in an "advise and consult" fund. A community foundation[61] is a public charity. If a donor makes a gift to an advise and consult fund within the community foundation, the community foundation will consult with the donor or his designee and consider his advice as to what distributions are appropriate, and to what distributees. The community foundation must retain the decision-making power, but there is a practical incentive for the community foundation to cooperate with legally proper suggestions made by the donor.

In certain circumstances, a gift to a community foundation will not be considered a completed gift. Regulation § 1.507-1(a) contains the rules on whether a completed gift has been made. It provides that a gift will be complete if the donor cannot impose any material restrictions or conditions that prevent the charity from freely and effectively employing the donated assets, or the income therefrom, in furtherance of its exempt purposes. Restrictions requiring retention of the property may be okay if they relate to the charity's exempt purpose (e.g., use of real property as a park).[62] The community foundation usually charges a fee for its services, which may go into its general operating fund, its unrestricted grant pool, or both.

The principal advantages of making a gift to a community foundation are that compliance with private foundation requirements is not necessary and the community foundation will administer the fund, relieving the donor of the trouble. The principal disadvantage is that the donor must surrender absolute control.

---

[61] Organized under IRC § 170(b)(1)(A)(vi) and Treas. Reg. § 1.170A-9(e)(10).

[62] A good source material on the technicalities is Stanley S. Weithorn, "Planning Considerations for Charitable Remainder and Lead Trusts," ALI-ABA Course of Study, Planning Techniques for Large Estates (1993).

¶ 38.07 INTERMEDIATE SANCTIONS

Section 4958 imposes sanctions (short of revocation of an exemption) for transactions resulting in private inurement. The IRS, in Notice 96-46,[63] summarizes some of its provisions.

---

[63] 1996-39 IRB 9.

Planning For Marriage and Other Family Arrangements

CHAPTER 39

Marital Property Agreements

¶ 39.01 INTRODUCTION

Marital property agreements can be entered into before marriage (prenuptial agreements) or after marriage (postnuptial agreements).

It is common for people entering into a marriage to sign a prenuptial agreement if one or both of the spouses have (or expect to have) a large estate, or if either or both spouses have children from a prior marriage. Postnuptial agreements are also done occasionally, for one reason or another.

Marital property agreements can accomplish a number of goals—

- They can provide for the ownership and management of property during the marriage.

- They can provide for the division of property on the termination of the marriage by death or divorce.[1]
- They can permit the spouses to decide between themselves which spouse will bear what debts.
- By addressing who owns the marital property, marital property agreements can provide asset protection and reduce taxes.

Marital property agreements are sometimes lengthy and are often filled with technical provisions addressing these and other points. But, by and large, marital property agreements exist to determine the division of property when the marriage terminates, which it inevitably will—by divorce or on the death of a spouse.

The requirements of marital property agreements are governed by state law, which is far from uniform.[2] However, certain common threads run through the state law patterns, so we can discuss and analyze the generally applicable rules, with the caveat that applicable state law must always be examined.

A detailed exposition of the law of marital property agreements is far beyond the scope of this chapter. However, we will deal with a few matters which have a special impact on estate planning.

¶ 39.02 VALIDITY OF THE MARITAL PROPERTY AGREEMENT

[1] Legal Representation of Both Parties

To be valid, a marital property agreement must be entered into voluntarily, with full disclosure of the facts or, in some states, with a voluntary waiver of full disclosure.[3] Such disclosure is necessary because in most marital property agreements, one or both parties will waive certain marital rights; otherwise, this type of agreement would not be necessary.

It is generally thought that a person must know what her marital rights are before she can voluntarily waive them. This usually means that each party must be represented by separate counsel. One lawyer should not represent both parties, and two lawyers in the same law firm should not represent the parties.

---

[1] "Divorce," in this chapter, includes annulment or other legal dissolution of the marriage.

[2] Approximately one-half of the states have adopted some version of the Unif. Premarital Agreement Act, 9B ULA 369 (1983) (UPAA). A few states have adopted the Unif. Marital Prop. Act, 9A ULA 97 (1983).

[3] UPAA § 6.

[2] Complete Disclosure of Financial Assets and Liabilities

Each party should fully disclose his property and financial obligations to avoid a claim of unenforceability later.[4] If state law requires, the parties may need to disclose their expectancies (e.g., contingent future interests in property) as well.

> **EXAMPLE:** Bride and Groom execute a prenuptial agreement. Bride does not list a trust of which she is the beneficiary. When Bride and Groom divorce, Groom comes in and says that if he had known Aunt Tillie had set up a trust for Bride, he would never have signed the agreement. Groom may be able to invalidate the agreement, or seek other remedies under state law.

Alternatively, some states allow either or both prospective spouses to waive disclosure, as long as the waiver is voluntary.[5] If the couple elects this avenue, it may be advisable to have the waiver contain a provision advising the waiving party of her right to disclosure of the other's property, and affirming that her waiver of such right is voluntary.

[3] Unconscionability

A party may be able to overturn a seemingly valid marital property agreement if (1) the agreement was unconscionable when it was entered into and (2) there was no disclosure or voluntary waiver of disclosure and no knowledge of the other party's property and financial obligations.[6] Unconscionability alone may be sufficient to overturn the agreement in some states. However, what is unconscionable is a difficult question to answer. Like beauty, the notion of unconscionability may vary with the beholder. Nevertheless, under the Uniform Premarital Agreement Act, unconscionability is determined as a matter of law.[7]

QUERY: Wealthy man marries bride with no assets. The marital agreement provides that if they divorce within the first five years, bride gets nothing. She voluntarily executes the agreement. Is that unconscionable?

[4] Special Property Rights

Depending on the law of the state involved, there may be certain property rights that must be specifically and specially waived or which cannot be

---

[4] UPAA § 6.

[5] UPAA § 6(a)(2)(ii).

[6] UPAA § 6(a)(2).

[7] UPAA § 6(c).

waived at all. For example, waiver of a surviving spouse's homestead right or a spouse's right to spousal support may require specific language, bold print, etc., to be enforceable. And, in certain states, alimony cannot be waived or limited in advance. Furthermore, under the Uniform Premarital Agreement Act, a court may order one spouse to provide spousal support notwithstanding contrary provisions in the agreement where the absence of such support would render the other spouse eligible for public assistance.[8] Last, child support cannot generally be waived or limited in a marital property agreement.[9]

[5] Multi-Jurisdictional Aspects and Change of Domicile

In preparing the marital property agreement, one must remember that the laws of another jurisdiction may be used to interpret it. For example, disclosure of assets may not be necessary in state A in order to make a prenuptial agreement enforceable. If the couple moves to state B, and one spouse dies there, the surviving spouse or children of the deceased spouse may sue for enforcement of the agreement in state B. If state B's law requires disclosure for enforcement of a prenuptial agreement, the agreement may not be enforceable in state B.

QUESTION: *What if the couple provides in the first instance that the law of state A will apply to the agreement?*

ANSWER: State B will usually respect this, except as to matters which are contradictory to its public policy. The drafter of a conflict-of-laws clause might also want to indicate that the law of state A applies, where possible, *without regard to its conflict-of-laws principles*, so that the application of state A conflicts law does not apply to provide that state B's law governs the interpretation of the agreement for a couple whose marital domicile is in state B.

To be respected, a marital agreement must be valid in the state whose law applies. Suppose bride and groom have residences in various states and countries. In such instance, it may be appropriate to get an affidavit from both the bride and the groom concerning their individual domiciles, to be sure that the agreement would be effective under the law of each of their domiciles as well as the marital domicile. Additionally, where the agreement concerns real property, the law of the situs (i.e., the place where the property is physically located) will, in general, ordinarily govern the validity of the agreement to the extent it concerns such real property. The law of the situs can also apply to any property (real or personal) located in a foreign jurisdiction.

---

[8] UPAA § 6(b).

[9] UPAA § 3(b).

The formal requirements, as well as the limits and capabilities of marital property agreements, vary considerably from state to state. Therefore, if there is significant real property in another state, it is wise to retain local counsel to review the agreement.

If a foreign (non-U.S.) jurisdiction is under consideration as a place of residence for the bride and groom or is the location where property covered by the agreement is or will be located, anything could happen. The U.S. Constitution will not limit the foreign jurisdiction to applying its laws only to real property within its limits or only to its own domiciliaries. The foreign jurisdiction may apply its own law to any property located within its borders, and may try to apply its law to other property of its residents or domiciliaries. On the other hand, a foreign judgment is not necessarily entitled to enforcement in the United States, as foreign jurisdictions are not protected by the United States Constitution's full faith and credit clause.[10] Accordingly, the judgment of a court in the foreign jurisdiction may be meaningless with respect to persons or property not found within its borders. The bottom line—a local attorney should be retained if it is important to have an agreement which is enforceable in a particular jurisdiction.

Finally, there is some planning potential in this area. A particular couple's set of facts may justify or require a choice of a particular marital domicile. For example, in Texas, separate property cannot be awarded to the nonowner spouse on divorce, court-ordered (as opposed to contractual) alimony is extremely limited, and spouses can agree either before or after marriage that no community property exists. Various rights of reimbursement may exist, but may be waived in a valid marital property agreement. Thus, for at least one of the parties, placing the marital domicile in such a state may be a desirable proposition.

[6] Agreement Signed Under Duress

The marital property agreement will not be enforceable if either person signed it under duress. What is duress? The classic textbook example involves a person signing a document with a gun to her head. Needless to say, the use of firearms as a negotiating tool is not advisable. However, different courts have held that certain factual configurations, short of threats or physical force, constituted duress in a prenuptial agreement situation. For example, in one case, a bride was about to walk down the aisle, when she was handed a prenuptial agreement which she had never seen before and told that she had to sign it as a condition of the marriage. She did, but a court later held that she signed under duress, and did not enforce the agreement.[11]

---

[10] Art. IV § 1.

[11] E.g., Lutgert v. Lutgert, 338 So. 2d 1111 (Fla. Ct. App. 1976); but see, e.g., Williams v. Williams, 720 SW2d 246 (Tex. App.—Houston (14th Dist.) 1986, no writ);

Most estate planners will not encounter many instances that extreme. However, it is best for the agreement to be executed while the wedding is still some distance away, so that there would be no undue humiliation to either prospective spouse if the wedding did not take place, and so that there is time to conduct the negotiations in a businesslike manner.

[7] Inclusion of Personal Matters

Some marital agreements go into such matters as the number of children the couple will have, who will do which household chores, how often the couple will engage in marital relations, etc. While these agreements may be good exercises in getting both parties' expectations out on the table, they are not specifically enforceable by a court, nor are damages probably recoverable for their breach. If the agreement must be filed in the public records, or exhibited in a judicial proceeding, it could cause the couple considerable embarrassment.

PRACTICE POINTER: If the couple wants to agree to items such as these, which are not legally enforceable, consider doing a side agreement, and having the primary document contain only the legal provisions.

[8] Property Division on Death or Divorce

The agreement may provide for disposition of property on death of a spouse, as well as on divorce. These two situations may well call for different dispositions.

¶ 39.03 PARTICULAR PROVISIONS IN THE MARITAL AGREEMENT

[1] Rights to Employee Benefits

Under some qualified plans, the surviving spouse has federally mandated rights.[12] For example, she may be entitled to a lifetime annuity if her husband dies before or after retiring, unless she consents in a specified fashion to a different disposition. So far, the courts have held that a person cannot waive his/her mandatory rights in the plan in a premarital agreement that does not

---

Howell v. Landry, 386 SE2d 610 (NC App. 1989) (enforcing agreements executed at eleventh hour).

[12] See Ch. 14 on employee benefits for a discussion.

itself qualify as a valid waiver under federal law.[13] Among other requirements, this means that the waiver must be signed during the applicable federal period. In order to waive the mandatory pre-retirement benefits, the participant (not the spouse) must be at least 35 years old, and the waiver must be signed during the couple's marriage. In order to waive a post-retirement annuity, the waiver cannot be signed until 90 days before the participant actually retires, even if the nonparticipant spouse has already waived a pre-retirement benefit. In either case, the waiver must be notarized and delivered to the plan administrator during the applicable time period.

What about an agreement that the employee's spouse will sign the waiver? The courts have held that prenuptial agreements providing that the spouse will execute the waiver are unenforceable with respect to the plan.[14] All of these cases hold that the plan administrator cannot recognize a consent that does not accord with statutory requirements, and that, if there is no consent, the administrator must pay the benefit in accordance with federal law, without regard to any agreement between the employee and the employee's spouse.

This may, however, leave open the possibility that the agreements are enforceable as a matter of state law—that is, the agreement may make the breaching spouse liable in damages under state law if she takes the mandatory federal benefit in violation of the agreement.

PRACTICE POINTER: One solution might be to provide in the agreement that if the non-employee spouse does not execute the waiver, the non-employee spouse must give up a dollar-for-dollar amount of other assets (or all of the other assets, or any other amount) the spouse would otherwise be entitled to get under the marital property agreement. This will put the non-employee spouse to an election as to whether he or she takes the benefits or other property. There is no authority on this type of agreement.

[2] Payment of Taxes

An important clause in the marital agreement might deal with how the couple is going to allocate payment of taxes between themselves.

---

[13] Ablamis v. Roper, 927 F2d 1450 (9th Cir. 1991); Fox Valley v. Brown, 897 F2d 275 (7th Cir. 1990); Hurwitz v. Shier, 789 F. Supp. 134 (SDNY 1992).

[14] E.g., Hurwitz v. Sher, 982 F2d 778 (2d Cir. 1992); Nellis v. Boeing Co., 15 EBC 1651 (D. Kan. 1992); Callahan v. Hutsell, Callahan & Buchine, P.S.C., 813 F. Supp. 541 (WD Ken. 1992), vacated on other grounds, 14 F3d 600 (6th Cir. 1993); but see In re Marriage of Rahn, 914 P2d 463 (Colo. 1995), cert. denied, 95 S. Ct. 684 (1996) (holding waiver of interest in qualified plan pursuant to prenuptial agreement enforceable in proceeding to dissolve marriage).

[a] Transfer Taxes

In general, each spouse will usually bear the transfer tax consequences of his/her own gifts. However, if Wife chooses to treat Husband's gifts as her own, pursuant to a gift-splitting election, the actual donor spouse, Husband, should probably bear the burden of the transfer taxes on Wife's deemed gift as between them. (Under federal law, each will be jointly and severally liable to the IRS for gift tax for all gifts made by either of them during the year.)[15]

[b] Income Taxes

Income taxes are a different matter. Determining whose income results in what taxes is complicated, due to the graduated rate system. If each spouse files a separate return, no issues should arise. However, if they file joint returns, a formula will be necessary to determine who owes what part of the tax. An endless variety of formulas exist. Here are a few that are commonly used:

- Wife pays tax at the highest marginal rate, as if her income were the last dollars the couple earned.
- Wife pays tax at the lowest marginal rate, as if her income were the first dollars the couple earned.
- The parties each compute their income tax as if they were single. Then Wife applies the following formula to determine her portion of the tax: the percentage of actual tax due which reflects Wife's separate tax divided by the sum of Husband's and Wife's separate taxes.
- The parties each compute their income tax as if they were single. Then Wife applies the following formula to determine her portion of the tax: the percentage of actual tax due which reflects Wife's taxable income as separately determined divided by the sum of Husband's and Wife's separate taxable incomes as individually determined.

The formulaic determinations can get very complicated where one spouse has an overall loss for the year and the other spouse has taxable income. The situation gets even more complex if these losses would have been suspended in the separate return of the spouse with the losses, remaining available for later use against that spouse's future separate income.

Of course, the parties could also agree to file only separate tax returns, although there can be tax disadvantages to this.

---

[15] IRC § 2513(d).

[c] Property Taxes

Division of property taxes is generally pretty straightforward. Usually, each spouse pays taxes on his/her own property, and they share taxes on joint property in proportion to their ownership interests.

[3] Debts

Marital property agreements frequently address debts. They may provide, for example, that the household expenses are shared equally, and that all other debts will be paid by the party incurring them. Or, the wife may agree to support the household and the husband, but may want any investments the husband makes or debts he incurs which are unrelated to support to be his own affair.

Spousal agreements as to who will pay the debts may not be effective against creditors.

> EXAMPLE: Agreement provides that each spouse will bear his/her own debts. Wife incurs a debt for groceries. Husband may be liable to the grocery store for that debt even if he knew nothing about it, either because it was a community debt or because it was for "necessaries." In such a case, the marital agreement can provide that as between themselves, Wife will pay, and if she does not, she will reimburse Husband if he has to pay.

[4] Privacy Concerns

If the agreement includes a schedule of exhibits listing the value of property and financial obligations, it may be worthwhile at the signing to execute copies with either blank schedules or with the values omitted. That way, if it is necessary to file or record the document for reasons other than litigating the validity of the document itself, the couple's financial privacy will be maintained to the maximum extent possible.

Many people are very private about the contents of their marital agreements, and even about the fact that they have such an agreement. This can sometimes be a problem, for example, when they are counting on the fact that the wife's ownership of property will keep it away from the husband's creditors. Sometimes, a creditor must have notice of a marital property agreement in order for it to be enforceable with respect to the creditor. In such instances, there is a conflict between the two goals of privacy and asset protection. In some states, filing the agreement in the deed records or other appropriate place will ordinarily serve as notice. In other states, a memorandum of agreement simply stating that a marital agreement exists may suffice.

[5] Provisions for Division of Property on Death

Sometimes, one sees an agreement that husband will leave, say, one-half of his estate to the wife. One needs to be careful about that kind of language. If "estate" is interpreted to mean the husband's probate estate, the agreement will not cover nonprobate assets or pre-death transfers.

For example, suppose the marital agreement provides that the wife will leave a certain amount or a certain percentage of her estate to the husband upon her death. Consider whether pre-death transfers or the rearrangement of assets in nonprobate form could render such a provision empty. In such a case, fraudulent conveyance laws might apply, but it would be best for the husband not to have to depend on that. It may be possible to minimize this problem by drafting—for example, by defining "estate" to include other types of property over which the wife has control and, perhaps, to cover gifts made within a certain period of her death.

Some drafters provide that one spouse's gifts to the other spouse will be considered an advancement against the donee-spouse's testamentary share of the donor spouse's estate. Although the concept sounds reasonable enough, it can be an emotionally difficult provision if the bride contemplates that with every birthday, anniversary, Valentine's Day, or other lifetime gift she receives from her husband, a debit is being entered somewhere reducing her testamentary share of her husband's estate. Sometimes, it is easier and better not to include such a provision and to rely on the donor-spouse to be cognizant that when a gift is made, the gift will be in addition to the donee-spouse's ultimate interest in the donor spouse's estate, probate or otherwise.

[6] Termination of Equitable Rights

In some states, equitable property rights between spouses exist. Such rights may include a right of reimbursement for (a) expenditures made by one spouse which benefit the other spouse's property or (b) expenditures made by the couple together which benefit only one of the spouses. Such rights may or may not be waivable in a particular state. If they can be waived, it is not at all certain that they should be. These issues require thought in each agreement.

[7] Community or Separate Property Characterization

An agreement that characterizes property as separate or community will have estate, as well as divorce, implications.

CHAPTER **40**

Special Issues for Blended Families

¶ 40.01 INTRODUCTION

In a second[1] marriage, if one or both spouses have children from a previous marriage, a number of significant issues exist. For illustration purposes, throughout this chapter, we'll use the following Example Bunch.

---

[1] For purposes of this chapter, the "second" marriage means any marriage following a previous marriage resulting in children (the "first marriage").

GLOBAL EXAMPLE

The Example Bunch. Here's a story of a lovely lady (Stepmom), who was bringing up three very lovely girls. ... Here's a story of a man named Stepdad, who was busy raising three boys of his own. Till one day, when this lady met this fellow, and they knew that it was much more than a hunch—that this group must somehow form a family—and, that's the way they all became the Example Bunch.

Among the foremost estate planning issues faced in a second marriage can be the general tendency to deny reality about the nature of the relationship between the members of the first and second families. The unfortunate truth is that some conflicts between the second wife and the children of the husband's first marriage (and vice versa) are inherent in the nature of their relationship.

Some of these conflicts are financial in nature. Stepdad's monetary resources are likely to be split—during lifetime, as he spends money on Stepmom (and possibly her kids) and his children and, on death, when he provides (or does not provide) for all of them. This diversion of money and other forms of wealth always has the potential to produce tension between Stepmom and the kids.

Other conflicts are emotional in nature. Even if Stepdad's children acknowledge Stepmom's sterling qualities, and are sincerely happy that their father has found a wonderful companion, they may also feel some resentment about someone taking their mother's place, as well as some insecurity about Dad's love for them vis-à-vis the new wife. Stepmom may also find herself competing with Stepdad's children for the time, love, and attention of their father.

These feelings, whether admitted or not, exist to some degree in virtually all blended families. This doesn't mean that anyone involved is a bad person, or is not trying his or her best to contribute to family harmony — these conflicts are just intrinsic aspects of the situation. Consider the Example Bunch. If Stepdad is raising three boys of his own in the same home with the couple, the situation could possibly be somewhat volatile. Add Stepmom's three very lovely girls as residents of the same home, mix in a couple of dissatisfied ex-spouses arriving on the scene periodically, and you have a recipe for a truly nuclear family.

No one really wants to come to terms with the possibility of the foregoing problems, but there are some estate planning advantages in approaching the situation with both eyes open. Conflicts may not surface until after Stepdad or Stepmom dies, but chances are they are there and they will. In any event, it is usually better to assume that they could. Accordingly, the wise planner will try to minimize chances for disagreement.

The following sections discuss some of the blended family estate planning issues and suggestions for their resolution. Throughout, it is supposed that Stepdad's plan is that, after his death, he wants to provide for Stepmom's support during her lifetime, and to have the property which is left after her death go to his own children. Variations on this theme abound, but for simplicity, let's say that's our paradigm.

¶ 40.02 QTIP TRUST

Frequently, the rest of the plan used in first marriages is to leave $600,000 to a bypass trust, and the rest of the estate in trust for the spouse's lifetime, remainder to the children. Is this a good plan in a second marriage? This plan works fine for tax purposes, but potential problems not usually present in first marriages exist.

[1] Disagreements on Investments and Apportionment

If the new spouse is restricted to an income interest, as is frequently the case, room for disagreement exists as to—

- Which receipts are considered income and which are considered principal under state law and the trust instrument;
- Which expenses are chargeable to income and which to principal; and
- How much of the trust assets should be invested in income-producing assets and how much in growth-producing assets.

These decisions involve that classic conflict-producer, the zero-sum situation—a dollar more income for Stepmom is a dollar less principal for Stepdad's kids. State law often does not provide a clear answer to the questions that arise, and trustee discretion is often involved.

If the trust is a QTIP or general power of appointment trust, the spouse must have the power to require the trustee to invest in assets which are productive of income.[2] It is not always clear how much income must be earned in order for the trust to be considered "productive of income." The closest laws that some states have on this point are statutory provisions addressing the allocation to income of proceeds from the sale of unproductive trust property. Such a statutory provision might say, for example, that, if a trustee is permitted to hold unproductive property, and the property has not produced at least a one percent return annually, then, on the eventual sale of the

---

[2] Treas. Reg. §§ 20.2056(b)-5(f)(4), 20.2056(b)-7(d)(2), 20.2056(b)-7(h), example 2.

property, an amount equal to a four percent return per year is allocated to the income beneficiary.[3] The trust instrument can and, in some cases, should be specific about this. For example, Stepdad could provide that Stepmom receives, annually, the greater of the income of the trust or (1) an amount giving her a total cumulative annual return of eight percent, (2) a dollar amount, adjusted by the consumer price index (CPI), or (3) any other appropriate amount.

Take the Example Bunch. If Stepmom is close in age to (or even younger than) Stepdad's children, and the estate plan makes the children wait until Stepmom dies before they get anything, they may in fact never receive anything or only receive their inheritance when they are themselves elderly. Of course, this is Stepdad's decision, and if this is what he wants, so be it. However, for the estate planner, this is a consideration that does not apply in first marriages, and it should be pointed out to Stepdad or Stepmom when planning wealth transfers in the context of a second marriage.

It may be a good idea, if possible, for Stepdad to leave his children their intended share of his assets outright or in a trust of which Stepmom is not a beneficiary, and leave other property (e.g., life insurance or employee benefits) directly to Stepmom (and vice versa, at Stepmom's death). This will result in estate tax at the first death, at least if the value of the estate passing to the children exceeds the unified credit, but will not create the problems inherent in joint interests. Alternatively, an irrevocable life insurance trust for the children would get them some money independent of Stepmom's or Stepdad's age and situation, without causing transfer tax problems.

There may be assets, however, which are not practical to leave to one group absolutely. An expensive house is an example.

What about leaving Stepdad's house outright to Stepmom? This disposition is simple and will qualify for the marital deduction. However, anything that goes outright to Stepmom is likely to end up in her children's hands on her death, rather than going to Stepdad's children. Stepdad may be perfectly happy to be generous to his wife, even at his children's expense, but he may not feel the same generosity when the question of ownership and use is between Stepmom's children vis-à-vis his.

One alternative might be to grant Stepmom (assumed to be the surviving spouse) use of the house for life, with fee ownership after her death passing to Stepdad's children. Most people (including,hopefully, Stepdad's kids) would think it "natural" to provide for the spouse's housing. And, unlike the situation which exists in the case of a pool of assets, there is no avenue for disagreement about what is income and principal or about what investments should be made. Nevertheless, since there is opportunity for disagreement concerning the payment of expenses relating to the house, it should be made clear (before Stepdad dies) what expenses are to be borne by whom. In absence

---

[3] E.g., Tex. Prop. Code Ann. § 113.110 (1990).

of some provision to the contrary, state law might provide that the spouse pays property taxes, insurance, and maintenance, and the children are liable for major repairs. Stepdad should also make clear who has the power to sell the house, and who gets the sales proceeds if the house is sold. Under the ordinary rules applicable to life estates, neither Stepmom nor Stepdad's kids could sell the entire house without the other's consent. And, if the kids are not all adults or if they don't have vested remainders, a court proceeding will usually be required to get the applicable consents on the kids' behalf. Putting the house in trust, with some extra money, would solve these problems, but can cause lack of eligibility for treatment under Sections 1034 and 121 on sale of the house.

WARNING: In the case of something like a qualified personal residence trust, where Stepmom may eventually have to pay rent to Stepdad's children, the amount of rent (or even Stepmom's continued occupancy of the house) can be a subject of dispute among the parties.

[2] Who Pays Estate Tax on QTIP Assets?

Another issue involved in using a QTIP trust in the context of a second marriage is the payment of estate tax on the QTIP assets.

Let's say Stepdad and Stepmom have a community property estate. The idea is that, on the death of the first spouse to die, the other spouse will have the income from the total community estate for life. On the surviving spouse's death, one-half of the total property remaining in both estates will pass one-half to Stepdad's children and one-half to Stepmom's children.

Scenario: Suppose Stepdad dies first, leaving his one-half of the community property to the QTIP trust. Then Stepmom dies. Some possible common estate plans will have outcomes as follows—

QTIP assets pass to Stepdad's children and Stepmom leaves her estate to her children by her will. Yes, the QTIP assets pass to Stepdad's children. However, the QTIP trust is included in Stepmom's gross estate. The tax payable by the QTIP trust is computed at the marginal rate on Stepmom's estate.[4] That is, the QTIP trust will bear the total estate tax payable by Stepmom's estate, less the total estate tax that would have been payable had the QTIP trust not been included in her estate. Other things being equal, this formula will result in more property going to Stepmom's children than to Stepdad's children. Additionally, if principal of the QTIP can be invaded for Stepmom's benefit, she has the opportunity during her lifetime to use part of the QTIP property, thus resulting in unequal amounts going to the different sets of children.

---

[4] IRC § 2207A(a)(1).

The QTIP trust will pass equally to all six children after Stepmom's death, and Stepmom is supposed to leave all of her remaining assets at her death equally to the six children. The problem here is that, after Stepdad dies, Stepmom is free to change her will and leave all of her property to her children, resulting in her children getting three-fourths of the total property, and Stepdad's children getting only one-fourth. Or, she might, in addition, use the QTIP property first for her own benefit, if the trust allows, so that Stepdad's children get even less of the total estate.

Both Stepdad's and Stepmom's entire estates are put into a joint revocable trust. During the lifetime of both spouses, either one can revoke it, in which case, each spouse gets his/her respective property back. At the death of the first spouse, it becomes irrevocable. The trust is then split into two trusts—one containing Stepmom's half of the property and the other containing Stepdad's. She has a power of appointment over her trust, so that she does not make a current gift of her half. The power of appointment consists of the right to vary each child's share by appointing it to the child himself or the child's descendants; she cannot vary the total amount received by each child's family group. During her remaining life, Stepmom receives income from both trusts, and perhaps discretionary distributions of principal. Discretionary distributions must be made pro rata from her trust and Stepdad's trust. On her death, the taxes from the QTIP trust and from her trust (which is included in her estate pursuant to Section 2036) are paid pro rata from each trust, and the remainder is left to all of the children or, in the case of her trust, to such members of each child's family group as she may have appointed. This plan will not sweep in money that Stepmom receives from independent sources after Stepdad's death, but it does take care of problems in the two above scenarios.

¶ 40.03 EMPLOYEE BENEFITS

If employee benefits exist, and a penalty tax under Section 4980A will be payable, the tax apportionment clause in the will should be carefully considered.[5]

Similarly, in some qualified plans, the participant spouse cannot deprive the nonparticipant spouse of an interest in the plan benefits without the nonparticipant's consent, which she or he may not choose to give when the time comes.[6] If this is the case, the nonparticipant may receive a certain amount of this property, regardless of the division of other property. That should be kept in mind in dividing the total pie.

---

[5] See Ch. 14 on employee benefits for a discussion of the penalty tax, and of the apportionment issue in this situation.

[6] See Ch. 14 on employee benefits and Ch. 39 on marital property agreements for a discussion of this.

In some plans, the employee spouse can effectively deprive the other spouse of these statutory rights by taking a lump sum distribution at retirement. Whether or not the employee spouse rolls it over, the non-employee spouse has no future rights in the money. Spousal consent in such plans is only required for distributions on death—not for lifetime distributions. This only applies to plans which do not require a qualified joint and survivor annuity or qualified pre-retirement survivor annuity on retirement or death.

Any rollover to an IRA will result in the spouse's federal rights in the plan, if any existed, to be lost.

¶ 40.04 STATUTORY SPOUSAL INTERESTS

The surviving spouse in most states will have certain enforceable rights in the deceased spouse's estate (for example, the right to elect a statutory share of the deceased spouse's property, or the right to live in the homestead). Hence, it is usually not possible to leave Stepmom less than a certain amount, absent a marital property agreement or other enforceable waiver of her rights. Attempts may be made to give away property during Stepdad's or Stepmom's lifetime or to put property in certain nonprobate forms in order to avoid the elective share. These techniques may have varying success, depending on the state involved. In some states, the elective share applies to certain nonprobate assets as well as probate assets and, in some states, transfers within a certain time before death are considered part of the marital estate for that purpose. A marital property agreement may be effective in waiving some or all of these rights.

¶ 40.05 ALIMONY

Alimony paid during the lifetime of the payor is taxable income to the payee,[7] and deductible by the payor,[8] if the couple structured it that way. The estate planner for a divorced person should check to see what, if any, obligation the divorce decree and property settlement agreement impose on the person's estate. For example, if Stepdad dies, the alimony obligation imposed under the divorce decree dissolving his first marriage may still remain an obligation of his estate. If so, it will be deductible for estate tax purposes as a claim against the estate if the promise or agreement underlying the alimony obligation was incurred for adequate consideration[9] or if the alimony obligation was decreed by a court with authority to impose the obligation without regard to the

---

[7] IRC § 71(a).

[8] IRC § 215(a).

[9] IRC § 2053(c)(1)(A).

agreement of the parties.[10] If the obligation was not imposed by court decree, but by a written settlement agreement relative to their marital or property rights, adequate consideration is deemed if the couple divorces within the three-year period beginning one year before the settlement agreement was executed.[11]

¶ 40.06 CHILD SUPPORT

Child support is usually not an obligation which is imposed by state law on the parent's estate, as the obligation to provide support for one's children normally ends at death. However, it is common for a divorcing couple to agree that child support payments will constitute obligations of a deceased payor's estate. Child support is not deductible for income tax purposes.[12] It may be deductible for estate tax purposes, subject to the analysis described above for alimony.

¶ 40.07 REQUIRED BEQUESTS

It is quite usual to have a provision in the divorce documents that requires the ex-husband (for example, Stepdad) to leave a certain amount of money or property to the children of the former marriage and/or to the former wife. For estates of decedents dying after July 18, 1984, if such a transfer of property would be considered a transfer for full consideration for purposes of the gift tax, it will also be free of estate tax.[13]

¶ 40.08 TAX APPORTIONMENT CLAUSES

If Stepdad is leaving property to both Stepmom and the children of the first marriage, he will need a fine-tuned clause apportioning expenses and taxes to the respective beneficiaries. A standard "all to the residue" clause, or the standard clause in the bypass-QTIP plan,[14] may not be appropriate.

---

[10] Harris v. Comm'r, 340 US 106 (1963).

[11] IRC § 2516(1), 2043.

[12] IRC §§ 215(a), 215(b), 71(c).

[13] IRC § 2043(b)(2).

[14] This clause is described in Chs. 4 and 49 on optimizing the tax benefits of married couples.

¶ 40.09 MARITAL PROPERTY AGREEMENT

A marital property agreement will often exist in a second marriage. It should be carefully examined.[15]

¶ 40.10 EXCLUSION OF GAIN ON SALE OF RESIDENCE

Section 121 allows a taxpayer to exclude up to $125,000 from the sale of her personal residence, if she is at least 55 years old on the date of the sale and has used the house as her principal residence for at least three of the five years preceding the sale, or meets other holding and use requirements. The section will not apply if either the taxpayer or her husband has made the election with respect to any other house.[16] Hence, if a couple who are both 55 or over are getting married, and both want to sell their houses, they must both sell before the marriage in order for both to take advantage of the exclusion. Similarly, if Stepdad (for example) has used the exclusion before, or was previously married to a wife who used it during the marriage, Stepmom cannot use the exclusion during the new marriage.[17] If one of the spouses closes the sale during the marriage, the other will be forever barred from using the exclusion.

What if Stepdad dies, the house was Stepdad's property, and Stepmom is over 55 and wants to sell the house and take advantage of the exclusion? If Stepdad met the holding and use requirements at the date of his death, and the house was held with Stepmom as joint tenants, tenants by the entirety, or community property, Stepmom can take advantage of the exclusion, if she is single on the date of sale.[18]

If only one spouse is over 55, the couple can take advantage of Section 121 if the house is held by that spouse, or by both spouses, as tenants in common, joint tenants, or community property.[19]

Section 1034 allows the rollover of gain on sale of a principal residence. Gain will be recognized only to the extent that the purchase price of the new house is less than the net sales price of the old house (i.e., to the extent that the taxpayer has net cash proceeds after the purchase of a new house). If both spouses sell their houses and move into a new residence, each can still roll over the gain from the previous house, except to the extent that the net sales price for his/her old house exceeds his/her contribution to the purchase price of the new house.[20] Basis of the new house is adjusted for unrecognized gain.[21]

---

[15] See Ch. 39 on marital property agreements for a discussion.

[16] IRC § 121(b)(2).

[17] IRC § 121(b)(2).

[18] IRC § 121(d)(2).

[19] IRC § 121(d)(1).

[20] See Rev. Rul. 75-238, 1975-1 CB 257. If one spouse actually pays for more than one-half of the house but the title is taken jointly, the rollover can be lost, if the spouse

EXAMPLE: Stepdad sells his old house for $500,000, which includes a $175,000 gain. Stepmom sells her old house for $400,000, which includes a $100,000 gain. Together, they buy a house that costs $800,000, each contributing $400,000 to the purchase price. Stepdad can exclude his gain, except to the extent that $500,000 (sales price of his old house) exceeds $400,000 (his contribution to the purchase of the new house), or $100,000. So, Stepdad can exclude $75,000 of gain, and Stepmom can exclude her entire $100,000 gain ($400,000 sale price of old home = $400,000 purchase price of new home). Stepdad's basis for his one-half of the new house will be $325,000 ($400,000 cost, less $75,000 excluded gain). Stepmom's basis for her one-half will be $300,000 ($400,000 purchase price less $100,000 excluded gain).

---

is only credited with one-half of the purchase price of the new house. See Snowa v. Comm'r, 1995 RIA TC Memo. ¶ 95,336, 70 TCM (CCH) 163 (1995).

[21] IRC § 1034(e).

CHAPTER 41

Special Issues For Unmarried Couples

¶ 41.01 INTRODUCTION

Today's living arrangements involve many couples, either of the same or opposite gender, who live together in a committed relationship similar to marriage. Many of these couples, for a variety of reasons, either cannot or do not choose to marry. A number of those individuals have wealth and need a special point of view taken in their estate planning.

For illustrative purposes, we will use the case of Morgan and Jody, who live together and are committed to a permanent relationship. Morgan is older than Jody, and is expected to die first.

¶ 41.02 SPECIAL TAX OPPORTUNITIES FOR UNMARRIED COUPLES

There are several tax planning opportunities available to unmarried couples that are not available to married couples. For example, Chapter 14 of the Internal Revenue Code generally does not apply to unrelated parties.[1]

[1] Grantor Retained Income Trusts (GRITs)

One of the old-style techniques in estate planning involved use of the grantor retained income trust (GRIT),[2] which is similar to the new-style qualified personal residence trust. Using this plan, Morgan establishes a trust for Jody, retaining an income interest for Morgan for a term of years. In doing so, Morgan makes a taxable gift of the value of the remainder interest.

> EXAMPLE: Property transferred to GRIT is $1,000,000 in cash. Morgan retains an interest for a term of years that results in the remainder interest being worth $400,000. Morgan, who is in the 55 percent gift tax bracket, pays a gift tax of $220,000 on the gift of the $400,000 remainder interest. The $1,000,000 is invested in growth stocks which pay no dividends. At the end of the term of years, the property is worth $2,000,000. The property passes to Jody tax-free at that time (assuming that Jody is not a skip person for generation-skipping transfer tax purposes with respect to Morgan). The gift tax cost is just over 10 percent of the $2,000,000 Jody ultimately received.

This technique is such a good deal for the taxpayer that it was generally shut down, except for personal residences, by Section 2702, which Congress enacted in 1990.[3] However, Section 2702 only applies to family members.[4] Unrelated parties, such as life companions, are still free to use old-style GRITs.

The use of this technique, however, can have the following catches—

Morgan's death during the term. If Morgan dies before the expiration of the income interest, the entire trust property will be included in Morgan's gross estate. Morgan's estate will, however, get a credit for the $220,000 of gift tax already paid. It is important that a term be chosen which Morgan expects to outlive.

---

[1] See Chs. 26, 27 and 31 for a discussion of chapter 14. But see Treas. Reg. § 25.2703-1(b), discussed in Ch. 27, substituting "natural objects of the taxpayer's bounty," for the statutory langage, "members of the transferor's family."

[2] See Ch. 24 for a discussion of GRITs.

[3] IRC § 2702.

[4] IRC §§ 2702(a), 2702(e).

Lack of income paid to Morgan. The GRIT feature that really packs a punch is the way it can be used to minimize income paid to Morgan, so that Jody ends up with the entire principal, plus most or all of the increase in value during the term. In essence, Morgan gets a gift tax offset for income that she does not actually receive. While GRITs were still permitted in family groups, the IRS had taken the position in some private rulings that: (1) the income interest would only be recognized if the donor had the right to compel the trustee to convert the trust property to income-producing property (à la QTIP trusts) and (2) the donor made an additional gift to the trust in each year in which she did not exercise her conversion right (à la *Dickman*).[5] The amount of the gift was the income that the donor could have gotten if she had exercised her rights. There are many who consider this a questionable proposition, but even supposing it is correct, the state law definition of productive property may include property with a fairly low rate of return. So, if the measure that Morgan could have demanded is, for example, four percent, the GRIT would still be a beneficial planning tool if it earned, including appreciation, more than four percent per year.

Chapter 24 on other actuarial techniques contains a comprehensive discussion of GRITs.

[2] Preferred Freezes

Another technique which was once widely used was the preferred stock freeze. Using this technique, Dad would form or recapitalize a family corporation, taking preferred stock for himself, and giving common stock to the kids. Dad's preferred stock would have a low, noncumulative dividend preference, and the kids would receive all of the growth in excess of the preferred dividend. Dad would retain a liquidation right in order to avoid making a gift on the formation or recapitalization of the company. The kids received all the appreciation in the company free of transfer tax. This technique was effectively shut down with respect to family groups by Section 2701, enacted in 1990.[6] Since Morgan and Jody are not related according to the definition used in Section 2701,[7] they are still free to do preferred freezes under the old rules.

---

[5] Dickman v. Comm'r, 465 US 330 (1984). The IRC § 7520 regulations provide that the actuarial tables can be used to value the income interest if the donor has the right to compel the trustee to invest in trust property which would be income-producing under local law. Treas. Reg. §§ 20.7520-3(b)(3)(v), example 2, 25.7520-3(b)(3)(v), example 2. See Ch. 24 for a further discussion of the *Dickman* issue.

[6] See Ch. 31 on preferred equity interests for a discussion of the rule.

[7] IRC §§ 2701(a)(1), 2701(e)(1).

[3] Buy-Sell Agreements and Unusual Restrictions (Section 2703)

Section 2703[8] provides that, in valuing property, certain buy-sell agreements and restrictions on the right to sell or use such property will be disregarded if such an agreement serves as a testamentary device to transfer property without adequate consideration to the "members of the decedent's family."[9] The regulations have changed this phrase to "natural objects of the person's bounty." The Treasury has declined to further define this term in the regulations, saying that the identity of those people depends on the facts and circumstances.[10] Arguably, a life companion could come within that category. If so, the regulation seems to clearly exceed the limits of the statute.

[4] Restrictions on Liquidation of Family Entities

Section 2704 of the Internal Revenue Code has created numerous issues in connection with restrictions on liquidation, liquidation rights, etc.[11] Since Section 2704(b) only applies to transfers to persons defined to be members of the transferor's family, if Morgan and Jody form a partnership together, they do not need to worry about Section 2704(b), which would otherwise disregard certain restrictions on liquidation of a business entity.[12]

[5] Charitable Remainder Trusts

Life companions who do not have children may be more likely to have charitable interests. Some might like to establish charitable remainder trusts during their lifetimes. If Jody and Morgan were spouses, Morgan could give assets to a charitable remainder trust with an annuity payable until the deaths of both husband and wife, which would qualify for the marital deduction.[13] Since that is not an option for companions, the following plan may make sense in many situations. Morgan establishes the charitable remainder trust during Morgan's life, with the annuity or unitrust interest passing to Morgan for life, then to Jody for Jody's life, then to charity. Morgan might reserve the power to revoke Jody's interest, so as not to make a current taxable gift to Jody on the funding of the trust. If Morgan in fact dies before Jody and has not revoked Jody's interest, then the value of the interest passing to Jody will be included in Morgan's gross estate and subject to estate tax at that time. The initial chari-

---

[8] See Ch. 27 for a discussion of IRC § 2703.

[9] IRC § 2703(b)(2).

[10] See Preamble to Final Regulations, 57 Fed. Reg. 4250 (Feb. 4, 1992).

[11] See Ch. 26 for a discussion of IRC § 2704.

[12] IRC §§ 2704(b)(1), 2704(c)(2).

[13] IRC § 2056(b)(8).

table deduction will be limited to the charity's actuarial interest, determined after both Morgan's and Jody's life expectancies.

See Chapter 33 for a detailed discussion of charitable remainder trusts.

[6] Techniques Using the Actuarial Tables

The premature death of a loved one is a tragedy. The emotional difficulties of preparing for an expected premature death are extreme. However, the estate planner cannot be blind to the fact that, unlike the typical situation, where a young person or middle-aged person views his or her demise as remote unless his death is sudden, a person with time to contemplate his own premature death generally has estate planning opportunities not otherwise available. For example, in certain segments of the unmarried population, AIDS is a factor which commonly impacts estate planning—particularly in considering the likelihood that the couple will attain their actuarial life expectancies. HIV can live in the body for many years before disabling symptoms appear. Even after a full-blown case of AIDS develops, the afflicted individual may live for several more years. Hence, a person recently diagnosed as HIV-positive may have an unusually long period (compared to a person afflicted with a different terminal condition) to plan his affairs. Techniques which require the use of the IRS actuarial tables are likely to be particularly appropriate in such a situation. Generally, a person who has recently developed AIDS will have a life expectancy long enough to use the actuarial tables, but his premature death will be sufficiently certain, barring medical advances, to predict with reasonable accuracy. This allows him the opportunity to use these tables, taking advantage of the probability that the tables will not be accurate when applied to his life.

For example, if Morgan recently tested positive for HIV or has been diagnosed with AIDS, the amount of Morgan's after-tax wealth transferable to Jody can be increased by having Morgan: (1) establish a charitable lead trust for Morgan's lifetime, with remainder to Jody; (2) sell property to Jody in exchange for a private annuity; or (3) use some other estate planning vehicle that takes advantage of property transfer techniques under which both the valuation of the property interest transferred depends on Morgan's life expectancy as determined under the IRS actuarial tables and the tax results are better if Morgan lives a shorter time than the actuarial tables predict.

See Chapter 11 on actuarial tables for a more detailed explanation.

¶ 41.03 TAX VARIATIONS FROM A MARRIAGE

Life companions are generally at a disadvantage compared to married couples when it comes to certain other tax provisions. What legal differences exist between the marital estate plan and an estate plan for life companions?

[1] No Marital Deduction

The marital deduction is not available for life companions. Hence, if Morgan makes gifts to Jody during Morgan's lifetime in excess of: (1) the annual exclusion and (2) tax-free payments of medical expenses and tuition, the gifts will be taxable. Such gifts will either use up Morgan's $600,000 exemption or give rise to gift tax. On Morgan's death, all property passing to Jody will be subject to the estate tax, once the balance of Morgan's $600,000 exemption is used.

[2] Generation-Skipping Transfer Tax

Since life companions are not legally related, their generation assignments are determined according to age, and not family[14] relationships. Hence, if Jody is more than 37$^{1}/_{2}$ years younger than Morgan, a transfer by Morgan to Jody will be a generation-skipping transfer. Similarly, if Jody has children, and Morgan wants to give or leave those children something, they may be included (because of their ages) in the generation of Morgan's grandchildren—not Morgan's children, as would be the case if Morgan and Jody were a married couple.

[3] Employee Benefits

[a] Spousal Benefits

Spouses have certain rights in some qualified plans, such as rights to receive lifetime annuities, unless they consent otherwise.[15] No such federally mandated rights exist in favor of life companions.

Some companies are starting to offer certain traditionally spousal benefits to employees' life companions. The IRS has privately ruled, in the context of such a plan providing health benefits to employees and their dependents, that the excess of the fair market value of the coverage provided to the employee's life companion over the amount paid by the employee was gross income subject to income and employment tax withholding, unless the life companion

---

[14] IRC § 2651. Many life companions consider themselves family. The use of the word "family" in this chapter is intended to denote relationships by blood, adoption, or legal marriage, rather than members of the family group, in the sociological sense of the word.

[15] See Ch. 14 on employee benefits for a description.

was recognized as a spouse under state law or a dependent under Section 152(a).[16]

Can a life companion be recognized under those tests? First, no state recognizes a marriage between two persons of the same gender; recognition of a life companion as a spouse is not possible, if no legal marriage under state law has taken place. Second, under Section 152(a)(9), a non-spouse "dependent" for a taxpayer in any year means an individual who receives over half of his support for the calendar year from the taxpayer, has the taxpayer's home as his or her principal place of abode, and is a member of the taxpayer's household. An individual is not recognized as a member of a taxpayer's household if at any time during the tax year the relationship between the individual and the taxpayer violates local law.[17] Hence, the dependent relationship will not be recognized if (1) the relationship between the employee and the life companion is illegal, (2) the life companion does not receive the requisite amount of support from the employee companion, or (3) the life companions do not maintain the same household.

[b] Penalty Tax on Large Plans

If Morgan has a large benefit in a qualified plan(s) or IRA(s), the benefit may be subject to the special estate tax on large accumulations in qualified plans.[18] If Morgan were married, the tax could be delayed until Morgan's surviving spouse either received an excess distribution or died with an excess accumulation.[19] Jody will not be eligible for this election. Hence, if an excess accumulation exists, this excise tax will be payable nine months after Morgan's death.

[c] Payout Requirements

If Morgan is planning to defer the payout of a qualified plan or IRA as long as possible, Morgan will not be able to take advantage of the surviving spouse exceptions to the general rules on payouts.[20] If Jody is the designated beneficiary on Morgan's required beginning date, the payout can be extended over the lives or life expectancies of Morgan and Jody; however, even if Jody is more than ten years younger than Morgan, the payout will only be calculated as if Jody were ten years younger than Morgan. If Morgan predeceases

---

[16] Priv. Ltr. Rul. 9603011 (Oct. 18, 1995); see also Priv. Ltr. Rul. 9717018 (Jan. 22, 1997), holding that cost of group-term life insurance on the life of a domestic partner was not excludable as a fringe benefit.

[17] IRC § 152(b)(5).

[18] IRC § 4980A. See Ch. 14 on employee benefits for a description.

[19] IRC § 4980A(d)(5).

[20] See Ch. 14 on employee benefits for a description of payout options.

Jody, the remaining payout to Jody can then be calculated using Jody's real age.

[d] Again, No Marital Deduction

As discussed above, no marital deduction is available for wealth transfers between Morgan and Jody. Accordingly, no marital deduction will be available for plan benefits passing to Jody. Hence, both the estate tax and the penalty tax on the plan benefit will be payable nine months after Morgan's death. If the plan does not pay Jody immediately, a large tax may become payable with Jody having no funds to pay it. In choosing a payout option, this issue should be considered.

¶ 41.04 NON-TAX-RELATED ASPECTS

[1] Health Care and Disability Documents

Life companions will want to give special consideration to executing financial durable powers of attorney, medical durable powers of attorney, living wills, designations of appointments of guardian, and designations of persons who can dispose of remains, naming the life companion as the appointee (if the companion is the person desired, of course).

One life companion may want to fund a revocable trust with his assets or establish a standby revocable trust with power to fund held by the other life companion, so that a person outside of the household cannot come in when the first life companion is disabled and administer the assets.

[2] Avoid Intestacy

It will be very important for life companions to have wills, or to title property in such a fashion that each life companion receives the desired property, since state intestacy laws will always give the property to blood or adoptive relatives. Some life companions like to use in terrorem clauses in their wills to discourage others from challenging the dispositions.

[3] Palimony

Depending on state law, it may be possible for life companions to contract with respect to the disposition and control of property in the event that one of them dies or they separate. Most jurisdictions will enforce contractual agreements regarding property if the contractual obligations arising under such agreements are based on rights that are substantially independent of the cohabitation arrangement. However, if the agreement is construed as an arrangement to provide sexual services for consideration, it is likely to be unenforceable as against public policy. Similarly, if the agreement contains rights arising from the cohabitation itself or other "marital"-type rights, it may not be enforceable under the law of some states.

[4] Children

One or both members of the couple may have children from a prior relationship. If that is the case, conflicts may exist regarding what property is left to the life companion versus what is left to the children. The same difficulty can exist in marriages where stepchildren are involved.[21] It should be assumed that conflicts will inhere in any arrangement in which the companion and the children share interests in the same property. For example, it would not be unusual, if Morgan gives Jody an interest in a house for Jody's life, with remainder to Morgan's children, for conflicts to arise between Jody and Morgan's children as to who bears expenses, what to do with proceeds of sale, etc.

One source of tension in the case of second marriages will not exist in the unmarried companion situation, however. A married couple has the opportunity to take advantage of the marital deduction, which requires leaving the qualifying part of the estate to the spouse (to the exclusion of the children) for the spouse's lifetime. The marital deduction is not available for unmarried life companions. Therefore, in the case of Morgan and Jody, although estate tax will have to be paid at Morgan's death, Morgan will have infinite choices as to how to structure the property split between Jody and Morgan's children, without regard to the rigidity of marital deduction trusts or the pressure to defer taxes with marital gifts.

---

[21] See Ch. 40 on special issues of blended families.

PART X

Advanced Maturity, Disability and Serious Illness

CHAPTER **42**

Special Issues of the Elderly

¶ 42.01 INTRODUCTION

The elderly constitute an important (and growing) segment of the estate planning public. They have their own set of special issues, which require sensitivity and expertise.

¶ 42.02 MEDICARE AND OTHER HEALTH INSURANCE

While health insurance is not strictly an estate planning issue, our elderly clients are likely to ask about this. For some, it will be important to know what Medicare covers and does not cover. Once they know that, they may be interested in major medical, Medigap and/or long-term care insurance.[1] The estate planner may direct them to knowledgeable sources concerning these issues.

---

[1] Major medical insurance generally covers stays in a hospital or skilled nursing facility after Medicare coverage has expired. Medigap policies cover Medicare's deductibles and co-payments and some services not covered by Medicare. Long-term care insurance pays for custodial care in a nursing home or in a home setting.

Medicare benefits which are "old-age" related[2] are entitlements — meaning, for our purposes, that they are not related to need. Medicare covers:

- People who are 65 years or older and entitled to Social Security or Railroad Retirement benefits ("eligible beneficiaries");
- Certain spouses, dependents, survivors, and former spouses of eligible beneficiaries; and
- Other special categories of people.

Medicare Part A (Hospital Insurance) covers certain expenses of hospital and skilled nursing facility care, hospice care, and home health care. Medicare Part B (Supplemental Medical Insurance) covers a percentage of certain charges for services not covered under Part A.

Part A coverage is automatic for all Medicare beneficiaries. A senior citizen must enroll and pay premiums to be entitled to Part B benefits. Statutory provisions regarding Medicare are contained in Title 42 USC § 1395 et seq.

There are many medical charges which Medicare does not generally cover, including charges for drugs, most dental services, hearing aids and related hearing tests, eyeglasses, contact lenses, related eye tests, and routine physicals.[3] Very importantly, Medicare does not cover nursing home services unless the patient has a post-hospitalization condition which requires daily skilled nursing care or other skilled rehabilitation services that as a practical matter can only be provided in a skilled nursing facility on an in-patient basis for a condition for which the patient was treated in the prior hospitalization.[4] Even then, coverage is limited to 100 days per spell of illness. Custodial care, which is what most people in a long-term nursing home situation need, is not covered.[5] In August 1996, Congress enacted favorable tax treatment for premiums on and proceeds of certain long-term care contracts and certain payments made for long-term care services. This is discussed in detail in Chapter 12.

¶ 42.03 MEDICAID

Unlike Medicare, Medicaid is a need-based program. Occasionally, an elderly person or that person's children want to establish "need" on the part of the

---

[2] Certain Medicare benefits are available in specific cases to persons under 65 years of age. Some of these cases are need-related.

[3] Medicare now allows beneficiaries to opt for managed care in certain circumstances. The managed care programs may provide coverage for some services not otherwise provided by Medicare. Unlike the general population, only a small minority of Medicare beneficiaries have chosen managed care.

[4] 42 USC § 1395d(a); 42 CFR § 409.61.

[5] Custodial care generally involves assistance with daily living tasks (such as bathing, dressing, and eating) and administration of routine health care services (such as giving two pills every four hours).

elderly person whose personal wealth otherwise prevents that person from meeting Medicaid's "need" standard. To this end, the elderly person transfers his or her assets to the children or to a trust. The expectation is that this asset transfer will reduce the elderly person's net worth to the point that Medicaid will then pay for the person's care, and thereby prevent the elderly person's assets from being depleted by the costs that Medicaid picks up. Does this work?

In brief, to qualify for Medicaid, a person must pass both an income test and an assets test—that is, neither that person's income nor available resources can be above the predetermined qualifying level. The amounts of the qualifying levels, which are quite low, depend on certain factors (such as, which state the person resides in, whether the person is married, or whether the person is institutionalized).[6]

In determining whether the person applying for Medicaid exceeds these levels, the person is entitled to exempt certain assets and income.[7] Accordingly, aside from those exempt assets, the Medicaid applicant must spend down his or her assets to be eligible for Medicaid. In this regard, assets transferred[8] for less than fair market value within 36 months before the filing of any Medicaid application are counted as assets owned on the date of transfer, and are deemed to have been spent down by the applicant after the transfer (at the rate of the average monthly cost of maintaining a Medicaid patient in her geographical area).[9] Therefore, a transfer made within 36 months before applying for Medicaid could render an elderly applicant ineligible for Medicaid for the rest of her life.

EXAMPLE: Grandma gives $1,000,000 to Son on January 1 of Year One. Within 36 months after the transfer, she applies for Medicaid. The average monthly cost of maintaining a Medicaid patient in Grandma's area is $2,000. It will take 500 months, or over 41 years, for Grandma to use up the $1,000,000 for purposes of Medicaid qualification. If Grandma had waited until 36 months had expired before she applied for Medicaid, the $1,000,000 would not have been a factor in her qualification.

For a person transferring property to an irrevocable trust, the look-back period is 60 months instead of 36, if there are any circumstances in which

---

[6] They can be found in 42 USC § 1396 et seq.

[7] In this regard, it surprises many people to learn that qualified plan benefits and IRAs are generally not exempt, but are considered available assets, to the extent that they can be accessed by the individual. Retirement plan income is also counted in determining eligibility for Medicaid. Planning for these assets requires special care. See Huber, "Pension Considerations in Medicaid Planning," Shepard's Elder Care/Law Newsletter (Apr. 1995).

[8] Certain specific transfers are exempt from these rules. 42 USC § 1396p(c). For purposes of this discussion, we will assume any transfer made is not an exempt transfer.

[9] 42 USC § 1396p(c)(1)(B). The average cost is a published number.

distributions from the trust could be made to or for the benefit of the person.[10] (A transfer to a revocable inter vivos trust does not trigger an ineligibility period, since it is not considered a transfer for Medicaid purposes.)

PRACTICE POINTER: Wait until the 36-month (or 60-month, if applicable) period has expired after a transfer has been made before applying for Medicaid, if the deemed asset calculation would cause a problem.

In some states, buying an annuity for the Medicaid applicant for fair market value with the applicant's excess funds may work. However, the law authorizes the Secretary of the Department of Health and Human Services to issue regulations permitting an annuity to be treated as a trust. In addition, amounts received from the annuity may cause the individual to fail the income test.

The Health Insurance Portability and Accountability Act of 1996[11] makes it a crime to dispose of assets for purposes of obtaining Medicaid eligibility if the transfer results in a period of ineligibility. Criminal liability is extended to anyone who counsels or aids another to violate this law; this provision would presumably include attorneys who advised or assisted in the criminal activity. The criminal sanction only applies, however, if a period of ineligibility is imposed under § 1917 of the Social Security Act. It is not clear what this means.

EXAMPLE: Suppose the average monthly cost of maintaining a Medicaid payment in Grandma's area is $3,000, and Grandma makes a transfer for the purpose of being eligible for Medicaid of $30,000, which renders her ineligible for ten months. Has a period of ineligibility been imposed at that point? Or, is a period of ineligibility imposed only if Grandma actually applies for Medicaid during the 10-month period? If it is the latter, then Medicaid planning can still be done by Grandma. In such a case, if Grandma forgets about the period of ineligibility and applies during the 10-month period, is she and/or the attorney who assisted with the transfer then criminally liable, based on a mens rea at the date of transfer?

Numerous ambiguities exist in the criminal statute. Pending a clarification, the status of Medicaid planning through transfer of a potential beneficiary's resources is uncertain.[12]

---

[10] 42 USC § 1396p(c)(1)(B)(i).

[11] Pub. L. No. 104-191.

[12] This statute does not affect planning by parents or other non-spouse relatives of a person to preserve the person's government benefits by giving or leaving property to the person in a discretionary trust. See Ch. 53 for a discussion.

Before a hospital, nursing home, or other medical care facility can take a Medicaid patient, it must be certified by the federal government as a Medicaid facility. Not all health care facilities want to be Medicaid facilities. A health care facility cannot charge the Medicaid patient any more than the amount fixed by the state. This means a person cannot use Medicaid payments to help finance a stay at a swank nursing home, unless the swank nursing home is willing to accept patients whom it can charge only the Medicaid amount. A facility that does qualify as a Medicaid facility may be just fine—however, it may not be a place that a person with a choice would want to stay. Therefore, before planning is done with respect to Medicaid benefits qualification, it would be best to determine whether an acceptable Medicaid facility is likely to have beds available.

¶ 42.04 HEALTH CARE AND DISABILITY DOCUMENTS

An elderly person is much more likely, statistically speaking, to become incapacitated for medical reasons than a young person is. Appropriate medical care and disability documents should therefore be prepared in anticipation of a client's medical incapacity.[13]

¶ 42.05 TRANSITIONING WEALTH AND MANAGEMENT

Estate planning techniques that require survival for a period of time in order to be effective (e.g., taxable gifts requiring three years to keep the gift tax paid from being included in the gross estate, life insurance policies which need to be transferred more than three years before death, and actuarial techniques which require survival for a term) should be thoroughly examined before employing them in an older person's estate plan.

Non-tax considerations are also important at this time. For example, transition of management of the family business to the younger generation should at least begin during the key person's lifetime, so that the business will not be faced with the shock of having the primary employee suddenly disappear.

¶ 42.06 EMOTIONAL ASPECTS OF ESTATE PLANNING FOR THE ELDERLY

Estate planning during the last stage of life can have a significant negative emotional impact on the elderly person. An elderly person who is being urged to transfer his wealth and make way for the younger generation can begin to

---

[13] See Ch. 43 on disability planning for a fuller discussion.

feel that he is being pushed aside, and is no longer considered valuable. It is often a good thing for the person who is gradually decreasing his involvement with the work-a-day world to permit himself (with the support of his family and advisors) to be a little self-indulgent in other ways.

Ideally, estate planning in these years should not put older folks through the trauma of feeling that they are no longer valued. Rather, it should gradually put them in a position to feel that they are able without guilt to travel, spend time with friends, relax, do whatever they enjoy, and savor the freedom from being tied down by day-to-day responsibilities.

¶ 42.07 FURTHER READING

An excellent source on government benefits available to the elderly is Regan, Entitlements, American College of Trust and Estate Counsel Foundation (1994 ed.)

Disability Planning

¶ 43.01 INTRODUCTION

The vast majority of us will be unable to communicate for at least a few days before we die. In some cases, sadly, effective communication can be cut off for an extended period of time, even years. Effective estate planning calls for consideration of this possibility.

Let's assume that Dad wants to address this possibility. His disability plan may involve consideration of some or all of the following: (1) the execution of certain financial documents (e.g., a durable power of attorney), (2) the execution of certain medical documents (e.g., a living will), (3) consideration of certain miscellaneous matters (e.g., designation of a guardian), and (4) the procurement of disability insurance.

¶ 43.02   IMPORTANT FINANCIAL DOCUMENTS

If Dad becomes incapacitated and has made no plans for that contingency, one of two things will happen. Either the family will figure out some jerry-rigged way to get by, or, if they cannot, a court will have to appoint a guardian for Dad. Informal means of dealing with incapacity can result in bigger problems down the road. And, guardianships tend to be expensive and cumbersome. Hence, it is wise to execute documents in advance that enable Dad's financial affairs to be efficiently handled by others in the event he becomes incapable of handling these affairs himself. Needless to say, the people that Dad entrusts with his business and financial affairs in such documents should be completely trustworthy.

The usual documents used to address the possibility of Dad's incapacity are a durable power of attorney, a revocable trust, or both.

[1] Durable Power of Attorney

Suppose Dad gives Mom a durable power of attorney. Legally speaking, Dad (the "principal") is authorizing Mom (the "agent") to manage his affairs to the extent provided by the power. A "general" power of attorney authorizes the agent to do anything the principal could do, to the extent permitted by law. A "limited" power of attorney gives the agent authority to perform specific actions. "Durable" means that the power of attorney is effective even if the principal becomes mentally incapacitated. However, even a durable power usually becomes ineffective on the qualification of a court-appointed guardian of the principal's estate.

[a] Practical Effectiveness of a Durable Power of Attorney

One of the chief problems with powers of attorney is that third parties often do not want to rely on them. Third parties may be especially reluctant to rely on a document which was not recently executed. They worry about whether the principal was competent when he signed the power, whether the power has been revoked, and whether the principal is dead. Many powers of attorney contain provisions to address these concerns—primarily, provisions that third parties may rely on the power in the absence of actual knowledge that it is no longer operative, as well as indemnification provisions protecting third parties who do in fact rely on the power to their detriment.

PRACTICE POINTER: Assuming that the principal is still competent, powers of attorney should be re-executed every few years to minimize this "reliability/validity" problem. If a statutory form of power of attorney is adopted or changes from the one originally used, it may also be advisable to re-execute.

[b] Gifts by Agent under Power of Attorney

Many states do not recognize the legal status of gifts made by an agent under a power of attorney except to the extent that the agent is specifically and expressly authorized to make gifts. Accordingly, if the principal wants the making of tax-planning gifts to be an option, the power of attorney should specifically authorize such gifts. Further, in this regard, the agent should also be specifically authorized to make gifts to himself, if that power is desired; otherwise, such a gift may be a breach of the agent's fiduciary duty of loyalty to the principal.

The IRS is watchful about unauthorized gifts made pursuant to a power of attorney. When the IRS believes that such gifts have been made, it takes the position that the unauthorized gifts are includable in the principal's estate under Section 2038.[1]

[c] Springing or Immediate Power of Attorney

Durable powers of attorney come in two kinds—"springing" and "immediate." A springing power of attorney becomes effective on the principal's disability. This is in concept what many people want, but it is a difficult document in practice. Why?—Suppose Dad granted a springing power of attorney to Mom. If Mom needs to use it to withdraw funds from the bank, Mom will have to convince the bank that Dad is disabled. This will require extrinsic proof. It may be wise to include provisions in Dad's springing power that a third party is entitled to rely on a letter signed by a doctor affirming Dad's incapacity, and that the third party will not have to investigate to see if the signature is genuine, or whether the signer is really a doctor.

An immediate power of attorney is effective upon execution. It can be extremely useful in situations where the principal's signature is needed, but she is not available.

EXAMPLE: Dad and Mom have been trying to sell their house for some time. While Mom is out of the country, Dad receives an offer which, after discussing with Mom, he decides to accept. Mom's signature is required

---

[1] E.g., Priv. Ltr. Rul. 9601002 (Sept. 22, 1995).

on the contract. If Dad has Mom's power of attorney, he should be able to sign on her behalf.

PRACTICE POINTER: If Dad signs an immediately effective power in favor of Son, but only wants it used during his incapacity, he can leave the instrument in the care of Attorney or other third person, with instructions to release it to Son on certain conditions relating to the determination of his incapacity. This should accomplish Dad's objective and eliminate the proof problems with springing powers (since the third party will only see an immediate power).

[d] Nondelegable Acts

The agent will not be able to perform acts that are legally nondelegable. For example the agent will normally not be able to: (1) make a will for the principal, (2) transfer the principal's funds to a new trust which would change the principal's dispositive plan (although the agent should be able to transfer funds to a trust previously established by the principal, if it is specifically authorized), (3) vote in a governmental election (although in a corporate election, he can vote shares of stock on behalf of the principal if the instrument is a valid proxy), (4) enter into marriage, (5) grant or obtain a divorce, or (6) revoke or amend a trust (in the absence of specific authorization). Additionally, a financial power of attorney will not give the agent the power to make the principal's medical decisions, unless it also qualifies as a health care power of attorney under applicable state law.

A power of attorney may not be sufficient, as a practical matter, to address a lengthy disability. Hence, if it looks like a long-term disability is looming, a revocable trust should be considered as a means of addressing incapacity problems.

[2] Funded Revocable Trust

For reasons that are not entirely logical, it is generally easier to get third parties to rely on a trustee's signature, rather than the signature of an agent under a power of attorney. If Dad puts his assets into a revocable trust before he is disabled, the entire mechanism for financially dealing with his disability will be in place. The trustee will manage the assets in accordance with the terms of the trust.

When a revocable trust is used, it is typical to have Dad serve as trustee or co-trustee of his revocable trust until he becomes disabled. The trust instrument should contain a clear definition of how disability is established. Frequently, the written judgment of two physicians, or two physicians and specified key family members, is used to determine incapacity or disability.

[3] Standby Revocable Trust With Durable Power of Attorney

Dad could, alternatively, establish a revocable trust, fund it with a nominal amount, and give the agent the authority to transfer assets to it. This eliminates the need for funding the trust with Dad's assets before disability. On Dad's disability, the agent's only function under the power of attorney will be to fund the trust.

It is a good idea to have a durable power of attorney authorizing further funding, even if a funded revocable trust is used. It is advisable for the same reason that one has a pour-over will with a funded trust— that is, if there are any assets which do not make it into the trust during Dad's competency, the agent can execute a transfer of these remaining assets to the trust.

¶ 43.03 IMPORTANT MEDICAL DOCUMENTS

Medical documents are often executed in the process of working on an estate plan. These are not financial documents, strictly speaking, although they certainly can have a financial impact in the situations in which they can be used. They include living wills, health care powers of attorney, organ donation forms, guardian designations, and designations of person to deal with remains.

[1] Living Will

"Living will" is a popular term in lay parlance; actually, the document is usually called a medical directive or a directive to physicians.

A living will generally says that, in specific circumstances, the signer does not want certain measures used to prolong his life. The living will's directives only come into play if the signer cannot communicate his desires, and the specific circumstances described in the document are present. The circumstances spelled out in the document may vary, depending on what the signer wants and on the law of the state in which the signer resides. In all cases, the person must be unable to communicate for himself, and his condition must be "hopeless"—either in the sense that his death is imminent, regardless of what lifesaving measures are taken, or in the sense that the person will never again regain the ability to live more than a vegetative or very low-quality existence.

QUESTION: *What lifesaving measures can be terminated or not initiated pursuant to a living will?*

ANSWER: It varies, depending on state law and the signer's desires. In all cases, the use of ventilators and dialysis machines (the two most common mechanical life-prolonging measures) can be stopped or prevented. In some cases, affirmative treatment such as surgery or antibiotics can be eliminated. In some states, food and hydration can be withheld if the patient has authorized it. However, it is usually not a good idea, even if it would be valid, to provide that no medication or treatment at all shall be given, since that would prevent the use of pain relievers and other measures affording a last measure of comfort to the patient. Most people prefer to be given pain-relieving medicines, anti-nausea medications, and other comfort-providing treatment, even if such palliative treatment should shorten their lives;[2] medical care documents often have such provisions.

Some living wills do not express a preference for withholding or terminating life support. Rather, they leave the decision to a designated party. There are advantages to this, in terms of dealing with situations where the timing of life support withdrawal has non-medical consequences. An example of such a situation is contained in *Lorenzen v. Employees Retirement Plan of the Sperry and Hutchison Company*.[3] In this case, the patient's physicians advised the spouse to request withdrawal of life support. She did so, without realizing that the patient was three days short of his normal retirement date under his pension plan. As a result, the surviving spouse received a pre-retirement benefit of about half of the ordinary retirement benefit that would have resulted if her husband had lived three more days. This case also illustrates the value of obtaining legal and/or financial advice in addition to medical advice before making a decision regarding the termination of life support.

[a] DNR Order

Sometimes, people confuse a living will with a Do Not Resuscitate Order, commonly known as a "DNR," which a doctor issues. They may erroneously believe that a living will is redundant, since the doctor can issue a DNR order if their condition becomes hopeless. In fact, a living will and a DNR order are not the same thing. A DNR order tells the medical staff that if the patient goes into life-threatening distress, they are not to try to resuscitate the patient. A person can remain in a coma for some time without undergoing an incident that will require resuscitation. A living will may help in such a situation, whereas a DNR order will not.

[b] Practical Matters

As a practical matter, a person with a sick spouse or relative may be reluctant to bring up the subject of a living will, or to bring the document to

---

[2] Why would such treatment shorten their lives? Certain analgesics and other comfort-providing medications are themselves toxins. If the patient's liver and kidneys are not working properly, the body cannot rid itself of these toxins effectively; hence, they can build up in the body and shorten the patient's life.

[3] 896 F2d 228 (7th Cir. 1990).

the hospital, before a decision on life support is imminent. As stated in ¶ 43.04, federal law requires hospitals to offer the choice of a living will to patients on admission, if circumstances allow. However, from a dispassionate point of view, the living will is ideally addressed before the person ever gets to the hospital, for a number of reasons. First, on admission to the hospital, the patient may not be conscious, or may be in a state of emergency not permitting time for consideration of the document. Secondly, a crisis necessitating a decision whether to put a person on life support may well arise suddenly, and there may be only a few minutes to make the decision. Moreover, persons who work at the hospital may be legally prohibited from witnessing a living will, causing a scramble for available witnesses, if witnesses are required by state law. Additionally, even with medical documents in place, it is usually much easier not to initiate life support than it is to have it removed. The extent to which this is true is largely a matter of hospital procedure, so it will vary depending on the hospital. In many hospitals, removing a patient from a life support machine is a major decision. The decision may require the approval of some or all of the following: the attending physician, the nurse in charge of the patient's care, the head nurse on the floor, the hospital chaplain, a pulmonologist or renal specialist (who is the ventilator or dialysis machine specialist), the hospital's general counsel, the hospital administrator, the patient's next of kin or medical powerholder, a second physician who is a specialist in the patient's disease or injury, and/or the head of the hospital ethics committee. By the time all of these people are located, the situation is explained to them, and they have come to an agreement, days or weeks may have passed.

In contrast, a decision *not* to start life support is usually made between (1) the patient, the next of kin or medical powerholder, and (2) the attending physician. It is not pleasant for a spouse or child to bring up the subject to a sick spouse or parent. Having the living will in place in advance of illness may ease the emotional burdens of all involved.

Additionally, a hospital's usual default treatment will be to put a patient whose physical condition warrants it on life support. What if there is no living will, or the hospital is hesitant to rely on one, for whatever reason? A court order to remove the patient from life support is a last resort possibility, of course, but seeking such an order may be a cumbersome endeavor. Alternatively, however, if the patient is at home, and does not want certain kinds of life support, a practical response may be to make arrangements for hospice care.[4] If the patient goes into distress, the appropriate hospice personnel can form an opinion as to whether it would be in conformity with the patient's intent to revive him. If so, they can call the ambulance or perform emergency treatment themselves before or while transporting the patient to the hospital.

---

[4] Hospice care, which consists of palliative measures and treatment designed to increase the patient's comfort and reduce pain and stress, is usually only available if the patient is expected to die shortly—often, within six months.

[c] Significance of Brain Death

Many people are confused about when a decision to continue or initiate life support is called for. That decision is only faced if the person is not already legally dead. The definition of legal death varies according to state law, but frequently includes cases in which the person's heart is still beating with the aid of a ventilator. For example, the complete absence of brain waves on an electroencephalogram for 48 consecutive hours (or some other definite period) will constitute legal death in many states. If the patient is legally dead, the hospital can (and, at some point, will) remove life support, without regard to the existence of a living will or the family's wishes.

[d] Person Who Wants Life Support

If the person knows in advance that he wants all measures taken to preserve his life, regardless of his prognosis, there may be no standard formal directive for expressing this wish. It, however, can be addressed in a medical power of attorney.

[e] To Sign or Not to Sign the Living Will

Usually, the estate planner's role is to explain the living will, not to recommend in favor of or against it. People often have strong feelings about this document. Some have been through lingering deaths of relatives, and believe that a living will may help avoid putting their families through such a trauma. Others have religious, moral, or ethical objections to living wills. Some may know of a case where a patient recovered after the doctors predicted that he would never come out of a coma.

In the absence of any documents such as a living will, the hospital will rely on whomever state law designates to make medical decisions for the patient. If this includes more than one person (e.g., all adult children of an unmarried patient), an impasse can occur if they do not all agree about the treatment decision. Moreover, for serious decisions like removal of life support, the hospital may not be able to make a treatment decision without a court order.

[f] Family Disagreements Concerning Continued Life Support

What if one child is designated the decision maker, but there is serious disagreement among the children as to whether Mom or Dad should be taken off life support? Theoretically, this is just the situation that a health care power of attorney was designed to address. However, as a practical matter, if close family members object to the powerholder's decision to remove life support, hospital personnel may administer life support to Mom or Dad in the absence of a court order to the contrary. Although this is frustrating for the power-holder, the hospital's position from a legal standpoint is not difficult to understand. If it errs by letting the person die, there is no going back and correcting the mistake.

[g] Children With Terminal Cases

Tragically, the question of withholding or terminating life support measures sometimes arises in the case of minors. Usually, the parents will have the right to make decisions regarding the health care of their child. However, when it gets to the point of withholding or terminating life support, the decision may be taken out of the parents' and hospital's hands and placed before the court. In some states, parents can avoid this problem by executing a living will on behalf of their minor child.

[2] Medical Power of Attorney

This document designates the person who can make medical decisions for the principal if he is unable to communicate. A medical power of attorney is broader than the living will, as it covers situations other than continuation/origination of life support.

> EXAMPLE: Jean is in an automobile accident. She has a cut on her face, and is unconscious. A person holding a medical power of attorney can decide whether to have a surgeon in the emergency unit repair the cut or to bring in a plastic surgeon.

Under some state laws, the signer is allowed to have only one agent at a time under a medical power of attorney. The one-agent rule allows medical personnel to rely on the decisions and instructions of that one person, so that the medical personnel are not confronted with arguments between two or more agents. The signer can, however, name successor agents to act, one at a time, in the order he or she desires.

Who should the agent be? Normally, husbands and wives will name each other as primary agents. It is not always easy to identify alternate agents. Some people prefer not to burden their children with such potentially difficult decisions, and choose a minister, close friend, or sibling. Others want to name one of their children, but are not sure which child to name, or in what order. Practical considerations should enter into this decision. For example, Dad could choose the child who lives in the same city that he does, the child who has a health care career, etc. These sorts of concrete considerations can reassure children who may feel that Dad must have liked the first agent best, the second one second best, and so on.

There are certain treatments that cannot be authorized by an agent. These vary according to state law, but may include such treatments as abortion, termination of life support when the patient is pregnant, electroshock therapy, and involuntary commitment to a mental institution.

Harvard Medical School has developed a form which lists numerous situations for the patient to consider in determining what kind of care she would like to have if she cannot speak for herself, and has boxes for her to check in each case. Other groups have developed similar non-state-specific forms. These forms are widely available.

Suppose Dad brings in a form like this. Should he sign it? This type of form can be a good indicator of Dad's intentions; however, if he signs a form like this, he should make sure that it will be valid under state law. Most states require the use of specific forms for medical powers and living wills. The use of a universal form may not comply with state law, and may operate as a revocation of a previously signed form which was valid under state law. Or, though the form may technically comply with state law, medical staff (not used to dealing with the universal form) may refuse to base their actions upon it. What if Dad lives in a state where the universal form is not valid, but he would still like to use it for the additional guidance it gives (compared to the valid state form)? Dad's lawyer might add a provision to the universal form indicating that the document is intended to set out nonbinding guidelines, and is not intended as a revocation of the previously executed document complying with state law.

[3] Organ Donation

A person can usually direct that his organs be made available for donation via a state-approved method. This may include executing a form that meets state law requirements or checking a box on a driver's license.

An organ donation decision can be excruciating for family members. So, if the person wants to donate his organs, it is wise to go ahead and indicate his intent himself in a manner recognized under applicable state law. Some people want to donate; others are hesitant. Some are afraid that the medical team will get trigger-happy, if they need an organ; while others have religious feelings which cause them to be in favor of or against the idea.

It is now illegal to charge the donor, his estate, or his family for removal (infelicitously known as "harvesting") of body parts. (Conversely, it is also illegal to pay for the donor's body parts.) Organs commonly removed are the corneas, heart, kidneys, liver, lungs, pancreas, skin, and bones (the most frequently used tissue).

Some final aspects of organ donation are as follows. Unlike the decision to withhold life support, parents can usually donate a deceased child's organs without court approval. While some clients may believe they are too old to donate their organs, in general, there is no specific age limitation on the usefulness of one's organs. Last, organ donation should not impact funeral and burial arrangements. Organ donation procedures leave the body otherwise intact, so organ removal does not preclude an open casket funeral.

[4] Designation of Person to Deal With Remains

In response to the needs of nontraditional couples, statutes enabling a person to designate an agent to deal with the person's remains upon his death are being enacted in various states. In the absence of such a statute, or if no designation exists in a state which allows one, the state's health laws usually set out a list of people who can make such decisions, in order of priority—usually the spouse, then adult children, then parents, etc. As a result, a deceased person's life companion may have no say at all in the burial or cremation arrangements, or may even be prohibited from attending the funeral. Now, in states that have enacted the appropriate legislation, a person can sign a document designating any person he chooses to control this category of decisions.

A designated survivor should know, before he accepts the responsibility of disposing of the remains, that he may become liable for payment for his chosen services.

¶ 43.04 ADDITIONAL HEALTH CARE DOCUMENT ISSUES

[1] Out-of-State Issues

Now, for the matter of the peripatetic signer. If a person spends a great deal of time in two or more jurisdictions, it is probably wise for that person to sign health care documents meeting the requirements of each jurisdiction. This way, if an Oklahoma resident, who frequently visits California, is hospitalized in California, a document satisfying California law can be brought to the hospital; presumably, hospital personnel will be accustomed to relying on such a document and will act in accordance with its directions.

Currently, as a matter of federal law, hospitals in the United States are required to ask incoming patients who are able to communicate whether they have living wills, and the hospitals are required to give them a living will form to complete if they want one.[5] However, a previously executed set of documents will come in handy if the person could not or did not sign one on admission to the hospital. In addition, the living will offered by the hospital only deals with withholding life support measures—it does not cover the myriad other decisions that a health care power does. Finally, if the patient does sign a document at the hospital, and it contains different provisions from those in prior documents, the later-signed hospital document will ordinarily control.

---

[5] 42 USC §§ 1395cc(f), 1396a(w).

[2] Location of the Documents

When they are needed, medical documents are often needed immediately. Because of their nature, it is best not to keep them at an attorney's office or in a safe deposit box. If the document is needed on Friday night, it may not be accessible until Monday morning if it is located in such a place. Accordingly, it is often advisable to give the medical documents to a person's doctor and/or to the medical care agents, in case they are needed.

One disadvantage of leaving the document with a person's doctor or medical care agent is that the signer may later change his mind—either about what he wants to do or about the people he wants to be the decision-makers. Medical personnel do not always require originals of these documents; they may be willing to rely on copies. Hence, an old document could be used by someone who does not know it has been superseded. While it is possible to round up all old originals and destroy them, there is not a way to be sure that all old copies have been destroyed.

[3] Designation of Guardian

[a] For the Signer

Despite whatever good preventive planning is done, there could arise a need at some point to designate a guardian of a person's estate and/or a guardian of the person. A guardian of the estate is charged with management of the ward's financial affairs. A guardian of the person is charged with the duties of caring for the ward's physical, mental, and emotional welfare—seeing that he has a place to live, food, clothing, schooling, etc.

Some states have designation statutes that allow a person to choose his guardian in advance. In a state which does not have such a statute, or in the case of a person who does not sign such a document in a state which does allow it, the guardian will usually be appointed by the court according to a statutory priority list—spouse, then adult child, then parent, etc. Within the same priority class, the court decides among eligible candidates.

[b] For the Signer's Children

A parent will usually be able to designate a guardian of the persons of his minor children, effective on his death, provided he is the last surviving parent at the time of his death. If he is not the last surviving parent, the surviving parent will generally be the natural guardian, unless he/she can be proven to be an unfit parent. In some cases, the surviving parent may have executed an agreement with the deceased parent indicating that the surviving parent would not accept guardianship of the couple's minor children. Usually, however, such an agreement is not enforceable, particularly if the surviving parent received consideration for executing the agreement. Finally, even if the surviving parent does not accept the guardianship of the children, the parent nevertheless remains financially liable for their support.

Most states do not have a statutory method for appointing a guardian of the person of the children in case of disability of the parent. This is usually handled informally by agreement of the relatives.

A guardian of the estate is the person who manages the child's financial matters. A guardian of the estate usually must be appointed by a court—the minor child's parent is not automatically the guardian. However, the parent is usually entitled to be appointed guardian of the estate unless there is a compelling reason that the parent should not serve in such capacity. Therefore, if Dad does not want Mom to handle assets that he will leave to the child, he should leave the assets in trust and name someone else as trustee.

¶ 43.05　DISABILITY INSURANCE

Disability insurance is a means of income replacement in case of disability. It does not provide for payment of medical bills—that is the function of health insurance.

Disability insurance is not strictly an estate planning matter. However, the estate planner can provide general guidance about what issues, in addition to price, are important in selecting a policy. For example, the following matters are pertinent:

- Whether payments begin after the insured becomes unable to engage in her own occupation, in any reasonably related occupation, or in any occupation at all.
- Whether the insured receives benefits even though she is able to work part-time.
- The period during which the insured must wait after an illness or accident before benefits begin; this term is called the "elimination period." Related to this is the effect of a delay between an accident and a disability as well as the effect where a disability ceases and then recurs.
- The period during which the benefits will be paid (e.g., benefits are often paid until the insured reaches retirement age).
- Whether benefits are limited, depending on the cause of the disability (e.g., there may be caps on benefits for specified conditions or diseases).
- Whether premiums need to be paid while the insured is disabled.
- Whether there are cost of living adjustments in benefit amounts.
- Whether the contract is renewable as long as premiums are paid.
- Whether the company has the right to cancel the contract, modify terms, or increase premiums unilaterally.

Pre-Mortem Planning

¶ 44.01 INTRODUCTION

When a person's death is expected to occur within a relatively short period, some of the techniques discussed in the balance of this chapter may be advisable.

> EXAMPLE: For purposes of this chapter, we will consider actions which might be appropriate for Tom, an individual who has been informed that he may not have long to live. All of the gift suggestions are, of course, subject to leaving enough in Tom's estate so that he is financially secure and comfortable for the remainder of his life.

¶ 44.02 EXECUTE FINANCIAL MANAGEMENT AND HEALTH CARE DOCUMENTS[1]

In the movies, a person is usually conscious and speaking until the last moment of his life. In real life, most of us in extremis will not be competent to handle our affairs for at least a few days before we die. Often, this period of incapacity is much longer.

Tom should arrange for a trusted person to handle his financial and personal affairs during any period in which he might not be capable of making necessary decisions on his own behalf. Appropriate documents for Tom to execute beforehand may include a durable financial power of attorney, a revocable trust, a health care power of attorney, a medical directive regarding life support, an organ donation form, and a designation of guardian. As discussed in Chapter 43, the form of these documents varies from state to state. So, Tom should be sure that his documents are appropriate not only for the state in which he lives, but any other state in which he is being treated or otherwise expects to spend substantial time.

¶ 44.03 MAKE A WILL

It goes without saying that Tom should get his will in order.

¶ 44.04 FUND A REVOCABLE TRUST[2]

Tom may want to fund a revocable trust, so that his beneficiaries will be spared the expense and trouble of probate. First, however, he should consult

---

[1] For a more complete discussion, see Ch. 43 on planning for disability.

[2] For a more complete discussion, see Ch. 7 on nontestamentary transfers.

with his tax advisor to consider situations in which transfers of certain assets to revocable trusts may not be advisable.[3]

¶ 44.05　TRANSFER ASSETS TO A FAMILY-OWNED ENTITY

Tom and his family may wish to consider transferring the family's business and investment assets to a family partnership, limited liability company, or other entity. Such an entity can prove invaluable for purposes of asset management and business succession planning, as well as probate avoidance for those assets held by the entity.[4] Valuation discounts may also be an advantage of holding assets in a business entity, although this technique may not be successful if it is the sole purpose of asset transfers to the entity.[5]

¶ 44.06　ASSUME MINORITY POSITIONS[6]

If Tom holds a controlling interest, a swing interest, or a veto interest in an entity, he could consider transferring the interests and retaining a less valuable interest. For example, if Tom holds stock in a corporation that has one class of stock, assuming no rights differing from state law apply, then: (1) if Tom owns 51 percent and Son owns 49 percent, Tom has a controlling interest; (2) if Tom owns 50 percent, Tom has a veto interest, or (3) if Tom has one-third, Mom has one-third, and Son has one-third, the IRS position may be that Tom has a swing interest, because he and Mom or Son can aggregate their interests and thereby control the corporation.

Even if Tom transfers sufficient stock to avoid having any of these interests in the corporation, this transfer technique may not work if the transfer occurs too close to death or if obtaining a discount is the only reason for the transfer. In 1990, the Tax Court refused to recognize such a transfer for purposes of estate tax valuation.[7] In this case, the taxpayer's gift of a 2 percent interest in a family business, which reduced her interest to 49 percent, was not successful in securing a minority discount in her estate when she made the gift 18 days before she died.

---

[3] See Ch. 6 for a discussion of these situations.

[4] For a more complete discussion, see Ch. 15 on family entities.

[5] Estate of Murphy, 1990 PH TC Memo. ¶ 90,472, 60 TCM (CCH) 645 (1990); but see Estate of Frank, 1995 RIA TC Memo. ¶ 95,132, TCM (CCH) 2255 (1995).

[6] For a more complete discussion, see Ch. 25 on valuation discounts.

[7] Estate of Murphy, 1990 P-H TC Memo. ¶ 90,472, 60 TCM (CCH) 645 (1990).

¶ 44.07 MAKE ANNUAL EXCLUSION GIFTS

Tom should consider making gifts wholly covered by the annual gift tax exclusion.[8] Such gifts will reduce his estate at no tax cost,[9] if a gift tax return is not required with respect to those gifts.

PRACTICE POINTER: If specific gifts to individuals are made in Tom's will, he should consider making these gifts during his life instead, to the extent of the available annual exclusions.

¶ 44.08 MAKE OTHER NONTAXABLE GIFTS

Tom might pay tuition and medical expenses of family members.[10] This technique would reduce his estate at no tax cost.

¶ 44.09 MAKE UNIFIED CREDIT GIFTS

Tom should consider making gifts up to the amount of his available unified credit, if there is enough time to get some income or appreciation of the gifted assets out of his estate.[11]

¶ 44.10 MAKE GIFTS REQUIRING PAYMENT OF GIFT TAX

Gifts requiring payment of gift tax may make sense, even if Tom is expected to live for less than three years. Such a technique will work well if the removal of the income and appreciation of the gifted assets from his estate is expected to outweigh the effects of both early payment of tax and the loss of any Section 1014 step-up in basis for the gifted property.[12]

¶ 44.11 MAKE CHARITABLE GIFTS

If charitable bequests are planned, Tom should consider making charitable gifts during his life instead. An income tax charitable deduction will be avail-

---

[8] For a more complete discussion, see Ch. 10 on tax-free gifts.

[9] Unless appreciated property is used to make these gifts — then, the step-up in basis on death will be lost.

[10] For a more complete discussion, see Ch. 10 on tax-free gifts.

[11] For a more complete discussion, see Ch. 8 on taxable gifts.

[12] For a more complete discussion, see Ch. 8 on taxable gifts.

able for these gifts during his life (subject to general limitations on deductions), and will not be available to his estate.[13] (An estate's or trust's income tax charitable deduction is limited to income of the estate or trust paid to charity—a charitable bequest itself does not qualify for an income tax charitable deduction from trust or estate income.)

A charitable gift in the form of a check that is mailed to a charity before the donor's death, but clears the bank in due course after the donor's death, is considered completed before the donor's death.[14] Accordingly, under such circumstances, an income tax charitable deduction for the amount of the check would be allowed on the decedent's final income tax return, assuming the donation to this charity otherwise qualifies for the income tax charitable deduction.

¶ 44.12 MAKE A SALE OR GIFT OF DEPRECIATED PROPERTY

Suppose Tom owns Blackacre, which has a value less than its basis. If Tom retains Blackacre, it will receive a step-down in basis at his death and the built-in loss will never be realized. What can Tom do to minimize this problem? If Tom gives the property during his lifetime to his wife, his wife will ordinarily take Tom's basis and then could realize the built-in loss when the property is sold after Tom's death.[15] The basis of the property will not be subject to adjustment on account of Tom's death because it is not in his estate.

What if Tom is not married or, for other reasons, does not wish to transfer the property to his spouse? Tom might consider selling Blackacre during his life to take advantage of the loss. This could be a good idea if the loss on the sale could be used to reduce Tom's income taxes and Blackacre can be sold to a party whose relationship to Tom does not require that the loss be disallowed under Section 267. If it is important to keep Blackacre in the family, the property could be sold to a family member who is not considered related under Section 267's loss disallowance rules, such as a daughter-in-law.

If a sale of Blackacre to a third party is neither feasible nor desirable, Tom might nevertheless sell it to a party related to him under the Section 267 loss disallowance rules. While, in such a case, Tom will not be able to deduct the loss on this sale, the related purchaser would be able to use Tom's disallowed loss to reduce all or a portion of any gain realized by the related purchaser on a future sale of the property for more than its value on the date of purchase from Tom.

---

[13] For a more complete discussion, see Ch. 32 on outright charitable gifts.

[14] Estate of Belcher, 83 TC 227 (1984); Treas. Reg. § 1.170A-1(b).

[15] IRC § 1041(b).

Alternatively, Tom might consider giving the property to a related party during his lifetime. For purposes of determining the donee's loss on a resale of the property, under Section 1015, the property's basis is its fair market value at the time of the gift. However, if the property is sold by the donee for more than its fair market value on the date of the gift, the donee is permitted to determine the amount of any gain realized on the sale of the property using Tom's basis in the property. In substance, part or all of Tom's original basis will be preserved and thereby reduce the donee's gain.

¶ 44.13 EXCHANGE PROPERTY FOR A PRIVATE ANNUITY[16]

If Tom is not "terminally ill,"[17] as defined in the regulations, a private annuity might be a good planning technique to consider.[18] In this situation, the actuarial tables, which are used to determine the value of the annuity received by Tom in exchange for one or more of his assets, may permit Tom to transfer the asset for less than its true value without gift tax consequences. If Tom lives 18 months or longer after the transaction, a rebuttable presumption will exist that Tom was not terminally ill on the date of the transaction and therefore that use of the actuarial tables to value the annuity was proper.[19]

¶ 44.14 FUND A CHARITABLE LEAD TRUST

Again, if there is a greater than fifty percent chance that Tom will live for at least a year, his funding of a charitable lead trust for his lifetime might work well. This is because he may receive a greater gift tax charitable deduction than will turn out to be warranted by the actual distributions made to the charitable beneficiary.[20]

---

[16] For a more complete discussion, see Ch. 23 on private annuities and Ch. 11 on gifts using the actuarial tables.

[17] For purposes of the applicable regulations, a person is "terminally ill" if he or she is known to have an incurable illness or other deteriorating physical condition, and there is at least a 50 percent probability that the person will die within one year. Treas. Reg. § 20.7520-3(b)(3)(i). See Ch. 11 for a discussion.

[18] For a more complete discussion, see Ch. 23 on private annuities and Ch. 11 on gifts using the actuarial tables.

[19] Treas. Reg. § 20.7520-3(b)(3)(i).

[20] For a more complete discussion, see Ch. 35 on charitable lead trusts and Ch. 11 on gifts using the actuarial tables.

¶ 44.15 USE AVAILABLE CARRYOVERS

Tom should use any capital loss, net operating loss, and charitable contribution carryovers, if possible. They will be lost at death, unless they can be used in his wife's joint return for the year of his death.

¶ 44.16 ACCELERATE POTENTIAL INCOME IN RESPECT OF A DECEDENT

Tom should think about accelerating income that, if paid after his death, will constitute income in respect of a decedent ("IRD"). If this income is accelerated so that it is reported on his last individual income tax returns, the income tax paid on that income will be removed from his estate.

> **EXAMPLE:** Tom sells property with a zero basis to his Son in exchange for an installment note with a face amount of $100,000 and adequate stated interest. If Tom dies with the installment note in his estate, the note will be subject to estate tax of $55,000, and income tax of $28,000, leaving $17,000 for his beneficiary. If, instead, he collects the note during his lifetime, there will be capital gains tax of $28,000, and estate tax of $39,600 (55 percent of the $72,000 after-tax proceeds of the note), saving $15,400 in estate tax.

¶ 44.17 TRANSFER LIFE INSURANCE

[1] Exclusion from Gross Estate

If Tom has life insurance, he might consider transferring the policies in a manner that causes the policies to escape estate taxation, but does not run afoul of the "transfer for value" rules.[21]

He should also consider exercising any options to buy additional life insurance, and maximizing any incidental insurance that might apply (for example, as an extra benefit of credit cards or mortgages).

[2] Viatical Settlements

If Tom has life insurance and is in need of cash, he can receive certain accelerated death benefits and viatical settlements during his lifetime, free of income taxes.[22]

---

[21] For a more complete discussion, see Ch. 12 on life insurance. The valuation of the policies should be considered in the analysis.

[22] IRC § 101(g).

¶ 44.18 BUY FLOWER BONDS

Flower bonds were formerly issued by the U.S. Treasury, and are still traded on the secondary market. These bonds are sold at a discount, reflecting the fact that they do not mature for a period and do not bear stated interest. They are redeemable at par in the purchaser's estate to the extent that they are used to pay estate taxes. They will also be valued at par for estate tax purposes, to the extent that they are or could be used to pay estate tax. The Treasury ceased issuing flower bonds some years ago, and only a few bonds remain outstanding. If a revocable trust owns the bonds, the trust should specifically direct that the bonds be used for payment of estate taxes in order for the redemption at par to be available.[23]

¶ 44.19 MAXIMIZE USE OF SPECIAL BUSINESS PROVISIONS[24]

In appropriate circumstances, Section 303 (stock redemptions), Section 2032A (special estate tax valuation for agricultural property), or Section 6166 (estate tax deferral for closely held businesses) can be useful. If any of these sections would be useful in Tom's case, Tom should do what arranging he can to insure that his estate meets the requirements of these sections and that the benefits available under these sections can be maximized.

For purposes of Section 303 and Section 2032A, any gifts made within three years before death (except "annual exclusion gifts" not required to be reported on a gift tax return and tax-free payments of medical and tuition expenses) are added back to the estate.[25] An estate will meet Section 6166's "thirty-five percent requirement" only if the estate meets the requirement both before and after gifts within three years of death are considered.[26]

The Tax Court recently held that Section 2032A and minority discounts cannot be used simultaneously for assets in the same entity.[27] In this case, the farm was one asset of a partnership holding many assets. The Section 2032A special use valuation of the farm was allowed, but the minority discount for

---

[23] Treas. Dep't. Circular No. 300, 4th Rev., § 306.28(b); 38 Fed. Reg. 7083.

[24] For a more complete discussion, see Ch. 19 on C corporations and Part XI on post-mortem elections.

[25] IRC §§ 2035(d)(3)(A), 2035(d)(3)(B).

[26] IRC § 2035(d)(4).

[27] Estate of Hoover v. Comm'r, 102 TC 777 (1994), rev'd, 69 F3d 1044 (10th Cir. 1995). The Tenth Circuit held that the $750,000 maximum reduction in value of qualified real property imposed by IRC § 2032A must be subtracted from the true fair market value of a minority interest in property, although the true fair market value is calculated using a minority discount. Warning: Hoover is not authority for the availability of a minority discount to reduce the special use value of property. See Maddox v. Comm'r, 93 TC 228 (1989).

the partnership interest was denied. Although the Tenth Circuit reversed the Tax Court, the Tax Court's holding remains important to the extent that the Tax Court may apply that view in cases appealable to other circuits.

PRACTICE POINTER: Don't transfer both a ranch and other property to an entity if you want to claim special use valuation on the ranch and minority discounts on the other property. What about taking a minority discount on the very property which is being specially valued?[28]

¶ 44.20 ACCEPT GIFTS

In certain cases, gifts to Tom will be appropriate.[29]

[1] Increase Basis in Appreciated Property Held by Donor

Family members might consider giving appreciated assets to Tom. At Tom's death, the appreciated assets will receive a Section 1014 stepped-up basis, under certain circumstances.

> EXAMPLE: Tom has a $400,000 estate, and has used none of his $600,000 unified credit. Wife owns, as her separate property, land that is worth $200,000 and has a zero basis. Wife gives the land to Tom. Tom dies and leaves the land to Daughter. Daughter will receive a stepped-up basis in the property, and no estate or gift tax will have been paid.

This technique doesn't work if Tom leaves the property to Wife (since she gave the land to him), unless Tom's death occurs more than a year after her gift to Tom.[30] It is not clear whether this rule applies if Tom leaves the property to a QTIP trust for Wife.

[2] Increase Tom's Estate to Maximize Use of Transfer Tax Benefits

This technique involves increasing Tom's estate, so that it will be large enough to utilize his transfer tax benefits. If Tom does not have enough property to utilize the unified credit,[31] Tom's wife could make gifts to him. This technique

---

[28] See the cases cited in n.27 above.

[29] For a more complete discussion, see Ch. 8 on taxable gifts.

[30] IRC § 1014(e).

[31] Or, if applicable, the generation-skipping transfer tax exemption, or any greater amount on which it might be desirable to pay tax at the point of Tom's death rather than later.

is especially useful if Tom's wife will have a taxable estate upon her death—gifts to Tom would then save estate tax for Tom's wife without resulting in estate tax for Tom.

¶ 44.21 PLAN FUNERAL ARRANGEMENTS

Tom may want to participate in making his own funeral arrangements, or at least make his wishes known on that subject. If he would like any particular person to make these decisions on his behalf, he can designate a person to deal with the disposition of his body in states which so permit.[32]

¶ 44.22 WITHDRAW FROM RETIREMENT PLANS

Tom will want to consider withdrawal from his qualified plans and IRAs, especially if he is not married. He may be able to avoid some or all of the excise tax imposed by Section 4980A, and accelerate the income in respect of a decedent. This advantage would need to be weighed against losing the opportunity to defer further payments and continue to earn income on the account tax-free for the permitted period.[33]

---

[32] See Ch. 43 on planning for disability for a further discussion.
[33] See Ch. 14 on employee benefits for an explanation.

PART XI

Planning for Post-Mortem Choices

CHAPTER **45**

Providing Liquidity for the Estate

¶ 45.01 LIFE INSURANCE

Life insurance is a generally recognized liquidity provider.[1] Use of an irrevocable insurance trust that can purchase property from the estate or lend money to the estate is a standard technique.

---

[1] See Ch. 12 for a complete discussion of life insurance.

¶ 45.02 RETIREMENT BENEFITS

A person should be careful about relying on retirement benefits to provide funds for estate taxes. For one thing, if the benefits are not payable in a lump sum, they can actually be the source of a liquidity problem, not the solution. This is because they will generate an estate tax and penalty tax, if applicable, whether or not the benefits are immediately payable. Moreover, even if the benefits are immediately available, not much is likely to be left after payment of the estate tax, income tax, penalty tax, and generation-skipping transfer tax (if applicable) associated with the benefits.[2]

¶ 45.03 EXTRACTING MONEY FROM ENTITIES

Often, a method of funding the estate tax will be to withdraw cash from business entities in which the estate holds an interest. This can be done by way of distributions, loans, or redemptions.

[1] Redemption of C Corporation Stock

Stock redemptions are tricky.[3] This chapter will assume knowledge of the rules of Sections 301 and 302 and will comment briefly on the special issues of estates. The general rule is that a stock redemption is taxed as a dividend—that is, as ordinary income, to the extent of the corporation's earnings and profits.[4] Certain exceptions exist for redemptions that qualify as capital transactions.[5] If the estate does redeem stock to pay taxes, it will ordinarily be important that the redemption receive capital transaction treatment.

Stock included in a decedent's estate takes a new basis equal to the stock's fair market value for estate tax purposes.[6] If a redemption by the estate is treated as a capital transaction, the estate would recognize gain only to the extent that the stock has appreciated after the date of death or alternate valuation date, as the case may be.

In some estates, Section 303 may be used as a means of gaining capital transaction treatment for a redemption of stock.[7] Section 302 may also be used to this same end, provided that the redemption can qualify as a complete termination of interest in the corporation. While Section 302 also provides

---

[2] See Ch. 14 on employee benefits.

[3] Ch. 19 on C corporations contains a more complete discussion of redemptions.

[4] IRC §§ 301, 316.

[5] IRC § 302.

[6] IRC § 1014.

[7] See Ch. 19 for a discussion.

other exceptions to ordinary income treatment, these other exceptions, which require a significant decrease in the actual and constructive ownership of stock in the corporation, will usually not apply. This is because stock attribution from the beneficiaries and their family members to the estate will often prevent the estate from having significantly decreased its constructive ownership in the family corporation as a result of the redemption.[8]

[a] Complete Termination of Interest—Section 302(b)(3)

The attribution rules mentioned above do not apply for purposes of the complete termination exception, under certain circumstances.[9]

[i] **Family attribution.** The family attribution rules described below can be waived by the estate if, after the redemption: (1) the estate has no interest in the corporation except as a creditor, and no person related to the estate (as defined below) is an officer, director, or employee of the company;[10] (2) the estate does not acquire any such interest within ten years after the date of the redemption, and it agrees to notify the IRS of any such acquisition and extend the statute of limitations accordingly;[11] (3) the stock redeemed was not acquired, directly or indirectly, within the 10-year period before the redemption, by the estate from any person whose shares would be attributed to the estate, unless the acquisition by the estate was not for the principal purpose of avoiding federal income tax;[12] (4) no person whose stock ownership would be attributable to the estate and who acquired any stock in the corporation, directly or indirectly, from the estate within the 10-year period before the redemption, still owns such stock at the time of the redemption, unless the stock so acquired is redeemed in the same transaction, or unless the purpose of the disposition by the estate was not to avoid federal income tax;[13] and (5) all persons related to the estate (as defined below) meet the above requirements and agree to be jointly and severally liable for the tax.[14]

[ii] **Attribution to entity from family members of beneficiaries.** Because of family attribution, stock owned by a beneficiary's family members is con-

---

[8] See Ch. 19 on C corporations for a detailed discussion of redemptions.

[9] IRC § 302(c)(1).

[10] IRC § 302(c)(2)(A)(i).

[11] IRC §§ 302(c)(2)(A)(ii), 302(c)(2)(A)(iii).

[12] IRC § 302(c)(2)(B).

[13] IRC § 302(c)(2)(B).

[14] IRC § 302(c)(2)(C).

sidered owned by the beneficiary.[15] Both stock actually owned and stock constructively owned by the beneficiary are considered owned by the estate.

> EXAMPLE: Dad's estate owns 20 percent of Family Corp. Son and Daughter are specific legatees of the estate. Son also owns 20 percent of the stock of the family corporation and Mom owns 60 percent. So, if Mom owns 60 percent of the stock, Mom's ownership will be attributed to Son.[16] Both the stock actually owned by Son (20 percent) and constructively owned by Son (60 percent) will be considered owned by the estate.[17] Therefore, if the estate redeems the 20 percent of the stock that it actually owns, it will be considered to own 100 percent of the stock both before and after the redemption.

The family attribution rules can be waived, as described above, if the estate and related persons meet the requirements.[18] In the above example, the waiver would prevent Mom's stock from being attributed to Son.

A "related person," with respect to the estate, is any person to whom ownership of stock in the corporation is attributable under the family attribution rules, if the stock is further attributable to the estate, under the entity attribution rules.[19] In other words, it includes any person whose ownership of stock is attributable to an estate beneficiary under the family attribution rules. This will be the spouse, children, grandchildren, and parents of any beneficiary.[20]

   [iii] Attribution to entity from beneficiaries. The difficulty with most estate redemptions is the fact that stock owned by beneficiaries of the estate is attributed to the estate.[21] Similarly, stock owned by a beneficiary of a trust is attributed to the trust if, under the maximum exercise of discretion in the beneficiary's favor, the beneficiary has an actuarial interest in the trust of more than five percent.[22] Entity attribution from beneficiaries cannot be waived. The entity attribution rules which cause the estate or trust to constructively own a beneficiary's stock can be avoided by distributing all of the beneficiary's beneficial interest in the entity to the beneficiary, so that the beneficiary is no longer considered a beneficiary of the entity.[23]

---

[15] IRC § 318(a)(1).

[16] IRC § 318(a)(1)(A)(ii).

[17] IRC § 318(a)(3)(A), 318(a)(5)(A).

[18] IRC § 302(c)(2)(A).

[19] IRC § 302(c)(2)(C)(ii)(II).

[20] IRC § 318(a)(1).

[21] IRC § 318(a)(3)(A). "Beneficiary" is defined in the regulations, and excludes certain persons who are beneficiaries in the state law sense. Treas. Reg. § 1.318-3.

[22] IRC § 318(a)(3)(B)(i).

[23] Treas. Reg. § 1.318-3(a) (dealing with estates) (also requiring that the beneficiary no longer have a claim against the estate arising out of his status as beneficiary

EXAMPLE: In the example above, even if the family attribution rules are waived, the 20 percent stock in the family corporation that Son actually owns will still be attributed to Dad's estate. If, however, Son's entire bequest is distributed to him, and the regulatory conditions are satisfied, Son is no longer considered a beneficiary of Dad's estate. Then, assuming no beneficiary owns stock in the corporation, if Dad's estate redeems its 20 percent, and the waiver of family attribution rules applies, Dad's estate will have a complete termination of interest.

[b] Redemption to Pay Death Taxes—Section 303

Section 303 provides that certain redemptions will be treated as capital transactions, regardless of how much stock the estate owns or is deemed to own after the redemption. Such a redemption is limited to amounts paid for death taxes and certain funeral and administrative expenses.[24] Other Section 303 requirements are described below.

[i] Time of redemption. The redemption distribution must occur after the individual's death and (1) within 90 days after the statute of limitations for assessment of the estate taxes has expired,[25] or (2) if a petition to the Tax Court for a deficiency in the estate tax has been filed, within 60 days after the decision of the Tax Court becomes final,[26] or (3) if a Section 6166 election has been made, within the time determined for the payment of estate tax installments, if this time is later.[27]

[ii] Qualifying percentage of stock. Stock of the redeeming corporation must constitute over 35 percent of the value of the gross estate, less the deductions allowable (not allowed) under Section 2053 (debts and administration expenses) and Section 2054 (casualty losses).[28] If two or more corporations are involved, they are treated as one corporation if the estate holds 20 percent or more in value of the outstanding stock of each corporation.[29]

EXAMPLE: If the estate holds 20 percent of the stock of Corporations *A*

---

and that there be only a remote possibility that the estate will need to recover property or payment from the beneficiary for any reason).

[24] IRC § 303(a).

[25] IRC § 303(b)(1)(A).

[26] IRC § 303(b)(1)(B).

[27] IRC § 303(b)(1)(C).

[28] IRC § 303(b)(2)(A). The significance of the word "allowable" is that the expenses can be taken against either the estate tax or income tax without affecting the computation.

[29] IRC § 303(b)(2)(B).

and *B*, and the stock of each corporation constitutes 18 percent of the estate, the stocks together constitute a qualifying percentage of the estate.

For purposes of the 20 percent requirement, stock held by the surviving spouse that was owned with the decedent as community property, tenants by the entirety, joint tenants, or tenants in common at the decedent's death is treated as included in the decedent's estate.[30]

[iii] **Relationship of shareholder to estate tax.** In a Section 303 redemption, the redeeming shareholder does not actually have to be the estate. However, the redeeming shareholder's interest in the taxable estate must be reduced directly by (or through a binding obligation to contribute to) the payment of death taxes or funeral and administration expenses.[31] Redemptions by the estate will usually qualify under this provision, since the estate is generally liable for these items. Redemptions by an individual may or may not qualify, depending on the circumstances.

> EXAMPLE: Dad's will leaves Son 100 shares of family stock (constituting 40 percent of the estate) as a specific bequest, bearing no expenses or taxes of the estate. The rest of the estate passes to Daughter pursuant to the residuary clause. If estate distributes the stock to Son and he redeems it, the redemption will not qualify for Section 303 treatment, since his interest in the estate was not reduced by the payment of the estate's expenses or taxes. If the residuary estate contains family stock, which is distributed to Daughter, Daughter's redemption of that stock will qualify under Section 303.

[iv] **Redemptions more than four years after death.** If stock is redeemed more than four years after the decedent's death, Section 303 will apply only to the extent of the lesser of (1) the aggregate of the death taxes and funeral and administration expenses remaining unpaid just before the redemption, and (2) such items which are paid within one year after the redemption.[32]

This is usually an issue when Section 6166 is used in conjunction with Section 303. In such a case, the estate tax payment is accomplished by serial redemptions. Each redemption will involve an amount of stock equal in value to the amount of estate tax and interest owed for the next Section 6166 installment. That amount of estate tax and interest is paid within one year after the redemption. If the redemption date is over four years after the decedent's death, and the entire proceeds of the redemption are not used to

---

[30] IRC § 303(b)(2)(B).

[31] IRC § 303(b)(3).

[32] IRC § 303(b)(4).

pay such amount within one year after the redemption, the proceeds not so paid will not qualify for Section 303 treatment.

Additionally, if at least 50 percent of the value of a closely held business interest eligible for Section 6166 is redeemed or otherwise disposed of, the due date of the deferred estate tax will be accelerated.[33] Stock redeemed under Section 303 is not considered redeemed for that purpose,[34] but only if all of the Section 303 redemption's proceeds are used to pay the deferred estate tax by the next installment due date, or within one year after the distribution, if earlier.[35] Hence, if 50 percent or more of the value of the business is redeemed or otherwise disposed of, and the taxpayers wish to avoid accelerating the tax, the interplay of the Section 6166 and Section 303 rules will effectively limit the amount of Section 303 redemptions to the federal estate tax due at each Section 6166 installment payment date. Payment of state death taxes does not qualify as payment of federal estate tax for this purpose, even if the estate received a federal estate tax credit for payment of the state death tax.[36]

[v] **Generation-skipping transfer tax.** If stock is the subject of a generation-skipping transfer occurring at and because of an individual's death, for Section 303 purposes: (1) the stock will be deemed to be included in the gross estate, (2) the generation-skipping transfer tax will be considered an estate tax, (3) the permissible redemption period will be measured from the date of the generation-skipping transfer, and (4) the relationship of stock to the estate will be measured solely with reference to the amount of generation-skipping transfer.[37]

[vi] **Public corporation.** There is no requirement that the stock redeemed pursuant to Section 303 be a closely held corporation. As long as it constitutes a sufficient portion of the decedent's estate, it can qualify. In fact, some public corporations use Section 303 redemption agreements as a form of employee benefit.

[vii] **Accumulated earnings tax.** Accumulation of earnings after a deceased stockholder's death to fund Section 303 redemption is not subject to the accumulated earnings tax.[38]

---

[33] IRC § 6166(g)(1)(A).

[34] IRC § 6166(g)(1)(B).

[35] IRC § 6166(g)(1)(B).

[36] Rev. Rul. 85-43, 1985-1 CB 356.

[37] IRC § 303(d).

[38] IRC §§ 537(a)(2), 537(b)(1).

[viii] Gifts made within three years of death. Pre-mortem planning for a Section 303 redemption might involve transferring other assets out of a person's estate so that the stock will constitute a sufficient percentage of the remaining estate. However, for purposes of qualifying for Section 303, gifts made within three years of death are included in the value of the decedent's estate.[39] Excluded, however, from this computation are (1) annual exclusion gifts of property other than life insurance policies, if a gift tax return is not required, and (2) tuition and medical payments qualifying for the gift tax exclusion.[40]

QUESTION: *What if the person purchases enough stock shortly before his death in order to qualify?*

ANSWER: There is no required holding period, so that should be okay.

[2] S Corporations

A redemption of S stock which is treated as a dividend is:

- *Nontaxable* to the extent of the accumulated adjustments account;
- Then *taxable* as ordinary income to the extent of earnings and profits from years the corporation had C corporation status;
- Then *nontaxable* to the extent of the shareholder's basis in the S stock; and
- Then *taxable* as capital gain to the extent of any excess.

Capital distributions in redemption of S corporation stock are taxed as capital gain to the extent of value received, less basis. The taxation of a redemption of S corporation stock will often be the same, regardless of whether the redemption is a dividend or a capital transaction.

QUESTION: *Does this mean the estate's stepped-up basis is not valuable if the estate and beneficiaries do not sell their stock?*

ANSWER: No. If the S corporation has appreciated assets, and the corporation liquidates, the redeeming shareholder will be able to take a capital loss.[41] Hence, the use of Section 303 is often only necessary with respect to a C corporation.[42]

---

[39] IRC § 2035(d)(3)(A).

[40] IRC §§ 2035(b)(2), 2035(d)(3)(A).

[41] See Ch. 18 for a description.

[42] See Ch. 18 on S corporations for a more complete discussion.

[3] Partnerships

A partnership distribution to an estate holding a partnership interest (or assignee interest) is not generally taxable, except to the extent that the distribution consists of money and exceeds the estate's basis in the partnership interest.[43] In that case, it is taxable as capital gain, except to the extent that it is attributable to the partnership's Section 751 assets.[44] Provided that the partnership has made a Section 754 election, the estate's Section 1014 fair market value basis in the partnership interest should allow the estate to receive partnership distributions of money to the extent of such fair market value basis without recognizing any gain. (The new basis provides direct gain recognition by the estate on the distribution, and the Section 754 election prevents recognition of pass-through gain if the partnership sells assets to raise money for the distribution.) Of course, the estate will be taxable on cash distributions in excess of that basis, as well as the estate's share of any partnership taxable income arising after the deceased partner died.[45]

It should be noted that the term "money" has a special definition here. Any decrease in a partner's share of partnership liabilities is considered a distribution of money to the partner. Such a reduction can result from the partnership's payment of the liability or the reduction of a partner's interest in partnership profits or loss, which effects a change in the partner's share of partnership liabilities. A partner is also deemed to receive a distribution of money if the partnership assumes the partner's individual liabilities.[46] Finally, in certain circumstances, a partner will be deemed to receive a distribution of money if the partnership distributes marketable securities.[47]

Chapter 16 on partnerships has some additional discussion of these issues.

¶ 45.04 BORROWING AND SELLING

Borrowing money, selling assets, and accumulating income, are all time-honored ways for estates to raise the cash needed to pay estate tax.

[1] Borrowing

If the estate borrows money to pay the estate tax, and the borrowing was necessary, the interest will be deductible for estate tax purposes.[48] Projected

---

[43] IRC § 731(a).

[44] IRC §§ 731(a), 751(a).

[45] IRC § 731(a)(1). See Ch. 16 on partnerships for a discussion.

[46] IRC § 752(b), 752(c).

[47] IRC § 731(c)(1). See Ch. 16 on partnerships.

[48] IRC § 2053(a).

interest to be paid after the date of filing the estate tax return is deductible,[49] unless it is incurred pursuant to a Section 6166 election to pay the estate tax in installments.[50] In that case, the deduction of the Section 6166 interest from the estate tax requires an amended return each year as interest is paid.[51]

What about deduction of the interest for income tax purposes? Generally, personal interest is not deductible.[52] Personal interest is any interest, except for five specific exceptions.[53] A regulation says that interest incurred on the tax deficiencies of individuals is generally personal interest, regardless of the source of the income (e.g., a business) generating the tax liability.[54] The Tax Court, however, has determined that the above regulation is invalid, holding that interest on an income tax deficiency attributable to income from an individual's business is deductible.[55] Hence, interest on any indebtedness incurred to pay an estate tax deficiency attributable to an estate's business might be deductible, under a similar theory.

In the case of an estate, interest payable pursuant to the Section 6166[56] election to defer payment of estate taxes is deductible on the estate's income tax return, if it is not deducted on the estate tax return.[57] What about non-Section 6166 interest? Interest paid on indebtedness properly allocable to a trade or business or to property held for the production of income is deductible as trade or business interest or investment interest, as the case may be.[58] To the extent that the estate owns investments and incurs interest to pay estate taxes attributable to the investments, the estate might be able to contend that this interest is deductible as investment interest, subject to the limitations on investment interest.

According to the IRS, interest paid to a beneficiary of a pecuniary bequest to account for delayed funding is not deductible for estate tax purposes, even if the interest was required by state law, at least where delayed funding

---

[49] See, e.g., Estate of Bahr v. Comm'r, 68 TC 74 (1977), acq., 1978-1 CB 1; Estate of Graegin v. Comm'r, 1988 PH TC Memo. ¶ 88,477, 56 TCM (CCH) 387 (1988) (allowing a deduction of interest projected to be paid 15 years in the future, on a dollar-for-dollar basis, with no discounting for the time lag).

[50] Rev. Rul. 80-250, 1980-2 CB 278.

[51] Rev. Proc. 81-27, 1981-2 CB 548, upheld as a reasonable procedure in Bailly Estate v. Comm'r, 81 TC 246 (1983).

[52] IRC § 163(h)(1).

[53] IRC § 163(h)(2).

[54] Temp. Reg. § 1.163-9T(b)(2).

[55] Redlark v. Comm'r, 106 TC 31 (1996).

[56] This section permits a 15-year deferral of tax on certain business interests and is in reality a method of borrowing from the U.S. government. It is explained in detail in Ch. 46.

[57] IRC § 163(h)(2)(E).

[58] IRC §§ 163(h)(2)(A), 163(h)(2)(B).

was not necessary.[59] Such a payment would be deductible for income tax purposes, if it both satisfied the general requirements of deductibility and would be included in the beneficiary's taxable income.[60]

[2] Selling Assets

The estate's new Section 1014 fair market value basis in most assets generally makes sales less painful, as gain (capital or otherwise) is generally eliminated, except to the extent of events occurring after the date of death. Selling expenses actually incurred in such sales are deductible on the estate tax return or the income tax return, at the seller's option.[61] In the case of income in respect of a decedent (IRD), the IRD income item does not receive a new basis at death,[62] and the selling expenses can be taken on both the estate tax return and the income tax return.[63]

Selling expenses are only deductible on the estate tax return if it is necessary to sell the asset(s) in order to pay debts, expenses and taxes.[64] In such a case, an expense may be deductible for estate tax purposes even if it is paid by the buyer.[65] Selling expenses are deductible on the income tax return, whether or not it is necessary to sell the asset.

It has been held that, if property is not actually sold, future estimated selling expenses cannot be deducted from the value in the estate. However, the courts have also accepted some valuation methods that take into account the negative effect which costs of sale have on the value of the asset, as discussed in Chapter 25.[66]

---

[59] Tech. Adv. Mem. 9604002 (Oct. 6, 1995).

[60] Rev. Rul. 73-322, 1973-1 CB 44.

[61] IRC §§ 642(g), 2053(a).

[62] IRC § 1014(c).

[63] IRC § 642(g).

[64] Treas. Reg. § 20.2053-3(d)(2).

[65] Priv. Ltr. Rul. 9235005 (May 27, 1992), taking the position that a "buyer's premium," which is a commission paid by the buyer at an auction, and which presumably affects the value that a buyer would be willing to pay, is included in the value of objects owned by the estate and sold at auction, and deductible if it otherwise meets the requirements for deduction of administration expenses.

[66] Estate of Koss v. Comm'r, 1994 RIA TC Memo. ¶ 94599, 68 TCM (CCH) 1356 (1994).

CHAPTER **46**

Deferred Payout of Estate Taxes

¶ 46.01 INTRODUCTION

Estate taxes are normally due nine months after date of death.[1] However, there are several provisions of the Internal Revenue Code allowing extended payouts of estate tax.

---

[1] IRC §§ 6151(a), 6075(a).

¶ 46.02 DEFERRAL OF TAX ON CLOSELY HELD BUSINESS INTEREST—SECTION 6166

The payment of estate tax on certain closely held businesses can be spread over two to ten annual installments.[2] In addition, payment of the first annual installment can be deferred for five years from the due date without regard to deferral.[3] The deferred tax will accrue interest during the deferral period.

[1] Amount Which Can Be Deferred

Under Section 6166, the deferral is limited to the estate tax attributable to the closely held business.

The amount of tax attributable to the closely held business is determined by multiplying the gross estate tax (as reduced by available credits) by a fraction the numerator of which is the value of the closely held business interest included in the gross estate and the denominator of which is the value of the gross estate (as reduced by the estate's allowable Section 2053 and Section 2054 deductions).[4]

> EXAMPLE: Gross estate is $1,000,000. No deductions or credits (except the unified credit) exist. The closely held business interest held by the estate is worth $600,000. Estate tax due is $153,000.[5] Amount of tax which can be deferred is $91,800 ($153,000 estate tax due × $600,000 value of interest/$1,000,000 gross estate value).

[2] Payment Schedule

The first payment of interest is due one year and nine months after the date of death.[6] Interest only is due for the first four years.[7] The principal can be paid in up to ten equal annual installments, the first one being made five years and nine months after the date of death.[8]

---

[2] IRC § 6166(a).

[3] Nine months after the date of death.

[4] IRC § 6166(a)(2); Reg. § 20.6166A-1(b).

[5] $345,000 less unified credit of $192,800.

[6] IRC §§ 6166(f)(1), 6151(a), 6075(a).

[7] IRC § 6166(f)(1), (a)(3).

[8] IRC §§ 6166(a)(1), 6166(a)(3).

[3] Section 6166 Election

The executor must elect the benefits of the deferred payout by the due date (including extensions) of the estate tax return.[9]

[4] Interest

With certain exceptions, interest is computed at four percent on the first $153,000 of tax (the "four percent portion"), which correlates to the tax on the first $1,000,000 in value of the business interest.[10] For tax in excess of the four percent portion, interest is computed at the prevailing rate for tax deficiencies for the period.[11]

[5] Qualification

Not every estate with an interest in a closely held business can qualify for Section 6166 deferred payout. The value of the interest in the closely held business which is includable in the gross estate must exceed 35 percent of the adjusted gross estate.[12] For this test only, certain residential property located on a farm is considered part of the closely held business.[13]

[a] "Closely Held Business" Defined

A "closely held business" means: (1) a sole proprietorship;[14] (2) a partnership, if the partnership has 15 or fewer partners[15] or the estate owns at least 20 percent capital interest in the partnership,[16] and (3) a corporation, if the corporation has 15 or fewer shareholders[17] or at least 20 percent of the cor-

---

[9] IRC § 6166(d).

[10] IRC § 6601(j). The computation is $345,800 (estate tax rate on the first $1,000,000) less $192,800 (unified credit). IRC § 6601(j)(2). The unified credit (which exempts $600,000 of value from estate tax) must be applied to the first $1,000,000, for the purposes of this calculation. Hence, the maximum value of a closely held business interest which will be eligible for the four percent rate is $400,000.

[11] IRC §§ 6601(a), 6621(b). The regular interest rate was computed differently in the past.

[12] IRC § 6166(a)(1). The "adjusted gross estate" is the gross estate, less amounts allowable as a deduction from the estate under IRC § 2053 or 2054 (expenses, debts, and casualty losses). IRC § 6166(b)(6).

[13] IRC § 6166(b)(3).

[14] IRC § 6166(b)(1)(A).

[15] IRC § 6166(b)(1)(B)(ii).

[16] IRC § 6166(b)(1)(B)(i).

[17] IRC § 6166(b)(1)(C)(ii).

poration's voting stock is included in the estate.[18]

[i] Attribution rules. For purposes of determining whether a business is closely held, the following special attribution rules apply:

- *Spousal ownership.* Stock or a partnership interest held by a husband or wife as community property (or the income from which is community income), joint tenants, tenants by the entirety, or tenants in common, is treated as owned by one person.[19]
- *Indirect ownership.* Property held, directly or indirectly, by or for a corporation, partnership, estate, or trust is deemed to be owned proportionately by or for its shareholders, partners, or beneficiaries;[20] a person is treated as the beneficiary of a trust only if the person has a present interest in the trust.[21]
- *Ownership by family members.* Interests held by members of the decedent's family are treated as interests owned by the decedent;[22] members of the decedent's family include only his siblings, spouse, ancestors, and lineal descendants.[23] The IRS view is that this attribution rule applies for the purpose of determining whether an entity has 15 or fewer owners, but does not apply for purposes of the 35 percent of gross estate test, the 20 percent test,[24] or the formula determining what amount of tax can be deferred.[25]

[ii] Attribution for the 20 percent ownership requirement. The executor can make a special election to consider all of the interests in a partnership or shares of any non-readily-tradable stock,[26] to the extent attributed to the decedent for purposes of determining the number of shareholders, as also attributed to the decedent for the purposes of determining whether at least 20 percent of the business is included in the estate.[27] If this election is made, the ten annual installments of estate tax must begin nine months after date of

---

[18] IRC § 6166(b)(1)(C)(i).

[19] IRC § 6166(b)(2)(B).

[20] IRC § 6166(b)(2)(C).

[21] IRC § 6166(b)(2)(C).

[22] IRC § 6166(b)(2)(D).

[23] IRC §§ 6166(b)(2)(D), 267(c)(4).

[24] Except as described in ¶ 46.02[5][a][ii] below.

[25] Priv. Ltr. Rul. 8428088 (Apr. 12, 1984).

[26] Non-readily-tradable stock is stock for which, as of the time of the decedent's death, there was no market on a stock exchange or in an over-the-counter market. IRC § 6166(b)(7)(B).

[27] IRC § 6166(b)(7)(A)(i).

death,[28] and the four percent interest rate on the first $1,000,000 in value does not apply.[29]

> EXAMPLE: Corporation X has 20 shareholders. Three are members of Grandpa's family. These three own 25 percent of Corporation X. Grandpa held ten percent of the stock at his death. The stock of Corporation X is not readily tradable. For purposes of determining whether the corporation is closely held, the 15-shareholder test will not be met. If the executor makes the special election, however, to treat the family members' interests as included in Grandpa's estate, the 20 percent ownership test will be met.

[b] "Active Business" Requirement

In all cases, the entity must carry on a trade or business.[30]

[i] "Active business" defined. The IRS has interpreted the trade or business requirement as intended to apply to a business such as a "manufacturing, mercantile or service enterprise, which conducts an active business, rather than being a passive owner of investment assets."[31] There has been some controversy over whether the ownership of real estate constitutes an active trade or business. The IRS has taken the position that a real estate business would qualify if the decedent personally or through an agent took part in the management of the business, and the business was active.[32] On the other hand, it is also clear that the IRS view is that passive ownership and management of rental property, as opposed to active conduct of a real estate rental service business, is not an active business.[33]

---

[28] IRC § 6166(b)(7)(A)(ii).

[29] IRC § 6166(b)(7)(A)(iii).

[30] IRC § 6166(b)(1).

[31] E.g., Tech. Adv. Mem. 8448006 (Aug. 20, 1984).

[32] E.g., Rev. Rul. 75-366, 1975-2 CB 472; Tech. Adv. Mem. 8432007 (Apr. 9, 1984); Tech. Adv. Mem. 8244003 (May 1, 1982); cf. Schindler v. United States, 87-2 USTC ¶ 13,735 (ND Ohio 1987) (landlord who rented to sharecroppers and was consulted on management matters but did not make decisions was not eligible for deferral); Tech. Adv. Mem. 9403004 (Oct. 8, 1993) (decedent who did not cultivate, operate or manage a ranch and received a fixed rental was not eligible); Priv. Ltr. Rul. 9621007 (Feb. 13, 1996), taking the position that (1) interviewing and selecting tenants, negotiating and enforcing leases, and resolving tenant complaints; (2) conducting administrative procedures, such as collecting rents, paying bills, and filing reports with governmental agencies; and (3) maintaining the properties did not constitute operation of a business. Instead these activities were viewed as those of an owner managing investment assets.

[33] Priv. Ltr. Rul. 9517006 (Jan. 18, 1995); Priv. Ltr. Rul. 9223028 (Mar. 4, 1992); Priv. Ltr. Rul. 9015009 (Jan. 5, 1990); Tech. Adv. Mem. 8451014 (Aug. 30, 1984); Priv. Ltr. Rul. 8240055 (July 7, 1982).

QUESTION: *If Dad owned a limited partnership interest in a partnership holding an active business, can his interest qualify for deferral?*

ANSWER: The answer should be yes, since the statute only requires that the business itself be active, not that the owner of the interest had to be active in the business. (After all, some interests held in a publicly traded corporation will qualify.) Oil and gas working interests are considered businesses, but royalty interests are not,[34] at least if the holder is not an active oil and gas operator.

[ii] Stock in holding companies. The executor can elect to treat the portion of any holding company stock which represents direct ownership of a business (or indirect ownership of a business through other holding companies) as stock of that business, provided that all of the stock is non-readily-tradable.[35] For this purpose, a "holding company" is any corporation which holds stock of another corporation.[36]

> **EXAMPLE:** Estate holds stock of Corporation *A*. Corporation *A*'s sole holdings are 100 percent of the stock of Corporation *B* and 60 percent of the stock of Corporation *C*. None of the stock is readily tradable. Absent an election, stock of Corporation *A* will not qualify for Section 6166 because Corporation *A* does not conduct a trade or business. The executor may elect to treat the estate as directly holding Corporation *A*'s interests in Corporations *B* and *C*.

If the holding company election is made, the ten annual principal installments of estate tax must begin nine months after date of death,[37] and the four percent interest rate on the first $1,000,000 in value does not apply.[38] Stock of the business company will be treated as voting stock to the extent that voting stock in the holding company owns the business company's voting stock.[39]

[iii] Passive assets excluded from value. For purposes of Section 6166, the value of a closely held business does not include the value attributable to passive assets.[40] A passive asset is any asset not used in a trade or business.[41]

---

[34] Rev. Rul. 61-55, 1961-1 CB 713; Tech. Adv. Mem. 8625005 (Mar. 6, 1986).

[35] IRC §§ 6166(b)(8)(A)(i), 6166(b)(8)(B); see also ¶ 46.02[5][a][ii] for the definition of non-readily-tradable stock.

[36] IRC § 6166(b)(8)(D)(i).

[37] IRC § 6166(b)(8)(A)(ii).

[38] IRC § 6166(b)(8)(A)(iii).

[39] IRC § 6166(b)(8)(C).

[40] IRC § 6166(b)(9)(A).

[41] IRC § 6166(b)(9)(B)(i).

Stock in another corporation is a passive asset, unless (1) the holding company election is made and (2) the stock of the other corporation qualifies for deferral.[42]

The following special exception exists, however, for multiple active corporations. Multiple corporations are treated as one corporation for purposes of determining their passive assets if (1) one corporation owns at least 20 percent in value of the voting stock of another corporation (or if the owner corporation owns less than 20 percent but the owned corporation has 15 or fewer shareholders), and (2) at least 80 percent of the value of the assets of each corporation (exclusive of the owner corporation's stock in the owned corporation) is attributable to trade or business assets.[43]

> EXAMPLE: Corporation A owns 20 percent in value of the voting stock of Corporation B. Corporation A also owns 10 percent of Corporation C, which has ten shareholders. Decedent dies owning stock of Corporation A. Eighty percent or more of the value of the assets of each corporation (exclusive of Corporation A's stock in Corporations B and C) is attributable to trade or business assets. These three corporations will be treated as one corporation for determining what percentage of value of Corporation A is attributable to passive assets. Thus, Corporation A's stock of Corporations B and C will not be considered passive assets, except to the extent that its share of the value of Corporations B and C is attributable to passive assets of those corporations.

[c] Business Must Constitute at Least 35 Percent of Estate

The closely held business interest must constitute at least 35 percent of the adjusted gross estate.[44] The "adjusted gross estate" is the gross estate, reduced by the amounts allowable as a deduction under Section 2053 or Section 2054.[45]

For purposes of the 35 percent requirement, if a person owned two or more closely held businesses, and 20 percent or more of the value of each is included in the estate, they will be treated as one business.[46] For purposes of the 20 percent requirement in the preceding sentence, the surviving spouse's interest in a business held by the decedent and surviving spouse as community property or as joint tenants, tenants by the entirety, or tenants in common will be treated as included in the decedent's estate.[47]

---

[42] IRC § 6166(b)(9)(B)(ii).

[43] IRC § 6166(b)(9)(B)(iii).

[44] IRC § 6166(a)(1).

[45] IRC § 6166(b)(6).

[46] IRC § 6166(c).

[47] IRC § 6166(c).

In addition, if the executor makes the election described in ¶ 46.02[5][a][ii] above, any interest attributed to the decedent pursuant to that election will be treated as included in the estate of the decedent for this purpose, as well.[48]

[6] Acceleration of Payment

Even if Section 6166 has been elected, certain events can accelerate the payment of tax. Let's say Dad has died, and Executor has elected to defer estate tax on Dad's interest in Fambus, the family business. Generally, if (1) any of the qualifying interest in Fambus is sold, distributed, exchanged, or disposed of, or the estate withdraws money or other property from Fambus, and (2) the aggregate of such transactions equals 50 percent or more of the value of the qualifying interest in Fambus, then the entire estate tax is accelerated.[49]

Redemptions pursuant to Section 303 are excepted from the above rule, if the entire amount distributed is used to pay estate taxes by the due date of the next annual installment or within the year after the redemption, whichever is earlier.[50] The interplay of Section 6166 and Section 303, when the 50 percent rule comes into play, means that Section 303 cannot be used for amounts in excess of the federal estate tax and the Section 303 redemptions must be done serially, so as to coincide with the Section 6166 annual installments.[51]

A distribution of stock in Fambus to the beneficiaries pursuant to Dad's will, the applicable laws of descent and distribution, or a trust created by Dad, is excepted from the acceleration requirement.[52] A similar transfer pursuant to the death of Dad's beneficiary is also excepted if the transferees are members of the transferor's family.[53] For this purpose, the members of a person's family are his siblings, spouse, ancestors and lineal descendants.[54]

In addition, certain other distributions and types of reorganizations are not events that trigger acceleration.[55]

Undistributed estate income remaining in the estate after the due date of the first installment must also be used to pay the tax.[56]

---

[48] IRC § 6166(b)(7)(A)(i).

[49] IRC § 6166(g)(1)(A).

[50] IRC § 6166(g)(1)(B).

[51] See Ch. 45 on liquidity for a discussion of combining a Section 303 redemption with an IRC § 6166 election.

[52] IRC § 6166(g)(1)(D).

[53] IRC § 6166(g)(1)(D).

[54] IRC §§ 6166(g)(1)(D), 267(c)(4).

[55] IRC § 6166(g)(1)(C).

[56] IRC § 6166(g)(2).

The executor is required to notify the IRS of all withdrawals and dispositions within 30 days of becoming aware of them, and to report each year on whether withdrawals, distributions, etc. have triggered acceleration.[57]

[7] Combination with Section 2032A

Section 6166 can be used in combination with Section 2032A.[58] The qualification and acceleration requirements are not the same for these two sections, and so each must be separately examined whenever an issue involving both matters arises.

[8] Generation-Skipping Transfer Tax

If a closely held business interest is the subject of a direct skip occurring at the same time as, and as a result of, the decedent's death, the GSTT is treated as additional estate tax for purposes of Section 6166.[59]

> EXAMPLE: Dad dies and leaves Fambus to Grandchild. If the estate tax on Fambus qualifies for deferral under Section 6166, then the GSTT on the direct skip can also be deferred.

> EXAMPLE: Dad is life tenant of a generation-skipping trust which holds Fambus. He dies, and Fambus passes to his children. The GSTT on the transfer cannot be deferred pursuant to Section 6166, because his death resulted in a taxable termination, not a direct skip.

[9] Deductibility of Interest on Deferred Tax Payments

Unlike interest owed to a bank, Section 6166 interest will be deductible on the estate's income tax return;[60] however, either kind of interest will be deductible for estate tax purposes,[61] which would probably be a more beneficial deduction for an estate at the maximum estate tax bracket.

In this regard, the amount of interest that may be deducted on the estate tax return is the amount of interest paid through that date. Interest that is expected to be incurred later due to the Section 6166 election is not deductible in advance.[62] Hence, each year, as interest is paid, an amended estate tax

---

[57] Treas. Reg. § 20.6166A-3(f)(1)(2).

[58] See Ch. 48 for a complete discussion of Section 2032A.

[59] IRC § 6166(i).

[60] IRC §§ 163(h)(2)(E), 163(h)(1).

[61] IRC § 2053; Estate of Bahr v. Comm'r, 68 TC 74 (1977), acq., 1978-1 CB 1.

[62] Rev. Rul. 80-250, 1980-2 CB 278.

return can be filed on which the interest paid is deducted.[63] For purposes of determining the deductibility of interest during the deferral period, the Tax Court has jurisdiction.[64] However, if the taxpayer elects to follow Revenue Procedure 81-27, and does not petition for Tax Court jurisdiction within the normal statutory period, the Tax Court cannot reopen the case to determine the interest deduction.

The IRS does not issue a refund, which would otherwise be due, since the additional interest will cause the previous tax paid to be too high. It will apply the overpayments of tax and interest to the next installments due or, if the estate elects in writing, to the next annual payment of interest.[65]

[10] Evaluation of Deferral Benefits

Section 6166 deferral is only an assured source of borrowing, and not necessarily at the most favorable rate. Accordingly, while Section 6166 benefits should be considered in relevant situations, it is by no means given that an estate which qualifies for Section 6166 treatment will want to elect its benefits. For example, the estate's personal representative should be aware that once the four percent interest rate amount is exhausted, interest is payable at the statutory deficiency rate. That rate may be higher than the rate at which the estate could borrow from a bank or other source.

[11] Remedies for IRS Denial of Section 6166 Election

One of the disadvantages of Section 6166 is that there is no judicial review of an IRS denial of the election. This is because there is no deficiency—the amount of tax due is agreed; only the timing is at issue. Where an estate has attempted to contest an IRS denial of the election, the Tax Court determined that it has no jurisdiction over the denial, even if a deficiency exists with respect to other issues.[66] In order to protest the IRS's denial of the election,

---

[63] Rev. Proc. 81-27, 1981-2 CB 548, upheld as a reasonable procedure by Bailly v. Comm'r, 81 TC 246, 251 (1983); Priv. Ltr. Rul. 9123024 (Mar. 8, 1991) (applying same rules to revocable trust subject to estate tax as would apply to estate).

[64] IRC § 7481(d).

[65] Tech. Adv. Mem. 9130001 (Feb. 5, 1991); but see Snyder v. United States, 630 F. Supp. 182 (D. Mo. 1986) and Eichheim v. United States, 88-1 USTC ¶ 13,764 (D. Colo. 1981), ordering a refund and reinstating deferral rights.

[66] Estate of Meyers v. Comm'r, 84 TC 560 (1985); Estate of Sherrod v. Comm'r, 82 TC 523 (1984), rev'd on other grounds, 774 F2d 1057, 85-2 USTC ¶ 13,630 (11th Cir. 1985); see also Estate of Bell v. Comm'r, 92 TC 714 (1989), aff'd, 928 F2d 901 (9th Cir. 1991) (holding that the Tax Court did have jurisdiction to determine the propriety of the IRS's denial of the continued benefits of IRC § 6166 to an estate, but only insofar as the Court's determination affects the amount of the estate's overpayment of tax).

the estate must pay the whole tax and file an action in district court or the Court of Federal Claims. However, if the tax has been paid (to establish jurisdiction for the refund action), there is no dispute about the amount due and owing, and the IRS's collection itself did not violate federal law, the denial of the Section 6166 election may be nonjusticiable.[67]

Where the IRS first accepts the election and then later rejects it, the courts have viewed the situation differently. In *Parrish v. Loeb*,[68] the district court held that the government was equitably estopped from denying the validity of a Section 6166 election, where during the three-year period before the attempted rejection, the IRS had accepted interest payments on the deferred tax and the estate had disposed of certain assets and distributed certain income in reliance on the election. The court held that it had jurisdiction, based on an estoppel theory dealing with the IRS's conduct.

Accordingly, in the absence of facts supporting the estoppel argument, an estate whose Section 6166 election is denied may only be able to gain access to the courts by arguing that the absence of a judicial forum to review the IRS's rejection of the election denies it due process. When presented, however, this argument has failed to convince a number of courts.[69]

[12] Keeping Estate Open With the Election

A Section 6166 election can provide a reason to keep an estate open until the tax is paid.[70]

[13] Planning to Qualify for the Section 6166 Election

If Section 6166 looks like a good option in a case where an owner of the family business is still living, the person may want to structure his estate to qualify. This kind of planning might involve, for example, giving away non-business

---

[67] Smith v. Booth, 60 AFTR2d 87-6110, 87-2 USTC ¶ 13,731 (5th Cir. 1987), rev'g 58 AFTR2d 86-6370, 86-2 USTC ¶ 13,748 (WD Tex. 1986); Schindler v. United States, 87-2 USTC ¶ 13,735 (ND Ohio 1987); Reiblich v. United States, 53 AFTR2d 84-1586 (4th Cir. 1984). Rocovich v. United States, 18 Cl. Ct. 418, 64 AFTR2d 89-5942 89-2 USTC ¶ 13,819 (1989), aff'd, 933 F.2d 991 (Fed. Cir. 1991). Compare Gettysburg Nat'l Bank v. United States, 70 AFTR2d 92-6229 92-2 USTC ¶ 60,108 (MD Pa. 1992), Eichheim, 88-1 USTC ¶ 13,764 (D.Colo. 1981); Delguzzi v. United States, 80-2 USTC ¶ 13,364 (DC Wash. 1980) (all dealing with judicial review of decision to accelerate the tax).

[68] 51 AFTR2d 83-1335, 83-1 USTC ¶ 13,507 (CD Ill. 1982).

[69] Green v. Cagle, 56 AFTR2d 85-6549, 85-2 USTC ¶ 13,634 (ND Tex. 1985), Rocovich v. United States, 18 Cl. Ct. 418, 64 AFTR2d 89-5942, 89-2 USTC ¶ 13,819, aff'd, 933 F2d 991 (Fed. Cir. 1991).

[70] Rev. Rul. 76-23, 1976-1 CB 264.

assets so that the business assets will constitute a greater percentage of the gross estate. In this regard, however, an estate will qualify only if the closely held business interest constitutes at least 35 percent of the adjusted gross estate (both with and without the inclusion in the estate of gifts made within three years of death). Annual exclusion gifts of property other than life insurance policies, and gifts qualifying for the tuition and medical expense exclusion are excluded from the computation.[71]

Planning to qualify before the person's death could also involve extracting from active businesses passive assets needed to pay estate taxes. This is so because the estate tax deferral on the value of the business will not include tax attributable to the passive assets; however, for purposes of determining whether 50 percent of the business assets have been disposed of or removed from the entity so as to accelerate the tax, the passive assets are included.[72]

If the business is in a holding company, consideration might also be given to eliminating the holding company so that the five-year deferral of principal installments and the four percent rate on the first $153,000 will not be lost by the necessity of making the holding company election.

¶ 46.03 OTHER DEFERRALS

Deferrals are also allowed for estate taxation of a remainder or reversionary interest,[73] and, in the discretion of the IRS, for hardship cases.[74]

This hardship exemption must be applied for. It allows the IRS to extend the time for payment of estate tax for up to 12 months from the due date of payment.[75]

Additionally, the IRS may, for reasonable cause, (1) extend the due date for payment of the estate tax up to 10 years after the initial due date of the estate tax and (2) extend the due date for payment of any part of a Section 6166 installment up to 12 months after the due date for the last installment.[76] Interest on the extended tax is payable at the deficiency rate.

---

[71] IRC § 2035(d)(4).

[72] IRC § 6166(b)(9)(A).

[73] IRC § 6163.

[74] IRC § 6161.

[75] IRC § 6161(a).

[76] IRC § 6161(a).

CHAPTER 47

Disclaimers

¶ 47.01 INTRODUCTION

Disclaimers offer a unique opportunity to accomplish estate planning after the death of an individual. Disclaimer law generally provides a nine-month window after a decedent's death for the decedent's beneficiaries to (in essence) make tax-free gifts, or otherwise make after-the-fact adjustments in the decedent's dispositive plan without adverse tax consequences. Specifically, within nine months after a decedent's death, a beneficiary who is entitled to an interest in property which is included in the decedent's gross estate may choose to disclaim her interest, without gift tax consequences to the beneficiary. Estate planning often involves drafting in anticipation of this powerful technique.

Ordinarily, if (for example) Child disclaims property of Mom's estate, the property will pass under state law to whomever would take the property if Child had died intestate immediately before Mom's death. However, the beneficiaries who will take disclaimed property can be varied in Mom's will or other applicable instrument. This adds a great deal of flexibility to the estate plan. However, for the disclaimer to work, Child cannot say who the beneficiaries will be and thus the disclaimed property must pass without direction by Child.[1]

In addition, if a beneficiary disclaims, the property must pass to another person, and the person disclaiming cannot benefit from the property disclaimed.[2] The only exception to this rule is a disclaimer by the surviving

---

[1] IRC § 2518(b)(4)(B).

[2] IRC § 2518(b)(4).

spouse. A surviving spouse's disclaimer will work even if the taker on disclaimer is a trust for her benefit.[3]

Disclaimers are often used to allow the survivor to make the estate planning decisions. For example, suppose Husband and Wife want to leave all of their property to each other outright, and let the survivor decide how much estate planning is done at the first death. The will may contain an outright gift of all property to the survivor, but plan for disclaimers in the following order:

- Amount of disclaimed property up to the deceased spouse's available unified credit passes to a bypass trust;
- Disclaimed property in excess of that amount, up to the GSTT exemption amount, passes to an exempt generation-skipping trust;
- Property further disclaimed passes to dynastic trusts or outright to descendants. In the alternative, the disclaimed property could pass to a disclaimer trust that benefits the surviving spouse but does not qualify for the estate tax marital deduction.

The survivor will thus have nine months after the death of the first spouse to die to effectuate an appropriate estate plan.[4]

Gifts can also be disclaimed, although this would be more unusual.

This chapter explains the technical requirements of disclaimers, focusing on disclaimers following an individual's death. In addition, it explores situations which merit planning to give the beneficiary additional choices provided by the option to disclaim. This planning involves special drafting to secure a different disposition on disclaimer than would otherwise occur under state law.

¶ 47.02 TECHNICAL REQUIREMENTS FOR DISCLAIMERS

If a person (i.e., a "disclaimant") makes a qualified disclaimer, the transfer tax laws apply with respect to the disclaimed interest in property as if the interest had never been transferred to the disclaimant.[5] (Note that the effect of this is that either more or less estate tax (and possibly generation-skipping transfer tax) may be payable as a result of the disclaimer.)

If the disclaimer is not a qualified disclaimer, the disclaimer is disregarded and the disclaimant is treated as having received the interest and assigned it to the person who takes the property under the non-qualified disclaimer.[6] The estate tax consequences with respect to the estate of the person who bequeathed the property that was the subject of the disclaimer will

---

[3] IRC § 2518(b)(4)(A).

[4] See Exhibit 47-A, Example 4, for representative language.

[5] IRC § 2518(a).

[6] Treas. Reg. § 25.2518-1(b).

be the same as if no disclaimer had been made. However, there may be gift and/or additional generation-skipping transfer tax that will also be payable as a result of the non-qualified disclaimer.

[1] Written Disclaimer Requirement

The disclaimer must be in writing.[7] The writing must identify the interest in the property that is being disclaimed and be signed by either the disclaimant or the disclaimant's legal representative.[8]

[2] Delivery of Written Disclaimer Within Disclaimer Period

The writing must be delivered[9] to the transferor of the interest, his legal representative, or the holder of legal title to the property to which the disclaimed interest relates.[10] The regulations add to the list of permissible recipients "the person in possession of such property."[11] In the case of a decedent, the delivery requirement will normally be accomplished by delivering the written disclaimer to the executor of the decedent's estate.

The delivery must be accomplished within nine months after the later of (1) the date on which the transfer creating the interest in the disclaimant is made, or (2) the day on which the disclaimant attains age 21. A disclaimer sent in an envelope which is postmarked within the nine-month period will be treated as timely delivered.[12] If the last day of the nine-month period falls on a Saturday, Sunday, or legal holiday, then delivery on the first succeeding day which is not a Saturday, Sunday, or legal holiday will be timely.[13]

[3] Taxable Transfer Which Starts the Disclaimer Period

The statute generally allows nine months after the "transfer creating the interest."[14] The regulations use the words "taxable transfer." The regulatory language has caused some confusion in cases where a completed gift or estate

---

[7] IRC § 2518(b)(1); Treas. Reg. § 25.2518-2(a)(2).

[8] Treas. Reg. § 25.2518-2(b)(1).

[9] IRC § 2518(b)(2) (imposes receipt requirement); Treas. Reg. § 25.2518-2(c)(1) (substitutes delivery requirement).

[10] IRC § 2518(b).

[11] Treas. Reg. § 25.2518-2(b)(2).

[12] Treas. Reg. §§ 25.2518-2(c)(2), 301.7502-1(c)(1), 301.7502-1(c)(2), 301.7502-1(d).

[13] Treas. Reg. §§ 25.2518-2(c)(2), 301.7502-1(c)(1), 301.7502-1(c)(2), 301.7502-1(d).

[14] IRC § 2518(b)(2)(A).

transfer was not actually subject to the gift tax (e.g., where the gift/estate tax had not yet been enacted or where the transferor was a nonresident alien). In such cases, the IRS has taken the position that a transfer triggering the disclaimer period is any transfer which would have been a completed gift under the gift tax laws, if they had applied to the transfer. Proposed regulations adopting this position were issued on August 21, 1996.[15] As proposed, these regulations will be effective for transfers made after the date they are published as final regulations in the Federal Register. However, the Treasury does not view these proposed regulations as prescribing any new rules.[16]

Transfers that appear to start the running of the disclaimer time limit occur at the following times in the following situations.[17]

[a] Transfer by Gift

The date of a transfer by gift is the date the gift is completed, whether or not gift tax is imposed.[18]

[b] Transfer Made at Death or Which Becomes Irrevocable at Death

The transfer occurs on the date of death. This is true regardless of when the transfer is effective under local law.[19]

[c] Inter Vivos Completed Gift Included in Donor's Estate

The transfer is deemed to have occurred on the date of the gift, despite its later inclusion in the donor's gross estate.[20]

> EXAMPLE: Dad transferred life insurance policy to an irrevocable life insurance trust (ILIT). He died two years later. Even though the policy proceeds are included in his estate, the disclaimer period began to run on the day he transferred the policy to the ILIT.

[d] General Power of Appointment

Suppose that A, B, and C are adults. If A gives B a general power of appointment over property, B has nine months from the date of creation of the

---

[15] 61 Fed. Reg. 43197 (Aug. 21, 1996).

[16] Preamble to Proposed Regulations.

[17] Treas. Reg. § 25.2518-2(c)(3).

[18] Treas. Reg. §§ 25.2518-2(c)(3), 25.2518-2(c)(5), example 6. See Ch. 2 for a discussion of when a gift is complete.

[19] Estate of Fleming v. Comm'r, 974 F2d 894 (7th Cir. 1992) (taxpayer unsuccessfully argued that the date the will was admitted to probate was the appropriate date).

[20] Treas. Reg. § 25.2518-2(c)(3).

power to disclaim the general power itself.[21] If *B* exercises the power or allows it to lapse, and *C* thereby becomes entitled to receive the property, *C* has nine months after the exercise or lapse to disclaim the property.[22]

What about a general power of appointment created before October 22, 1942? A power created on or before October 21, 1942 only results in inclusion of the subject property in the powerholder's estate to the extent that the power is exercised.[23]

Application of this rule may depend on the facts. The IRS has privately ruled that *D*, a beneficiary of a pre-1942 trust, who had partially released a general power of appointment granted under that trust, had not parted with dominion and control over the trust property since *D* had retained a limited power over the property. Therefore, *C*, a beneficiary, could make a timely disclaimer of his interest in the trust within nine months after *D*'s death.[24]

[e] Limited Power of Appointment Held by Non-Creator of Power

Where property is subject to a limited power of appointment, the taxable transfer starting the disclaimer period occurs on the date the power was created or authorized, whether the disclaimant is the donee, an object, or a taker in default of appointment.[25]

EXAMPLE: *A*, *B*, *C*, and *D* are adults. On January 1 of Year One, *A* gives *B* a limited power of appointment over property. *C* is the taker in default of appointment. *B* appoints property to *D*. *B*, *C*, and *D* all have until September 1 of Year One to disclaim any power over or interest in the property (of course, in *B*'s case, once he has appointed the property to *D*, it is too late for him to disclaim his power of appointment).

[f] Life Estate and Remainder

Where property passes to beneficiary for life, with remainder to another, the taxable transfer triggering the disclaimer period occurs on the date of the original taxable transfer with respect to both the life tenant and any remainder beneficiaries, whether their interests are vested or contingent.[26]

---

[21] Treas. Reg. § 25.2518-2(c)(3).

[22] Treas. Reg. § 25.2518-2(c)(3).

[23] IRC § 2041(a)(1).

[24] Priv. Ltr. Rul. 9447021 (Aug. 22, 1994).

[25] Treas. Reg. § 25.2518-2(c)(3). If the powerholder is the creator, then the transfer is not complete, and the triggering transfer will occur on the grantor's death or earlier exercise, as described in ¶ 47.02[3][b] above.

[26] Treas. Reg. § 25.2518-2(c)(3).

[g] QTIP Property

With respect to property which is subject to a QTIP election, the disclaimer period begins when the QTIP interest is created by the predeceasing spouse or the donor spouse, and not on the surviving spouse's death.[27] This rule applies to the spouse income beneficiary as well as any remainder beneficiaries. With respect to the remainder beneficiaries, this is a surprising result, since for virtually all other tax purposes, the transfer is considered to take place on the survivor's death. Someone might challenge the regulation that prescribes this rule, which is arguably invalid.

[h] Multiple Disclaimers of Same Property

Where property transferred in a single transfer is disclaimed by more than one person, with respect to all disclaimants, the transfer occurs on the date of the transfer creating the interest in the first disclaimant.[28]

EXAMPLE: Property passes from Decedent to Son or, if Son disclaims, to Daughter. Son disclaims eight months after Decedent's death. Daughter has only one month to disclaim.[29]

[i] Contingent Interests Created After 1932 and Before 1977

Section 2518 governs the disclaiming of contingent interests created after 1976.[30] Slightly different rules apply to the disclaiming of contingent interests created before 1977.

[i] Date disclaimer period begins.

The United States Supreme Court has ruled that the creation of the contingent remainder interest, and not the vesting of the remainder, triggers the period during which a beneficiary may disclaim the contingent remainder interest in a trust created after the federal gift tax was imposed, but before the enactment of Section 2518.[31] This is the same standard adopted in the regulations for interests created after 1976.

[ii] Length of disclaimer period.

However, the nine-month period of Section 2518 is not the same for pre–Section 2518 cases. The disclaimer of an

---

[27] Treas. Reg. § 25.2518-2(c)(3).

[28] Treas. Reg. § 25.2518-2(c)(3).

[29] Daughter could, of course, have disclaimed her contingent interest within the previous eight months. If she did not know that Son was disclaiming, however, she may not have seen a reason to disclaim.

[30] Tax Reform Act of 1976, Pub. L. No. 94-455, §§ 2009(b)(1), 2009(e)(2), 90 Stat. 1525 (1976).

[31] Jewett v. Comm'r, 455 US 305 (1982).

interest created before 1977 is not a taxable transfer if it is made "within a reasonable time after knowledge of the existence of the [taxable] transfer," and is unequivocal and effective under local law.[32]

[j]　Contingent Interests Created Before 1932

In *Estate of Irvine v. United States*,[33] the Supreme Court addressed the question of the proper time for disclaiming remainder interests created before 1932, the year in which the gift tax became effective.

In 1917, Lucius Ordway created an irrevocable trust. The trust was to terminate upon the death of Ordway's last surviving child, at which time the trust property was to be distributed among Ordway's then living grandchildren. Soon after the death of the last child in 1979, two of the grandchildren disclaimed their remainder interests in the trust. The grandchildren had known about their trust interests for 47 years.

The Supreme Court, resolving a conflict in the circuits on the issue, found that the beneficiaries were required to disclaim within a reasonable time after obtaining knowledge of their interests (or perhaps the enactment of the gift tax, if later), even though the gift tax had not been enacted at the creation of the trust in 1917. The Court found that waiting to disclaim for 47 years after obtaining knowledge of the interests did not constitute a "reasonable" delay, so the disclaimers were not timely, and were treated as gifts.

As explained above, the proposed regulations provide that the transfer in such a case is the date of the original transfer.

[k]　Joint Tenancy With Right of Survivorship

Two issues exist with respect to the disclaimer of joint tenancy property. One is whether the period for disclaiming begins on the creation of the joint tenancy or on the first joint tenant's death. The other issue is whether the surviving tenant can disclaim the one-half survivorship interest in property that was originally contributed by him. Both are discussed below at ¶ 47.02[13].

[4]　Filing Requirements

Federal law does not require a disclaimer to be filed in the court records, as long as the disclaimer is effective under local law to pass property without direction by the disclaimant to the qualified alternate takers described in Section 2518(b)(4). On the other hand, federal law will require that the dis-

---

[32] Treas. Reg. § 25.2511-1(c)(2).

[33] 114 S. Ct. 1473 (1994).

claimer be filed if local law requires a filing for the disclaimer to operate to pass the disclaimed property (either as a disclaimer or an assignment under local law).[34]

[5] Irrevocability

To be effective, a disclaimer must be both irrevocable and unconditional.[35]

[6] No Acceptance of Benefits

A disclaimer cannot be a qualified disclaimer if the disclaimant accepts, expressly or impliedly, the disclaimed property or any of its benefits.[36]

[a] What Constitutes Acceptance?

Acceptance is manifested by an affirmative act consistent with ownership of the interest in property, including (1) use of the property, (2) receipt of income from the property, (3) the management of or direction of others to act with respect to the property, (4) the acceptance of consideration in return for making the disclaimer, and (5) the exercise of a power of appointment to any extent (this is considered acceptance of the entire power).[37]

A nonbinding statement of intention to make the disclaimant whole may, however, be okay. In one private letter ruling, a decedent's children and grandchildren proposed to disclaim their interests under a trust as well as under the laws of intestacy, so that the property would pass to the decedent's spouse outright. As part of this transaction, the spouse proposed to execute estate planning documents giving her descendants rights similar to those they would have had if the decedent's estate plan had been left intact. The IRS found that since the spouse was not obligated to execute her later estate plan, there was no consideration for the disclaimers, and the disclaimers would not be considered gifts.[38]

---

[34] Treas. Reg. § 25.2518-1(c)(1)(i). Note that this rule applies to disclaimers of interests in property created before 1982; the portion of the regulation addressing interests created in 1982 or later has been reserved. Treas. Reg. § 25.2518-1(c)(1)(ii).

[35] Treas. Reg. § 25.2518-2(a)(1).

[36] IRC § 2518(b)(3); Treas. Reg. § 25.2518-2(d)(1).

[37] Treas. Reg. § 25.2518-2(d)(1); see also Priv. Ltr. Rul. 9232014 (May 5, 1992); Priv. Ltr. Rul. 9232004 (Mar. 12, 1992).

[38] Priv. Ltr. Rul. 9427030 (Apr. 12, 1994); compare Estate of Monroe v. Comm'r, 104 TC 352 (1995) (disclaimers disqualified even though no consideration promised where disclaimants believed that person who took as a result of disclaimer would take care of them).

[b] What Does Not Constitute Acceptance?

[i] Exercise of non-discretionary powers as a fiduciary. A beneficiary who is also a fiduciary with respect to certain property may exercise powers to preserve or maintain the property in his fiduciary capacity without being considered to have accepted the property (unless he exercises, as fiduciary, a wholly discretionary power to direct enjoyment of the disclaimed property or to allocate enjoyment of the property among a designated class).[39]

> EXAMPLE: Beneficiary *A* disclaims any interest in a testamentary trust. He continues to serve as executor of the estate. He may exercise powers as executor without accepting benefits, except discretionary powers to vary the enjoyment of the disclaimed property.

[ii] Receipt of benefits by beneficiary under age 21. A beneficiary who is under age 21 (or the custodian of property for such a beneficiary) may take action with regard to (and receive benefits from) property prior to the beneficiary's 21st birthday without being considered to have accepted the property.[40]

[iii] Automatic vesting at death. Acceptance does not include merely taking delivery of an instrument of title or the vesting of an interest in property in the disclaimant immediately upon the death of a decedent pursuant to local law.[41]

> EXAMPLE: *D* died intestate on November 6, 1991, owning 449.25 shares of *X* Corporation stock, which passed to *W*. *W* took no action with respect to this stock. On December 31, 1991, *X* Corporation declared a dividend. *D*'s son deposited the dividend check into *W*'s checking account without telling her. The IRS ruled that *W* could make a qualified disclaimer of 250 shares of the stock, since she had not taken any action that constituted acceptance of the stock or the income.[42]

[iv] Acceptance of one of multiple separate interests. Acceptance of one interest in property will not by itself constitute acceptance of any other separate interest created by the transferor and held by the disclaimant in the same property.[43]

---

[39] Treas. Reg. § 25.2518-2(d)(2).

[40] Treas. Reg. § 25.2518-2(d)(3).

[41] Treas. Reg. § 25.2518-2(d)(1).

[42] Priv. Ltr. Rul. 9243024 (July 23, 1992).

[43] Treas. Reg. § 25.2518-2(d)(1).

[v] **Residence in joint tenancy property.** In the case of residential property held in joint tenancy by some or all of the residents, a surviving joint tenant will not be considered to have accepted an interest in the property passing from the deceased joint tenant merely because she resides in the property before disclaiming.[44]

If she was a co-tenant before the decedent's death, she should not be considered to have accepted the property even if she continues to occupy the property after she disclaims, since she is exercising rights incident to her interest as a co-tenant.

[vi] **Payment of taxes on property.** A donee who uses personal funds to pay property taxes due on Blackacre (but does not reside on Blackacre) has not exercised dominion and control to an extent that would prevent him from disclaiming Blackacre.[45]

[vii] **Execution of will exercising power of appointment over property.** If the donee of a general power of appointment executes a will which provides for the exercise of the power, but then disclaims the power within nine months of the creation of the power, he or she will not be deemed to have accepted the power.[46] This is because a testamentary power cannot be exercised by the will of a living person, which by definition has not taken effect.

[7] Passage of Property Without Direction by the Disclaimant

For a disclaimer to be qualified, the disclaimed property must pass without direction on the part of the disclaimant.[47]

[a] Agreement Regarding Passage of Property

If there is an express or implied agreement that the disclaimed property will pass to a person specified by the disclaimant, the disclaimer will not be a qualified disclaimer.[48]

Can several parties agree to disclaim so that, for example, Mom can get the property? Apparently, the IRS thinks so.[49] In Priv. Ltr. Rul. 9509003, to

---

[44] Treas. Reg. § 25.2518-2(d)(1). See ¶ 47.02[13] for further discussion of disclaimers of property held in joint tenancy.

[45] Treas. Reg. § 25.2518-2(d)(4), example 3.

[46] Treas. Reg. § 25.2518-2(d)(4), example 7.

[47] IRC § 2518(b)(4).

[48] Treas. Reg. § 25.2518-2(e)(1).

[49] Priv. Ltr. Rul. 9509003 (Nov. 3, 1994).

achieve a desired result, a family group all disclaimed together, and the IRS ruled that the disclaimers qualified. In contrast, Beneficiary *A* cannot disclaim property which Beneficiary *B* would then take, if Beneficiary *A* has conditioned his disclaimer on Beneficiary *B*'s agreement to give the property to a third person.

[b] Disclaimant's Power of Appointment Over the Disclaimed Property

If the disclaimant, either alone or in conjunction with another, has a power of appointment over the disclaimed property after disclaiming, then the disclaimer will not be a qualified disclaimer unless the power is limited by an ascertainable standard.[50]

[c] Fiduciary Power Over Property

The disclaimant may hold a fiduciary power as trustee or executor to distribute the disclaimed property among beneficiaries after the disclaimer, so long as the power is subject to an ascertainable standard.[51]

[d] Surviving Spouse's Power to Direct Beneficial Enjoyment

The surviving spouse can have an interest in disclaimed property. However, she cannot retain a power to control who enjoys the property, unless the power is limited to an ascertainable standard.[52]

[e] Deed in Lieu of Disclaimer

A written transfer of the transferor's entire interest in property will be treated as a qualified disclaimer, even if it does not constitute a disclaimer under local law, provided that the transfer—

- Meets the general requirements of Sections 2518(b)(2) and 2518(b)(3) and
- Is effective to transfer the property to a person or persons who would have received the property had the transferor made a qualified disclaimer.[53]

---

[50] Treas. Reg. § 25.2518-2(e)(1)(i).

[51] Treas. Reg. § 25.2518-2(e)(1).

[52] Treas. Reg. § 25.2518-2(e)(2).

[53] IRC § 2518(c)(3).

Section 2518(c)(3) was added to the Internal Revenue Code in 1981.[54] Its general purpose is to allow a transfer which does not qualify as a disclaimer under local law to constitute a qualified disclaimer under federal law, as long as the disclaimer operates as a valid transfer under local law to the persons who would have received the property had it been a qualified disclaimer under local law.[55]

[i] **Partial disclaimers.** Section 2518(c)(3) as written applies to a transfer of the transferor's entire interest in the property. However, the legislative history of this section provides that a transfer of an otherwise qualifying undivided portion of the transferor's entire interest is treated as a qualified disclaimer of that undivided portion.[56]

[ii] **Spousal disclaimers.** The general rule is that "a transfer will not be considered a transfer of the entire interest in the property if, by reason of the transfer, some or all of the beneficial enjoyment in the property returns to the transferor or the transferor has any power after the transfer to control the beneficial enjoyment from the property."[57] However, Section 2518(b)(4) allows a spouse to disclaim property and be the recipient of the property after the disclaimer. Thus, despite the ambiguity created by the Blue Book passage regarding the ability of a surviving spouse to transfer property under this section, retain a beneficial interest in the property transferred, and have the transfer treated as a qualified disclaimer, the law has been applied to uphold that result under Section 2518(c)(3).[58]

[iii] **"No probate" agreement.** An agreement not to probate a will entered into by the disclaimant and others (including the person who takes as a result of the disclaimer) may be considered to have the effect of directing how the disclaimed property will pass. In such circumstances, the agreement could prevent the disclaimer from qualifying under Section 2518, where persons other than those who would take as a result of a qualified disclaimer become entitled to the property in question.[59]

---

[54] Economic Recovery Tax Act of 1981, Pub. L. No. 97-34, 95 Stat. 172 § 426(a) (1981).

[55] General Explanation of the Economic Recovery Tax Act of 1981, HR 4242, 97th Congress, 1st Sess., tit. IV, at 267 (1981) (Blue Book).

[56] Blue Book at 267.

[57] Blue Book at 267. The transfer and transferor in these sentences refer to the would-be disclaimer and disclaimant.

[58] See ¶ 47.02[7][e][ii] below.

[59] See Priv. Ltr. Rul. 9610004 (Nov. 8, 1995) (finding a taxable gift rather than a qualified disclaimer, because effect of agreement was to pass disclaimed property to

Technical Advice Memorandum 9228004[60] provides a good example of the practical application of this principle. Decedent, a Texas resident, left Husband an income interest in a trust which did not qualify for QTIP treatment. Decedent's sons held the remainder interest. Husband and the sons agreed not to probate Decedent's will. Sons, individually and on behalf of their own children, then disclaimed most of the property of the estate that passed to them by intestacy. Since Decedent's descendants were then treated as having predeceased her, the disclaimed property passed to Husband, and Decedent's estate claimed a marital deduction. The IRS ruled that the agreement not to probate the will was itself a qualified disclaimer under Section 2518(c)(3). The IRS found that under Texas law, the will operates to vest property in the devisees immediately, regardless of whether the will is ultimately probated. In making the agreement not to probate the will, the spouse effectively transferred what he would have received under the will (the trust income interest) to the persons who would have received the property had he disclaimed (the sons, who were the remainder beneficiaries). Since the agreement not to probate the will was treated as a qualified disclaimer, and the sons' disclaimers for themselves and their children were also qualified disclaimers, the property ultimately received by Husband was deemed to have passed directly from Decedent, and the estate was entitled to claim the marital deduction.

Note that, in this ruling, the IRS correctly pointed out that the entire transaction could have been accomplished with disclaimers alone—Husband disclaims income interest in trust, so remainder beneficiaries receive fee simple title; remainder beneficiaries then disclaim property in excess of what they want to keep.

[iv] Deed in lieu of disclaimer. In Private Letter Ruling 9135043,[61] the IRS ruled that a deed operated as a qualified disclaimer under Section 2518(c)(3). Decedent had owned real property with Husband as joint tenants with rights of survivorship. Husband had furnished all of the consideration for the property, and paid all of the mortgage payments and other expenses of the property. Under local (Massachusetts) law, Husband could not disclaim the property, since he had furnished the consideration. Within nine months of Decedent's death, Husband executed a deed transferring Decedent's interest

---

surviving spouse rather than to disclaimant's issue who would take upon execution of qualified disclaimer) and DePaoli v. Comm'r, 62 F3d 1259 (10th Cir. 1995), rev'g 1993 RIA TC Memo. ¶ 93, 577, 66 TCM (CCH) 1493 (1993) (same fact situation, but opposite result, because under state law, decedent's wife rather than his illegitimate issue would have taken if his legitimate son had executed a qualified disclaimer).

[60] March 31, 1992.

[61] June 3, 1991.

in the property to Daughter, who would have received the property had Husband been able to disclaim. The deed qualified under Section 2518(c)(3).

Disclaimers of jointly held property are discussed more fully at ¶ 47.02[13].

[v] Tax Court interpretation—sole defect in disclaimer must be local law characterization of transfer. In 1993, the Tax Court adopted a narrow interpretation of Section 2518(c)(3) in *Estate of Bennett v. Commissioner*.[62] Bennett left the bulk of his estate to a trust. The trust did not qualify for QTIP treatment because the trustee could terminate the trust in favor of persons other than the spouse; the trustee could allocate receipts and expenses between income and principal in any manner; and distributions during the spouse's lifetime could be made to persons other than the surviving spouse. In a very involved series of transactions, the trustees disclaimed certain of their powers, and some of the beneficiaries other than the surviving spouse disclaimed their interests. Several of these disclaimers did not qualify under local (Kansas) law, and were not properly made under independent federal requirements. The estate argued that even though the disclaimers did not comply with the federal requirements, they should be viewed as qualified disclaimers under Section 2518(c)(3). The Tax Court stated:

> Section 2518(c)(3) should not be viewed as a catch-all provision to save defective or disqualified [under local law] disclaimers but as an entirely new relief provision under which, after a disclaimer has been disqualified, the would-be disclaimant makes an actual written transfer to the person who otherwise would have received the property had the disclaimer been valid under local law. The relief of section 2518(c)(3) was designed to eliminate the gift tax consequences for the beneficiary who had made a disclaimer that was disqualified and who then made an actual written transfer to another individual.[63]

The Tax Court found that the beneficiaries' disclaimers were not qualified disclaimers under the basic provisions of Section 2518, nor did they qualify under Section 2518(c)(3) since they were not "actual written transfers" made within the nine-month period. Thus, the Tax Court has held that Section 2518(c)(3) relief is appropriate only if the sole defect in a disclaimer which is otherwise proper for federal purposes is its local law characterization as a transfer instead of a disclaimer.

[f] Passage of Property to Disclaimant's Charity

It is not uncommon for a person to want to disclaim in favor of his private foundation. Of course, the instrument would have to be drafted to provide this

---

[62] 100 TC 42 (1993).

[63] 100 TC 42 at 76.

disposition on disclaimer. Even if this is done, is there still a problem with the disclaimant's being able to participate in decisions regarding distribution of the funds? The IRS thinks so.

Under the facts addressed in a private letter ruling in 1992, Decedent left property outright to his sons. If any son disclaimed his share, the disclaimed property was to pass to a charity selected by a designated person other than the disclaimant. During his life, Decedent had established Foundation, which could receive the disclaimed property, and which included Decedent's children on its board. Foundation proposed to amend its bylaws prior to the execution of the disclaimers to provide that any disclaimed property designated to pass to Foundation would be held in a separate fund, governed by a committee of the board that would not include the disclaimants. The IRS ruled that the disclaimers could be qualified disclaimers, since the disclaimants would have no power to direct the beneficial enjoyment of the disclaimed property, and that Decedent's estate could be entitled to an estate tax charitable deduction for the amounts disclaimed.[64] The clear implication is that in the absence of the amendment to the bylaws, a qualified disclaimer could not have been made.

PRACTICE POINTER: If the charitable beneficiary who takes pursuant to a disclaimer is a private foundation or other charity, and the disclaimant is entitled to participate in decisions regarding its distributions, the disclaimer may not be valid. This is because it may be viewed as a disclaimer accompanied by a retention of the right to direct payment of the transferred property. To avoid this, the disclaimed property should pass into a separate fund, and the disclaimant should have no ability to participate in directing its disposition.[65] However, the disclaimant can be permitted to make non-binding recommendations regarding the disposition of the fund.[66]

[8] Passage of Property to Another Person

[a] General Rule

The disclaimed property must pass to a person other than the disclaimant.[67] Technical Advice Memorandum 9417002[68] provides a good example of local law defeating the intended outcome of disclaimers. In this ruling, Daugh-

---

[64] Priv. Ltr. Rul. 9235022 (May 29, 1992).

[65] See Priv. Ltr. Rul. 9350033 (Sept. 22, 1993); Priv. Ltr. Rul. 9350032 (Sept. 22, 1993); Priv. Ltr. Rul. 9320008 (Feb. 2, 1993); Priv. Ltr. Rul. 9319022 (Feb. 9, 1993); Priv. Ltr. Rul. 9317039 (Feb. 2, 1993).

[66] See Priv. Ltr. Rul. 9532027 (May 12, 1995), in which disclaimants were permitted to advise but could not control use of disclaimed funds).

[67] IRC § 2518(b)(4)(B).

[68] June 23, 1993.

ter disclaimed her interest as a residuary beneficiary of Father's estate with respect to certain shares in a closely held corporation. Father's will provided that if Daughter did not survive him, his property would pass to Daughter's Husband and children. Daughter's Husband disclaimed any interest he had in the disclaimed property, and as a result Daughter transferred the shares to her children. The IRS found that local (Mississippi) law would provide that where no provision is made in a will for disclaimers (as opposed to prior death), the disclaimed property would pass under the Mississippi laws of intestacy, rather than as if Daughter had predeceased Father. Since Daughter had not disclaimed her intestate interest in Father's estate, she received the shares from Father under the laws of intestacy, and her transfer of the shares to her children was actually a taxable gift by her.

WARNING: Although this result would not have occurred in all states, in light of varying state laws dealing with disclaimers, this ruling does point out that it is important in planning to consider all possible consequences of a disclaimer.

[b] Exception for Surviving Spouse Disclaimant

Property disclaimed by the surviving spouse can pass to her or for her benefit.[69] The disclaimed property may not pass to a third person for the benefit of the disclaimant unless the disclaimant is the surviving spouse.[70]

Disclaimer's effect on bypass trust. If the language in a dispositive document provides that a bypass trust (or other gift) is to be funded with the greatest amount that can pass free of estate tax, a disclaimer by the surviving spouse of other property automatically reduces the credit shelter trust.

> EXAMPLE: Dad, who never made taxable gifts, has an estate of $3,000,000. Dad's will leaves the "maximum amount that can pass free of estate tax" to a bypass trust. The balance of the estate is left to Mom, or if she does not survive, to dynastic trusts for the children. Mom decides she wants to disclaim $400,000, so that Dad's GSTT exemption can be fully used. If Mom disclaims $400,000, the "maximum amount that can pass free of estate tax" to the bypass trust will now be $200,000, resulting in the bypass trust receiving $200,000, the dynastic trusts for the children receiving $400,000, and Mom receiving the rest of the estate. In order for the dynastic trusts to will receive $1,000,000, Mom must disclaim $1,000,000. Then, the bypass trust will receive nothing, and the dynastic trusts will receive $1,000,000. If Mom wants the dynastic trusts to be fully funded (i.e., to have $1,000,000 after-tax), and they are trusts which bear a portion of the estate tax, she will need to disclaim an amount which results in their receiving an after-tax amount of $1,000,000. If Dad

---

[69] IRC § 2518(b)(4)(A).

[70] Treas. Reg. § 25.2518-2(e)(1)(ii), 25.2518-2(e)(2).

never made taxable gifts, and the will disposes of all the property in the taxable estate, this amount will be $1,259,649.

PRACTICE POINTER: If the aim is to keep the bypass trust intact, and allow Mom the flexibility to disclaim amounts in excess of the credit-sheltered amount, while remaining a beneficiary of the bypass trust, the funding clause for the bypass bequest should generally provide that the bequest should be computed without regard to disclaimers of other property made by the surviving spouse. (If Mom disclaims her interest in the bypass trust itself, then the formula does take into account the disclaimer, allowing Mom to disclaim that amount altogether.) The following is a sample clause: "If my wife disclaims any property passing to her by reason of my death, other than her interest in the bypass trust, the amount passing to the bypass trust shall be computed as if such disclaimer had not been made."

PRACTICE POINTER: Sometimes, people like the idea of the tax benefits of the bypass trust, but are nervous about trusts. They want to leave everything to the surviving spouse in case the surviving spouse wants to receive it outright when the time comes; however, they like the idea of giving the surviving spouse the option of taking advantage of the tax benefits. In such a case, the surviving spouse can be given the option to disclaim the remaining amount of the deceased spouse's unified credit in favor of a trust which provides that she can invade it if necessary. The surviving spouse cannot have a power of appointment over a trust which contains property she has disclaimed.[71] If the trust is drafted with a power of appointment, she can disclaim it separately from other interests.[72] If the surviving spouse is trustee of the trust which will hold the disclaimed property, her powers to direct the beneficial enjoyment must be limited to an ascertainable standard, or the disclaimer will not be qualified.[73] If the trust is drafted with broader powers, the surviving spouse may have to decline to serve as trustee, since fiduciary powers may not be disclaimable under state law, and may not be partially disclaimable under federal law.

[9] Execution of Disclaimer by Proper Person

The disclaimer must be signed by the disclaimant or the disclaimant's legal representative.[74] A parent, for example, cannot disclaim on behalf of a minor child unless he is the child's legal representative.

---

[71] Treas. Reg. §§ 25.2518-2(e)(2), 25.2518-2(e)(5), example 5.

[72] Treas. Reg. § 25.2518-3(a)(1)(iii).

[73] Treas. Reg. § 25.2518-3(a)(1)(iii). See Exhibit 47-A, Example 2, for representative language.

[74] Treas. Reg. § 25.2518-2(b)(1).

[a] Executor

An executor who is authorized to disclaim property under local law and who is authorized to act for the estate at the time the disclaimer is executed may make a qualified disclaimer.[75] This is the case even where the result of the disclaimer is to cause property to pass to the executor in her individual capacity.[76] An executor who is not authorized to disclaim under local law cannot execute a qualified disclaimer (since the disclaimer would not operate to pass the property as required under Section 2518(b)(4)).[77] In some cases, local law may require obtaining court approval.[78]

[b] Guardian Ad Litem

A guardian ad litem may make a qualified disclaimer on behalf of minor beneficiaries,[79] if he is authorized to do so under local law.

[c] Legal Guardian

A parent acting as the minor child's legal guardian has been ruled able to make a qualified disclaimer on behalf of the minor child in the manner and to the extent provided under local law.[80] This is a ruling under Texas law, which required that a guardian could only act with court approval.

[d] Charity

A charity might want to disclaim a bequest, for example, of contaminated real estate. It can do so if state law permits. For example, a charity was able to make a qualified disclaimer through a court order when the state (Oklahoma) Attorney General joined in the court action to represent the charity's interests.[81]

---

[75] Tech. Adv. Mem. 8015014 (Dec. 28, 1979).

[76] Priv. Ltr. Rul. 8749041 (Sept. 4, 1987).

[77] Tech. Adv. Mem. 8148018 (July 31, 1981); Tech. Adv. Mem. 7937011 (May 31, 1979).

[78] Priv. Ltr. Rul. 8338116 (Jun. 23, 1983) (New Jersey).

[79] Priv. Ltr. Rul. 9310020 (Dec. 14, 1992); Priv. Ltr. Rul. 9251019 (Sept. 18, 1992).

[80] Priv. Ltr. Rul. 9228004 (Mar. 31, 1992) (stating that under Texas law, a personal representative may disclaim for a minor child with the approval of the probate court).

[81] Priv. Ltr. Rul. 9222041 (Feb. 28, 1992).

[e] Attorney-in-Fact

A power in an agent to disclaim, being similar to the power to make a gift, is probably required to be specifically authorized in most states. If it is specifically authorized, the attorney-in-fact should be able to disclaim.[82] An attorney for the executor of an estate was found to have authority under state law (Oregon) to make a qualified disclaimer on behalf of the executor.[83]

[f] Trustee

Generally, interests in trusts must be disclaimed by the beneficiaries. This requirement can necessitate a court proceeding to deal with interests of minors, the unborn, and unascertained persons. Can the trustee disclaim on their behalf? No, as a general rule, a trustee's disclaimer would be ineffective. A trustee is not a proper person to execute a disclaimer on behalf of a trust or on behalf of the beneficiary of a trust, unless (1) the trust instrument authorizes the trustee to disclaim or (2) the affected beneficiary consents to the disclaimer.[84]

[i] Fiduciary powers disclaimed. In *Cleaveland v. United States*,[85] the district court held that a trustee could disclaim a power of invasion if the beneficiaries did not object. This case should not be relied on as authority that trustees can disclaim their fiduciary powers without the consent (at least implied) of the beneficiaries.[86]

[ii] Authorized by trust agreement. In Revenue Ruling 90-110,[87] the IRS ruled that a trustee could not disclaim the power to invade trust property for the benefit of a certain beneficiary. The beneficiary did not consent to the disclaimer, nor did the governing instrument authorize the trustee to disclaim on the beneficiary's behalf. The IRS implied, however, that if either local law or the governing instrument authorized the trustee to disclaim on behalf of the beneficiary, such a disclaimer could be treated as a qualified disclaimer.[88]

---

[82] See Priv. Ltr. Rul. 9015017 (Jan. 10, 1990).

[83] Estate of Allen v. Comm'r, 1989 PH TC Memo. ¶ 89, 111, 56 TCM (CCH) 1494 (1989).

[84] George G. Bogert, The Law of Trusts and Trustees § 150 (Rev. 2d ed. 1979); Restatement (Second) of Trusts, § 102(4) (1959).

[85] 62 AFTR2d 88-5992, 88-1 USTC (CCH) ¶ 13,766 (CD Ill. 1988).

[86] See, e.g., Estate of Bennett v. Comm'r, 100 TC 42 (1993), in which the Tax Court held that the trustees' attempted disclaimers of certain fiduciary powers amounted to an ineffective renunciation of their trusteeship.

[87] 1990-2 CB 209.

[88] See also Tech. Adv. Mem. 9135003 (May 23, 1991).

[iii] **Joined by beneficiary.** In Private Letter Ruling 9247026,[89] a trustee disclaimed a trust's interest in an employee benefit plan only after all possible beneficiaries of the trust had executed their own disclaimers with respect to plan property. The trustee's disclaimer was a qualified disclaimer, resulting in the property's passing to beneficiaries outside the plan.[90]

PLANNING POINT: The estate planner may wish to consider including provisions in wills, trusts or beneficiary designations which permit a trustee to disclaim and provide a method of disclaimer. The specific authorization may overcome an argument that the trustee has no power to disclaim without the consent of the affected beneficiary.[91] Consider also whether all trustees should have this power, or merely a disinterested trustee. If a trustee with an interest in the trust has the ability to disclaim as trustee in favor of himself individually, the disclaimer would be invalid unless the beneficiary-trustee were the surviving spouse. As a practical matter, a trustee needs to consider the question of potential liability to the beneficiaries of disclaiming their interests.

[10] No Consideration for Disclaimer

The disclaimant cannot receive any consideration for executing the disclaimer. This will be considered an acceptance of the benefits of the disclaimed property.[92]

An agreement to disclaim in order that another person will take the property is apparently okay. One letter ruling, for example, involved A, a California resident, who died in 1991 with a will drafted in 1968. The will required A's Wife to elect to (1) contribute all of her community property to the trust created under A's will (in exchange for receiving a life interest in A's property and Wife's property held in the trust) or (2) keep her community property as allowed under California law and be treated as if she had predeceased A under the will. In 1968 Wife had executed a consent to take under the will, but after A's death intended to elect against the will. The will provided that if Wife predeceased A, A's property passed into trusts for A's children, or if a child was not living, outright to the child's descendants. All of A's children proposed to disclaim their interests under the will, so that the property would pass to A's grandchildren. The grandchildren (adults acting on their own, minors through a guardian ad litem) would then disclaim their

---

[89] Aug. 24, 1992.

[90] See also Priv. Ltr. Rul. 9521032 (Feb. 28, 1995), in which a trustee's disclaimer of a power of invasion was qualified where the trustee was also the sole beneficiary.

[91] See Rev. Rul. 90-110, 1990-2 CB 209; Priv. Ltr. Rul. 9521032 (Feb. 28, 1995); Tech. Adv. Mem. 9135003 (May 23, 1991).

[92] Treas. Reg. § 25.2518-2(d)(4), example 2.

interests, so that the property would pass by intestacy outright to Wife. The IRS ruled that if Wife's election against the will were valid, then the subsequent disclaimers could be qualified disclaimers, and the property passing to Wife by intestacy would be eligible for the estate tax marital deduction in A's estate.[93]

What if the "consideration" is paid pursuant to a nonbinding agreement or understanding? The answer seems to be fact-specific. For example, disclaimers were held to be invalid in *Monroe v. Commissioner*.[94] In this case, Louise Monroe made numerous cash bequests in her will. The remainder of Louise's estate, including any renounced legacies, was left to Edgar, her surviving husband. Edgar decided to request disclaimers from 29 of the legatees named in Louise's will. The disclaimers would result in the disclaimed property passing to Edgar. All of the legatees who were asked to disclaim their bequests did so. Shortly thereafter, they received personal checks signed by Edgar, bearing the notation "gift," in amounts approximately equal to or greater than the amounts of their respective disclaimed bequests. The Tax Court determined that 28 of the disclaimers were invalid due to their being executed for consideration, and reduced the marital deduction accordingly. The estate argued that the disclaimers and the later gifts that were received by the disclaimants from Edgar were independent, unrelated transactions, because there was no agreement or promise to any legatee to exchange consideration for a disclaimer.

The Tax Court found that even if no binding agreement existed, the evidence suggested that the disclaimants expected, for one reason or another, that they would receive compensation for their disclaimed bequests in the form of a gift or legacy from Edgar. Also, the testimony of many of the disclaimants suggested that they feared the consequences if they refused to disclaim.

The Tax Court concluded that, although the disclaimants may not have explicitly bargained with Edgar for consideration in return for executing their disclaimers, nonetheless, each disclaimant was induced or, in some instances, coerced, into executing a disclaimer. Under those circumstances, the consideration for their disclaimers was the implied promise that they would be better off if they did what Edgar wanted them to do than if they refused to do so. Thus, their disclaimers were not qualified.

In another situation, the IRS determined that several disclaimants had acted in concert in making their disclaimers in order to reduce the estate tax liability of the decedent's estate. But, in the absence of an underlying agreement, any expectancy the disclaiming descendants might have had in inheriting an enhanced estate due to the decreased estate tax was "purely specu-

---

[93] Priv. Ltr. Rul. 9310020 (Dec. 14, 1992).

[94] 104 TC 352 (1995).

lative," and therefore did not constitute the acceptance of any consideration in return for the making of the disclaimers.[96]

[11] Partial Disclaimers

Certain partial disclaimers are permissible.

[a] Undivided Portion of Property

A disclaimer of an "undivided portion" of all or any separate interests in property will be treated as a qualified disclaimer if it otherwise meets the requirements of a qualified disclaimer.[96] An "undivided portion" is a fraction or percentage of each and every substantial interest or right owned by the disclaimant in the property and must extend over the entire term of the disclaimant's interest in the property (including other property into which the disclaimed property is converted).[97]

> EXAMPLE: Dad dies owning a farm. Dad leaves Child an income interest for life in the farm, remainder to Grandchild. Child can disclaim 40 percent of his income interest; that would be an undivided portion of all of his interests in the farm, extending over the entire term of those interests.[98] Child could not disclaim a term of years out of his income interest, since that is not all or an undivided portion of that interest.[99]

> EXAMPLE: Dad dies and establishes a testamentary trust. Child gets income for life, remainder to Grandchild. Child cannot make a qualified disclaimer of all of the income in excess of $100,000 per year. The disclaimed amount would not be an undivided portion of the interest.[100]

A disclaimer of some specific rights while retaining other rights with respect to an interest in the property is not a disclaimer of an undivided portion of the disclaimant's interest in the property.[101]

It was once widely suggested that, when Dad left property in fee simple to Child, Child should disclaim the remainder interest and keep the income interest. Then, when Child died, none of the property would be included in Child's estate. The regulations provide that such a disclaimer will not be

---

[96] Priv. Ltr. Rul. 9509003 (Nov. 3, 1994).

[96] IRC § 2518(c)(1).

[97] Treas. Reg. § 25.2518-3(b).

[98] Treas. Reg. § 25.2518-3(d), example 4.

[99] Treas. Reg. § 25.2518-3(a)(1)(i); see also Treas. Reg. § 25.2518-3(d), example 11.

[100] Treas. Reg. § 25.2518-3(d), example 12.

[101] Treas. Reg. § 25.2518-3(b).

qualified.[102] This rule does not apply to interests in a trust in which separate interests are not merged.[103]

WARNING: Is planning with non-merged interests a good idea? In this regard, we have to be careful of the nominal interest rules.

[b] Nominal Interest

If Dad creates a "nominal interest" in property which prevents the merger of Child's interests in the property, Child's disclaimer of any of his interests will be qualified only if Child disclaims all interests which would be merged but for the existence of the nominal interest.[104]

A "nominal interest" is an interest in property created by the transferor that—

- Is actuarially valued at less than five percent of the value of the property at the time of the taxable transfer,
- Prevents the merger under local law of two or more other interests created by the transferor in the property, and
- Can be shown under the applicable facts and circumstances to have been created primarily to prevent the merger of the other interests.[105]

EXAMPLE: Dad devises Blackacre to Child for life, then to Gardener for one month, remainder to Child's estate. Assume that without Gardener's interest, state law would have merged Child's interests into fee simple title. Gardener's interest is likely a "nominal interest."[106]

[c] Power of Appointment

A power of appointment over property is considered a separate interest, all or an undivided portion of which may be disclaimed.[107] However, any right to direct beneficial enjoyment of the subject property retained by the disclaimant after the disclaimer must be limited by an ascertainable standard.[108]

---

[102] Treas. Reg. § 25.2518-3(b).

[103] Treas. Reg. § 25.2518-3(d), example 8; see also Priv. Ltr. Rul. 9526018 (Mar. 30, 1995); Priv. Ltr. Rul. 9526019 (Mar. 31, 1995).

[104] Treas. Reg. § 25.2518-3(a)(1)(i).

[105] Treas. Reg. § 25.2518-3(a)(1)(iv).

[106] Treas. Reg. § 25.2518-3(d), example 13; see also Treas. Reg. § 25.2518-3(d), example 14.

[107] Treas. Reg. § 25.2518-3(a)(1)(iii).

[108] Treas. Reg. § 25.2518-3(a)(1)(iii).

EXAMPLE: Mom is trustee of an irrevocable trust created by Dad. All trust income is to be paid to Mom and Child. Mom, as trustee, may invade principal for her support. Mom also holds a testamentary limited power of appointment over the trust; if she does not exercise the power, the trust property passes to Child on her death. If Mom disclaims her power to invade principal for her support, but retains the testamentary power of appointment, the disclaimer will not be qualified. If Mom disclaims the testamentary power of appointment, that can be a qualified disclaimer, since the power and interest she has retained in the trust are limited by an ascertainable standard.[109]

In Private Letter Ruling 9236018,[110] Daughter was named trustee of a trust established by Decedent. All trust income was payable to Daughter, and she had a lifetime and testamentary general power of appointment. The IRS ruled that Daughter could make a qualified disclaimer of a fractional share of both the lifetime and testamentary general powers of appointment. After the disclaimer, Daughter's only power over the disclaimed portion of the trust was the non-discretionary power to pay all income to herself for life.

[d] Interest in a Trust

A person can make a qualified disclaimer of income from specific property held in a trust, while retaining the right to receive income from other properties held in the trust. A person can also make a qualified disclaimer of an income interest and a remainder interest in specific trust assets, while retaining interests in other trust property. However, in either case, the disclaimer qualifies only if the property to which the disclaimer relates is removed from the trust.[111]

EXAMPLE: Dad dies, leaving shares in Corporation X and Corporation Y to a trust. The trust pays all income to Son and Daughter equally for 10 years, at which time the trust terminates in equal shares in favor of Son and Daughter. Son disclaims his income interest in the Corporation X shares. Son's disclaimer is not qualified if the shares remain in trust. This would be true even if Son were only an income beneficiary of the trust.[112] If Son disclaimed both his income and remainder interest in the shares of Corporation X, and by local law, the shares were removed from the trust and paid to Daughter, his disclaimer could be a qualified disclaimer.[113]

---

[109] Treas. Reg. § 25.2518-3(d), example 9.

[110] June 5, 1992.

[111] Treas. Reg. § 25.2518-3(a)(2).

[112] Treas. Reg. § 25.2518-3(d), examples 5, 7.

[113] Treas. Reg. § 25.2518-3(d), example 6.

[e] Severable Property

A disclaimer of "severable property" may be a qualified disclaimer.

[i] Definition. "Severable property" is property which can be divided into separate parts, each of which maintains a complete and independent existence after severance.[114]

EXAMPLE: Dad dies, leaving a life estate in Blackacre to Mom, remainder to Child. Mom can disclaim her life interest in Blackacre if Blackacre passes, without any direction on the part of Mom, to Mom or others.[115]

EXAMPLE: A dies owning 200 shares of Corporation X, paintings, jewelry and silver. The Corporation X shares are left to B, and the paintings, jewelry and silver are left to C. B disclaims 50 shares of stock, and C disclaims the jewelry and two paintings. Each disclaimer may be a qualified disclaimer, since the property is severable property.[116] If B disclaimed only his remainder interest in the shares of stock, that would not be a qualified disclaimer of severable property.[117] This is distinguished from the above example because in the above example, Mom's sole interest in Blackacre was an income interest. Here, however, B has a fee interest in the property.

EXAMPLE: X dies owning a 500-acre farm, which he leaves to Y. Y can make a qualified disclaimer of 300 identified acres.[118]

[ii] Local law. What if local law does not recognize a purported disclaimer of severable property? Then, in order to be a qualified disclaimer, the disclaimer must operate under local law to transfer the property to another person without direction on the part of the disclaimant.[119]

[f] Qualified Pecuniary Disclaimer

A pecuniary disclaimer of a dollar amount of property out of a larger fund is possible, but tricky.

---

[114] Treas. Reg. § 25.2518-3(a)(1)(ii).

[115] Treas. Reg. § 25.2518-3(a)(2); see also Priv. Ltr. Rul. 9232004 (Mar. 12, 1992).

[116] Treas. Reg. § 25.2518-3(d), example 1.

[117] Treas. Reg. § 25.2518-3(b), 25.2518-3(d), example 2; see also Priv. Ltr. Rul. 9310020 (Dec. 14, 1992).

[118] Treas. Reg. § 25.2518-3(d), example 3.

[119] Treas. Reg. § 25.2518-3(a)(1)(ii).

[i] **Formula disclaimer permissible.** The pecuniary disclaimer may be expressed in terms of a formula.

EXAMPLE: Dad bequeaths his residuary estate to Child; if Child disclaims, the disclaimed property passes to Wife. Child may make a qualified disclaimer of a fractional share of Dad's residuary estate, the numerator being the smallest amount which would allow Dad's estate to pass free of estate tax, and the denominator being the value of the entire residuary estate.[120]

In Private Letter Ruling 9232024, Dad created a testamentary marital and bypass trust, providing that if Mom disclaimed property from the marital trust, the disclaimed property would pass to a disclaimer trust identical to the bypass trust, except that Mom would not be trustee. In order to use Dad's generation-skipping transfer tax exemption, Wife disclaimed, using the following formula amount from the Marital Trust: "The fraction of the marital trust that I disclaim is as follows: (1) The numerator of the fraction is the amount which will result in the Family [bypass] Trust and the Disclaimer Trust having an aggregate value, after taking into account all taxes, administration expenses, claims, debts and other expenses that are properly chargeable against either the Family Trust or the Disclaimer Trust by reason of my spouse's death, of $1,333,333 and (2) the denominator of the fraction is the value of the property, as finally determined for federal estate tax purposes in my spouse's estate, that would have passed to the Marital Trust at my spouse's death absent this disclaimer."

The IRS ruled, in this ruling, that the spouse's disclaimer could be a qualified disclaimer.[121] (Note that pursuant to the will described in the ruling, one-fourth of the disclaimed property was to pass to the son of the disclaimant, and three-fourths was to pass to the decedent's grandchildren after the spouse's death.)

[ii] **Segregation of disclaimed property and its share of income earned prior to disclaimer.** Following a pecuniary disclaimer, the amount disclaimed and any income attributable to the disclaimed amount earned prior to the date of the disclaimer must be segregated from the portion of the gift or bequest that was not disclaimed.[122]

---

[120] Treas. Reg. § 25.2518-3(d), example 20.

[121] Priv. Ltr. Rul. 9232024 (May 11, 1992); see also Estate of McInnes v. Comm'r, 1992 RIA TC Memo. ¶ 92, 558, 64 TCM (CCH) 840 (1992); Priv. Ltr. Rul. 9513011 (Dec. 29, 1994); Priv. Ltr. Rul. 9447033 (Aug. 26, 1994); Priv. Ltr. Rul. 9227006 (Mar. 20, 1992).

[122] Treas. Reg. § 25.2518-3(c).

Manner of funding. The segregation of assets must be performed in a manner similar to funding marital deduction bequests.[123] The segregation may be done based on the fair market value of the assets on the date of the disclaimer.[124] Alternatively, the segregation may be done based on values that are fairly representative of value changes that may have occurred between the date of transfer and the date of the disclaimer.[125]

Distribution from bequest before disclaimer. If a distribution of a pecuniary amount from the bequest or gift is made to the disclaimant prior to the disclaimer, that distribution is treated as a distribution of corpus from the bequest or gift, and the disclaimant is treated as having accepted a proportionate share of income earned by the bequest or gift.[126]

Disclaimant's share of income. The proportionate share of income which the disclaimant is considered to have accepted is determined using the following formula:

(amount of distributions received by disclaimant before disclaimer/value of bequest or gift on date of transfer)×total income earned by gift or bequest between date of transfer and date of disclaimer.[127]

EXAMPLE: Dad bequeaths a stock account worth $100,000 to Son. Four months after Dad's death, Son withdraws stocks worth $40,000. Eight months after Dad's death, Son disclaims $60,000 of the account. The account's fair market value on the date of the disclaimer equals its date of death value, but the account earned $20,000 income between Dad's date of death and the date of the disclaimer. Son is considered to have accepted $8,000 of the income (($40,000/$100,000)×$20,000).[128] Presumably, some of the income would have been earned after the $40,000 distribution, but that does not affect the amount Son is considered to have accepted.

In Private Letter Ruling 9244012,[129] the decedent's spouse allowed the decedent's executor to pay the balance due on state and federal personal income taxes for the decedent and his spouse for the year of decedent's death. The spouse had agreed that if the estate paid any portion of tax that was attributable to her income, she would reimburse the estate, with market rate interest. The spouse was found to owe the estate an amount of this income tax, so she executed a promissory note to the estate and paid it a short time later.

---

[123] Treas. Reg. § 25.2518-3(c).

[124] Treas. Reg. § 25.2518-3(c).

[125] Treas. Reg. § 25.2518-3(c).

[126] Treas. Reg. § 25.2518-3(c).

[127] Treas. Reg. § 25.2518-3(c).

[128] Treas. Reg. § 25.2518-3(d), example 17.

[129] July 29, 1992.

When the spouse wanted to disclaim a number of shares of stock from her residuary bequest, the IRS ruled that the amount disclaimed could not include the shares of stock with respect to which she was considered to have accepted the dividend income (by reason of having obtained the loan for taxes). The ruling states that the number of shares the spouse could not disclaim was determined by the following formula:

(amount of loan to spouse/total dividend income earned on shares at time of loan) × number of shares held by estate.

[iii] **Segregation of income earned by disclaimed property after the disclaimer.** After the disclaimer has occurred and the disclaimed property and its share of income earned prior to the disclaimer has been segregated as described above, all income earned by the disclaimed property should be segregated from the non-disclaimed property and its income.

> EXAMPLE: *A* bequeaths her residuary estate of $1,000,000 to *B*. Six months after *A*'s death, *B* disclaims $200,000. No distributions have been made to *B* during administration. On the date of the disclaimer, the value of the residuary estate and all income earned to the date of the disclaimer is $1,500,000. As soon as *B* disclaims, *A*'s executor places $300,000 ($200,000/$1,000,000 × $1,500,000) in a separate fund. After that segregation, all income earned by the $300,000 is segregated from the property retained by *B*. *B*'s disclaimer can be a qualified disclaimer.[130] Note that if all of the income earned by the estate prior to the date of the disclaimer had been distributed to *B*, *B* could not have made a qualified disclaimer.[131]

[g] **Powers of Beneficiary with Respect to Trust**

A beneficiary of a trust who has the power to change the trustee or the right to serve as trustee either presently or in the future may disclaim such powers.[132]

[12] Voidable Disclaimer by a Debtor

The fact that a disclaimer is voidable by the disclaimant's creditors does not prevent it from being a qualified disclaimer.[133] However, a disclaimer which is

---

[130] Treas. Reg. § 25.2518-3(d), example 19.

[131] Treas. Reg. § 25.2518-3(d), example 18.

[132] Priv. Ltr. Rul. 9526018 (Mar. 30, 1995).

[133] Treas. Reg. § 25.2518-1(c)(2).

wholly void or which is actually voided by the creditors is not a qualified disclaimer.[134]

Chapter 53 of this book, concerning asset protection, has a full discussion of disclaimers by a debtor.

[13] Joint Tenancy With Right of Survivorship

Two issues exist with respect to the disclaimer of joint tenancy property. One is whether the period for disclaiming begins on the creation of the joint tenancy or on the first joint tenant's death. The other issue is whether the surviving tenant can disclaim the one-half survivorship interest in property that was originally contributed by him.

[a] The Regulation

Treasury Regulation § 25.2518-2(c)(4) addresses disclaimers of jointly held property. This regulation states the general rule that such disclaimers must be made within nine months after the transfer creating the joint tenancy.[135] The regulation also states that no disclaimer may be made of joint tenancy property to the extent consideration for the property was furnished by the disclaimant.[136]

[b] The Regulation Declared Invalid

Taxpayers have successfully challenged the regulation on both counts.[137]

[i] Event triggering disclaimer period. On the first issue, the courts have held that so long as joint tenants with right of survivorship have the right to partition the property, it is impossible to determine who will ultimately receive the property, so the surviving joint tenant has nine months following the first joint tenant's death to make a qualified disclaimer of the deceased joint tenant's one-half of the property. Consequently, Treasury Regulation § 25.2518-

---

[134] Treas. Reg. § 25.2518-1(c)(2).

[135] Treas. Reg. § 25.2518-2(c)(4)(i) (declared erroneous by IRS, action on decision 1990-06 (Feb. 7, 1990)).

[136] An exception is provided for joint tenancies between spouses and tenancies by the entirety created after 1976 and before 1982 (if no election to treat the creation of such tenancy as a gift was made under prior IRC § 2515). Treas. Reg. § 25.2518-2(c)(4)(ii).

[137] Kennedy v. Comm'r, 804 F2d 1332 (7th Cir. 1986); McDonald v. Comm'r, 853 F2d 1494 (8th Cir. 1988); Darcy v. Comm'r, 872 F2d 84 (4th Cir. 1989).

2(c)(4)(i) has been found invalid since the regulation fails to account for the rights of joint tenants to partition.[138]

[ii] Disclaimer of property contributed by disclaimant. On the second issue, Section 2040 provides that if spouses hold property as joint tenants with right of survivorship, then one-half of the property is included in the first spouse to die's estate, regardless of who actually furnished the consideration. In such a situation, the Tax Court has ruled that the surviving spouse can disclaim the one-half that is included in the estate of the deceased spouse, even if the surviving spouse originally furnished that consideration.[139]

It is important to note that these cases involve situations in which the joint tenant could partition the property and receive one-half of it. This is in contrast to a situation where the gift is not complete until an actual transfer to the other spouse or the first spouse's death.

EXAMPLE: *B* furnishes all consideration for an account held by *B* and *C* as joint tenants. The transfer is not a completed gift, since either *B* or *C* has the right to withdraw the entire account at any time. *C* never exercises this right. *B* dies. Local law provides that (a) all parties to a joint account have an unlimited power of withdrawal, but (b) until such a withdrawal occurs, a joint account belongs, during the lifetime of all parties, to the parties in proportion to the net contributions by each of the sums on deposit. *C* has nine months after *B*'s death to disclaim the property in the account.[140] The key to this example is that the creation of the joint account is not a transfer subject to estate or gift tax.

The IRS responded to the *Kennedy, McDonald,* and *Dancy* decisions, in which taxpayers successfully challenged Treasury Regulation § 25.2518-2(c)(4), by issuing an Action on Decision.[141] The Action on Decision provides that "[w]here a joint tenant has the right to sever the joint tenancy or cause the property to be partitioned under state law, the Service will no longer litigate that the transfer relative to which the timeliness of the disclaimer is measured refers to the transfer creating the joint tenancy. The IRS will also no longer contend that a joint tenant cannot make a qualified disclaimer of any portion of the joint interest attributable to consideration furnished by that joint tenant. Treas. Reg. § 25.2518-2(c)(4)(i) will be revised accordingly." The

---

[138] Kennedy v. Comm'r, 804 F2d 1332, 1335 (7th Cir. 1986).

[139] McDonald v. Comm'r, 1989 PH TC Memo. ¶ 89, 140, 56 TCM (CCH) 1598 (1989). The Eighth Circuit followed the reasoning of the Seventh Circuit in *Kennedy.*

[140] Treas. Reg. § 25.2518-2(c)(5).

[141] AOD 1990-06 (Feb. 7, 1990).

IRS has followed this principle in various recent private letter rulings dealing with disclaimers of jointly held property.[142]

[iii] Proposed Regulations. Proposed Regulations, which would change the invalid regulation, were issued August 21, 1996.[143] They would apply the following proposed rules—

Proposed Rule #1: Interests that are unilaterally severable. The rules discussed in this paragraph do not apply to joint bank accounts and joint brokerage accounts. With respect to other property, in the case of an interest in a joint tenancy with right of survivorship or a tenancy by the entirety that either joint tenant can sever unilaterally under local law, the time in which to make a qualified disclaimer of the interest to which the survivor succeeds by operation of law upon the death of the first joint tenant to die begins to run on the death of the first joint tenant to die. Except for cases described in #3 below, the interest that may be disclaimed is the interest to which the disclaimant succeeds by right of survivorship, regardless of the portion of the property attributable to consideration furnished by the disclaimant and regardless of the portion of the property that is included in the decedent's gross estate under Section 2040.[144]

Proposed Rule #2: Interests that are not unilaterally severable. Except as provided in Proposed Rule #3 below, if an interest in joint property with right of survivorship or an interest held as a tenant by the entirety is not unilaterally severable under local law, the period in which to make a qualified disclaimer of the interest or any portion of the interest begins on the transaction creating the tenancy. A co-tenant who cannot unilaterally sever the interest under applicable local law cannot make a qualified disclaimer of any portion of the joint interest to the extent attributable to consideration furnished by that tenant.[145]

Proposed Rule #3: Tenancies in real property between spouses created after 1954 and before 1982 and certain tenancies in real property between spouses created on or after July 14, 1988. In the case of a joint tenancy between spouses or a tenancy by the entirety in real property created after 1954 and before 1982 where no election was made under Section 2515, or a joint tenancy between spouses or a tenancy by the entirety in real property created on or

---

[142] Tech. Adv. Mem. 9427003 (Mar. 30, 1994); Priv. Ltr. Rul. 9420031 (Feb. 22, 1994); Priv. Ltr. Rul. 9411014 (Dec. 15, 1993); Priv. Ltr. Rul. 9336011 (June 8, 1993) (also dealing with disclaimers of pay-on-death accounts); Priv. Ltr. Rul. 9232014 (May 5, 1992); Priv. Ltr. Rul. 9218015 (Feb. 5, 1992) (dealing with Texas community property with rights of survivorship); Priv. Ltr. Rul. 9214022 (Jan. 6, 1992); Priv. Ltr. Rul. 9113011 (Dec. 24, 1990); Priv. Ltr. Rul. 9038031 (June 25, 1990).

[143] 61 Fed. Reg. 43197 (Aug. 21, 1996).

[144] Prop. Reg. § 25.2518-2(c)(4)(i).

[145] Prop. Reg. § 25.2518-2(c)(4)(ii).

after July 14, 1988, to which Section 2523(i)(3) applies (relating to the creation of a tenancy where the spouse of the donor is not a United States citizen), the surviving spouse can make a qualified disclaimer within nine months after the death of the first spouse to die. The surviving spouse may disclaim any portion of the joint interest that is includable in the decedent's gross estate under Section 2040.[146]

Proposed Rule #4: Special rule for joint bank and brokerage accounts established between spouses or between persons other than husband and wife. In the case of a transfer to a joint bank account or a joint brokerage account, if a transferor may unilaterally withdraw the transferor's own contributions from the account without the consent of the other co-tenant, the transfer creating the survivor's interest in a decedent's share of the account occurs on the death of the deceased co-tenant. Accordingly, if a surviving joint tenant desires to make a qualified disclaimer with respect to funds contributed by a deceased co-tenant, the disclaimer period begins on the co-tenant's death. The surviving joint tenant may not disclaim any portion of the joint account attributable to consideration furnished by that surviving joint tenant.[147]

The proposed regulations would be effective for disclaimers made after the date of publication as final regulations in the Federal Register.[148]

[c] Tenancy by the Entirety

For disclaimer purposes, the IRS has treated property held by a husband and wife as tenants by the entirety the same as property held by spouses as joint tenants with right of survivorship.[149]

[d] Bottom Line on Disclaiming Joint Tenancy Interests

The time for disclaiming survivorship interests is nine months after the first joint tenant's date of death, unless the creation of the tenancy is a completed gift and the joint tenants have no right to partition. In that case, the triggering event is the creation of the joint tenancy.[150]

---

[146] Prop. Reg. § 25.2518-2(c)(4)(iii).

[147] Prop. Reg. § 25.2518-2(c)(4)(iv).

[148] Prop. Reg. § 25.2518-2(c)(4)(v).

[149] Priv. Ltr. Rul. 9106016 (Nov. 8, 1990) (Missouri); Priv. Ltr. Rul. 9208003 (Oct. 28, 1991) (Arkansas); Priv. Ltr. Rul. 9427003, (Mar. 30, 1994) (Maryland); Priv. Ltr. Rul. 9529001 (Mar. 22, 1995) (Pennsylvania).

[150] For an alternative analysis, see Stuart Rosenblum & Stephen M. Pollan, Disclaiming Jointly Held Real Estate, NYLJ, (Sept. 16, 1992), discussing an approach used in Hoffman v. United States, 56 AFTR2d 6553, 85-2 USTC (CCH) ¶ 13,630 (D. Neb. 1985).

¶ 47.03 DISCLAIMERS FOR SPECIFIC PURPOSES

The following sections contain representative examples of situations in which disclaimers can accomplish, or have (or could have, if proper measures were taken) accomplished, useful purposes.

[1] Disclaimers to Allow Non-Qualifying Gifts to Qualify for Marital Deduction

Disclaimers of nonqualifying beneficial interests and powers can save the marital deduction. Examine the following scenarios—

Disclaimers by descendants qualify trust for QTIP treatment. If *A* leaves his property to a trust which benefits his spouse and descendants, the descendants can disclaim their interests in the trust. If the trust would then contain qualifying provisions, it can qualify for the marital deduction.

Wife's disclaimer of tainted power qualifies trust for QTIP treatment. If a trust otherwise qualifies for QTIP treatment, but the spouse has a lifetime power of appointment, then a disclaimer of the power of appointment could save the marital deduction. For example, in 1992, the IRS ruled on a situation in which *A* left his property to a trust which paid all income to Wife for life. The trust also gave Wife the right to "disclaim or renounce" her interest in all or any portion of the trust at any time and from time to time. Any property so disclaimed or renounced would pass to a specified qualified charity. The IRS ruled that, since the power to disclaim or renounce was not limited by the time limits allowed for qualified disclaimers under federal or local law, Wife's power amounted to a lifetime power to appoint trust property to a person other than the surviving spouse, so the trust could not qualify for QTIP treatment. However, the IRS also ruled that Wife's proposed disclaimer of this lifetime power of appointment could remove this taint and allow the trust to qualify for the estate tax marital deduction.[151]

Children's disclaimer of interest in split-interest trust allows marital deduction. If a married grantor dies within the retained interest term of a QPRT, GRAT, or GRIT, and language is not included which would allow the interest included in the grantor's estate to qualify for the marital deduction, a disclaimer may be helpful. For example, under the facts of one ruling, a decedent had established a lifetime GRIT (Grantor Retained Income Trust), but died prior to the expiration of its 6-year term. Under the terms of the agreement, the trust property was to pass pursuant to the decedent's general power of appointment, and in default of appointment, to the decedent's children, or if they were not living, to the children's estates. Each child and grandchild proposed to disclaim his interest in the GRIT. Under local (South Carolina)

---

[151] Priv. Ltr. Rul. 9226059 (Mar. 31, 1992); see also Priv. Ltr. Rul. 9329025 (Apr. 28, 1993).

law, the GRIT property would then pass to the surviving spouse under the laws of intestacy. The IRS ruled that the disclaimers were qualified disclaimers, and that the transfer to the surviving spouse would qualify for the estate tax marital deduction.[152] If the decedent had not retained a power of appointment, thereby making the gift of the remainder interest in case of his death during the six-year term incomplete, it would presumably have been too late for the descendants to disclaim, unless the decedent died within nine months after creating the GRIT.

DRAFTING TIP: Include a power of appointment in case of death of a grantor during the retained interest term of a QPRT, GRAT, GRUT, or GRIT, to facilitate disclaimers; however, limit the power of appointment over a GRAT or GRUT to the portion of the trust which would be otherwise includable in the grantor's estate.

[2] Disclaimers to Utilize Decedent's Unified Credit

If the marital bequest is overfunded, a disclaimer can allow the surviving spouse to take advantage of the deceased's spouse's exemption amount. Although drafting in anticipation of such a disclaimer is helpful, the result may be able to be accomplished under state law disposition. Examine the following scenarios—

Wife disclaims property under laws of intestacy. Decedent had no will. Local law provided that Wife received $20,000 plus one-half of the balance of Decedent's estate, with the balance passing to Decedent's descendants. Wife proposed to disclaim a formula amount so that when the disclaimed amount was added to the property already passing to Decedent's descendants, Decedent's unified credit would be fully utilized. The IRS approved this formula disclaimer.[153]

Wife disclaims outright gift in favor of usufruct. A, a Louisiana decedent, died in 1991 with a will which the IRS interpreted as passing all of A's property to his wife outright. A's wife proposed to disclaim the amount which could pass free of estate tax, so that under state law and the governing instrument, that amount would pass to the children, with a usufruct in her. The IRS ruled that A's wife's disclaimer was a qualified disclaimer.[154]

---

[152] Priv. Ltr. Rul. 9340052 (July 12, 1993).

[153] Priv. Ltr. Rul. 9338010 (June 21, 1993).

[154] Priv. Ltr. Rul. 9245021 (Aug. 7, 1992).

[3] Disclaimers to Minimize Generation-Skipping Transfer Tax

[a] Use Decedent's GSTT Exemption

Dad may see the advantages of using the $1,000,000 generation-skipping transfer tax (GSTT) exemption, but be reluctant to commit his estate to actually paying estate taxes if Mom survives him.

DRAFTING TIP: Dad can provide that if Mom disclaims, Dad's remaining exemption amount can pass to a dynastic trust. This way, Mom can decide whether to fund the entire GSTT exemption based on facts available at her death.

EXAMPLE: Mom and Dad have over $1,000,000 in property, and may inherit large sums from their parents in the future. They want the survivor to have the ability to benefit from all marital property if he or she needs it. The will may provide for a bypass trust and a marital gift, but could also include a dynastic trust that would receive property disclaimed by the survivor. The surviving spouse thus has the ability to determine the best financial and tax results after the death of the other spouse.[155]

Likewise, a child may wish to disclaim, thereby allowing property to pass to a descendant or a trust for a descendant, and thus use the GSTT exemption. The IRS has approved a combination of marital and child disclaimers which have such a result.[156]

Efficient use of the GSTT exemption may require separation of trusts into independent shares. In such a case, the separate share rules of the GSTT come into play in determining whether the shares will be recognized.[157]

[b] Maximize Benefits of Trusts That Are Grandfathered From GSTT

Disclaimers can be used to take maximum advantage of grandfathered trusts. Examine the following scenarios—

Disclaimer of interests in grandfathered revocable trust allows GSTT-free gifts to grandchildren. Decedent had created a revocable trust in 1950. She had last amended it in 1984, after which she became incapacitated. During Decedent's incapacity, her children (as trustee of the trust and under durable powers of attorney) had made trust distributions to her, followed by gifts for their own and their descendants' benefit. After Decedent's death, her children proposed to disclaim their interests in the trust, allowing trust property to pass to Decedent's grandchildren with no GSTT. The IRS ruled that the disclaim-

---

[155] See Exhibit 47-A, Example 3, for representative language.

[156] E.g., Priv. Ltr. Rul. 9244012 (July 29, 1992); see also Priv. Ltr. Rul. 9323027 (Mar. 16, 1993); Priv. Ltr. Rul. 9236018 (June 5, 1992).

[157] See Ch. 5 for a discussion of the separate share rules.

ers could be qualified disclaimers, and that they would not result in the trust's loss of grandfathering from GSTT, due to Decedent's disability at all times from October 22, 1986 to her death.[158] The previous gifts made by the children (in their fiduciary capacity as agent) to themselves were not considered acceptances of the property, since they were considered gifts made by Decedent.

Pre-1942 general powers of appointment. A pre-1942 general power of appointment can provide a new period for disclaiming interests in an old trust. Private Letter Ruling 9245011[159] is a good illustrative model of disclaimer planning with respect to a pre-1942 general power of appointment. In this ruling, prior to 1942, *G* created Trust *A*, for the benefit of his wife, which granted his wife a testamentary general power of appointment, with provisions in default of appointment in favor of his descendants, and Trust *B*, for the benefit of his children, which gave his children a lifetime power, acting together, to distribute trust property to themselves for any reason. *G*'s children were also trustees of Trust *A*, with the right to distribute property to *G*'s wife for any reason. The following was proposed: (1) *G*'s wife would release her testamentary general power over Trust *A*; (2) within nine months of this release, *G*'s children would: (a) disclaim their interests in Trust *A*, (b) release their power to make discretionary distributions to *G*'s wife from Trust *A*, and (c) release their power to invade Trust *B* for their own benefit; (3) *G*'s grandchildren then, also within nine months of *G*'s wife's release of her general power, would disclaim a portion of their interests in Trust *A*; and (4) Trust *A* would then continue to be held for *G*'s wife and grandchildren, and Trust *B* would continue to be held for the benefit of the children and grandchildren.

The IRS ruled that these releases and disclaimers operated together to create trusts that were grandfathered from GSTT at no transfer tax cost to *G*'s wife, children or grandchildren.

G's wife's release of her general power had no transfer tax consequence since the power was created prior to 1942. However, her release (rather than the initial establishment of the trust) triggered the running of the period of time for other trust beneficiaries to disclaim their interests, since Treasury Regulation § 25.2518-2(c)(3) states that a disclaimer must be made within nine months of the lapse of a general power of appointment. *G*'s children disclaimed their interests in Trust *A*, and also released their fiduciary power to invade the trust for *G*'s wife's benefit, since under Treasury Regulation § 25.2518-2(e)(i), a fiduciary's disclaimer of a beneficial interest in a trust is not a qualified disclaimer if the fiduciary retains a discretionary power to allocate enjoyment of the interest.[160]

---

[158] Priv. Ltr. Rul. 9340027 (June 30, 1993).

[159] July 31, 1992.

[160] See also Priv. Ltr. Rul. 9445014 (Aug. 10, 1994); Priv. Ltr. Rul. 9244012 (July 29, 1992); Priv. Ltr. Rul. 9226013 (Mar. 23, 1992).

Grandfathering from GSTT was not affected, since amounts remaining in trust after the lapse of a general power of appointment are treated as additions if the lapse was treated as a taxable transfer under Chapter 11 or 12, and in this case it was not.[161]

[4] Disclaimers to Generate Estate Tax so That Alternate Valuation May Be Used

This is one of the most interesting features of disclaimers. Suppose that an estate will pass tax-free, due to the marital deduction. The value of the assets in the estate is lower on the alternate valuation date than on the date of death. Under the will structure, the bypass trust will not be fully funded if date of death values are used. The alternate valuation date can be elected only if the election decreases both the value of the gross estate, and the sum of the estate tax and the GSTT with respect to property includable in the decedent's gross estate.[162] A small disclaimer can solve the problem.

> EXAMPLE: Mother leaves a pecuniary marital formula bequest to Father, to be funded at date of distribution values, and the balance of her estate to a bypass trust. At Mother's date of death, her estate was worth $1,500,000, so that, at date of death values, Father should receive $900,000 and the bypass trust $600,000. By the alternate valuation date, Mother's estate has dropped in value to $1,000,000. Using date of death values to determine the amount of the bequests and date of distribution values for funding, Father will still receive $900,000, but the bypass trust will only receive $100,000. In order to utilize the alternate valuation date, both the gross estate and the estate tax must be reduced. The estate tax cannot be reduced from zero, so estate tax must be generated, in order to accomplish the mandatory reduction. If Father disclaims a small amount of the pecuniary marital bequest, estate tax would be generated, and the estate could use the alternate valuation date, thus allowing the Bypass Trust to be funded with $600,000 +, and reducing the marital bequest to $400,000 −. In this regard, see ¶ 47.02[8][b] above for language required to permit this sort of disclaimer (bypass trust not reduced by disclaimer of marital bequest).

[5] Disclaimers to Minimize or Defer Tax on Employee Benefits

Another interesting aspect of disclaimers is that they can be used to minimize or defer tax on employee benefits.

---

[161] Treas. Reg. § 26.2601-1(b)(1)(v)(A); see also Priv. Ltr. Rul. 9424062 (Mar. 23, 1994); Priv. Ltr. Rul. 9424063 (Mar. 23, 1994); Priv. Ltr. Rul. 9425014 (Mar. 23, 1994) (applying this principle under Texas law); Priv. Ltr. Rul. 9340053 (July 12, 1993); Priv. Ltr. Rul. 9318020 (Feb. 4, 1993).

[162] IRC § 2032(c).

EXAMPLE: Husband has an employee benefit plan for which he has executed the following beneficiary designation: Wife, then the bypass trust, then the marital trust, then children. The designation also provides that if any beneficiary disclaims, the property passes to the next named beneficiary. This allows Husband's survivors to determine where the proceeds will do the most good and receive the most favorable tax treatment. This plan requires careful drafting to be sure that an authorized person can disclaim the interests, and that the plan administrator will respect the designation. The difficulties, if any, will usually arise with the plan itself, or with state law, as the IRS has approved disclaimers with such drafting.[163]

Does such a disclaimer work to shift income tax on the disclaimed benefits to the recipient? It seems so, and the IRS has agreed with that position in private letter rulings such as the following—

- *Spouse not subject to income tax on disclaimed benefits.* A left a qualified plan payable to Spouse, or if she were not living, to children. Spouse disclaimed 44.3 percent of the amount in the plan. The disclaimed property passed to the children in equal shares. The IRS ruled that since the disclaimer was a qualified disclaimer under Section 2518, the spouse would only be taxed for income tax purposes on the amount she actually received, and the children would be subject to income tax on the balance.[164] The IRS also found on the same facts that the surviving spouse would not be considered the person entitled to receive the disclaimed benefits under Section 691(a).[165]

- *Disclaimers allow benefits to pass to spouse.* A died, leaving an inter vivos trust as the beneficiary of his employee benefit plan. A's spouse and descendants disclaimed all of their interests in the plan under the trust. The trustee then filed a disclaimer on behalf of the trust and all of its beneficiaries with the trustees of the benefit plan, so that under the terms of the plan itself, the proceeds due would be payable to A's spouse. The spouse rolled over the amount distributed to her from the plan to an IRA. The IRS ruled that the disclaimers were qualified, and that the spouse would not be subject to immediate income tax on amounts received as a result of the disclaimers from the plan which she rolled over into the IRA.[166]

---

[163] E.g., Priv. Ltr. Rul. 9320015 (Feb. 17, 1993).

[164] Priv. Ltr. Rul. 9303027 (Oct. 27, 1992).

[165] Priv. Ltr. Rul. 9319029 (Feb. 12, 1993); see also Priv. Ltr. Rul. 9226058 (Mar. 31, 1992).

[166] Priv. Ltr. Rul. 9247026 (Aug. 24, 1992).

[6] Qualify Trust as a Qualified Subchapter S Trust

A qualified subchapter S trust (QSST) can only have one permissible distributee during the income beneficiary's lifetime. A trust which does not qualify as a QSST due to the existence of extra beneficiaries may be able to qualify if the extra beneficiaries disclaim their interests. This may require a court proceeding in the case of minor or unborn descendants. The IRS takes the position that a trust has more than one principal and income beneficiary during the lifetime of the current beneficiary if the trust instrument designates unborn persons as potential beneficiaries during the current beneficiary's lifetime, even if no such persons have yet been born.[187] Hence, to qualify such a trust as a QSST, a disclaimer must be made on behalf of unborn persons who could receive benefits during the current beneficiary's life.

[7] Disclaimers to Make a Tax-Free Charitable Gift of Estate's Assets

Maybe Mom would like to make a charitable gift in her estate, but is reluctant to put such a bequest in her will without being sure whether Child will have enough property. Mom can give Child an option by providing that her estate goes to Child, or if Child disclaims, to a charity. Of course, Child could accept the bequest, and give it to charity himself. That would not be as good a result, however, since Mom's estate would not get a charitable estate tax deduction in that scenario.

Disclaimers can help in charitable planning in the following ways—

Eliminate disqualifying interest in split-interest trust. If Son leaves an income interest to his mother, followed by a remainder interest to charity, his mother can disclaim her interest, and allow the property to pass tax-free to charity.

Disclaimer permits reformation of non-qualifying trust. In Private Letter Ruling 9347013,[188] the IRS approved the reformation of a charitable trust to qualify for the estate tax charitable deduction as a charitable remainder unitrust. Decedent left her property to two trusts which provided for payments of all income and discretionary amounts of principal to her children, with payment of trust property at a child's death to a qualified charity. Each child disclaimed his or her rights to principal distributions. The estate then proceeded with a reformation of the children's income interests into unitrust interests. The disclaimers combined with the reformation qualified the remainder interest in the trusts for the estate tax charitable deduction.[189]

---

[187] Rev. Rul. 89-45, 1989-1 CB 267.

[188] Aug. 19, 1993.

[189] See also Priv. Ltr. Rul. 9610005 (Nov. 9, 1995); Priv. Ltr. Rul. 9529042 (Apr. 28, 1995); Priv. Ltr. Rul. 9527040 (Apr. 11, 1995); Priv. Ltr. Rul. 9341003 (July 13, 1993).

Disclaimers could have saved charitable deduction. Decedent left the residue of his estate to charity. However, he left a codicil which allowed his executors to make gifts (each gift not to exceed one percent of his gross estate) to persons who had contributed to Decedent's well-being during his life. The Tax Court found that Decedent's estate was not entitled to a charitable deduction for the property passing to charity, since the one percent gifts could have exhausted the entire estate. The opinion suggests that by the due date of the federal estate tax return, and before the power was exercised, the executor could have obtained a complete renunciation of the power to invade the charitable bequest (presumably by court order). Since such a renunciation would be treated as a disclaimer under Section 2055(a), effective as of the decedent's date of death, the executors would be deemed to never have held the power, and the charitable deduction could have been claimed.[170]

---

[170] Estate of Marine v. Comm'r, 97 TC 368 (1991).

¶ 47.04 REFERENCE MATERIALS

[1] Exhibit 47–A: Simple Disclaimer Form

(CAPTION)

DISCLAIMER

I, (DISCLAIMANT), in accordance with the provisions of Section 37A of the Texas Probate Code, do hereby disclaim my interest in any and all property passing under Section .... of the Last Will and Testament of (DECEDENT), Deceased (the "Will"), said disclaimed property being more particularly described as follows:

[include an appropriate description of the property; if real property is disclaimed, for title purposes it is a good idea to include a proper legal description in the disclaimer]

The Will is dated the .... day of ...., 19....., and was admitted to probate in Probate Court Number .... of .... County, Texas, under the above cause number.

Dated this .... day of ...., 19......

....
(DISCLAIMANT)

THE STATE OF TEXAS

COUNTY OF ....

This instrument was acknowledged before me on the .... day of ...., 19..... by (DISCLAIMANT).

....
Notary Public in and for the State of Texas

I received this disclaimer on the .... day of ...., 19......

....
(EXECUTOR), Independent Executor of the Estate of (DECEDENT), Deceased

EXAMPLE 1. This provision leaves property to son, but if son disclaims the property, it passes to a communities foundation so that son can have some input into how the property is used.

Should my son survive me for thirty (30) days, I bequeath to my son, outright and free of trust, cash in the amount of (AMOUNT) ($XXXXX.XX). Should my son survive me for thirty (30) days, but disclaim all or any part of the property passing pursuant to this section, trustee shall pay over and deliver such disclaimed property to the .... Foundation, ..., Texas, to be held and administered in accordance with the terms and provisions of paragraphs (i) and (ii) of this section. Should my son not survive me for thirty (30) days, I bequeath the property described above in this section in accordance with the terms and provisions of this will dealing with the disposition of my residuary estate.

(i) Should my son disclaim all or any part of the property passing pursuant to this section, such disclaimed property shall be held by the .... Foundation in an advised fund.

(ii) The charitable uses and purposes to which the .... Foundation shall devote the property passing pursuant to this section shall be decided by the .... Foundation, in its sole discretion. However, I request the .... Foundation to seek the advice and counsel of my son, so long as he shall be living, available, and willing to give advice and counsel, from time to time, regarding the .... Foundation's use of the property constituting this gift.

EXAMPLE 2. The following is a set of provisions that provide an outright residuary bequest to a surviving spouse, with a standby disclaimer bypass trust which can be funded by the survivor's disclaimer. With these provisions, the survivor has the ability to determine how much, if any, of the deceased's spouse's property will pass to the bypass trust.

Disposition of Residuary Estate

(a) Should my (spouse) survive me, I devise and bequeath my entire residuary estate to (him/her).

(b) Should my (spouse) survive me, but disclaim all or a part of (his/her) interest in property otherwise passing to my (spouse) pursuant to the preceding paragraph, the property so disclaimed shall pass to the trustee of THE BYPASS TRUST, to be held, administered and disposed of in accordance with the terms and provisions of section ....

THE BYPASS TRUST. Trustee shall hold, administer and dispose of any property passing to THE BYPASS TRUST in a separate trust, of which my (spouse) shall be the income beneficiary, in accordance with the following terms and provisions.

(a) So long as my (spouse) is living, trustee shall pay such part or all of the income or corpus, or both, of the trust as trustee shall deem proper for the health, education, maintenance and support of my (spouse) and children, accumulating and adding to corpus any income not so used.

(b) On my (spouse)'s death, trustee shall continue to hold, or pay over and deliver, the corpus of the trust then on hand in accordance with the terms and provisions of this Article dealing with the disposition of my residuary estate, as if my (spouse) had not survived me, and my death had occurred immediately after the death of my (spouse).

Note that all distributions from the bypass trust are subject to an ascertainable standard (so that the spouse can be trustee, if desired), and that the spouse has no testamentary power of appointment over the property.

EXAMPLE 3. This set of provisions assumes that a pecuniary bypass trust has already been established earlier in the will. These provisions provide an outright residuary bequest to a surviving spouse, and further provide that amounts disclaimed by the surviving spouse will pass to dynastic trusts for descendants. With these provisions, the survivor has the ability to determine how much, if any, of the deceased's spouse's property will pass to these dynastic trusts, as follows.

1. If the spouse makes no disclaimer, at least a portion of the deceased spouse's GSTT exemption amount can be allocated to the bypass trust. If the residuary marital gift were to a QTIP trust, the balance of the GSTT exemption could be allocated to that trust (see Example 4).

2. The spouse could disclaim an amount in favor of the dynastic trusts sufficient to fund them with the amount of the deceased spouse's GSTT exemption that is not allocated to the bypass trust. NOTE: Be sure to consider the source for payment of the estate tax on amounts disclaimed. If the tax is to be paid from the disclaimed property, the disclaimer must provide a formula to allow for the amount of tax to be disclaimed also. Additionally, the bypass trust must be drafted so as not to be reduced by disclaimer of the marital bequest, if the spouse wants to keep the entire bypass trust.

3. The spouse could disclaim an amount in favor of the dynastic trusts sufficient to fund them with the entire amount of the deceased spouse's GSTT exemption (in which case no amount of the exemption would be allocated to the bypass trust). NOTE: The tax considerations described above would apply in this case also.

Disposition of Residuary Estate

(a) Should my (spouse) survive me, I devise and bequeath my entire residuary estate to (him/her).

(b) Should my (spouse) survive me, but disclaim all or a part of (his/her) interest in property otherwise passing to my (spouse) pursuant to the preceding paragraph, the property so disclaimed shall pass to the trustee hereinafter named, to be allocated, per stirpes, among those of my descendants who are living thirty (30) days after my death. Trustee shall hold each descendant's share so allocated in a separate trust named for such descendant followed by the words "DYNASTIC TRUST." The descendant for whom such trust is named shall be the income beneficiary of such trust, which shall be administered and disposed of in accordance with the terms and provisions of section ....

EXAMPLE 4. This set of provisions assumes no tax planning has happened earlier in the will. It starts with an outright residuary bequest to the surviving spouse, then uses disclaimers to fund the bypass, a QTIP trust to utilize the decedent's unused GSTT exemption, and then dynastic trusts for descendants. The surviving spouse will have the ability to accept all property outright under the will, or use disclaimers to fund all or any part of the tax-oriented gifts. The tax allocation clause should be drafted to provide for payment of taxes from the appropriate sources.

Disposition of Residuary Estate

(a) Should my (spouse) survive me, I devise and bequeath my entire residuary estate to (him/her).

(b) Should my (spouse) survive me, but disclaim all or a part of (his/her) interest in property otherwise passing to my (spouse) pursuant to the preceding paragraph, the property so disclaimed shall pass as follows:

(i) I devise and bequeath an amount of such disclaimed property to the trustee of THE BYPASS TRUST (to be held, administered and disposed of in accordance with the terms and provisions of section ....) until the value of all property passing to such trust pursuant to this section is equal to the lesser of (i) all property passing pursuant to this section or (ii) the Exemption Amount. In making the computations necessary to determine the amount of this gift, values as finally determined for federal estate tax purposes in my estate shall control. Should my (spouse) disclaim property valued in excess of the Exemption Amount, then my executor shall have the power and the sole discretion to satisfy this gift out of such disclaimed property in cash or in kind or partly in cash and partly in kind and to select the assets so disclaimed which shall constitute this gift, provided that my executor shall value such assets at their respective fair market values as of the date or dates of distribution.

(ii) I devise and bequeath the property so disclaimed in excess of the Exemption Amount to the trustee of THE QTIP TRUST, to be held, administered and disposed of in accordance with the terms and provisions of section ....

(c) Should my (spouse) survive me, but disclaim all or a part of (his/her) interest in property otherwise passing to THE BYPASS TRUST or THE QTIP TRUST, or both, pursuant to the preceding paragraph, the property so disclaimed shall pass to the trustee hereinafter named, to be allocated, per stirpes, among those of my descendants who are living thirty (30) days after my death. Trustee shall hold each descendant's share so allocated in a separate trust named for such descendant followed by the words "DYNASTIC TRUST." The descendant for whom such trust is named shall be the income beneficiary of such trust, which shall be administered and disposed of in accordance with the terms and provisions of section ....

(d) The "exemption amount" shall mean the maximum amount which would result in no federal estate tax payable by my estate, if such tax were computed by giving effect to all relevant tax credits (including but not limited to (i) the unified credit provided by section 2010 of the Internal Revenue Code, (ii) the credit for state death taxes provided by section 2011 of the Internal Revenue Code and (iii) any credit or reduction in adjusted taxable gifts provided by chapter 14 of the Internal Revenue Code) and all other factors pertinent to the computation of the federal estate tax in my estate, but only to the extent that the use of any such credit or reduction or the consideration of any such factor does not increase the amount of death taxes otherwise payable to any taxing authority by reason of my death. For purposes of the preceding sentence only, "federal estate tax" does not include any tax imposed on an excess retirement accumulation as defined in section 4980A of the Internal Revenue Code. The exemption amount shall be computed without regard to disclaimers of other assets.

CHAPTER **48**

Special Use Valuation of Farms and Ranches

¶ 48.01 INTRODUCTION

Section 2032A provides for favorable estate tax valuation of agricultural real property, as well as certain other real property. Section 2032A's special valuation rules theoretically apply to real estate used in any business, valuing the real property at its actual use as opposed to its highest and best use.[1] However, Section 2032A is, as a practical matter, mostly used to value agricultural real property, because the valuation of such property is based on a formula that will usually produce a very low taxable value.[2] The special formula used to value agricultural real estate is not applicable to any other kind of real property. Where special use valuation is used for a farm or ranch, the special valuation benefits generally will be lost if the property does not (1) stay in the family and (2) continue to be used for agricultural purposes by a materially participating family member for at least 10 years after the decedent's death.

The maximum valuation decrease on account of the special valuation election is $750,000.[3] Thus, the maximum value of farmland that can be bequeathed by a married couple to their family tax-free is $2,700,000.[4] Hence, this is not a technique that can result in mega-savings; however, in a small estate, it can mean the difference between the family's being able to keep the farm or having to sell it.

---

[1] IRC § 2032A(e)(8).

[2] IRC § 2032A(e)(7).

[3] IRC § 2032A(a)(2).

[4] ($600,000 unified credit and $750,000 special use reduction)×2 people.

¶ 48.02 QUALIFICATION

In oversimplified terms, at least 50 percent of the decedent's estate must consist of property used for farming by the decedent or a member of his family. Twenty-five percent of the estate must consist of real property used in the farming business. The decedent or a member of his family must have owned and materially participated in the farming business for five out of the eight years preceding the decedent's death, subject to certain exceptions. The property must pass to a member of the decedent's family. That family member is known as the "qualified heir." The qualified heir must continue to farm the property for ten years after the decedent's death. A proper election and a tax recapture agreement must also be filed.

A more detailed explanation of the qualification requirements follows.

[1] Requirement: U.S. Decedent

The decedent must have been a United States citizen or resident.[5]

[2] Requirement: File an Election and Tax Recapture Agreement

[a] Election

The executor must make an irrevocable election to apply special use valuation on the estate tax return.[6]

[b] Recapture Agreement

If special use valuation is elected, a tax recapture agreement must be filed with the estate tax return.[7] Additionally, for the special use value to apply for generation-skipping transfer tax purposes, the recapture agreement must specifically provide for the signatories' consent to the imposition of, and personal liability for, additional generation-skipping transfer tax in the event recapture of estate tax is imposed.[8]

The agreement must provide that each signer will be personally liable for a "recapture tax" if the ranch is sold or ceases to be used as a ranch in the recapture period (generally, the 10-year period after decedent's death).[9]

---

[5] IRC § 2032A(a)(1)(A).

[6] IRC § 2032A(d)(1).

[7] IRC § 2032A(d)(1).

[8] Treas. Reg. § 26.2642-2(b)(1).

[9] IRC §§ 2032A(a)(1)(B), 2032A(d)(2), 2032A(c)(1).

The real property for which special use valuation is elected must be designated in the recapture agreement.[10]

The agreement must be signed by everyone in being who has an interest in the specially valued property.[11] This means everyone, including minors and people with remote contingent interests.[12] If a minor or incapacitated person has an interest, a court-appointed representative or other person who can bind the child will have to sign the agreement on the person's behalf.[13] A parent who has not been appointed by the court as personal representative of the child's estate cannot make this agreement for the child unless local law permits the parent to bind the child.[14] Potential objects of a power of appointment are not required to sign, but the holder of the power and the takers in default of appointment are.[15]

[c] Correction of Defective Election or Agreement

The IRS has, from the beginning, interpreted the requirements of both the election and the tax recapture agreement very strictly. In reaction, Congress enacted a provision allowing a taxpayer to correct a defective election and agreement after audit, if the item(s) to be corrected were timely filed and substantially complied with the requirements.[16] If the election and agreement do not meet the requirements, but substantially comply, then the executor has up to 90 days after being notified of the failure to meet the requirements to bring the election or agreement into compliance.[17] The IRS has been quite strict in its interpretation of what constitutes substantial compliance.[18]

[3] Requirement: Fifty Percent of Estate Is Qualified Use Property Passing to a Qualified Heir

At least 50 percent of the "adjusted estate" must consist of the "net value of property"—

---

[10] IRC § 2032A(b)(1)(D).

[11] IRC § 2032A(d)(2).

[12] Treas. Reg. § 20.2032A-8(c)(2).

[13] Treas. Reg. § 20.2032A-8(c)(3).

[14] Treas. Reg. § 20.2032A-8(c)(3).

[15] Treas. Reg. § 20.2032A-8(c)(2).

[16] IRC § 2032A(d)(3) (enacted by Tax Reform Act of 1984, § 1025).

[17] IRC § 2032A(d)(3).

[18] For a description of rulings allowing and disallowing perfection, see Zumbach, 445-2d T.M., Section 2032A — Special Use Valuation.

- Used for a "qualified use" by the decedent or a "member of the decedent's family," and
- Acquired from or passed from the decedent to a "qualified heir" of the decedent.[19]

[a] "Adjusted Estate" Defined

The "adjusted estate" is the value of the gross estate without regard to the special use valuation rules, reduced by unpaid mortgages on, or indebtedness in respect of, property in the gross estate.[20]

[b] "Net Value of Property" Defined

The "net value" of any real or personal property is its estate tax value without regard to the special use valuation rules, reduced by mortgages on, and debts in respect of, such property.[21]

[c] "Qualified Use" Defined

A "qualified use" is farming, which also includes ranching, horticulture, raising timber, and some associated processing.[22] A qualified use requires an equity interest in the activity. Accordingly, while cash rentals are generally not considered equity interests, crop share rentals can be if the landlord participates in the economic risk of the activity.

A cash rental of the property to a family member of the decedent before his death is permitted, however.[23] But, after the decedent's death, the qualified use requirement cannot be satisfied by a cash rental, even to a member of the qualified heir's family, except during the grace period or under the exception allowing the surviving spouse to rent for cash to a family member.[24]

[d] "Qualified Heir" Defined

[i] In general. A "qualified heir," with respect to any property, is a member of the decedent's family who acquired the property from the dece-

---

[19] IRC § 2032A(b)(1).

[20] IRC §§ 2032A(b)(3)(A), 2053(a)(4).

[21] IRC §§ 2032A(b)(3)(B), 2053(a)(4).

[22] IRC §§ 2032A(b)(2)(A), 2032A(e)(4), 2032(e)(5). In theory, any trade or business is a qualified use. IRC § 2032A(b)(2)(B). However, this chapter will only consider the qualified use of farming, as defined in the statute.

[23] Treas. Reg. § 20.2032A-3(b)(1).

[24] IRC § 2032A(c)(1)(B); Priv. Ltr. Rul. 8240015 (June 29, 1982).

dent.[25] The qualified heir is deemed to have acquired the property from the decedent if—

- The property passes from the decedent to the qualified heir under the rule of Section 1014;
- The qualified heir acquires the property from the estate; or
- The qualified heir acquires the property from a trust, to the extent that the property was included in the decedent's gross estate.[26]

If the qualified heir later disposes of specially valued real property to a member of his own family, the transferee will thereafter be treated as the qualified heir.[27]

[ii] Qualified heir where special use property held in trust. Generally, the qualified heir must have a present interest in the trust holding the special use property. If all income beneficiaries of a discretionary trust are qualified heirs, they will be considered as having present interests in the trust property.[28] The fact that the trustee can delay trust distributions until state and federal taxes have been paid does not prevent the beneficiaries from having a present interest.[29]

If a bequest creates successive interests, an election may be made only if all interests in the qualified use property are held by qualified heirs.

Practitioners must be forewarned of the problems caused by Treasury Regulation § 20.2032A-8(a)(2), which provides that a remainder interest cannot be subject to divestment in favor of a non-family member.[30] The IRS has interpreted this regulation to mean that a special power of appointment over the remainder interest, to the extent that it can be exercised in favor of a non-family member, renders an interest subject to divestment in favor of a non-family member. Therefore, according to the IRS, the remainder is not held by a qualified heir and the property does not qualify for Section 2032A treatment.[31] The IRS has also taken the position, under this regulation, that a disclaimer of the power to appoint the property to persons who are not qualified heirs would not be effective to avoid the successive interest requirement.[32] The Tax Court and two circuit courts have held that Treasury Regulation § 20.2032A-8(a)(2) was invalid, to the extent that it disallows special

---

[25] IRC § 2032A(e)(1).

[26] IRC § 2032A(e)(9).

[27] IRC § 2032A(e)(9).

[28] IRC § 2032A(g).

[29] Tech. Adv. Mem. 8532007 (Apr. 22, 1985).

[30] Treas. Reg. § 20.2032A-8(a)(2).

[31] Rev. Rul. 82-140, 1982-2 CB 208.

[32] Thompson Estate v. Comm'r, 864 F2d 1128 (4th Cir. 1989).

use valuation simply because of a special power of appointment exercisable in favor of a non-qualified heir.[33]

What if the property passes pursuant to directions in the dispositive document, and not pursuant to a power of appointment? In such situations, the IRS has taken the similar position that, where there is a remote chance that specially valued property could pass to a qualified heir, the property will not qualify under the above regulation.[34] The Tax Court has ruled that Reg. § 20.2032A-8(a)(2) is invalid to the extent of its application in cases where a remote contingent gift to non-qualified heirs exists.[35]

[e] "Member of the Decedent's Family" Defined

A member of Karen's family is one of the following:

- Karen's ancestor;
- Karen's spouse;
- A lineal descendant of Karen's parents;
- A lineal descendant of Karen's husband; or
- The spouse of any person who is a lineal descendant of Karen's parents or a lineal descendant of Karen's husband.[36]

[4] Requirement: Twenty-Five Percent of Adjusted Estate is Qualified Real Property

At least 25 percent of the adjusted estate must consist of the net value of real property that was:[37]

- Acquired from the decedent[38] by a qualified heir and
- Meets the eight-year material participation test described below.

---

[33] Thompson Estate v. Comm'r, 864 F2d 1128 (4th Cir. 1989); Clinard Estate v. Comm'r, 86 TC 1180 (1986); Smoot Estate v. Comm'r, 892 F2d 597 (7th Cir. 1989), aff'g 664 F Supp 293 (CD Ill. 1987).

[34] E.g., Priv. Ltr. Rul. 8332012 (Apr. 22, 1983). However, see Tech. Adv. Mem. 8643005 (July 18, 1986) and Tech. Adv. Mem. 9038002 (June 8, 1990), allowing special use valuation when the chance that a non-qualified heir would ever take the property was "exceedingly remote" (actuarially valued at a maximum of 0.00001 percent and at 0.1126 percent, respectively).

[35] Davis Estate v. Comm'r, 86 TC 1156 (1986). Clinard Estate v. Comm'r, 86 TC 1180 (1986). Pliske Estate v. Comm'r, 51 TCM 1543 (1986).

[36] IRC § 2032A(e)(2).

[37] IRC § 2032A(b)(1)(B).

[38] "Acquired from the decedent" has the meaning described in ¶ 48.02[3][d][i] above.

[5] Requirement: Before Decedent's Death the Property Was Owned and Put to a Qualified Use by Decedent or Family Member

During the eight-year period ending on the date of decedent's death, there must have been periods aggregating at least five years during which the real property was owned and used for farming by the decedent or a member of the decedent's family.[39]

Real property devoted to farming also includes residential buildings and related improvements on the decedent's real property that are occupied on a regular basis by the owner or lessee of the real property (or by the employees of the owner or lessee) for the purpose of operating or maintaining the real property, and roads, buildings, and other structures and improvements functionally related to the farm.[40] A farm residence occupied by the decedent owner of the specially valued property is considered occupied for the purpose of operating the farm even though a family member other than the decedent was the person materially participating in the operation of the farm.[41]

Real property valued under Section 2032A may be owned directly or may be owned indirectly through ownership of an interest in a corporation, a partnership, or a trust.[42] Where the ownership is indirect, however, the decedent's interest in the corporation, partnership, or trust must, in addition to meeting the tests for qualification under Section 2032A, qualify under the tests of Section 6166(b)(1) as an interest in a closely held business both on the date of the decedent's death and for sufficient other time (combined with periods of direct ownership) to equal at least five years of the relevant eight-year period.[43]

Directly owned real property that is leased by a decedent to a separate closely held business is considered qualified real property, but only if the separate business qualifies as a closely held business under Section 6166(b)(1) with respect to the decedent on the date of his or her death and for sufficient other time (combined with periods during which the property was operated as a proprietorship) to equal at least five years of the relevant eight-year period.[44] For example, real property owned by the decedent and leased to a farming corporation or partnership owned and operated entirely by the decedent and fewer than 15 members of the decedent's family is eligible for special use valuation.

---

[39] IRC § 2032A(b)(1)(C)(i).

[40] IRC § 2032A(e)(3).

[41] Treas. Reg. § 20.2032A-3(b)(2).

[42] Treas. Reg. § 20.2032A-3(b)(1).

[43] See Ch. 46 for a description of the requirements of IRC § 6166(b)(1).

[44] IRC § 6166(b)(1).

All specially valued property must be used in a trade or business.[45] The term "separate closely held business" applies only to an active business such as a manufacturing, mercantile, or service enterprise, or to the raising of agricultural or horticultural commodities, as distinguished from passive investment activities.[46] The mere passive rental of property to a party other than a member of the decedent's family will not qualify.[47] The decedent or a member of the decedent's family must own an equity interest in the farm operation.[48] A trade or business is not necessarily present even though an office and regular hours are maintained for management of income-producing assets.[49] Additionally, no trade or business is present if the activities are not engaged in for profit.[50]

[6] Requirement: Material Participation—General Rule

During the eight-year period ending on the date of decedent's death, there must have been periods aggregating at least five years during which the decedent or a member of the decedent's family materially participated in the operation of the farm.[51] This is a requirement that is often difficult to meet. Material participation requires a high level of involvement. Material participation by a family member must occur while the person is a family member.[52]

[a] Full-Time Versus Part-Time Involvement

Generally, material participation is determined in a manner similar to that used for purposes of determining whether a person is self-employed.[53] Accordingly, substantially full-time employment on the farm (at least 35 hours per week) or employment to whatever lesser extent is necessary to fully manage the farm constitutes material participation.[54]

In the absence of this objective level of involvement, the participant's activities must qualify under the Section 1402(a)(1) (self-employment) regu-

---

[45] Treas. Reg. § 20.2032A-3(b)(1); IRC § 6166(b)(1).

[46] IRC § 6166(b)(1).

[47] IRC § 6166(b)(1).

[48] IRC § 6166(b)(1).

[49] IRC § 6166(b)(1).

[50] IRC § 6166(b)(1).

[51] IRC § 2032A(b)(1)(C)(ii).

[52] Treas. Reg. § 20.2032A-3(e)(1).

[53] IRC §§ 1402(a)(1), 2032A(b)(1)(C)(ii), 2032A(e)(6).

[54] Treas. Reg. § 20.2032A-3(e)(1).

lations.[55] If the participant is self-employed and has not paid self-employment taxes, material participation will be presumed not to have taken place unless the participant informs the IRS why the self-employment tax was not paid and pays all such taxes due, along with penalties and interest.[56] If the land is formed by any nonfamily member or entity under crop share arrangement, the participant's involvement must be pursuant to a formal arrangement providing for actual participation in the production or management of production. Provision of capital itself is not sufficient; at least some actual physical work must be performed if production is the test, and significant participation in management decisions is required if management of production is the test.[57] The Farmer's Tax Guide, published by the IRS, provides that one way to satisfy the test is to work 100 hours or more spread over a period of five weeks or more in activities connected with crop production.[58]

[b] Factors Considered

Physical work and participation in management decisions are the principal factors considered.[59] At a minimum, the participant must regularly advise or consult with other managing parties on the business operation and must participate in making a substantial number of the decisions. Production activities on the land should be inspected regularly by the participant, and funds should be advanced and financial responsibility assumed for a substantial portion of the expense involved in the farming and operation.

Other factors are listed in the regulations.[60]

[c] Activities of an Agent or Employee

Material participation cannot be accomplished through an employee or agent,[61] although an employee or agent who is a family member can qualify as a material participant.[62]

[d] Ownership by Entity—Required Arrangement

[i] General rules. Where the real property is indirectly owned, material participation must be pursuant to an arrangement between the entity and the

---

[55] IRC § 2032A(e)(6).

[56] IRC § 2032A(e)(6).

[57] Treas. Reg. § 1.1402(a)-4(b)(3)(ii).

[58] U.S. Dep't. of Treasury, Internal Revenue Service, Pub. No. 225, Farmer's Tax Guide.

[59] Treas. Reg. § 20.2032A-3(e)(2).

[60] Treas. Reg. § 20.2032A-3(e).

[61] Treas. Reg. § 1.1402(a)-4(b)(5).

[62] Treas. Reg. § 20.2032A-3(e)(1).

materially participating decedent or family member, specifying the services to be performed.[63] Holding an office in which certain material functions are inherent may constitute the necessary arrangement for material participation.[64]

[ii] Ownership by trust. According to Treasury Regulation 20.2032A-3(f)(1), where property is owned by a trust, the necessary arrangement will generally be found in one or more of the following four situations:

Trustee materially participates. The arrangement may result from appointment of the decedent/family member as a trustee.

Employee of closely held business owned by trust materially participates. The arrangement may result from an employer-employee relationship in which the decedent/family member is employed by a qualified closely held business owned by the trust in a position requiring his or her material participation in its activities.

Independent contractor with trustee materially participates. The decedent/family member may enter into a contract with the trustee to manage, or take part in managing, the real property for the trust.

Beneficiary materially participates. Where the trust agreement expressly grants the management rights to the decedent/family member beneficial owner, that grant is sufficient to constitute the arrangement required.

[iii] Ownership by estate. Material participation can be determined in the same manner as if the property were held by a trust.[65]

[e] Ownership by Entity—Required Activities

Where property is owned by a qualified closely held business, the same participation standards apply under Section 2032A as where the property is directly owned.[66] In the case of a corporation, a partnership, or a trust where the participating decedent and/or family members are employees, the activities of such individuals must be such that if they were not employees their activities would subject them to self-employment taxes.[67]

Where property is owned by a corporation, a partnership, or a trust, participation in the management and operation of the real property itself as a component of the closely held business is the determinative factor.[68] It is not enough to nominally hold a position as a corporate officer or director and

---

[63] Treas. Reg. § 20.2032A-3(e)(1).

[64] Treas. Reg. § 20.2032A-3(e)(1).

[65] Treas. Reg. § 20.2032A-3(f)(2).

[66] Treas. Reg. § 20.2032A-3(f)(2).

[67] Treas. Reg. § 20.2032A-3(f)(2).

[68] Treas. Reg. § 20.2032A-3(f)(2).

receive a salary or to merely be listed as a partner and share in partnership profits and losses.[69] Note that this is the rule even though, as partners, the participants pay self-employment income taxes on their distributive shares of partnership earnings.[70]

When real property is directly owned and is leased to a corporation or partnership in which the decedent owned an interest, which qualifies as an interest in a trade or business within the meaning of Section 6166(b)(1), the presence of material participation is determined by looking at the activities of the decedent/family member with regard to the property, in whatever capacity rendered.[71] During any periods when qualified real property is held by an estate, material participation is to be determined in the same manner as if the property were owned by a trust.[72]

[7] Material Participation—Special Rule for Elderly or Disabled Decedent

If the decedent did not meet the normal material participation test, but was receiving old-age Social Security benefits for a continuous period ending on his death, or had a mental or physical impairment rendering him unable to materially participate for a continuous period ending on his death, then the eight-year test period referenced above ends on the date on which the longer of those continuous periods began, rather than on the decedent's death.[73] That is, the material participation requirements must have been met at the time when the disability or receipt of old age benefits began.

If a person does not cease to materially participate, he may not be eligible for Social Security benefits. The Social Security exception enables a person who is renting land to a third party to retire, receive Social Security benefits, and still take advantage of special use valuation. If a person ceases to materially participate, and does not meet this test, his estate will be ineligible for special use valuation unless a family member materially participates.

WARNING: If a person retires and then resumes material participation, a new eight-year period will begin, and the previous years of retirement may render the property ineligible for special use valuation.

---

[69] Treas. Reg. § 20.2032A-3(f)(2).

[70] Treas. Reg. § 20.2032A-3(f)(2).

[71] Treas. Reg. § 20.2032A-3(f)(2).

[72] Treas. Reg. § 20.2032A-3(f)(2).

[73] IRC §§ 2032A(b)(4)(A), 2032A(b)(4)(B).

¶ 48.03 DETERMINING THE SPECIAL USE VALUE

"Qualified real property" means real property which is eligible for special use valuation.[74] The special use value of qualified real property is determined using the following steps:[75]

Step One. Determine the average[76] annual gross cash rental for comparable land used for farming purposes in the farm's locality. Then, determine the average annual state and local real estate taxes for the comparable land. Subtract the taxes from the rental.[77] In applying this calculation the following rules apply:

- If there is no comparable land from which the average annual gross cash rental may be determined, but there is comparable land from which the average net share rental may be determined, the crop share rental can be substituted for the cash rental.[78]
- If there is no comparable land from which the average annual gross cash rental or net share rental can be determined, the formula valuation is not available.[79] Traditional valuation based on actual use is still available.[80]
- If the average cash or share rental is available, continue with the formula.
- Only arm's-length rentals can be considered.[81]

Step Two. Determine the average annual effective interest rate for all new Federal Land Bank loans made in the locality.[82] This is a figure that is published annually by the IRS in a revenue ruling.[83]

Step Three. Divide the number determined in Step One by the number determined in Step Two.[84]

Step Four. Determine the actual fair market value of the farm, without regard to the special use valuation.

---

[74] IRC § 2032A(b).

[75] IRC § 2032A(e)(7)(A).

[76] Each of the average computations in Steps One and Two is made on the basis of the five calendar years ending before the date of the decedent's death. IRC § 2032A(e)(7)(A).

[77] IRC § 2032A(d)(7)(A)(i).

[78] IRC § 2032A(e)(7)(B).

[79] IRC § 2032A(d)(7)(C).

[80] IRC § 2032A(d)(7)(C).

[81] Treas. Reg. § 20.2032A-4(b)(2)(ii).

[82] IRC § 2032A(d)(7)(ii).

[83] E.g., Rev. Rul. 97-13, 1997-16 IRB 4.

[84] IRC § 2032A(d)(7)(A).

Step Five. Subtract $750,000 from the number determined in *Step Four.*[85]

Step Six. Select the higher of the numbers determined in *Step Three* and *Step Five.* This is the special use valuation.

¶ 48.04 RECAPTURE TAX

If, within 10 years after the decedent's death and before the qualified heir's death, (1) the qualified heir disposes of any interest in the property (other than a disposition to a member of his family), or (2) the qualified heir ceases to use the qualified real property for a qualified use, then a recapture tax is imposed.[86] The IRS position is that in the post-death period, the qualified heir (not a member of the qualified heir's family) must satisfy the qualified use requirement.[87]

[1] Cessation of Qualified Use

Either of the two following circumstances will constitute cessation of qualified use.[88]

[a] Cessation of Farming Activity

The general rule is that if the property is not used for farming,[89] qualified use status for the property will cease. However, if the qualified heir begins to use the qualified real property within two years after the decedent's death, any failure to use the property before the commencement date does not count. However, in this instance, the 10-year qualified use period is extended by the period of nonuse.[90]

> **EXAMPLE:** Decedent's son rented the farm from Dad on a cash basis before Dad's death. Son will have two years after Dad's death to convert his lease to a crop share lease.

[b] Cessation of Material Participation

[i] *General rule.* The qualified use will cease if, during any period of eight years ending after the date of the decedent's death and before the date of the

---

[85] IRC § 2032A(a)(2).

[86] IRC § 2032A(c)(1).

[87] Priv. Ltr. Rul. 8652005 (Sept. 12, 1986).

[88] IRC § 2032A(c)(6).

[89] IRC § 2032A(c)(6)(A).

[90] IRC § 2032A(c)(7)(A).

qualified heir's death, there have been periods aggregating more than three years during which:

- The decedent held the property and there was no material participation by the decedent or any member of his family in the operation of the farm; or
- The property was held by a qualified heir and there is no material participation by the qualified heir or any member of his family in the operation of the farm.[91]

[ii] Exception for active management by eligible qualified heir. If a qualified heir is an "eligible qualified heir," active management by the eligible qualified heir, or the fiduciary of an eligible qualified heir who is under 21 or disabled, meets the material participation test.[92]

1. *"Eligible Qualified Heir" Defined.* An "eligible qualified heir" is a qualified heir who (1) is the decedent's surviving spouse, (2) has not attained the age of 21, (3) is disabled, or (4) is a student.[93] A "student" in a particular calendar year is a person who, during each of five calendar months during the year, (1) is a full-time student at an educational organization which normally maintains a regular faculty and curriculum and normally has a regularly enrolled body of students in attendance at the place where its educational activities are regularly carried on, or (2) is pursuing a full-time course of institutional on-farm training under the supervision of an accredited agent of such an educational organization or of a state or a political subdivision of a state.[94]

2. *"Active Management" Defined.* "Active management" means making the management decisions of a business other than the daily operating decisions.[95] A surviving spouse can rent the farm on a cash basis to her family members without the rental being considered a cessation of a qualified use.[96] The active management requirement can be met even if no self-employment tax is payable.[97] Active management by the surviving spouse can be tacked to the deceased spouse's material participation to satisfy the five-out-of-eight year requirement.[98]

---

[91] IRC § 2032A(c)(6)(B).

[92] IRC § 2032A(c)(7)(B).

[93] IRC § 2032A(c)(7)(C).

[94] IRC §§ 151(c)(4), 2032A(c)(7)(D).

[95] IRC § 2032A(e)(12).

[96] IRC § 2032A(b)(5)(A).

[97] S. Rep. No. 144, 97th Cong., 1st Sess., 134 (1981).

[98] IRC § 2032A(b)(5)(C).

[2] Disposition of Special Use Property

[a] General Rule

If the qualified real property is disposed of, except to a member of the family, the qualified use ceases.

[b] Exceptions

[i] Involuntary conversions. If a specially valued property is replaced by other farming property as a result of an involuntary conversion under Section 1033, no recapture tax will be imposed if the cost of the replacement property equals or exceeds the amount realized on the conversion.[99] If all of the proceeds are not reinvested, a partial recapture tax applies.[100] The replacement property will then be substituted for the specially valued property for most purposes.[101]

[ii] Like-kind exchanges. If an interest in the specially valued property is exchanged solely for like-kind qualified exchange property under Section 1031, no recapture tax is imposed on the exchange.[102] "Qualified exchange property" is real property that will be used for the same purposes as the exchanged property.[103] If non-qualified exchange property is received in the exchange, a partial tax will be imposed to the extent that the fair market value of that property equals or exceeds the fair market value of the exchanged property.

[3] Amount of Recapture Tax

The amount of the recapture tax on a disposition or cessation of use of the entire specially valued property is equal to the lesser of (1) the increase in the estate tax which would have been owed if the property had not been specially valued, plus interest, or (2) the excess of the amount realized (or the fair market value of the property, in a disposition which is not at arm's-length) over the special value of the property.[104]

Other important aspects of the recapture tax are as follows:

---

[99] IRC § 2032A(h)(1)(A).

[100] IRC § 2032A(h)(1)(B).

[101] IRC § 2032A(h)(2).

[102] IRC § 2032A(i)(1)(A).

[103] IRC § 2032A(i)(3).

[104] IRC § 2032A(c)(2).

- A marital deduction is allowed for property that actually passes to the surviving spouse.[105]
- The tax is due six months after the date of the disposition or cessation.[106]
- Both the qualified heir (unless he has furnished bond to the Treasury in accordance with a statutory procedure)[107] and each person who signed the recapture agreement are personally liable for the tax; the statute of limitations on assessment is extended for the appropriate period.[108]
- A partial disposition will attract a partial tax.[109]
- If the qualified heir disposes of, severs, or disposes of the right to sever timber on qualifying woodlands, that will be treated as a partial disposition of the property.[110]
- Other special rules apply to timber operations.[111]
- The recapture tax is not eligible for deferred payout under Section 6166(a)(1).[112]
- If the special use valuation originally applied for generation-skipping transfer tax purposes, the amount which is exempt from generation-skipping transfer tax with respect to the property is redetermined as of the transferor's date of death; any available GSTT exemption not yet allocated is automatically allocated to the property.[113]

¶ 48.05 COMBINING SPECIAL USE VALUATION WITH OTHER DISCOUNTS

The special use valuation is independent of other discounts. Accordingly, it would seem logical that other discounts should apply, in addition to special use valuation, when the situation warrants it. However, the Tax Court has held that a Section 2032A discount could not apply in addition to minority and marketability discounts.[114] In the *Hoover* case, a partnership held real estate and a great deal of other property. The court granted the special use

---

[105] Tech. Adv. Mem. 8652005 (Sept. 12, 1986).

[106] IRC § 2032A(c)(4).

[107] IRC §§ 2032A(c)(5), (e)(11).

[108] IRC § 2032A(f).

[109] IRC § 2032A(c)(2)(D).

[110] IRC § 2032A(c)(2)(E).

[111] IRC § 2032A(e)(13).

[112] Tech. Adv. Mem. 8652005 (Sept. 12, 1986).

[113] Treas. Reg. § 26.2642-4(a)(4)(i).

[114] Maddox Estate v. Comm'r, 93 TC 228 (1989); Hoover Estate v. Comm'r, 102 TC 777 (1994), rev'd, 102 F2d 842 (10th Cir. 1995).

valuation, but denied any other discount. In this case, the other discounts were far more valuable than the Section 2032A discount. The case was reversed by the Tenth Circuit, which allowed the estate to use a minority discount to value its interest in the partnership before applying the $750,000 reduction limitation. However, it might be the better part of valor not to put property other than special use valuation candidates into the same entity with property to be specially valued.

¶ 48.06 BASIS OF SPECIALLY VALUED PROPERTY

The income tax basis of specially valued property is its special use value.[115] However, if the executor or trustee holding specially valued property transfers it to a qualified heir in a taxable transaction, the gain is limited to the excess of the fair market value at date of transfer over fair market value at date of death.[116] The transferee's basis would then be the special use value plus gain recognized by the estate.[117]

PRACTICE POINTER: If the recapture tax is imposed, the qualified heir may elect that the specially valued property will receive a new basis immediately before the disposition or cessation of the qualified use. The increase in basis will be the difference between special use value and fair market value on date of death (or alternate valuation date).[118] The cost of this election is that interest must be paid on the recapture tax from the original due date, at the normal rate on underpayments.[119]

¶ 48.07 SPECIAL USE COMMUNITY PROPERTY

What if the qualified real property was held by the decedent and surviving spouse as community property? In this case, the surviving spouse's interest in the property will be taken into account to the extent necessary to provide the same result under Section 2032A which would have obtained if the property had not been community property.[120] This means that the entire value of community property held by the decedent and his wife will be counted in the decedent's estate for purposes of satisfying the percentage tests. The IRS has

---

[115] IRC § 1014(a)(3).
[116] IRC § 1040(a).
[117] IRC § 1040(c).
[118] IRC § 1016(c).
[119] IRC § 1016(c)(5).
[120] IRC § 2032A(e)(10).

privately ruled that the $750,000 limitation on reduction in value is applicable to the decedent's one-half community share.[121]

> **EXAMPLE:** Deceased Husband and surviving Wife owned a farm worth $2,000,000 as community property. Husband's estate is worth $3,000,000. Hence, his estate will need to use both halves of the community property to qualify for the 50 percent test. Suppose that the formula results in a valuation of decedent's $1,000,000 half of the farm at $200,000. The $750,000 is applied to the decedent's one-half, so the special value is $250,000.

¶ 48.08   PLANNING TO QUALIFY

Using Section 2032A in an estate plan may require various funding decisions.[122] Additionally, in creating an estate plan, some persons may want to make gifts of farm property in order to qualify for Section 2032A. Gifts made within three years before death will be added to the estate for purposes of determining whether the estate qualifies for Section 2032A.[123] Annual exclusion gifts and Section 2503(e) gifts of tuition and medical expenses are not added back to the estate.[124]

---

[121] E.g., Priv. Ltr. Rul. 8227014 (Mar. 31, 1982).

[122] See Chapter 49 for a discussion.

[123] IRC § 2035(d)(3)(B).

[124] IRC § 2035(b).

Wills With Marital Deduction Provisions— Drafting, Funding, and Apportionment

¶ 49.01 INTRODUCTION

The most tax-efficient disposition of property involves careful drafting of the dispositive documents, and careful administration once death has occurred, to take advantage of opportunities in funding bequests.

¶ 49.02 FORMULA WILLS

[1] Definition

Today, many wills (or revocable trusts) of married couples follow a standard pattern. As a general rule, these wills provide that, on the death of the first spouse, the maximum amount which can pass free of tax (without regard to the marital deduction) is left to a "bypass trust," so-called because it is drafted so as to escape inclusion in (i.e., "bypass") the surviving spouse's estate. The remaining estate is left in a form that qualifies for the marital deduction—often, a QTIP trust. The ultimate beneficiaries of the two trusts are usually the same. The estate plan will frequently be designed to utilize the maximum generation-skipping transfer tax exemption. This will often result in two marital deduction gifts—a QTIP trust which is exempt from generation-skipping transfer tax and a second marital deduction gift which is not exempt. A dispositive plan following the "bypass trust—exempt QTIP trust—non-exempt QTIP trust" pattern will be called a "formula will" in this chapter, although the disposition could also be in the form of a revocable trust. In a $2,000,000 estate with no prior use of any exemptions, a formula will would result in $600,000 passing to the bypass trust, $400,000 passing to the exempt marital deduction trust, and $1,000,000 passing to the non-exempt marital deduction bequest. This chapter is generally applicable to all estates, but will focus particularly on the problems and opportunities involved with a formula will.

[2] Types of Bypass and Marital Deduction Bequests

[a] Marital Deduction Bequests

Before 1964, it was fashionable for will drafters to draft the marital deduction gift in the form of a pecuniary bequest,[1] and to further provide that it would be funded with assets valued at their estate tax values. Then, on the death of the first spouse, this marital bequest was funded with property that had actually decreased in value since the date of death. Under such a provision, the marital deduction gift could be satisfied with property having an aggregate lower value than was used to determine the amount of the marital deduction on the estate tax return.

The IRS responded to this practice with Revenue Procedure 64-19,[2] which provided that a pecuniary bequest would not qualify for the marital deduction unless it was required by the will to be funded in one of certain specified ways, all of which were designed to prevent the executor from having any discretion to allocate a disproportionately large amount of depreciation or small amount of appreciation to the marital bequest. The following are forms of gifts that can qualify for the marital deduction after Revenue Procedure 64-19.

[i] **Bequest of cash.** Revenue Procedure 64-19 does not apply to a pecuniary bequest which is required to be satisfied in cash.

---

[1] A "pecuniary" bequest is a bequest of cash or property with a specific dollar value.

[2] 1964-1 (Part I) CB 682.

[ii] Bequest of specific property. Revenue Procedure 64-19 does not apply to a bequest of specific property.

[iii] Date of distribution bequest. In this chapter, a "date of distribution bequest" refers to a bequest that can be satisfied in cash or in kind, as long as the bequest must be funded with assets valued at their respective values on the date or dates of their distribution. Revenue Procedure 64-19 does not apply to a date of distribution bequest. The following is a sample date of distribution bequest clause:

> My executor shall have the power and the sole discretion to satisfy this bequest in cash or in kind or partly in cash and partly in kind and to select the assets which shall constitute this bequest, provided that my executor shall value such assets at their respective fair market values as of the date or dates of distribution.

[iv] Minimum net worth bequest. In this chapter, a "minimum net worth bequest" refers to a pecuniary bequest that can be satisfied with assets valued at their adjusted estate tax values, so long as the bequest is required to be funded with assets which, in the aggregate, have a fair market value at date, or dates, of distribution at least equal to the value of the bequest as finally determined for federal estate tax purposes.[3] The following is a sample minimum net worth bequest clause:

> My executor shall value the property distributed in satisfaction of this bequest at the lesser of the adjusted basis of such property for federal income tax purposes or the fair market value of such property as of the date or dates of distribution.

[v] Fairly representative bequest. In this chapter, a "fairly representative bequest" refers to a pecuniary bequest that can be satisfied at adjusted estate tax values, so long as the property used to fund the bequest is fairly representative of the total appreciation and depreciation in the value of all property available for distribution in satisfaction of the bequest.[4] The following is a sample fairly representative bequest clause:

> My executor shall value the property distributed in satisfaction of this bequest at the adjusted basis of such property for federal income tax purposes; provided, however, that my executor must select property of my estate that, in the aggregate, is fairly representative of the total of all appreciation or depreciation in the value of all property available for distribution in satisfaction of this bequest between the date of valuation for federal estate tax purposes and the date or dates of distribution.

---

[3] Such a bequest will meet the requirements of Rev. Proc. 64-19.

[4] Such a bequest will meet the requirements of Rev. Proc. 64-19.

[vi] Bequest of a fractional share of the estate. In this chapter, a "true fractional share bequest" refers to a bequest of a fractional share of the estate, under which each beneficiary shares proportionately in the appreciation or depreciation in the value of each asset to the date, or dates, of distribution.[5] A sample clause effecting such a bequest is as follows:

> I give a fractional share of my estate of which (A) the numerator is the smallest amount that, if allowed as a federal estate tax marital deduction, would result in the least possible federal estate tax being payable by reason of my death, and (B) the denominator is the value of my residuary estate as finally determined for federal estate tax purposes.

The amount actually received by the marital bequest will vary, depending on whether the denominator of the fraction is the gross residue, or the net residue.

EXAMPLE: Decedent's estate is $3,000,000. Formula will exists. Expenses chargeable against the bypass bequest are $300,000. The marital deduction amount is $2,400,000, whether or not the gross residue or the net residue is the denominator, as long as the expense items are actually charged to the bypass share. The marital deduction is determined as follows:

$$\frac{\$2,400,000}{\$3,000,000} \times \$3,000,000, \text{ or } \frac{\$2,400,000}{\$2,700,000} \times \$2,700,000 = \$2,400,000$$

Even though the marital deduction for estate tax purposes is $2,400,000 either way, the fraction will make a difference in the amount the marital bequest eventually receives. Suppose that the net $2,700,000 in the estate increases to $4,000,000 before distribution. If the bequest is a fraction of the gross residue, the amount to which the marital deduction bequest is entitled will be $3,200,000, determined as follows:

$$\frac{\$2,400,000}{\$3,000,000} \times \$4,000,000 = \$3,200,000$$

If the bequest is a fraction of the net residue, after expenses and taxes, the marital bequest will be entitled to $3,600,000, determined as follows:

If the denominator is the gross residue, less will pass to the marital bequest. The drafter should consider whether a "gross residue fraction" or "net residue fraction" is better in each particular case. Which fraction is better will depend on whether it is desirable to maximize or minimize the amount the marital bequest receives.

---

[5] Such a bequest is not affected by Rev. Proc. 64-19.

[vii] Residuary bequest. In this chapter, a "residuary bequest" refers both to (1) a bequest of the entire estate and (2) a bequest of the entire rest, residue, and remainder of the estate after all other bequests are satisfied.[6]

[b] Pecuniary Bypass Bequest

[i] Applicability of Revenue Procedure 64-19-type requirements. If the bypass gift is in the form of a pecuniary bequest, followed by a residuary marital or charitable bequest, language conforming to Revenue Procedure 64-19 needs to be included in the bequest.[7] The requirements of Revenue Procedure 64-19 are not applicable to the bypass bequest itself, if it is not accompanied by a marital or charitable bequest, since there is no policy reason to protect the amount of the bypass bequest. However, as a matter of protecting the marital deduction or charitable bequest, such language is required in the bypass bequest.[8] If the bypass bequest can be satisfied at estate tax values and no Revenue Procedure 64-19-type requirement is applicable, then the executor would have discretion to decrease the amount of the residuary marital deduction bequest by funding the bypass bequest with appreciated property. The following are examples of how this concept appliest to bypass bequest language.

[ii] Minimum worth bequest. The executor will have the same discretion (as that noted in the preceding paragraph) to stuff the bypass trust with appreciated property if a Revenue Procedure 64-19-type minimum worth gift is used. In order to protect the marital deduction gift, a "maximum worth" type bypass gift would have to be used instead.

[iii] Date of distribution bequest. A date of distribution bypass bequest allows protection of the bypass bequest at the expense of the marital deduction bequest in the case of a generally depreciated estate, but does not disqualify the marital deduction gift. The IRS has in fact ruled that a specific pecuniary bequest that must be satisfied at date of distribution values will not disqualify a residuary marital deduction gift (provided that the distribution is not unreasonably postponed).[9] This is because even though a general depreciation in assets could result in funding the specific bequest at the expense of the marital

---

[6] Such a bequest is not affected by Rev. Proc. 64-19 if preresiduary bequests qualify under the following rules.

[7] See Rev. Rul. 90-3, 1990-1 CB 174 (holding that date of distribution bypass bequest did not disqualify residuary marital bequest), and Rev. Rul. 81-20, 1981-1 CB 471, (reaching same result with a residuary charitable bequest).

[8] Rev. Rul. 90-3, 1990-1 CB 174; Rev. Rul. 81-20, 1981-1 CB 471.

[9] Rev. Rul. 90-3, 1990-1 CB 174.

deduction bequest, such funding would not be a result of the executor's exercise of discretion.[10]

[iv] Fairly representative bequest. A "fairly representative" type bypass bequest should not allow the executor to affect the amounts of the bypass trust and marital bequests, and thus should protect the marital bequest. The IRS has ruled that such a bequest does not disqualify the marital deduction.[11]

[c] Residuary Bypass Bequest

If the pecuniary bequest is the marital bequest, and the bypass trust is the residuary gift, Revenue Procedure 64-19 language is required by its own terms.

[3] Administration and Valuation of Different Types of Bequests

[a] Bequest of Cash or Specific Property

Both a bequest of cash and a bequest of specific property are easy to administer. No valuations are required for cash. And, for a specific property bequest, only the estate tax valuation is required.

[b] Date of Distribution Bequest

Date of distribution bequests are easy to administer. For assets funding such bequests; two valuation determinations are required—one for estate tax value and the other for date of distribution value.

[c] Minimum or Maximum Worth Bequest

This type of bequest is easy to administer. For assets funding a minimum or maximum worth bequest, an estate tax value is required and a date of distribution value is required (for assets worth less than their income tax basis in the case of minimum worth bequests or for assets worth more than their income tax basis in the case of maximum worth bequests). This type of bequest allows overfunding of the marital deduction bequest.

[d] Fairly Representative Bequest

A fairly representative bequest requires revaluation of all assets that are available for distribution to fund the bequest each time a distribution is made.

---

[10] Rev. Rul. 90-3, 1990-1 CB 174.

[11] Priv. Ltr. Rul. 9007016 (Nov. 16, 1989).

The fraction representing the fair representation of total appreciation and depreciation can change as the estate is administered, causing difficulties with administration.

> EXAMPLE: Pecuniary marital deduction fairly representative bequest, at estate tax value, is $400,000. Residuary bypass trust, at estate tax value, is $600,000. Therefore, appreciation (or depreciation) is to be distributed on a 40-60 basis. One year after death, the estate is worth $1,100,000. A distribution of $200,000 is made to the bypass trust. Thenceforth, the appreciation should be shared on a new basis. What is that basis?
>
> - *One approach:* Before the distribution, the marital and bypass gifts were entitled, respectively, to 4/10ths and 6/10ths of the $100,000 of appreciation. After the distribution, each is entitled to $400,000 of the remaining $800,000 of original principal of the estate, or 1/2 of all future appreciation and depreciation.
> - *Another approach:* Before the distribution, the marital and bypass gifts were entitled, respectively, to $440,000 and $660,000. After the distribution, they are entitled to $440,000 and $460,000, respectively, resulting in their being entitled to 44/90ths and 46/90ths, respectively, of future appreciation and depreciation.[12]

QUERY: If the estate values are changed on audit, and interim distributions have been made, a new fraction will have to be generated which compensates for earlier distributions.

[e] Fractional Share Bequest

No revaluations are required. In a true fractional share bequest, the fraction changes as described in [d] above, not only with non-pro rata distributions, but also with payment of expenses and taxes, and with revaluations on audit.

> EXAMPLE: Suppose two fractional share bequests of 50 percent of the estate exist—a marital deduction bequest and a bequest to a third party. The estate tax value of each bequest is $2,000,000. Taxes and expenses of $1,000,000, which are to be paid from the third party's share, are paid nine months later. After the payment, the values of the third party bequest and the marital bequest are $1,000,000 and $2,000,000, respectively. Since the taxes and expenses were charged against the third party's

---

[12] This approach has been endorsed by Richard D. Covey (R. Covey, Marital Deduction and Credit Shelter Dispositions and the Use of Formula Provisions, 81-82 (1984)), and Jeffrey N. Pennell (Pennell, 239-4th T.M., Estate Tax Marital Deduction, VIII.H.2.d. (discussing true fractional share funding), VIII.1.a. (discussing pick-and-choose fractional share funding).

share of the estate, the shares have switched from $1/2 - 1/2$ to $1/3 - 2/3$. Is appreciation shared $1/3 - 2/3$ starting from date of death? Or, is appreciation shared $1/2 - 1/2$ from death until payment of the taxes and expenses and then shared $1/3 - 2/3$ thereafter? There is no certain answer. Similar complications arise with non-pro rata distributions and changes of value on audit that are present in the fairly representative bequest.

If the fractional share bequest must be satisfied with an undivided interest in each asset available for distribution, it is not a pecuniary bequest. Such funding may be required unless the will or local law authorizes non-pro rata funding.[13] What if the executor is allowed to satisfy the bequest with a fraction of the estate represented by 100 percent of specific assets (a "pick-and-choose fractional share bequest")? Such a bequest may be considered a pecuniary fairly representative bequest, requiring revaluation of all assets available for funding at each non-pro rata distribution and with estate tax changes on audit. The law on the various consequences of funding such a bequest is uncertain.[14]

[f] Residuary Bequest

This type of bequest is easy to administer. No additional valuation of assets funding the residue is required after estate tax valuation.

[4] Income Tax Consequences on Funding Various Types of Bequests[15]

[a] Treatment of Funding as a Sale

Funding a date of distribution or minimum worth pecuniary bequest with property will be considered a sale by the estate for income tax purposes.[16] Other types of bequests (other than a bequest of a specific sum of money[17] or of specific property which is allowed to be paid or credited in fewer than four installments) may, at the estate's election, be treated as a sale for income tax purposes.[18] Accordingly, while in the case of a fractional share, residuary, or fairly representative bequest, funding with appreciated assets is not automati-

---

[13] See Rev. Rul. 69-486, 1969-2 CB 159.

[14] See Pennell (843 T.M., Estate Tax Marital Deduction, VIII.I.2.b).

[15] See Ch. 6 on income taxation of estates and trusts for a fuller discussion.

[16] Reg. § 1.1014-4(a)(3).

[17] A specific sum of money does not include a formula pecuniary bequest. Reg. § 1.663(a)-1(b)(1).

[18] IRC § 643(e)(3).

cally treated as a sale, the executor can elect to treat such funding as a sale.[19] This election cannot be made on an asset-by-asset basis, but must be applied to all distributions during a taxable year.[20] The election cannot be made with respect to a Section 663(a) bequest (i.e., an amount paid or permanently set aside for charity or a bequest of a specific sum of money or specific property).[21]

[b] Consequences of Sale Treatment

[i] **Realization of gain or loss.** When the funding of a bequest is treated as a sale, the estate will realize gain or loss equal to the difference between the value of the asset used to fund the bequest and that asset's basis in the hands of the estate.

> EXAMPLE: Will provides date of distribution bequest of $100,000. XYZ stock, which constitutes long-term capital gain property, was worth $50,000 for estate tax purposes, and thus acquired a basis of $50,000 in the hands of the estate under Section 1014. The stock is now worth $100,000. If the executor funds the bequest with the XYZ stock, the estate realizes a $50,000 long-term capital gain, which generates an income tax of $14,000 (at 28 percent).

Depending on the nature of the asset used to fund the bequest, all or a portion of the gain realized by the estate may be taxed as ordinary income. That would be the case, for example, if some of the gain were treated as recapture income.

[ii] **Assignment of income issues.** Funding a pecuniary bequest with employee benefits and other income in respect of a decedent results in acceleration of income and taxation of the value of the income to the estate.[22]

[iii] **Losses on funding bequests.** When an estate transfers depreciated property in satisfaction of a pecuniary bequest, the estate ordinarily recognizes a capital loss. And, the deduction of the loss on a sale between an estate and a beneficiary is not disallowed under Section 267, which (though it applies to trusts) does not apply to estates.

A capital loss realized by an estate is generally excluded from distributable net income.[23] As such, it cannot be passed through to the beneficiary (and therefore deducted on the beneficiary's own income tax return), except in the

---

[19] IRC § 643(e)(3).

[20] IRC § 643(e)(3)(B).

[21] IRC § 643(e)(4).

[22] IRC § 691(a) (2); see Estate of Noel v. Comm'r, 50 TC 702 (1968).

[23] IRC § 643(a)(3).

year in which the estate terminates.[24] However, until then, such losses can be carried over to succeeding taxable years of the estate.[25] In the year the estate terminates, any unused capital loss carryover will inure to the benefit of the beneficiaries "succeeding to the property of the estate." These are the beneficiaries who bear the burden of any loss in the estate's value—ordinarily the residuary legatees.[26] Nonresiduary legatees, such as those receiving some formula pecuniary and fractional share bequests, are included if their bequests are determined by the value of the estate as reduced by losses.[27]

[iv] **Beneficiary's basis in distributed asset.** In the case of a distribution treated as a sale, the distributed asset will receive a new basis. The new basis will be its adjusted basis in the hands of the estate immediately before the distribution, adjusted for any gain or loss recognized by the estate.[28] In the case of any distribution that is not treated as a sale, the distributee will receive a carryover basis in the asset from the estate.[29] Except for income in respect of a decedent, this will equal the value of the asset as included in the gross estate less any adjustment for depreciation, depletion, and other post-death events, because that value determined the estate's basis in the asset under Section 1014.

[v] **Consequences by type of bequest.** The following summarizes the income tax consequences on funding according to the type of bequest received:

- *Cash.* Whether or not a distribution of cash in satisfaction of a bequest is a sale, basis of property "transferred" will be the same as the value "received," so no gain or loss will result on funding.
- *Bequest of specific property.* Funding will not constitute a sale.
- *Date of distribution bequest.* Funding will be treated as a sale. Amount realized by estate will be fair market value of funding asset at date of distribution.
- *Minimum worth bequest.* Funding will be treated as a sale. Amount realized by estate will be lesser of fair market value of funding asset at date of distribution, or its adjusted basis in the estate. Hence, loss, but not gain, can be recognized.
- *Fairly representative bequest.* Since assets are used to satisfy bequest at adjusted estate tax values, basis will be the same as funding value.

---

[24] IRC § 642(h).

[25] IRC § 1212(b).

[26] IRC § 642(h); Treas. Reg. § 1.642(h)-3(a), (c).

[27] Treas. Reg. § 1.642(h)-3(c).

[28] IRC § 643(e)(1).

[29] IRC § 643(e)(1).

- *Fractional share bequest.* Funding a fractional share bequest will not automatically constitute a sale.
- *Residuary bequest.* Funding a residuary bequest will not automatically constitute a sale.

[c] Carrying Out Estate Distributable Net Income to the Distributee

To the extent that funding a bequest carries out distributable net income, the funding has the following income tax consequences: (1) the estate receives a distribution deduction and (2) the distributee will recognize income. If the distribution is made in property, then, for this purpose, the amount distributed is deemed to be the lesser of the fair market value of the funding asset or its basis in the hands of the estate (adjusted by recognized gain).[30] Funding of Section 663(a) bequests does not carry out distributable net income.[31] What bequests carry out distributable net income?

[i] **Specific amount of money bequest.** The funding of a "specific amount of money bequest" does not carry out distributable net income unless the bequest is required to be satisfied in more than three installments.[32] To qualify as a "specific amount of money bequest," the amount of money must be ascertainable (1) under the terms of a testator's will as of the date of death or (2) under the terms of an inter vivos trust as of the date of inception of the trust.[33]

[ii] **Specific property bequest.** The funding of a specific property bequest does not carry out distributable net income. To qualify as a specific property bequest, the property must be ascertainable (1) under the terms of a testator's will as of the date of death or (2) under the terms of an inter vivos trust as of the date of inception of the trust.[34]

[iii] **Formula pecuniary bequests of any type.** Although bequests of fixed dollar amounts do not normally carry out distributable net income, the Treasury's position is that formula bequests that can be satisfied with property selected by the executor do not come under this exception, and therefore such bequests do carry out distributable net income. This is because, in the case of formula bequests, the identity of the property and the amount of the bequest are dependent on the exercise of the executor's discretion as well as on the

---

[30] IRC § 643(e)(2), (e)(3)(A)(iii).

[31] IRC § 643(e)(4).

[32] IRC § 663(a).

[33] Treas. Reg. § 1.663(a)-1.

[34] Treas. Reg. § 1.663(a)-1.

payment of administration expenses and other charges, neither of which are determinable facts existing on the date of the decedent's death.[35]

[iv] **Residuary and fractional share bequests.** Distributions in satisfaction of these bequests carry out distributable net income.

[v] **Real estate distributions.** Distribution of real estate owned by a decedent, title to which under local law passes directly from the decedent to the heirs or devisees is not a distribution which carries out distributable net income.[36]

[d] Non-Pro Rata Funding

If the distributees' consent is required for non-pro rata funding of a bequest, either by reason of applicable state law or the governing instrument, a non-pro rata distribution (with the distributees' consent) will be treated as a distribution of fractional pro rata interests of the distributed property, followed by an exchange of the interests among the beneficiaries.[37] This deemed exchange will be taxable unless an exception under the general income tax rules applicable to exchanges exists. Conversely, if non-pro rata funding is permitted without the consent of the distributees, no taxable exchange is deemed to take place among the distributees.[38]

¶ 49.03 PECUNIARY BEQUEST: SHOULD IT BE THE MARITAL OR THE BYPASS?

In a formula will where the pecuniary-residuary pattern is used, what factors should be considered in deciding which gift should be the pecuniary bequest and which should be the residuary?

One factor to take into account is that funding a pecuniary bequest with appreciated property could result in gain recognition.[39] Another factor to consider is that the residuary estate will generally be entitled to all of the income of the estate (other than income from a gift of specific property), even if the pecuniary gift is much larger in amount than the residue.[40] However, in some states, and, under many wills, interest is payable on pecuniary bequests at a designated rate after a certain time.

---

[35] Treas. Reg. § 1.663(a)-1(b)(1).

[36] Treas. Reg. § 1.661(a)-2(e).

[37] Rev. Rul. 69-486, 1969-2 CB 159.

[38] See, e.g., Priv. Ltr. Rul. 9618280 (June 21, 1996).

[39] See discussion in ¶ 49.02[4] above.

[40] 6 W. Bowe—D. Parker, Page on Wills § 59.15 (1962).

The following general rules of thumb provide a starting point for analysis.

[1] Increasing Estate

Generally, in an estate which is expected to appreciate or earn substantial income after death, either the marital deduction should be the pecuniary bequest or the smaller gift should be the pecuniary bequest.

[a] Case for the Smaller Gift Being the Pecuniary Bequest

In an appreciating estate, there is less danger of having to trigger gain by being forced to fund the pecuniary bequest with appreciated assets. Fewer assets need to be reappraised at date of distribution. Both these considerations can be mitigated by early funding, because there is less likely to be a change in value if very little time has elapsed between date of estate tax valuation and date of distribution.

[b] Case for the Marital Deduction Gift Being the Pecuniary Bequest

In an estate with an increasing value, this pattern will result in the maximum amount passing to the bypass trust. The fact that a marital deduction gift is not entitled to income from estate assets before distribution during a reasonable period of administration will not disqualify the marital deduction gift; however, such a fact may affect the valuation of the marital deduction.[41] The opportunity to make significant tax-free transfers of property to the bypass trust in the form of income and appreciation of the estate may well be worth a possible increase in estate tax caused by a potential valuation of the marital deduction pecuniary gift at less than face.

[2] Decreasing Estate

In a depreciating or money-losing estate, the opposite rules of thumb would apply.

[3] Estate With Section 2032A Property

In an estate where Section 2032A property is expected to be a significant factor, a date of distribution marital bequest and residuary bypass trust will be advantageous.[42]

---

[41] Treas. Reg. § 20.2056(b)-5(f)(9). This sentence does not appear to apply to property held in a revocable trust.

[42] See discussion at ¶ 49.04[6] below.

¶ 49.04 FUNDING ASPECTS OF PARTICULAR ASSETS

[1] Funding With Income in Respect of a Decedent

[a] Is Section 691(c) Deduction Lost on Funding the Marital Bequest With an IRD Item?

If income in respect of a decedent (IRD) is specifically bequeathed to a surviving spouse or marital deduction trust in a taxable estate, these items are excluded from the gross estate and the marital deduction for Section 691(c) purposes. Accordingly, the Section 691(c) income tax deduction for estate taxes paid on such IRD items will be lost.[43] Payments to a surviving spouse under the provisions of a survivorship annuity are treated similarly.[44] The IRS has tried to extend this exclusion to IRD items that, while not specifically bequeathed to the marital trust, are in fact used to fund it.

The Tax Court, however, has found that such a rule would be inconsistent with the statute and regulations as written.[45] Under the Tax Court's interpretation of Section 691(c) and Treasury Regulation § 1.691(c)-1(a), if IRD items receivable by the estate are used to fund a marital deduction bequest in the discretion of the executor, the Section 691(c) deduction for estate taxes may be taken by the recipient of the property even though no estate tax was actually generated by that particular property. This holding appears to be appropriate, at least if there were sufficient assets in the estate other than income in respect of a decedent which could have been used to fund the bequest.

[b] Opportunity to Fund at Gross Value of IRD Item

If an IRD item is used to fund a marital bequest, the marital deduction will be allowed at the gross (pre-income tax) value, but the amount included in the surviving spouse's estate will be the net (after-income tax) value.[46]

[2] Funding With Employee Benefits

The income portion of employee benefits is taxed as income in respect of a decedent.[47] This characterization has the following ramifications:

Assignment of income. If the right to a stream of employee benefits is used

---

[43] Rev. Rul. 67-242, 1967-2 CB 227.

[44] Treas. Reg. § 1.691(d)-1(e), example (2).

[45] Estate of Kincaid v. Comm'r, 85 TC 25 (1985).

[46] Priv. Ltr. Rul. 8929046 (Apr. 25, 1989).

[47] See ¶ 49.04[1] above for discussion of IRD items.

to fund a bequest where funding is treated as a sale, this will result in acceleration of taxation of the income.[48]

> EXAMPLE: A dies. His estate is entitled to an annuity of $20,000 per year for ten years from an employee benefit trust. His executor distributes the right to the annuity in satisfaction of a date of distribution bequest. This distribution will be treated as an assignment of income, and the estate will recognize income equal to the current value of the annuity, despite the fact that it has not received the payments. Thereafter, the distributee will receive a basis of the current value of the annuity and will be taxed on the payments under the regular annuity rules.[49]

Qualification of annuity for marital deduction. Some annuity payments do not qualify for the marital deduction, and therefore should be used to satisfy the bypass gift, to the extent possible. The qualification of annuity payments for the marital deduction is a complex area of the law.[50]

Nonemployee spouse's interest. If the nonemployee spouse dies first, and the nonemployee spouse's interest under the plan passes only to the surviving spouse, it will qualify for the marital deduction. If not (e.g., if it is bequeathed to a QTIP trust), the result is uncertain.[51]

[3] Funding With Assets Which Do Not Qualify for the Marital Deduction

Certain assets do not qualify for the marital deduction.[52] These include annuities that cannot qualify for Section 2056(b)(6) or Section 2056(b)(7)(C) treatment, other non-deductible terminable interests, and interests that are not includable in the decedent's gross estate. If there is any possibility under the dispositive instrument that the marital deduction bequest could be satisfied with nondeductible terminable interests, the marital deduction will be reduced by the value of those items.[53] Hence, these items should be specifically ex-

---

[48] IRC § 691(a)(2). This consequence also occurs if the right to employee benefits in a lump sum is used to fund such a bequest. However, this is not quite so potentially devastating, since at least the money to pay the tax is available.

[49] IRC § 72; Treas. Reg. §§ 1.72-1 et seq.

[50] See Ch. 14 on employee benefits and Ch. 13 on commercial annuities for a discussion.

[51] If the plan is a qualified plan, the predeceasing nonparticipant spouse does not have a devisable interest in the plan. Boggs v. Boggs, 117 S. Ct. 1754 (1997). If the nonemployee spouse's interest is still considered includable in his or her gross estate, the interest automatically passing to the surviving participant spouse should qualify for the marital deduction.

[52] IRC § 2056(b)(2).

[53] IRC § 2056(b)(2).

cluded from the marital deduction gift through use of a clause similar to the following:

This gift shall be reduced to the extent that it cannot be satisfied with qualifying assets. In no event shall there be included in this gift any property or the proceeds of any property which will not qualify for the federal estate tax marital deduction.

[4] Funding With Assets That are Subject to Foreign Death Taxes

Any available Section 2014 foreign death tax credit will be lost to the extent that assets subject to foreign death taxes could be used to fund a marital deduction gift.[54] To avoid this situation, a clause similar to the following should be used:

> Property which is subject to foreign death taxes shall be used to satisfy this bequest only to the extent that other assets are insufficient.

If, despite the marital deduction and the unified credit, the estate owes United States estate tax, then a lower overall tax on the death of the first spouse to die will result if property which is subject to foreign death taxes is required to be used to fund the bypass bequest. If, on the other hand, the estate is not taxable, a foreign death tax credit will not be available. In this instance, the exclusion of property subject to foreign death taxes from the marital deduction bequest would only make a difference if the credit were available for 100 percent of the foreign death tax. In such a case, more property could be put into the bypass trust than the bypass amount, thus causing more property to bypass the surviving spouse's estate, but not causing a tax on the estate of the first spouse to die.

[5] Funding With Items Associated With Phantom Values

Items that are associated with values that do not exist in reality, but are included in the estate only for tax purposes, can present a problem. For example, assume that an amount representing unpaid dividends and deemed interest on the unpaid dividends is included in the estate under Section 2701. Even if the applicable retained interest in the corporation is used to fund the marital gift to the surviving spouse, it is very unclear whether the specially included amount will be treated as passing to the surviving spouse for purposes of the marital deduction. This is because the surviving spouse may have no right under state law to collect the dividends and will almost certainly have no right to the amount represented by the deemed compounded interest on the unpaid dividends.

---

[54] Treas. Reg. § 20.2014-3(b)(2).

[6] Funding With Section 2032A Special Use Property

As discussed in the following subsections, Section 2032A presents special opportunities, even when no estate tax is due at the death of the first spouse.

[a] Pecuniary Bequests

QUESTION: *Can we stuff lots of specially valued property into the bypass trust by funding a pecuniary bypass bequest with property at its special use value?*

ANSWER: No, not if it is a date of distribution bequest, since date of distribution value reflects actual fair market value.[55]

QUESTION: *So, if special use property funds a date of distribution bequest, is gain recognized on the difference between special use value and actual fair market value?*

ANSWER: No. Gain from funding a pecuniary bequest with Section 2032A property is limited to the amount by which the value on the date of distribution exceeds the actual fair market value[56] on the estate tax valuation date.[57]

QUESTION: *How about stuffing the bypass bequest by using a pecuniary date of distribution marital bequest?*

ANSWER: This works.[58] The bottom line is that, by electing Section 2032A valuation, the bypass bequest can be increased, but only if the bypass bequest is not a date of distribution bequest.

> EXAMPLE: Estate consists of a ranch. Fair market value is $1,000,000. Special valuation is $400,000. A formula will exists. No change in value occurs before distribution. A fractional share or fairly representative bequest will allow the entire ranch to pass to the residuary trust, leaving zero to the marital gift. This is because the formula requires the amount necessary, based on estate tax value, to reduce the estate tax to zero, to be allocated to the bypass bequest ($400,000 out of a $400,000 estate), and no post-death appreciation has occurred to increase value on funding. However, if the bypass bequest is a date-of-distribution bequest, only 40 percent of the ranch can be used to satisfy the date-of-distribution bypass bequest, and 60 percent will go to the marital gift. Why? The

---

[55] See Tech. Adv. Mem. 8314001 (Sept. 22, 1982); Tech. Adv. Mem. 8314005 (Dec. 14, 1982); Simpson v. United States, 71A AFTR2d 93-5082, 92-2 USTC ¶ 60,118 (DNM 1992).

[56] Not the IRC § 2032A value.

[57] IRC § 1040.

[58] See authorities cited in n.55.

formula will result in the bypass date-of-distribution bequest being entitled to receive $400,000 (the entire estate, at estate tax value). However, when the bypass bequest is funded, it will be funded at $400,000, based on actual fair market value, which will be 40 percent of the actual fair market value of the estate. Conversely, if the marital bequest is the pecuniary date-of-distribution bequest, the formula will result in its being entitled to zero, so the entire ranch will pass to the residuary bypass trust.

[b] Maximum Section 2032A Election

When the amount of property that could otherwise qualify for Section 2032A special use valuation exceeds the exemption amount, should Section 2032A be elected for the amount passing to the marital gift?

It depends on the desired result. The maximum election will increase the fair market value of property passing to the bypass trust, with the consequences illustrated in the following example.

EXAMPLE: Estate consists of ranch worth $2,000,000. Special use valuation is $1,250,000. Formula will based on estate tax values will result in $650,000 to the marital deduction bequest and $600,000 passing to the bypass bequest. Hence, if maximum Section 2032A valuation is elected, date of distribution marital bequest can receive $650,000 in actual value of ranch property, and residuary bypass trust can receive $1,350,000 in actual value. If the election were only made up to $600,000, then the gross estate would be $1,400,000, the marital trust would receive $800,000 in actual value ($1,400,000 total estate less $600,000 exemption), and the bypass trust would receive $1,200,000, which is the actual value of the remaining estate.

[c] Funding of Marital Bequest With Section 2032A Property

Will funding the marital gift with qualifying property to the maximum extent possible maximize the amount that can qualify for special use in the surviving spouse's estate, up to the valuation limit?

Yes, as illustrated in the following example.

EXAMPLE: Estate has ranch valued at $1,000,000 and specially valued at $600,000, and other assets worth $1,000,000. Surviving spouse has zero estate. She is entitled to $1,000,000 under the formula will. If the marital bequest is funded with ranchland with an actual value of $1,000,000, that amount will be available to be specially valued at $600,000 again in her estate, resulting in zero tax on both of their estates. If instead, she receives other assets worth $1,000,000, tax on her estate will be incurred.

[d] Recapture Tax on Cessation of Qualified Use

The Section 2032A recapture tax will come into play on a cessation of qualified use or a disposition to a person who is not a qualified heir. The marital deduction will apply to property actually passing to the surviving spouse from the original decedent in such an event.[59]

> EXAMPLE: Qualified heir leaves farm property to his wife (not the original decedent's wife) outright. She ceases to use the property for a qualified use. The fact that the bequest to her qualified for the marital deduction will not affect the recapture tax. However, if, under the terms of the original decedent's will, the farm would have passed to the original decedent's wife had the special use valuation not been elected, the marital deduction for the amount actually passing to her in the absence of the special use election will be allowed in computing the recapture tax. This can happen, for example, under a formula clause in which the spouse's share would have been greater if the farm property had been valued at its actual fair market value.

[7] Funding With Section 6166 Property

It may be desirable to fund a nonmarital bequest with Section 6166 property (that is, property qualifying for the payment of estate tax in installments) in a taxable estate, so that the tax advantages are not lost, particularly if the deferral might not be available at the surviving spouse's death.

[8] Funding With Ownership in Business Entity

If the estate owns a controlling interest in a business entity, funding the marital deduction bequest with a *noncontrolling* interest in such entity involves special considerations. These considerations receive detailed attention elsewhere in this book.[60]

[9] Funding With Appreciating or Income-Producing Property

Generally speaking, the executor will want to fund the marital deduction bequest with property which is not as likely to appreciate, or earn as much income, as property going into the bypass trust.

¶ 49.05 OPTIMUM TIME OF FUNDING

[1] Funding a Bypass Trust

The bypass trust should be funded as soon as possible, to prevent it from being reduced or wiped out, if (1) the bypass trust is a form of bequest that bears losses and depreciation before other bequests, (2) the estate is decreasing in

---

[59] E.g., Tech. Adv. Mem. 8240015 (June 29, 1982).

[60] See Ch. 25 for a discussion.

value, and (3) the election of the alternate valuation date under Section 2032 will not solve the problem.

PRACTICE POINTER: Even in the case of an estate that is not decreasing in value, early funding of a pecuniary bypass trust will give the bypass trust a chance to start earning income and appreciating at the earliest possible date.

[2] Funding Pecuniary Bequests

If the pecuniary bequest constitutes a large part of the estate, early funding will minimize the time available for appreciation, and thus reduce the chance that the executor will be forced to fund the pecuniary bequest with appreciated assets. On the other hand, if the pecuniary bequest is the marital bequest, late funding will allow the maximum income and appreciation to pass to the bypass trust. Even though the pecuniary bequest must be paid interest at a statutory rate if it is not funded by a certain time, state law interest rates are generally not high. If funding is unreasonably delayed, state law may provide penalties and the marital deduction may be decreased.

¶ 49.06   GSTT ISSUES

The GSTT regulations have some very complex funding requirements for (1) exempt gifts/bequests and (2) exempt gifts/bequests given by the same instruments as non-exempt gifts/bequests. Chapter 5 of this book discusses these regulations in detail.

One aim of the GSTT regulations is to prevent overfunding of exempt bequests. Suppose the will contains either an exempt nonmarital bequest and a nonexempt marital bequest or an exempt bequest and any other nonexempt bequest. The same funding/overfunding issues apply as in the case of a bypass bequest and a marital bequest; and, indeed, the exempt bequest will often be the bypass bequest. Additional issues posed by the GSTT regulations follow, assuming, for illustration, that a bequest of $1,000,000 is made, which is intended to be fully exempt.

If the exempt bequest is a pecuniary bequest, it will be fully exempt if it is either funded with cash, funded at date of distribution value, or funded with assets at fairly representative values.[61] For pecuniary bequests funded in other ways, the applicable fraction will be the exemption allocated, divided by the value of property actually funding the bequest.

If the exempt bequest is the residuary bequest, the bequest will be fully exempt if it follows a pecuniary bequest that is either (1) satisfied in cash and

---

[61] Treas. Reg. § 26.2642-2(b)(2).

carries appropriate interest or (2) satisfied in kind at date of distribution values or fairly representative values.[62] Otherwise, a discounted value of the cash funding the bequest and the date of distribution values of other property funding the bequest will be used in calculating the applicable fraction.[63]

A pecuniary gift and another gift made in the same instrument will be treated as separate shares for GSTT purposes if (1) the pecuniary amount carries appropriate interest, (2) the trustee pays or sets aside the pecuniary amount within 15 months after the transferor's death, or (3) the pecuniary amount is satisfied with assets at date of distribution or fairly representative values.

PRACTICE POINTER: If a GSTT exemption gift/bequest is involved and a pecuniary/residuary format is used, use a pecuniary formula which complies with Revenue Procedure 64-19 concepts, and provide that the pecuniary bequest bears appropriate interest.

¶ 49.07   APPORTIONMENT AND DEDUCTION OF EXPENSES AND TAXES

The apportionment of expenses and taxes, and the decision to deduct expenses against the estate tax or the income tax, is extremely important.

> **EXAMPLE:** Suppose estate is valued at $1,000,000. A formula will exists. Expenses which could be deducted against either the estate tax or the income tax are $100,000. The beneficiaries of the bypass trust and the marital deduction bequest are the same. Estate income is $100,000. For simplicity, a flat income tax rate of 39.6 percent is assumed.

[1] What if All Expenses are Allocated to Marital Bequest?

[a] Consequences

This allocation will result in the full exemption amount passing to the bypass trust. In the case of expenses that are not deducted against the estate tax, it will result in an estate tax being due. An interrelated computation is required to figure this estate tax and the resulting amount passing to the marital deduction trust. In most cases, deduction against the estate tax will result in loss of deduction against income tax.[64]

---

[62] Treas. Reg. § 26.2642-2(b)(3).

[63] Treas. Reg. § 26.2642-2(b)(3).

[64] IRC § 642(g).

[b] Analysis Using the Global Example

Numbers received by each trust represent amounts of principal. In the Global Example:

- *Bypass trust.* The bypass trust would receive $600,000.
- *Expenses deducted on Form 706.* If all expenses are deducted against the estate tax, income tax will be $39,600, and estate tax will be zero. Marital trust would receive $300,000.
- *Expenses deducted on Form 1041.* If all expenses are deducted against the income tax, income tax is zero. Assuming that expenses are payable out of the marital trust rather than the bypass trust, the marital trust would receive $240,983.61, and estate tax would be $59,016.39.

[2] What if All Expenses and Taxes are Apportioned to Bypass Trust?

[a] Consequences

This apportionment results in less than the full exemption amount passing to the bypass trust. In the case of expenses which are deducted against the estate tax, there is no compensating tax advantage. In the case of expenses which are not deducted against the estate tax, this apportionment results in no estate tax (as long as the expenses are less than the exemption amount), but also results in less passing to the bypass trust than could otherwise so pass.

[b] Analysis Using the Global Example

In the global example:

- *Bypass trust.* Bypass trust receives $500,000.
- *Marital trust.* Marital trust receives $400,000.
- *Expenses deducted on Form 706.* If the expenses are deducted against the estate tax, income tax is $39,600, and estate tax is zero.
- *Expenses deducted on Form 1041.* If the expenses are deducted against the income tax, income tax is zero, and estate tax is zero.

[3] What if Apportionment Is Determined by a Formula?

It is possible to devise formula clauses which reach various desired tax results. For example, there is a standard way to apportion taxes and expenses at the first death of two spouses when: (1) the goal is to have zero estate tax at the first death, and to get as much property into the bypass trust as possible consistently with zero estate tax; (2) all property is initially passing to a bypass trust or marital deduction gift; and (3) the ultimate beneficiaries of all trusts after the surviving spouse's death are the same. Such a clause allocates items which are chargeable to principal and deducted for estate tax purposes to the marital deduction bequest, other principal items to the non-marital bequest, and items which are properly chargeable to income under state law to income.[65]

The model apportionment results in no estate tax (as long as the expenses do not exceed the exemption amount), and the least income tax consistent with no estate tax. It also results in less property passing to the bypass trust than the maximum amount that could otherwise so pass. Many people don't want to pay any extra current income tax, even if paying a little more income tax at the first death would mean more money passing tax-free at the survivor's death.

It is important to remember that formula apportionment clauses that are designed to be tax-efficient are usually premised on the assumption that the same people will take the property, no matter how the taxes are apportioned. If different people will be taking different property, the tax clause needs to be customized in every situation.

Let's suppose we have the standard clause described above.

[a] Consequences

A typical formula apportionment clause might provide that all items that are deducted for estate tax purposes are allocated to the marital deduction bequest,[66] and all other items are allocated to the bypass trust.

[b] Analysis Using the Global Example

In the global example:

- *Bypass trust.* Bypass trust will receive either $500,000 or $600,000, depending on where expenses are deducted.
- *Marital deduction gift.* Marital trust will receive either $300,000 or $400,000, depending on where expenses are deducted.
- *Expenses deducted on Form 706.* If the expenses are deducted against the estate tax, estate tax is zero, income tax is $39,600, the bypass trust receives $600,000 and the marital bequest receives $300,000.
- *Expenses deducted on Form 1041.* If the expenses are deducted against the income tax, income tax is zero, estate tax is zero, the marital trust receives $400,000 and the bypass receives $500,000.

---

[65] The income allocation is subject to the issues of the Hubert case, described below.

[66] For the reason noted in ¶ 49.07[2][a] above.

[c] Drafting Considerations for Phrasing of Apportionment Formula

A phrase such as "I give my wife an amount equal to the maximum marital deduction allowable to my estate" could be interpreted to require the executor to deduct all expenses which are otherwise deductible for both income and estate tax purposes on the estate's income tax return (since this should result in such expenses being charged to the bypass bequest rather than the marital bequest). Because of this, the drafter should ensure that provision is made allowing the executor to choose to deduct expenses which are deductible for both income and estate tax purposes in whichever way appears better, and to have the marital deduction gift computed accordingly. The same idea applies if a standard clause is included providing that the fiduciary will exercise no power in a manner which would cause a loss of or decrease in the marital deduction. Use of a clause similar to the following is advisable:

> Except as otherwise permitted herein, neither my executor nor my trustee shall exercise any power or discretion in such a manner as to result in a loss of or decrease in the marital deduction available to my estate; provided, however, that nothing in this will shall be construed as a direction by me to my executor to exercise any election or option which may be available under any tax or other law in such a manner as will result in a larger amount passing to my spouse in a manner which qualifies for the estate tax marital deduction than if the contrary election were made.

[4] What if Apportionment is in Discretion of Executor?

If the executor has discretion to decide where to deduct items of expense which are properly chargeable to principal, how does the executor decide which items to deduct against the estate tax vis-à-vis the estate's income tax? Assuming that the will has been drafted with formula will clauses which maximize tax benefits, funding decisions will have the following consequences.

[a] Deduction for Estate Tax Purposes

The deduction on the Form 706: (1) will reduce the marital deduction bequest, (2) will not affect the estate tax (since the amount would be deductible either as an expense or as a marital deduction), (3) will increase the income tax, and (4) will allow maximum use of the bypass trust.

[b] Deduction for Income Tax Purposes

The deduction on the Form 1041: (1) will reduce the bypass trust, (2) will not affect the estate tax (unless the expenses exceed the amount of the bypass gift), and (3) will reduce the income tax.

[5] What if Apportionment Is Determined by Law (in Absence of Will Provision)?

[a] State Law Provision

Generally, in the absence of a provision in the dispositive document, the apportionment of taxes and expenses will depend on state law.

[b] Federal Law Provision

In some cases, federal law applies. These cases include: (1) insurance on the life of the decedent,[67] (2) property over which the decedent had a general power of appointment,[68] (3) QTIP property,[69] and (4) property included in the decedent's estate under Section 2036.[70]

[6] What About Apportioning Administrative Expenses to Income?

The income of the estate may be able to be charged with administrative expenses if such an apportionment is proper under the dispositive document and state law.

Why would we want to make this allocation? If any nondeductible expenses are properly allocable to income, then it will be more tax-efficient to have those expenses allocated to income of the estate, and not to principal. If those expenses were charged to principal, they would either reduce the bypass trust or generate an estate tax, since they would have to be paid out of the bypass trust or the marital deduction gift.

If an apportionment clause provides that all expenses are to be borne out of the residue of the estate, then state law may require that the expenses be borne out of principal, thereby reducing either the bypass trust or the marital deduction gift.[71] Hence, the apportionment clause should provide that expenses attributable to income should be borne out of income.

> **EXAMPLE:** Bypass trust is valued at $600,000. Marital deduction trust is $400,000. Expense of preparing the estate's income tax return is $2,500. It has been generally thought that the $2,500 can be deducted from the

---

[67] IRC § 2206.

[68] IRC § 2207.

[69] IRC § 2207A.

[70] IRC § 2207B.

[71] See, e.g., Sobota Estate v. Comm'r, 1996 RIA TC Memo. ¶ 96,294, 71 TCM 3217 (1996).

estate's income as a matter of fiduciary accounting, and does not have to be subtracted from either the $600,000 bypass bequest or the marital bequest.

The U.S. Supreme Court has adopted the position that administrative expenses which are properly charged to income of the marital deduction bequest do not reduce the marital deduction in certain circumstances.[72] The Supreme Court, ruling favorably in the particular taxpayer's case, held that whether charging administrative expenses against the marital deduction would reduce the marital deduction depended on the facts and circumstances.[73]

[7] What About Apportionment Among Generation-Skipping Trusts?

The tax apportionment clause should provide that the property which is subject to generation-skipping transfer tax should bear taxes before exempt property does.

[8] Tax Apportionment—Special Problems Related to Marital Deduction

[a] Section 4980A

The Section 4980A excise tax has been replaced with respect to decedents dying after 1996. For decedents dying before 1997, it created special apportionment problems.

[i] Apportionment to marital bequest. For decedents dying and distributions made before 1997, Section 4980A imposed a 15 percent excise tax on certain large annual distributions from qualified employee benefit plans and individual retirement accounts ("4980A plans") and a special estate tax of 15 percent of certain excess retirement accumulations in such plans upon the death of the plan participant.[74] This special estate tax is added to the estate tax otherwise payable under the estate tax provisions of the Internal Revenue Code. No unified (or other) credit or marital deduction is allowable for use in

---

[72] Comm'r v. Estate of Hubert, 117 S. Ct. 1124, 79 AFTR2d 97-1394 (1997).

[73] Comm'r v. Estate of Hubert, 117 S. Ct. 1124, 79 AFTR2d 97-1394 (1997). See Ch. 50 for a discussion of this issue.

[74] See Ch. 14 on employee benefits for a discussion.

computing the 15 percent estate tax.[75] However, if the spouse of the participant is the beneficiary of most of the deceased spouse's interests in 4980A plans, and the spouse elects not to have the 15 percent estate tax apply, then the 15 percent estate tax is not imposed.[76] Instead, all of the predeceasing spouse's interest in such plans will be aggregated with those of the surviving spouse for purposes of future imposition of the Section 4980A taxes.

No federal apportionment rule applies with respect to the 15 percent estate tax.[77] Under state law, the testator may be able to direct by will that the 15 percent estate tax will not be imposed on probate assets.[78] However, the executor will probably be prevented from seeking direct reimbursement for estate taxes from the plan administrator under both Section 514 of the Employer Retirement Income Security Act (ERISA) and the specific limitations on alienation of interest in qualified plan trusts.

Because the participant's spouse may elect in some cases to avoid the 15 percent estate tax (but then have to aggregate payments from the decedent's 4980A plans with payments from his or her own 4980A plans for purposes of the 15 percent lifetime excise tax), there may be an incentive for the surviving spouse not to elect to avoid the 15 percent estate tax if that tax is apportioned to other beneficiaries. It was appropriate to consider having the 15 percent special estate tax imposed upon the surviving spouse where that spouse would be receiving all the payments from 4980A plans. This will not increase the regular estate tax, since the special 15 percent estate tax can be deducted under Section 2053(a) for regular estate tax purposes, thereby preventing an increase in the regular estate tax caused by a reduction in the regular estate tax marital deduction.

[ii] **Older apportionment formulas.** Old-style marital deduction clauses may speak in terms of funding the marital deduction bequest with the least amount which would produce a zero estate tax. Since the unified credit cannot be applied against this tax,[79] it will not be possible to reduce the estate tax to zero unless the spouse makes the deferral election described above. If the spouse does not so elect (so that the Section 4980A tax will not permit reduction of the estate tax to zero) and the will contains one of these formulas, the executor may be faced with getting a will construction to see whether he is supposed to fund the bypass trust with no assets or with an amount that would result in no additional estate tax beyond the penalty tax.

---

[75] IRC § 4980A(d)(2).

[76] IRC § 4980A(5).

[77] Temp. Reg. Q. d-8A.

[78] E.g., Tex. Prob. Code Ann. § 322A.

[79] IRC § 4980A(d)(2).

[b] Chapter 14 Considerations

State apportionment laws apportion tax, generally, to the recipients of property. However, the application of such laws to apportion taxes imposed by Sections 2701 and 2704, each of which can add "phantom" amounts to the gross estate which no one in fact receives, is highly uncertain. Will drafters may want to specifically address the tax on such items.

[c] The Compounding Effect of Any Tax Borne by Marital Deduction

The estate tax can increase enormously if the burden of tax is borne by property that would otherwise qualify for the marital deduction. This is because of the spiraling effect of such a payment.

EXAMPLE: Estate is $1,000,000. Formula will exists. Expenses of $100,000 which are not deducted on Form 706 are charged to the marital bequest. This payment decreases the amount received by the spouse by $100,000. This amount will be transferred to the government as a tax payment, for which there is no estate tax deduction. Because the marital deduction is reduced by $100,000, the taxable estate increases by $100,000. An increase in the taxable estate of $100,000, in turn, means a further increase in tax of $37,000. This increase in tax, is again borne by the marital deduction property, further reducing the marital deduction, causing a further increase in estate tax, and so on.

Thus, a stated tax rate of 55 percent converts to an effective rate of taxation of 122 percent when the marital bequest bears the tax, as illustrated by the following. Assume Estate has $10,000,000, and the will contains a non-marital bequest of $3,000,000. The will provides that the marital bequest bears all taxes. While the initial tax on $3,000,000 is $1,098,000, the spiraling tax effect will cause the estate tax to increase by $1,098,000 × 122.22 percent, for a total tax of $2,439,976.

Although in some cases it will be the testator's intent that the property otherwise passing to the surviving spouse bear the tax on specific bequests or nonprobate property, the consequences should be considered.

[d] Making Less Than Full QTIP Election

Making a partial QTIP election or no QTIP election can generate an estate tax. If different beneficiaries are involved, and all taxes are charged to the non-QTIP beneficiaries (based on the expectation at time of will drafting that the full QTIP election would be made), the non-QTIP beneficiaries' bequests can be wiped out.

QUESTION: *Can executor have the discretion to allocate taxes to the QTIP trust if the QTIP election is not made?*

ANSWER: The question has not been totally resolved. It is discussed in detail in Chapter 50.

QUESTION: *Can property for which the QTIP election is not made pass to a different trust, or even to different beneficiaries?*

ANSWER: The IRS position generally is that such a provision in a will disqualifies the gift for the marital deduction, even if the executor actually makes a 100 percent QTIP election, since the discretion in the executor to make or not make the QTIP election could vary the amount of property passing to the QTIP trust, which is not allowable.[80]

The final regulations were effective for decedents dying after March 1, 1994. The Tax Court has announced that it will no longer disallow the marital deduction for interests which are contingent on the QTIP election in the case of decedents dying before the final regulations became effective, and the IRS has acquiesced with respect to such decedents.[81] However, the court specifically declined to comment on the validity of the final regulation's contrary position with respect to decedents dying after its effective date.[82] Temporary and proposed regulations amending the above final regulation were subsequently released on February 14, 1997, effective for decedents whose estate tax returns are due after February 18, 1997.[83] These provisions say that a marital deduction will not be denied solely because the surviving spouse's mandatory income interest (or life estate) is contingent on the executor's QTIP election.

¶ 49.08 ADDITIONAL READING

An excellent additional source for the issues addressed in this chapter is Pennell, 843 T.M., Estate Tax Marital Deduction.

---

[80] See Treas. Reg. §§ 20.2056(b)-7(d)(3), 20.2056(b)-7(h), example 6; Priv. Ltr. Rul. 8901003 (Sept. 9, 1988); Tech. Adv. Mem. 8611006 (Nov. 29, 1985). The Tax Court agreed with the IRS in three cases: Estate of Clayton v. Comm'r, 97 TC 329 (1991), rev'd, 976 F2d 1486 (5th Cir. 1992); Estate of Robertson v. Comm'r, 98 TC 678 (1992), rev'd, 15 F3d 779 (8th Cir. 1994); Estate of Spencer v. Comm'r, 1992 RIA TC Memo. ¶ 92, 579, 64 TCM 937 (1992), rev'd, 3 F3d 226 (6th Cir. 1995). All three of these decisions were reversed. However, the final regulations, which maintain the IRS position, were adopted after the reversals, and specifically mentioned two of the reversals.

[81] Estate of Clack v. Comm'r, 106 TC (1996), acq. in result, 1996-29 IRB 4.

[82] Estate of Clack v. Comm'r, 106 TC (1996), acq. in result, 1996-29 IRB 4.

[83] Temp. Reg. §§ 20.2056-7T(d)(3)(ii), 20.2056-7T(h), example 6(ii), 20.2044-1T, example 8, TD 8714, as corrected by Ann. 97-49, 1997-20 IRB 8.

CHAPTER **50**

Other Post-Mortem Elections

¶ 50.01 INTRODUCTION

In the post-mortem period, the executor has the opportunity to make a number of significant tax elections.

¶ 50.02 QTIP ELECTION

The executor must decide whether to make a full, partial, or no QTIP election.

[1] Manner of Election

The QTIP election is made on the decedent's Form 706 by listing the property for which the QTIP election is made on Part 2 of Schedule M and computing the tax accordingly. A formula election is permissible and will result in a partial QTIP election.[1] The formula should be self-adjusting for changes on audit. The following is a sample election using a self-adjusting formula—

> An election is being made with respect to a fraction of the entire marital trust. This fraction is defined by the following formula: X/Y, where X = the lowest amount necessary to produce the least amount of federal estate tax possible payable by the estate; and Y = the value of the marital trust, as finally determined for federal estate tax purposes.

It may be wise to use formula elections in all cases because a QTIP election is irrevocable, and therefore cannot later be changed, in the absence of a formula, to reflect audit results.[2] The following is a sample election clause taking into account changes occurring during an audit and reading them back into the formula—

> An election is made to claim a QTIP marital deduction for a fraction of the value of property passing to the marital trust, as computed above. If, for any reason, any amount reported in this Form 706 should differ from the amount as finally determined for federal estate tax purposes, then the amount of property subject to the election shall change in accordance with the above formula.

[2] When Not to Make a Full QTIP Election

For the reasons discussed in the following subsections, it may be desirable to make only a partial QTIP election or to make no QTIP election at all.

---

[1] Treas. Reg. § 20.2056(b)-7(b)(2)(i).

[2] IRC § 2056(b)(7)(B)(v); Treas. Reg. § 20.2056(b)-7(b)(4)(ii).

[a] To Preserve Bypass Trust

Less than a full QTIP election can preserve the full credit shelter when that is not otherwise done.

EXAMPLE: Entire $2,000,000 estate is left to a trust which would qualify as QTIP. The executor could make a partial election for $^{14}/_{20}$ of the trust, so that the $600,000 portion will be exempt from estate tax at the survivor's death.

[b] To Equalize Estates

Less than a full QTIP election can equalize the estates of both spouses. Equalization will allow the run-up through the brackets in both estates. The maximum advantage of this is reached when the partial QTIP election results in $3,000,000 being included in the predeceasing spouse's estate.

EXAMPLE: Husband dies. His estate is $10,000,000. Wife has no estate. Entire estate is left to a trust that could qualify for QTIP. If the full QTIP election is made, Husband's estate tax will be zero and Wife's estate in excess of $3,000,000 will be taxed at 55 percent. If a QTIP election is made for $^{7}/_{10}$ of the trust, $3,000,000 of Husband's estate and $3,000,000 of Wife's estate will be taxed at less than 55 percent.

[c] To Avoid Surcharge

Equalization may avoid the potential surcharge of an additional 5 percent estate tax under Section 2001(c)(3). Here, the goal is to reduce both estates to $10,000,000 or less.

EXAMPLE: Husband dies. His estate is $12,000,000. Wife has no estate. Entire estate is left to a trust which would qualify for QTIP. If full QTIP election is made, $2,000,000 will be taxed at 60 percent. If a $^{10}/_{12}$ election is made, the top bracket in either estate (assuming Wife's estate does not increase to over $10,000,000) will be 55 percent or less.

[d] To Allow Use of Credit for Tax on Prior Transfers (TPT Credit)

Making less than the full QTIP election in a decedent's estate can enable the surviving spouse's estate to take advantage of the Section 2013 credit for tax on prior transfers.[3]

---

[3] Under pre-QTIP law, the IRS ruled that the executors could not waive the marital deduction and avail the estate of the TPT credit. Rev. Rul. 59-123, 1959-1 CB 248. The IRS has acknowledged that a surviving spouse can disclaim property and avail the estate of the TPT credit. Tech. Adv. Mem. 8512004 (Dec. 11, 1984). The principle of Rev. Rul. 59-123 should not apply to prevent an executor from making a partial QTIP election and taking a TPT credit, since the whole point of the QTIP

PRACTICE POINTER: In the case of a married decedent, it may be advantageous to extend the due date of the estate tax return for the full 15 months after death. If the surviving spouse dies during this period (and she was eligible to use the actuarial tables on the date of death of the predeceasing spouse),[4] it may be desirable not to make the QTIP election in the predeceasing spouse's estate and to use the Section 2013 credit in the surviving spouse's estate. As indicated by the following example, this technique can result in significant tax savings.

The regulations state that if the second spouse to die has an income interest in property for which the Section 2013 credit is claimed, the credit will only be available if the interest is able to be valued on the basis of recognized valuation principles.[5] An income interest that would have been eligible for the QTIP deduction (had QTIP treatment been elected) should be eligible for valuation under the TPT credit.

The Section 7520 regulations provide that the limitations on use of the actuarial tables apply for purposes of Section 2013, except in the case where the value of the estate tax in the first decedent's estate depended on the value of the life interest received by the second decedent.

What if Wife is terminally ill on Husband's death? The regulations say that the actuarial tables cannot be used to value Wife's interest in a trust established by Husband for purposes of the Section 2013 credit.[6] However, there is pre-regulatory case law to the contrary.[7] The theory is that the use of the actuarial tables for purposes of the Section 2013 credit is not subject to abuse.

If Husband is terminally ill, and he could make an actuarial transfer based on a life expectancy he knows is incorrect, there is room for planning; the regulations have implicitly adopted the position that if Husband is expected to die within one year, such planning would be abusive and will not be permitted. However, Husband is not going to time his death to occur when his Wife is terminally ill, just so that the life estate property he leaves her will be able to be actuarially valued on a favorable basis. A strong argument can be

---

election is to allow the executor to choose how much of the bequest to qualify for the marital deduction.

[4] Treas. Reg. § 20.7520-3(b)(3). See Ch. 11 for a discussion of the availability of the actuarial tables.

[5] Treas. Reg. § 20.2013-4(a).

[6] Treas. Reg. § 20.7520-3(b)(3).

[7] Merchants Nat'l Bank of Topeka v. United States, 31 AFTR2d 73-1446, 73-1 USTC ¶ 12,917 (D. Kan. 1973), modified on reh'g, 369 F. Supp. 1080 (D. Kan. 1973); Continental Ill. Nat'l Bank & Trust Co. of Chicago v. United States, 32 AFTR2d 73-6235, 73-2 USTC ¶ 12,946 (ND Ill. 1973), aff'd, 504 F2d 586 (7th Cir. 1974); Mercantile-Safe Deposit & Trust Co. v. United States, 368 F. Supp. 32 (D. Md. 1974).

made that the actuarial tables should apply for purposes of the Section 2013 credit, regardless of the physical condition of the surviving spouse.

In the case of simultaneous deaths, both the regulations and pre-regulatory case law agree that the actuarial tables cannot be used.[8]

[e] To Allow Alternate Valuation

Making less than the full QTIP election can create a taxable estate in order to take advantage of the election to value the estate as of the alternate valuation date. Specifically, in a depreciating estate, a unified credit residuary trust can be reduced, or even wiped out. Therefore, in a proper case, it may be desirable to render the estate taxable (by not making the full QTIP election) to take advantage of the alternate valuation date and salvage the unified credit trust.

> EXAMPLE: Suppose total estate is $2,000,000 and a formula will with a pecuniary date of distribution marital bequest and a residuary bypass trust is present. At date of death values, the marital deduction bequest would receive $1,400,000 and the bypass trust would receive $600,000. Six months later, before funding, estate value has dropped to $1,400,000. Under the general rules, the marital deduction bequest would then be funded with $1,400,000 and the bypass trust would be zero. The alternate valuation is not generally available if the gross estate and the estate tax would not thereby be reduced.[9] The executor can take advantage of the alternate valuation by making a partial QTIP election, which results in a taxable estate of, say, $1,000. Then, the marital deduction portion of the QTIP will be $799,000; the nonqualified portion of the QTIP will be $601,000. Estate tax on $1,000 will be incurred.

[f] To Freeze the Survivor's Estate

Making a partial or zero QTIP election can freeze the surviving spouse's estate. This can be desirable in the case of highly appreciating assets.

> EXAMPLE: Taxable estate of predeceasing spouse is $3,000,000. It is expected to increase to $30,000,000 at the expected date of the surviving spouse's death in 10 years. By not making the QTIP election, $1,092,000 of estate tax can be paid now, as opposed to $16,500,000 later.

---

[8] Treas. Reg. § 20.7520-3(b)(3)(iii), 20.7520-3(b)(4), example 2; Old Kent Bank & Trust Co. v. United States, 292 F. Supp. 48 (WD Mich. 1968), rev'd on other issues, 430 F2d 392 (6th Cir. 1970); Lion Estate v. Comm'r, 52 TC 601 (1969), aff'd, 438 F2d 56 (4th Cir. 1971); Carter Estate v. Comm'r, 921 F2d 63, (5th Cir. 1991), rev'g 90-1 USTC ¶ 60,003 (ED La. 1989); Marks Estate v. Comm'r, 94 TC 720 (1990).

[9] IRC § 2032(c)(2).

[3] Forming Separate Trusts With Partial QTIP Election

If a partial QTIP election is made and the governing instrument allows it, the trustee should consider dividing the trust assets into separate trusts. This must be done with respect to a fractional or percentage share of the property so that the elective portion reflects its proportionate share of the increase or decrease in value of the entire property at the date of division.[10]

The separate trusts do not have to be funded with a pro rata portion of each asset.[11] However, the fiduciary must be required to divide the trusts on the basis of the fair market value of the assets of the trust at the date of division.[12] The division into separate trusts must be accomplished by the end of the period of estate administration.[13]

Establishment of separate trusts would allow, for example, the pursuit of different investment objectives in the two trusts (e.g., putting appreciating assets in the non-QTIP trust). It also allows principal invasion for the spouse from the QTIP trust; however, the regulations also allow invasions to be treated as made from the non-elected portion of a trust which is not separated.[14] One obvious way of doing this is to establish separate trusts for QTIP and non-QTIP amounts in the governing instrument. Alternatively, language could be included in the dispositive instrument authorizing an executor, trustee, or beneficiary (via power of appointment) to establish separate trusts of the QTIP and non-QTIP amounts.

[4] Disclaimers and Gifts Instead of QTIP Election

On occasions where no QTIP election or a partial QTIP election would be appropriate, a disclaimer[15] in favor of a nonqualifying marital trust should also be considered. Or, an acceptance by the surviving spouse, followed by a gift from the surviving spouse to the proposed beneficiaries, is another alternative.

---

[10] Treas. Reg. § 20.2056(b)-7(b)(2)(i).

[11] Treas. Reg. § 20.2056(b)-7(b)(2)(ii)(B).

[12] Treas. Reg. § 20.2056(b)-7(b)(2)(ii)(C).

[13] Treas. Reg. § 20.2056(b)-7(b)(2)(ii)(A).

[14] Treas. Reg. §§ 20.2044-1(d)(3), 25.2519-1(c)(3).

[15] Disclaimers are fully discussed in Ch. 47.

¶ 50.03 REVERSE QTIP ELECTION

[1] Protecting Predeceased Spouse's Generation-Skipping Transfer Tax Exemption

A very important element of generation-skipping transfer tax planning is the reverse QTIP election.[16] The executor of the decedent's estate may elect to treat QTIP property for purposes of the GSTT as if the QTIP election had not been made. The effect of the election is to treat the predeceasing spouse, rather than the surviving spouse, as the transferor of the QTIP trust.[17] Partial reverse QTIP elections are not permitted under the terms of the statute as written, but the QTIP trust can be split into two trusts, one of which will be subject to the reverse QTIP election and the other of which will not be subject to the election. However, this division of the QTIP trust must meet certain requirements.[18]

> **EXAMPLE:** If the reverse QTIP election is not made, the surviving spouse will be the transferor of the QTIP trust for generation-skipping transfer tax purposes. Suppose Husband predeceases Wife. Husband's will transfers his entire $2,000,000 estate to a QTIP trust which provides income to Wife, remainder to grandchildren. If Wife is treated as transferor of all the QTIP property for generation-skipping transfer tax purposes, Husband's $1,000,000 generation-skipping transfer tax exemption will be wasted. However, if the reverse QTIP election is made, Husband will be treated as the transferor, and his generation-skipping transfer tax exemption can be used on this trust.

PRACTICE POINTER: Make the reverse QTIP election if the generation-skipping transfer tax exemption of the first spouse to die is not otherwise used. Note that, in general, the reverse QTIP election is sensible only to the extent that no other gift is available to absorb the exemption. This is because all of the income of a QTIP trust must be paid to the surviving spouse rather than accumulated.

[2] Tax Apportionment

The generation-skipping transfer tax exemption allocated to a QTIP trust of which the predeceasing spouse is a transferor will be at least partially wasted if the estate tax is paid from the QTIP trust. For example, suppose Husband established QTIP trust with $1,000,000 and allocated $1,000,000 of exemption to the trust. When Wife dies, $550,000 is recoverable from the QTIP property;

---

[16] IRC § 2652(a)(3).

[17] IRC § 2652(a)(3). See Ch. 5 on the generation-skipping transfer tax for a fuller discussion.

[18] Reg. §§ 26.2652-2(a), 26.2654-1(b)(1).

hence, $1,000,000 of exemption was used to shelter only $450,000 of property. However, if Husband had originally allocated only $450,000 of his exemption to the trust, the inclusion ratio for the trust would be [11]/[20], and nothing would appear to change that on Wife's death. If Wife or Husband directs that the tax be paid from another source, the regulations state that such a provision will not be considered a constructive addition to the trust.[19] The following sample clause addresses this problem—

---

[19] Treas. Reg. §§ 26.2601-1(b)(1)(v)(C), 26.2652-1(a)(3).

Notwithstanding any other provision of this will to the contrary, if:

    (a) a valid election is made to qualify all or a part of The Marital Trust for the marital deduction under section 2056(b)(7)of the Internal Revenue Code; and

    (b) a valid election is made to treat me as the "transferor" of less than all of the property to be allocated to The Marital Trust for generation-skipping transfer tax purposes pursuant to section 2652(a)(3) of the Internal Revenue Code,

        then my executor shall divide (on a fractional share basis) the property that would otherwise constitute The Marital Trust into separate trusts. One of the separate trusts so established shall be The Exempt Marital Trust, to hold the property to which all or any part of my generation-skipping transfer tax exemption allowed pursuant to section 2631 of the Internal Revenue Code is allocated, and the other trust so established shall be The Non-Exempt Marital Trust, to hold the property which is not exempt from such tax. Any estate, gift or other transfer tax attributable to (or that would later be recoverable from) The Exempt Marital Trust, under section 2207A of the Internal Revenue Code or otherwise, by reason of the death of my spouse, shall instead be charged first, entirely, or to the extent possible, to The Non-Exempt Marital Trust.

[3] Making the Reverse QTIP Election

The reverse QTIP election is made by checking the box on Form 706, Schedule R, Part 1, and including a notice of allocation of the exemption with the Form 706 of the first spouse to die.

[4] Separate Trusts

As noted above, a partial election for a single trust is not available. It will often be desirable to keep exempt trusts separate from non-exempt trusts. This would allow, for example, the pursuit of different investment objectives (e.g., putting appreciating assets in the exempt trust), the inclusion of lower generations as beneficiaries of the exempt trust, and principal invasion for the spouse and children (after the spouse's death) to be made from the non-exempt trust.

If separate trusts are desired to avoid creating a partially exempt trust, the executor must split the trust or establish separate QTIP trusts before funding.

> EXAMPLE: Marital deduction trust is $2,000,000. Reverse QTIP election is made with respect to entire trust, resulting in inclusion ratio of 50 percent. Thereafter, 50 percent of any transfers from the trust will be subject to generation-skipping transfer tax. If the trust is separated into trusts with inclusion ratios of 0 and 1, generation-skipping transfer tax can be minimized.

[5] Funding of Exemption Amount

Section 2642 provides that the generation-skipping transfer tax exemption allocation will be made at the time of transfer to the trust (or direct skip) instead of date of death if the requirements prescribed by the IRS respecting allocation of post-death changes in value are not met.[20]

[6] Other Consequences of the Reverse QTIP Election

Other consequences of the special election will also ensue. For instance, if QTIP trust is established for Wife, remainder to Grandchild, and the reverse QTIP election is not made, then Wife will be the transferor for GSTT purposes, and the transfer on her death will be a direct skip. If the election is made, so that Husband is the transferor, the transfer on Wife's death will be a taxable termination. The value of property in the trust for purposes of allocating the generation-skipping transfer tax exemption will be determined at Wife's death or Husband's death, depending on who is the transferor. Also, if the trust beneficiaries are not family members, the generation assignments of all beneficiaries may differ depending on who the transferor is.

The reverse QTIP election can be disadvantageous if a child of the predeceasing spouse is alive at date of death of the predeceasing spouse but dies before the surviving spouse dies, and the child's share passes on the surviving spouse's death to the child's children. In such a case, if no election had been made, the surviving spouse would have been the transferor and there would be no generation-skipping transfer. This is because, in the case of a direct skip, the descendants of a predeceased child will be considered "stepped-up" to the

---

[20] The regulations are discussed in Ch. 5 on the generation-skipping transfer tax. They are Treas. Reg. §§ 26.2642-2(b) and 26.2654-1.

next generation.[21] However, if the election is made, the predeceasing spouse is deemed the transferor, and there will be a taxable termination at the time.

[7] Formula Will Application

A formula will often provides a bypass trust, a QTIP trust to absorb the excess generation-skipping tax exemption, and another marital deduction bequest. Normally, on death, for a decedent who has never made a taxable gift, the executor will (1) allocate $600,000 of the exemption to the bypass trust, (2) establish a QTIP trust for the remaining $400,000, (3) make a reverse QTIP election for that trust, (4) allocate the remaining exemption to that trust, and (5) leave the remaining marital deduction bequest as non-exempt.

¶ 50.04 TAXABLE YEAR

The executor can elect a non-calendar year for an estate (but not for a trust). One advantage of a fiscal year is that it can defer payment of income tax on up to eleven months of estate income for the period of estate administration. However, the practicality of determining income on a non-calendar year basis may or may not present difficulties. The taxable year is elected by filing a timely income tax return for the first year of the estate. If a timely election is not made, a calendar year will be automatically chosen.

¶ 50.05 WAIVER OF EXECUTOR'S COMMISSIONS

If the will or state law provides commissions, the executor may elect to accept or waive them. If the executor is the sole beneficiary, or the sole residuary beneficiary, it might make sense to take the commissions, since dollars taken as a beneficiary may be taxed at 55 percent, while dollars taken as compensation may be taxed at 39.6 percent. Or, it might not. For example, if the executor is the surviving spouse, taking the commission would change tax-free dollars qualifying for the marital deduction to dollars taxable as income.

¶ 50.06 SECTION 754 ELECTION FOR DECEDENT'S SHARE OF PARTNERSHIP PROPERTY

An election to step up the decedent's share of the inside basis of a partnership's or limited liability company's assets must be made on the income tax return filed by the partnership or LLC for the year of death, unless the entity already

---

[21] IRC § 2612(c)(2).

has an election in effect. If it does, a new election does not have to be filed.[22] This election is made by the partnership or LLC, rather than the executor.

The executor's role is to request that the partnership make the election if it would benefit the estate. Since the election will require the partnership to keep a separate set of books with respect to the estate's interest, the partnership may decide not to make the election or, as a condition of making the election, may require the estate to reimburse the partnership for the costs incurred as a result of making the election.

¶ 50.07 ALTERNATE VALUATION DATE

The executor can elect to value the assets as of the earlier of either six months after the date of death or the date of disposition of the assets.[23] The alternate valuation date cannot be elected if its only effect is to increase the basis of the estate assets—it has to lower both the value of the gross estate and the combined estate tax and GSTT.[24]

The election must be made on an estate tax return, which is filed no later than one year after the due date (including extensions) for filing the return.[25]

To the extent that actuarially valued interests are included in an estate, post-death changes in the interest rates can make the alternate valuation date desirable or undesirable. For example, the right to receive an annuity will be worth less if interest rates increase after death. Hence, the alternate valuation date could reduce the estate tax on such an interest.[26]

¶ 50.08 ADMINISTRATION OF THE SURVIVING SPOUSE'S ESTATE WHEN THE SURVIVING SPOUSE WAS THE BENEFICIARY OF A QTIP

Assuming there is no will provision to the contrary, the executor should be aware of the right to recover the estate tax incurred by the surviving spouse's estate on the QTIP assets from the QTIP trust or the persons who have received distributions from the QTIP trust.[27] If the will does not otherwise address the issue, the amount recoverable is the difference between the total tax paid and the tax that would have been payable had the QTIP property not

---

[22] Reg. § 1.754-1(b)(1).

[23] IRC § 2032(a).

[24] IRC § 2032(c).

[25] IRC § 2032(d).

[26] Priv. Ltr. Rul. 9637006 (May 10, 1996) (right to receive stream of lottery payments).

[27] IRC § 2207A.

been included in the survivor's estate.[28] Interest and penalties are also recoverable.[29] The will, however, may impose a different allocation.[30]

If a right of recovery exists, the executor will ordinarily have a duty to be aware of the right of recovery. If the executor does not try to recover the tax, the executor may incur liability. And, in such event, if the beneficiaries of the estate have a right to compel the executor to enforce the recovery, or to surcharge the executor, they may be deemed to have made gifts to the QTIP trust (or the beneficiaries thereof), or to the executor, when the right to compel the recovery or surcharge the executor is no longer enforceable.[31] Finally, a delay in the exercise of the right of recovery may be treated as an interest-free loan subject to Section 7872.[32]

¶ 50.09　MISCELLANEOUS ELECTIONS

The following other elections must also be considered in appropriate cases:

- *Gift-splitting.* The executor may consent to gift-splitting with respect to gifts made before the decedent's death.[33]
- *Dower, curtesy, etc.* A surviving spouse may exercise state law rights of dower, curtesy, election against the will, etc.
- *Joint return.* The executor may join the surviving spouse in filing a joint income tax return for the year in which the decedent died.[34]
- *Medical expense deduction.* The decedent's unreimbursed medical expenses outstanding at his death may be deducted on the decedent's final income tax return (if they are paid out of his estate within one year after his death)[35] or on the federal estate tax return.[36]
- *Series EE bond redemption value.* If Series EE U.S. savings bonds are included in the cash-method taxpayer's estate, the executor can elect to report the increase in the redemption value of the bonds as income on the decedent's final income tax return.[37] This election is an alternative to having the income taxed to the estate or the beneficiaries (either on redemption of the bonds or on the holder's election). Whether this

---

[28] IRC § 2207A(a)(1).

[29] IRC § 2207A(d).

[30] IRC § 2207A(a)(2).

[31] Treas. Reg. § 20.2207A-1(a)(2).

[32] Treas. Reg. § 20.2207A-1(a)(2).

[33] Reg. § 25.2513-2(c).

[34] IRC § 6013(a).

[35] IRC § 213(c).

[36] IRC § 2053(a)(3).

[37] IRC § 454(a).

election should be made will depend on the specific circumstances. If the executor makes the election to include the income on the final return, the income tax will be deductible from the estate as a debt for estate tax purposes. If a beneficiary or the estate recognizes income from the bonds, the income will be considered income in respect of a decedent and the estate tax paid on that income will be deductible for income tax purposes. If the executor elects to begin reporting all income on a current basis, the reporting must continue in subsequent years.

¶ 50.10 DELAYED FUNDING

According to the IRS, the executor cannot deduct statutory interest paid to a legatee to compensate that legatee for the belated funding of a pecuniary bequest. The IRS's position is that, even if the delayed funding was necessary to the administration of the estate, the statutory interest paid to the legatee was merely a manner of allocating estate income, and therefore was not in the nature of compensation for a loan (i.e., interest).[38]

¶ 50.11 REFORMATIONS

Certain post-mortem reformations of nonqualified charitable split-interest gifts are permissible.[39] However, no statutory provision exists allowing reformation of a trust in order to retroactively qualify the trust for the estate tax marital deduction. The IRS's position on such reformations is that the reformation is not relevant for estate tax purposes, even if it is binding on the beneficiaries.[40]

---

[38] Priv. Ltr. Rul. 9604002 (Oct. 6, 1995).

[39] IRC § 2055.

[40] See, e.g., Estate of Rapp v. Comm'r, 1996 RIA TC Memo. ¶ 96, 010, 71 TCM (CCH) 1709 (Jan. 18, 1996) (court held interest not reformable under state law, so IRS position not addressed by court).